S H O W C A S E   P R E S E N T S

BATMAN

V O L U M E   T W O

BATMAN CREATED BY BOB KANE

Dan DiDio Senior VP-Executive Editor

Julius Schwartz Editor-original series

Bob Joy Editor-collected edition

Robbin Brosterman Senior Art Director

Paul Levitz President & Publisher

Georg Brewer VP-Design & DC Direct Creative

Richard Bruning Senior VP-Creative Director

Patrick Caldon Executive VP-Finance & Operations

Chris Caramalis VP-Finance

John Cunningham VP-Marketing

Terri Cunningham VP-Managing Editor

Alison Gill VP-Manufacturing

Hank Kanalz VP-General Manager, WildStorm

Jim Lee Editorial Director-WildStorm

Paula Lowitt Senior VP-Business & Legal Affairs

MaryEllen McLaughlin VP-Advertising & Custom Publishing

John Nee VP-Business Development

Gregory Noveck Senior VP-Creative Affairs

Sue Pohja VP-Book Trade Sales

Cheryl Rubin Senior VP-Brand Management

Jeff Trojan VP-Business Development, DC Direct

Bob Wayne VP-Sales

Cover illustration by Carmine Infantino and Joe Giella.
Cover colored by Tonya and Richard Horie.

SHOWCASE PRESENTS: BATMAN VOL. TWO
Published by DC Comics. Cover and compilation
copyright © 2007 DC Comics. All Rights Reserved.

Originally published in single magazine form in DETECTIVE COMICS 343-358,
BATMAN 175, 177-181, 183-184, 188 © 1965-1966 DC Comics.
All Rights Reserved. All characters, their distinctive likenesses and related
elements featured in this publication are trademarks of DC Comics

DC Comics, 1700 Broadway, New York, NY 10019
A Warner Bros. Entertainment Company
Printed in Canada. First Printing.
ISBN: 1-4012-1362-6
ISBN 13: 978-1-4012-1362-6

TABLE OF CONTENTS

ALL COVERS PENCILLED BY **CARMINE INFANTINO** AND INKED BY **JOE GIELLA** AND
ALL INTERIORS PENCILLED BY **SHELDON MOLDOFF** AND INKED BY **JOE GIELLA** UNLESS OTHERWISE NOTED.

UNTIL THE 1970S IT WAS NOT COMMON PRACTICE IN THE COMIC BOOK INDUSTRY TO CREDIT ALL STORIES. IN THE PREPARATION OF THIS COLLECTION WE HAVE USED OUR BEST EFFORTS TO REVIEW ANY SURVIVING RECORDS AND CONSULT ANY AVAILABLE DATABASES AND KNOWLEDGEABLE PARTIES. WE REGRET THE INNATE LIMITATIONS OF THIS PROCESS AND ANY MISSING OR MIS-ASSIGNED ATTRIBUTIONS THAT MAY OCCUR. ANY ADDITIONAL INFORMATION ON CREDITS SHOULD BE DIRECTED TO: EDITOR, COLLECTED EDITIONS, C/O DC COMICS.

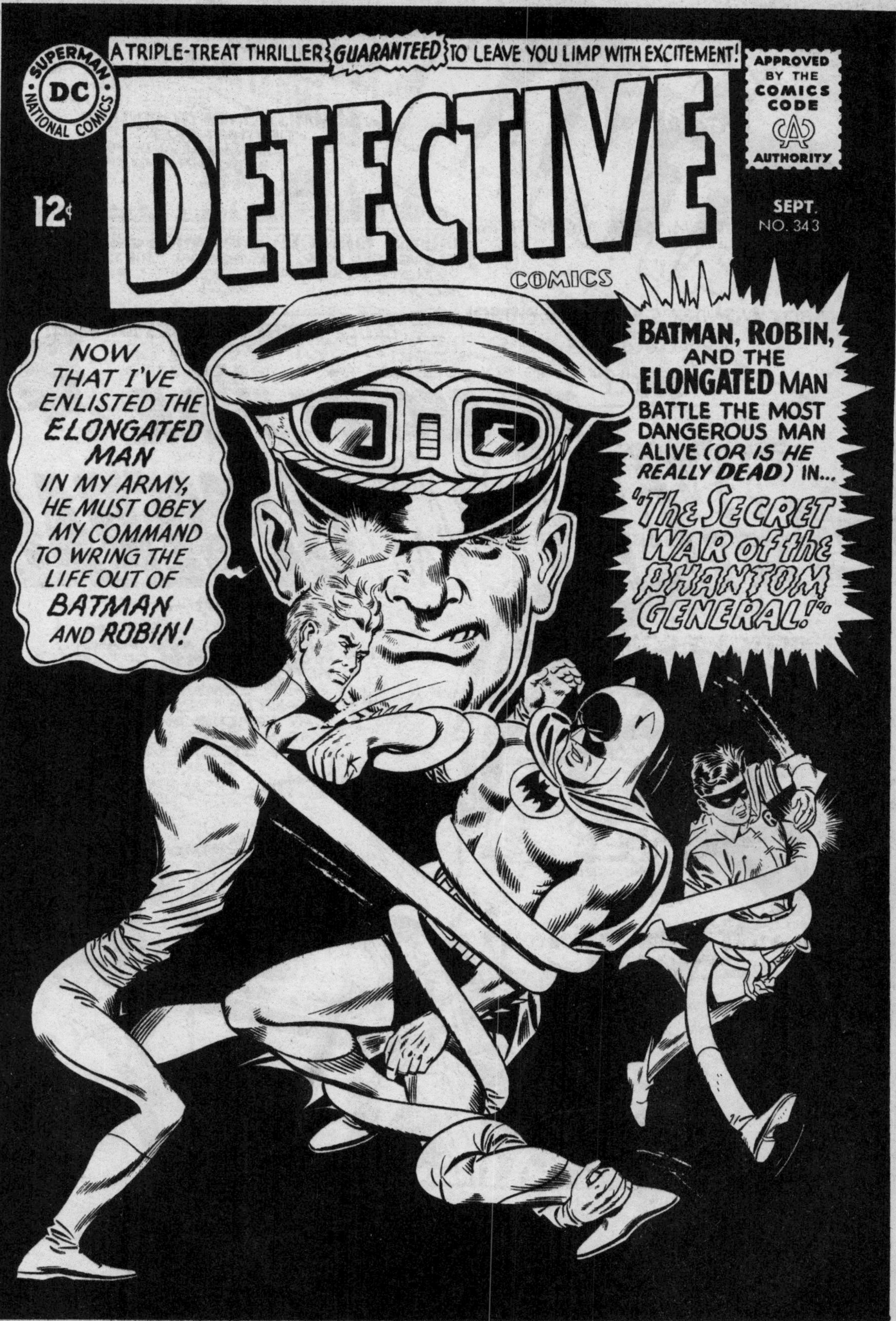
SUPERMAN DC NATIONAL COMICS
A TRIPLE-TREAT THRILLER GUARANTEED TO LEAVE YOU LIMP WITH EXCITEMENT!
APPROVED BY THE COMICS CODE AUTHORITY
DETECTIVE COMICS
12¢
SEPT. NO. 343
NOW THAT I'VE ENLISTED THE ELONGATED MAN IN MY ARMY, HE MUST OBEY MY COMMAND TO WRING THE LIFE OUT OF BATMAN AND ROBIN!
BATMAN, ROBIN, AND THE ELONGATED MAN BATTLE THE MOST DANGEROUS MAN ALIVE (OR IS HE REALLY DEAD) IN... "The SECRET WAR of the PHANTOM GENERAL!"

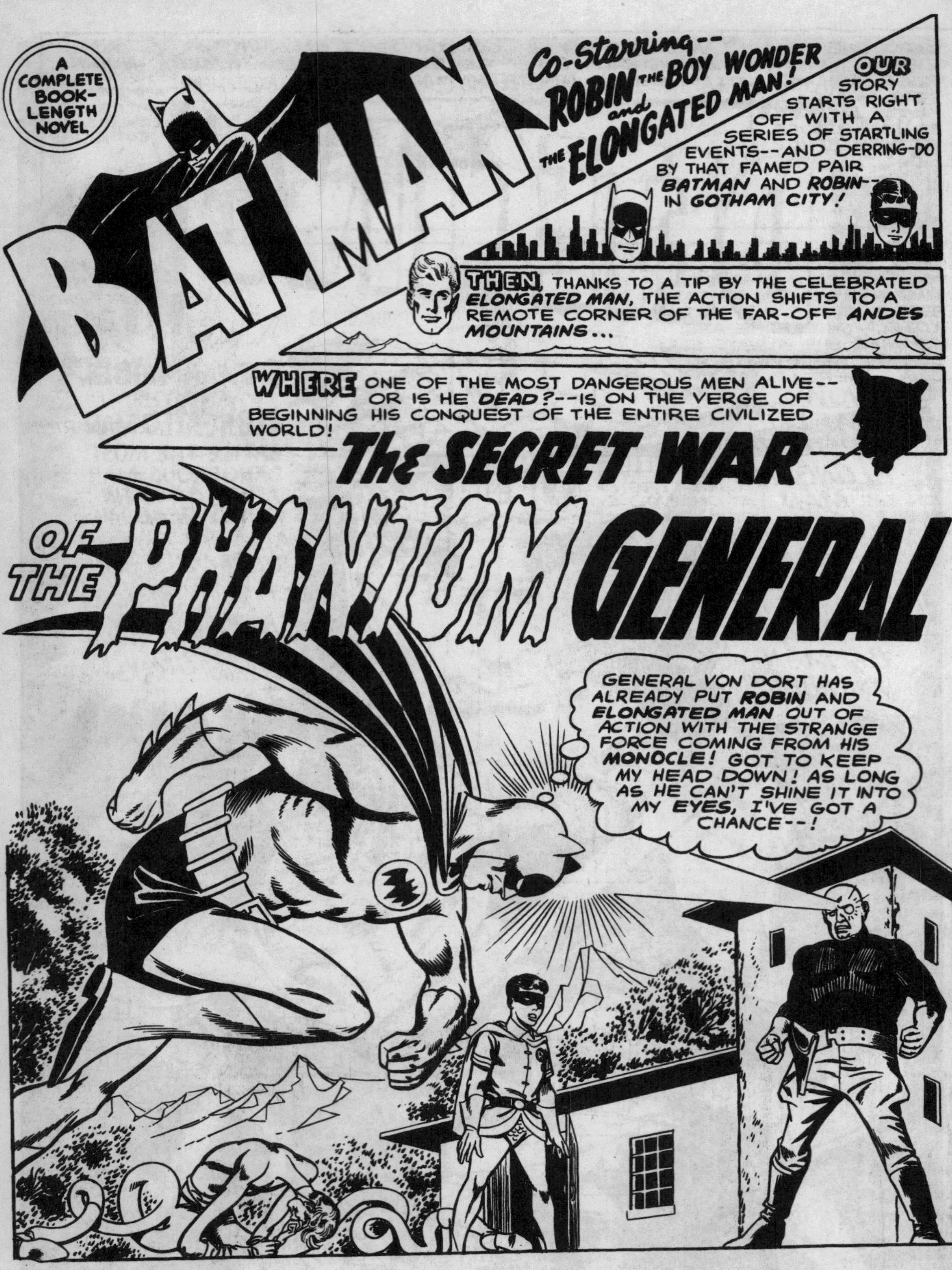
A COMPLETE BOOK-LENGTH NOVEL
BATMAN
Co-Starring-- ROBIN THE BOY WONDER and THE ELONGATED MAN!
OUR STORY STARTS RIGHT OFF WITH A SERIES OF STARTLING EVENTS--AND DERRING-DO BY THAT FAMED PAIR BATMAN AND ROBIN-- IN GOTHAM CITY!
THEN, THANKS TO A TIP BY THE CELEBRATED ELONGATED MAN, THE ACTION SHIFTS TO A REMOTE CORNER OF THE FAR-OFF ANDES MOUNTAINS...
WHERE ONE OF THE MOST DANGEROUS MEN ALIVE-- OR IS HE DEAD?--IS ON THE VERGE OF BEGINNING HIS CONQUEST OF THE ENTIRE CIVILIZED WORLD!
The SECRET WAR OF THE PHANTOM GENERAL
GENERAL VON DORT HAS ALREADY PUT ROBIN AND ELONGATED MAN OUT OF ACTION WITH THE STRANGE FORCE COMING FROM HIS MONOCLE! GOT TO KEEP MY HEAD DOWN! AS LONG AS HE CAN'T SHINE IT INTO MY EYES, I'VE GOT A CHANCE--!

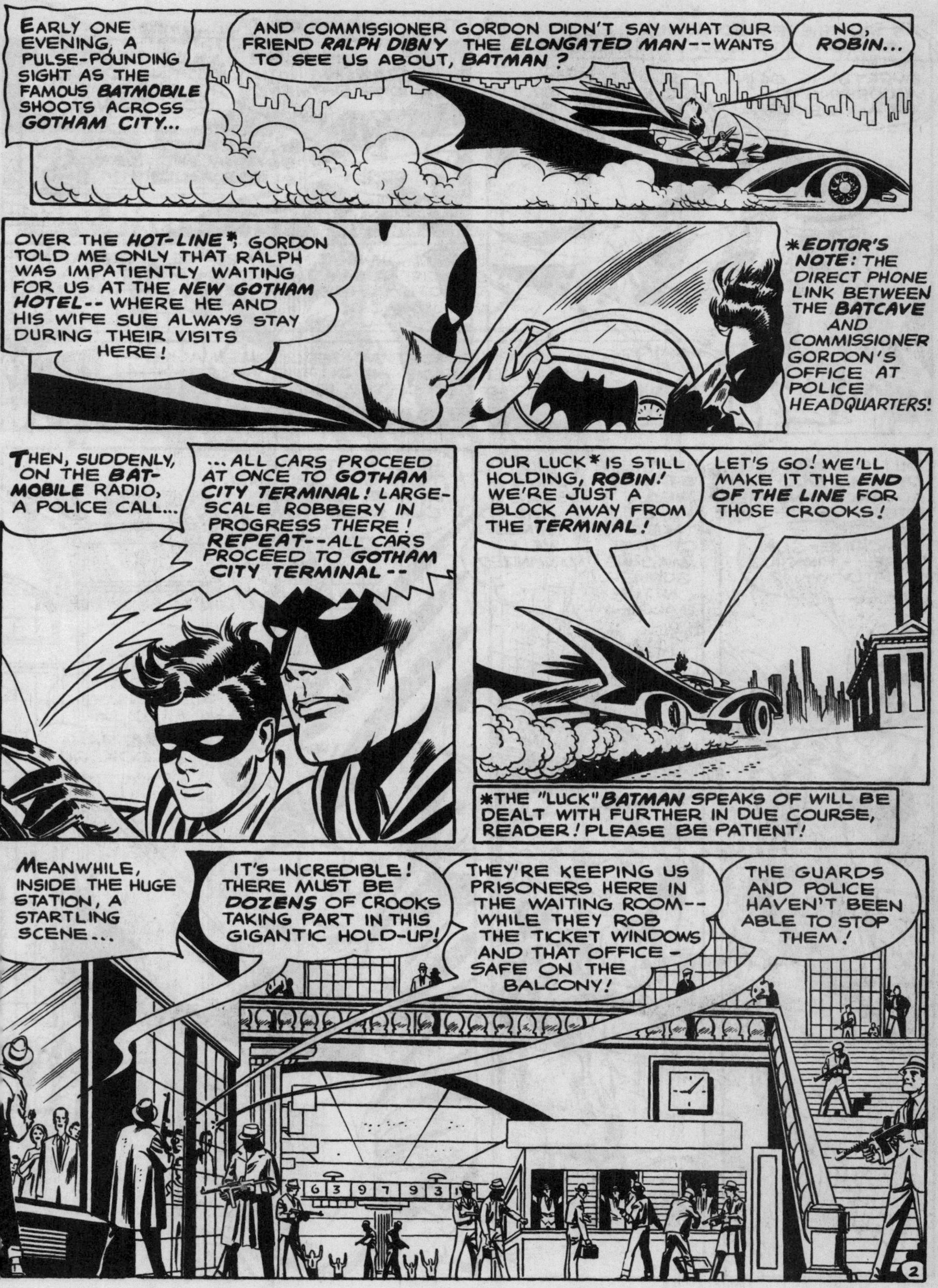

EARLY ONE EVENING, A PULSE-POUNDING SIGHT AS THE FAMOUS BATMOBILE SHOOTS ACROSS GOTHAM CITY...
AND COMMISSIONER GORDON DIDN'T SAY WHAT OUR FRIEND RALPH DIBNY THE ELONGATED MAN--WANTS TO SEE US ABOUT, BATMAN ?
NO, ROBIN...
OVER THE HOT-LINE*, GORDON TOLD ME ONLY THAT RALPH WAS IMPATIENTLY WAITING FOR US AT THE NEW GOTHAM HOTEL-- WHERE HE AND HIS WIFE SUE ALWAYS STAY DURING THEIR VISITS HERE!
*EDITOR'S NOTE: THE DIRECT PHONE LINK BETWEEN THE BATCAVE AND COMMISSIONER GORDON'S OFFICE AT POLICE HEADQUARTERS!
THEN, SUDDENLY, ON THE BAT-MOBILE RADIO, A POLICE CALL...
...ALL CARS PROCEED AT ONCE TO GOTHAM CITY TERMINAL! LARGE-SCALE ROBBERY IN PROGRESS THERE! REPEAT--ALL CARS PROCEED TO GOTHAM CITY TERMINAL--
OUR LUCK* IS STILL HOLDING, ROBIN! WE'RE JUST A BLOCK AWAY FROM THE TERMINAL!
LET'S GO! WE'LL MAKE IT THE END OF THE LINE FOR THOSE CROOKS!
*THE "LUCK" BATMAN SPEAKS OF WILL BE DEALT WITH FURTHER IN DUE COURSE, READER! PLEASE BE PATIENT!
MEANWHILE, INSIDE THE HUGE STATION, A STARTLING SCENE...
IT'S INCREDIBLE! THERE MUST BE DOZENS OF CROOKS TAKING PART IN THIS GIGANTIC HOLD-UP!
THEY'RE KEEPING US PRISONERS HERE IN THE WAITING ROOM--WHILE THEY ROB THE TICKET WINDOWS AND THAT OFFICE-SAFE ON THE BALCONY!
THE GUARDS AND POLICE HAVEN'T BEEN ABLE TO STOP THEM!
6 3 9 7 9 3 1
2

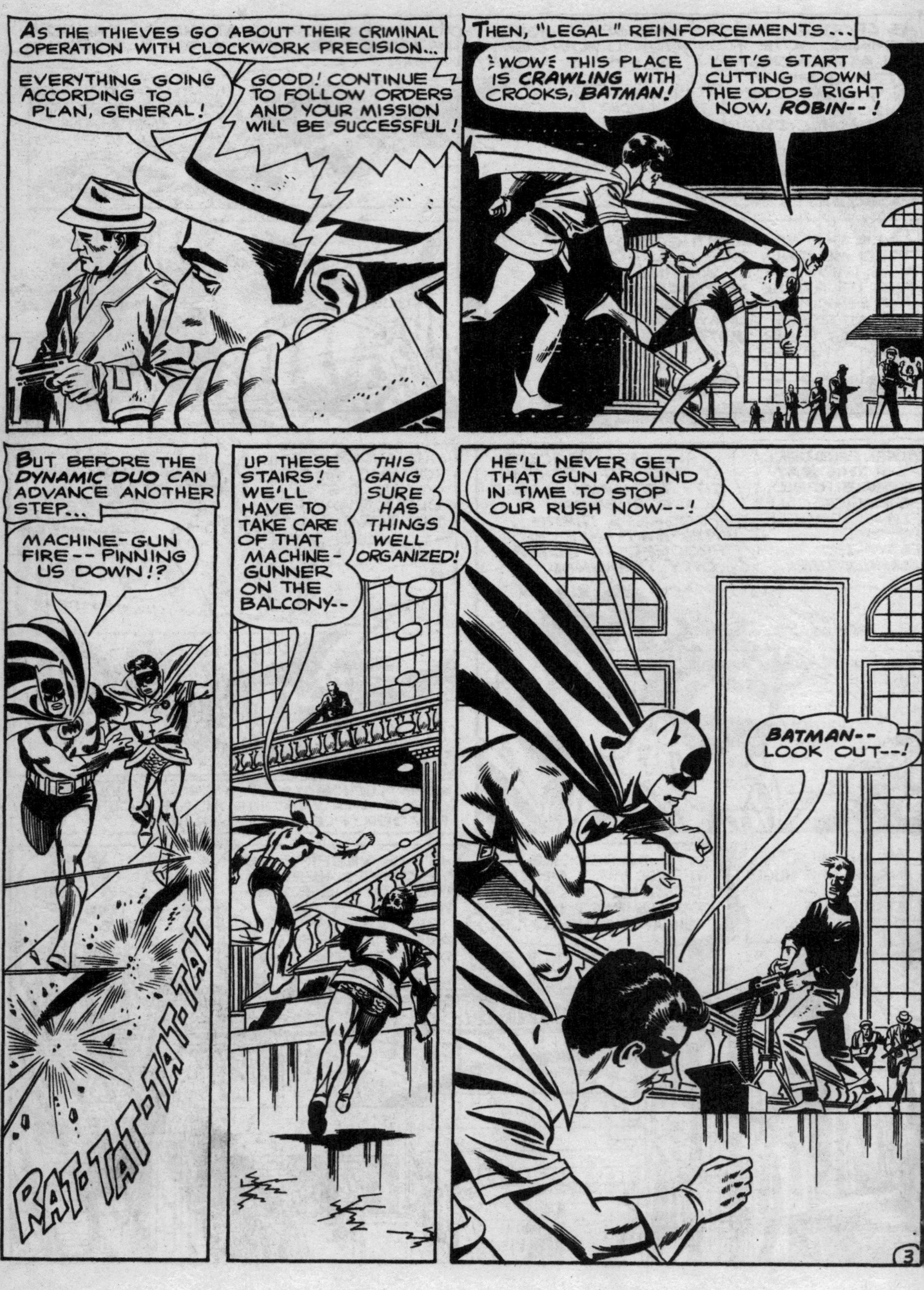
AS THE THIEVES GO ABOUT THEIR CRIMINAL OPERATION WITH CLOCKWORK PRECISION...
EVERYTHING GOING ACCORDING TO PLAN, GENERAL!
GOOD! CONTINUE TO FOLLOW ORDERS AND YOUR MISSION WILL BE SUCCESSFUL!
THEN, "LEGAL" REINFORCEMENTS...
WOW! THIS PLACE IS CRAWLING WITH CROOKS, BATMAN!
LET'S START CUTTING DOWN THE ODDS RIGHT NOW, ROBIN--!
BUT BEFORE THE DYNAMIC DUO CAN ADVANCE ANOTHER STEP...
MACHINE-GUN FIRE--PINNING US DOWN!?
RAT-TAT-TAT-TAT
UP THESE STAIRS! WE'LL HAVE TO TAKE CARE OF THAT MACHINE-GUNNER ON THE BALCONY--
THIS GANG SURE HAS THINGS WELL ORGANIZED!
HE'LL NEVER GET THAT GUN AROUND IN TIME TO STOP OUR RUSH NOW--!
BATMAN--LOOK OUT--!
3

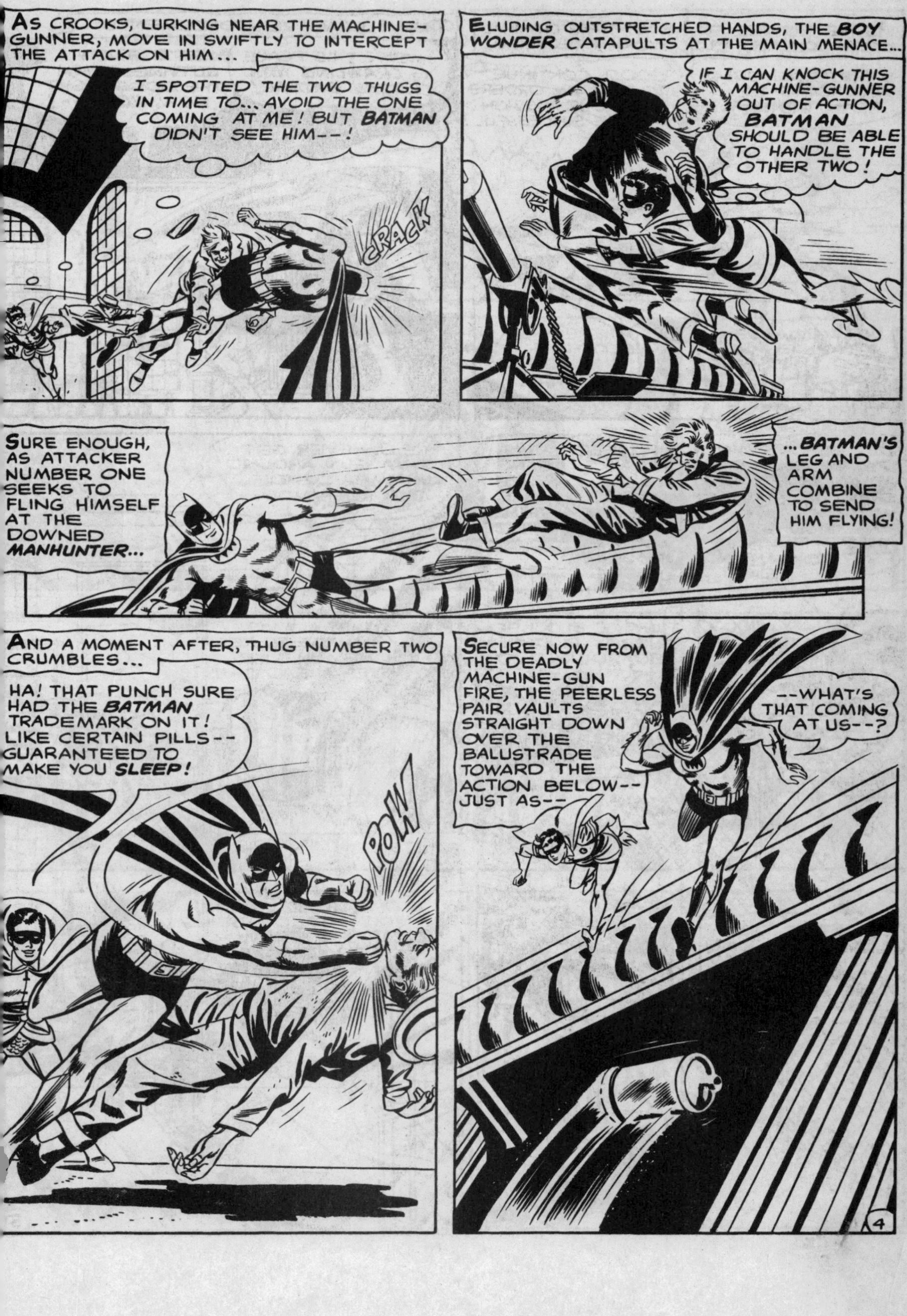
AS CROOKS, LURKING NEAR THE MACHINE-GUNNER, MOVE IN SWIFTLY TO INTERCEPT THE ATTACK ON HIM...
I SPOTTED THE TWO THUGS IN TIME TO... AVOID THE ONE COMING AT ME! BUT BATMAN DIDN'T SEE HIM--!
CRACK
ELUDING OUTSTRETCHED HANDS, THE BOY WONDER CATAPULTS AT THE MAIN MENACE...
IF I CAN KNOCK THIS MACHINE-GUNNER OUT OF ACTION, BATMAN SHOULD BE ABLE TO HANDLE THE OTHER TWO!
SURE ENOUGH, AS ATTACKER NUMBER ONE SEEKS TO FLING HIMSELF AT THE DOWNED MANHUNTER...
...BATMAN'S LEG AND ARM COMBINE TO SEND HIM FLYING!
AND A MOMENT AFTER, THUG NUMBER TWO CRUMBLES...
HA! THAT PUNCH SURE HAD THE BATMAN TRADEMARK ON IT! LIKE CERTAIN PILLS--GUARANTEED TO MAKE YOU SLEEP!
POW
SECURE NOW FROM THE DEADLY MACHINE-GUN FIRE, THE PEERLESS PAIR VAULTS STRAIGHT DOWN OVER THE BALUSTRADE TOWARD THE ACTION BELOW--JUST AS--
--WHAT'S THAT COMING AT US--?
4

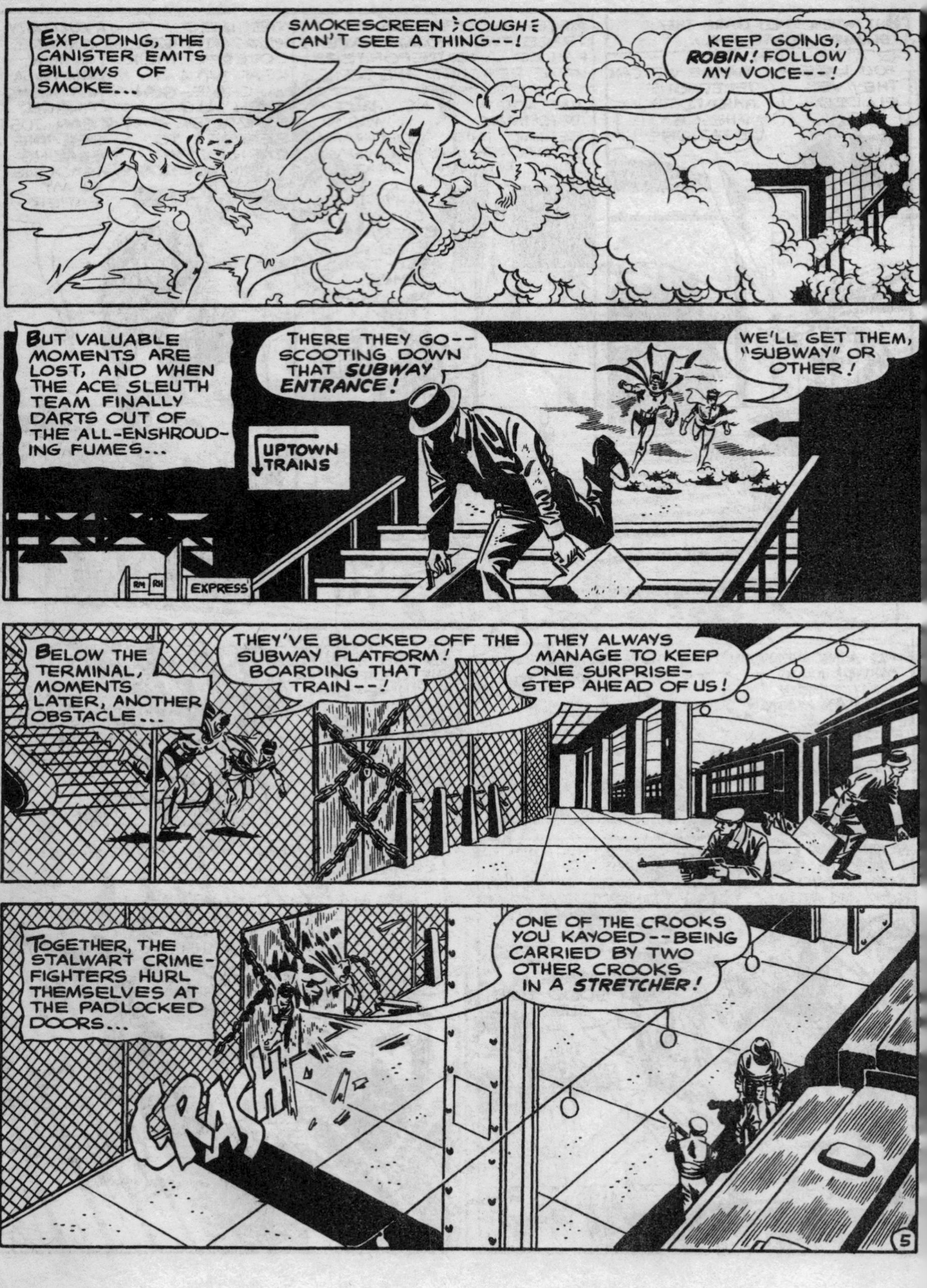
EXPLODING, THE CANISTER EMITS BILLOWS OF SMOKE...
SMOKESCREEN ;COUGH: CAN'T SEE A THING--!
KEEP GOING, ROBIN! FOLLOW MY VOICE--!
BUT VALUABLE MOMENTS ARE LOST, AND WHEN THE ACE SLEUTH TEAM FINALLY DARTS OUT OF THE ALL-ENSHROUDING FUMES...
UPTOWN TRAINS
EXPRESS
THERE THEY GO--SCOOTING DOWN THAT SUBWAY ENTRANCE!
WE'LL GET THEM, "SUBWAY" OR OTHER!
BELOW THE TERMINAL, MOMENTS LATER, ANOTHER OBSTACLE...
THEY'VE BLOCKED OFF THE SUBWAY PLATFORM! BOARDING THAT TRAIN--!
THEY ALWAYS MANAGE TO KEEP ONE SURPRISE-STEP AHEAD OF US!
TOGETHER, THE STALWART CRIME-FIGHTERS HURL THEMSELVES AT THE PADLOCKED DOORS...
ONE OF THE CROOKS YOU KAYOED--BEING CARRIED BY TWO OTHER CROOKS IN A STRETCHER!
CRASH
5

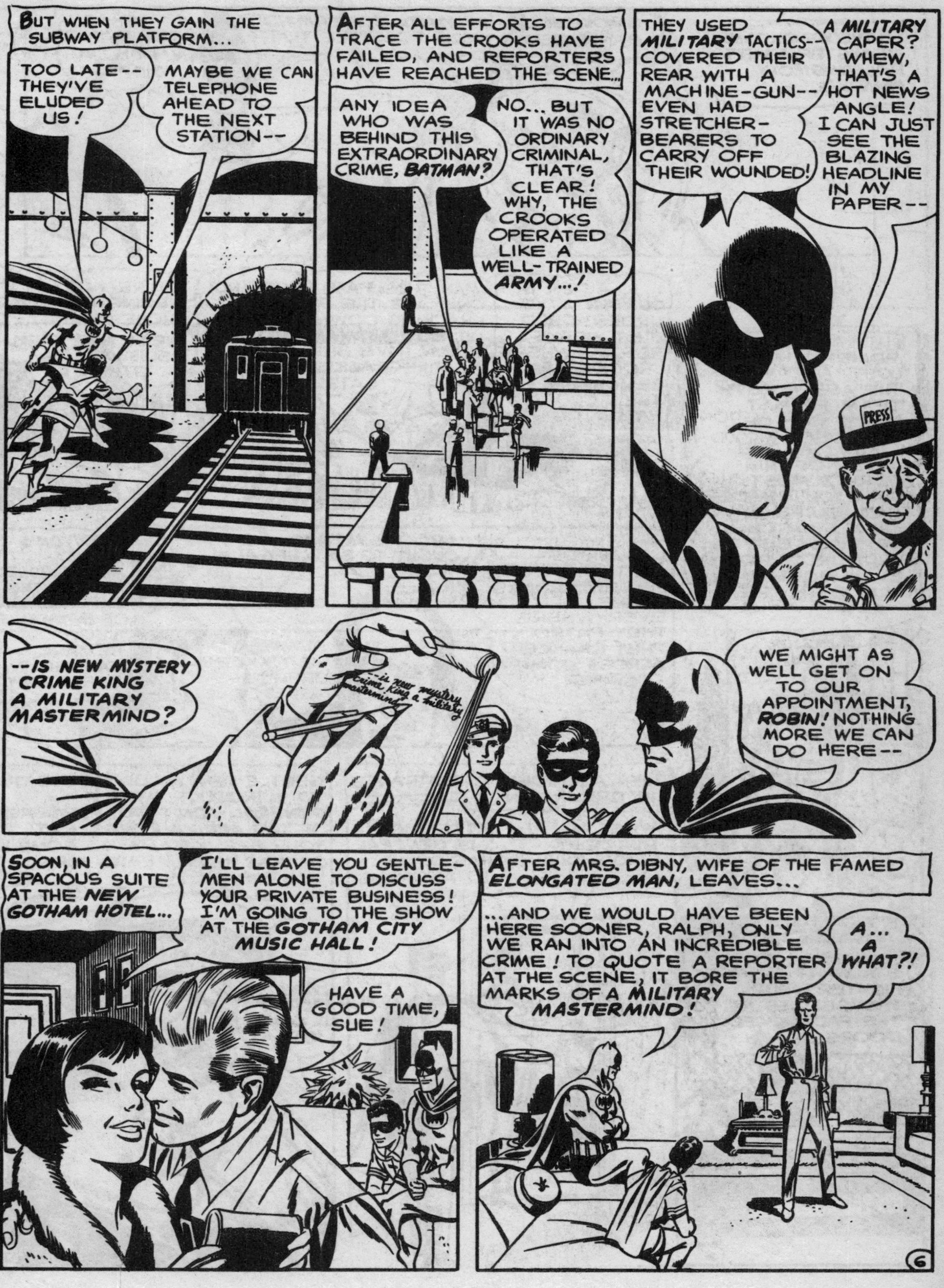
BUT WHEN THEY GAIN THE SUBWAY PLATFORM...
TOO LATE-- THEY'VE ELUDED US!
MAYBE WE CAN TELEPHONE AHEAD TO THE NEXT STATION--
AFTER ALL EFFORTS TO TRACE THE CROOKS HAVE FAILED, AND REPORTERS HAVE REACHED THE SCENE...
ANY IDEA WHO WAS BEHIND THIS EXTRAORDINARY CRIME, BATMAN?
NO... BUT IT WAS NO ORDINARY CRIMINAL, THAT'S CLEAR! WHY, THE CROOKS OPERATED LIKE A WELL-TRAINED ARMY...!
THEY USED MILITARY TACTICS--COVERED THEIR REAR WITH A MACHINE-GUN--EVEN HAD STRETCHER-BEARERS TO CARRY OFF THEIR WOUNDED!
A MILITARY CAPER? WHEW, THAT'S A HOT NEWS ANGLE! I CAN JUST SEE THE BLAZING HEADLINE IN MY PAPER--
PRESS
--IS NEW MYSTERY CRIME KING A MILITARY MASTERMIND?
--is new mystery crime king a military mastermind
WE MIGHT AS WELL GET ON TO OUR APPOINTMENT, ROBIN! NOTHING MORE WE CAN DO HERE--
SOON, IN A SPACIOUS SUITE AT THE NEW GOTHAM HOTEL...
I'LL LEAVE YOU GENTLEMEN ALONE TO DISCUSS YOUR PRIVATE BUSINESS! I'M GOING TO THE SHOW AT THE GOTHAM CITY MUSIC HALL!
HAVE A GOOD TIME, SUE!
AFTER MRS. DIBNY, WIFE OF THE FAMED ELONGATED MAN, LEAVES...
...AND WE WOULD HAVE BEEN HERE SOONER, RALPH, ONLY WE RAN INTO AN INCREDIBLE CRIME! TO QUOTE A REPORTER AT THE SCENE, IT BORE THE MARKS OF A MILITARY MASTERMIND!
A... A WHAT?!
6

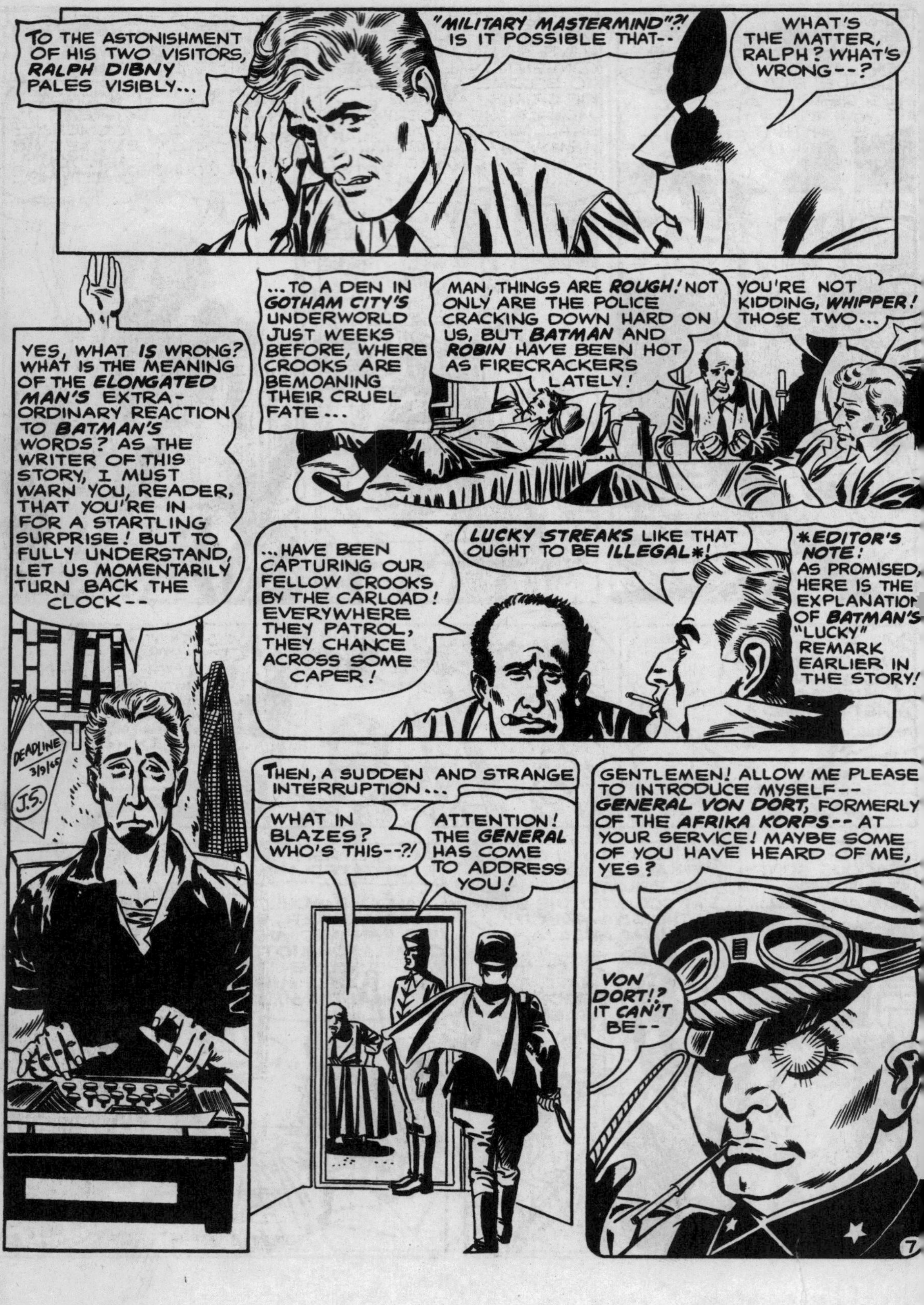

TO THE ASTONISHMENT OF HIS TWO VISITORS, RALPH DIBNY PALES VISIBLY...
"MILITARY MASTERMIND"?! IS IT POSSIBLE THAT--
WHAT'S THE MATTER, RALPH? WHAT'S WRONG--?
YES, WHAT IS WRONG? WHAT IS THE MEANING OF THE ELONGATED MAN'S EXTRA-ORDINARY REACTION TO BATMAN'S WORDS? AS THE WRITER OF THIS STORY, I MUST WARN YOU, READER, THAT YOU'RE IN FOR A STARTLING SURPRISE! BUT TO FULLY UNDERSTAND, LET US MOMENTARILY TURN BACK THE CLOCK--
DEADLINE 3/9/65
J.S.
...TO A DEN IN GOTHAM CITY'S UNDERWORLD JUST WEEKS BEFORE, WHERE CROOKS ARE BEMOANING THEIR CRUEL FATE...
MAN, THINGS ARE ROUGH! NOT ONLY ARE THE POLICE CRACKING DOWN HARD ON US, BUT BATMAN AND ROBIN HAVE BEEN HOT AS FIRECRACKERS LATELY!
YOU'RE NOT KIDDING, WHIPPER! THOSE TWO...
...HAVE BEEN CAPTURING OUR FELLOW CROOKS BY THE CARLOAD! EVERYWHERE THEY PATROL, THEY CHANCE ACROSS SOME CAPER!
LUCKY STREAKS LIKE THAT OUGHT TO BE ILLEGAL*!
*EDITOR'S NOTE: AS PROMISED, HERE IS THE EXPLANATION OF BATMAN'S "LUCKY" REMARK EARLIER IN THE STORY!
THEN, A SUDDEN AND STRANGE INTERRUPTION...
WHAT IN BLAZES? WHO'S THIS--?!
ATTENTION! THE GENERAL HAS COME TO ADDRESS YOU!
GENTLEMEN! ALLOW ME PLEASE TO INTRODUCE MYSELF-- GENERAL VON DORT, FORMERLY OF THE AFRIKA KORPS-- AT YOUR SERVICE! MAYBE SOME OF YOU HAVE HEARD OF ME, YES?
VON DORT!? IT CAN'T BE--
7

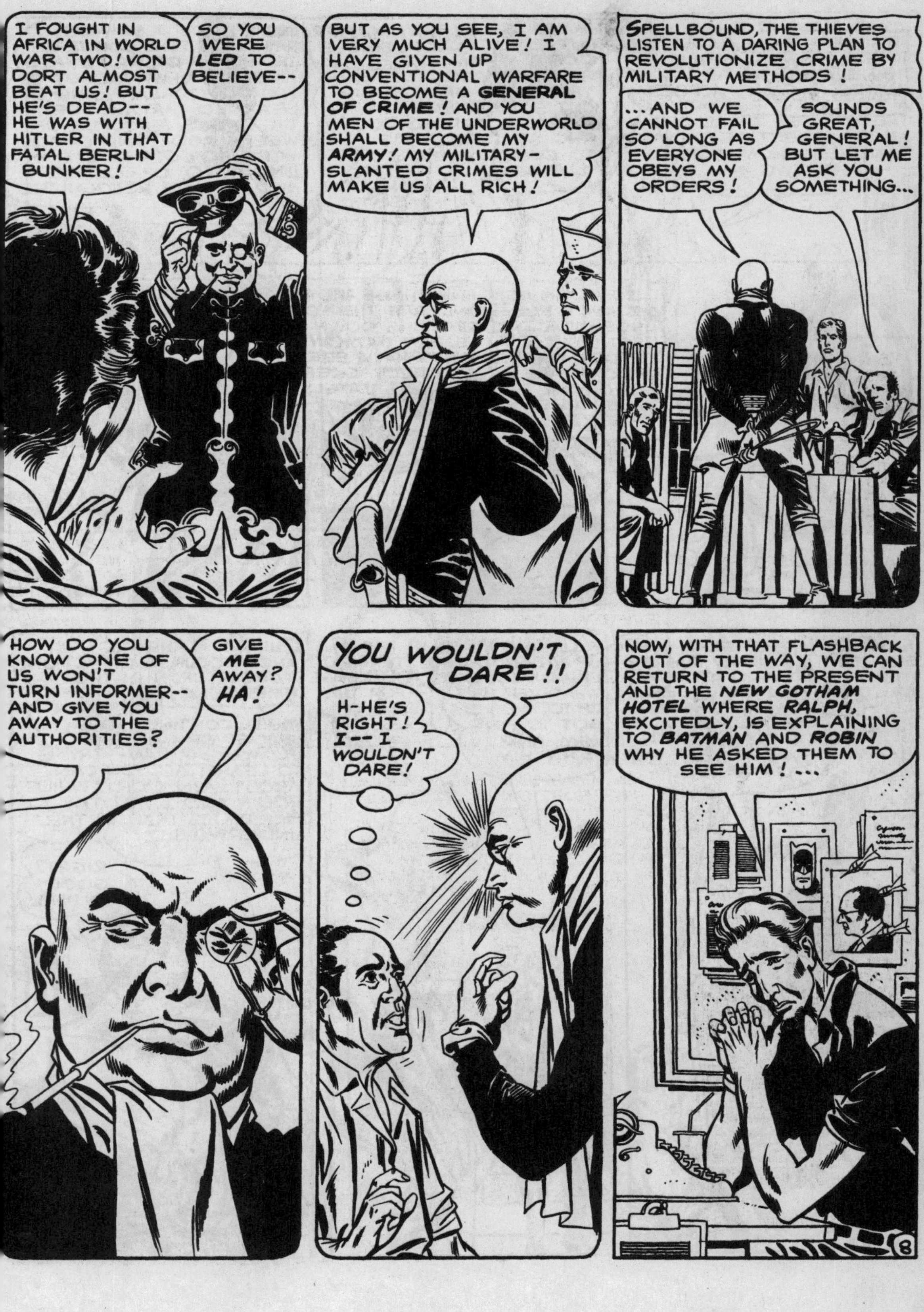
I FOUGHT IN AFRICA IN WORLD WAR TWO! VON DORT ALMOST BEAT US! BUT HE'S DEAD-- HE WAS WITH HITLER IN THAT FATAL BERLIN BUNKER!
SO YOU WERE LED TO BELIEVE--
BUT AS YOU SEE, I AM VERY MUCH ALIVE! I HAVE GIVEN UP CONVENTIONAL WARFARE TO BECOME A GENERAL OF CRIME! AND YOU MEN OF THE UNDERWORLD SHALL BECOME MY ARMY! MY MILITARY-SLANTED CRIMES WILL MAKE US ALL RICH!
SPELLBOUND, THE THIEVES LISTEN TO A DARING PLAN TO REVOLUTIONIZE CRIME BY MILITARY METHODS!
...AND WE CANNOT FAIL SO LONG AS EVERYONE OBEYS MY ORDERS!
SOUNDS GREAT, GENERAL! BUT LET ME ASK YOU SOMETHING...
HOW DO YOU KNOW ONE OF US WON'T TURN INFORMER-- AND GIVE YOU AWAY TO THE AUTHORITIES?
GIVE ME AWAY? HA!
YOU WOULDN'T DARE!!
H-HE'S RIGHT! I-- I WOULDN'T DARE!
NOW, WITH THAT FLASHBACK OUT OF THE WAY, WE CAN RETURN TO THE PRESENT AND THE NEW GOTHAM HOTEL WHERE RALPH, EXCITEDLY, IS EXPLAINING TO BATMAN AND ROBIN WHY HE ASKED THEM TO SEE HIM! ...
8

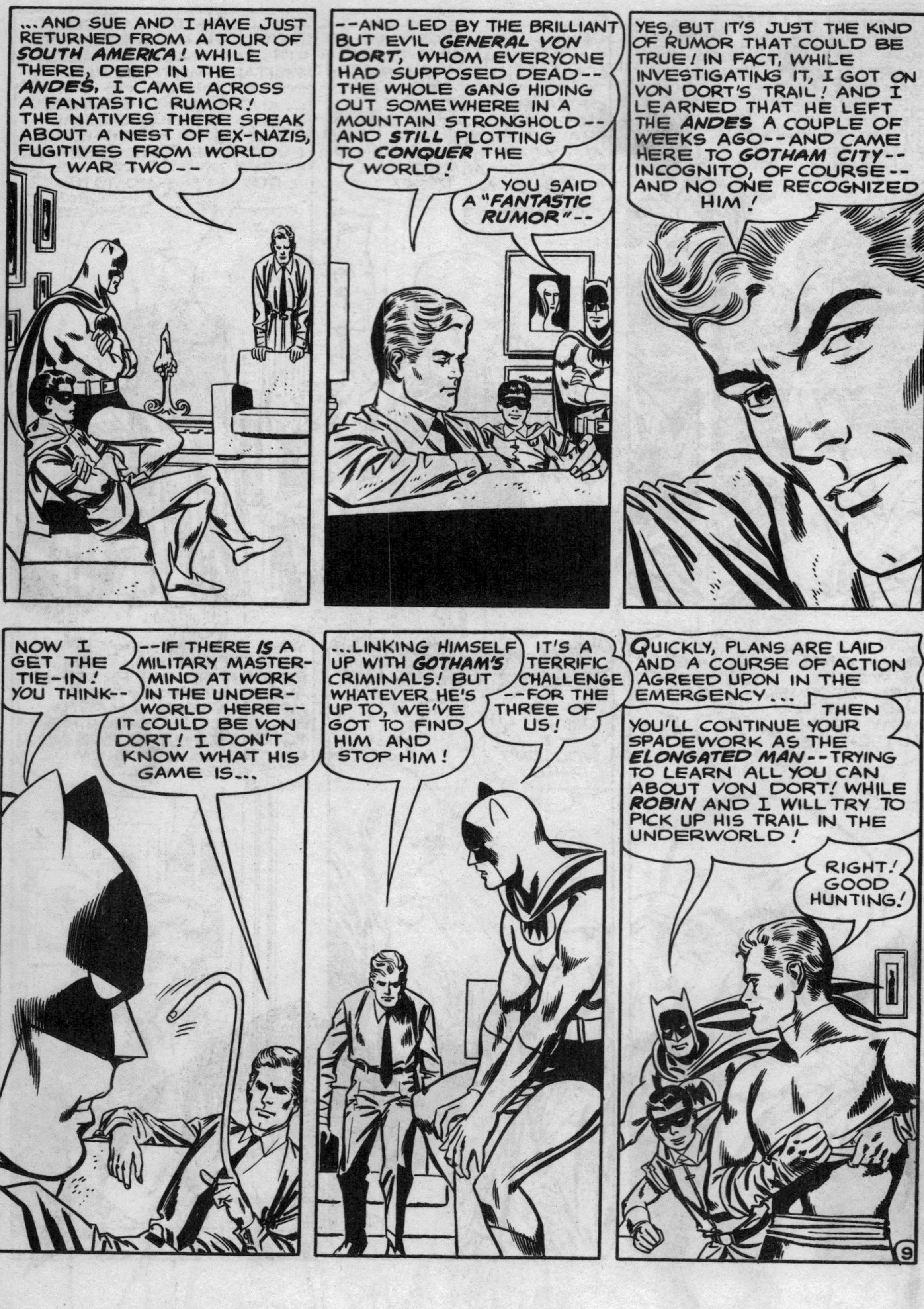
...AND SUE AND I HAVE JUST RETURNED FROM A TOUR OF SOUTH AMERICA! WHILE THERE, DEEP IN THE ANDES, I CAME ACROSS A FANTASTIC RUMOR! THE NATIVES THERE SPEAK ABOUT A NEST OF EX-NAZIS, FUGITIVES FROM WORLD WAR TWO--
--AND LED BY THE BRILLIANT BUT EVIL GENERAL VON DORT, WHOM EVERYONE HAD SUPPOSED DEAD--THE WHOLE GANG HIDING OUT SOMEWHERE IN A MOUNTAIN STRONGHOLD--AND STILL PLOTTING TO CONQUER THE WORLD!
YOU SAID A "FANTASTIC RUMOR"--
YES, BUT IT'S JUST THE KIND OF RUMOR THAT COULD BE TRUE! IN FACT, WHILE INVESTIGATING IT, I GOT ON VON DORT'S TRAIL! AND I LEARNED THAT HE LEFT THE ANDES A COUPLE OF WEEKS AGO--AND CAME HERE TO GOTHAM CITY--INCOGNITO, OF COURSE--AND NO ONE RECOGNIZED HIM!
NOW I GET THE TIE-IN! YOU THINK--
--IF THERE IS A MILITARY MASTER-MIND AT WORK IN THE UNDER-WORLD HERE--IT COULD BE VON DORT! I DON'T KNOW WHAT HIS GAME IS...
...LINKING HIMSELF UP WITH GOTHAM'S CRIMINALS! BUT WHATEVER HE'S UP TO, WE'VE GOT TO FIND HIM AND STOP HIM!
IT'S A TERRIFIC CHALLENGE --FOR THE THREE OF US!
QUICKLY, PLANS ARE LAID AND A COURSE OF ACTION AGREED UPON IN THE EMERGENCY...
THEN YOU'LL CONTINUE YOUR SPADEWORK AS THE ELONGATED MAN--TRYING TO LEARN ALL YOU CAN ABOUT VON DORT! WHILE ROBIN AND I WILL TRY TO PICK UP HIS TRAIL IN THE UNDERWORLD!
RIGHT! GOOD HUNTING!
9

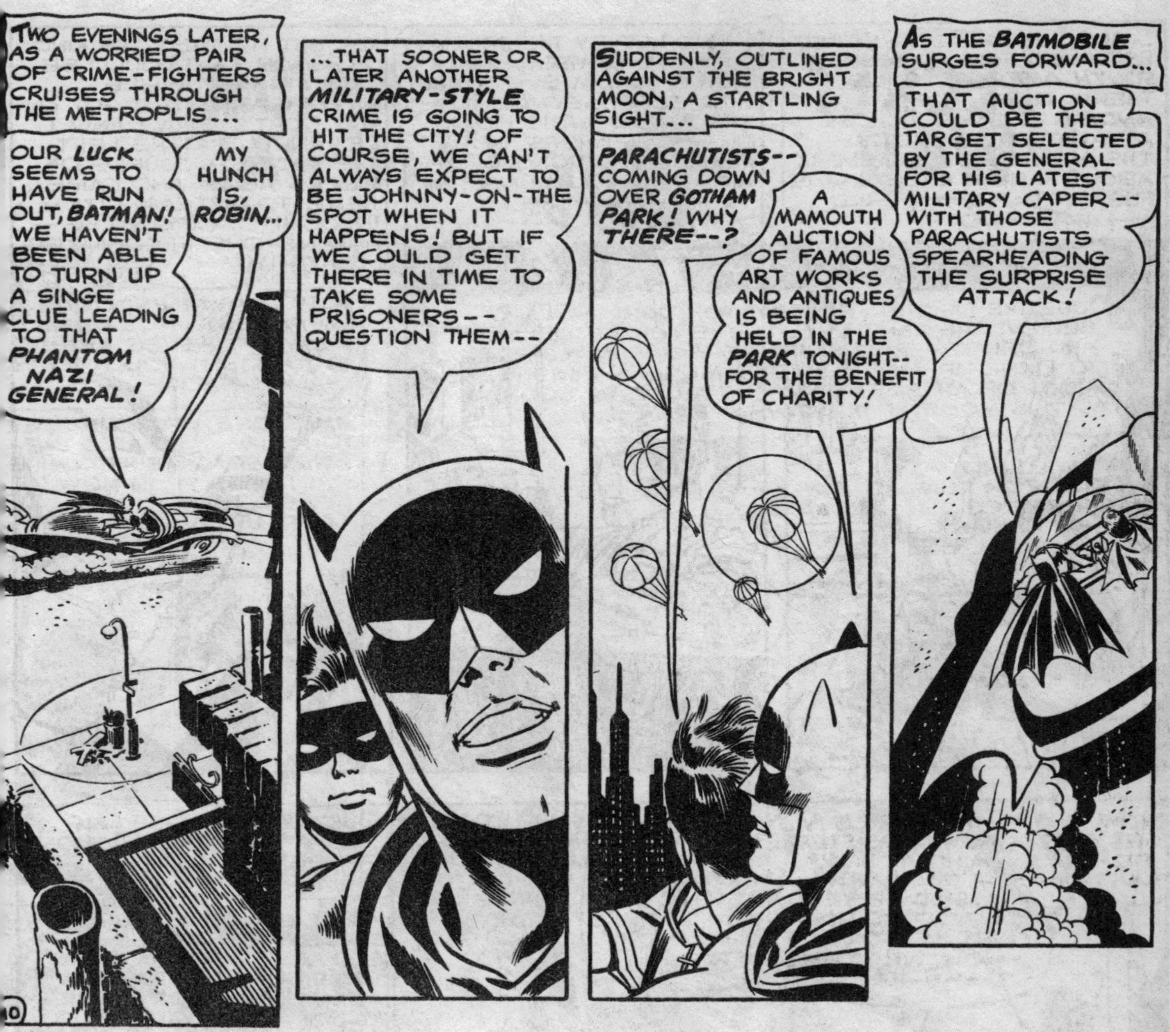
TWO EVENINGS LATER, AS A WORRIED PAIR OF CRIME-FIGHTERS CRUISES THROUGH THE METROPLIS...
OUR LUCK SEEMS TO HAVE RUN OUT, BATMAN! WE HAVEN'T BEEN ABLE TO TURN UP A SINGE CLUE LEADING TO THAT PHANTOM NAZI GENERAL!
MY HUNCH IS, ROBIN...
...THAT SOONER OR LATER ANOTHER MILITARY-STYLE CRIME IS GOING TO HIT THE CITY! OF COURSE, WE CAN'T ALWAYS EXPECT TO BE JOHNNY-ON-THE SPOT WHEN IT HAPPENS! BUT IF WE COULD GET THERE IN TIME TO TAKE SOME PRISONERS-- QUESTION THEM--
SUDDENLY, OUTLINED AGAINST THE BRIGHT MOON, A STARTLING SIGHT...
PARACHUTISTS-- COMING DOWN OVER GOTHAM PARK! WHY THERE--?
A MAMOUTH AUCTION OF FAMOUS ART WORKS AND ANTIQUES IS BEING HELD IN THE PARK TONIGHT-- FOR THE BENEFIT OF CHARITY!
AS THE BATMOBILE SURGES FORWARD...
THAT AUCTION COULD BE THE TARGET SELECTED BY THE GENERAL FOR HIS LATEST MILITARY CAPER-- WITH THOSE PARACHUTISTS SPEARHEADING THE SURPRISE ATTACK!

BATMAN

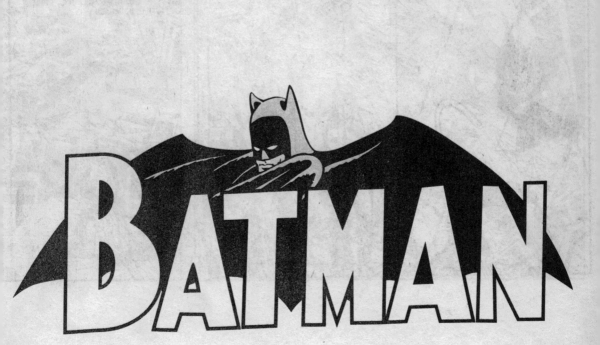

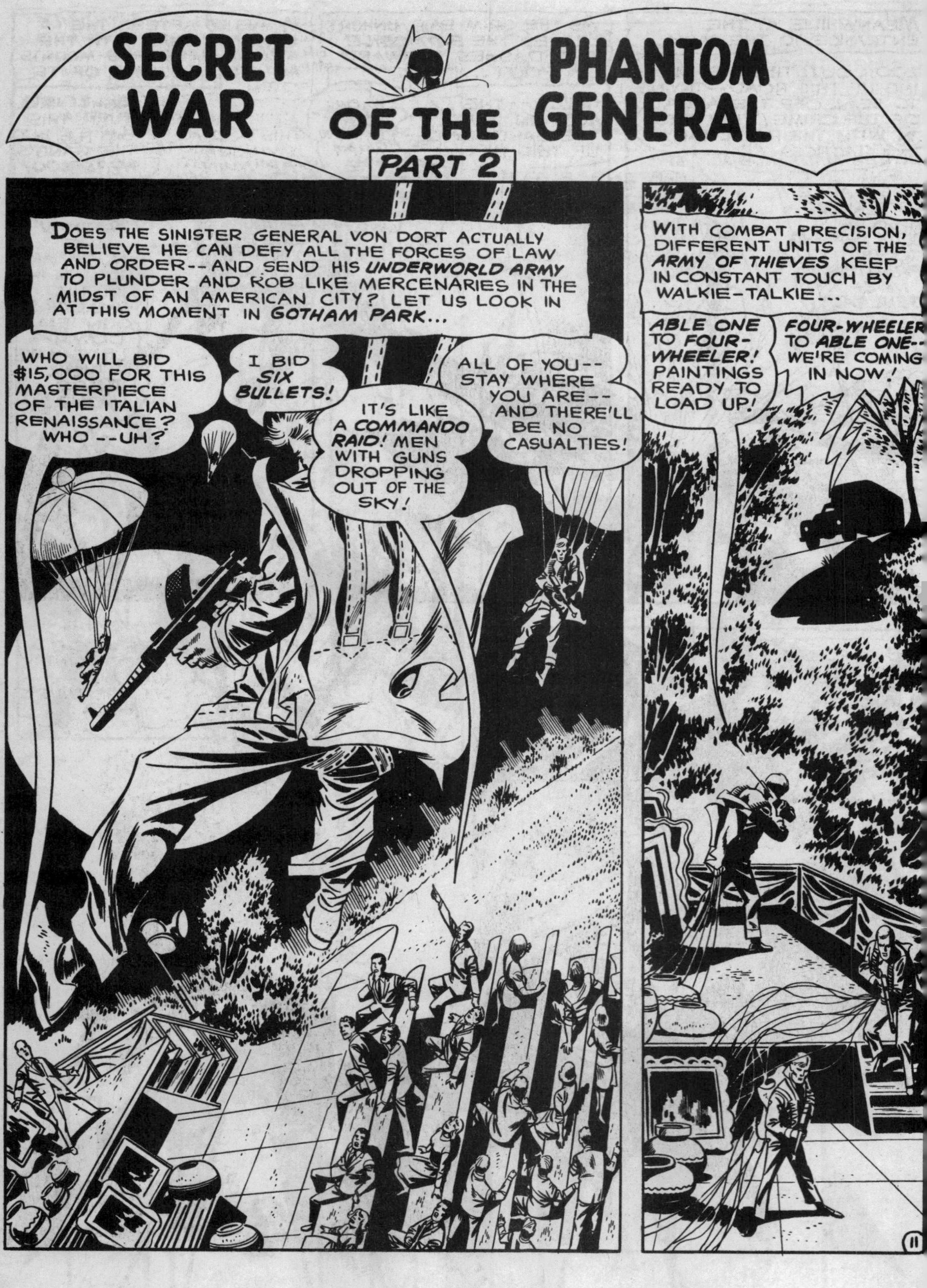
SECRET WAR OF THE PHANTOM GENERAL
PART 2
DOES THE SINISTER GENERAL VON DORT ACTUALLY BELIEVE HE CAN DEFY ALL THE FORCES OF LAW AND ORDER--AND SEND HIS UNDERWORLD ARMY TO PLUNDER AND ROB LIKE MERCENARIES IN THE MIDST OF AN AMERICAN CITY? LET US LOOK IN AT THIS MOMENT IN GOTHAM PARK...
WHO WILL BID $15,000 FOR THIS MASTERPIECE OF THE ITALIAN RENAISSANCE? WHO--UH?
I BID SIX BULLETS!
IT'S LIKE A COMMANDO RAID! MEN WITH GUNS DROPPING OUT OF THE SKY!
ALL OF YOU--STAY WHERE YOU ARE--AND THERE'LL BE NO CASUALTIES!
WITH COMBAT PRECISION, DIFFERENT UNITS OF THE ARMY OF THIEVES KEEP IN CONSTANT TOUCH BY WALKIE-TALKIE...
ABLE ONE TO FOUR-WHEELER! PAINTINGS READY TO LOAD UP!
FOUR-WHEELER TO ABLE ONE--WE'RE COMING IN NOW!
11

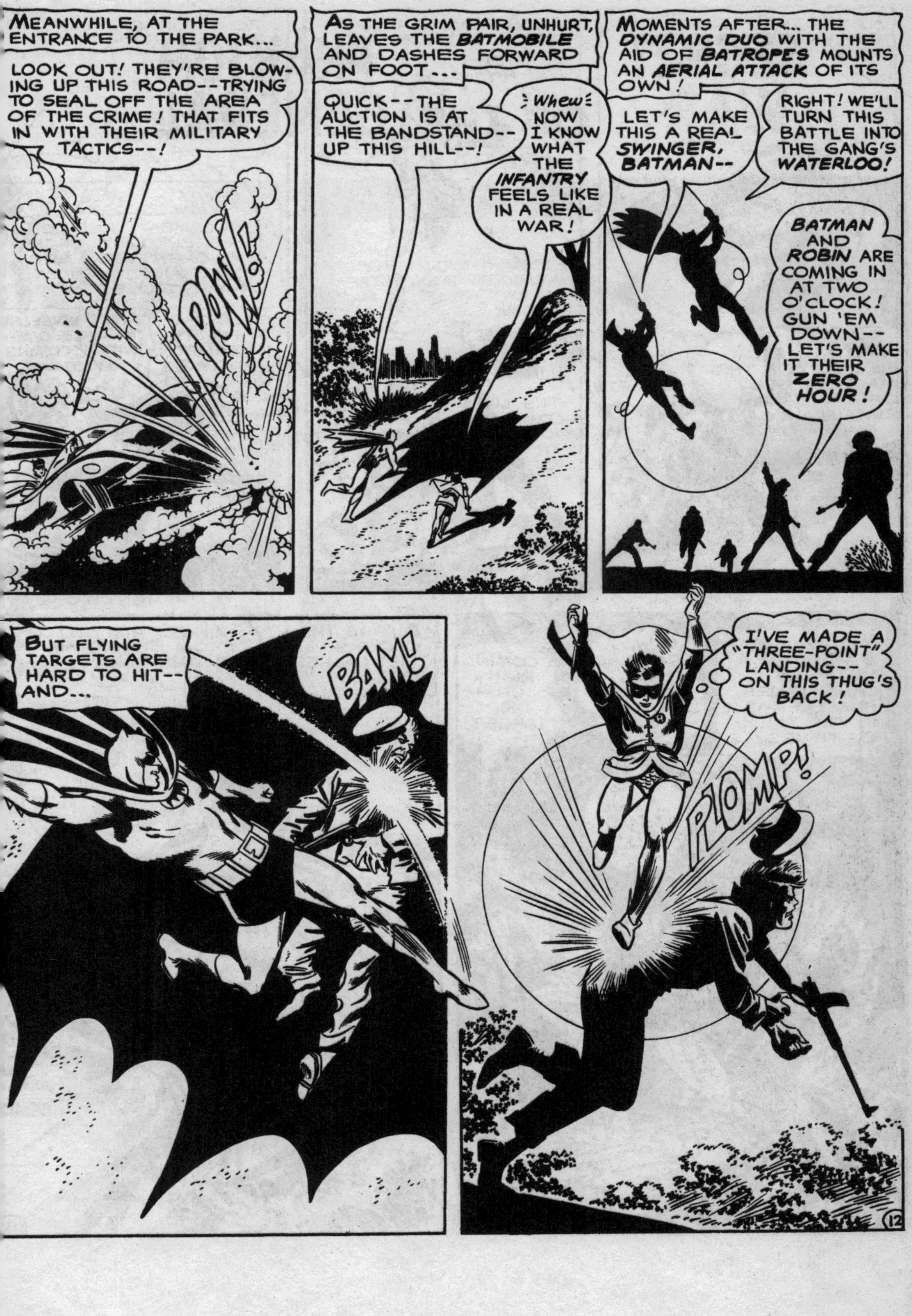
MEANWHILE, AT THE ENTRANCE TO THE PARK...
LOOK OUT! THEY'RE BLOWING UP THIS ROAD--TRYING TO SEAL OFF THE AREA OF THE CRIME! THAT FITS IN WITH THEIR MILITARY TACTICS--!
POW!
AS THE GRIM PAIR, UNHURT, LEAVES THE BATMOBILE AND DASHES FORWARD ON FOOT...
QUICK--THE AUCTION IS AT THE BANDSTAND--UP THIS HILL--!
Whew NOW I KNOW WHAT THE INFANTRY FEELS LIKE IN A REAL WAR!
MOMENTS AFTER... THE DYNAMIC DUO WITH THE AID OF BATROPES MOUNTS AN AERIAL ATTACK OF ITS OWN!
LET'S MAKE THIS A REAL SWINGER, BATMAN--
RIGHT! WE'LL TURN THIS BATTLE INTO THE GANG'S WATERLOO!
BATMAN AND ROBIN ARE COMING IN AT TWO O'CLOCK! GUN 'EM DOWN--LET'S MAKE IT THEIR ZERO HOUR!
BUT FLYING TARGETS ARE HARD TO HIT--AND...
BAM!
I'VE MADE A "THREE-POINT" LANDING--ON THIS THUG'S BACK!
PLOMP!
12

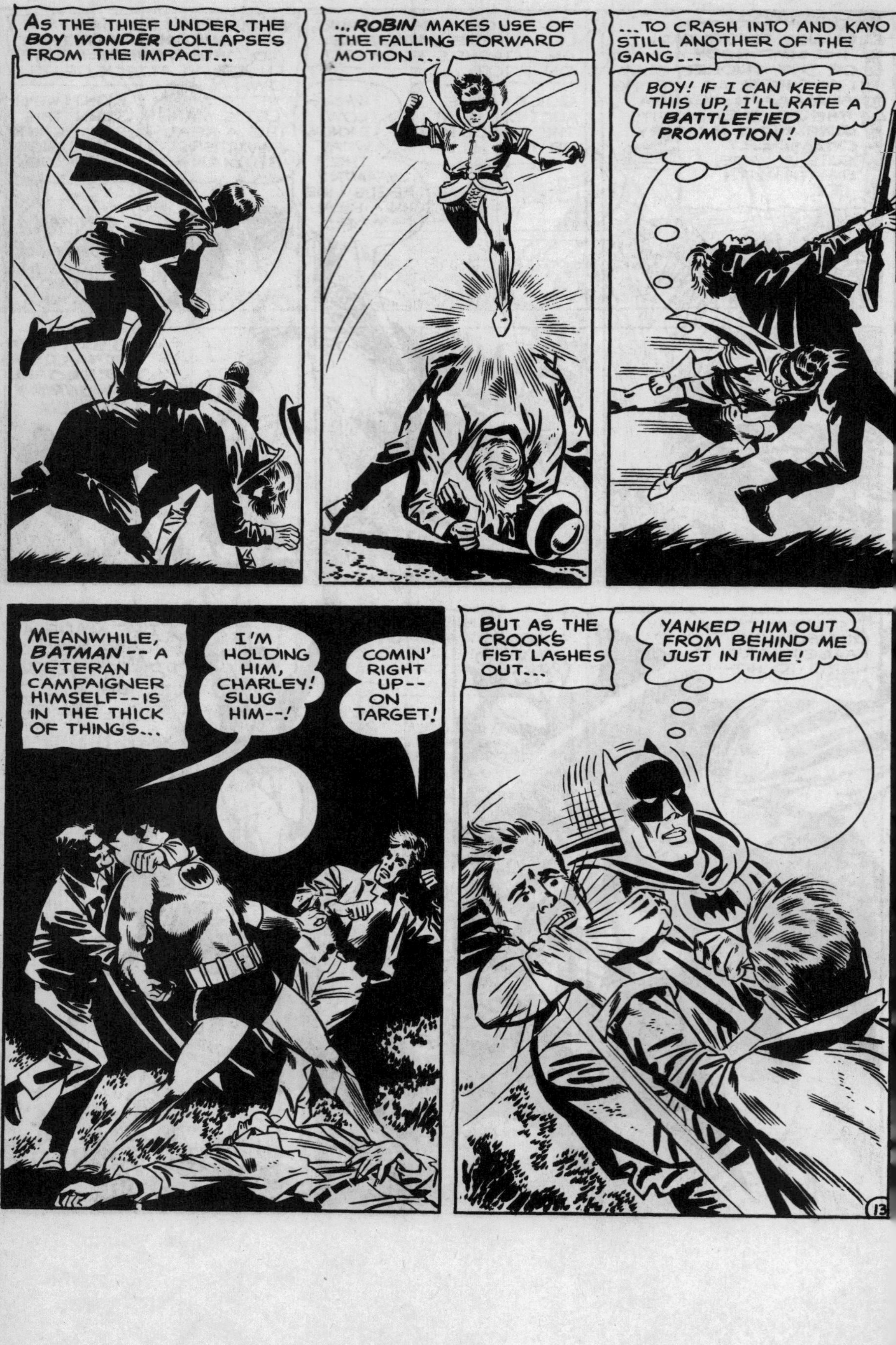
AS THE THIEF UNDER THE BOY WONDER COLLAPSES FROM THE IMPACT...
...ROBIN MAKES USE OF THE FALLING FORWARD MOTION...
...TO CRASH INTO AND KAYO STILL ANOTHER OF THE GANG...
BOY! IF I CAN KEEP THIS UP, I'LL RATE A BATTLEFIED PROMOTION!
MEANWHILE, BATMAN--A VETERAN CAMPAIGNER HIMSELF--IS IN THE THICK OF THINGS...
I'M HOLDING HIM, CHARLEY! SLUG HIM--!
COMIN' RIGHT UP--ON TARGET!
BUT AS THE CROOK'S FIST LASHES OUT...
YANKED HIM OUT FROM BEHIND ME JUST IN TIME!
13

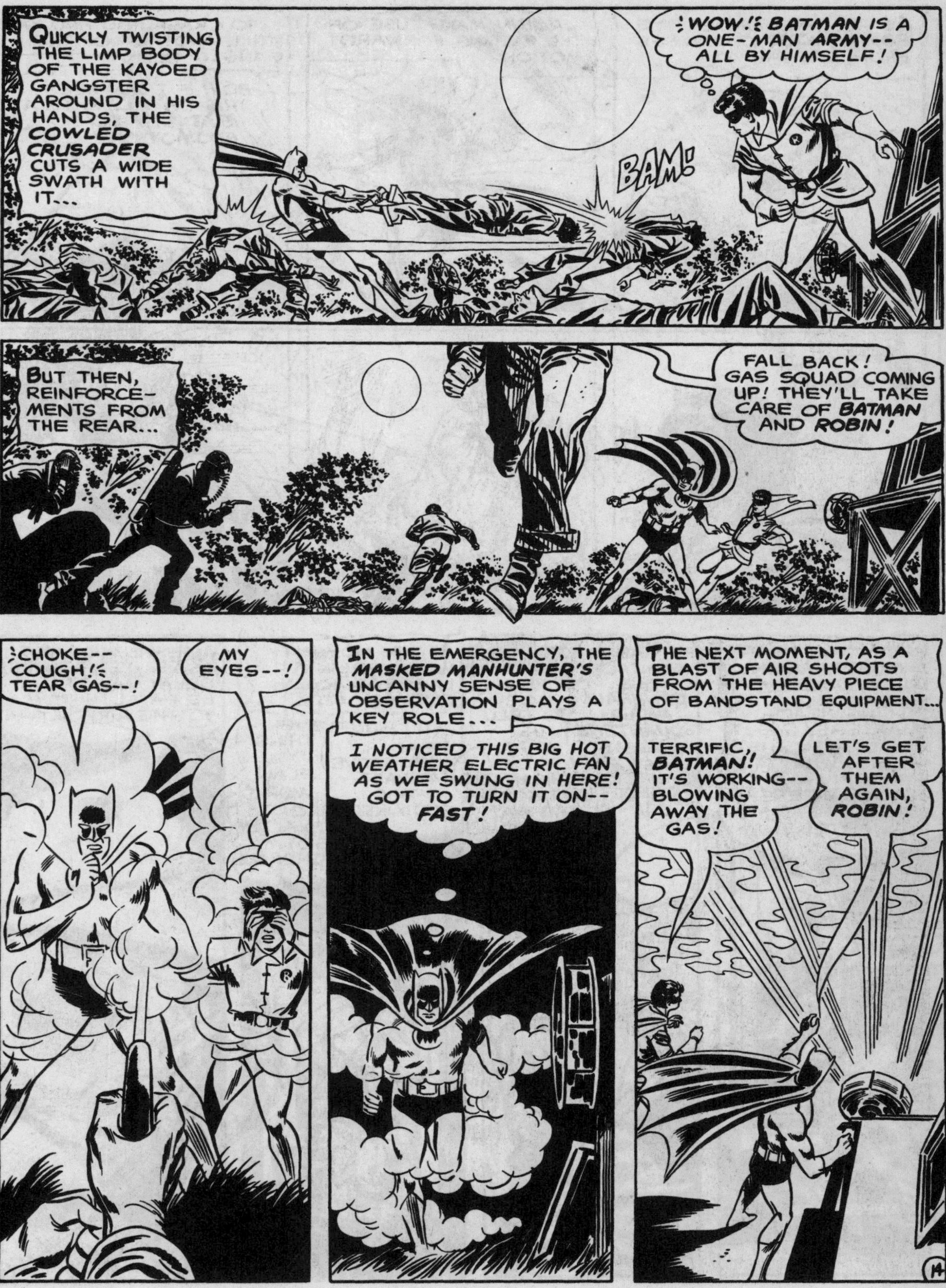
QUICKLY TWISTING THE LIMP BODY OF THE KAYOED GANGSTER AROUND IN HIS HANDS, THE COWLED CRUSADER CUTS A WIDE SWATH WITH IT...
WOW! BATMAN IS A ONE-MAN ARMY-- ALL BY HIMSELF!
BAM!
BUT THEN, REINFORCE-MENTS FROM THE REAR...
FALL BACK! GAS SQUAD COMING UP! THEY'LL TAKE CARE OF BATMAN AND ROBIN!
CHOKE-- COUGH! TEAR GAS--!
MY EYES--!
IN THE EMERGENCY, THE MASKED MANHUNTER'S UNCANNY SENSE OF OBSERVATION PLAYS A KEY ROLE...
I NOTICED THIS BIG HOT WEATHER ELECTRIC FAN AS WE SWUNG IN HERE! GOT TO TURN IT ON-- FAST!
THE NEXT MOMENT, AS A BLAST OF AIR SHOOTS FROM THE HEAVY PIECE OF BANDSTAND EQUIPMENT...
TERRIFIC, BATMAN! IT'S WORKING-- BLOWING AWAY THE GAS!
LET'S GET AFTER THEM AGAIN, ROBIN!
14

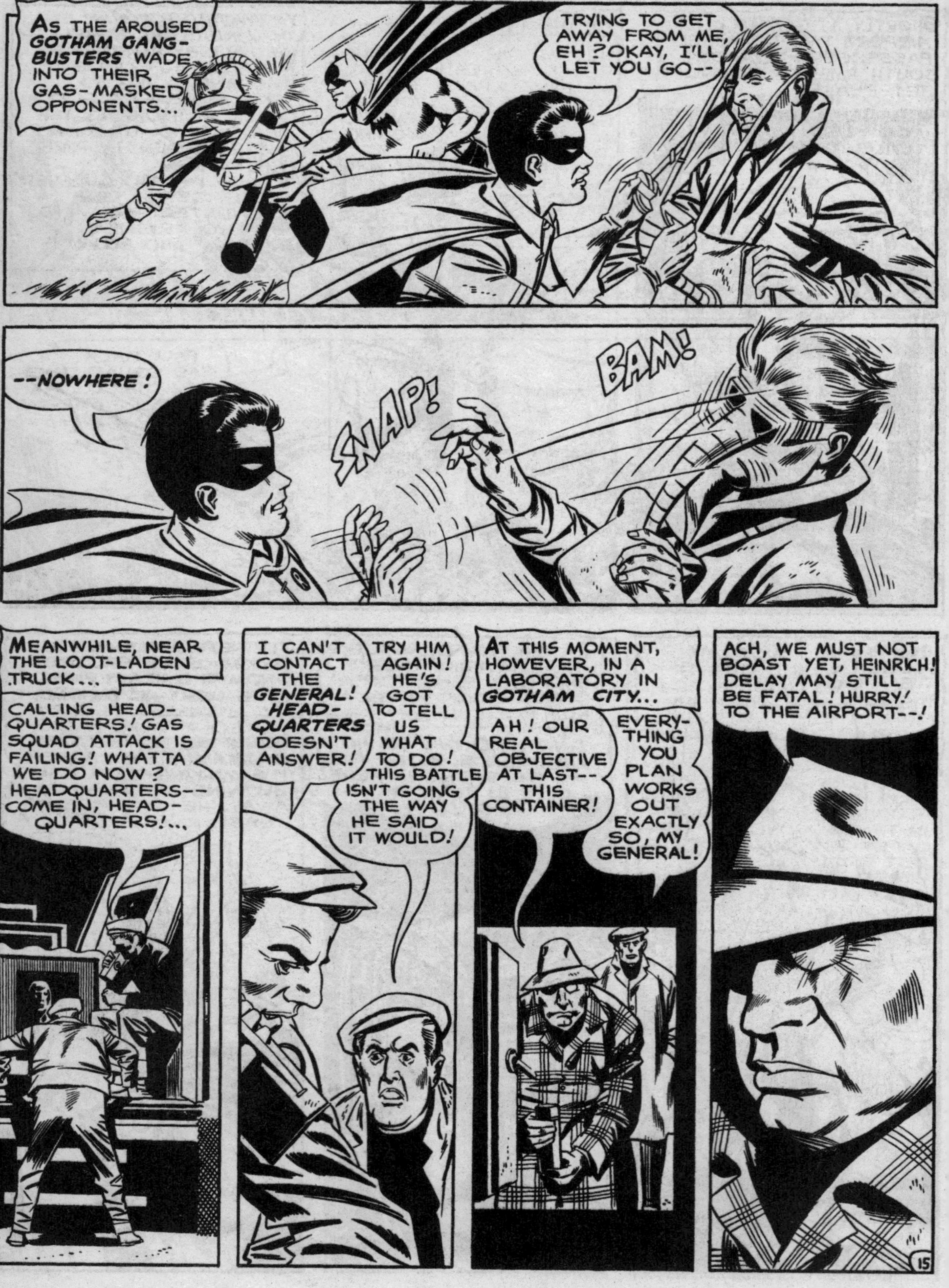
AS THE AROUSED GOTHAM GANG-BUSTERS WADE INTO THEIR GAS-MASKED OPPONENTS...
TRYING TO GET AWAY FROM ME, EH ? OKAY, I'LL LET YOU GO--
--NOWHERE !
SNAP!
BAM!
MEANWHILE, NEAR THE LOOT-LADEN TRUCK...
CALLING HEAD-QUARTERS! GAS SQUAD ATTACK IS FAILING! WHATTA WE DO NOW ? HEADQUARTERS--COME IN, HEAD-QUARTERS!...
I CAN'T CONTACT THE GENERAL! HEAD-QUARTERS DOESN'T ANSWER!
TRY HIM AGAIN! HE'S GOT TO TELL US WHAT TO DO! THIS BATTLE ISN'T GOING THE WAY HE SAID IT WOULD!
AT THIS MOMENT, HOWEVER, IN A LABORATORY IN GOTHAM CITY...
AH! OUR REAL OBJECTIVE AT LAST-- THIS CONTAINER!
EVERY-THING YOU PLAN WORKS OUT EXACTLY SO, MY GENERAL!
ACH, WE MUST NOT BOAST YET, HEINRICH! DELAY MAY STILL BE FATAL! HURRY! TO THE AIRPORT--!
15

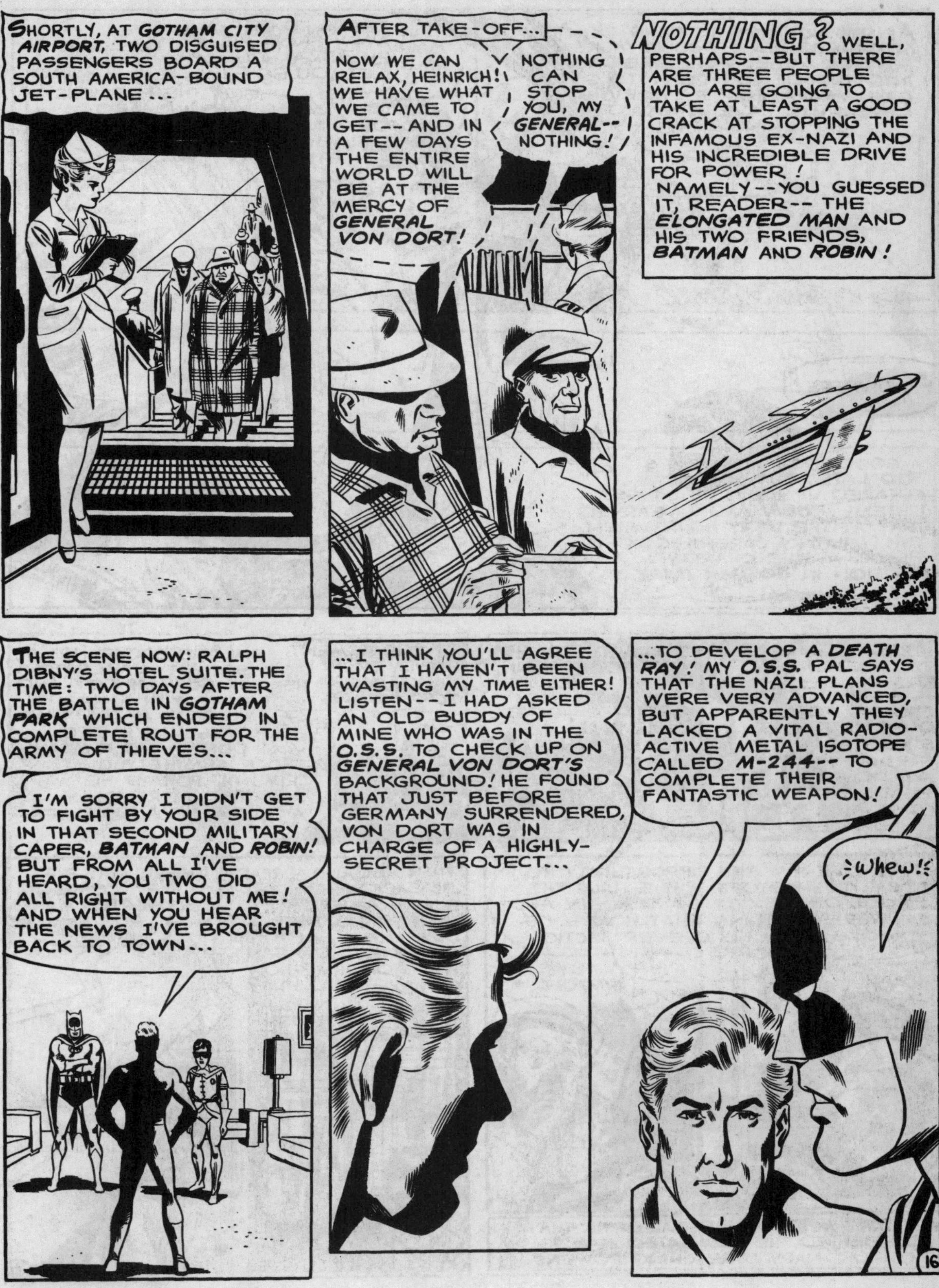
SHORTLY, AT GOTHAM CITY AIRPORT, TWO DISGUISED PASSENGERS BOARD A SOUTH AMERICA-BOUND JET-PLANE ...
AFTER TAKE-OFF...
NOW WE CAN RELAX, HEINRICH! WE HAVE WHAT WE CAME TO GET-- AND IN A FEW DAYS THE ENTIRE WORLD WILL BE AT THE MERCY OF GENERAL VON DORT!
NOTHING CAN STOP YOU, MY GENERAL-- NOTHING!
NOTHING? WELL, PERHAPS--BUT THERE ARE THREE PEOPLE WHO ARE GOING TO TAKE AT LEAST A GOOD CRACK AT STOPPING THE INFAMOUS EX-NAZI AND HIS INCREDIBLE DRIVE FOR POWER! NAMELY--YOU GUESSED IT, READER-- THE ELONGATED MAN AND HIS TWO FRIENDS, BATMAN AND ROBIN!
THE SCENE NOW: RALPH DIBNY'S HOTEL SUITE. THE TIME: TWO DAYS AFTER THE BATTLE IN GOTHAM PARK WHICH ENDED IN COMPLETE ROUT FOR THE ARMY OF THIEVES...
I'M SORRY I DIDN'T GET TO FIGHT BY YOUR SIDE IN THAT SECOND MILITARY CAPER, BATMAN AND ROBIN! BUT FROM ALL I'VE HEARD, YOU TWO DID ALL RIGHT WITHOUT ME! AND WHEN YOU HEAR THE NEWS I'VE BROUGHT BACK TO TOWN...
...I THINK YOU'LL AGREE THAT I HAVEN'T BEEN WASTING MY TIME EITHER! LISTEN--I HAD ASKED AN OLD BUDDY OF MINE WHO WAS IN THE O.S.S. TO CHECK UP ON GENERAL VON DORT'S BACKGROUND! HE FOUND THAT JUST BEFORE GERMANY SURRENDERED, VON DORT WAS IN CHARGE OF A HIGHLY-SECRET PROJECT...
...TO DEVELOP A DEATH RAY! MY O.S.S. PAL SAYS THAT THE NAZI PLANS WERE VERY ADVANCED, BUT APPARENTLY THEY LACKED A VITAL RADIO-ACTIVE METAL ISOTOPE CALLED M-244-- TO COMPLETE THEIR FANTASTIC WEAPON!
Whew!
16

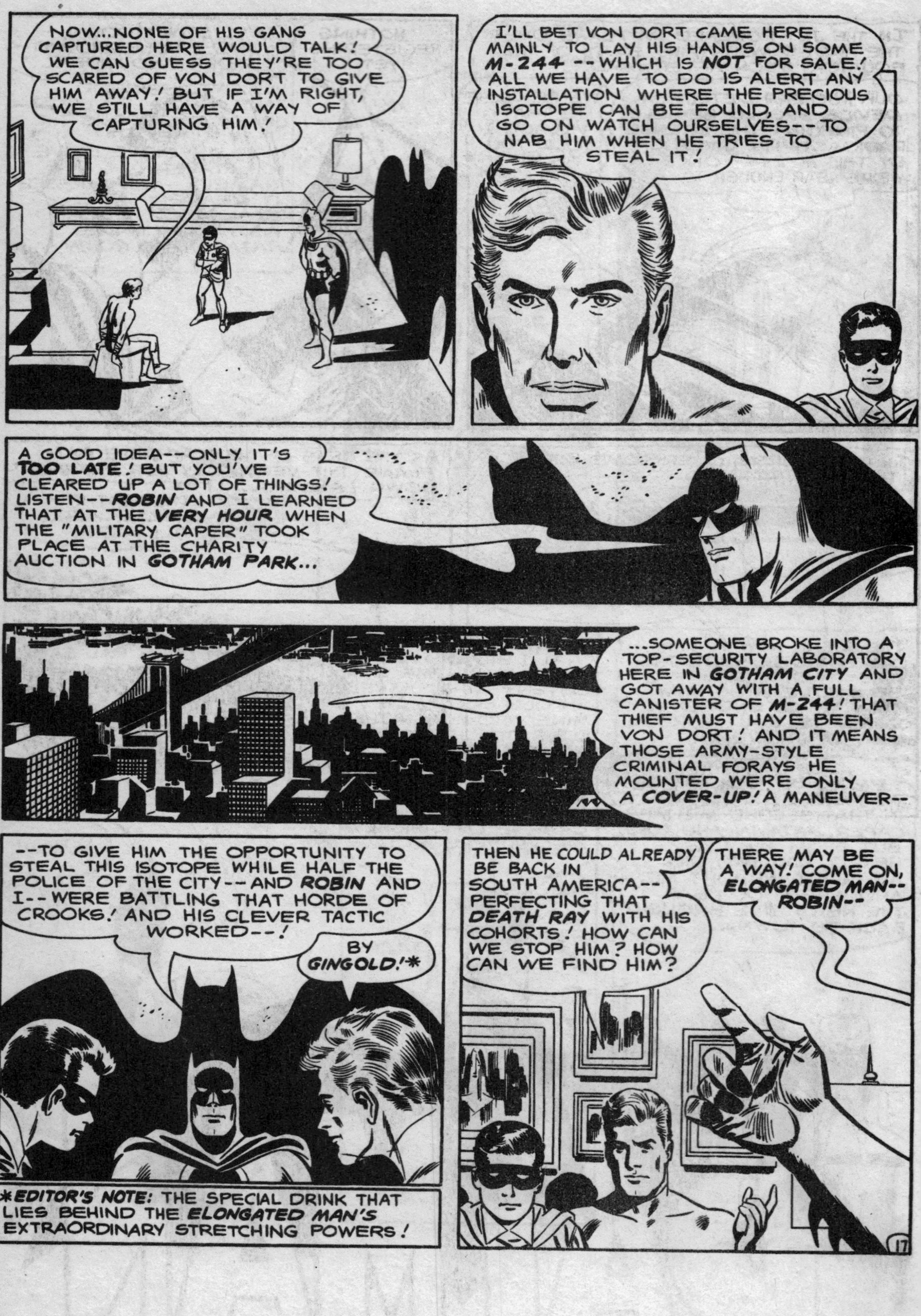
NOW...NONE OF HIS GANG CAPTURED HERE WOULD TALK! WE CAN GUESS THEY'RE TOO SCARED OF VON DORT TO GIVE HIM AWAY! BUT IF I'M RIGHT, WE STILL HAVE A WAY OF CAPTURING HIM!
I'LL BET VON DORT CAME HERE MAINLY TO LAY HIS HANDS ON SOME M-244 --WHICH IS NOT FOR SALE! ALL WE HAVE TO DO IS ALERT ANY INSTALLATION WHERE THE PRECIOUS ISOTOPE CAN BE FOUND, AND GO ON WATCH OURSELVES--TO NAB HIM WHEN HE TRIES TO STEAL IT!
A GOOD IDEA--ONLY IT'S TOO LATE! BUT YOU'VE CLEARED UP A LOT OF THINGS! LISTEN--ROBIN AND I LEARNED THAT AT THE VERY HOUR WHEN THE "MILITARY CAPER" TOOK PLACE AT THE CHARITY AUCTION IN GOTHAM PARK...
...SOMEONE BROKE INTO A TOP-SECURITY LABORATORY HERE IN GOTHAM CITY AND GOT AWAY WITH A FULL CANISTER OF M-244! THAT THIEF MUST HAVE BEEN VON DORT! AND IT MEANS THOSE ARMY-STYLE CRIMINAL FORAYS HE MOUNTED WERE ONLY A COVER-UP! A MANEUVER--
--TO GIVE HIM THE OPPORTUNITY TO STEAL THIS ISOTOPE WHILE HALF THE POLICE OF THE CITY--AND ROBIN AND I--WERE BATTLING THAT HORDE OF CROOKS! AND HIS CLEVER TACTIC WORKED--!
BY GINGOLD!*
*EDITOR'S NOTE: THE SPECIAL DRINK THAT LIES BEHIND THE ELONGATED MAN'S EXTRAORDINARY STRETCHING POWERS!
THEN HE COULD ALREADY BE BACK IN SOUTH AMERICA--PERFECTING THAT DEATH RAY WITH HIS COHORTS! HOW CAN WE STOP HIM? HOW CAN WE FIND HIM?
THERE MAY BE A WAY! COME ON, ELONGATED MAN--ROBIN--
17

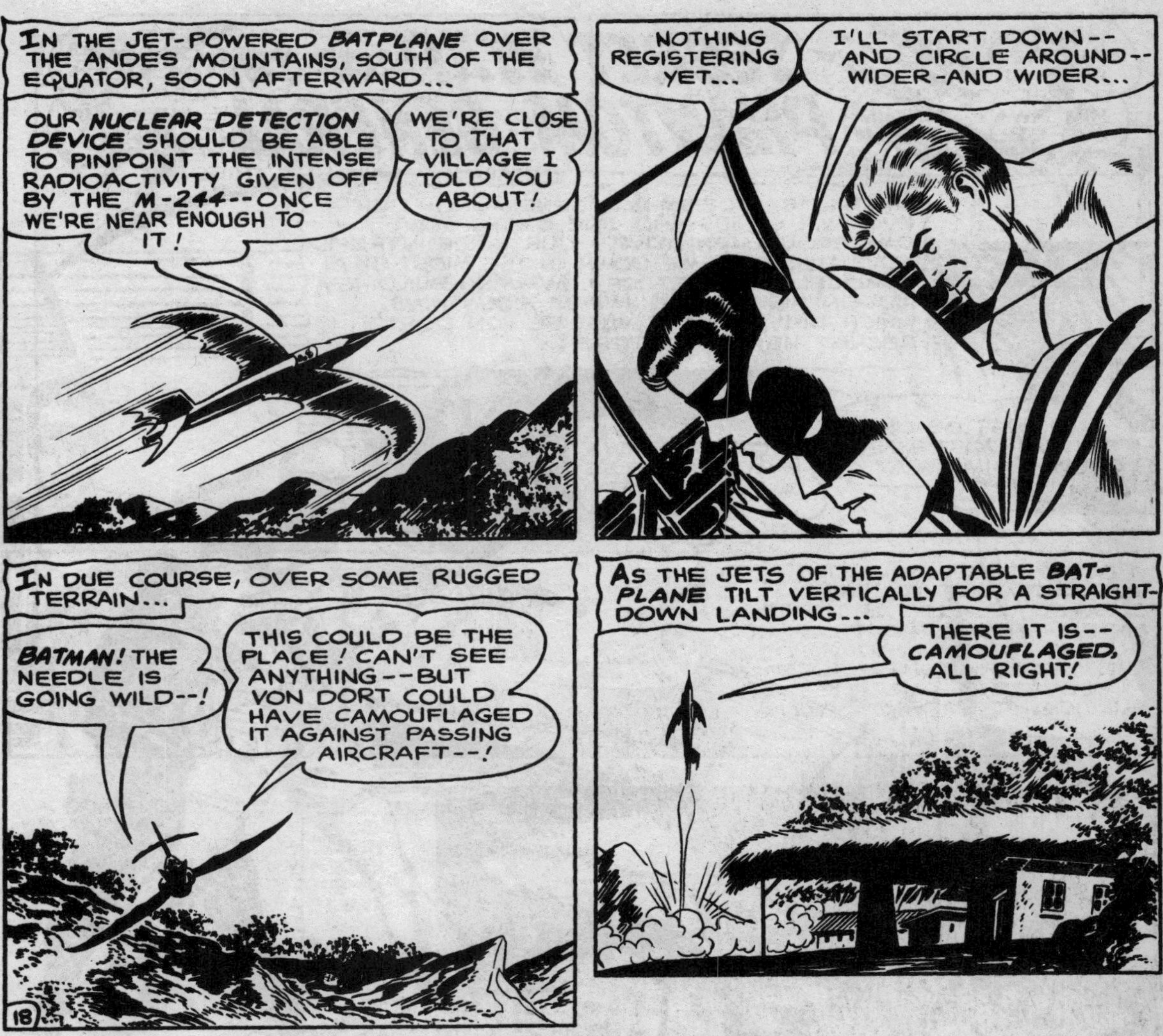
IN THE JET-POWERED BATPLANE OVER THE ANDES MOUNTAINS, SOUTH OF THE EQUATOR, SOON AFTERWARD...
OUR NUCLEAR DETECTION DEVICE SHOULD BE ABLE TO PINPOINT THE INTENSE RADIOACTIVITY GIVEN OFF BY THE M-244--ONCE WE'RE NEAR ENOUGH TO IT!
WE'RE CLOSE TO THAT VILLAGE I TOLD YOU ABOUT!
NOTHING REGISTERING YET...
I'LL START DOWN--AND CIRCLE AROUND--WIDER-AND WIDER...
IN DUE COURSE, OVER SOME RUGGED TERRAIN...
BATMAN! THE NEEDLE IS GOING WILD--!
THIS COULD BE THE PLACE! CAN'T SEE ANYTHING--BUT VON DORT COULD HAVE CAMOUFLAGED IT AGAINST PASSING AIRCRAFT--!
18
AS THE JETS OF THE ADAPTABLE BAT-PLANE TILT VERTICALLY FOR A STRAIGHT-DOWN LANDING...
THERE IT IS--CAMOUFLAGED, ALL RIGHT!

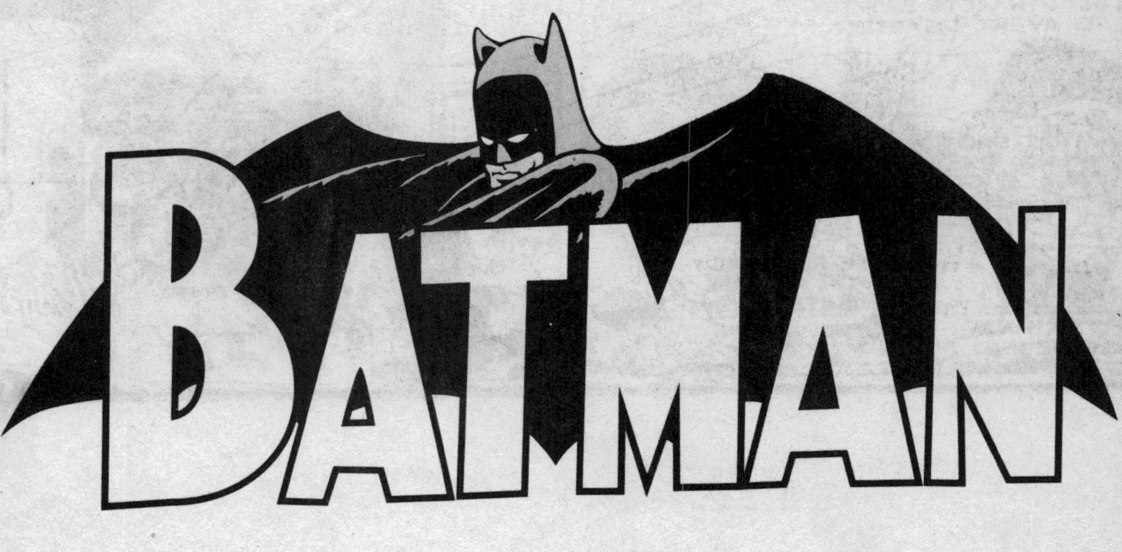
BATMAN

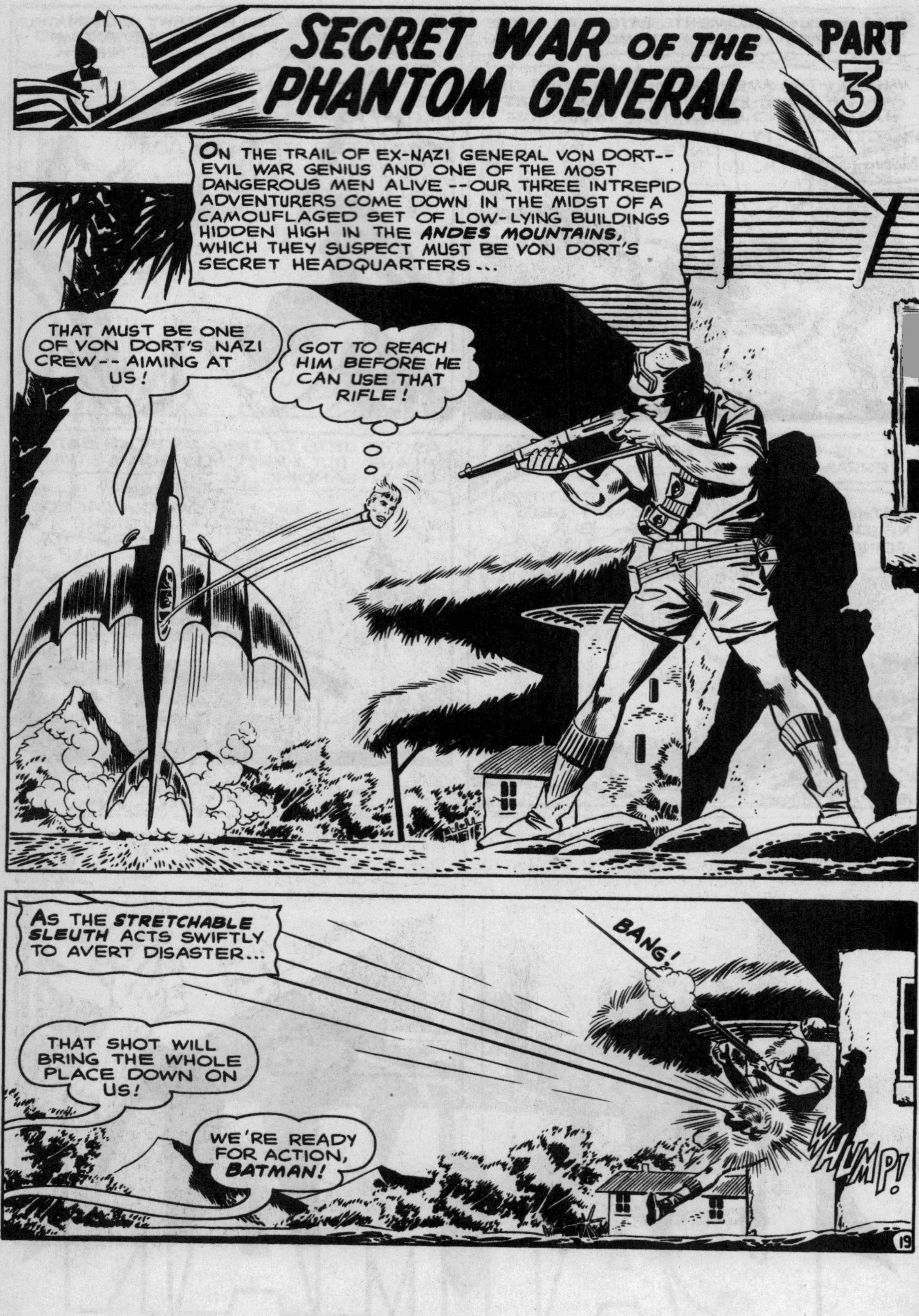
SECRET WAR OF THE PHANTOM GENERAL
PART 3
ON THE TRAIL OF EX-NAZI GENERAL VON DORT-- EVIL WAR GENIUS AND ONE OF THE MOST DANGEROUS MEN ALIVE --OUR THREE INTREPID ADVENTURERS COME DOWN IN THE MIDST OF A CAMOUFLAGED SET OF LOW-LYING BUILDINGS HIDDEN HIGH IN THE ANDES MOUNTAINS, WHICH THEY SUSPECT MUST BE VON DORT'S SECRET HEADQUARTERS...
THAT MUST BE ONE OF VON DORT'S NAZI CREW-- AIMING AT US!
GOT TO REACH HIM BEFORE HE CAN USE THAT RIFLE!
AS THE STRETCHABLE SLEUTH ACTS SWIFTLY TO AVERT DISASTER...
BANG!
THAT SHOT WILL BRING THE WHOLE PLACE DOWN ON US!
WE'RE READY FOR ACTION, BATMAN!
WHUMP!
19

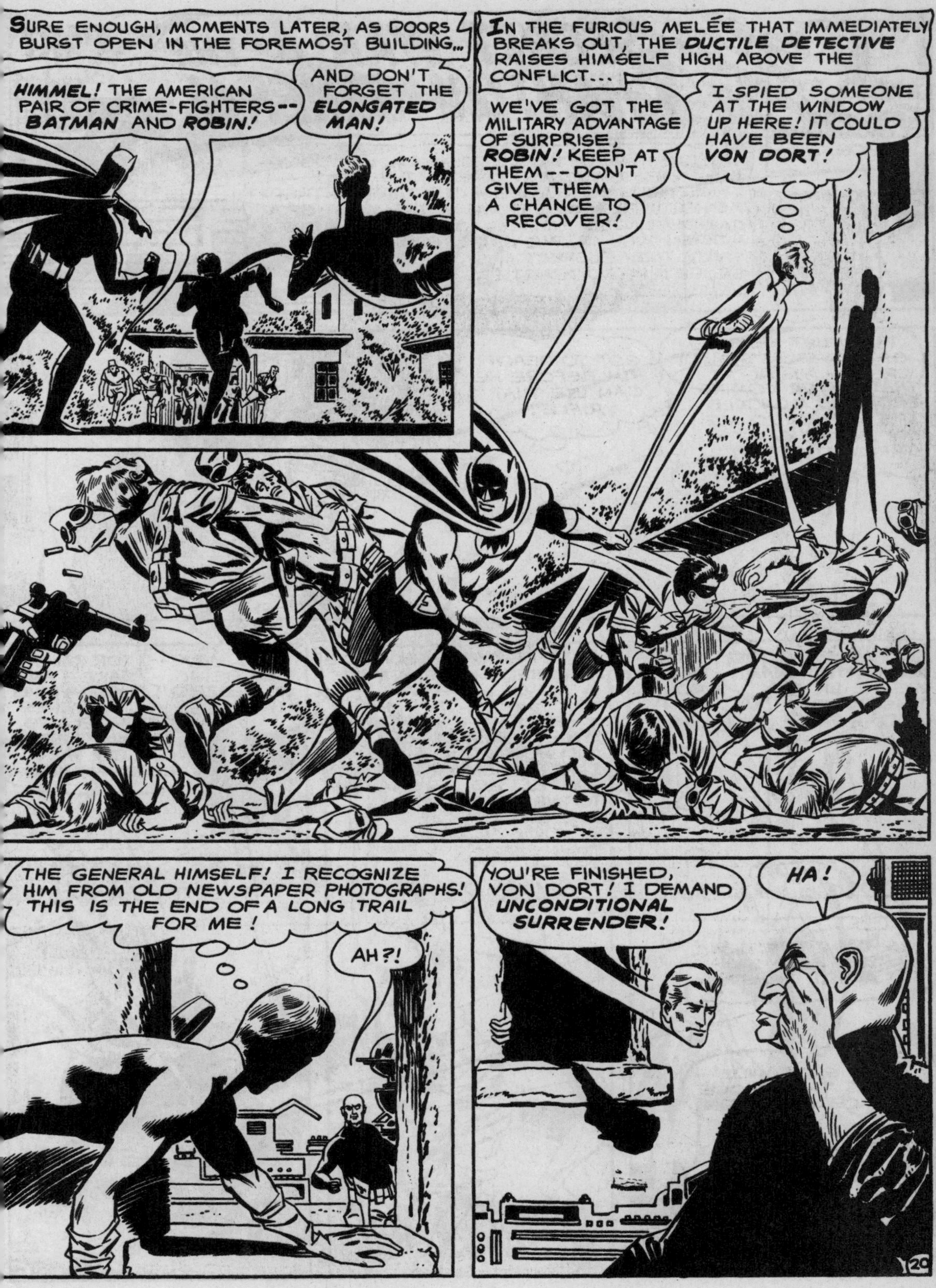
SURE ENOUGH, MOMENTS LATER, AS DOORS BURST OPEN IN THE FOREMOST BUILDING...
HIMMEL! THE AMERICAN PAIR OF CRIME-FIGHTERS-- BATMAN AND ROBIN!
AND DON'T FORGET THE ELONGATED MAN!
IN THE FURIOUS MELÉE THAT IMMEDIATELY BREAKS OUT, THE DUCTILE DETECTIVE RAISES HIMSELF HIGH ABOVE THE CONFLICT...
WE'VE GOT THE MILITARY ADVANTAGE OF SURPRISE, ROBIN! KEEP AT THEM -- DON'T GIVE THEM A CHANCE TO RECOVER!
I SPIED SOMEONE AT THE WINDOW UP HERE! IT COULD HAVE BEEN VON DORT!
THE GENERAL HIMSELF! I RECOGNIZE HIM FROM OLD NEWSPAPER PHOTOGRAPHS! THIS IS THE END OF A LONG TRAIL FOR ME!
AH?!
YOU'RE FINISHED, VON DORT! I DEMAND UNCONDITIONAL SURRENDER!
HA!
20

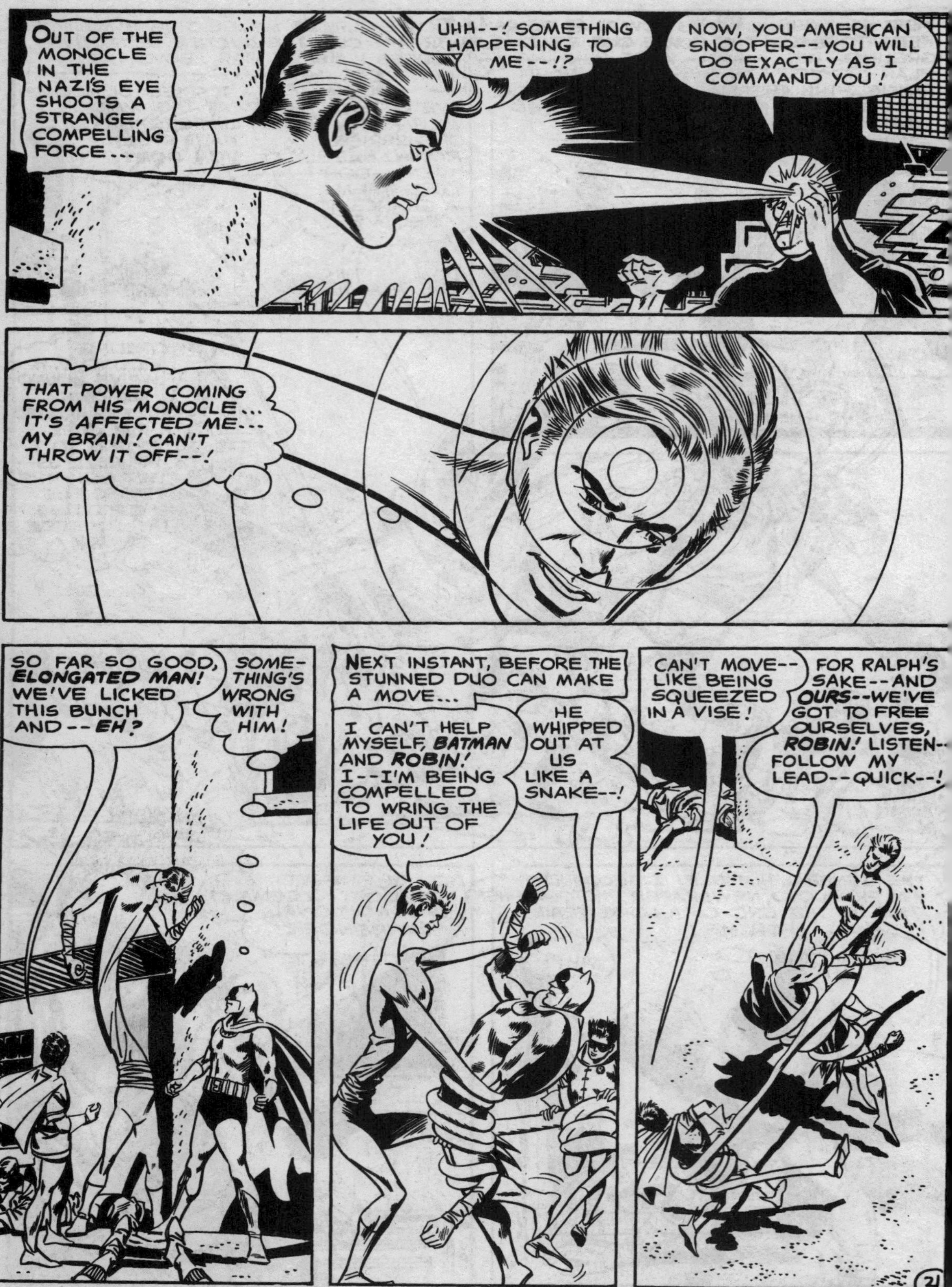
OUT OF THE MONOCLE IN THE NAZI'S EYE SHOOTS A STRANGE, COMPELLING FORCE...
UHH--! SOMETHING HAPPENING TO ME--!?
NOW, YOU AMERICAN SNOOPER--YOU WILL DO EXACTLY AS I COMMAND YOU!
THAT POWER COMING FROM HIS MONOCLE... IT'S AFFECTED ME--- MY BRAIN! CAN'T THROW IT OFF--!
SO FAR SO GOOD, ELONGATED MAN! WE'VE LICKED THIS BUNCH AND--EH?
SOME-THING'S WRONG WITH HIM!
NEXT INSTANT, BEFORE THE STUNNED DUO CAN MAKE A MOVE...
I CAN'T HELP MYSELF, BATMAN AND ROBIN! I--I'M BEING COMPELLED TO WRING THE LIFE OUT OF YOU!
HE WHIPPED OUT AT US LIKE A SNAKE--!
CAN'T MOVE-- LIKE BEING SQUEEZED IN A VISE!
FOR RALPH'S SAKE--AND OURS--WE'VE GOT TO FREE OURSELVES, ROBIN! LISTEN-- FOLLOW MY LEAD--QUICK--!
21

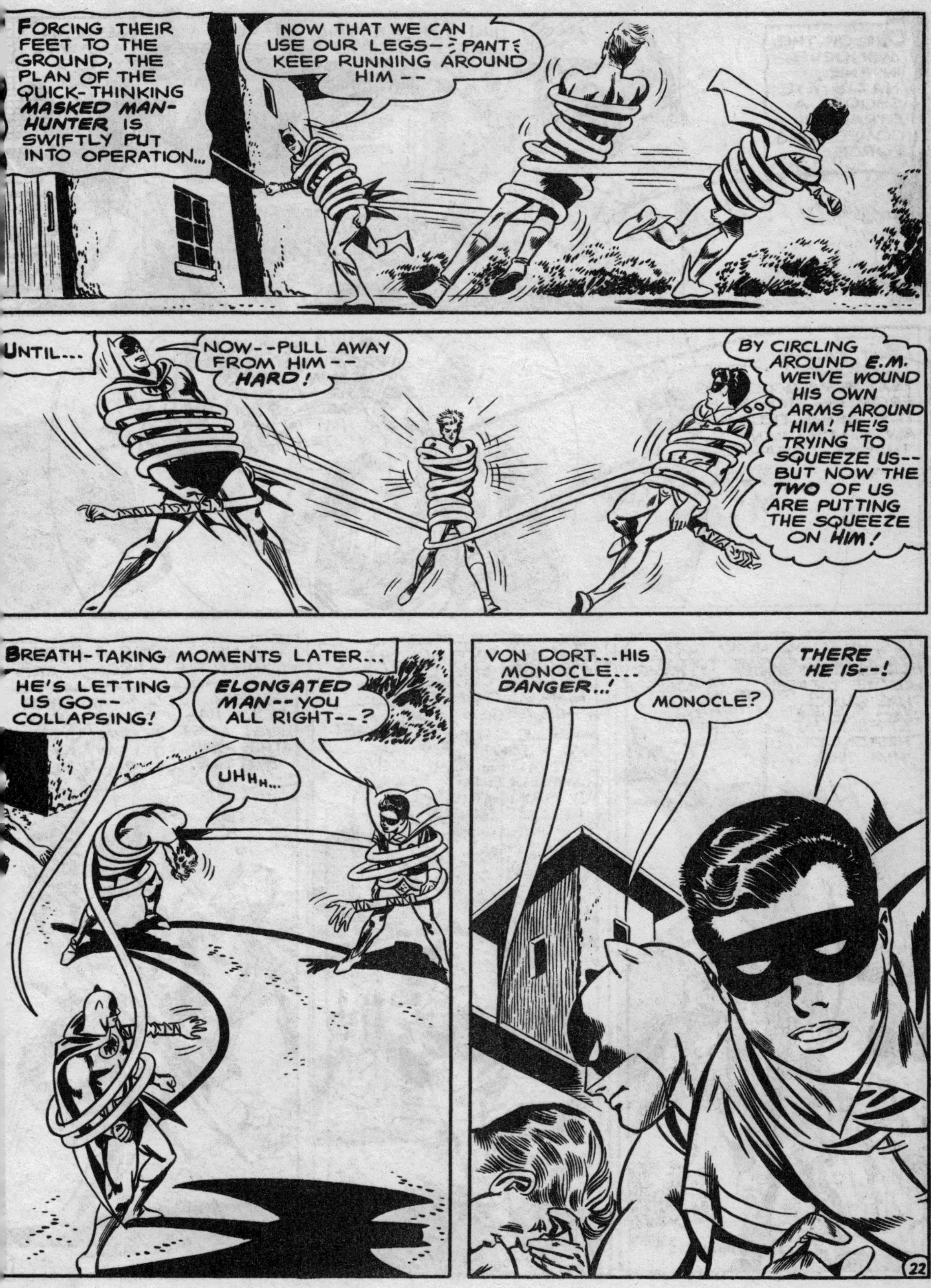
FORCING THEIR FEET TO THE GROUND, THE PLAN OF THE QUICK-THINKING MASKED MAN-HUNTER IS SWIFTLY PUT INTO OPERATION...
NOW THAT WE CAN USE OUR LEGS-- PANT KEEP RUNNING AROUND HIM --
UNTIL...
NOW--PULL AWAY FROM HIM-- HARD!
BY CIRCLING AROUND E.M. WE'VE WOUND HIS OWN ARMS AROUND HIM! HE'S TRYING TO SQUEEZE US-- BUT NOW THE TWO OF US ARE PUTTING THE SQUEEZE ON HIM!
BREATH-TAKING MOMENTS LATER...
HE'S LETTING US GO-- COLLAPSING!
ELONGATED MAN--YOU ALL RIGHT--?
UHHH...
VON DORT...HIS MONOCLE... DANGER...!
MONOCLE?
THERE HE IS--!
22

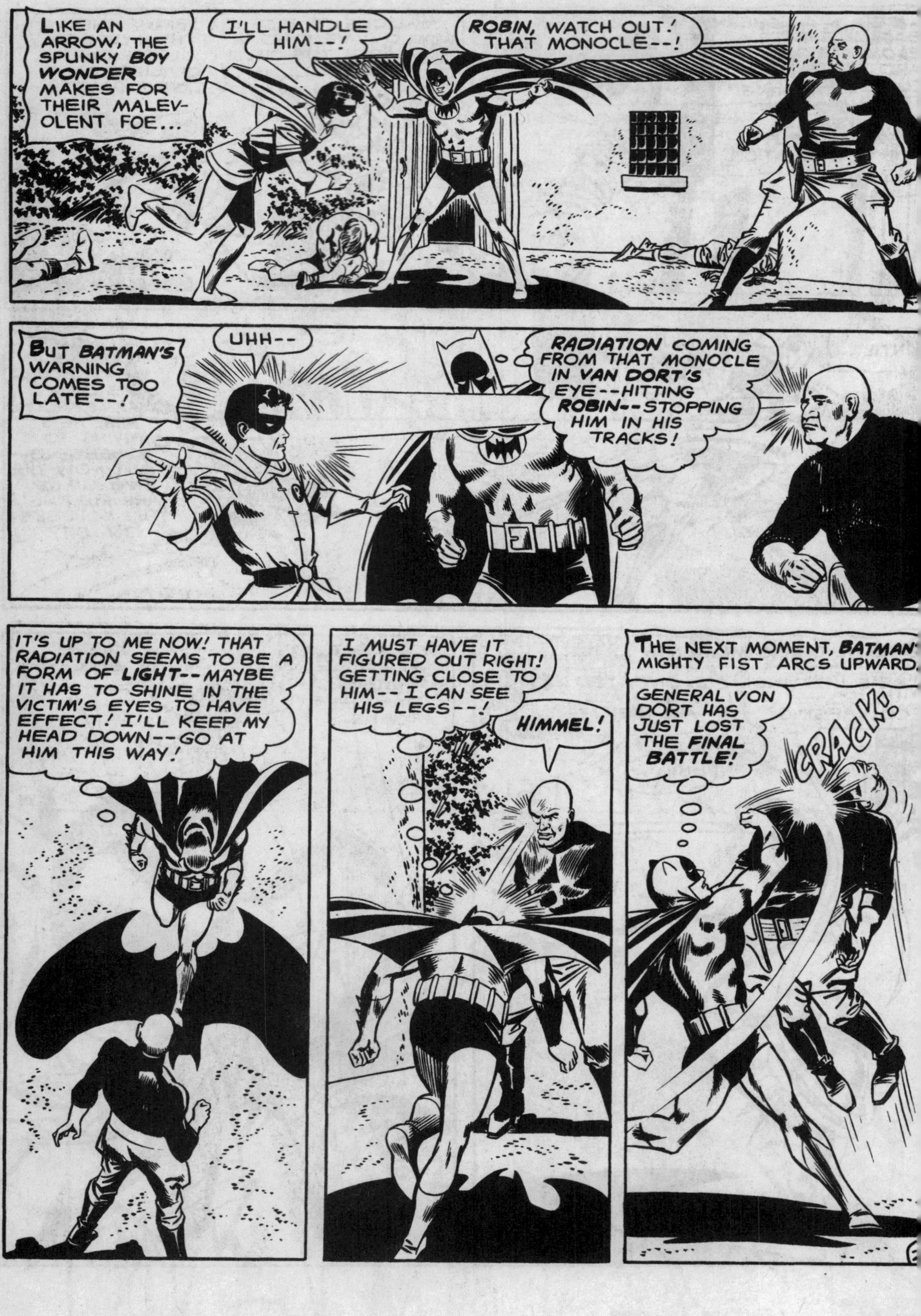
LIKE AN ARROW, THE SPUNKY BOY WONDER MAKES FOR THEIR MALEVOLENT FOE...
I'LL HANDLE HIM--!
ROBIN, WATCH OUT! THAT MONOCLE--!
BUT BATMAN'S WARNING COMES TOO LATE--!
UHH--
RADIATION COMING FROM THAT MONOCLE IN VAN DORT'S EYE--HITTING ROBIN--STOPPING HIM IN HIS TRACKS!
IT'S UP TO ME NOW! THAT RADIATION SEEMS TO BE A FORM OF LIGHT--MAYBE IT HAS TO SHINE IN THE VICTIM'S EYES TO HAVE EFFECT! I'LL KEEP MY HEAD DOWN--GO AT HIM THIS WAY!
I MUST HAVE IT FIGURED OUT RIGHT! GETTING CLOSE TO HIM--I CAN SEE HIS LEGS--!
HIMMEL!
THE NEXT MOMENT, BATMAN'S MIGHTY FIST ARCS UPWARD.
GENERAL VON DORT HAS JUST LOST THE FINAL BATTLE!
CRACK!

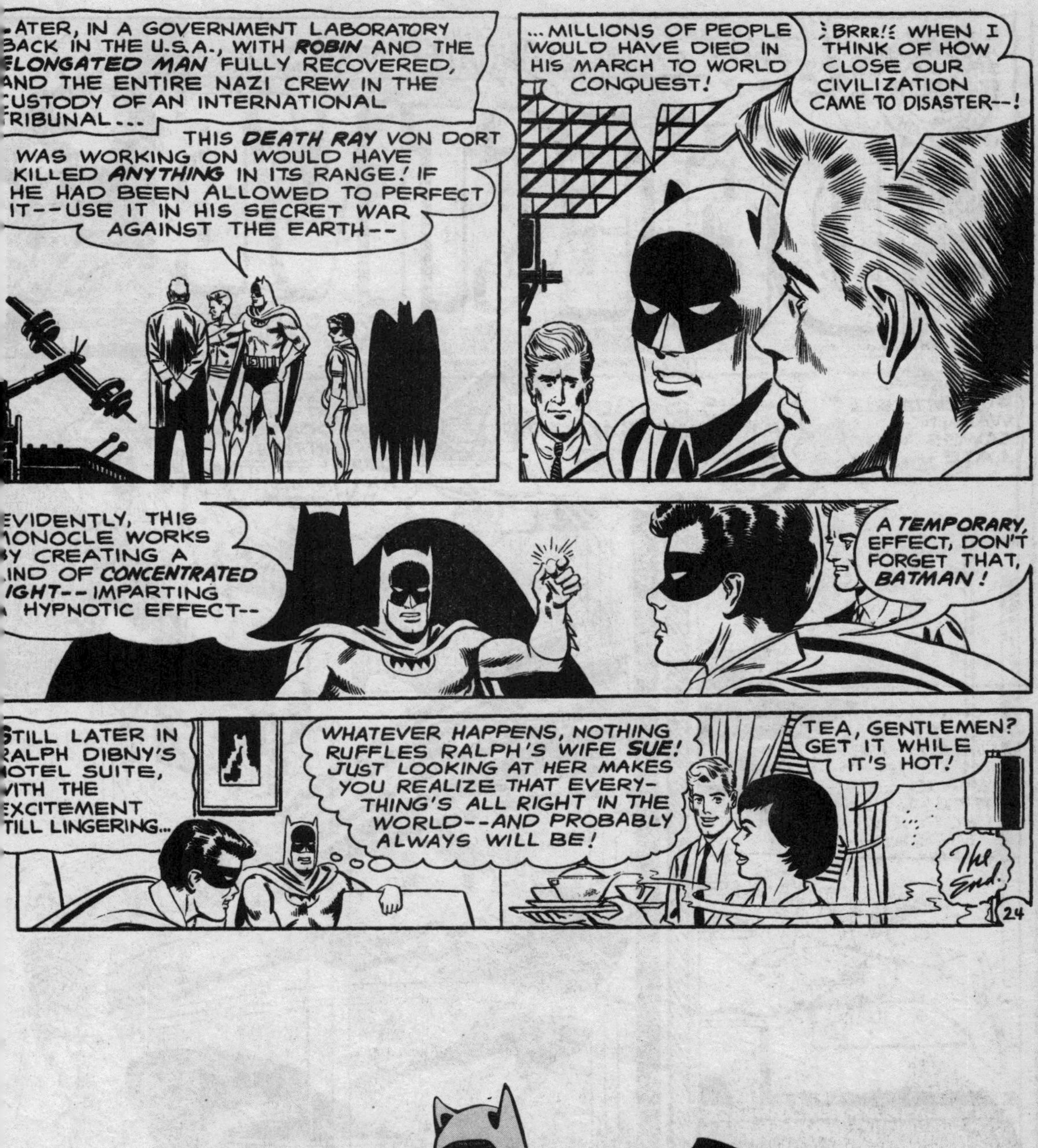
ATER, IN A GOVERNMENT LABORATORY BACK IN THE U.S.A., WITH ROBIN AND THE ELONGATED MAN FULLY RECOVERED, AND THE ENTIRE NAZI CREW IN THE CUSTODY OF AN INTERNATIONAL TRIBUNAL...
THIS DEATH RAY VON DORT WAS WORKING ON WOULD HAVE KILLED ANYTHING IN ITS RANGE! IF HE HAD BEEN ALLOWED TO PERFECT IT--USE IT IN HIS SECRET WAR AGAINST THE EARTH--
...MILLIONS OF PEOPLE WOULD HAVE DIED IN HIS MARCH TO WORLD CONQUEST!
BRRR!! WHEN I THINK OF HOW CLOSE OUR CIVILIZATION CAME TO DISASTER--!
VIDENTLY, THIS MONOCLE WORKS BY CREATING A KIND OF CONCENTRATED IGHT--IMPARTING A HYPNOTIC EFFECT--
A TEMPORARY EFFECT, DON'T FORGET THAT, BATMAN!
TILL LATER IN RALPH DIBNY'S HOTEL SUITE, WITH THE EXCITEMENT TILL LINGERING...
WHATEVER HAPPENS, NOTHING RUFFLES RALPH'S WIFE SUE! JUST LOOKING AT HER MAKES YOU REALIZE THAT EVERYTHING'S ALL RIGHT IN THE WORLD--AND PROBABLY ALWAYS WILL BE!
TEA, GENTLEMEN? GET IT WHILE IT'S HOT!
The End
24

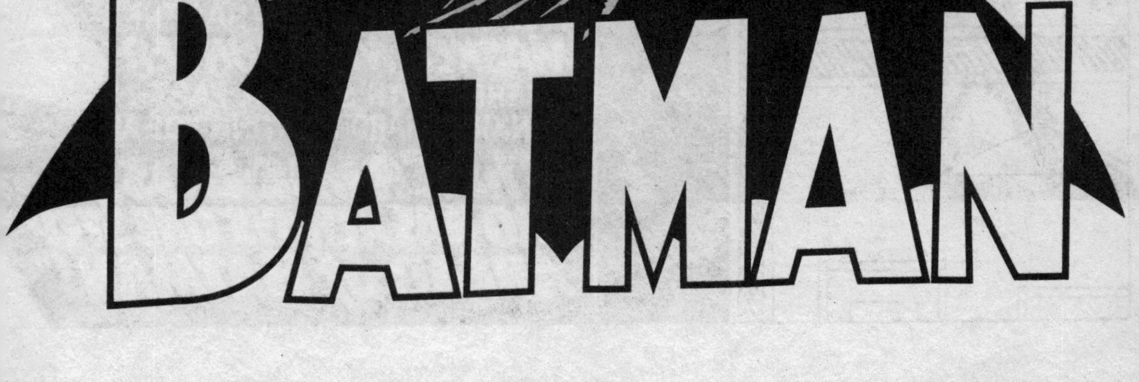
BATMAN

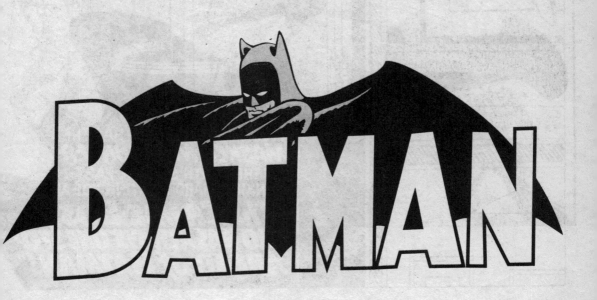

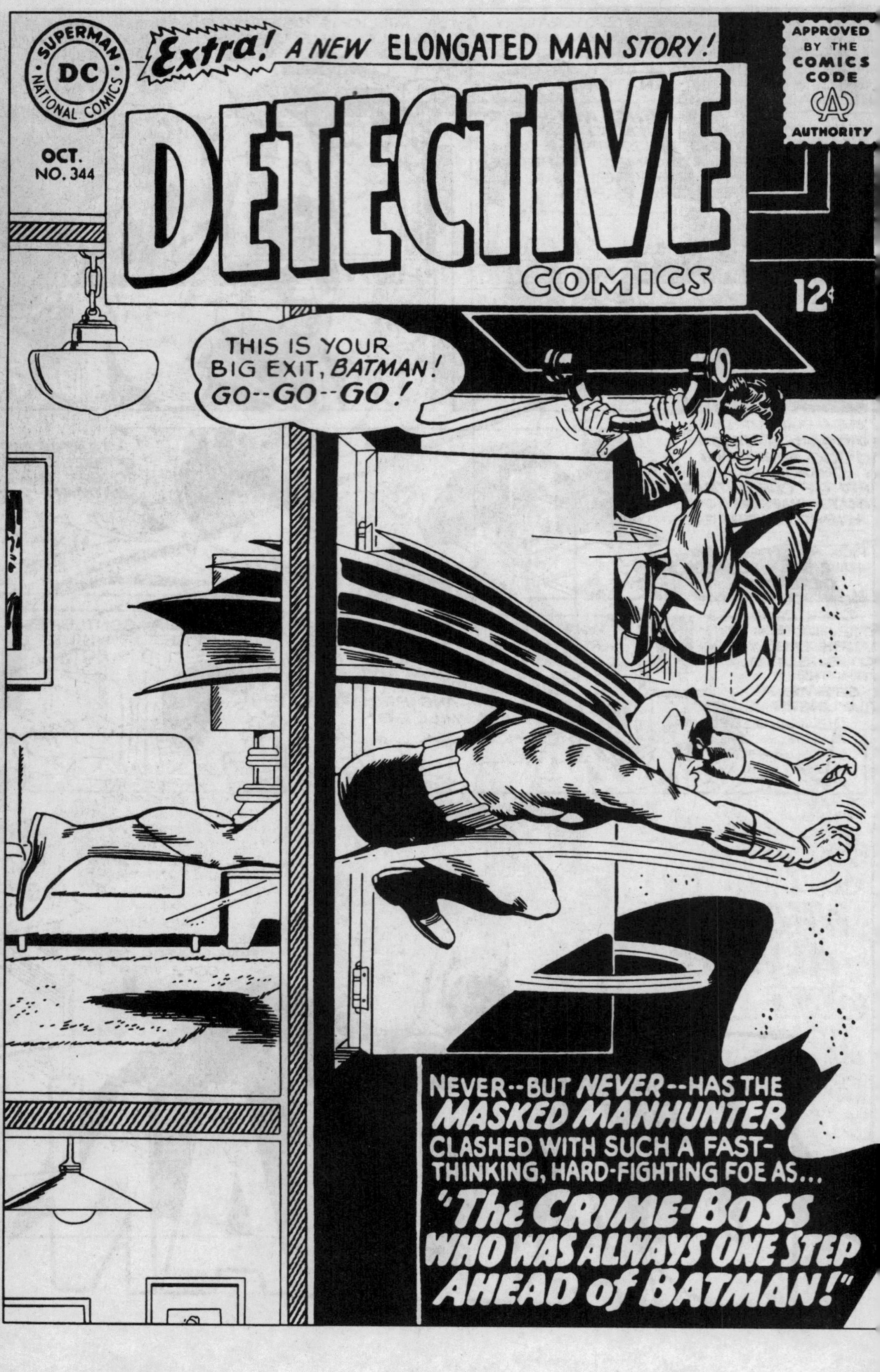
SUPERMAN DC NATIONAL COMICS
Extra! A NEW ELONGATED MAN STORY!
APPROVED BY THE COMICS CODE AUTHORITY
OCT. NO. 344
DETECTIVE COMICS
12¢
THIS IS YOUR BIG EXIT, BATMAN! GO--GO--GO!
NEVER--BUT NEVER--HAS THE MASKED MANHUNTER CLASHED WITH SUCH A FAST-THINKING, HARD-FIGHTING FOE AS...
"The CRIME-BOSS WHO WAS ALWAYS ONE STEP AHEAD of BATMAN!"

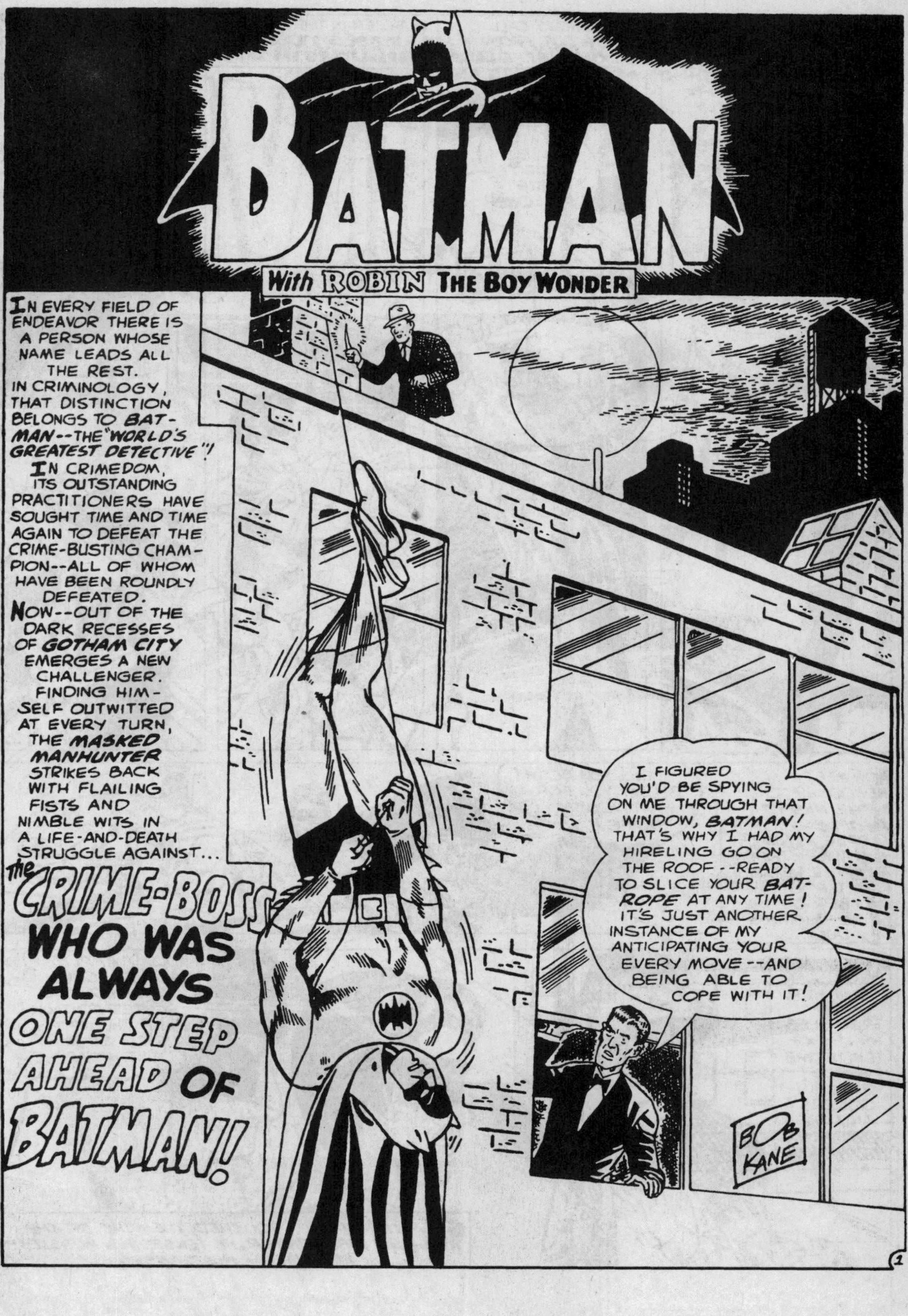
BATMAN
With ROBIN THE BOY WONDER
IN EVERY FIELD OF ENDEAVOR THERE IS A PERSON WHOSE NAME LEADS ALL THE REST. IN CRIMINOLOGY, THAT DISTINCTION BELONGS TO BATMAN--THE "WORLD'S GREATEST DETECTIVE"! IN CRIMEDOM, ITS OUTSTANDING PRACTITIONERS HAVE SOUGHT TIME AND TIME AGAIN TO DEFEAT THE CRIME-BUSTING CHAMPION--ALL OF WHOM HAVE BEEN ROUNDLY DEFEATED. NOW--OUT OF THE DARK RECESSES OF GOTHAM CITY EMERGES A NEW CHALLENGER. FINDING HIMSELF OUTWITTED AT EVERY TURN, THE MASKED MANHUNTER STRIKES BACK WITH FLAILING FISTS AND NIMBLE WITS IN A LIFE-AND-DEATH STRUGGLE AGAINST...
The CRIME-BOSS WHO WAS ALWAYS ONE STEP AHEAD OF BATMAN!
I FIGURED YOU'D BE SPYING ON ME THROUGH THAT WINDOW, BATMAN! THAT'S WHY I HAD MY HIRELING GO ON THE ROOF--READY TO SLICE YOUR BAT-ROPE AT ANY TIME! IT'S JUST ANOTHER INSTANCE OF MY ANTICIPATING YOUR EVERY MOVE--AND BEING ABLE TO COPE WITH IT!
BOB KANE
1

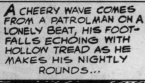

A CHEERY WAVE COMES FROM A PATROLMAN ON A LONELY BEAT, HIS FOOT-FALLS ECHOING WITH HOLLOW TREAD AS HE MAKES HIS NIGHTLY ROUNDS...

A FRIENDLY CALL RINGS OUT FROM A MILKMAN IN THE EARLY MORNING HOURS AS HE MAKES HIS DELIVERIES...

ALL QUIET HERE, FELLOWS!

EARLIER IN THE EVENING, A NEWSBOY TOSSES A PAPER TO HIS FAVORITE CUSTOMERS...

GOOD HUNTING, BATMAN AND ROBIN!

THESE ARE THE NIGHT PEOPLE OF GOTHAM CITY, THE DENIZENS OF THE DARK HOURS WHEN CRIME RUNS RAMPANT IN THE MURKY DEPTHS OF CITY LIFE, WHEN THE SLEEK, GRIM BAT-MOBILE PROWLS LIKE A LIVING WATCH-DOG ALONG THE CURBS AND ALLEYS OF ITS LABYRINTHINE WAYS...

NOW MEET A NEWCOMER TO THESE NIGHT PEOPLE -- "APPLE ALICE" -- WHO ALWAYS HAS AN APPLE READY FOR THE YOUNGER MEMBER OF THE CRIME-BUSTING DUO...

BLESS YOU BOTH! BLESS YOU FOR WHAT YOU'RE DOING!

BUT ON THIS PARTICULAR NIGHT HER HAND TREMBLES AS IT EX-TENDS THE APPLE! HER CHIN QUIVERS! AND SHE SPEAKS NO WORD AT ALL!

ODD! "APPLE ALICE" LOOKS TERRIFIED--TOO SCARED TO TALK! AND THE WAY SHE'S STARING AT THAT APPLE--

SUSPICION HAVING TOUCHED THE MIND OF THE MASKED MANHUNTER, HE TENSES HIS MUSCLES-- HEIGHTENS HIS SENSES...

2

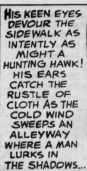

HIS KEEN EYES DEVOUR THE SIDEWALK AS INTENTLY AS MIGHT A HUNTING HAWK! HIS EARS CATCH THE RUSTLE OF CLOTH AS THE COLD WIND SWEEPS AN ALLEYWAY WHERE A MAN LURKS IN THE SHADOWS...

SOMEONE'S MIGHTY ANXIOUS TO SEE THAT WE DO THE EXPECTED THING...

BATMAN'S QUICK WITS WORK AT FRENZIED SPEED! OUT OF THE CORNER OF HIS MOUTH HE SNAPS A WHISPERED COMMAND AT ROBIN.

DON'T BITE INTO THAT APPLE! JUST PRETEND TO DO SO -- AND KEEL OVER IN PAIN!

EYES SPARKLING SO BRIGHTLY THAT THEY DIM THE OVERHEAD STREET LAMPS -- FOR THE TEEN-AGE THUNDERBOLT SCENTS MYSTERY AND A NEW CASE -- HE GOES INTO HIS "ACT"...

OH! OHHHH!

ROBIN'S IN AGONY! GOT TO RUSH HIM TO A HOSPITAL!

CAREENING AROUND A CORNER, THE BATMOBILE HURTLES THROUGH THE NIGHT-TIME HOURS...

BRRR...

I'LL THROW IN THE SPECIAL SOUND EFFECTS GIMMICK THAT SIMULATES THE NOISE OF A MOTOR RECEDING INTO THE DISTANCE!

THEN FEET RAM HARD INTO PERFECT BRAKES -- AND TWO GRIM FIGURES RISE TO SEND THEIR BATROPES CURLING HIGH...

I DIDN'T GET A CHANCE TO ASK -- WHAT'S UP?

I'M NOT SURE! IT'S ONLY A FEELING I HAVE THAT THERE IS SOMETHING -- TERRIBLY WRONG!

THEIR FEET ARE AS STEADY AS THOSE OF MOUNTAIN GOATS AS THEY PICK THEIR UNERRING WAY ALONG THE EDGE OF A BUILDING ROOFTOP...

I SAW THAT MAN BELOW WATCHING "APPLE ALICE" GIVE YOU AN APPLE! AND SHE WAS FRIGHTENED --

BECAUSE IT WAS "DOCTORED", eh? SHE HAD TO GIVE IT TO ME -- OR ELSE!

3

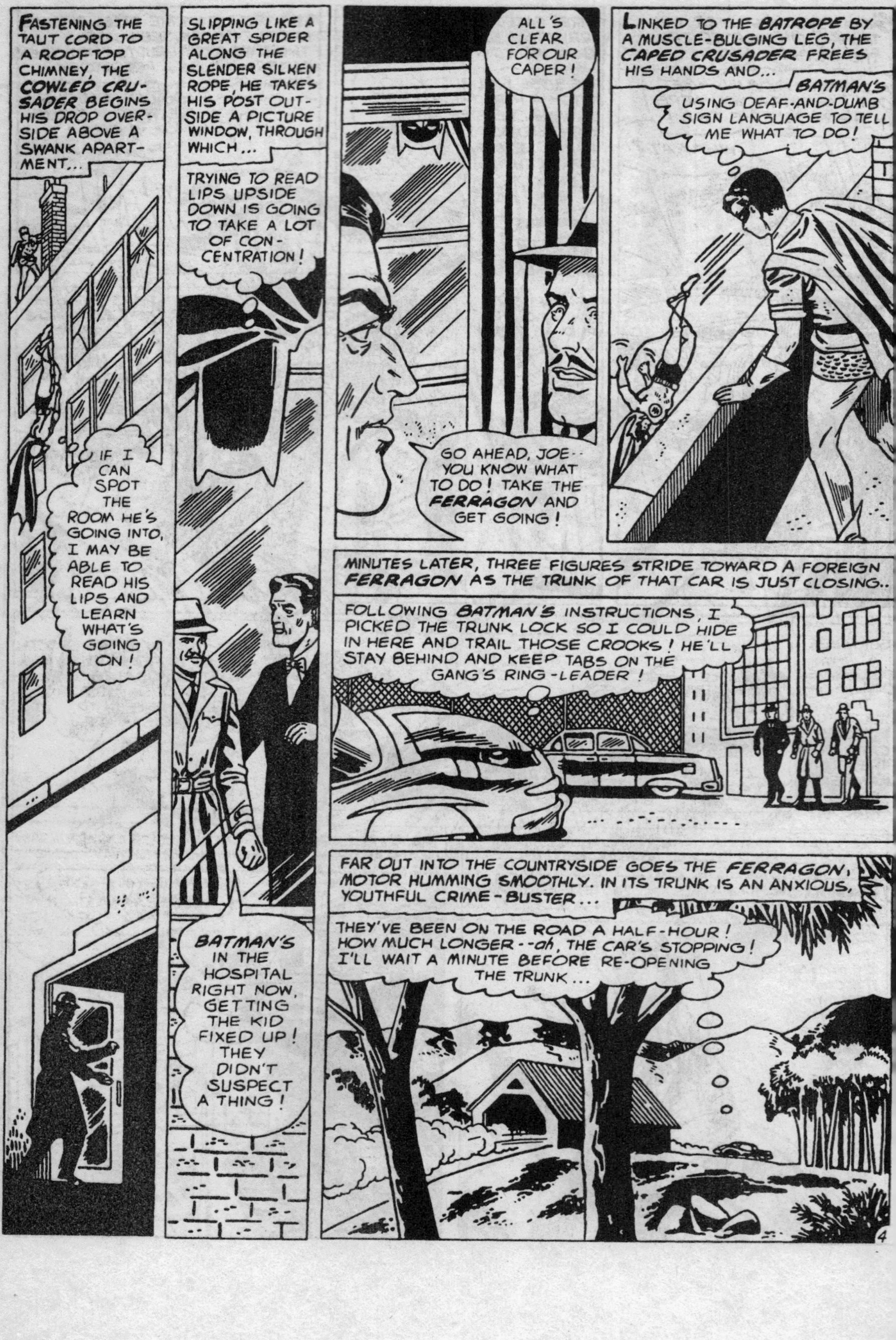
FASTENING THE TAUT CORD TO A ROOFTOP CHIMNEY, THE COWLED CRUSADER BEGINS HIS DROP OVERSIDE ABOVE A SWANK APARTMENT...
IF I CAN SPOT THE ROOM HE'S GOING INTO, I MAY BE ABLE TO READ HIS LIPS AND LEARN WHAT'S GOING ON!
SLIPPING LIKE A GREAT SPIDER ALONG THE SLENDER SILKEN ROPE, HE TAKES HIS POST OUTSIDE A PICTURE WINDOW, THROUGH WHICH...
TRYING TO READ LIPS UPSIDE DOWN IS GOING TO TAKE A LOT OF CONCENTRATION!
BATMAN'S IN THE HOSPITAL RIGHT NOW, GETTING THE KID FIXED UP! THEY DIDN'T SUSPECT A THING!
ALL'S CLEAR FOR OUR CAPER!
GO AHEAD, JOE-- YOU KNOW WHAT TO DO! TAKE THE FERRAGON AND GET GOING!
LINKED TO THE BATROPE BY A MUSCLE-BULGING LEG, THE CAPED CRUSADER FREES HIS HANDS AND...
BATMAN'S USING DEAF-AND-DUMB SIGN LANGUAGE TO TELL ME WHAT TO DO!
MINUTES LATER, THREE FIGURES STRIDE TOWARD A FOREIGN FERRAGON AS THE TRUNK OF THAT CAR IS JUST CLOSING..
FOLLOWING BATMAN'S INSTRUCTIONS, I PICKED THE TRUNK LOCK SO I COULD HIDE IN HERE AND TRAIL THOSE CROOKS! HE'LL STAY BEHIND AND KEEP TABS ON THE GANG'S RING-LEADER!
FAR OUT INTO THE COUNTRYSIDE GOES THE FERRAGON, MOTOR HUMMING SMOOTHLY. IN ITS TRUNK IS AN ANXIOUS, YOUTHFUL CRIME-BUSTER...
THEY'VE BEEN ON THE ROAD A HALF-HOUR! HOW MUCH LONGER--ah, THE CAR'S STOPPING! I'LL WAIT A MINUTE BEFORE RE-OPENING THE TRUNK...
4

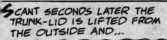

SCANT SECONDS LATER THE TRUNK-LID IS LIFTED FROM THE OUTSIDE AND...

ALL RIGHT, *ROBIN* -- GET OUT ! WE KNEW YOU WERE IN THERE ALL THE TIME !

WHAAAT ?!

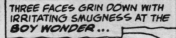

THREE FACES GRIN DOWN WITH IRRITATING SMUGNESS AT THE *BOY WONDER*...

THE BOSS FIGURED YOU'D HITCH A RIDE THERE ! HE'S ALWAYS ONE STEP AHEAD OF EVERYBODY ! HE ISN'T NAMED *JOHNNY WITTS* FOR NOTHING ! HE'S GOT PLENTY OF 'EM ! NOW -- MOVE !

OKAY !

LEG MUSCLES LIKE STEEL SPRINGS UNCOIL -- AS THE *TEEN-AGE THUNDERBOLT* ERUPTS FROM THE CAR TRUNK LIKE A PREDATORY PANTHER ...

YOU CAN TELL THE REST TO A JUDGE, MISTER !

POW!

CAUGHT BY SURPRISE AT THE DETERMINED DARING OF THE YOUTHFUL YEGG-CATCHER, THE GUN-MAN REELS BACK-WARDS...

OCK!

IN A FOLLOW-UP MANEUVER, THE *BOY WONDER* CATCHES THE MAN IN THE TRENCHCOAT IN A CLEVER LEG-LOCK...

TWO DOWN -- ONE MORE ON HIS WAY !

5

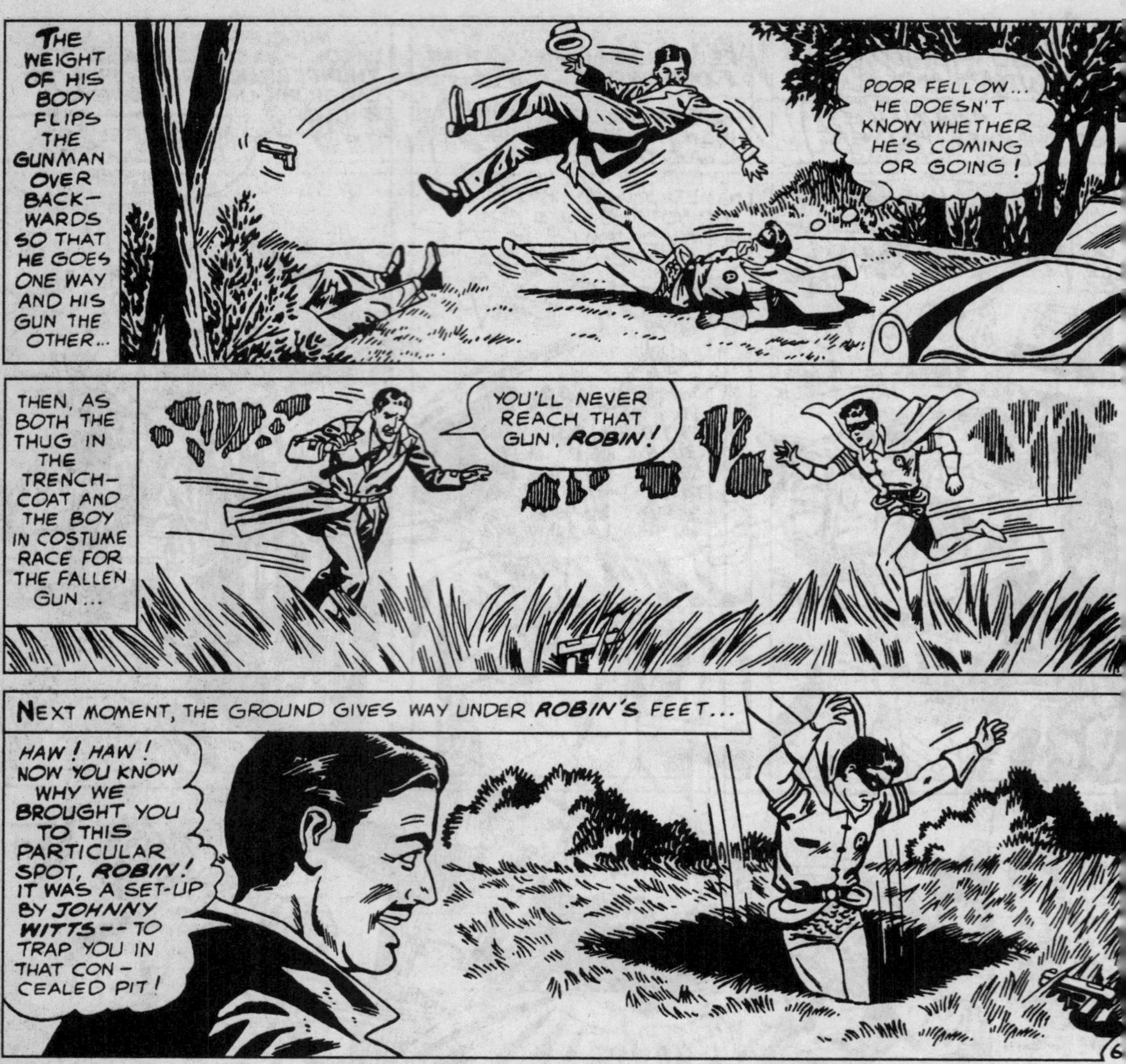
THE WEIGHT OF HIS BODY FLIPS THE GUNMAN OVER BACK-WARDS SO THAT HE GOES ONE WAY AND HIS GUN THE OTHER...
POOR FELLOW... HE DOESN'T KNOW WHETHER HE'S COMING OR GOING!
THEN, AS BOTH THE THUG IN THE TRENCH-COAT AND THE BOY IN COSTUME RACE FOR THE FALLEN GUN...
YOU'LL NEVER REACH THAT GUN, ROBIN!
NEXT MOMENT, THE GROUND GIVES WAY UNDER ROBIN'S FEET...
HAW! HAW! NOW YOU KNOW WHY WE BROUGHT YOU TO THIS PARTICULAR SPOT, ROBIN! IT WAS A SET-UP BY JOHNNY WITTS-- TO TRAP YOU IN THAT CON-CEALED PIT!
6

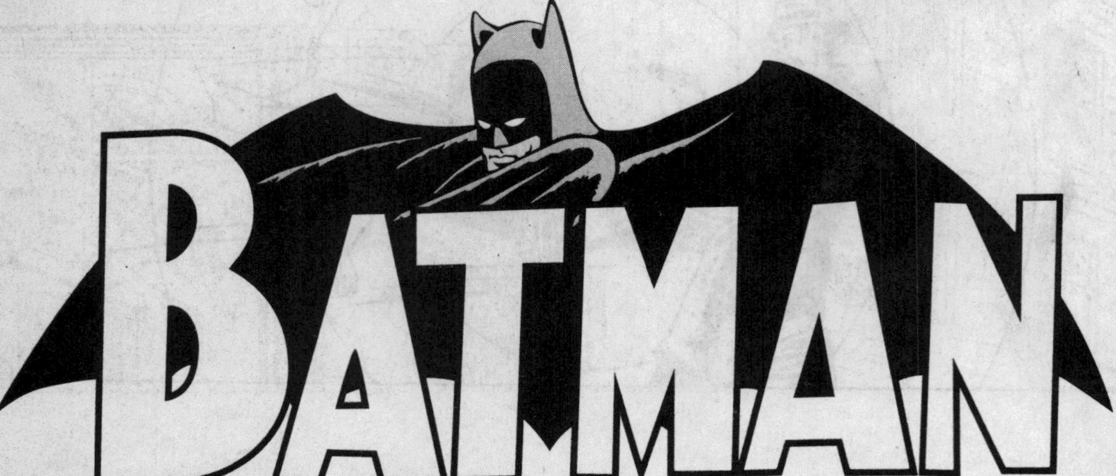
BATMAN

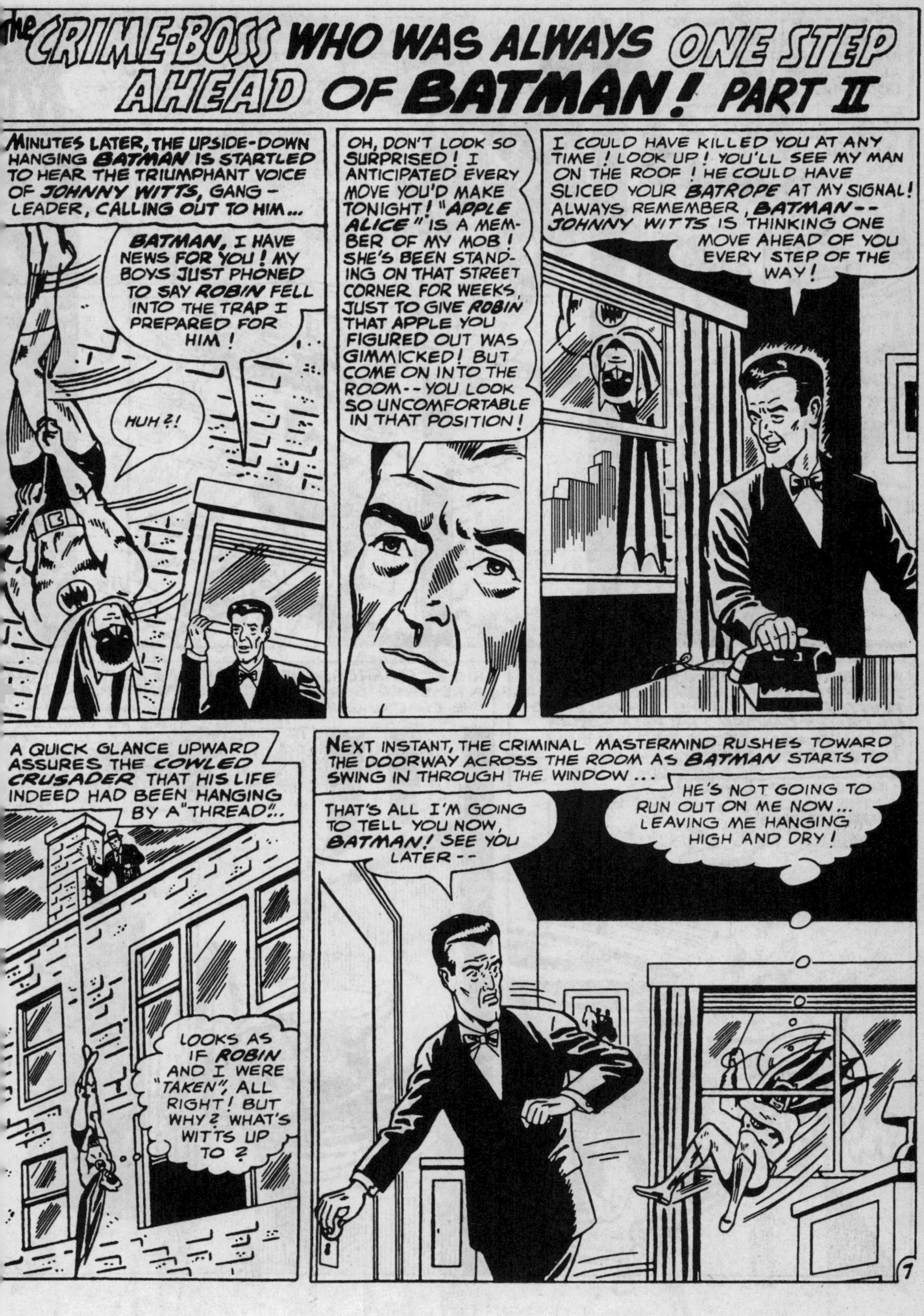
The CRIME-BOSS WHO WAS ALWAYS ONE STEP AHEAD OF BATMAN! PART II
MINUTES LATER, THE UPSIDE-DOWN HANGING BATMAN IS STARTLED TO HEAR THE TRIUMPHANT VOICE OF JOHNNY WITTS, GANG-LEADER, CALLING OUT TO HIM...
BATMAN, I HAVE NEWS FOR YOU! MY BOYS JUST PHONED TO SAY ROBIN FELL INTO THE TRAP I PREPARED FOR HIM!
HUH?!
OH, DON'T LOOK SO SURPRISED! I ANTICIPATED EVERY MOVE YOU'D MAKE TONIGHT! "APPLE ALICE" IS A MEMBER OF MY MOB! SHE'S BEEN STANDING ON THAT STREET CORNER FOR WEEKS, JUST TO GIVE ROBIN THAT APPLE YOU FIGURED OUT WAS GIMMICKED! BUT COME ON INTO THE ROOM--YOU LOOK SO UNCOMFORTABLE IN THAT POSITION!
I COULD HAVE KILLED YOU AT ANY TIME! LOOK UP! YOU'LL SEE MY MAN ON THE ROOF! HE COULD HAVE SLICED YOUR BATROPE AT MY SIGNAL! ALWAYS REMEMBER, BATMAN--JOHNNY WITTS IS THINKING ONE MOVE AHEAD OF YOU EVERY STEP OF THE WAY!
A QUICK GLANCE UPWARD ASSURES THE COWLED CRUSADER THAT HIS LIFE INDEED HAD BEEN HANGING BY A "THREAD"!..
LOOKS AS IF ROBIN AND I WERE "TAKEN", ALL RIGHT! BUT WHY? WHAT'S WITTS UP TO?
NEXT INSTANT, THE CRIMINAL MASTERMIND RUSHES TOWARD THE DOORWAY ACROSS THE ROOM AS BATMAN STARTS TO SWING IN THROUGH THE WINDOW...
THAT'S ALL I'M GOING TO TELL YOU NOW, BATMAN! SEE YOU LATER--
HE'S NOT GOING TO RUN OUT ON ME NOW... LEAVING ME HANGING HIGH AND DRY!
7

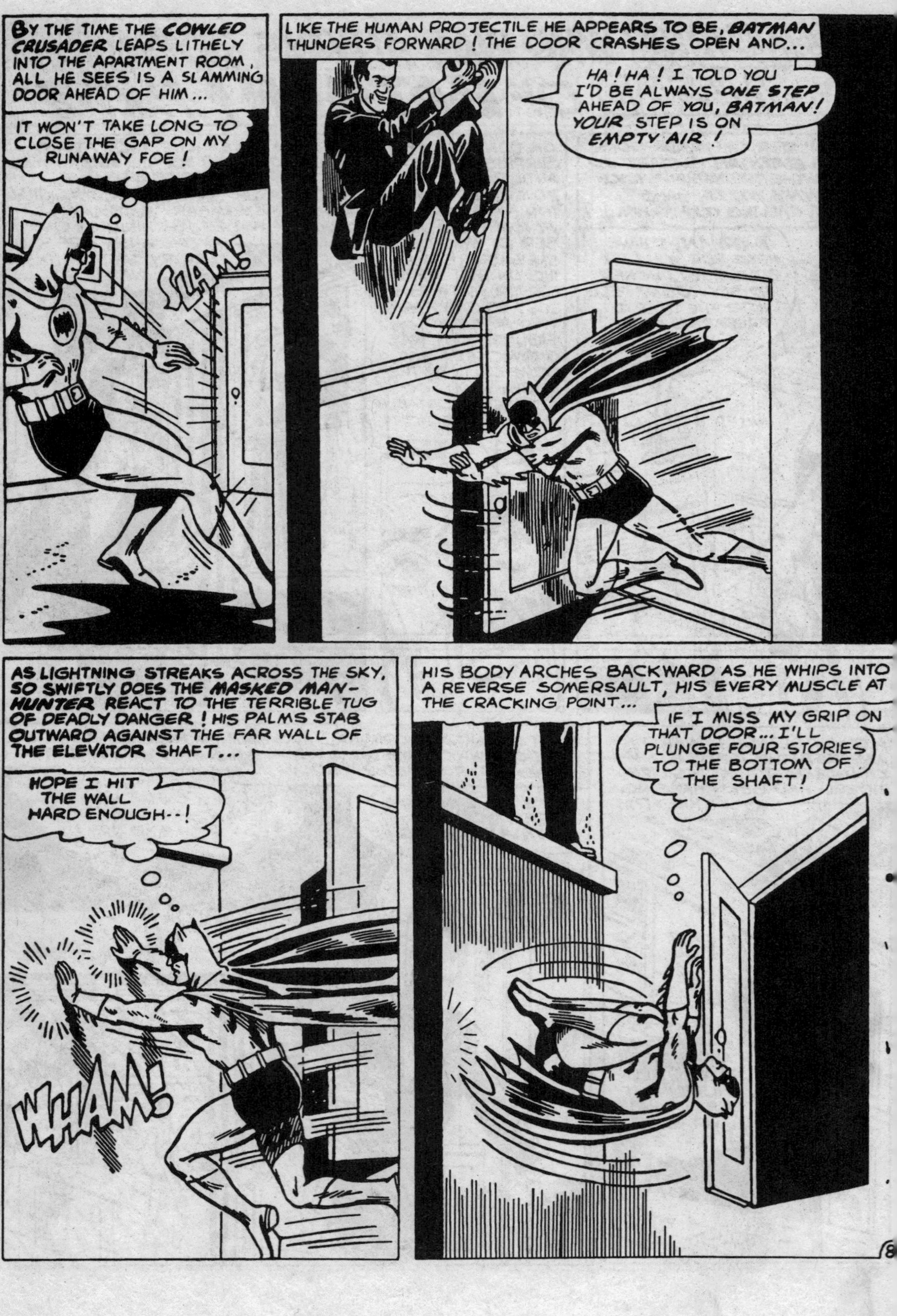
BY THE TIME THE COWLED CRUSADER LEAPS LITHELY INTO THE APARTMENT ROOM, ALL HE SEES IS A SLAMMING DOOR AHEAD OF HIM...
IT WON'T TAKE LONG TO CLOSE THE GAP ON MY RUNAWAY FOE!
SLAM!
LIKE THE HUMAN PROJECTILE HE APPEARS TO BE, BATMAN THUNDERS FORWARD! THE DOOR CRASHES OPEN AND...
HA! HA! I TOLD YOU I'D BE ALWAYS ONE STEP AHEAD OF YOU, BATMAN! YOUR STEP IS ON EMPTY AIR!
AS LIGHTNING STREAKS ACROSS THE SKY, SO SWIFTLY DOES THE MASKED MAN-HUNTER REACT TO THE TERRIBLE TUG OF DEADLY DANGER! HIS PALMS STAB OUTWARD AGAINST THE FAR WALL OF THE ELEVATOR SHAFT...
HOPE I HIT THE WALL HARD ENOUGH--!
WHAM!
HIS BODY ARCHES BACKWARD AS HE WHIPS INTO A REVERSE SOMERSAULT, HIS EVERY MUSCLE AT THE CRACKING POINT...
IF I MISS MY GRIP ON THAT DOOR... I'LL PLUNGE FOUR STORIES TO THE BOTTOM OF THE SHAFT!
8

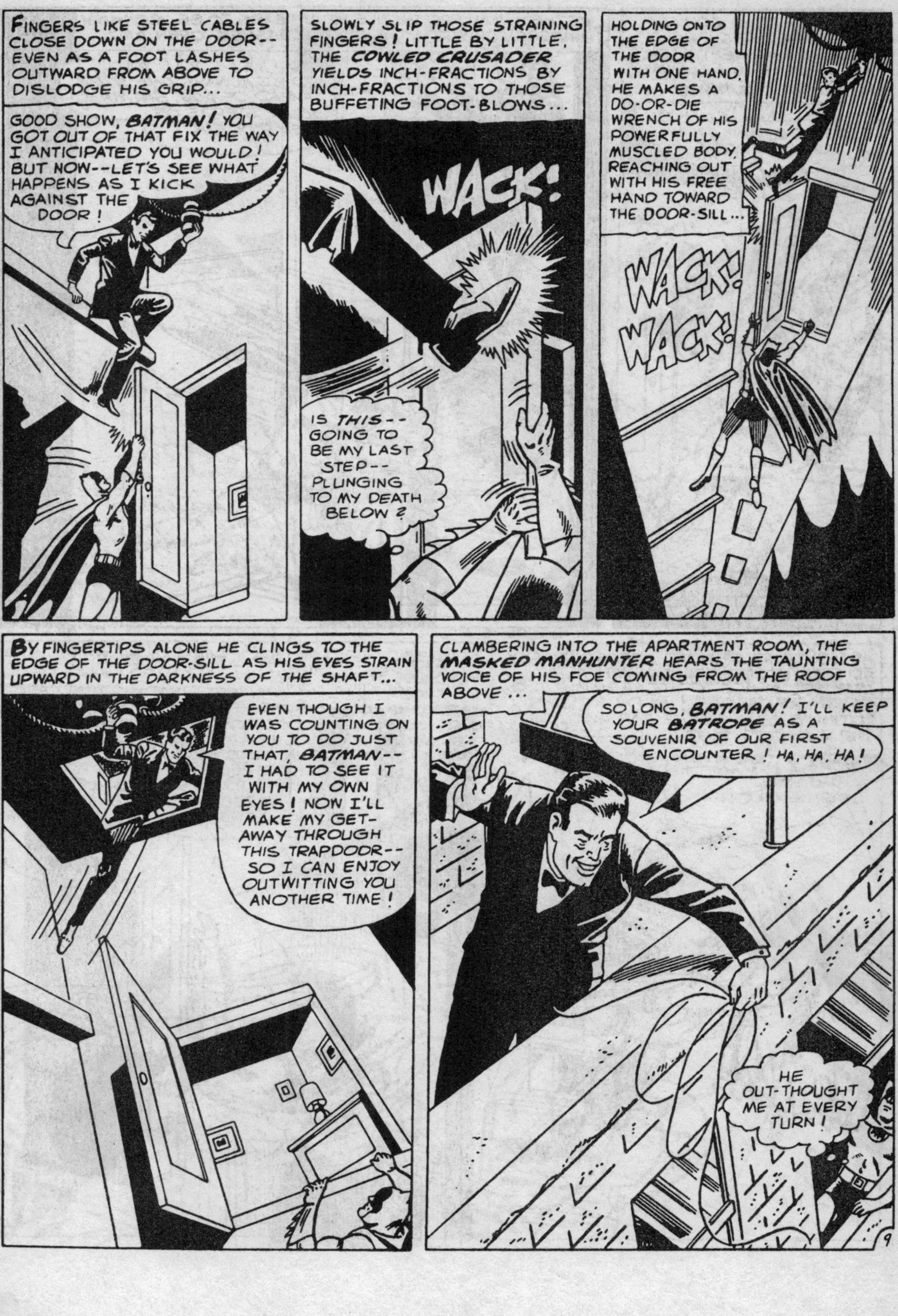
FINGERS LIKE STEEL CABLES CLOSE DOWN ON THE DOOR-- EVEN AS A FOOT LASHES OUTWARD FROM ABOVE TO DISLODGE HIS GRIP...
GOOD SHOW, BATMAN! YOU GOT OUT OF THAT FIX THE WAY I ANTICIPATED YOU WOULD! BUT NOW--LET'S SEE WHAT HAPPENS AS I KICK AGAINST THE DOOR!
SLOWLY SLIP THOSE STRAINING FINGERS! LITTLE BY LITTLE, THE COWLED CRUSADER YIELDS INCH-FRACTIONS BY INCH-FRACTIONS TO THOSE BUFFETING FOOT-BLOWS...
WACK!
IS THIS-- GOING TO BE MY LAST STEP-- PLUNGING TO MY DEATH BELOW?
HOLDING ONTO THE EDGE OF THE DOOR WITH ONE HAND, HE MAKES A DO-OR-DIE WRENCH OF HIS POWERFULLY MUSCLED BODY, REACHING OUT WITH HIS FREE HAND TOWARD THE DOOR-SILL...
WACK! WACK!
BY FINGERTIPS ALONE HE CLINGS TO THE EDGE OF THE DOOR-SILL AS HIS EYES STRAIN UPWARD IN THE DARKNESS OF THE SHAFT...
EVEN THOUGH I WAS COUNTING ON YOU TO DO JUST THAT, BATMAN-- I HAD TO SEE IT WITH MY OWN EYES! NOW I'LL MAKE MY GET-AWAY THROUGH THIS TRAPDOOR-- SO I CAN ENJOY OUTWITTING YOU ANOTHER TIME!
CLAMBERING INTO THE APARTMENT ROOM, THE MASKED MANHUNTER HEARS THE TAUNTING VOICE OF HIS FOE COMING FROM THE ROOF ABOVE...
SO LONG, BATMAN! I'LL KEEP YOUR BATROPE AS A SOUVENIR OF OUR FIRST ENCOUNTER! HA, HA, HA!
HE OUT-THOUGHT ME AT EVERY TURN!
9

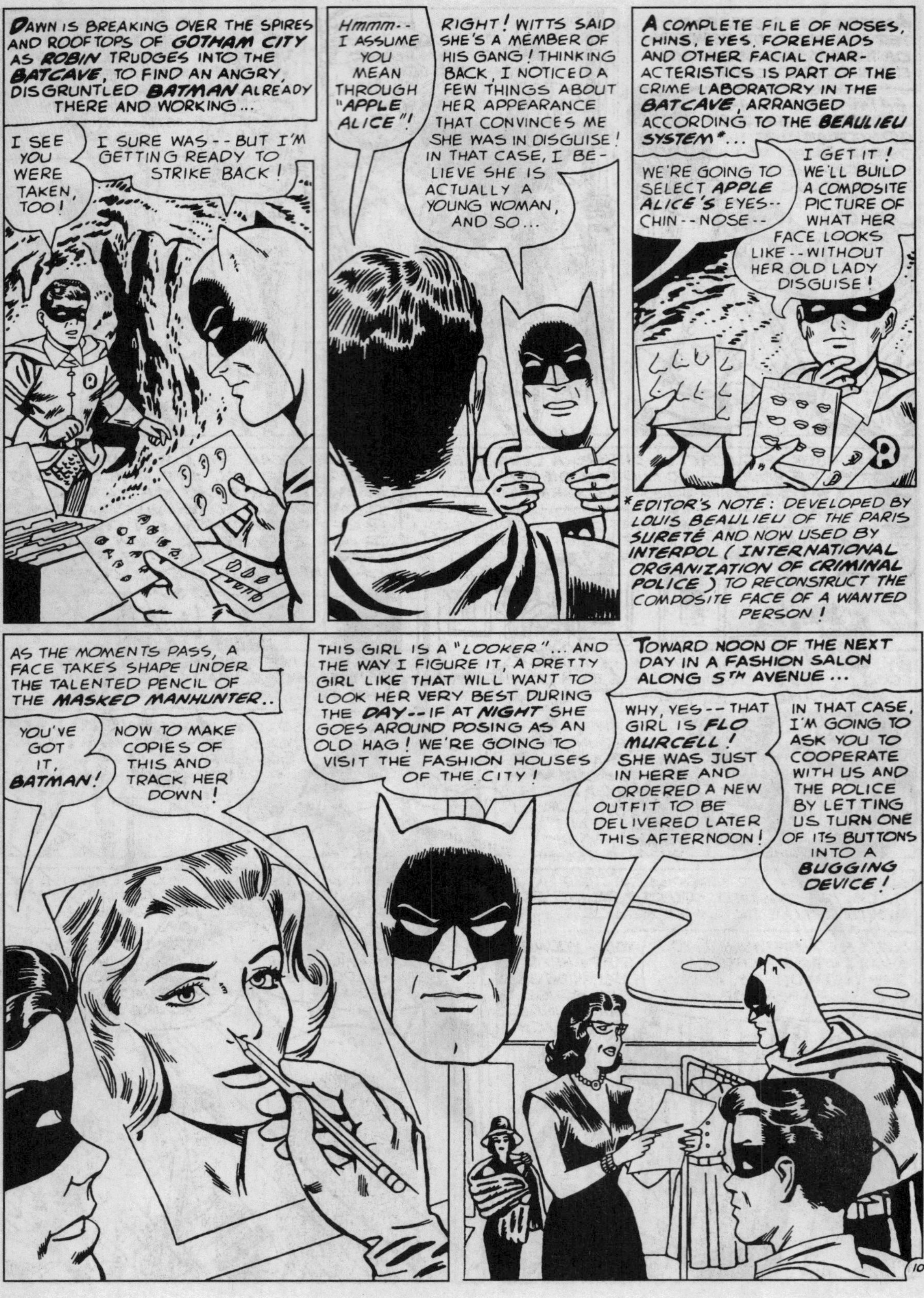
DAWN IS BREAKING OVER THE SPIRES AND ROOFTOPS OF GOTHAM CITY AS ROBIN TRUDGES INTO THE BATCAVE, TO FIND AN ANGRY, DISGRUNTLED BATMAN ALREADY THERE AND WORKING...
I SEE YOU WERE TAKEN, TOO!
I SURE WAS--BUT I'M GETTING READY TO STRIKE BACK!
Hmmm--I ASSUME YOU MEAN THROUGH "APPLE ALICE"!
RIGHT! WITTS SAID SHE'S A MEMBER OF HIS GANG! THINKING BACK, I NOTICED A FEW THINGS ABOUT HER APPEARANCE THAT CONVINCES ME SHE WAS IN DISGUISE! IN THAT CASE, I BELIEVE SHE IS ACTUALLY A YOUNG WOMAN, AND SO...
A COMPLETE FILE OF NOSES, CHINS, EYES, FOREHEADS AND OTHER FACIAL CHARACTERISTICS IS PART OF THE CRIME LABORATORY IN THE BATCAVE, ARRANGED ACCORDING TO THE BEAULIEU SYSTEM*...
WE'RE GOING TO SELECT APPLE ALICE'S EYES--CHIN--NOSE--
I GET IT! WE'LL BUILD A COMPOSITE PICTURE OF WHAT HER FACE LOOKS LIKE--WITHOUT HER OLD LADY DISGUISE!
*EDITOR'S NOTE: DEVELOPED BY LOUIS BEAULIEU OF THE PARIS SURETÉ AND NOW USED BY INTERPOL (INTERNATIONAL ORGANIZATION OF CRIMINAL POLICE) TO RECONSTRUCT THE COMPOSITE FACE OF A WANTED PERSON!
AS THE MOMENTS PASS, A FACE TAKES SHAPE UNDER THE TALENTED PENCIL OF THE MASKED MANHUNTER..
YOU'VE GOT IT, BATMAN!
NOW TO MAKE COPIES OF THIS AND TRACK HER DOWN!
THIS GIRL IS A "LOOKER"... AND THE WAY I FIGURE IT, A PRETTY GIRL LIKE THAT WILL WANT TO LOOK HER VERY BEST DURING THE DAY--IF AT NIGHT SHE GOES AROUND POSING AS AN OLD HAG! WE'RE GOING TO VISIT THE FASHION HOUSES OF THE CITY!
TOWARD NOON OF THE NEXT DAY IN A FASHION SALON ALONG 5TH AVENUE...
WHY, YES--THAT GIRL IS FLO MURCELL! SHE WAS JUST IN HERE AND ORDERED A NEW OUTFIT TO BE DELIVERED LATER THIS AFTERNOON!
IN THAT CASE, I'M GOING TO ASK YOU TO COOPERATE WITH US AND THE POLICE BY LETTING US TURN ONE OF ITS BUTTONS INTO A BUGGING DEVICE!
10

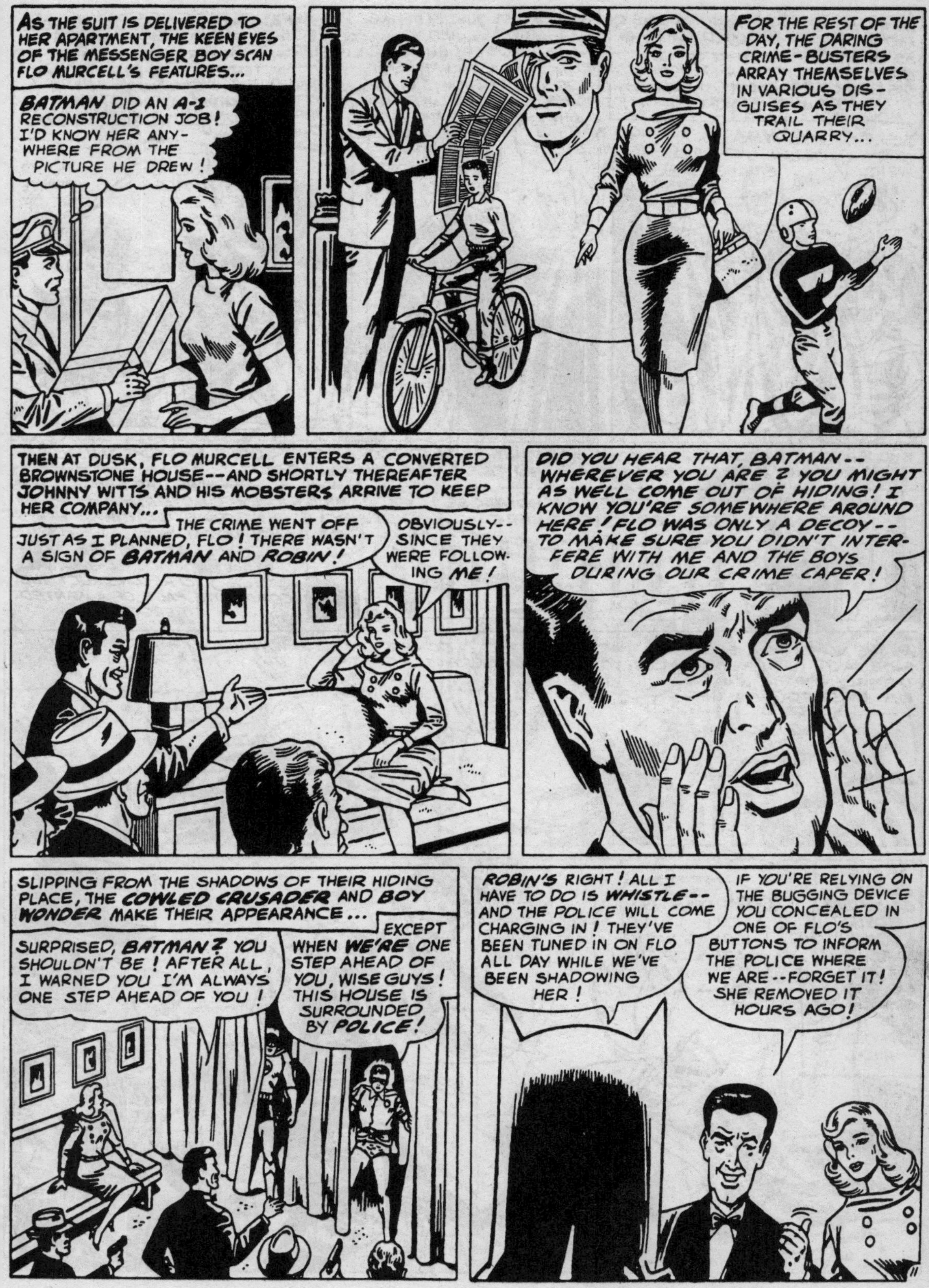
AS THE SUIT IS DELIVERED TO HER APARTMENT, THE KEEN EYES OF THE MESSENGER BOY SCAN FLO MURCELL'S FEATURES...
BATMAN DID AN A-1 RECONSTRUCTION JOB! I'D KNOW HER ANYWHERE FROM THE PICTURE HE DREW!
FOR THE REST OF THE DAY, THE DARING CRIME-BUSTERS ARRAY THEMSELVES IN VARIOUS DISGUISES AS THEY TRAIL THEIR QUARRY...
THEN AT DUSK, FLO MURCELL ENTERS A CONVERTED BROWNSTONE HOUSE--AND SHORTLY THEREAFTER JOHNNY WITTS AND HIS MOBSTERS ARRIVE TO KEEP HER COMPANY...
THE CRIME WENT OFF JUST AS I PLANNED, FLO! THERE WASN'T A SIGN OF BATMAN AND ROBIN!
OBVIOUSLY--SINCE THEY WERE FOLLOWING ME!
DID YOU HEAR THAT, BATMAN--WHEREVER YOU ARE? YOU MIGHT AS WELL COME OUT OF HIDING! I KNOW YOU'RE SOMEWHERE AROUND HERE! FLO WAS ONLY A DECOY--TO MAKE SURE YOU DIDN'T INTERFERE WITH ME AND THE BOYS DURING OUR CRIME CAPER!
SLIPPING FROM THE SHADOWS OF THEIR HIDING PLACE, THE COWLED CRUSADER AND BOY WONDER MAKE THEIR APPEARANCE...
SURPRISED, BATMAN? YOU SHOULDN'T BE! AFTER ALL, I WARNED YOU I'M ALWAYS ONE STEP AHEAD OF YOU!
EXCEPT WHEN WE'RE ONE STEP AHEAD OF YOU, WISE GUYS! THIS HOUSE IS SURROUNDED BY POLICE!
ROBIN'S RIGHT! ALL I HAVE TO DO IS WHISTLE--AND THE POLICE WILL COME CHARGING IN! THEY'VE BEEN TUNED IN ON FLO ALL DAY WHILE WE'VE BEEN SHADOWING HER!
IF YOU'RE RELYING ON THE BUGGING DEVICE YOU CONCEALED IN ONE OF FLO'S BUTTONS TO INFORM THE POLICE WHERE WE ARE--FORGET IT! SHE REMOVED IT HOURS AGO!
11

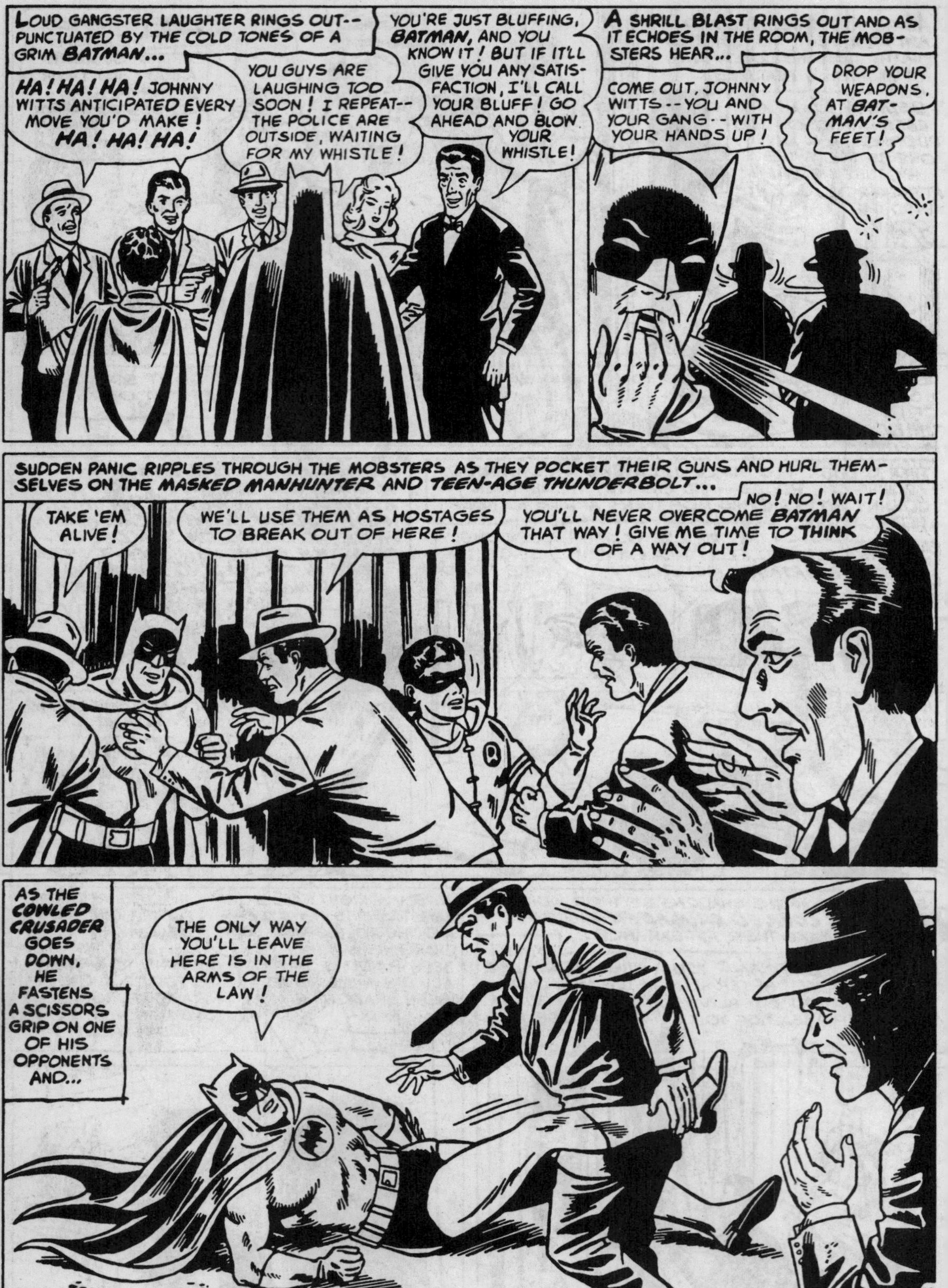
LOUD GANGSTER LAUGHTER RINGS OUT-- PUNCTUATED BY THE COLD TONES OF A GRIM BATMAN...
HA! HA! HA! JOHNNY WITTS ANTICIPATED EVERY MOVE YOU'D MAKE! HA! HA! HA!
YOU GUYS ARE LAUGHING TOO SOON! I REPEAT-- THE POLICE ARE OUTSIDE, WAITING FOR MY WHISTLE!
YOU'RE JUST BLUFFING, BATMAN, AND YOU KNOW IT! BUT IF IT'LL GIVE YOU ANY SATISFACTION, I'LL CALL YOUR BLUFF! GO AHEAD AND BLOW YOUR WHISTLE!
A SHRILL BLAST RINGS OUT AND AS IT ECHOES IN THE ROOM, THE MOBSTERS HEAR...
COME OUT, JOHNNY WITTS--YOU AND YOUR GANG--WITH YOUR HANDS UP!
DROP YOUR WEAPONS, AT BATMAN'S FEET!
SUDDEN PANIC RIPPLES THROUGH THE MOBSTERS AS THEY POCKET THEIR GUNS AND HURL THEMSELVES ON THE MASKED MANHUNTER AND TEEN-AGE THUNDERBOLT...
TAKE 'EM ALIVE!
WE'LL USE THEM AS HOSTAGES TO BREAK OUT OF HERE!
NO! NO! WAIT! YOU'LL NEVER OVERCOME BATMAN THAT WAY! GIVE ME TIME TO THINK OF A WAY OUT!
AS THE COWLED CRUSADER GOES DOWN, HE FASTENS A SCISSORS GRIP ON ONE OF HIS OPPONENTS AND...
THE ONLY WAY YOU'LL LEAVE HERE IS IN THE ARMS OF THE LAW!
12

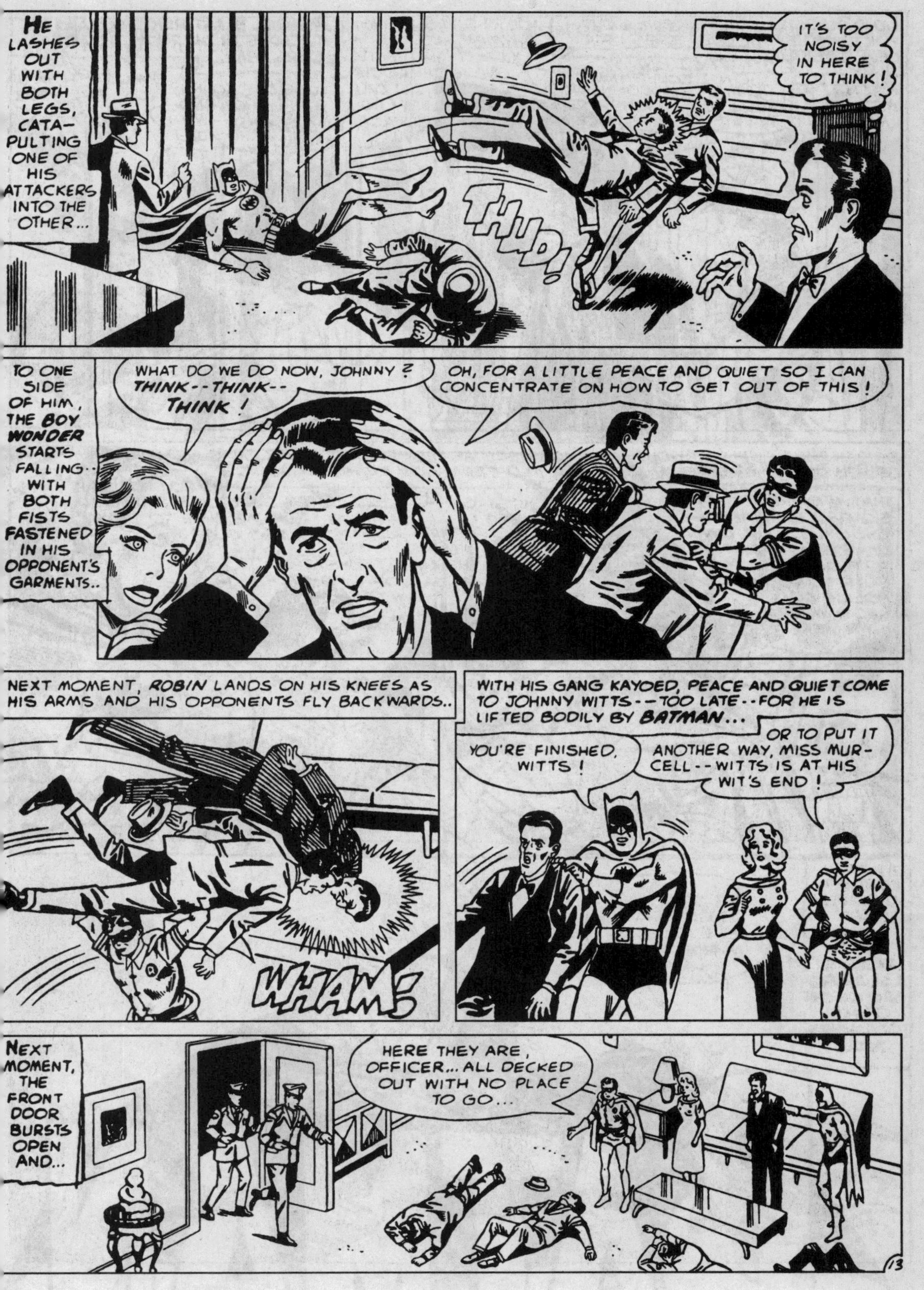
HE LASHES OUT WITH BOTH LEGS, CATA-PULTING ONE OF HIS ATTACKERS INTO THE OTHER...
IT'S TOO NOISY IN HERE TO THINK!
THUD!
TO ONE SIDE OF HIM, THE BOY WONDER STARTS FALLING.. WITH BOTH FISTS FASTENED IN HIS OPPONENT'S GARMENTS..
WHAT DO WE DO NOW, JOHNNY? THINK--THINK--THINK!
OH, FOR A LITTLE PEACE AND QUIET SO I CAN CONCENTRATE ON HOW TO GET OUT OF THIS!
NEXT MOMENT, ROBIN LANDS ON HIS KNEES AS HIS ARMS AND HIS OPPONENTS FLY BACKWARDS..
WHAM!
WITH HIS GANG KAYOED, PEACE AND QUIET COME TO JOHNNY WITTS--TOO LATE--FOR HE IS LIFTED BODILY BY BATMAN...
YOU'RE FINISHED, WITTS!
OR TO PUT IT ANOTHER WAY, MISS MUR-CELL--WITTS IS AT HIS WIT'S END!
NEXT MOMENT, THE FRONT DOOR BURSTS OPEN AND...
HERE THEY ARE, OFFICER... ALL DECKED OUT WITH NO PLACE TO GO...
13

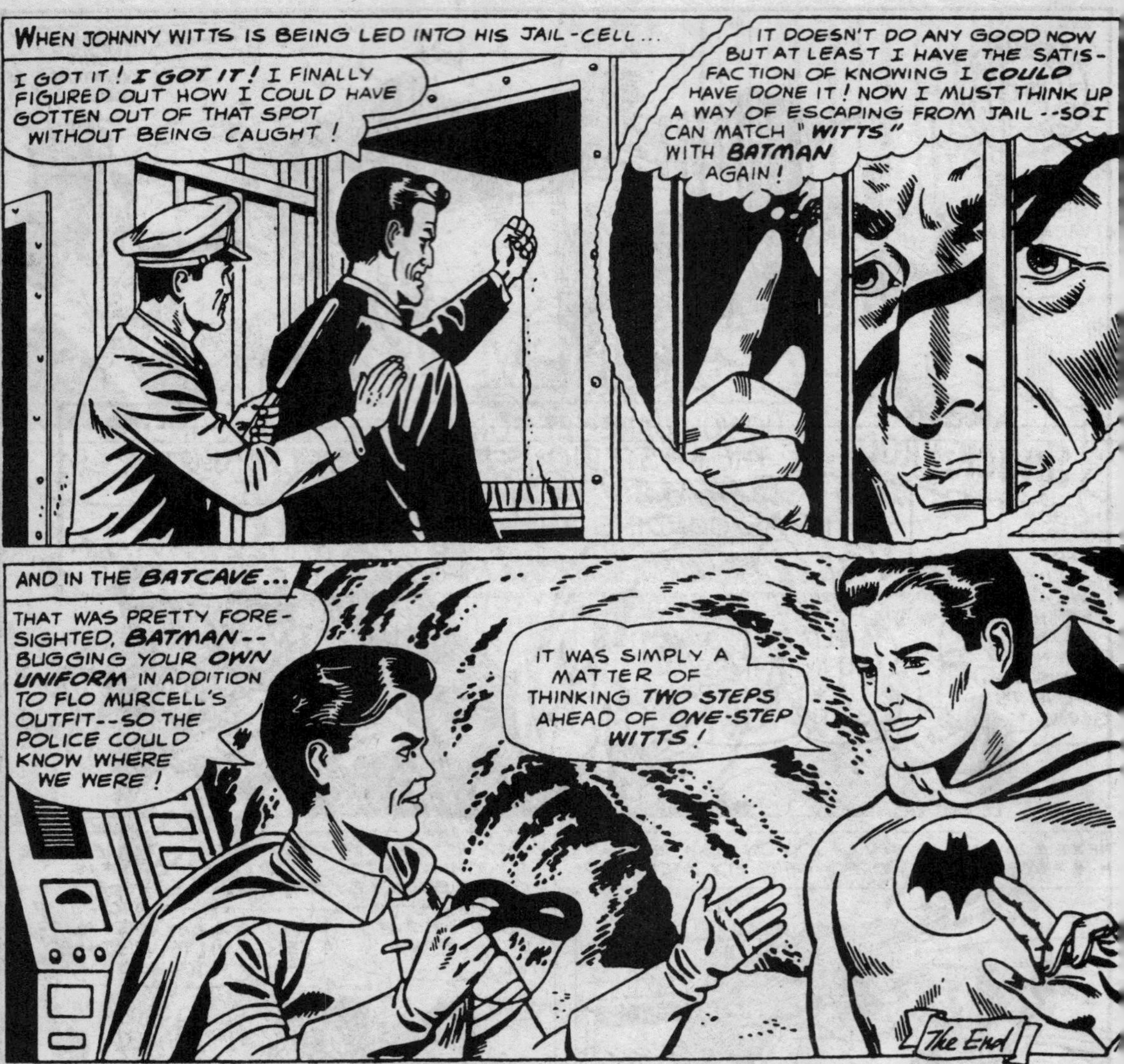
WHEN JOHNNY WITTS IS BEING LED INTO HIS JAIL-CELL...
I GOT IT! I GOT IT! I FINALLY FIGURED OUT HOW I COULD HAVE GOTTEN OUT OF THAT SPOT WITHOUT BEING CAUGHT!
IT DOESN'T DO ANY GOOD NOW BUT AT LEAST I HAVE THE SATISFACTION OF KNOWING I COULD HAVE DONE IT! NOW I MUST THINK UP A WAY OF ESCAPING FROM JAIL--SO I CAN MATCH "WITTS" WITH BATMAN AGAIN!
AND IN THE BATCAVE...
THAT WAS PRETTY FORE-SIGHTED, BATMAN--BUGGING YOUR OWN UNIFORM IN ADDITION TO FLO MURCELL'S OUTFIT--SO THE POLICE COULD KNOW WHERE WE WERE!
IT WAS SIMPLY A MATTER OF THINKING TWO STEPS AHEAD OF ONE-STEP WITTS!
The End

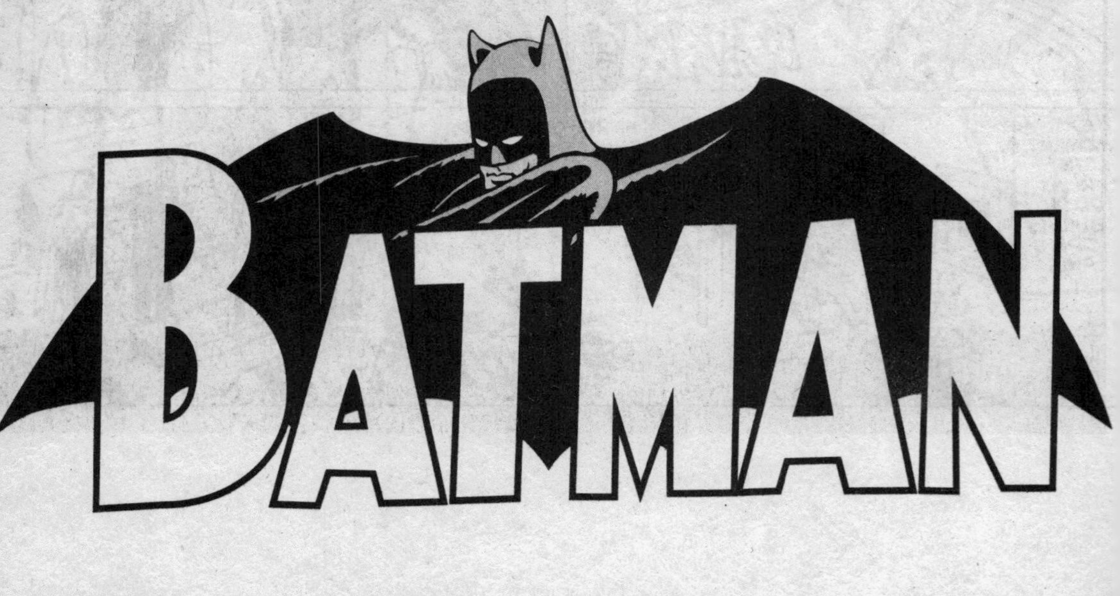
BATMAN

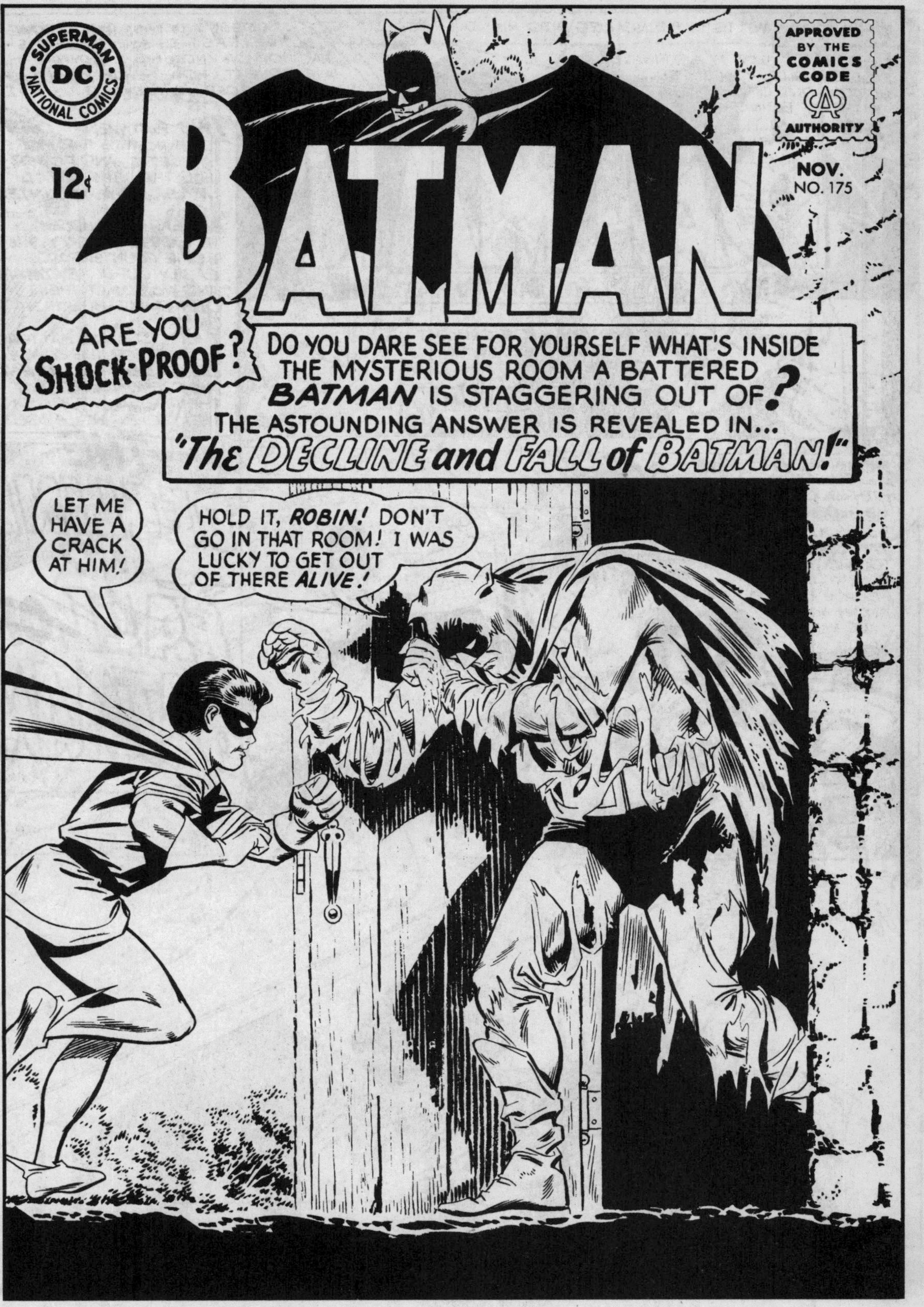
SUPERMAN DC NATIONAL COMICS
APPROVED BY THE COMICS CODE AUTHORITY
BATMAN
12¢
NOV. NO. 175
ARE YOU SHOCK-PROOF?
DO YOU DARE SEE FOR YOURSELF WHAT'S INSIDE THE MYSTERIOUS ROOM A BATTERED BATMAN IS STAGGERING OUT OF? THE ASTOUNDING ANSWER IS REVEALED IN... "The DECLINE and FALL of BATMAN!"
LET ME HAVE A CRACK AT HIM!
HOLD IT, ROBIN! DON'T GO IN THAT ROOM! I WAS LUCKY TO GET OUT OF THERE ALIVE!

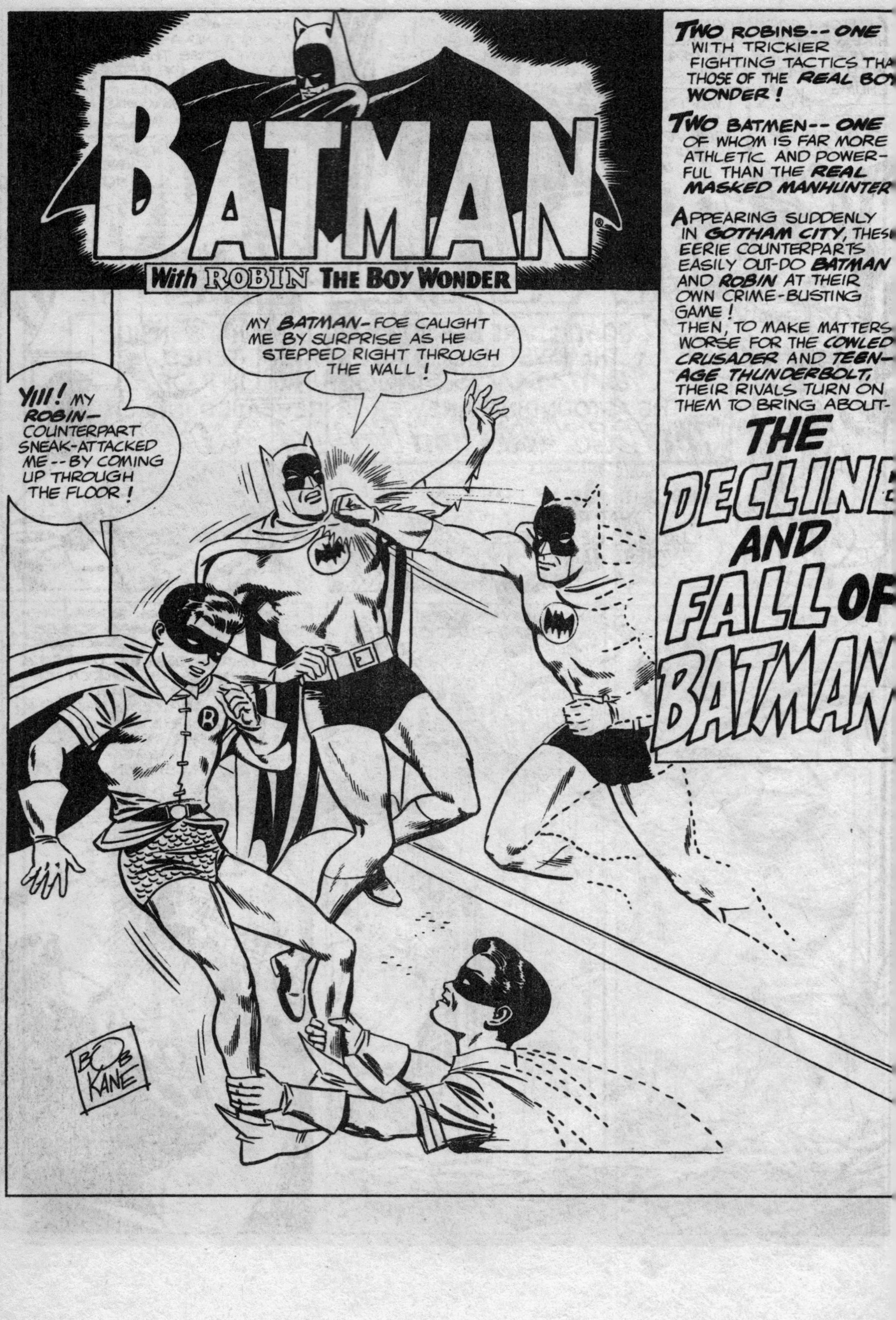
BATMAN
With ROBIN THE BOY WONDER
TWO ROBINS-- ONE WITH TRICKIER FIGHTING TACTICS THA THOSE OF THE REAL BOY WONDER!
TWO BATMEN-- ONE OF WHOM IS FAR MORE ATHLETIC AND POWERFUL THAN THE REAL MASKED MANHUNTER
APPEARING SUDDENLY IN GOTHAM CITY, THES EERIE COUNTERPARTS EASILY OUT-DO BATMAN AND ROBIN AT THEIR OWN CRIME-BUSTING GAME! THEN, TO MAKE MATTERS WORSE FOR THE COWLED CRUSADER AND TEEN-AGE THUNDERBOLT, THEIR RIVALS TURN ON THEM TO BRING ABOUT-
THE DECLINE AND FALL OF BATMAN
YIII! MY ROBIN-COUNTERPART SNEAK-ATTACKED ME--BY COMING UP THROUGH THE FLOOR!
MY BATMAN-FOE CAUGHT ME BY SURPRISE AS HE STEPPED RIGHT THROUGH THE WALL!
BOB KANE

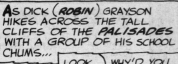

As DICK (*ROBIN*) GRAYSON HIKES ACROSS THE TALL CLIFFS OF THE *PALISADES* WITH A GROUP OF HIS SCHOOL CHUMS....

LOOK, THERE'S THE OLD CARVER PLACE!

WHY'D YOU STEER US HERE, DICK? IT'S SUPPOSED TO BE HAUNTED!

NOT A GHOST OF A CHANCE! HOW ABOUT ONE OF YOU FELLOWS TAKING A PICTURE OF ME WITH THAT HOUSE AS A BACKGROUND!

I'LL DO IT, DICK--LONG AS I CAN KEEP MY DISTANCE!

THERE IS NO SUSPICION IN YOUNG DICK'S MIND AS HE STRIKES A HAMMY POSE THAT HE IS STARTING A CHAIN OF EERIE, ALMOST INCREDIBLE PERILS FOR HIM-SELF AS *ROBIN*, AND FOR *BATMAN* AS WELL...

MAKE SURE YOU GET THE HOUSE IN!

I'M FOCUSING RIGHT NOW... HOLD IT!

FOR EVEN AS THE CAMERA CLICKS--FAMILIAR GLOVED HANDS APPEAR AT THE WINDOW OF AN UPPER FLOOR..

IN THE WAYNE MANSION THAT NIGHT AFTER DINNER--THE TABLE IS SET FOR ONLY TWO PLACES, SINCE BRUCE (*BATMAN*) WAYNE IS OFF ON A *JUSTICE LEAGUE* CASE..

GOT TO GET TO MY DARK ROOM, AUNT HARRIET, AND SEE IF MY PICTURES ARE DEVELOPED YET!

ALONE IN HIS DARK ROOM, DICK GRAYSON IS STUNNED TO SEE...

WH--WHAT'S *THIS* ? LOOKS LIKE SOMEONE IN THE WINDOW OF THAT HAUNTED HOUSE ... SOMEONE AWFULLY FAMILIAR! I'D BETTER PUT THIS SLIDE ON A SCREEN AND SEE WHAT THAT FIGURE LOOKS LIKE BLOWN UP!

2

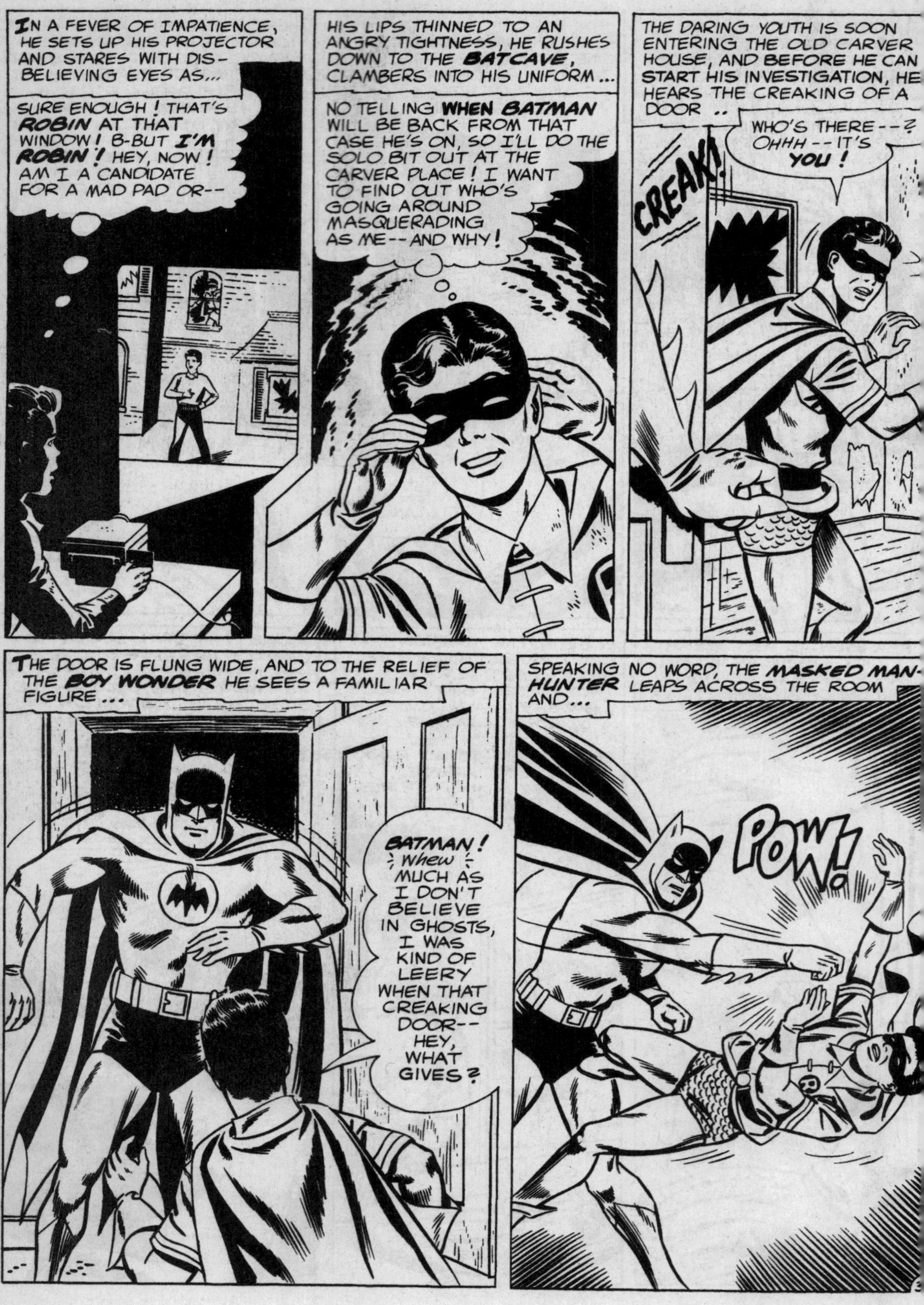
IN A FEVER OF IMPATIENCE, HE SETS UP HIS PROJECTOR AND STARES WITH DISBELIEVING EYES AS...
SURE ENOUGH! THAT'S ROBIN AT THAT WINDOW! B-BUT I'M ROBIN! HEY, NOW! AM I A CANDIDATE FOR A MAD PAD OR--
HIS LIPS THINNED TO AN ANGRY TIGHTNESS, HE RUSHES DOWN TO THE BATCAVE, CLAMBERS INTO HIS UNIFORM...
NO TELLING WHEN BATMAN WILL BE BACK FROM THAT CASE HE'S ON, SO I'LL DO THE SOLO BIT OUT AT THE CARVER PLACE! I WANT TO FIND OUT WHO'S GOING AROUND MASQUERADING AS ME--AND WHY!
THE DARING YOUTH IS SOON ENTERING THE OLD CARVER HOUSE, AND BEFORE HE CAN START HIS INVESTIGATION, HE HEARS THE CREAKING OF A DOOR..
CREAK!
WHO'S THERE--? OHHH--IT'S YOU!
THE DOOR IS FLUNG WIDE, AND TO THE RELIEF OF THE BOY WONDER HE SEES A FAMILIAR FIGURE...
BATMAN! Whew MUCH AS I DON'T BELIEVE IN GHOSTS, I WAS KIND OF LEERY WHEN THAT CREAKING DOOR--HEY, WHAT GIVES?
SPEAKING NO WORD, THE MASKED MAN-HUNTER LEAPS ACROSS THE ROOM AND...
POW!

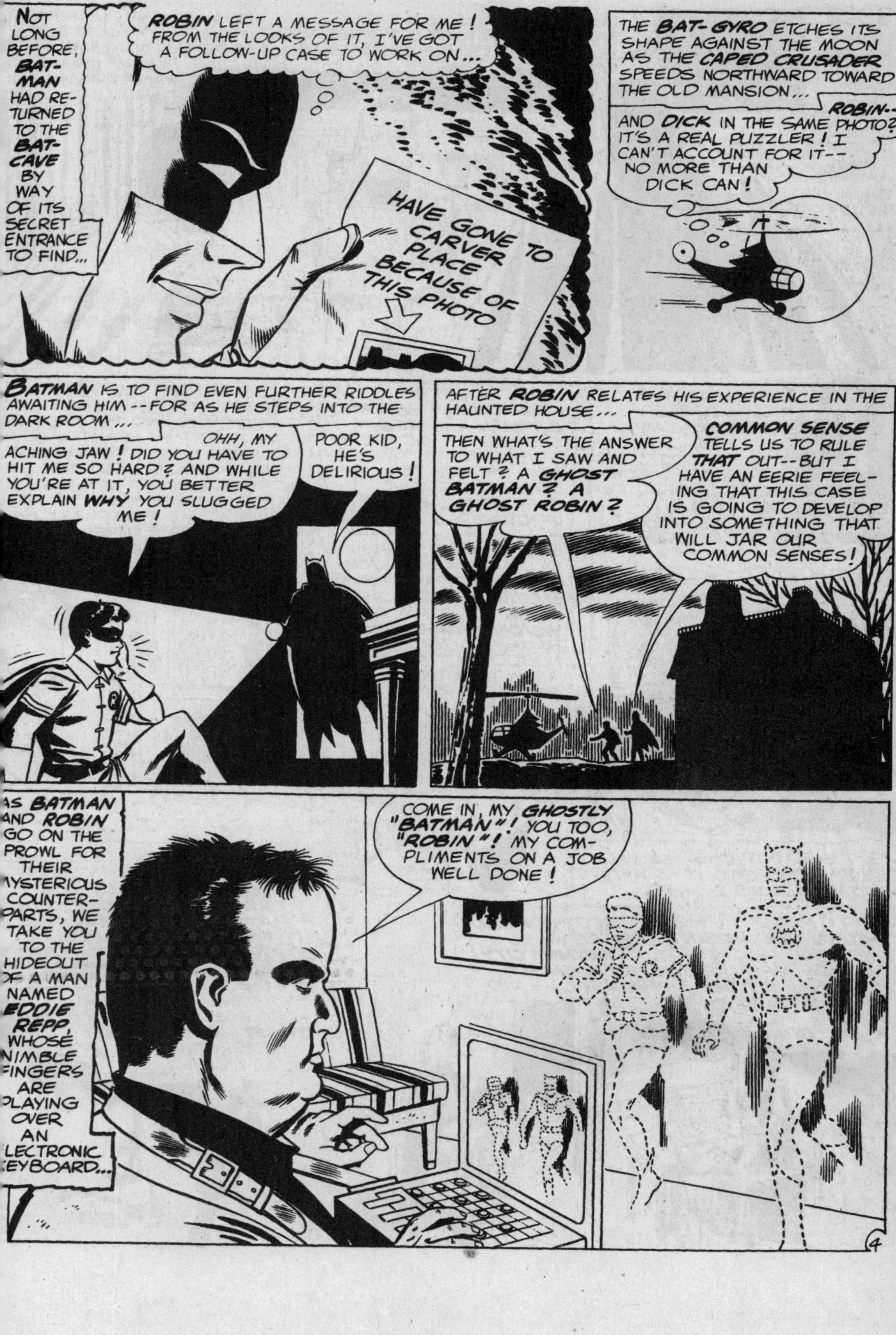
NOT LONG BEFORE, BATMAN HAD RETURNED TO THE BAT-CAVE BY WAY OF ITS SECRET ENTRANCE TO FIND...
ROBIN LEFT A MESSAGE FOR ME! FROM THE LOOKS OF IT, I'VE GOT A FOLLOW-UP CASE TO WORK ON...
HAVE GONE TO CARVER PLACE BECAUSE OF THIS PHOTO
THE BAT-GYRO ETCHES ITS SHAPE AGAINST THE MOON AS THE CAPED CRUSADER SPEEDS NORTHWARD TOWARD THE OLD MANSION...
ROBIN--AND DICK IN THE SAME PHOTO? IT'S A REAL PUZZLER! I CAN'T ACCOUNT FOR IT--NO MORE THAN DICK CAN!
BATMAN IS TO FIND EVEN FURTHER RIDDLES AWAITING HIM--FOR AS HE STEPS INTO THE DARK ROOM...
OHH, MY ACHING JAW! DID YOU HAVE TO HIT ME SO HARD? AND WHILE YOU'RE AT IT, YOU BETTER EXPLAIN WHY YOU SLUGGED ME!
POOR KID, HE'S DELIRIOUS!
AFTER ROBIN RELATES HIS EXPERIENCE IN THE HAUNTED HOUSE...
THEN WHAT'S THE ANSWER TO WHAT I SAW AND FELT? A GHOST BATMAN? A GHOST ROBIN?
COMMON SENSE TELLS US TO RULE THAT OUT--BUT I HAVE AN EERIE FEELING THAT THIS CASE IS GOING TO DEVELOP INTO SOMETHING THAT WILL JAR OUR COMMON SENSES!
AS BATMAN AND ROBIN GO ON THE PROWL FOR THEIR MYSTERIOUS COUNTERPARTS, WE TAKE YOU TO THE HIDEOUT OF A MAN NAMED EDDIE REPP, WHOSE NIMBLE FINGERS ARE PLAYING OVER AN ELECTRONIC KEYBOARD...
COME IN, MY GHOSTLY "BATMAN"! YOU TOO, "ROBIN"! MY COMPLIMENTS ON A JOB WELL DONE!
4

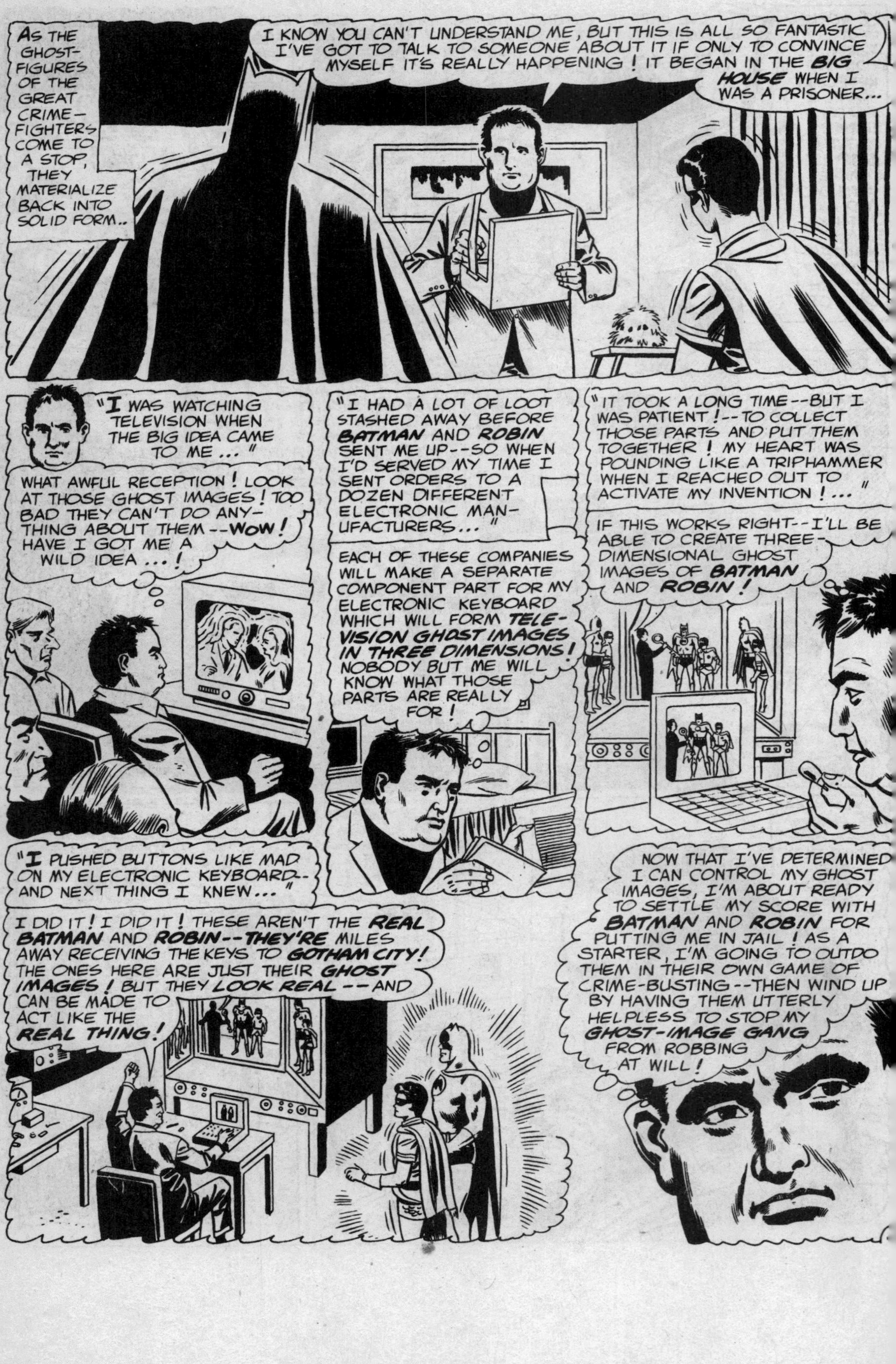
AS THE GHOST-FIGURES OF THE GREAT CRIME-FIGHTERS COME TO A STOP, THEY MATERIALIZE BACK INTO SOLID FORM..
I KNOW YOU CAN'T UNDERSTAND ME, BUT THIS IS ALL SO FANTASTIC I'VE GOT TO TALK TO SOMEONE ABOUT IT IF ONLY TO CONVINCE MYSELF IT'S REALLY HAPPENING! IT BEGAN IN THE BIG HOUSE WHEN I WAS A PRISONER...
"I WAS WATCHING TELEVISION WHEN THE BIG IDEA CAME TO ME..."
WHAT AWFUL RECEPTION! LOOK AT THOSE GHOST IMAGES! TOO BAD THEY CAN'T DO ANYTHING ABOUT THEM--WOW! HAVE I GOT ME A WILD IDEA...!
"I HAD A LOT OF LOOT STASHED AWAY BEFORE BATMAN AND ROBIN SENT ME UP--SO WHEN I'D SERVED MY TIME I SENT ORDERS TO A DOZEN DIFFERENT ELECTRONIC MANUFACTURERS..."
EACH OF THESE COMPANIES WILL MAKE A SEPARATE COMPONENT PART FOR MY ELECTRONIC KEYBOARD WHICH WILL FORM TELEVISION GHOST IMAGES IN THREE DIMENSIONS! NOBODY BUT ME WILL KNOW WHAT THOSE PARTS ARE REALLY FOR!
"IT TOOK A LONG TIME--BUT I WAS PATIENT!--TO COLLECT THOSE PARTS AND PUT THEM TOGETHER! MY HEART WAS POUNDING LIKE A TRIPHAMMER WHEN I REACHED OUT TO ACTIVATE MY INVENTION!..."
IF THIS WORKS RIGHT--I'LL BE ABLE TO CREATE THREE-DIMENSIONAL GHOST IMAGES OF BATMAN AND ROBIN!
"I PUSHED BUTTONS LIKE MAD ON MY ELECTRONIC KEYBOARD--AND NEXT THING I KNEW..."
I DID IT! I DID IT! THESE AREN'T THE REAL BATMAN AND ROBIN--THEY'RE MILES AWAY RECEIVING THE KEYS TO GOTHAM CITY! THE ONES HERE ARE JUST THEIR GHOST IMAGES! BUT THEY LOOK REAL--AND CAN BE MADE TO ACT LIKE THE REAL THING!
NOW THAT I'VE DETERMINED I CAN CONTROL MY GHOST IMAGES, I'M ABOUT READY TO SETTLE MY SCORE WITH BATMAN AND ROBIN FOR PUTTING ME IN JAIL! AS A STARTER, I'M GOING TO OUTDO THEM IN THEIR OWN GAME OF CRIME-BUSTING--THEN WIND UP BY HAVING THEM UTTERLY HELPLESS TO STOP MY GHOST-IMAGE GANG FROM ROBBING AT WILL!

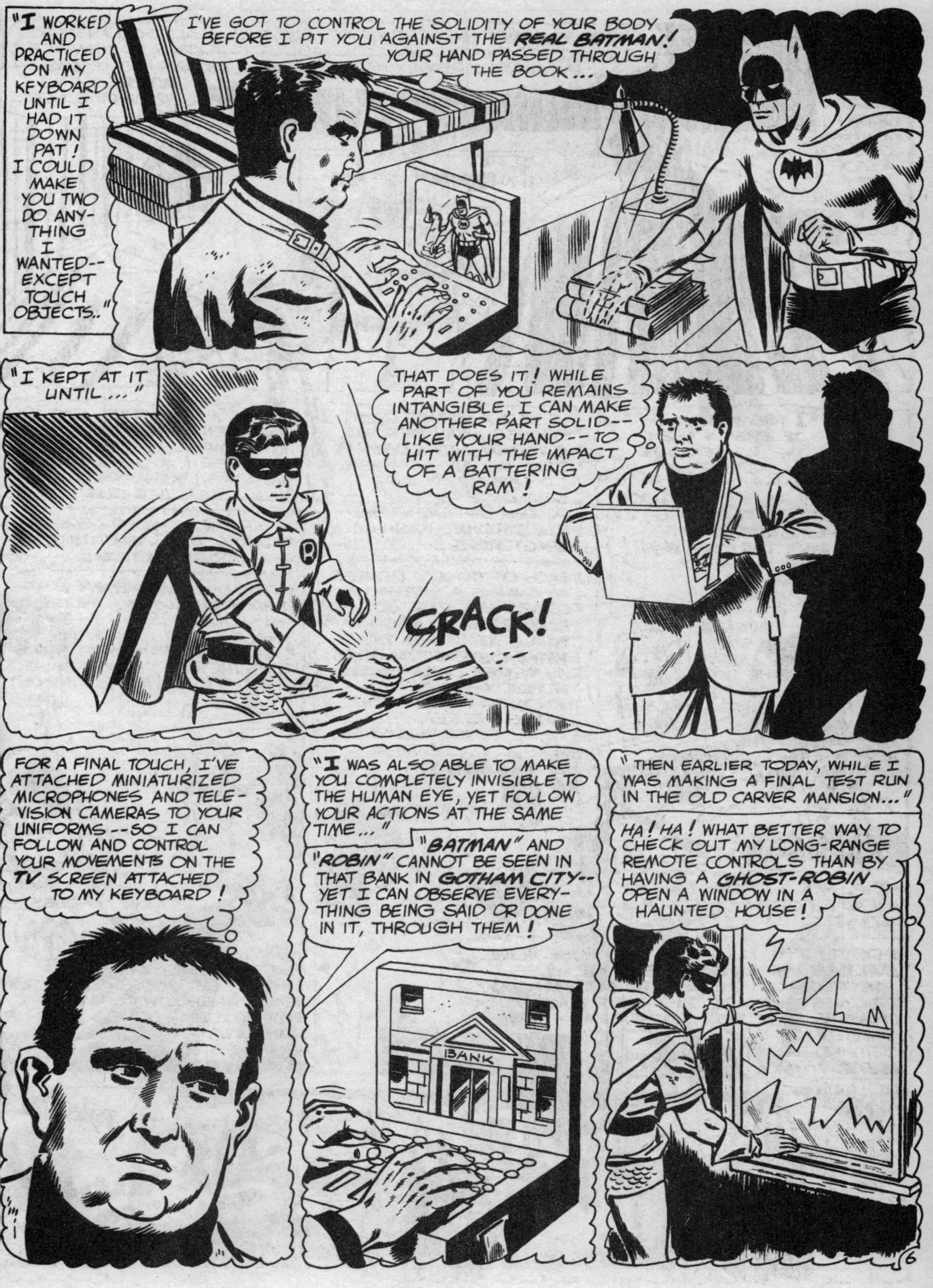
"I WORKED AND PRACTICED ON MY KEYBOARD UNTIL I HAD IT DOWN PAT! I COULD MAKE YOU TWO DO ANYTHING I WANTED--EXCEPT TOUCH OBJECTS.."
I'VE GOT TO CONTROL THE SOLIDITY OF YOUR BODY BEFORE I PIT YOU AGAINST THE REAL BATMAN! YOUR HAND PASSED THROUGH THE BOOK...
"I KEPT AT IT UNTIL..."
THAT DOES IT! WHILE PART OF YOU REMAINS INTANGIBLE, I CAN MAKE ANOTHER PART SOLID--LIKE YOUR HAND--TO HIT WITH THE IMPACT OF A BATTERING RAM!
CRACK!
FOR A FINAL TOUCH, I'VE ATTACHED MINIATURIZED MICROPHONES AND TELEVISION CAMERAS TO YOUR UNIFORMS--SO I CAN FOLLOW AND CONTROL YOUR MOVEMENTS ON THE TV SCREEN ATTACHED TO MY KEYBOARD!
"I WAS ALSO ABLE TO MAKE YOU COMPLETELY INVISIBLE TO THE HUMAN EYE, YET FOLLOW YOUR ACTIONS AT THE SAME TIME..."
"BATMAN" AND "ROBIN" CANNOT BE SEEN IN THAT BANK IN GOTHAM CITY--YET I CAN OBSERVE EVERYTHING BEING SAID OR DONE IN IT, THROUGH THEM!
BANK
"THEN EARLIER TODAY, WHILE I WAS MAKING A FINAL TEST RUN IN THE OLD CARVER MANSION..."
HA! HA! WHAT BETTER WAY TO CHECK OUT MY LONG-RANGE REMOTE CONTROLS THAN BY HAVING A GHOST-ROBIN OPEN A WINDOW IN A HAUNTED HOUSE!
6

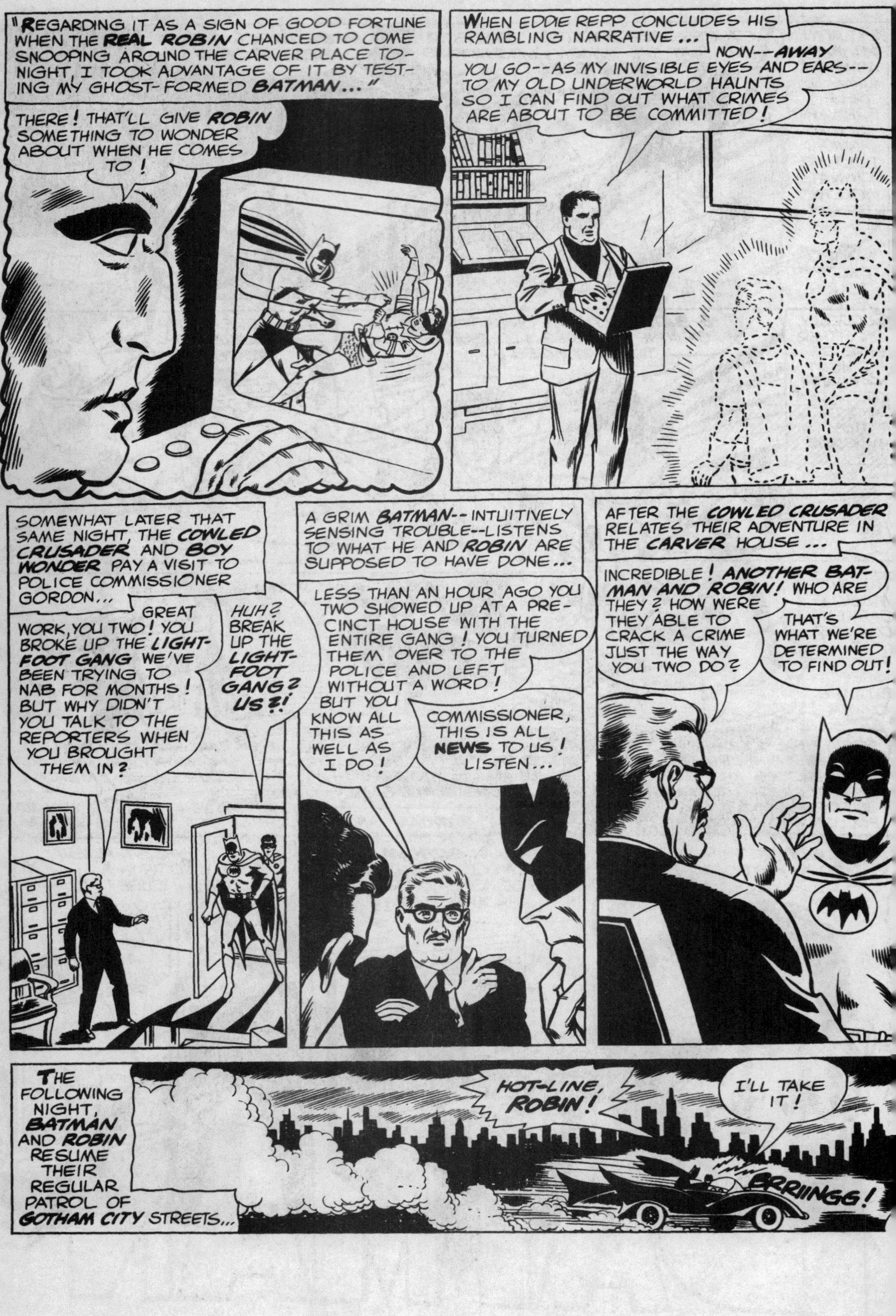
"REGARDING IT AS A SIGN OF GOOD FORTUNE WHEN THE REAL ROBIN CHANCED TO COME SNOOPING AROUND THE CARVER PLACE TONIGHT, I TOOK ADVANTAGE OF IT BY TESTING MY GHOST-FORMED BATMAN..."
THERE! THAT'LL GIVE ROBIN SOMETHING TO WONDER ABOUT WHEN HE COMES TO!
WHEN EDDIE REPP CONCLUDES HIS RAMBLING NARRATIVE...
NOW--AWAY YOU GO--AS MY INVISIBLE EYES AND EARS--TO MY OLD UNDERWORLD HAUNTS SO I CAN FIND OUT WHAT CRIMES ARE ABOUT TO BE COMMITTED!
SOMEWHAT LATER THAT SAME NIGHT, THE COWLED CRUSADER AND BOY WONDER PAY A VISIT TO POLICE COMMISSIONER GORDON...
GREAT WORK, YOU TWO! YOU BROKE UP THE LIGHT-FOOT GANG WE'VE BEEN TRYING TO NAB FOR MONTHS! BUT WHY DIDN'T YOU TALK TO THE REPORTERS WHEN YOU BROUGHT THEM IN?
HUH? BREAK UP THE LIGHT-FOOT GANG? US?!
A GRIM BATMAN--INTUITIVELY SENSING TROUBLE--LISTENS TO WHAT HE AND ROBIN ARE SUPPOSED TO HAVE DONE...
LESS THAN AN HOUR AGO YOU TWO SHOWED UP AT A PRECINCT HOUSE WITH THE ENTIRE GANG! YOU TURNED THEM OVER TO THE POLICE AND LEFT WITHOUT A WORD!
BUT YOU KNOW ALL THIS AS WELL AS I DO!
COMMISSIONER, THIS IS ALL NEWS TO US! LISTEN...
AFTER THE COWLED CRUSADER RELATES THEIR ADVENTURE IN THE CARVER HOUSE...
INCREDIBLE! ANOTHER BATMAN AND ROBIN! WHO ARE THEY? HOW WERE THEY ABLE TO CRACK A CRIME JUST THE WAY YOU TWO DO?
THAT'S WHAT WE'RE DETERMINED TO FIND OUT!
THE FOLLOWING NIGHT, BATMAN AND ROBIN RESUME THEIR REGULAR PATROL OF GOTHAM CITY STREETS...
HOT-LINE, ROBIN!
I'LL TAKE IT!
BRRIINGG!

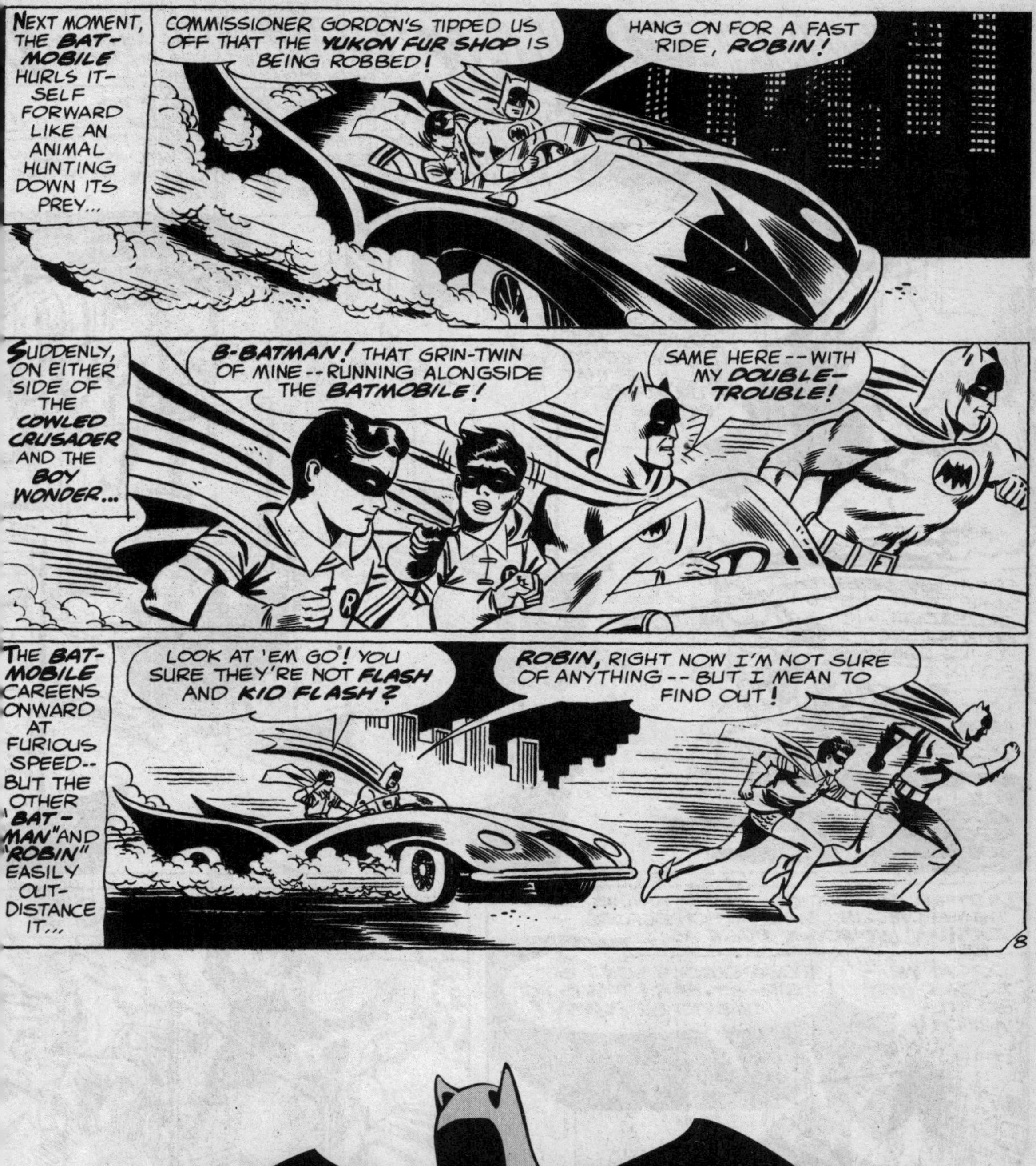
NEXT MOMENT, THE BAT-MOBILE HURLS IT-SELF FORWARD LIKE AN ANIMAL HUNTING DOWN ITS PREY...
COMMISSIONER GORDON'S TIPPED US OFF THAT THE YUKON FUR SHOP IS BEING ROBBED!
HANG ON FOR A FAST RIDE, ROBIN!
SUDDENLY, ON EITHER SIDE OF THE COWLED CRUSADER AND THE BOY WONDER...
B-BATMAN! THAT GRIN-TWIN OF MINE--RUNNING ALONGSIDE THE BATMOBILE!
SAME HERE--WITH MY DOUBLE-TROUBLE!
THE BAT-MOBILE CAREENS ONWARD AT FURIOUS SPEED--BUT THE OTHER "BAT-MAN" AND "ROBIN" EASILY OUT-DISTANCE IT...
LOOK AT 'EM GO! YOU SURE THEY'RE NOT FLASH AND KID FLASH?
ROBIN, RIGHT NOW I'M NOT SURE OF ANYTHING--BUT I MEAN TO FIND OUT!
8

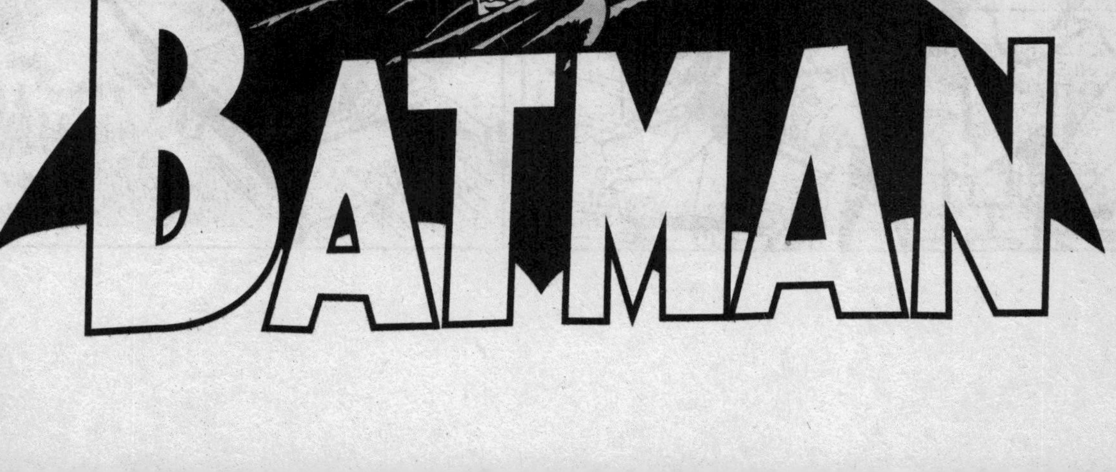
BATMAN

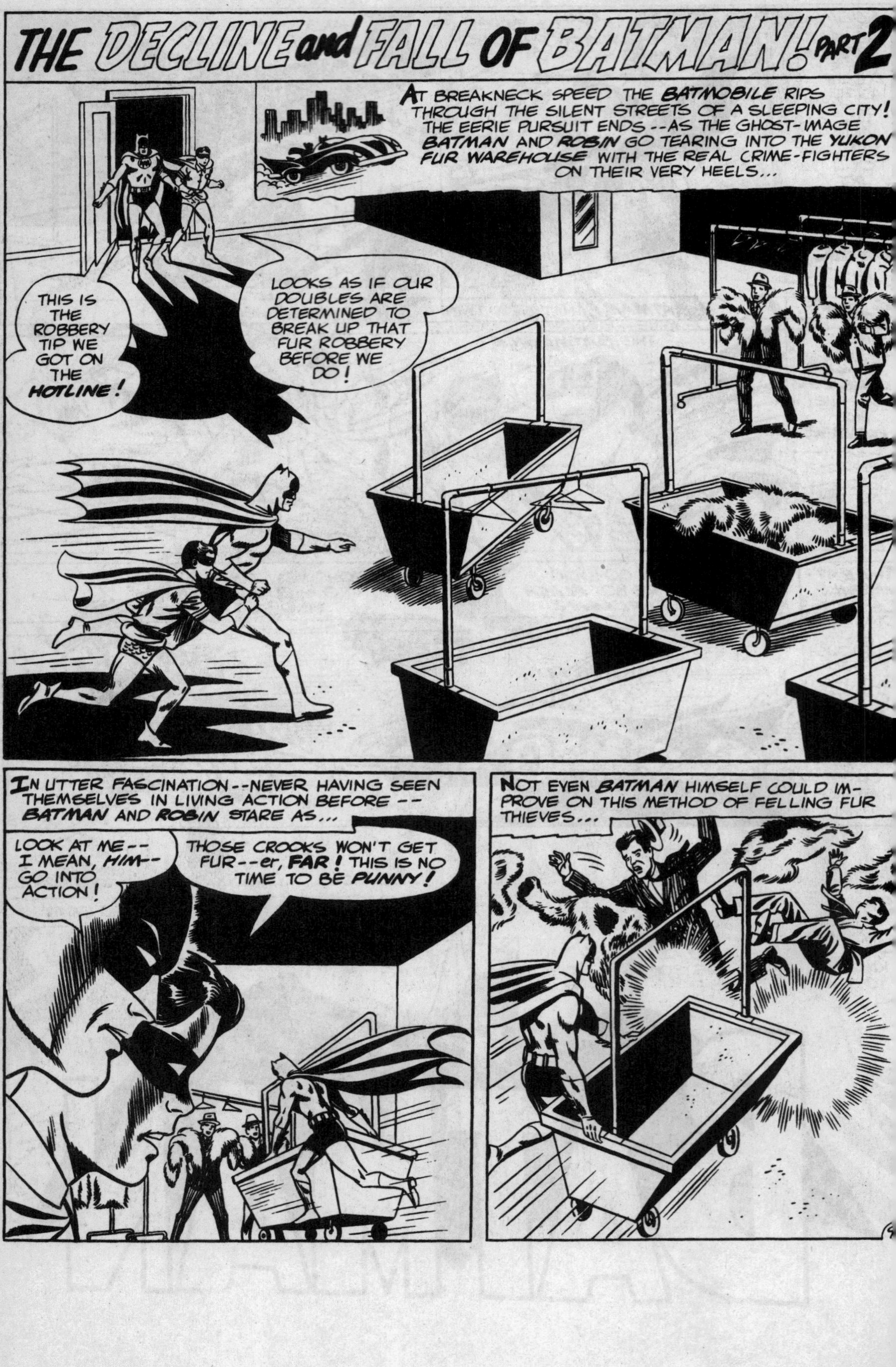
THE DECLINE and FALL OF BATMAN! PART 2
AT BREAKNECK SPEED THE BATMOBILE RIPS THROUGH THE SILENT STREETS OF A SLEEPING CITY! THE EERIE PURSUIT ENDS--AS THE GHOST-IMAGE BATMAN AND ROBIN GO TEARING INTO THE YUKON FUR WAREHOUSE WITH THE REAL CRIME-FIGHTERS ON THEIR VERY HEELS...
THIS IS THE ROBBERY TIP WE GOT ON THE HOTLINE!
LOOKS AS IF OUR DOUBLES ARE DETERMINED TO BREAK UP THAT FUR ROBBERY BEFORE WE DO!
IN UTTER FASCINATION--NEVER HAVING SEEN THEMSELVES IN LIVING ACTION BEFORE--BATMAN AND ROBIN STARE AS...
LOOK AT ME--I MEAN, HIM--GO INTO ACTION!
THOSE CROOKS WON'T GET FUR--er, FAR! THIS IS NO TIME TO BE PUNNY!
NOT EVEN BATMAN HIMSELF COULD IMPROVE ON THIS METHOD OF FELLING FUR THIEVES...

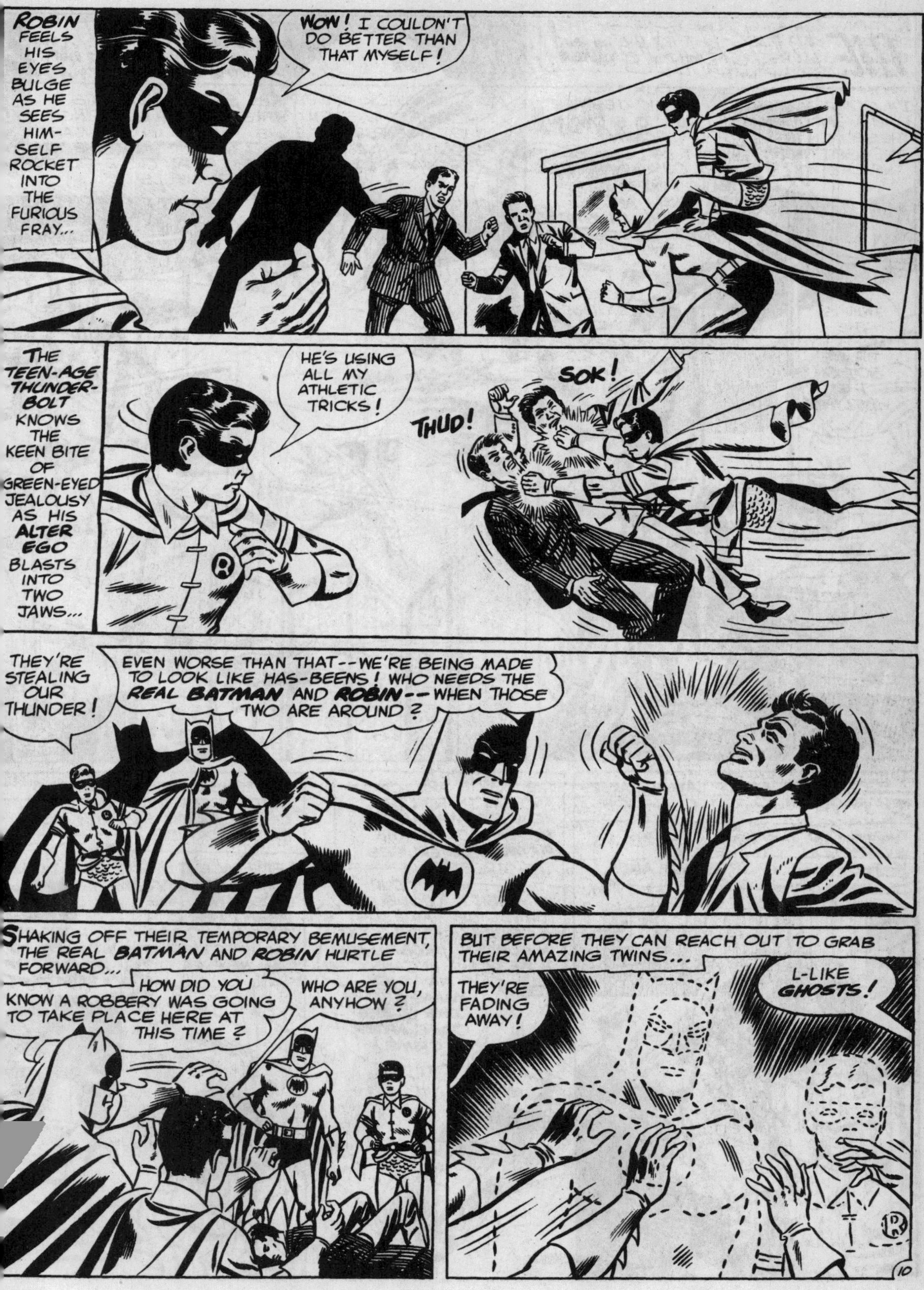
ROBIN FEELS HIS EYES BULGE AS HE SEES HIMSELF ROCKET INTO THE FURIOUS FRAY...
WOW! I COULDN'T DO BETTER THAN THAT MYSELF!
THE TEEN-AGE THUNDER-BOLT KNOWS THE KEEN BITE OF GREEN-EYED JEALOUSY AS HIS ALTER EGO BLASTS INTO TWO JAWS...
HE'S USING ALL MY ATHLETIC TRICKS!
SOK!
THUD!
THEY'RE STEALING OUR THUNDER!
EVEN WORSE THAN THAT--WE'RE BEING MADE TO LOOK LIKE HAS-BEENS! WHO NEEDS THE REAL BATMAN AND ROBIN--WHEN THOSE TWO ARE AROUND?
SHAKING OFF THEIR TEMPORARY BEMUSEMENT, THE REAL BATMAN AND ROBIN HURTLE FORWARD...
HOW DID YOU KNOW A ROBBERY WAS GOING TO TAKE PLACE HERE AT THIS TIME?
WHO ARE YOU, ANYHOW?
BUT BEFORE THEY CAN REACH OUT TO GRAB THEIR AMAZING TWINS...
THEY'RE FADING AWAY!
L-LIKE GHOSTS!
10

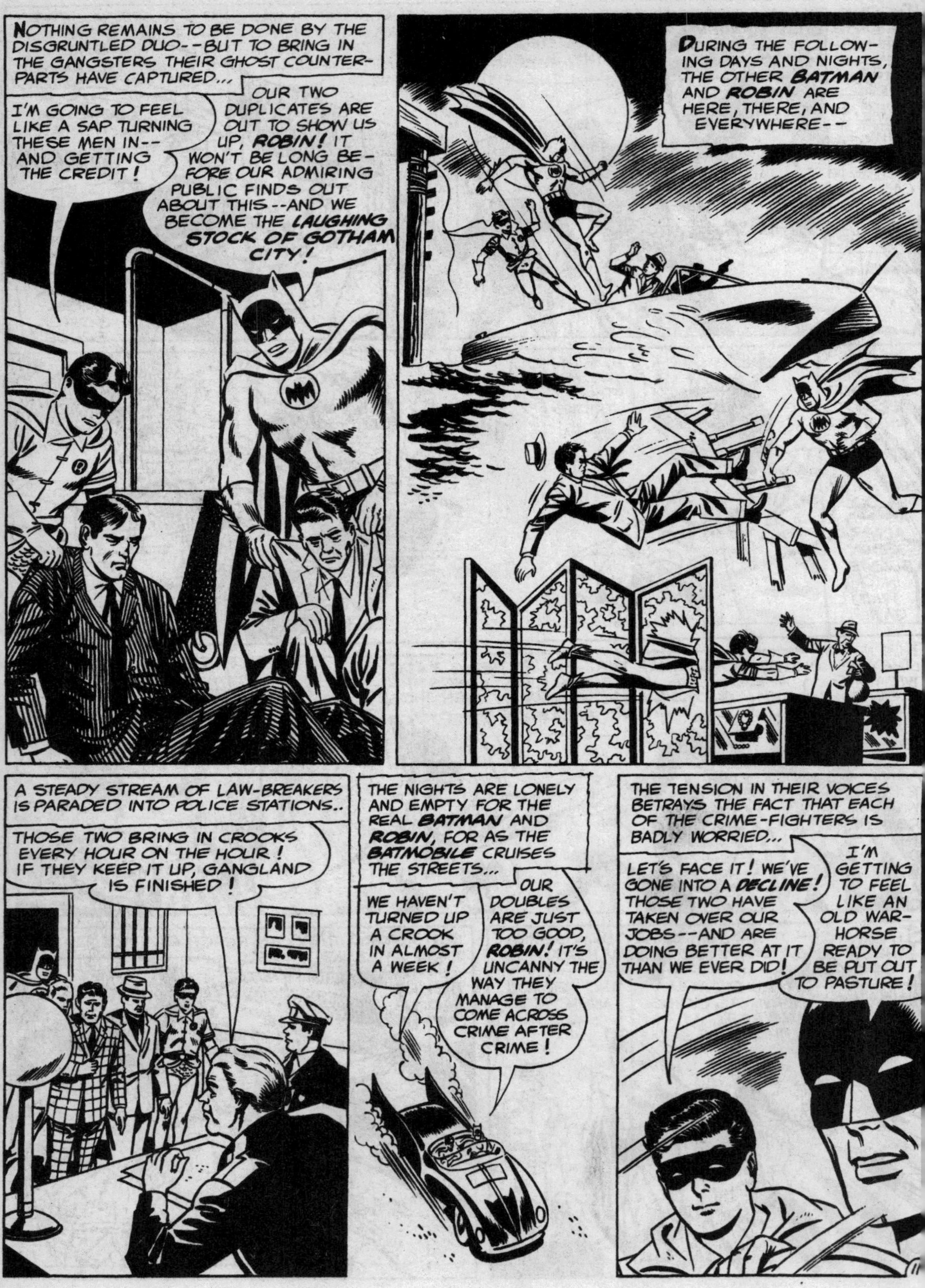
NOTHING REMAINS TO BE DONE BY THE DISGRUNTLED DUO--BUT TO BRING IN THE GANGSTERS THEIR GHOST COUNTERPARTS HAVE CAPTURED...
I'M GOING TO FEEL LIKE A SAP TURNING THESE MEN IN--AND GETTING THE CREDIT!
OUR TWO DUPLICATES ARE OUT TO SHOW US UP, ROBIN! IT WON'T BE LONG BEFORE OUR ADMIRING PUBLIC FINDS OUT ABOUT THIS--AND WE BECOME THE LAUGHING STOCK OF GOTHAM CITY!
DURING THE FOLLOWING DAYS AND NIGHTS, THE OTHER BATMAN AND ROBIN ARE HERE, THERE, AND EVERYWHERE--
A STEADY STREAM OF LAW-BREAKERS IS PARADED INTO POLICE STATIONS..
THOSE TWO BRING IN CROOKS EVERY HOUR ON THE HOUR! IF THEY KEEP IT UP, GANGLAND IS FINISHED!
THE NIGHTS ARE LONELY AND EMPTY FOR THE REAL BATMAN AND ROBIN, FOR AS THE BATMOBILE CRUISES THE STREETS...
WE HAVEN'T TURNED UP A CROOK IN ALMOST A WEEK!
OUR DOUBLES ARE JUST TOO GOOD, ROBIN! IT'S UNCANNY THE WAY THEY MANAGE TO COME ACROSS CRIME AFTER CRIME!
THE TENSION IN THEIR VOICES BETRAYS THE FACT THAT EACH OF THE CRIME-FIGHTERS IS BADLY WORRIED...
LET'S FACE IT! WE'VE GONE INTO A DECLINE! THOSE TWO HAVE TAKEN OVER OUR JOBS--AND ARE DOING BETTER AT IT THAN WE EVER DID!
I'M GETTING TO FEEL LIKE AN OLD WAR-HORSE READY TO BE PUT OUT TO PASTURE!

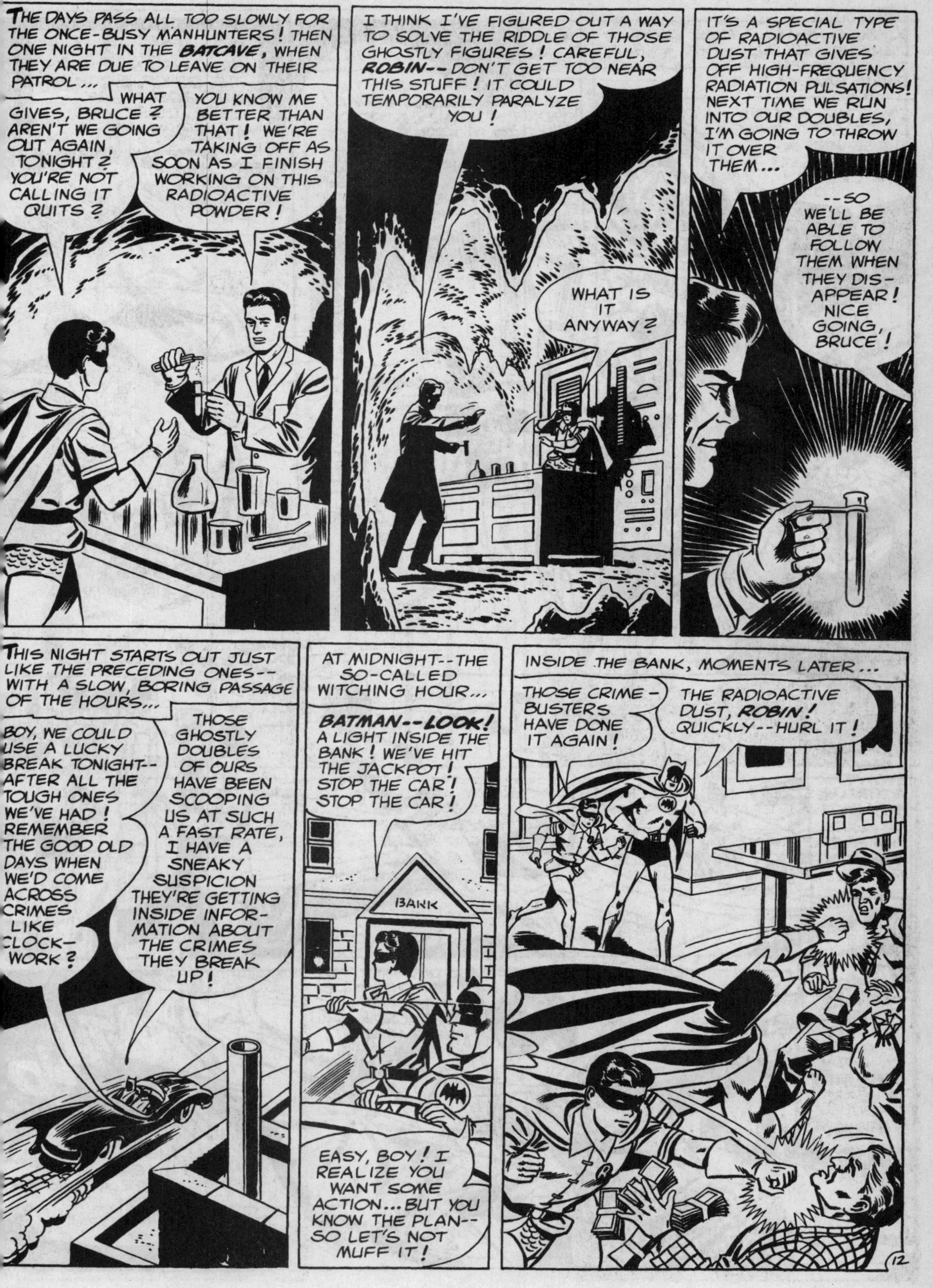
THE DAYS PASS ALL TOO SLOWLY FOR THE ONCE-BUSY MANHUNTERS! THEN ONE NIGHT IN THE BATCAVE, WHEN THEY ARE DUE TO LEAVE ON THEIR PATROL...
WHAT GIVES, BRUCE? AREN'T WE GOING OUT AGAIN, TONIGHT? YOU'RE NOT CALLING IT QUITS?
YOU KNOW ME BETTER THAN THAT! WE'RE TAKING OFF AS SOON AS I FINISH WORKING ON THIS RADIOACTIVE POWDER!
I THINK I'VE FIGURED OUT A WAY TO SOLVE THE RIDDLE OF THOSE GHOSTLY FIGURES! CAREFUL, ROBIN-- DON'T GET TOO NEAR THIS STUFF! IT COULD TEMPORARILY PARALYZE YOU!
WHAT IS IT ANYWAY?
IT'S A SPECIAL TYPE OF RADIOACTIVE DUST THAT GIVES OFF HIGH-FREQUENCY RADIATION PULSATIONS! NEXT TIME WE RUN INTO OUR DOUBLES, I'M GOING TO THROW IT OVER THEM...
--SO WE'LL BE ABLE TO FOLLOW THEM WHEN THEY DIS-APPEAR! NICE GOING, BRUCE!
THIS NIGHT STARTS OUT JUST LIKE THE PRECEDING ONES-- WITH A SLOW, BORING PASSAGE OF THE HOURS...
BOY, WE COULD USE A LUCKY BREAK TONIGHT-- AFTER ALL THE TOUGH ONES WE'VE HAD! REMEMBER THE GOOD OLD DAYS WHEN WE'D COME ACROSS CRIMES LIKE CLOCK-WORK?
THOSE GHOSTLY DOUBLES OF OURS HAVE BEEN SCOOPING US AT SUCH A FAST RATE, I HAVE A SNEAKY SUSPICION THEY'RE GETTING INSIDE INFOR-MATION ABOUT THE CRIMES THEY BREAK UP!
AT MIDNIGHT--THE SO-CALLED WITCHING HOUR...
BATMAN--LOOK! A LIGHT INSIDE THE BANK! WE'VE HIT THE JACKPOT! STOP THE CAR! STOP THE CAR!
BANK
EASY, BOY! I REALIZE YOU WANT SOME ACTION...BUT YOU KNOW THE PLAN-- SO LET'S NOT MUFF IT!
INSIDE THE BANK, MOMENTS LATER...
THOSE CRIME-BUSTERS HAVE DONE IT AGAIN!
THE RADIOACTIVE DUST, ROBIN! QUICKLY--HURL IT!
12

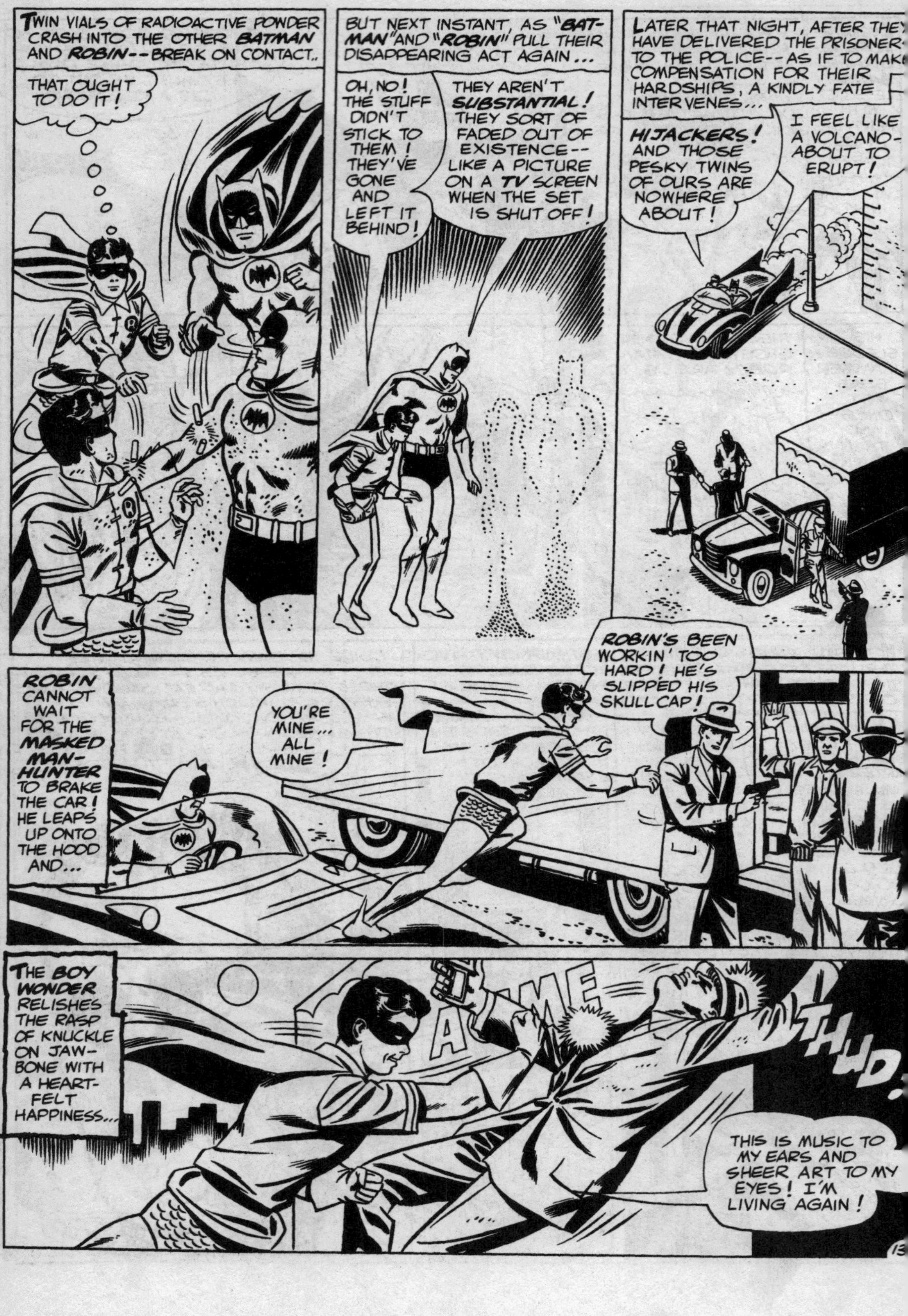
TWIN VIALS OF RADIOACTIVE POWDER CRASH INTO THE OTHER BATMAN AND ROBIN--BREAK ON CONTACT..
THAT OUGHT TO DO IT!
BUT NEXT INSTANT, AS "BATMAN" AND "ROBIN" PULL THEIR DISAPPEARING ACT AGAIN...
OH, NO! THE STUFF DIDN'T STICK TO THEM! THEY'VE GONE AND LEFT IT BEHIND!
THEY AREN'T SUBSTANTIAL! THEY SORT OF FADED OUT OF EXISTENCE--LIKE A PICTURE ON A TV SCREEN WHEN THE SET IS SHUT OFF!
HIJACKERS! AND THOSE PESKY TWINS OF OURS ARE NOWHERE ABOUT!
I FEEL LIKE A VOLCANO--ABOUT TO ERUPT!
ROBIN CANNOT WAIT FOR THE MASKED MAN-HUNTER TO BRAKE THE CAR! HE LEAPS UP ONTO THE HOOD AND...
YOU'RE MINE... ALL MINE!
ROBIN'S BEEN WORKIN' TOO HARD! HE'S SLIPPED HIS SKULLCAP!
THE BOY WONDER RELISHES THE RASP OF KNUCKLE ON JAW-BONE WITH A HEART-FELT HAPPINESS...
THUD!
THIS IS MUSIC TO MY EARS AND SHEER ART TO MY EYES! I'M LIVING AGAIN!
13

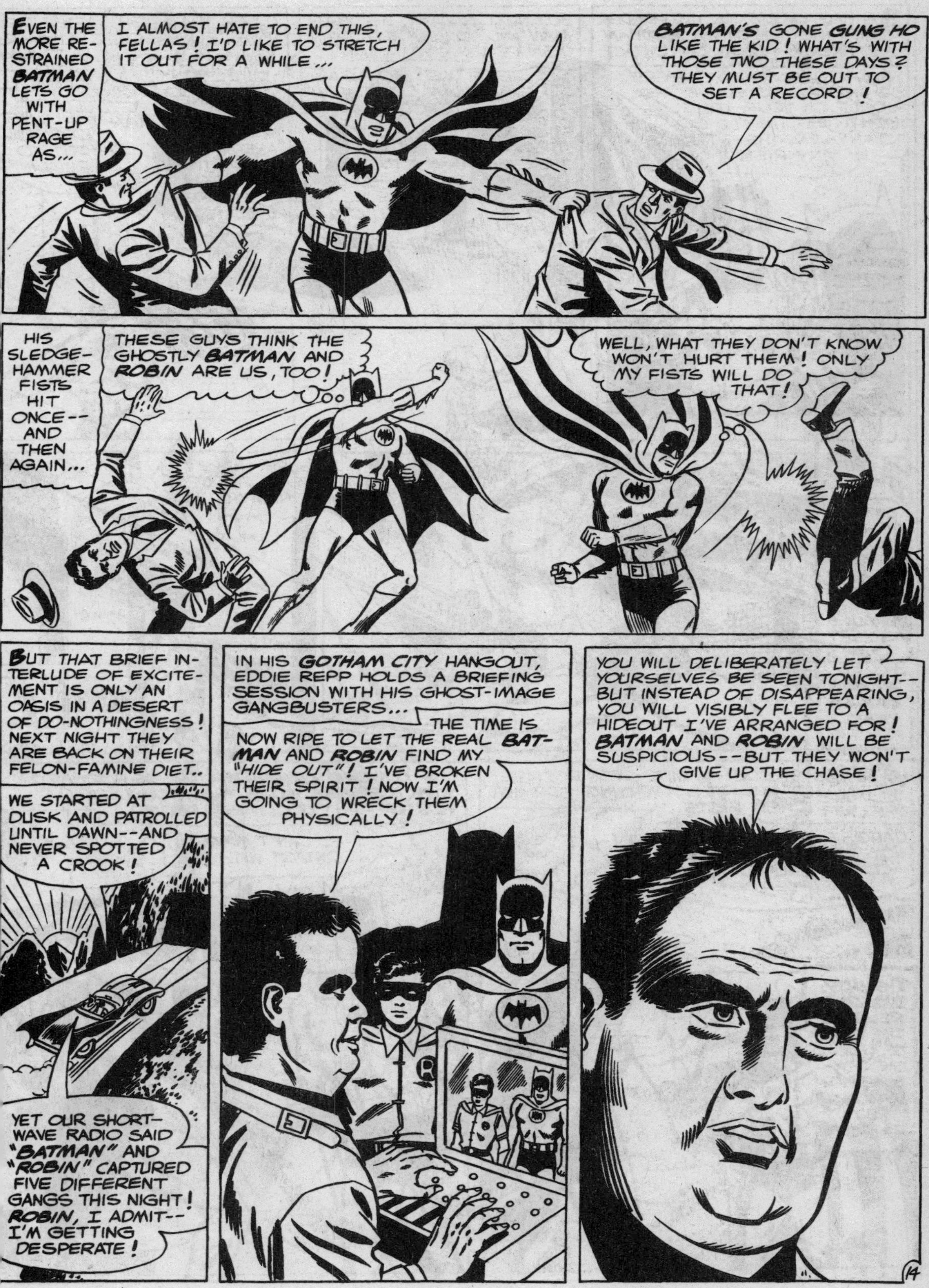
EVEN THE MORE RE-STRAINED BATMAN LETS GO WITH PENT-UP RAGE AS...
I ALMOST HATE TO END THIS, FELLAS! I'D LIKE TO STRETCH IT OUT FOR A WHILE...
BATMAN'S GONE GUNG HO LIKE THE KID! WHAT'S WITH THOSE TWO THESE DAYS? THEY MUST BE OUT TO SET A RECORD!
HIS SLEDGE-HAMMER FISTS HIT ONCE--AND THEN AGAIN...
THESE GUYS THINK THE GHOSTLY BATMAN AND ROBIN ARE US, TOO!
WELL, WHAT THEY DON'T KNOW WON'T HURT THEM! ONLY MY FISTS WILL DO THAT!
BUT THAT BRIEF IN-TERLUDE OF EXCITE-MENT IS ONLY AN OASIS IN A DESERT OF DO-NOTHINGNESS! NEXT NIGHT THEY ARE BACK ON THEIR FELON-FAMINE DIET..
WE STARTED AT DUSK AND PATROLLED UNTIL DAWN--AND NEVER SPOTTED A CROOK!
YET OUR SHORT-WAVE RADIO SAID "BATMAN" AND "ROBIN" CAPTURED FIVE DIFFERENT GANGS THIS NIGHT! ROBIN, I ADMIT--I'M GETTING DESPERATE!
IN HIS GOTHAM CITY HANGOUT, EDDIE REPP HOLDS A BRIEFING SESSION WITH HIS GHOST-IMAGE GANGBUSTERS...
THE TIME IS NOW RIPE TO LET THE REAL BAT-MAN AND ROBIN FIND MY "HIDE OUT"! I'VE BROKEN THEIR SPIRIT! NOW I'M GOING TO WRECK THEM PHYSICALLY!
YOU WILL DELIBERATELY LET YOURSELVES BE SEEN TONIGHT--BUT INSTEAD OF DISAPPEARING, YOU WILL VISIBLY FLEE TO A HIDEOUT I'VE ARRANGED FOR! BATMAN AND ROBIN WILL BE SUSPICIOUS--BUT THEY WON'T GIVE UP THE CHASE!
14

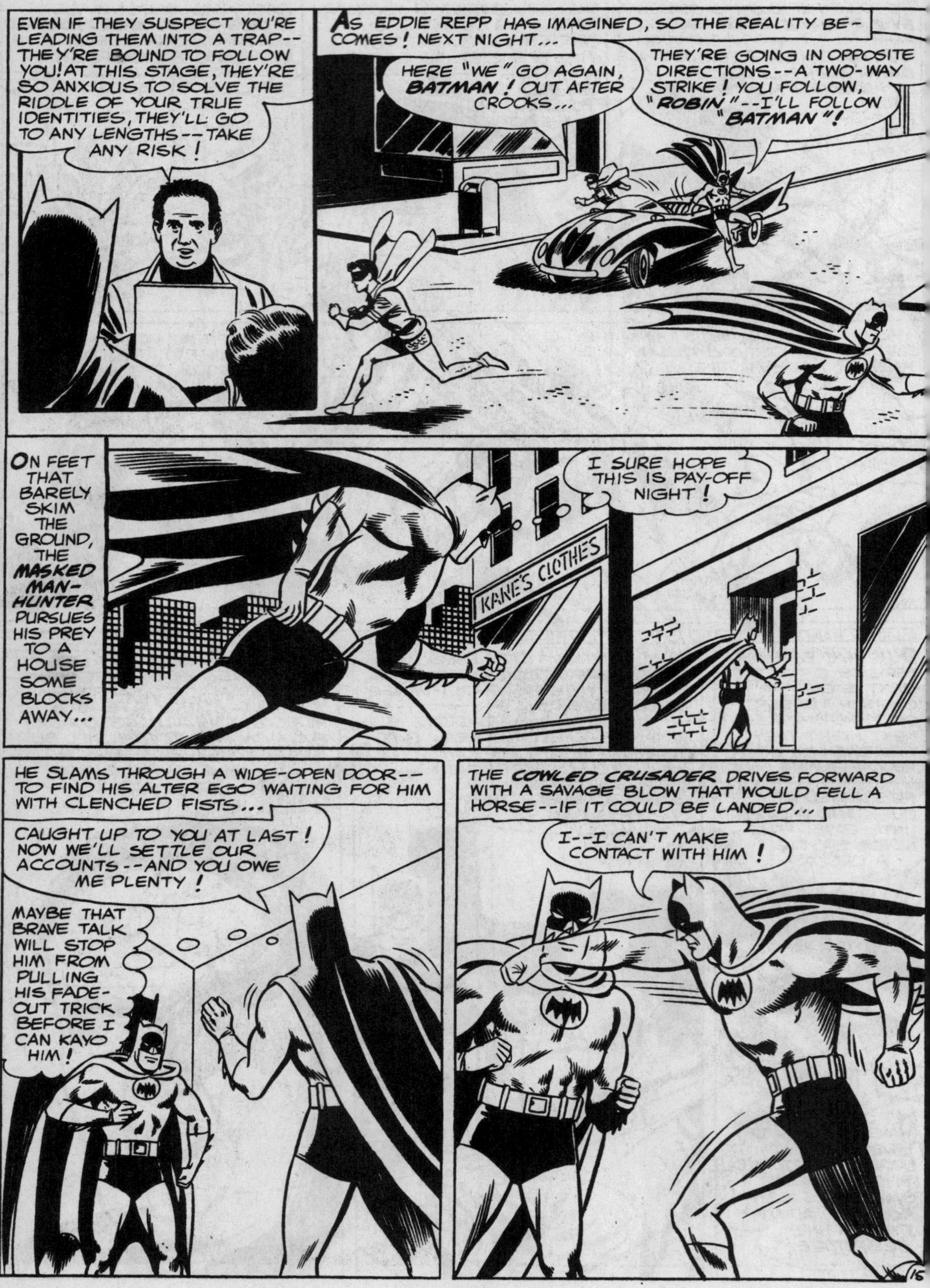
EVEN IF THEY SUSPECT YOU'RE LEADING THEM INTO A TRAP--THEY'RE BOUND TO FOLLOW YOU! AT THIS STAGE, THEY'RE SO ANXIOUS TO SOLVE THE RIDDLE OF YOUR TRUE IDENTITIES, THEY'LL GO TO ANY LENGTHS--TAKE ANY RISK!
AS EDDIE REPP HAS IMAGINED, SO THE REALITY BECOMES! NEXT NIGHT...
HERE "WE" GO AGAIN, BATMAN! OUT AFTER CROOKS...
THEY'RE GOING IN OPPOSITE DIRECTIONS--A TWO-WAY STRIKE! YOU FOLLOW, "ROBIN"--I'LL FOLLOW "BATMAN"!
ON FEET THAT BARELY SKIM THE GROUND, THE MASKED MAN-HUNTER PURSUES HIS PREY TO A HOUSE SOME BLOCKS AWAY...
I SURE HOPE THIS IS PAY-OFF NIGHT!
KANE'S CLOTHES
HE SLAMS THROUGH A WIDE-OPEN DOOR--TO FIND HIS ALTER EGO WAITING FOR HIM WITH CLENCHED FISTS...
CAUGHT UP TO YOU AT LAST! NOW WE'LL SETTLE OUR ACCOUNTS--AND YOU OWE ME PLENTY!
MAYBE THAT BRAVE TALK WILL STOP HIM FROM PULLING HIS FADE-OUT TRICK BEFORE I CAN KAYO HIM!
THE COWLED CRUSADER DRIVES FORWARD WITH A SAVAGE BLOW THAT WOULD FELL A HORSE--IF IT COULD BE LANDED...
I--I CAN'T MAKE CONTACT WITH HIM!
15

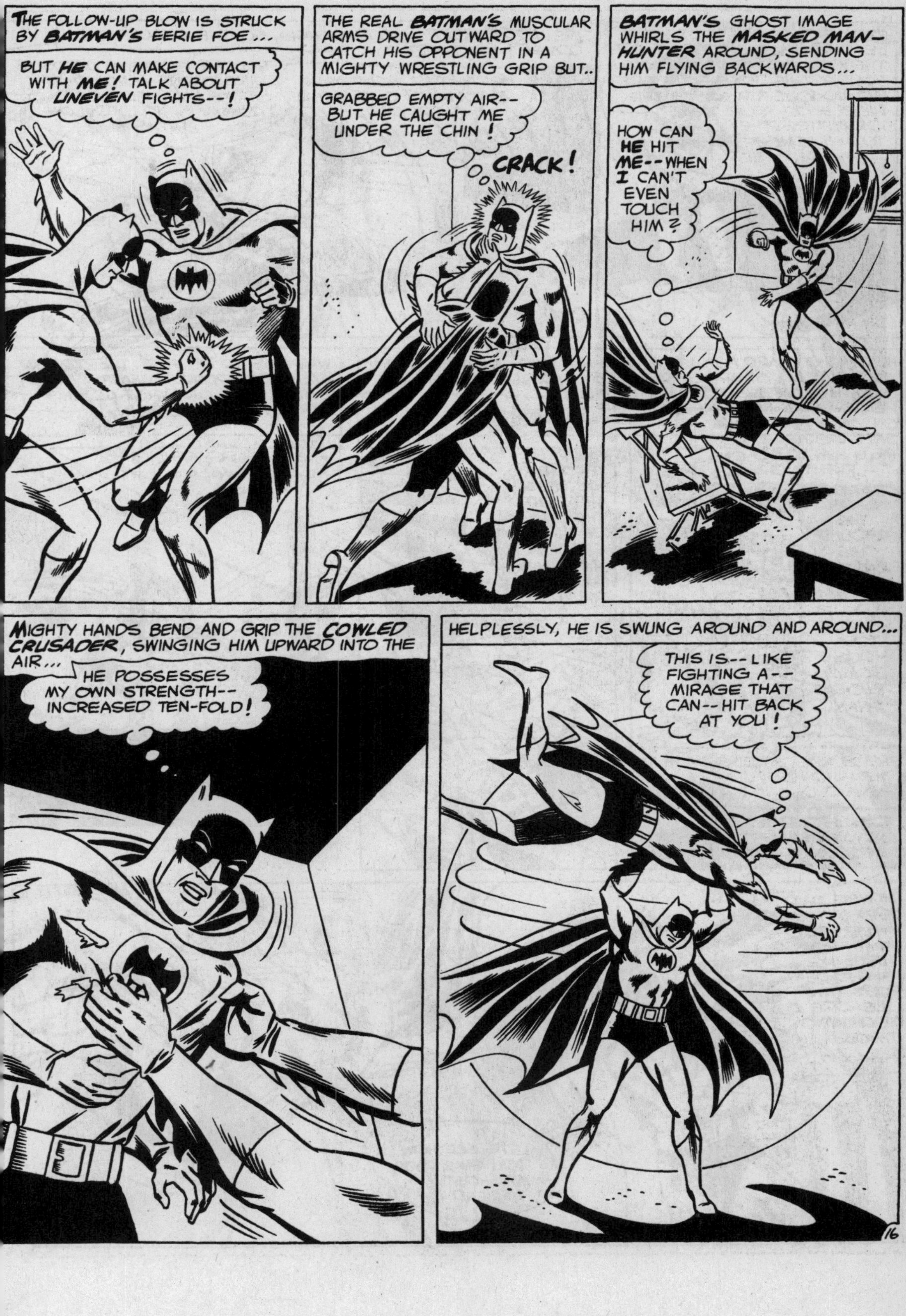
THE FOLLOW-UP BLOW IS STRUCK BY BATMAN'S EERIE FOE...
BUT HE CAN MAKE CONTACT WITH ME! TALK ABOUT UNEVEN FIGHTS--!
THE REAL BATMAN'S MUSCULAR ARMS DRIVE OUTWARD TO CATCH HIS OPPONENT IN A MIGHTY WRESTLING GRIP BUT..
GRABBED EMPTY AIR-- BUT HE CAUGHT ME UNDER THE CHIN!
CRACK!
BATMAN'S GHOST IMAGE WHIRLS THE MASKED MAN-HUNTER AROUND, SENDING HIM FLYING BACKWARDS...
HOW CAN HE HIT ME--WHEN I CAN'T EVEN TOUCH HIM?
MIGHTY HANDS BEND AND GRIP THE COWLED CRUSADER, SWINGING HIM UPWARD INTO THE AIR...
HE POSSESSES MY OWN STRENGTH-- INCREASED TEN-FOLD!
HELPLESSLY, HE IS SWUNG AROUND AND AROUND...
THIS IS--LIKE FIGHTING A-- MIRAGE THAT CAN--HIT BACK AT YOU!
16

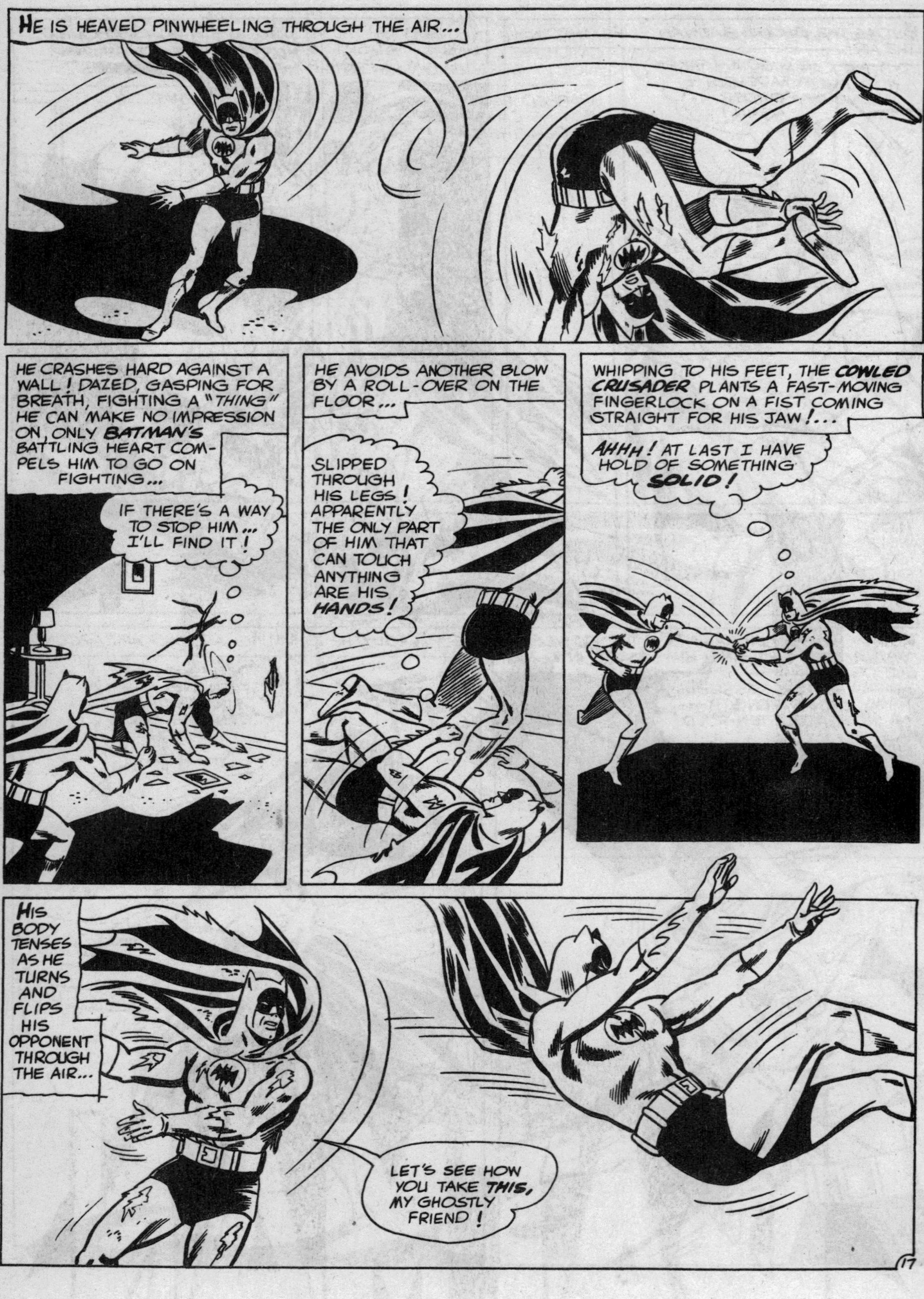
HE IS HEAVED PINWHEELING THROUGH THE AIR...
HE CRASHES HARD AGAINST A WALL! DAZED, GASPING FOR BREATH, FIGHTING A "THING" HE CAN MAKE NO IMPRESSION ON, ONLY BATMAN'S BATTLING HEART COMPELS HIM TO GO ON FIGHTING...
IF THERE'S A WAY TO STOP HIM... I'LL FIND IT!
HE AVOIDS ANOTHER BLOW BY A ROLL-OVER ON THE FLOOR...
SLIPPED THROUGH HIS LEGS! APPARENTLY THE ONLY PART OF HIM THAT CAN TOUCH ANYTHING ARE HIS HANDS!
WHIPPING TO HIS FEET, THE COWLED CRUSADER PLANTS A FAST-MOVING FINGERLOCK ON A FIST COMING STRAIGHT FOR HIS JAW!...
AHHH! AT LAST I HAVE HOLD OF SOMETHING SOLID!
HIS BODY TENSES AS HE TURNS AND FLIPS HIS OPPONENT THROUGH THE AIR...
LET'S SEE HOW YOU TAKE THIS, MY GHOSTLY FRIEND!
17

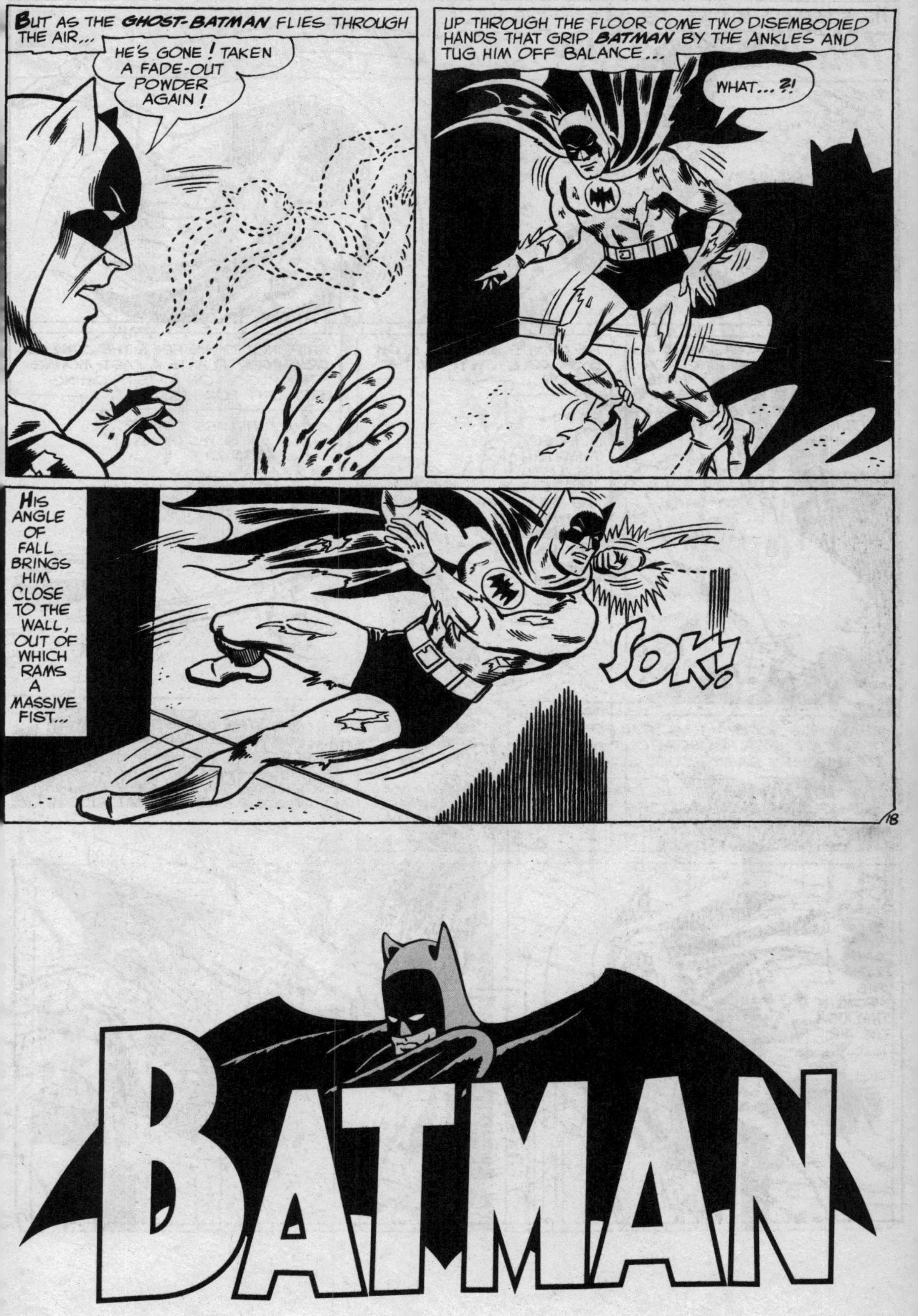
BUT AS THE GHOST-BATMAN FLIES THROUGH THE AIR...
HE'S GONE! TAKEN A FADE-OUT POWDER AGAIN!
UP THROUGH THE FLOOR COME TWO DISEMBODIED HANDS THAT GRIP BATMAN BY THE ANKLES AND TUG HIM OFF BALANCE...
WHAT...?!
HIS ANGLE OF FALL BRINGS HIM CLOSE TO THE WALL, OUT OF WHICH RAMS A MASSIVE FIST...
SOK!
18

BATMAN

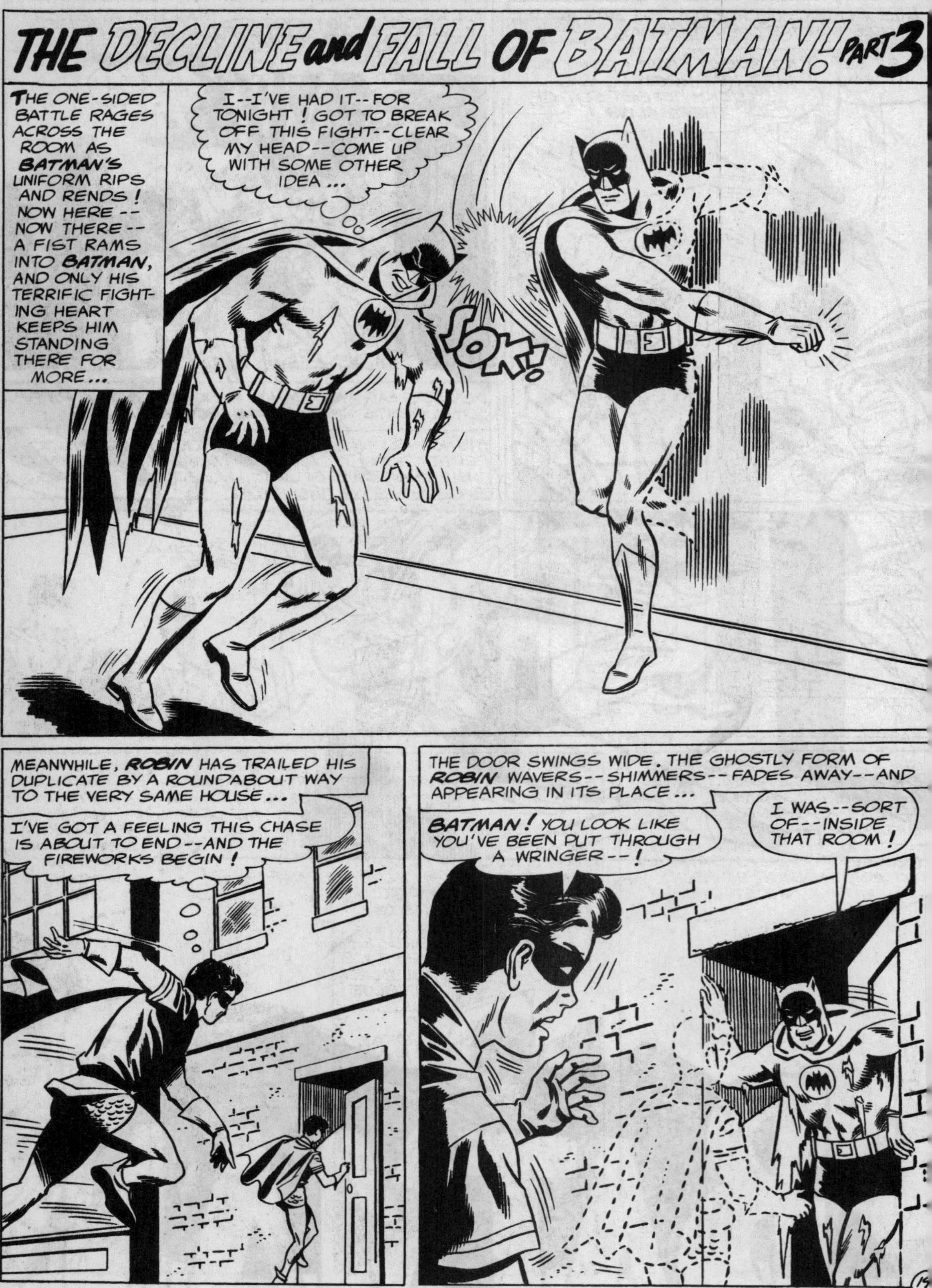
THE DECLINE and FALL OF BATMAN! PART 3
THE ONE-SIDED BATTLE RAGES ACROSS THE ROOM AS BATMAN'S UNIFORM RIPS AND RENDS! NOW HERE -- NOW THERE -- A FIST RAMS INTO BATMAN, AND ONLY HIS TERRIFIC FIGHTING HEART KEEPS HIM STANDING THERE FOR MORE...
I--I'VE HAD IT--FOR TONIGHT! GOT TO BREAK OFF THIS FIGHT--CLEAR MY HEAD--COME UP WITH SOME OTHER IDEA...
SOK!
MEANWHILE, ROBIN HAS TRAILED HIS DUPLICATE BY A ROUNDABOUT WAY TO THE VERY SAME HOUSE...
I'VE GOT A FEELING THIS CHASE IS ABOUT TO END--AND THE FIREWORKS BEGIN!
THE DOOR SWINGS WIDE. THE GHOSTLY FORM OF ROBIN WAVERS--SHIMMERS--FADES AWAY--AND APPEARING IN ITS PLACE...
BATMAN! YOU LOOK LIKE YOU'VE BEEN PUT THROUGH A WRINGER--!
I WAS--SORT OF--INSIDE THAT ROOM!

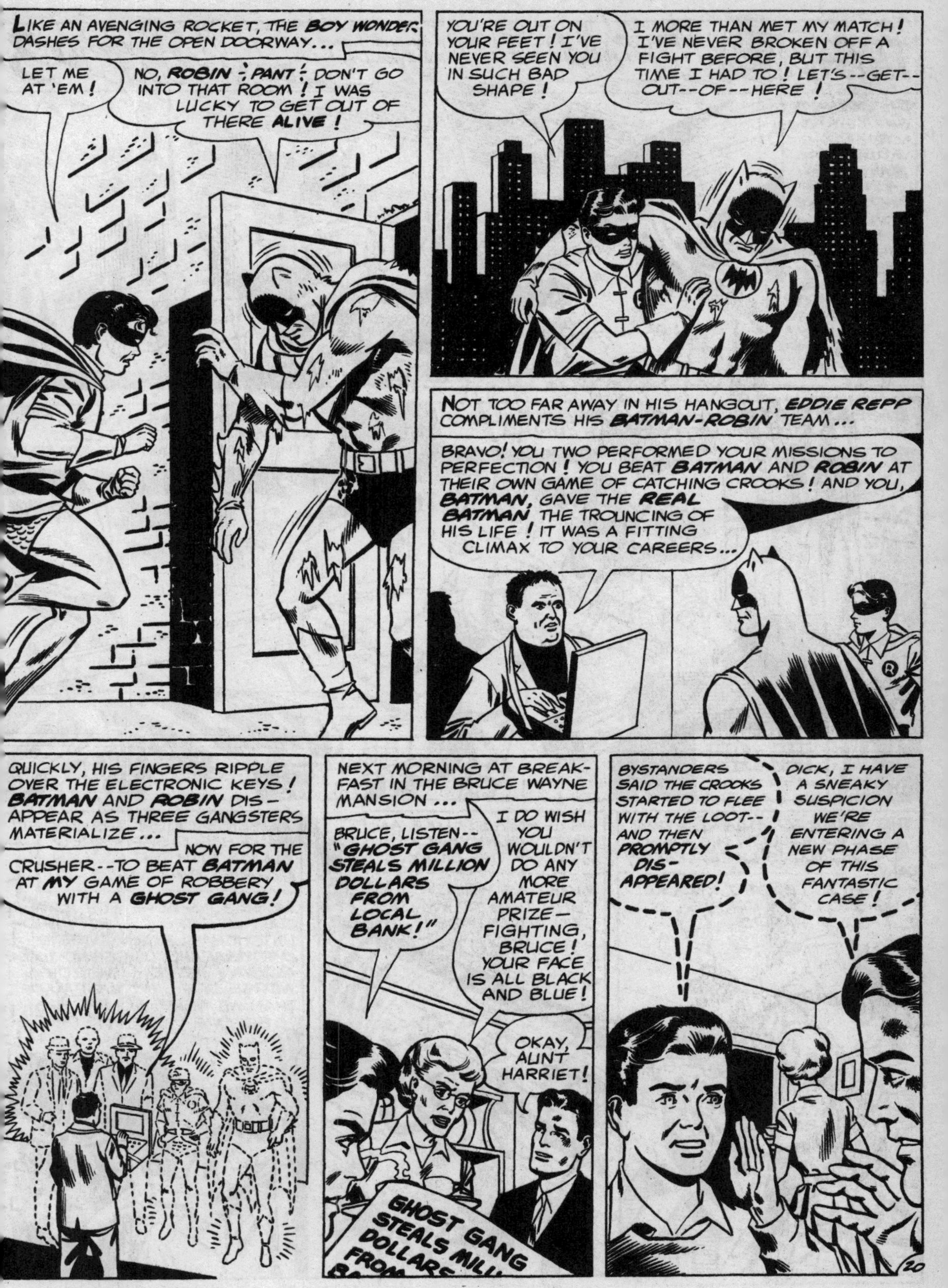
LIKE AN AVENGING ROCKET, THE BOY WONDER DASHES FOR THE OPEN DOORWAY...
LET ME AT 'EM!
NO, ROBIN -PANT- DON'T GO INTO THAT ROOM! I WAS LUCKY TO GET OUT OF THERE ALIVE!
YOU'RE OUT ON YOUR FEET! I'VE NEVER SEEN YOU IN SUCH BAD SHAPE!
I MORE THAN MET MY MATCH! I'VE NEVER BROKEN OFF A FIGHT BEFORE, BUT THIS TIME I HAD TO! LET'S--GET--OUT--OF--HERE!
NOT TOO FAR AWAY IN HIS HANGOUT, EDDIE REPP COMPLIMENTS HIS BATMAN-ROBIN TEAM...
BRAVO! YOU TWO PERFORMED YOUR MISSIONS TO PERFECTION! YOU BEAT BATMAN AND ROBIN AT THEIR OWN GAME OF CATCHING CROOKS! AND YOU, BATMAN, GAVE THE REAL BATMAN THE TROUNCING OF HIS LIFE! IT WAS A FITTING CLIMAX TO YOUR CAREERS...
QUICKLY, HIS FINGERS RIPPLE OVER THE ELECTRONIC KEYS! BATMAN AND ROBIN DISAPPEAR AS THREE GANGSTERS MATERIALIZE...
NOW FOR THE CRUSHER--TO BEAT BATMAN AT MY GAME OF ROBBERY WITH A GHOST GANG!
NEXT MORNING AT BREAKFAST IN THE BRUCE WAYNE MANSION...
BRUCE, LISTEN-- "GHOST GANG STEALS MILLION DOLLARS FROM LOCAL BANK!"
I DO WISH YOU WOULDN'T DO ANY MORE AMATEUR PRIZE-FIGHTING, BRUCE! YOUR FACE IS ALL BLACK AND BLUE!
OKAY, AUNT HARRIET!
GHOST GANG STEALS MILL DOLLARS FROM
BYSTANDERS SAID THE CROOKS STARTED TO FLEE WITH THE LOOT--AND THEN PROMPTLY DISAPPEARED!
DICK, I HAVE A SNEAKY SUSPICION WE'RE ENTERING A NEW PHASE OF THIS FANTASTIC CASE!
20

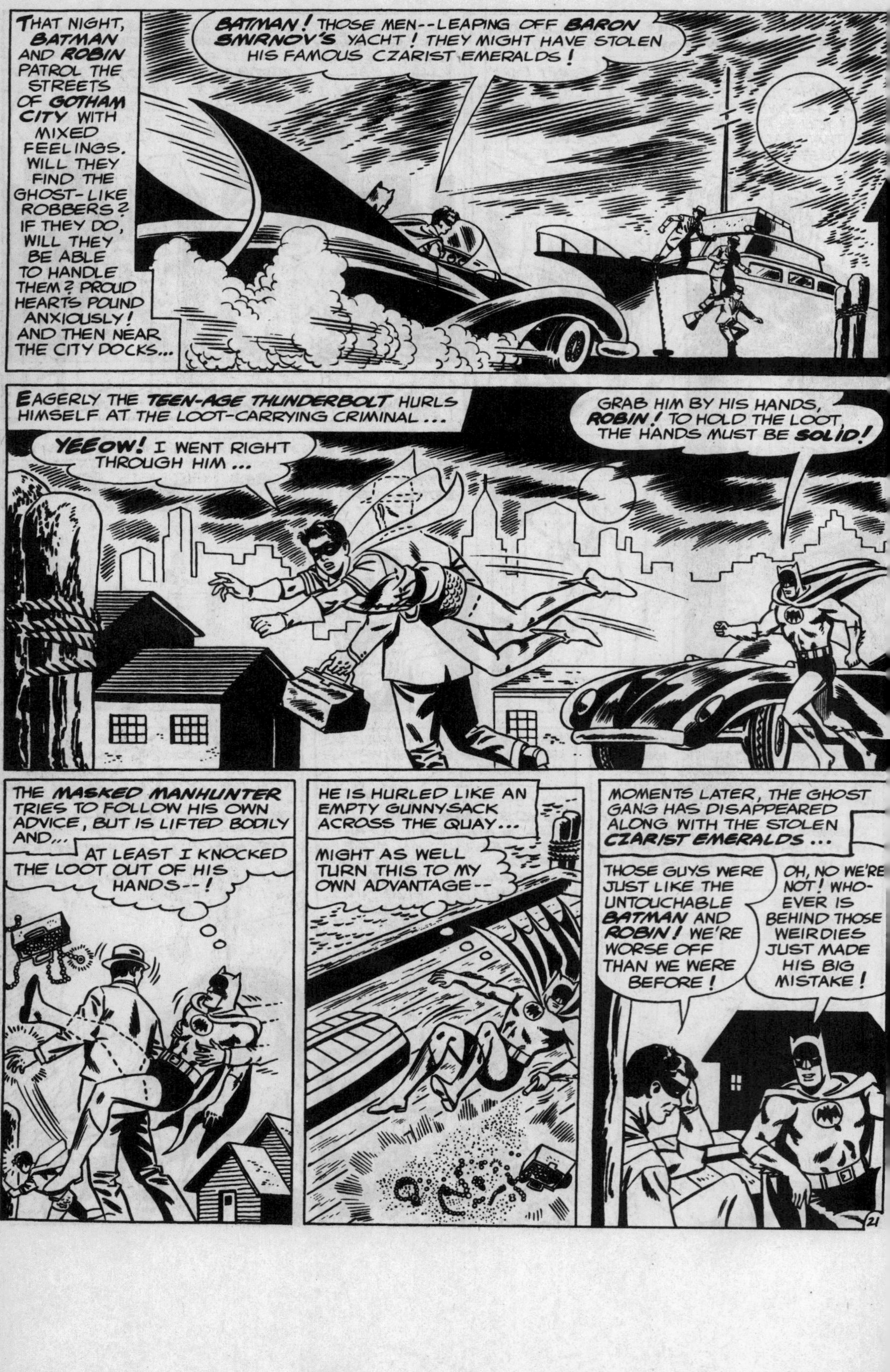
THAT NIGHT, BATMAN AND ROBIN PATROL THE STREETS OF GOTHAM CITY WITH MIXED FEELINGS. WILL THEY FIND THE GHOST-LIKE ROBBERS? IF THEY DO, WILL THEY BE ABLE TO HANDLE THEM? PROUD HEARTS POUND ANXIOUSLY! AND THEN NEAR THE CITY DOCKS...
BATMAN! THOSE MEN--LEAPING OFF BARON SMIRNOV'S YACHT! THEY MIGHT HAVE STOLEN HIS FAMOUS CZARIST EMERALDS!
EAGERLY THE TEEN-AGE THUNDERBOLT HURLS HIMSELF AT THE LOOT-CARRYING CRIMINAL...
YEEOW! I WENT RIGHT THROUGH HIM...
GRAB HIM BY HIS HANDS, ROBIN! TO HOLD THE LOOT, THE HANDS MUST BE SOLID!
THE MASKED MANHUNTER TRIES TO FOLLOW HIS OWN ADVICE, BUT IS LIFTED BODILY AND...
AT LEAST I KNOCKED THE LOOT OUT OF HIS HANDS--!
HE IS HURLED LIKE AN EMPTY GUNNYSACK ACROSS THE QUAY...
MIGHT AS WELL TURN THIS TO MY OWN ADVANTAGE--
MOMENTS LATER, THE GHOST GANG HAS DISAPPEARED ALONG WITH THE STOLEN CZARIST EMERALDS...
THOSE GUYS WERE JUST LIKE THE UNTOUCHABLE BATMAN AND ROBIN! WE'RE WORSE OFF THAN WE WERE BEFORE!
OH, NO WE'RE NOT! WHO-EVER IS BEHIND THOSE WEIRDIES JUST MADE HIS BIG MISTAKE!
21

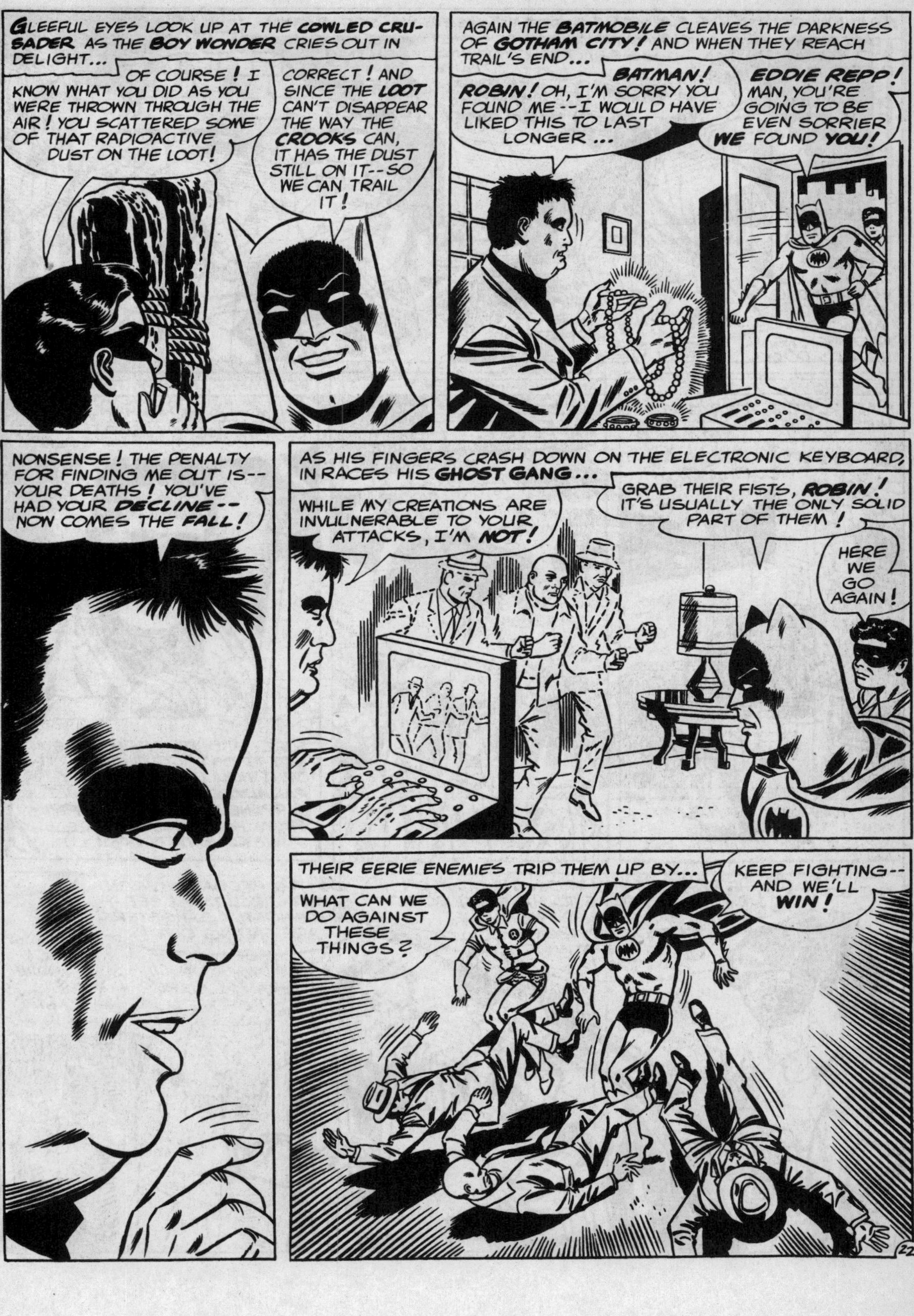
GLEEFUL EYES LOOK UP AT THE COWLED CRUSADER AS THE BOY WONDER CRIES OUT IN DELIGHT...
OF COURSE! I KNOW WHAT YOU DID AS YOU WERE THROWN THROUGH THE AIR! YOU SCATTERED SOME OF THAT RADIOACTIVE DUST ON THE LOOT!
CORRECT! AND SINCE THE LOOT CAN'T DISAPPEAR THE WAY THE CROOKS CAN, IT HAS THE DUST STILL ON IT--SO WE CAN TRAIL IT!
AGAIN THE BATMOBILE CLEAVES THE DARKNESS OF GOTHAM CITY! AND WHEN THEY REACH TRAIL'S END...
BATMAN! ROBIN! OH, I'M SORRY YOU FOUND ME--I WOULD HAVE LIKED THIS TO LAST LONGER...
EDDIE REPP! MAN, YOU'RE GOING TO BE EVEN SORRIER WE FOUND YOU!
NONSENSE! THE PENALTY FOR FINDING ME OUT IS--YOUR DEATHS! YOU'VE HAD YOUR DECLINE--NOW COMES THE FALL!
AS HIS FINGERS CRASH DOWN ON THE ELECTRONIC KEYBOARD, IN RACES HIS GHOST GANG...
WHILE MY CREATIONS ARE INVULNERABLE TO YOUR ATTACKS, I'M NOT!
GRAB THEIR FISTS, ROBIN! IT'S USUALLY THE ONLY SOLID PART OF THEM!
HERE WE GO AGAIN!
THEIR EERIE ENEMIES TRIP THEM UP BY...
WHAT CAN WE DO AGAINST THESE THINGS?
KEEP FIGHTING--AND WE'LL WIN!
22

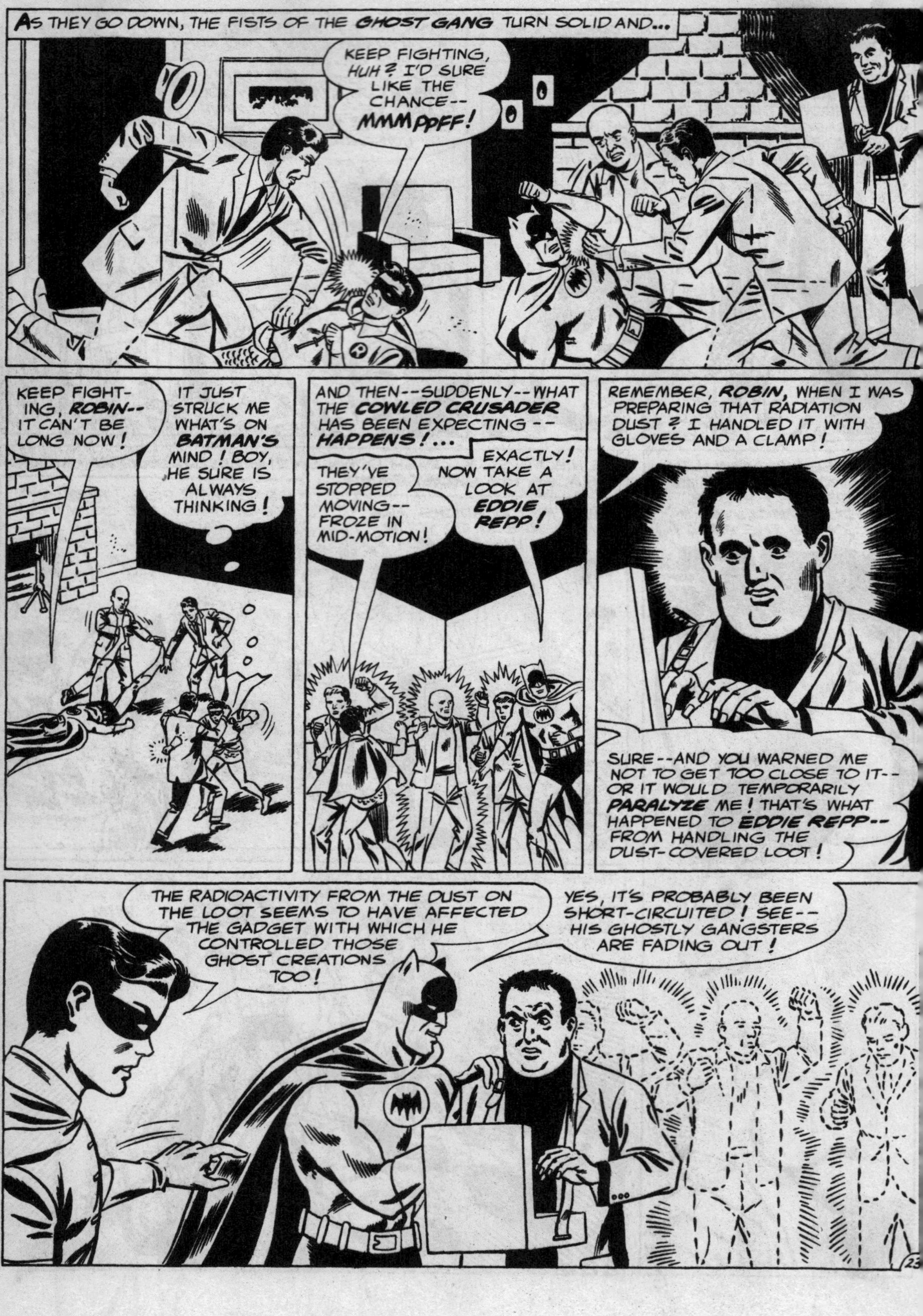
AS THEY GO DOWN, THE FISTS OF THE GHOST GANG TURN SOLID AND...
KEEP FIGHTING, HUH? I'D SURE LIKE THE CHANCE-- MMMPPFF!
KEEP FIGHT-ING, ROBIN-- IT CAN'T BE LONG NOW!
IT JUST STRUCK ME WHAT'S ON BATMAN'S MIND! BOY, HE SURE IS ALWAYS THINKING!
AND THEN--SUDDENLY--WHAT THE COWLED CRUSADER HAS BEEN EXPECTING--HAPPENS!...
THEY'VE STOPPED MOVING-- FROZE IN MID-MOTION!
EXACTLY! NOW TAKE A LOOK AT EDDIE REPP!
REMEMBER, ROBIN, WHEN I WAS PREPARING THAT RADIATION DUST? I HANDLED IT WITH GLOVES AND A CLAMP!
SURE--AND YOU WARNED ME NOT TO GET TOO CLOSE TO IT--OR IT WOULD TEMPORARILY PARALYZE ME! THAT'S WHAT HAPPENED TO EDDIE REPP--FROM HANDLING THE DUST-COVERED LOOT!
THE RADIOACTIVITY FROM THE DUST ON THE LOOT SEEMS TO HAVE AFFECTED THE GADGET WITH WHICH HE CONTROLLED THOSE GHOST CREATIONS TOO!
YES, IT'S PROBABLY BEEN SHORT-CIRCUITED! SEE--HIS GHOSTLY GANGSTERS ARE FADING OUT!
23

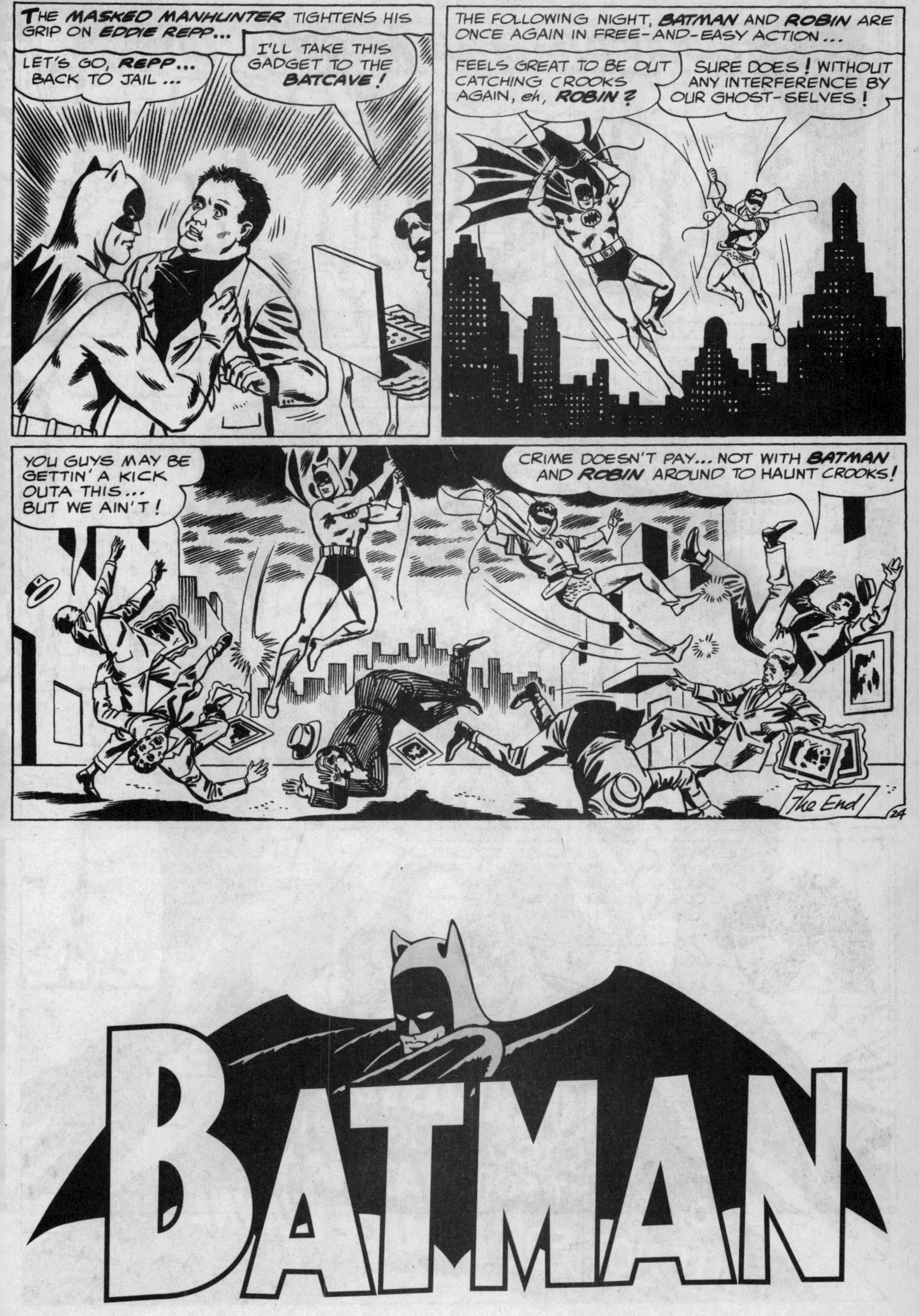
THE MASKED MANHUNTER TIGHTENS HIS GRIP ON EDDIE REPP...
LET'S GO, REPP... BACK TO JAIL...
I'LL TAKE THIS GADGET TO THE BATCAVE!
THE FOLLOWING NIGHT, BATMAN AND ROBIN ARE ONCE AGAIN IN FREE-AND-EASY ACTION...
FEELS GREAT TO BE OUT CATCHING CROOKS AGAIN, eh, ROBIN?
SURE DOES! WITHOUT ANY INTERFERENCE BY OUR GHOST-SELVES!
YOU GUYS MAY BE GETTIN' A KICK OUTA THIS... BUT WE AIN'T!
CRIME DOESN'T PAY... NOT WITH BATMAN AND ROBIN AROUND TO HAUNT CROOKS!
The End
24

BATMAN

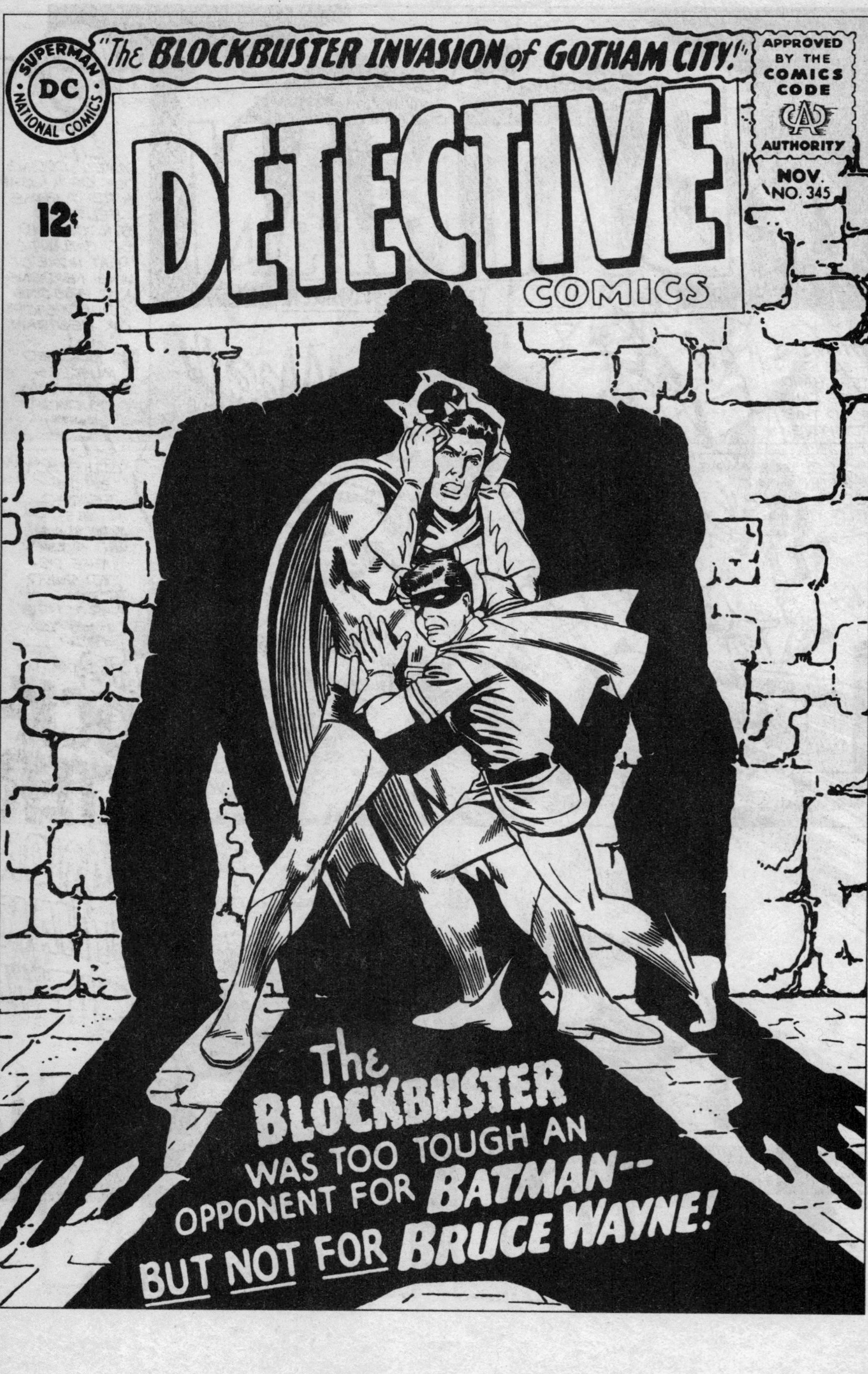

"The BLOCKBUSTER INVASION of GOTHAM CITY!"
SUPERMAN DC NATIONAL COMICS
APPROVED BY THE COMICS CODE AUTHORITY
DETECTIVE COMICS
12¢
NOV. NO. 345
The BLOCKBUSTER WAS TOO TOUGH AN OPPONENT FOR BATMAN-- BUT NOT FOR BRUCE WAYNE!

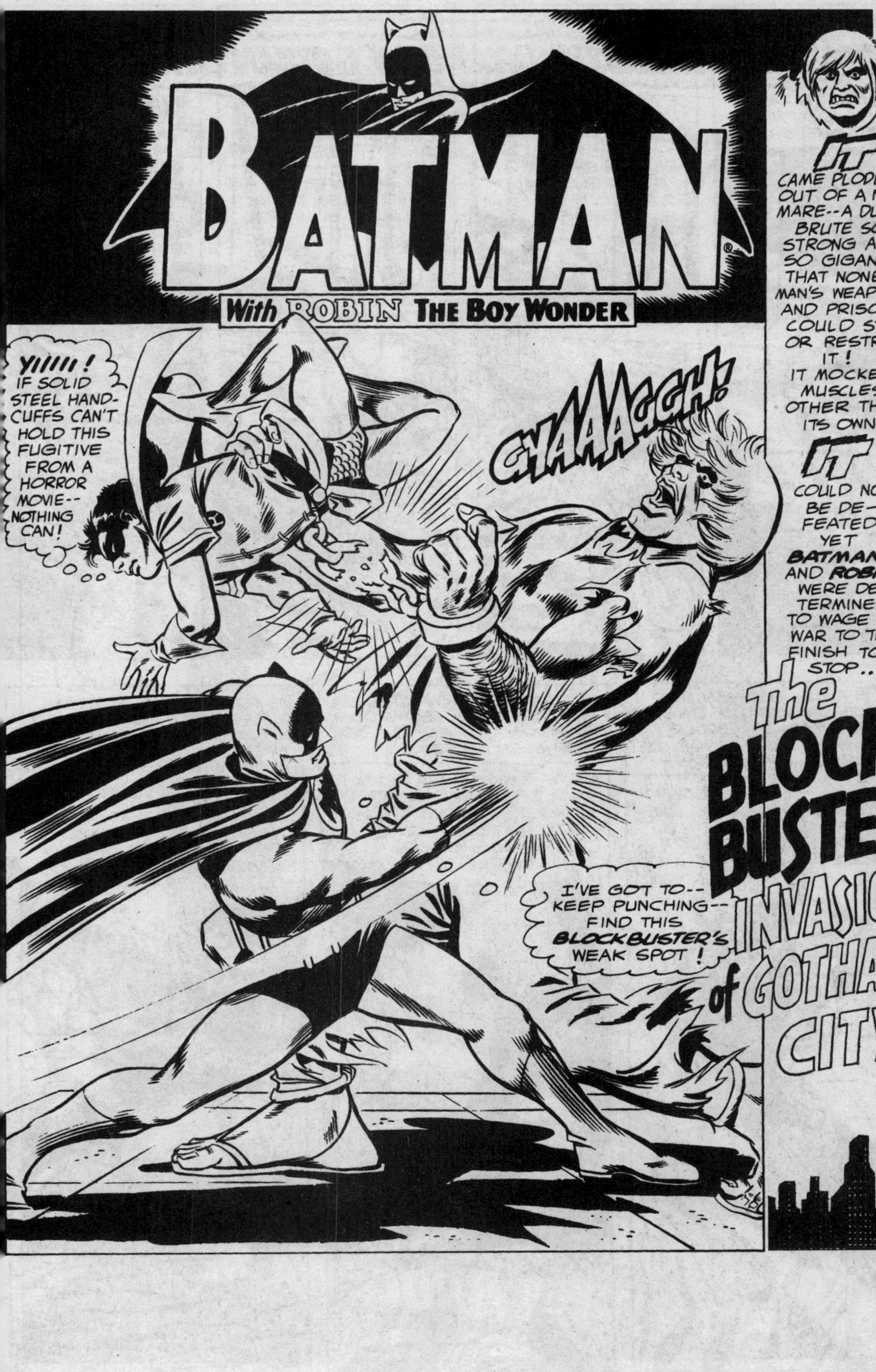
BATMAN
With ROBIN THE BOY WONDER
IT CAME PLODDING OUT OF A NIGHTMARE--A DUMB BRUTE SO STRONG AND SO GIGANTIC THAT NONE OF MAN'S WEAPONS AND PRISONS COULD STOP OR RESTRAIN IT! IT MOCKED MUSCLES OTHER THAN ITS OWN!
IT COULD NOT BE DEFEATED--YET BATMAN AND ROBIN WERE DETERMINED TO WAGE A WAR TO THE FINISH TO STOP...
YIIIII! IF SOLID STEEL HANDCUFFS CAN'T HOLD THIS FUGITIVE FROM A HORROR MOVIE--NOTHING CAN!
GYAAAGGH!
I'VE GOT TO--KEEP PUNCHING--FIND THIS BLOCKBUSTER'S WEAK SPOT!
THE BLOCK-BUSTER INVASION OF GOTHAM CITY!

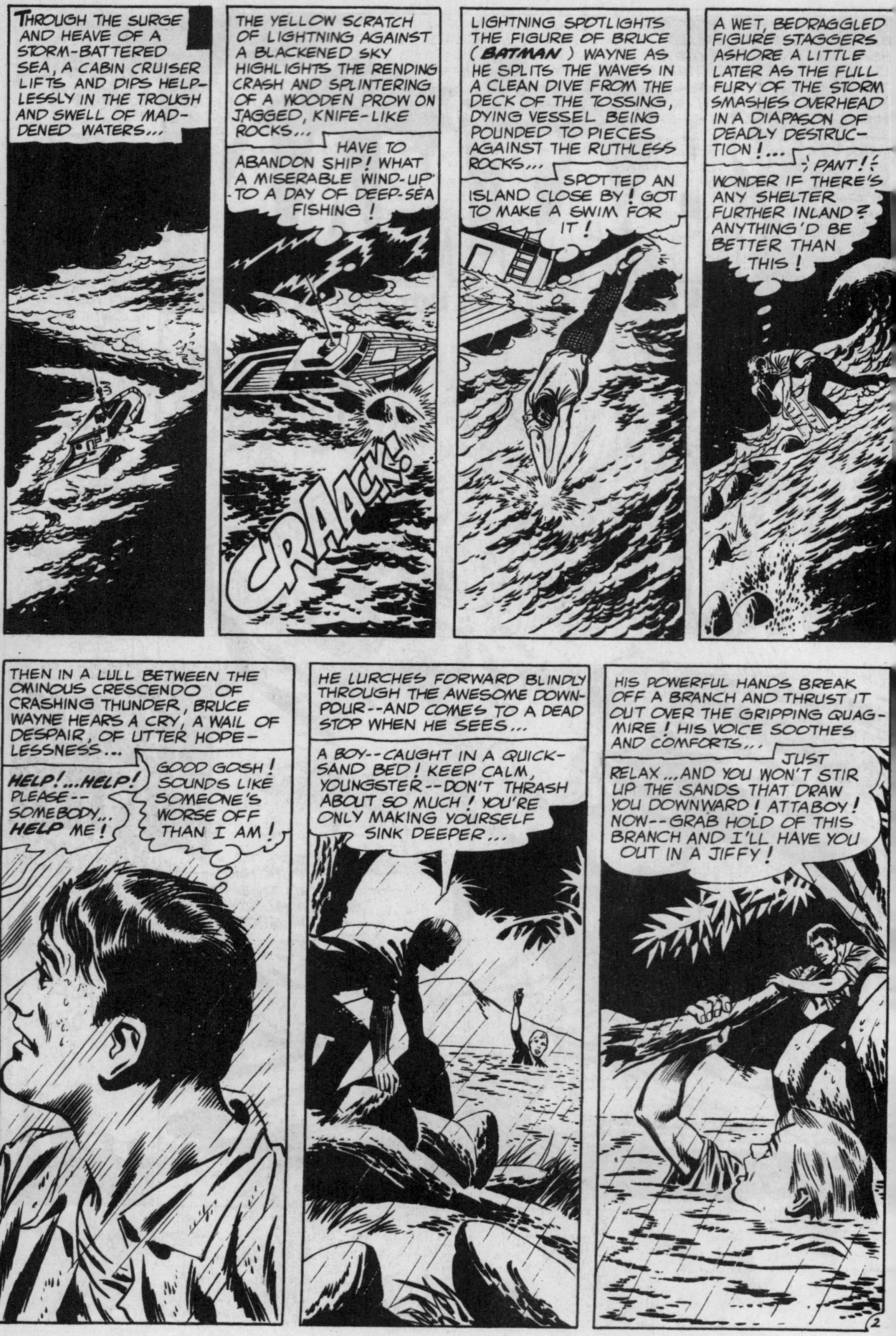
THROUGH THE SURGE AND HEAVE OF A STORM-BATTERED SEA, A CABIN CRUISER LIFTS AND DIPS HELPLESSLY IN THE TROUGH AND SWELL OF MADDENED WATERS...
THE YELLOW SCRATCH OF LIGHTNING AGAINST A BLACKENED SKY HIGHLIGHTS THE RENDING CRASH AND SPLINTERING OF A WOODEN PROW ON JAGGED, KNIFE-LIKE ROCKS...
HAVE TO ABANDON SHIP! WHAT A MISERABLE WIND-UP TO A DAY OF DEEP-SEA FISHING!
CRAACK!
LIGHTNING SPOTLIGHTS THE FIGURE OF BRUCE (BATMAN) WAYNE AS HE SPLITS THE WAVES IN A CLEAN DIVE FROM THE DECK OF THE TOSSING, DYING VESSEL BEING POUNDED TO PIECES AGAINST THE RUTHLESS ROCKS...
SPOTTED AN ISLAND CLOSE BY! GOT TO MAKE A SWIM FOR IT!
A WET, BEDRAGGLED FIGURE STAGGERS ASHORE A LITTLE LATER AS THE FULL FURY OF THE STORM SMASHES OVERHEAD IN A DIAPASON OF DEADLY DESTRUCTION!...
;PANT!; WONDER IF THERE'S ANY SHELTER FURTHER INLAND? ANYTHING'D BE BETTER THAN THIS!
THEN IN A LULL BETWEEN THE OMINOUS CRESCENDO OF CRASHING THUNDER, BRUCE WAYNE HEARS A CRY, A WAIL OF DESPAIR, OF UTTER HOPELESSNESS...
HELP!...HELP! PLEASE--SOMEBODY... HELP ME!
GOOD GOSH! SOUNDS LIKE SOMEONE'S WORSE OFF THAN I AM!
HE LURCHES FORWARD BLINDLY THROUGH THE AWESOME DOWNPOUR--AND COMES TO A DEAD STOP WHEN HE SEES...
A BOY--CAUGHT IN A QUICKSAND BED! KEEP CALM, YOUNGSTER--DON'T THRASH ABOUT SO MUCH! YOU'RE ONLY MAKING YOURSELF SINK DEEPER...
HIS POWERFUL HANDS BREAK OFF A BRANCH AND THRUST IT OUT OVER THE GRIPPING QUAGMIRE! HIS VOICE SOOTHES AND COMFORTS...
JUST RELAX...AND YOU WON'T STIR UP THE SANDS THAT DRAW YOU DOWNWARD! ATTABOY! NOW--GRAB HOLD OF THIS BRANCH AND I'LL HAVE YOU OUT IN A JIFFY!
2

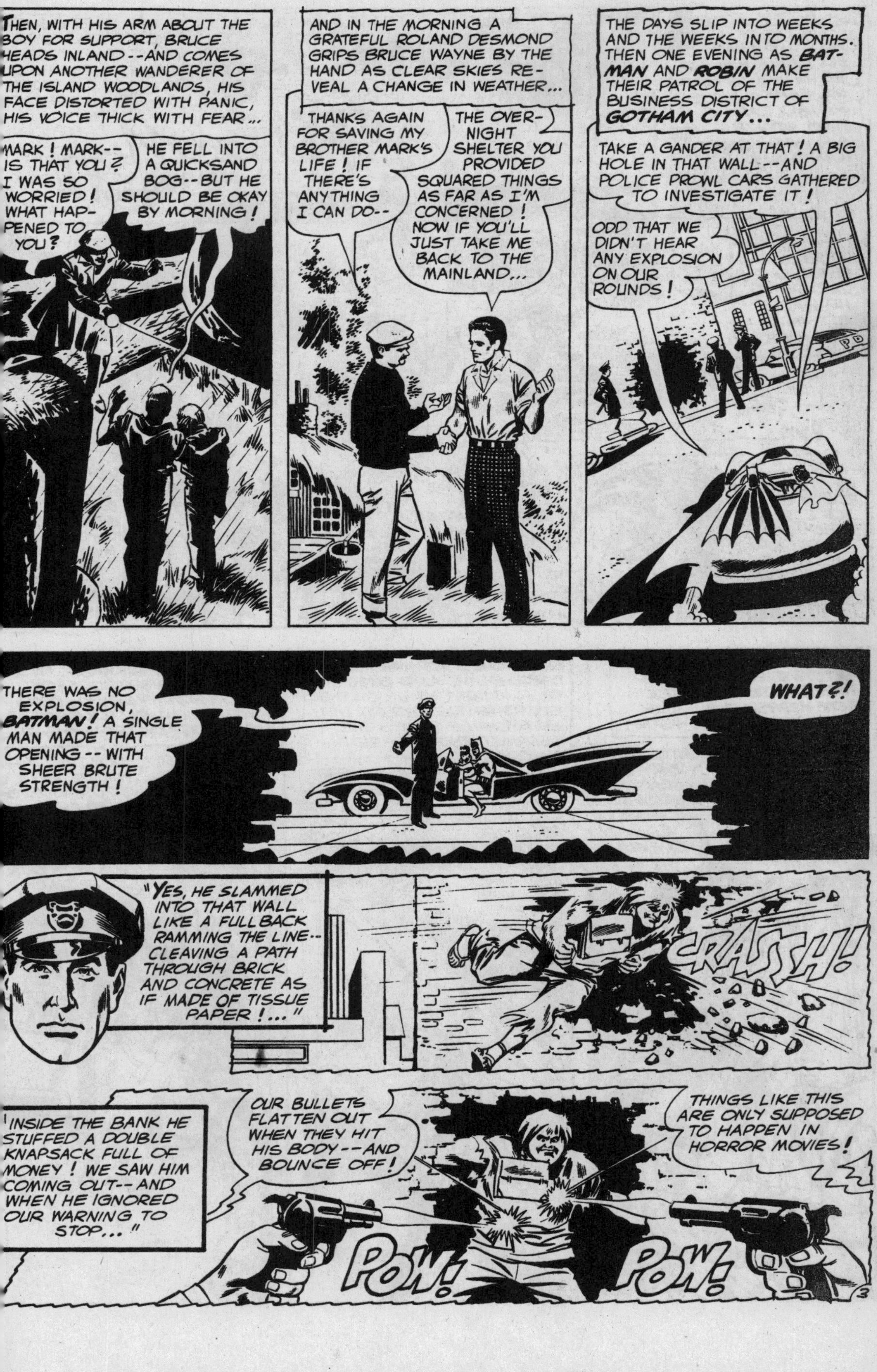
THEN, WITH HIS ARM ABOUT THE BOY FOR SUPPORT, BRUCE HEADS INLAND--AND COMES UPON ANOTHER WANDERER OF THE ISLAND WOODLANDS, HIS FACE DISTORTED WITH PANIC, HIS VOICE THICK WITH FEAR...
MARK! MARK--IS THAT YOU? I WAS SO WORRIED! WHAT HAPPENED TO YOU?
HE FELL INTO A QUICKSAND BOG--BUT HE SHOULD BE OKAY BY MORNING!
AND IN THE MORNING A GRATEFUL ROLAND DESMOND GRIPS BRUCE WAYNE BY THE HAND AS CLEAR SKIES REVEAL A CHANGE IN WEATHER...
THANKS AGAIN FOR SAVING MY BROTHER MARK'S LIFE! IF THERE'S ANYTHING I CAN DO--
THE OVERNIGHT SHELTER YOU PROVIDED SQUARED THINGS AS FAR AS I'M CONCERNED! NOW IF YOU'LL JUST TAKE ME BACK TO THE MAINLAND...
THE DAYS SLIP INTO WEEKS AND THE WEEKS INTO MONTHS. THEN ONE EVENING AS BATMAN AND ROBIN MAKE THEIR PATROL OF THE BUSINESS DISTRICT OF GOTHAM CITY...
TAKE A GANDER AT THAT! A BIG HOLE IN THAT WALL--AND POLICE PROWL CARS GATHERED TO INVESTIGATE IT!
ODD THAT WE DIDN'T HEAR ANY EXPLOSION ON OUR ROUNDS!
PD
THERE WAS NO EXPLOSION, BATMAN! A SINGLE MAN MADE THAT OPENING--WITH SHEER BRUTE STRENGTH!
WHAT?!
"YES, HE SLAMMED INTO THAT WALL LIKE A FULLBACK RAMMING THE LINE--CLEAVING A PATH THROUGH BRICK AND CONCRETE AS IF MADE OF TISSUE PAPER!..."
CRASSH!
"INSIDE THE BANK HE STUFFED A DOUBLE KNAPSACK FULL OF MONEY! WE SAW HIM COMING OUT--AND WHEN HE IGNORED OUR WARNING TO STOP..."
OUR BULLETS FLATTEN OUT WHEN THEY HIT HIS BODY--AND BOUNCE OFF!
THINGS LIKE THIS ARE ONLY SUPPOSED TO HAPPEN IN HORROR MOVIES!
POW!
POW!
3

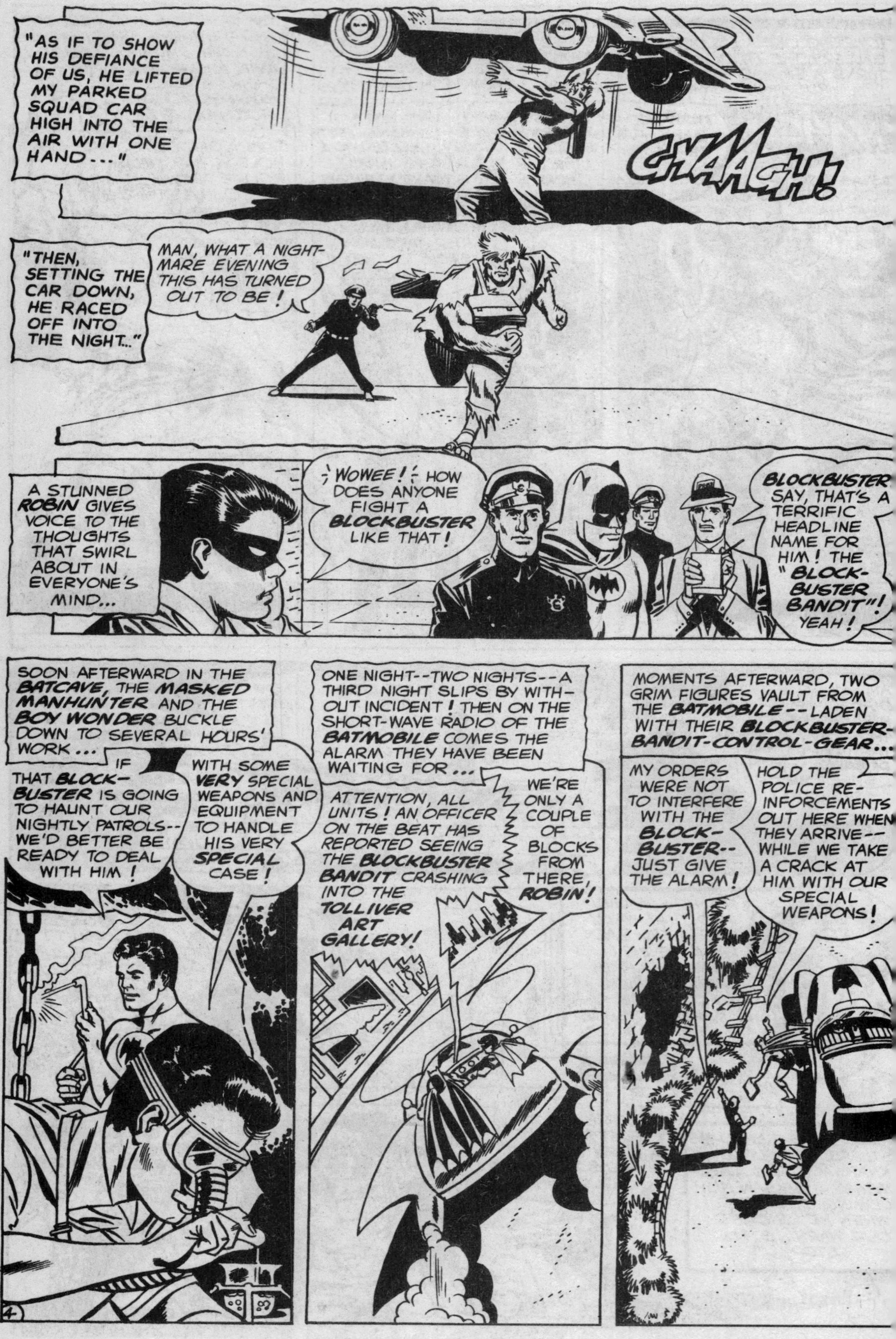
"AS IF TO SHOW HIS DEFIANCE OF US, HE LIFTED MY PARKED SQUAD CAR HIGH INTO THE AIR WITH ONE HAND..."
GHAAGH!
"THEN, SETTING THE CAR DOWN, HE RACED OFF INTO THE NIGHT..."
MAN, WHAT A NIGHT-MARE EVENING THIS HAS TURNED OUT TO BE!
A STUNNED ROBIN GIVES VOICE TO THE THOUGHTS THAT SWIRL ABOUT IN EVERYONE'S MIND...
WOWEE! HOW DOES ANYONE FIGHT A BLOCKBUSTER LIKE THAT!
BLOCKBUSTER SAY, THAT'S A TERRIFIC HEADLINE NAME FOR HIM! THE "BLOCK-BUSTER BANDIT"! YEAH!
SOON AFTERWARD IN THE BATCAVE, THE MASKED MANHUNTER AND THE BOY WONDER BUCKLE DOWN TO SEVERAL HOURS' WORK...
IF THAT BLOCK-BUSTER IS GOING TO HAUNT OUR NIGHTLY PATROLS-- WE'D BETTER BE READY TO DEAL WITH HIM!
WITH SOME VERY SPECIAL WEAPONS AND EQUIPMENT TO HANDLE HIS VERY SPECIAL CASE!
4
ONE NIGHT--TWO NIGHTS--A THIRD NIGHT SLIPS BY WITH-OUT INCIDENT! THEN ON THE SHORT-WAVE RADIO OF THE BATMOBILE COMES THE ALARM THEY HAVE BEEN WAITING FOR...
ATTENTION, ALL UNITS! AN OFFICER ON THE BEAT HAS REPORTED SEEING THE BLOCKBUSTER BANDIT CRASHING INTO THE TOLLIVER ART GALLERY!
WE'RE ONLY A COUPLE OF BLOCKS FROM THERE, ROBIN!
MOMENTS AFTERWARD, TWO GRIM FIGURES VAULT FROM THE BATMOBILE--LADEN WITH THEIR BLOCKBUSTER-BANDIT-CONTROL-GEAR...
MY ORDERS WERE NOT TO INTERFERE WITH THE BLOCK-BUSTER-- JUST GIVE THE ALARM!
HOLD THE POLICE RE-INFORCEMENTS OUT HERE WHEN THEY ARRIVE-- WHILE WE TAKE A CRACK AT HIM WITH OUR SPECIAL WEAPONS!

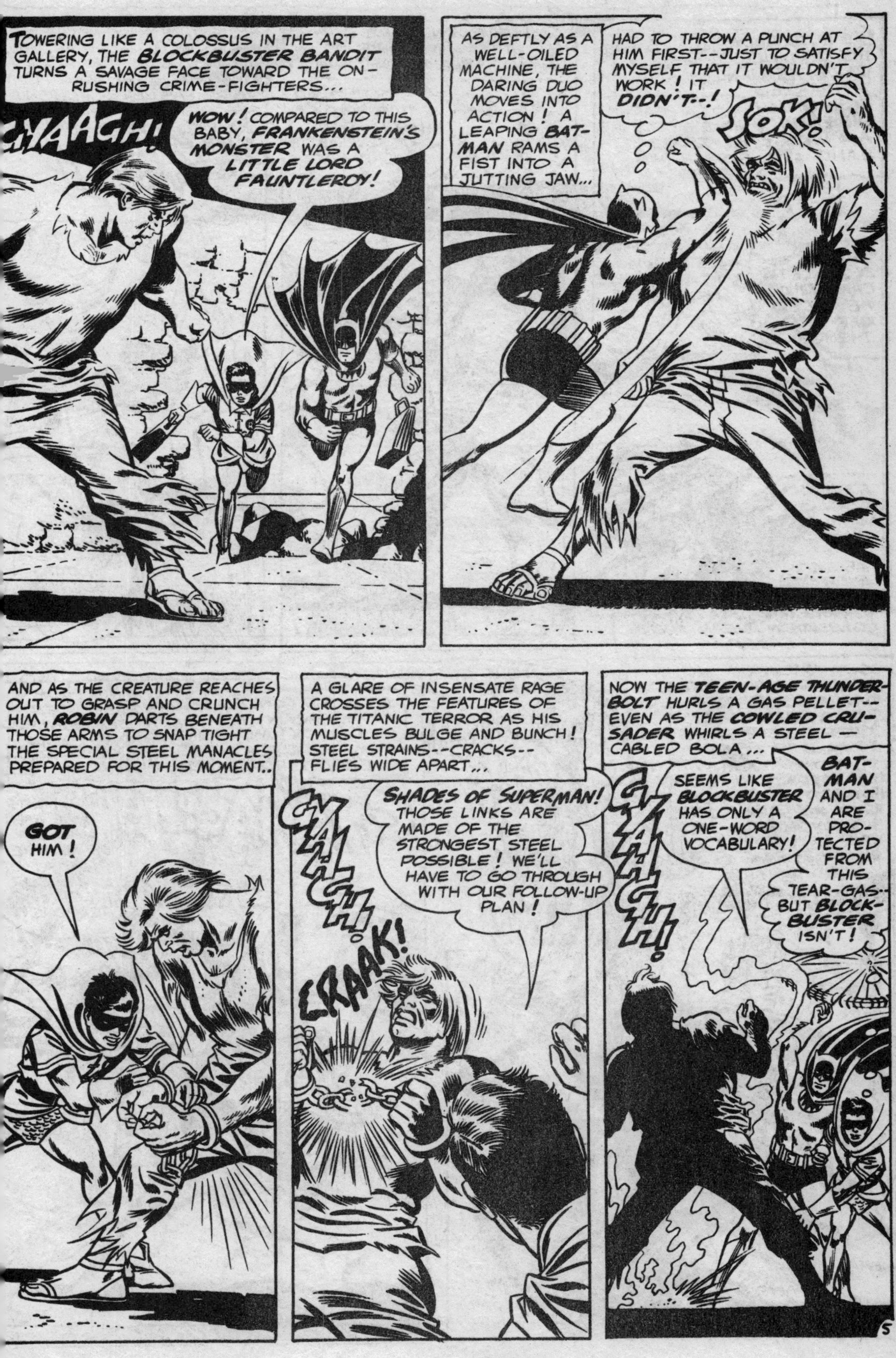
TOWERING LIKE A COLOSSUS IN THE ART GALLERY, THE BLOCKBUSTER BANDIT TURNS A SAVAGE FACE TOWARD THE ON-RUSHING CRIME-FIGHTERS...
GYAAGH!
WOW! COMPARED TO THIS BABY, FRANKENSTEIN'S MONSTER WAS A LITTLE LORD FAUNTLEROY!
AS DEFTLY AS A WELL-OILED MACHINE, THE DARING DUO MOVES INTO ACTION! A LEAPING BATMAN RAMS A FIST INTO A JUTTING JAW...
HAD TO THROW A PUNCH AT HIM FIRST--JUST TO SATISFY MYSELF THAT IT WOULDN'T WORK! IT DIDN'T--!
SOK!
AND AS THE CREATURE REACHES OUT TO GRASP AND CRUNCH HIM, ROBIN DARTS BENEATH THOSE ARMS TO SNAP TIGHT THE SPECIAL STEEL MANACLES PREPARED FOR THIS MOMENT..
GOT HIM!
A GLARE OF INSENSATE RAGE CROSSES THE FEATURES OF THE TITANIC TERROR AS HIS MUSCLES BULGE AND BUNCH! STEEL STRAINS--CRACKS--FLIES WIDE APART...
GYAAGH!
SHADES OF SUPERMAN! THOSE LINKS ARE MADE OF THE STRONGEST STEEL POSSIBLE! WE'LL HAVE TO GO THROUGH WITH OUR FOLLOW-UP PLAN!
CRAAK!
NOW THE TEEN-AGE THUNDERBOLT HURLS A GAS PELLET--EVEN AS THE COWLED CRUSADER WHIRLS A STEEL-CABLED BOLA...
GYAAGH!
SEEMS LIKE BLOCKBUSTER HAS ONLY A ONE-WORD VOCABULARY!
BATMAN AND I ARE PROTECTED FROM THIS TEAR-GAS--BUT BLOCKBUSTER ISN'T!
5

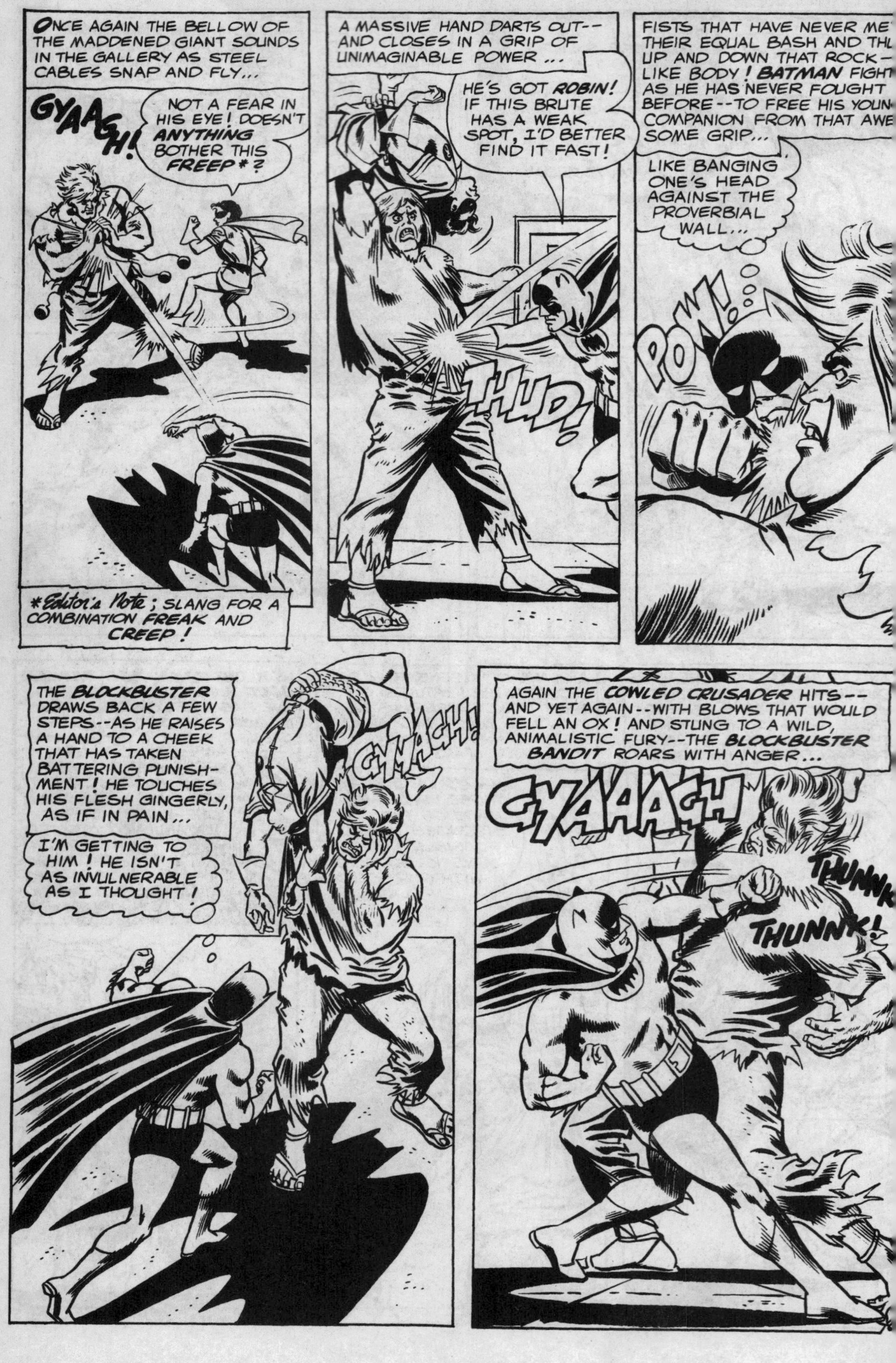
ONCE AGAIN THE BELLOW OF THE MADDENED GIANT SOUNDS IN THE GALLERY AS STEEL CABLES SNAP AND FLY...
GYAAGH!
NOT A FEAR IN HIS EYE! DOESN'T ANYTHING BOTHER THIS FREEP*?
*Editor's Note; SLANG FOR A COMBINATION FREAK AND CREEP!
A MASSIVE HAND DARTS OUT-- AND CLOSES IN A GRIP OF UNIMAGINABLE POWER...
HE'S GOT ROBIN! IF THIS BRUTE HAS A WEAK SPOT, I'D BETTER FIND IT FAST!
THUD!
FISTS THAT HAVE NEVER ME THEIR EQUAL BASH AND TH UP AND DOWN THAT ROCK-LIKE BODY! BATMAN FIGHT AS HE HAS NEVER FOUGHT BEFORE--TO FREE HIS YOUN COMPANION FROM THAT AWE SOME GRIP...
LIKE BANGING ONE'S HEAD AGAINST THE PROVERBIAL WALL...
POW!
THE BLOCKBUSTER DRAWS BACK A FEW STEPS--AS HE RAISES A HAND TO A CHEEK THAT HAS TAKEN BATTERING PUNISHMENT! HE TOUCHES HIS FLESH GINGERLY, AS IF IN PAIN...
I'M GETTING TO HIM! HE ISN'T AS INVULNERABLE AS I THOUGHT!
GYAACH!
AGAIN THE COWLED CRUSADER HITS-- AND YET AGAIN--WITH BLOWS THAT WOULD FELL AN OX! AND STUNG TO A WILD, ANIMALISTIC FURY--THE BLOCKBUSTER BANDIT ROARS WITH ANGER...
GYAAACH
THUNNK
THUNNK!

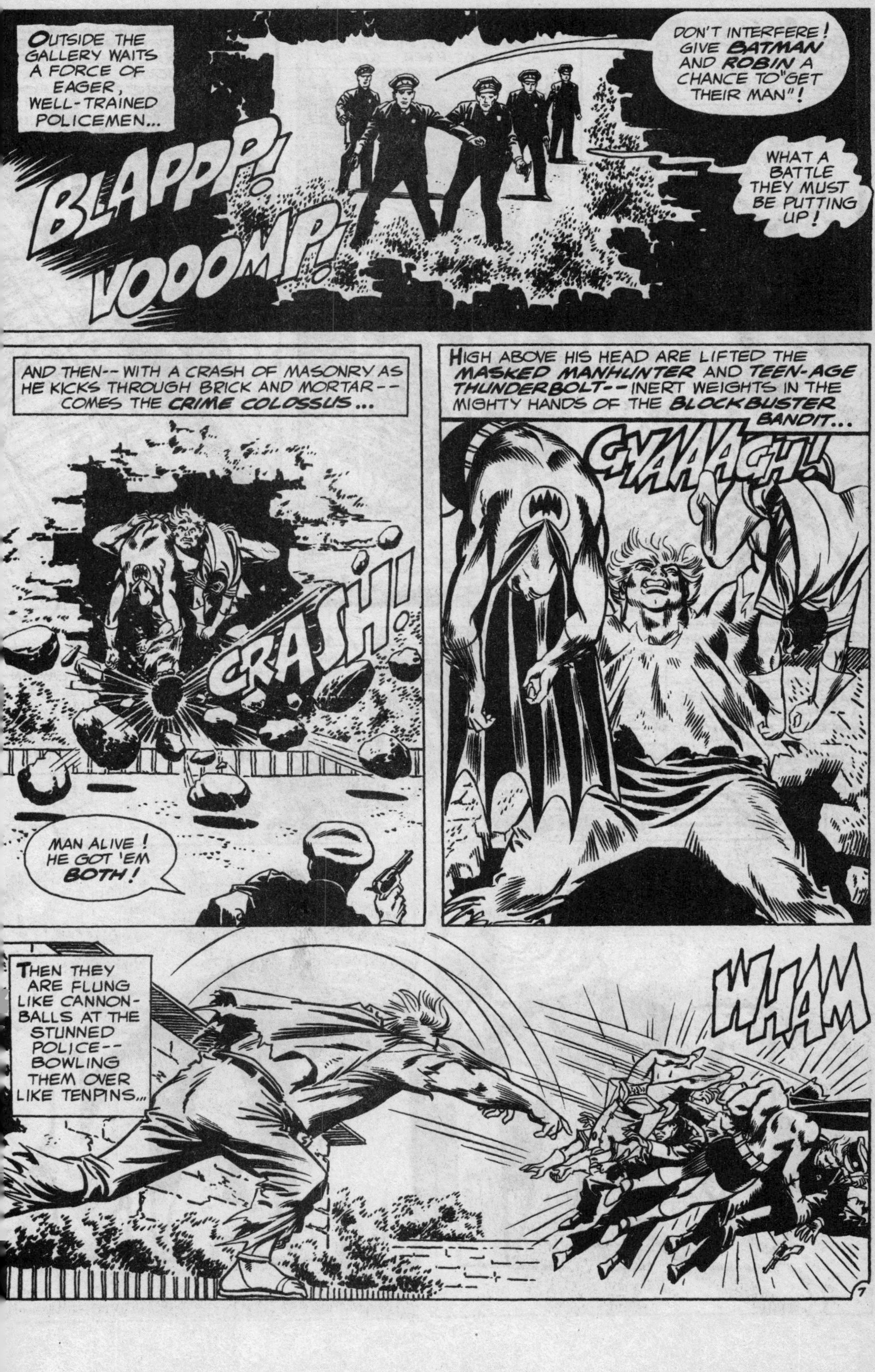
OUTSIDE THE GALLERY WAITS A FORCE OF EAGER, WELL-TRAINED POLICEMEN...
DON'T INTERFERE! GIVE BATMAN AND ROBIN A CHANCE TO "GET THEIR MAN"!
WHAT A BATTLE THEY MUST BE PUTTING UP!
BLAPPP!
VOOOMP!
AND THEN--WITH A CRASH OF MASONRY AS HE KICKS THROUGH BRICK AND MORTAR--COMES THE CRIME COLOSSUS...
CRASH!
MAN ALIVE! HE GOT 'EM BOTH!
HIGH ABOVE HIS HEAD ARE LIFTED THE MASKED MANHUNTER AND TEEN-AGE THUNDERBOLT--INERT WEIGHTS IN THE MIGHTY HANDS OF THE BLOCKBUSTER BANDIT...
GYAAAGH!
THEN THEY ARE FLUNG LIKE CANNON-BALLS AT THE STUNNED POLICE--BOWLING THEM OVER LIKE TENPINS...
WHAM
7

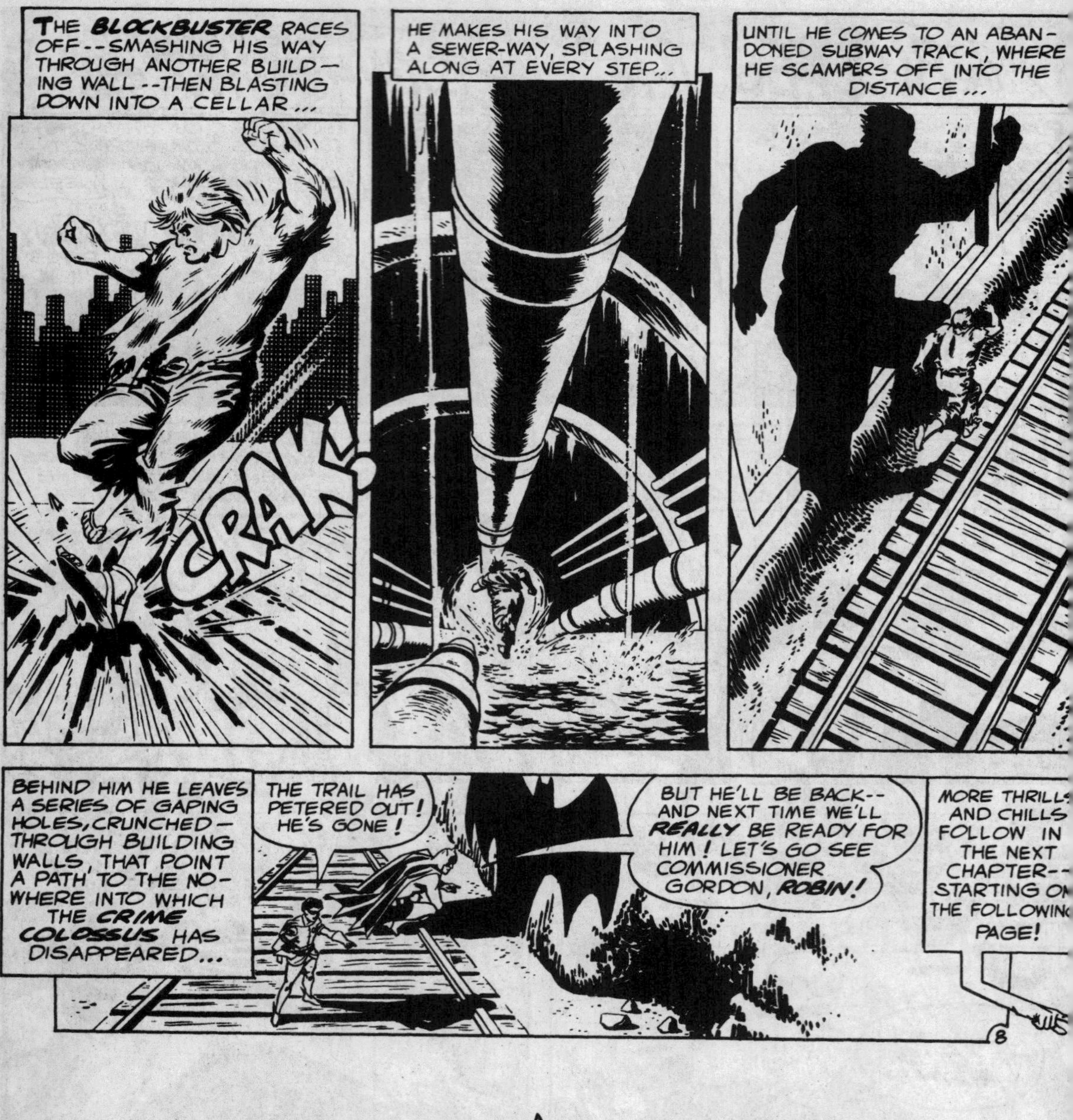
THE BLOCKBUSTER RACES OFF--SMASHING HIS WAY THROUGH ANOTHER BUILDING WALL--THEN BLASTING DOWN INTO A CELLAR...
CRAK!
HE MAKES HIS WAY INTO A SEWER-WAY, SPLASHING ALONG AT EVERY STEP...
UNTIL HE COMES TO AN ABANDONED SUBWAY TRACK, WHERE HE SCAMPERS OFF INTO THE DISTANCE...
BEHIND HIM HE LEAVES A SERIES OF GAPING HOLES, CRUNCHED-THROUGH BUILDING WALLS, THAT POINT A PATH TO THE NOWHERE INTO WHICH THE CRIME COLOSSUS HAS DISAPPEARED...
THE TRAIL HAS PETERED OUT! HE'S GONE!
BUT HE'LL BE BACK--AND NEXT TIME WE'LL REALLY BE READY FOR HIM! LET'S GO SEE COMMISSIONER GORDON, ROBIN!
MORE THRILLS AND CHILLS FOLLOW IN THE NEXT CHAPTER--STARTING ON THE FOLLOWING PAGE!
8

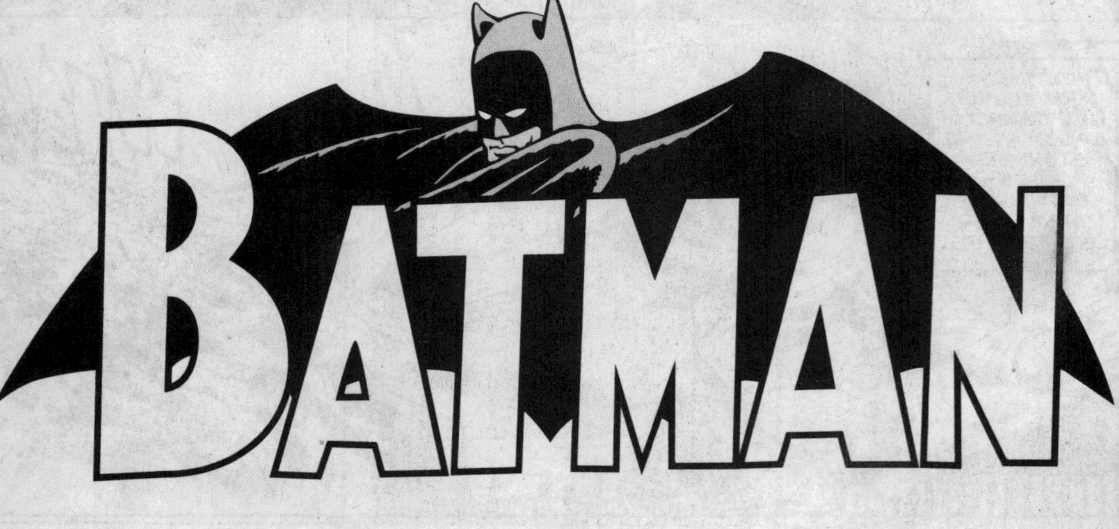
BATMAN

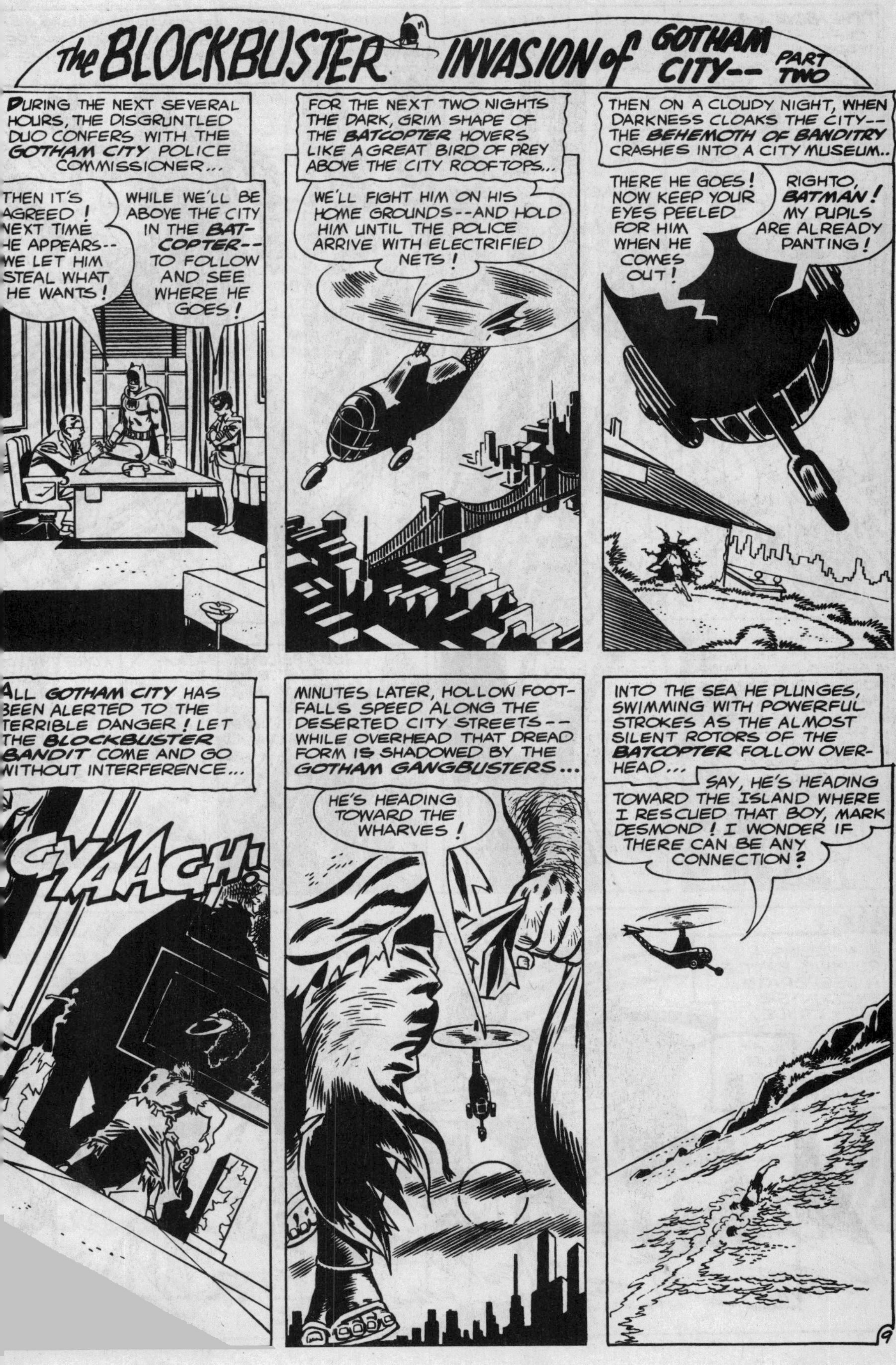
The BLOCKBUSTER INVASION of GOTHAM CITY-- PART TWO
DURING THE NEXT SEVERAL HOURS, THE DISGRUNTLED DUO CONFERS WITH THE GOTHAM CITY POLICE COMMISSIONER...
THEN IT'S AGREED! NEXT TIME HE APPEARS-- WE LET HIM STEAL WHAT HE WANTS!
WHILE WE'LL BE ABOVE THE CITY IN THE BAT-COPTER-- TO FOLLOW AND SEE WHERE HE GOES!
FOR THE NEXT TWO NIGHTS THE DARK, GRIM SHAPE OF THE BATCOPTER HOVERS LIKE A GREAT BIRD OF PREY ABOVE THE CITY ROOFTOPS...
WE'LL FIGHT HIM ON HIS HOME GROUNDS--AND HOLD HIM UNTIL THE POLICE ARRIVE WITH ELECTRIFIED NETS!
THEN ON A CLOUDY NIGHT, WHEN DARKNESS CLOAKS THE CITY-- THE BEHEMOTH OF BANDITRY CRASHES INTO A CITY MUSEUM..
THERE HE GOES! NOW KEEP YOUR EYES PEELED FOR HIM WHEN HE COMES OUT!
RIGHTO, BATMAN! MY PUPILS ARE ALREADY PANTING!
ALL GOTHAM CITY HAS BEEN ALERTED TO THE TERRIBLE DANGER! LET THE BLOCKBUSTER BANDIT COME AND GO WITHOUT INTERFERENCE...
GYAAGH!
MINUTES LATER, HOLLOW FOOT-FALLS SPEED ALONG THE DESERTED CITY STREETS-- WHILE OVERHEAD THAT DREAD FORM IS SHADOWED BY THE GOTHAM GANGBUSTERS...
HE'S HEADING TOWARD THE WHARVES!
INTO THE SEA HE PLUNGES, SWIMMING WITH POWERFUL STROKES AS THE ALMOST SILENT ROTORS OF THE BATCOPTER FOLLOW OVER-HEAD...
SAY, HE'S HEADING TOWARD THE ISLAND WHERE I RESCUED THAT BOY, MARK DESMOND! I WONDER IF THERE CAN BE ANY CONNECTION?
9

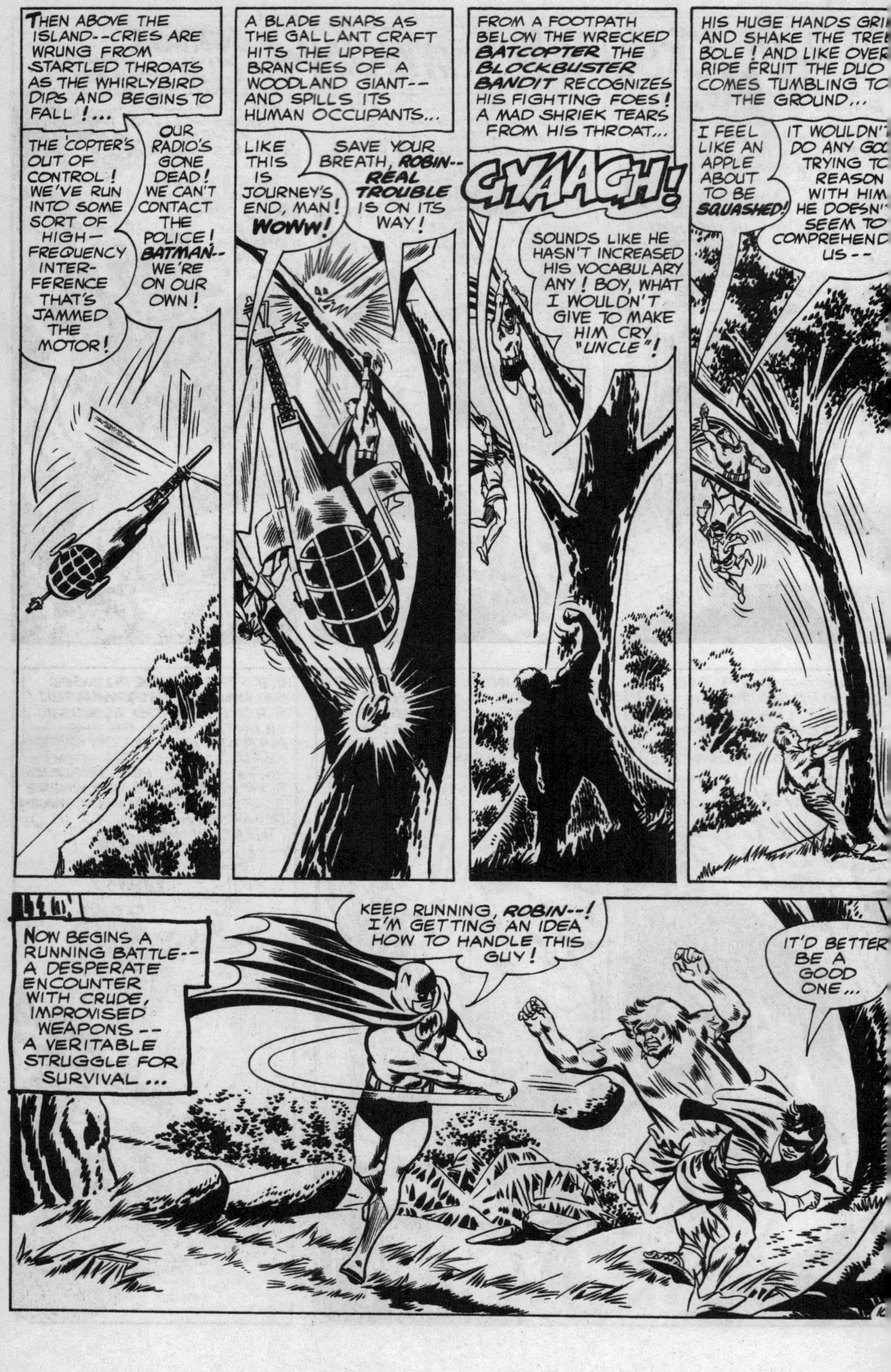
THEN ABOVE THE ISLAND--CRIES ARE WRUNG FROM STARTLED THROATS AS THE WHIRLYBIRD DIPS AND BEGINS TO FALL!...
THE 'COPTER'S OUT OF CONTROL! WE'VE RUN INTO SOME SORT OF HIGH-FREQUENCY INTERFERENCE THAT'S JAMMED THE MOTOR!
OUR RADIO'S GONE DEAD! WE CAN'T CONTACT THE POLICE! BATMAN-- WE'RE ON OUR OWN!
A BLADE SNAPS AS THE GALLANT CRAFT HITS THE UPPER BRANCHES OF A WOODLAND GIANT-- AND SPILLS ITS HUMAN OCCUPANTS...
LIKE THIS IS JOURNEY'S END, MAN! WOWW!
SAVE YOUR BREATH, ROBIN-- REAL TROUBLE IS ON ITS WAY!
FROM A FOOTPATH BELOW THE WRECKED BATCOPTER THE BLOCKBUSTER BANDIT RECOGNIZES HIS FIGHTING FOES! A MAD SHRIEK TEARS FROM HIS THROAT...
GYAAGH!
SOUNDS LIKE HE HASN'T INCREASED HIS VOCABULARY ANY! BOY, WHAT I WOULDN'T GIVE TO MAKE HIM CRY "UNCLE"!
HIS HUGE HANDS GRI AND SHAKE THE TRE BOLE! AND LIKE OVER RIPE FRUIT THE DUO COMES TUMBLING TO THE GROUND...
I FEEL LIKE AN APPLE ABOUT TO BE SQUASHED!
IT WOULDN'T DO ANY GO TRYING TO REASON WITH HIM HE DOESN' SEEM TO COMPREHEND US--
NOW BEGINS A RUNNING BATTLE-- A DESPERATE ENCOUNTER WITH CRUDE, IMPROVISED WEAPONS-- A VERITABLE STRUGGLE FOR SURVIVAL...
KEEP RUNNING, ROBIN--! I'M GETTING AN IDEA HOW TO HANDLE THIS GUY!
IT'D BETTER BE A GOOD ONE...

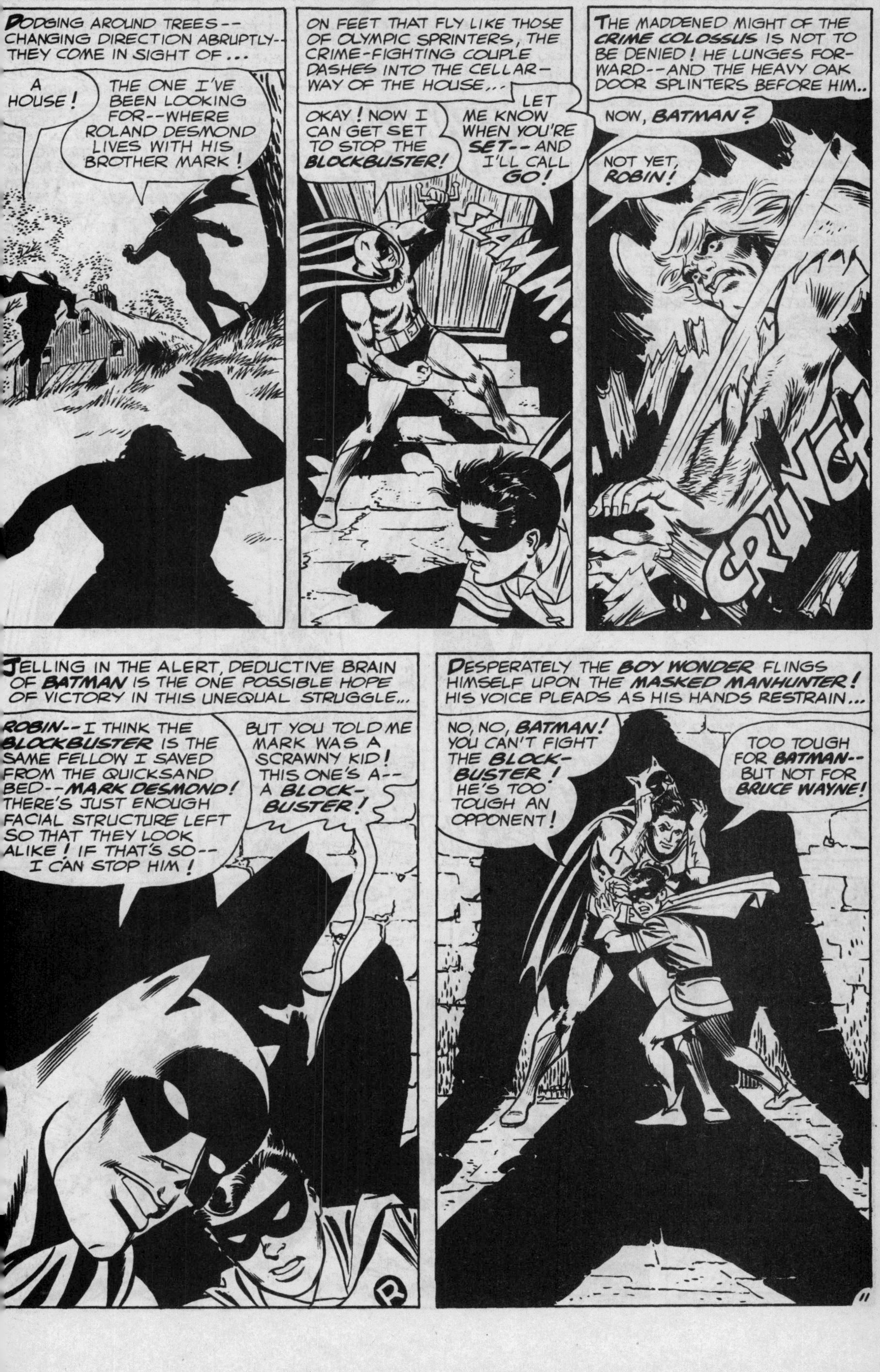
DODGING AROUND TREES-- CHANGING DIRECTION ABRUPTLY-- THEY COME IN SIGHT OF ...
A HOUSE!
THE ONE I'VE BEEN LOOKING FOR--WHERE ROLAND DESMOND LIVES WITH HIS BROTHER MARK!
ON FEET THAT FLY LIKE THOSE OF OLYMPIC SPRINTERS, THE CRIME-FIGHTING COUPLE DASHES INTO THE CELLAR-WAY OF THE HOUSE...
OKAY! NOW I CAN GET SET TO STOP THE BLOCKBUSTER!
LET ME KNOW WHEN YOU'RE SET-- AND I'LL CALL GO!
SLAM
THE MADDENED MIGHT OF THE CRIME COLOSSUS IS NOT TO BE DENIED! HE LUNGES FORWARD--AND THE HEAVY OAK DOOR SPLINTERS BEFORE HIM..
NOW, BATMAN?
NOT YET, ROBIN!
CRUNCH
JELLING IN THE ALERT, DEDUCTIVE BRAIN OF BATMAN IS THE ONE POSSIBLE HOPE OF VICTORY IN THIS UNEQUAL STRUGGLE...
ROBIN--I THINK THE BLOCKBUSTER IS THE SAME FELLOW I SAVED FROM THE QUICKSAND BED--MARK DESMOND! THERE'S JUST ENOUGH FACIAL STRUCTURE LEFT SO THAT THEY LOOK ALIKE! IF THAT'S SO-- I CAN STOP HIM!
BUT YOU TOLD ME MARK WAS A SCRAWNY KID! THIS ONE'S A-- A BLOCK-BUSTER!
DESPERATELY THE BOY WONDER FLINGS HIMSELF UPON THE MASKED MANHUNTER! HIS VOICE PLEADS AS HIS HANDS RESTRAIN...
NO, NO, BATMAN! YOU CAN'T FIGHT THE BLOCK-BUSTER! HE'S TOO TOUGH AN OPPONENT!
TOO TOUGH FOR BATMAN-- BUT NOT FOR BRUCE WAYNE!
11

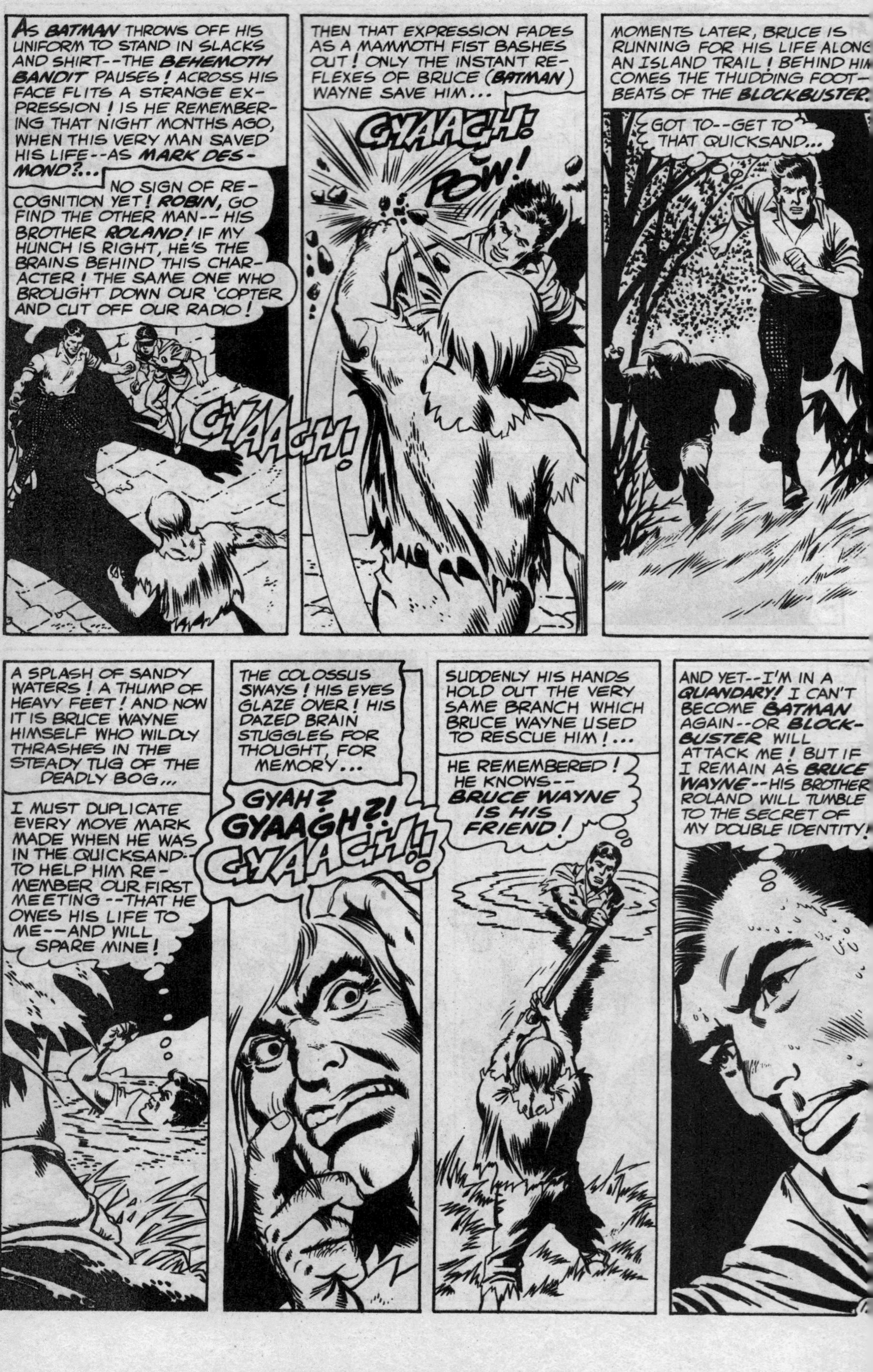
AS BATMAN THROWS OFF HIS UNIFORM TO STAND IN SLACKS AND SHIRT--THE BEHEMOTH BANDIT PAUSES! ACROSS HIS FACE FLITS A STRANGE EXPRESSION! IS HE REMEMBERING THAT NIGHT MONTHS AGO, WHEN THIS VERY MAN SAVED HIS LIFE--AS MARK DESMOND?...
NO SIGN OF RECOGNITION YET! ROBIN, GO FIND THE OTHER MAN--HIS BROTHER ROLAND! IF MY HUNCH IS RIGHT, HE'S THE BRAINS BEHIND THIS CHARACTER! THE SAME ONE WHO BROUGHT DOWN OUR 'COPTER AND CUT OFF OUR RADIO!
GYAAGH!
THEN THAT EXPRESSION FADES AS A MAMMOTH FIST BASHES OUT! ONLY THE INSTANT REFLEXES OF BRUCE (BATMAN) WAYNE SAVE HIM...
GYAAGH!
POW!
MOMENTS LATER, BRUCE IS RUNNING FOR HIS LIFE ALONG AN ISLAND TRAIL! BEHIND HIM COMES THE THUDDING FOOTBEATS OF THE BLOCKBUSTER.
GOT TO--GET TO THAT QUICKSAND...
A SPLASH OF SANDY WATERS! A THUMP OF HEAVY FEET! AND NOW IT IS BRUCE WAYNE HIMSELF WHO WILDLY THRASHES IN THE STEADY TUG OF THE DEADLY BOG...
I MUST DUPLICATE EVERY MOVE MARK MADE WHEN HE WAS IN THE QUICKSAND--TO HELP HIM REMEMBER OUR FIRST MEETING--THAT HE OWES HIS LIFE TO ME--AND WILL SPARE MINE!
THE COLOSSUS SWAYS! HIS EYES GLAZE OVER! HIS DAZED BRAIN STUGGLES FOR THOUGHT, FOR MEMORY...
GYAH? GYAAGH?! GYAAGH!
SUDDENLY HIS HANDS HOLD OUT THE VERY SAME BRANCH WHICH BRUCE WAYNE USED TO RESCUE HIM!...
HE REMEMBERED! HE KNOWS--BRUCE WAYNE IS HIS FRIEND!
AND YET--I'M IN A QUANDARY! I CAN'T BECOME BATMAN AGAIN--OR BLOCKBUSTER WILL ATTACK ME! BUT IF I REMAIN AS BRUCE WAYNE--HIS BROTHER ROLAND WILL TUMBLE TO THE SECRET OF MY DOUBLE IDENTITY!

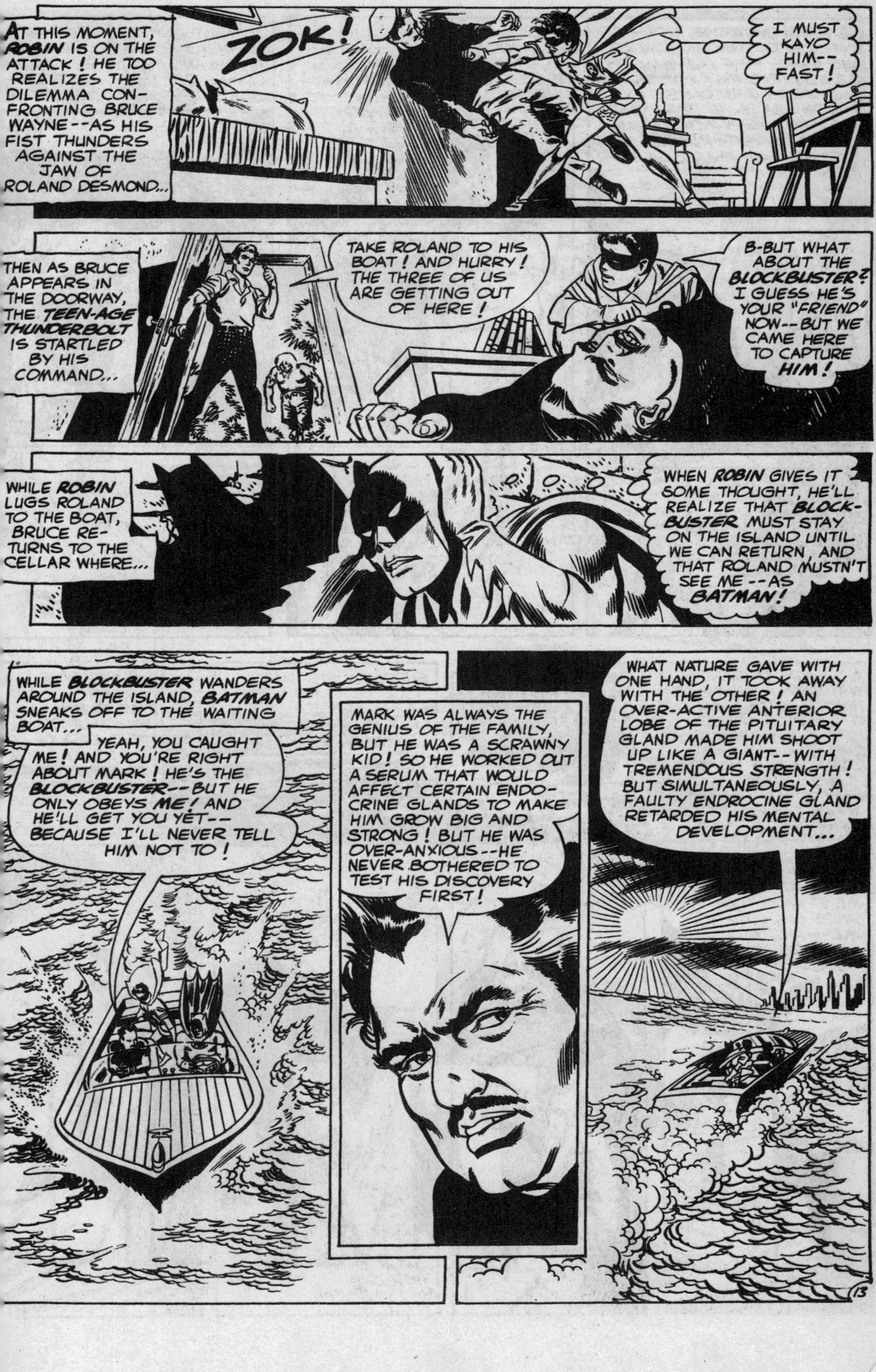
AT THIS MOMENT, ROBIN IS ON THE ATTACK! HE TOO REALIZES THE DILEMMA CONFRONTING BRUCE WAYNE--AS HIS FIST THUNDERS AGAINST THE JAW OF ROLAND DESMOND...
ZOK!
I MUST KAYO HIM--FAST!
THEN AS BRUCE APPEARS IN THE DOORWAY, THE TEEN-AGE THUNDERBOLT IS STARTLED BY HIS COMMAND...
TAKE ROLAND TO HIS BOAT! AND HURRY! THE THREE OF US ARE GETTING OUT OF HERE!
B-BUT WHAT ABOUT THE BLOCKBUSTER? I GUESS HE'S YOUR "FRIEND" NOW--BUT WE CAME HERE TO CAPTURE HIM!
WHILE ROBIN LUGS ROLAND TO THE BOAT, BRUCE RETURNS TO THE CELLAR WHERE...
WHEN ROBIN GIVES IT SOME THOUGHT, HE'LL REALIZE THAT BLOCKBUSTER MUST STAY ON THE ISLAND UNTIL WE CAN RETURN, AND THAT ROLAND MUSTN'T SEE ME--AS BATMAN!
WHILE BLOCKBUSTER WANDERS AROUND THE ISLAND, BATMAN SNEAKS OFF TO THE WAITING BOAT...
YEAH, YOU CAUGHT ME! AND YOU'RE RIGHT ABOUT MARK! HE'S THE BLOCKBUSTER--BUT HE ONLY OBEYS ME! AND HE'LL GET YOU YET--BECAUSE I'LL NEVER TELL HIM NOT TO!
MARK WAS ALWAYS THE GENIUS OF THE FAMILY, BUT HE WAS A SCRAWNY KID! SO HE WORKED OUT A SERUM THAT WOULD AFFECT CERTAIN ENDOCRINE GLANDS TO MAKE HIM GROW BIG AND STRONG! BUT HE WAS OVER-ANXIOUS--HE NEVER BOTHERED TO TEST HIS DISCOVERY FIRST!
WHAT NATURE GAVE WITH ONE HAND, IT TOOK AWAY WITH THE OTHER! AN OVER-ACTIVE ANTERIOR LOBE OF THE PITUITARY GLAND MADE HIM SHOOT UP LIKE A GIANT--WITH TREMENDOUS STRENGTH! BUT SIMULTANEOUSLY, A FAULTY ENDROCINE GLAND RETARDED HIS MENTAL DEVELOPMENT...
13

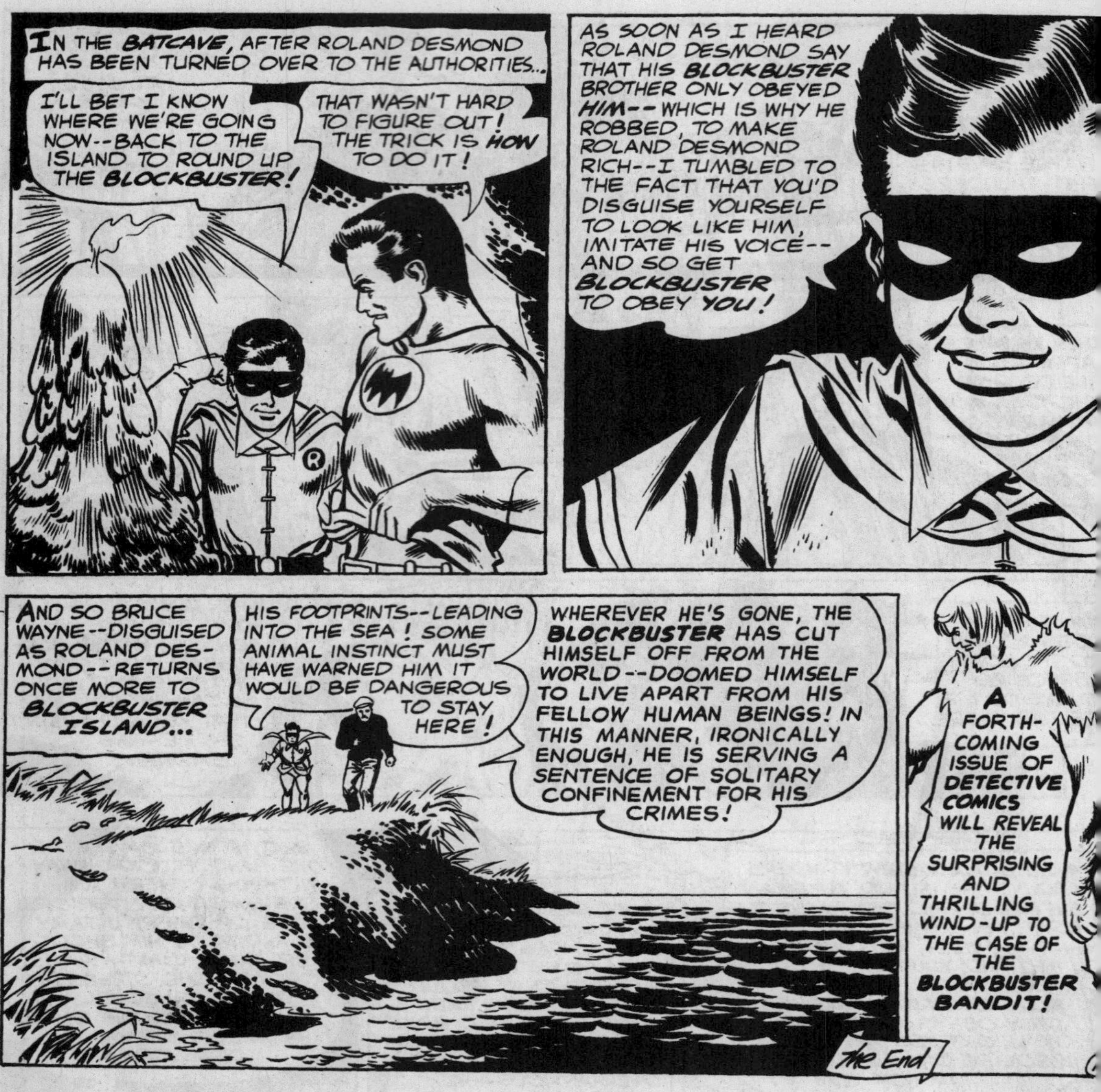
IN THE BATCAVE, AFTER ROLAND DESMOND HAS BEEN TURNED OVER TO THE AUTHORITIES...
I'LL BET I KNOW WHERE WE'RE GOING NOW--BACK TO THE ISLAND TO ROUND UP THE BLOCKBUSTER!
THAT WASN'T HARD TO FIGURE OUT! THE TRICK IS HOW TO DO IT!
AS SOON AS I HEARD ROLAND DESMOND SAY THAT HIS BLOCKBUSTER BROTHER ONLY OBEYED HIM--WHICH IS WHY HE ROBBED, TO MAKE ROLAND DESMOND RICH--I TUMBLED TO THE FACT THAT YOU'D DISGUISE YOURSELF TO LOOK LIKE HIM, IMITATE HIS VOICE--AND SO GET BLOCKBUSTER TO OBEY YOU!
AND SO BRUCE WAYNE--DISGUISED AS ROLAND DESMOND--RETURNS ONCE MORE TO BLOCKBUSTER ISLAND...
HIS FOOTPRINTS--LEADING INTO THE SEA! SOME ANIMAL INSTINCT MUST HAVE WARNED HIM IT WOULD BE DANGEROUS TO STAY HERE!
WHEREVER HE'S GONE, THE BLOCKBUSTER HAS CUT HIMSELF OFF FROM THE WORLD--DOOMED HIMSELF TO LIVE APART FROM HIS FELLOW HUMAN BEINGS! IN THIS MANNER, IRONICALLY ENOUGH, HE IS SERVING A SENTENCE OF SOLITARY CONFINEMENT FOR HIS CRIMES!
A FORTHCOMING ISSUE OF DETECTIVE COMICS WILL REVEAL THE SURPRISING AND THRILLING WIND-UP TO THE CASE OF THE BLOCKBUSTER BANDIT!
The End

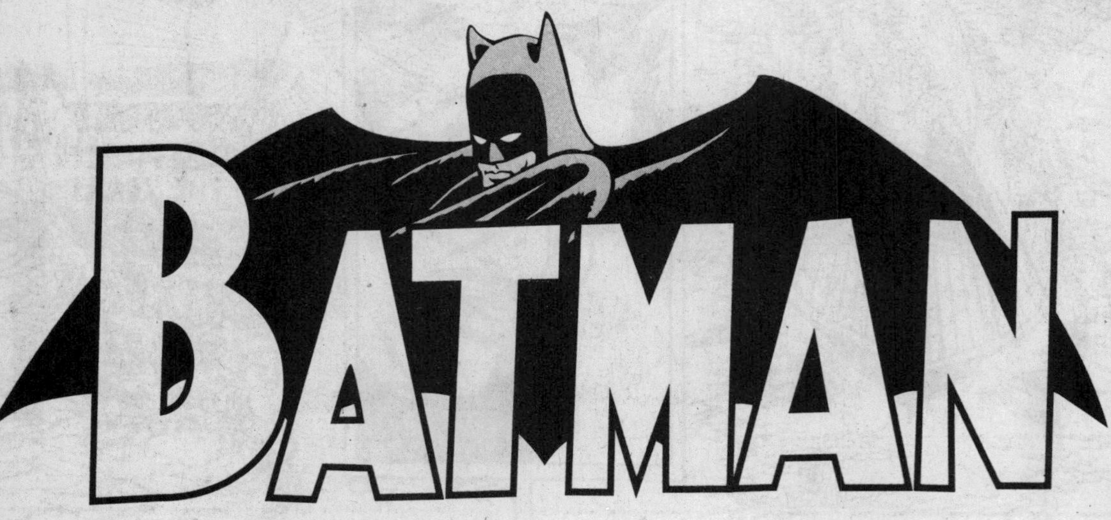
BATMAN

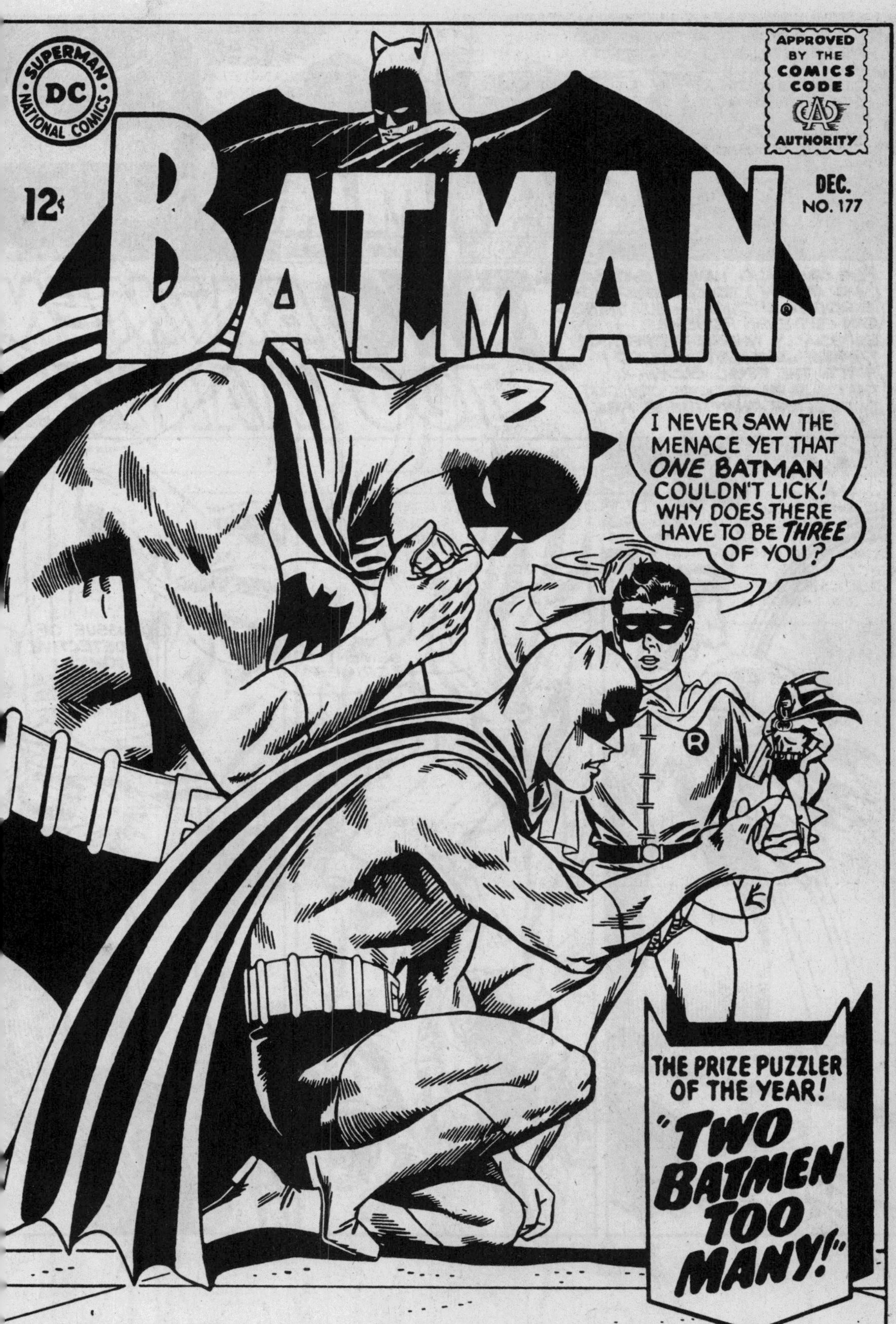
SUPERMAN
DC
NATIONAL COMICS
APPROVED BY THE COMICS CODE AUTHORITY
12¢
BATMAN
DEC.
NO. 177
I NEVER SAW THE MENACE YET THAT ONE BATMAN COULDN'T LICK! WHY DOES THERE HAVE TO BE THREE OF YOU?
THE PRIZE PUZZLER OF THE YEAR!
"TWO BATMEN TOO MANY!"

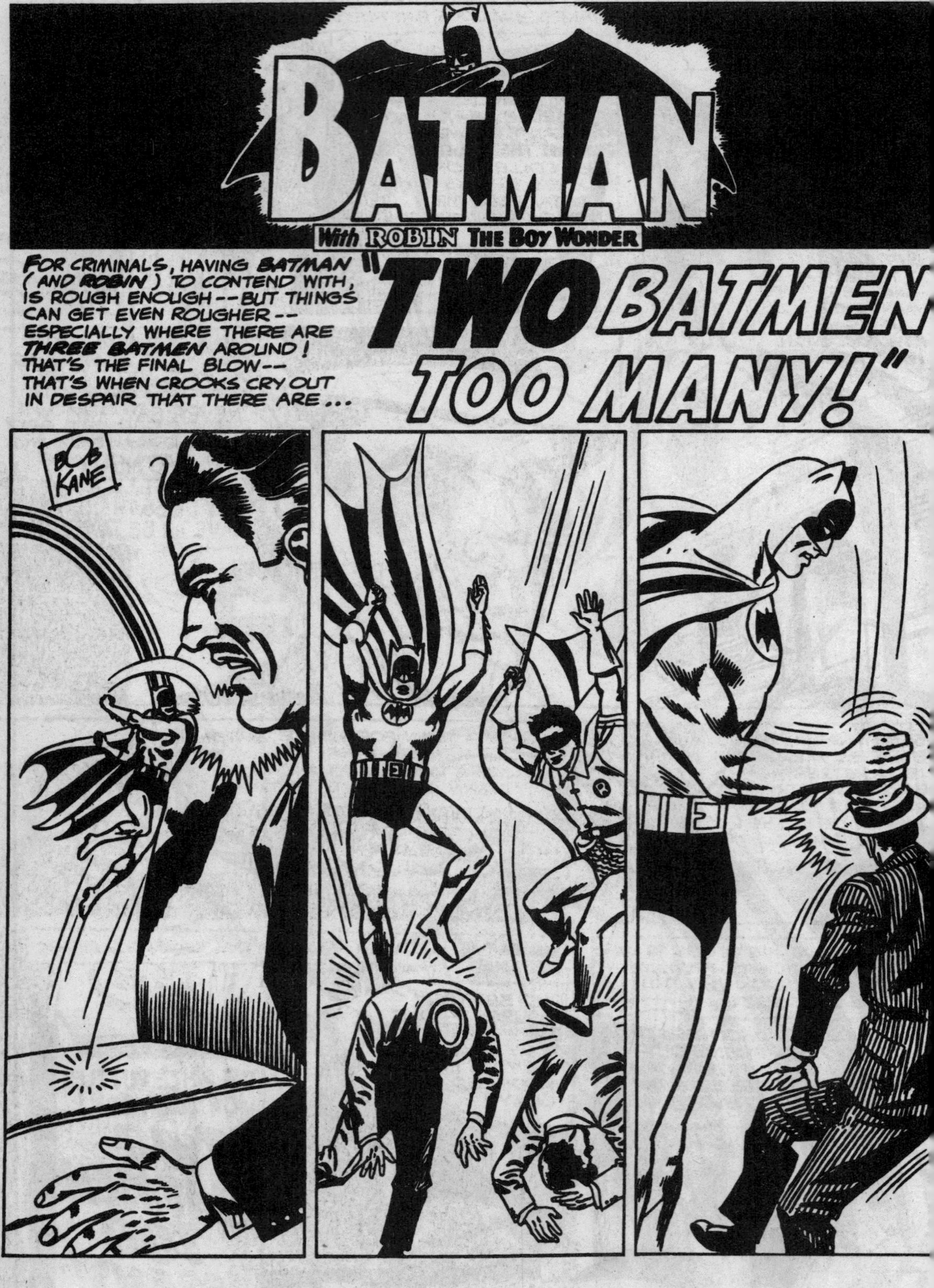
BATMAN
With ROBIN THE BOY WONDER
FOR CRIMINALS, HAVING BATMAN (AND ROBIN) TO CONTEND WITH, IS ROUGH ENOUGH--BUT THINGS CAN GET EVEN ROUGHER--ESPECIALLY WHERE THERE ARE THREE BATMEN AROUND! THAT'S THE FINAL BLOW--THAT'S WHEN CROOKS CRY OUT IN DESPAIR THAT THERE ARE...
"TWO BATMEN TOO MANY!"
BOB KANE

THIS IS ED *"NUMBERS"* GARVEY, A MAN AT WAR-- A MAN BESIEGED BY *"BATS"*--EVEN AT HIS HOME !

A BAT-SHAPED KITE ! ANY- BODY ELSE'D THINK A KID LOST IT--BUT I'M POSITIVE *BATMAN* PUT IT THERE--AS ANOTHER MANEUVER IN HIS *PSYCHOLOGICAL WAR* AGAINST ME !

AND EVEN A WALK THROUGH A *GOTHAM CITY* ALLEYWAY TAKES HIM TO A BATTLEGROUND OF *"BATS"* !

LAUNDRY--MAKING A BAT-SHAPED SHADOW ! ANOTHER *"COINCIDENCE"* RIGGED BY *BATMAN!* HE CAN'T *PROVE* I STOLE THE KIMBER GEM COLLECTION, SO HE'S TRYING TO STAMPEDE ME INTO SURRENDERING IT...

I WAS DOING PLENTY OKAY IN THE *NUMBERS RACKET,* UNTIL I BE- CAME OBSESSED WITH THE IDEA OF STEALING THE KIMBER GEM SET ! THE IDEA WAS DRIVING ME AS BATTY AS *BATMAN* IS DRIVING ME NOW !

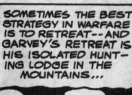

SOMETIMES THE BEST STRATEGY IN WARFARE IS TO RETREAT--AND GARVEY'S RETREAT IS HIS ISOLATED HUNT- ING LODGE IN THE MOUNTAINS...

IF I STAY OUTA TOWN FOR AWHILE, *BATMAN* MAY LAY OFF ME! HEY--THAT SOUNDS LIKE A LANDSLIDE AHEAD ! I HOPE MY CABIN ISN'T IN ITS PATH--

R-RUMBLE!

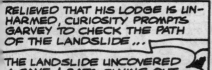

RELIEVED THAT HIS LODGE IS UN- HARMED, CURIOSITY PROMPTS GARVEY TO CHECK THE PATH OF THE LANDSLIDE ...

THE LANDSLIDE UNCOVERED A CAVE ! BATS FLYING OUT-- REMIND ME OF A *BAT-CAVE!* UGH--CAN'T I EVER STOP THINKING ABOUT *BATMAN* ?

AS GARVEY'S TORCH PROBES THE CAVERN'S DARK DEPTHS...

TWO SEATED FIGURES --ONE BIG--ONE LITTLE ! THEY LOOK LIKE THEY'VE BEEN MODELED FROM CLAY !

2

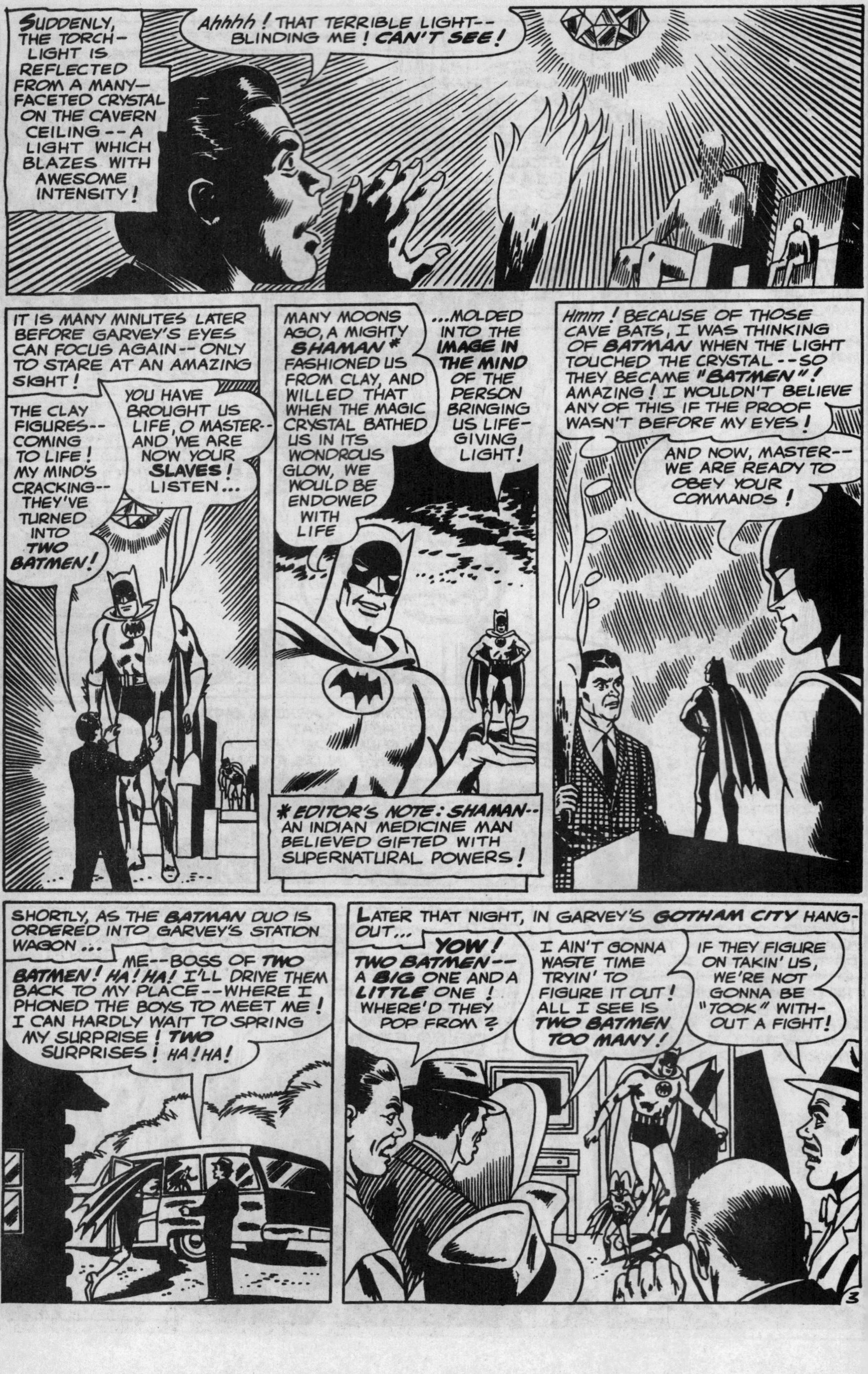
SUDDENLY, THE TORCH-LIGHT IS REFLECTED FROM A MANY-FACETED CRYSTAL ON THE CAVERN CEILING -- A LIGHT WHICH BLAZES WITH AWESOME INTENSITY!
Ahhhh! THAT TERRIBLE LIGHT-- BLINDING ME! CAN'T SEE!
IT IS MANY MINUTES LATER BEFORE GARVEY'S EYES CAN FOCUS AGAIN -- ONLY TO STARE AT AN AMAZING SIGHT!
THE CLAY FIGURES-- COMING TO LIFE! MY MIND'S CRACKING-- THEY'VE TURNED INTO TWO BATMEN!
YOU HAVE BROUGHT US LIFE, O MASTER-- AND WE ARE NOW YOUR SLAVES! LISTEN...
MANY MOONS AGO, A MIGHTY SHAMAN* FASHIONED US FROM CLAY, AND WILLED THAT WHEN THE MAGIC CRYSTAL BATHED US IN ITS WONDROUS GLOW, WE WOULD BE ENDOWED WITH LIFE
...MOLDED INTO THE IMAGE IN THE MIND OF THE PERSON BRINGING US LIFE-GIVING LIGHT!
*EDITOR'S NOTE: SHAMAN-- AN INDIAN MEDICINE MAN BELIEVED GIFTED WITH SUPERNATURAL POWERS!
Hmm! BECAUSE OF THOSE CAVE BATS, I WAS THINKING OF BATMAN WHEN THE LIGHT TOUCHED THE CRYSTAL -- SO THEY BECAME "BATMEN"! AMAZING! I WOULDN'T BELIEVE ANY OF THIS IF THE PROOF WASN'T BEFORE MY EYES!
AND NOW, MASTER-- WE ARE READY TO OBEY YOUR COMMANDS!
SHORTLY, AS THE BATMAN DUO IS ORDERED INTO GARVEY'S STATION WAGON...
ME--BOSS OF TWO BATMEN! HA! HA! I'LL DRIVE THEM BACK TO MY PLACE--WHERE I PHONED THE BOYS TO MEET ME! I CAN HARDLY WAIT TO SPRING MY SURPRISE! TWO SURPRISES! HA! HA!
LATER THAT NIGHT, IN GARVEY'S GOTHAM CITY HANG-OUT...
YOW! TWO BATMEN-- A BIG ONE AND A LITTLE ONE! WHERE'D THEY POP FROM?
I AIN'T GONNA WASTE TIME TRYIN' TO FIGURE IT OUT! ALL I SEE IS TWO BATMEN TOO MANY!
IF THEY FIGURE ON TAKIN' US, WE'RE NOT GONNA BE "TOOK" WITH-OUT A FIGHT!
3

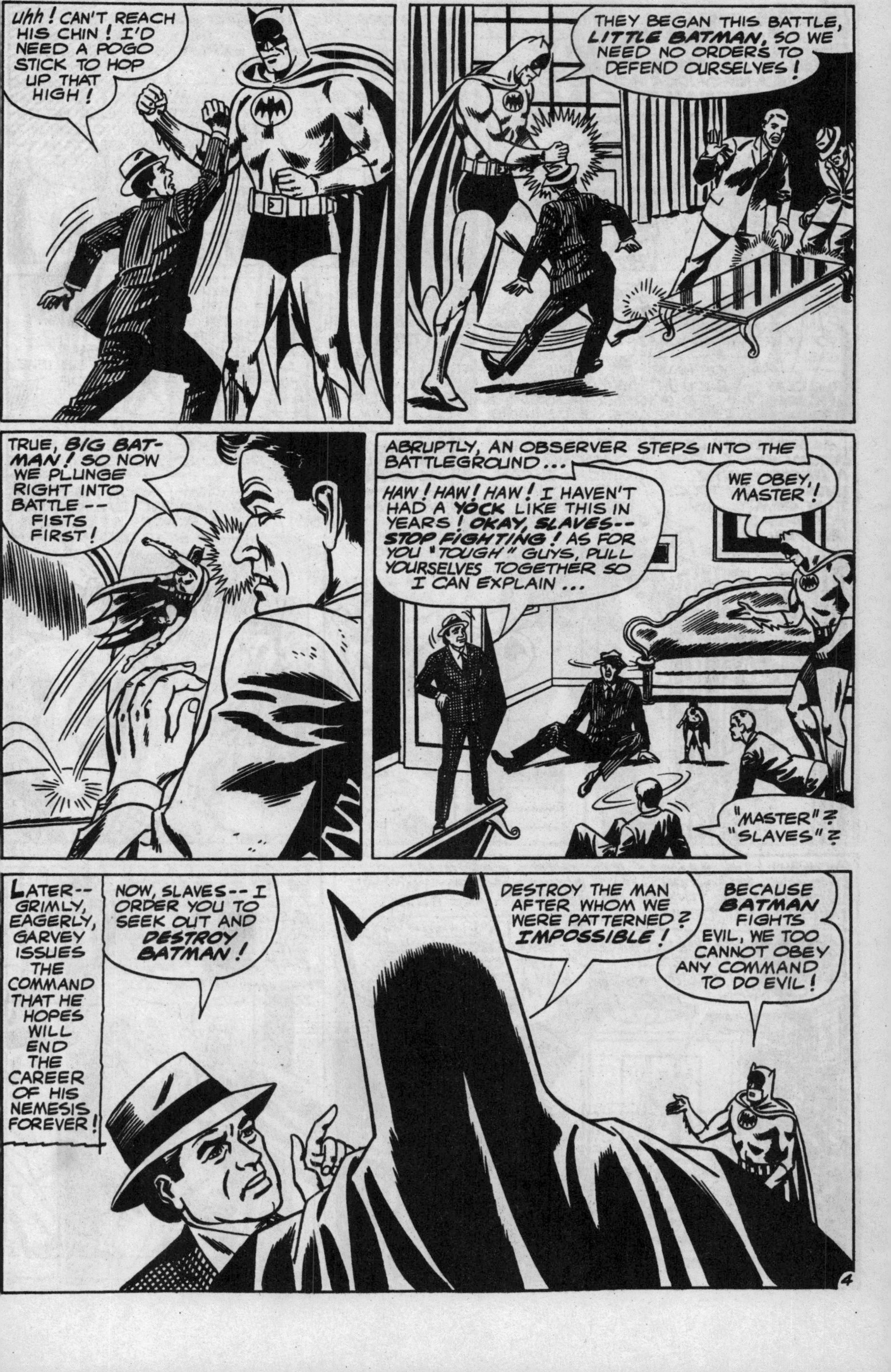
UHH! CAN'T REACH HIS CHIN! I'D NEED A POGO STICK TO HOP UP THAT HIGH!
THEY BEGAN THIS BATTLE, LITTLE BATMAN, SO WE NEED NO ORDERS TO DEFEND OURSELVES!
TRUE, BIG BATMAN! SO NOW WE PLUNGE RIGHT INTO BATTLE -- FISTS FIRST!
ABRUPTLY, AN OBSERVER STEPS INTO THE BATTLEGROUND...
HAW! HAW! HAW! I HAVEN'T HAD A YOCK LIKE THIS IN YEARS! OKAY, SLAVES-- STOP FIGHTING! AS FOR YOU "TOUGH" GUYS, PULL YOURSELVES TOGETHER SO I CAN EXPLAIN...
WE OBEY, MASTER!
"MASTER"? "SLAVES"?
LATER-- GRIMLY, EAGERLY, GARVEY ISSUES THE COMMAND THAT HE HOPES WILL END THE CAREER OF HIS NEMESIS FOREVER!
NOW, SLAVES-- I ORDER YOU TO SEEK OUT AND DESTROY BATMAN!
DESTROY THE MAN AFTER WHOM WE WERE PATTERNED? IMPOSSIBLE!
BECAUSE BATMAN FIGHTS EVIL, WE TOO CANNOT OBEY ANY COMMAND TO DO EVIL!
4

Hmm! THIS COMPLICATES MATTERS-- BUT I'VE SOLVED TOUGHER PROBLEMS! OFFHAND, I DON'T KNOW HOW TO MAKE USE OF BIG BATMAN, BUT I GOT ME A NIFTY IDEA HOW TO PUT LITTLE BATMAN TO WORK FOR US!

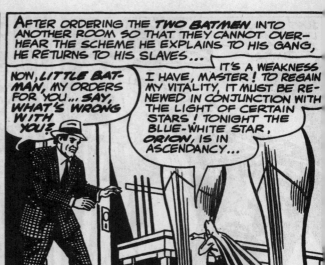

AFTER ORDERING THE *TWO BATMEN* INTO ANOTHER ROOM SO THAT THEY CANNOT OVER-HEAR THE SCHEME HE EXPLAINS TO HIS GANG, HE RETURNS TO HIS SLAVES...

NOW, LITTLE BATMAN, MY ORDERS FOR YOU... SAY, WHAT'S WRONG WITH YOU?

IT'S A WEAKNESS I HAVE, MASTER! TO REGAIN MY VITALITY, IT MUST BE RENEWED IN CONJUNCTION WITH THE LIGHT OF CERTAIN STARS! TONIGHT THE BLUE-WHITE STAR, ORION, IS IN ASCENDANCY...

...SO YOU MUST LET ORION SHINE UPON A BLUE-WHITE GEM-- THEN TOUCH THAT GEM TO MY FOREHEAD TO REVITALIZE MY LIFE-FORCE!

A BLUE-WHITE DIAMOND? A CINCH! I CAN PUT MY HANDS ON ONE IN A JIFFY! WAIT HERE!

SHORTLY, GARVEY RETURNS WITH A MAGNIFICENT BLUE-WHITE DIAMOND, AND BEGINS THE REQUIRED RITUAL...

AH! I CAN FEEL STELLAR ENERGY FLOWING THROUGH ME! NOW I AM READY, MASTER!

OKAY! SOON AS I PUT THIS DIAMOND BACK IN ITS HIDING PLACE, WE'LL GET STARTED!

MIDNIGHT! THE *BANGLE BROTHERS CARNIVAL* IS DARK AND DESERTED-- BUT BEHIND THE PAY-WAGON'S LOCKED DOOR, THE DAY'S RECEIPTS ARE BEING TALLIED. SUDDENLY...

GOOD EVENING, GENTLEMEN! I'M HERE TO OFFER MY SERVICES IN YOUR CARNIVAL!

WOW! A MIDGET--THE SMALLEST MIDGET THAT EVER LIVED! NAW! IT'S A TRICK! IT CAN'T BE REAL!

OF COURSE I'M REAL! I CAN BE YOUR STAR ATTRACTION! I NOT ONLY LOOK LIKE BATMAN, BUT I CAN DO ANYTHING HE DOES! I'VE EVEN GOT MY OWN BAT-ROPE! WATCH THIS--!

JUST BECAUSE I'M LITTLE, DON'T THINK I'M A SMALL—TIMER!

CONVINCED? READY TO SIGN ME UP NOW?

AND HOW! STAY PUT! DON'T MOVE! FIRST I WANT TO GET MY BROTHER IN HERE TO SEE YOU!

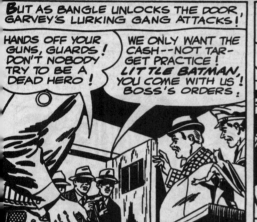

BUT AS BANGLE UNLOCKS THE DOOR, GARVEY'S LURKING GANG ATTACKS!'

HANDS OFF YOUR GUNS, GUARDS! DON'T NOBODY TRY TO BE A DEAD HERO!

WE ONLY WANT THE CASH--NOT TAR-GET PRACTICE! LITTLE BATMAN, YOU COME WITH US! BOSS'S ORDERS.

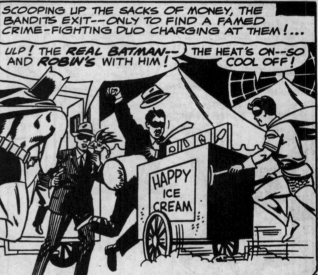

SCOOPING UP THE SACKS OF MONEY, THE BANDITS EXIT--ONLY TO FIND A FAMED CRIME-FIGHTING DUO CHARGING AT THEM!...

ULP! THE REAL BATMAN-- AND ROBIN'S WITH HIM!

THE HEAT'S ON--SO COOL OFF!

HAPPY ICE CREAM

/6

BATMAN

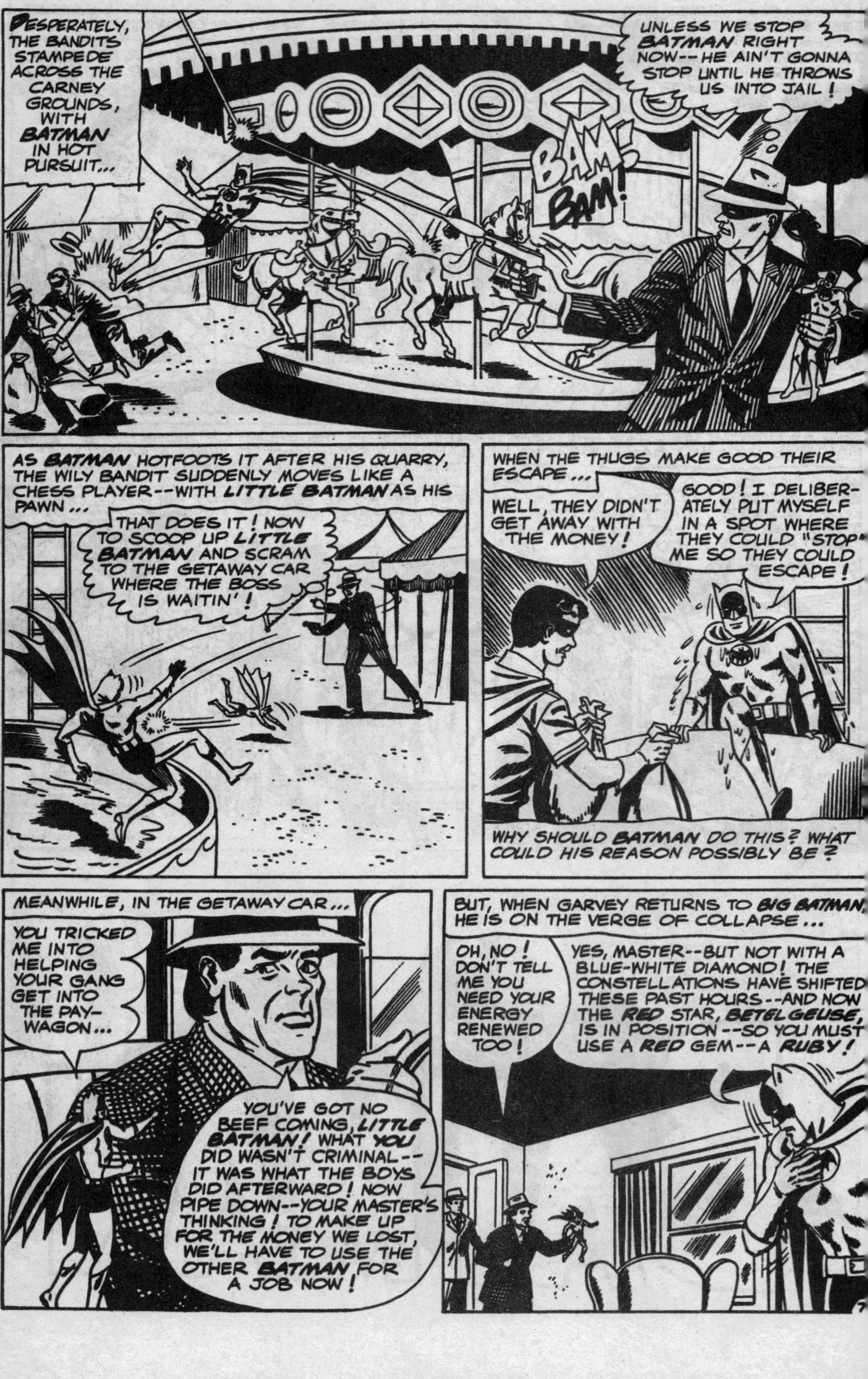
DESPERATELY, THE BANDITS STAMPEDE ACROSS THE CARNEY GROUNDS, WITH BATMAN IN HOT PURSUIT...
UNLESS WE STOP BATMAN RIGHT NOW-- HE AIN'T GONNA STOP UNTIL HE THROWS US INTO JAIL!
BAM! BAM!
AS BATMAN HOTFOOTS IT AFTER HIS QUARRY, THE WILY BANDIT SUDDENLY MOVES LIKE A CHESS PLAYER--WITH LITTLE BATMAN AS HIS PAWN...
THAT DOES IT! NOW TO SCOOP UP LITTLE BATMAN AND SCRAM TO THE GETAWAY CAR WHERE THE BOSS IS WAITIN'!
WHEN THE THUGS MAKE GOOD THEIR ESCAPE...
WELL, THEY DIDN'T GET AWAY WITH THE MONEY!
GOOD! I DELIBERATELY PUT MYSELF IN A SPOT WHERE THEY COULD "STOP" ME SO THEY COULD ESCAPE!
WHY SHOULD BATMAN DO THIS? WHAT COULD HIS REASON POSSIBLY BE?
MEANWHILE, IN THE GETAWAY CAR...
YOU TRICKED ME INTO HELPING YOUR GANG GET INTO THE PAY-WAGON...
YOU'VE GOT NO BEEF COMING, LITTLE BATMAN! WHAT YOU DID WASN'T CRIMINAL-- IT WAS WHAT THE BOYS DID AFTERWARD! NOW PIPE DOWN--YOUR MASTER'S THINKING! TO MAKE UP FOR THE MONEY WE LOST, WE'LL HAVE TO USE THE OTHER BATMAN FOR A JOB NOW!
BUT, WHEN GARVEY RETURNS TO BIG BATMAN, HE IS ON THE VERGE OF COLLAPSE...
OH, NO! DON'T TELL ME YOU NEED YOUR ENERGY RENEWED TOO!
YES, MASTER--BUT NOT WITH A BLUE-WHITE DIAMOND! THE CONSTELLATIONS HAVE SHIFTED THESE PAST HOURS--AND NOW THE RED STAR, BETELGEUSE, IS IN POSITION--SO YOU MUST USE A RED GEM--A RUBY!
7

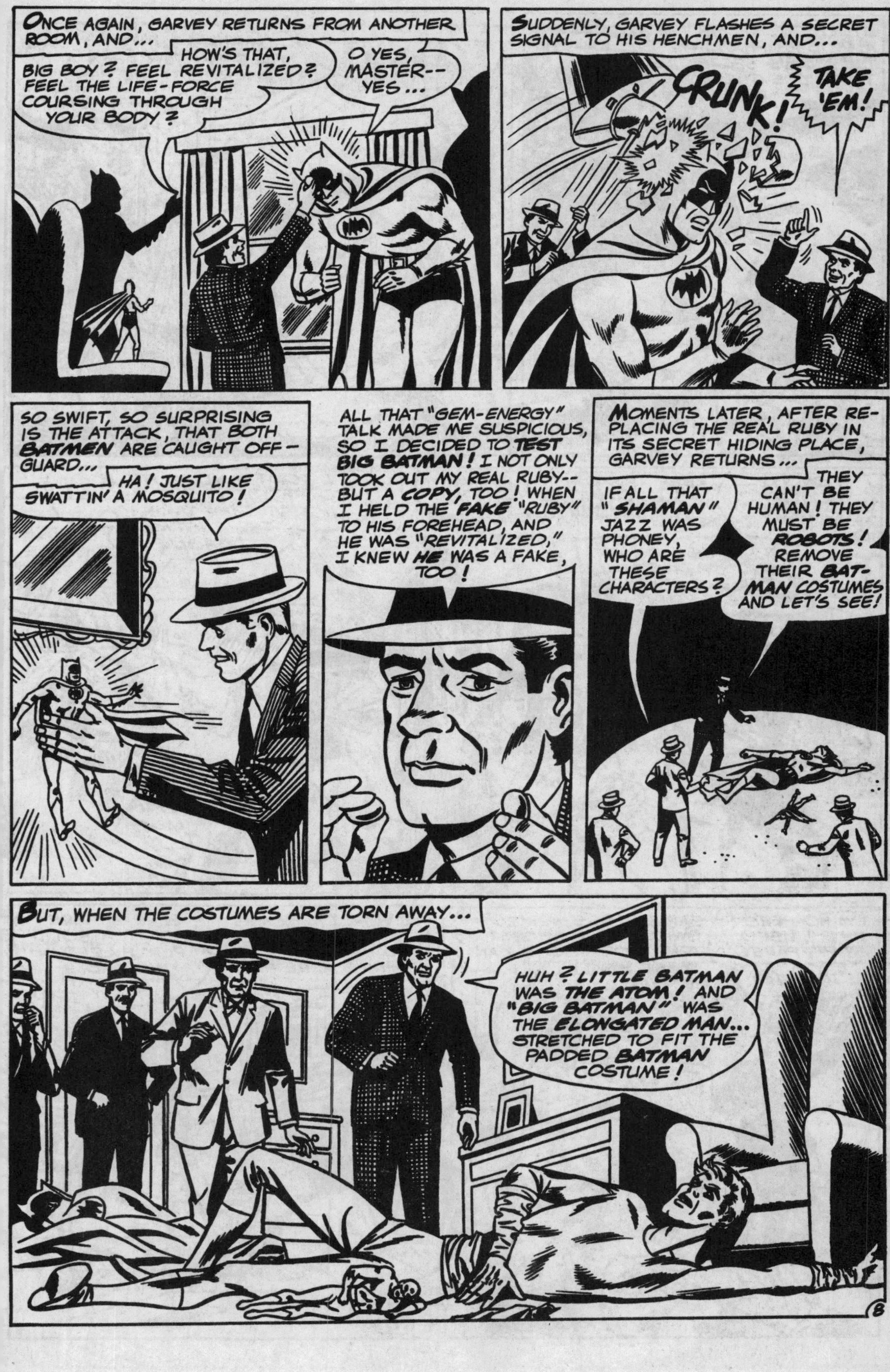
ONCE AGAIN, GARVEY RETURNS FROM ANOTHER ROOM, AND...
HOW'S THAT, BIG BOY? FEEL REVITALIZED? FEEL THE LIFE-FORCE COURSING THROUGH YOUR BODY?
O YES, MASTER-- YES...
SUDDENLY, GARVEY FLASHES A SECRET SIGNAL TO HIS HENCHMEN, AND...
CRUNK!
TAKE 'EM!
SO SWIFT, SO SURPRISING IS THE ATTACK, THAT BOTH BATMEN ARE CAUGHT OFF-GUARD...
HA! JUST LIKE SWATTIN' A MOSQUITO!
ALL THAT "GEM-ENERGY" TALK MADE ME SUSPICIOUS, SO I DECIDED TO TEST BIG BATMAN! I NOT ONLY TOOK OUT MY REAL RUBY-- BUT A COPY, TOO! WHEN I HELD THE FAKE "RUBY" TO HIS FOREHEAD, AND HE WAS "REVITALIZED," I KNEW HE WAS A FAKE, TOO!
MOMENTS LATER, AFTER RE-PLACING THE REAL RUBY IN ITS SECRET HIDING PLACE, GARVEY RETURNS...
IF ALL THAT "SHAMAN" JAZZ WAS PHONEY, WHO ARE THESE CHARACTERS?
THEY CAN'T BE HUMAN! THEY MUST BE ROBOTS! REMOVE THEIR BAT-MAN COSTUMES AND LET'S SEE!
BUT, WHEN THE COSTUMES ARE TORN AWAY...
HUH? LITTLE BATMAN WAS THE ATOM! AND "BIG BATMAN" WAS THE ELONGATED MAN... STRETCHED TO FIT THE PADDED BATMAN COSTUME!
8

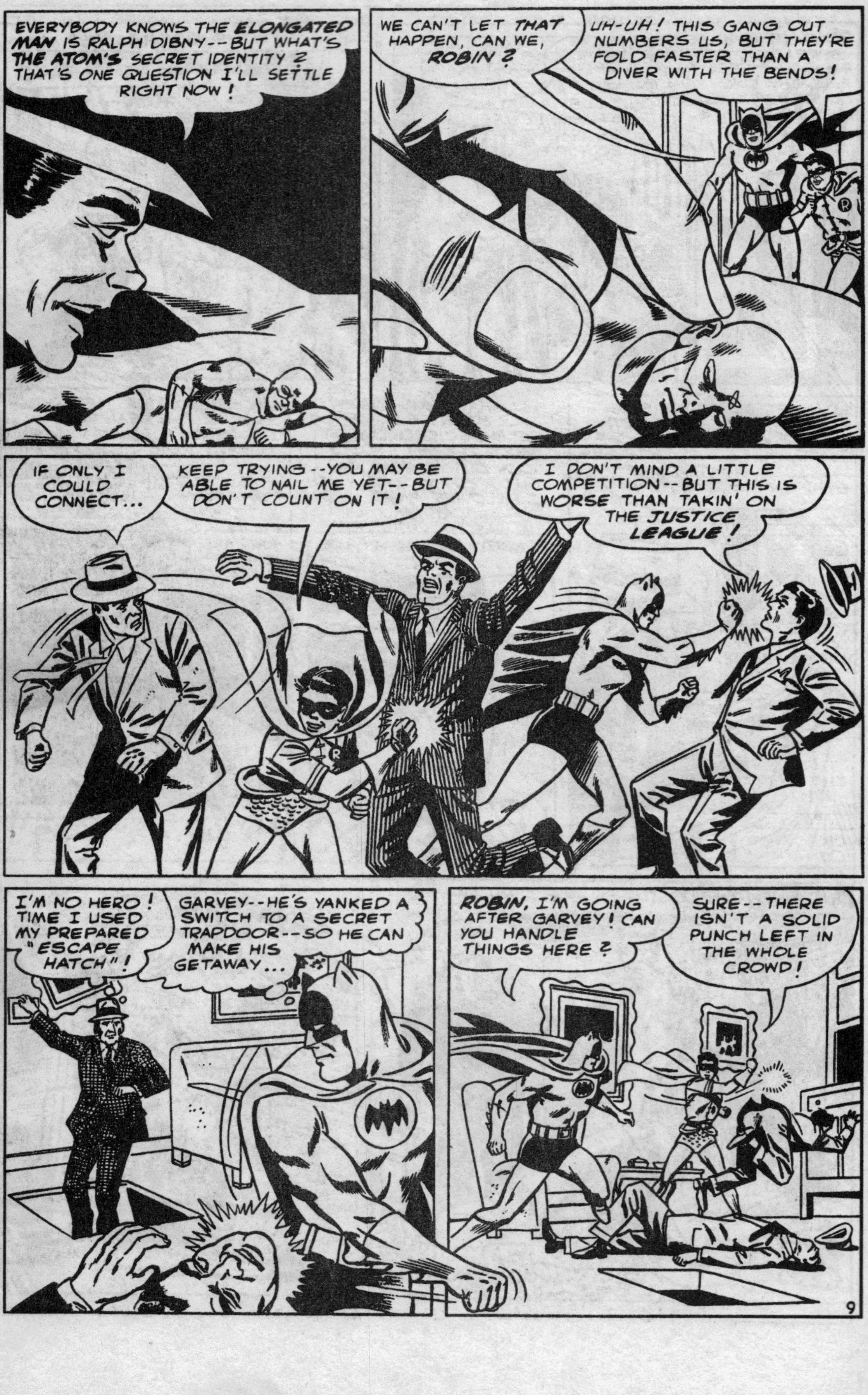
EVERYBODY KNOWS THE ELONGATED MAN IS RALPH DIBNY--BUT WHAT'S THE ATOM'S SECRET IDENTITY ? THAT'S ONE QUESTION I'LL SETTLE RIGHT NOW !
WE CAN'T LET THAT HAPPEN, CAN WE, ROBIN ?
UH-UH! THIS GANG OUT NUMBERS US, BUT THEY'RE FOLD FASTER THAN A DIVER WITH THE BENDS!
IF ONLY I COULD CONNECT...
KEEP TRYING--YOU MAY BE ABLE TO NAIL ME YET--BUT DON'T COUNT ON IT!
I DON'T MIND A LITTLE COMPETITION--BUT THIS IS WORSE THAN TAKIN' ON THE JUSTICE LEAGUE!
I'M NO HERO! TIME I USED MY PREPARED "ESCAPE HATCH"!
GARVEY--HE'S YANKED A SWITCH TO A SECRET TRAPDOOR--SO HE CAN MAKE HIS GETAWAY...
ROBIN, I'M GOING AFTER GARVEY! CAN YOU HANDLE THINGS HERE ?
SURE--THERE ISN'T A SOLID PUNCH LEFT IN THE WHOLE CROWD!
9

TO BATMAN'S ASTONISHMENT, HE DROPS INTO A SPREADING NETWORK OF TRACKS...

I'LL BE DARNED! A SECTION OF AN OLD SUBWAY RUNS RIGHT UNDER HIS HOUSE! AND THERE GOES GARVEY--ON AN ELECTRIFIED GO-CART!

TOO LATE, THE *MASKED MAN-HUNTER* HURLS HIMSELF AT THE SPEEDING VEHICLE...

LAY OFF, *BATMAN*-- THIS IS A PRIVATE CAR! NO FREE RIDERS TODAY!

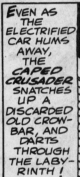

EVEN AS THE ELECTRIFIED CAR HUMS AWAY, THE *CAPED CRUSADER* SNATCHES UP A DISCARDED OLD CROW-BAR, AND DARTS THROUGH THE LABYRINTH!

I'VE GOT ONE ADVANTAGE--HIS CAR *HAS* TO STAY ON THE TRACK--BUT I'M ON FOOT! I CAN CROSS OVER, TAKE A SHORT-CUT, AND INTERCEPT HIM!

LIKE A HUNTER, *BATMAN* STALKS HIS FLEET QUARRY--AND THEN THRUSTS HIS WEAPON FORWARD WITH THE SPEED OF A SPEAR...

TOO BAD, GARVEY-- BUT IT LOOKS LIKE YOU'VE JUST BEEN...

...DERAILED!

EEEYAH!

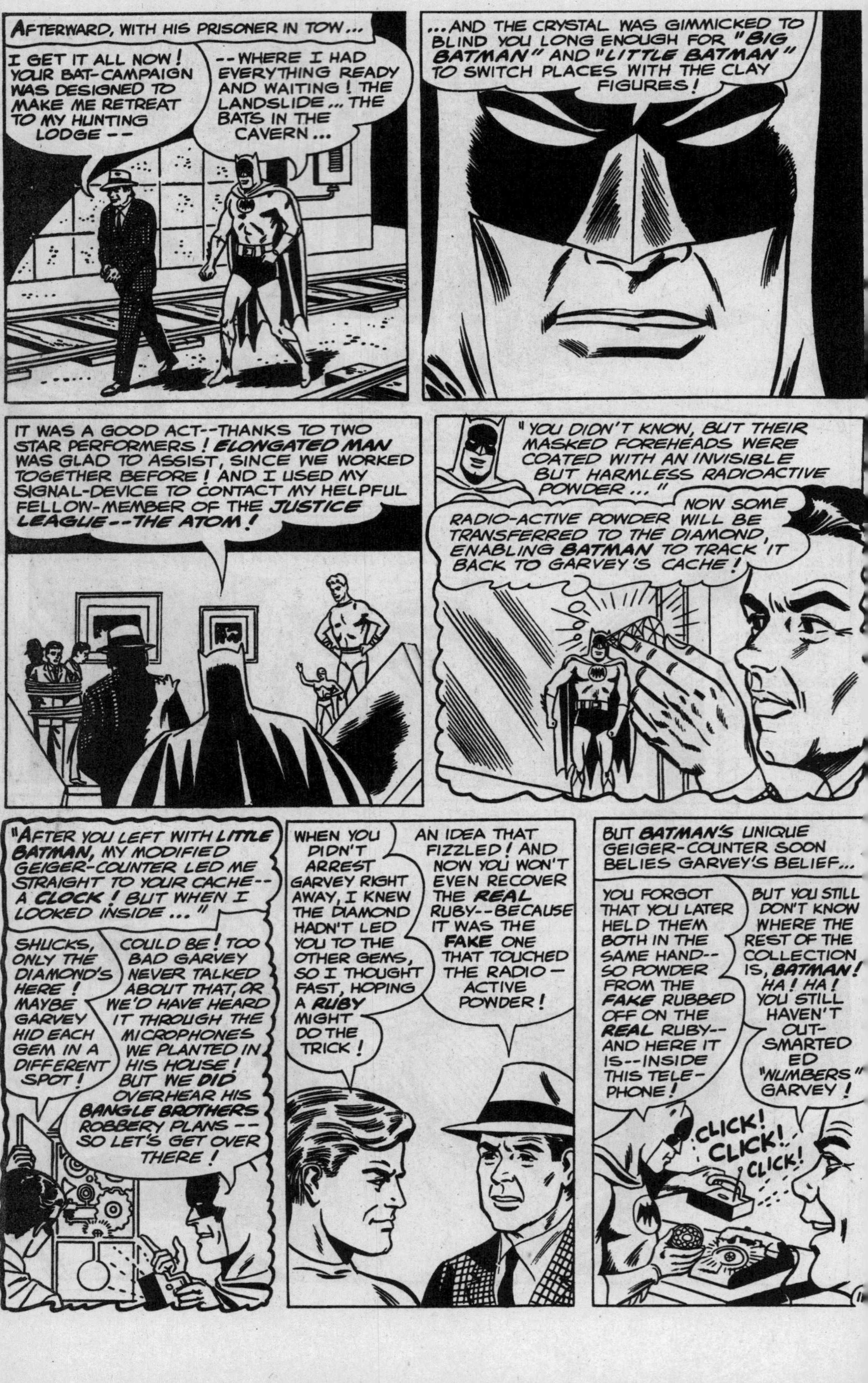
AFTERWARD, WITH HIS PRISONER IN TOW...
I GET IT ALL NOW! YOUR BAT-CAMPAIGN WAS DESIGNED TO MAKE ME RETREAT TO MY HUNTING LODGE --
-- WHERE I HAD EVERYTHING READY AND WAITING! THE LANDSLIDE... THE BATS IN THE CAVERN...
...AND THE CRYSTAL WAS GIMMICKED TO BLIND YOU LONG ENOUGH FOR "BIG BATMAN" AND "LITTLE BATMAN" TO SWITCH PLACES WITH THE CLAY FIGURES!
IT WAS A GOOD ACT--THANKS TO TWO STAR PERFORMERS! ELONGATED MAN WAS GLAD TO ASSIST, SINCE WE WORKED TOGETHER BEFORE! AND I USED MY SIGNAL-DEVICE TO CONTACT MY HELPFUL FELLOW-MEMBER OF THE JUSTICE LEAGUE--THE ATOM!
"YOU DIDN'T KNOW, BUT THEIR MASKED FOREHEADS WERE COATED WITH AN INVISIBLE BUT HARMLESS RADIOACTIVE POWDER..."
NOW SOME RADIO-ACTIVE POWDER WILL BE TRANSFERRED TO THE DIAMOND, ENABLING BATMAN TO TRACK IT BACK TO GARVEY'S CACHE!
"AFTER YOU LEFT WITH LITTLE BATMAN, MY MODIFIED GEIGER-COUNTER LED ME STRAIGHT TO YOUR CACHE--A CLOCK! BUT WHEN I LOOKED INSIDE..."
SHUCKS, ONLY THE DIAMOND'S HERE! MAYBE GARVEY HID EACH GEM IN A DIFFERENT SPOT!
COULD BE! TOO BAD GARVEY NEVER TALKED ABOUT THAT, OR WE'D HAVE HEARD IT THROUGH THE MICROPHONES WE PLANTED IN HIS HOUSE! BUT WE DID OVERHEAR HIS BANGLE BROTHERS ROBBERY PLANS -- SO LET'S GET OVER THERE!
WHEN YOU DIDN'T ARREST GARVEY RIGHT AWAY, I KNEW THE DIAMOND HADN'T LED YOU TO THE OTHER GEMS, SO I THOUGHT FAST, HOPING A RUBY MIGHT DO THE TRICK!
AN IDEA THAT FIZZLED! AND NOW YOU WON'T EVEN RECOVER THE REAL RUBY--BECAUSE IT WAS THE FAKE ONE THAT TOUCHED THE RADIO-ACTIVE POWDER!
BUT BATMAN'S UNIQUE GEIGER-COUNTER SOON BELIES GARVEY'S BELIEF...
YOU FORGOT THAT YOU LATER HELD THEM BOTH IN THE SAME HAND--SO POWDER FROM THE FAKE RUBBED OFF ON THE REAL RUBY--AND HERE IT IS--INSIDE THIS TELE-PHONE!
BUT YOU STILL DON'T KNOW WHERE THE REST OF THE COLLECTION IS, BATMAN! HA! HA! YOU STILL HAVEN'T OUT-SMARTED ED "NUMBERS" GARVEY!
CLICK! CLICK! CLICK!

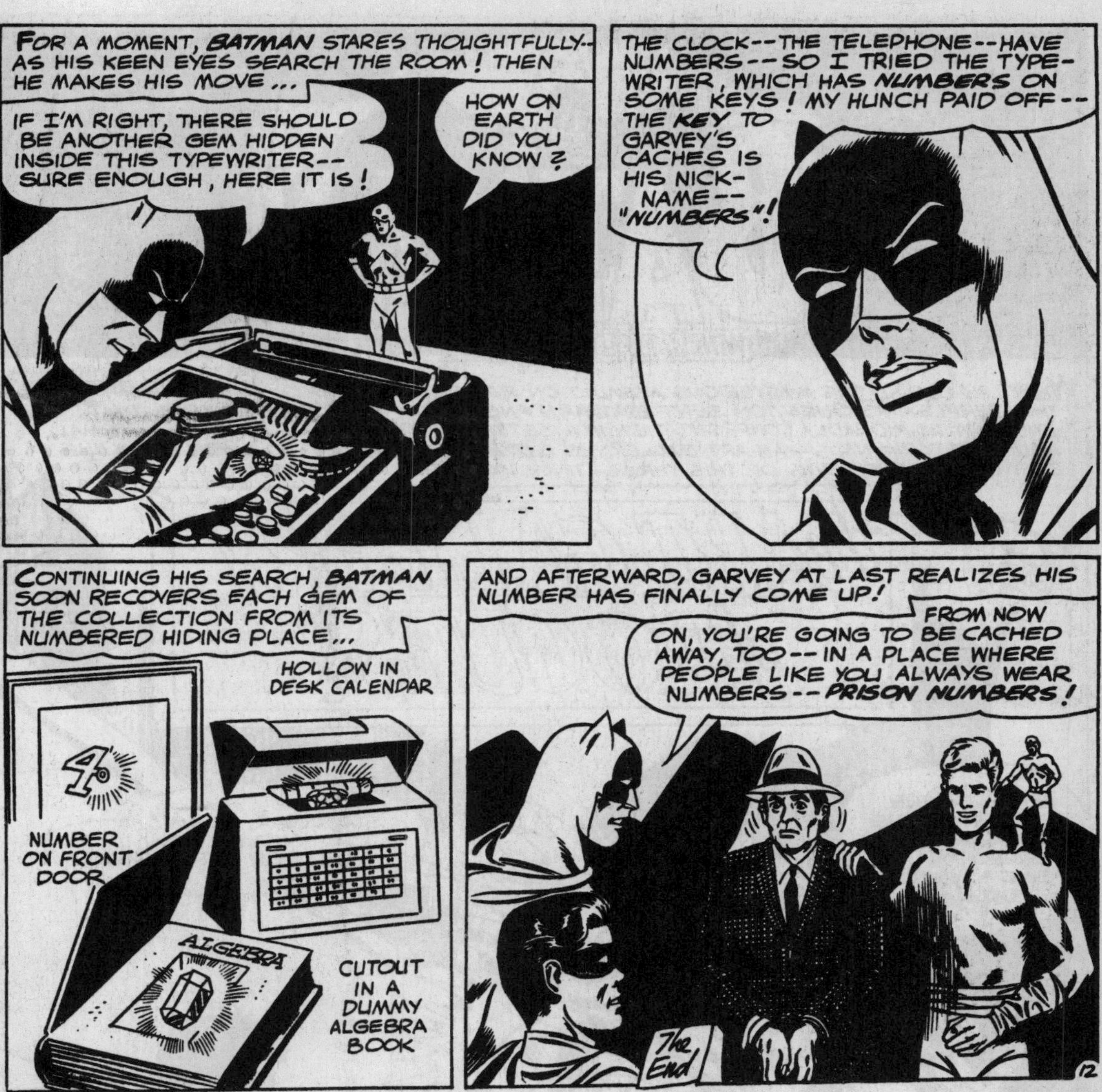
FOR A MOMENT, BATMAN STARES THOUGHTFULLY-- AS HIS KEEN EYES SEARCH THE ROOM! THEN HE MAKES HIS MOVE...
IF I'M RIGHT, THERE SHOULD BE ANOTHER GEM HIDDEN INSIDE THIS TYPEWRITER-- SURE ENOUGH, HERE IT IS!
HOW ON EARTH DID YOU KNOW?
THE CLOCK--THE TELEPHONE--HAVE NUMBERS--SO I TRIED THE TYPEWRITER, WHICH HAS NUMBERS ON SOME KEYS! MY HUNCH PAID OFF-- THE KEY TO GARVEY'S CACHES IS HIS NICKNAME--"NUMBERS"!
CONTINUING HIS SEARCH, BATMAN SOON RECOVERS EACH GEM OF THE COLLECTION FROM ITS NUMBERED HIDING PLACE...
HOLLOW IN DESK CALENDAR
NUMBER ON FRONT DOOR
ALGEBRA
CUTOUT IN A DUMMY ALGEBRA BOOK
AND AFTERWARD, GARVEY AT LAST REALIZES HIS NUMBER HAS FINALLY COME UP!
FROM NOW ON, YOU'RE GOING TO BE CACHED AWAY, TOO--IN A PLACE WHERE PEOPLE LIKE YOU ALWAYS WEAR NUMBERS--PRISON NUMBERS!
The End
12

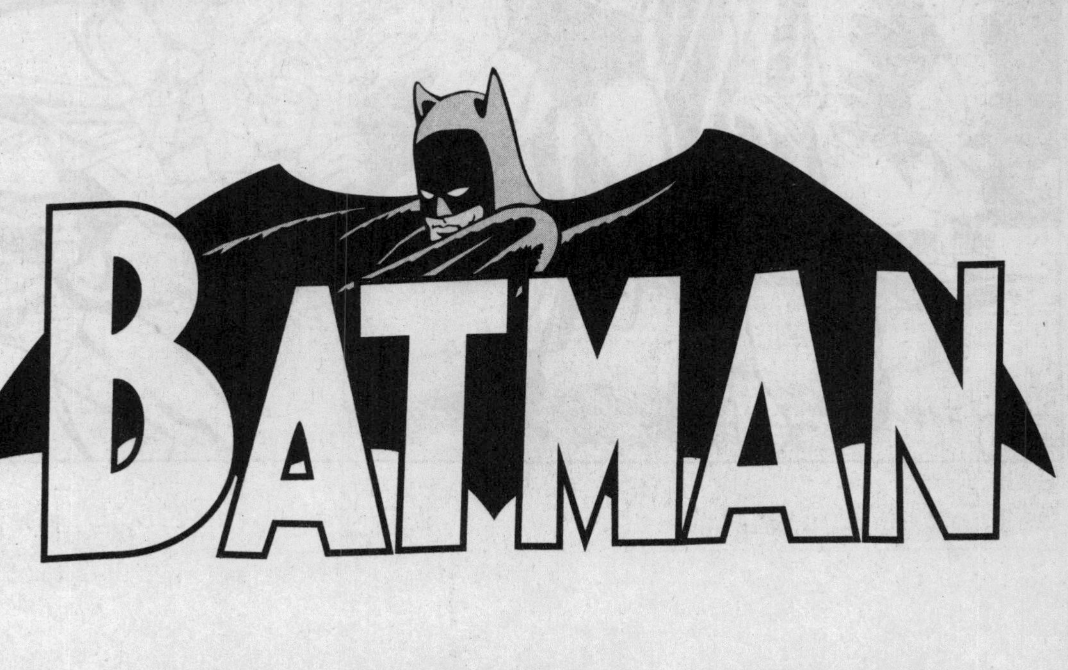
BATMAN

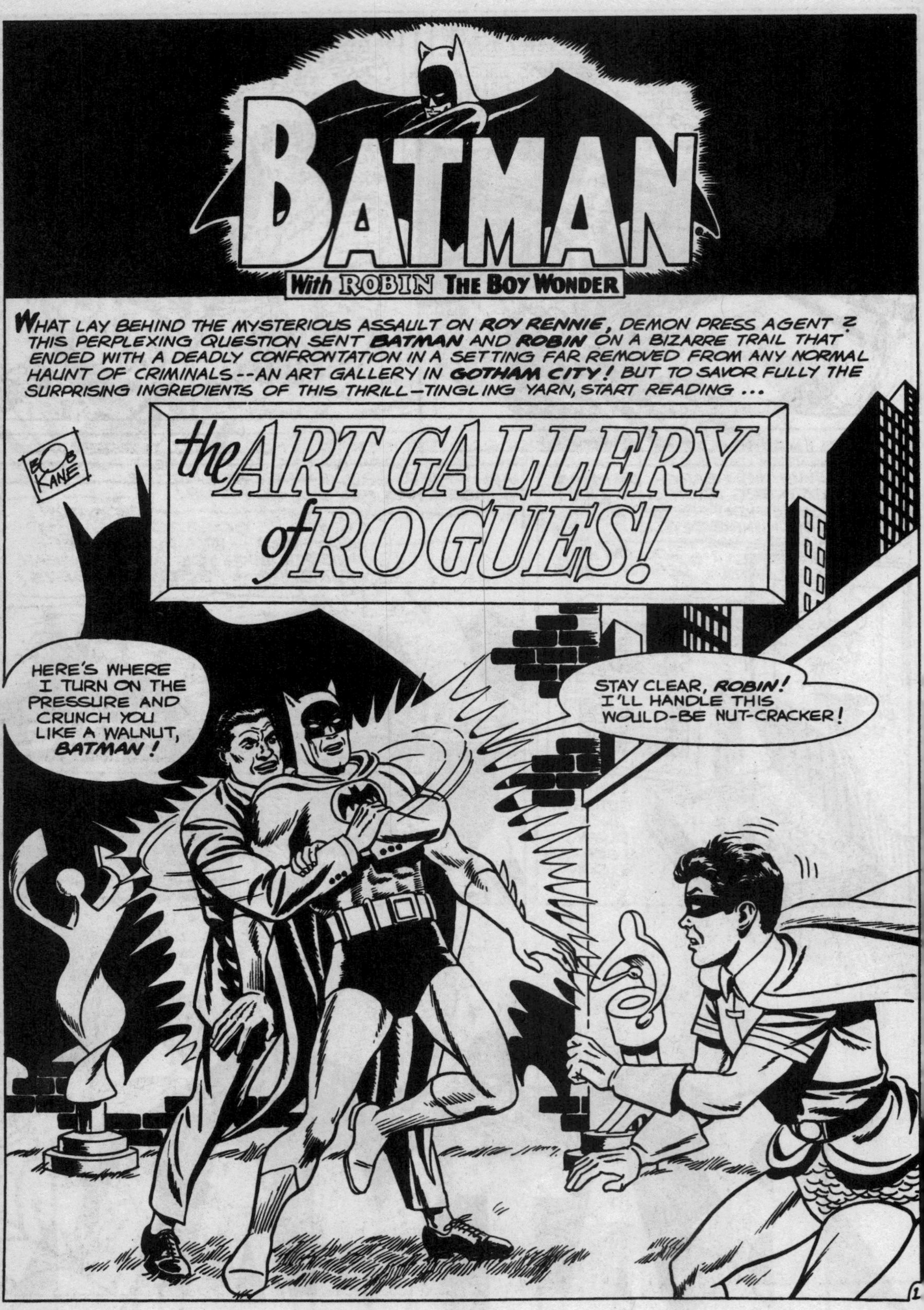
BATMAN
With ROBIN THE BOY WONDER
WHAT LAY BEHIND THE MYSTERIOUS ASSAULT ON ROY RENNIE, DEMON PRESS AGENT ? THIS PERPLEXING QUESTION SENT BATMAN AND ROBIN ON A BIZARRE TRAIL THAT ENDED WITH A DEADLY CONFRONTATION IN A SETTING FAR REMOVED FROM ANY NORMAL HAUNT OF CRIMINALS--AN ART GALLERY IN GOTHAM CITY! BUT TO SAVOR FULLY THE SURPRISING INGREDIENTS OF THIS THRILL-TINGLING YARN, START READING ...
the ART GALLERY of ROGUES!
BOB KANE
HERE'S WHERE I TURN ON THE PRESSURE AND CRUNCH YOU LIKE A WALNUT, BATMAN!
STAY CLEAR, ROBIN! I'LL HANDLE THIS WOULD-BE NUT-CRACKER!
1

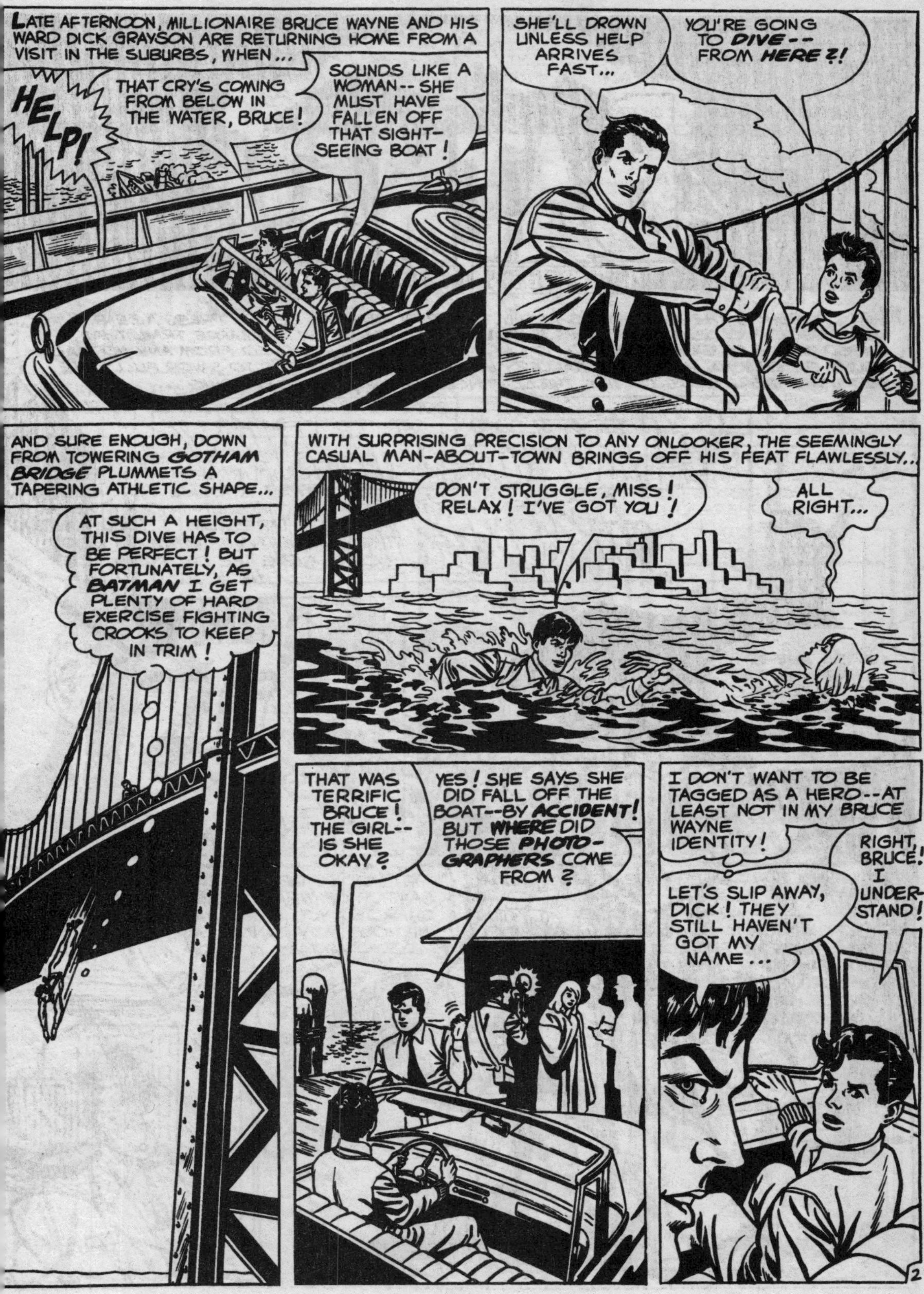
LATE AFTERNOON, MILLIONAIRE BRUCE WAYNE AND HIS WARD DICK GRAYSON ARE RETURNING HOME FROM A VISIT IN THE SUBURBS, WHEN...
HELP!
THAT CRY'S COMING FROM BELOW IN THE WATER, BRUCE!
SOUNDS LIKE A WOMAN-- SHE MUST HAVE FALLEN OFF THAT SIGHT-SEEING BOAT!
SHE'LL DROWN UNLESS HELP ARRIVES FAST...
YOU'RE GOING TO DIVE-- FROM HERE?!
AND SURE ENOUGH, DOWN FROM TOWERING GOTHAM BRIDGE PLUMMETS A TAPERING ATHLETIC SHAPE...
AT SUCH A HEIGHT, THIS DIVE HAS TO BE PERFECT! BUT FORTUNATELY, AS BATMAN I GET PLENTY OF HARD EXERCISE FIGHTING CROOKS TO KEEP IN TRIM!
WITH SURPRISING PRECISION TO ANY ONLOOKER, THE SEEMINGLY CASUAL MAN-ABOUT-TOWN BRINGS OFF HIS FEAT FLAWLESSLY...
DON'T STRUGGLE, MISS! RELAX! I'VE GOT YOU!
ALL RIGHT...
THAT WAS TERRIFIC BRUCE! THE GIRL-- IS SHE OKAY?
YES! SHE SAYS SHE DID FALL OFF THE BOAT--BY ACCIDENT! BUT WHERE DID THOSE PHOTOGRAPHERS COME FROM?
I DON'T WANT TO BE TAGGED AS A HERO--AT LEAST NOT IN MY BRUCE WAYNE IDENTITY!
LET'S SLIP AWAY, DICK! THEY STILL HAVEN'T GOT MY NAME...
RIGHT, BRUCE! I UNDERSTAND!
2

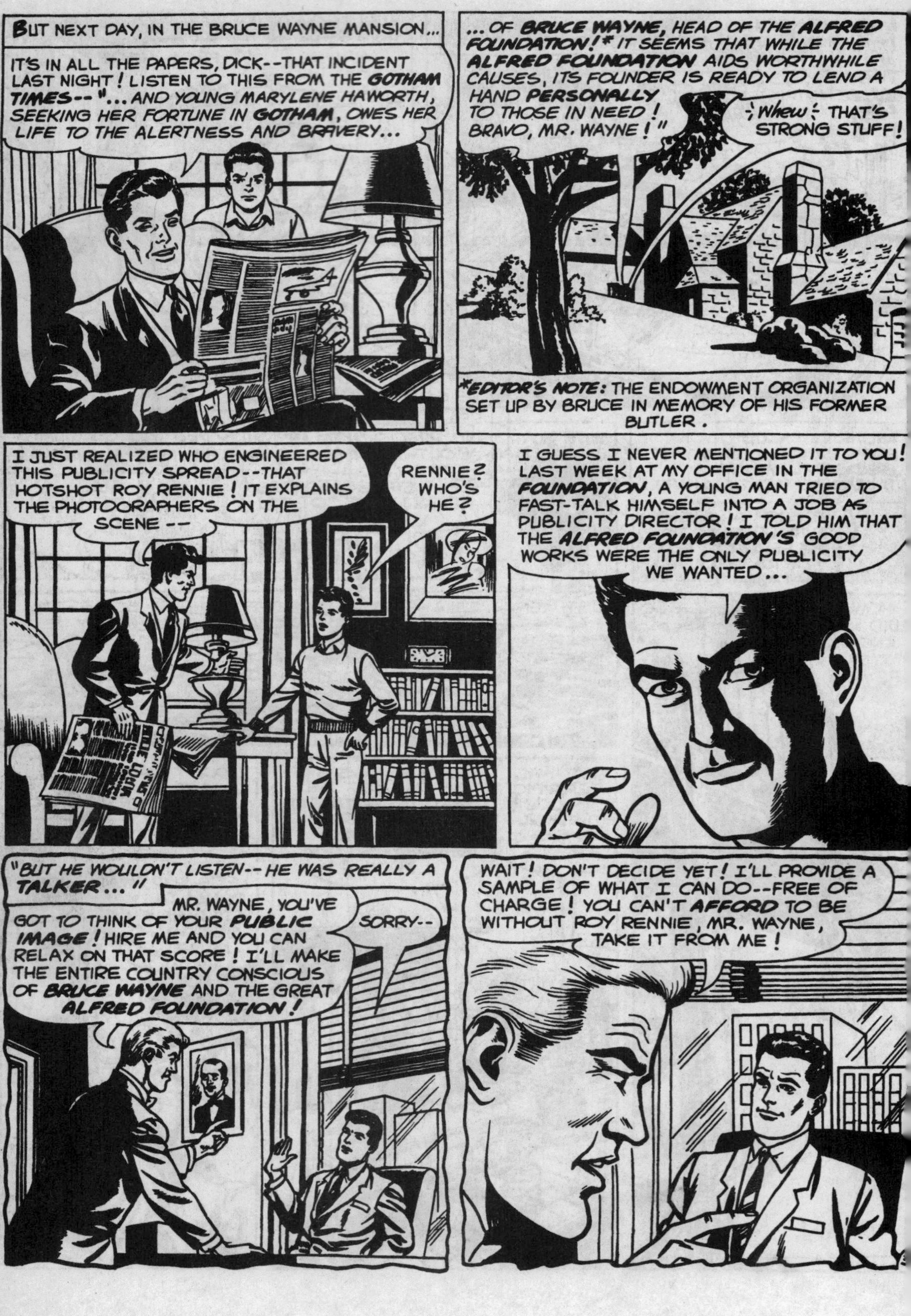
BUT NEXT DAY, IN THE BRUCE WAYNE MANSION...
IT'S IN ALL THE PAPERS, DICK--THAT INCIDENT LAST NIGHT! LISTEN TO THIS FROM THE GOTHAM TIMES-- "...AND YOUNG MARYLENE HAWORTH, SEEKING HER FORTUNE IN GOTHAM, OWES HER LIFE TO THE ALERTNESS AND BRAVERY...
...OF BRUCE WAYNE, HEAD OF THE ALFRED FOUNDATION!* IT SEEMS THAT WHILE THE ALFRED FOUNDATION AIDS WORTHWHILE CAUSES, ITS FOUNDER IS READY TO LEND A HAND PERSONALLY TO THOSE IN NEED! BRAVO, MR. WAYNE!"
WHEW! THAT'S STRONG STUFF!
*EDITOR'S NOTE: THE ENDOWMENT ORGANIZATION SET UP BY BRUCE IN MEMORY OF HIS FORMER BUTLER.
I JUST REALIZED WHO ENGINEERED THIS PUBLICITY SPREAD--THAT HOTSHOT ROY RENNIE! IT EXPLAINS THE PHOTOGRAPHERS ON THE SCENE --
RENNIE? WHO'S HE?
I GUESS I NEVER MENTIONED IT TO YOU! LAST WEEK AT MY OFFICE IN THE FOUNDATION, A YOUNG MAN TRIED TO FAST-TALK HIMSELF INTO A JOB AS PUBLICITY DIRECTOR! I TOLD HIM THAT THE ALFRED FOUNDATION'S GOOD WORKS WERE THE ONLY PUBLICITY WE WANTED...
"BUT HE WOULDN'T LISTEN-- HE WAS REALLY A TALKER..."
MR. WAYNE, YOU'VE GOT TO THINK OF YOUR PUBLIC IMAGE! HIRE ME AND YOU CAN RELAX ON THAT SCORE! I'LL MAKE THE ENTIRE COUNTRY CONSCIOUS OF BRUCE WAYNE AND THE GREAT ALFRED FOUNDATION!
SORRY--
WAIT! DON'T DECIDE YET! I'LL PROVIDE A SAMPLE OF WHAT I CAN DO--FREE OF CHARGE! YOU CAN'T AFFORD TO BE WITHOUT ROY RENNIE, MR. WAYNE, TAKE IT FROM ME!

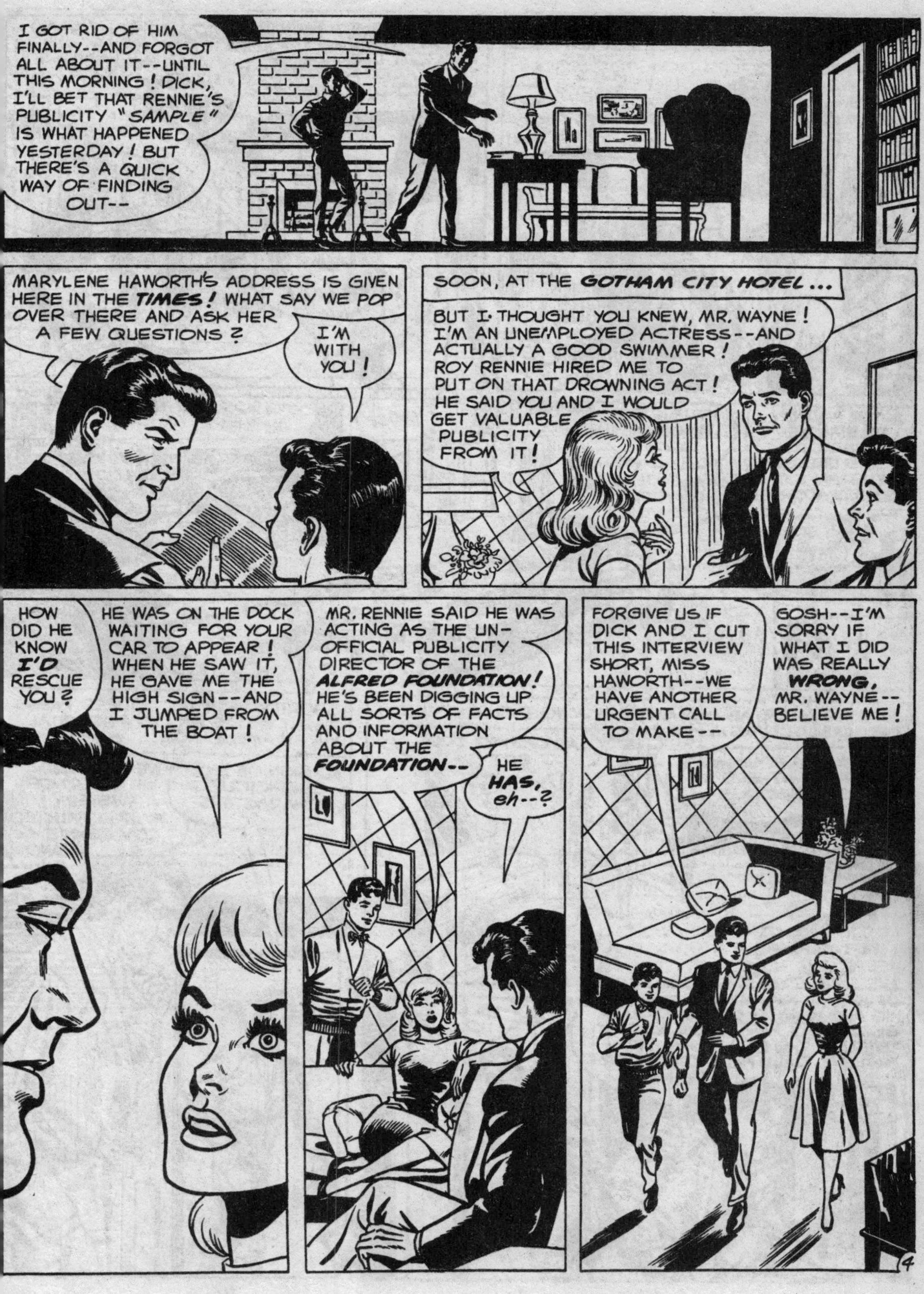
I GOT RID OF HIM FINALLY--AND FORGOT ALL ABOUT IT--UNTIL THIS MORNING! DICK, I'LL BET THAT RENNIE'S PUBLICITY "SAMPLE" IS WHAT HAPPENED YESTERDAY! BUT THERE'S A QUICK WAY OF FINDING OUT--
MARYLENE HAWORTH'S ADDRESS IS GIVEN HERE IN THE TIMES! WHAT SAY WE POP OVER THERE AND ASK HER A FEW QUESTIONS?
I'M WITH YOU!
SOON, AT THE GOTHAM CITY HOTEL...
BUT I THOUGHT YOU KNEW, MR. WAYNE! I'M AN UNEMPLOYED ACTRESS--AND ACTUALLY A GOOD SWIMMER! ROY RENNIE HIRED ME TO PUT ON THAT DROWNING ACT! HE SAID YOU AND I WOULD GET VALUABLE PUBLICITY FROM IT!
HOW DID HE KNOW I'D RESCUE YOU?
HE WAS ON THE DOCK WAITING FOR YOUR CAR TO APPEAR! WHEN HE SAW IT, HE GAVE ME THE HIGH SIGN--AND I JUMPED FROM THE BOAT!
MR. RENNIE SAID HE WAS ACTING AS THE UN-OFFICIAL PUBLICITY DIRECTOR OF THE ALFRED FOUNDATION! HE'S BEEN DIGGING UP ALL SORTS OF FACTS AND INFORMATION ABOUT THE FOUNDATION--
HE HAS, eh--?
FORGIVE US IF DICK AND I CUT THIS INTERVIEW SHORT, MISS HAWORTH--WE HAVE ANOTHER URGENT CALL TO MAKE--
GOSH--I'M SORRY IF WHAT I DID WAS REALLY WRONG, MR. WAYNE--BELIEVE ME!
4

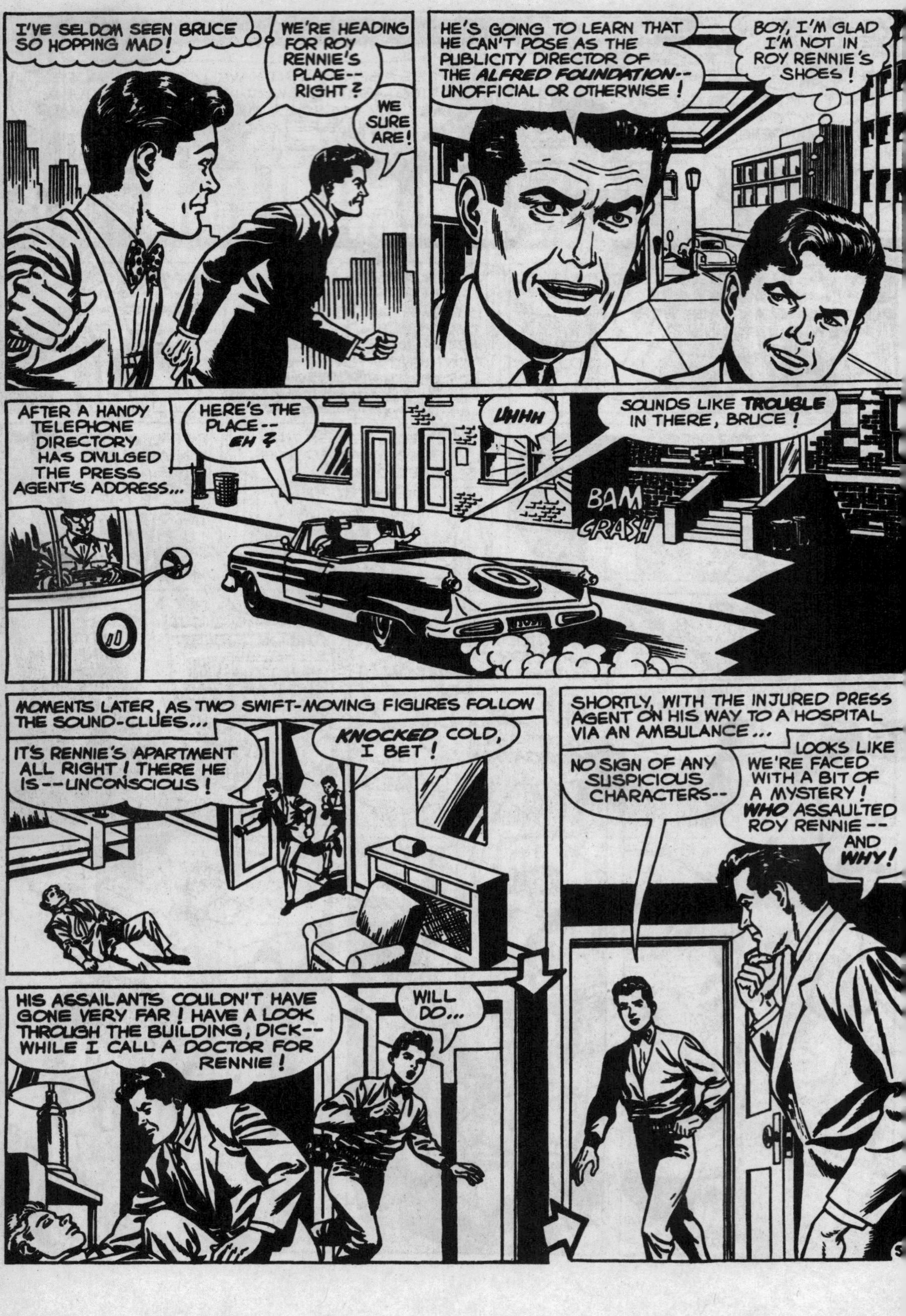
I'VE SELDOM SEEN BRUCE SO HOPPING MAD!
WE'RE HEADING FOR ROY RENNIE'S PLACE-- RIGHT?
WE SURE ARE!
HE'S GOING TO LEARN THAT HE CAN'T POSE AS THE PUBLICITY DIRECTOR OF THE ALFRED FOUNDATION-- UNOFFICIAL OR OTHERWISE!
BOY, I'M GLAD I'M NOT IN ROY RENNIE'S SHOES!
AFTER A HANDY TELEPHONE DIRECTORY HAS DIVULGED THE PRESS AGENT'S ADDRESS...
HERE'S THE PLACE-- EH?
UHHH
SOUNDS LIKE TROUBLE IN THERE, BRUCE!
BAM
CRASH
MOMENTS LATER, AS TWO SWIFT-MOVING FIGURES FOLLOW THE SOUND-CLUES...
IT'S RENNIE'S APARTMENT ALL RIGHT! THERE HE IS--UNCONSCIOUS!
KNOCKED COLD, I BET!
HIS ASSAILANTS COULDN'T HAVE GONE VERY FAR! HAVE A LOOK THROUGH THE BUILDING, DICK-- WHILE I CALL A DOCTOR FOR RENNIE!
WILL DO...
SHORTLY, WITH THE INJURED PRESS AGENT ON HIS WAY TO A HOSPITAL VIA AN AMBULANCE...
NO SIGN OF ANY SUSPICIOUS CHARACTERS--
LOOKS LIKE WE'RE FACED WITH A BIT OF A MYSTERY! WHO ASSAULTED ROY RENNIE-- AND WHY!

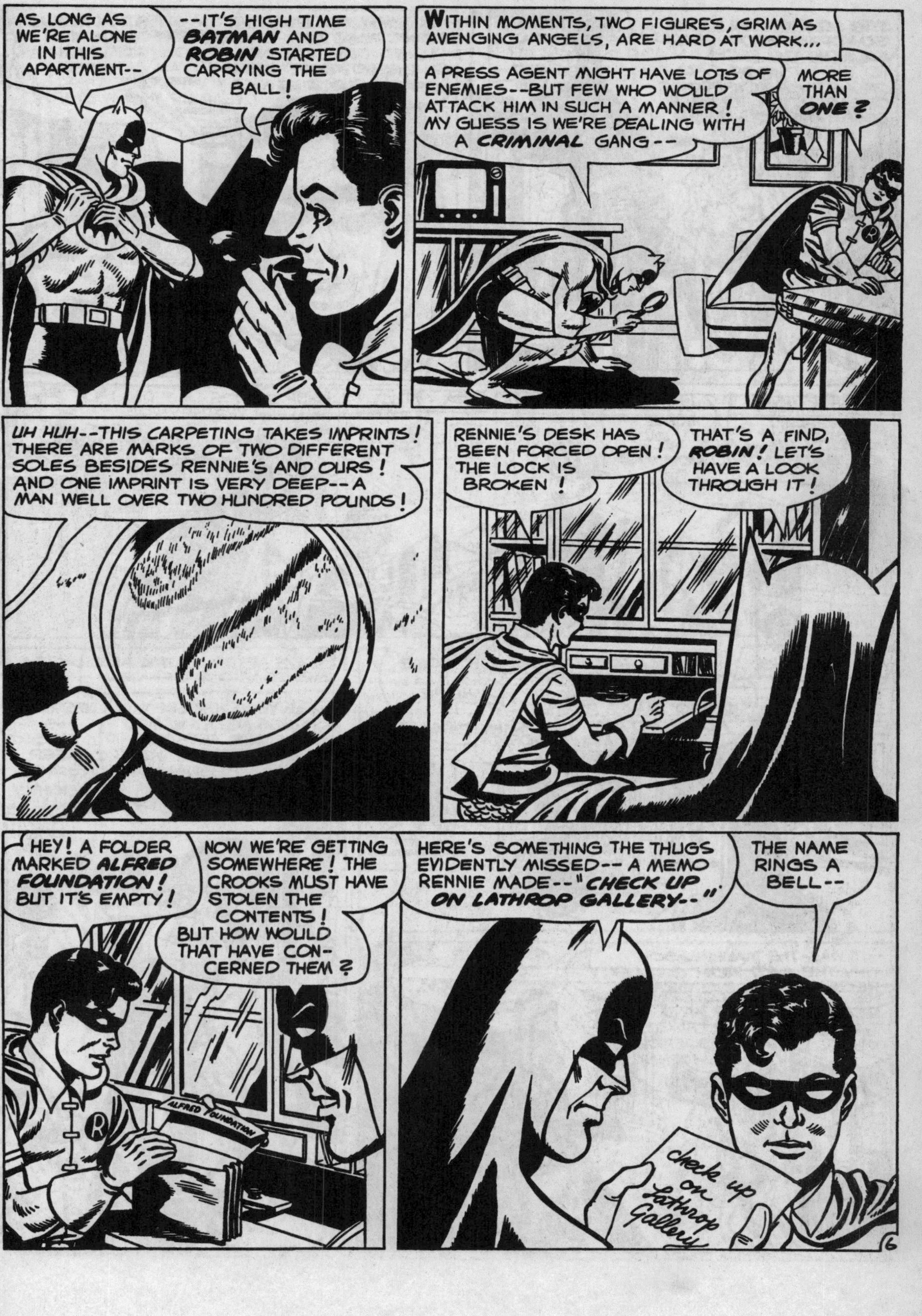
AS LONG AS WE'RE ALONE IN THIS APARTMENT--
--IT'S HIGH TIME BATMAN AND ROBIN STARTED CARRYING THE BALL!
WITHIN MOMENTS, TWO FIGURES, GRIM AS AVENGING ANGELS, ARE HARD AT WORK...
A PRESS AGENT MIGHT HAVE LOTS OF ENEMIES--BUT FEW WHO WOULD ATTACK HIM IN SUCH A MANNER! MY GUESS IS WE'RE DEALING WITH A CRIMINAL GANG--
MORE THAN ONE?
UH HUH--THIS CARPETING TAKES IMPRINTS! THERE ARE MARKS OF TWO DIFFERENT SOLES BESIDES RENNIE'S AND OURS! AND ONE IMPRINT IS VERY DEEP--A MAN WELL OVER TWO HUNDRED POUNDS!
RENNIE'S DESK HAS BEEN FORCED OPEN! THE LOCK IS BROKEN!
THAT'S A FIND, ROBIN! LET'S HAVE A LOOK THROUGH IT!
HEY! A FOLDER MARKED ALFRED FOUNDATION! BUT IT'S EMPTY!
ALFRED FOUNDATION
NOW WE'RE GETTING SOMEWHERE! THE CROOKS MUST HAVE STOLEN THE CONTENTS!
BUT HOW WOULD THAT HAVE CONCERNED THEM?
HERE'S SOMETHING THE THUGS EVIDENTLY MISSED--A MEMO RENNIE MADE--"CHECK UP ON LATHROP GALLERY--"
THE NAME RINGS A BELL--
check up on Lathrop Gallery
6

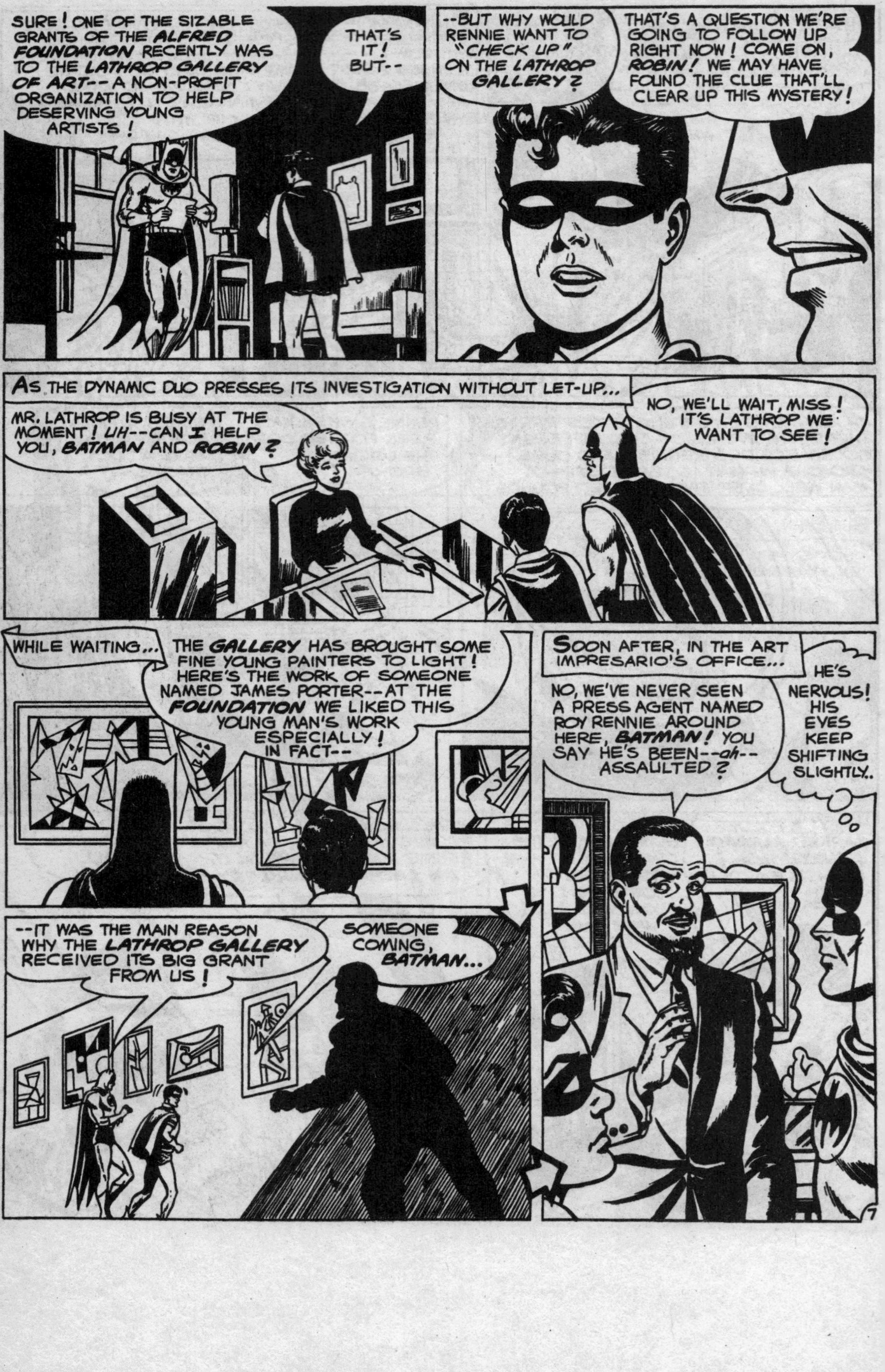

SURE! ONE OF THE SIZABLE GRANTS OF THE ALFRED FOUNDATION RECENTLY WAS TO THE LATHROP GALLERY OF ART-- A NON-PROFIT ORGANIZATION TO HELP DESERVING YOUNG ARTISTS!
THAT'S IT! BUT--
--BUT WHY WOULD RENNIE WANT TO "CHECK UP" ON THE LATHROP GALLERY?
THAT'S A QUESTION WE'RE GOING TO FOLLOW UP RIGHT NOW! COME ON, ROBIN! WE MAY HAVE FOUND THE CLUE THAT'LL CLEAR UP THIS MYSTERY!
AS THE DYNAMIC DUO PRESSES ITS INVESTIGATION WITHOUT LET-UP...
MR. LATHROP IS BUSY AT THE MOMENT! UH--CAN I HELP YOU, BATMAN AND ROBIN?
NO, WE'LL WAIT, MISS! IT'S LATHROP WE WANT TO SEE!
WHILE WAITING...
THE GALLERY HAS BROUGHT SOME FINE YOUNG PAINTERS TO LIGHT! HERE'S THE WORK OF SOMEONE NAMED JAMES PORTER--AT THE FOUNDATION WE LIKED THIS YOUNG MAN'S WORK ESPECIALLY! IN FACT--
--IT WAS THE MAIN REASON WHY THE LATHROP GALLERY RECEIVED ITS BIG GRANT FROM US!
SOMEONE COMING, BATMAN...
SOON AFTER, IN THE ART IMPRESARIO'S OFFICE...
NO, WE'VE NEVER SEEN A PRESS AGENT NAMED ROY RENNIE AROUND HERE, BATMAN! YOU SAY HE'S BEEN--ah--ASSAULTED?
HE'S NERVOUS! HIS EYES KEEP SHIFTING SLIGHTLY..
7

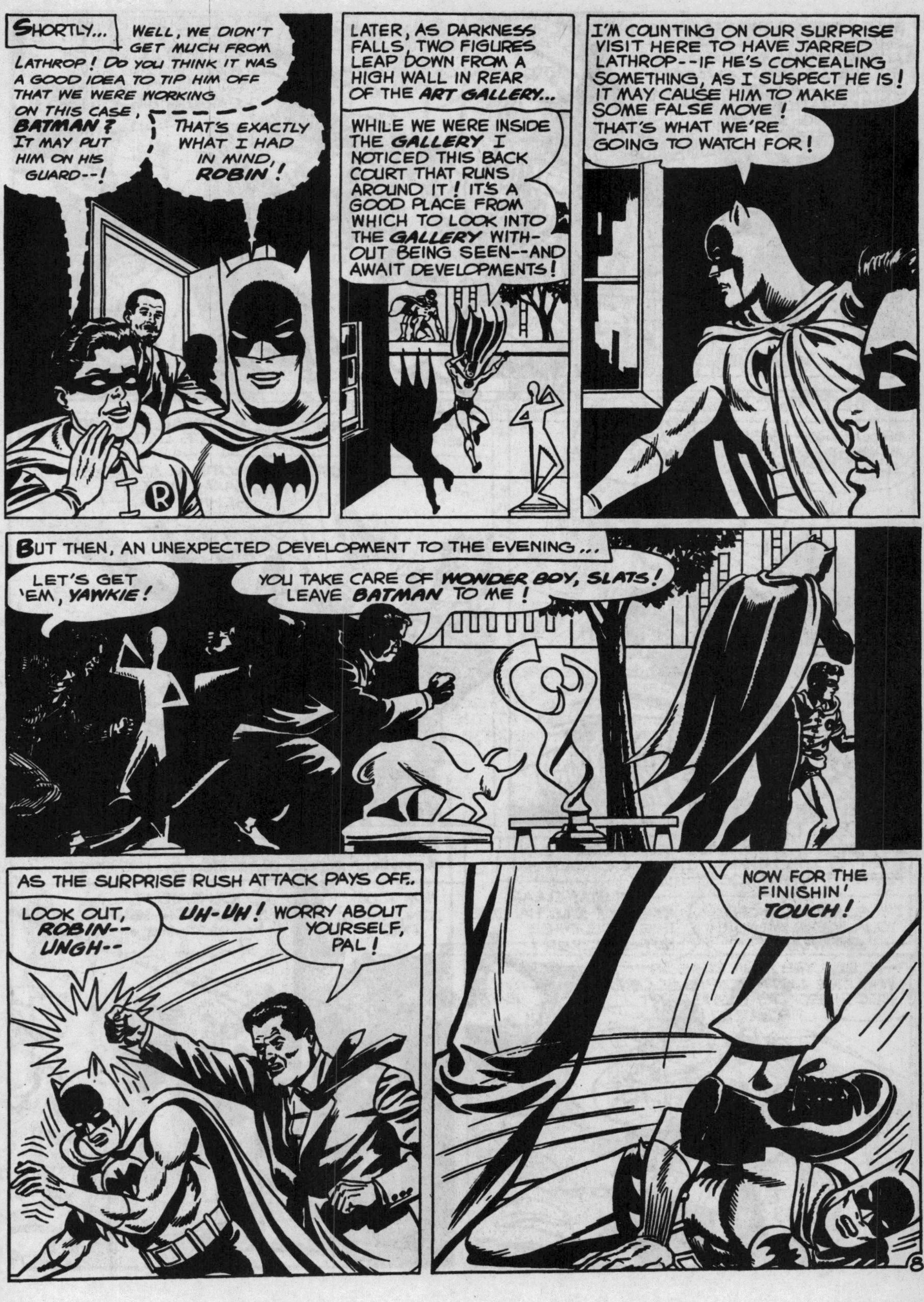
SHORTLY...
WELL, WE DIDN'T GET MUCH FROM LATHROP! DO YOU THINK IT WAS A GOOD IDEA TO TIP HIM OFF THAT WE WERE WORKING ON THIS CASE, BATMAN? IT MAY PUT HIM ON HIS GUARD--!
THAT'S EXACTLY WHAT I HAD IN MIND, ROBIN!
LATER, AS DARKNESS FALLS, TWO FIGURES LEAP DOWN FROM A HIGH WALL IN REAR OF THE ART GALLERY...
WHILE WE WERE INSIDE THE GALLERY I NOTICED THIS BACK COURT THAT RUNS AROUND IT! IT'S A GOOD PLACE FROM WHICH TO LOOK INTO THE GALLERY WITH-OUT BEING SEEN--AND AWAIT DEVELOPMENTS!
I'M COUNTING ON OUR SURPRISE VISIT HERE TO HAVE JARRED LATHROP--IF HE'S CONCEALING SOMETHING, AS I SUSPECT HE IS! IT MAY CAUSE HIM TO MAKE SOME FALSE MOVE! THAT'S WHAT WE'RE GOING TO WATCH FOR!
BUT THEN, AN UNEXPECTED DEVELOPMENT TO THE EVENING...
LET'S GET 'EM, YAWKIE!
YOU TAKE CARE OF WONDER BOY, SLATS! LEAVE BATMAN TO ME!
AS THE SURPRISE RUSH ATTACK PAYS OFF..
LOOK OUT, ROBIN-- UNGH--
UH-UH! WORRY ABOUT YOURSELF, PAL!
NOW FOR THE FINISHIN' TOUCH!
8

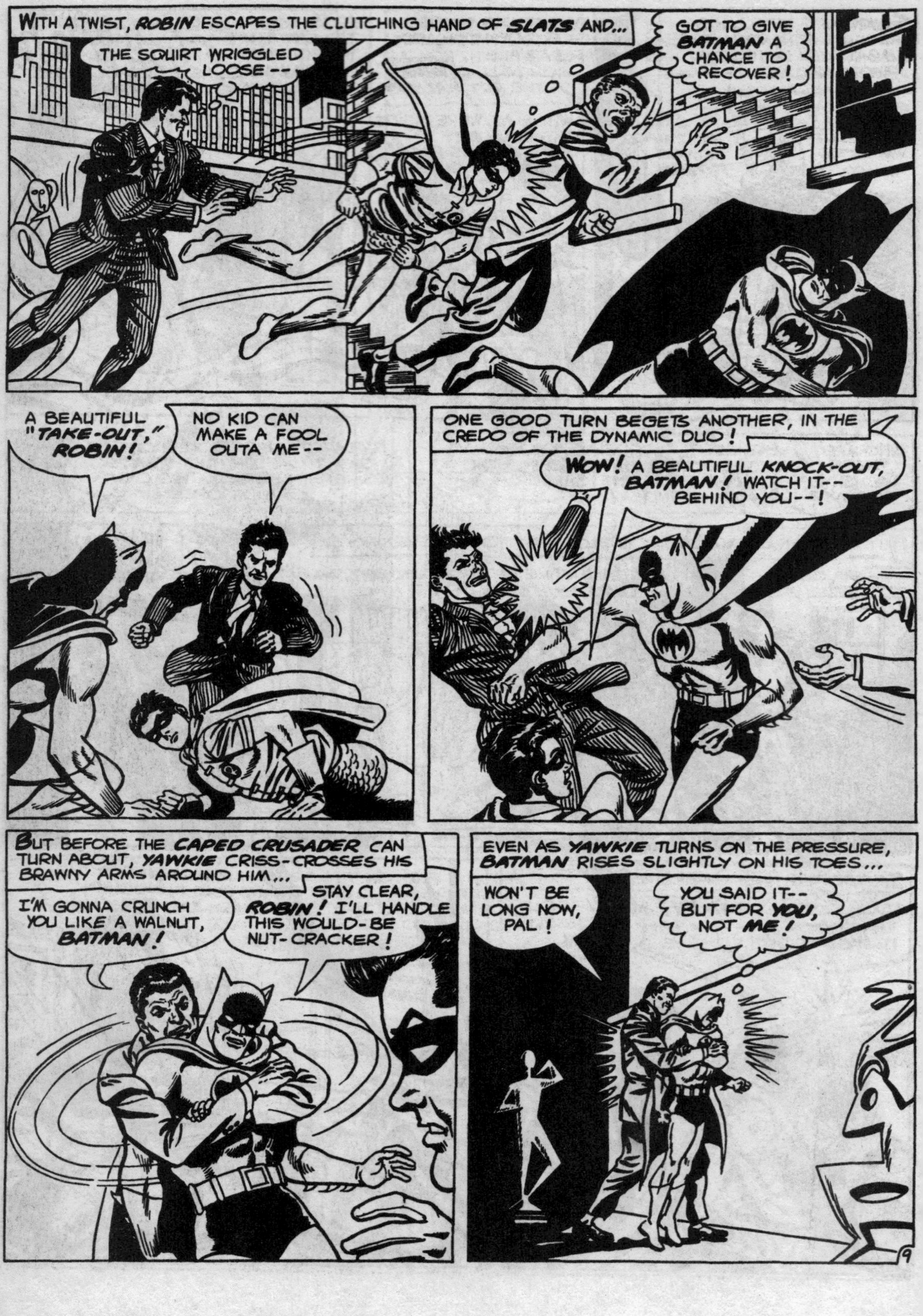
WITH A TWIST, ROBIN ESCAPES THE CLUTCHING HAND OF SLATS AND...
THE SQUIRT WRIGGLED LOOSE --
GOT TO GIVE BATMAN A CHANCE TO RECOVER!
A BEAUTIFUL "TAKE-OUT," ROBIN!
NO KID CAN MAKE A FOOL OUTA ME --
ONE GOOD TURN BEGETS ANOTHER, IN THE CREDO OF THE DYNAMIC DUO!
WOW! A BEAUTIFUL KNOCK-OUT, BATMAN! WATCH IT-- BEHIND YOU--!
BUT BEFORE THE CAPED CRUSADER CAN TURN ABOUT, YAWKIE CRISS-CROSSES HIS BRAWNY ARMS AROUND HIM...
I'M GONNA CRUNCH YOU LIKE A WALNUT, BATMAN!
STAY CLEAR, ROBIN! I'LL HANDLE THIS WOULD-BE NUT-CRACKER!
EVEN AS YAWKIE TURNS ON THE PRESSURE, BATMAN RISES SLIGHTLY ON HIS TOES...
WON'T BE LONG NOW, PAL!
YOU SAID IT-- BUT FOR YOU, NOT ME!
9

SUMMONING UP ALL HIS RESERVE STRENGTH, THE EMBATTLED DETECTIVE PIVOTS AROUND,...

THEN BACKFOOTS HIMSELF AND HIS BURDEN TOWARD A NEARBY WALL --

FROM THAT SOUND I'D SAY THAT TAKES CARE OF *YAWKIE!*

THUD!

WHO ARE THESE TWO GUYS, ANYWAY?

LATHROP'S HIRELINGS, PROBABLY! I SPOTTED HIM WATCHING THE FIGHT FROM THE GALLERY WINDOW --

LATHROP JUST DUCKED OUT OF SIGHT! AFTER HIM-- THIS IS WHERE WE CRACK THIS CASE WIDE OPEN!

INSIDE THE HALF-DARKENED GALLERY...

THAT DOOR-- IT JUST CLOSED!

FASTER, *ROBIN!* HE'S IN THERE!

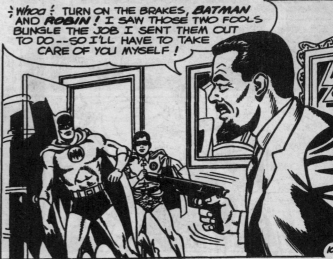

÷ *WHOA!* TURN ON THE BRAKES, *BATMAN* AND *ROBIN!* I SAW THOSE TWO FOOLS BUNGLE THE JOB I SENT THEM OUT TO DO --SO I'LL HAVE TO TAKE CARE OF YOU MYSELF!

10

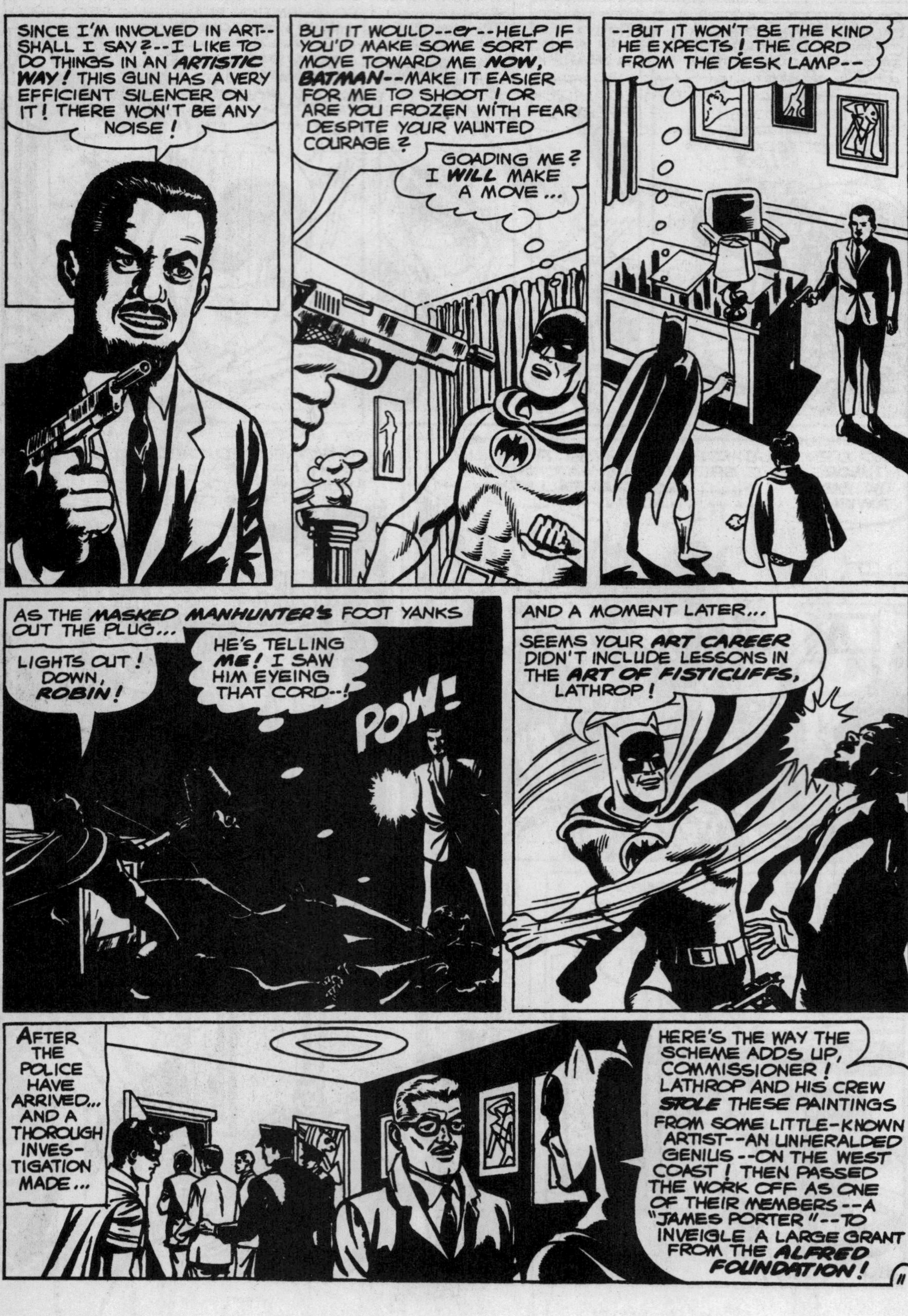
SINCE I'M INVOLVED IN ART--SHALL I SAY?--I LIKE TO DO THINGS IN AN ARTISTIC WAY! THIS GUN HAS A VERY EFFICIENT SILENCER ON IT! THERE WON'T BE ANY NOISE!
BUT IT WOULD--er--HELP IF YOU'D MAKE SOME SORT OF MOVE TOWARD ME NOW, BATMAN--MAKE IT EASIER FOR ME TO SHOOT! OR ARE YOU FROZEN WITH FEAR DESPITE YOUR VAUNTED COURAGE?
GOADING ME? I WILL MAKE A MOVE...
--BUT IT WON'T BE THE KIND HE EXPECTS! THE CORD FROM THE DESK LAMP--
AS THE MASKED MANHUNTER'S FOOT YANKS OUT THE PLUG...
LIGHTS OUT! DOWN, ROBIN!
HE'S TELLING ME! I SAW HIM EYEING THAT CORD--!
POW!
AND A MOMENT LATER...
SEEMS YOUR ART CAREER DIDN'T INCLUDE LESSONS IN THE ART OF FISTICUFFS, LATHROP!
AFTER THE POLICE HAVE ARRIVED... AND A THOROUGH INVESTIGATION MADE...
HERE'S THE WAY THE SCHEME ADDS UP, COMMISSIONER! LATHROP AND HIS CREW STOLE THESE PAINTINGS FROM SOME LITTLE-KNOWN ARTIST--AN UNHERALDED GENIUS--ON THE WEST COAST! THEN PASSED THE WORK OFF AS ONE OF THEIR MEMBERS--A "JAMES PORTER"--TO INVEIGLE A LARGE GRANT FROM THE ALFRED FOUNDATION!
11

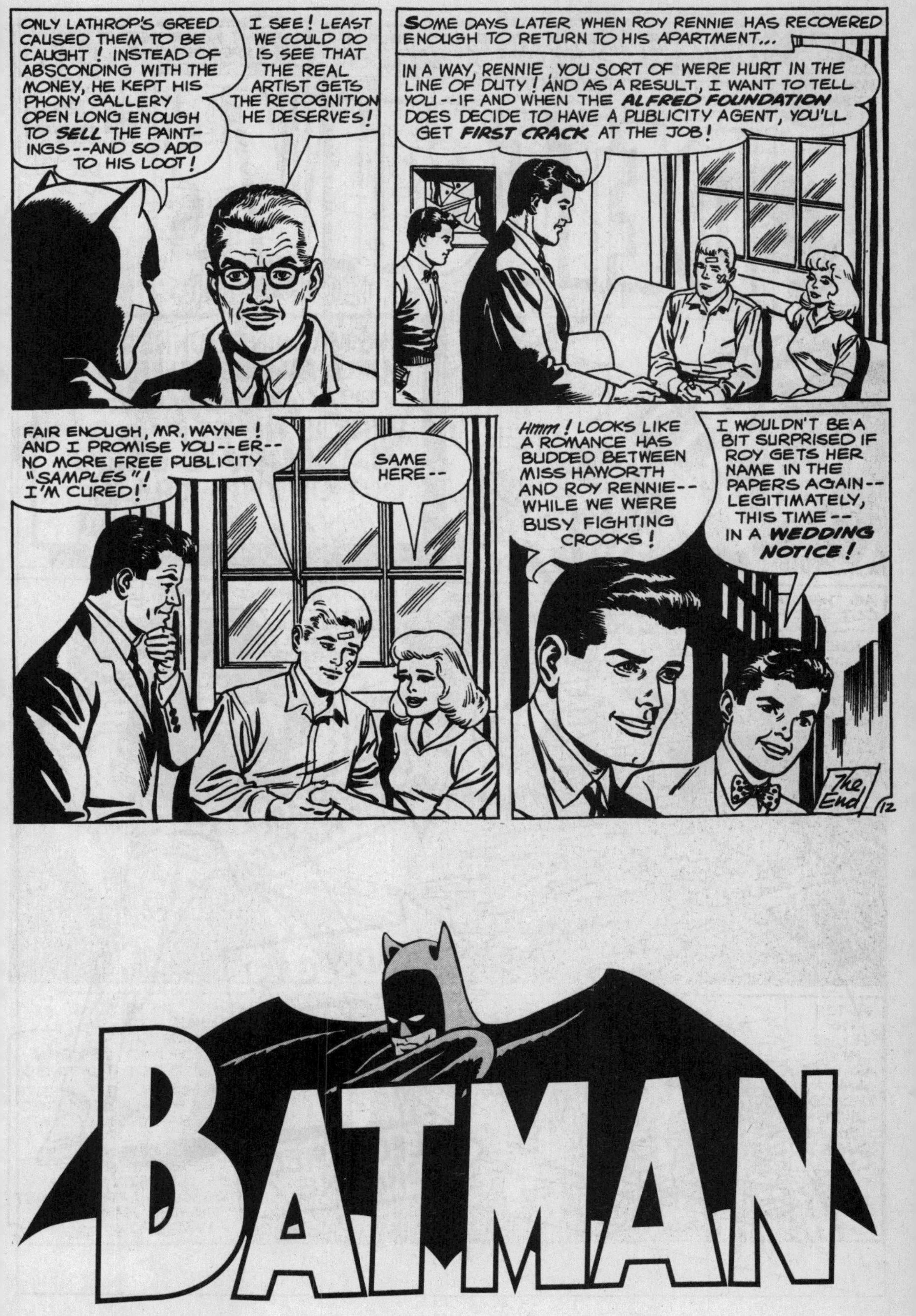
ONLY LATHROP'S GREED CAUSED THEM TO BE CAUGHT! INSTEAD OF ABSCONDING WITH THE MONEY, HE KEPT HIS PHONY GALLERY OPEN LONG ENOUGH TO SELL THE PAINTINGS--AND SO ADD TO HIS LOOT!
I SEE! LEAST WE COULD DO IS SEE THAT THE REAL ARTIST GETS THE RECOGNITION HE DESERVES!
SOME DAYS LATER WHEN ROY RENNIE HAS RECOVERED ENOUGH TO RETURN TO HIS APARTMENT...
IN A WAY, RENNIE, YOU SORT OF WERE HURT IN THE LINE OF DUTY! AND AS A RESULT, I WANT TO TELL YOU--IF AND WHEN THE ALFRED FOUNDATION DOES DECIDE TO HAVE A PUBLICITY AGENT, YOU'LL GET FIRST CRACK AT THE JOB!
FAIR ENOUGH, MR. WAYNE! AND I PROMISE YOU--ER--NO MORE FREE PUBLICITY "SAMPLES"! I'M CURED!
SAME HERE--
HMM! LOOKS LIKE A ROMANCE HAS BUDDED BETWEEN MISS HAWORTH AND ROY RENNIE--WHILE WE WERE BUSY FIGHTING CROOKS!
I WOULDN'T BE A BIT SURPRISED IF ROY GETS HER NAME IN THE PAPERS AGAIN--LEGITIMATELY, THIS TIME--IN A WEDDING NOTICE!
The End
12

BATMAN

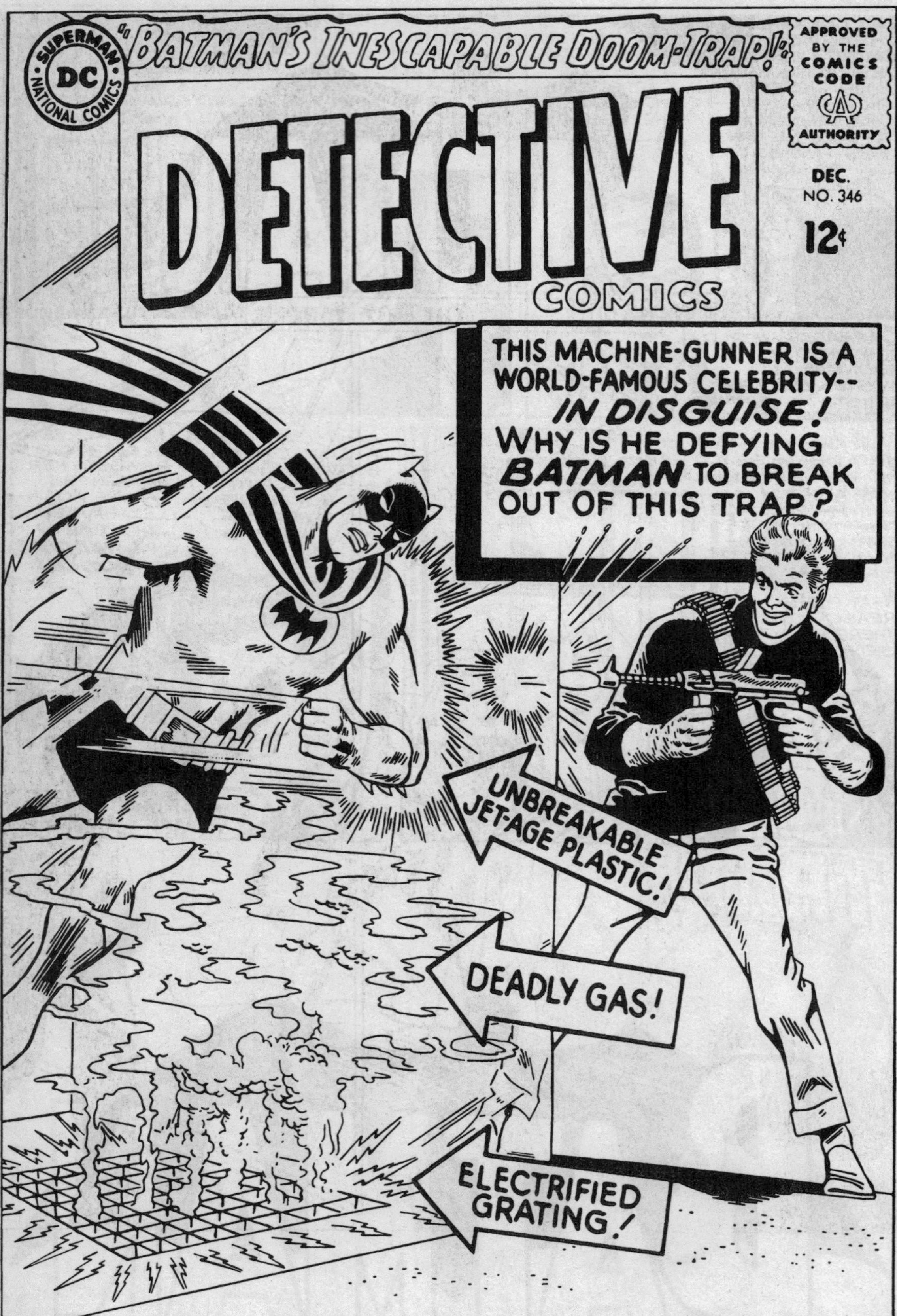
"BATMAN'S INESCAPABLE DOOM-TRAP!"
DETECTIVE COMICS
DEC. NO. 346
12¢
THIS MACHINE-GUNNER IS A WORLD-FAMOUS CELEBRITY-- IN DISGUISE! WHY IS HE DEFYING BATMAN TO BREAK OUT OF THIS TRAP?
UNBREAKABLE JET-AGE PLASTIC!
DEADLY GAS!
ELECTRIFIED GRATING!

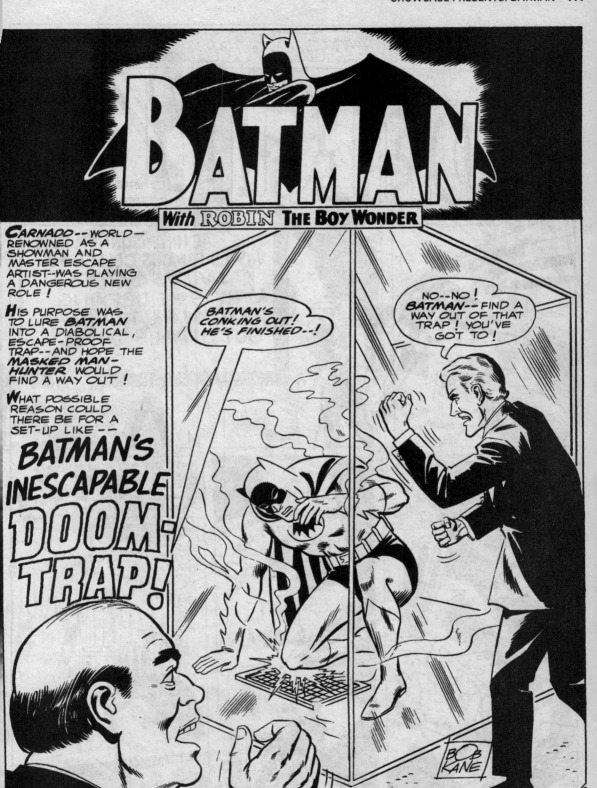

BATMAN

With ROBIN The BOY WONDER

CARNADO--WORLD-- RENOWNED AS A SHOWMAN AND MASTER ESCAPE ARTIST--WAS PLAYING A DANGEROUS NEW ROLE!

HIS PURPOSE WAS TO LURE BATMAN INTO A DIABOLICAL, ESCAPE-PROOF TRAP--AND HOPE THE MASKED MAN-HUNTER WOULD FIND A WAY OUT!

WHAT POSSIBLE REASON COULD THERE BE FOR A SET-UP LIKE --

BATMAN'S INESCAPABLE DOOM-TRAP!

BATMAN'S CONKING OUT! HE'S FINISHED--!

NO--NO! BATMAN-- FIND A WAY OUT OF THAT TRAP! YOU'VE GOT TO!

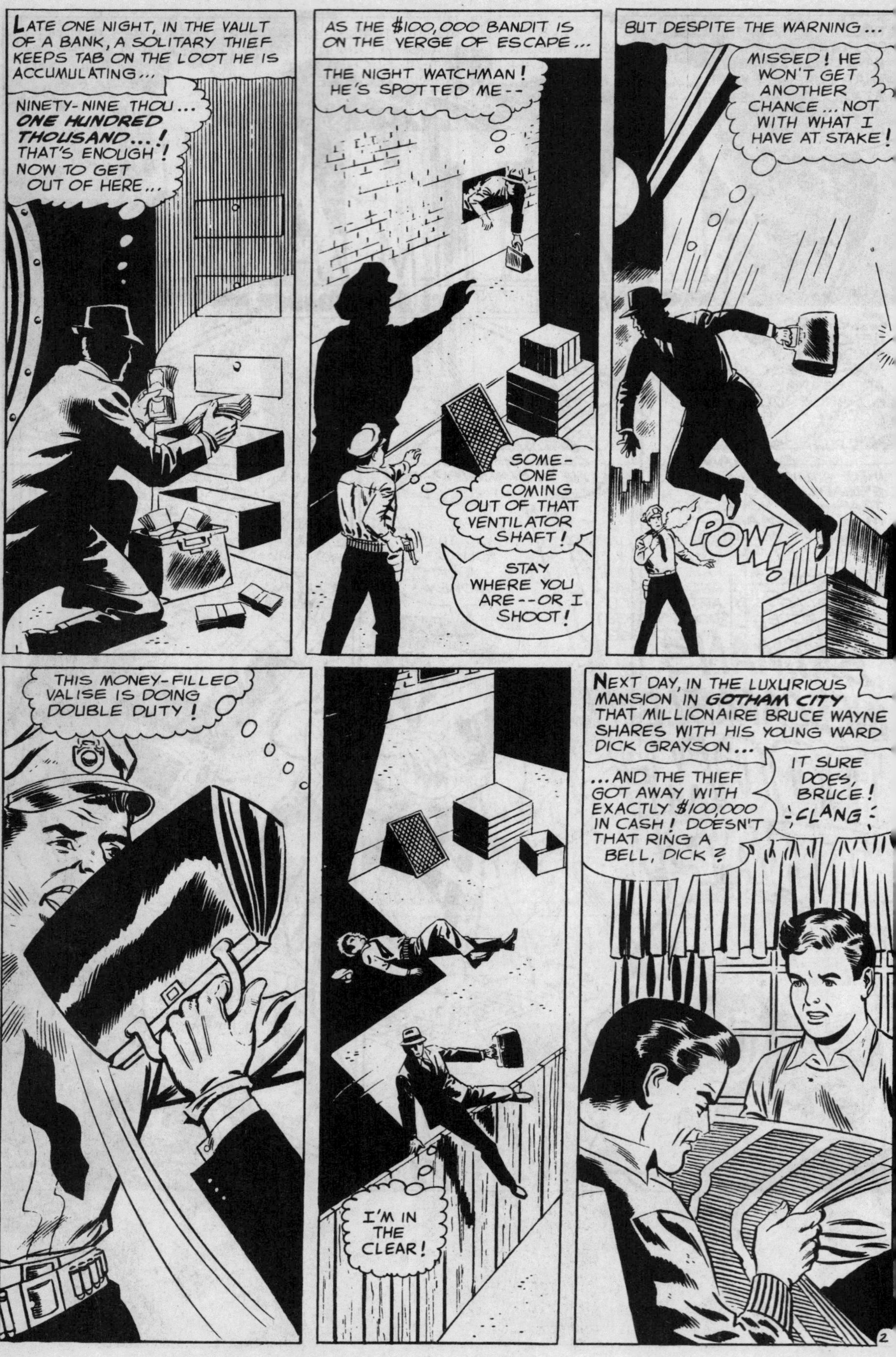
LATE ONE NIGHT, IN THE VAULT OF A BANK, A SOLITARY THIEF KEEPS TAB ON THE LOOT HE IS ACCUMULATING...
NINETY-NINE THOU... ONE HUNDRED THOUSAND...! THAT'S ENOUGH! NOW TO GET OUT OF HERE...
AS THE $100,000 BANDIT IS ON THE VERGE OF ESCAPE...
THE NIGHT WATCHMAN! HE'S SPOTTED ME--
SOME-ONE COMING OUT OF THAT VENTILATOR SHAFT!
STAY WHERE YOU ARE--OR I SHOOT!
BUT DESPITE THE WARNING...
MISSED! HE WON'T GET ANOTHER CHANCE... NOT WITH WHAT I HAVE AT STAKE!
POW!
THIS MONEY-FILLED VALISE IS DOING DOUBLE DUTY!
I'M IN THE CLEAR!
NEXT DAY, IN THE LUXURIOUS MANSION IN GOTHAM CITY THAT MILLIONAIRE BRUCE WAYNE SHARES WITH HIS YOUNG WARD DICK GRAYSON...
...AND THE THIEF GOT AWAY WITH EXACTLY $100,000 IN CASH! DOESN'T THAT RING A BELL, DICK?
IT SURE DOES, BRUCE! CLANG
2

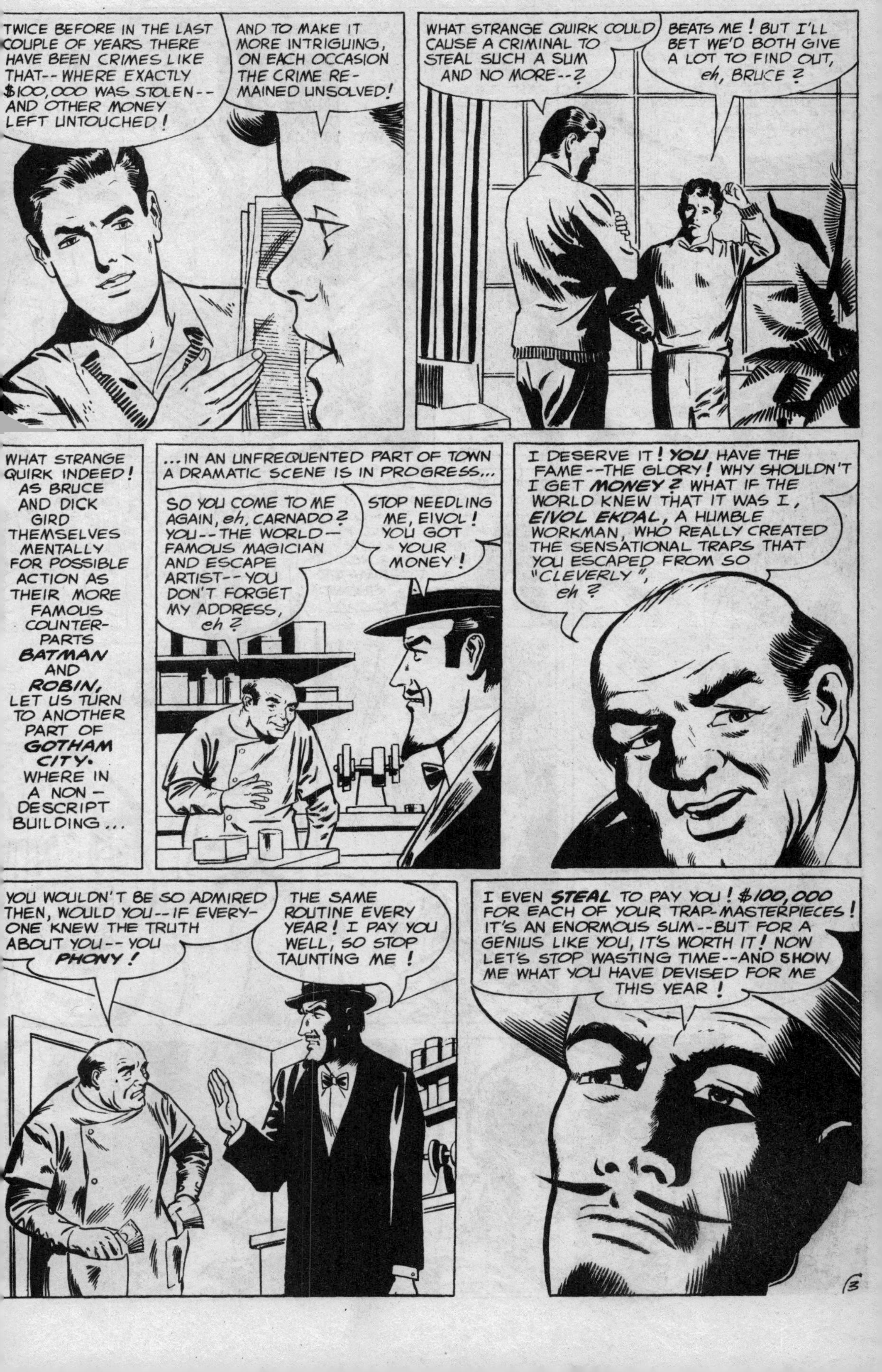
TWICE BEFORE IN THE LAST COUPLE OF YEARS THERE HAVE BEEN CRIMES LIKE THAT--WHERE EXACTLY $100,000 WAS STOLEN--AND OTHER MONEY LEFT UNTOUCHED!
AND TO MAKE IT MORE INTRIGUING, ON EACH OCCASION THE CRIME REMAINED UNSOLVED!
WHAT STRANGE QUIRK COULD CAUSE A CRIMINAL TO STEAL SUCH A SUM AND NO MORE--?
BEATS ME! BUT I'LL BET WE'D BOTH GIVE A LOT TO FIND OUT, eh, BRUCE?
WHAT STRANGE QUIRK INDEED! AS BRUCE AND DICK GIRD THEMSELVES MENTALLY FOR POSSIBLE ACTION AS THEIR MORE FAMOUS COUNTERPARTS BATMAN AND ROBIN, LET US TURN TO ANOTHER PART OF GOTHAM CITY. WHERE IN A NON-DESCRIPT BUILDING...
...IN AN UNFREQUENTED PART OF TOWN A DRAMATIC SCENE IS IN PROGRESS...
SO YOU COME TO ME AGAIN, eh, CARNADO? YOU--THE WORLD-FAMOUS MAGICIAN AND ESCAPE ARTIST--YOU DON'T FORGET MY ADDRESS, eh?
STOP NEEDLING ME, EIVOL! YOU GOT YOUR MONEY!
I DESERVE IT! YOU HAVE THE FAME--THE GLORY! WHY SHOULDN'T I GET MONEY? WHAT IF THE WORLD KNEW THAT IT WAS I, EIVOL EKDAL, A HUMBLE WORKMAN, WHO REALLY CREATED THE SENSATIONAL TRAPS THAT YOU ESCAPED FROM SO "CLEVERLY", eh?
YOU WOULDN'T BE SO ADMIRED THEN, WOULD YOU--IF EVERYONE KNEW THE TRUTH ABOUT YOU--YOU PHONY!
THE SAME ROUTINE EVERY YEAR! I PAY YOU WELL, SO STOP TAUNTING ME!
I EVEN STEAL TO PAY YOU! $100,000 FOR EACH OF YOUR TRAP-MASTERPIECES! IT'S AN ENORMOUS SUM--BUT FOR A GENIUS LIKE YOU, IT'S WORTH IT! NOW LET'S STOP WASTING TIME--AND SHOW ME WHAT YOU HAVE DEVISED FOR ME THIS YEAR!
3

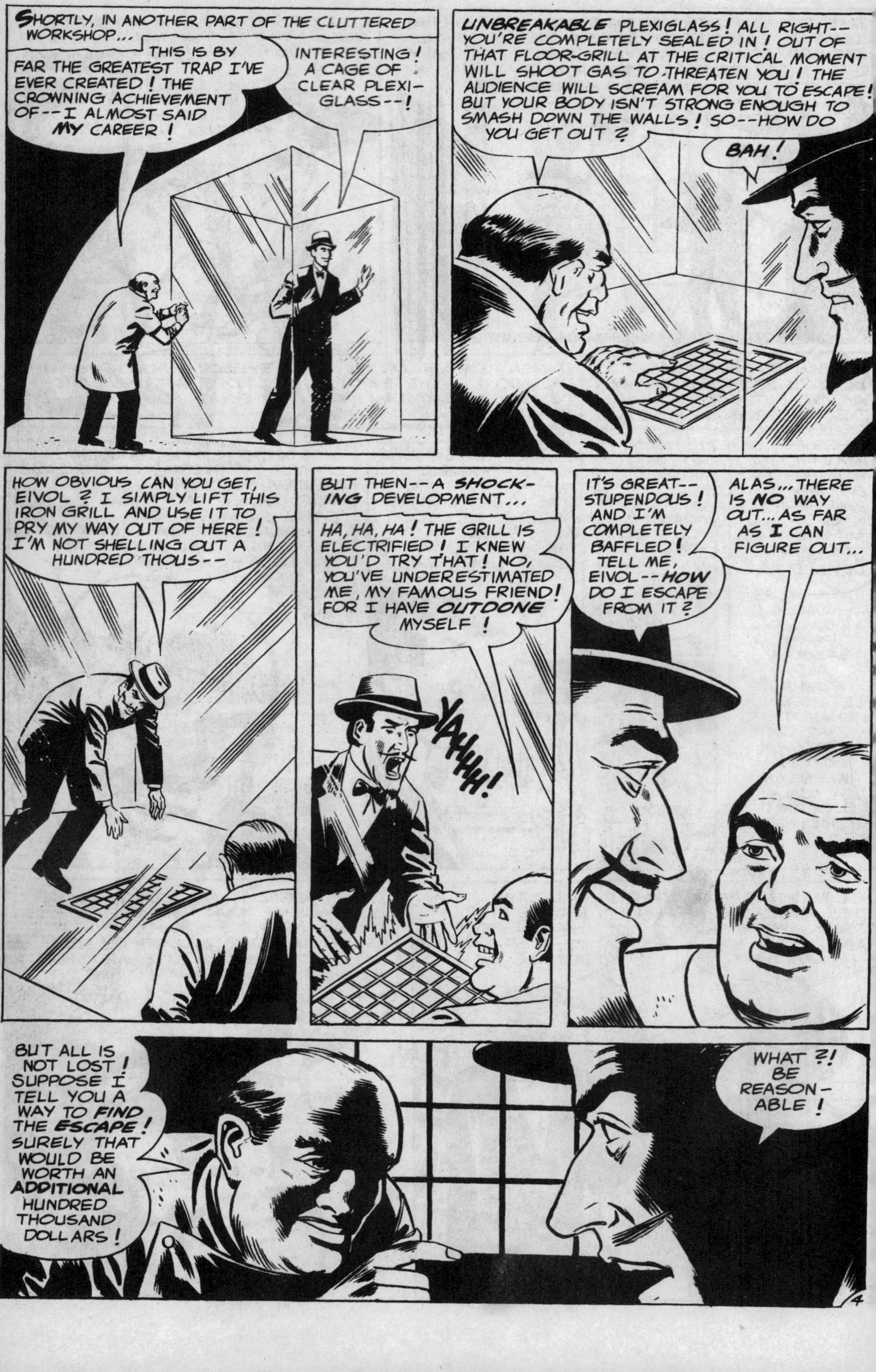
SHORTLY, IN ANOTHER PART OF THE CLUTTERED WORKSHOP...
THIS IS BY FAR THE GREATEST TRAP I'VE EVER CREATED! THE CROWNING ACHIEVEMENT OF--I ALMOST SAID MY CAREER!
INTERESTING! A CAGE OF CLEAR PLEXI-GLASS--!
UNBREAKABLE PLEXIGLASS! ALL RIGHT--YOU'RE COMPLETELY SEALED IN! OUT OF THAT FLOOR-GRILL AT THE CRITICAL MOMENT WILL SHOOT GAS TO THREATEN YOU! THE AUDIENCE WILL SCREAM FOR YOU TO ESCAPE! BUT YOUR BODY ISN'T STRONG ENOUGH TO SMASH DOWN THE WALLS! SO--HOW DO YOU GET OUT?
BAH!
HOW OBVIOUS CAN YOU GET, EIVOL? I SIMPLY LIFT THIS IRON GRILL AND USE IT TO PRY MY WAY OUT OF HERE! I'M NOT SHELLING OUT A HUNDRED THOUS--
BUT THEN--A SHOCKING DEVELOPMENT...
HA, HA, HA! THE GRILL IS ELECTRIFIED! I KNEW YOU'D TRY THAT! NO, YOU'VE UNDERESTIMATED ME, MY FAMOUS FRIEND! FOR I HAVE OUTDONE MYSELF!
YAHHH!
IT'S GREAT--STUPENDOUS! AND I'M COMPLETELY BAFFLED! TELL ME, EIVOL--HOW DO I ESCAPE FROM IT?
ALAS... THERE IS NO WAY OUT... AS FAR AS I CAN FIGURE OUT...
BUT ALL IS NOT LOST! SUPPOSE I TELL YOU A WAY TO FIND THE ESCAPE! SURELY THAT WOULD BE WORTH AN ADDITIONAL HUNDRED THOUSAND DOLLARS!
WHAT?! BE REASON-ABLE!
4

TAKE IT OR LEAVE IT, CARNADO!

IF I THOUGHT IT'D WORK, I'D BASH THE SECRET OUT OF HIM! GUESS I'LL HAVE TO PULL ANOTHER CRIME--STEAL THE MONEY! I MUST HAVE THAT TRAP! AUDIENCES ARE BEGINNING TO BE BORED WITH ME ...

...I MUST GIVE THEM SOMETHING NEW AND STARTLING--THAT WILL LIFT THEM OUT OF THEIR SEATS!

ALL RIGHT, EIVOL, IT'S A DEAL! NOW SPILL IT-- HOW DO I GO ABOUT LEARNING THE ESCAPE?

YOU BILL YOURSELF AS THE *WORLD'S GREATEST ESCAPE ARTIST*, BUT *YOU* AND I KNOW THERE IS *SOMEONE ELSE* WHO REALLY DESERVES THAT TITLE! OF COURSE I MEAN--*BATMAN*! NO MATTER HOW IMPOSSIBLE IT'S SEEMED, *BATMAN* HAS ALWAYS MANAGED TO SAFELY WORK HIS WAY OUT OF THE MOST DIABOLIC TRAPS THAT HIS ENEMIES HAVE DEVISED FOR HIM!

IT HASN'T DAWNED ON YOU YET, CARNADO? ALL WE'VE GOT TO DO IS LURE *BATMAN* INTO *THIS TRAP*--AND THEN *WATCH* HOW HE ESCAPES! WHEN *HE* FINDS OUT, *YOU* 'LL FIND OUT! SIMPLE?

BY GEORGE, YOU'VE GOT IT! I HOPE *BATMAN* COMES THROUGH FOR US--

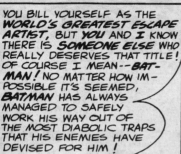

YES, THAT'S TRUE! BUT HOW DOES THAT HELP--

OF COURSE HE WILL--ESPECIALLY IF WE GIVE HIM A PUSH IN THE RIGHT DIRECTION! WE'LL HAVE TO ARRANGE THINGS EXACTLY RIGHT TO BRING THIS OFF WITHOUT A HITCH! NOW BEND AN EAR ...

THE NEXT NIGHT... AS A SLEEK VEHICLE PROWLS THROUGH *GOTHAM CITY*, CARRYING TWO FAMILIAR MASKED FIGURES...

I GUESS IT WAS JUST A FORLORN HOPE, *ROBIN*! NO SIGN YET OF THAT STRANGE $100,000 BURGLAR ...

LISTEN--THAT SOUND-- LIKE GLASS BREAKING-- JUST AHEAD OF US!

CRASH!!

5

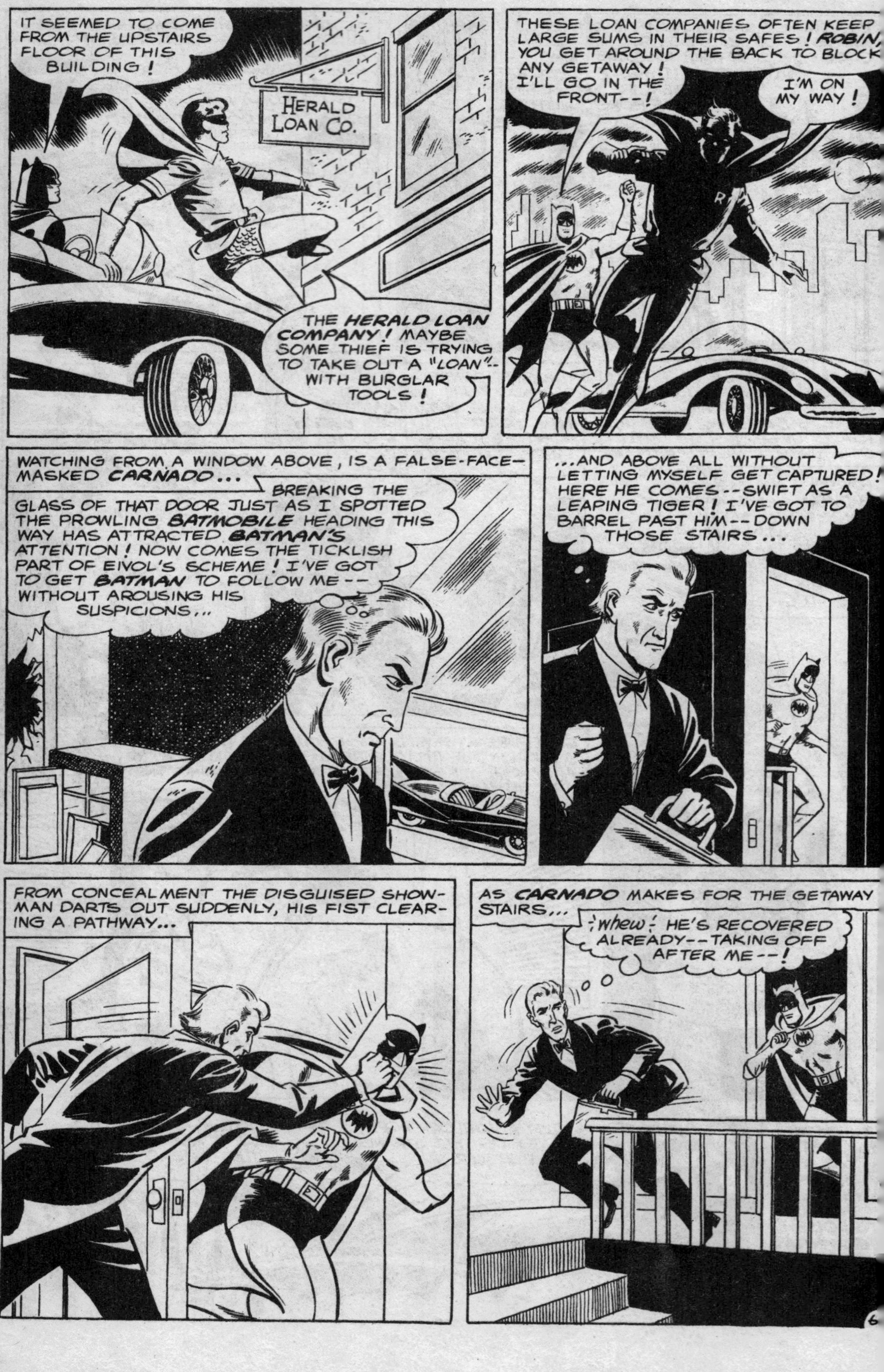
IT SEEMED TO COME FROM THE UPSTAIRS FLOOR OF THIS BUILDING!
HERALD LOAN CO.
THE HERALD LOAN COMPANY! MAYBE SOME THIEF IS TRYING TO TAKE OUT A "LOAN"-- WITH BURGLAR TOOLS!
THESE LOAN COMPANIES OFTEN KEEP LARGE SUMS IN THEIR SAFES! ROBIN, YOU GET AROUND THE BACK TO BLOCK ANY GETAWAY! I'LL GO IN THE FRONT--!
I'M ON MY WAY!
WATCHING FROM A WINDOW ABOVE, IS A FALSE-FACE-MASKED CARNADO...
BREAKING THE GLASS OF THAT DOOR JUST AS I SPOTTED THE PROWLING BATMOBILE HEADING THIS WAY HAS ATTRACTED BATMAN'S ATTENTION! NOW COMES THE TICKLISH PART OF EIVOL'S SCHEME! I'VE GOT TO GET BATMAN TO FOLLOW ME -- WITHOUT AROUSING HIS SUSPICIONS...
...AND ABOVE ALL WITHOUT LETTING MYSELF GET CAPTURED! HERE HE COMES--SWIFT AS A LEAPING TIGER! I'VE GOT TO BARREL PAST HIM--DOWN THOSE STAIRS...
FROM CONCEALMENT THE DISGUISED SHOWMAN DARTS OUT SUDDENLY, HIS FIST CLEARING A PATHWAY...
AS CARNADO MAKES FOR THE GETAWAY STAIRS...
-whew- HE'S RECOVERED ALREADY--TAKING OFF AFTER ME--!
6

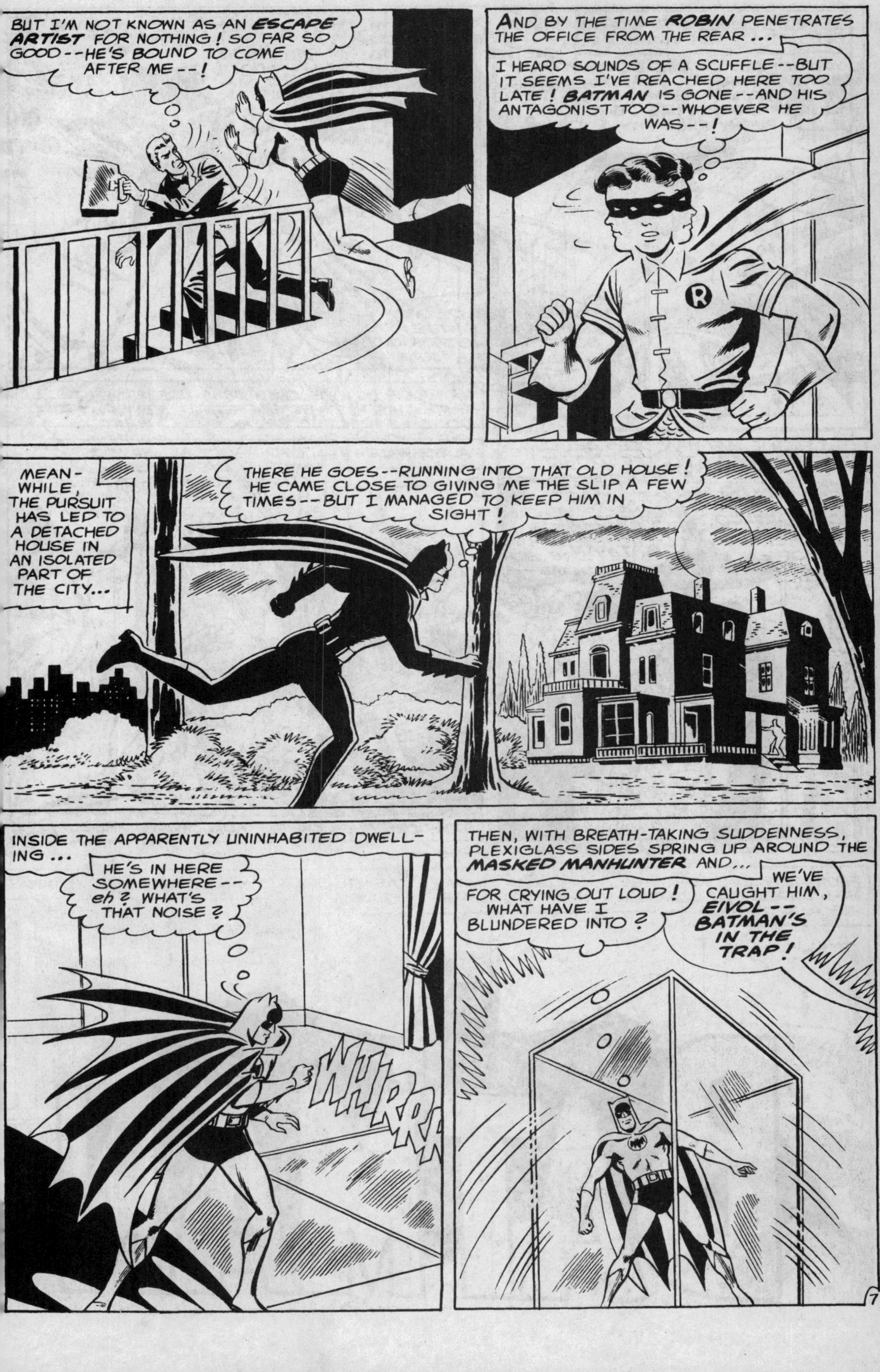
BUT I'M NOT KNOWN AS AN ESCAPE ARTIST FOR NOTHING! SO FAR SO GOOD--HE'S BOUND TO COME AFTER ME--!
AND BY THE TIME ROBIN PENETRATES THE OFFICE FROM THE REAR...
I HEARD SOUNDS OF A SCUFFLE--BUT IT SEEMS I'VE REACHED HERE TOO LATE! BATMAN IS GONE--AND HIS ANTAGONIST TOO--WHOEVER HE WAS--!
MEANWHILE, THE PURSUIT HAS LED TO A DETACHED HOUSE IN AN ISOLATED PART OF THE CITY...
THERE HE GOES--RUNNING INTO THAT OLD HOUSE! HE CAME CLOSE TO GIVING ME THE SLIP A FEW TIMES--BUT I MANAGED TO KEEP HIM IN SIGHT!
INSIDE THE APPARENTLY UNINHABITED DWELLING...
HE'S IN HERE SOMEWHERE--eh? WHAT'S THAT NOISE?
WHIRRR
THEN, WITH BREATH-TAKING SUDDENNESS, PLEXIGLASS SIDES SPRING UP AROUND THE MASKED MANHUNTER AND...
FOR CRYING OUT LOUD! WHAT HAVE I BLUNDERED INTO?
WE'VE CAUGHT HIM, EIVOL--BATMAN'S IN THE TRAP!
7

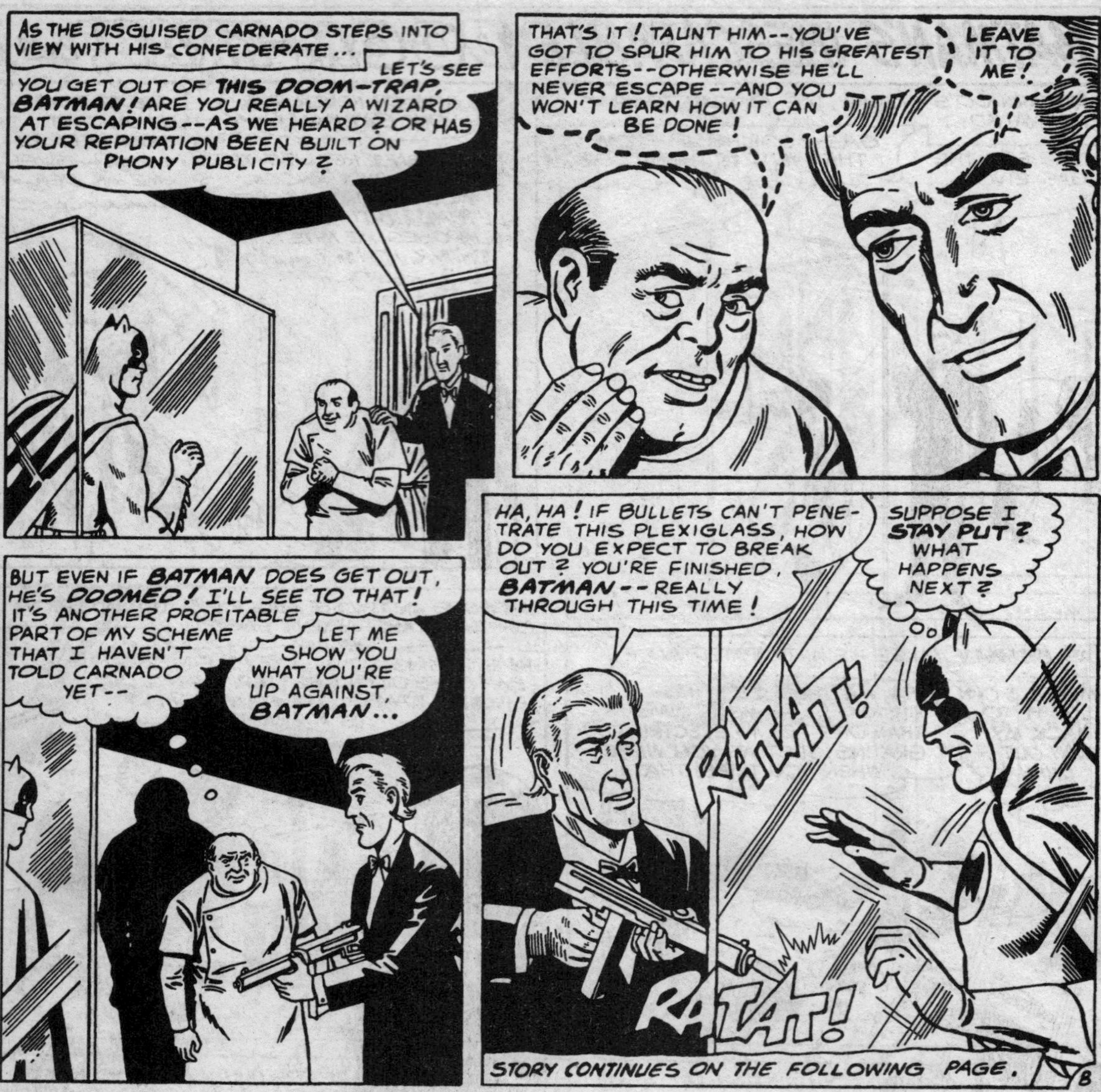
AS THE DISGUISED CARNADO STEPS INTO VIEW WITH HIS CONFEDERATE ...
LET'S SEE YOU GET OUT OF THIS DOOM-TRAP, BATMAN! ARE YOU REALLY A WIZARD AT ESCAPING--AS WE HEARD? OR HAS YOUR REPUTATION BEEN BUILT ON PHONY PUBLICITY?
THAT'S IT! TAUNT HIM--YOU'VE GOT TO SPUR HIM TO HIS GREATEST EFFORTS--OTHERWISE HE'LL NEVER ESCAPE--AND YOU WON'T LEARN HOW IT CAN BE DONE!
LEAVE IT TO ME!
BUT EVEN IF BATMAN DOES GET OUT, HE'S DOOMED! I'LL SEE TO THAT! IT'S ANOTHER PROFITABLE PART OF MY SCHEME THAT I HAVEN'T TOLD CARNADO YET--
LET ME SHOW YOU WHAT YOU'RE UP AGAINST, BATMAN...
HA, HA! IF BULLETS CAN'T PENETRATE THIS PLEXIGLASS, HOW DO YOU EXPECT TO BREAK OUT? YOU'RE FINISHED, BATMAN--REALLY THROUGH THIS TIME!
SUPPOSE I STAY PUT? WHAT HAPPENS NEXT?
RATATAT!
RATAT!
STORY CONTINUES ON THE FOLLOWING PAGE.
B

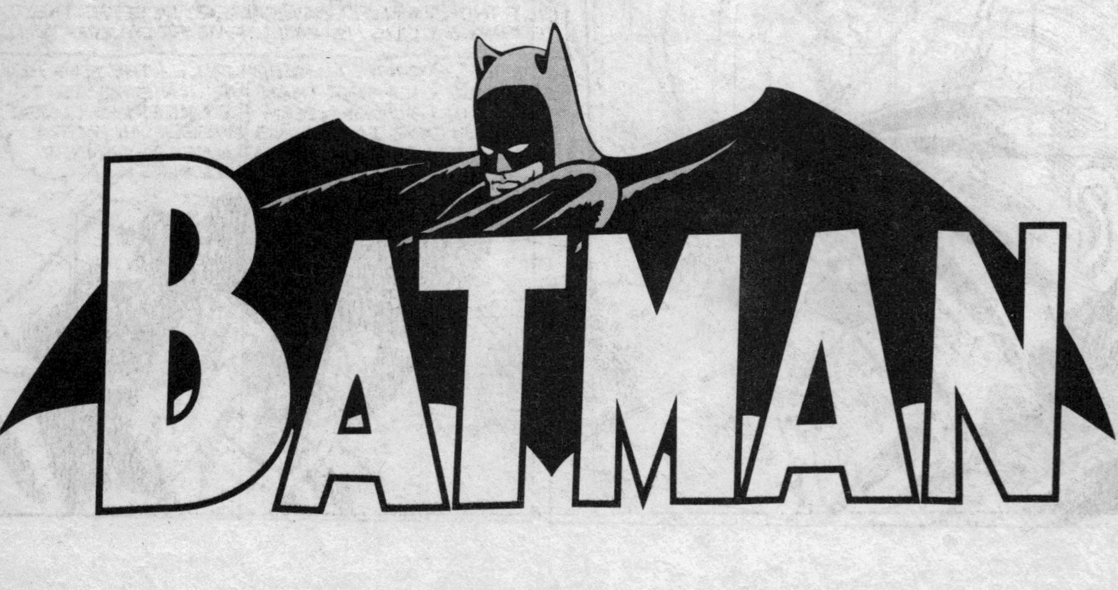
BATMAN

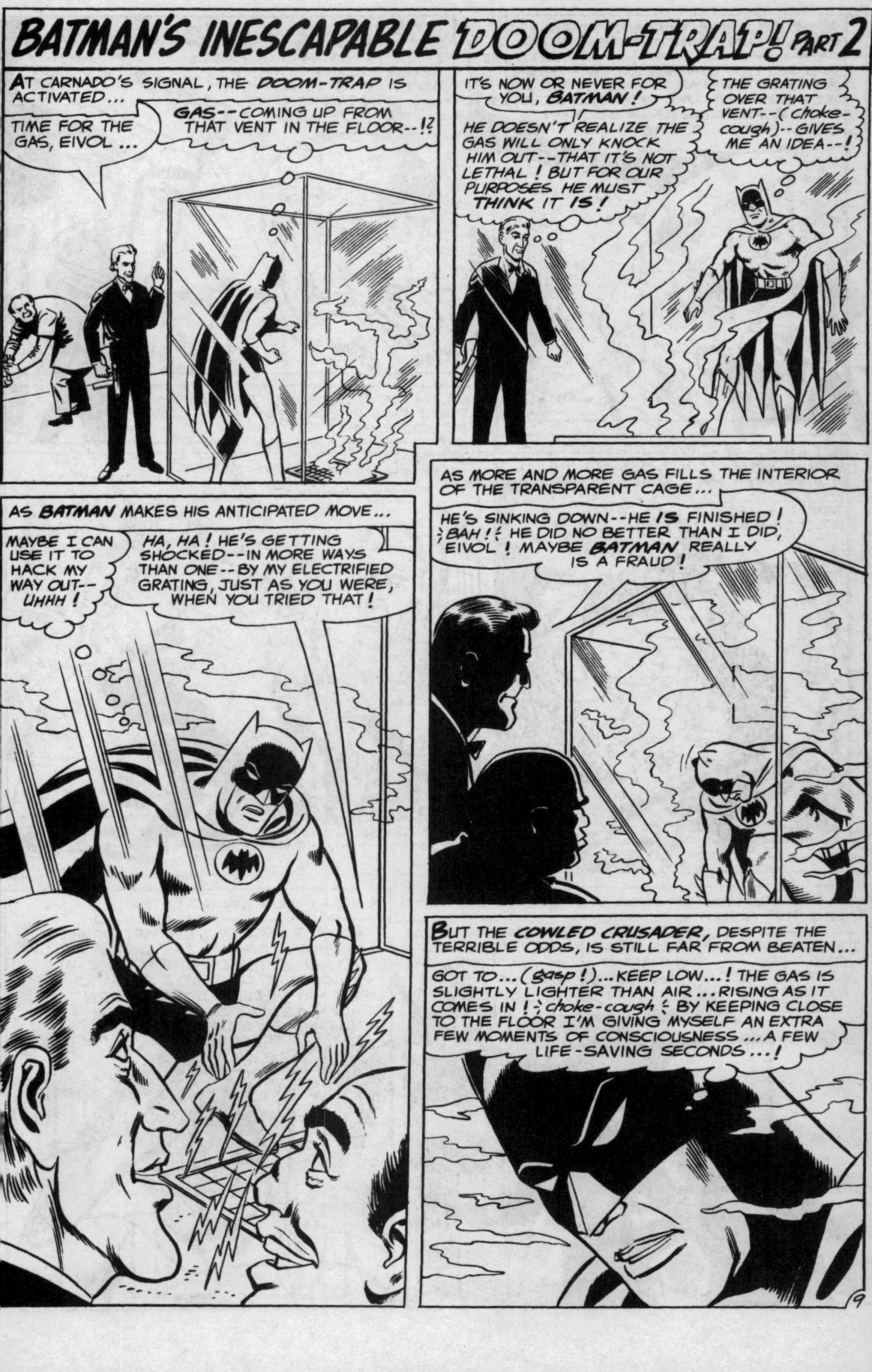
BATMAN'S INESCAPABLE DOOM-TRAP! PART 2
AT CARNADO'S SIGNAL, THE DOOM-TRAP IS ACTIVATED...
TIME FOR THE GAS, EIVOL...
GAS--COMING UP FROM THAT VENT IN THE FLOOR--!?
IT'S NOW OR NEVER FOR YOU, BATMAN!
HE DOESN'T REALIZE THE GAS WILL ONLY KNOCK HIM OUT--THAT IT'S NOT LETHAL! BUT FOR OUR PURPOSES HE MUST THINK IT IS!
THE GRATING OVER THAT VENT--(choke-cough)--GIVES ME AN IDEA--!
AS BATMAN MAKES HIS ANTICIPATED MOVE...
MAYBE I CAN USE IT TO HACK MY WAY OUT--UHHH!
HA, HA! HE'S GETTING SHOCKED--IN MORE WAYS THAN ONE--BY MY ELECTRIFIED GRATING, JUST AS YOU WERE, WHEN YOU TRIED THAT!
AS MORE AND MORE GAS FILLS THE INTERIOR OF THE TRANSPARENT CAGE...
HE'S SINKING DOWN--HE IS FINISHED! BAH! HE DID NO BETTER THAN I DID, EIVOL! MAYBE BATMAN REALLY IS A FRAUD!
BUT THE COWLED CRUSADER, DESPITE THE TERRIBLE ODDS, IS STILL FAR FROM BEATEN...
GOT TO...(gasp!)...KEEP LOW...! THE GAS IS SLIGHTLY LIGHTER THAN AIR...RISING AS IT COMES IN! choke-cough BY KEEPING CLOSE TO THE FLOOR I'M GIVING MYSELF AN EXTRA FEW MOMENTS OF CONSCIOUSNESS...A FEW LIFE-SAVING SECONDS...!
9

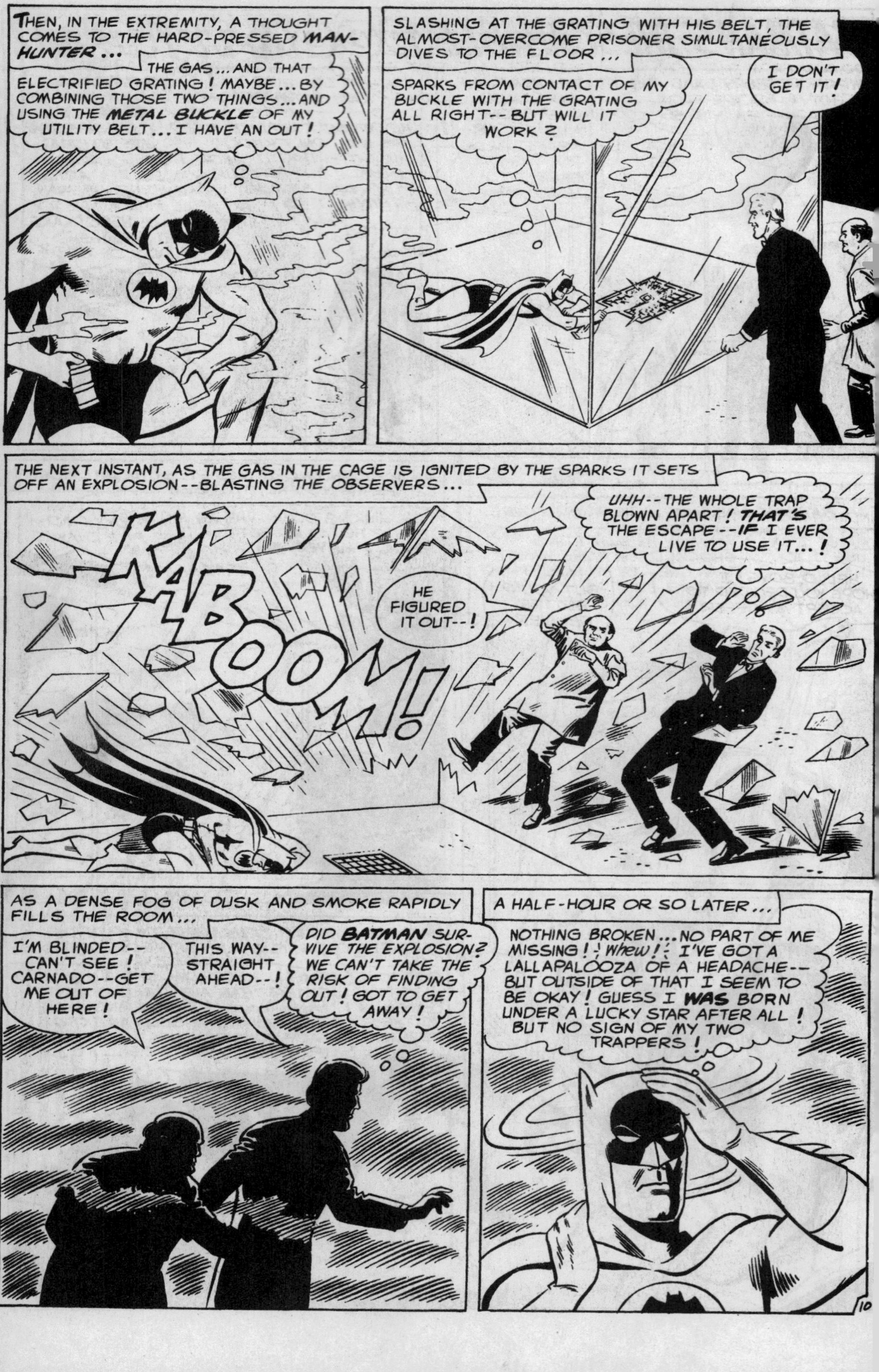

THEN, IN THE EXTREMITY, A THOUGHT COMES TO THE HARD-PRESSED MAN-HUNTER ...
THE GAS ... AND THAT ELECTRIFIED GRATING! MAYBE ... BY COMBINING THOSE TWO THINGS ... AND USING THE METAL BUCKLE OF MY UTILITY BELT ... I HAVE AN OUT!
SLASHING AT THE GRATING WITH HIS BELT, THE ALMOST-OVERCOME PRISONER SIMULTANEOUSLY DIVES TO THE FLOOR ...
SPARKS FROM CONTACT OF MY BUCKLE WITH THE GRATING ALL RIGHT-- BUT WILL IT WORK?
I DON'T GET IT!
THE NEXT INSTANT, AS THE GAS IN THE CAGE IS IGNITED BY THE SPARKS IT SETS OFF AN EXPLOSION--BLASTING THE OBSERVERS ...
KABOOOM!
HE FIGURED IT OUT--!
UHH--THE WHOLE TRAP BLOWN APART! THAT'S THE ESCAPE--IF I EVER LIVE TO USE IT ...!
AS A DENSE FOG OF DUSK AND SMOKE RAPIDLY FILLS THE ROOM ...
I'M BLINDED-- CAN'T SEE! CARNADO--GET ME OUT OF HERE!
THIS WAY-- STRAIGHT AHEAD--!
DID BATMAN SURVIVE THE EXPLOSION? WE CAN'T TAKE THE RISK OF FINDING OUT! GOT TO GET AWAY!
A HALF-HOUR OR SO LATER ...
NOTHING BROKEN ... NO PART OF ME MISSING! WHEW! I'VE GOT A LALLAPALOOZA OF A HEADACHE-- BUT OUTSIDE OF THAT I SEEM TO BE OKAY! GUESS I WAS BORN UNDER A LUCKY STAR AFTER ALL! BUT NO SIGN OF MY TWO TRAPPERS!
10

NEXT DAY IN EIVOL'S WORKSHOP...

THERE YOU ARE, PAL--YOUR $100,000 FROM THAT LOAN COMPANY ROBBERY! AND I'VE GOT MY ESCAPE FROM THAT TRAP--EVEN IF IT IS A BIT DANGEROUS! SO WE CAN SAY ALL IS HUNKY-DORY, eh?

NOT YET!

THERE'S NOTHING IN THE PAPERS ABOUT BATMAN BEING KILLED OR EVEN INJURED--AND THAT MEANS HE GOT AWAY UNHARMED LAST NIGHT! AND IT ALSO MEANS-- THAT WE CAN EXPECT HIM HERE ANY-TIME NOW!

WHAT!? HOW COULD HE POSSIBLY FIND US? I WAS EVEN DIS-GUISED--AND NO ONE KNOWS YOU--

WE LEFT NO CLUES AT THAT ABANDONED HOUSE--WE WERE PARTICULARLY CAREFUL ABOUT THAT!

NO CLUES THAT WE KNOW OF! LISTEN, CARNADO! BATMAN IS NOT KNOWN AS THE WORLD'S GREATEST DETECTIVE FOR NOTHING! AND HE PROVED HIMSELF AS AN ESCAPE ARTIST! SOMEHOW--SOMEWAY, HE'LL FIND A WAY TO TRAIL US HERE! CARE TO BET ANOTHER $100,000 ON THAT?

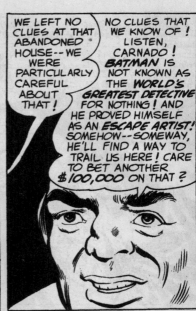

I THOUGHT NOT! OH, WELL DON'T WORRY-- I'M PREPARED! I INVITED A COUPLE OF UNDERWORLD FRIENDS OF MINE--AND HERE THEY ARE NOW RIGHT ON TIME!

HELLO, BOYS! I HOPE YOU DECIDED TO ACCEPT MY OFFER?

YEAH, EIVOL! BUT YOU'D BETTER DELIVER!

YOU GET HALF NOW-- THE REST OVER BATMAN'S DEAD BODY!

THAT LITTLE EIVOL IS A CONNIVER! HE'S GOT THOSE TWO HOODLUMS TO PAY HIM $100,000-- FOR A SURE-FIRE CHANCE TO FINISH OFF BATMAN!

AS THE STAGE IS SET FOR A KILLING BY THE CUNNING LITTLE WORKSHOP OWNER...

...AND THAT WAY YOU'LL GET BATMAN IN A CROSS-FIRE BETWEEN YOU! NOW YOU'D BETTER GET IN YOUR HIDING PLACES-- THE MUMMY CASE AND SUIT OF ARMOR! THEY'RE PROPS USED IN A MAGIC ACT! FOLLOW THE INSTRUCTIONS I GAVE YOU, AND THEY'LL WORK!

11

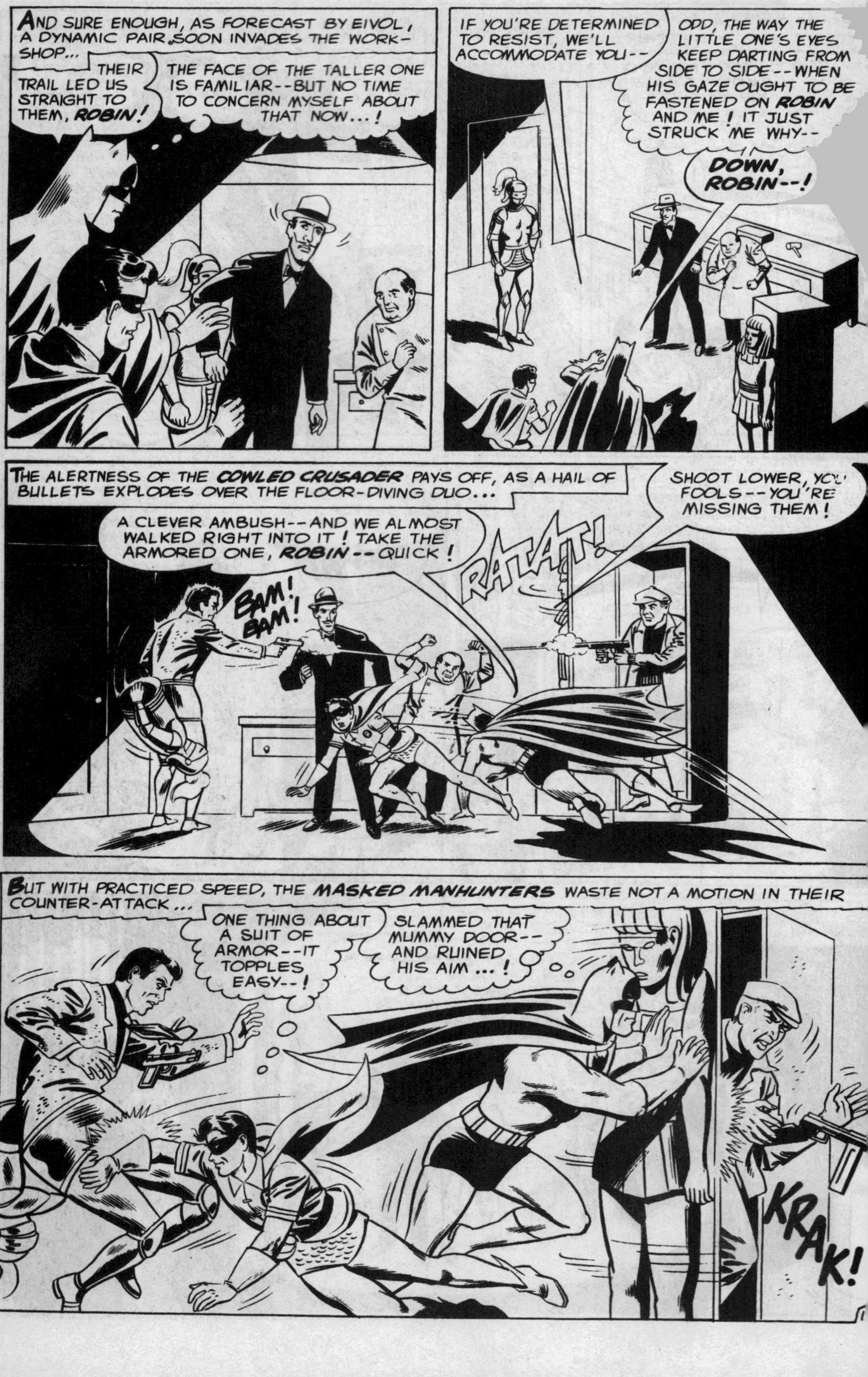
AND SURE ENOUGH, AS FORECAST BY EIVOL, A DYNAMIC PAIR SOON INVADES THE WORK-SHOP...
THEIR TRAIL LED US STRAIGHT TO THEM, ROBIN!
THE FACE OF THE TALLER ONE IS FAMILIAR--BUT NO TIME TO CONCERN MYSELF ABOUT THAT NOW...!
IF YOU'RE DETERMINED TO RESIST, WE'LL ACCOMMODATE YOU--
ODD, THE WAY THE LITTLE ONE'S EYES KEEP DARTING FROM SIDE TO SIDE--WHEN HIS GAZE OUGHT TO BE FASTENED ON ROBIN AND ME! IT JUST STRUCK 'ME WHY--
DOWN, ROBIN--!
THE ALERTNESS OF THE COWLED CRUSADER PAYS OFF, AS A HAIL OF BULLETS EXPLODES OVER THE FLOOR-DIVING DUO...
SHOOT LOWER, YOU FOOLS--YOU'RE MISSING THEM!
A CLEVER AMBUSH--AND WE ALMOST WALKED RIGHT INTO IT! TAKE THE ARMORED ONE, ROBIN--QUICK!
RATATAT!
BAM! BAM!
BUT WITH PRACTICED SPEED, THE MASKED MANHUNTERS WASTE NOT A MOTION IN THEIR COUNTER-ATTACK...
ONE THING ABOUT A SUIT OF ARMOR--IT TOPPLES EASY--!
SLAMMED THAT MUMMY DOOR--AND RUINED HIS AIM...!
KRAK!

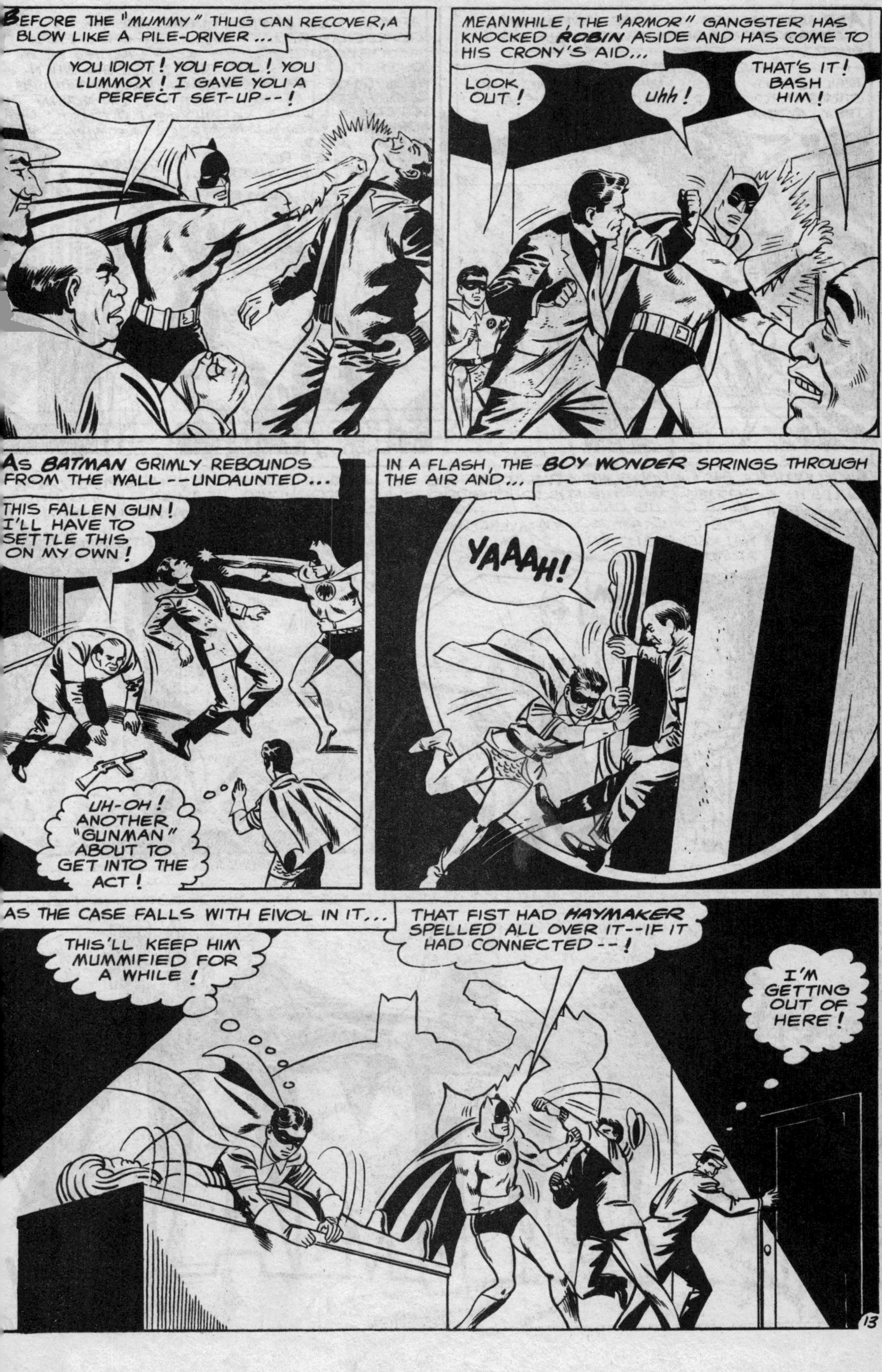
BEFORE THE "MUMMY" THUG CAN RECOVER, A BLOW LIKE A PILE-DRIVER ...
YOU IDIOT! YOU FOOL! YOU LUMMOX! I GAVE YOU A PERFECT SET-UP--!
MEANWHILE, THE "ARMOR" GANGSTER HAS KNOCKED ROBIN ASIDE AND HAS COME TO HIS CRONY'S AID...
LOOK OUT!
UHH!
THAT'S IT! BASH HIM!
AS BATMAN GRIMLY REBOUNDS FROM THE WALL--UNDAUNTED...
THIS FALLEN GUN! I'LL HAVE TO SETTLE THIS ON MY OWN!
UH-OH! ANOTHER "GUNMAN" ABOUT TO GET INTO THE ACT!
IN A FLASH, THE BOY WONDER SPRINGS THROUGH THE AIR AND...
YAAAH!
AS THE CASE FALLS WITH EIVOL IN IT...
THIS'LL KEEP HIM MUMMIFIED FOR A WHILE!
THAT FIST HAD HAYMAKER SPELLED ALL OVER IT--IF IT HAD CONNECTED--!
I'M GETTING OUT OF HERE!
13

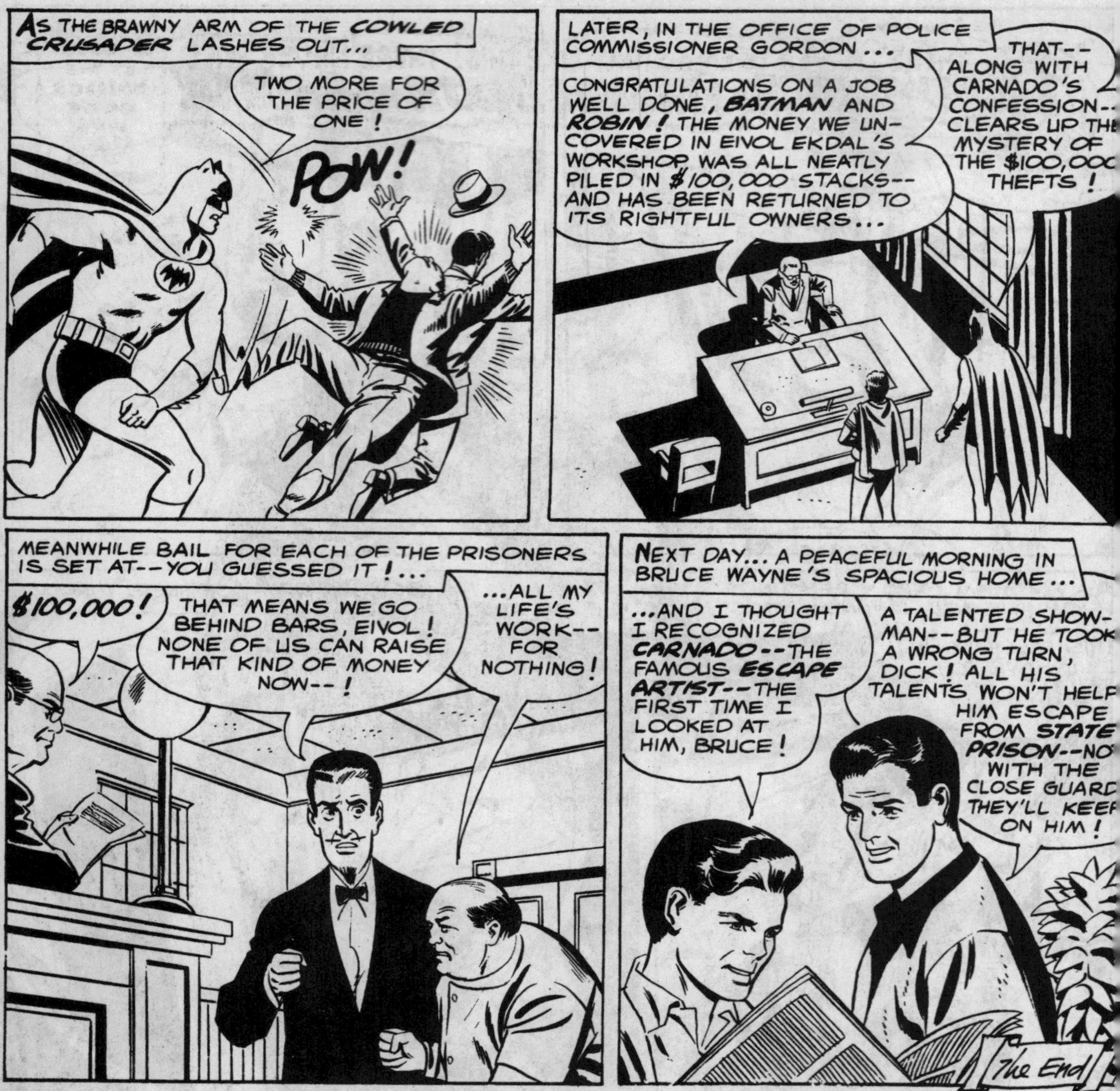
AS THE BRAWNY ARM OF THE COWLED CRUSADER LASHES OUT...
TWO MORE FOR THE PRICE OF ONE!
POW!
LATER, IN THE OFFICE OF POLICE COMMISSIONER GORDON...
CONGRATULATIONS ON A JOB WELL DONE, BATMAN AND ROBIN! THE MONEY WE UN-COVERED IN EIVOL EKDAL'S WORKSHOP WAS ALL NEATLY PILED IN $100,000 STACKS-- AND HAS BEEN RETURNED TO ITS RIGHTFUL OWNERS...
THAT-- ALONG WITH CARNADO'S CONFESSION-- CLEARS UP THE MYSTERY OF THE $100,00 THEFTS!
MEANWHILE BAIL FOR EACH OF THE PRISONERS IS SET AT--YOU GUESSED IT!...
$100,000!
THAT MEANS WE GO BEHIND BARS, EIVOL! NONE OF US CAN RAISE THAT KIND OF MONEY NOW--!
...ALL MY LIFE'S WORK-- FOR NOTHING!
NEXT DAY... A PEACEFUL MORNING IN BRUCE WAYNE'S SPACIOUS HOME...
...AND I THOUGHT I RECOGNIZED CARNADO--THE FAMOUS ESCAPE ARTIST--THE FIRST TIME I LOOKED AT HIM, BRUCE!
A TALENTED SHOW-MAN--BUT HE TOOK A WRONG TURN, DICK! ALL HIS TALENTS WON'T HELP HIM ESCAPE FROM STATE PRISON--NO WITH THE CLOSE GUARD THEY'LL KEEP ON HIM!
The End

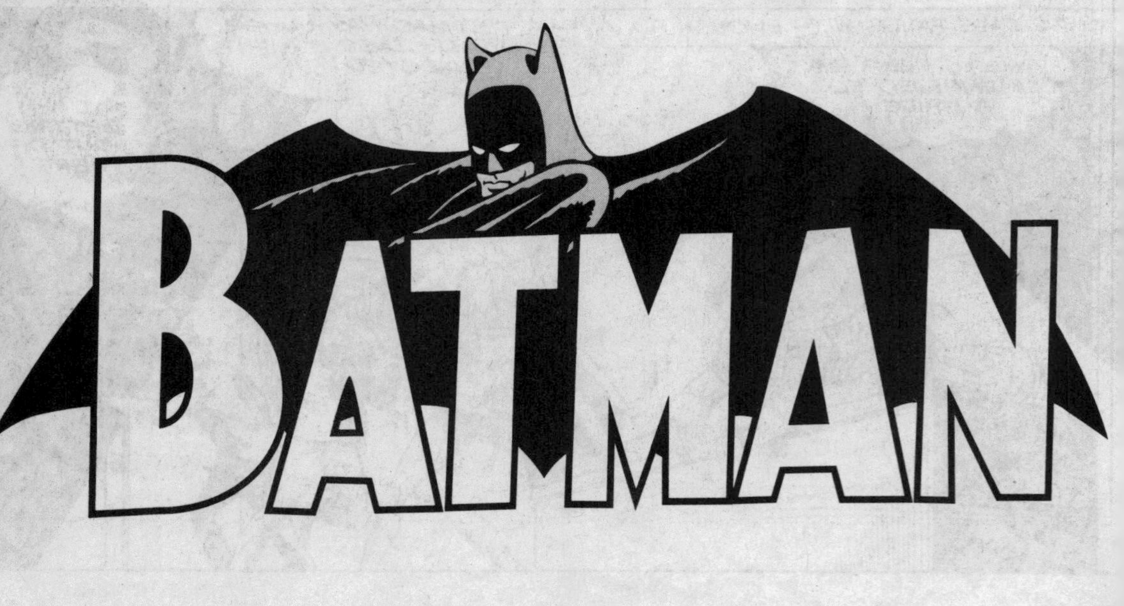
BATMAN

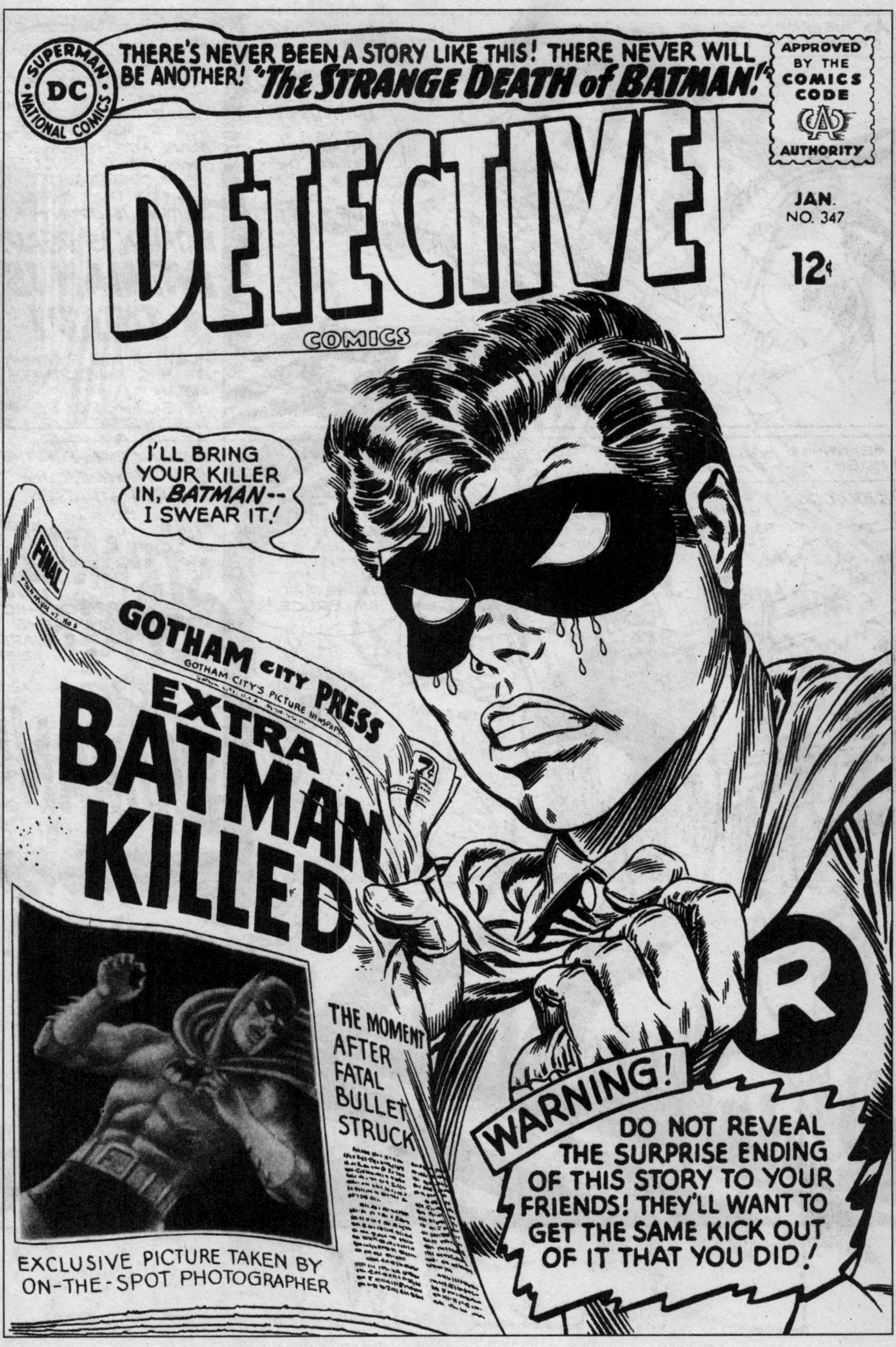
THERE'S NEVER BEEN A STORY LIKE THIS! THERE NEVER WILL BE ANOTHER! "The STRANGE DEATH of BATMAN!"
SUPERMAN DC NATIONAL COMICS
APPROVED BY THE COMICS CODE AUTHORITY
DETECTIVE COMICS
JAN. NO. 347
12¢
I'LL BRING YOUR KILLER IN, BATMAN-- I SWEAR IT!
FINAL
GOTHAM CITY PRESS
GOTHAM CITY'S PICTURE NEWSPAPER
EXTRA
BATMAN KILLED
THE MOMENT AFTER FATAL BULLET STRUCK
EXCLUSIVE PICTURE TAKEN BY ON-THE-SPOT PHOTOGRAPHER
WARNING!
DO NOT REVEAL THE SURPRISE ENDING OF THIS STORY TO YOUR FRIENDS! THEY'LL WANT TO GET THE SAME KICK OUT OF IT THAT YOU DID!

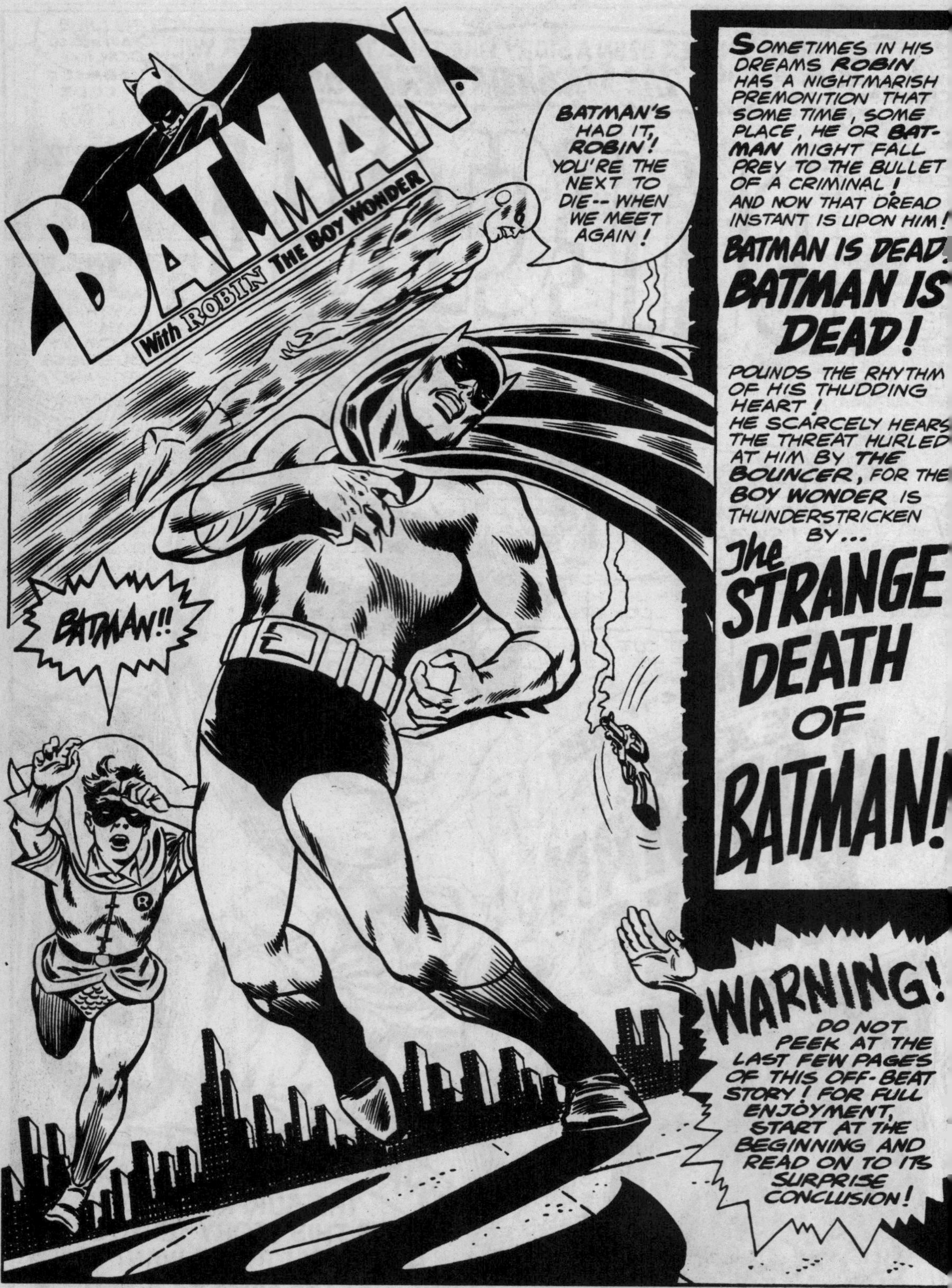
BATMAN
With ROBIN THE BOY WONDER
BATMAN'S HAD IT, ROBIN! YOU'RE THE NEXT TO DIE-- WHEN WE MEET AGAIN!
SOMETIMES IN HIS DREAMS ROBIN HAS A NIGHTMARISH PREMONITION THAT SOME TIME, SOME PLACE, HE OR BATMAN MIGHT FALL PREY TO THE BULLET OF A CRIMINAL! AND NOW THAT DREAD INSTANT IS UPON HIM!
BATMAN IS DEAD! BATMAN IS DEAD!
POUNDS THE RHYTHM OF HIS THUDDING HEART! HE SCARCELY HEARS THE THREAT HURLED AT HIM BY THE BOUNCER, FOR THE BOY WONDER IS THUNDERSTRICKEN BY...
The STRANGE DEATH OF BATMAN!
BATMAN!!
WARNING! DO NOT PEEK AT THE LAST FEW PAGES OF THIS OFF-BEAT STORY! FOR FULL ENJOYMENT, START AT THE BEGINNING AND READ ON TO ITS SURPRISE CONCLUSION!

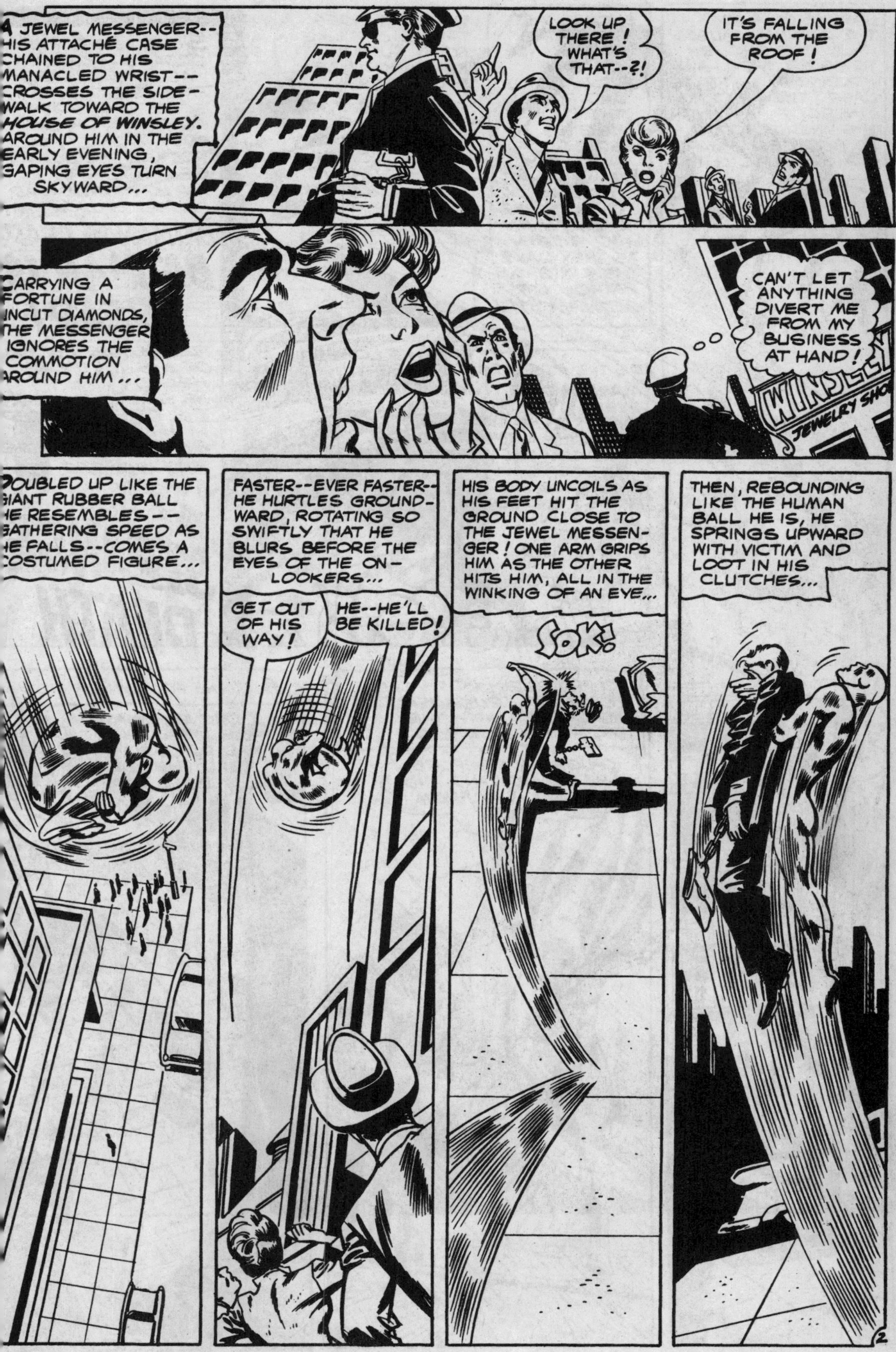
A JEWEL MESSENGER-- HIS ATTACHÉ CASE CHAINED TO HIS MANACLED WRIST-- CROSSES THE SIDE-WALK TOWARD THE *HOUSE OF WINSLEY*. AROUND HIM IN THE EARLY EVENING, GAPING EYES TURN SKYWARD...
LOOK UP THERE! WHAT'S THAT--?!
IT'S FALLING FROM THE ROOF!
CARRYING A FORTUNE IN UNCUT DIAMONDS, THE MESSENGER IGNORES THE COMMOTION AROUND HIM...
CAN'T LET ANYTHING DIVERT ME FROM MY BUSINESS AT HAND!
DOUBLED UP LIKE THE GIANT RUBBER BALL HE RESEMBLES-- GATHERING SPEED AS HE FALLS--COMES A COSTUMED FIGURE...
FASTER--EVER FASTER-- HE HURTLES GROUND-WARD, ROTATING SO SWIFTLY THAT HE BLURS BEFORE THE EYES OF THE ON-LOOKERS...
GET OUT OF HIS WAY!
HE--HE'LL BE KILLED!
HIS BODY UNCOILS AS HIS FEET HIT THE GROUND CLOSE TO THE JEWEL MESSEN-GER! ONE ARM GRIPS HIM AS THE OTHER HITS HIM, ALL IN THE WINKING OF AN EYE...
SOK!
THEN, REBOUNDING LIKE THE HUMAN BALL HE IS, HE SPRINGS UPWARD WITH VICTIM AND LOOT IN HIS CLUTCHES...

LANDING ON A ROOF, THE CRIMINAL PAUSES ONLY LONG ENOUGH TO SEVER THE CHAIN HOLDING THE ATTACHÉ CASE! THEN HITTING THE ROOF HARD WITH HIS UNIQUE BOOTS, HE BOUNCES UPWARD IN A GRACEFUL CURVE...

NOW FOR MY ROOF-TO-ROOF GETAWAY!

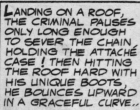

SUCH IS THE STARTLING APPEARANCE OF *THE BOUNCER*! AND FROM THEN ON BEGINS A SERIES OF FABULOUS CRIMES THAT CRY A CHALLENGE TO *BATMAN* AND *ROBIN* AS THEY MAKE THEIR NIGHTLY PATROL OF *GOTHAM CITY*...

THERE HE GOES, TAKING OFF LIKE SOME SUPER-KANGAROO! WE SPOTTED HIM TOO LATE!

WE'LL CATCH UP TO HIM ANOTHER NIGHT, *ROBIN*! SOONER OR LATER HIS PATH AND OURS WILL MEET!

AS THE *MASKED MANHUNTER* AVERS, IT IS INEVITABLE THAT CRIMINAL AND CRIME-BUSTERS SHOULD CROSS PATHS! AND SO ON A RAINY EVENING IN LATE AUTUMN, NEAR A WHARFSIDE WAREHOUSE...

HERE HE COMES! AS IF DEFYING US TO NAB HIM!

ALL I ASK IS ONE CRACK AT HIM -- AND WE'LL SEE HOW MUCH BOUNCE TO THE OUNCE HE HAS!

SO PRECISELY DOES THE *COWLED CRUSADER* TIME HIS ONRUSH WITH THE DROPPING *BOUNCER* ...

CAUGHT HIM BEFORE HE COULD LAND AND BOUND AWAY FROM ME!

BUT THE FOLLOW-UP INSTAN

I DROVE HIM AWAY FROM ME -- AS IF I HAD PUNCHED A REAL RUBBER BALL!

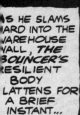

AS HE SLAMS HARD INTO THE WAREHOUSE WALL, *THE BOUNCER'S* RESILIENT BODY FLATTENS FOR A BRIEF INSTANT...

HERE'S WHERE THE *"PUNCH BALL"* STRIKES BACK...

THUMP!

RESUMING HIS SHAPE, HE RICOCHETS OFF THE WALL AND INTO THE TEEN-AGE THUNDERBOLT...

THIS IS NO KID GAME WE'RE PLAYING, *ROBIN!*

ZWING!

AWWWPP!

LIKE A MADDENED HANDBALL, *THE BOUNCER* MOVES FROM WALL TO WALL...

IF HE EVER SLOWS DOWN-- I'LL TAKE THE BOUNCE OUT OF HIM BY DOUBLE-PUNCHING HIM FROM OPPOSITE DIRECTIONS!

WHAP! THUMP! WHAAKK! GOES THE *BOUNCER* AS HE RICOCHETS BACK AND FORTH WITH EYE-BLINDING SPEED -- UNTIL A WELL-CHOSEN MOMENT WHEN...

HE CURVED-BALL ME...

THUD!

THIS TIME AS *THE BOUNCER* HITS A WALL, HE CONTROLS HIS ANGLE OF CONTACT TO PROPEL HIM UPWARD INTO THE SKY, LEAVING HIS FOES DAZED, STAGGERED BY THE SWIFTNESS OF HIS ONSLAUGHT...

THE BALL GAME'S OVER! HE SHUT US OUT--

HE GOT ALL THE HITS-- AND WE MADE ALL THE ERRORS!

4

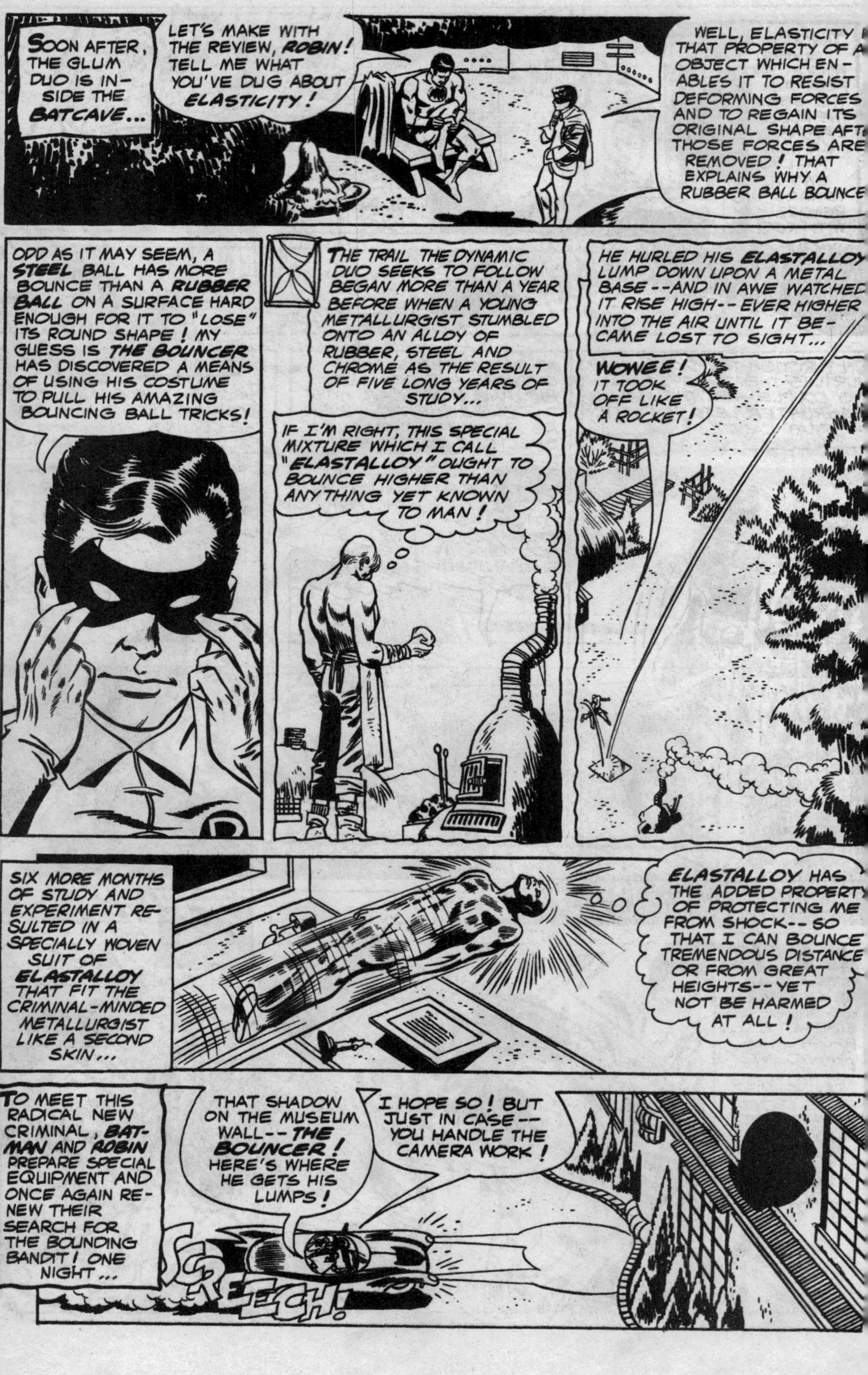
SOON AFTER, THE GLUM DUO IS INSIDE THE BATCAVE...
LET'S MAKE WITH THE REVIEW, ROBIN! TELL ME WHAT YOU'VE DUG ABOUT ELASTICITY!
WELL, ELASTICITY IS THAT PROPERTY OF AN OBJECT WHICH ENABLES IT TO RESIST DEFORMING FORCES AND TO REGAIN ITS ORIGINAL SHAPE AFTER THOSE FORCES ARE REMOVED! THAT EXPLAINS WHY A RUBBER BALL BOUNCES
ODD AS IT MAY SEEM, A STEEL BALL HAS MORE BOUNCE THAN A RUBBER BALL ON A SURFACE HARD ENOUGH FOR IT TO "LOSE" ITS ROUND SHAPE! MY GUESS IS THE BOUNCER HAS DISCOVERED A MEANS OF USING HIS COSTUME TO PULL HIS AMAZING BOUNCING BALL TRICKS!
THE TRAIL THE DYNAMIC DUO SEEKS TO FOLLOW BEGAN MORE THAN A YEAR BEFORE WHEN A YOUNG METALLURGIST STUMBLED ONTO AN ALLOY OF RUBBER, STEEL AND CHROME AS THE RESULT OF FIVE LONG YEARS OF STUDY...
IF I'M RIGHT, THIS SPECIAL MIXTURE WHICH I CALL "ELASTALLOY" OUGHT TO BOUNCE HIGHER THAN ANYTHING YET KNOWN TO MAN!
HE HURLED HIS ELASTALLOY LUMP DOWN UPON A METAL BASE--AND IN AWE WATCHED IT RISE HIGH--EVER HIGHER INTO THE AIR UNTIL IT BECAME LOST TO SIGHT...
WOWEE! IT TOOK OFF LIKE A ROCKET!
SIX MORE MONTHS OF STUDY AND EXPERIMENT RESULTED IN A SPECIALLY WOVEN SUIT OF ELASTALLOY THAT FIT THE CRIMINAL-MINDED METALLURGIST LIKE A SECOND SKIN...
ELASTALLOY HAS THE ADDED PROPERTY OF PROTECTING ME FROM SHOCK--SO THAT I CAN BOUNCE TREMENDOUS DISTANCES OR FROM GREAT HEIGHTS--YET NOT BE HARMED AT ALL!
TO MEET THIS RADICAL NEW CRIMINAL, BATMAN AND ROBIN PREPARE SPECIAL EQUIPMENT AND ONCE AGAIN RENEW THEIR SEARCH FOR THE BOUNDING BANDIT! ONE NIGHT...
THAT SHADOW ON THE MUSEUM WALL--THE BOUNCER! HERE'S WHERE HE GETS HIS LUMPS!
I HOPE SO! BUT JUST IN CASE--YOU HANDLE THE CAMERA WORK!
SCREECH!

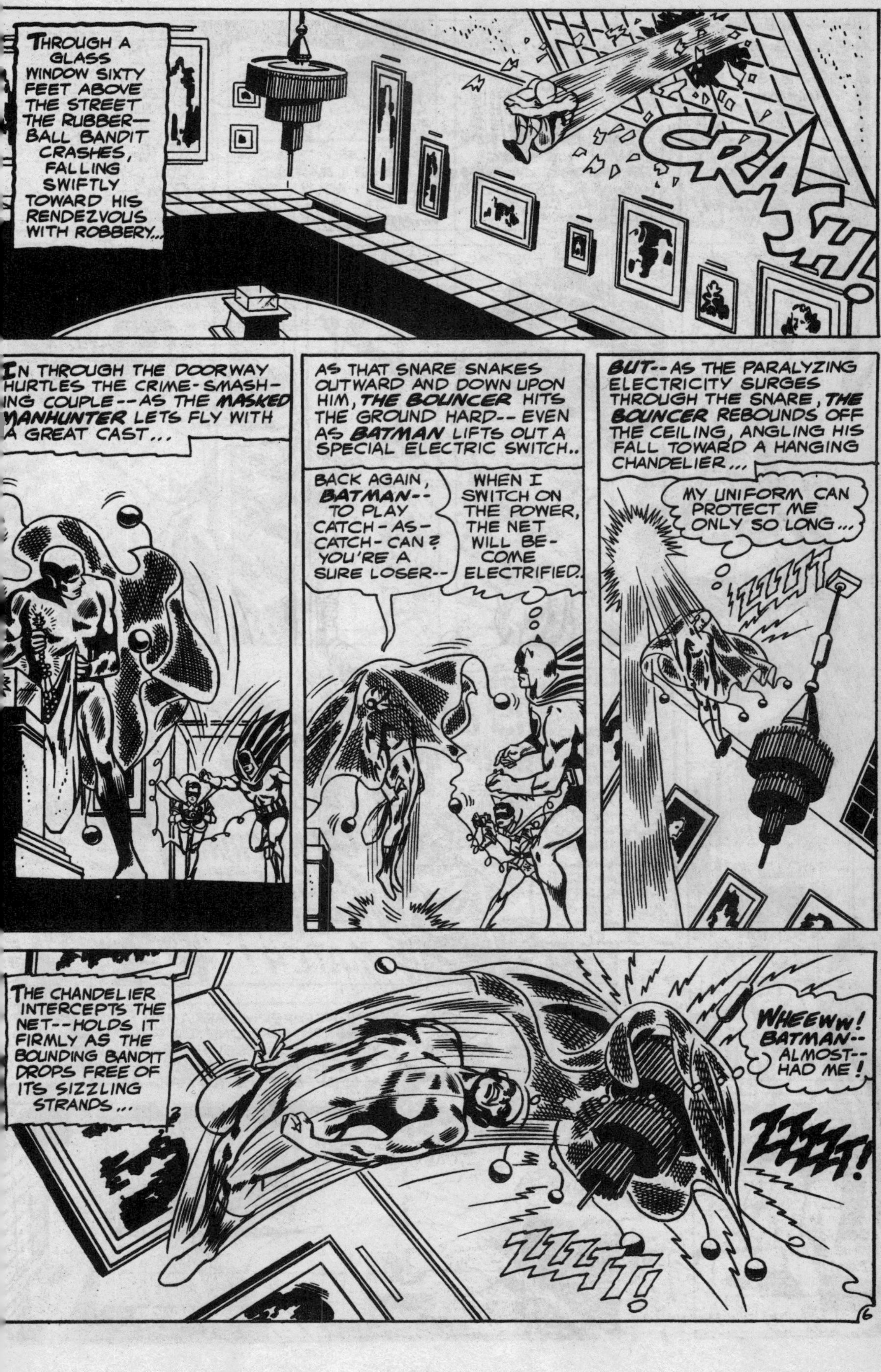
THROUGH A GLASS WINDOW SIXTY FEET ABOVE THE STREET THE RUBBER-BALL BANDIT CRASHES, FALLING SWIFTLY TOWARD HIS RENDEZVOUS WITH ROBBERY...
CRASH!
IN THROUGH THE DOORWAY HURTLES THE CRIME-SMASHING COUPLE--AS THE MASKED MANHUNTER LETS FLY WITH A GREAT CAST...
AS THAT SNARE SNAKES OUTWARD AND DOWN UPON HIM, THE BOUNCER HITS THE GROUND HARD-- EVEN AS BATMAN LIFTS OUT A SPECIAL ELECTRIC SWITCH..
BACK AGAIN, BATMAN-- TO PLAY CATCH-AS-CATCH-CAN? YOU'RE A SURE LOSER--
WHEN I SWITCH ON THE POWER, THE NET WILL BECOME ELECTRIFIED.
BUT--AS THE PARALYZING ELECTRICITY SURGES THROUGH THE SNARE, THE BOUNCER REBOUNDS OFF THE CEILING, ANGLING HIS FALL TOWARD A HANGING CHANDELIER...
MY UNIFORM CAN PROTECT ME ONLY SO LONG...
ZZZTT
THE CHANDELIER INTERCEPTS THE NET--HOLDS IT FIRMLY AS THE BOUNDING BANDIT DROPS FREE OF ITS SIZZLING STRANDS...
WHEEWW! BATMAN-- ALMOST-- HAD ME!
ZZZZT!
ZZZTT!
6

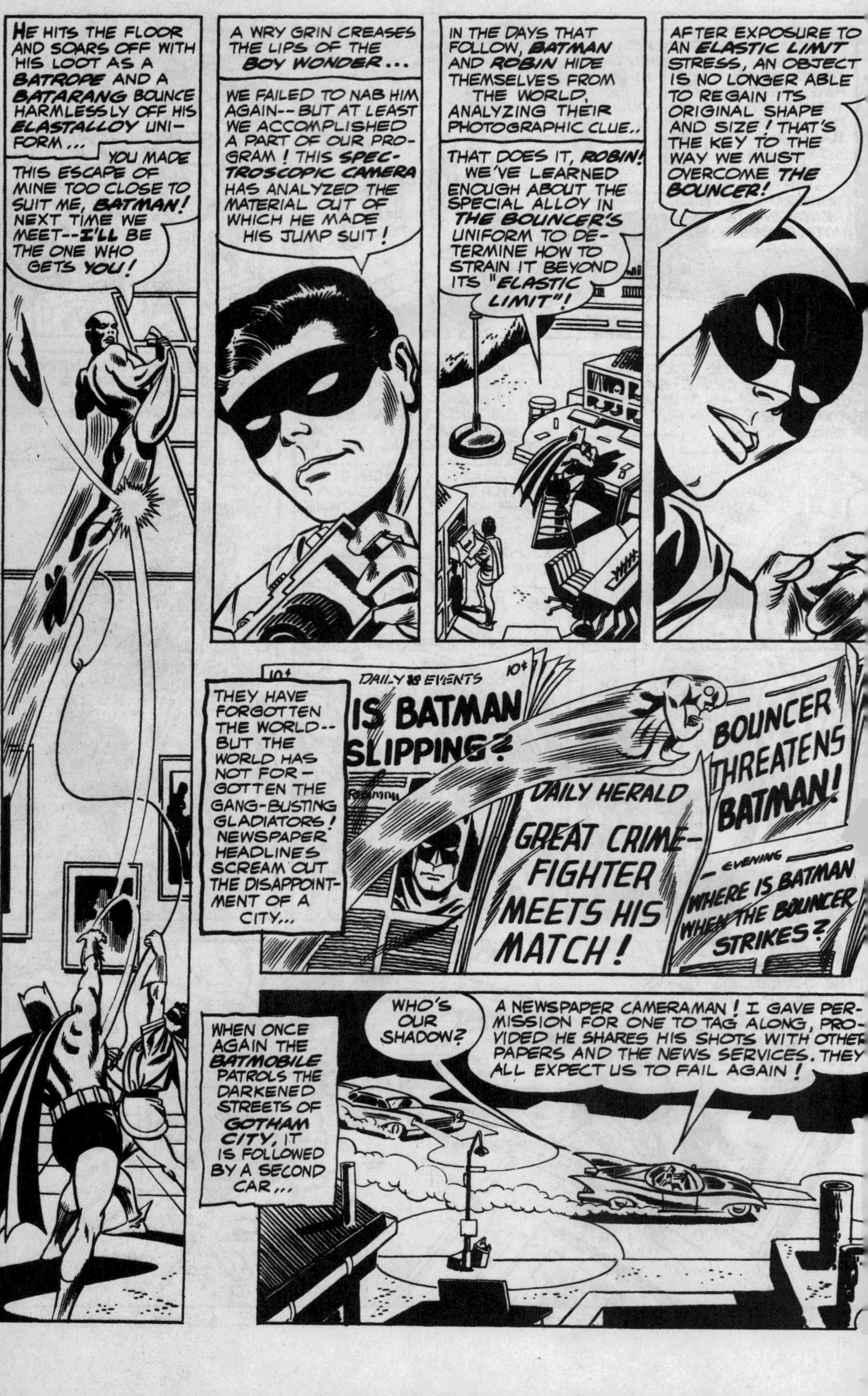
HE HITS THE FLOOR AND SOARS OFF WITH HIS LOOT AS A BATROPE AND A BATARANG BOUNCE HARMLESSLY OFF HIS ELASTALLOY UNIFORM...
YOU MADE THIS ESCAPE OF MINE TOO CLOSE TO SUIT ME, BATMAN! NEXT TIME WE MEET--I'LL BE THE ONE WHO GETS YOU!
A WRY GRIN CREASES THE LIPS OF THE BOY WONDER...
WE FAILED TO NAB HIM AGAIN--BUT AT LEAST WE ACCOMPLISHED A PART OF OUR PROGRAM! THIS SPECTROSCOPIC CAMERA HAS ANALYZED THE MATERIAL OUT OF WHICH HE MADE HIS JUMP SUIT!
IN THE DAYS THAT FOLLOW, BATMAN AND ROBIN HIDE THEMSELVES FROM THE WORLD, ANALYZING THEIR PHOTOGRAPHIC CLUE...
THAT DOES IT, ROBIN! WE'VE LEARNED ENOUGH ABOUT THE SPECIAL ALLOY IN THE BOUNCER'S UNIFORM TO DETERMINE HOW TO STRAIN IT BEYOND ITS "ELASTIC LIMIT"!
AFTER EXPOSURE TO AN ELASTIC LIMIT STRESS, AN OBJECT IS NO LONGER ABLE TO REGAIN ITS ORIGINAL SHAPE AND SIZE! THAT'S THE KEY TO THE WAY WE MUST OVERCOME THE BOUNCER!
THEY HAVE FORGOTTEN THE WORLD--BUT THE WORLD HAS NOT FORGOTTEN THE GANG-BUSTING GLADIATORS! NEWSPAPER HEADLINES SCREAM OUT THE DISAPPOINTMENT OF A CITY...
10¢
DAILY EVENTS 10¢
IS BATMAN SLIPPING?
BOUNCER THREATENS BATMAN!
DAILY HERALD
GREAT CRIME-FIGHTER MEETS HIS MATCH!
EVENING
WHERE IS BATMAN WHEN THE BOUNCER STRIKES?
WHEN ONCE AGAIN THE BATMOBILE PATROLS THE DARKENED STREETS OF GOTHAM CITY, IT IS FOLLOWED BY A SECOND CAR...
WHO'S OUR SHADOW?
A NEWSPAPER CAMERAMAN! I GAVE PERMISSION FOR ONE TO TAG ALONG, PROVIDED HE SHARES HIS SHOTS WITH OTHER PAPERS AND THE NEWS SERVICES. THEY ALL EXPECT US TO FAIL AGAIN!

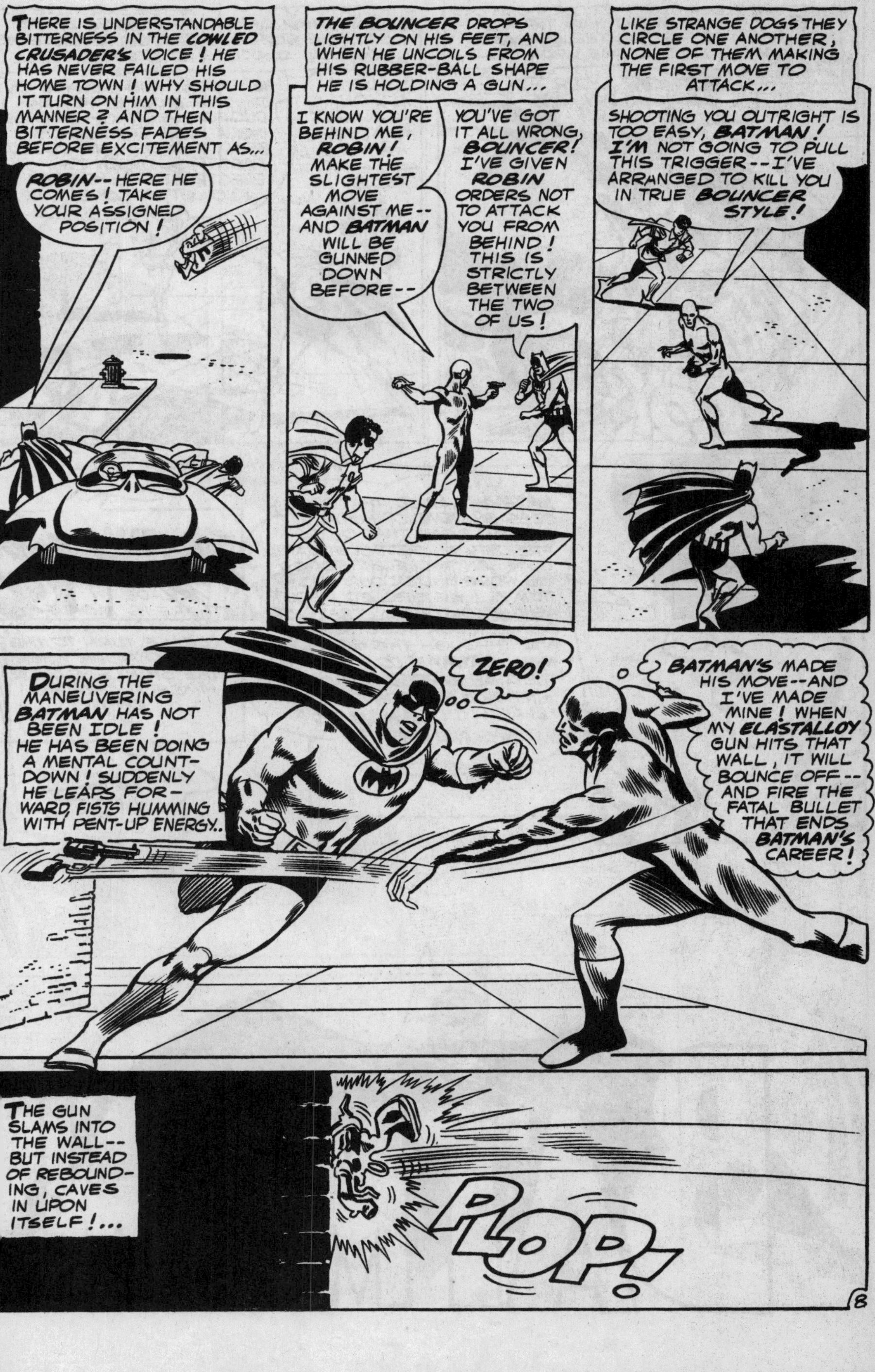
THERE IS UNDERSTANDABLE BITTERNESS IN THE COWLED CRUSADER'S VOICE! HE HAS NEVER FAILED HIS HOME TOWN! WHY SHOULD IT TURN ON HIM IN THIS MANNER? AND THEN BITTERNESS FADES BEFORE EXCITEMENT AS...
ROBIN--HERE HE COMES! TAKE YOUR ASSIGNED POSITION!
THE BOUNCER DROPS LIGHTLY ON HIS FEET, AND WHEN HE UNCOILS FROM HIS RUBBER-BALL SHAPE HE IS HOLDING A GUN...
I KNOW YOU'RE BEHIND ME, ROBIN! MAKE THE SLIGHTEST MOVE AGAINST ME--AND BATMAN WILL BE GUNNED DOWN BEFORE--
YOU'VE GOT IT ALL WRONG, BOUNCER! I'VE GIVEN ROBIN ORDERS NOT TO ATTACK YOU FROM BEHIND! THIS IS STRICTLY BETWEEN THE TWO OF US!
LIKE STRANGE DOGS THEY CIRCLE ONE ANOTHER, NONE OF THEM MAKING THE FIRST MOVE TO ATTACK...
SHOOTING YOU OUTRIGHT IS TOO EASY, BATMAN! I'M NOT GOING TO PULL THIS TRIGGER--I'VE ARRANGED TO KILL YOU IN TRUE BOUNCER STYLE!
DURING THE MANEUVERING BATMAN HAS NOT BEEN IDLE! HE HAS BEEN DOING A MENTAL COUNT-DOWN! SUDDENLY HE LEAPS FOR-WARD, FISTS HUMMING WITH PENT-UP ENERGY..
ZERO!
BATMAN'S MADE HIS MOVE--AND I'VE MADE MINE! WHEN MY ELASTALLOY GUN HITS THAT WALL, IT WILL BOUNCE OFF--AND FIRE THE FATAL BULLET THAT ENDS BATMAN'S CAREER!
THE GUN SLAMS INTO THE WALL--BUT INSTEAD OF REBOUNDING, CAVES IN UPON ITSELF!...
PLOP!
8

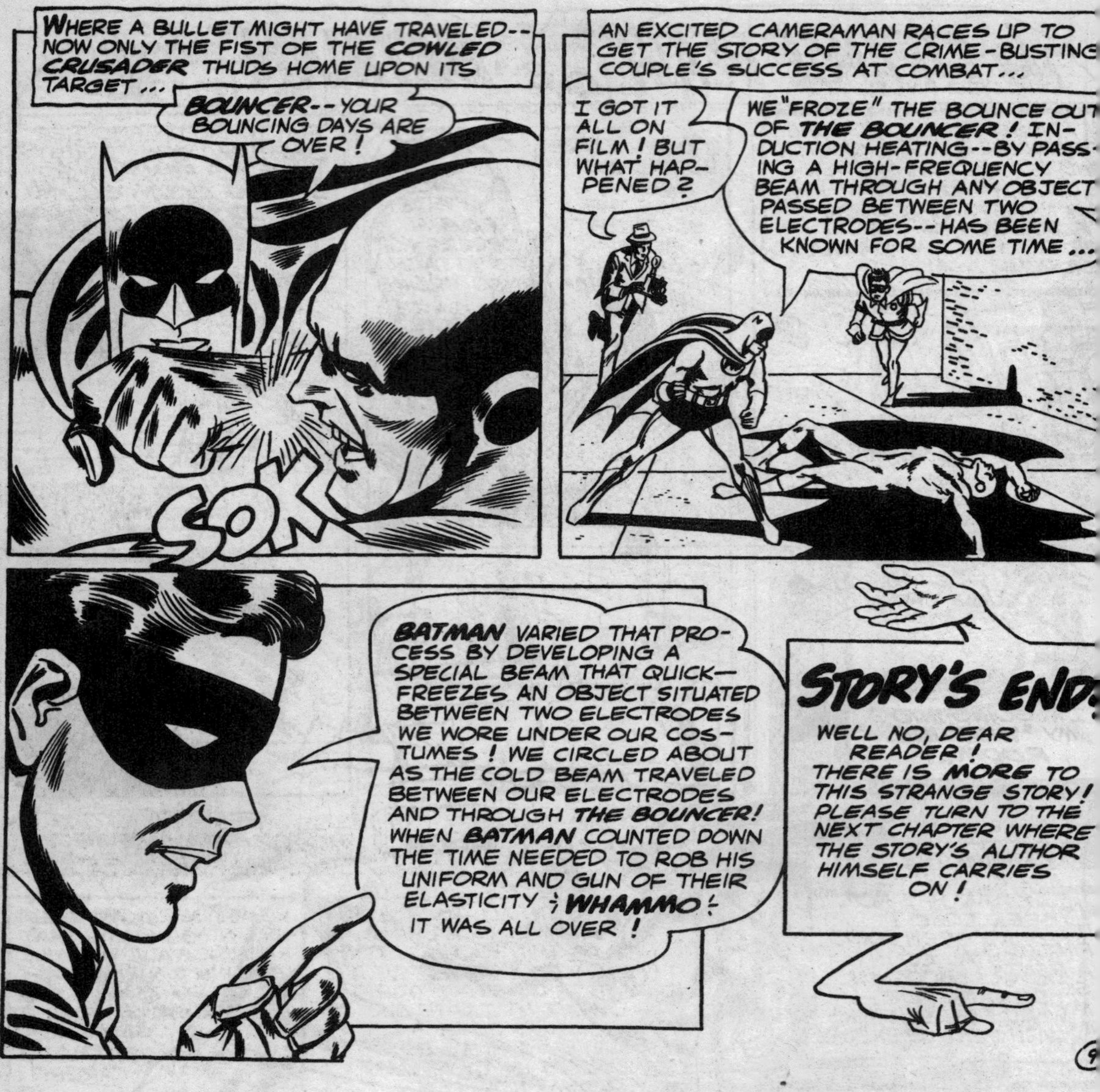
WHERE A BULLET MIGHT HAVE TRAVELED-- NOW ONLY THE FIST OF THE COWLED CRUSADER THUDS HOME UPON ITS TARGET...
BOUNCER--YOUR BOUNCING DAYS ARE OVER!
SOK
AN EXCITED CAMERAMAN RACES UP TO GET THE STORY OF THE CRIME-BUSTING COUPLE'S SUCCESS AT COMBAT...
I GOT IT ALL ON FILM! BUT WHAT HAPPENED?
WE "FROZE" THE BOUNCE OUT OF THE BOUNCER! INDUCTION HEATING--BY PASSING A HIGH-FREQUENCY BEAM THROUGH ANY OBJECT PASSED BETWEEN TWO ELECTRODES--HAS BEEN KNOWN FOR SOME TIME...
BATMAN VARIED THAT PROCESS BY DEVELOPING A SPECIAL BEAM THAT QUICK-FREEZES AN OBJECT SITUATED BETWEEN TWO ELECTRODES WE WORE UNDER OUR COSTUMES! WE CIRCLED ABOUT AS THE COLD BEAM TRAVELED BETWEEN OUR ELECTRODES AND THROUGH THE BOUNCER! WHEN BATMAN COUNTED DOWN THE TIME NEEDED TO ROB HIS UNIFORM AND GUN OF THEIR ELASTICITY -- WHAMMO! -- IT WAS ALL OVER!
STORY'S END?
WELL NO, DEAR READER! THERE IS MORE TO THIS STRANGE STORY! PLEASE TURN TO THE NEXT CHAPTER WHERE THE STORY'S AUTHOR HIMSELF CARRIES ON!

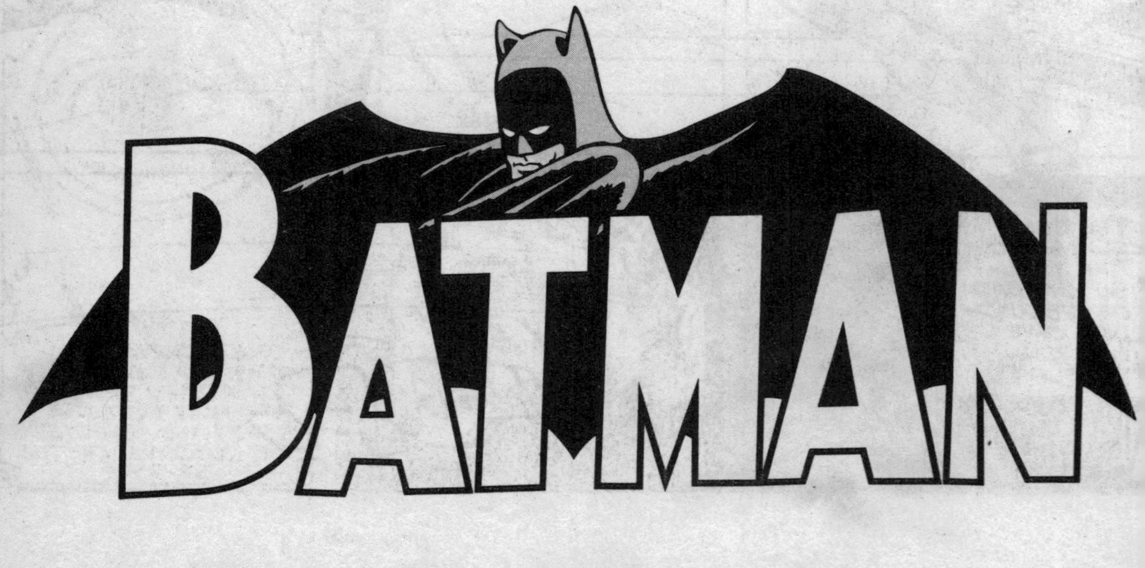
BATMAN

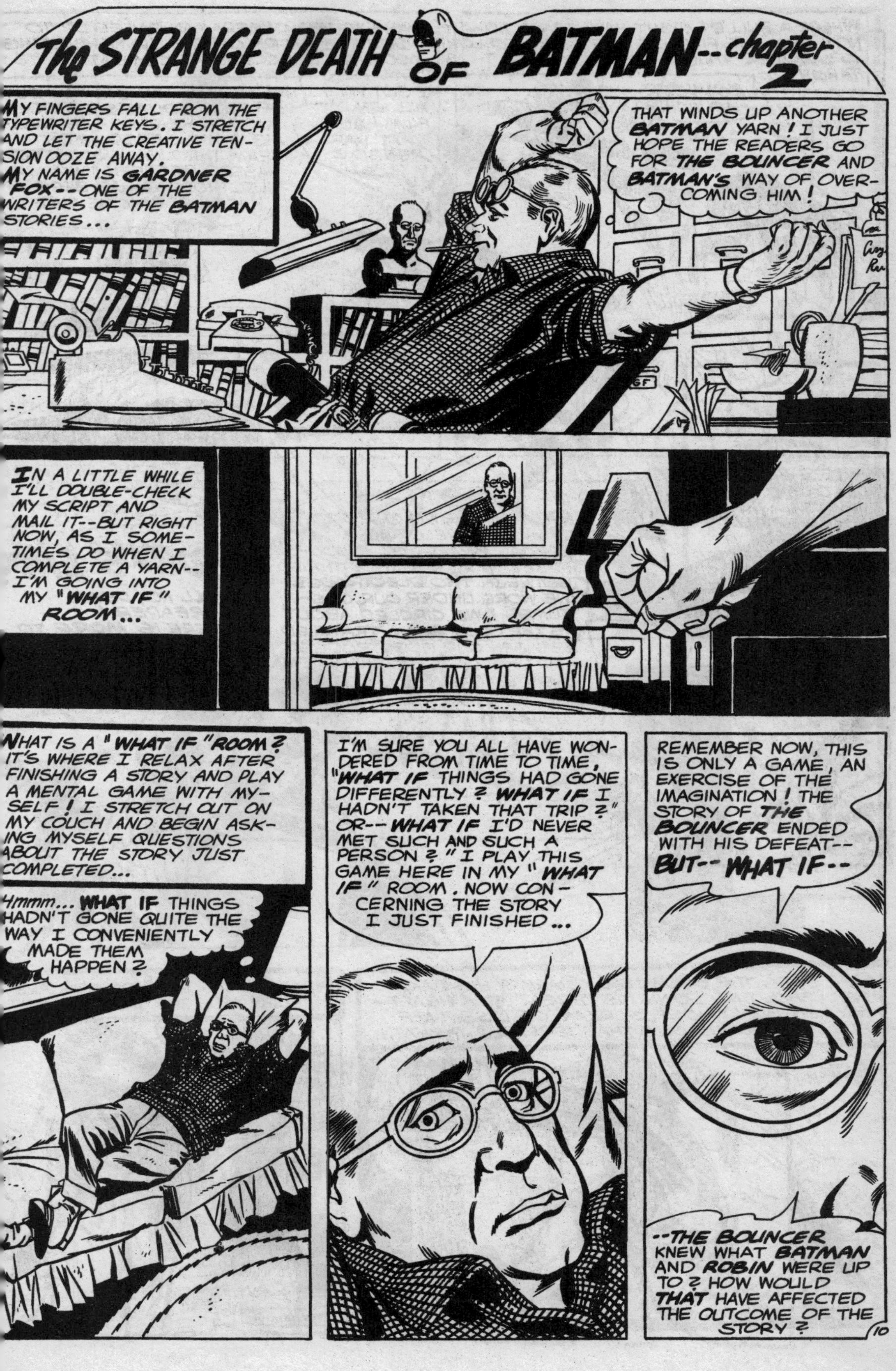
the STRANGE DEATH OF BATMAN--chapter 2
MY FINGERS FALL FROM THE TYPEWRITER KEYS. I STRETCH AND LET THE CREATIVE TENSION OOZE AWAY. MY NAME IS GARDNER FOX--ONE OF THE WRITERS OF THE BATMAN STORIES...
THAT WINDS UP ANOTHER BATMAN YARN! I JUST HOPE THE READERS GO FOR THE BOUNCER AND BATMAN'S WAY OF OVERCOMING HIM!
IN A LITTLE WHILE I'LL DOUBLE-CHECK MY SCRIPT AND MAIL IT--BUT RIGHT NOW, AS I SOMETIMES DO WHEN I COMPLETE A YARN--I'M GOING INTO MY "WHAT IF" ROOM...
WHAT IS A "WHAT IF" ROOM? IT'S WHERE I RELAX AFTER FINISHING A STORY AND PLAY A MENTAL GAME WITH MYSELF! I STRETCH OUT ON MY COUCH AND BEGIN ASKING MYSELF QUESTIONS ABOUT THE STORY JUST COMPLETED...
HMMM... WHAT IF THINGS HADN'T GONE QUITE THE WAY I CONVENIENTLY MADE THEM HAPPEN?
I'M SURE YOU ALL HAVE WONDERED FROM TIME TO TIME, "WHAT IF THINGS HAD GONE DIFFERENTLY? WHAT IF I HADN'T TAKEN THAT TRIP?" OR--WHAT IF I'D NEVER MET SUCH AND SUCH A PERSON?" I PLAY THIS GAME HERE IN MY "WHAT IF" ROOM. NOW CONCERNING THE STORY I JUST FINISHED...
REMEMBER NOW, THIS IS ONLY A GAME, AN EXERCISE OF THE IMAGINATION! THE STORY OF THE BOUNCER ENDED WITH HIS DEFEAT--BUT--WHAT IF--
--THE BOUNCER KNEW WHAT BATMAN AND ROBIN WERE UP TO? HOW WOULD THAT HAVE AFFECTED THE OUTCOME OF THE STORY?
10

COME BACK WITH ME NOW IN MY IMAGINATION TO THAT CRITICAL MOMENT WHEN *THE BOUNCER* FOUND HIMSELF BETWEEN *BAT-MAN* AND *ROBIN*, WAITING FOR THEIR FREEZER-BEAM TO DESTROY THE ELASTICITY OF THE *ELASTALLOY* UNIFORM...

WHAT'S THIS? MY HEARTBEAT-- SLOWING DOWN! I AM ONE OF THOSE MEDICAL CURIOSITIES WHO POSSESSES A *TRIPLE HEART**! THUS I CAN ALWAYS HEAR IT BEATING...

* *AUTHOR'S NOTE* SUCH RARE INSTANCES HAVE BEEN REPORTED BY *THE EPHEMERIDES* AND IN VARIOUS MEDICAL BOOKS AND JOURNALS

NATURALLY, IF SUCH WERE THE CASE, *THE BOUNCER* WOULD NOT WAIT FOR *BATMAN* TO FREEZE HIS UNIFORM! HE WOULD HURL HIS *ELASTALLOY* GUN BEFORE IT BECAME AFFECTED BY THE COLD...

MY OWN EXPERIMENTS HAVE TAUGHT ME MY HEART ONLY SLOWS DOWN WHEN IT IS VERY COLD! AND SINCE THE *ELASTALLOY* COMPOUND WILL ALSO BE AFFECTED BY INTENSE COLD-- I'D BETTER ACT NOW!

FAST IS *BATMAN* AS HE LEAPS IN--BUT EVEN FASTER IS THE BULLET FROM THE *ELASTALLOY* GUN AS IT BOUNCES OFF THE WALL...

BLAM

OFF GOES *THE BOUNCER*, SOARING HIGH AND FAR, SHOUTING DOWN HIS THREAT AT A HEART-BROKEN BOY WHOSE SCREAM OF DISBELIEF ALMOST DROWNS OUT THAT TERRIBLE THREAT...

BATMAN!!

BATMAN'S HAD IT, ROBIN! YOU'RE THE *NEXT* TO DIE--WHEN WE MEET AGAIN!

NEXT DAY THE NEWSPAPERS ARE FILLED WITH THE TRAGIC EVENT...

I'LL BRING YOUR KILLER IN, *BATMAN*, I SWEAR IT!

EXTRA BATMAN KILLED!

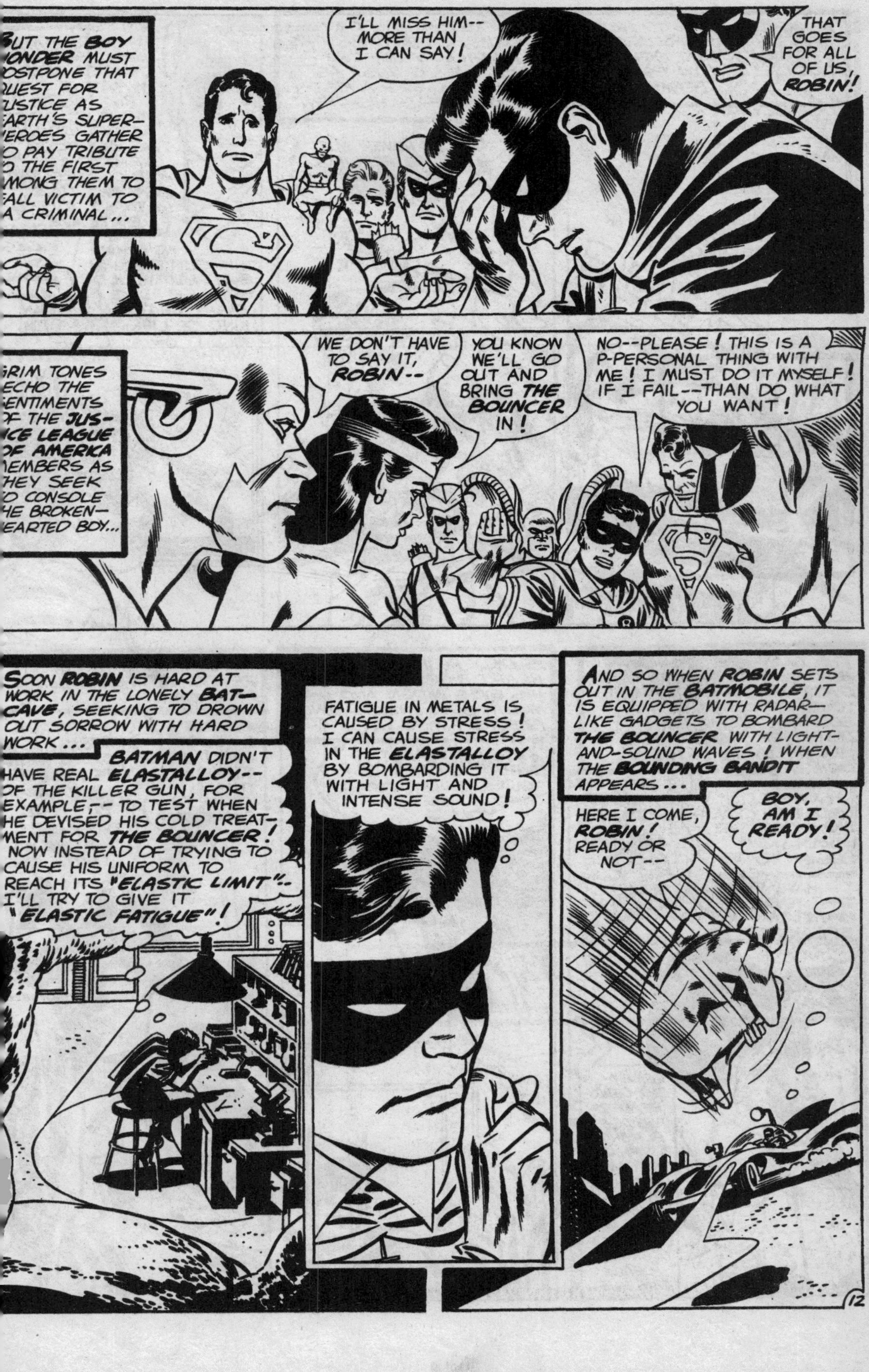
BUT THE BOY WONDER MUST POSTPONE THAT QUEST FOR JUSTICE AS EARTH'S SUPER-HEROES GATHER TO PAY TRIBUTE TO THE FIRST AMONG THEM TO FALL VICTIM TO A CRIMINAL...
I'LL MISS HIM-- MORE THAN I CAN SAY!
THAT GOES FOR ALL OF US, ROBIN!
GRIM TONES ECHO THE SENTIMENTS OF THE JUSTICE LEAGUE OF AMERICA MEMBERS AS THEY SEEK TO CONSOLE THE BROKEN-HEARTED BOY...
WE DON'T HAVE TO SAY IT, ROBIN--
YOU KNOW WE'LL GO OUT AND BRING THE BOUNCER IN!
NO--PLEASE! THIS IS A P-PERSONAL THING WITH ME! I MUST DO IT MYSELF! IF I FAIL--THAN DO WHAT YOU WANT!
SOON ROBIN IS HARD AT WORK IN THE LONELY BAT-CAVE, SEEKING TO DROWN OUT SORROW WITH HARD WORK...
BATMAN DIDN'T HAVE REAL ELASTALLOY-- OF THE KILLER GUN, FOR EXAMPLE,-- TO TEST WHEN HE DEVISED HIS COLD TREATMENT FOR THE BOUNCER! NOW INSTEAD OF TRYING TO CAUSE HIS UNIFORM TO REACH ITS "ELASTIC LIMIT"- I'LL TRY TO GIVE IT "ELASTIC FATIGUE"!
FATIGUE IN METALS IS CAUSED BY STRESS! I CAN CAUSE STRESS IN THE ELASTALLOY BY BOMBARDING IT WITH LIGHT AND INTENSE SOUND!
AND SO WHEN ROBIN SETS OUT IN THE BATMOBILE, IT IS EQUIPPED WITH RADAR-LIKE GADGETS TO BOMBARD THE BOUNCER WITH LIGHT-AND-SOUND WAVES! WHEN THE BOUNDING BANDIT APPEARS...
HERE I COME, ROBIN! READY OR NOT--
BOY, AM I READY!
12

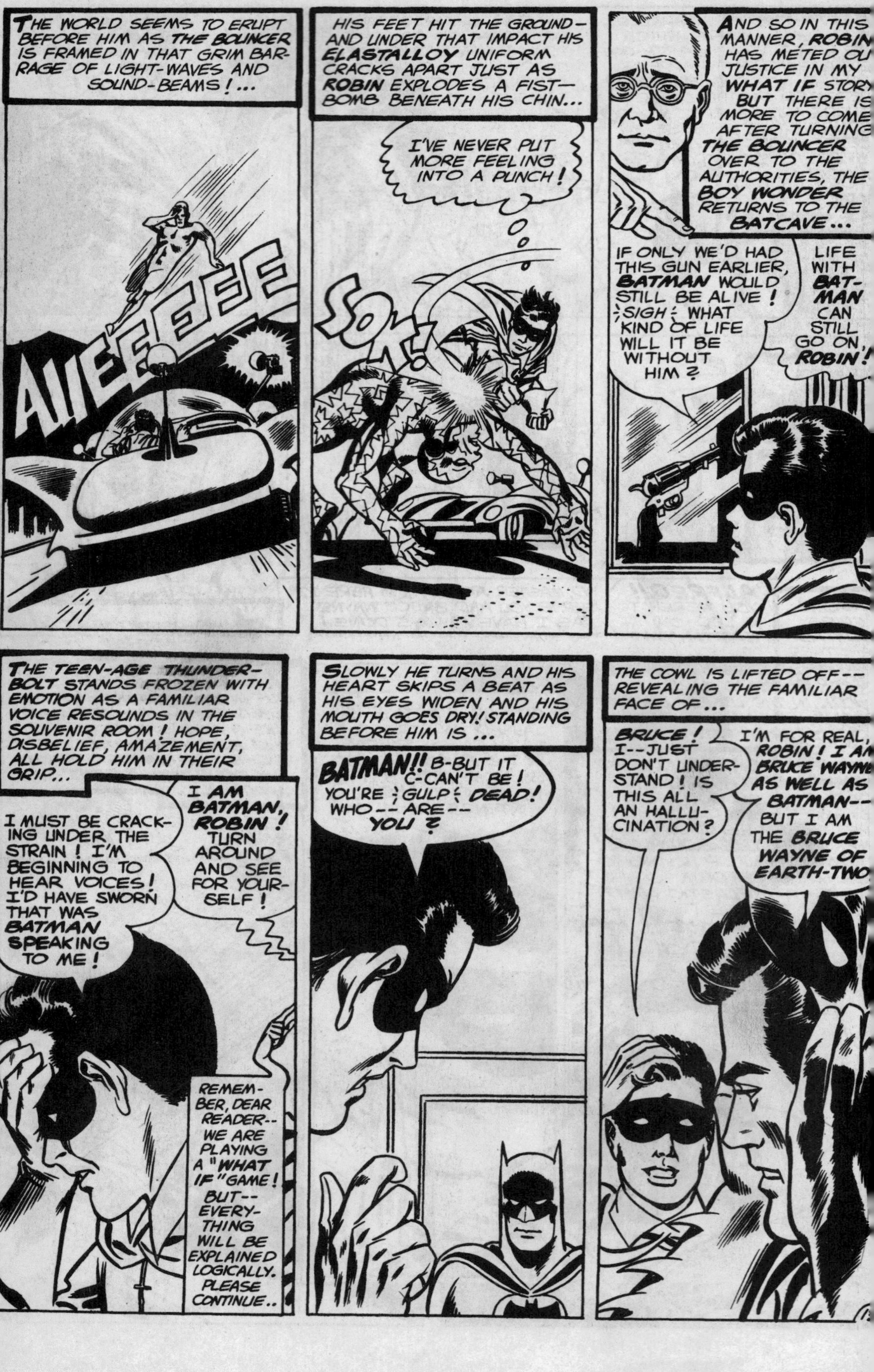
THE WORLD SEEMS TO ERUPT BEFORE HIM AS THE BOUNCER IS FRAMED IN THAT GRIM BARRAGE OF LIGHT-WAVES AND SOUND-BEAMS!...
AIIEEEEE
HIS FEET HIT THE GROUND-- AND UNDER THAT IMPACT HIS ELASTALLOY UNIFORM CRACKS APART JUST AS ROBIN EXPLODES A FIST-BOMB BENEATH HIS CHIN...
I'VE NEVER PUT MORE FEELING INTO A PUNCH!
SOK!
AND SO IN THIS MANNER, ROBIN HAS METED OU JUSTICE IN MY WHAT IF STORY BUT THERE IS MORE TO COME AFTER TURNING THE BOUNCER OVER TO THE AUTHORITIES, THE BOY WONDER RETURNS TO THE BATCAVE...
IF ONLY WE'D HAD THIS GUN EARLIER, BATMAN WOULD STILL BE ALIVE! ;SIGH; WHAT KIND OF LIFE WILL IT BE WITHOUT HIM?
LIFE WITH BATMAN CAN STILL GO ON, ROBIN!
THE TEEN-AGE THUNDERBOLT STANDS FROZEN WITH EMOTION AS A FAMILIAR VOICE RESOUNDS IN THE SOUVENIR ROOM! HOPE, DISBELIEF, AMAZEMENT, ALL HOLD HIM IN THEIR GRIP...
I MUST BE CRACKING UNDER THE STRAIN! I'M BEGINNING TO HEAR VOICES! I'D HAVE SWORN THAT WAS BATMAN SPEAKING TO ME!
I AM BATMAN, ROBIN! TURN AROUND AND SEE FOR YOURSELF!
REMEMBER, DEAR READER-- WE ARE PLAYING A "WHAT IF" GAME! BUT-- EVERYTHING WILL BE EXPLAINED LOGICALLY. PLEASE CONTINUE..
SLOWLY HE TURNS AND HIS HEART SKIPS A BEAT AS HIS EYES WIDEN AND HIS MOUTH GOES DRY! STANDING BEFORE HIM IS...
BATMAN!! B-BUT IT C-CAN'T BE! YOU'RE ;GULP; DEAD! WHO--ARE--YOU?
THE COWL IS LIFTED OFF-- REVEALING THE FAMILIAR FACE OF...
BRUCE! I--JUST DON'T UNDERSTAND! IS THIS ALL AN HALLUCINATION?
I'M FOR REAL, ROBIN! I AM BRUCE WAYNE AS WELL AS BATMAN-- BUT I AM THE BRUCE WAYNE OF EARTH-TWO

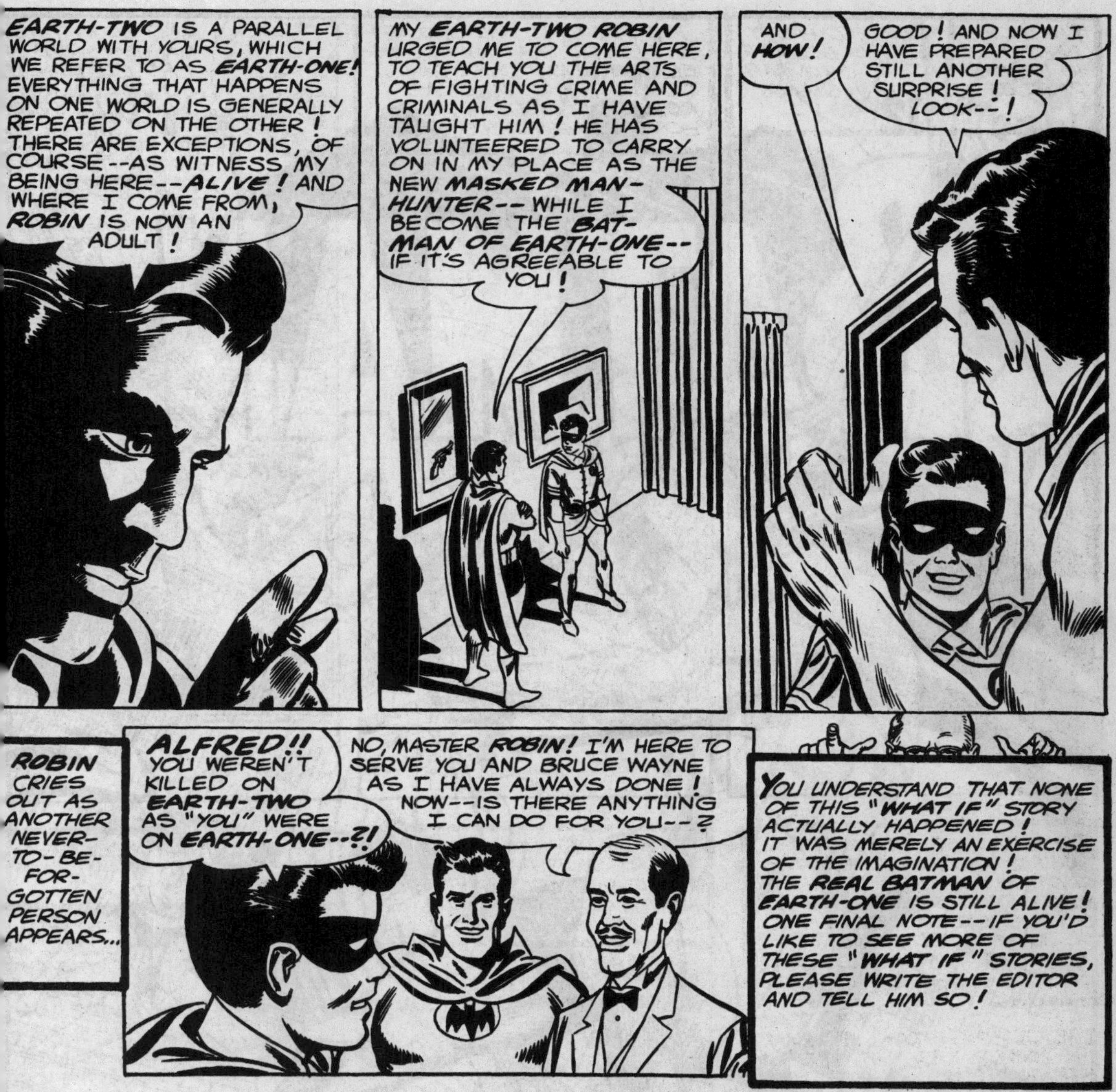
EARTH-TWO IS A PARALLEL WORLD WITH YOURS, WHICH WE REFER TO AS EARTH-ONE! EVERYTHING THAT HAPPENS ON ONE WORLD IS GENERALLY REPEATED ON THE OTHER! THERE ARE EXCEPTIONS, OF COURSE--AS WITNESS MY BEING HERE--ALIVE! AND WHERE I COME FROM, ROBIN IS NOW AN ADULT!
MY EARTH-TWO ROBIN URGED ME TO COME HERE, TO TEACH YOU THE ARTS OF FIGHTING CRIME AND CRIMINALS AS I HAVE TAUGHT HIM! HE HAS VOLUNTEERED TO CARRY ON IN MY PLACE AS THE NEW MASKED MAN-HUNTER--WHILE I BECOME THE BAT-MAN OF EARTH-ONE--IF IT'S AGREEABLE TO YOU!
AND HOW!
GOOD! AND NOW I HAVE PREPARED STILL ANOTHER SURPRISE! LOOK--!
ROBIN CRIES OUT AS ANOTHER NEVER-TO-BE-FOR-GOTTEN PERSON APPEARS...
ALFRED!! YOU WEREN'T KILLED ON EARTH-TWO AS "YOU" WERE ON EARTH-ONE--?!
NO, MASTER ROBIN! I'M HERE TO SERVE YOU AND BRUCE WAYNE AS I HAVE ALWAYS DONE! NOW--IS THERE ANYTHING I CAN DO FOR YOU--?
YOU UNDERSTAND THAT NONE OF THIS "WHAT IF" STORY ACTUALLY HAPPENED! IT WAS MERELY AN EXERCISE OF THE IMAGINATION! THE REAL BATMAN OF EARTH-ONE IS STILL ALIVE! ONE FINAL NOTE--IF YOU'D LIKE TO SEE MORE OF THESE "WHAT IF" STORIES, PLEASE WRITE THE EDITOR AND TELL HIM SO!

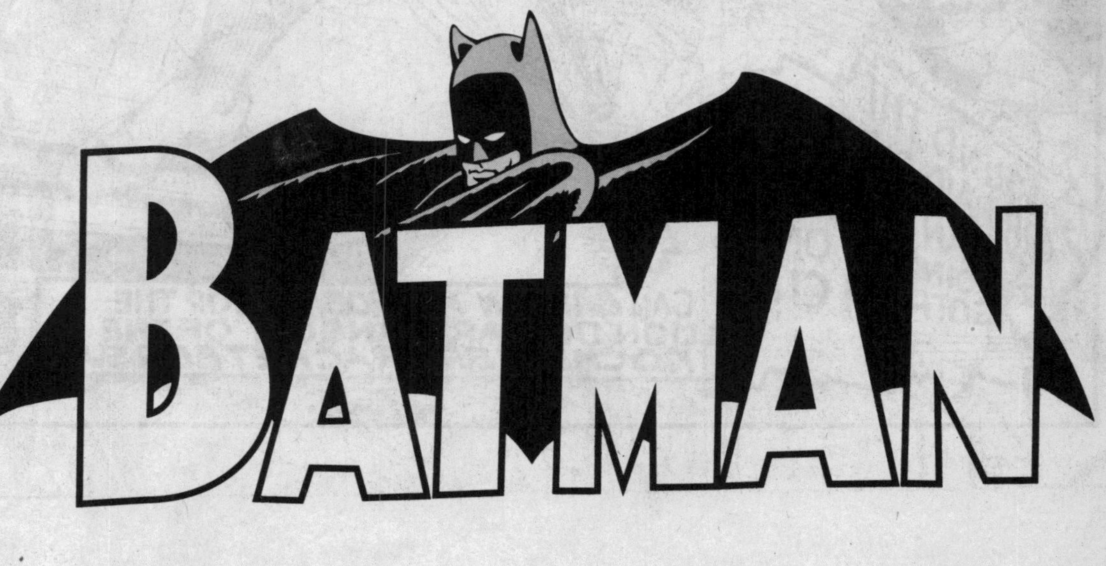
BATMAN

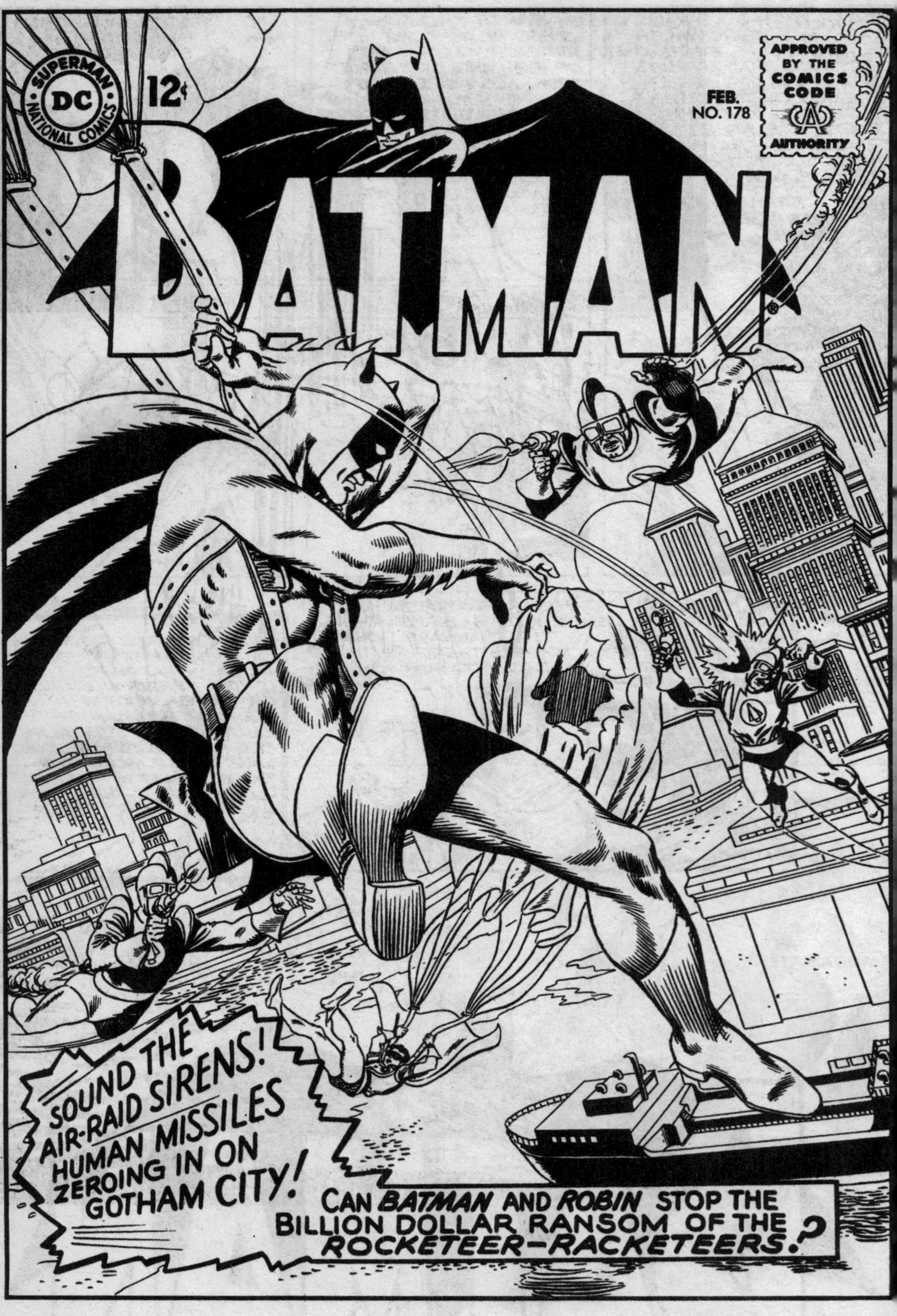
SUPERMAN DC NATIONAL COMICS
12¢
APPROVED BY THE COMICS CODE AUTHORITY
FEB. NO. 178
BATMAN
SOUND THE AIR-RAID SIRENS! HUMAN MISSILES ZEROING IN ON GOTHAM CITY!
CAN BATMAN AND ROBIN STOP THE BILLION DOLLAR RANSOM OF THE ROCKETEER-RACKETEERS?

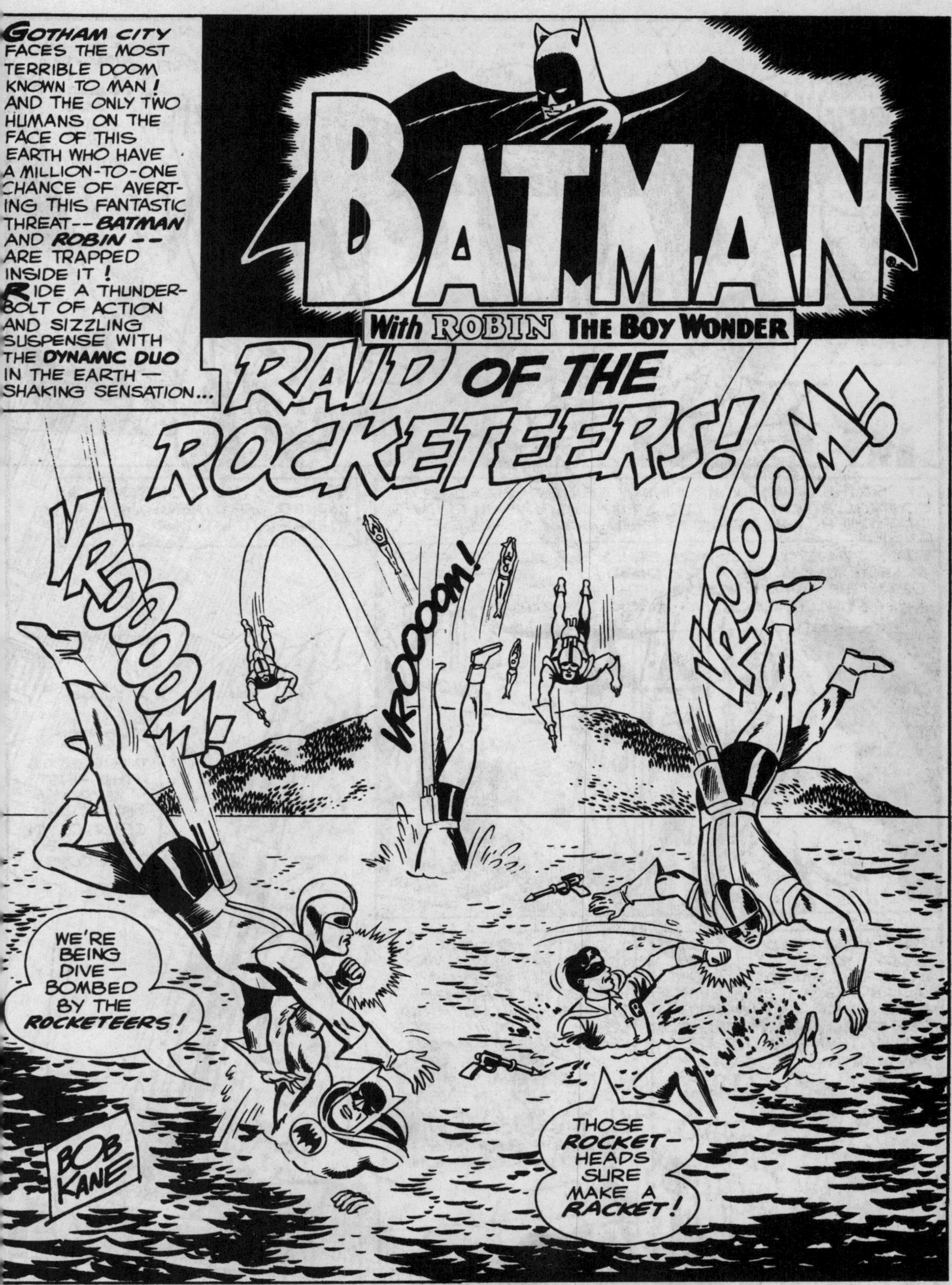
GOTHAM CITY FACES THE MOST TERRIBLE DOOM KNOWN TO MAN! AND THE ONLY TWO HUMANS ON THE FACE OF THIS EARTH WHO HAVE A MILLION-TO-ONE CHANCE OF AVERTING THIS FANTASTIC THREAT--BATMAN AND ROBIN--ARE TRAPPED INSIDE IT! RIDE A THUNDERBOLT OF ACTION AND SIZZLING SUSPENSE WITH THE DYNAMIC DUO IN THE EARTH-SHAKING SENSATION...
BATMAN
With ROBIN THE BOY WONDER
RAID OF THE ROCKETEERS!
VROOOOM!
VROOOOM!
VROOOM!
WE'RE BEING DIVE-BOMBED BY THE ROCKETEERS!
BOB KANE
THOSE ROCKET-HEADS SURE MAKE A RACKET!

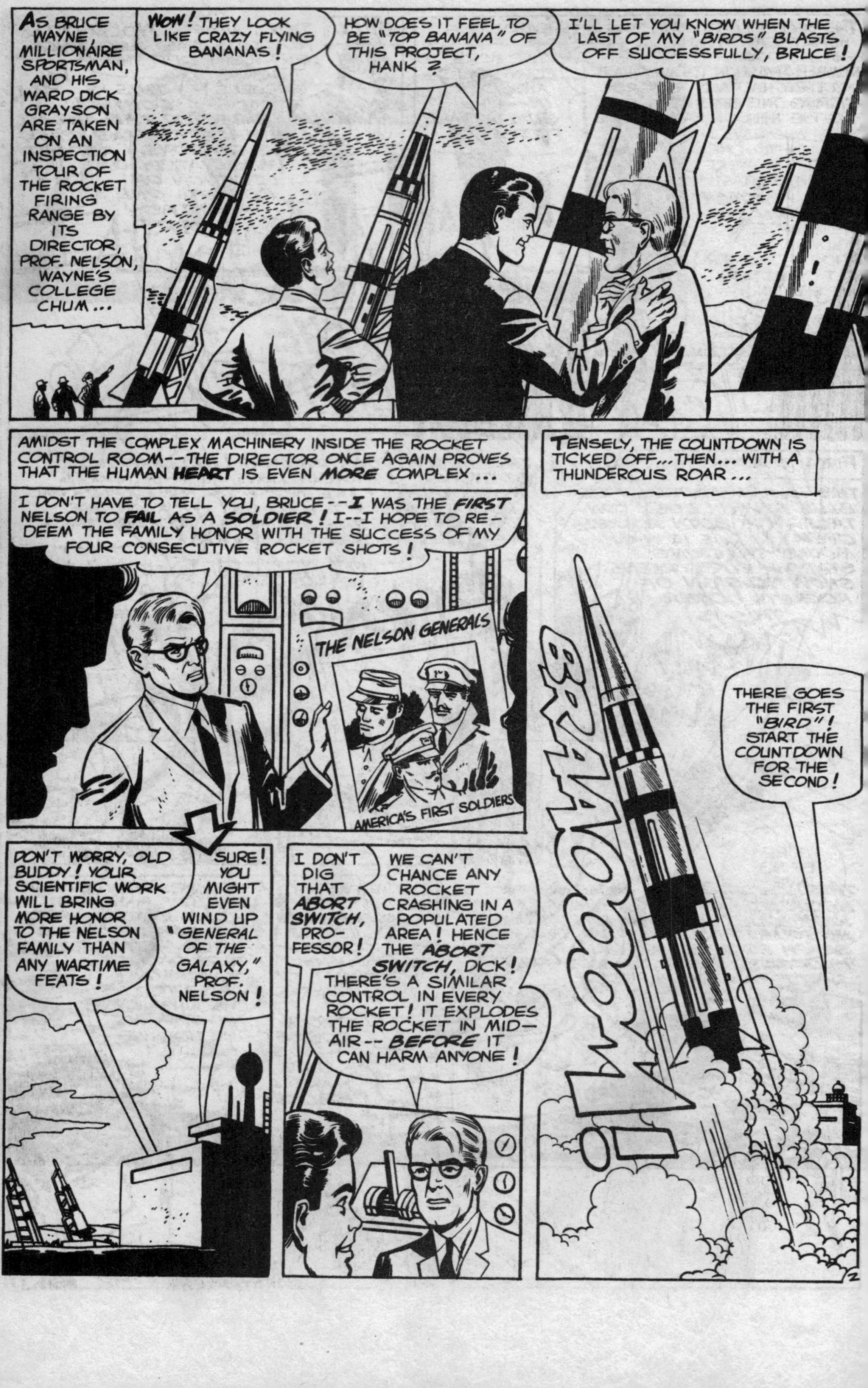
AS BRUCE WAYNE, MILLIONAIRE SPORTSMAN, AND HIS WARD DICK GRAYSON ARE TAKEN ON AN INSPECTION TOUR OF THE ROCKET FIRING RANGE BY ITS DIRECTOR, PROF. NELSON, WAYNE'S COLLEGE CHUM...
WOW! THEY LOOK LIKE CRAZY FLYING BANANAS!
HOW DOES IT FEEL TO BE "TOP BANANA" OF THIS PROJECT, HANK?
I'LL LET YOU KNOW WHEN THE LAST OF MY "BIRDS" BLASTS OFF SUCCESSFULLY, BRUCE!
AMIDST THE COMPLEX MACHINERY INSIDE THE ROCKET CONTROL ROOM--THE DIRECTOR ONCE AGAIN PROVES THAT THE HUMAN HEART IS EVEN MORE COMPLEX...
I DON'T HAVE TO TELL YOU, BRUCE--I WAS THE FIRST NELSON TO FAIL AS A SOLDIER! I--I HOPE TO REDEEM THE FAMILY HONOR WITH THE SUCCESS OF MY FOUR CONSECUTIVE ROCKET SHOTS!
THE NELSON GENERALS
AMERICA'S FIRST SOLDIERS
DON'T WORRY, OLD BUDDY! YOUR SCIENTIFIC WORK WILL BRING MORE HONOR TO THE NELSON FAMILY THAN ANY WARTIME FEATS!
SURE! YOU MIGHT EVEN WIND UP "GENERAL OF THE GALAXY," PROF. NELSON!
I DON'T DIG THAT ABORT SWITCH, PROFESSOR!
WE CAN'T CHANCE ANY ROCKET CRASHING IN A POPULATED AREA! HENCE THE ABORT SWITCH, DICK! THERE'S A SIMILAR CONTROL IN EVERY ROCKET! IT EXPLODES THE ROCKET IN MID-AIR--BEFORE IT CAN HARM ANYONE!
TENSELY, THE COUNTDOWN IS TICKED OFF...THEN...WITH A THUNDEROUS ROAR...
BRAAOOOM!
THERE GOES THE FIRST "BIRD"! START THE COUNTDOWN FOR THE SECOND!
2

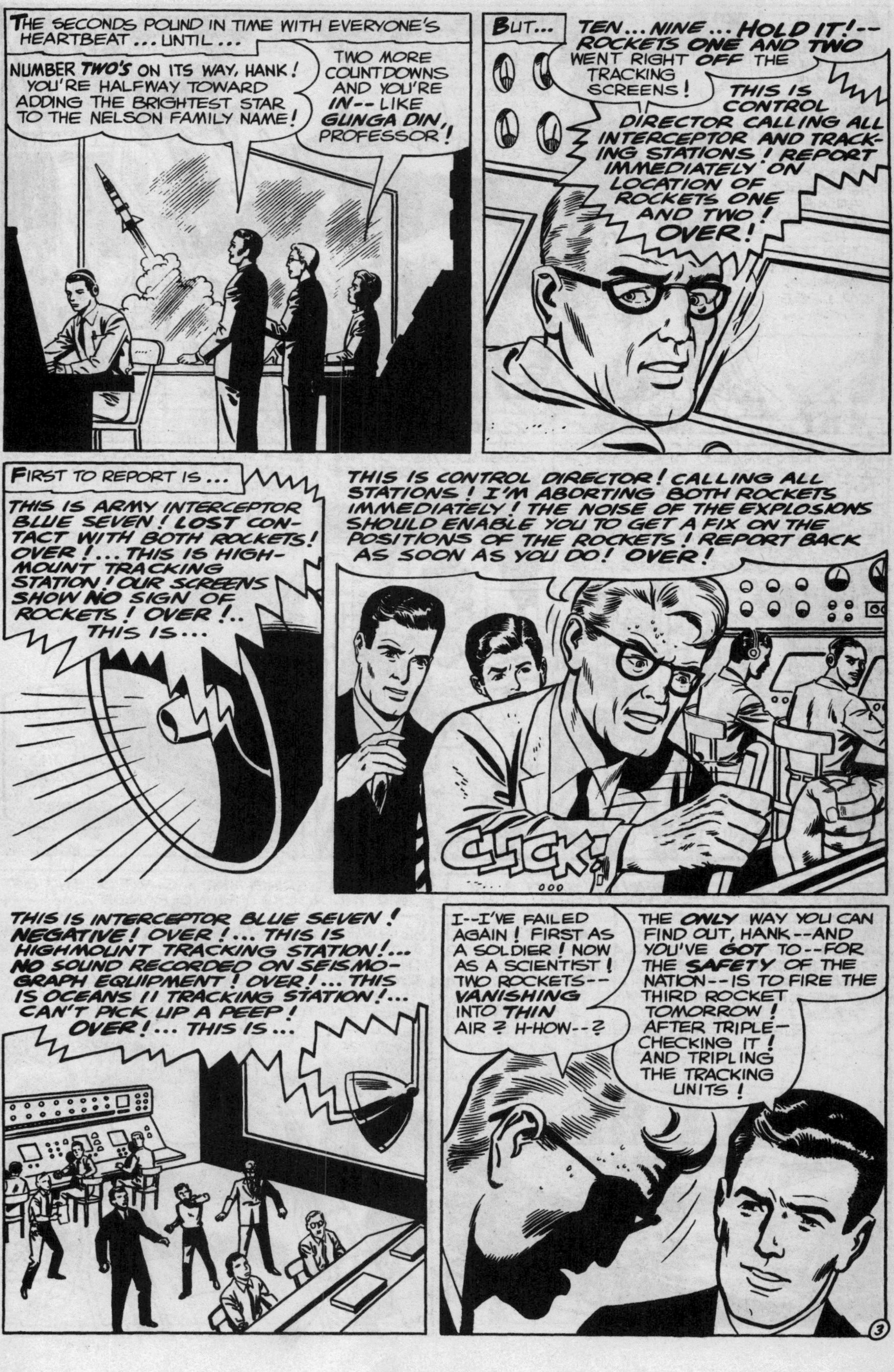
THE SECONDS POUND IN TIME WITH EVERYONE'S HEARTBEAT ... UNTIL ...
NUMBER TWO'S ON ITS WAY, HANK! YOU'RE HALFWAY TOWARD ADDING THE BRIGHTEST STAR TO THE NELSON FAMILY NAME!
TWO MORE COUNTDOWNS AND YOU'RE IN--LIKE GUNGA DIN, PROFESSOR!
BUT...
TEN ... NINE ... HOLD IT!--ROCKETS ONE AND TWO WENT RIGHT OFF THE TRACKING SCREENS!
THIS IS CONTROL DIRECTOR CALLING ALL INTERCEPTOR AND TRACKING STATIONS! REPORT IMMEDIATELY ON LOCATION OF ROCKETS ONE AND TWO! OVER!
FIRST TO REPORT IS ...
THIS IS ARMY INTERCEPTOR BLUE SEVEN! LOST CONTACT WITH BOTH ROCKETS! OVER! ... THIS IS HIGHMOUNT TRACKING STATION! OUR SCREENS SHOW NO SIGN OF ROCKETS! OVER!.. THIS IS...
THIS IS CONTROL DIRECTOR! CALLING ALL STATIONS! I'M ABORTING BOTH ROCKETS IMMEDIATELY! THE NOISE OF THE EXPLOSIONS SHOULD ENABLE YOU TO GET A FIX ON THE POSITIONS OF THE ROCKETS! REPORT BACK AS SOON AS YOU DO! OVER!
CLICK!
THIS IS INTERCEPTOR BLUE SEVEN! NEGATIVE! OVER! ... THIS IS HIGHMOUNT TRACKING STATION!... NO SOUND RECORDED ON SEISMOGRAPH EQUIPMENT! OVER! ... THIS IS OCEANS 11 TRACKING STATION!... CAN'T PICK UP A PEEP! OVER! ... THIS IS ...
I--I'VE FAILED AGAIN! FIRST AS A SOLDIER! NOW AS A SCIENTIST! TWO ROCKETS--VANISHING INTO THIN AIR? H-HOW--?
THE ONLY WAY YOU CAN FIND OUT, HANK--AND YOU'VE GOT TO--FOR THE SAFETY OF THE NATION--IS TO FIRE THE THIRD ROCKET TOMORROW! AFTER TRIPLE-CHECKING IT! AND TRIPLING THE TRACKING UNITS!
3

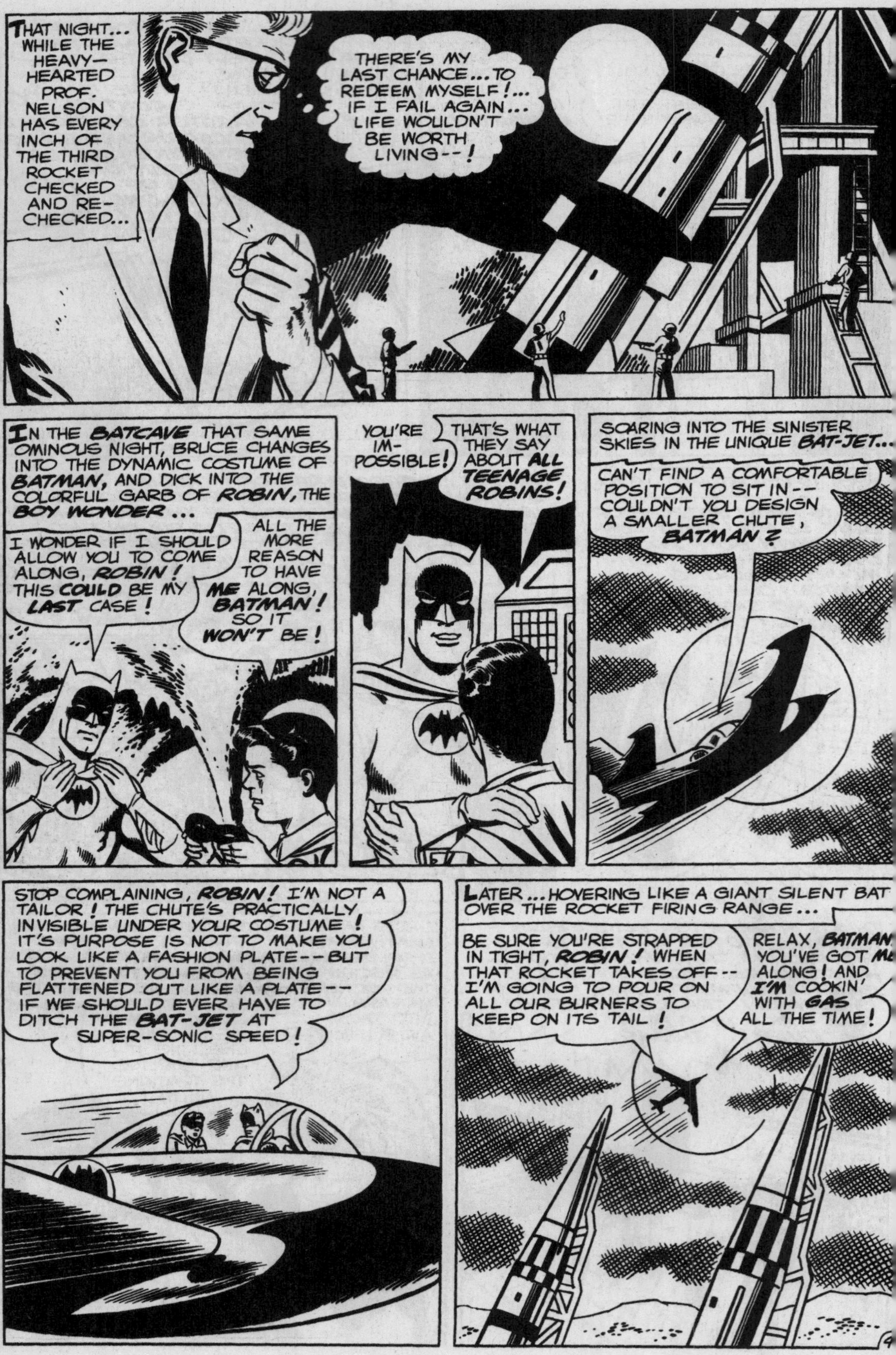
THAT NIGHT... WHILE THE HEAVY-HEARTED PROF. NELSON HAS EVERY INCH OF THE THIRD ROCKET CHECKED AND RE-CHECKED...
THERE'S MY LAST CHANCE... TO REDEEM MYSELF!... IF I FAIL AGAIN... LIFE WOULDN'T BE WORTH LIVING--!
IN THE BATCAVE THAT SAME OMINOUS NIGHT, BRUCE CHANGES INTO THE DYNAMIC COSTUME OF BATMAN, AND DICK INTO THE COLORFUL GARB OF ROBIN, THE BOY WONDER...
I WONDER IF I SHOULD ALLOW YOU TO COME ALONG, ROBIN! THIS COULD BE MY LAST CASE!
ALL THE MORE REASON TO HAVE ME ALONG, BATMAN! SO IT WON'T BE!
YOU'RE IM-POSSIBLE!
THAT'S WHAT THEY SAY ABOUT ALL TEENAGE ROBINS!
SOARING INTO THE SINISTER SKIES IN THE UNIQUE BAT-JET...
CAN'T FIND A COMFORTABLE POSITION TO SIT IN--COULDN'T YOU DESIGN A SMALLER CHUTE, BATMAN?
STOP COMPLAINING, ROBIN! I'M NOT A TAILOR! THE CHUTE'S PRACTICALLY INVISIBLE UNDER YOUR COSTUME! IT'S PURPOSE IS NOT TO MAKE YOU LOOK LIKE A FASHION PLATE--BUT TO PREVENT YOU FROM BEING FLATTENED OUT LIKE A PLATE--IF WE SHOULD EVER HAVE TO DITCH THE BAT-JET AT SUPER-SONIC SPEED!
LATER... HOVERING LIKE A GIANT SILENT BAT OVER THE ROCKET FIRING RANGE...
BE SURE YOU'RE STRAPPED IN TIGHT, ROBIN! WHEN THAT ROCKET TAKES OFF--I'M GOING TO POUR ON ALL OUR BURNERS TO KEEP ON ITS TAIL!
RELAX, BATMAN! YOU'VE GOT ME ALONG! AND I'M COOKIN' WITH GAS ALL THE TIME!
4

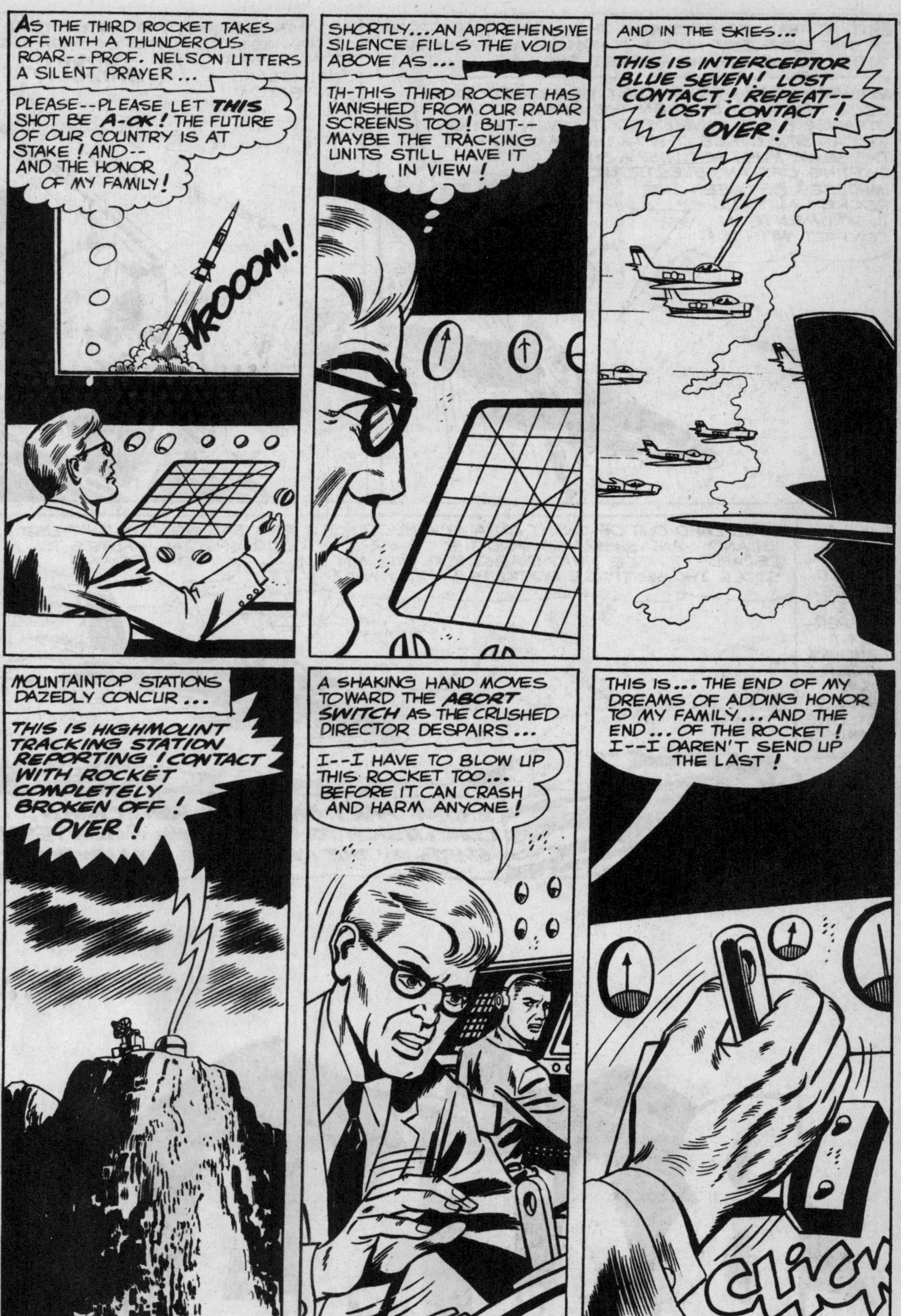
AS THE THIRD ROCKET TAKES OFF WITH A THUNDEROUS ROAR--PROF. NELSON UTTERS A SILENT PRAYER...
PLEASE--PLEASE LET THIS SHOT BE A-OK! THE FUTURE OF OUR COUNTRY IS AT STAKE! AND--AND THE HONOR OF MY FAMILY!
VROOOM!
SHORTLY...AN APPREHENSIVE SILENCE FILLS THE VOID ABOVE AS...
TH-THIS THIRD ROCKET HAS VANISHED FROM OUR RADAR SCREENS TOO! BUT--MAYBE THE TRACKING UNITS STILL HAVE IT IN VIEW!
AND IN THE SKIES...
THIS IS INTERCEPTOR BLUE SEVEN! LOST CONTACT! REPEAT--LOST CONTACT! OVER!
MOUNTAINTOP STATIONS DAZEDLY CONCUR...
THIS IS HIGHMOUNT TRACKING STATION REPORTING! CONTACT WITH ROCKET COMPLETELY BROKEN OFF! OVER!
A SHAKING HAND MOVES TOWARD THE ABORT SWITCH AS THE CRUSHED DIRECTOR DESPAIRS...
I--I HAVE TO BLOW UP THIS ROCKET TOO... BEFORE IT CAN CRASH AND HARM ANYONE!
THIS IS... THE END OF MY DREAMS OF ADDING HONOR TO MY FAMILY... AND THE END... OF THE ROCKET! I--I DAREN'T SEND UP THE LAST!
CLICK
5

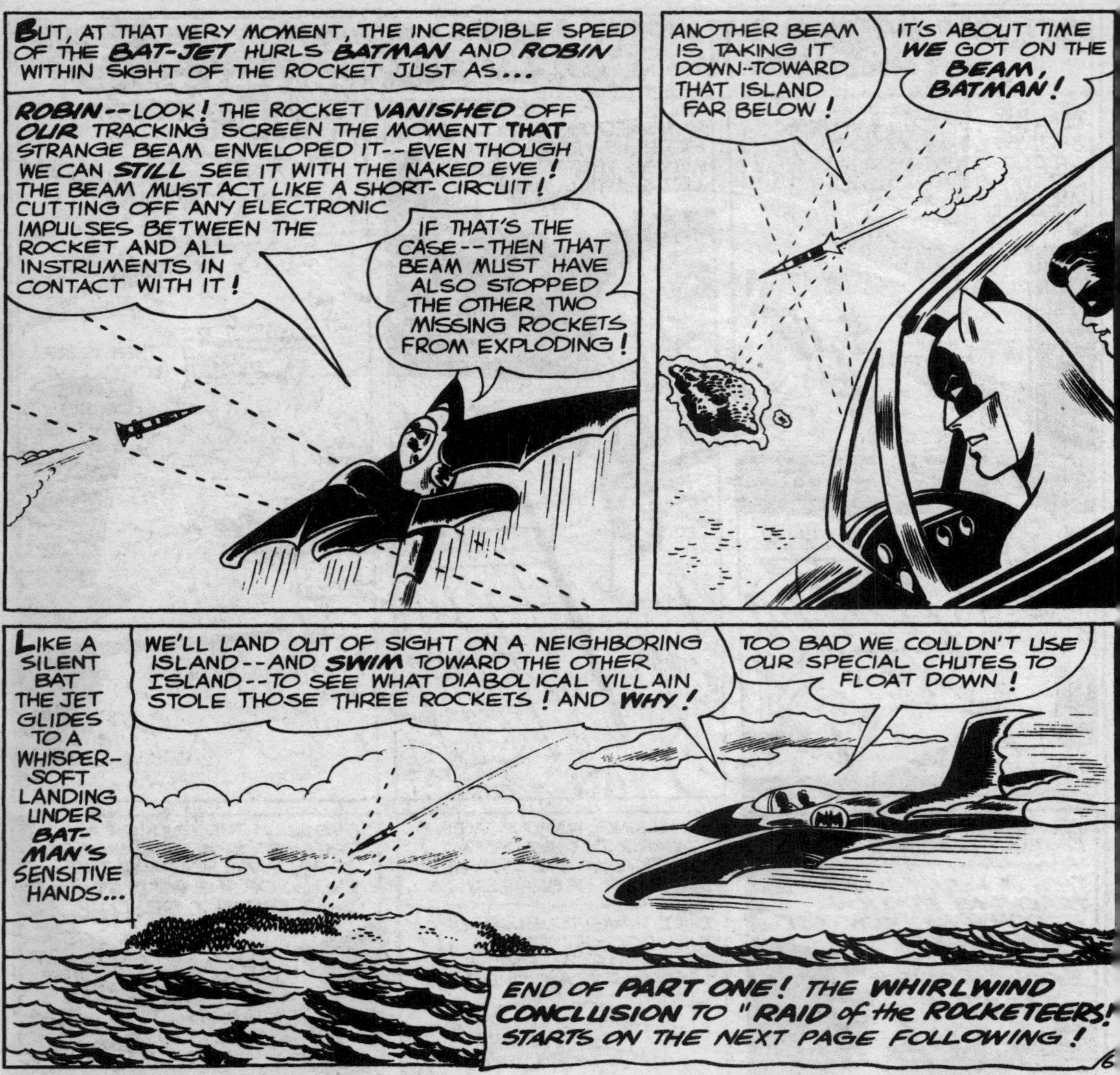
BUT, AT THAT VERY MOMENT, THE INCREDIBLE SPEED OF THE BAT-JET HURLS BATMAN AND ROBIN WITHIN SIGHT OF THE ROCKET JUST AS...
ROBIN--LOOK! THE ROCKET VANISHED OFF OUR TRACKING SCREEN THE MOMENT THAT STRANGE BEAM ENVELOPED IT--EVEN THOUGH WE CAN STILL SEE IT WITH THE NAKED EYE! THE BEAM MUST ACT LIKE A SHORT-CIRCUIT! CUTTING OFF ANY ELECTRONIC IMPULSES BETWEEN THE ROCKET AND ALL INSTRUMENTS IN CONTACT WITH IT!
IF THAT'S THE CASE--THEN THAT BEAM MUST HAVE ALSO STOPPED THE OTHER TWO MISSING ROCKETS FROM EXPLODING!
ANOTHER BEAM IS TAKING IT DOWN--TOWARD THAT ISLAND FAR BELOW!
IT'S ABOUT TIME WE GOT ON THE BEAM, BATMAN!
LIKE A SILENT BAT THE JET GLIDES TO A WHISPER-SOFT LANDING UNDER BATMAN'S SENSITIVE HANDS...
WE'LL LAND OUT OF SIGHT ON A NEIGHBORING ISLAND--AND SWIM TOWARD THE OTHER ISLAND--TO SEE WHAT DIABOLICAL VILLAIN STOLE THOSE THREE ROCKETS! AND WHY!
TOO BAD WE COULDN'T USE OUR SPECIAL CHUTES TO FLOAT DOWN!
END OF PART ONE! THE WHIRLWIND CONCLUSION TO "RAID of the ROCKETEERS!" STARTS ON THE NEXT PAGE FOLLOWING!
6

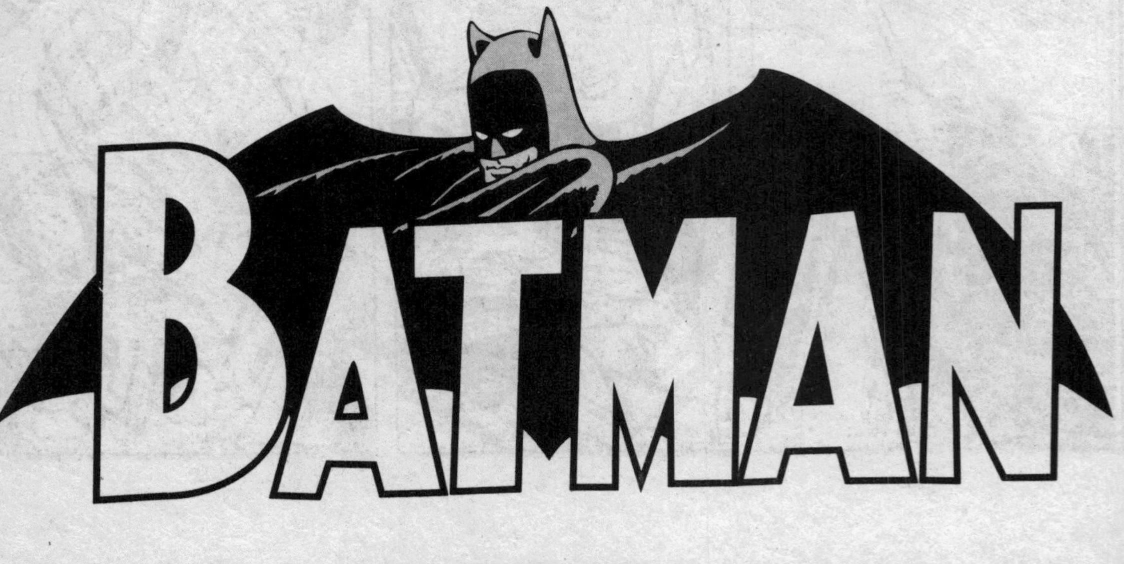
BATMAN

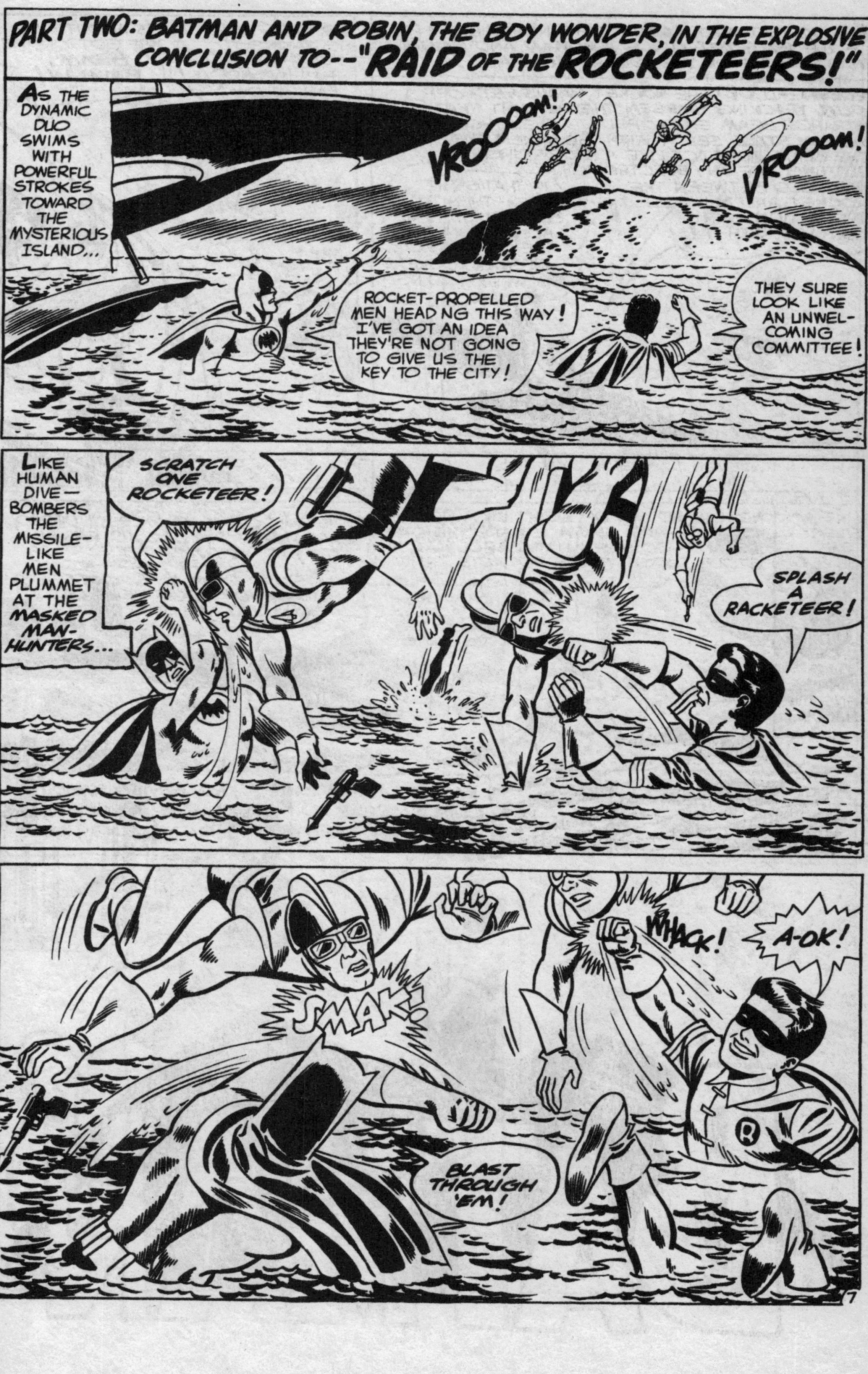
PART TWO: BATMAN AND ROBIN, THE BOY WONDER, IN THE EXPLOSIVE CONCLUSION TO--"RAID OF THE ROCKETEERS!"
AS THE DYNAMIC DUO SWIMS WITH POWERFUL STROKES TOWARD THE MYSTERIOUS ISLAND...
VROOOOOM!
VROOOOM!
ROCKET-PROPELLED MEN HEAD NG THIS WAY! I'VE GOT AN IDEA THEY'RE NOT GOING TO GIVE US THE KEY TO THE CITY!
THEY SURE LOOK LIKE AN UNWEL-COMING COMMITTEE!
LIKE HUMAN DIVE-BOMBERS THE MISSILE-LIKE MEN PLUMMET AT THE MASKED MAN-HUNTERS...
SCRATCH ONE ROCKETEER!
SPLASH A RACKETEER!
SMAK!
WHACK!
A-OK!
BLAST THROUGH 'EM!
7

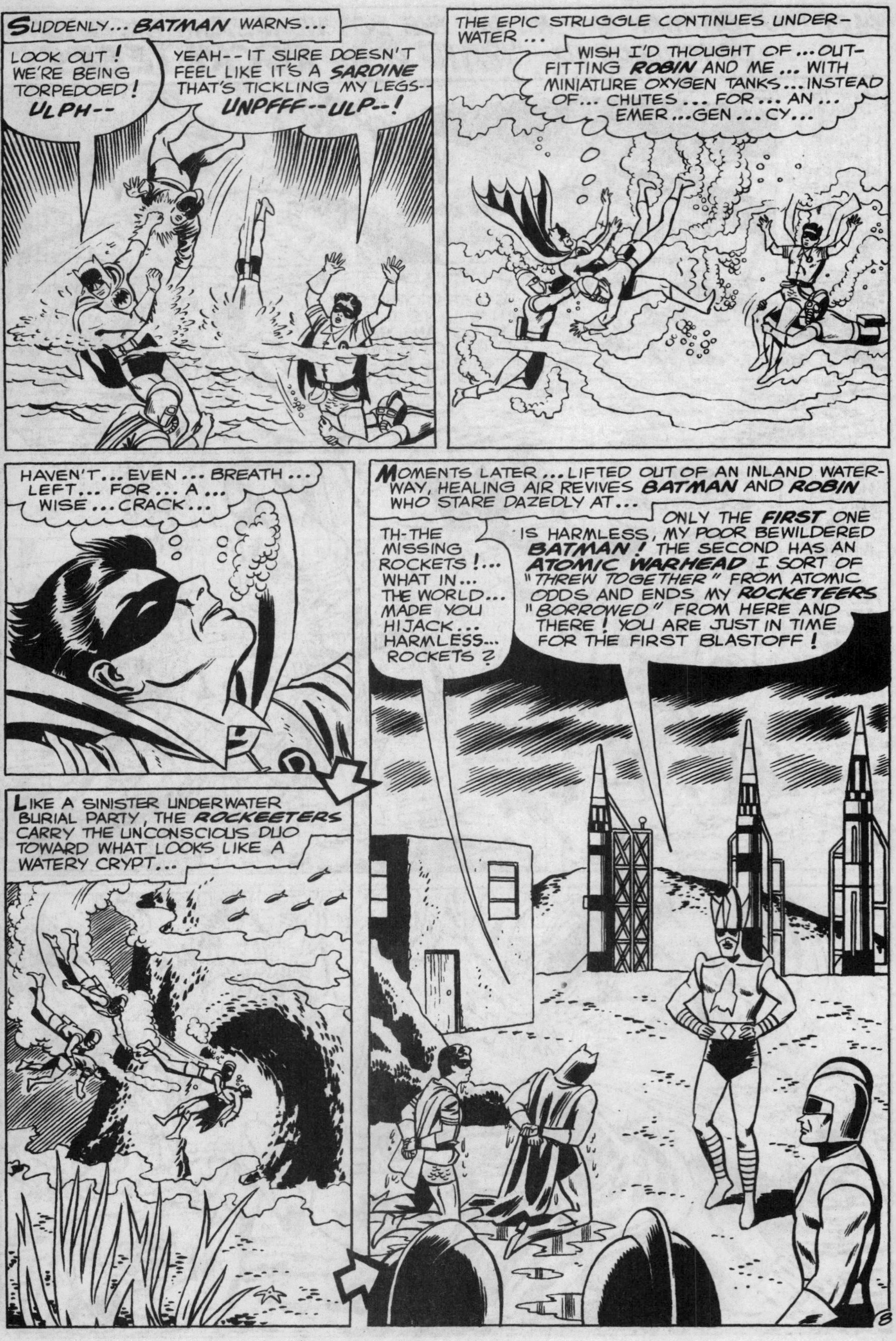
SUDDENLY... BATMAN WARNS...
LOOK OUT! WE'RE BEING TORPEDOED! ULPH--
YEAH--IT SURE DOESN'T FEEL LIKE IT'S A SARDINE THAT'S TICKLING MY LEGS-- UNPFFF--ULP--!
THE EPIC STRUGGLE CONTINUES UNDER-WATER...
WISH I'D THOUGHT OF ...OUT-FITTING ROBIN AND ME... WITH MINIATURE OXYGEN TANKS...INSTEAD OF... CHUTES... FOR... AN... EMER...GEN...CY...
HAVEN'T... EVEN... BREATH... LEFT... FOR... A... WISE... CRACK...
LIKE A SINISTER UNDERWATER BURIAL PARTY, THE ROCKEETERS CARRY THE UNCONSCIOUS DUO TOWARD WHAT LOOKS LIKE A WATERY CRYPT...
MOMENTS LATER... LIFTED OUT OF AN INLAND WATER-WAY, HEALING AIR REVIVES BATMAN AND ROBIN WHO STARE DAZEDLY AT...
TH-THE MISSING ROCKETS!... WHAT IN... THE WORLD... MADE YOU HIJACK... HARMLESS... ROCKETS?
ONLY THE FIRST ONE IS HARMLESS, MY POOR BEWILDERED BATMAN! THE SECOND HAS AN ATOMIC WARHEAD I SORT OF "THREW TOGETHER" FROM ATOMIC ODDS AND ENDS MY ROCKETEERS "BORROWED" FROM HERE AND THERE! YOU ARE JUST IN TIME FOR THE FIRST BLASTOFF!
8

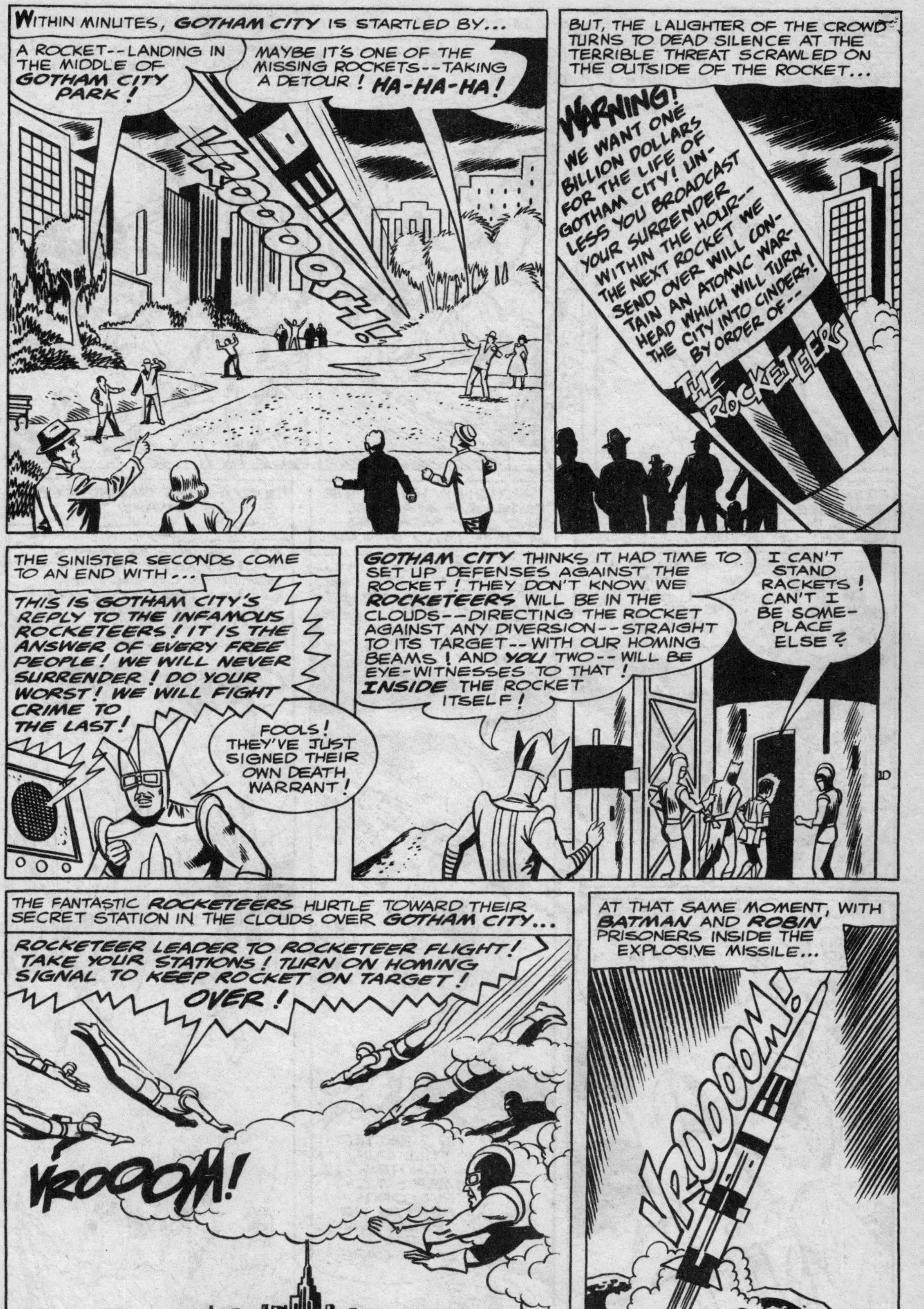
WITHIN MINUTES, GOTHAM CITY IS STARTLED BY...
A ROCKET--LANDING IN THE MIDDLE OF GOTHAM CITY PARK!
MAYBE IT'S ONE OF THE MISSING ROCKETS--TAKING A DETOUR! HA-HA-HA!
VROOOOOOOSH!
BUT, THE LAUGHTER OF THE CROWD TURNS TO DEAD SILENCE AT THE TERRIBLE THREAT SCRAWLED ON THE OUTSIDE OF THE ROCKET...
WARNING! WE WANT ONE BILLION DOLLARS FOR THE LIFE OF GOTHAM CITY! UNLESS YOU BROADCAST YOUR SURRENDER WITHIN THE HOUR--THE NEXT ROCKET WE SEND OVER WILL CONTAIN AN ATOMIC WARHEAD WHICH WILL TURN THE CITY INTO CINDERS! BY ORDER OF--
THE ROCKETEERS
THE SINISTER SECONDS COME TO AN END WITH...
THIS IS GOTHAM CITY'S REPLY TO THE INFAMOUS ROCKETEERS! IT IS THE ANSWER OF EVERY FREE PEOPLE! WE WILL NEVER SURRENDER! DO YOUR WORST! WE WILL FIGHT CRIME TO THE LAST!
FOOLS! THEY'VE JUST SIGNED THEIR OWN DEATH WARRANT!
GOTHAM CITY THINKS IT HAD TIME TO SET UP DEFENSES AGAINST THE ROCKET! THEY DON'T KNOW WE ROCKETEERS WILL BE IN THE CLOUDS--DIRECTING THE ROCKET AGAINST ANY DIVERSION--STRAIGHT TO ITS TARGET--WITH OUR HOMING BEAMS! AND YOU TWO--WILL BE EYE-WITNESSES TO THAT! INSIDE THE ROCKET ITSELF!
I CAN'T STAND RACKETS! CAN'T I BE SOME-PLACE ELSE?
THE FANTASTIC ROCKETEERS HURTLE TOWARD THEIR SECRET STATION IN THE CLOUDS OVER GOTHAM CITY...
ROCKETEER LEADER TO ROCKETEER FLIGHT! TAKE YOUR STATIONS! TURN ON HOMING SIGNAL TO KEEP ROCKET ON TARGET! OVER!
VROOOOM!
AT THAT SAME MOMENT, WITH BATMAN AND ROBIN PRISONERS INSIDE THE EXPLOSIVE MISSILE...
VROOOOOM!
9

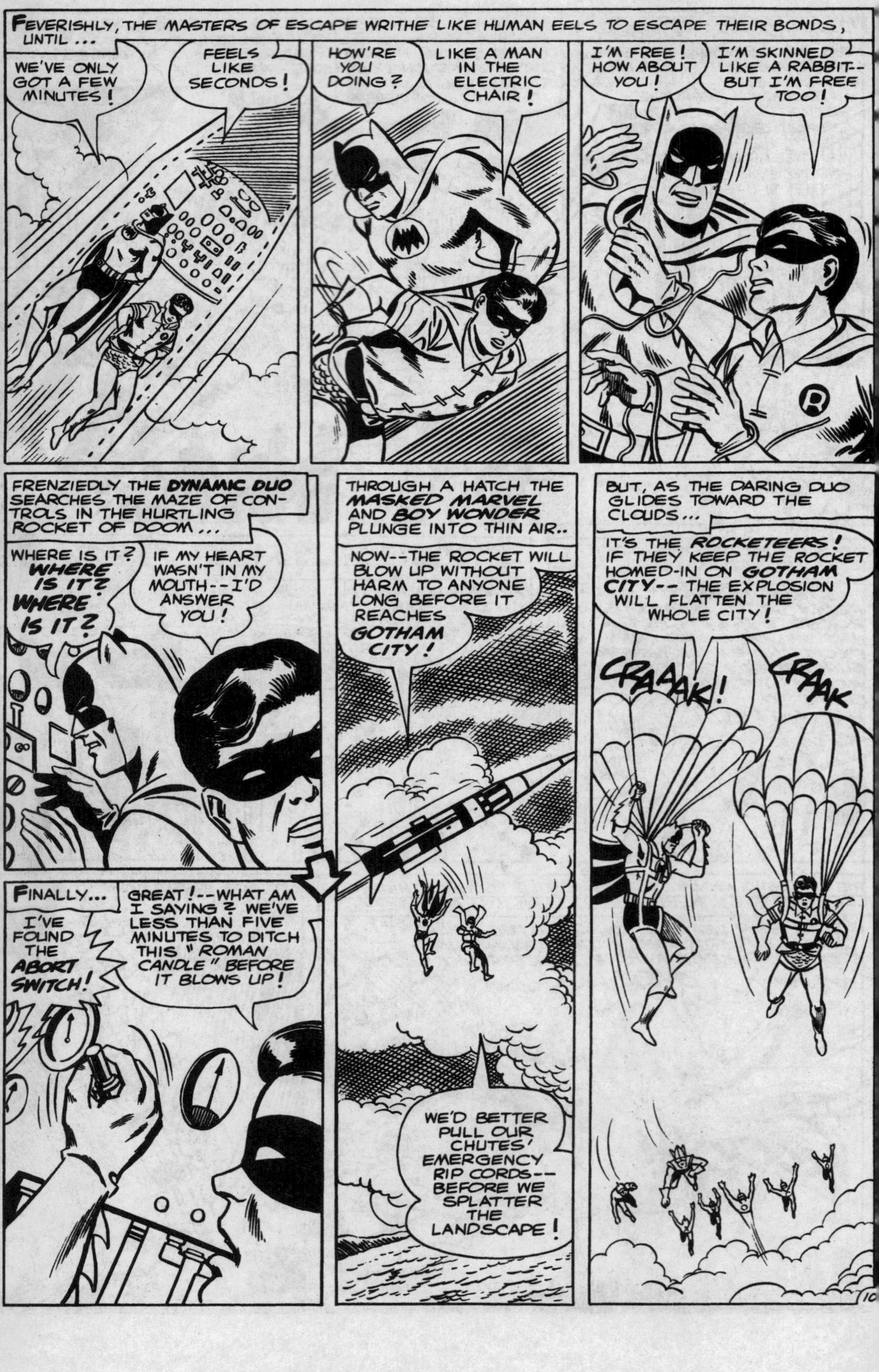
FEVERISHLY, THE MASTERS OF ESCAPE WRITHE LIKE HUMAN EELS TO ESCAPE THEIR BONDS, UNTIL ...
WE'VE ONLY GOT A FEW MINUTES!
FEELS LIKE SECONDS!
HOW'RE YOU DOING?
LIKE A MAN IN THE ELECTRIC CHAIR!
I'M FREE! HOW ABOUT YOU!
I'M SKINNED LIKE A RABBIT-- BUT I'M FREE TOO!
FRENZIEDLY THE DYNAMIC DUO SEARCHES THE MAZE OF CONTROLS IN THE HURTLING ROCKET OF DOOM ...
WHERE IS IT? WHERE IS IT? WHERE IS IT?
IF MY HEART WASN'T IN MY MOUTH--I'D ANSWER YOU!
FINALLY...
I'VE FOUND THE ABORT SWITCH!
GREAT!--WHAT AM I SAYING? WE'VE LESS THAN FIVE MINUTES TO DITCH THIS "ROMAN CANDLE" BEFORE IT BLOWS UP!
THROUGH A HATCH THE MASKED MARVEL AND BOY WONDER PLUNGE INTO THIN AIR..
NOW--THE ROCKET WILL BLOW UP WITHOUT HARM TO ANYONE LONG BEFORE IT REACHES GOTHAM CITY!
WE'D BETTER PULL OUR CHUTES' EMERGENCY RIP CORDS--BEFORE WE SPLATTER THE LANDSCAPE!
BUT, AS THE DARING DUO GLIDES TOWARD THE CLOUDS...
IT'S THE ROCKETEERS! IF THEY KEEP THE ROCKET HOMED-IN ON GOTHAM CITY-- THE EXPLOSION WILL FLATTEN THE WHOLE CITY!
CRAAAK!
CRAAAK

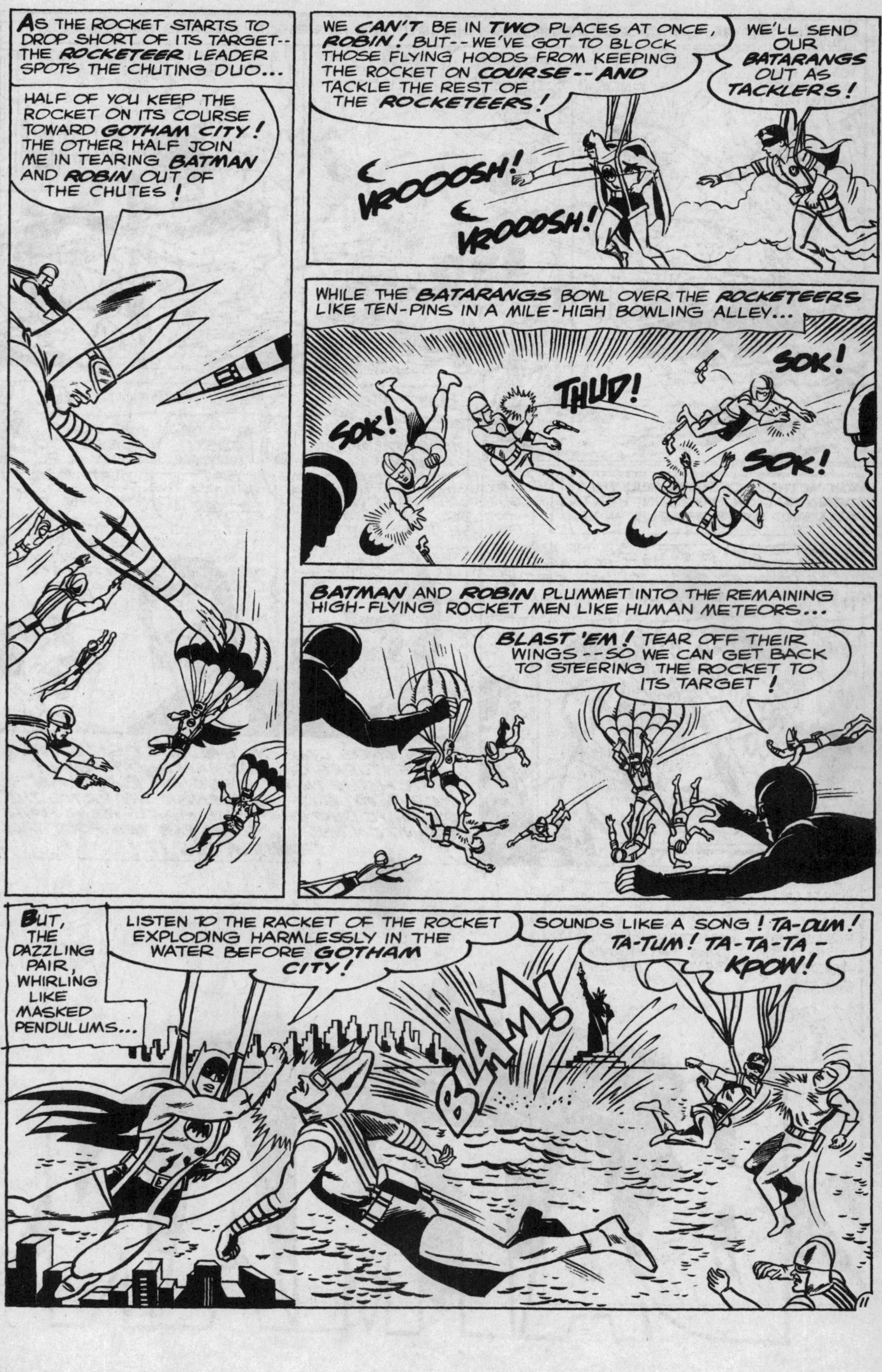
AS THE ROCKET STARTS TO DROP SHORT OF ITS TARGET-- THE ROCKETEER LEADER SPOTS THE CHUTING DUO...
HALF OF YOU KEEP THE ROCKET ON ITS COURSE TOWARD GOTHAM CITY! THE OTHER HALF JOIN ME IN TEARING BATMAN AND ROBIN OUT OF THE CHUTES!
WE CAN'T BE IN TWO PLACES AT ONCE, ROBIN! BUT--WE'VE GOT TO BLOCK THOSE FLYING HOODS FROM KEEPING THE ROCKET ON COURSE--AND TACKLE THE REST OF THE ROCKETEERS!
WE'LL SEND OUR BATARANGS OUT AS TACKLERS!
VROOOOSH!
VROOOOSH!
WHILE THE BATARANGS BOWL OVER THE ROCKETEERS LIKE TEN-PINS IN A MILE-HIGH BOWLING ALLEY...
SOK!
THUD!
SOK!
SOK!
BATMAN AND ROBIN PLUMMET INTO THE REMAINING HIGH-FLYING ROCKET MEN LIKE HUMAN METEORS...
BLAST 'EM! TEAR OFF THEIR WINGS--SO WE CAN GET BACK TO STEERING THE ROCKET TO ITS TARGET!
BUT, THE DAZZLING PAIR, WHIRLING LIKE MASKED PENDULUMS...
LISTEN TO THE RACKET OF THE ROCKET EXPLODING HARMLESSLY IN THE WATER BEFORE GOTHAM CITY!
SOUNDS LIKE A SONG! TA-DUM! TA-TUM! TA-TA-TA-KPOW!
BLAM!
11

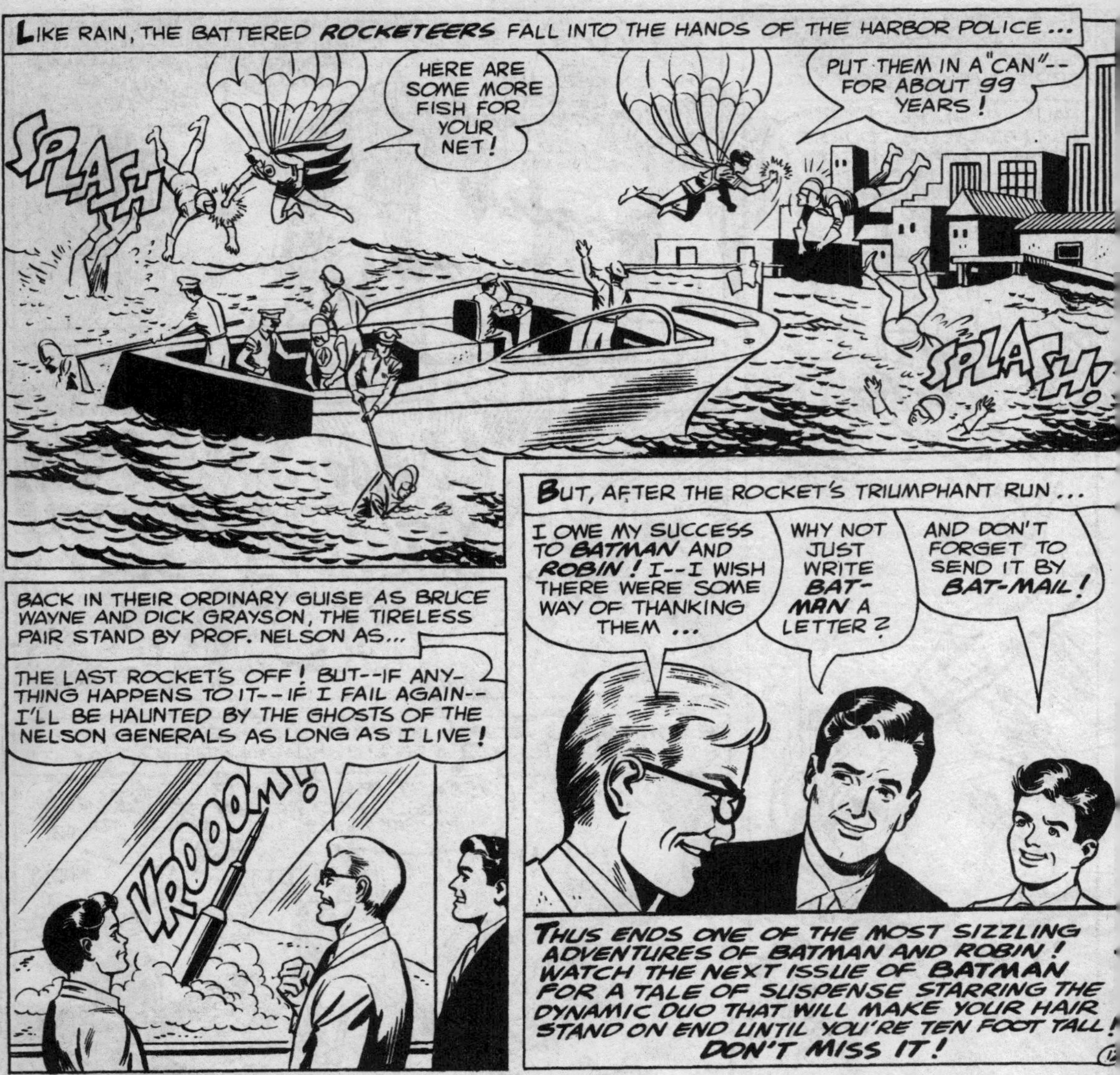
LIKE RAIN, THE BATTERED ROCKETEERS FALL INTO THE HANDS OF THE HARBOR POLICE...
SPLASH
HERE ARE SOME MORE FISH FOR YOUR NET!
PUT THEM IN A "CAN"-- FOR ABOUT 99 YEARS!
SPLASH!
BACK IN THEIR ORDINARY GUISE AS BRUCE WAYNE AND DICK GRAYSON, THE TIRELESS PAIR STAND BY PROF. NELSON AS...
THE LAST ROCKET'S OFF! BUT--IF ANYTHING HAPPENS TO IT--IF I FAIL AGAIN--I'LL BE HAUNTED BY THE GHOSTS OF THE NELSON GENERALS AS LONG AS I LIVE!
VROOOOM!
BUT, AFTER THE ROCKET'S TRIUMPHANT RUN...
I OWE MY SUCCESS TO BATMAN AND ROBIN! I--I WISH THERE WERE SOME WAY OF THANKING THEM...
WHY NOT JUST WRITE BATMAN A LETTER?
AND DON'T FORGET TO SEND IT BY BAT-MAIL!
THUS ENDS ONE OF THE MOST SIZZLING ADVENTURES OF BATMAN AND ROBIN! WATCH THE NEXT ISSUE OF BATMAN FOR A TALE OF SUSPENSE STARRING THE DYNAMIC DUO THAT WILL MAKE YOUR HAIR STAND ON END UNTIL YOU'RE TEN FOOT TALL! DON'T MISS IT!

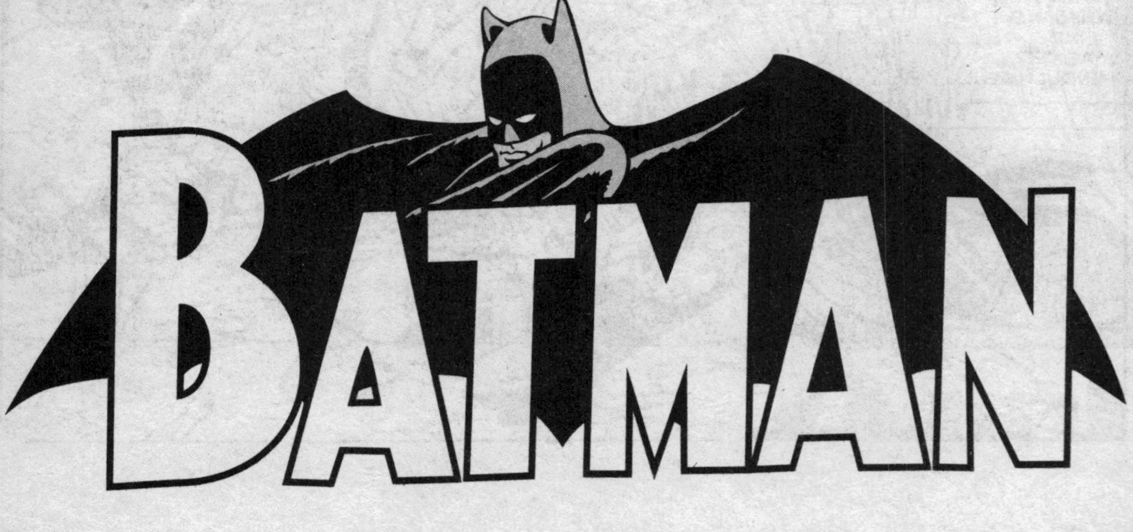
BATMAN

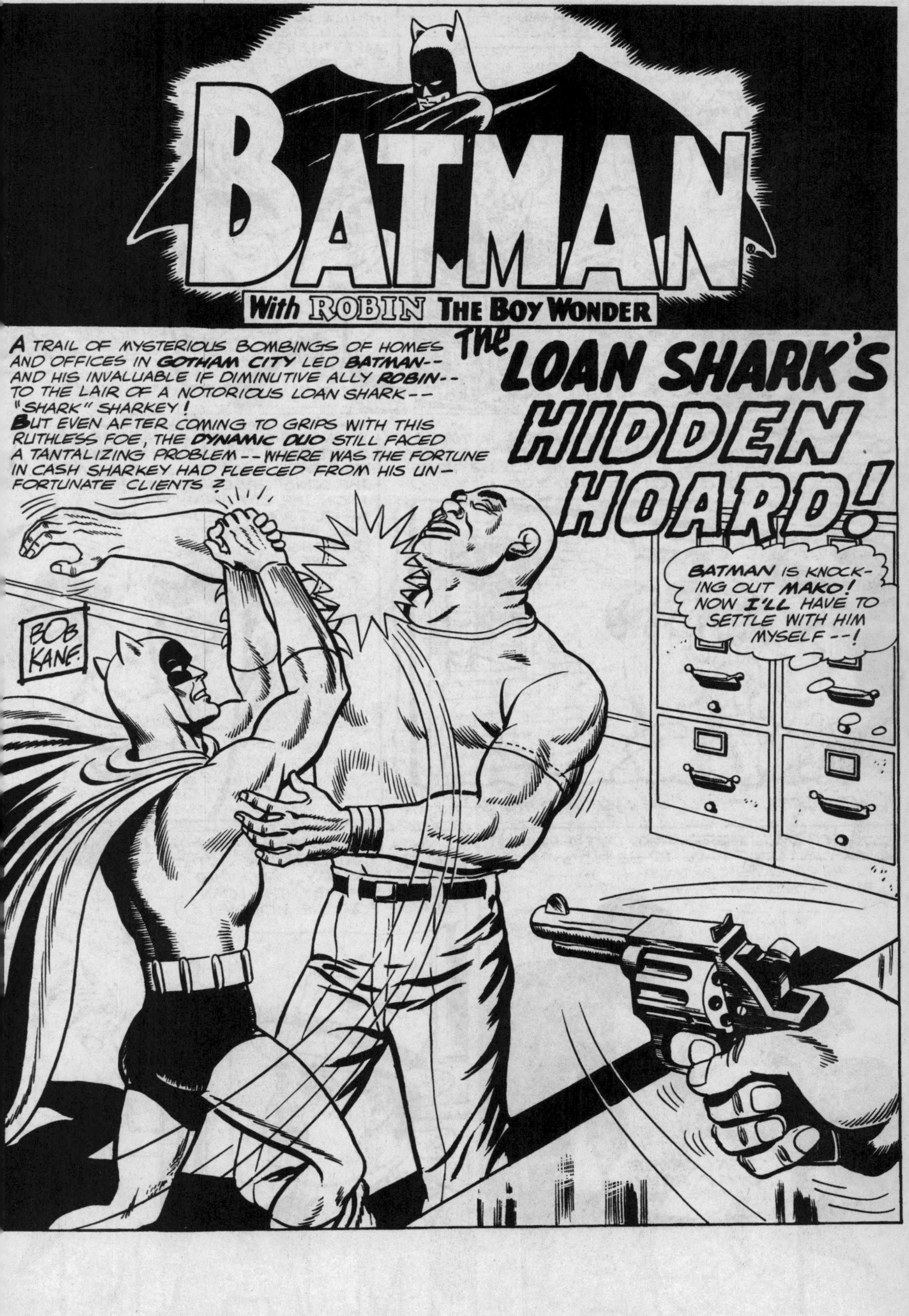
BATMAN
With ROBIN THE BOY WONDER
A TRAIL OF MYSTERIOUS BOMBINGS OF HOMES AND OFFICES IN GOTHAM CITY LED BATMAN-- AND HIS INVALUABLE IF DIMINUTIVE ALLY ROBIN-- TO THE LAIR OF A NOTORIOUS LOAN SHARK-- "SHARK" SHARKEY!
BUT EVEN AFTER COMING TO GRIPS WITH THIS RUTHLESS FOE, THE DYNAMIC DUO STILL FACED A TANTALIZING PROBLEM--WHERE WAS THE FORTUNE IN CASH SHARKEY HAD FLEECED FROM HIS UNFORTUNATE CLIENTS?
The LOAN SHARK'S HIDDEN HOARD!
BATMAN IS KNOCKING OUT MAKO! NOW I'LL HAVE TO SETTLE WITH HIM MYSELF--!
BOB KANE

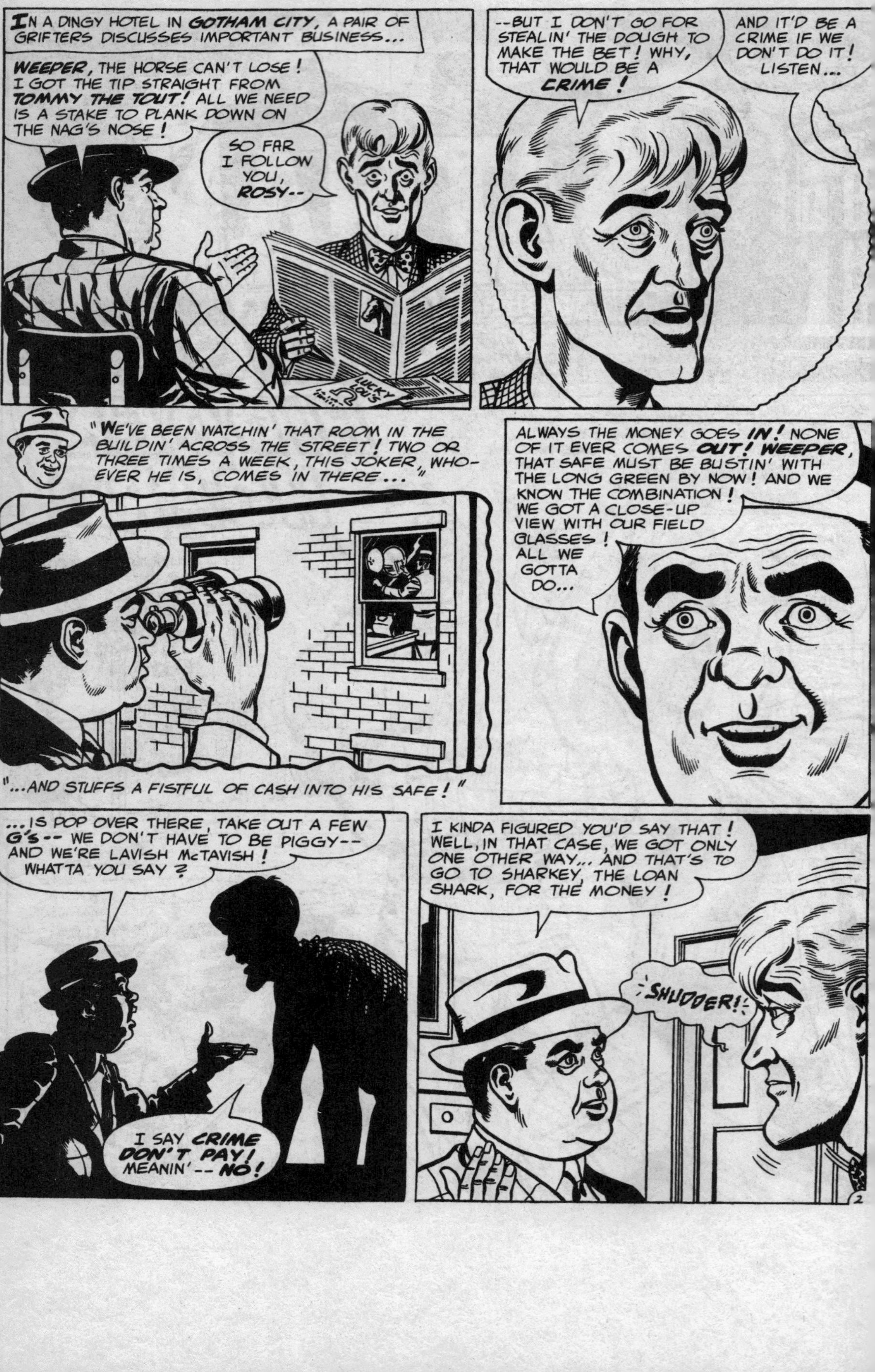
IN A DINGY HOTEL IN GOTHAM CITY, A PAIR OF GRIFTERS DISCUSSES IMPORTANT BUSINESS...
WEEPER, THE HORSE CAN'T LOSE! I GOT THE TIP STRAIGHT FROM TOMMY THE TOUT! ALL WE NEED IS A STAKE TO PLANK DOWN ON THE NAG'S NOSE!
SO FAR I FOLLOW YOU, ROSY--
LUCKY LOU'S
--BUT I DON'T GO FOR STEALIN' THE DOUGH TO MAKE THE BET! WHY, THAT WOULD BE A CRIME!
AND IT'D BE A CRIME IF WE DON'T DO IT! LISTEN...
"WE'VE BEEN WATCHIN' THAT ROOM IN THE BUILDIN' ACROSS THE STREET! TWO OR THREE TIMES A WEEK, THIS JOKER, WHO-EVER HE IS, COMES IN THERE..."
"...AND STUFFS A FISTFUL OF CASH INTO HIS SAFE!"
ALWAYS THE MONEY GOES IN! NONE OF IT EVER COMES OUT! WEEPER, THAT SAFE MUST BE BUSTIN' WITH THE LONG GREEN BY NOW! AND WE KNOW THE COMBINATION! WE GOT A CLOSE-UP VIEW WITH OUR FIELD GLASSES! ALL WE GOTTA DO...
...IS POP OVER THERE, TAKE OUT A FEW G'S-- WE DON'T HAVE TO BE PIGGY-- AND WE'RE LAVISH McTAVISH! WHATTA YOU SAY?
I SAY CRIME DON'T PAY! MEANIN' -- NO!
I KINDA FIGURED YOU'D SAY THAT! WELL, IN THAT CASE, WE GOT ONLY ONE OTHER WAY... AND THAT'S TO GO TO SHARKEY, THE LOAN SHARK, FOR THE MONEY!
SHUDDER!
2

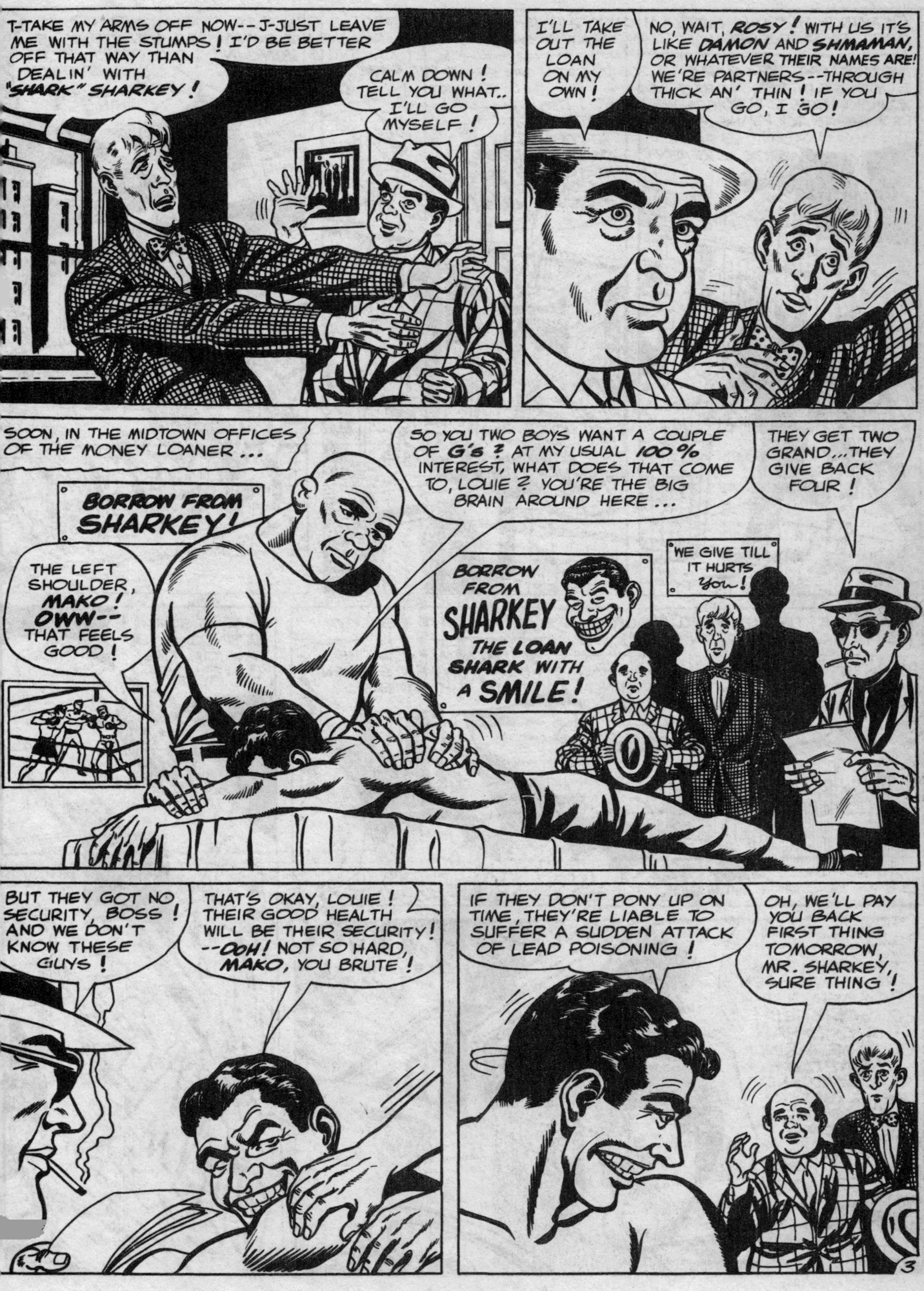
T-TAKE MY ARMS OFF NOW--J-JUST LEAVE ME WITH THE STUMPS! I'D BE BETTER OFF THAT WAY THAN DEALIN' WITH "SHARK" SHARKEY!
CALM DOWN! TELL YOU WHAT.. I'LL GO MYSELF!
I'LL TAKE OUT THE LOAN ON MY OWN!
NO, WAIT, ROSY! WITH US IT'S LIKE DAMON AND SHMAMAN, OR WHATEVER THEIR NAMES ARE! WE'RE PARTNERS--THROUGH THICK AN' THIN! IF YOU GO, I GO!
SOON, IN THE MIDTOWN OFFICES OF THE MONEY LOANER...
BORROW FROM SHARKEY!
SO YOU TWO BOYS WANT A COUPLE OF G's? AT MY USUAL 100% INTEREST, WHAT DOES THAT COME TO, LOUIE? YOU'RE THE BIG BRAIN AROUND HERE...
THEY GET TWO GRAND... THEY GIVE BACK FOUR!
THE LEFT SHOULDER, MAKO! OWW-- THAT FEELS GOOD!
BORROW FROM SHARKEY THE LOAN SHARK WITH A SMILE!
WE GIVE TILL IT HURTS You!
BUT THEY GOT NO SECURITY, BOSS! AND WE DON'T KNOW THESE GUYS!
THAT'S OKAY, LOUIE! THEIR GOOD HEALTH WILL BE THEIR SECURITY! --OOH! NOT SO HARD, MAKO, YOU BRUTE!
IF THEY DON'T PONY UP ON TIME, THEY'RE LIABLE TO SUFFER A SUDDEN ATTACK OF LEAD POISONING!
OH, WE'LL PAY YOU BACK FIRST THING TOMORROW, MR. SHARKEY, SURE THING!
3

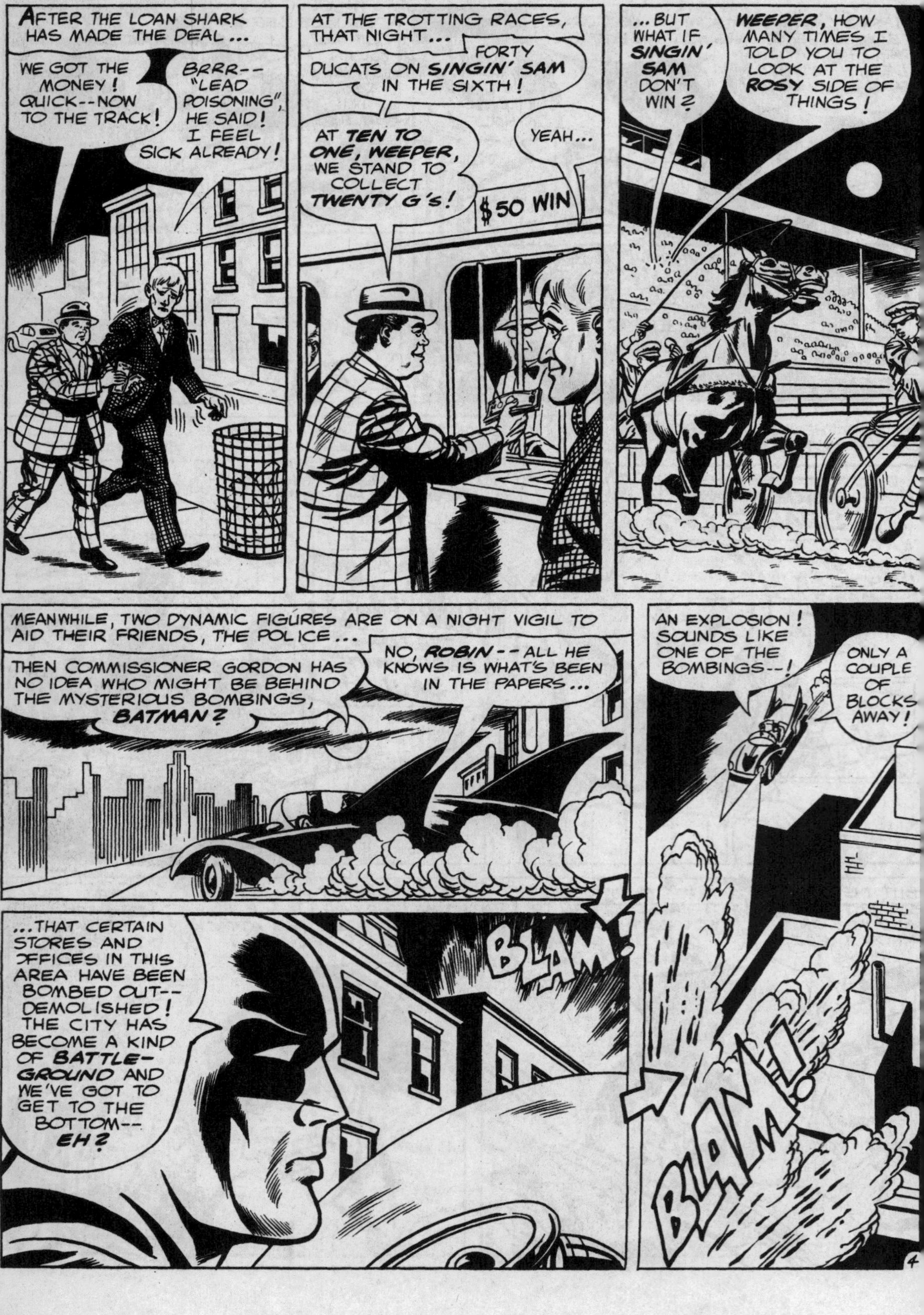

AFTER THE LOAN SHARK HAS MADE THE DEAL...
WE GOT THE MONEY! QUICK--NOW TO THE TRACK!
BRRR--"LEAD POISONING", HE SAID! I FEEL SICK ALREADY!
AT THE TROTTING RACES, THAT NIGHT...
FORTY DUCATS ON SINGIN' SAM IN THE SIXTH!
AT TEN TO ONE, WEEPER, WE STAND TO COLLECT TWENTY G's!
YEAH...
$50 WIN
...BUT WHAT IF SINGIN' SAM DON'T WIN?
WEEPER, HOW MANY TIMES I TOLD YOU TO LOOK AT THE ROSY SIDE OF THINGS!
MEANWHILE, TWO DYNAMIC FIGURES ARE ON A NIGHT VIGIL TO AID THEIR FRIENDS, THE POLICE...
THEN COMMISSIONER GORDON HAS NO IDEA WHO MIGHT BE BEHIND THE MYSTERIOUS BOMBINGS, BATMAN?
NO, ROBIN--ALL HE KNOWS IS WHAT'S BEEN IN THE PAPERS...
...THAT CERTAIN STORES AND OFFICES IN THIS AREA HAVE BEEN BOMBED OUT--DEMOLISHED! THE CITY HAS BECOME A KIND OF BATTLE-GROUND AND WE'VE GOT TO GET TO THE BOTTOM--EH?
BLAM!
AN EXPLOSION! SOUNDS LIKE ONE OF THE BOMBINGS--!
ONLY A COUPLE OF BLOCKS AWAY!
BLAM!
4

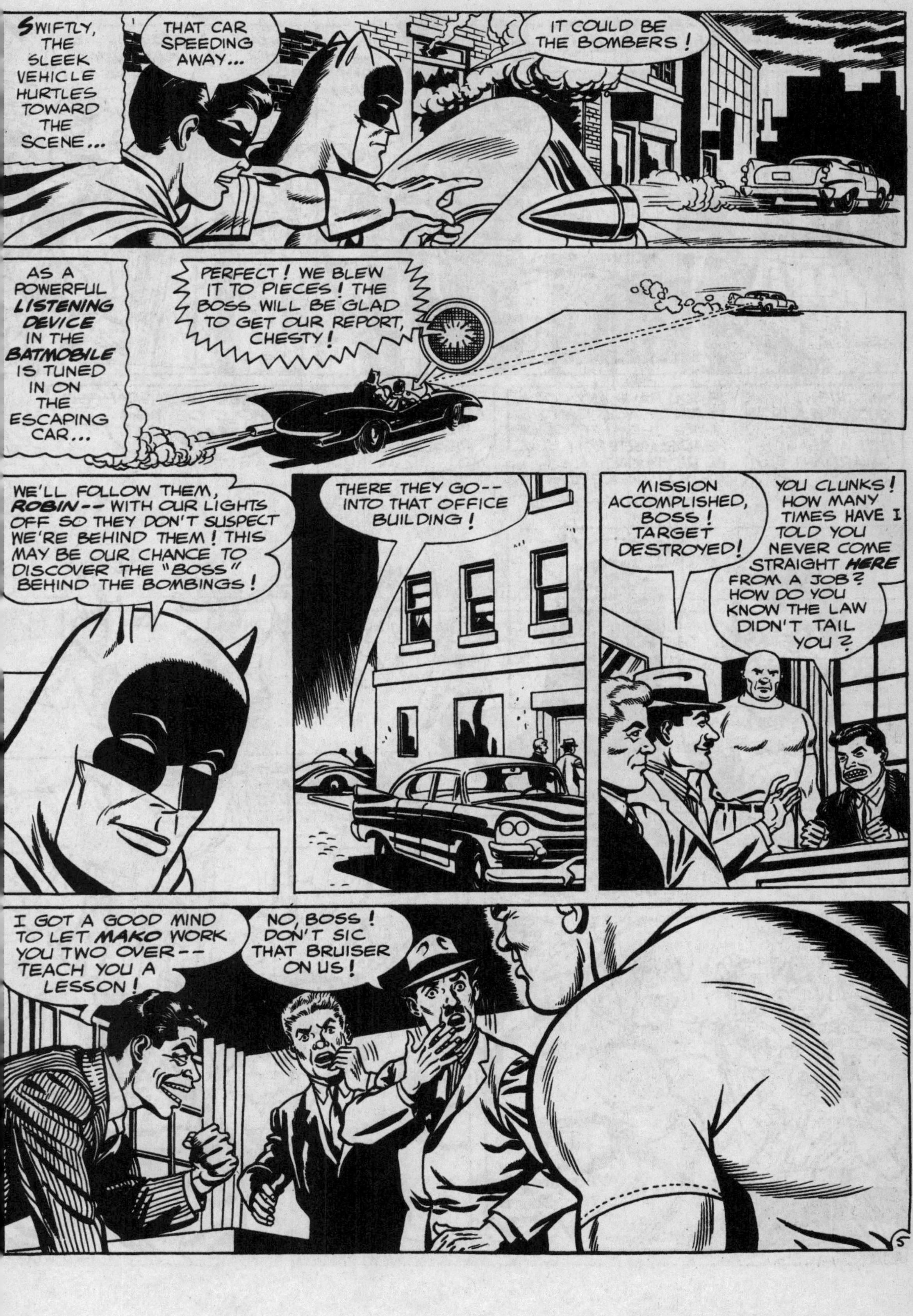
SWIFTLY, THE SLEEK VEHICLE HURTLES TOWARD THE SCENE...
THAT CAR SPEEDING AWAY...
IT COULD BE THE BOMBERS!
AS A POWERFUL LISTENING DEVICE IN THE BATMOBILE IS TUNED IN ON THE ESCAPING CAR...
PERFECT! WE BLEW IT TO PIECES! THE BOSS WILL BE GLAD TO GET OUR REPORT, CHESTY!
WE'LL FOLLOW THEM, ROBIN-- WITH OUR LIGHTS OFF SO THEY DON'T SUSPECT WE'RE BEHIND THEM! THIS MAY BE OUR CHANCE TO DISCOVER THE "BOSS" BEHIND THE BOMBINGS!
THERE THEY GO-- INTO THAT OFFICE BUILDING!
MISSION ACCOMPLISHED, BOSS! TARGET DESTROYED!
YOU CLUNKS! HOW MANY TIMES HAVE I TOLD YOU NEVER COME STRAIGHT HERE FROM A JOB? HOW DO YOU KNOW THE LAW DIDN'T TAIL YOU?
I GOT A GOOD MIND TO LET MAKO WORK YOU TWO OVER-- TEACH YOU A LESSON!
NO, BOSS! DON'T SIC THAT BRUISER ON US!
5

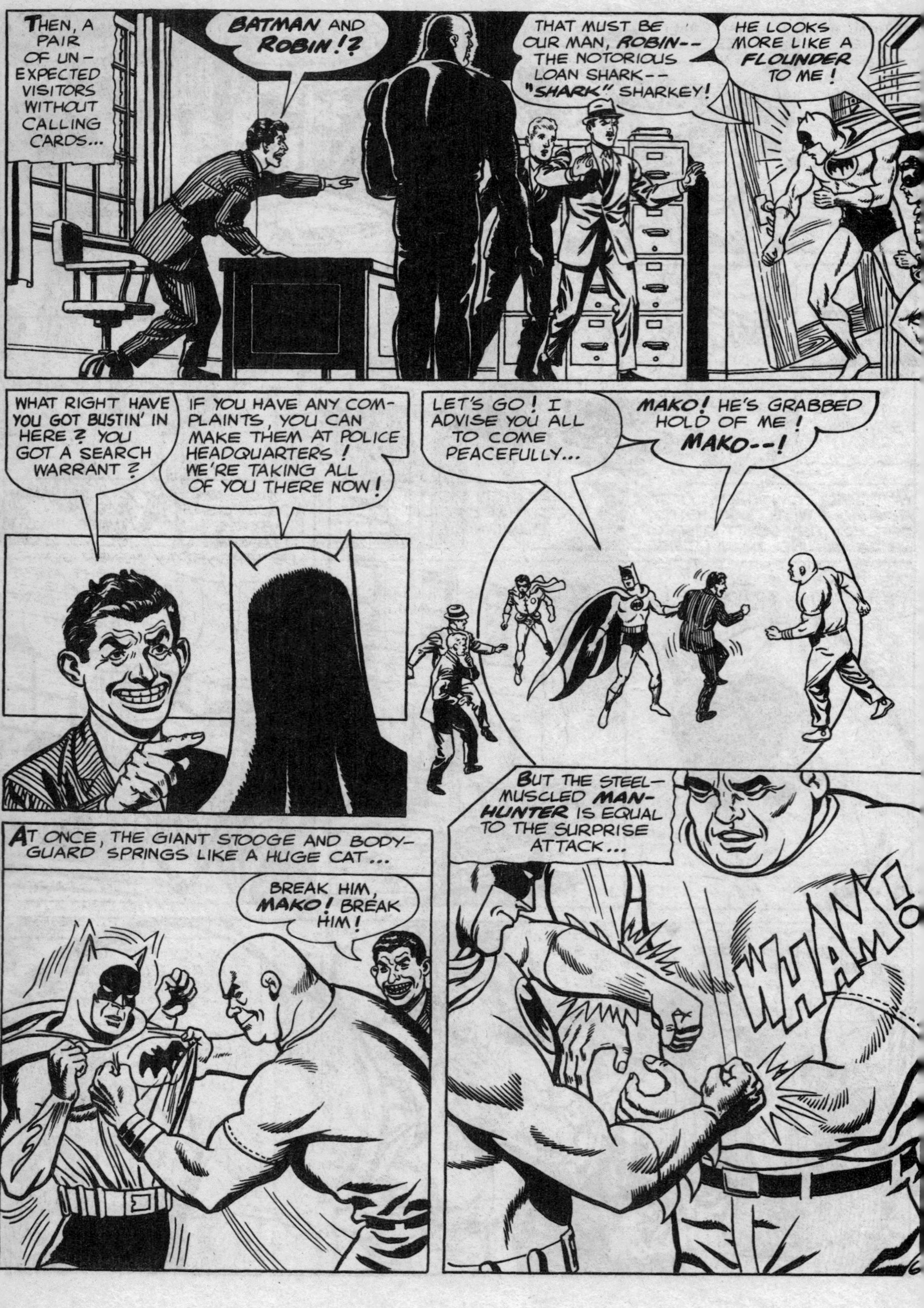
THEN, A PAIR OF UN-EXPECTED VISITORS WITHOUT CALLING CARDS...
BATMAN AND ROBIN!?
THAT MUST BE OUR MAN, ROBIN-- THE NOTORIOUS LOAN SHARK-- "SHARK" SHARKEY!
HE LOOKS MORE LIKE A FLOUNDER TO ME!
WHAT RIGHT HAVE YOU GOT BUSTIN' IN HERE? YOU GOT A SEARCH WARRANT?
IF YOU HAVE ANY COM-PLAINTS, YOU CAN MAKE THEM AT POLICE HEADQUARTERS! WE'RE TAKING ALL OF YOU THERE NOW!
LET'S GO! I ADVISE YOU ALL TO COME PEACEFULLY...
MAKO! HE'S GRABBED HOLD OF ME! MAKO--!
AT ONCE, THE GIANT STOOGE AND BODY-GUARD SPRINGS LIKE A HUGE CAT...
BREAK HIM, MAKO! BREAK HIM!
BUT THE STEEL-MUSCLED MAN-HUNTER IS EQUAL TO THE SURPRISE ATTACK...
WHAM!
6

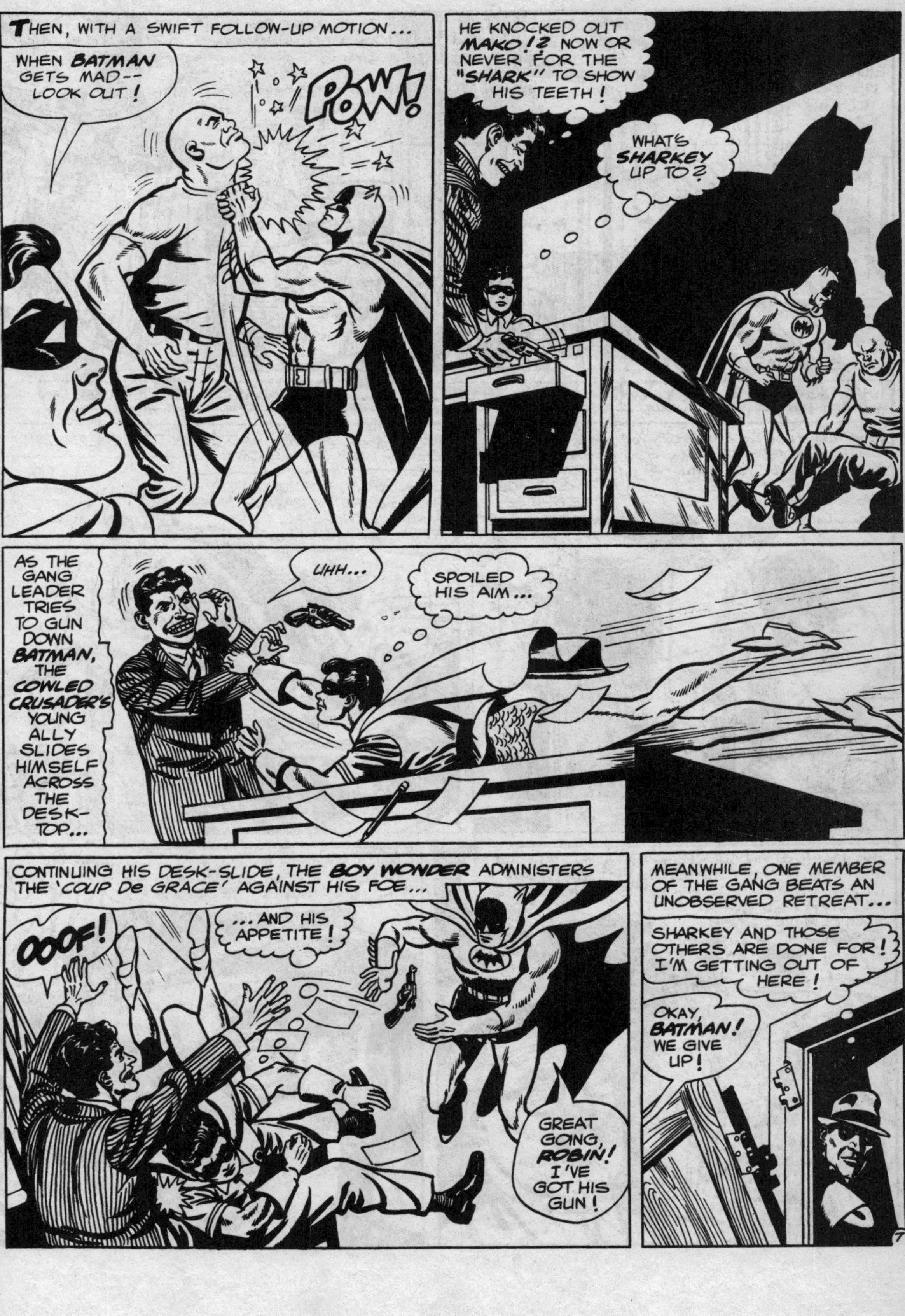
THEN, WITH A SWIFT FOLLOW-UP MOTION...
WHEN BATMAN GETS MAD-- LOOK OUT!
POW!
HE KNOCKED OUT MAKO!? NOW OR NEVER FOR THE "SHARK" TO SHOW HIS TEETH!
WHAT'S SHARKEY UP TO?
AS THE GANG LEADER TRIES TO GUN DOWN BATMAN, THE COWLED CRUSADER'S YOUNG ALLY SLIDES HIMSELF ACROSS THE DESK-TOP...
UHH...
SPOILED HIS AIM...
CONTINUING HIS DESK-SLIDE, THE BOY WONDER ADMINISTERS THE 'COUP De GRACE' AGAINST HIS FOE...
OOOF!
...AND HIS APPETITE!
GREAT GOING, ROBIN! I'VE GOT HIS GUN!
MEANWHILE, ONE MEMBER OF THE GANG BEATS AN UNOBSERVED RETREAT...
SHARKEY AND THOSE OTHERS ARE DONE FOR! I'M GETTING OUT OF HERE!
OKAY, BATMAN! WE GIVE UP!
7

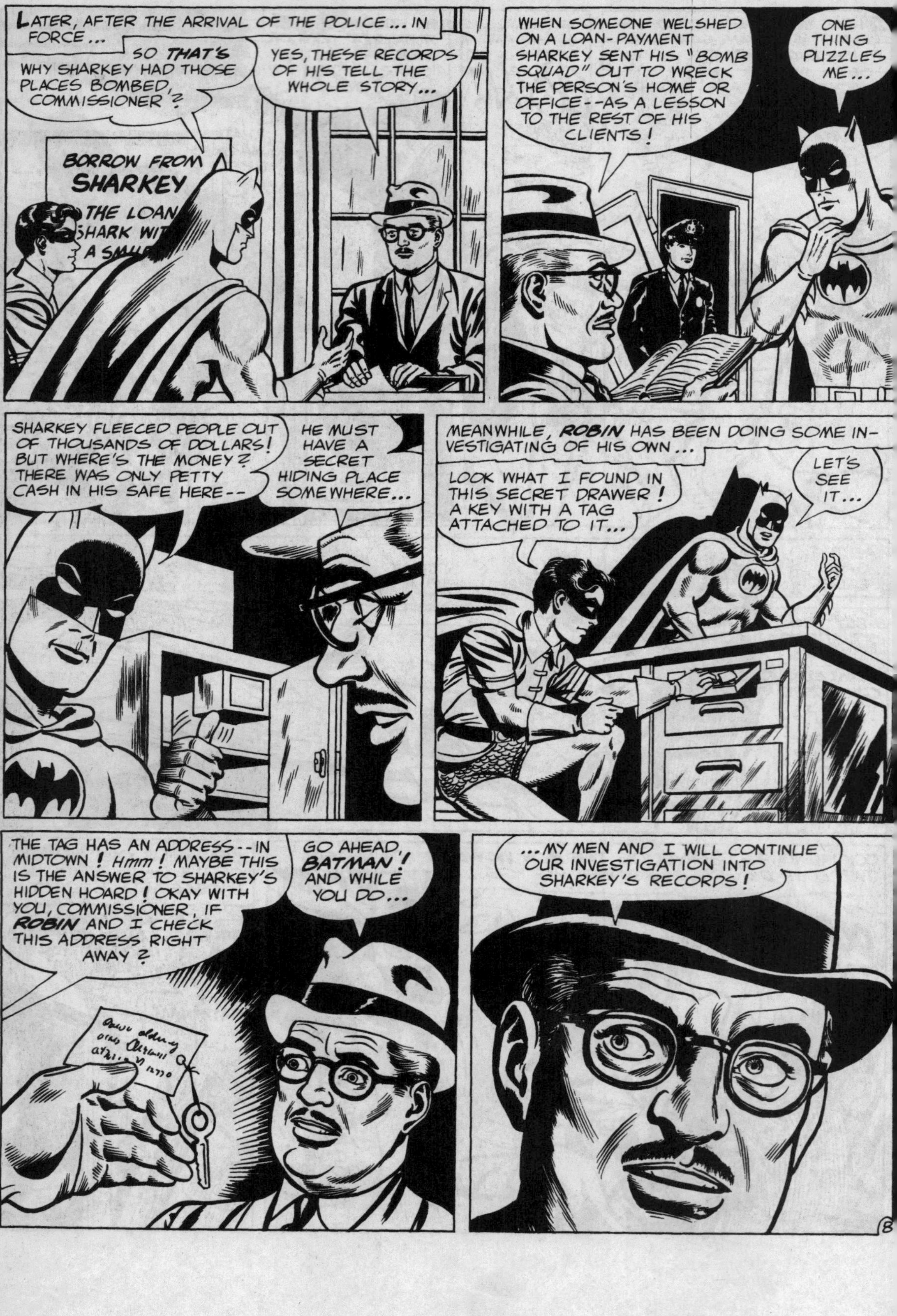
LATER, AFTER THE ARRIVAL OF THE POLICE ... IN FORCE ...
SO THAT'S WHY SHARKEY HAD THOSE PLACES BOMBED, COMMISSIONER ?
YES, THESE RECORDS OF HIS TELL THE WHOLE STORY...
BORROW FROM SHARKEY THE LOAN SHARK WIT A SMI
WHEN SOMEONE WELSHED ON A LOAN-PAYMENT SHARKEY SENT HIS "BOMB SQUAD" OUT TO WRECK THE PERSON'S HOME OR OFFICE--AS A LESSON TO THE REST OF HIS CLIENTS !
ONE THING PUZZLES ME ...
SHARKEY FLEECED PEOPLE OUT OF THOUSANDS OF DOLLARS ! BUT WHERE'S THE MONEY ? THERE WAS ONLY PETTY CASH IN HIS SAFE HERE--
HE MUST HAVE A SECRET HIDING PLACE SOMEWHERE...
MEANWHILE, ROBIN HAS BEEN DOING SOME INVESTIGATING OF HIS OWN ...
LOOK WHAT I FOUND IN THIS SECRET DRAWER ! A KEY WITH A TAG ATTACHED TO IT...
LET'S SEE IT...
THE TAG HAS AN ADDRESS--IN MIDTOWN ! Hmm ! MAYBE THIS IS THE ANSWER TO SHARKEY'S HIDDEN HOARD ! OKAY WITH YOU, COMMISSIONER, IF ROBIN AND I CHECK THIS ADDRESS RIGHT AWAY ?
GO AHEAD, BATMAN ! AND WHILE YOU DO...
...MY MEN AND I WILL CONTINUE OUR INVESTIGATION INTO SHARKEY'S RECORDS !
8

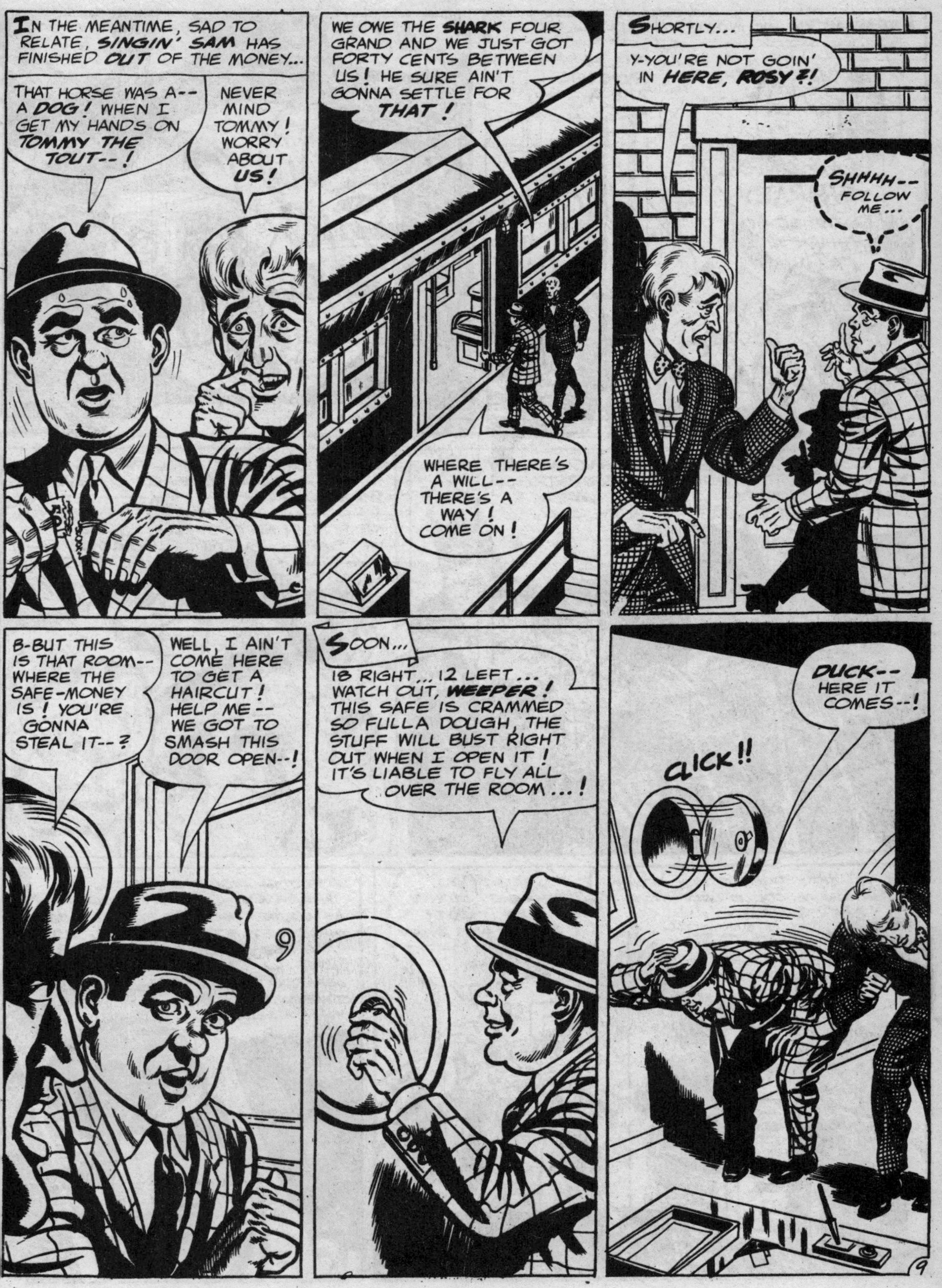
IN THE MEANTIME, SAD TO RELATE, SINGIN' SAM HAS FINISHED OUT OF THE MONEY...
THAT HORSE WAS A-- A DOG! WHEN I GET MY HANDS ON TOMMY THE TOUT--!
NEVER MIND TOMMY! WORRY ABOUT US!
WE OWE THE SHARK FOUR GRAND AND WE JUST GOT FORTY CENTS BETWEEN US! HE SURE AIN'T GONNA SETTLE FOR THAT!
WHERE THERE'S A WILL-- THERE'S A WAY! COME ON!
SHORTLY...
Y-YOU'RE NOT GOIN' IN HERE, ROSY?!
SHHHH-- FOLLOW ME...
B-BUT THIS IS THAT ROOM-- WHERE THE SAFE-MONEY IS! YOU'RE GONNA STEAL IT--?
WELL, I AIN'T COME HERE TO GET A HAIRCUT! HELP ME-- WE GOT TO SMASH THIS DOOR OPEN--!
SOON...
18 RIGHT... 12 LEFT... WATCH OUT, WEEPER! THIS SAFE IS CRAMMED SO FULLA DOUGH, THE STUFF WILL BUST RIGHT OUT WHEN I OPEN IT! IT'S LIABLE TO FLY ALL OVER THE ROOM...!
DUCK-- HERE IT COMES--!
CLICK!!
9

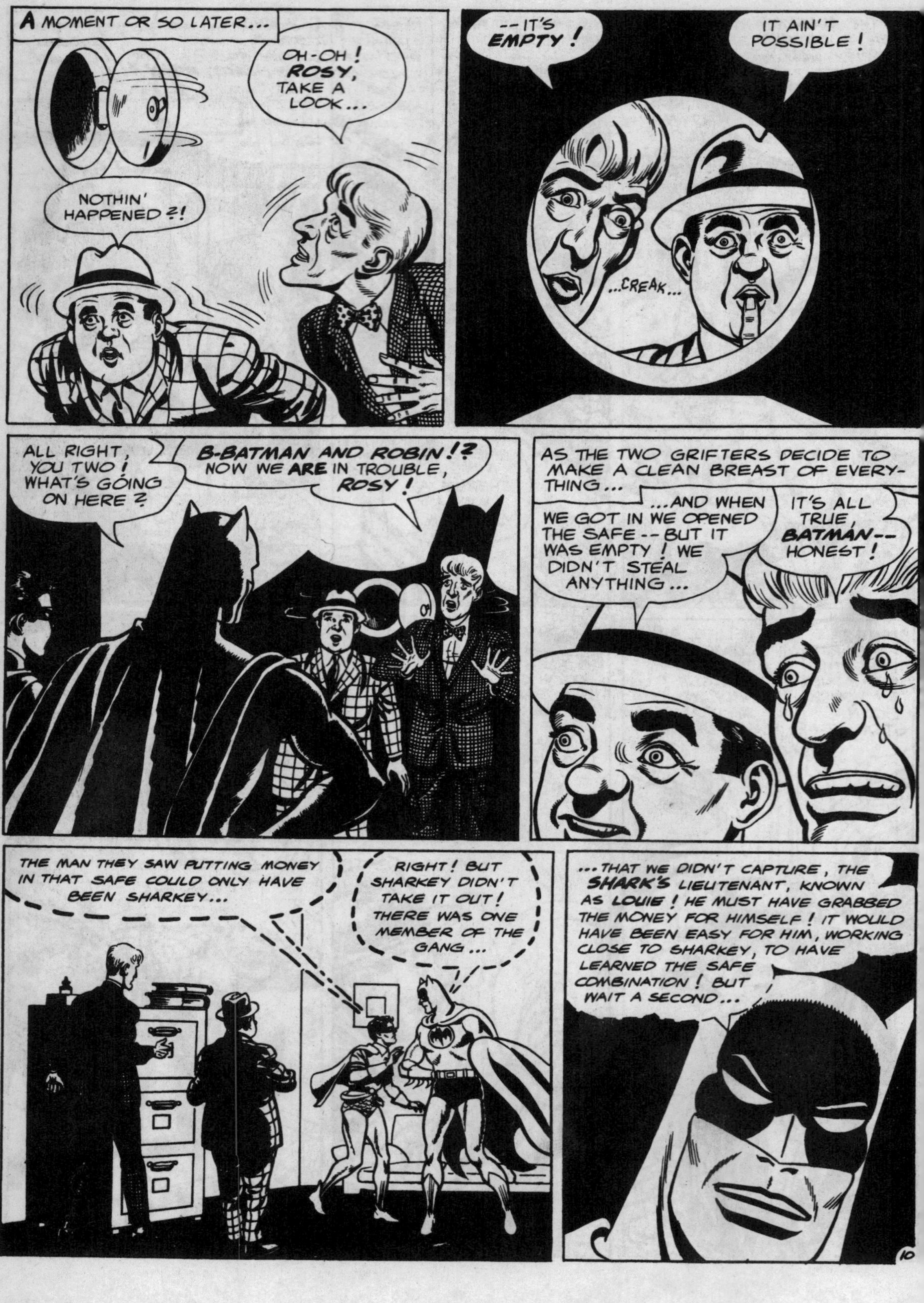
A MOMENT OR SO LATER...
OH-OH! ROSY, TAKE A LOOK...
NOTHIN' HAPPENED ?!
--IT'S EMPTY!
IT AIN'T POSSIBLE!
...CREAK...
ALL RIGHT, YOU TWO! WHAT'S GOING ON HERE ?
B-BATMAN AND ROBIN!? NOW WE ARE IN TROUBLE, ROSY!
AS THE TWO GRIFTERS DECIDE TO MAKE A CLEAN BREAST OF EVERY-THING...
...AND WHEN WE GOT IN WE OPENED THE SAFE -- BUT IT WAS EMPTY! WE DIDN'T STEAL ANYTHING...
IT'S ALL TRUE, BATMAN-- HONEST!
THE MAN THEY SAW PUTTING MONEY IN THAT SAFE COULD ONLY HAVE BEEN SHARKEY...
RIGHT! BUT SHARKEY DIDN'T TAKE IT OUT! THERE WAS ONE MEMBER OF THE GANG...
...THAT WE DIDN'T CAPTURE, THE SHARK'S LIEUTENANT, KNOWN AS LOUIE! HE MUST HAVE GRABBED THE MONEY FOR HIMSELF! IT WOULD HAVE BEEN EASY FOR HIM, WORKING CLOSE TO SHARKEY, TO HAVE LEARNED THE SAFE COMBINATION! BUT WAIT A SECOND...
10

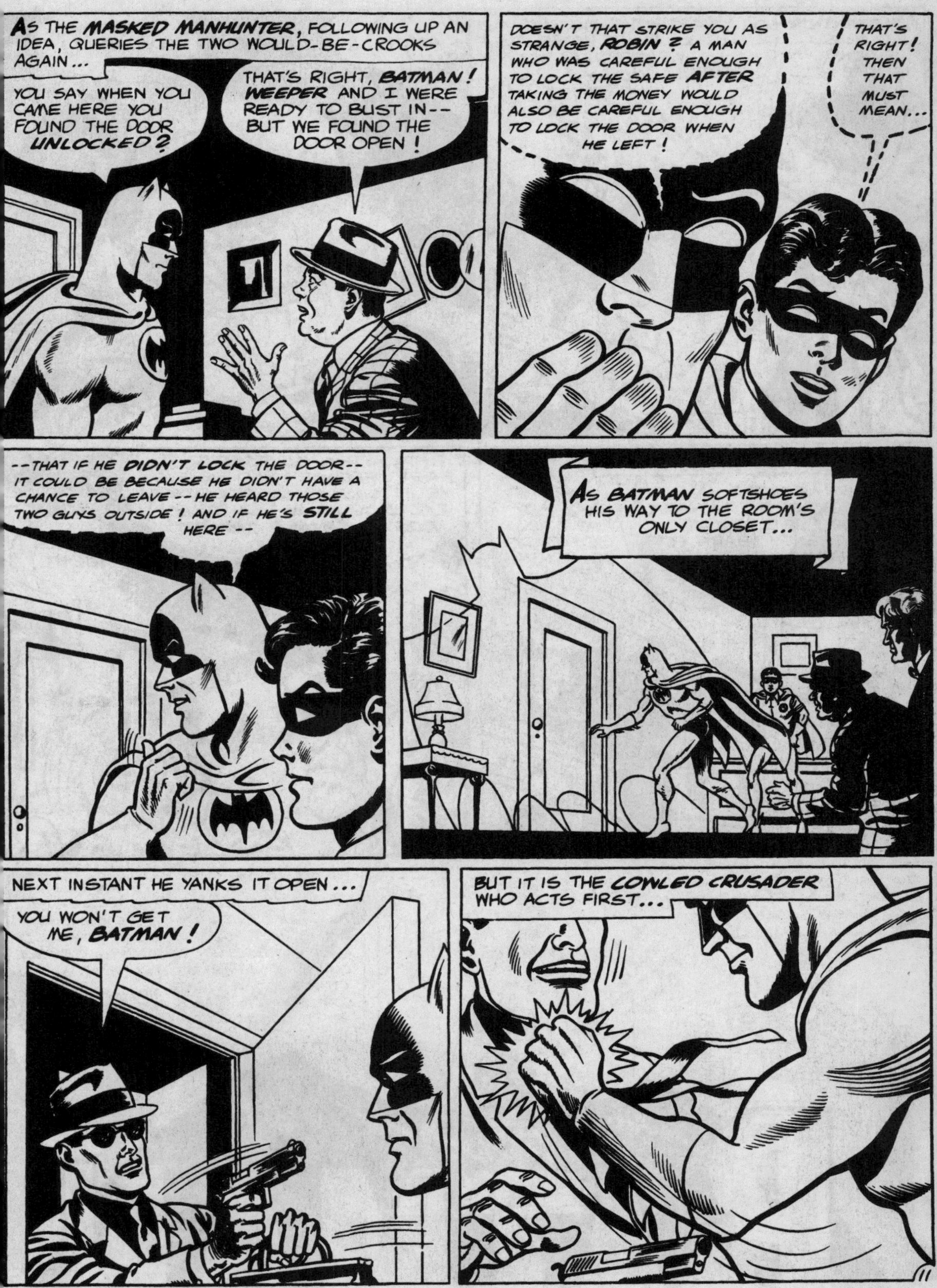
AS THE MASKED MANHUNTER, FOLLOWING UP AN IDEA, QUERIES THE TWO WOULD-BE-CROOKS AGAIN...
YOU SAY WHEN YOU CAME HERE YOU FOUND THE DOOR UNLOCKED?
THAT'S RIGHT, BATMAN! WEEPER AND I WERE READY TO BUST IN-- BUT WE FOUND THE DOOR OPEN!
DOESN'T THAT STRIKE YOU AS STRANGE, ROBIN? A MAN WHO WAS CAREFUL ENOUGH TO LOCK THE SAFE AFTER TAKING THE MONEY WOULD ALSO BE CAREFUL ENOUGH TO LOCK THE DOOR WHEN HE LEFT!
THAT'S RIGHT! THEN THAT MUST MEAN...
--THAT IF HE DIDN'T LOCK THE DOOR-- IT COULD BE BECAUSE HE DIDN'T HAVE A CHANCE TO LEAVE--HE HEARD THOSE TWO GUYS OUTSIDE! AND IF HE'S STILL HERE--
AS BATMAN SOFTSHOES HIS WAY TO THE ROOM'S ONLY CLOSET...
NEXT INSTANT HE YANKS IT OPEN...
YOU WON'T GET ME, BATMAN!
BUT IT IS THE COWLED CRUSADER WHO ACTS FIRST...

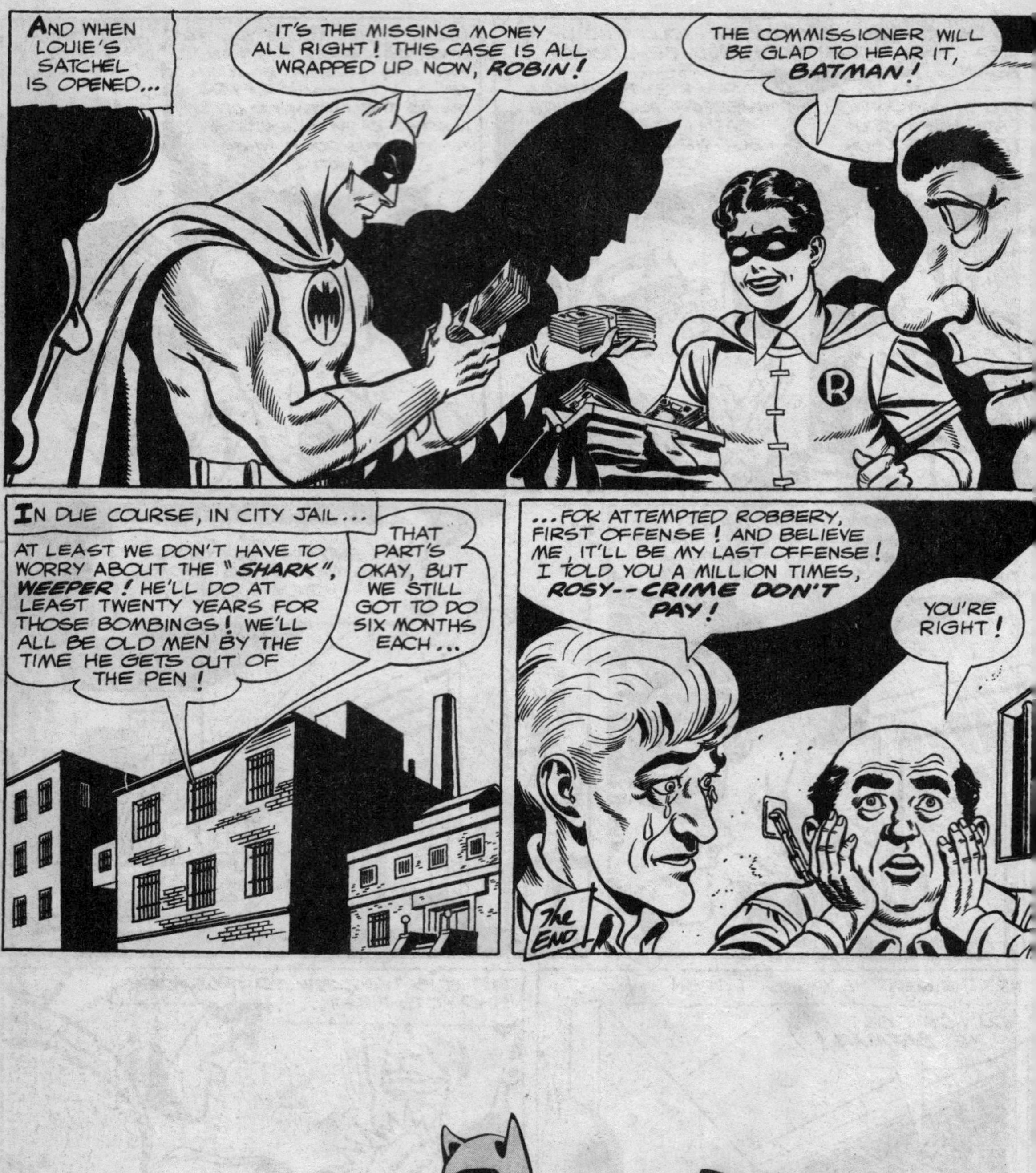
AND WHEN LOUIE'S SATCHEL IS OPENED...
IT'S THE MISSING MONEY ALL RIGHT! THIS CASE IS ALL WRAPPED UP NOW, ROBIN!
THE COMMISSIONER WILL BE GLAD TO HEAR IT, BATMAN!
IN DUE COURSE, IN CITY JAIL...
AT LEAST WE DON'T HAVE TO WORRY ABOUT THE "SHARK", WEEPER! HE'LL DO AT LEAST TWENTY YEARS FOR THOSE BOMBINGS! WE'LL ALL BE OLD MEN BY THE TIME HE GETS OUT OF THE PEN!
THAT PART'S OKAY, BUT WE STILL GOT TO DO SIX MONTHS EACH...
...FOR ATTEMPTED ROBBERY, FIRST OFFENSE! AND BELIEVE ME, IT'LL BE MY LAST OFFENSE! I TOLD YOU A MILLION TIMES, ROSY--CRIME DON'T PAY!
YOU'RE RIGHT!
The End

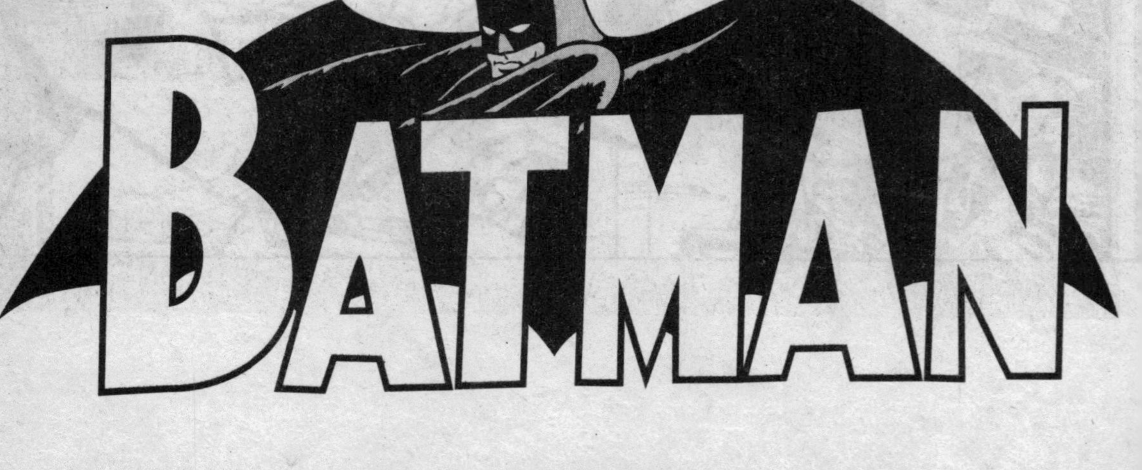
BATMAN

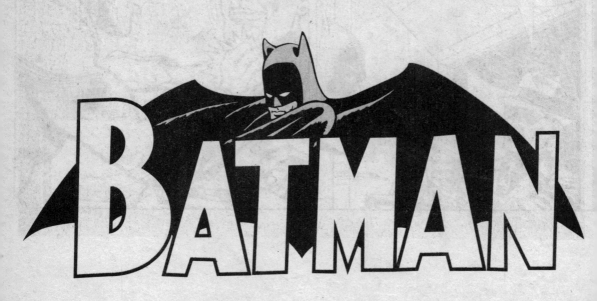

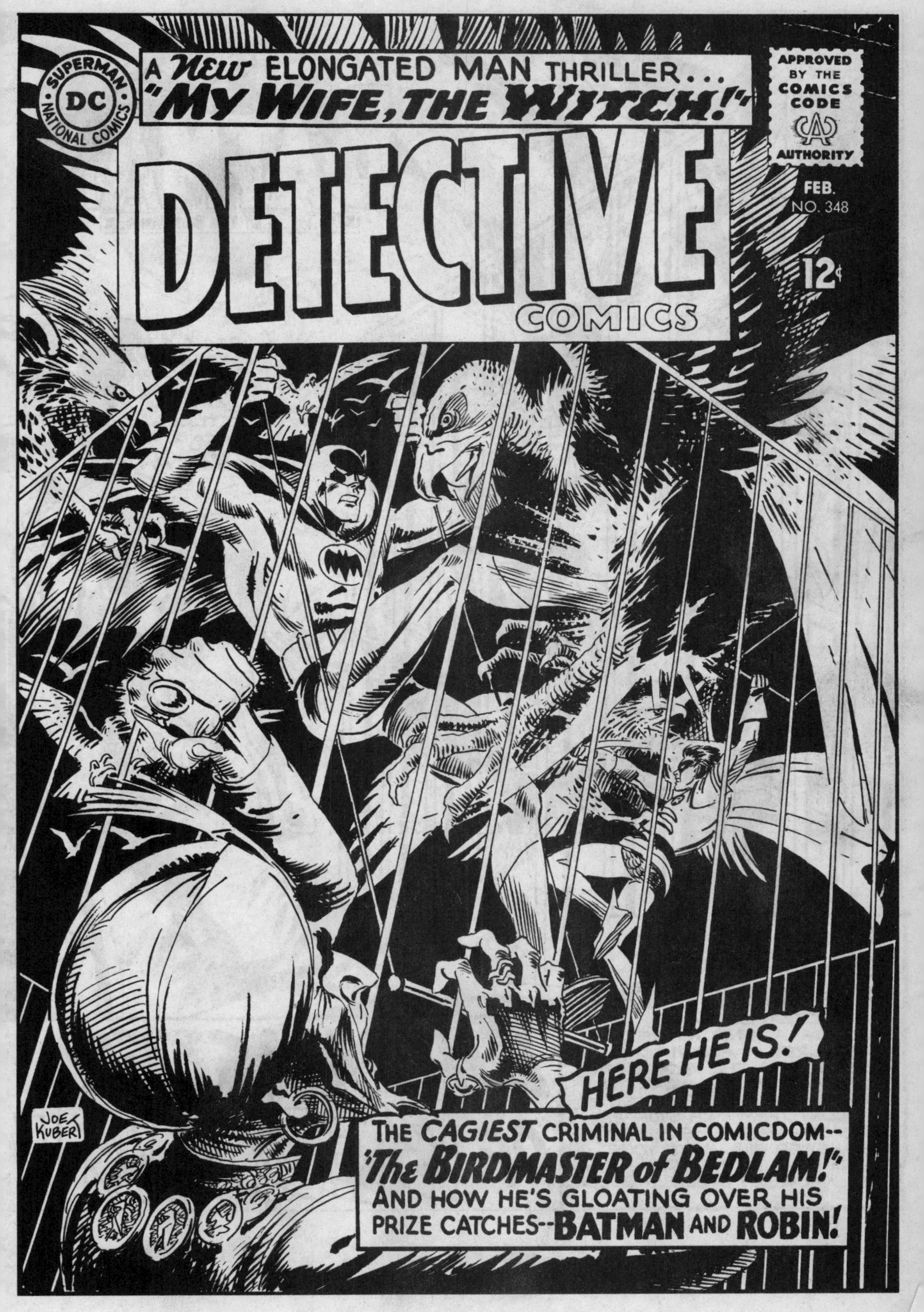
SUPERMAN DC NATIONAL COMICS
A NEW ELONGATED MAN THRILLER...
"MY WIFE, THE WITCH!"
APPROVED BY THE COMICS CODE AUTHORITY
DETECTIVE COMICS
FEB. NO. 348
12¢
HERE HE IS!
JOE KUBERT
THE CAGIEST CRIMINAL IN COMICDOM--
"The BIRDMASTER of BEDLAM!"
AND HOW HE'S GLOATING OVER HIS
PRIZE CATCHES--BATMAN AND ROBIN!

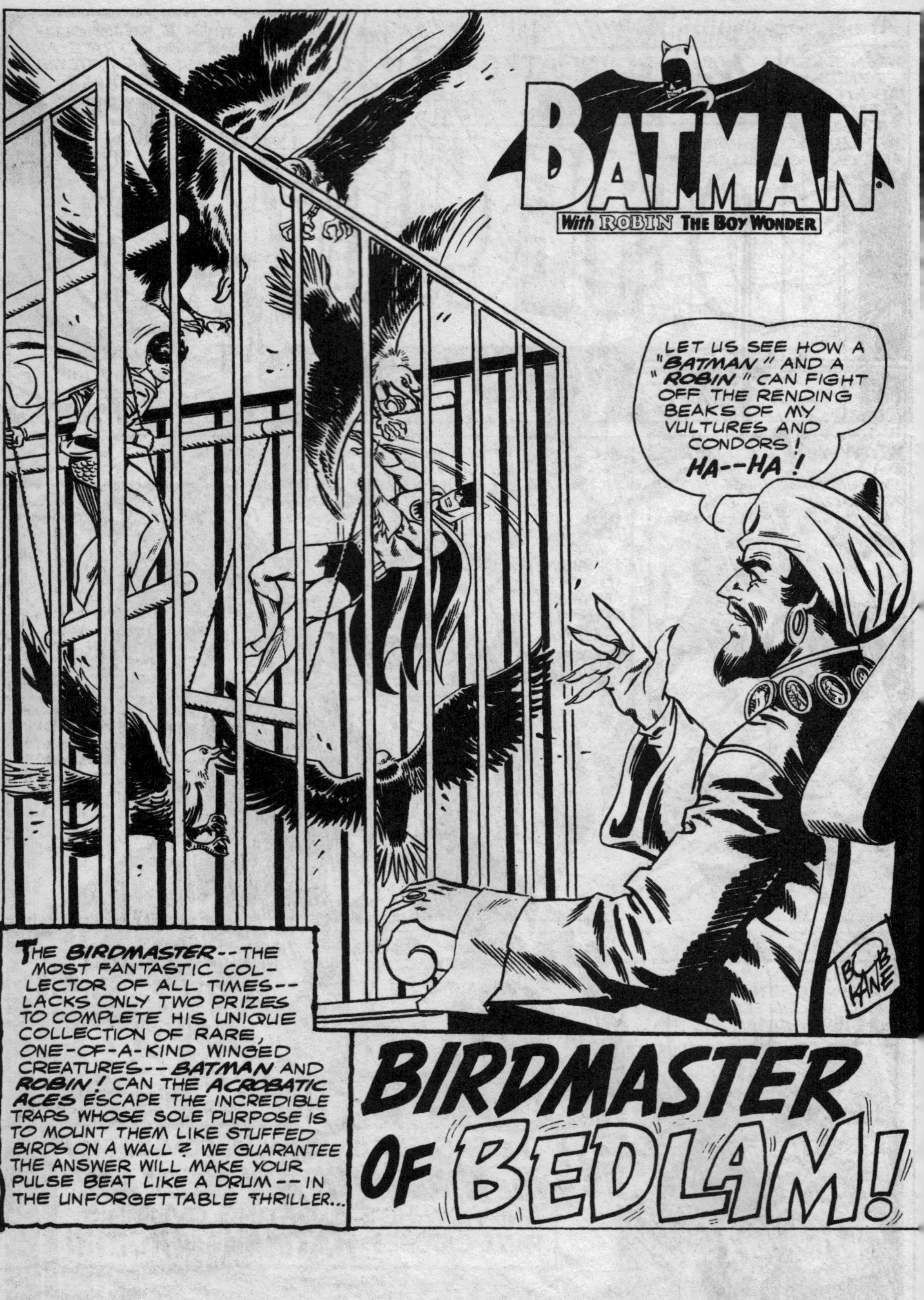
BATMAN
With ROBIN THE BOY WONDER
LET US SEE HOW A "BATMAN" AND A "ROBIN" CAN FIGHT OFF THE RENDING BEAKS OF MY VULTURES AND CONDORS! HA--HA!
THE BIRDMASTER--THE MOST FANTASTIC COLLECTOR OF ALL TIMES--LACKS ONLY TWO PRIZES TO COMPLETE HIS UNIQUE COLLECTION OF RARE, ONE-OF-A-KIND WINGED CREATURES--BATMAN AND ROBIN! CAN THE ACROBATIC ACES ESCAPE THE INCREDIBLE TRAPS WHOSE SOLE PURPOSE IS TO MOUNT THEM LIKE STUFFED BIRDS ON A WALL? WE GUARANTEE THE ANSWER WILL MAKE YOUR PULSE BEAT LIKE A DRUM--IN THE UNFORGETTABLE THRILLER...
BIRDMASTER OF BEDLAM!
BOB KANE

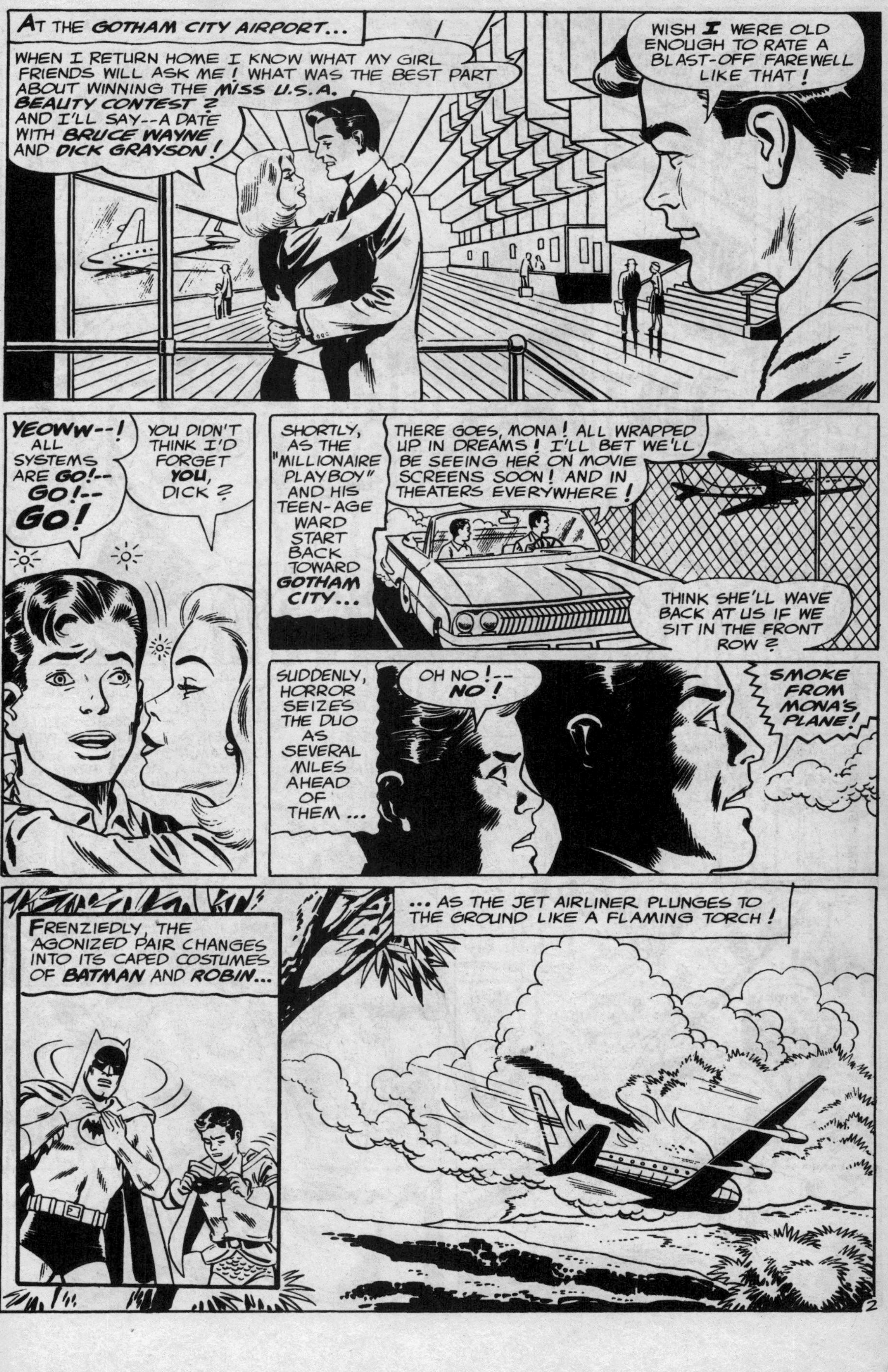
AT THE GOTHAM CITY AIRPORT...
WHEN I RETURN HOME I KNOW WHAT MY GIRL FRIENDS WILL ASK ME! WHAT WAS THE BEST PART ABOUT WINNING THE MISS U.S.A. BEAUTY CONTEST? AND I'LL SAY--A DATE WITH BRUCE WAYNE AND DICK GRAYSON!
WISH I WERE OLD ENOUGH TO RATE A BLAST-OFF FAREWELL LIKE THAT!
YEOWW--! ALL SYSTEMS ARE GO!--GO!--GO!
YOU DIDN'T THINK I'D FORGET YOU, DICK?
SHORTLY, AS THE "MILLIONAIRE PLAYBOY" AND HIS TEEN-AGE WARD START BACK TOWARD GOTHAM CITY...
THERE GOES, MONA! ALL WRAPPED UP IN DREAMS! I'LL BET WE'LL BE SEEING HER ON MOVIE SCREENS SOON! AND IN THEATERS EVERYWHERE!
THINK SHE'LL WAVE BACK AT US IF WE SIT IN THE FRONT ROW?
SUDDENLY, HORROR SEIZES THE DUO AS SEVERAL MILES AHEAD OF THEM...
OH NO!--NO!
SMOKE FROM MONA'S PLANE!
FRENZIEDLY, THE AGONIZED PAIR CHANGES INTO ITS CAPED COSTUMES OF BATMAN AND ROBIN...
...AS THE JET AIRLINER PLUNGES TO THE GROUND LIKE A FLAMING TORCH!
2

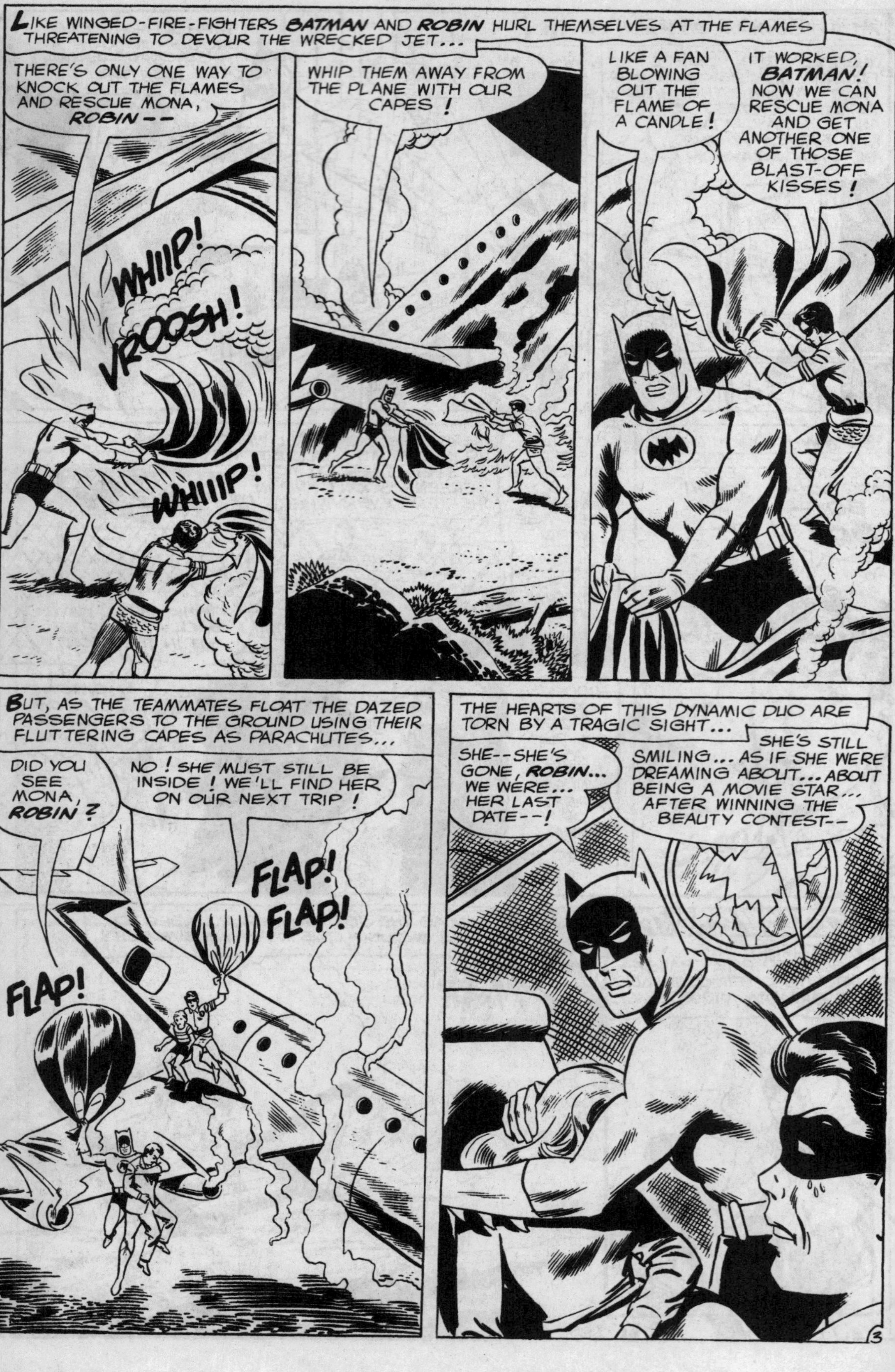
LIKE WINGED-FIRE-FIGHTERS BATMAN AND ROBIN HURL THEMSELVES AT THE FLAMES THREATENING TO DEVOUR THE WRECKED JET...
THERE'S ONLY ONE WAY TO KNOCK OUT THE FLAMES AND RESCUE MONA, ROBIN--
WHIIP!
VROOSH!
WHIIIP!
WHIP THEM AWAY FROM THE PLANE WITH OUR CAPES!
LIKE A FAN BLOWING OUT THE FLAME OF A CANDLE!
IT WORKED, BATMAN! NOW WE CAN RESCUE MONA AND GET ANOTHER ONE OF THOSE BLAST-OFF KISSES!
BUT, AS THE TEAMMATES FLOAT THE DAZED PASSENGERS TO THE GROUND USING THEIR FLUTTERING CAPES AS PARACHUTES...
DID YOU SEE MONA, ROBIN?
NO! SHE MUST STILL BE INSIDE! WE'LL FIND HER ON OUR NEXT TRIP!
FLAP! FLAP!
FLAP!
THE HEARTS OF THIS DYNAMIC DUO ARE TORN BY A TRAGIC SIGHT...
SHE--SHE'S GONE, ROBIN... WE WERE... HER LAST DATE--!
SHE'S STILL SMILING... AS IF SHE WERE DREAMING ABOUT... ABOUT BEING A MOVIE STAR... AFTER WINNING THE BEAUTY CONTEST--
3

AS RESCUE CREWS SPEED UP, *BATMAN* QUESTIONS THE PILOT AND IS STUNNED TO HEAR...

THE SHIP WAS ATTACKED BY BIRDS, *BATMAN!* BUZZARDS!-- VULTURES!-- CONDORS!--

SMASHING MY WIND-SHIELD! DROPPING THE AIR PRESSURE! FOUL-ING THE AFTER-BURNERS! CROSSING THE CONTROLS!

BIRDS--ATTACKING LIKE *KAMIKAZE* FIGHTER PLANES! I--I NEVER SAW ANYTHING LIKE IT!

WE WERE TOO FAR AWAY TO SEE ANY BIRDS FROM WHERE WE WERE WHEN WE SAW THE PLANE GO DOWN! BUT-- IF THERE REALLY WERE SUCH AN ATTACK-- WHY ISN'T THERE ANY EVIDENCE OF IT?

BEATS ME, *BATMAN!* NOT A SINGLE BODY OF A DEAD BIRD AROUND! YET-- SOME *MUST* HAVE BEEN KILLED ATTACKING THE PLANE--IF THERE WERE SUCH AN ATTACK!

WHILE THE FAMED DETECTIVE IS GIVING HIS REPORT TO THE AUTHORITIES SHORTLY, AT THE AIRFIELD'S COM-MUNICATION'S CENTER, WHICH IS IN CONTACT WITH ALL APPROACHING AIRCRAFT...

THIS IS FLIGHT *309!* OUTBOUND FOR BOSTON! ATTACKED BY SAVAGE BIRDS! GOING DOWN!...

MAY DAY! MAY DAY! MAY DAY! BIRDS FORCING ME DOWN!

THIS IS FLIGHT *451!* ATTACKED BY BIRDS! GOING DOWN WITHOUT POWER!

FLIGHT *117!* INBOUND TO GOTHAM CITY-- ATTACKING BIRDS--!

FLIGHT EMERGENCY CALLS SUDDENLY CEASE AND...

CRASH!

AND THEN--LIKE WINGED NIGHTMARES CHILLING EVERYONE'S BLOOD--A SINISTER FLOCK APPEARS TO THE INCREDULOUS SPECTATORS...

ATTENTION! THIS IS THE *BIRDMASTER!* THE SOUNDS OF FALLING AIRCRAFT PROVE THAT *I* CONTROL THE AIRWAYS! I WARN YOU! MY FLOCKS WILL DESTROY ANYONE DARING TO TRESPASS IN MY REALM! ATTENTION! THIS IS THE *BIRDMASTER!*

ROBIN! MONA DIDN'T DIE *ACCIDENTALLY!* SHE WAS *MURDERED!*

AND WE'RE LIS-TENING TO THE TAPED VOICE OF THE KILLER! CARRIED BY HIS INFERNAL BIRDS! TAUNTING US!

4

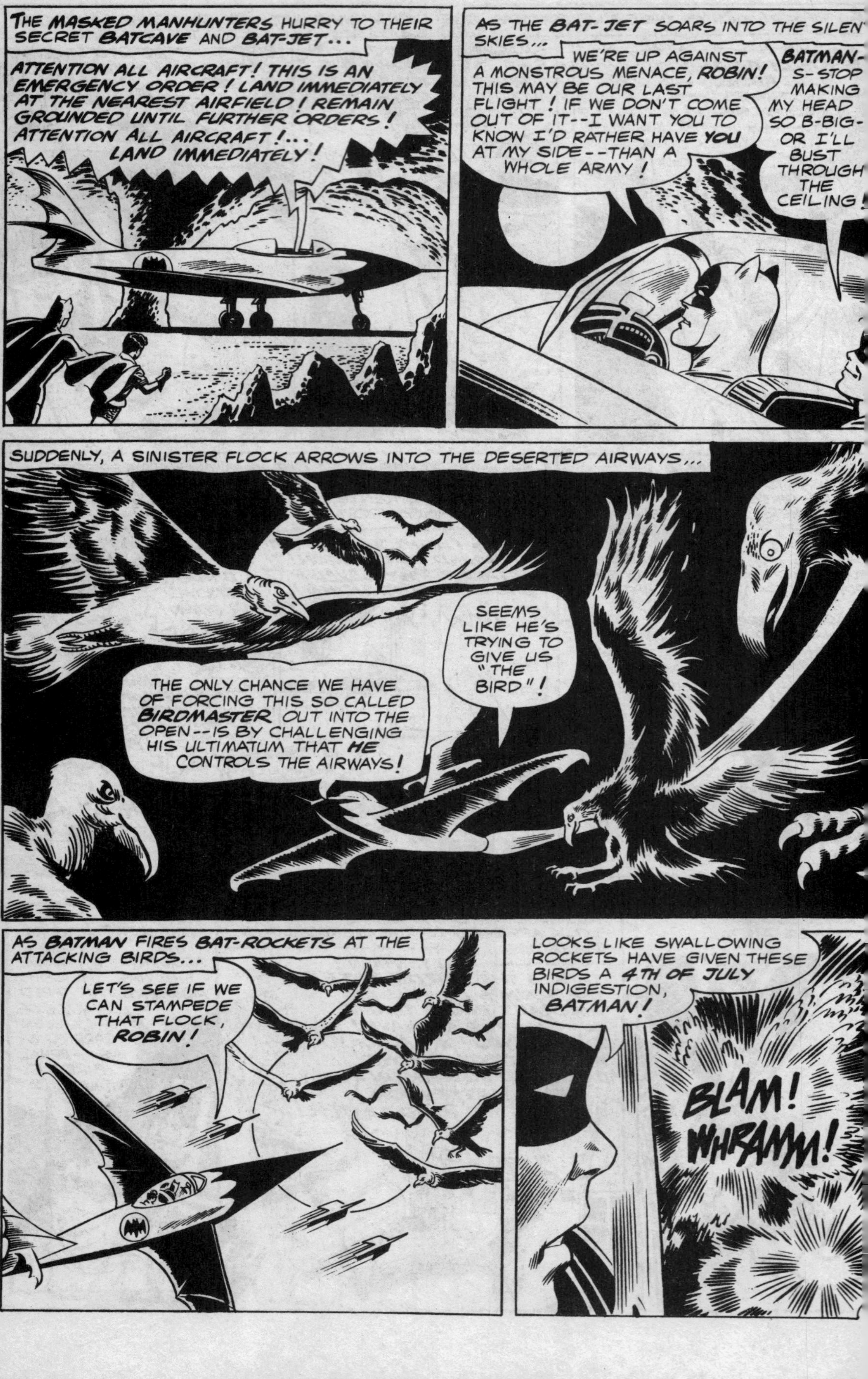
THE MASKED MANHUNTERS HURRY TO THEIR SECRET BATCAVE AND BAT-JET...
ATTENTION ALL AIRCRAFT! THIS IS AN EMERGENCY ORDER! LAND IMMEDIATELY AT THE NEAREST AIRFIELD! REMAIN GROUNDED UNTIL FURTHER ORDERS! ATTENTION ALL AIRCRAFT!... LAND IMMEDIATELY!
AS THE BAT-JET SOARS INTO THE SILEN
SKIES...
WE'RE UP AGAINST A MONSTROUS MENACE, ROBIN! THIS MAY BE OUR LAST FLIGHT! IF WE DON'T COME OUT OF IT--I WANT YOU TO KNOW I'D RATHER HAVE YOU AT MY SIDE--THAN A WHOLE ARMY!
BATMAN-S-STOP MAKING MY HEAD SO B-BIG-OR I'LL BUST THROUGH THE CEILING!
SUDDENLY, A SINISTER FLOCK ARROWS INTO THE DESERTED AIRWAYS...
THE ONLY CHANCE WE HAVE OF FORCING THIS SO CALLED BIRDMASTER OUT INTO THE OPEN--IS BY CHALLENGING HIS ULTIMATUM THAT HE CONTROLS THE AIRWAYS!
SEEMS LIKE HE'S TRYING TO GIVE US "THE BIRD"!
AS BATMAN FIRES BAT-ROCKETS AT THE ATTACKING BIRDS...
LET'S SEE IF WE CAN STAMPEDE THAT FLOCK, ROBIN!
LOOKS LIKE SWALLOWING ROCKETS HAVE GIVEN THESE BIRDS A 4TH OF JULY INDIGESTION, BATMAN!
BLAM! WHRAMM!

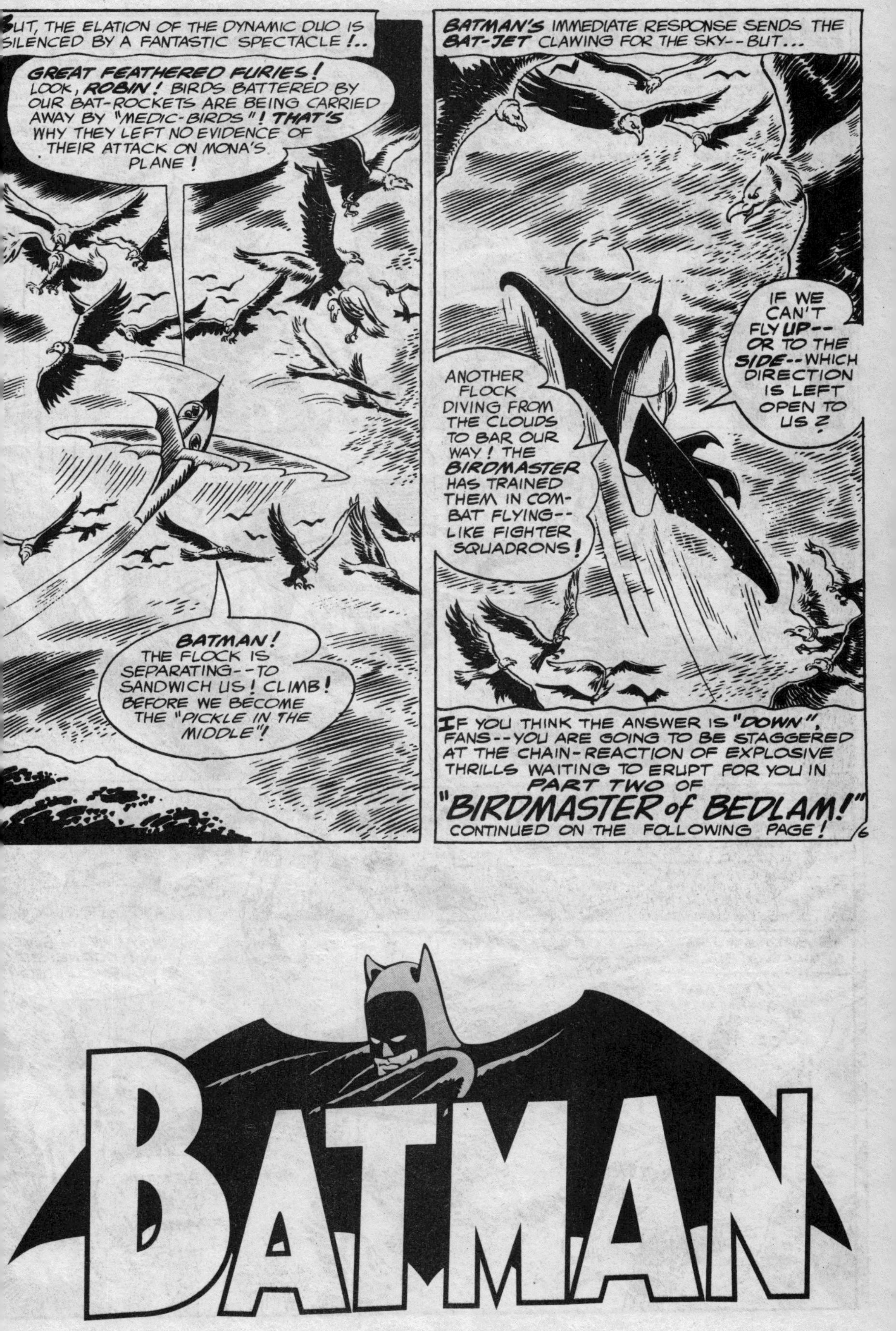
BUT, THE ELATION OF THE DYNAMIC DUO IS SILENCED BY A FANTASTIC SPECTACLE!..
GREAT FEATHERED FURIES! LOOK, ROBIN! BIRDS BATTERED BY OUR BAT-ROCKETS ARE BEING CARRIED AWAY BY "MEDIC-BIRDS"! THAT'S WHY THEY LEFT NO EVIDENCE OF THEIR ATTACK ON MONA'S PLANE!
BATMAN! THE FLOCK IS SEPARATING--TO SANDWICH US! CLIMB! BEFORE WE BECOME THE "PICKLE IN THE MIDDLE"!
BATMAN'S IMMEDIATE RESPONSE SENDS THE BAT-JET CLAWING FOR THE SKY--BUT...
ANOTHER FLOCK DIVING FROM THE CLOUDS TO BAR OUR WAY! THE BIRDMASTER HAS TRAINED THEM IN COMBAT FLYING--LIKE FIGHTER SQUADRONS!
IF WE CAN'T FLY UP--OR TO THE SIDE--WHICH DIRECTION IS LEFT OPEN TO US?
IF YOU THINK THE ANSWER IS "DOWN", FANS--YOU ARE GOING TO BE STAGGERED AT THE CHAIN-REACTION OF EXPLOSIVE THRILLS WAITING TO ERUPT FOR YOU IN PART TWO OF "BIRDMASTER of BEDLAM!"
CONTINUED ON THE FOLLOWING PAGE!
6

BATMAN

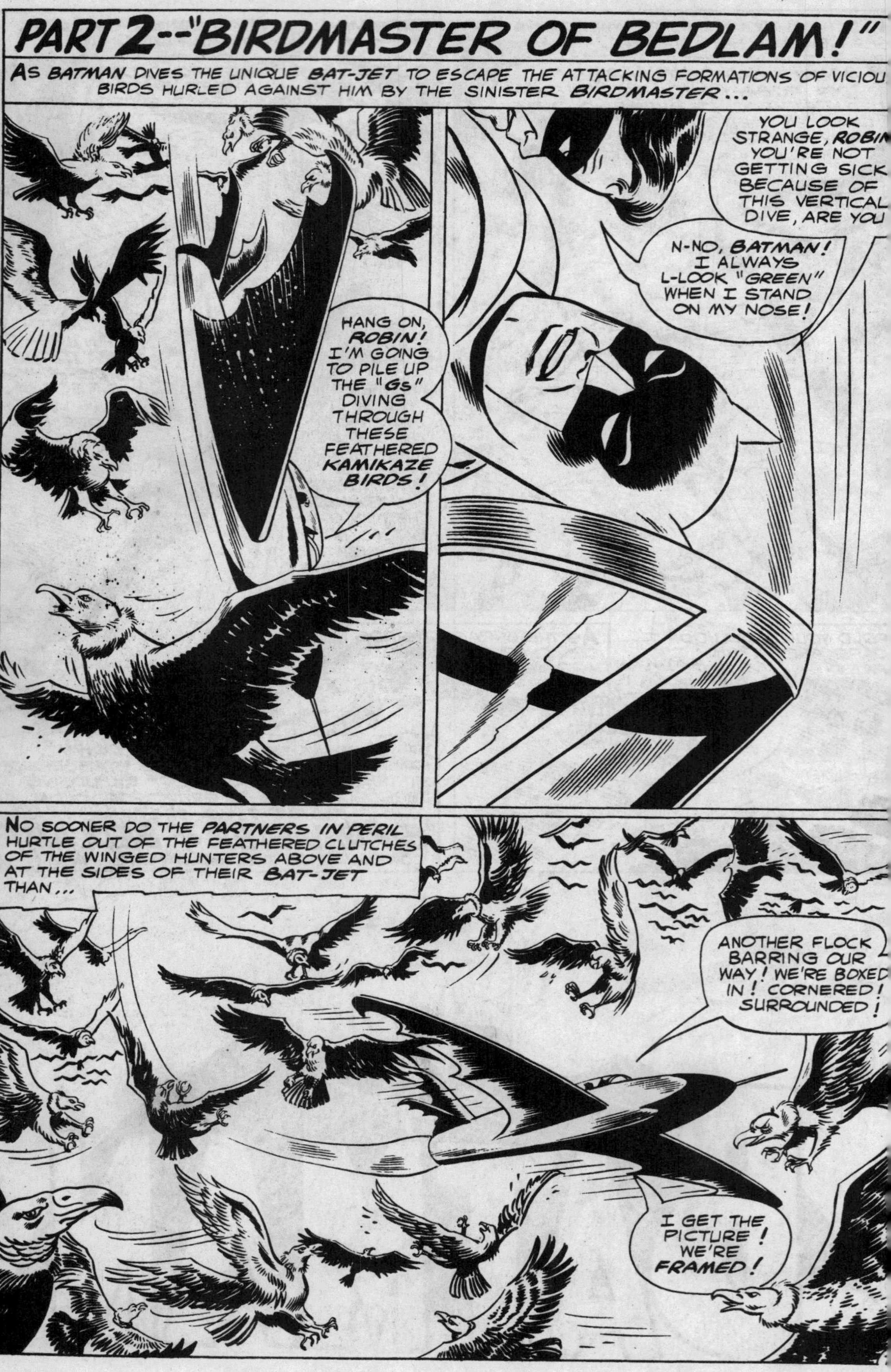
PART 2--"BIRDMASTER OF BEDLAM!"
AS BATMAN DIVES THE UNIQUE BAT-JET TO ESCAPE THE ATTACKING FORMATIONS OF VICIOU BIRDS HURLED AGAINST HIM BY THE SINISTER BIRDMASTER...
HANG ON, ROBIN! I'M GOING TO PILE UP THE "Gs" DIVING THROUGH THESE FEATHERED KAMIKAZE BIRDS!
YOU LOOK STRANGE, ROBI YOU'RE NOT GETTING SICK BECAUSE OF THIS VERTICAL DIVE, ARE YOU
N-NO, BATMAN! I ALWAYS L-LOOK "GREEN" WHEN I STAND ON MY NOSE!
NO SOONER DO THE PARTNERS IN PERIL HURTLE OUT OF THE FEATHERED CLUTCHES OF THE WINGED HUNTERS ABOVE AND AT THE SIDES OF THEIR BAT-JET THAN...
ANOTHER FLOCK BARRING OUR WAY! WE'RE BOXED IN! CORNERED! SURROUNDED!
I GET THE PICTURE! WE'RE FRAMED!

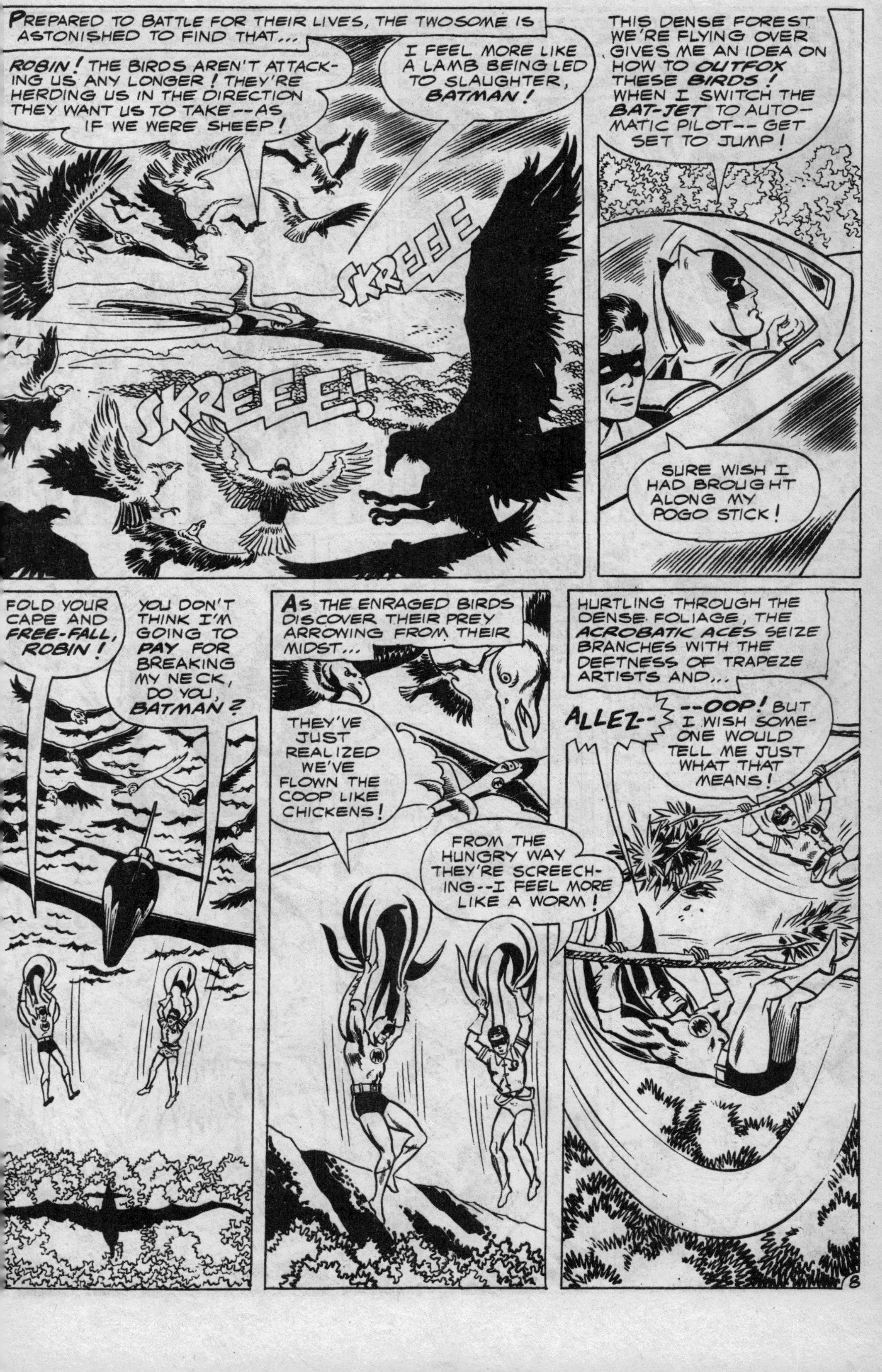
PREPARED TO BATTLE FOR THEIR LIVES, THE TWOSOME IS ASTONISHED TO FIND THAT...
ROBIN! THE BIRDS AREN'T ATTACKING US ANY LONGER! THEY'RE HERDING US IN THE DIRECTION THEY WANT US TO TAKE--AS IF WE WERE SHEEP!
I FEEL MORE LIKE A LAMB BEING LED TO SLAUGHTER, BATMAN!
SKREEE
SKREEE!
THIS DENSE FOREST WE'RE FLYING OVER GIVES ME AN IDEA ON HOW TO OUTFOX THESE BIRDS! WHEN I SWITCH THE BAT-JET TO AUTOMATIC PILOT-- GET SET TO JUMP!
SURE WISH I HAD BROUGHT ALONG MY POGO STICK!
FOLD YOUR CAPE AND FREE-FALL, ROBIN!
YOU DON'T THINK I'M GOING TO PAY FOR BREAKING MY NECK, DO YOU, BATMAN?
AS THE ENRAGED BIRDS DISCOVER THEIR PREY ARROWING FROM THEIR MIDST...
THEY'VE JUST REALIZED WE'VE FLOWN THE COOP LIKE CHICKENS!
FROM THE HUNGRY WAY THEY'RE SCREECHING--I FEEL MORE LIKE A WORM!
HURTLING THROUGH THE DENSE FOLIAGE, THE ACROBATIC ACES SEIZE BRANCHES WITH THE DEFTNESS OF TRAPEZE ARTISTS AND...
ALLEZ--
--OOP! BUT I WISH SOMEONE WOULD TELL ME JUST WHAT THAT MEANS!
8

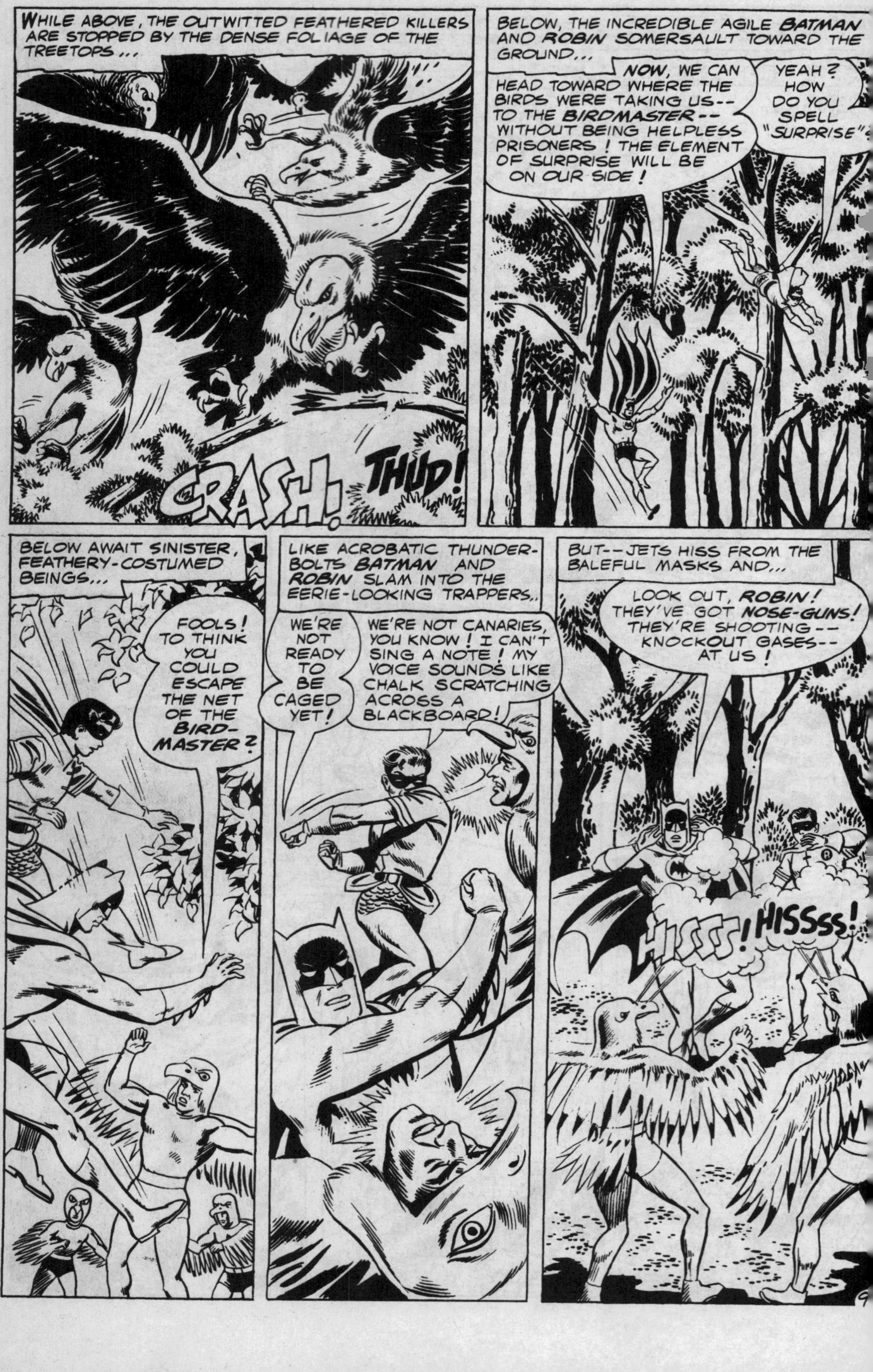
WHILE ABOVE, THE OUTWITTED FEATHERED KILLERS ARE STOPPED BY THE DENSE FOLIAGE OF THE TREETOPS...
CRASH!
THUD!
BELOW, THE INCREDIBLE AGILE BATMAN AND ROBIN SOMERSAULT TOWARD THE GROUND...
NOW, WE CAN HEAD TOWARD WHERE THE BIRDS WERE TAKING US-- TO THE BIRDMASTER-- WITHOUT BEING HELPLESS PRISONERS! THE ELEMENT OF SURPRISE WILL BE ON OUR SIDE!
YEAH? HOW DO YOU SPELL "SURPRISE"?
BELOW AWAIT SINISTER, FEATHERY-COSTUMED BEINGS...
FOOLS! TO THINK YOU COULD ESCAPE THE NET OF THE BIRD-MASTER?
LIKE ACROBATIC THUNDER-BOLTS BATMAN AND ROBIN SLAM INTO THE EERIE-LOOKING TRAPPERS..
WE'RE NOT READY TO BE CAGED YET!
WE'RE NOT CANARIES, YOU KNOW! I CAN'T SING A NOTE! MY VOICE SOUNDS LIKE CHALK SCRATCHING ACROSS A BLACKBOARD!
BUT--JETS HISS FROM THE BALEFUL MASKS AND...
LOOK OUT, ROBIN! THEY'VE GOT NOSE-GUNS! THEY'RE SHOOTING-- KNOCKOUT GASES-- AT US!
HISSS!
HISSSS!
9

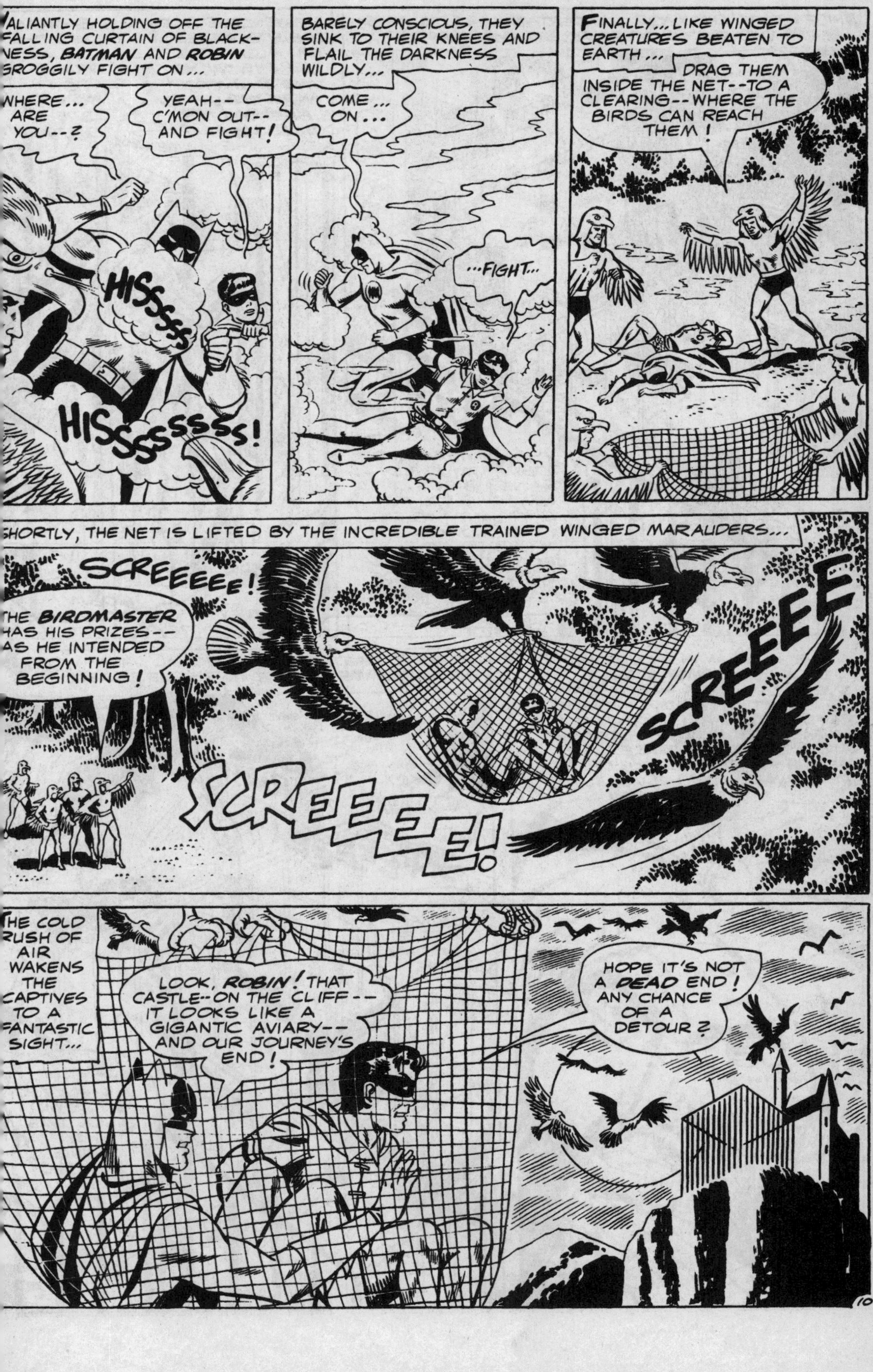
VALIANTLY HOLDING OFF THE FALLING CURTAIN OF BLACKNESS, BATMAN AND ROBIN GROGGILY FIGHT ON...
WHERE... ARE YOU--?
YEAH-- C'MON OUT-- AND FIGHT!
HISSSSSS
HISSSSSSSSS!
BARELY CONSCIOUS, THEY SINK TO THEIR KNEES AND FLAIL THE DARKNESS WILDLY...
COME... ON...
...FIGHT...
FINALLY... LIKE WINGED CREATURES BEATEN TO EARTH...
DRAG THEM INSIDE THE NET--TO A CLEARING--WHERE THE BIRDS CAN REACH THEM!
SHORTLY, THE NET IS LIFTED BY THE INCREDIBLE TRAINED WINGED MARAUDERS...
SCREEEEEE!
THE BIRDMASTER HAS HIS PRIZES-- AS HE INTENDED FROM THE BEGINNING!
SCREEEEEE
SCREEEEE!
THE COLD RUSH OF AIR WAKENS THE CAPTIVES TO A FANTASTIC SIGHT...
LOOK, ROBIN! THAT CASTLE--ON THE CLIFF-- IT LOOKS LIKE A GIGANTIC AVIARY-- AND OUR JOURNEY'S END!
HOPE IT'S NOT A DEAD END! ANY CHANCE OF A DETOUR?
10

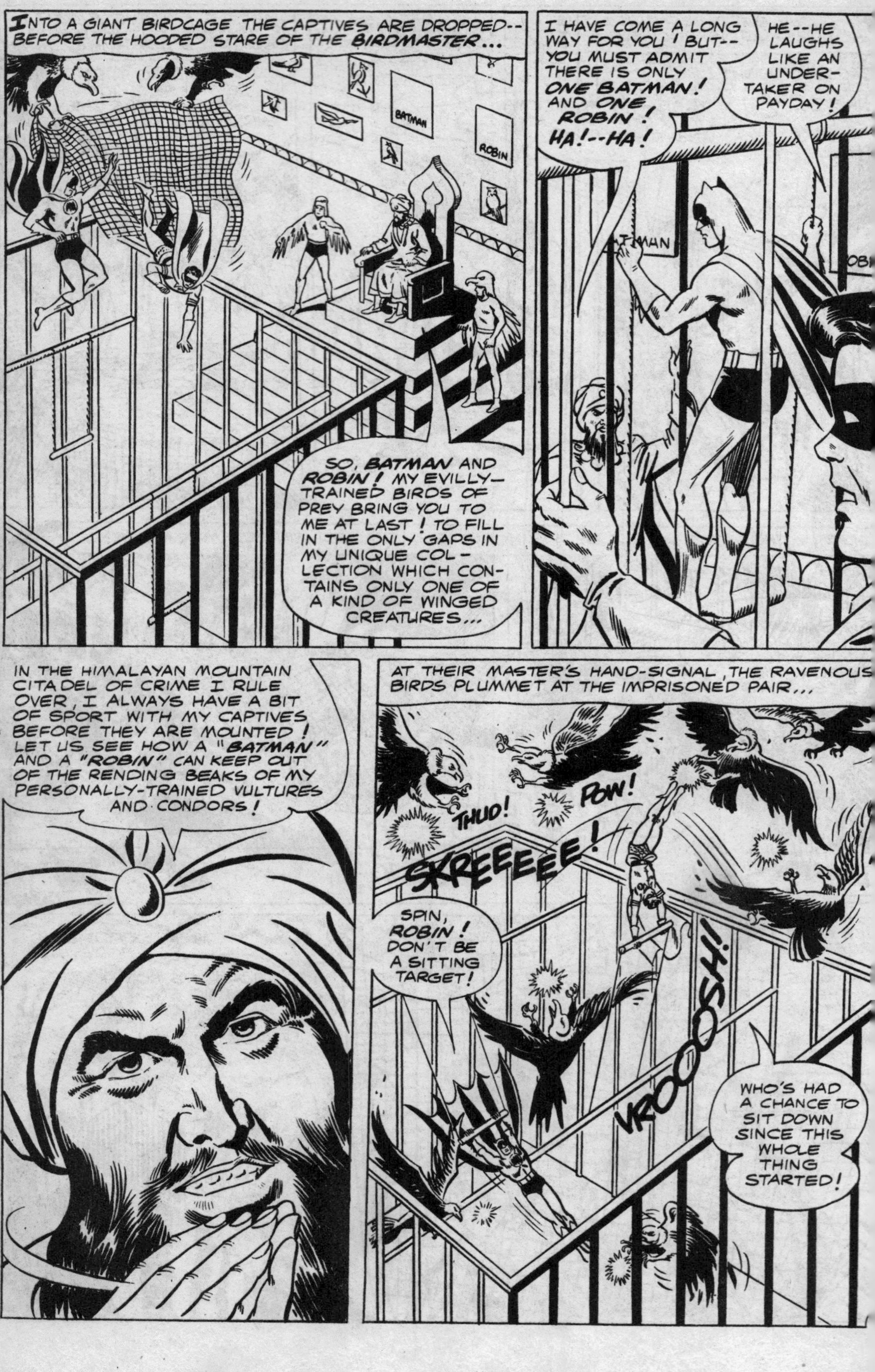
INTO A GIANT BIRDCAGE THE CAPTIVES ARE DROPPED-- BEFORE THE HOODED STARE OF THE BIRDMASTER...
BATMAN
ROBIN
SO, BATMAN AND ROBIN! MY EVILLY-TRAINED BIRDS OF PREY BRING YOU TO ME AT LAST! TO FILL IN THE ONLY GAPS IN MY UNIQUE COLLECTION WHICH CONTAINS ONLY ONE OF A KIND OF WINGED CREATURES...
I HAVE COME A LONG WAY FOR YOU! BUT-- YOU MUST ADMIT THERE IS ONLY ONE BATMAN! AND ONE ROBIN! HA!--HA!
HE--HE LAUGHS LIKE AN UNDERTAKER ON PAYDAY!
IN THE HIMALAYAN MOUNTAIN CITADEL OF CRIME I RULE OVER, I ALWAYS HAVE A BIT OF SPORT WITH MY CAPTIVES BEFORE THEY ARE MOUNTED! LET US SEE HOW A "BATMAN" AND A "ROBIN" CAN KEEP OUT OF THE RENDING BEAKS OF MY PERSONALLY-TRAINED VULTURES AND CONDORS!
AT THEIR MASTER'S HAND-SIGNAL, THE RAVENOUS BIRDS PLUMMET AT THE IMPRISONED PAIR...
THUD!
POW!
SKREEEEEE!
SPIN, ROBIN! DON'T BE A SITTING TARGET!
WHOOSH!
VROOOOSH!
WHO'S HAD A CHANCE TO SIT DOWN SINCE THIS WHOLE THING STARTED!

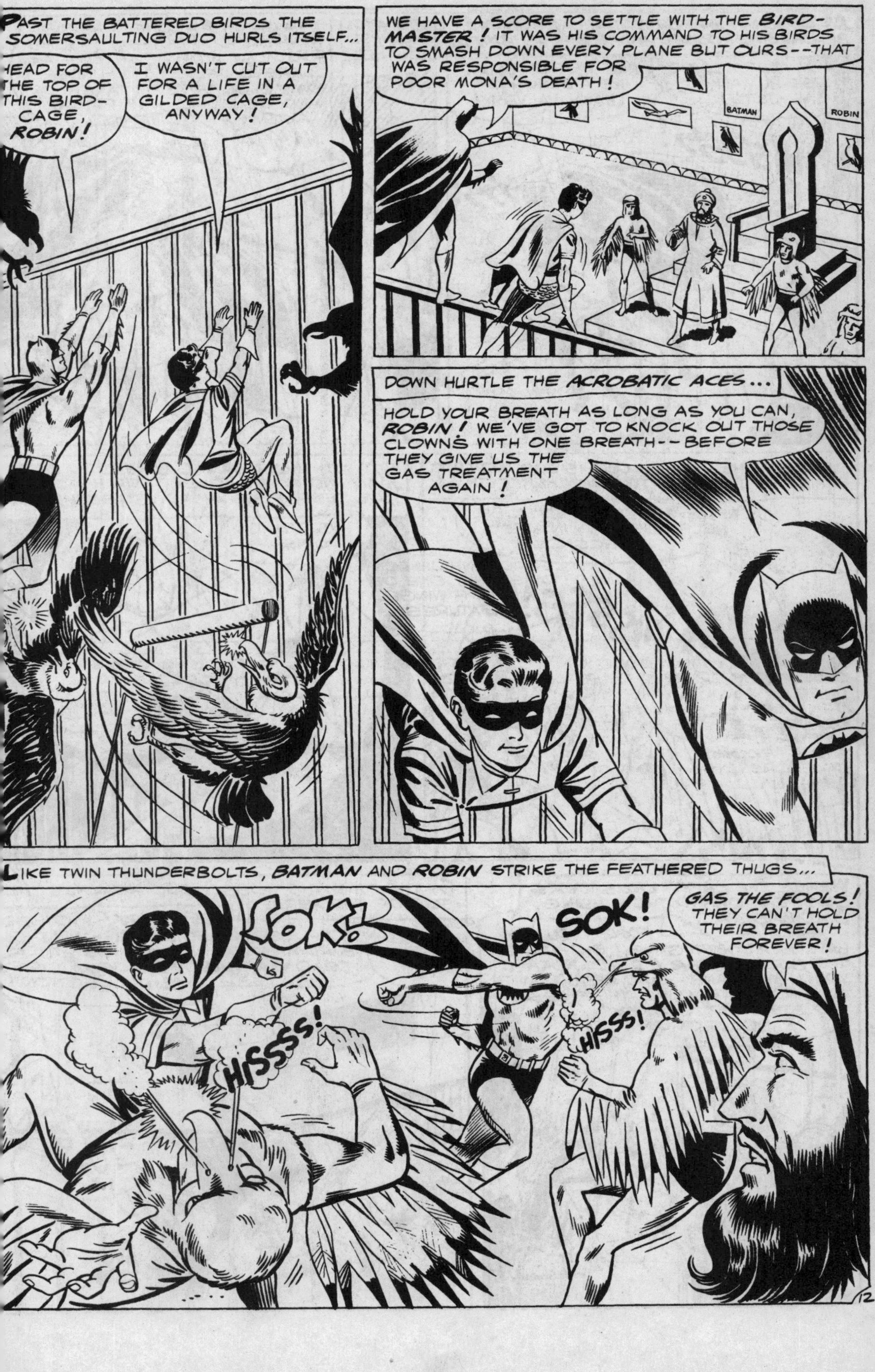
PAST THE BATTERED BIRDS THE SOMERSAULTING DUO HURLS ITSELF...
HEAD FOR THE TOP OF THIS BIRD-CAGE, ROBIN!
I WASN'T CUT OUT FOR A LIFE IN A GILDED CAGE, ANYWAY!
WE HAVE A SCORE TO SETTLE WITH THE BIRD-MASTER! IT WAS HIS COMMAND TO HIS BIRDS TO SMASH DOWN EVERY PLANE BUT OURS--THAT WAS RESPONSIBLE FOR POOR MONA'S DEATH!
BATMAN
ROBIN
DOWN HURTLE THE ACROBATIC ACES...
HOLD YOUR BREATH AS LONG AS YOU CAN, ROBIN! WE'VE GOT TO KNOCK OUT THOSE CLOWNS WITH ONE BREATH--BEFORE THEY GIVE US THE GAS TREATMENT AGAIN!
LIKE TWIN THUNDERBOLTS, BATMAN AND ROBIN STRIKE THE FEATHERED THUGS...
SOK!
SOK!
GAS THE FOOLS! THEY CAN'T HOLD THEIR BREATH FOREVER!
HISSSS!
HISSS!
12

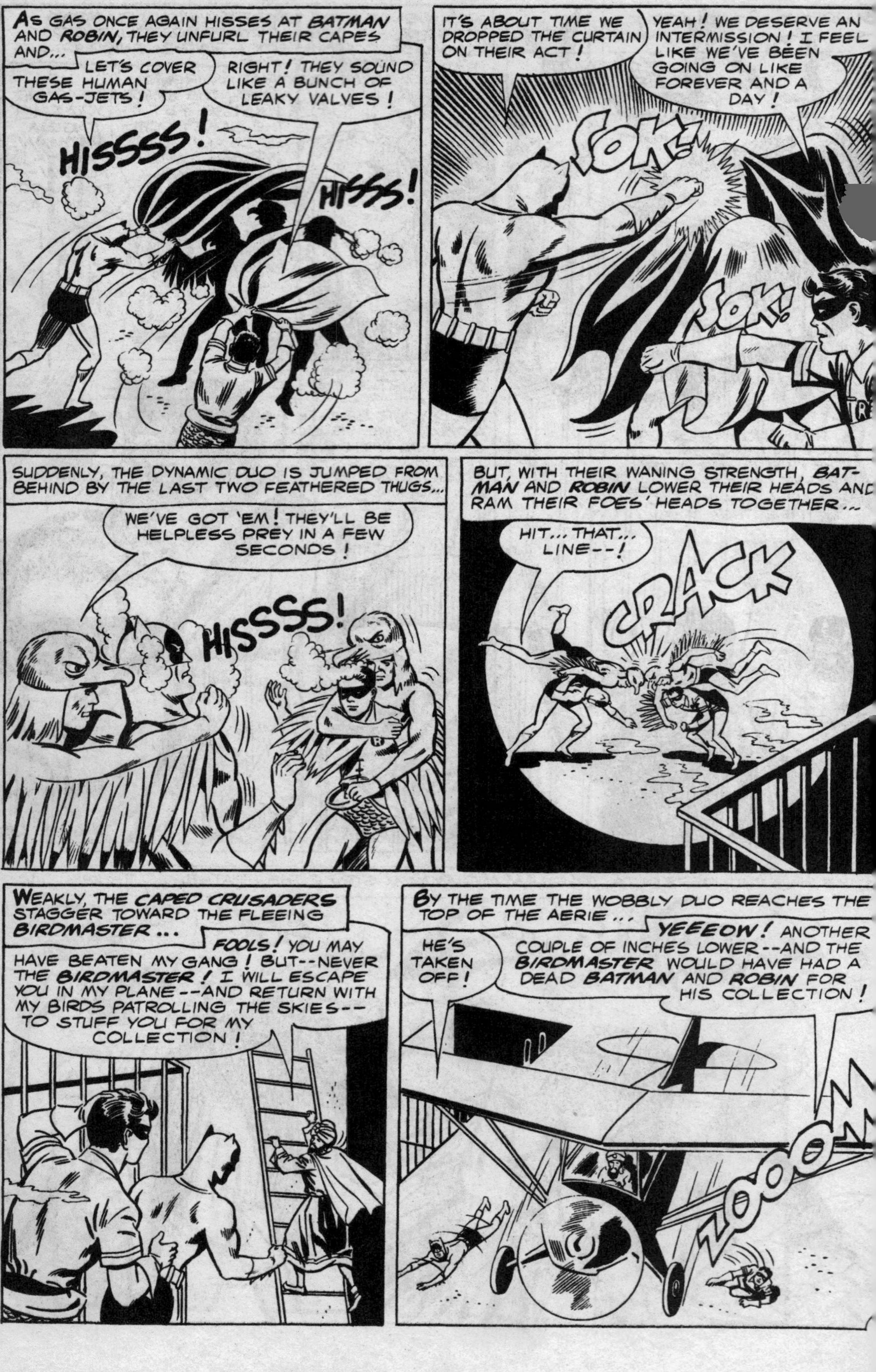
AS GAS ONCE AGAIN HISSES AT BATMAN AND ROBIN, THEY UNFURL THEIR CAPES AND...
LET'S COVER THESE HUMAN GAS-JETS!
RIGHT! THEY SOUND LIKE A BUNCH OF LEAKY VALVES!
HISSSS!
HISSS!
IT'S ABOUT TIME WE DROPPED THE CURTAIN ON THEIR ACT!
YEAH! WE DESERVE AN INTERMISSION! I FEEL LIKE WE'VE BEEN GOING ON LIKE FOREVER AND A DAY!
SOK!
SOK!
SUDDENLY, THE DYNAMIC DUO IS JUMPED FROM BEHIND BY THE LAST TWO FEATHERED THUGS...
WE'VE GOT 'EM! THEY'LL BE HELPLESS PREY IN A FEW SECONDS!
HISSSS!
BUT, WITH THEIR WANING STRENGTH, BATMAN AND ROBIN LOWER THEIR HEADS AND RAM THEIR FOES' HEADS TOGETHER...
HIT... THAT... LINE--!
CRACK
WEAKLY, THE CAPED CRUSADERS STAGGER TOWARD THE FLEEING BIRDMASTER...
FOOLS! YOU MAY HAVE BEATEN MY GANG! BUT--NEVER THE BIRDMASTER! I WILL ESCAPE YOU IN MY PLANE--AND RETURN WITH MY BIRDS PATROLLING THE SKIES--TO STUFF YOU FOR MY COLLECTION!
BY THE TIME THE WOBBLY DUO REACHES THE TOP OF THE AERIE...
HE'S TAKEN OFF!
YEEEOW! ANOTHER COUPLE OF INCHES LOWER--AND THE BIRDMASTER WOULD HAVE HAD A DEAD BATMAN AND ROBIN FOR HIS COLLECTION!
ZOOOOM

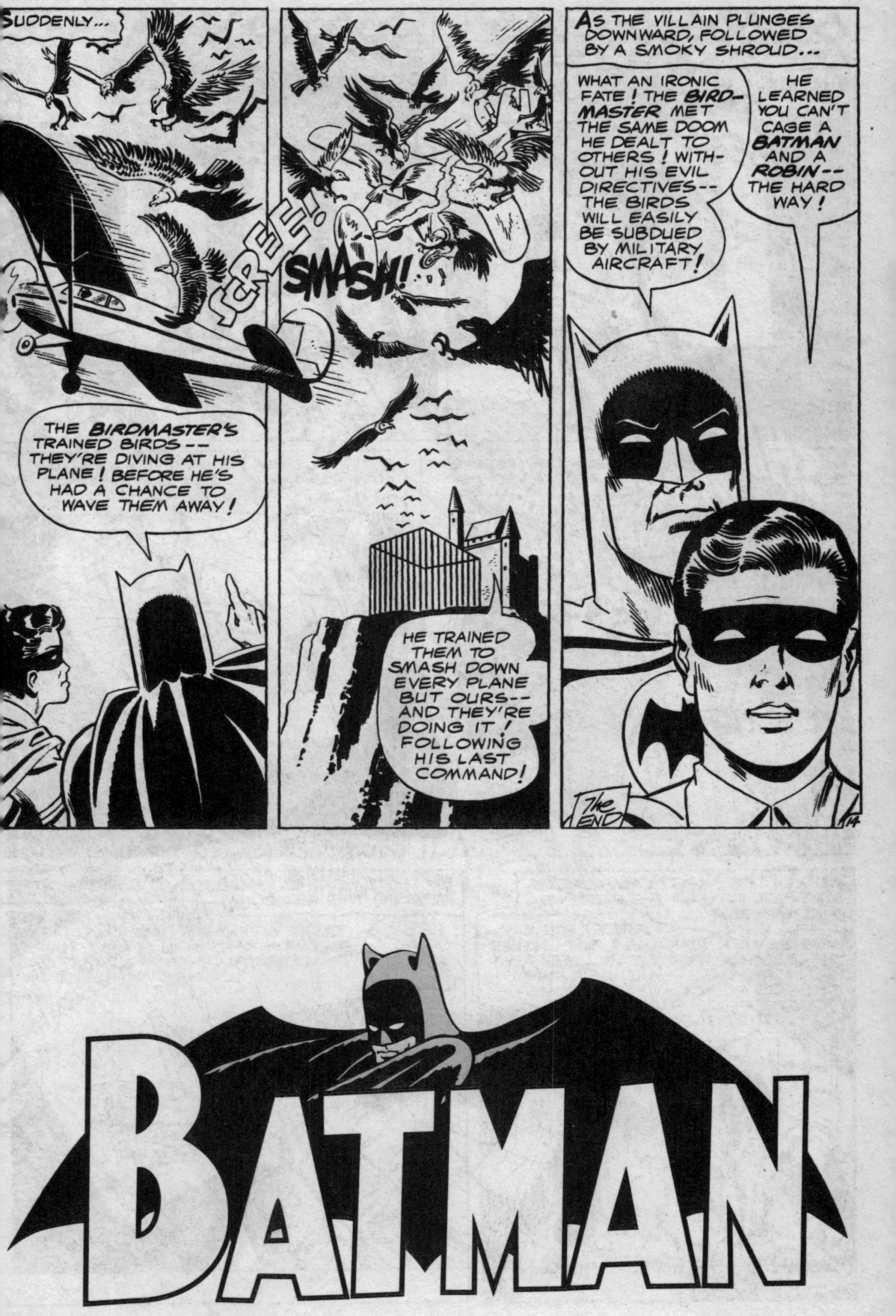
SUDDENLY...
SCREEE!
THE BIRDMASTER'S TRAINED BIRDS -- THEY'RE DIVING AT HIS PLANE! BEFORE HE'S HAD A CHANCE TO WAVE THEM AWAY!
SMASH!
HE TRAINED THEM TO SMASH DOWN EVERY PLANE BUT OURS-- AND THEY'RE DOING IT! FOLLOWING HIS LAST COMMAND!
AS THE VILLAIN PLUNGES DOWNWARD, FOLLOWED BY A SMOKY SHROUD...
WHAT AN IRONIC FATE! THE BIRD-MASTER MET THE SAME DOOM HE DEALT TO OTHERS! WITH-OUT HIS EVIL DIRECTIVES-- THE BIRDS WILL EASILY BE SUBDUED BY MILITARY AIRCRAFT!
HE LEARNED YOU CAN'T CAGE A BATMAN AND A ROBIN-- THE HARD WAY!
The END
14

BATMAN

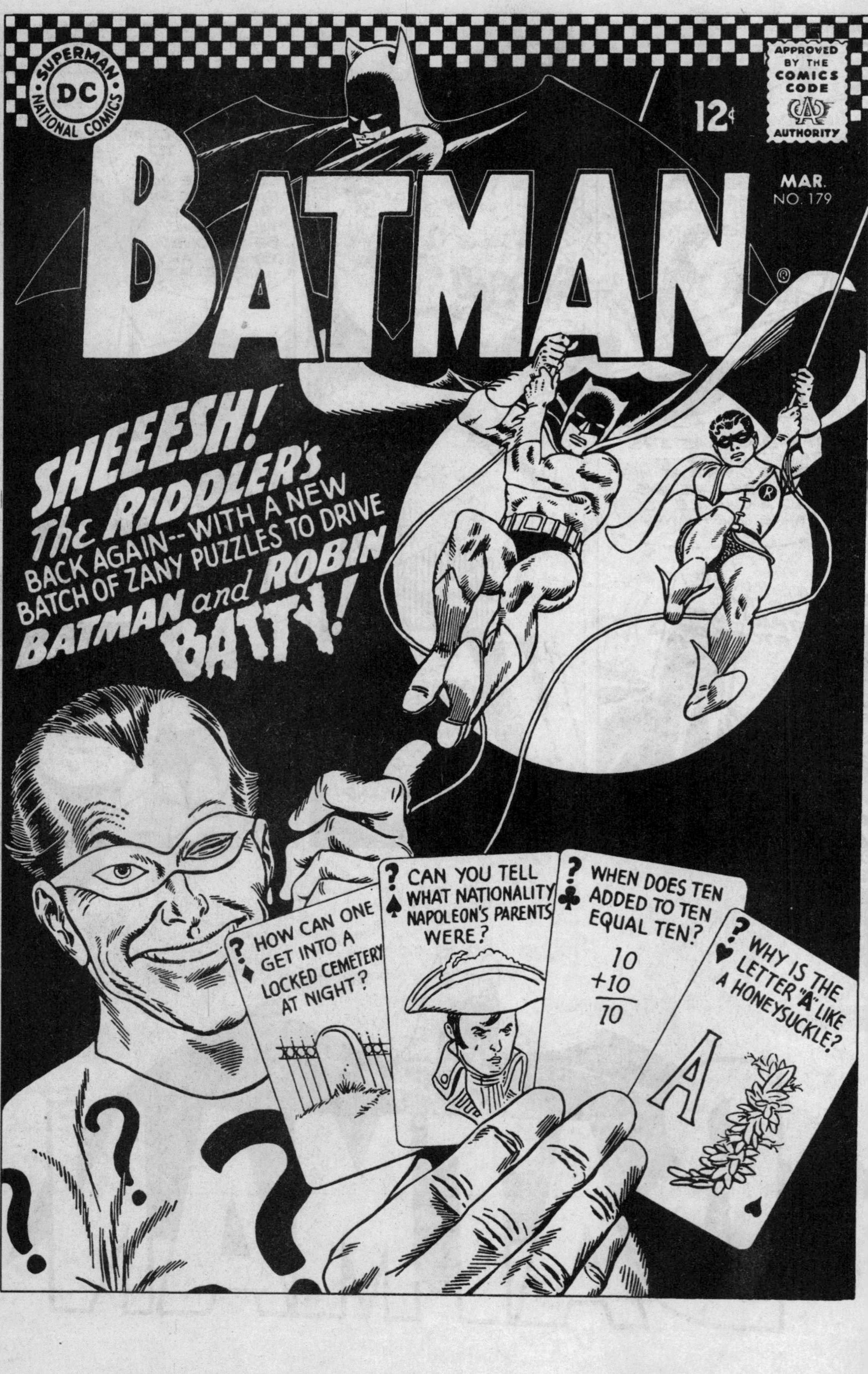
SUPERMAN DC NATIONAL COMICS
APPROVED BY THE COMICS CODE AUTHORITY
12¢
BATMAN
MAR. NO. 179
SHEEESH! The RIDDLER's BACK AGAIN-- WITH A NEW BATCH OF ZANY PUZZLES TO DRIVE BATMAN and ROBIN BATTY!
HOW CAN ONE GET INTO A LOCKED CEMETERY AT NIGHT?
CAN YOU TELL WHAT NATIONALITY NAPOLEON'S PARENTS WERE?
WHEN DOES TEN ADDED TO TEN EQUAL TEN?
10 +10 10
WHY IS THE LETTER "A" LIKE A HONEYSUCKLE?
A

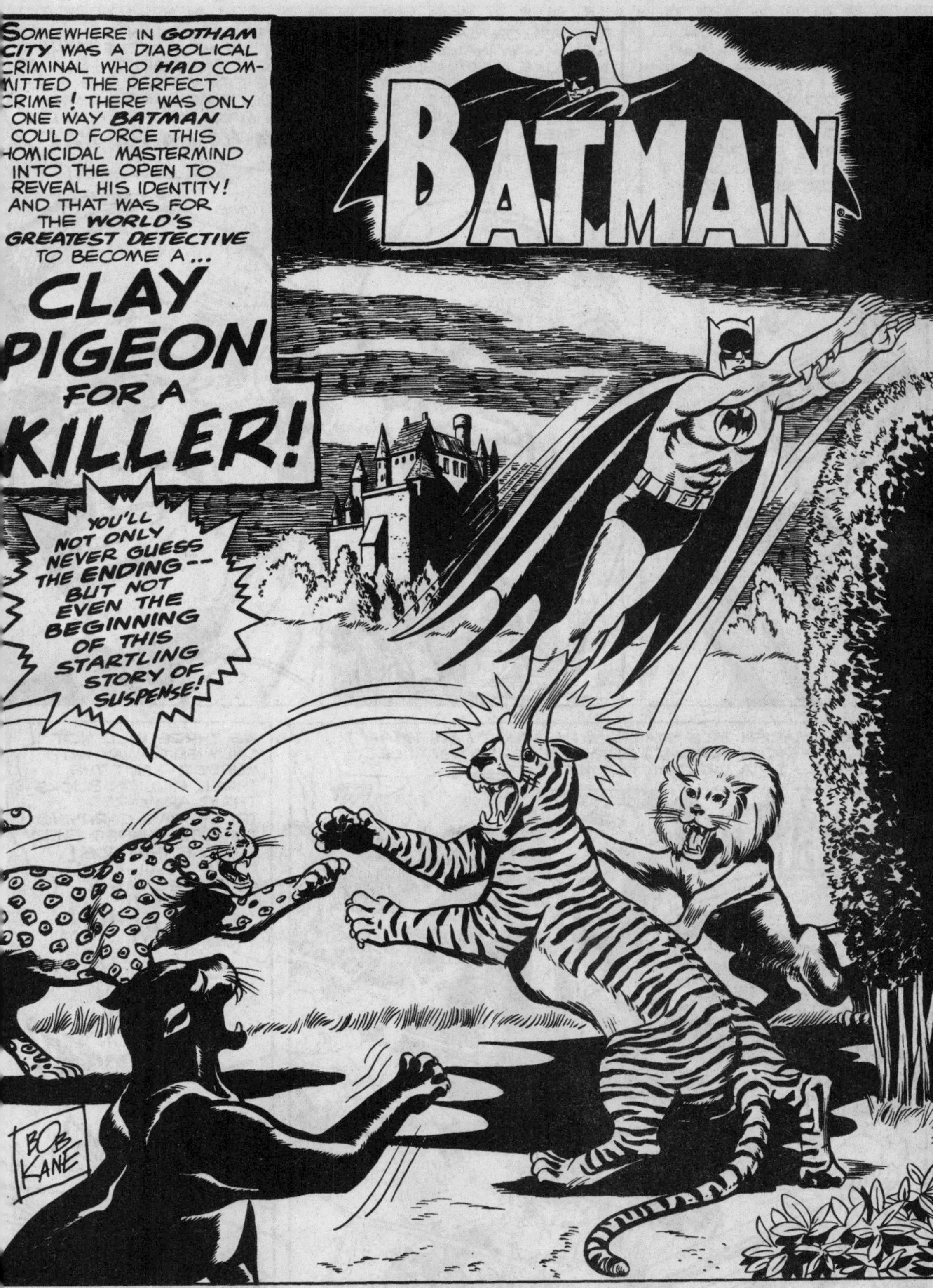
BATMAN
SOMEWHERE IN GOTHAM CITY WAS A DIABOLICAL CRIMINAL WHO HAD COMMITTED THE PERFECT CRIME! THERE WAS ONLY ONE WAY BATMAN COULD FORCE THIS HOMICIDAL MASTERMIND INTO THE OPEN TO REVEAL HIS IDENTITY! AND THAT WAS FOR THE WORLD'S GREATEST DETECTIVE TO BECOME A...
CLAY PIGEON FOR A KILLER!
YOU'LL NOT ONLY NEVER GUESS THE ENDING-- BUT NOT EVEN THE BEGINNING OF THIS STARTLING STORY OF SUSPENSE!
BOB KANE

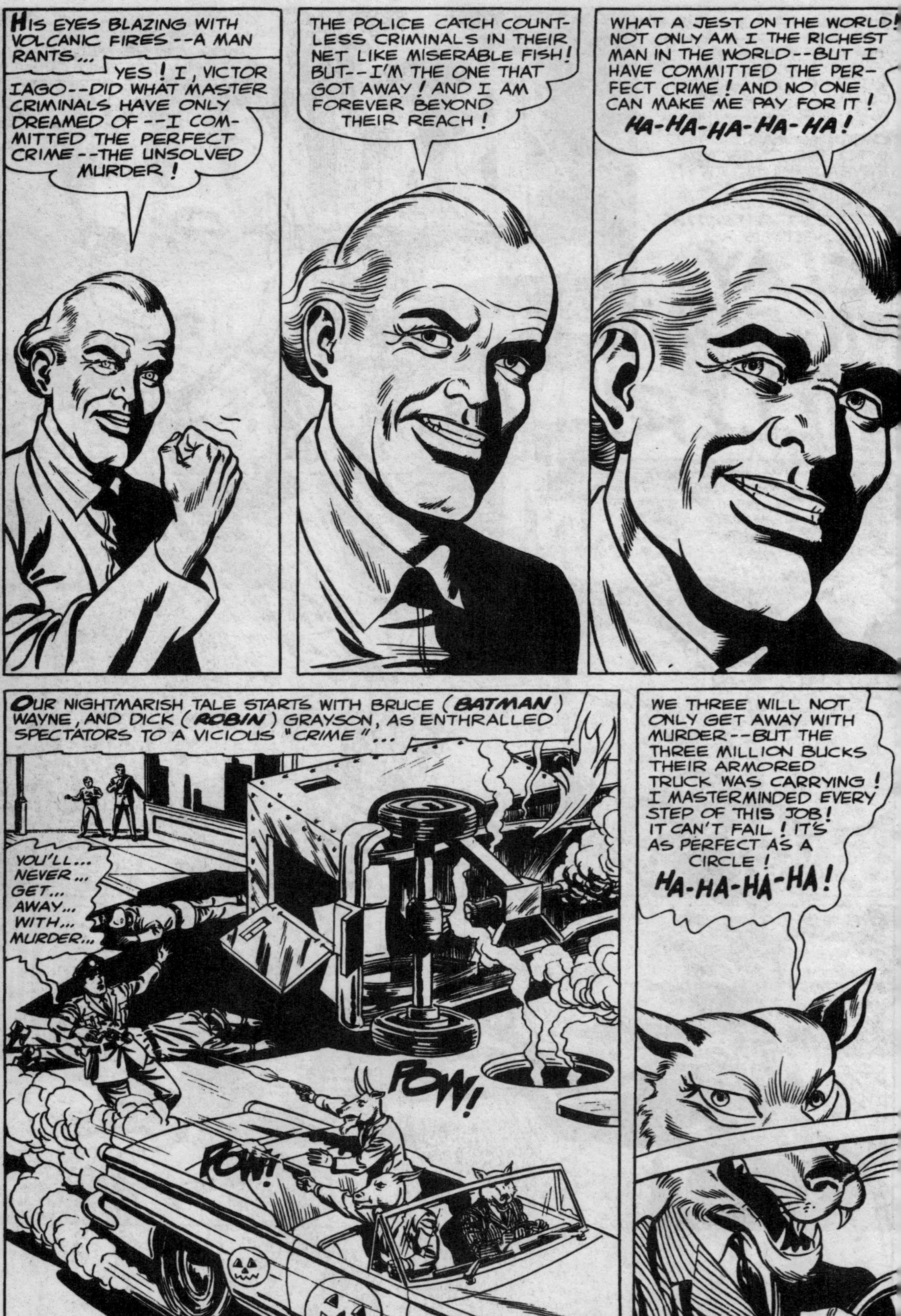
HIS EYES BLAZING WITH VOLCANIC FIRES--A MAN RANTS...
YES! I, VICTOR IAGO--DID WHAT MASTER CRIMINALS HAVE ONLY DREAMED OF--I COMMITTED THE PERFECT CRIME--THE UNSOLVED MURDER!
THE POLICE CATCH COUNTLESS CRIMINALS IN THEIR NET LIKE MISERABLE FISH! BUT--I'M THE ONE THAT GOT AWAY! AND I AM FOREVER BEYOND THEIR REACH!
WHAT A JEST ON THE WORLD! NOT ONLY AM I THE RICHEST MAN IN THE WORLD--BUT I HAVE COMMITTED THE PERFECT CRIME! AND NO ONE CAN MAKE ME PAY FOR IT!
HA-HA-HA-HA-HA!
OUR NIGHTMARISH TALE STARTS WITH BRUCE (BATMAN) WAYNE, AND DICK (ROBIN) GRAYSON, AS ENTHRALLED SPECTATORS TO A VICIOUS "CRIME"...
YOU'LL... NEVER... GET... AWAY... WITH... MURDER...
POW!
POW!
WE THREE WILL NOT ONLY GET AWAY WITH MURDER--BUT THE THREE MILLION BUCKS THEIR ARMORED TRUCK WAS CARRYING! I MASTERMINDED EVERY STEP OF THIS JOB! IT CAN'T FAIL! IT'S AS PERFECT AS A CIRCLE!
HA-HA-HA-HA!

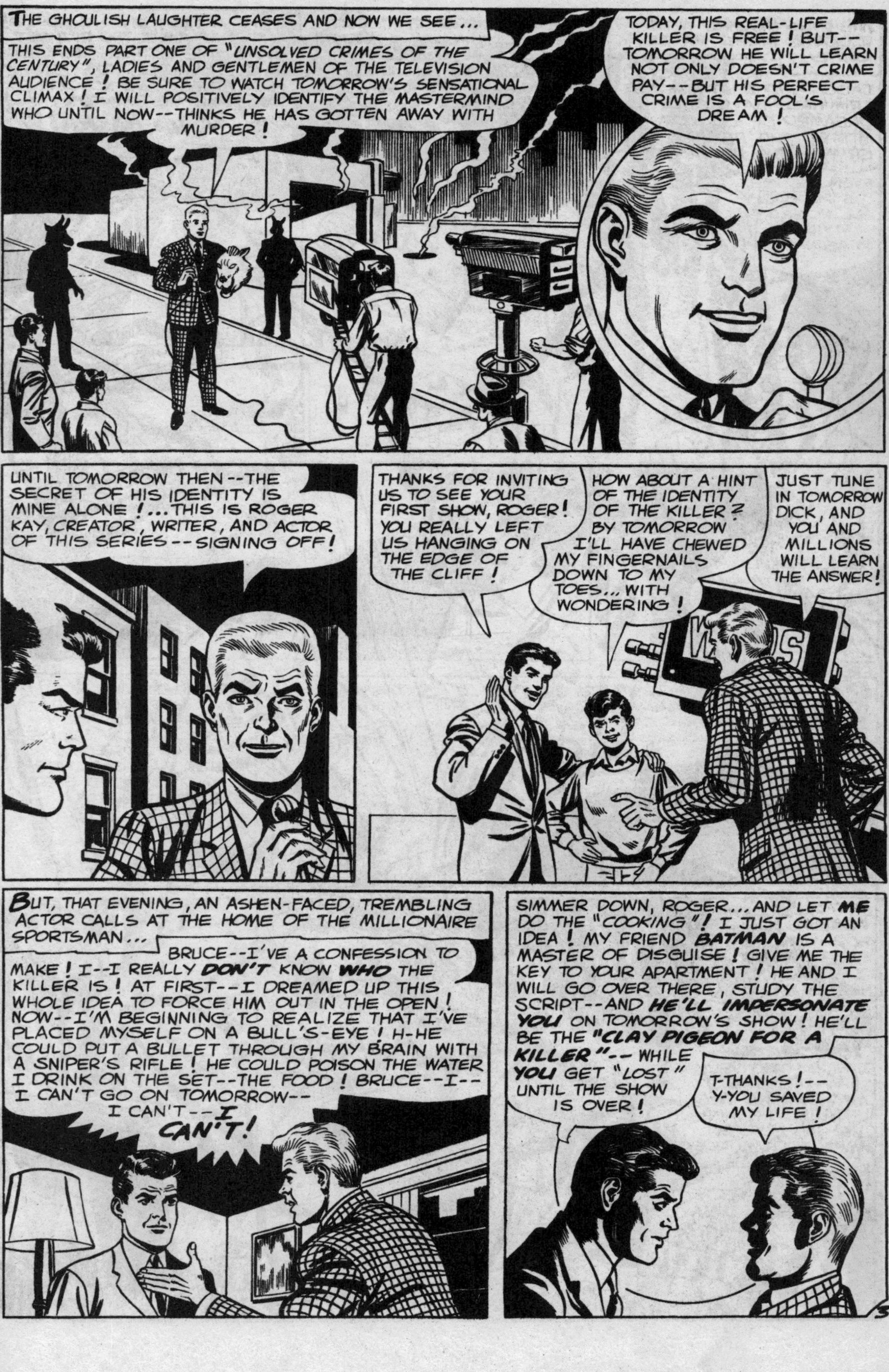
THE GHOULISH LAUGHTER CEASES AND NOW WE SEE...
THIS ENDS PART ONE OF "UNSOLVED CRIMES OF THE CENTURY", LADIES AND GENTLEMEN OF THE TELEVISION AUDIENCE! BE SURE TO WATCH TOMORROW'S SENSATIONAL CLIMAX! I WILL POSITIVELY IDENTIFY THE MASTERMIND WHO UNTIL NOW--THINKS HE HAS GOTTEN AWAY WITH MURDER!
TODAY, THIS REAL-LIFE KILLER IS FREE! BUT--TOMORROW HE WILL LEARN NOT ONLY DOESN'T CRIME PAY--BUT HIS PERFECT CRIME IS A FOOL'S DREAM!
UNTIL TOMORROW THEN--THE SECRET OF HIS IDENTITY IS MINE ALONE!...THIS IS ROGER KAY, CREATOR, WRITER, AND ACTOR OF THIS SERIES--SIGNING OFF!
THANKS FOR INVITING US TO SEE YOUR FIRST SHOW, ROGER! YOU REALLY LEFT US HANGING ON THE EDGE OF THE CLIFF!
HOW ABOUT A HINT OF THE IDENTITY OF THE KILLER? BY TOMORROW I'LL HAVE CHEWED MY FINGERNAILS DOWN TO MY TOES... WITH WONDERING!
JUST TUNE IN TOMORROW DICK, AND YOU AND MILLIONS WILL LEARN THE ANSWER!
BUT, THAT EVENING, AN ASHEN-FACED, TREMBLING ACTOR CALLS AT THE HOME OF THE MILLIONAIRE SPORTSMAN...
BRUCE--I'VE A CONFESSION TO MAKE! I--I REALLY DON'T KNOW WHO THE KILLER IS! AT FIRST--I DREAMED UP THIS WHOLE IDEA TO FORCE HIM OUT IN THE OPEN! NOW--I'M BEGINNING TO REALIZE THAT I'VE PLACED MYSELF ON A BULL'S-EYE! H-HE COULD PUT A BULLET THROUGH MY BRAIN WITH A SNIPER'S RIFLE! HE COULD POISON THE WATER I DRINK ON THE SET--THE FOOD! BRUCE--I--I CAN'T GO ON TOMORROW--I CAN'T--I CAN'T!
SIMMER DOWN, ROGER... AND LET ME DO THE "COOKING"! I JUST GOT AN IDEA! MY FRIEND BATMAN IS A MASTER OF DISGUISE! GIVE ME THE KEY TO YOUR APARTMENT! HE AND I WILL GO OVER THERE, STUDY THE SCRIPT--AND HE'LL IMPERSONATE YOU ON TOMORROW'S SHOW! HE'LL BE THE "CLAY PIGEON FOR A KILLER"--WHILE YOU GET "LOST" UNTIL THE SHOW IS OVER!
T-THANKS!--Y-YOU SAVED MY LIFE!
3

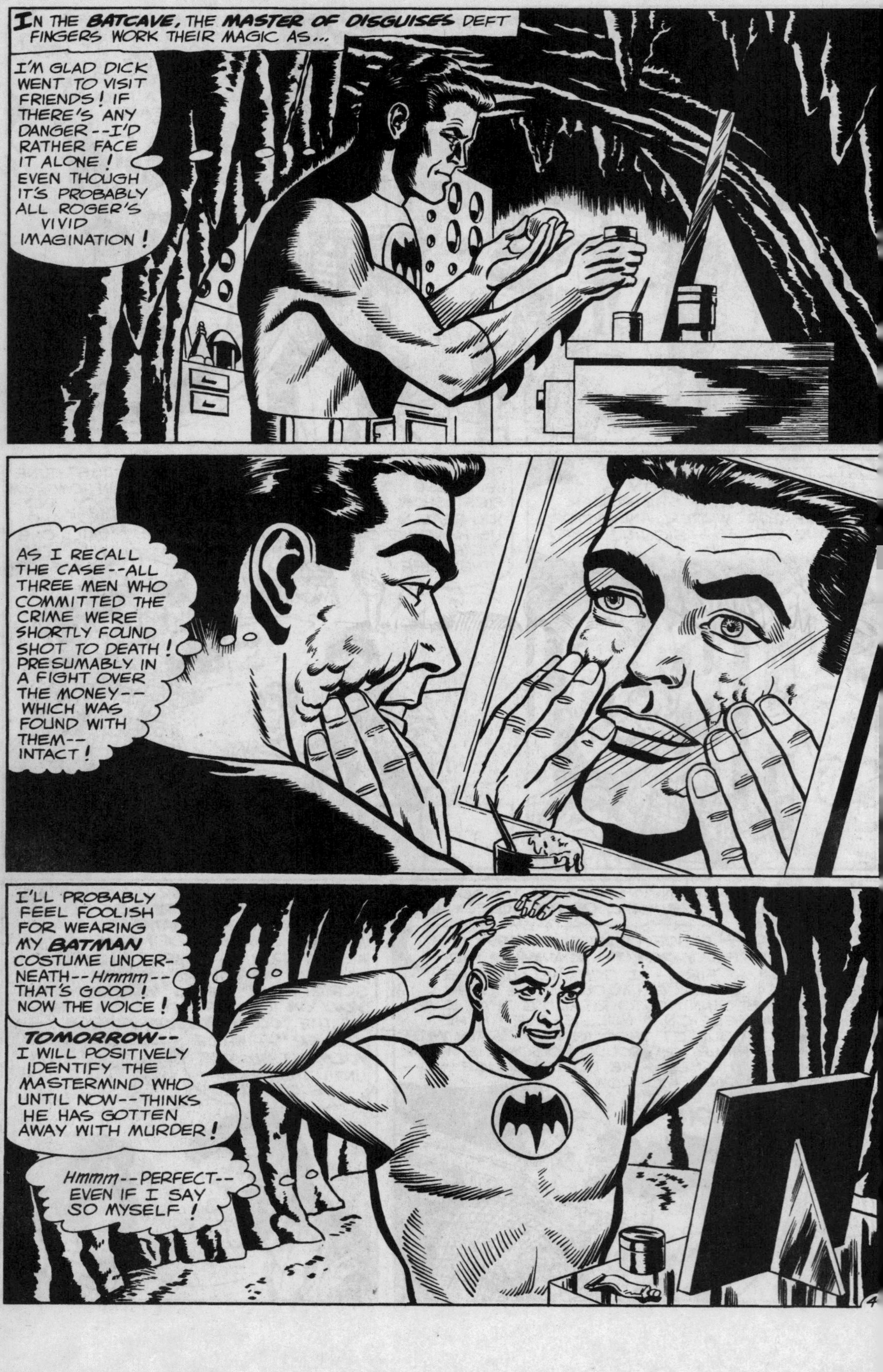
IN THE BATCAVE, THE MASTER OF DISGUISES DEFT FINGERS WORK THEIR MAGIC AS...
I'M GLAD DICK WENT TO VISIT FRIENDS! IF THERE'S ANY DANGER--I'D RATHER FACE IT ALONE! EVEN THOUGH IT'S PROBABLY ALL ROGER'S VIVID IMAGINATION!
AS I RECALL THE CASE--ALL THREE MEN WHO COMMITTED THE CRIME WERE SHORTLY FOUND SHOT TO DEATH! PRESUMABLY IN A FIGHT OVER THE MONEY--WHICH WAS FOUND WITH THEM--INTACT!
I'LL PROBABLY FEEL FOOLISH FOR WEARING MY BATMAN COSTUME UNDERNEATH--Hmmm--THAT'S GOOD! NOW THE VOICE!
TOMORROW--I WILL POSITIVELY IDENTIFY THE MASTERMIND WHO UNTIL NOW--THINKS HE HAS GOTTEN AWAY WITH MURDER!
Hmmm--PERFECT--EVEN IF I SAY SO MYSELF!
4

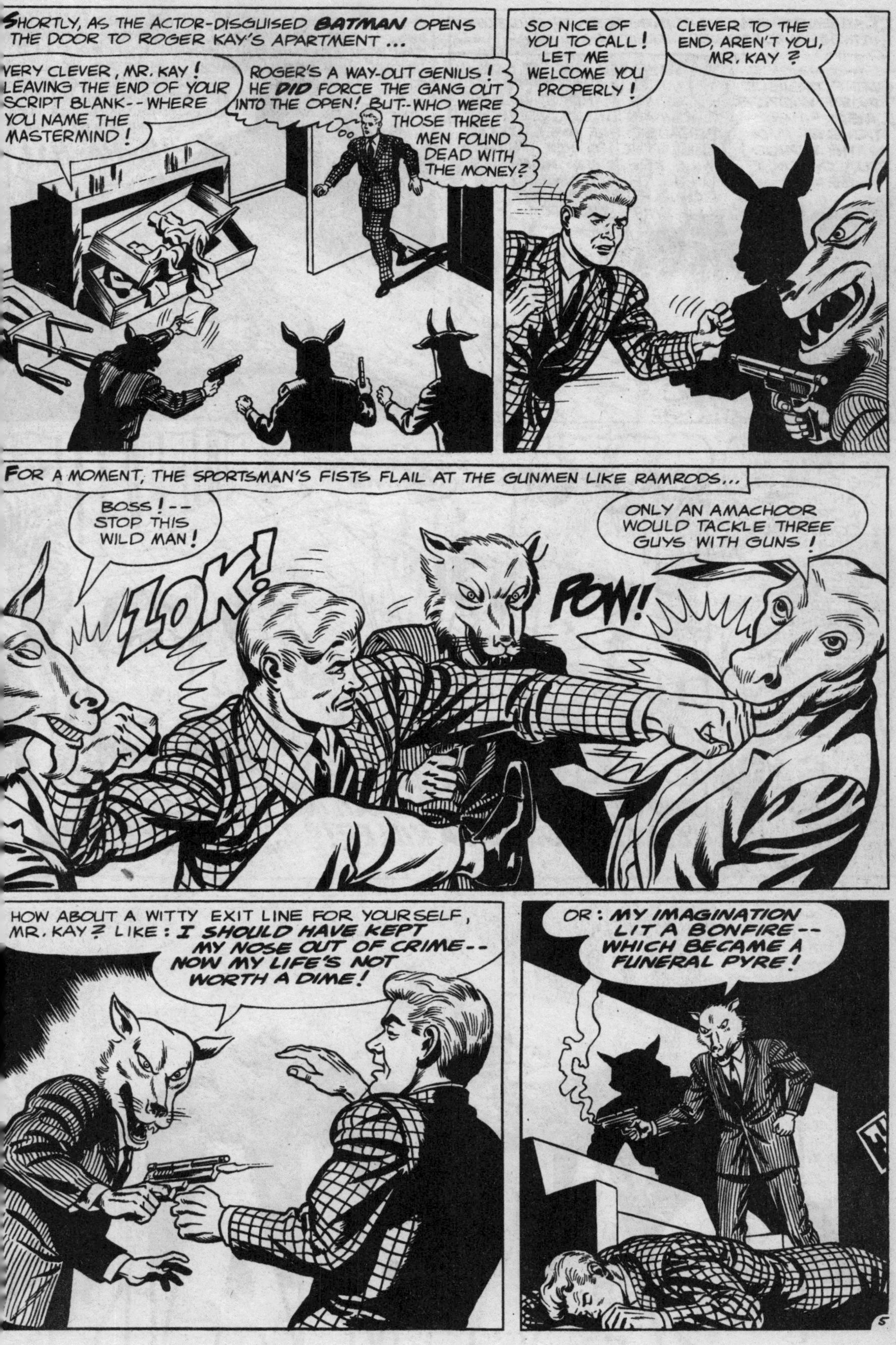
SHORTLY, AS THE ACTOR-DISGUISED BATMAN OPENS THE DOOR TO ROGER KAY'S APARTMENT ...
VERY CLEVER, MR. KAY! LEAVING THE END OF YOUR SCRIPT BLANK--WHERE YOU NAME THE MASTERMIND!
ROGER'S A WAY-OUT GENIUS! HE DID FORCE THE GANG OUT INTO THE OPEN! BUT--WHO WERE THOSE THREE MEN FOUND DEAD WITH THE MONEY?
SO NICE OF YOU TO CALL! LET ME WELCOME YOU PROPERLY!
CLEVER TO THE END, AREN'T YOU, MR. KAY?
FOR A MOMENT, THE SPORTSMAN'S FISTS FLAIL AT THE GUNMEN LIKE RAMRODS...
BOSS!-- STOP THIS WILD MAN!
ZOK!
ONLY AN AMACHOOR WOULD TACKLE THREE GUYS WITH GUNS!
POW!
HOW ABOUT A WITTY EXIT LINE FOR YOURSELF, MR. KAY? LIKE: I SHOULD HAVE KEPT MY NOSE OUT OF CRIME-- NOW MY LIFE'S NOT WORTH A DIME!
OR: MY IMAGINATION LIT A BONFIRE-- WHICH BECAME A FUNERAL PYRE!

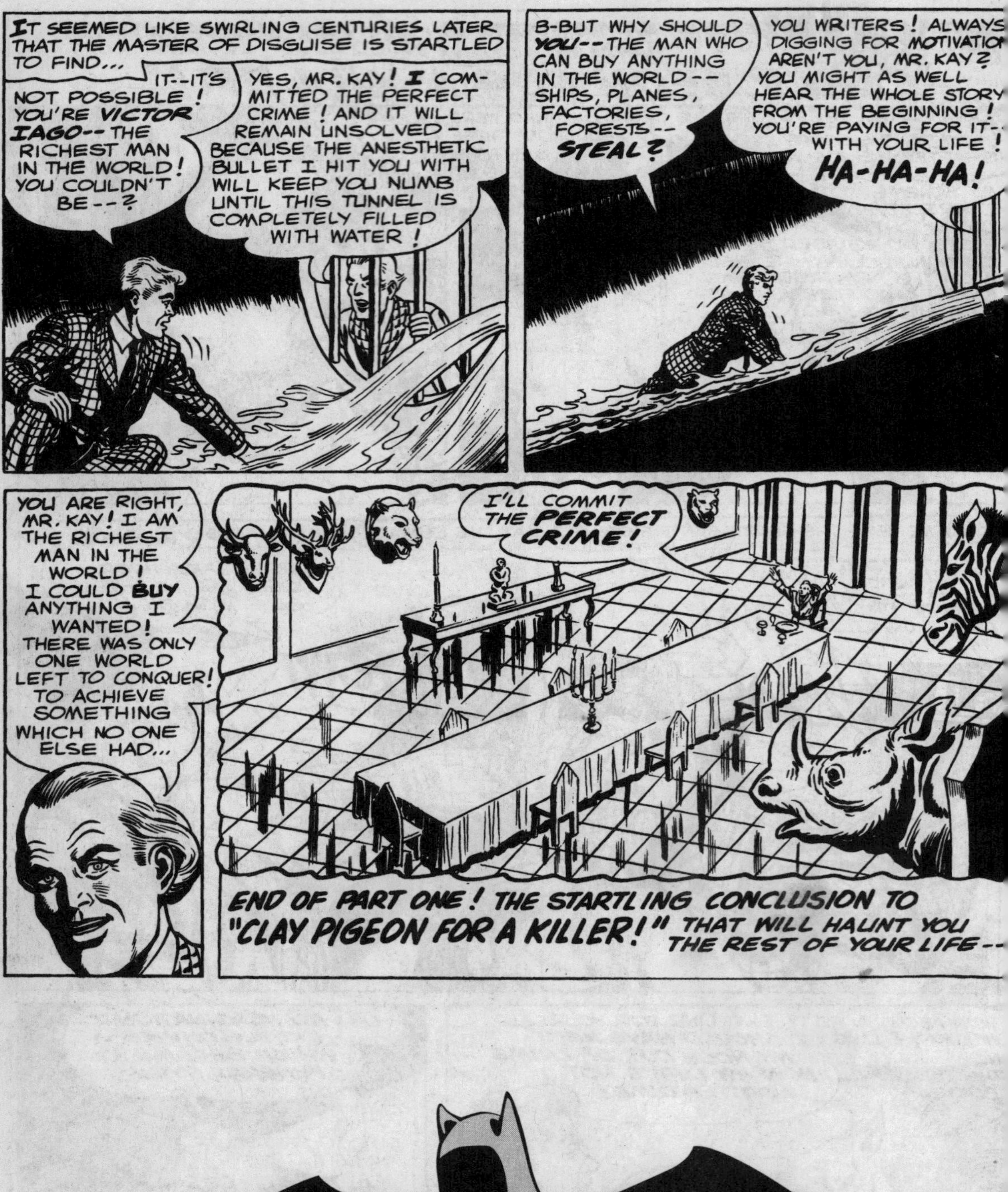
IT SEEMED LIKE SWIRLING CENTURIES LATER THAT THE MASTER OF DISGUISE IS STARTLED TO FIND...
IT--IT'S NOT POSSIBLE! YOU'RE VICTOR IAGO-- THE RICHEST MAN IN THE WORLD! YOU COULDN'T BE--?
YES, MR. KAY! I COMMITTED THE PERFECT CRIME! AND IT WILL REMAIN UNSOLVED--BECAUSE THE ANESTHETIC BULLET I HIT YOU WITH WILL KEEP YOU NUMB UNTIL THIS TUNNEL IS COMPLETELY FILLED WITH WATER!
B-BUT WHY SHOULD YOU--THE MAN WHO CAN BUY ANYTHING IN THE WORLD--SHIPS, PLANES, FACTORIES, FORESTS--STEAL?
YOU WRITERS! ALWAYS DIGGING FOR MOTIVATION AREN'T YOU, MR. KAY? YOU MIGHT AS WELL HEAR THE WHOLE STORY FROM THE BEGINNING! YOU'RE PAYING FOR IT--WITH YOUR LIFE!
HA-HA-HA!
YOU ARE RIGHT, MR. KAY! I AM THE RICHEST MAN IN THE WORLD! I COULD BUY ANYTHING I WANTED! THERE WAS ONLY ONE WORLD LEFT TO CONQUER! TO ACHIEVE SOMETHING WHICH NO ONE ELSE HAD...
I'LL COMMIT THE PERFECT CRIME!
END OF PART ONE! THE STARTLING CONCLUSION TO "CLAY PIGEON FOR A KILLER!" THAT WILL HAUNT YOU THE REST OF YOUR LIFE--

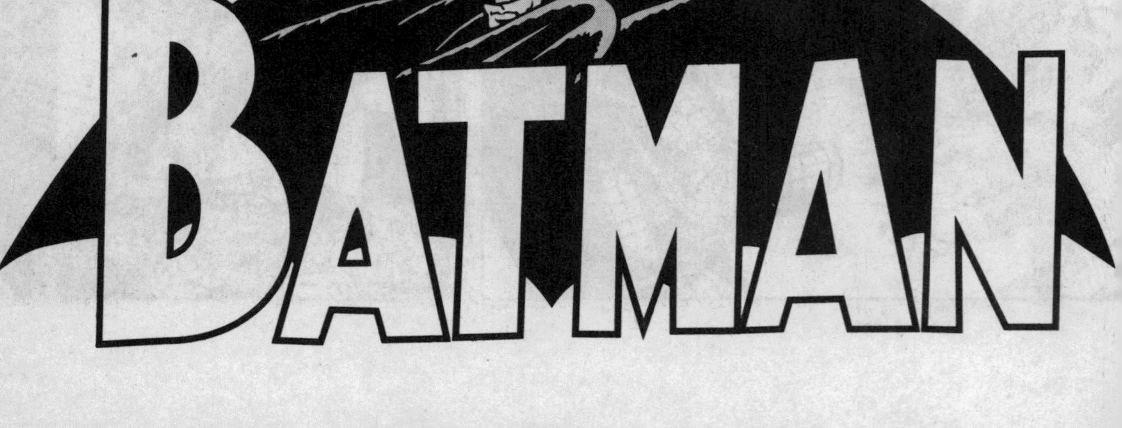
BATMAN

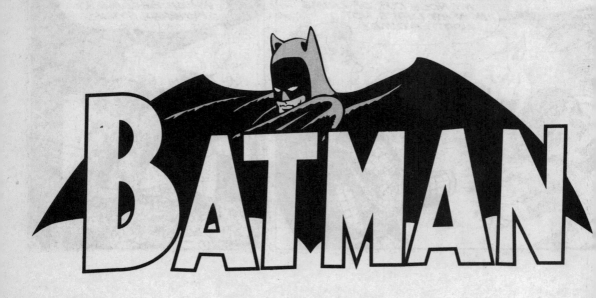

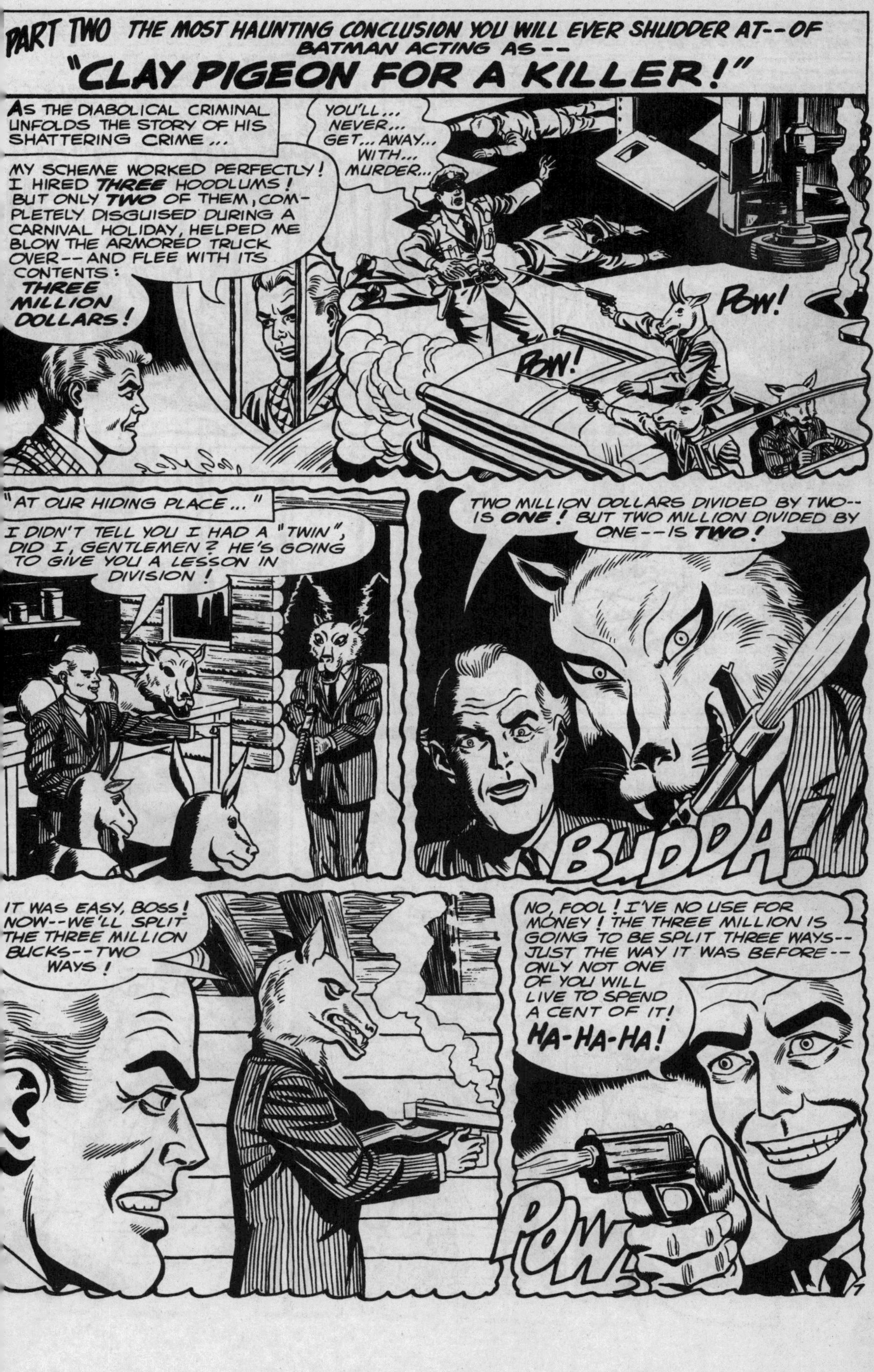
PART TWO THE MOST HAUNTING CONCLUSION YOU WILL EVER SHUDDER AT--OF BATMAN ACTING AS--
"CLAY PIGEON FOR A KILLER!"
AS THE DIABOLICAL CRIMINAL UNFOLDS THE STORY OF HIS SHATTERING CRIME ...
YOU'LL... NEVER... GET... AWAY... WITH... MURDER...
MY SCHEME WORKED PERFECTLY! I HIRED THREE HOODLUMS! BUT ONLY TWO OF THEM, COMPLETELY DISGUISED DURING A CARNIVAL HOLIDAY, HELPED ME BLOW THE ARMORED TRUCK OVER--AND FLEE WITH ITS CONTENTS: THREE MILLION DOLLARS!
POW!
POW!
"AT OUR HIDING PLACE ..."
I DIDN'T TELL YOU I HAD A "TWIN", DID I, GENTLEMEN? HE'S GOING TO GIVE YOU A LESSON IN DIVISION!
TWO MILLION DOLLARS DIVIDED BY TWO--IS ONE! BUT TWO MILLION DIVIDED BY ONE--IS TWO!
BUDDA!
IT WAS EASY, BOSS! NOW--WE'LL SPLIT THE THREE MILLION BUCKS--TWO WAYS!
NO, FOOL! I'VE NO USE FOR MONEY! THE THREE MILLION IS GOING TO BE SPLIT THREE WAYS--JUST THE WAY IT WAS BEFORE--ONLY NOT ONE OF YOU WILL LIVE TO SPEND A CENT OF IT! HA-HA-HA!
POW!

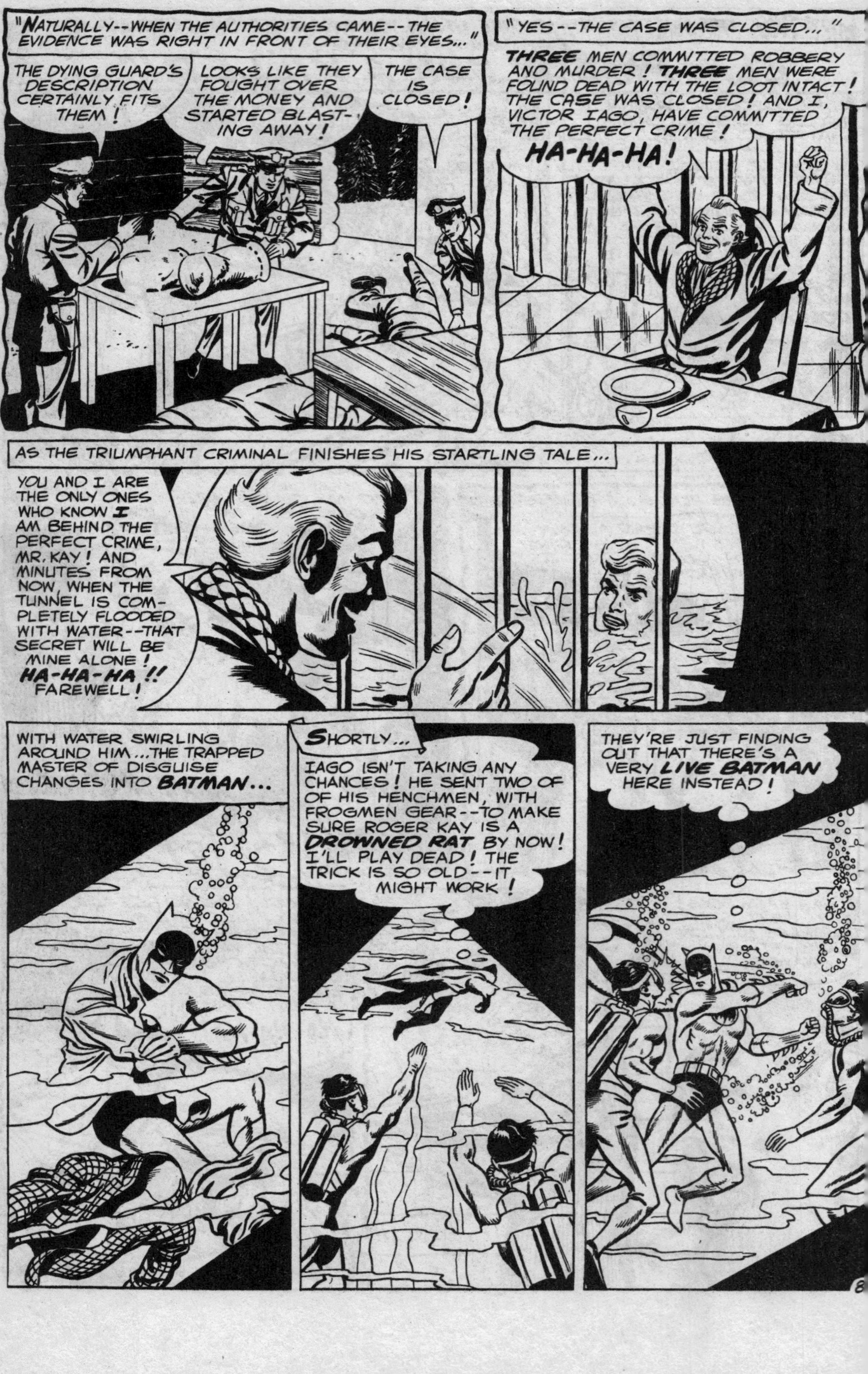
"NATURALLY--WHEN THE AUTHORITIES CAME--THE EVIDENCE WAS RIGHT IN FRONT OF THEIR EYES..."
THE DYING GUARD'S DESCRIPTION CERTAINLY FITS THEM!
LOOKS LIKE THEY FOUGHT OVER THE MONEY AND STARTED BLASTING AWAY!
THE CASE IS CLOSED!
"YES--THE CASE WAS CLOSED..."
THREE MEN COMMITTED ROBBERY AND MURDER! THREE MEN WERE FOUND DEAD WITH THE LOOT INTACT! THE CASE WAS CLOSED! AND I, VICTOR IAGO, HAVE COMMITTED THE PERFECT CRIME!
HA-HA-HA!
AS THE TRIUMPHANT CRIMINAL FINISHES HIS STARTLING TALE...
YOU AND I ARE THE ONLY ONES WHO KNOW I AM BEHIND THE PERFECT CRIME, MR. KAY! AND MINUTES FROM NOW, WHEN THE TUNNEL IS COMPLETELY FLOODED WITH WATER--THAT SECRET WILL BE MINE ALONE! HA-HA-HA!! FAREWELL!
WITH WATER SWIRLING AROUND HIM...THE TRAPPED MASTER OF DISGUISE CHANGES INTO BATMAN...
SHORTLY...
IAGO ISN'T TAKING ANY CHANCES! HE SENT TWO OF HIS HENCHMEN, WITH FROGMEN GEAR--TO MAKE SURE ROGER KAY IS A DROWNED RAT BY NOW! I'LL PLAY DEAD! THE TRICK IS SO OLD--IT MIGHT WORK!
THEY'RE JUST FINDING OUT THAT THERE'S A VERY LIVE BATMAN HERE INSTEAD!
8

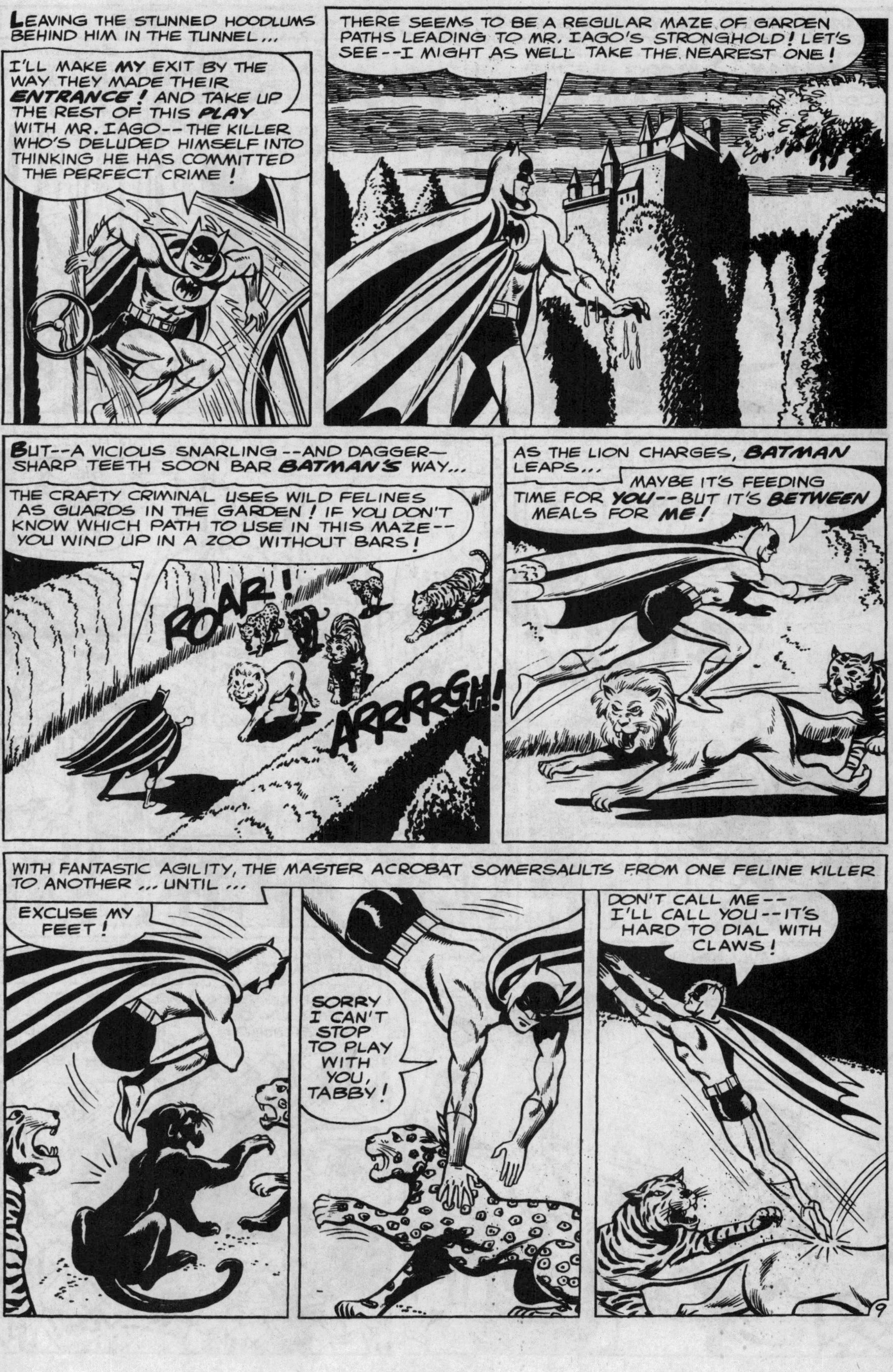
LEAVING THE STUNNED HOODLUMS BEHIND HIM IN THE TUNNEL...
I'LL MAKE MY EXIT BY THE WAY THEY MADE THEIR ENTRANCE! AND TAKE UP THE REST OF THIS PLAY WITH MR. IAGO--THE KILLER WHO'S DELUDED HIMSELF INTO THINKING HE HAS COMMITTED THE PERFECT CRIME!
THERE SEEMS TO BE A REGULAR MAZE OF GARDEN PATHS LEADING TO MR. IAGO'S STRONGHOLD! LET'S SEE--I MIGHT AS WELL TAKE THE NEAREST ONE!
BUT--A VICIOUS SNARLING--AND DAGGER-SHARP TEETH SOON BAR BATMAN'S WAY...
THE CRAFTY CRIMINAL USES WILD FELINES AS GUARDS IN THE GARDEN! IF YOU DON'T KNOW WHICH PATH TO USE IN THIS MAZE--YOU WIND UP IN A ZOO WITHOUT BARS!
ROAR!
ARRRRGH!
AS THE LION CHARGES, BATMAN LEAPS...
MAYBE IT'S FEEDING TIME FOR YOU--BUT IT'S BETWEEN MEALS FOR ME!
WITH FANTASTIC AGILITY, THE MASTER ACROBAT SOMERSAULTS FROM ONE FELINE KILLER TO ANOTHER... UNTIL...
EXCUSE MY FEET!
SORRY I CAN'T STOP TO PLAY WITH YOU, TABBY!
DON'T CALL ME--I'LL CALL YOU--IT'S HARD TO DIAL WITH CLAWS!
9

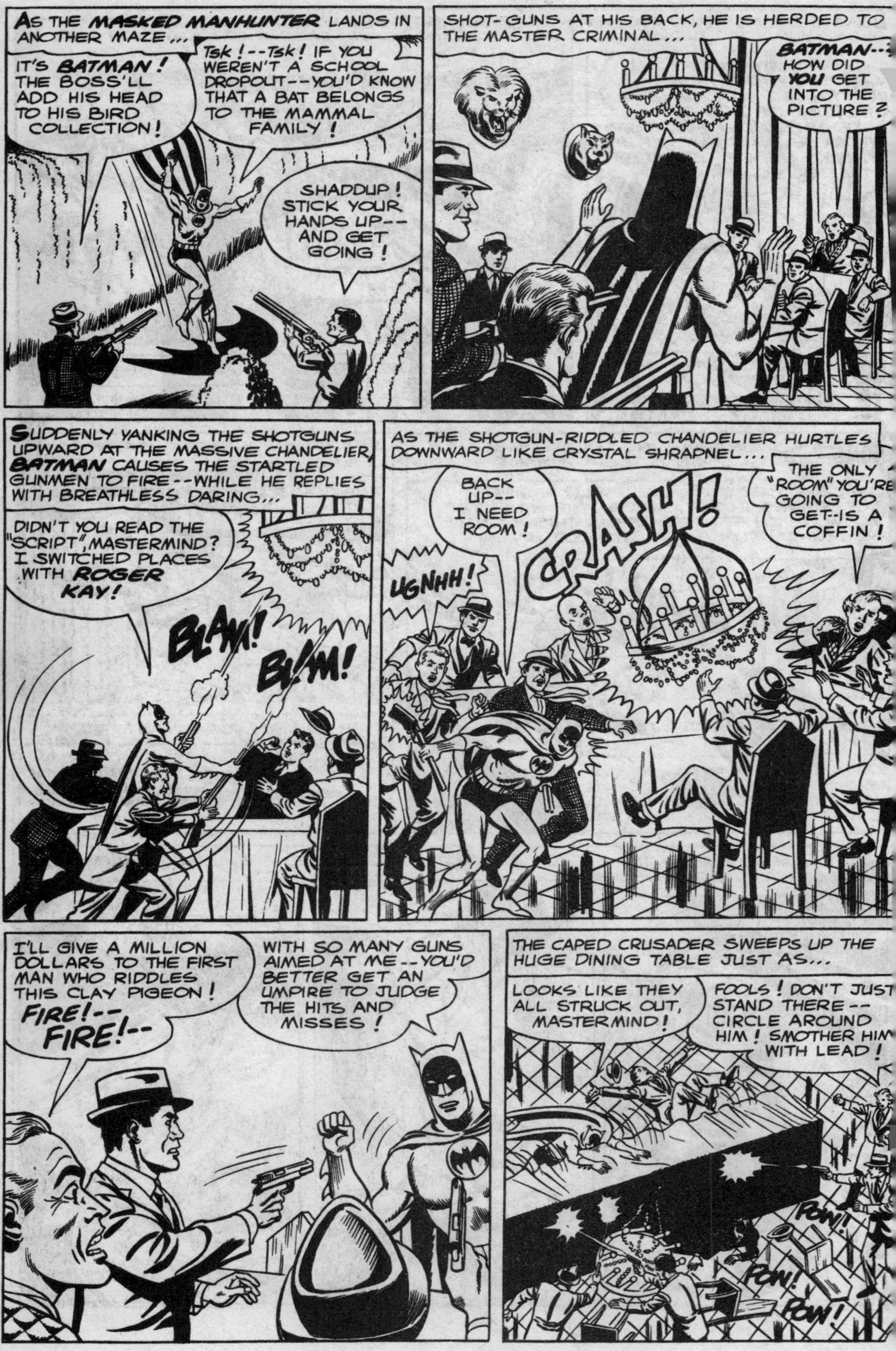
AS THE MASKED MANHUNTER LANDS IN ANOTHER MAZE...
IT'S BATMAN! THE BOSS'LL ADD HIS HEAD TO HIS BIRD COLLECTION!
Tsk!--Tsk! IF YOU WEREN'T A SCHOOL DROPOUT--YOU'D KNOW THAT A BAT BELONGS TO THE MAMMAL FAMILY!
SHADDUP! STICK YOUR HANDS UP--AND GET GOING!
SHOT-GUNS AT HIS BACK, HE IS HERDED TO THE MASTER CRIMINAL...
BATMAN--! HOW DID YOU GET INTO THE PICTURE?
SUDDENLY YANKING THE SHOTGUNS UPWARD AT THE MASSIVE CHANDELIER, BATMAN CAUSES THE STARTLED GUNMEN TO FIRE--WHILE HE REPLIES WITH BREATHLESS DARING...
DIDN'T YOU READ THE "SCRIPT", MASTERMIND? I SWITCHED PLACES WITH ROGER KAY!
BLAM!
BLAM!
AS THE SHOTGUN-RIDDLED CHANDELIER HURTLES DOWNWARD LIKE CRYSTAL SHRAPNEL...
BACK UP--I NEED ROOM!
THE ONLY "ROOM" YOU'RE GOING TO GET--IS A COFFIN!
CRASH!
UGNHH!
I'LL GIVE A MILLION DOLLARS TO THE FIRST MAN WHO RIDDLES THIS CLAY PIGEON! FIRE!--FIRE!--
WITH SO MANY GUNS AIMED AT ME--YOU'D BETTER GET AN UMPIRE TO JUDGE THE HITS AND MISSES!
THE CAPED CRUSADER SWEEPS UP THE HUGE DINING TABLE JUST AS...
LOOKS LIKE THEY ALL STRUCK OUT, MASTERMIND!
FOOLS! DON'T JUST STAND THERE--CIRCLE AROUND HIM! SMOTHER HIM WITH LEAD!
POW!
POW!
POW!

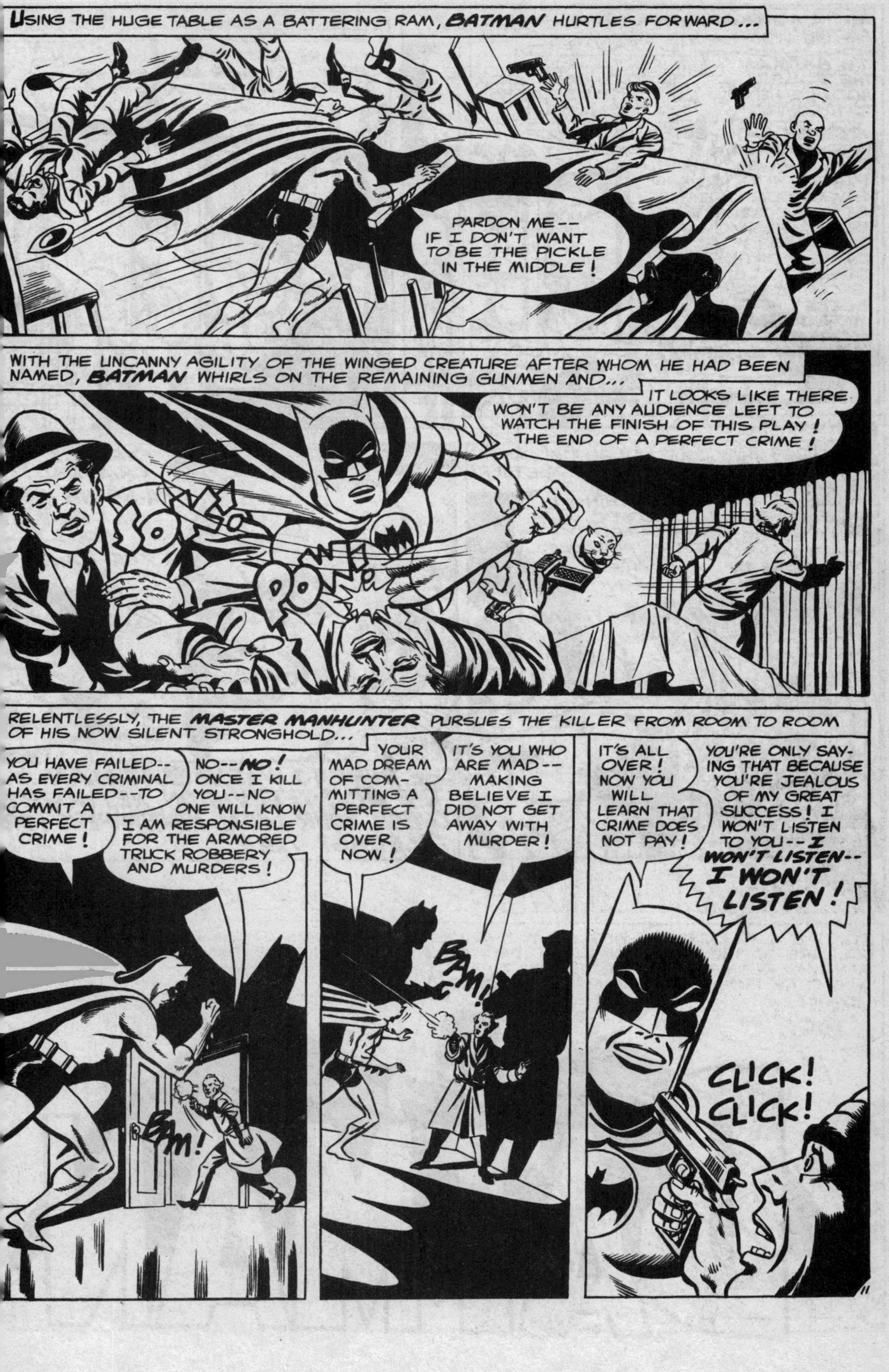
USING THE HUGE TABLE AS A BATTERING RAM, BATMAN HURTLES FORWARD...
PARDON ME-- IF I DON'T WANT TO BE THE PICKLE IN THE MIDDLE!
WITH THE UNCANNY AGILITY OF THE WINGED CREATURE AFTER WHOM HE HAD BEEN NAMED, BATMAN WHIRLS ON THE REMAINING GUNMEN AND...
IT LOOKS LIKE THERE WON'T BE ANY AUDIENCE LEFT TO WATCH THE FINISH OF THIS PLAY! THE END OF A PERFECT CRIME!
SOCK
POW
RELENTLESSLY, THE MASTER MANHUNTER PURSUES THE KILLER FROM ROOM TO ROOM OF HIS NOW SILENT STRONGHOLD...
YOU HAVE FAILED-- AS EVERY CRIMINAL HAS FAILED--TO COMMIT A PERFECT CRIME!
NO--NO! ONCE I KILL YOU--NO ONE WILL KNOW I AM RESPONSIBLE FOR THE ARMORED TRUCK ROBBERY AND MURDERS!
BAM!
YOUR MAD DREAM OF COMMITTING A PERFECT CRIME IS OVER NOW!
IT'S YOU WHO ARE MAD-- MAKING BELIEVE I DID NOT GET AWAY WITH MURDER!
BAM!
IT'S ALL OVER! NOW YOU WILL LEARN THAT CRIME DOES NOT PAY!
YOU'RE ONLY SAYING THAT BECAUSE YOU'RE JEALOUS OF MY GREAT SUCCESS! I WON'T LISTEN TO YOU--I WON'T LISTEN--I WON'T LISTEN!
CLICK! CLICK!

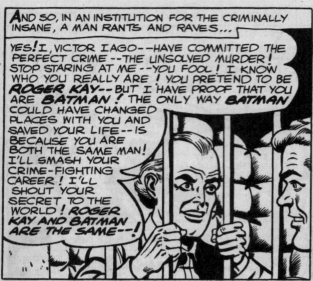

AND SO, IN AN INSTITUTION FOR THE CRIMINALLY INSANE, A MAN RANTS AND RAVES...

YES! I, VICTOR IAGO--HAVE COMMITTED THE PERFECT CRIME--THE UNSOLVED MURDER! STOP STARING AT ME--YOU FOOL! I KNOW WHO YOU REALLY ARE! YOU PRETEND TO BE *ROGER KAY*--BUT I HAVE PROOF THAT YOU ARE *BATMAN!* THE ONLY WAY *BATMAN* COULD HAVE CHANGED PLACES WITH YOU AND SAVED YOUR LIFE--IS BECAUSE YOU ARE BOTH THE SAME MAN! I'LL SMASH YOUR CRIME-FIGHTING CAREER! I'LL SHOUT YOUR SECRET TO THE WORLD! ROGER KAY AND BATMAN ARE THE SAME--!

SUDDENLY, STEPPING NEXT TO ROGER KAY...

HOW ARE YOU GOING TO EXPLAIN SEEING *ROGER KAY* AND ME TOGETHER AT THE SAME TIME-- IN THE SAME PLACE!

IT'S TRUE! THEY COULDN'T BE THE SAME MAN--IF I SEE THEM BOTH TOGETHER! OR AM I IMAGINING IT? AM I IMAGINING THE WHOLE THING? DID I IMAGINE I COULD DO WHAT CRIMINALS HAVE DREAMED OF -- COMMIT THE PERFECT CRIME?

PERFECT CRIMINAL?-- HA-HA-HA-HA! I'M A PERFECT FOOL!-- HA-HA-HA!!

The End.

BE SURE TO WATCH *BATMAN* ON THE *ABC* TELEVISION NETWORK! CHECK YOUR LOCAL NEWSPAPERS FOR TELECAST TIME!

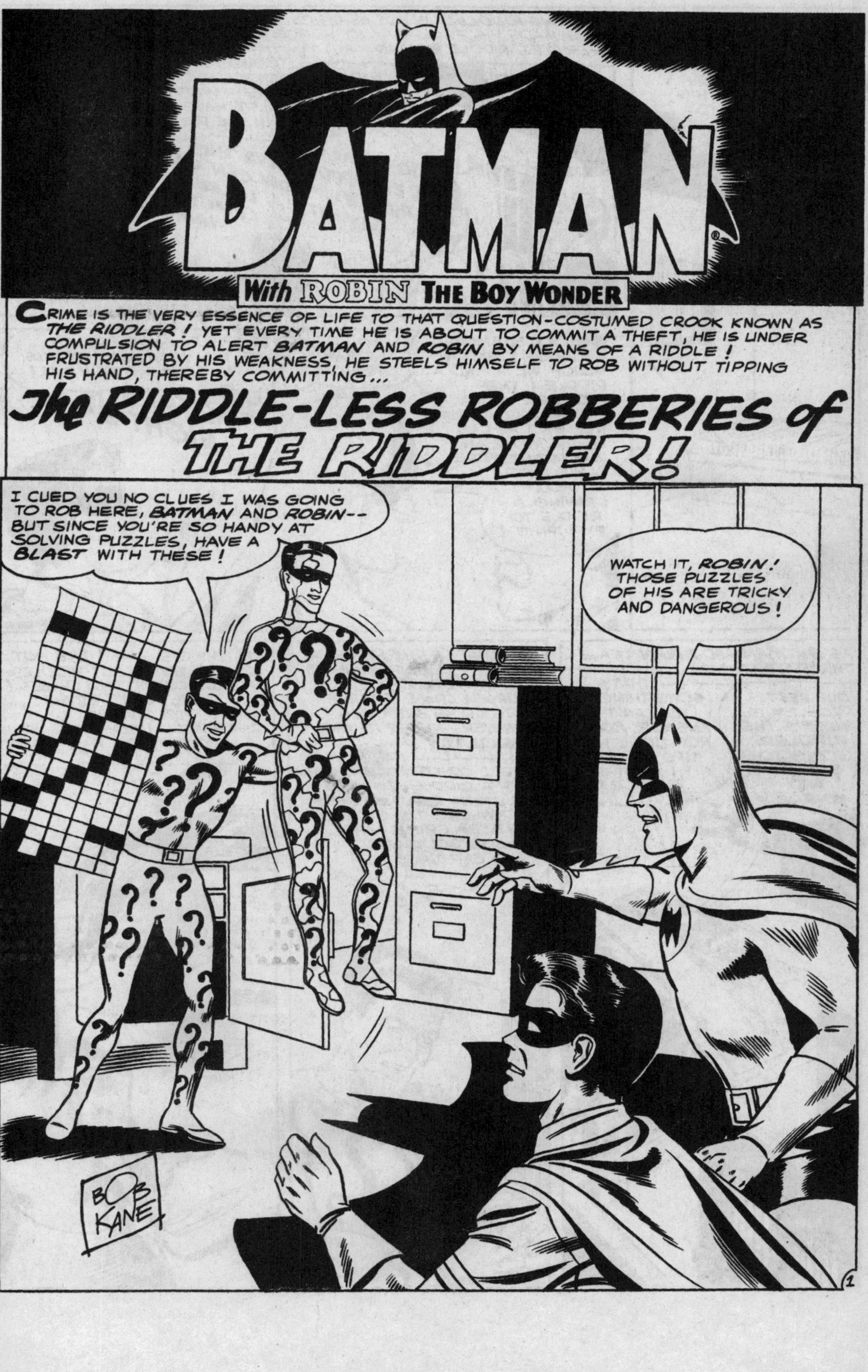
BATMAN
With ROBIN THE BOY WONDER
CRIME IS THE VERY ESSENCE OF LIFE TO THAT QUESTION-COSTUMED CROOK KNOWN AS THE RIDDLER! YET EVERY TIME HE IS ABOUT TO COMMIT A THEFT, HE IS UNDER COMPULSION TO ALERT BATMAN AND ROBIN BY MEANS OF A RIDDLE! FRUSTRATED BY HIS WEAKNESS, HE STEELS HIMSELF TO ROB WITHOUT TIPPING HIS HAND, THEREBY COMMITTING...
The RIDDLE-LESS ROBBERIES of THE RIDDLER!
I CUED YOU NO CLUES I WAS GOING TO ROB HERE, BATMAN AND ROBIN-- BUT SINCE YOU'RE SO HANDY AT SOLVING PUZZLES, HAVE A BLAST WITH THESE!
WATCH IT, ROBIN! THOSE PUZZLES OF HIS ARE TRICKY AND DANGEROUS!
BOB KANE
1

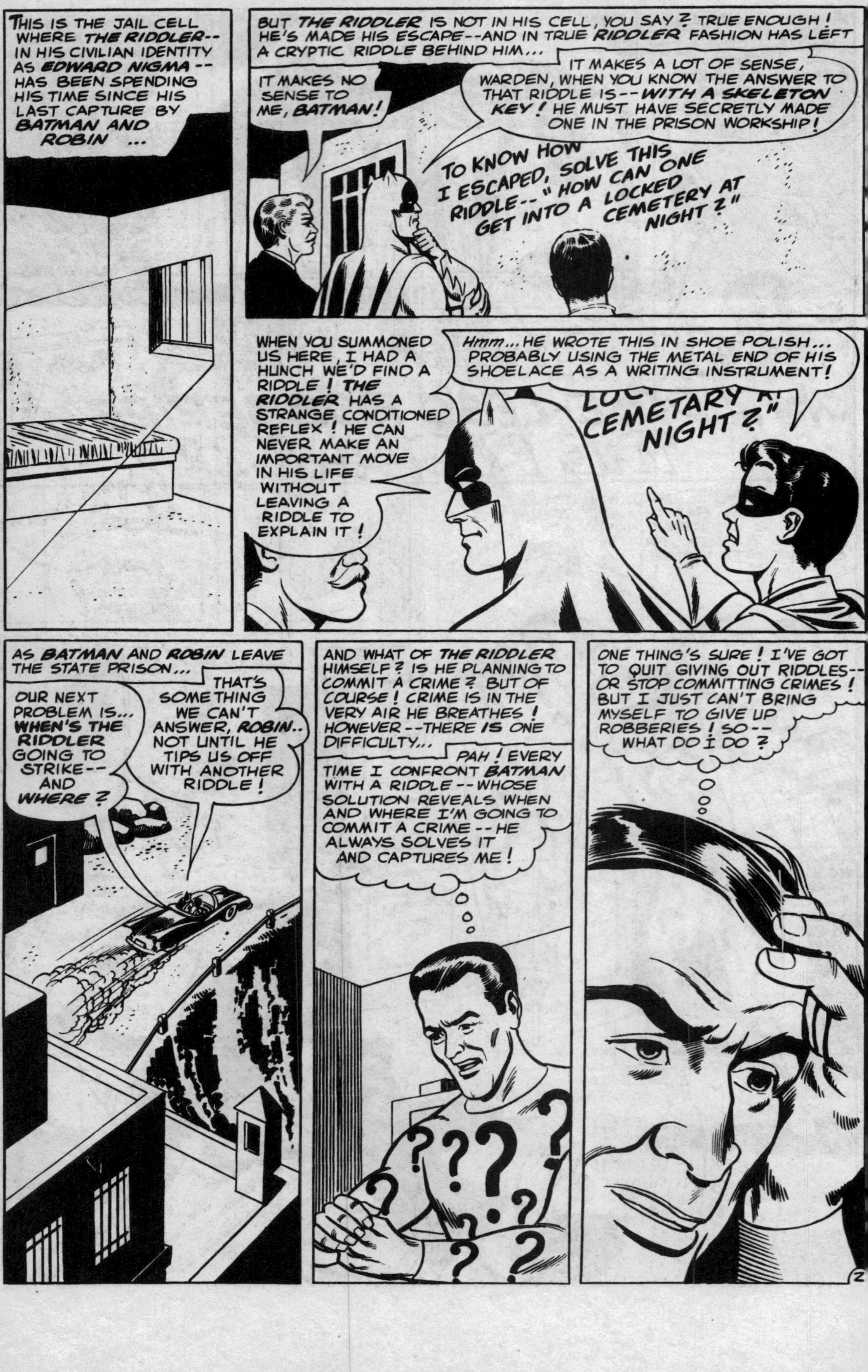
THIS IS THE JAIL CELL WHERE THE RIDDLER-- IN HIS CIVILIAN IDENTITY AS EDWARD NIGMA -- HAS BEEN SPENDING HIS TIME SINCE HIS LAST CAPTURE BY BATMAN AND ROBIN ...
BUT THE RIDDLER IS NOT IN HIS CELL, YOU SAY? TRUE ENOUGH! HE'S MADE HIS ESCAPE--AND IN TRUE RIDDLER FASHION HAS LEFT A CRYPTIC RIDDLE BEHIND HIM...
IT MAKES NO SENSE TO ME, BATMAN!
IT MAKES A LOT OF SENSE, WARDEN, WHEN YOU KNOW THE ANSWER TO THAT RIDDLE IS--WITH A SKELETON KEY! HE MUST HAVE SECRETLY MADE ONE IN THE PRISON WORKSHIP!
TO KNOW HOW I ESCAPED, SOLVE THIS RIDDLE-- "HOW CAN ONE GET INTO A LOCKED CEMETERY AT NIGHT?"
WHEN YOU SUMMONED US HERE, I HAD A HUNCH WE'D FIND A RIDDLE! THE RIDDLER HAS A STRANGE CONDITIONED REFLEX! HE CAN NEVER MAKE AN IMPORTANT MOVE IN HIS LIFE WITHOUT LEAVING A RIDDLE TO EXPLAIN IT!
Hmm... HE WROTE THIS IN SHOE POLISH... PROBABLY USING THE METAL END OF HIS SHOELACE AS A WRITING INSTRUMENT!
CEMETARY AT NIGHT?"
AS BATMAN AND ROBIN LEAVE THE STATE PRISON...
OUR NEXT PROBLEM IS... WHEN'S THE RIDDLER GOING TO STRIKE-- AND WHERE?
THAT'S SOMETHING WE CAN'T ANSWER, ROBIN.. NOT UNTIL HE TIPS US OFF WITH ANOTHER RIDDLE!
AND WHAT OF THE RIDDLER HIMSELF? IS HE PLANNING TO COMMIT A CRIME? BUT OF COURSE! CRIME IS IN THE VERY AIR HE BREATHES! HOWEVER--THERE IS ONE DIFFICULTY...
PAH! EVERY TIME I CONFRONT BATMAN WITH A RIDDLE--WHOSE SOLUTION REVEALS WHEN AND WHERE I'M GOING TO COMMIT A CRIME--HE ALWAYS SOLVES IT AND CAPTURES ME!
ONE THING'S SURE! I'VE GOT TO QUIT GIVING OUT RIDDLES-- OR STOP COMMITTING CRIMES! BUT I JUST CAN'T BRING MYSELF TO GIVE UP ROBBERIES! SO-- WHAT DO I DO?
2

A HOPEFUL SMILE CURVES HIS GRIM LIPS...

SIMPLE-- RIDICULOUSLY SIMPLE! I'LL STOP GIVING RIDDLES TO MY CRIMES!

THEN GLOOM SETTLES ON HIM ONCE AGAIN...

SURE! THAT'S EASY TO SAY! BUT CAN I REALLY PREVENT MYSELF FROM HANDING OUT THOSE RIDDLES? I--I'LL NEVER KNOW UNTIL I TRY! AND SO-- A ROBBERY IS INDICATED!

THAT NIGHT UNDER COVER OF A MIDNIGHT BLACKNESS, HE JIMMIES A LOCK "GUARANTEED" TO BE BURGLAR-PROOF...

SOON NOW--VERY SOON-- I'LL KNOW THE TRUTH ABOUT MYSELF! WILL I FILL MY HANDS WITH PRECIOUS GEMS? OR--; GULP! WELL, I WON'T THINK ABOUT THAT!

MOMENTS LATER, INSIDE THE *HOUSE OF THAYER*, HE CUTS OUT A SECTION OF GLASS FROM A DISPLAY CASE BENEATH HIS EYES GLITTERS A SULTAN'S FORTUNE IN GEMS...

NOW COMES MY MOMENT OF TRUTH! I DIDN'T SEND ANY RIDDLE TO *BATMAN*-- YET *HERE* I AM COMMITTING A ROBBERY! I'M ALMOST BEGINNING-- TO HOPE!

DESPERATELY HIS HANDS STAB INTO THE OPENING OF THE DISPLAY CASE. HIS FINGERS SPREAD LIKE TALONS TO SWOOP AND STEAL! AND THEN...

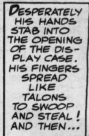

I--I CAN'T *TOUCH* THEM! MY FINGERS HAVE STIFFENED SO I CAN'T EVEN MOVE THEM! MY SUB-CONSCIOUS MIND-- *WILL NOT LET ME STEAL!!*

HE STAGGERS THROUGH THE JEWELRY STORE, WILD LAUGHTER THROBBING IN HIS THROAT...

HA! HA! HA! I'M STYMIED! I CAN'T COMMIT A CRIME WITHOUT ALERTING *BATMAN* AND *ROBIN* WITH A RIDDLE! WHAT A JOKE ON ME! ALL MY LIFE I'VE SENT OUT RIDDLES AND ROBBED! NOW I CAN'T DO ONE-- WITHOUT THE OTHER! *HA! HA! HA!*

A HAUNTED LOOK TOUCHES HIS EYES! HE STARES BLINDLY WITH THE SAGGING LOOK OF A BEATEN MAN...

IF I CAN'T ROB--I'M DONE FOR! MY LIFE IS RUINED!

3

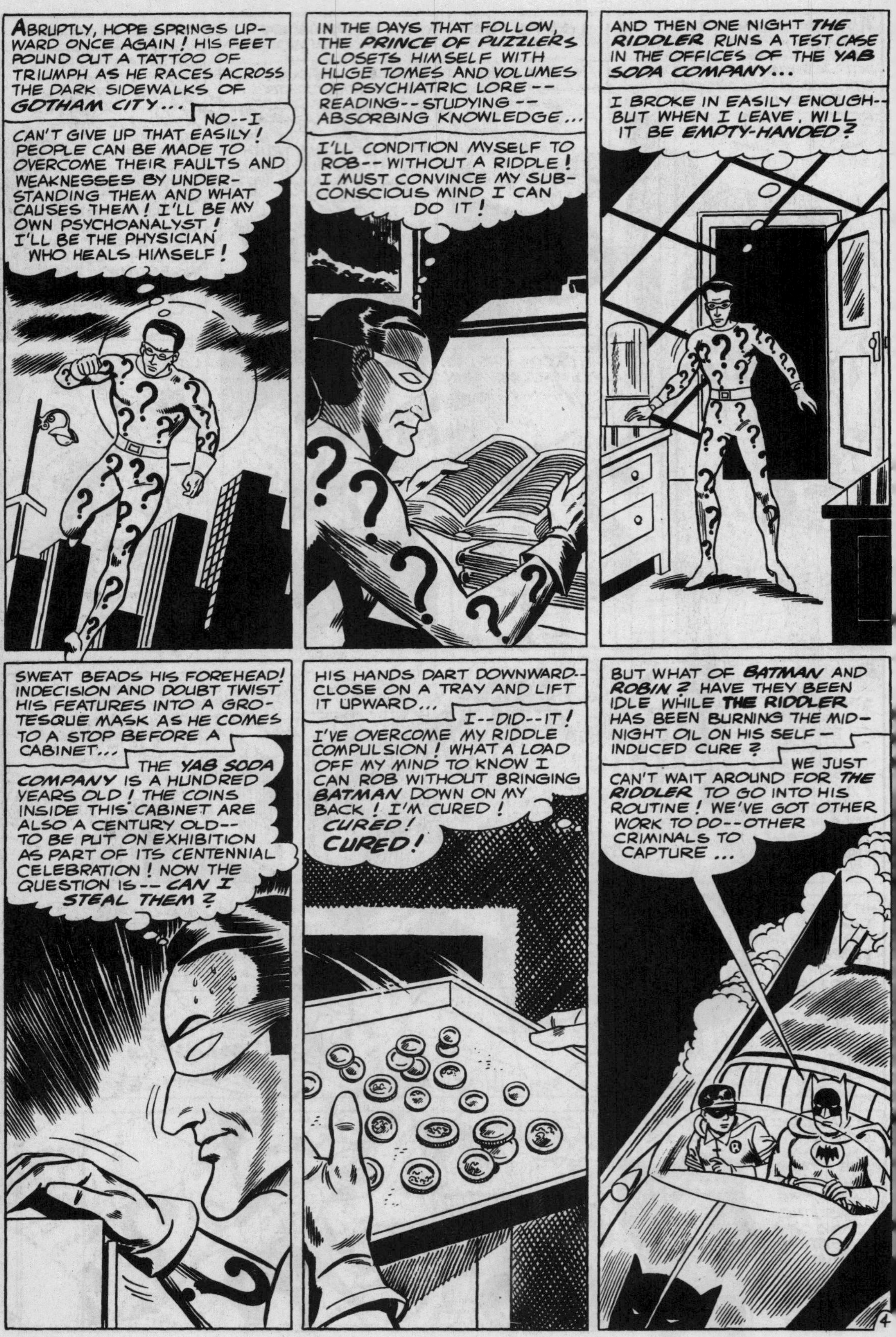
ABRUPTLY, HOPE SPRINGS UPWARD ONCE AGAIN! HIS FEET POUND OUT A TATTOO OF TRIUMPH AS HE RACES ACROSS THE DARK SIDEWALKS OF GOTHAM CITY...
NO--I CAN'T GIVE UP THAT EASILY! PEOPLE CAN BE MADE TO OVERCOME THEIR FAULTS AND WEAKNESSES BY UNDERSTANDING THEM AND WHAT CAUSES THEM! I'LL BE MY OWN PSYCHOANALYST! I'LL BE THE PHYSICIAN WHO HEALS HIMSELF!
IN THE DAYS THAT FOLLOW, THE PRINCE OF PUZZLERS CLOSETS HIMSELF WITH HUGE TOMES AND VOLUMES OF PSYCHIATRIC LORE -- READING-- STUDYING -- ABSORBING KNOWLEDGE...
I'LL CONDITION MYSELF TO ROB-- WITHOUT A RIDDLE! I MUST CONVINCE MY SUBCONSCIOUS MIND I CAN DO IT!
AND THEN ONE NIGHT THE RIDDLER RUNS A TEST CASE IN THE OFFICES OF THE YAB SODA COMPANY...
I BROKE IN EASILY ENOUGH-- BUT WHEN I LEAVE, WILL IT BE EMPTY-HANDED?
SWEAT BEADS HIS FOREHEAD! INDECISION AND DOUBT TWIST HIS FEATURES INTO A GROTESQUE MASK AS HE COMES TO A STOP BEFORE A CABINET...
THE YAB SODA COMPANY IS A HUNDRED YEARS OLD! THE COINS INSIDE THIS CABINET ARE ALSO A CENTURY OLD-- TO BE PUT ON EXHIBITION AS PART OF ITS CENTENNIAL CELEBRATION! NOW THE QUESTION IS-- CAN I STEAL THEM?
HIS HANDS DART DOWNWARD-- CLOSE ON A TRAY AND LIFT IT UPWARD...
I--DID--IT! I'VE OVERCOME MY RIDDLE COMPULSION! WHAT A LOAD OFF MY MIND TO KNOW I CAN ROB WITHOUT BRINGING BATMAN DOWN ON MY BACK! I'M CURED! CURED! CURED!
BUT WHAT OF BATMAN AND ROBIN? HAVE THEY BEEN IDLE WHILE THE RIDDLER HAS BEEN BURNING THE MIDNIGHT OIL ON HIS SELF-INDUCED CURE?
WE JUST CAN'T WAIT AROUND FOR THE RIDDLER TO GO INTO HIS ROUTINE! WE'VE GOT OTHER WORK TO DO--OTHER CRIMINALS TO CAPTURE...
4

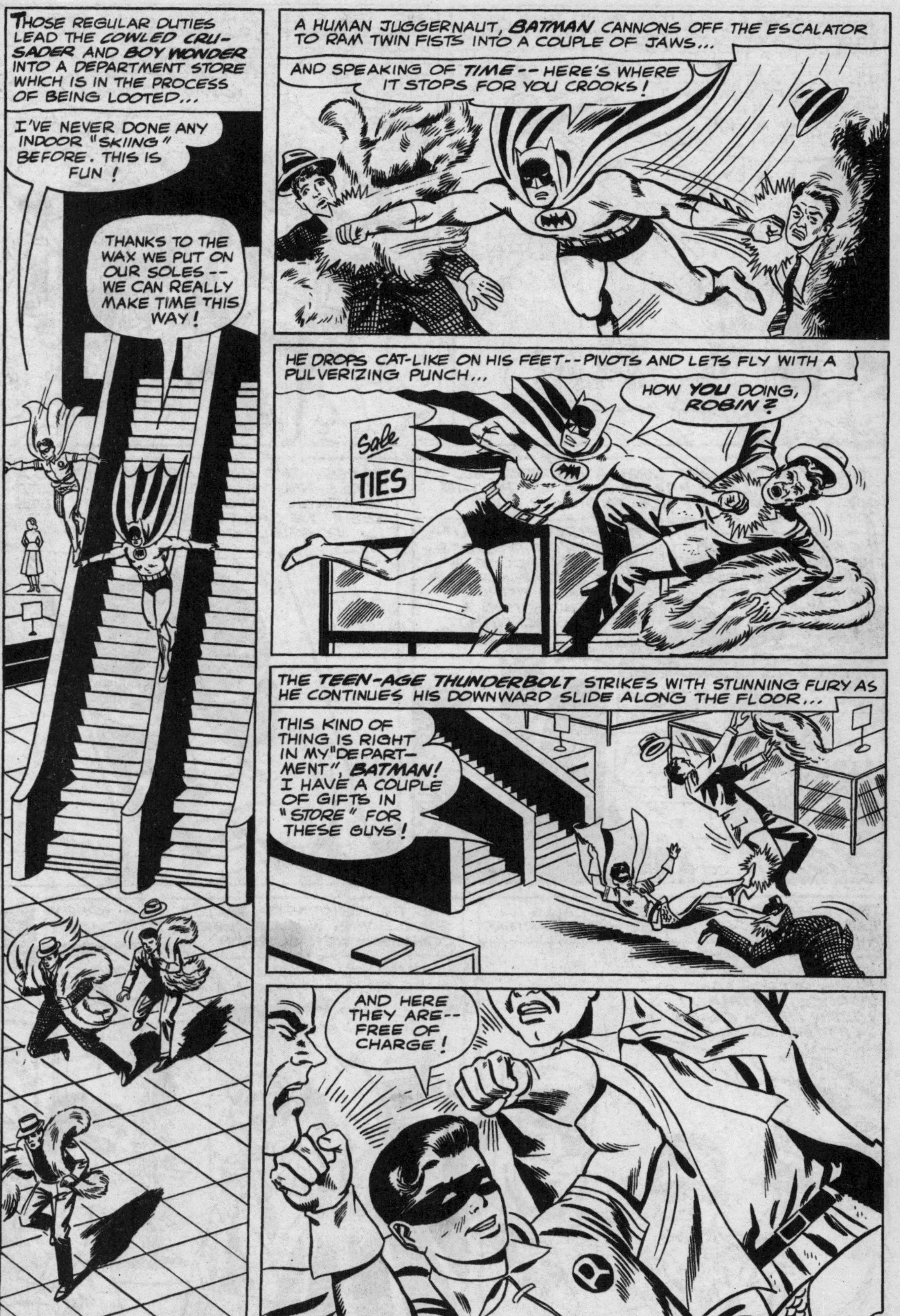
THOSE REGULAR DUTIES LEAD THE COWLED CRU-SADER AND BOY WONDER INTO A DEPARTMENT STORE WHICH IS IN THE PROCESS OF BEING LOOTED...
I'VE NEVER DONE ANY INDOOR "SKIING" BEFORE. THIS IS FUN!
THANKS TO THE WAX WE PUT ON OUR SOLES -- WE CAN REALLY MAKE TIME THIS WAY!
A HUMAN JUGGERNAUT, BATMAN CANNONS OFF THE ESCALATOR TO RAM TWIN FISTS INTO A COUPLE OF JAWS...
AND SPEAKING OF TIME -- HERE'S WHERE IT STOPS FOR YOU CROOKS!
HE DROPS CAT-LIKE ON HIS FEET--PIVOTS AND LETS FLY WITH A PULVERIZING PUNCH...
HOW YOU DOING, ROBIN?
Sale
TIES
THE TEEN-AGE THUNDERBOLT STRIKES WITH STUNNING FURY AS HE CONTINUES HIS DOWNWARD SLIDE ALONG THE FLOOR...
THIS KIND OF THING IS RIGHT IN MY "DEPART-MENT", BATMAN! I HAVE A COUPLE OF GIFTS IN "STORE" FOR THESE GUYS!
AND HERE THEY ARE-- FREE OF CHARGE!
5

LATER, THOSE SAME DUTIES BRING THEM INTO ACTION ON A RESCUE MISSION IN A DESERTED AREA OF A CRAGGY GORGE...

YOU HAD A NASTY FALL...BUT YOU'RE SAFE NOW! WE'LL HAVE YOU IN A HOSPITAL BED WITHIN A FEW MINUTES!

YOU FELLOWS ARE TERRIFIC!

AND LATER STILL, TO HELP IN SAVING PEOPLE TRAPPED INSIDE A BLAZING APARTMENT HOUSE...

THIS IS THE LAST OF THEM, ROBIN!

WE'RE CERTAINLY HAVING OUR-SELVES A HOT TIME IN TOWN TONIGHT!

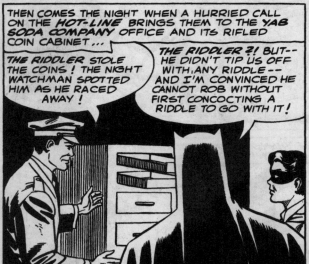

THEN COMES THE NIGHT WHEN A HURRIED CALL ON THE HOT-LINE BRINGS THEM TO THE YAB SODA COMPANY OFFICE AND ITS RIFLED COIN CABINET...

THE RIDDLER STOLE THE COINS! THE NIGHT WATCHMAN SPOTTED HIM AS HE RACED AWAY!

THE RIDDLER?! BUT-- HE DIDN'T TIP US OFF WITH ANY RIDDLE-- AND I'M CONVINCED HE CANNOT ROB WITHOUT FIRST CONCOCTING A RIDDLE TO GO WITH IT!

UNLESS--THE RIDDLER DID GIVE US A RIDDLE--BUT SO CLEVERLY CONCEALED WE WEREN'T EVEN AWARE OF IT! LET'S SEE IF WE CAN FIGURE OUT WHAT IT POSSIBLY COULD HAVE BEEN--

THE MASKED MANHUNTER RECALLS AN EARLIER NIGHT AT POLICE HEADQUARTERS WHEN...

THIS NINE-INCH-LONG ENVELOPE AND BLANK LETTER CAME FOR YOU, BATMAN! LOOKS LIKE A CRANK LETTER TO ME!

AND THE NIGHT AFTERWARD, WHEN A HONEY-SUCKLE VINE WAS DELIVERED TO POLICE COMMISSIONER GORDON...

WHAT DO YOU MAKE OF IT?

WELL, IT SMELLS KIND OF NICE! I ALWAYS DID LIKE HONEYSUCKLE!

6

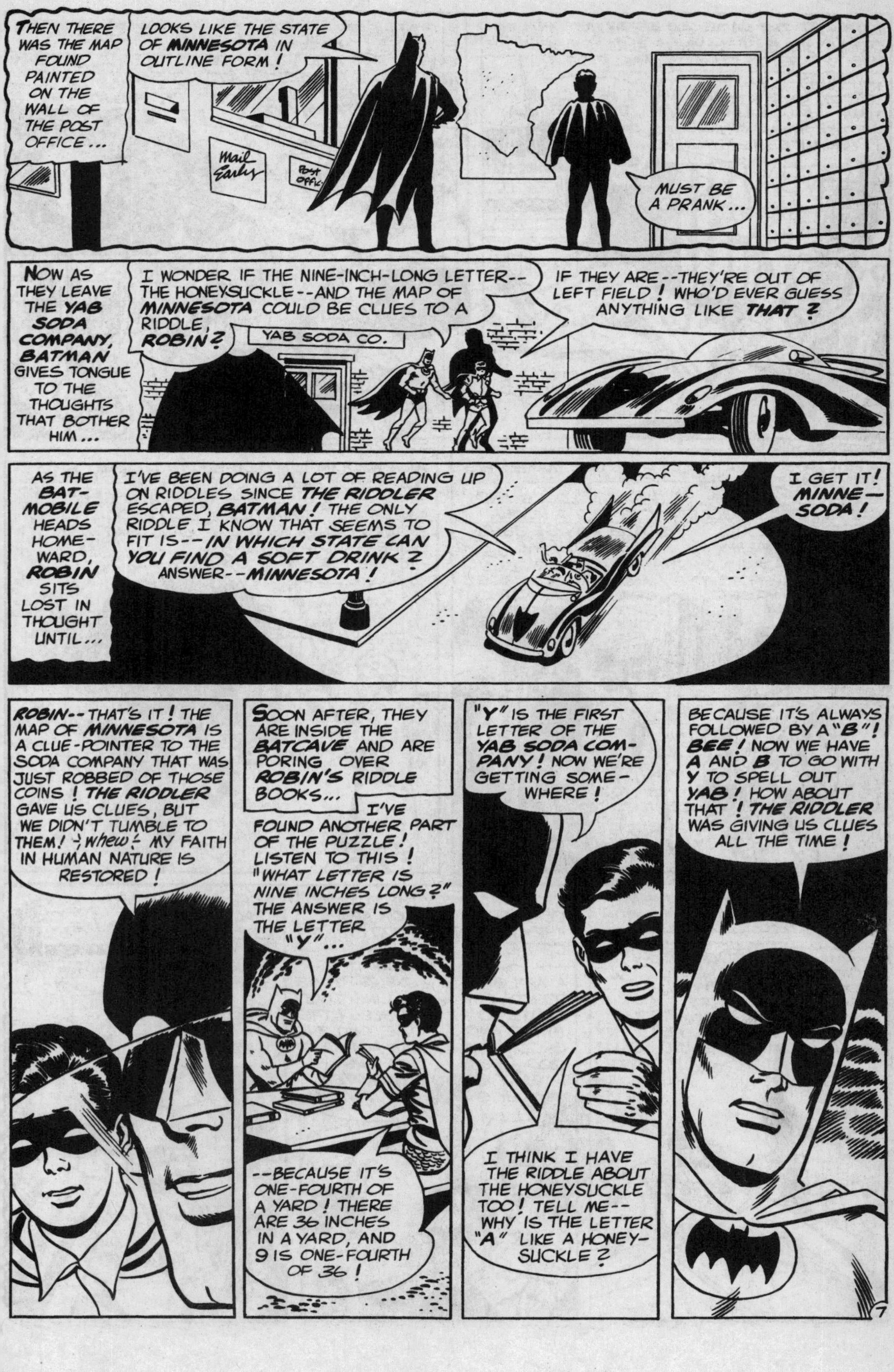
THEN THERE WAS THE MAP FOUND PAINTED ON THE WALL OF THE POST OFFICE...
LOOKS LIKE THE STATE OF MINNESOTA IN OUTLINE FORM!
Mail Early
Post Office
MUST BE A PRANK...
NOW AS THEY LEAVE THE YAB SODA COMPANY, BATMAN GIVES TONGUE TO THE THOUGHTS THAT BOTHER HIM...
I WONDER IF THE NINE-INCH-LONG LETTER-- THE HONEYSUCKLE--AND THE MAP OF MINNESOTA COULD BE CLUES TO A RIDDLE, ROBIN?
YAB SODA CO.
IF THEY ARE--THEY'RE OUT OF LEFT FIELD! WHO'D EVER GUESS ANYTHING LIKE THAT?
AS THE BAT-MOBILE HEADS HOME-WARD, ROBIN SITS LOST IN THOUGHT UNTIL...
I'VE BEEN DOING A LOT OF READING UP ON RIDDLES SINCE THE RIDDLER ESCAPED, BATMAN! THE ONLY RIDDLE I KNOW THAT SEEMS TO FIT IS--IN WHICH STATE CAN YOU FIND A SOFT DRINK? ANSWER--MINNESOTA!
I GET IT! MINNE-SODA!
ROBIN--THAT'S IT! THE MAP OF MINNESOTA IS A CLUE-POINTER TO THE SODA COMPANY THAT WAS JUST ROBBED OF THOSE COINS! THE RIDDLER GAVE US CLUES, BUT WE DIDN'T TUMBLE TO THEM! -whew- MY FAITH IN HUMAN NATURE IS RESTORED!
SOON AFTER, THEY ARE INSIDE THE BATCAVE AND ARE PORING OVER ROBIN'S RIDDLE BOOKS...
I'VE FOUND ANOTHER PART OF THE PUZZLE! LISTEN TO THIS! "WHAT LETTER IS NINE INCHES LONG?" THE ANSWER IS THE LETTER "Y"...
--BECAUSE IT'S ONE-FOURTH OF A YARD! THERE ARE 36 INCHES IN A YARD, AND 9 IS ONE-FOURTH OF 36!
"Y" IS THE FIRST LETTER OF THE YAB SODA COMPANY! NOW WE'RE GETTING SOME-WHERE!
I THINK I HAVE THE RIDDLE ABOUT THE HONEYSUCKLE TOO! TELL ME--WHY IS THE LETTER "A" LIKE A HONEY-SUCKLE?
BECAUSE IT'S ALWAYS FOLLOWED BY A "B"! BEE! NOW WE HAVE A AND B TO GO WITH Y TO SPELL OUT YAB! HOW ABOUT THAT! THE RIDDLER WAS GIVING US CLUES ALL THE TIME!
7

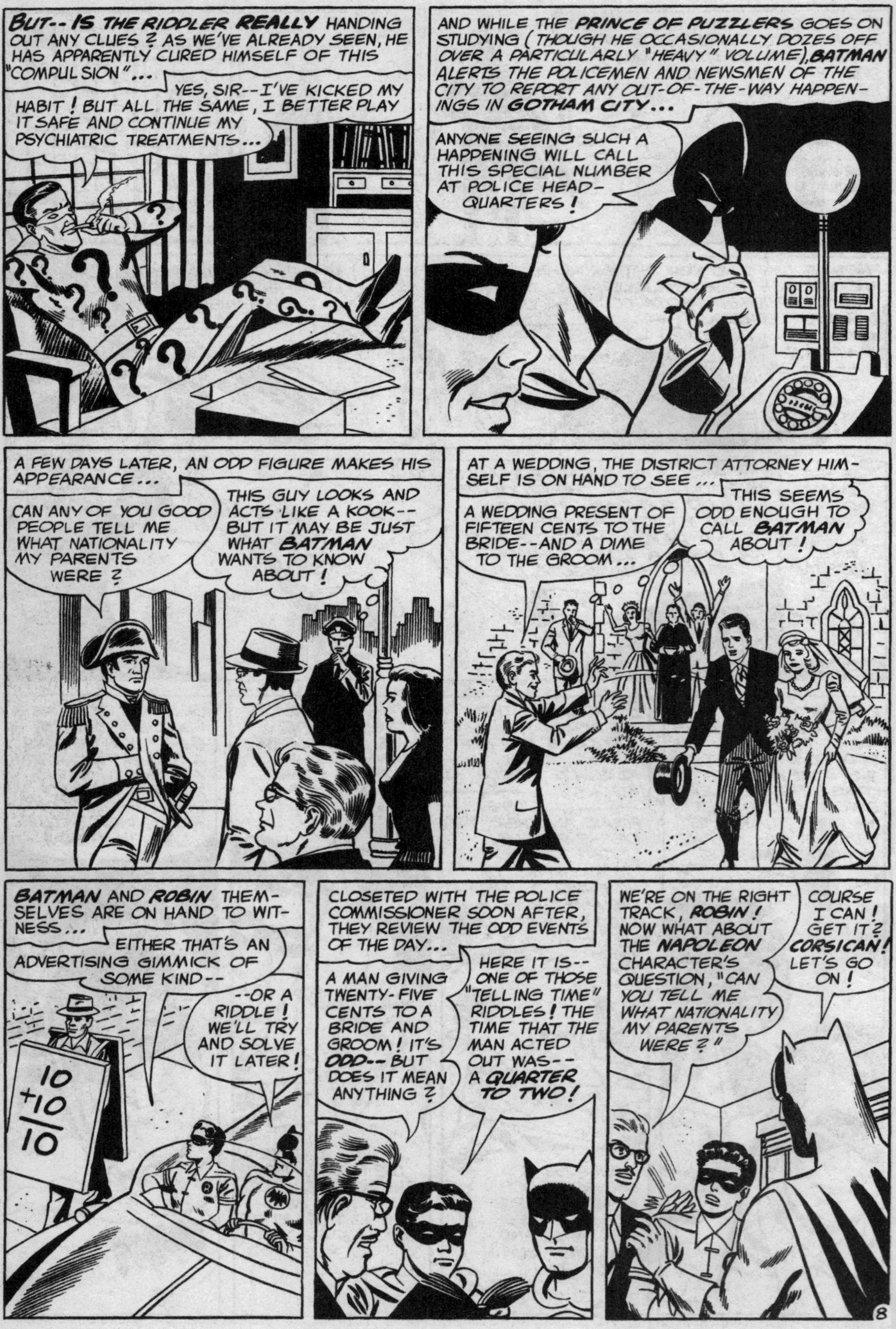
BUT-- IS THE RIDDLER REALLY HANDING OUT ANY CLUES? AS WE'VE ALREADY SEEN, HE HAS APPARENTLY CURED HIMSELF OF THIS "COMPULSION"...
YES, SIR--I'VE KICKED MY HABIT! BUT ALL THE SAME, I BETTER PLAY IT SAFE AND CONTINUE MY PSYCHIATRIC TREATMENTS...
AND WHILE THE PRINCE OF PUZZLERS GOES ON STUDYING (THOUGH HE OCCASIONALLY DOZES OFF OVER A PARTICULARLY "HEAVY" VOLUME), BATMAN ALERTS THE POLICEMEN AND NEWSMEN OF THE CITY TO REPORT ANY OUT-OF-THE-WAY HAPPENINGS IN GOTHAM CITY...
ANYONE SEEING SUCH A HAPPENING WILL CALL THIS SPECIAL NUMBER AT POLICE HEAD-QUARTERS!
A FEW DAYS LATER, AN ODD FIGURE MAKES HIS APPEARANCE...
CAN ANY OF YOU GOOD PEOPLE TELL ME WHAT NATIONALITY MY PARENTS WERE?
THIS GUY LOOKS AND ACTS LIKE A KOOK--BUT IT MAY BE JUST WHAT BATMAN WANTS TO KNOW ABOUT!
AT A WEDDING, THE DISTRICT ATTORNEY HIMSELF IS ON HAND TO SEE...
A WEDDING PRESENT OF FIFTEEN CENTS TO THE BRIDE--AND A DIME TO THE GROOM...
THIS SEEMS ODD ENOUGH TO CALL BATMAN ABOUT!
BATMAN AND ROBIN THEMSELVES ARE ON HAND TO WITNESS...
EITHER THAT'S AN ADVERTISING GIMMICK OF SOME KIND--
--OR A RIDDLE! WE'LL TRY AND SOLVE IT LATER!
10 +10 10
CLOSETED WITH THE POLICE COMMISSIONER SOON AFTER, THEY REVIEW THE ODD EVENTS OF THE DAY...
A MAN GIVING TWENTY-FIVE CENTS TO A BRIDE AND GROOM! IT'S ODD--BUT DOES IT MEAN ANYTHING?
HERE IT IS--ONE OF THOSE "TELLING TIME" RIDDLES! THE TIME THAT THE MAN ACTED OUT WAS--A QUARTER TO TWO!
WE'RE ON THE RIGHT TRACK, ROBIN! NOW WHAT ABOUT THE NAPOLEON CHARACTER'S QUESTION, "CAN YOU TELL ME WHAT NATIONALITY MY PARENTS WERE?"
COURSE I CAN! GET IT? CORSICAN! LET'S GO ON!
8

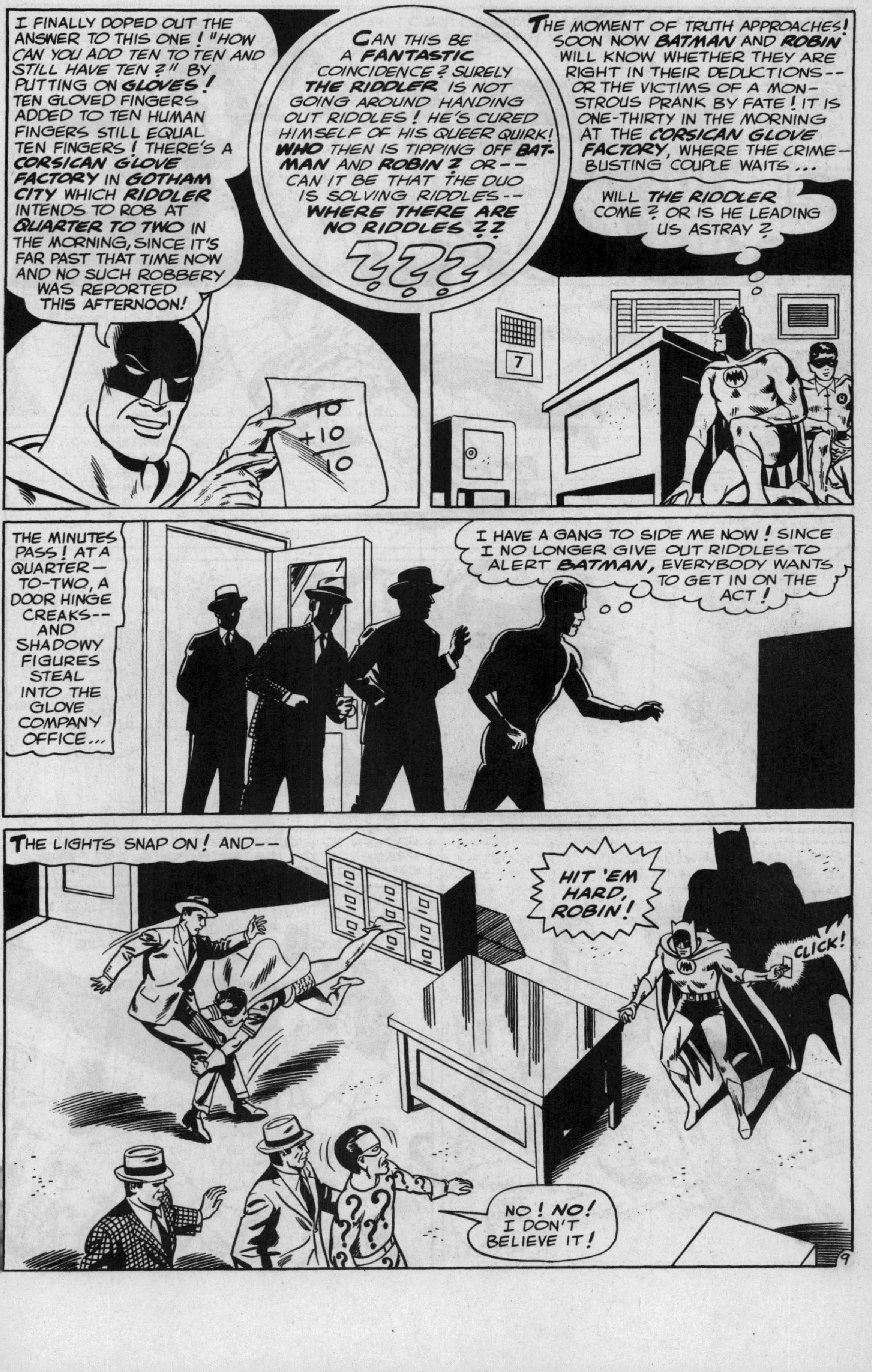
I FINALLY DOPED OUT THE ANSWER TO THIS ONE! "HOW CAN YOU ADD TEN TO TEN AND STILL HAVE TEN?" BY PUTTING ON GLOVES! TEN GLOVED FINGERS ADDED TO TEN HUMAN FINGERS STILL EQUAL TEN FINGERS! THERE'S A CORSICAN GLOVE FACTORY IN GOTHAM CITY WHICH RIDDLER INTENDS TO ROB AT QUARTER TO TWO IN THE MORNING, SINCE IT'S FAR PAST THAT TIME NOW AND NO SUCH ROBBERY WAS REPORTED THIS AFTERNOON!
10
+10
10
CAN THIS BE A FANTASTIC COINCIDENCE? SURELY THE RIDDLER IS NOT GOING AROUND HANDING OUT RIDDLES! HE'S CURED HIMSELF OF HIS QUEER QUIRK! WHO THEN IS TIPPING OFF BATMAN AND ROBIN? OR-- CAN IT BE THAT THE DUO IS SOLVING RIDDLES-- WHERE THERE ARE NO RIDDLES??
???
THE MOMENT OF TRUTH APPROACHES! SOON NOW BATMAN AND ROBIN WILL KNOW WHETHER THEY ARE RIGHT IN THEIR DEDUCTIONS-- OR THE VICTIMS OF A MONSTROUS PRANK BY FATE! IT IS ONE-THIRTY IN THE MORNING AT THE CORSICAN GLOVE FACTORY, WHERE THE CRIME-BUSTING COUPLE WAITS ...
WILL THE RIDDLER COME? OR IS HE LEADING US ASTRAY?
7
THE MINUTES PASS! AT A QUARTER-TO-TWO, A DOOR HINGE CREAKS-- AND SHADOWY FIGURES STEAL INTO THE GLOVE COMPANY OFFICE...
I HAVE A GANG TO SIDE ME NOW! SINCE I NO LONGER GIVE OUT RIDDLES TO ALERT BATMAN, EVERYBODY WANTS TO GET IN ON THE ACT!
THE LIGHTS SNAP ON! AND--
HIT 'EM HARD, ROBIN!
CLICK!
NO! NO! I DON'T BELIEVE IT!
9

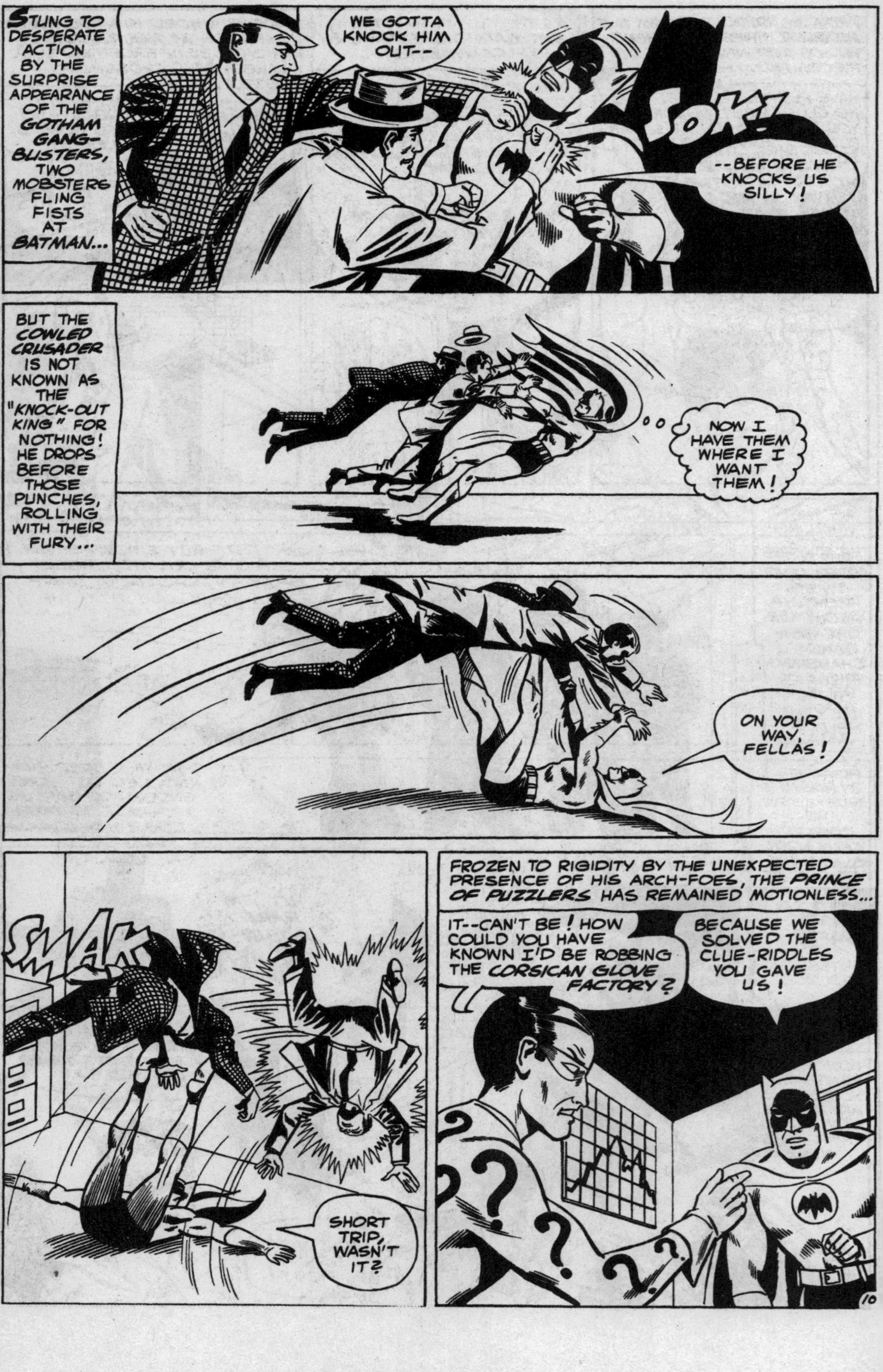
STUNG TO DESPERATE ACTION BY THE SURPRISE APPEARANCE OF THE GOTHAM GANG-BUSTERS, TWO MOBSTERS FLING FISTS AT BATMAN...
WE GOTTA KNOCK HIM OUT--
SOK!
--BEFORE HE KNOCKS US SILLY!
BUT THE COWLED CRUSADER IS NOT KNOWN AS THE "KNOCK-OUT KING" FOR NOTHING! HE DROPS BEFORE THOSE PUNCHES, ROLLING WITH THEIR FURY...
NOW I HAVE THEM WHERE I WANT THEM!
ON YOUR WAY, FELLAS!
SWAK
SHORT TRIP, WASN'T IT?
FROZEN TO RIGIDITY BY THE UNEXPECTED PRESENCE OF HIS ARCH-FOES, THE PRINCE OF PUZZLERS HAS REMAINED MOTIONLESS...
IT--CAN'T BE! HOW COULD YOU HAVE KNOWN I'D BE ROBBING THE CORSICAN GLOVE FACTORY?
BECAUSE WE SOLVED THE CLUE-RIDDLES YOU GAVE US!
10

FROM HIS TRICKY UNIFORM *THE RIDDLER* WHIPS OUT A HANDFUL OF JIGSAW PUZZLE PIECES AND...

YOU GUYS HAVE FLIPPED-- I CUED YOU NO CLUES! BUT AS LONG AS YOU'RE SO HANDY AT SOLVING PUZZLES, HAVE A *BLAST* PUTTING THIS JIGSAW TOGETHER!

AS THE CUT-OUTS HIT HIM, *BATMAN* IS BATTERED BY EXPLOSIVE BLASTS...

BAM!
BAM!
BAM!

HAVING KAYOED HIS FOE, ROBIN CHARGES AT *THE RIDDLER*-- ONLY TO BE INTERCEPTED BY A LARGE-SIZED CROSSWORD PUZZLE...

MMPPFFF! GLUPP!!

NOW, NOW, *ROBIN*-- NO CROSS WORDS, PLEASE!

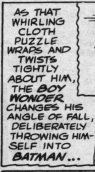

AS THAT WHIRLING CLOTH PUZZLE WRAPS AND TWISTS TIGHTLY ABOUT HIM, THE *BOY WONDER* CHANGES HIS ANGLE OF FALL, DELIBERATELY THROWING HIMSELF INTO *BATMAN*...

BAM!
BAM!
BAM!

THE RIDDLER'S CROSSING US UP WITH HIS PERILOUS PUZZLES-- BUT I'LL MATCH HIM TRICK FOR TRICK!

POWERED BY *ROBIN'S* SIDE-SWIPE, THE *COWLED CRUSADER* SLAMS THE *PRINCE OF PUZZLERS* INTO THE VERY SAFE HE INTENDED TO ROB...

THAT WILL KEEP HIM KNOCKED OUT LONG ENOUGH TO GIVE US A CHANCE TO OVERCOME HIS PUZZLES!

WHEN THE *MASKED MANHUNTERS* RECOVER...

NOW WHAT'S THIS NONSENSE ABOUT NOT GIVING OUT ANY RIDDLE CLUES? HOW DO YOU THINK WE GOT HERE?

I--I CAN'T IMAGINE! ALL I KNOW IS I DIDN'T GIVE YOU ANY RIDDLES! I'VE TRAINED MYSELF NOT TO!

11

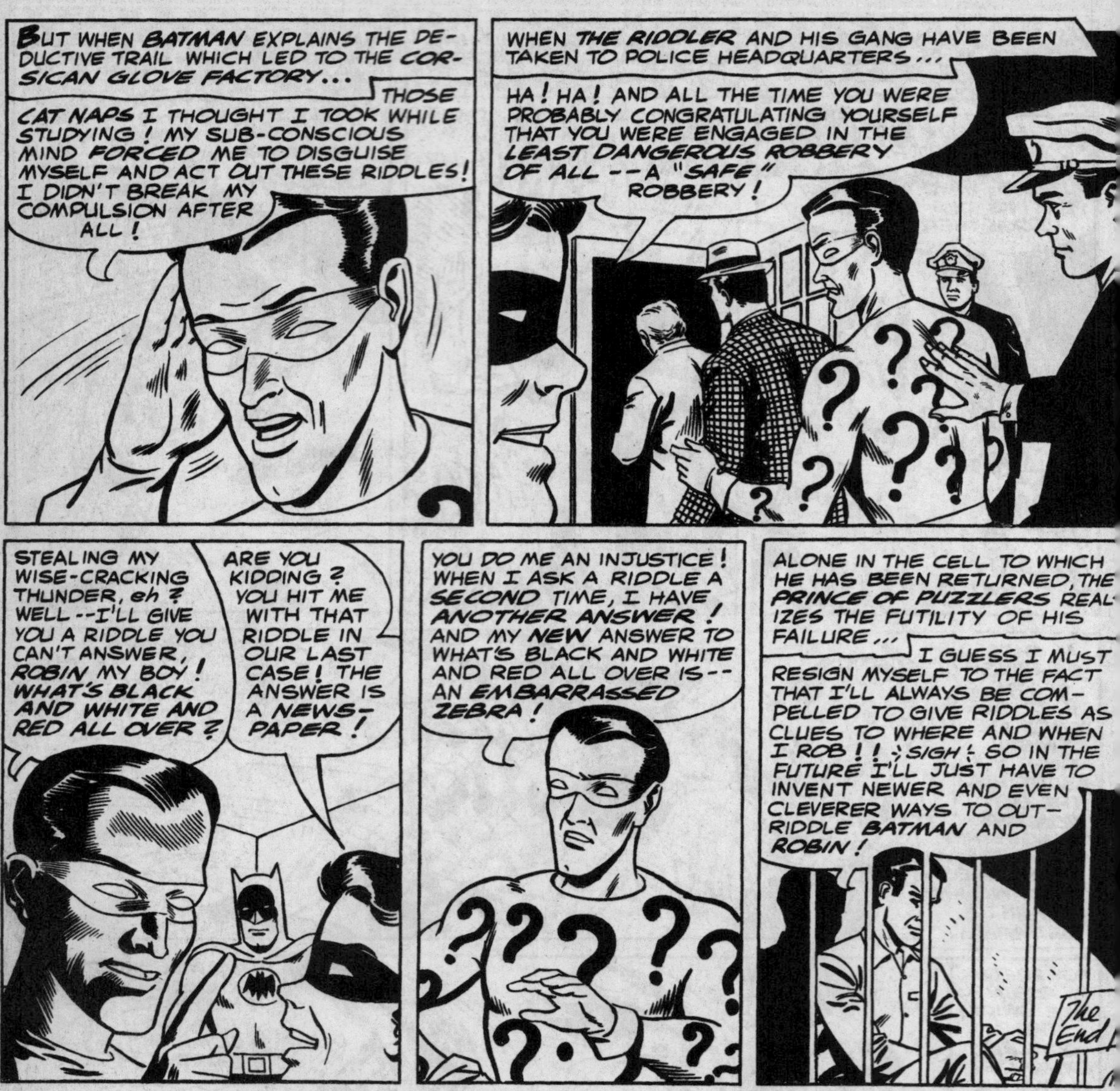
BUT WHEN BATMAN EXPLAINS THE DEDUCTIVE TRAIL WHICH LED TO THE CORSICAN GLOVE FACTORY...
THOSE CAT NAPS I THOUGHT I TOOK WHILE STUDYING! MY SUB-CONSCIOUS MIND FORCED ME TO DISGUISE MYSELF AND ACT OUT THESE RIDDLES! I DIDN'T BREAK MY COMPULSION AFTER ALL!
WHEN THE RIDDLER AND HIS GANG HAVE BEEN TAKEN TO POLICE HEADQUARTERS...
HA! HA! AND ALL THE TIME YOU WERE PROBABLY CONGRATULATING YOURSELF THAT YOU WERE ENGAGED IN THE LEAST DANGEROUS ROBBERY OF ALL -- A "SAFE" ROBBERY!
STEALING MY WISE-CRACKING THUNDER, eh? WELL--I'LL GIVE YOU A RIDDLE YOU CAN'T ANSWER, ROBIN MY BOY! WHAT'S BLACK AND WHITE AND RED ALL OVER?
ARE YOU KIDDING? YOU HIT ME WITH THAT RIDDLE IN OUR LAST CASE! THE ANSWER IS A NEWSPAPER!
YOU DO ME AN INJUSTICE! WHEN I ASK A RIDDLE A SECOND TIME, I HAVE ANOTHER ANSWER! AND MY NEW ANSWER TO WHAT'S BLACK AND WHITE AND RED ALL OVER IS--AN EMBARRASSED ZEBRA!
ALONE IN THE CELL TO WHICH HE HAS BEEN RETURNED, THE PRINCE OF PUZZLERS REALIZES THE FUTILITY OF HIS FAILURE...
I GUESS I MUST RESIGN MYSELF TO THE FACT THAT I'LL ALWAYS BE COMPELLED TO GIVE RIDDLES AS CLUES TO WHERE AND WHEN I ROB!! -SIGH- SO IN THE FUTURE I'LL JUST HAVE TO INVENT NEWER AND EVEN CLEVERER WAYS TO OUT-RIDDLE BATMAN AND ROBIN!
The End

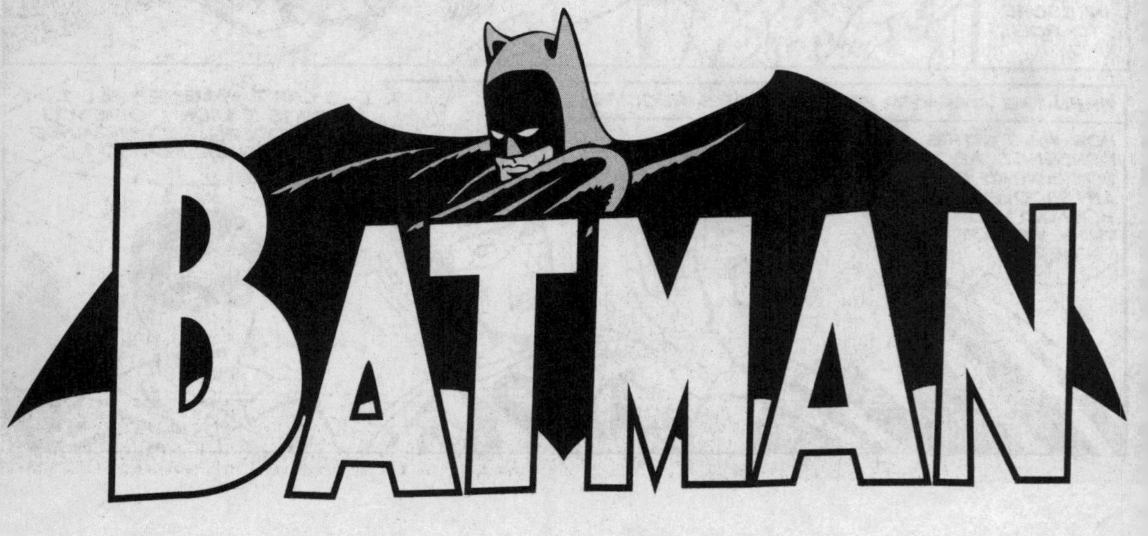
BATMAN

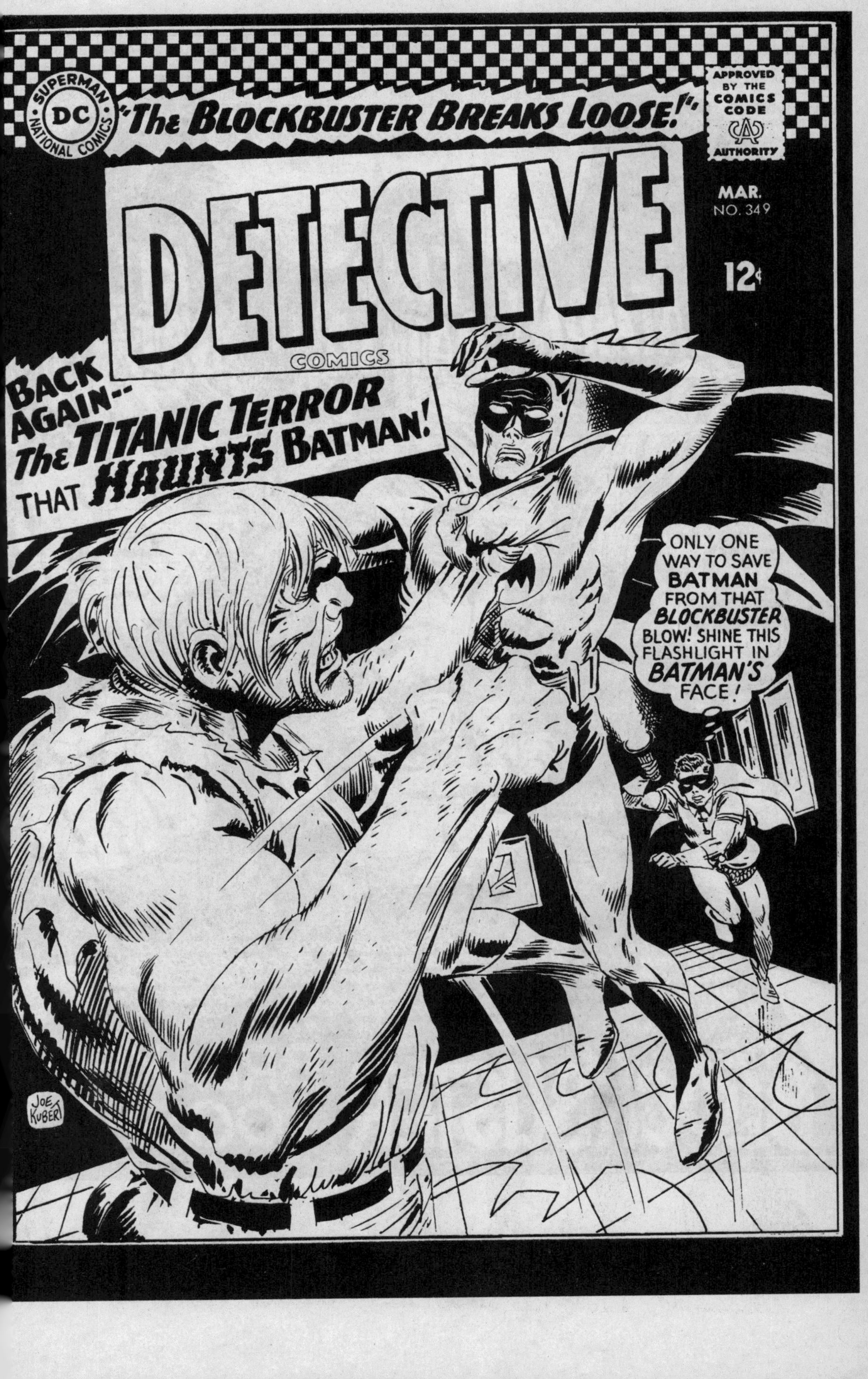
SUPERMAN DC NATIONAL COMICS
"The BLOCKBUSTER BREAKS LOOSE!"
APPROVED BY THE COMICS CODE AUTHORITY
DETECTIVE COMICS
MAR. NO. 349
12¢
BACK AGAIN... The TITANIC TERROR THAT HAUNTS BATMAN!
ONLY ONE WAY TO SAVE BATMAN FROM THAT BLOCKBUSTER BLOW! SHINE THIS FLASHLIGHT IN BATMAN'S FACE!
JOE KUBERT

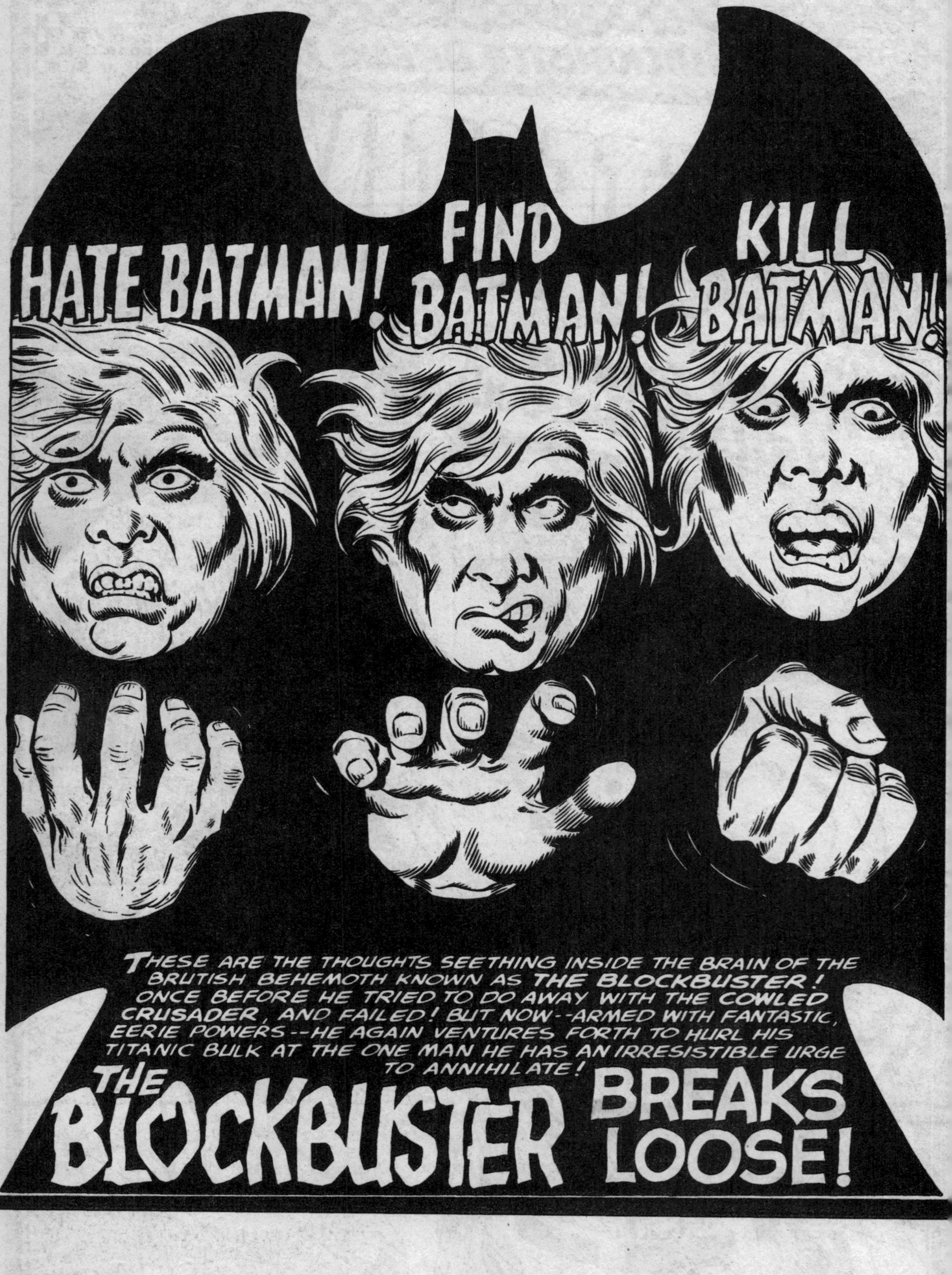
HATE BATMAN!
FIND BATMAN!
KILL BATMAN!
THESE ARE THE THOUGHTS SEETHING INSIDE THE BRAIN OF THE BRUTISH BEHEMOTH KNOWN AS THE BLOCKBUSTER! ONCE BEFORE HE TRIED TO DO AWAY WITH THE COWLED CRUSADER, AND FAILED! BUT NOW--ARMED WITH FANTASTIC, EERIE POWERS--HE AGAIN VENTURES FORTH TO HURL HIS TITANIC BULK AT THE ONE MAN HE HAS AN IRRESISTIBLE URGE TO ANNIHILATE!
THE BLOCKBUSTER BREAKS LOOSE!

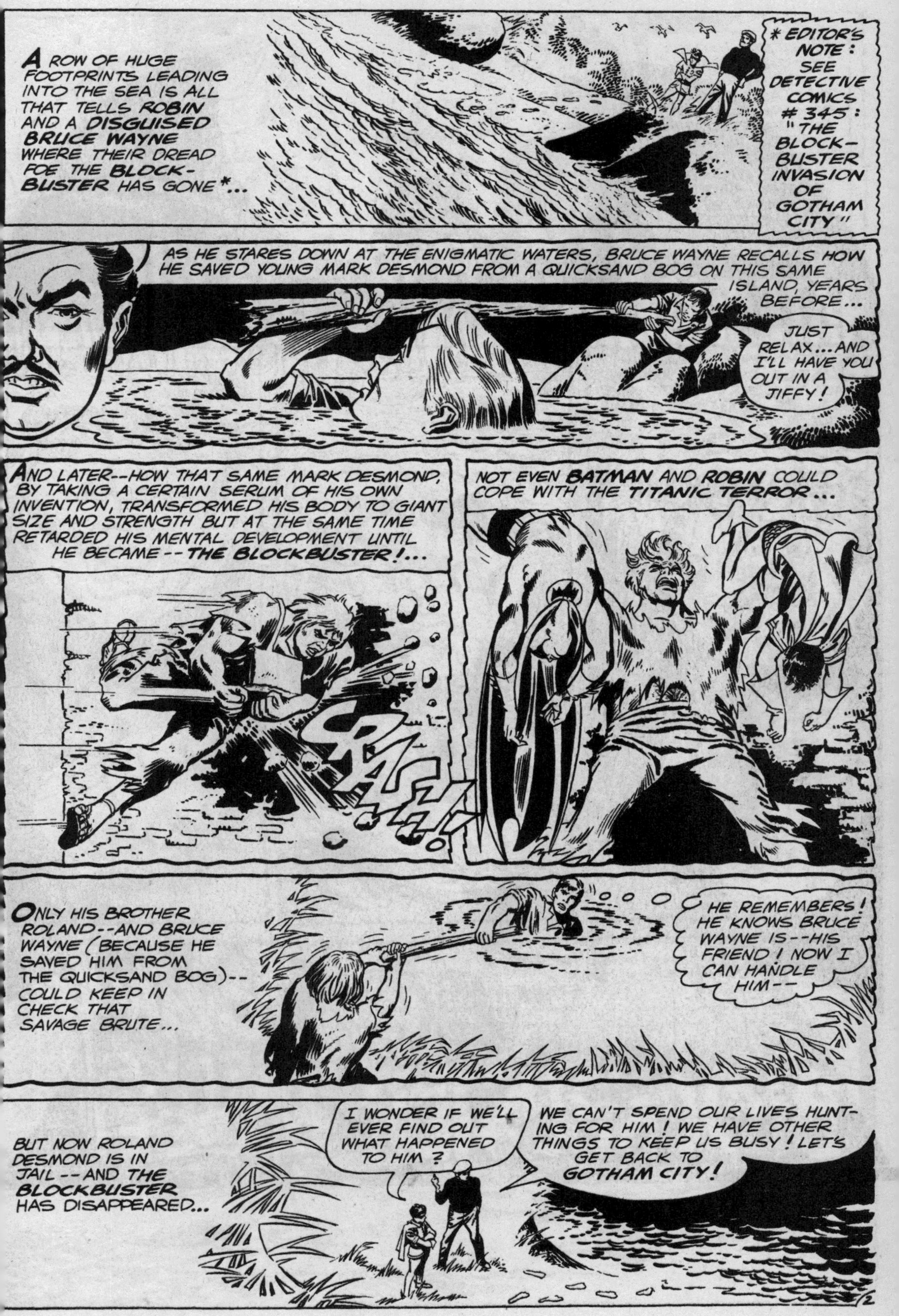
A ROW OF HUGE FOOTPRINTS LEADING INTO THE SEA IS ALL THAT TELLS ROBIN AND A DISGUISED BRUCE WAYNE WHERE THEIR DREAD FOE THE BLOCK-BUSTER HAS GONE*...
* EDITOR'S NOTE: SEE DETECTIVE COMICS # 345: "THE BLOCK-BUSTER INVASION OF GOTHAM CITY"
AS HE STARES DOWN AT THE ENIGMATIC WATERS, BRUCE WAYNE RECALLS HOW HE SAVED YOUNG MARK DESMOND FROM A QUICKSAND BOG ON THIS SAME ISLAND, YEARS BEFORE...
JUST RELAX... AND I'LL HAVE YOU OUT IN A JIFFY!
AND LATER--HOW THAT SAME MARK DESMOND, BY TAKING A CERTAIN SERUM OF HIS OWN INVENTION, TRANSFORMED HIS BODY TO GIANT SIZE AND STRENGTH BUT AT THE SAME TIME RETARDED HIS MENTAL DEVELOPMENT UNTIL HE BECAME --THE BLOCKBUSTER!...
CRASH!
NOT EVEN BATMAN AND ROBIN COULD COPE WITH THE TITANIC TERROR...
ONLY HIS BROTHER ROLAND--AND BRUCE WAYNE (BECAUSE HE SAVED HIM FROM THE QUICKSAND BOG)--COULD KEEP IN CHECK THAT SAVAGE BRUTE...
HE REMEMBERS! HE KNOWS BRUCE WAYNE IS--HIS FRIEND! NOW I CAN HANDLE HIM--
BUT NOW ROLAND DESMOND IS IN JAIL--AND THE BLOCKBUSTER HAS DISAPPEARED...
I WONDER IF WE'LL EVER FIND OUT WHAT HAPPENED TO HIM?
WE CAN'T SPEND OUR LIVES HUNTING FOR HIM! WE HAVE OTHER THINGS TO KEEP US BUSY! LET'S GET BACK TO GOTHAM CITY!
2

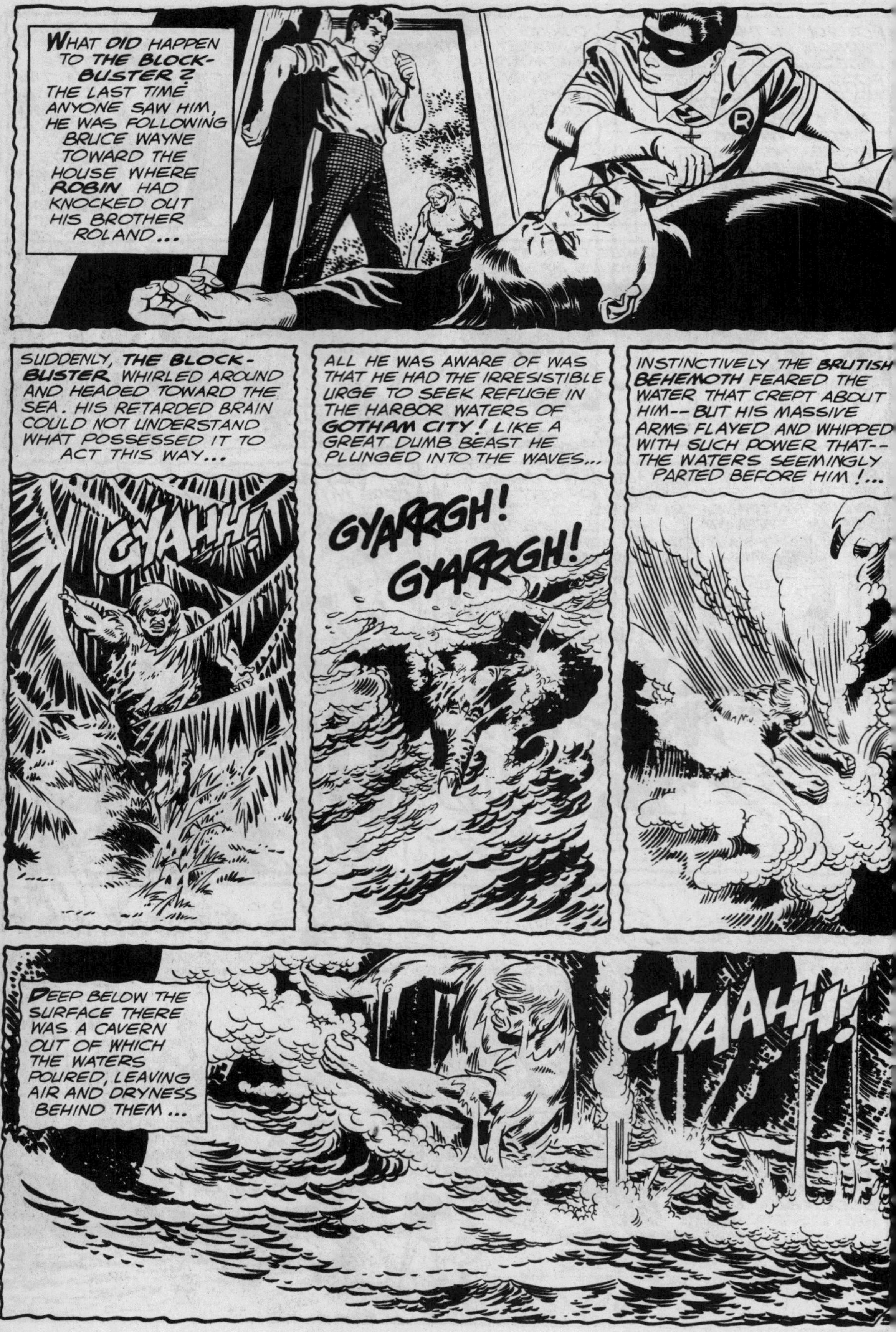
WHAT DID HAPPEN TO THE BLOCK-BUSTER ? THE LAST TIME ANYONE SAW HIM, HE WAS FOLLOWING BRUCE WAYNE TOWARD THE HOUSE WHERE ROBIN HAD KNOCKED OUT HIS BROTHER ROLAND...
SUDDENLY, THE BLOCK-BUSTER WHIRLED AROUND AND HEADED TOWARD THE SEA. HIS RETARDED BRAIN COULD NOT UNDERSTAND WHAT POSSESSED IT TO ACT THIS WAY...
GYAHH!
ALL HE WAS AWARE OF WAS THAT HE HAD THE IRRESISTIBLE URGE TO SEEK REFUGE IN THE HARBOR WATERS OF GOTHAM CITY! LIKE A GREAT DUMB BEAST HE PLUNGED INTO THE WAVES...
GYARRGH! GYARRGH!
INSTINCTIVELY THE BRUTISH BEHEMOTH FEARED THE WATER THAT CREPT ABOUT HIM-- BUT HIS MASSIVE ARMS FLAYED AND WHIPPED WITH SUCH POWER THAT-- THE WATERS SEEMINGLY PARTED BEFORE HIM !...
DEEP BELOW THE SURFACE THERE WAS A CAVERN OUT OF WHICH THE WATERS POURED, LEAVING AIR AND DRYNESS BEHIND THEM...
GYAAHH!

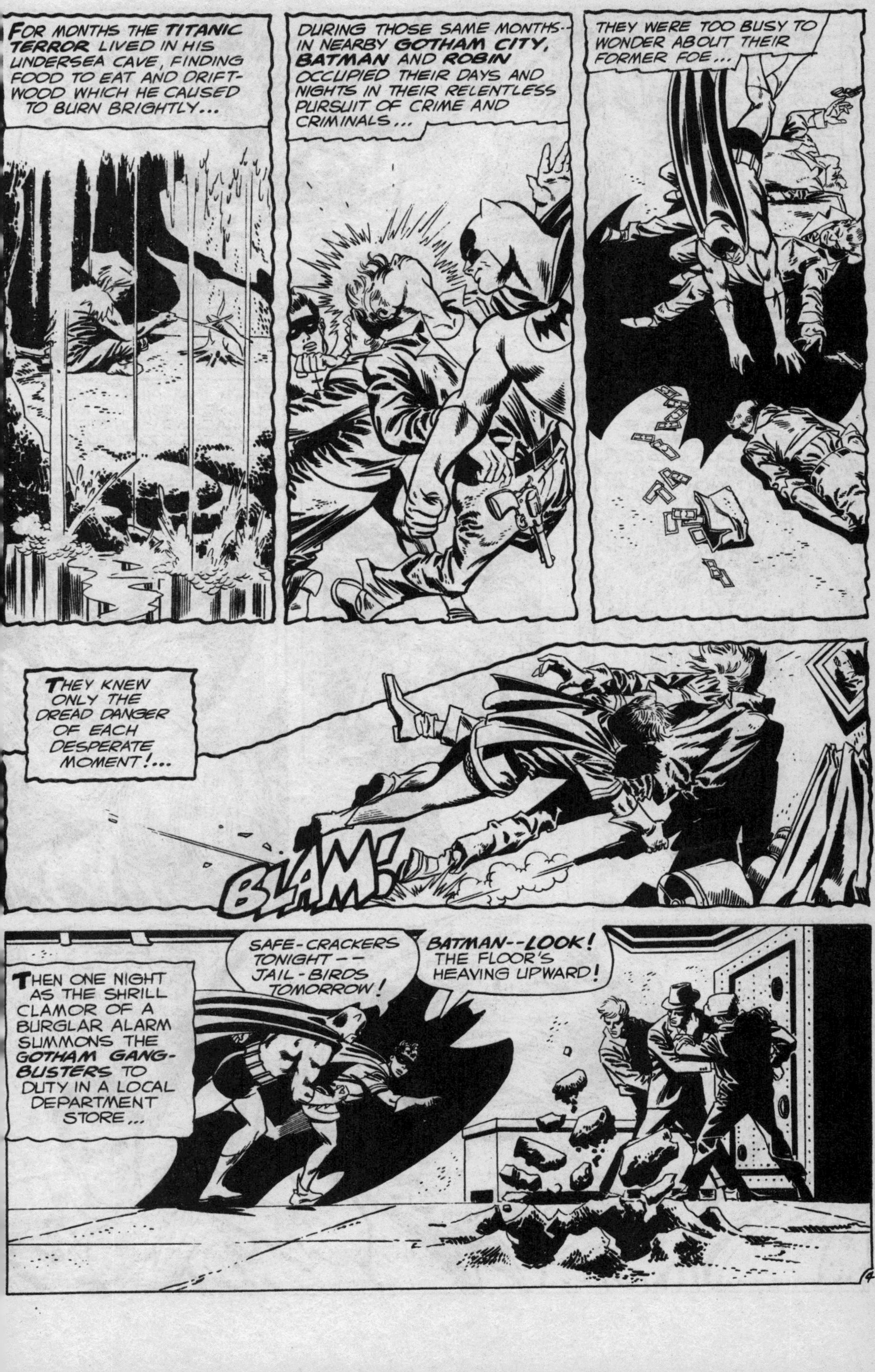
FOR MONTHS THE TITANIC TERROR LIVED IN HIS UNDERSEA CAVE, FINDING FOOD TO EAT AND DRIFT-WOOD WHICH HE CAUSED TO BURN BRIGHTLY...
DURING THOSE SAME MONTHS-- IN NEARBY GOTHAM CITY, BATMAN AND ROBIN OCCUPIED THEIR DAYS AND NIGHTS IN THEIR RELENTLESS PURSUIT OF CRIME AND CRIMINALS...
THEY WERE TOO BUSY TO WONDER ABOUT THEIR FORMER FOE...
THEY KNEW ONLY THE DREAD DANGER OF EACH DESPERATE MOMENT!...
BLAM!
THEN ONE NIGHT AS THE SHRILL CLAMOR OF A BURGLAR ALARM SUMMONS THE GOTHAM GANG-BUSTERS TO DUTY IN A LOCAL DEPARTMENT STORE...
SAFE-CRACKERS TONIGHT -- JAIL-BIRDS TOMORROW!
BATMAN--LOOK! THE FLOOR'S HEAVING UPWARD!
4

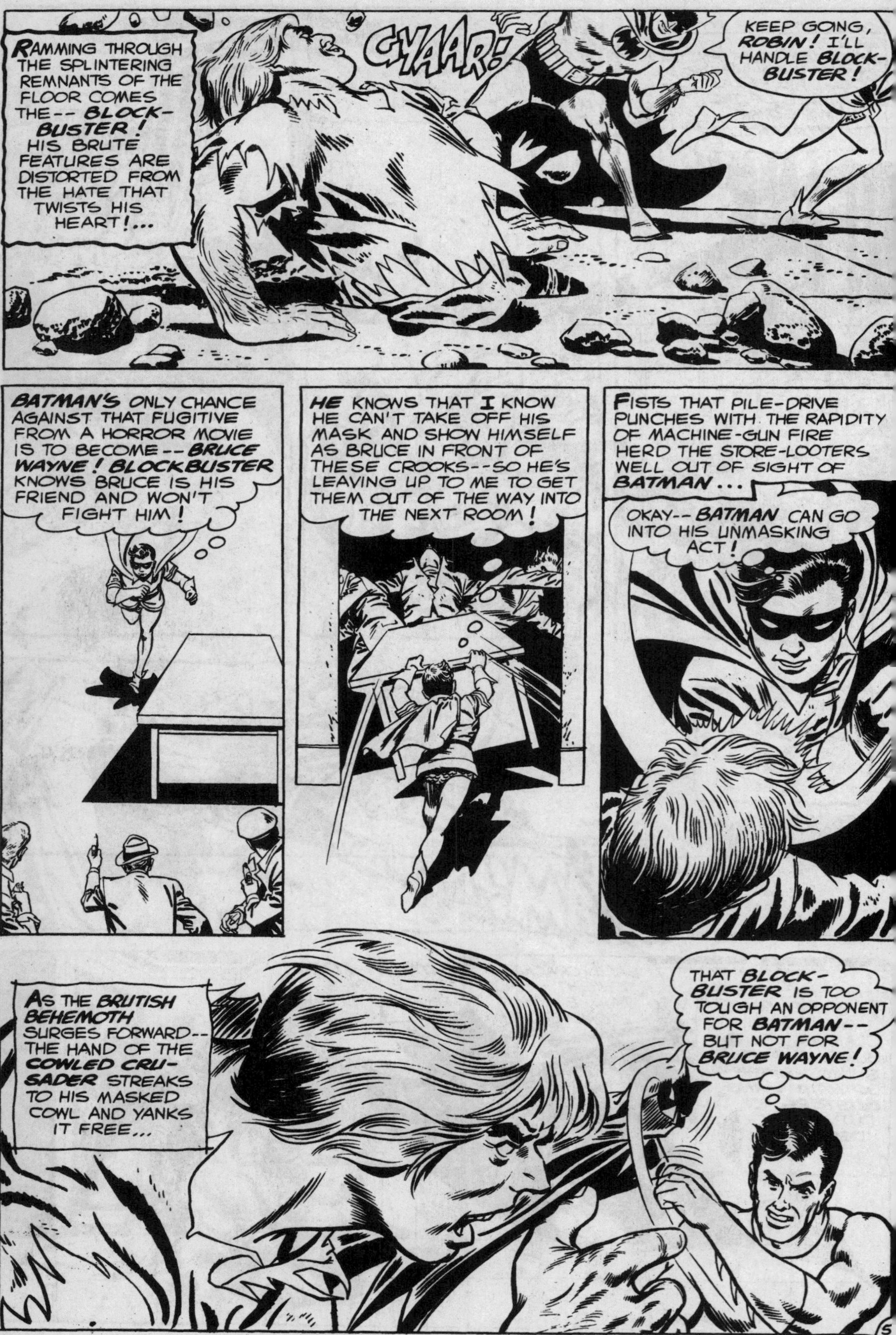
RAMMING THROUGH THE SPLINTERING REMNANTS OF THE FLOOR COMES THE-- BLOCK-BUSTER! HIS BRUTE FEATURES ARE DISTORTED FROM THE HATE THAT TWISTS HIS HEART!...
GYAAR!
KEEP GOING, ROBIN! I'LL HANDLE BLOCK-BUSTER!
BATMAN'S ONLY CHANCE AGAINST THAT FUGITIVE FROM A HORROR MOVIE IS TO BECOME-- BRUCE WAYNE! BLOCKBUSTER KNOWS BRUCE IS HIS FRIEND AND WON'T FIGHT HIM!
HE KNOWS THAT I KNOW HE CAN'T TAKE OFF HIS MASK AND SHOW HIMSELF AS BRUCE IN FRONT OF THESE CROOKS--SO HE'S LEAVING UP TO ME TO GET THEM OUT OF THE WAY INTO THE NEXT ROOM!
FISTS THAT PILE-DRIVE PUNCHES WITH THE RAPIDITY OF MACHINE-GUN FIRE HERD THE STORE-LOOTERS WELL OUT OF SIGHT OF BATMAN...
OKAY-- BATMAN CAN GO INTO HIS UNMASKING ACT!
AS THE BRUTISH BEHEMOTH SURGES FORWARD-- THE HAND OF THE COWLED CRUSADER STREAKS TO HIS MASKED COWL AND YANKS IT FREE...
THAT BLOCK-BUSTER IS TOO TOUGH AN OPPONENT FOR BATMAN-- BUT NOT FOR BRUCE WAYNE!
5

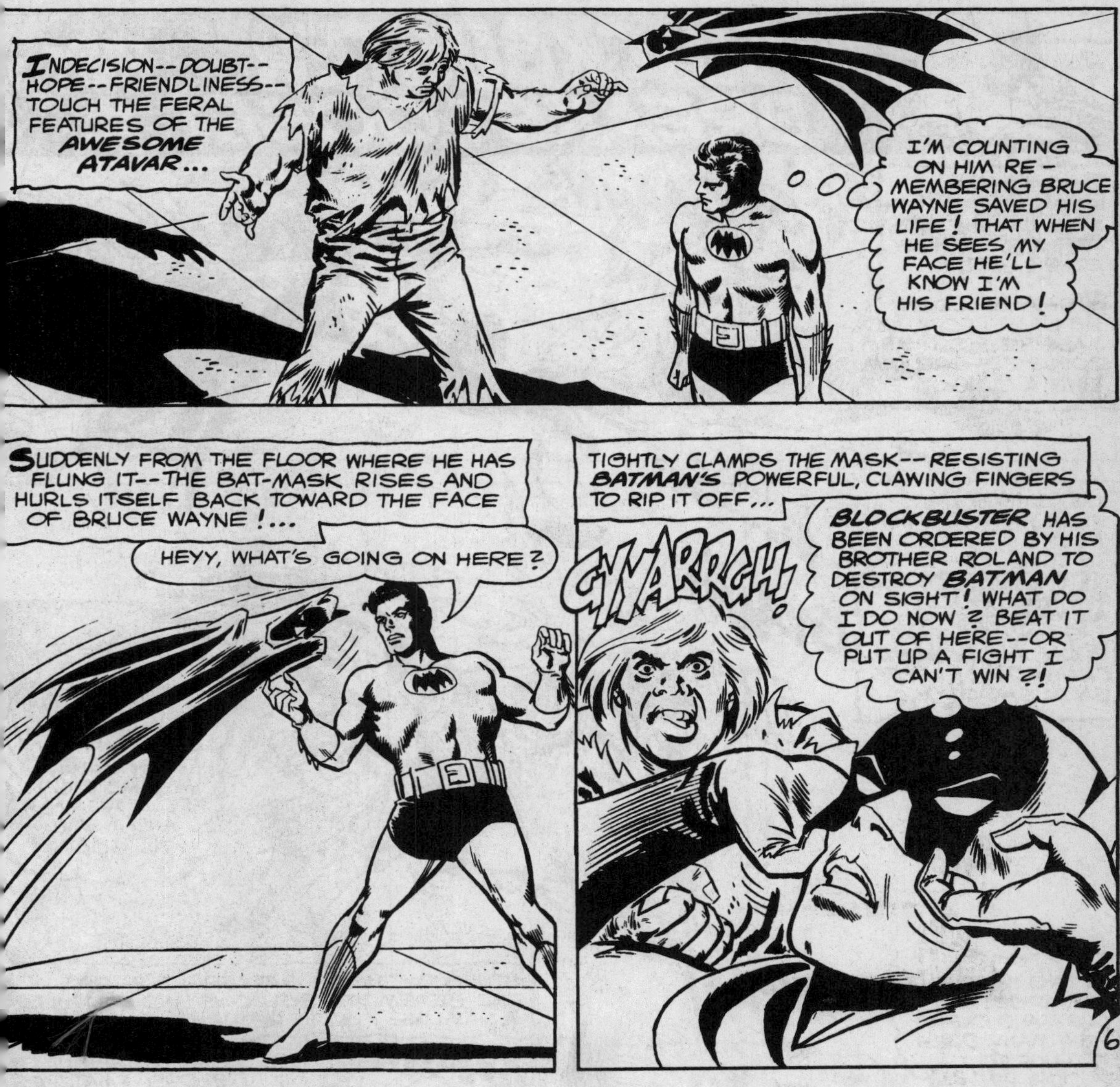
INDECISION--DOUBT--HOPE--FRIENDLINESS--TOUCH THE FERAL FEATURES OF THE AWESOME ATAVAR...
I'M COUNTING ON HIM RE-MEMBERING BRUCE WAYNE SAVED HIS LIFE! THAT WHEN HE SEES MY FACE HE'LL KNOW I'M HIS FRIEND!
SUDDENLY FROM THE FLOOR WHERE HE HAS FLUNG IT--THE BAT-MASK RISES AND HURLS ITSELF BACK TOWARD THE FACE OF BRUCE WAYNE!...
HEYY, WHAT'S GOING ON HERE?
TIGHTLY CLAMPS THE MASK--RESISTING BATMAN'S POWERFUL, CLAWING FINGERS TO RIP IT OFF...
GYARRGH!
BLOCKBUSTER HAS BEEN ORDERED BY HIS BROTHER ROLAND TO DESTROY BATMAN ON SIGHT! WHAT DO I DO NOW? BEAT IT OUT OF HERE--OR PUT UP A FIGHT I CAN'T WIN?!
6

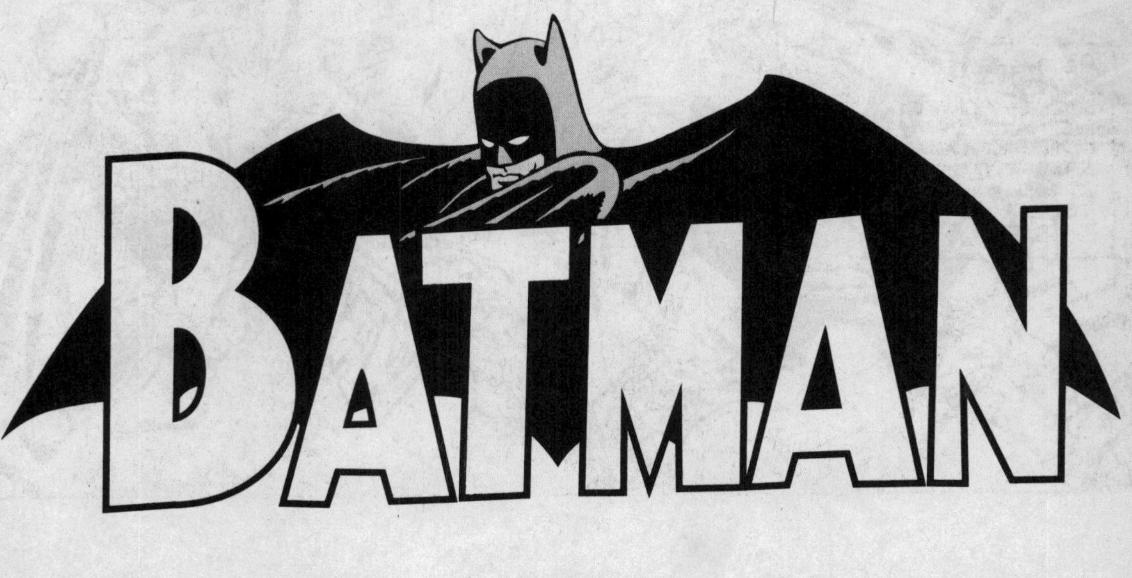
BATMAN

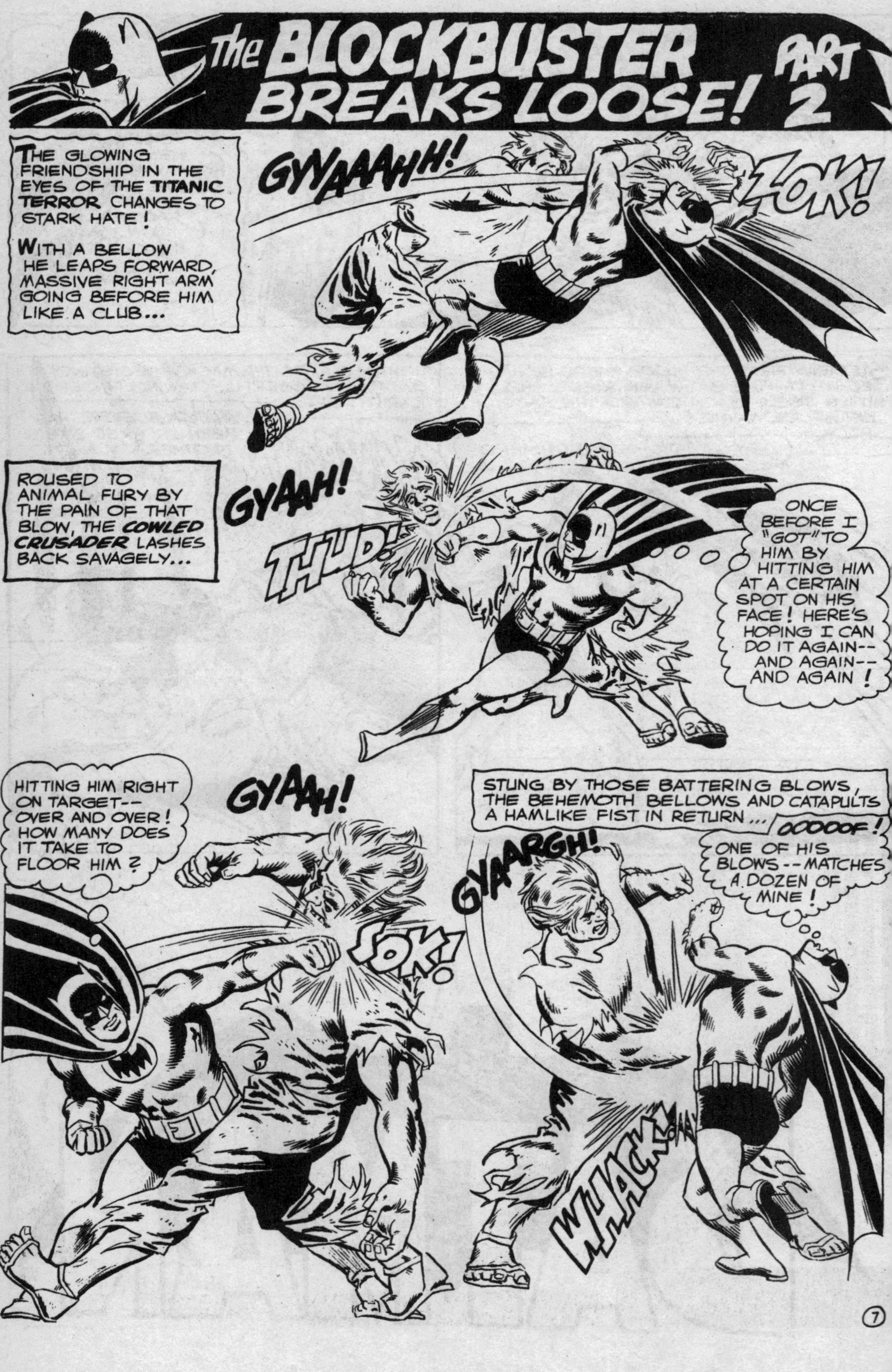
The BLOCKBUSTER BREAKS LOOSE! PART 2
THE GLOWING FRIENDSHIP IN THE EYES OF THE TITANIC TERROR CHANGES TO STARK HATE!
WITH A BELLOW HE LEAPS FORWARD, MASSIVE RIGHT ARM GOING BEFORE HIM LIKE A CLUB...
GYYAAAHH!
ZOK!
ROUSED TO ANIMAL FURY BY THE PAIN OF THAT BLOW, THE COWLED CRUSADER LASHES BACK SAVAGELY...
GYAAH!
THUD!
ONCE BEFORE I "GOT" TO HIM BY HITTING HIM AT A CERTAIN SPOT ON HIS FACE! HERE'S HOPING I CAN DO IT AGAIN-- AND AGAIN-- AND AGAIN!
HITTING HIM RIGHT ON TARGET-- OVER AND OVER! HOW MANY DOES IT TAKE TO FLOOR HIM?
GYAAH!
SOK!
STUNG BY THOSE BATTERING BLOWS, THE BEHEMOTH BELLOWS AND CATAPULTS A HAMLIKE FIST IN RETURN...
OOOOOF!
GYAARGH!
ONE OF HIS BLOWS--MATCHES A DOZEN OF MINE!
WHACK
7

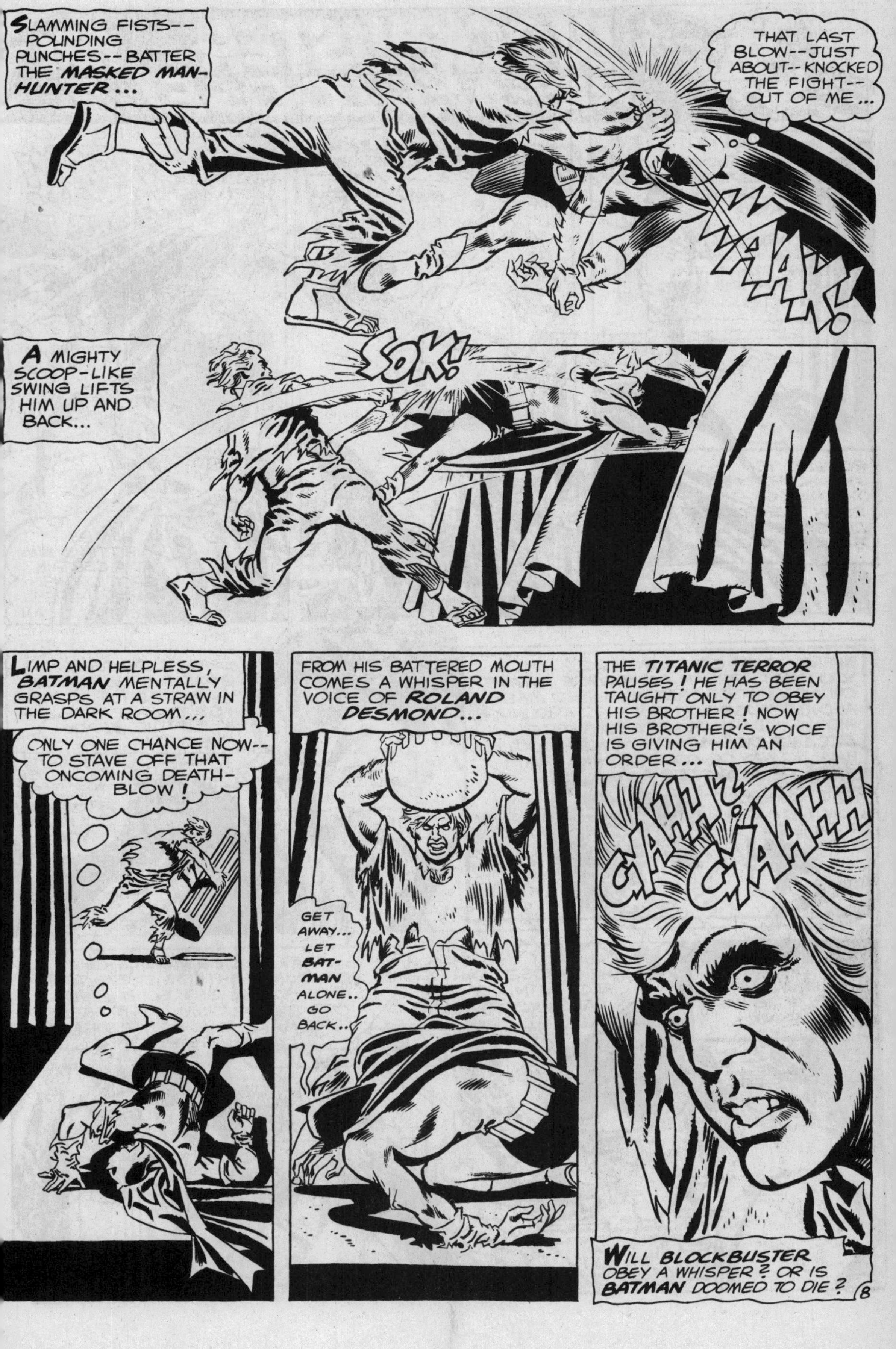
SLAMMING FISTS-- POUNDING PUNCHES--BATTER THE MASKED MAN-HUNTER...
THAT LAST BLOW--JUST ABOUT--KNOCKED THE FIGHT-- OUT OF ME...
WAAK!
A MIGHTY SCOOP-LIKE SWING LIFTS HIM UP AND BACK...
SOK!
LIMP AND HELPLESS, BATMAN MENTALLY GRASPS AT A STRAW IN THE DARK ROOM...
ONLY ONE CHANCE NOW-- TO STAVE OFF THAT ONCOMING DEATH-BLOW!
FROM HIS BATTERED MOUTH COMES A WHISPER IN THE VOICE OF ROLAND DESMOND...
GET AWAY... LET BAT-MAN ALONE.. GO BACK...
THE TITANIC TERROR PAUSES! HE HAS BEEN TAUGHT ONLY TO OBEY HIS BROTHER! NOW HIS BROTHER'S VOICE IS GIVING HIM AN ORDER...
GAHH? GAAHH
WILL BLOCKBUSTER OBEY A WHISPER? OR IS BATMAN DOOMED TO DIE?
8

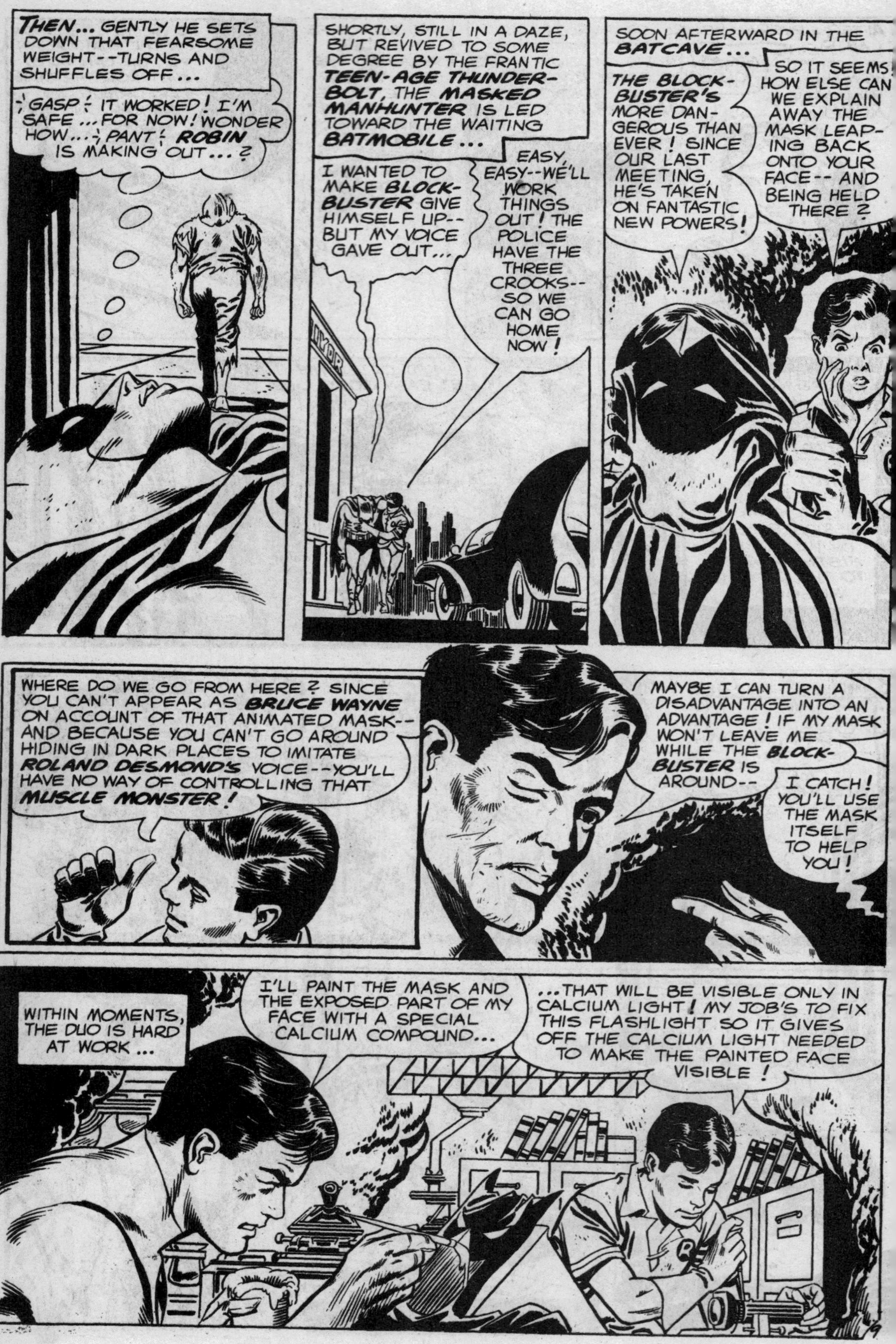
THEN... GENTLY HE SETS DOWN THAT FEARSOME WEIGHT--TURNS AND SHUFFLES OFF...
-GASP- IT WORKED! I'M SAFE ... FOR NOW! WONDER HOW...-PANT- ROBIN IS MAKING OUT...?
SHORTLY, STILL IN A DAZE, BUT REVIVED TO SOME DEGREE BY THE FRANTIC TEEN-AGE THUNDERBOLT, THE MASKED MANHUNTER IS LED TOWARD THE WAITING BATMOBILE...
I WANTED TO MAKE BLOCKBUSTER GIVE HIMSELF UP--BUT MY VOICE GAVE OUT...
EASY, EASY--WE'LL WORK THINGS OUT! THE POLICE HAVE THE THREE CROOKS--SO WE CAN GO HOME NOW!
SOON AFTERWARD IN THE BATCAVE...
THE BLOCKBUSTER'S MORE DANGEROUS THAN EVER! SINCE OUR LAST MEETING, HE'S TAKEN ON FANTASTIC NEW POWERS!
SO IT SEEMS! HOW ELSE CAN WE EXPLAIN AWAY THE MASK LEAPING BACK ONTO YOUR FACE-- AND BEING HELD THERE?
WHERE DO WE GO FROM HERE? SINCE YOU CAN'T APPEAR AS BRUCE WAYNE ON ACCOUNT OF THAT ANIMATED MASK--AND BECAUSE YOU CAN'T GO AROUND HIDING IN DARK PLACES TO IMITATE ROLAND DESMOND'S VOICE--YOU'LL HAVE NO WAY OF CONTROLLING THAT MUSCLE MONSTER!
MAYBE I CAN TURN A DISADVANTAGE INTO AN ADVANTAGE! IF MY MASK WON'T LEAVE ME WHILE THE BLOCKBUSTER IS AROUND--
I CATCH! YOU'LL USE THE MASK ITSELF TO HELP YOU!
WITHIN MOMENTS, THE DUO IS HARD AT WORK...
I'LL PAINT THE MASK AND THE EXPOSED PART OF MY FACE WITH A SPECIAL CALCIUM COMPOUND...
...THAT WILL BE VISIBLE ONLY IN CALCIUM LIGHT! MY JOB'S TO FIX THIS FLASHLIGHT SO IT GIVES OFF THE CALCIUM LIGHT NEEDED TO MAKE THE PAINTED FACE VISIBLE!

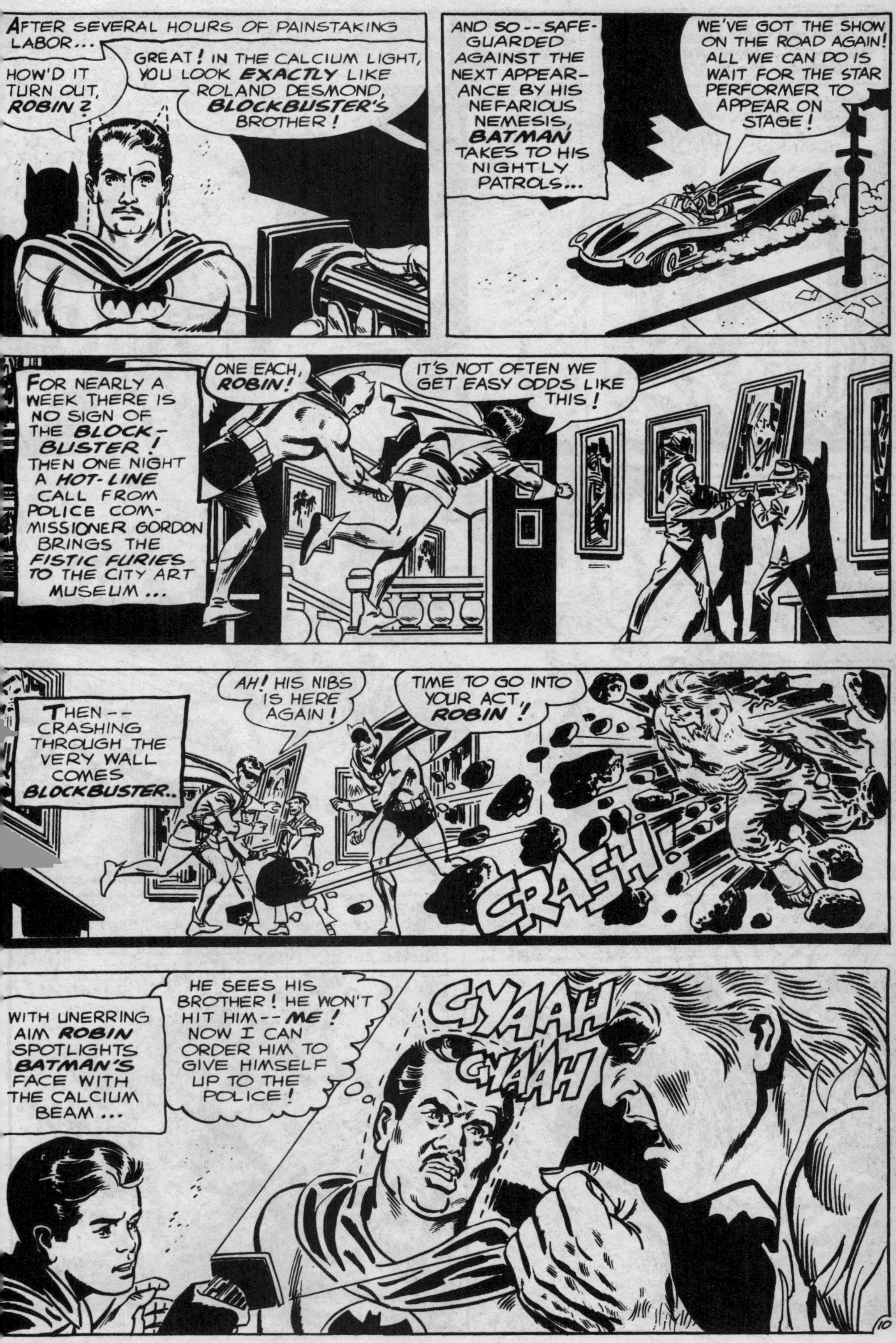
AFTER SEVERAL HOURS OF PAINSTAKING LABOR...
HOW'D IT TURN OUT, ROBIN?
GREAT! IN THE CALCIUM LIGHT, YOU LOOK EXACTLY LIKE ROLAND DESMOND, BLOCKBUSTER'S BROTHER!
AND SO--SAFE-GUARDED AGAINST THE NEXT APPEARANCE BY HIS NEFARIOUS NEMESIS, BATMAN TAKES TO HIS NIGHTLY PATROLS...
WE'VE GOT THE SHOW ON THE ROAD AGAIN! ALL WE CAN DO IS WAIT FOR THE STAR PERFORMER TO APPEAR ON STAGE!
FOR NEARLY A WEEK THERE IS NO SIGN OF THE BLOCK-BUSTER! THEN ONE NIGHT A HOT-LINE CALL FROM POLICE COMMISSIONER GORDON BRINGS THE FISTIC FURIES TO THE CITY ART MUSEUM...
ONE EACH, ROBIN!
IT'S NOT OFTEN WE GET EASY ODDS LIKE THIS!
THEN--CRASHING THROUGH THE VERY WALL COMES BLOCKBUSTER..
AH! HIS NIBS IS HERE AGAIN!
TIME TO GO INTO YOUR ACT, ROBIN!
CRASH!
WITH UNERRING AIM ROBIN SPOTLIGHTS BATMAN'S FACE WITH THE CALCIUM BEAM...
HE SEES HIS BROTHER! HE WON'T HIT HIM--ME! NOW I CAN ORDER HIM TO GIVE HIMSELF UP TO THE POLICE!
GYAAH GYAAH
10

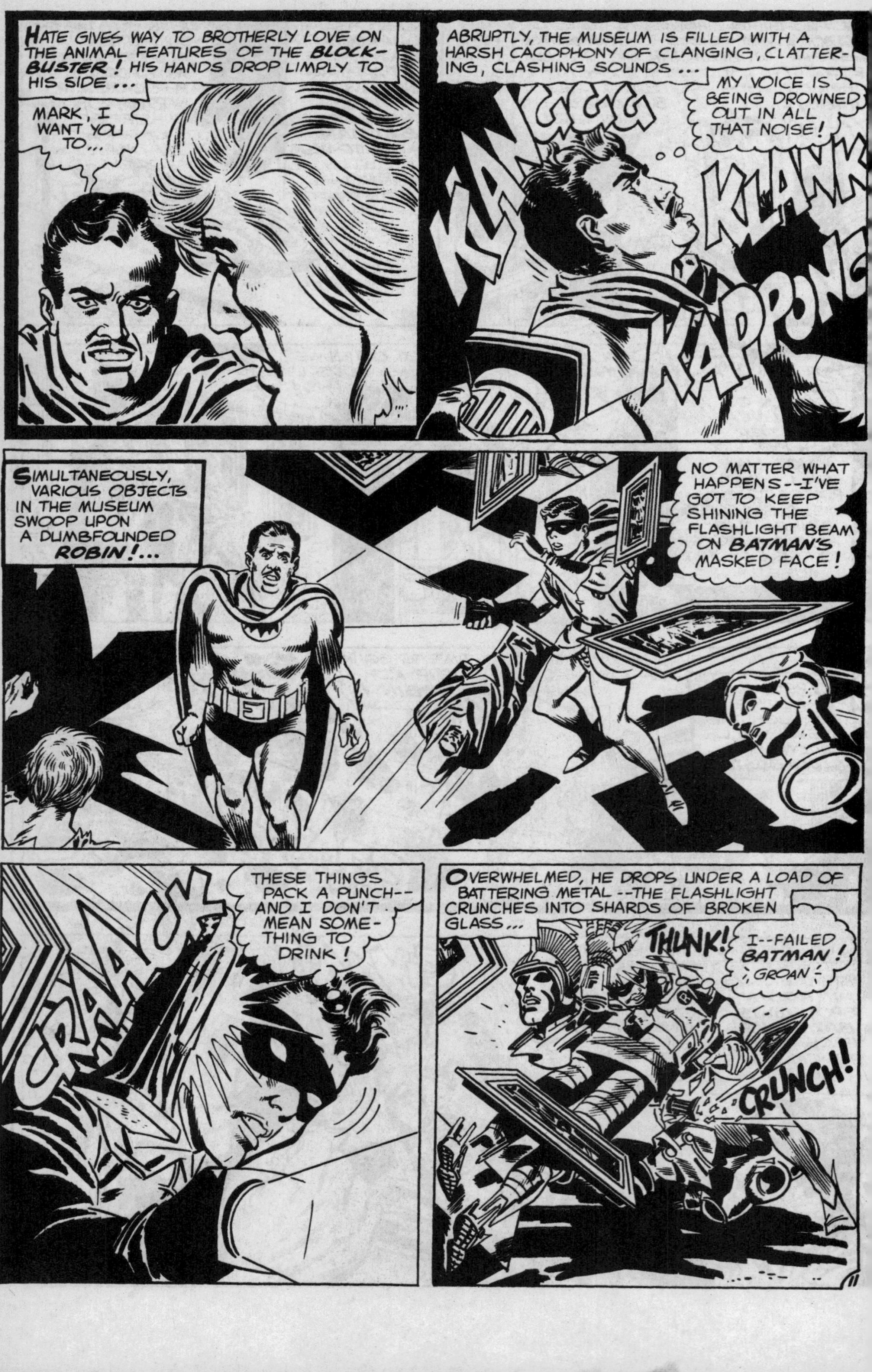
HATE GIVES WAY TO BROTHERLY LOVE ON THE ANIMAL FEATURES OF THE BLOCK-BUSTER! HIS HANDS DROP LIMPLY TO HIS SIDE...
MARK, I WANT YOU TO...
ABRUPTLY, THE MUSEUM IS FILLED WITH A HARSH CACOPHONY OF CLANGING, CLATTERING, CLASHING SOUNDS...
MY VOICE IS BEING DROWNED OUT IN ALL THAT NOISE!
KLANGGG
KLANK
KAPPONG
SIMULTANEOUSLY, VARIOUS OBJECTS IN THE MUSEUM SWOOP UPON A DUMBFOUNDED ROBIN!...
NO MATTER WHAT HAPPENS--I'VE GOT TO KEEP SHINING THE FLASHLIGHT BEAM ON BATMAN'S MASKED FACE!
CRAACK
THESE THINGS PACK A PUNCH--AND I DON'T MEAN SOMETHING TO DRINK!
OVERWHELMED, HE DROPS UNDER A LOAD OF BATTERING METAL--THE FLASHLIGHT CRUNCHES INTO SHARDS OF BROKEN GLASS...
THUNK!
I--FAILED BATMAN! GROAN
CRUNCH!
11

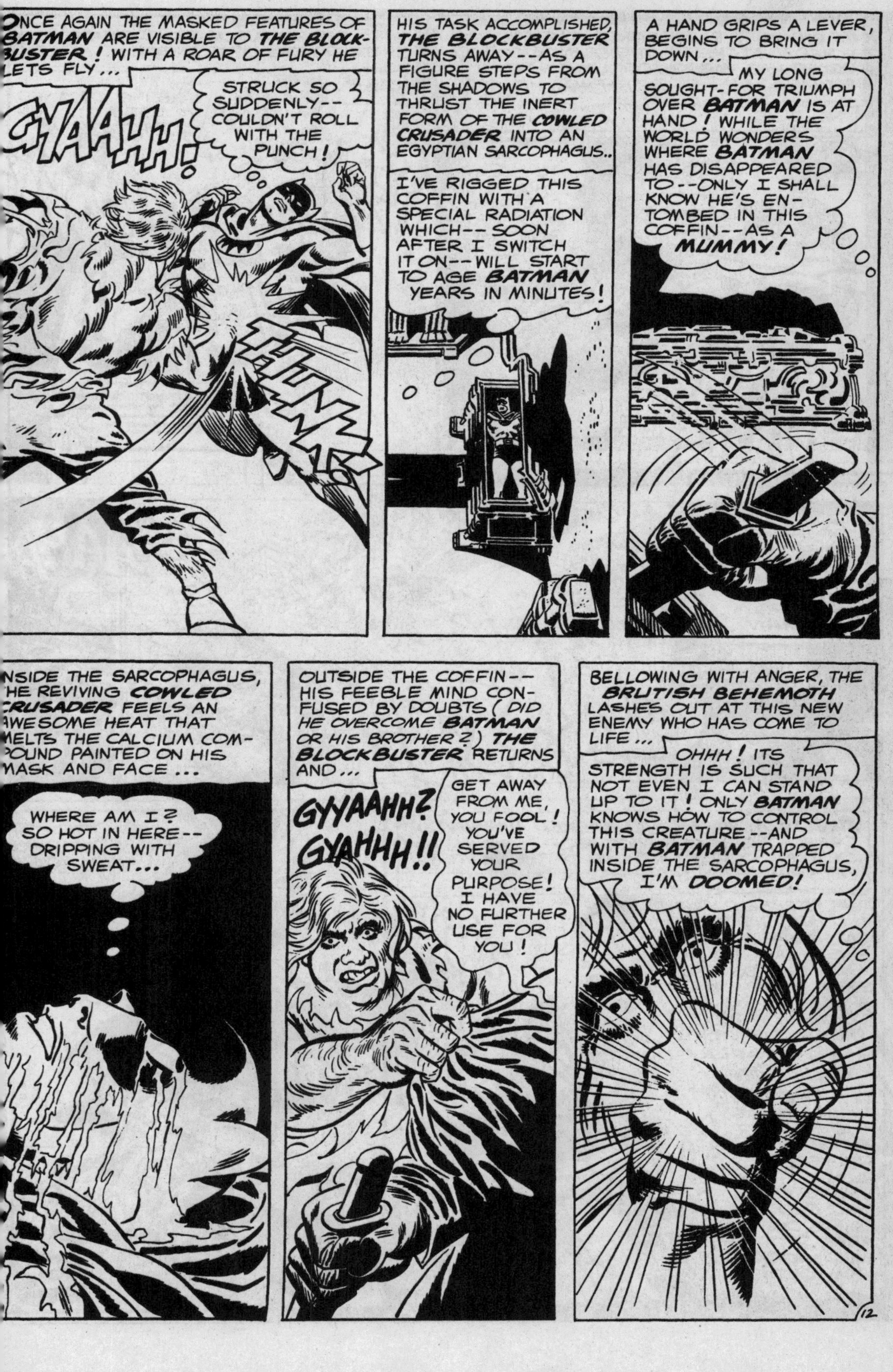
ONCE AGAIN THE MASKED FEATURES OF BATMAN ARE VISIBLE TO THE BLOCKBUSTER! WITH A ROAR OF FURY HE LETS FLY...
STRUCK SO SUDDENLY-- COULDN'T ROLL WITH THE PUNCH!
GYAAHH!
THUNK!
HIS TASK ACCOMPLISHED, THE BLOCKBUSTER TURNS AWAY--AS A FIGURE STEPS FROM THE SHADOWS TO THRUST THE INERT FORM OF THE COWLED CRUSADER INTO AN EGYPTIAN SARCOPHAGUS..
I'VE RIGGED THIS COFFIN WITH A SPECIAL RADIATION WHICH-- SOON AFTER I SWITCH IT ON--WILL START TO AGE BATMAN YEARS IN MINUTES!
A HAND GRIPS A LEVER, BEGINS TO BRING IT DOWN...
MY LONG SOUGHT-FOR TRIUMPH OVER BATMAN IS AT HAND! WHILE THE WORLD WONDERS WHERE BATMAN HAS DISAPPEARED TO--ONLY I SHALL KNOW HE'S ENTOMBED IN THIS COFFIN--AS A MUMMY!
INSIDE THE SARCOPHAGUS, THE REVIVING COWLED CRUSADER FEELS AN AWESOME HEAT THAT MELTS THE CALCIUM COMPOUND PAINTED ON HIS MASK AND FACE...
WHERE AM I? SO HOT IN HERE-- DRIPPING WITH SWEAT...
OUTSIDE THE COFFIN-- HIS FEEBLE MIND CONFUSED BY DOUBTS (DID HE OVERCOME BATMAN OR HIS BROTHER?) THE BLOCKBUSTER RETURNS AND...
GYYAAHH? GYAHHH!!
GET AWAY FROM ME, YOU FOOL! YOU'VE SERVED YOUR PURPOSE! I HAVE NO FURTHER USE FOR YOU!
BELLOWING WITH ANGER, THE BRUTISH BEHEMOTH LASHES OUT AT THIS NEW ENEMY WHO HAS COME TO LIFE...
OHHH! ITS STRENGTH IS SUCH THAT NOT EVEN I CAN STAND UP TO IT! ONLY BATMAN KNOWS HOW TO CONTROL THIS CREATURE--AND WITH BATMAN TRAPPED INSIDE THE SARCOPHAGUS, I'M DOOMED!
12

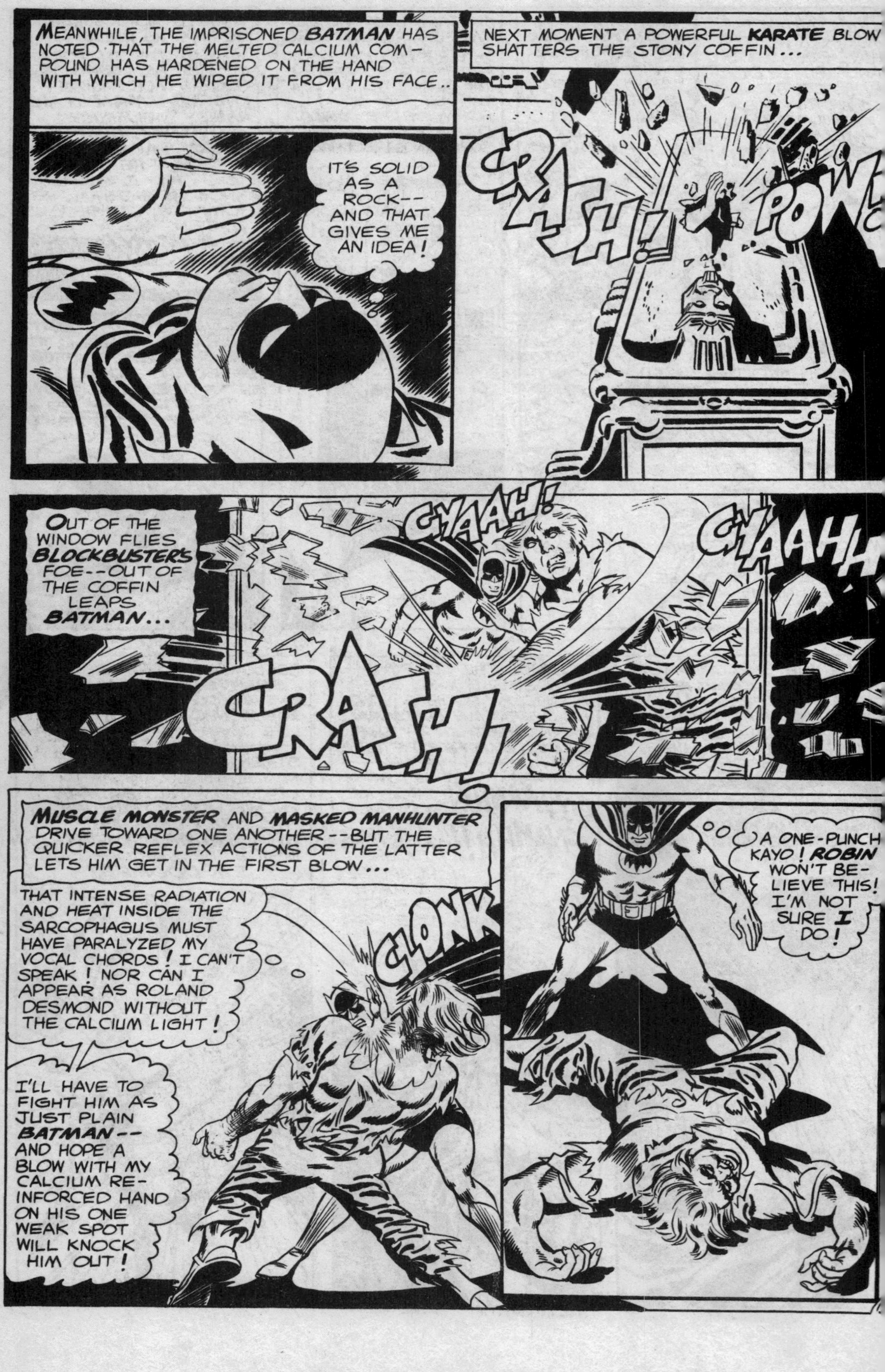
MEANWHILE, THE IMPRISONED BATMAN HAS NOTED THAT THE MELTED CALCIUM COMPOUND HAS HARDENED ON THE HAND WITH WHICH HE WIPED IT FROM HIS FACE..
IT'S SOLID AS A ROCK-- AND THAT GIVES ME AN IDEA!
NEXT MOMENT A POWERFUL KARATE BLOW SHATTERS THE STONY COFFIN...
CRASH!
POW
OUT OF THE WINDOW FLIES BLOCKBUSTER'S FOE--OUT OF THE COFFIN LEAPS BATMAN...
GYAAH!
GYAAHH
CRASH
MUSCLE MONSTER AND MASKED MANHUNTER DRIVE TOWARD ONE ANOTHER--BUT THE QUICKER REFLEX ACTIONS OF THE LATTER LETS HIM GET IN THE FIRST BLOW...
THAT INTENSE RADIATION AND HEAT INSIDE THE SARCOPHAGUS MUST HAVE PARALYZED MY VOCAL CHORDS! I CAN'T SPEAK! NOR CAN I APPEAR AS ROLAND DESMOND WITHOUT THE CALCIUM LIGHT!
I'LL HAVE TO FIGHT HIM AS JUST PLAIN BATMAN-- AND HOPE A BLOW WITH MY CALCIUM RE-INFORCED HAND ON HIS ONE WEAK SPOT WILL KNOCK HIM OUT!
CLONK
A ONE-PUNCH KAYO! ROBIN WON'T BE-LIEVE THIS! I'M NOT SURE I DO!

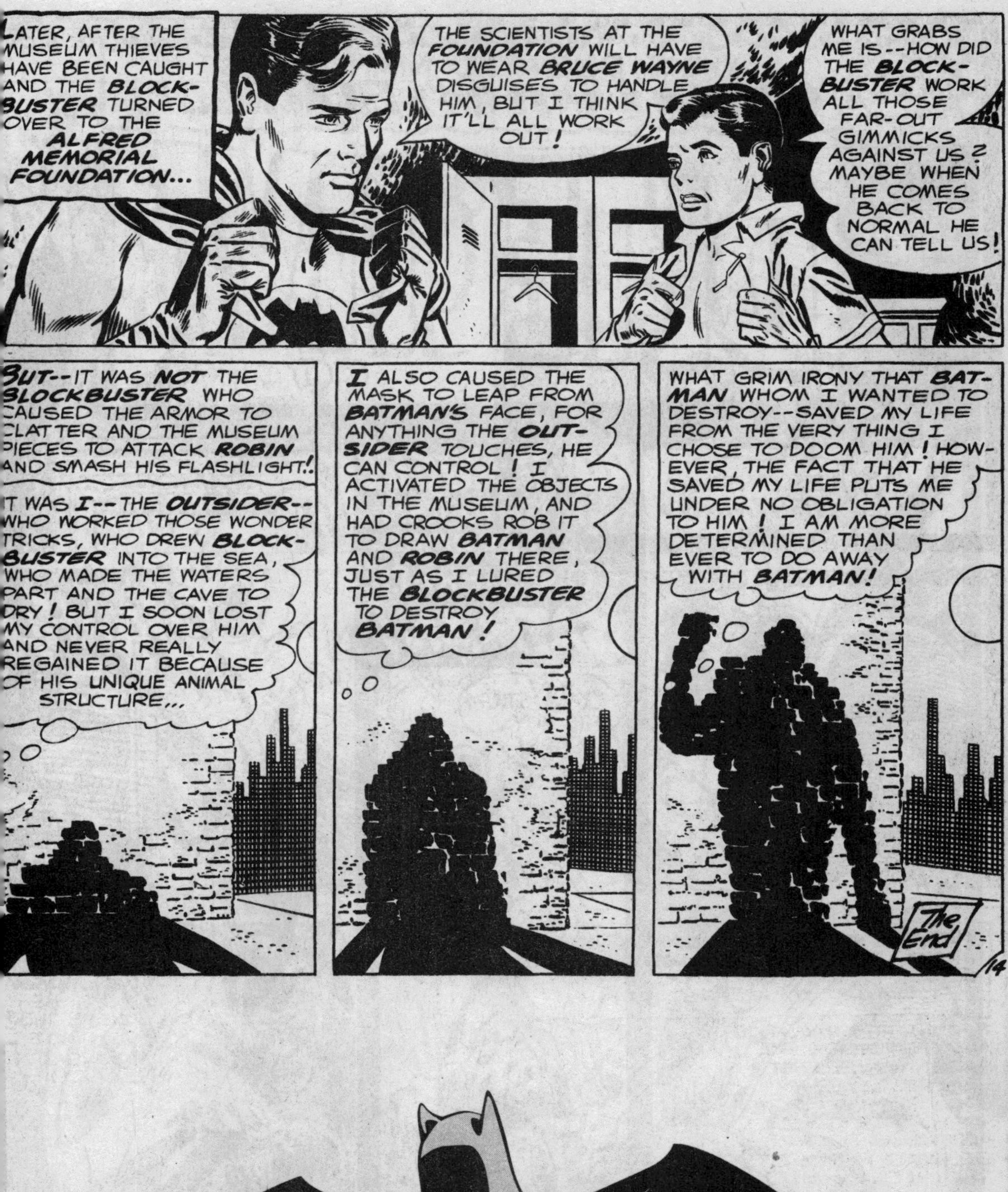
LATER, AFTER THE MUSEUM THIEVES HAVE BEEN CAUGHT AND THE BLOCK-BUSTER TURNED OVER TO THE ALFRED MEMORIAL FOUNDATION...
THE SCIENTISTS AT THE FOUNDATION WILL HAVE TO WEAR BRUCE WAYNE DISGUISES TO HANDLE HIM, BUT I THINK IT'LL ALL WORK OUT!
WHAT GRABS ME IS--HOW DID THE BLOCK-BUSTER WORK ALL THOSE FAR-OUT GIMMICKS AGAINST US? MAYBE WHEN HE COMES BACK TO NORMAL HE CAN TELL US!
BUT--IT WAS NOT THE BLOCKBUSTER WHO CAUSED THE ARMOR TO CLATTER AND THE MUSEUM PIECES TO ATTACK ROBIN AND SMASH HIS FLASHLIGHT!
IT WAS I--THE OUTSIDER--WHO WORKED THOSE WONDER TRICKS, WHO DREW BLOCK-BUSTER INTO THE SEA, WHO MADE THE WATERS PART AND THE CAVE TO DRY! BUT I SOON LOST MY CONTROL OVER HIM AND NEVER REALLY REGAINED IT BECAUSE OF HIS UNIQUE ANIMAL STRUCTURE...
I ALSO CAUSED THE MASK TO LEAP FROM BATMAN'S FACE, FOR ANYTHING THE OUT-SIDER TOUCHES, HE CAN CONTROL! I ACTIVATED THE OBJECTS IN THE MUSEUM, AND HAD CROOKS ROB IT TO DRAW BATMAN AND ROBIN THERE, JUST AS I LURED THE BLOCKBUSTER TO DESTROY BATMAN!
WHAT GRIM IRONY THAT BAT-MAN WHOM I WANTED TO DESTROY--SAVED MY LIFE FROM THE VERY THING I CHOSE TO DOOM HIM! HOW-EVER, THE FACT THAT HE SAVED MY LIFE PUTS ME UNDER NO OBLIGATION TO HIM! I AM MORE DETERMINED THAN EVER TO DO AWAY WITH BATMAN!
The End
14

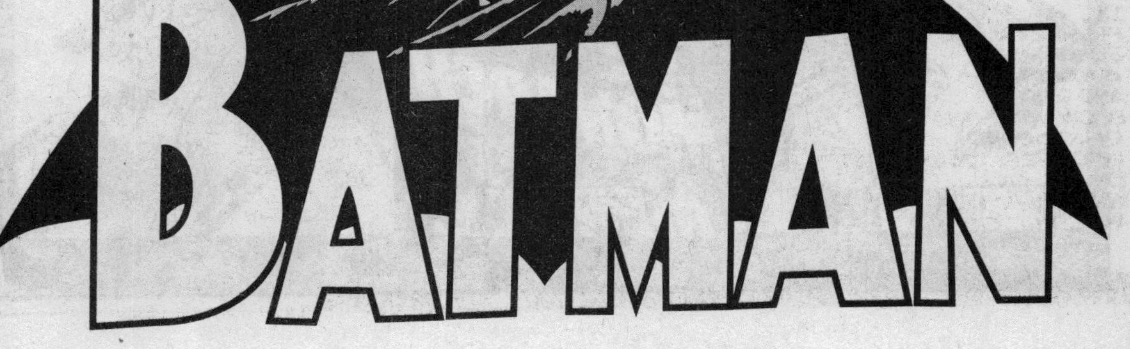
BATMAN

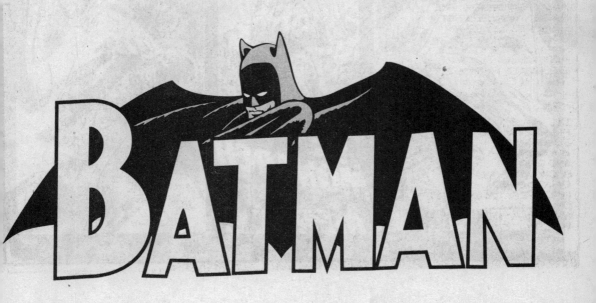

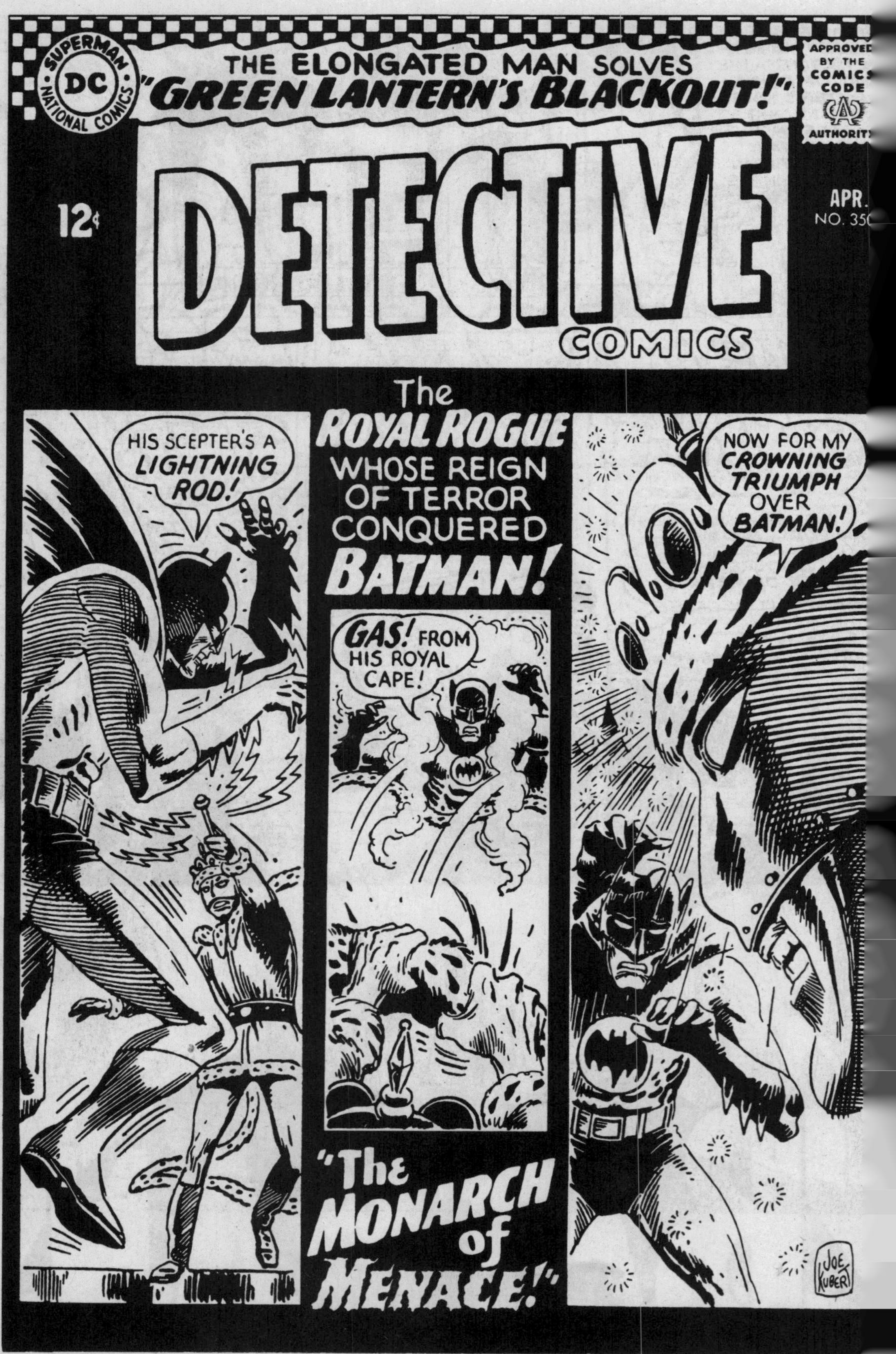
SUPERMAN DC NATIONAL COMICS
THE ELONGATED MAN SOLVES
"GREEN LANTERN'S BLACKOUT!"
APPROVED BY THE COMICS CODE AUTHORITY
12¢
DETECTIVE COMICS
APR.
NO. 350
The ROYAL ROGUE WHOSE REIGN OF TERROR CONQUERED BATMAN!
HIS SCEPTER'S A LIGHTNING ROD!
GAS! FROM HIS ROYAL CAPE!
NOW FOR MY CROWNING TRIUMPH OVER BATMAN!
"The MONARCH of MENACE!"
JOE KUBERT

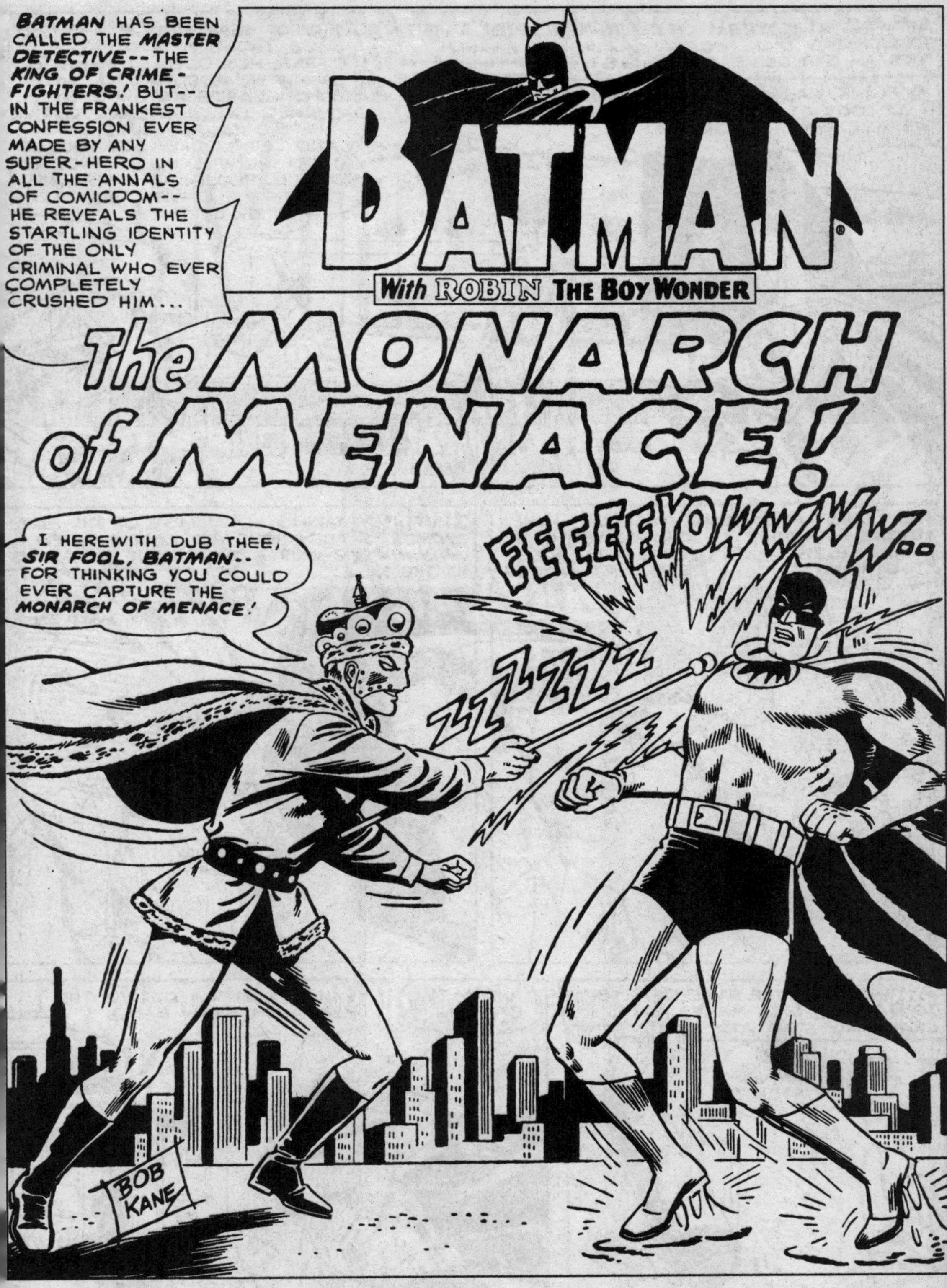
BATMAN HAS BEEN CALLED THE MASTER DETECTIVE--THE KING OF CRIME-FIGHTERS! BUT--IN THE FRANKEST CONFESSION EVER MADE BY ANY SUPER-HERO IN ALL THE ANNALS OF COMICDOM--HE REVEALS THE STARTLING IDENTITY OF THE ONLY CRIMINAL WHO EVER COMPLETELY CRUSHED HIM...
BATMAN
With ROBIN THE BOY WONDER
The MONARCH of MENACE!
I HEREWITH DUB THEE, SIR FOOL, BATMAN--FOR THINKING YOU COULD EVER CAPTURE THE MONARCH OF MENACE!
EEEEEYOWWWW..
ZZZZZZ
BOB KANE

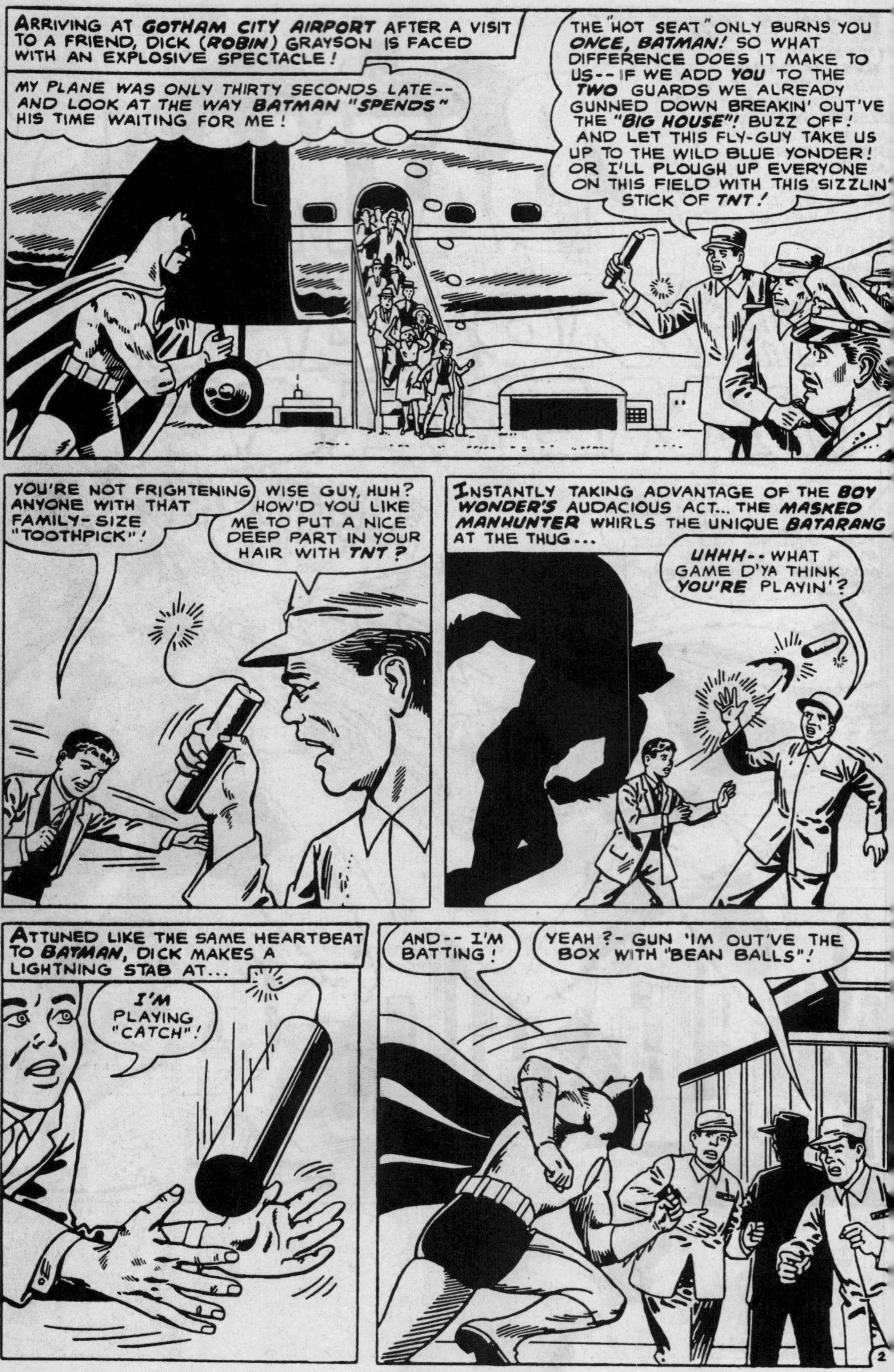
ARRIVING AT GOTHAM CITY AIRPORT AFTER A VISIT TO A FRIEND, DICK (ROBIN) GRAYSON IS FACED WITH AN EXPLOSIVE SPECTACLE!
MY PLANE WAS ONLY THIRTY SECONDS LATE-- AND LOOK AT THE WAY BATMAN "SPENDS" HIS TIME WAITING FOR ME!
THE "HOT SEAT" ONLY BURNS YOU ONCE, BATMAN! SO WHAT DIFFERENCE DOES IT MAKE TO US-- IF WE ADD YOU TO THE TWO GUARDS WE ALREADY GUNNED DOWN BREAKIN' OUT'VE THE "BIG HOUSE"! BUZZ OFF! AND LET THIS FLY-GUY TAKE US UP TO THE WILD BLUE YONDER! OR I'LL PLOUGH UP EVERYONE ON THIS FIELD WITH THIS SIZZLIN' STICK OF TNT!
YOU'RE NOT FRIGHTENING ANYONE WITH THAT FAMILY-SIZE "TOOTHPICK"!
WISE GUY, HUH? HOW'D YOU LIKE ME TO PUT A NICE DEEP PART IN YOUR HAIR WITH TNT?
INSTANTLY TAKING ADVANTAGE OF THE BOY WONDER'S AUDACIOUS ACT... THE MASKED MANHUNTER WHIRLS THE UNIQUE BATARANG AT THE THUG...
UHHH-- WHAT GAME D'YA THINK YOU'RE PLAYIN'?
ATTUNED LIKE THE SAME HEARTBEAT TO BATMAN, DICK MAKES A LIGHTNING STAB AT...
I'M PLAYING "CATCH"!
AND-- I'M BATTING!
YEAH?- GUN 'IM OUT'VE THE BOX WITH "BEAN BALLS"!
2

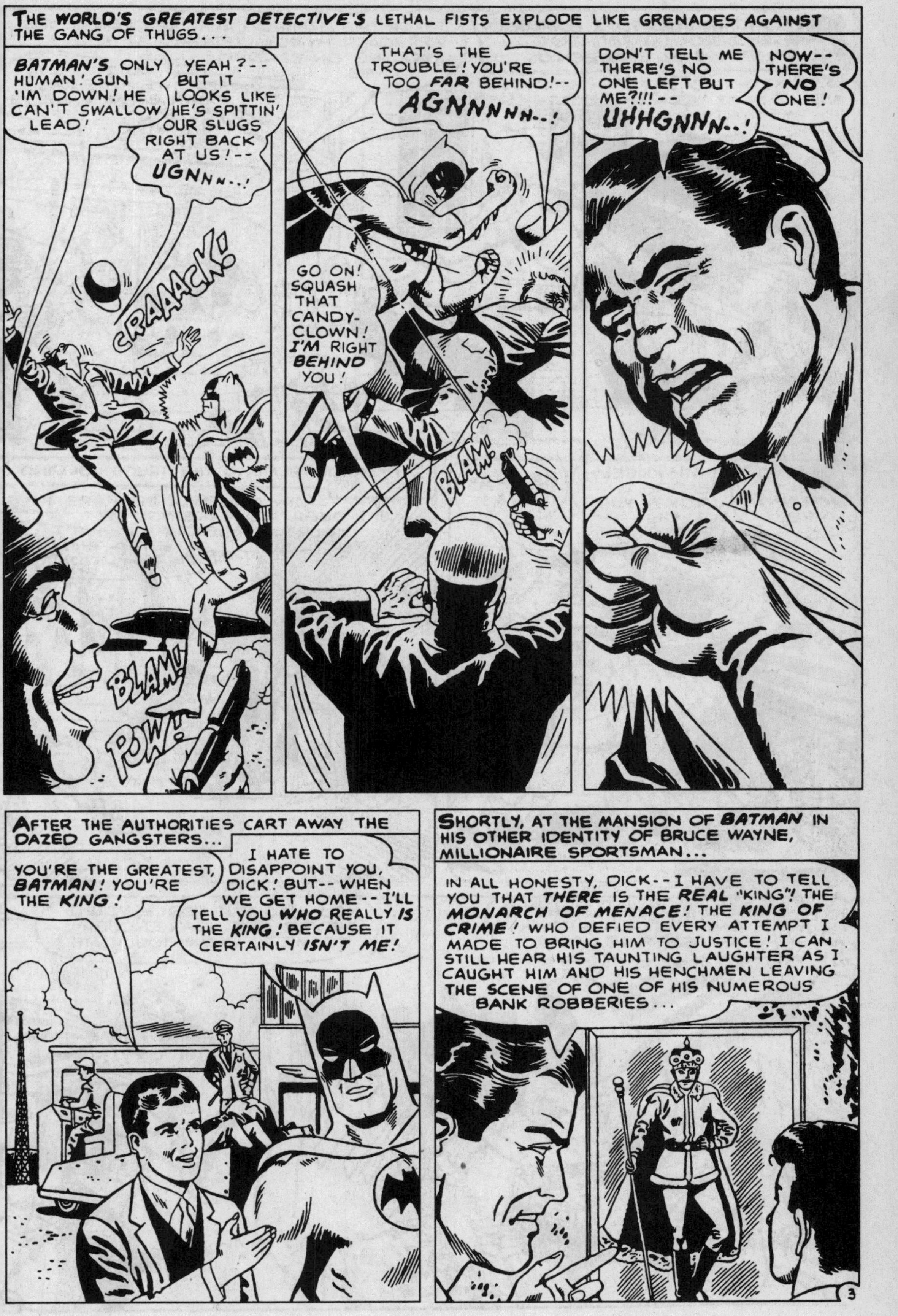
THE WORLD'S GREATEST DETECTIVE'S LETHAL FISTS EXPLODE LIKE GRENADES AGAINST THE GANG OF THUGS...
BATMAN'S ONLY HUMAN! GUN 'IM DOWN! HE CAN'T SWALLOW LEAD!
YEAH?-- BUT IT LOOKS LIKE HE'S SPITTIN' OUR SLUGS RIGHT BACK AT US!-- UGNNN..!
CRAAACK!
BLAM!
POW!
THAT'S THE TROUBLE! YOU'RE TOO FAR BEHIND!-- AGNNNNNN..!
GO ON! SQUASH THAT CANDY-CLOWN! I'M RIGHT BEHIND YOU!
BLAM!
DON'T TELL ME THERE'S NO ONE LEFT BUT ME?!!! -- UHHGNNN..!
NOW-- THERE'S NO ONE!
AFTER THE AUTHORITIES CART AWAY THE DAZED GANGSTERS...
YOU'RE THE GREATEST, BATMAN! YOU'RE THE KING!
I HATE TO DISAPPOINT YOU, DICK! BUT-- WHEN WE GET HOME-- I'LL TELL YOU WHO REALLY IS THE KING! BECAUSE IT CERTAINLY ISN'T ME!
SHORTLY, AT THE MANSION OF BATMAN IN HIS OTHER IDENTITY OF BRUCE WAYNE, MILLIONAIRE SPORTSMAN...
IN ALL HONESTY, DICK-- I HAVE TO TELL YOU THAT THERE IS THE REAL "KING"! THE MONARCH OF MENACE! THE KING OF CRIME! WHO DEFIED EVERY ATTEMPT I MADE TO BRING HIM TO JUSTICE! I CAN STILL HEAR HIS TAUNTING LAUGHTER AS I CAUGHT HIM AND HIS HENCHMEN LEAVING THE SCENE OF ONE OF HIS NUMEROUS BANK ROBBERIES...
3

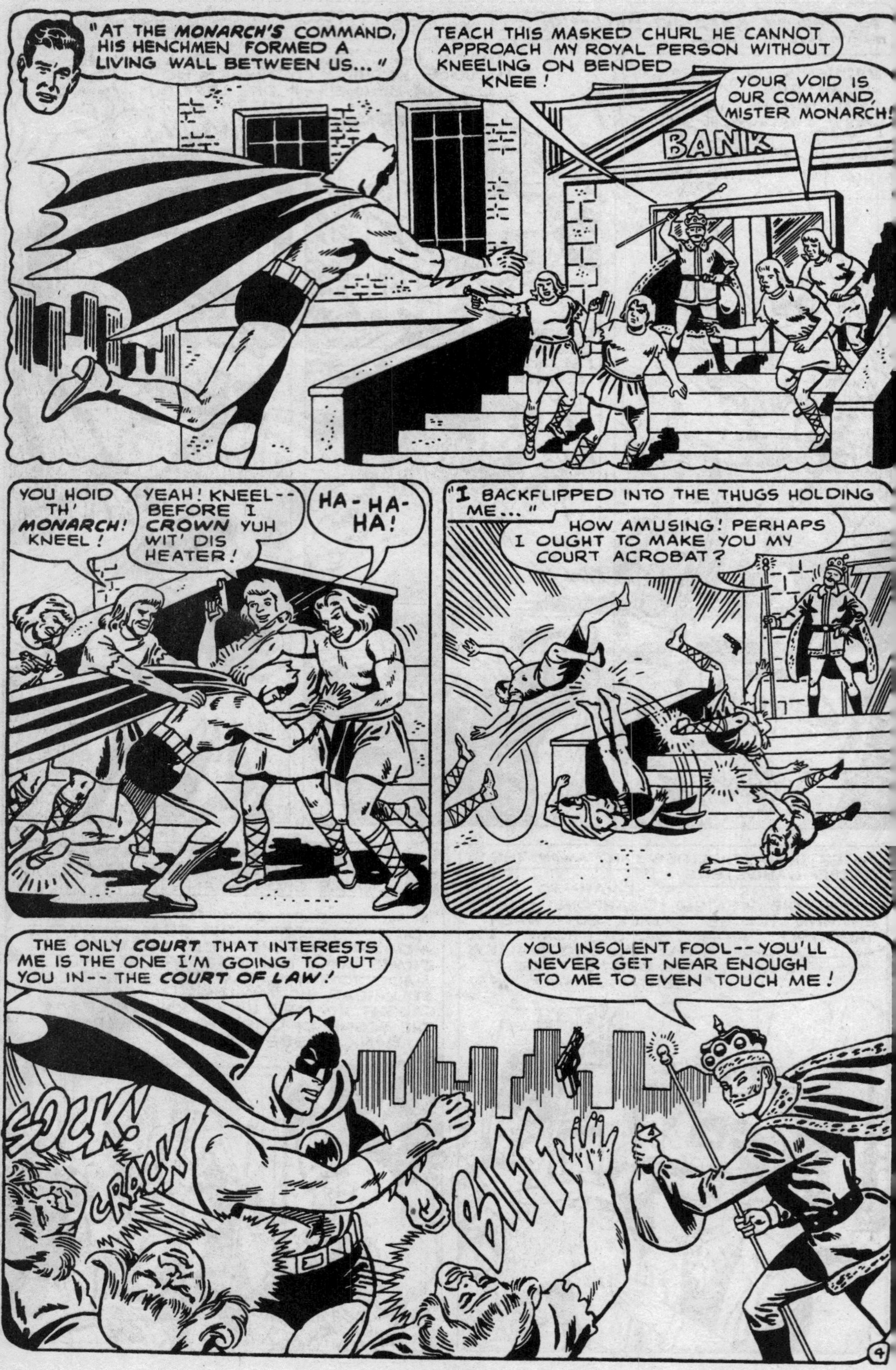
"AT THE MONARCH'S COMMAND, HIS HENCHMEN FORMED A LIVING WALL BETWEEN US..."
TEACH THIS MASKED CHURL HE CANNOT APPROACH MY ROYAL PERSON WITHOUT KNEELING ON BENDED KNEE!
YOUR VOID IS OUR COMMAND, MISTER MONARCH!
BANK
YOU HOID TH' MONARCH! KNEEL!
YEAH! KNEEL--BEFORE I CROWN YUH WIT' DIS HEATER!
HA-HA-HA!
"I BACKFLIPPED INTO THE THUGS HOLDING ME..."
HOW AMUSING! PERHAPS I OUGHT TO MAKE YOU MY COURT ACROBAT?
THE ONLY COURT THAT INTERESTS ME IS THE ONE I'M GOING TO PUT YOU IN--THE COURT OF LAW!
YOU INSOLENT FOOL--YOU'LL NEVER GET NEAR ENOUGH TO ME TO EVEN TOUCH ME!
SOCK!
CRACK
BIFF
4

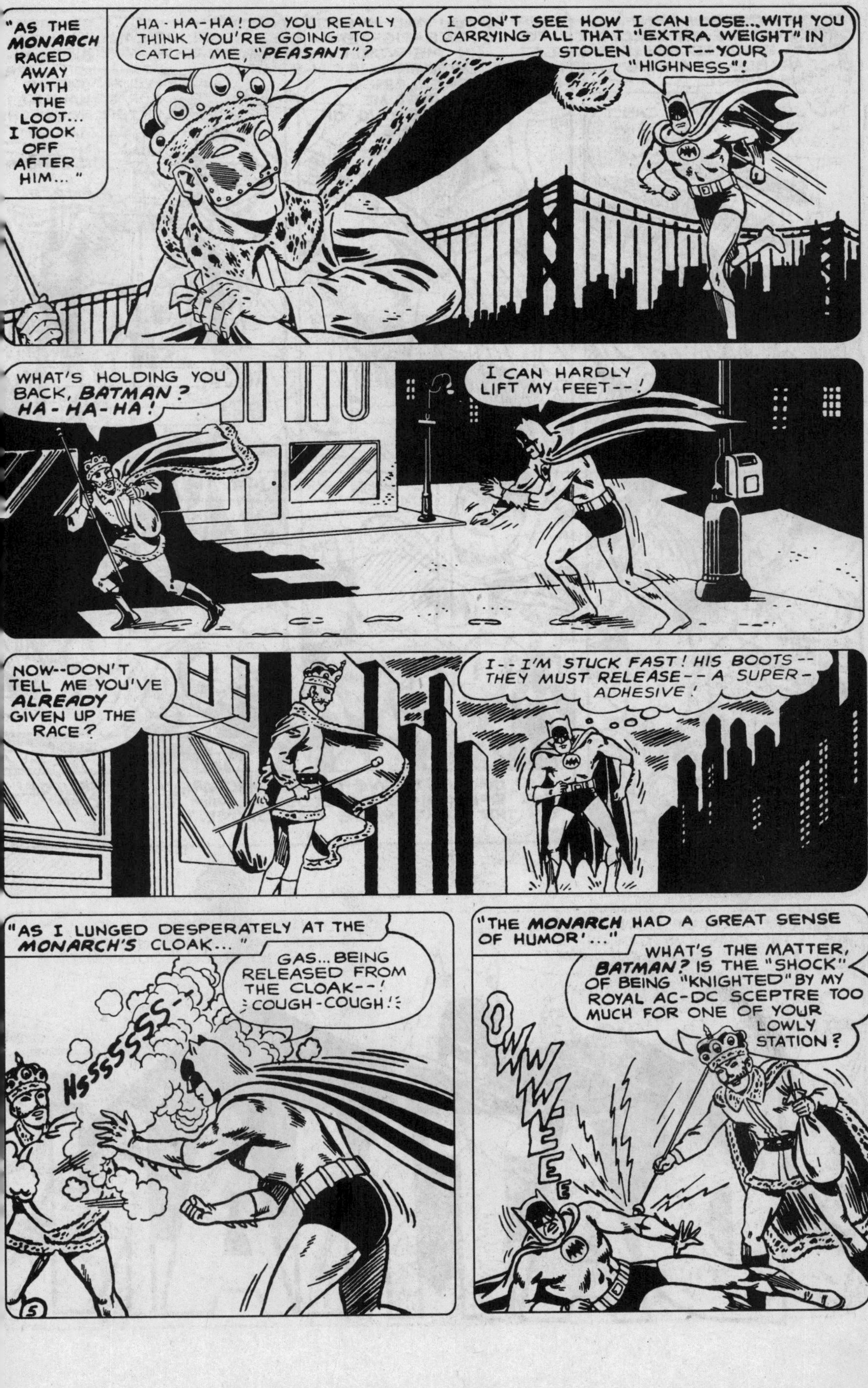
"AS THE MONARCH RACED AWAY WITH THE LOOT... I TOOK OFF AFTER HIM..."
HA-HA-HA! DO YOU REALLY THINK YOU'RE GOING TO CATCH ME, "PEASANT"?
I DON'T SEE HOW I CAN LOSE...WITH YOU CARRYING ALL THAT "EXTRA WEIGHT" IN STOLEN LOOT--YOUR "HIGHNESS"!
WHAT'S HOLDING YOU BACK, BATMAN? HA-HA-HA!
I CAN HARDLY LIFT MY FEET--!
NOW--DON'T TELL ME YOU'VE ALREADY GIVEN UP THE RACE?
I--I'M STUCK FAST! HIS BOOTS--THEY MUST RELEASE--A SUPER-ADHESIVE!
"AS I LUNGED DESPERATELY AT THE MONARCH'S CLOAK..."
GAS...BEING RELEASED FROM THE CLOAK--! COUGH-COUGH!
HSSSSSSS-
5
"THE MONARCH HAD A GREAT SENSE OF HUMOR'..."
WHAT'S THE MATTER, BATMAN? IS THE "SHOCK" OF BEING "KNIGHTED" BY MY ROYAL AC-DC SCEPTRE TOO MUCH FOR ONE OF YOUR LOWLY STATION?
OWWWEEE

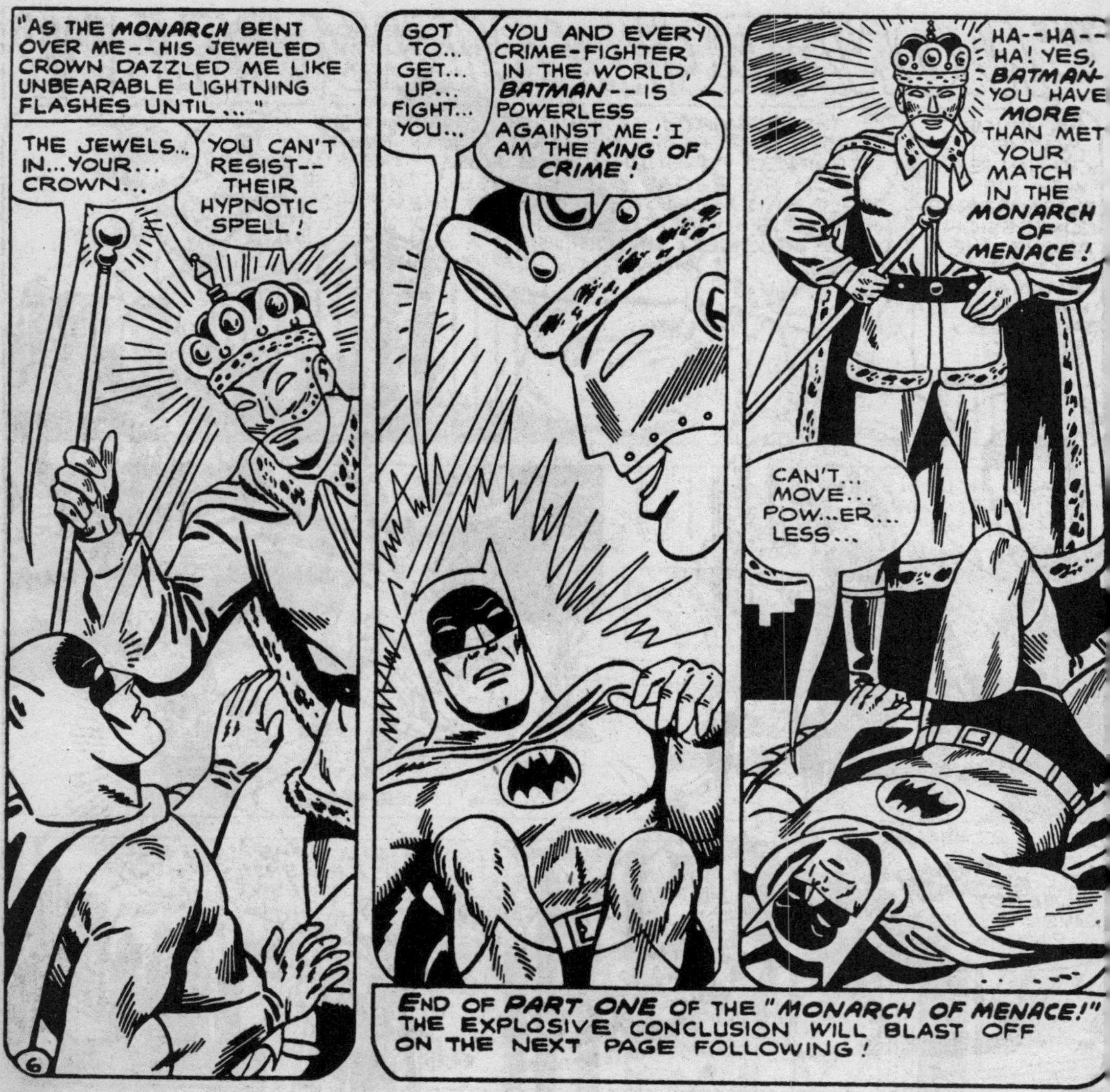
"AS THE MONARCH BENT OVER ME--HIS JEWELED CROWN DAZZLED ME LIKE UNBEARABLE LIGHTNING FLASHES UNTIL..."
THE JEWELS... IN...YOUR... CROWN...
YOU CAN'T RESIST--THEIR HYPNOTIC SPELL!
6
GOT TO... GET... UP... FIGHT... YOU...
YOU AND EVERY CRIME-FIGHTER IN THE WORLD, BATMAN--IS POWERLESS AGAINST ME! I AM THE KING OF CRIME!
HA--HA--HA! YES, BATMAN--YOU HAVE MORE THAN MET YOUR MATCH IN THE MONARCH OF MENACE!
CAN'T... MOVE... POW...ER... LESS...
END OF PART ONE OF THE "MONARCH OF MENACE!" THE EXPLOSIVE CONCLUSION WILL BLAST OFF ON THE NEXT PAGE FOLLOWING!

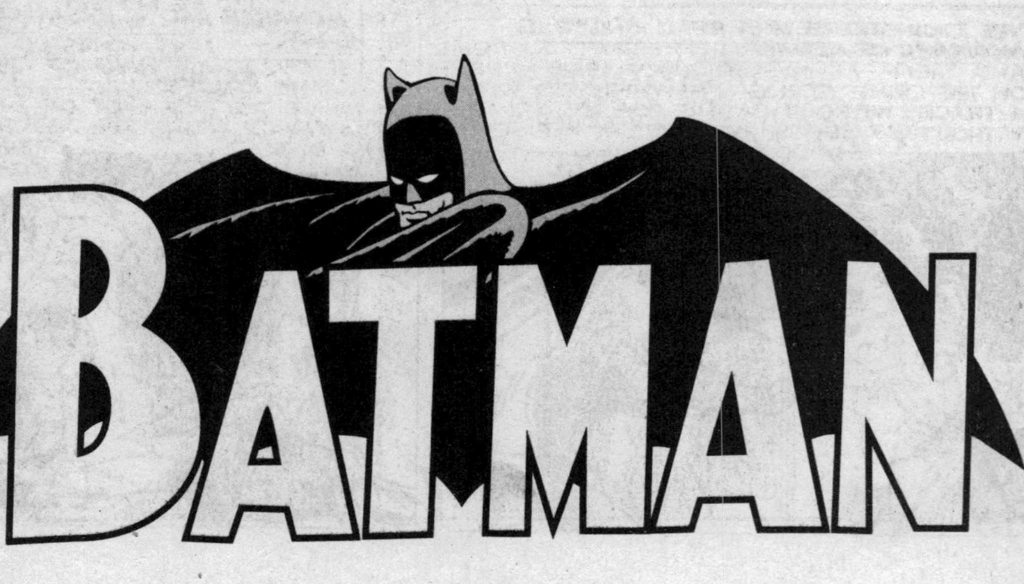
BATMAN

THE MONARCH of MENACE! PART 2

AS BRUCE WAYNE CONTINUES WITH HIS EXTRAORDINARY CONFESSION ABOUT THE ONLY CRIMINAL WHO HAD TAUNTINGLY BESTED HIM...

THE *MONARCH* COMMITTED ONE DARING CRIME AFTER ANOTHER! HIS STICKY FOOTPRINTS TRAPPED PURSUERS LIKE FLIES! THE FUMES FROM HIS REGAL CLOAK DAZED THEM! HIS ELECTRIC SCEPTRE STUNNED THEM! HIS CROWN JEWELS HYPNOTIZED THEM INTO HELPLESSNESS! HE REIGNED UNTOUCHED! A *KING OF CRIME!* A A *MONARCH OF MENACE!*

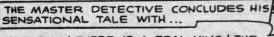

THE MASTER DETECTIVE CONCLUDES HIS SENSATIONAL TALE WITH...

YES, DICK! THERE *IS* A REAL KING! THE *MONARCH OF MENACE!* HE REIGNED SUPREME! AND THEN--AS MYSTERIOUSLY AS HE APPEARED ON THE CRIME SCENE--HE VANISHED WITHOUT A TRACE! WITHOUT PAYING FOR HIS CRIMES! WITHOUT MY BEING ABLE TO LAY A FINGER ON HIM!

THIS ALL HAPPENED A LONG TIME AGO, BEFORE YOU JOINED ME IN FIGHTING CRIME! BUT--NOW YOU SEE WHY I CAN'T HONESTLY BE CALLED THE *KING OF CRIME-FIGHTERS!* NOT WHILE THE *MONARCH OF MENACE* WENT FREE AS A BIRD!

I HOPE HE COMES BACK SOME DAY, BRUCE! I'LL PUT THAT "BIRD" IN A "CAGE"!

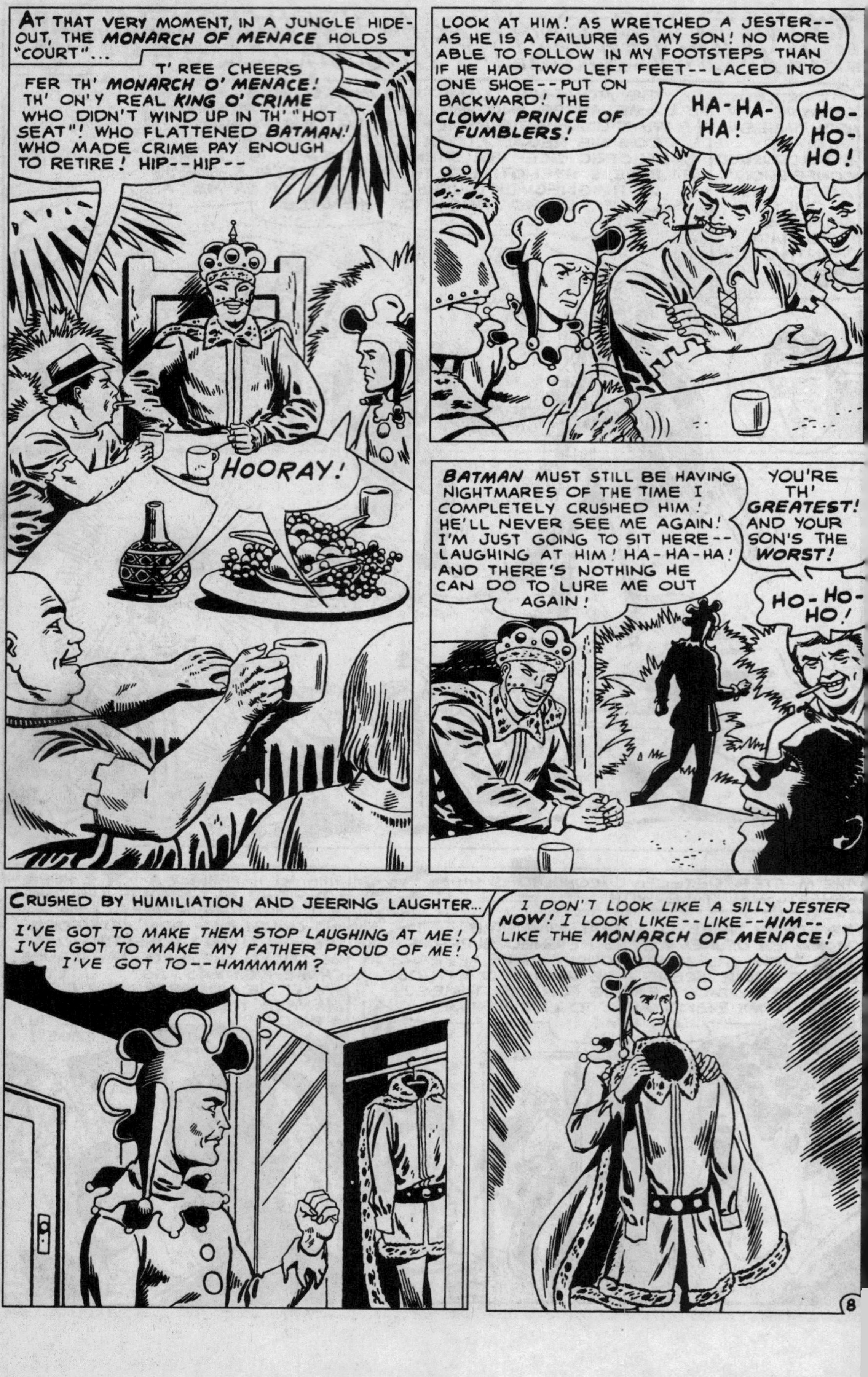
AT THAT VERY MOMENT, IN A JUNGLE HIDE-OUT, THE MONARCH OF MENACE HOLDS "COURT"...
T' REE CHEERS FER TH' MONARCH O' MENACE! TH' ON'Y REAL KING O' CRIME WHO DIDN'T WIND UP IN TH' "HOT SEAT"! WHO FLATTENED BATMAN! WHO MADE CRIME PAY ENOUGH TO RETIRE! HIP--HIP--
HOORAY!
LOOK AT HIM! AS WRETCHED A JESTER--AS HE IS A FAILURE AS MY SON! NO MORE ABLE TO FOLLOW IN MY FOOTSTEPS THAN IF HE HAD TWO LEFT FEET--LACED INTO ONE SHOE--PUT ON BACKWARD! THE CLOWN PRINCE OF FUMBLERS!
HA-HA-HA!
HO-HO-HO!
BATMAN MUST STILL BE HAVING NIGHTMARES OF THE TIME I COMPLETELY CRUSHED HIM! HE'LL NEVER SEE ME AGAIN! I'M JUST GOING TO SIT HERE--LAUGHING AT HIM! HA-HA-HA! AND THERE'S NOTHING HE CAN DO TO LURE ME OUT AGAIN!
YOU'RE TH' GREATEST! AND YOUR SON'S THE WORST!
HO-HO-HO!
CRUSHED BY HUMILIATION AND JEERING LAUGHTER...
I'VE GOT TO MAKE THEM STOP LAUGHING AT ME! I'VE GOT TO MAKE MY FATHER PROUD OF ME! I'VE GOT TO--HMMMMM?
I DON'T LOOK LIKE A SILLY JESTER NOW! I LOOK LIKE--LIKE--HIM--LIKE THE MONARCH OF MENACE!
8

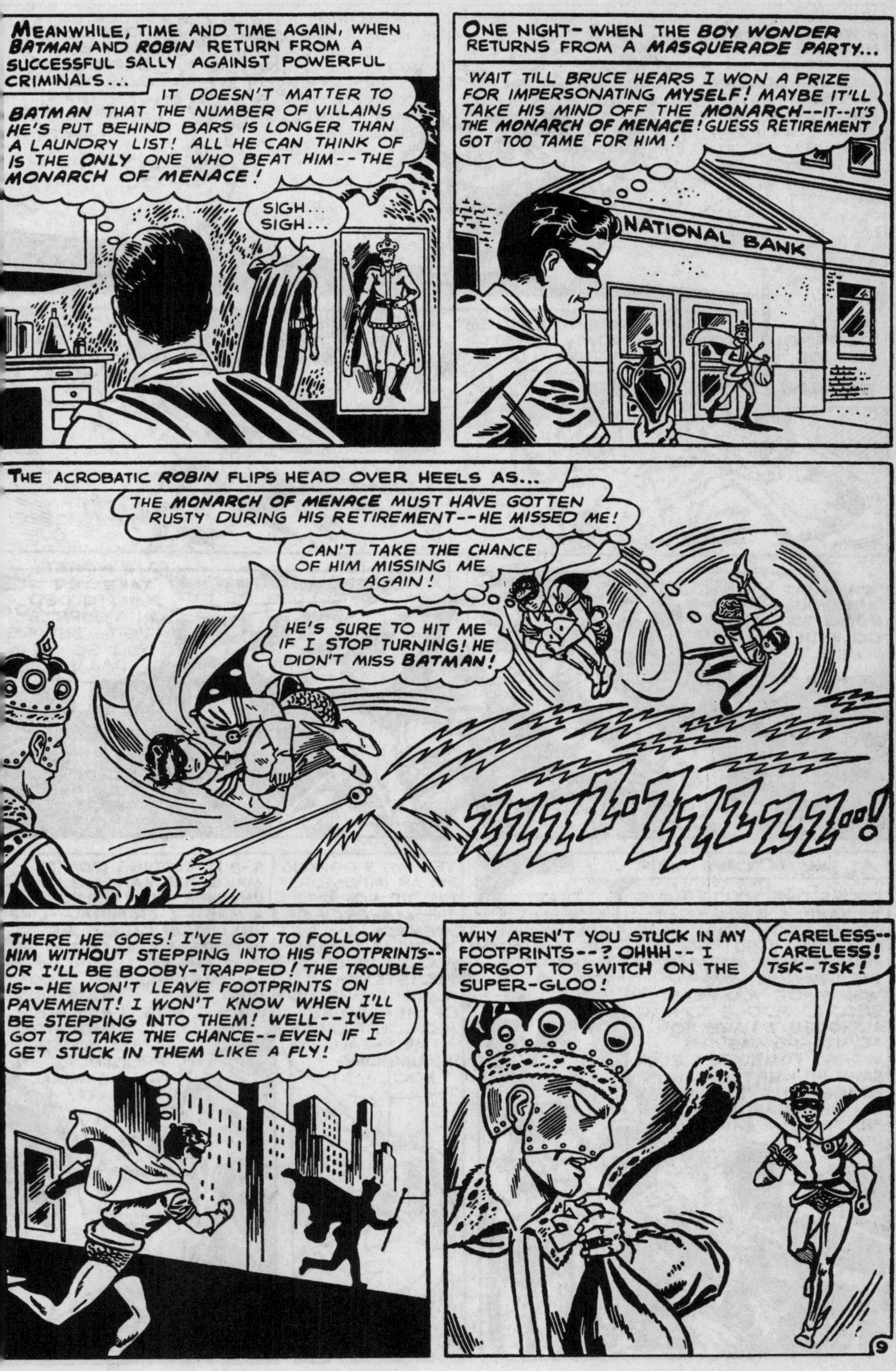
MEANWHILE, TIME AND TIME AGAIN, WHEN BATMAN AND ROBIN RETURN FROM A SUCCESSFUL SALLY AGAINST POWERFUL CRIMINALS...
IT DOESN'T MATTER TO BATMAN THAT THE NUMBER OF VILLAINS HE'S PUT BEHIND BARS IS LONGER THAN A LAUNDRY LIST! ALL HE CAN THINK OF IS THE ONLY ONE WHO BEAT HIM--THE MONARCH OF MENACE!
SIGH... SIGH...
ONE NIGHT- WHEN THE BOY WONDER RETURNS FROM A MASQUERADE PARTY...
WAIT TILL BRUCE HEARS I WON A PRIZE FOR IMPERSONATING MYSELF! MAYBE IT'LL TAKE HIS MIND OFF THE MONARCH--IT--IT'S THE MONARCH OF MENACE! GUESS RETIREMENT GOT TOO TAME FOR HIM!
NATIONAL BANK
THE ACROBATIC ROBIN FLIPS HEAD OVER HEELS AS...
THE MONARCH OF MENACE MUST HAVE GOTTEN RUSTY DURING HIS RETIREMENT--HE MISSED ME!
CAN'T TAKE THE CHANCE OF HIM MISSING ME AGAIN!
HE'S SURE TO HIT ME IF I STOP TURNING! HE DIDN'T MISS BATMAN!
ZZZZZ-ZZZZZZZ-ZZZZZZoo!
THERE HE GOES! I'VE GOT TO FOLLOW HIM WITHOUT STEPPING INTO HIS FOOTPRINTS--OR I'LL BE BOOBY-TRAPPED! THE TROUBLE IS--HE WON'T LEAVE FOOTPRINTS ON PAVEMENT! I WON'T KNOW WHEN I'LL BE STEPPING INTO THEM! WELL--I'VE GOT TO TAKE THE CHANCE--EVEN IF I GET STUCK IN THEM LIKE A FLY!
WHY AREN'T YOU STUCK IN MY FOOTPRINTS--? OHHH-- I FORGOT TO SWITCH ON THE SUPER-GLOO!
CARELESS--CARELESS! TSK-TSK!
9

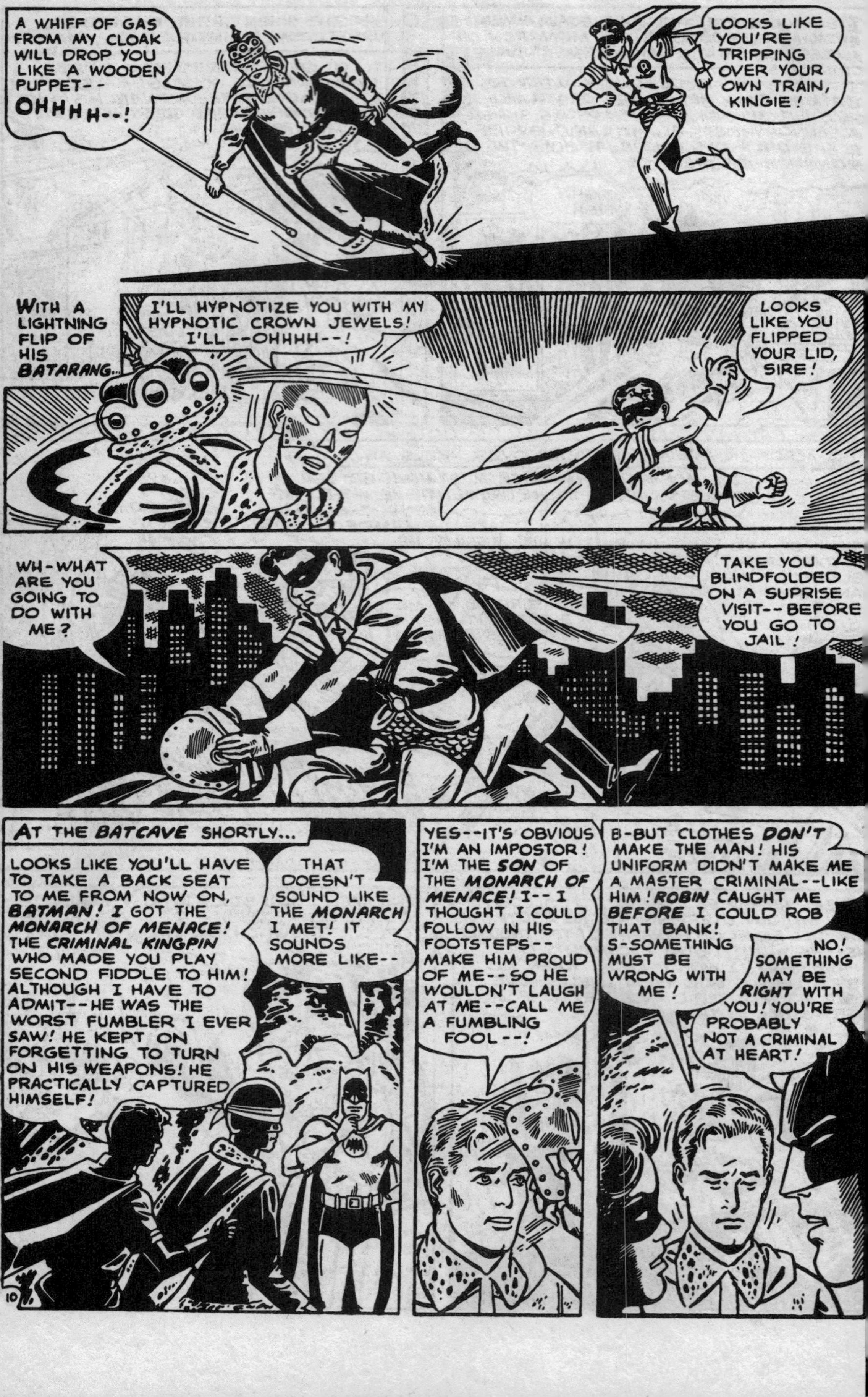
A WHIFF OF GAS FROM MY CLOAK WILL DROP YOU LIKE A WOODEN PUPPET-- OHHHH--!
LOOKS LIKE YOU'RE TRIPPING OVER YOUR OWN TRAIN, KINGIE!
WITH A LIGHTNING FLIP OF HIS BATARANG...
I'LL HYPNOTIZE YOU WITH MY HYPNOTIC CROWN JEWELS! I'LL--OHHHH--!
LOOKS LIKE YOU FLIPPED YOUR LID, SIRE!
WH-WHAT ARE YOU GOING TO DO WITH ME?
TAKE YOU BLINDFOLDED ON A SUPRISE VISIT--BEFORE YOU GO TO JAIL!
AT THE BATCAVE SHORTLY...
LOOKS LIKE YOU'LL HAVE TO TAKE A BACK SEAT TO ME FROM NOW ON, BATMAN! I GOT THE MONARCH OF MENACE! THE CRIMINAL KINGPIN WHO MADE YOU PLAY SECOND FIDDLE TO HIM! ALTHOUGH I HAVE TO ADMIT--HE WAS THE WORST FUMBLER I EVER SAW! HE KEPT ON FORGETTING TO TURN ON HIS WEAPONS! HE PRACTICALLY CAPTURED HIMSELF!
THAT DOESN'T SOUND LIKE THE MONARCH I MET! IT SOUNDS MORE LIKE--
YES--IT'S OBVIOUS I'M AN IMPOSTOR! I'M THE SON OF THE MONARCH OF MENACE! I--I THOUGHT I COULD FOLLOW IN HIS FOOTSTEPS--MAKE HIM PROUD OF ME--SO HE WOULDN'T LAUGH AT ME--CALL ME A FUMBLING FOOL--!
B-BUT CLOTHES DON'T MAKE THE MAN! HIS UNIFORM DIDN'T MAKE ME A MASTER CRIMINAL--LIKE HIM! ROBIN CAUGHT ME BEFORE I COULD ROB THAT BANK! S-SOMETHING MUST BE WRONG WITH ME!
NO! SOMETHING MAY BE RIGHT WITH YOU! YOU'RE PROBABLY NOT A CRIMINAL AT HEART!
10

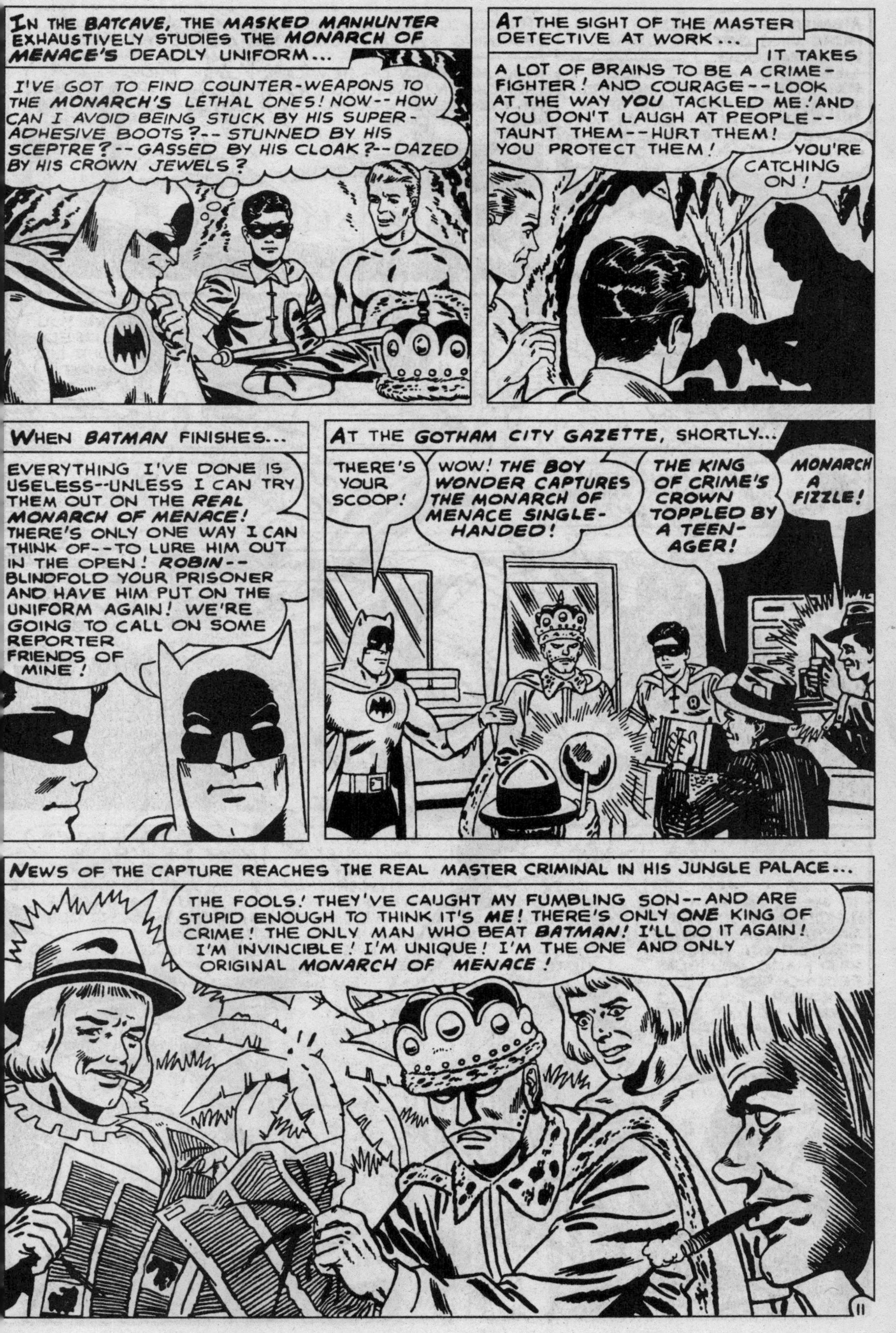
IN THE BATCAVE, THE MASKED MANHUNTER EXHAUSTIVELY STUDIES THE MONARCH OF MENACE'S DEADLY UNIFORM...
I'VE GOT TO FIND COUNTER-WEAPONS TO THE MONARCH'S LETHAL ONES! NOW--HOW CAN I AVOID BEING STUCK BY HIS SUPER-ADHESIVE BOOTS?--STUNNED BY HIS SCEPTRE?--GASSED BY HIS CLOAK?--DAZED BY HIS CROWN JEWELS?
AT THE SIGHT OF THE MASTER DETECTIVE AT WORK...
IT TAKES A LOT OF BRAINS TO BE A CRIME-FIGHTER! AND COURAGE--LOOK AT THE WAY YOU TACKLED ME! AND YOU DON'T LAUGH AT PEOPLE--TAUNT THEM--HURT THEM! YOU PROTECT THEM!
YOU'RE CATCHING ON!
WHEN BATMAN FINISHES...
EVERYTHING I'VE DONE IS USELESS--UNLESS I CAN TRY THEM OUT ON THE REAL MONARCH OF MENACE! THERE'S ONLY ONE WAY I CAN THINK OF--TO LURE HIM OUT IN THE OPEN! ROBIN--BLINDFOLD YOUR PRISONER AND HAVE HIM PUT ON THE UNIFORM AGAIN! WE'RE GOING TO CALL ON SOME REPORTER FRIENDS OF MINE!
AT THE GOTHAM CITY GAZETTE, SHORTLY...
THERE'S YOUR SCOOP!
WOW! THE BOY WONDER CAPTURES THE MONARCH OF MENACE SINGLE-HANDED!
THE KING OF CRIME'S CROWN TOPPLED BY A TEEN-AGER!
MONARCH A FIZZLE!
NEWS OF THE CAPTURE REACHES THE REAL MASTER CRIMINAL IN HIS JUNGLE PALACE...
THE FOOLS! THEY'VE CAUGHT MY FUMBLING SON--AND ARE STUPID ENOUGH TO THINK IT'S ME! THERE'S ONLY ONE KING OF CRIME! THE ONLY MAN WHO BEAT BATMAN! I'LL DO IT AGAIN! I'M INVINCIBLE! I'M UNIQUE! I'M THE ONE AND ONLY ORIGINAL MONARCH OF MENACE!
11

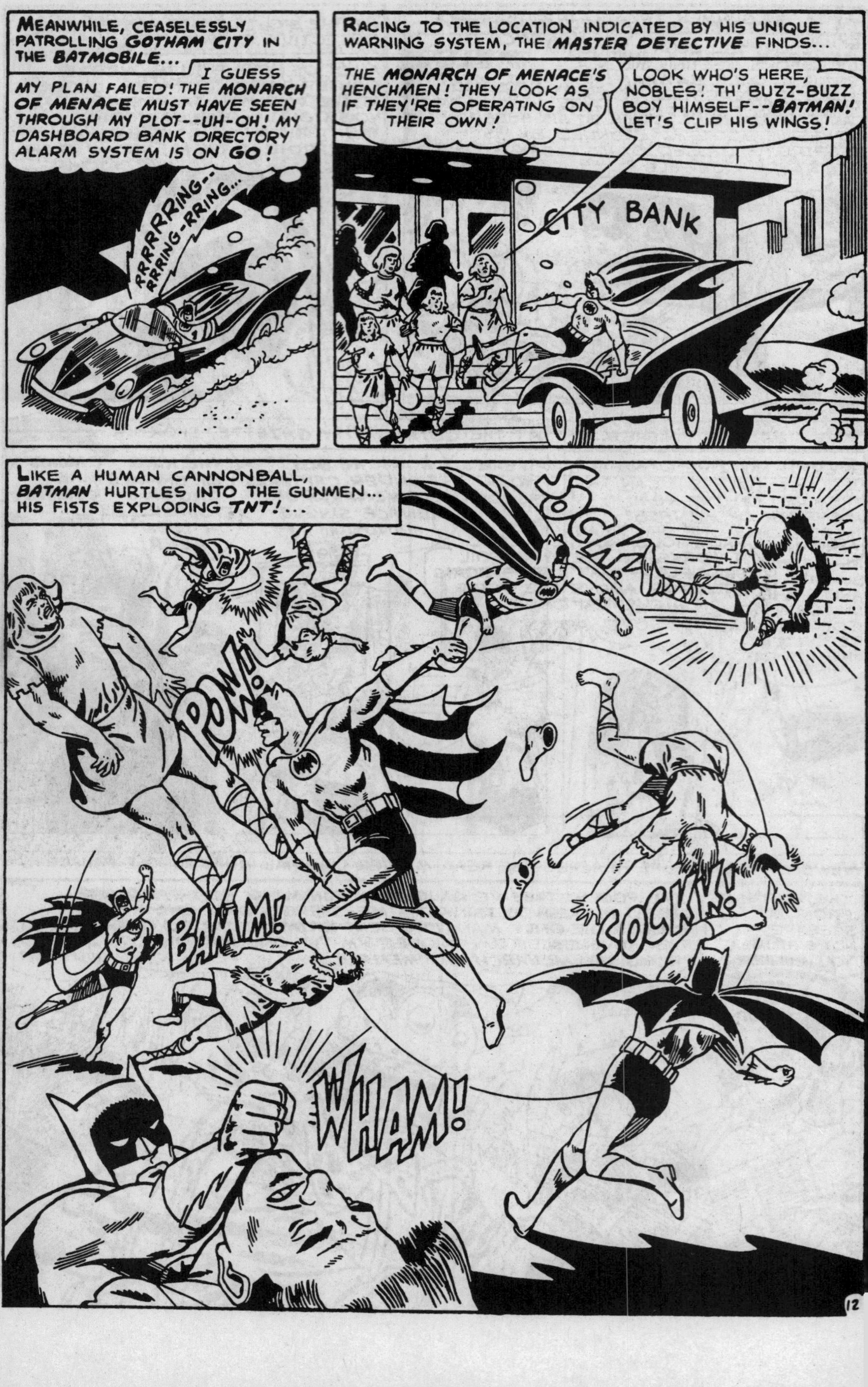
MEANWHILE, CEASELESSLY PATROLLING GOTHAM CITY IN THE BATMOBILE...
I GUESS MY PLAN FAILED! THE MONARCH OF MENACE MUST HAVE SEEN THROUGH MY PLOT--UH-OH! MY DASHBOARD BANK DIRECTORY ALARM SYSTEM IS ON GO!
RRRRRRING-- RRRING-RRING...
RACING TO THE LOCATION INDICATED BY HIS UNIQUE WARNING SYSTEM, THE MASTER DETECTIVE FINDS...
THE MONARCH OF MENACE'S HENCHMEN! THEY LOOK AS IF THEY'RE OPERATING ON THEIR OWN!
LOOK WHO'S HERE, NOBLES! TH' BUZZ-BUZZ BOY HIMSELF--BATMAN! LET'S CLIP HIS WINGS!
CITY BANK
LIKE A HUMAN CANNONBALL, BATMAN HURTLES INTO THE GUNMEN... HIS FISTS EXPLODING TNT!...
SOCK!
POW!
BAMM!
SOCK!
WHAM!
12

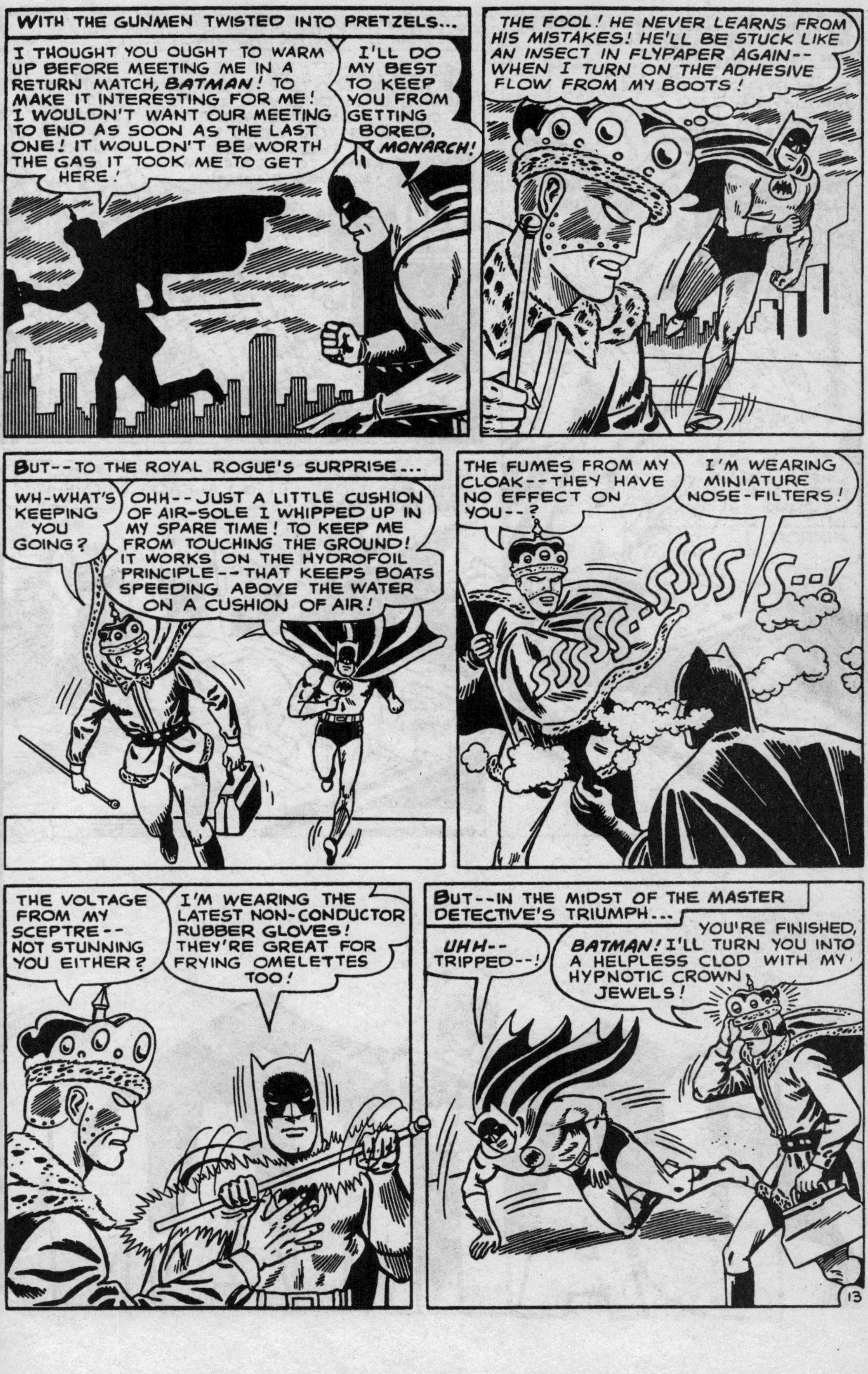
WITH THE GUNMEN TWISTED INTO PRETZELS...
I THOUGHT YOU OUGHT TO WARM UP BEFORE MEETING ME IN A RETURN MATCH, BATMAN! TO MAKE IT INTERESTING FOR ME! I WOULDN'T WANT OUR MEETING TO END AS SOON AS THE LAST ONE! IT WOULDN'T BE WORTH THE GAS IT TOOK ME TO GET HERE!
I'LL DO MY BEST TO KEEP YOU FROM GETTING BORED, MONARCH!
THE FOOL! HE NEVER LEARNS FROM HIS MISTAKES! HE'LL BE STUCK LIKE AN INSECT IN FLYPAPER AGAIN-- WHEN I TURN ON THE ADHESIVE FLOW FROM MY BOOTS!
BUT--TO THE ROYAL ROGUE'S SURPRISE...
WH-WHAT'S KEEPING YOU GOING?
OHH--JUST A LITTLE CUSHION OF AIR-SOLE I WHIPPED UP IN MY SPARE TIME! TO KEEP ME FROM TOUCHING THE GROUND! IT WORKS ON THE HYDROFOIL PRINCIPLE--THAT KEEPS BOATS SPEEDING ABOVE THE WATER ON A CUSHION OF AIR!
THE FUMES FROM MY CLOAK--THEY HAVE NO EFFECT ON YOU--?
I'M WEARING MINIATURE NOSE-FILTERS!
SSSSS--SSSSSS--!
THE VOLTAGE FROM MY SCEPTRE--NOT STUNNING YOU EITHER?
I'M WEARING THE LATEST NON-CONDUCTOR RUBBER GLOVES! THEY'RE GREAT FOR FRYING OMELETTES TOO!
BUT--IN THE MIDST OF THE MASTER DETECTIVE'S TRIUMPH...
UHH--TRIPPED--!
YOU'RE FINISHED, BATMAN! I'LL TURN YOU INTO A HELPLESS CLOD WITH MY HYPNOTIC CROWN JEWELS!
13

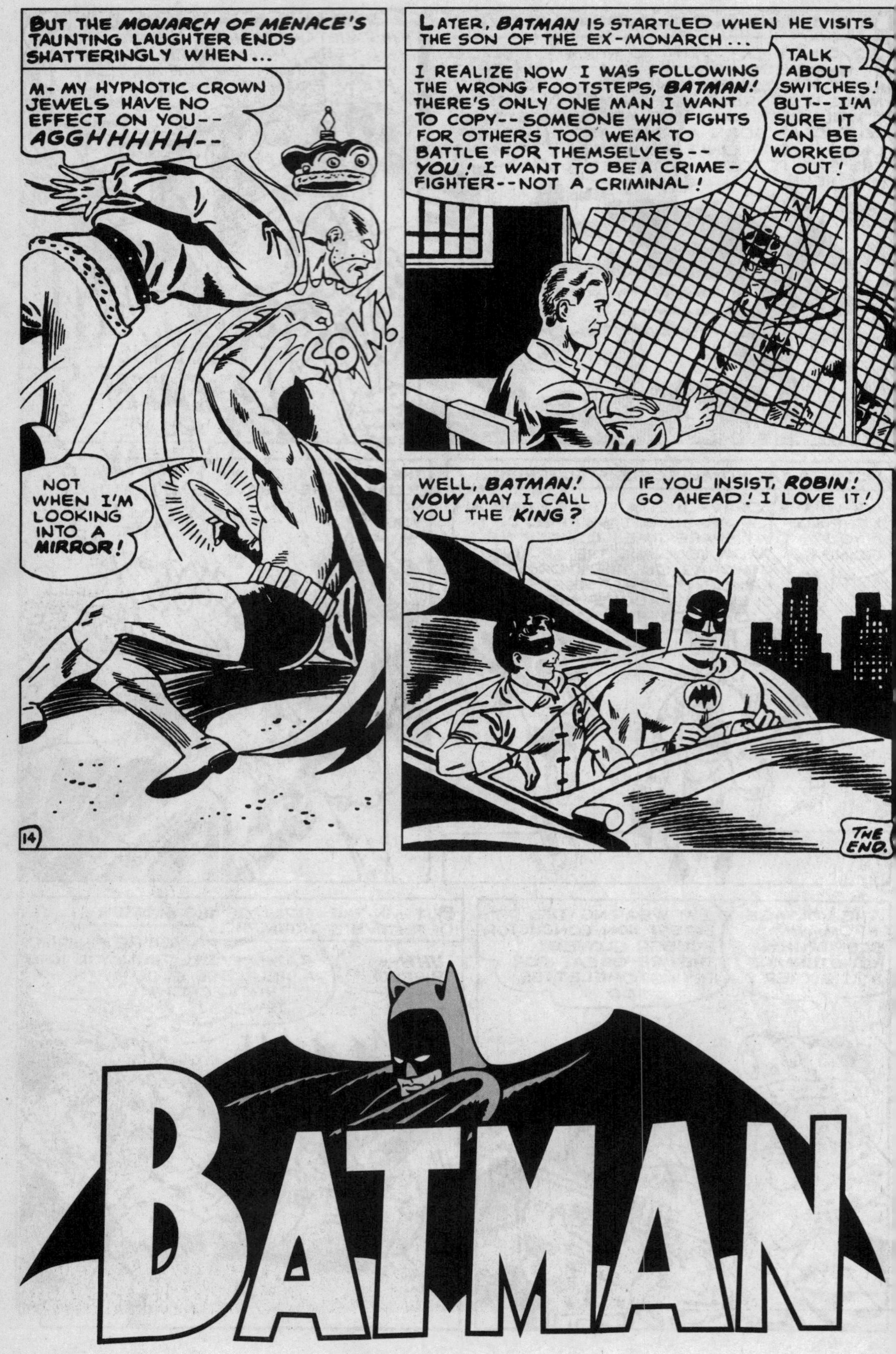
BUT THE MONARCH OF MENACE'S TAUNTING LAUGHTER ENDS SHATTERINGLY WHEN...
M-MY HYPNOTIC CROWN JEWELS HAVE NO EFFECT ON YOU-- AGGHHHHHH--
SOCK!
NOT WHEN I'M LOOKING INTO A MIRROR!
14
LATER, BATMAN IS STARTLED WHEN HE VISITS THE SON OF THE EX-MONARCH...
I REALIZE NOW I WAS FOLLOWING THE WRONG FOOTSTEPS, BATMAN! THERE'S ONLY ONE MAN I WANT TO COPY-- SOMEONE WHO FIGHTS FOR OTHERS TOO WEAK TO BATTLE FOR THEMSELVES-- YOU! I WANT TO BE A CRIME-FIGHTER--NOT A CRIMINAL!
TALK ABOUT SWITCHES! BUT-- I'M SURE IT CAN BE WORKED OUT!
WELL, BATMAN! NOW MAY I CALL YOU THE KING?
IF YOU INSIST, ROBIN! GO AHEAD! I LOVE IT!
THE END.

BATMAN

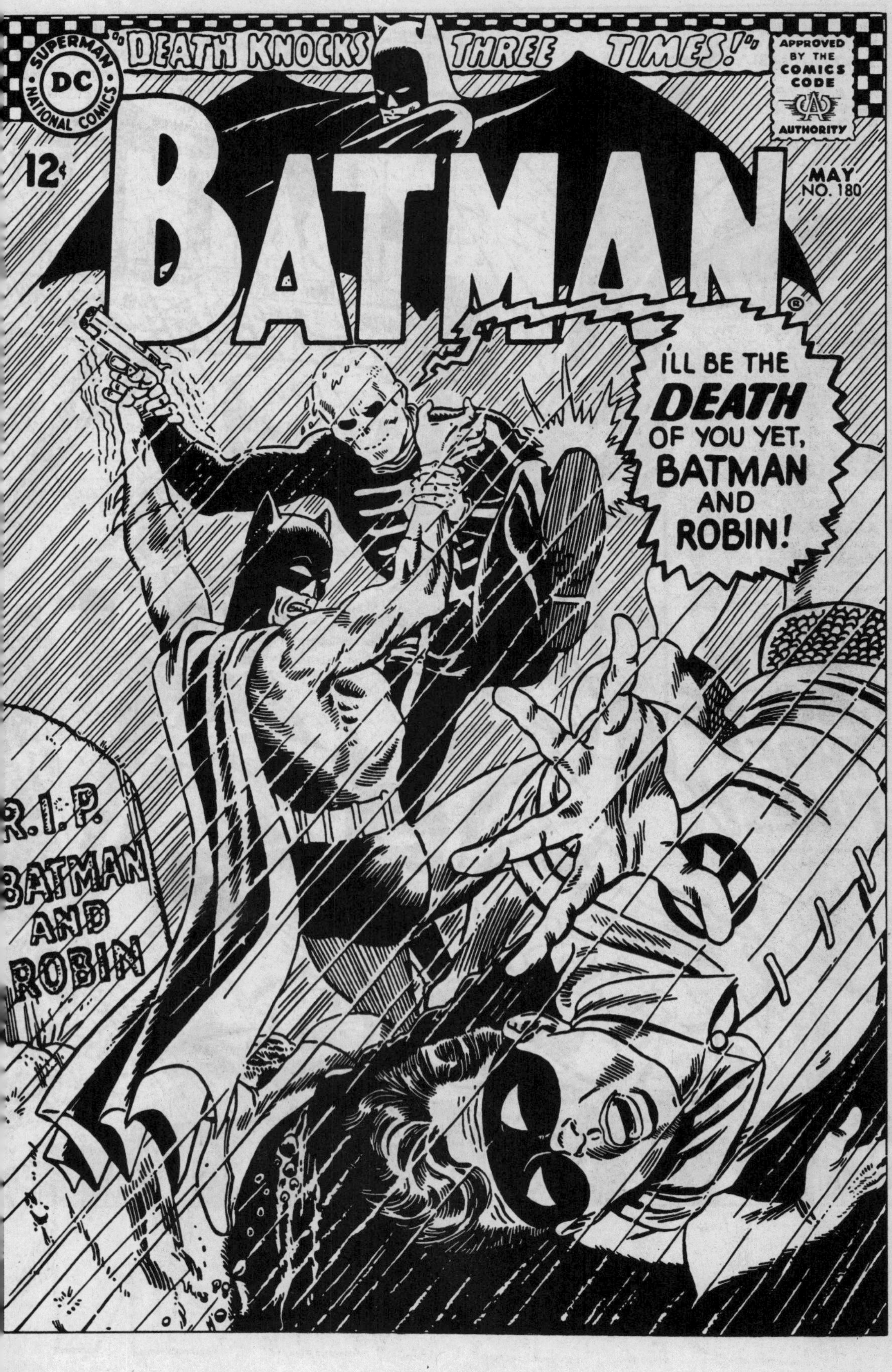
"DEATH KNOCKS THREE TIMES!"
SUPERMAN DC NATIONAL COMICS
APPROVED BY THE COMICS CODE AUTHORITY
12¢
BATMAN
MAY NO. 180
I'LL BE THE DEATH OF YOU YET, BATMAN AND ROBIN!
R.I.P. BATMAN AND ROBIN

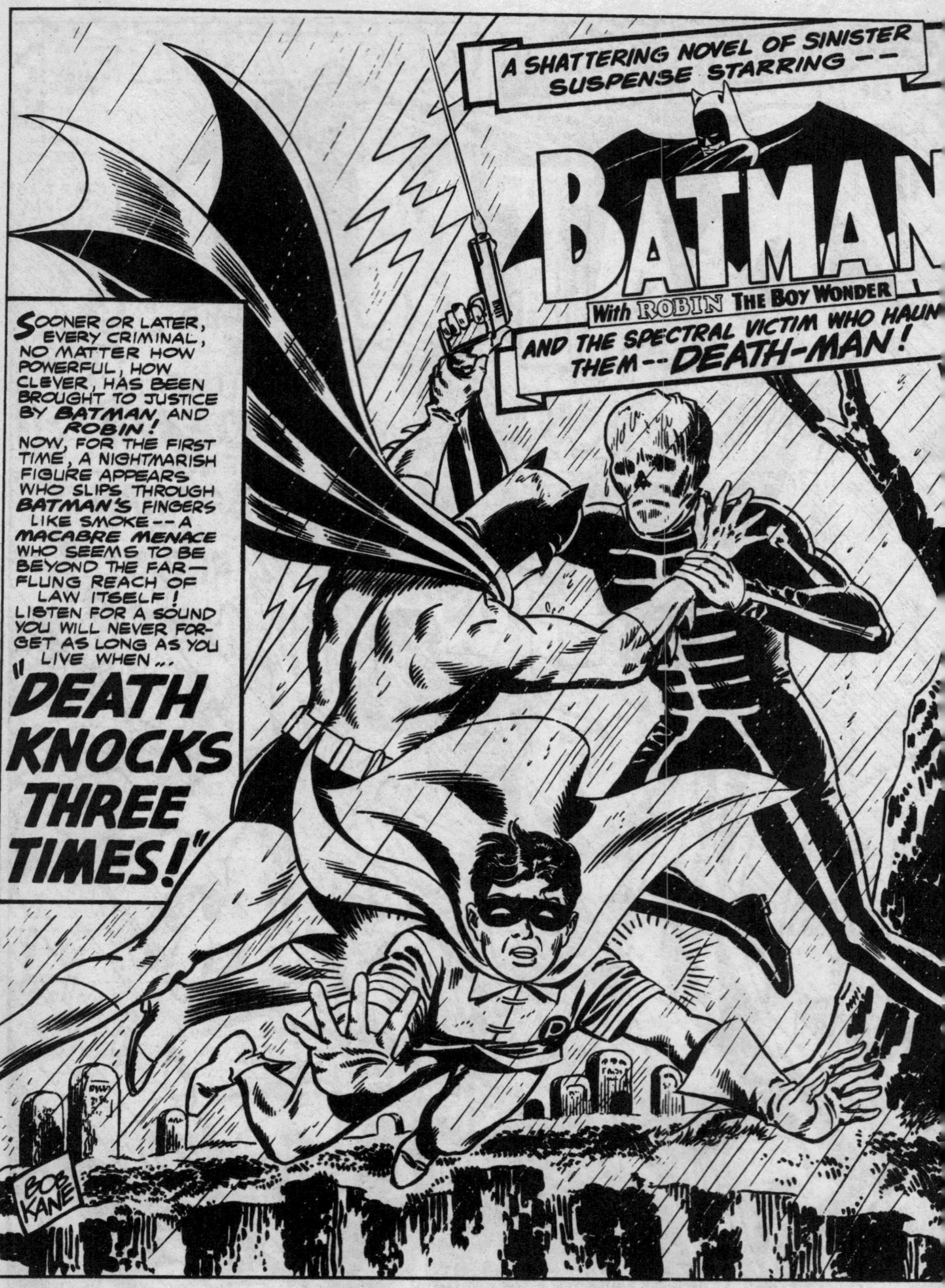
A SHATTERING NOVEL OF SINISTER SUSPENSE STARRING --
BATMAN
With ROBIN THE BOY WONDER
AND THE SPECTRAL VICTIM WHO HAUN
THEM -- DEATH-MAN!
SOONER OR LATER, EVERY CRIMINAL, NO MATTER HOW POWERFUL, HOW CLEVER, HAS BEEN BROUGHT TO JUSTICE BY BATMAN AND ROBIN! NOW, FOR THE FIRST TIME, A NIGHTMARISH FIGURE APPEARS WHO SLIPS THROUGH BATMAN'S FINGERS LIKE SMOKE -- A MACABRE MENACE WHO SEEMS TO BE BEYOND THE FAR-FLUNG REACH OF LAW ITSELF! LISTEN FOR A SOUND YOU WILL NEVER FORGET AS LONG AS YOU LIVE WHEN...
"DEATH KNOCKS THREE TIMES!"
BOB KANE

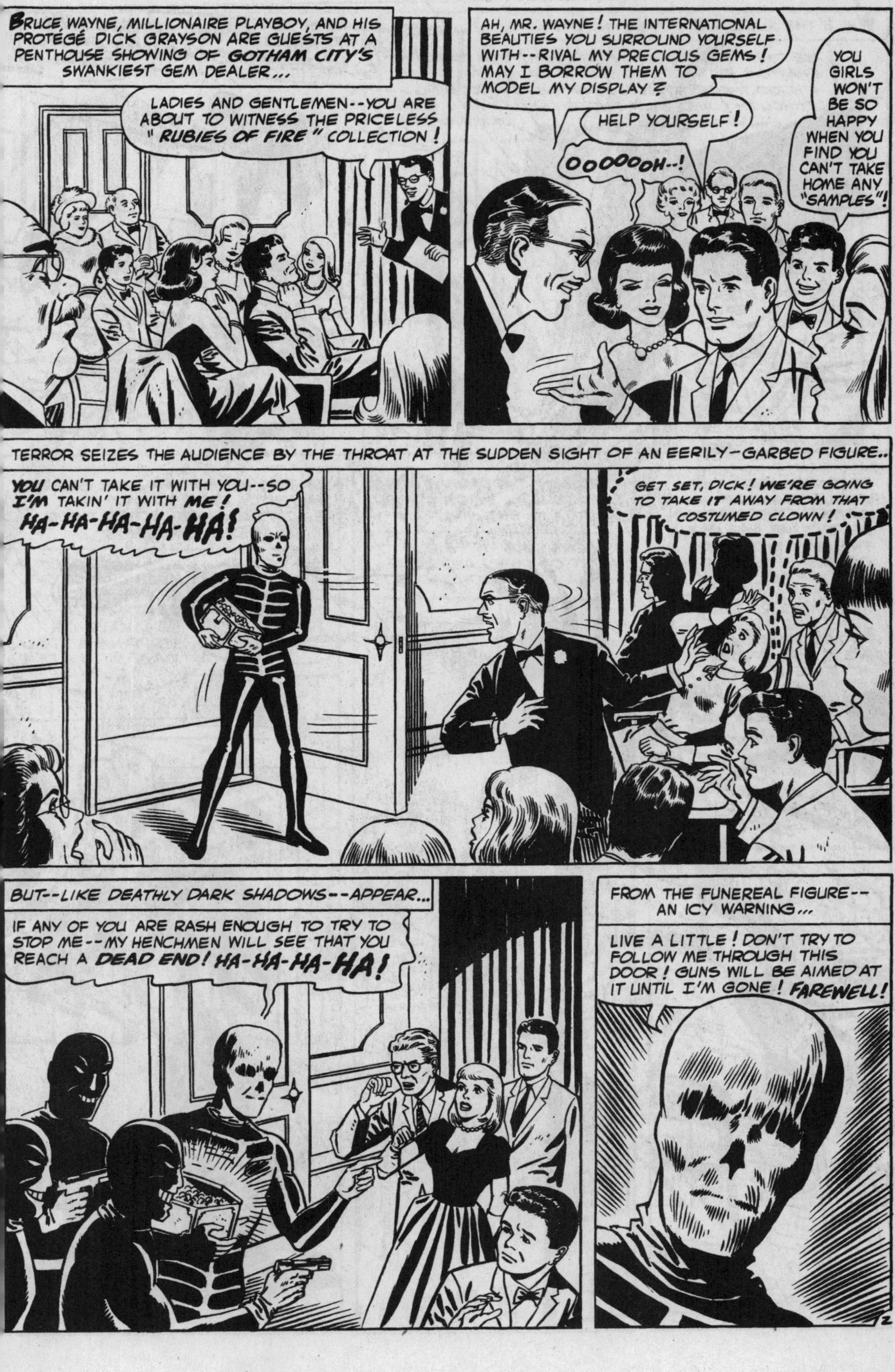
BRUCE WAYNE, MILLIONAIRE PLAYBOY, AND HIS PROTÉGÉ DICK GRAYSON ARE GUESTS AT A PENTHOUSE SHOWING OF GOTHAM CITY'S SWANKIEST GEM DEALER...
LADIES AND GENTLEMEN--YOU ARE ABOUT TO WITNESS THE PRICELESS "RUBIES OF FIRE" COLLECTION!
AH, MR. WAYNE! THE INTERNATIONAL BEAUTIES YOU SURROUND YOURSELF WITH--RIVAL MY PRECIOUS GEMS! MAY I BORROW THEM TO MODEL MY DISPLAY?
HELP YOURSELF!
OOOOOOH--!
YOU GIRLS WON'T BE SO HAPPY WHEN YOU FIND YOU CAN'T TAKE HOME ANY "SAMPLES"!
TERROR SEIZES THE AUDIENCE BY THE THROAT AT THE SUDDEN SIGHT OF AN EERILY-GARBED FIGURE..
YOU CAN'T TAKE IT WITH YOU--SO I'M TAKIN' IT WITH ME! HA-HA-HA-HA-HA!
GET SET, DICK! WE'RE GOING TO TAKE IT AWAY FROM THAT COSTUMED CLOWN!
BUT--LIKE DEATHLY DARK SHADOWS--APPEAR...
IF ANY OF YOU ARE RASH ENOUGH TO TRY TO STOP ME--MY HENCHMEN WILL SEE THAT YOU REACH A DEAD END! HA-HA-HA-HA!
FROM THE FUNEREAL FIGURE-- AN ICY WARNING...
LIVE A LITTLE! DON'T TRY TO FOLLOW ME THROUGH THIS DOOR! GUNS WILL BE AIMED AT IT UNTIL I'M GONE! FAREWELL!
2

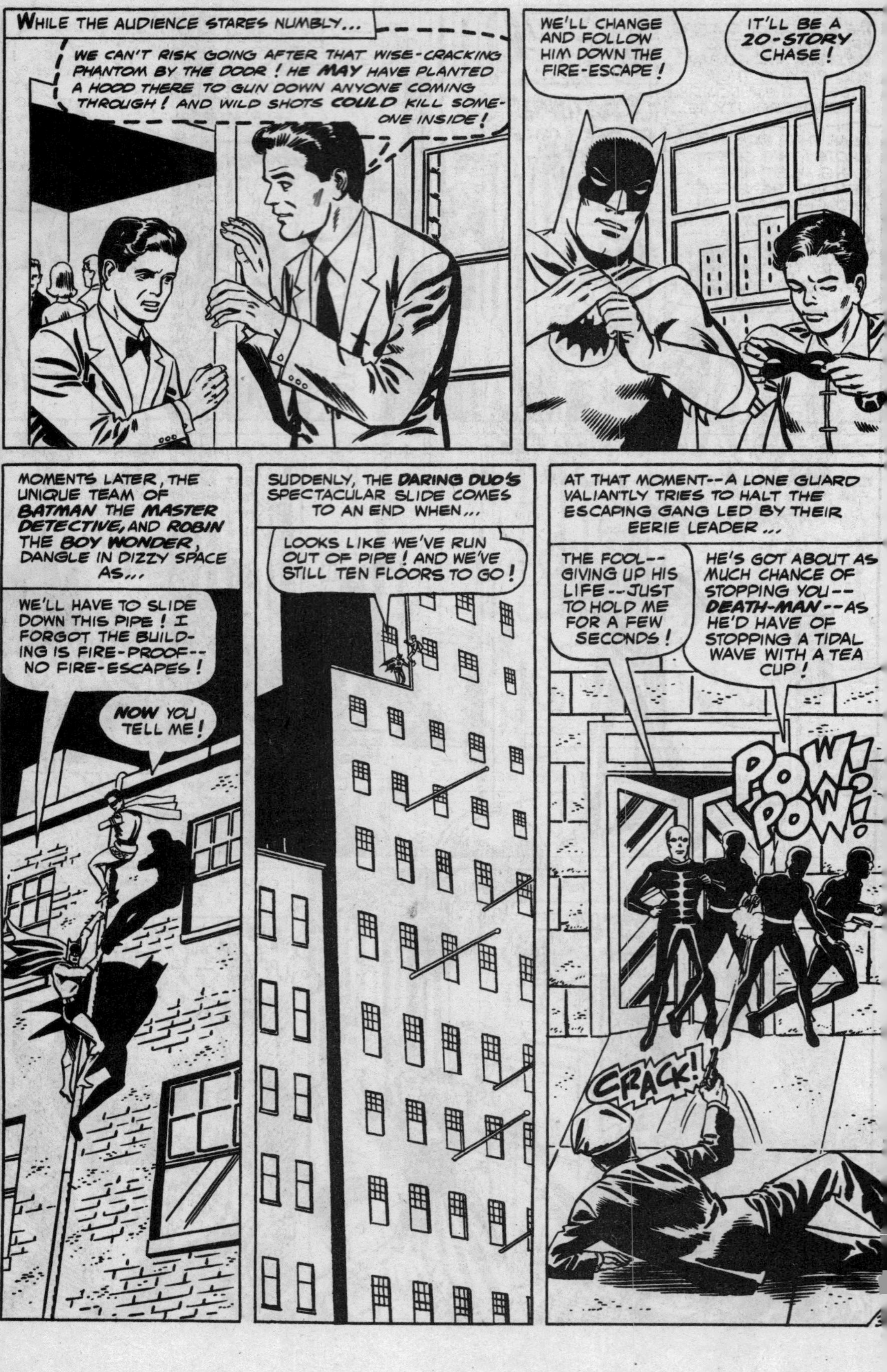
WHILE THE AUDIENCE STARES NUMBLY...
WE CAN'T RISK GOING AFTER THAT WISE-CRACKING PHANTOM BY THE DOOR! HE MAY HAVE PLANTED A HOOD THERE TO GUN DOWN ANYONE COMING THROUGH! AND WILD SHOTS COULD KILL SOMEONE INSIDE!
WE'LL CHANGE AND FOLLOW HIM DOWN THE FIRE-ESCAPE!
IT'LL BE A 20-STORY CHASE!
MOMENTS LATER, THE UNIQUE TEAM OF BATMAN THE MASTER DETECTIVE, AND ROBIN THE BOY WONDER, DANGLE IN DIZZY SPACE AS...
WE'LL HAVE TO SLIDE DOWN THIS PIPE! I FORGOT THE BUILDING IS FIRE-PROOF--NO FIRE-ESCAPES!
NOW YOU TELL ME!
SUDDENLY, THE DARING DUO'S SPECTACULAR SLIDE COMES TO AN END WHEN...
LOOKS LIKE WE'VE RUN OUT OF PIPE! AND WE'VE STILL TEN FLOORS TO GO!
AT THAT MOMENT--A LONE GUARD VALIANTLY TRIES TO HALT THE ESCAPING GANG LED BY THEIR EERIE LEADER...
THE FOOL--GIVING UP HIS LIFE--JUST TO HOLD ME FOR A FEW SECONDS!
HE'S GOT ABOUT AS MUCH CHANCE OF STOPPING YOU--DEATH-MAN--AS HE'D HAVE OF STOPPING A TIDAL WAVE WITH A TEA CUP!
POW! POW! POW!
CRACK!

THE SOUNDS OF GUNFIRE FROM BELOW STING *BATMAN* AND *ROBIN* INTO RISKING THEIR LIVES TO THEIR INCREDIBLE ACROBATIC AGILITY AS...

HEAR THAT, *ROBIN* ? SHOTS ! THAT GRISLY GANG MUST HAVE REACHED THE STREET AND ARE SHOOTING THEIR WAY OUT ! WE'VE GOT TO TAKE THE FASTEST WAY DOWN TO TRY TO STOP THEM ! VIA THOSE FLAGPOLES !

POW! POW!

GO!-- GO!-- GO!-- *BATMAN!*

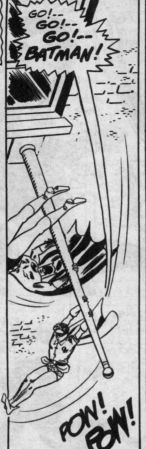

POW! POW!

A SINGLE, WOUNDED GUARD--HOLDING THE GANG BACK--

POW! POW!

HE COULD USE FOUR HELPING HANDS--!

POW! POW!

AS THE RUTHLESS FIGURE OF DEATH LEADS HIS SINISTER GANG PAST THE SLUMPED GUARD-- FLAPPING CAPES LIKE GIANT WINGS SEEM TO HOVER OVER THEM ...

BATMAN... TAKE... OVER...

A LITTLE MORE TARGET PRACTICE WON'T HOLD US UP MUCH ! AN EXTRA RUBY TO THE MAN WHO "KNOCKS" THOSE CLAY PIGEONS OUT OF THE AIR FIRST !

POW! POW!

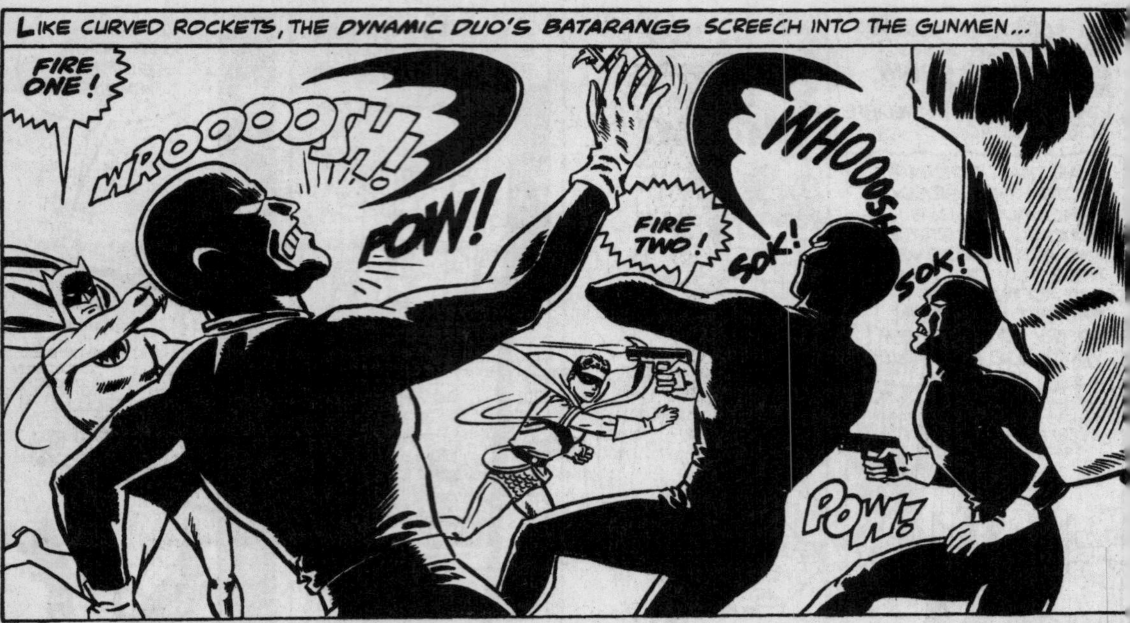
LIKE CURVED ROCKETS, THE DYNAMIC DUO'S BATARANGS SCREECH INTO THE GUNMEN...
FIRE ONE!
WROOOOSH!
POW!
WHOOOSH
FIRE TWO!
SOK!
SOK!
POW!

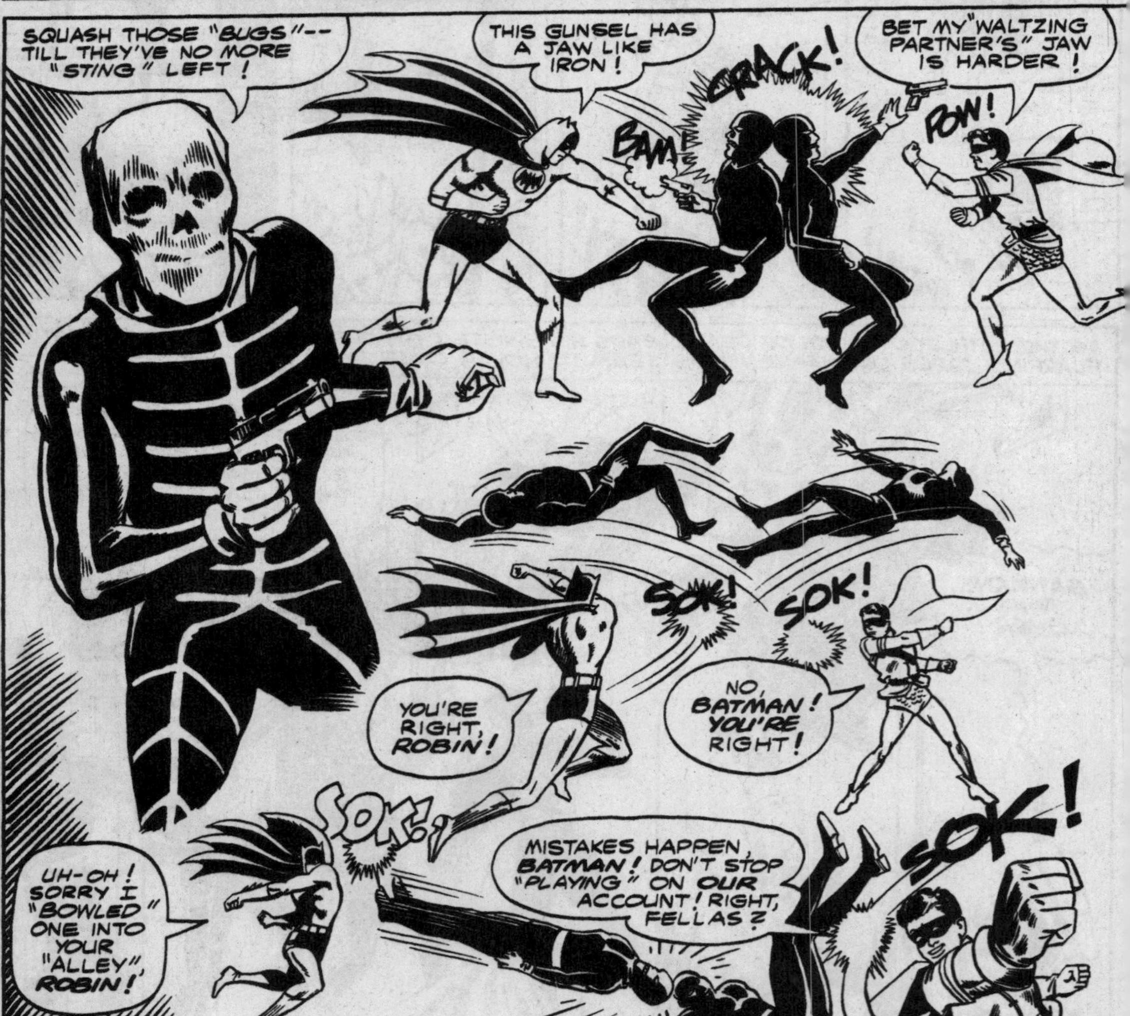
SQUASH THOSE "BUGS"-- TILL THEY'VE NO MORE "STING" LEFT!
THIS GUNSEL HAS A JAW LIKE IRON!
CRACK!
BET MY "WALTZING PARTNER'S" JAW IS HARDER!
BAM
POW!
SOK!
SOK!
YOU'RE RIGHT, ROBIN!
NO, BATMAN! YOU'RE RIGHT!
SOK!
SOK!
UH-OH! SORRY I "BOWLED" ONE INTO YOUR "ALLEY", ROBIN!
MISTAKES HAPPEN, BATMAN! DON'T STOP "PLAYING" ON OUR ACCOUNT! RIGHT, FELLAS?

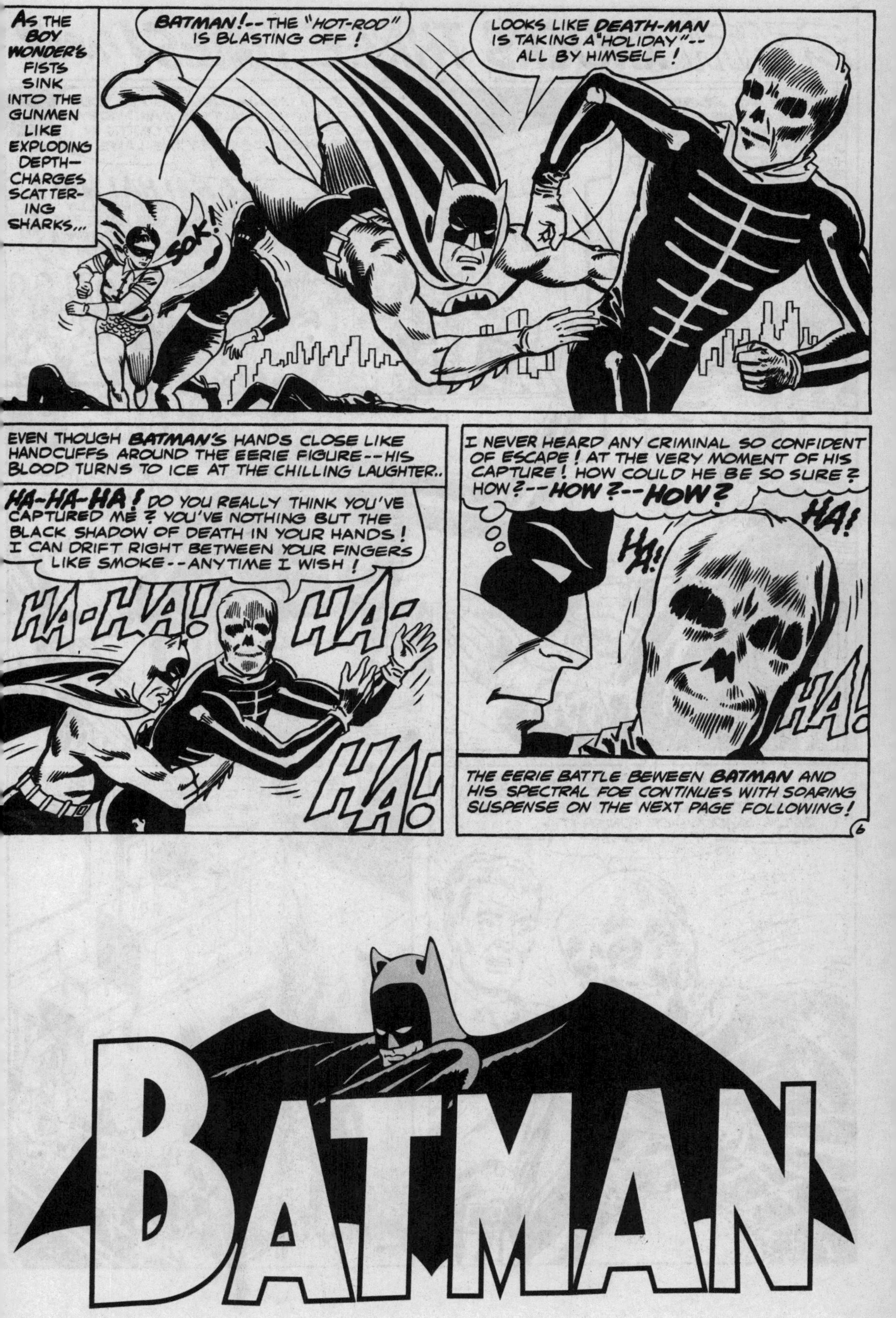
AS THE BOY WONDER'S FISTS SINK INTO THE GUNMEN LIKE EXPLODING DEPTH-CHARGES SCATTERING SHARKS...
BATMAN!--THE "HOT-ROD" IS BLASTING OFF!
LOOKS LIKE DEATH-MAN IS TAKING A "HOLIDAY"--ALL BY HIMSELF!
SOK!
EVEN THOUGH BATMAN'S HANDS CLOSE LIKE HANDCUFFS AROUND THE EERIE FIGURE--HIS BLOOD TURNS TO ICE AT THE CHILLING LAUGHTER..
HA-HA-HA! DO YOU REALLY THINK YOU'VE CAPTURED ME? YOU'VE NOTHING BUT THE BLACK SHADOW OF DEATH IN YOUR HANDS! I CAN DRIFT RIGHT BETWEEN YOUR FINGERS LIKE SMOKE--ANYTIME I WISH!
HA-HA! HA-
HA!
I NEVER HEARD ANY CRIMINAL SO CONFIDENT OF ESCAPE! AT THE VERY MOMENT OF HIS CAPTURE! HOW COULD HE BE SO SURE? HOW?--HOW?--HOW?
HA!
HA!
HA!
THE EERIE BATTLE BEWEEN BATMAN AND HIS SPECTRAL FOE CONTINUES WITH SOARING SUSPENSE ON THE NEXT PAGE FOLLOWING!
6

BATMAN

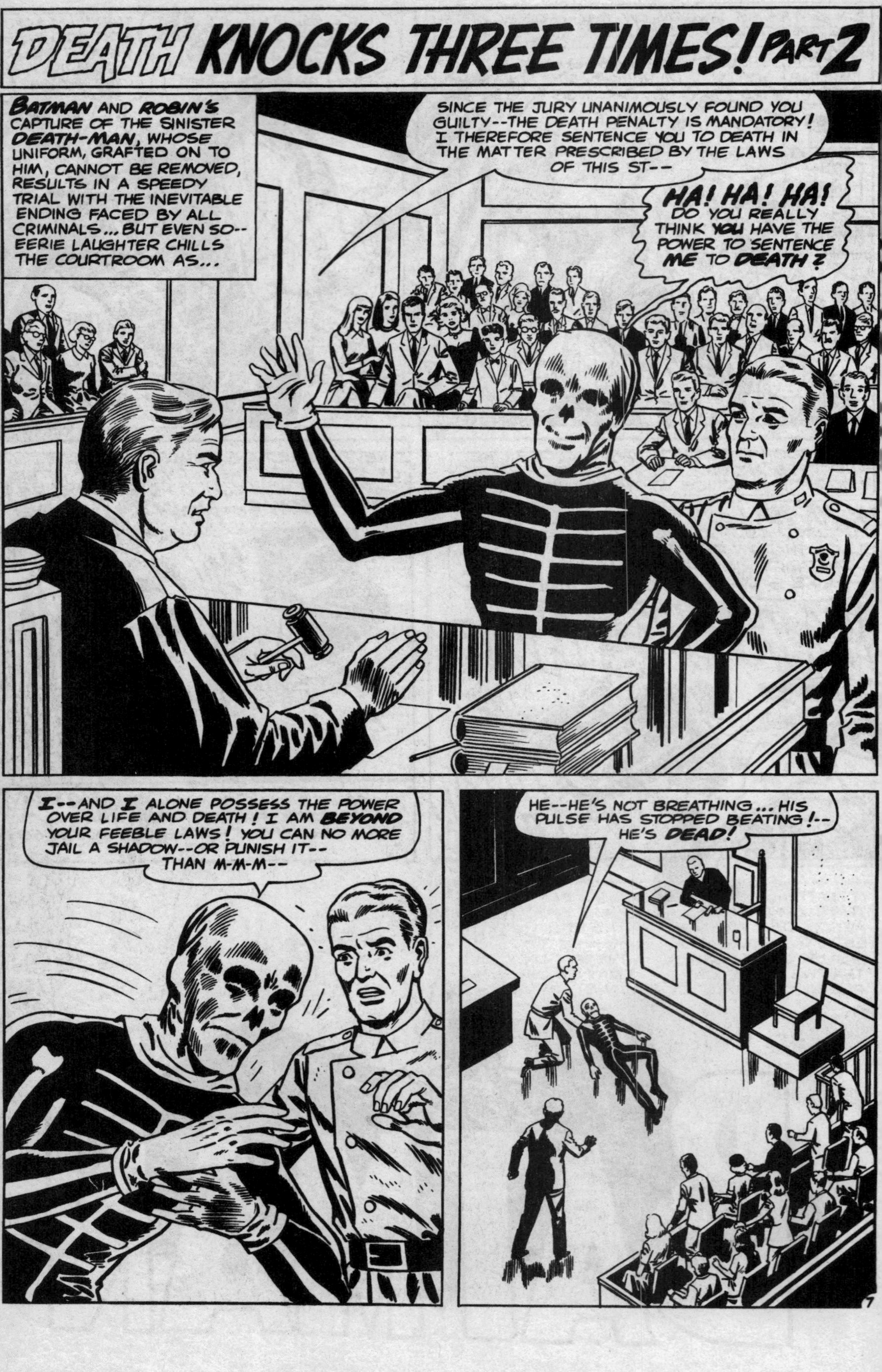
DEATH KNOCKS THREE TIMES! PART 2
BATMAN AND ROBIN'S CAPTURE OF THE SINISTER DEATH-MAN, WHOSE UNIFORM, GRAFTED ON TO HIM, CANNOT BE REMOVED, RESULTS IN A SPEEDY TRIAL WITH THE INEVITABLE ENDING FACED BY ALL CRIMINALS... BUT EVEN SO-- EERIE LAUGHTER CHILLS THE COURTROOM AS...
SINCE THE JURY UNANIMOUSLY FOUND YOU GUILTY--THE DEATH PENALTY IS MANDATORY! I THEREFORE SENTENCE YOU TO DEATH IN THE MATTER PRESCRIBED BY THE LAWS OF THIS ST--
HA! HA! HA! DO YOU REALLY THINK YOU HAVE THE POWER TO SENTENCE ME TO DEATH?
I--AND I ALONE POSSESS THE POWER OVER LIFE AND DEATH! I AM BEYOND YOUR FEEBLE LAWS! YOU CAN NO MORE JAIL A SHADOW--OR PUNISH IT-- THAN M-M-M--
HE--HE'S NOT BREATHING... HIS PULSE HAS STOPPED BEATING!--HE'S DEAD!
7

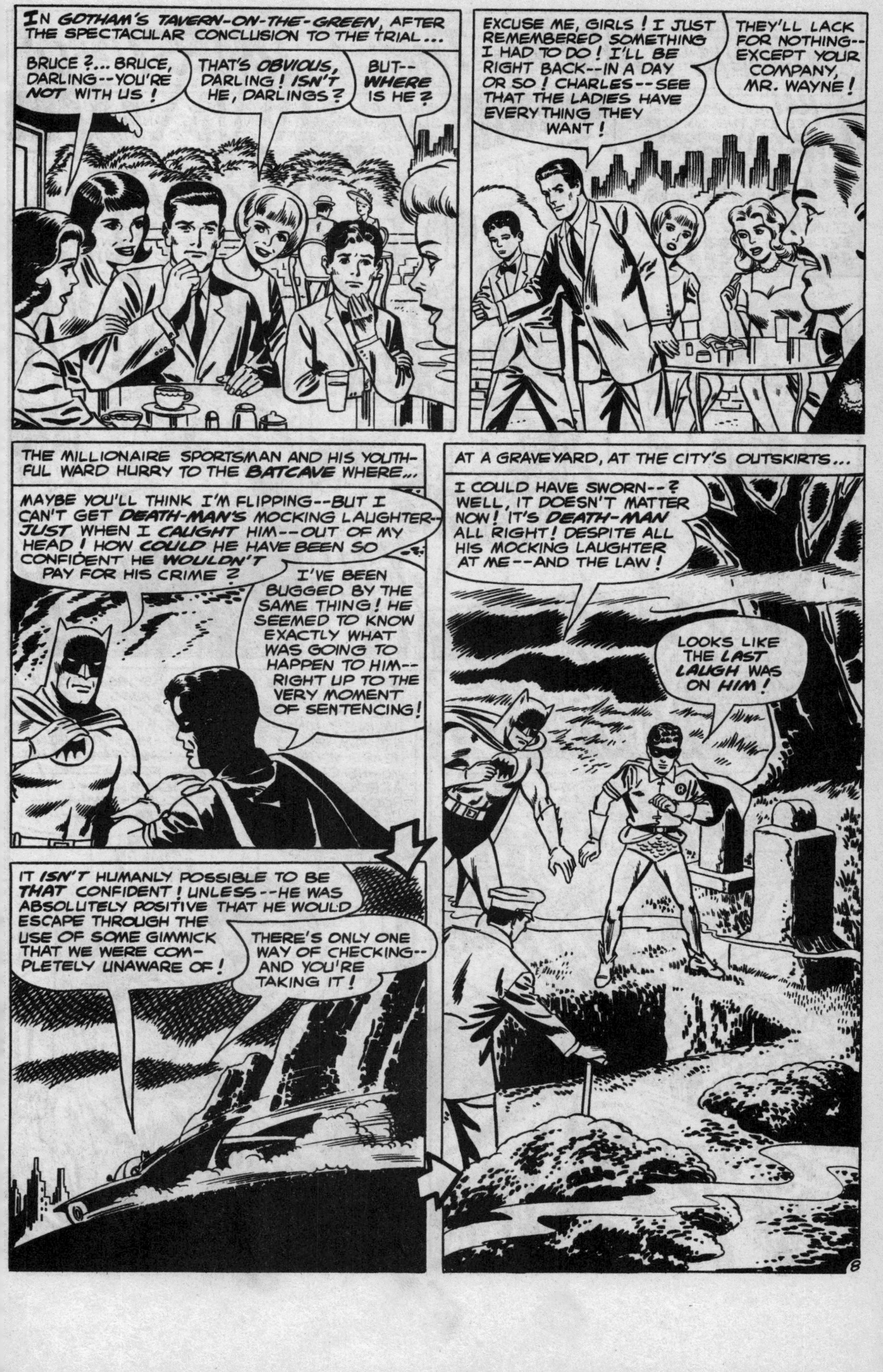
IN GOTHAM'S TAVERN-ON-THE-GREEN, AFTER THE SPECTACULAR CONCLUSION TO THE TRIAL...
BRUCE ?... BRUCE, DARLING--YOU'RE NOT WITH US !
THAT'S OBVIOUS, DARLING ! ISN'T HE, DARLINGS ?
BUT-- WHERE IS HE ?
EXCUSE ME, GIRLS ! I JUST REMEMBERED SOMETHING I HAD TO DO ! I'LL BE RIGHT BACK--IN A DAY OR SO ! CHARLES--SEE THAT THE LADIES HAVE EVERYTHING THEY WANT !
THEY'LL LACK FOR NOTHING--EXCEPT YOUR COMPANY, MR. WAYNE !
THE MILLIONAIRE SPORTSMAN AND HIS YOUTHFUL WARD HURRY TO THE BATCAVE WHERE...
MAYBE YOU'LL THINK I'M FLIPPING--BUT I CAN'T GET DEATH-MAN'S MOCKING LAUGHTER--JUST WHEN I CAUGHT HIM--OUT OF MY HEAD ! HOW COULD HE HAVE BEEN SO CONFIDENT HE WOULDN'T PAY FOR HIS CRIME ?
I'VE BEEN BUGGED BY THE SAME THING ! HE SEEMED TO KNOW EXACTLY WHAT WAS GOING TO HAPPEN TO HIM--RIGHT UP TO THE VERY MOMENT OF SENTENCING !
IT ISN'T HUMANLY POSSIBLE TO BE THAT CONFIDENT ! UNLESS--HE WAS ABSOLUTELY POSITIVE THAT HE WOULD ESCAPE THROUGH THE USE OF SOME GIMMICK THAT WE WERE COMPLETELY UNAWARE OF !
THERE'S ONLY ONE WAY OF CHECKING--AND YOU'RE TAKING IT !
AT A GRAVEYARD, AT THE CITY'S OUTSKIRTS...
I COULD HAVE SWORN--? WELL, IT DOESN'T MATTER NOW ! IT'S DEATH-MAN ALL RIGHT ! DESPITE ALL HIS MOCKING LAUGHTER AT ME--AND THE LAW !
LOOKS LIKE THE LAST LAUGH WAS ON HIM !
8

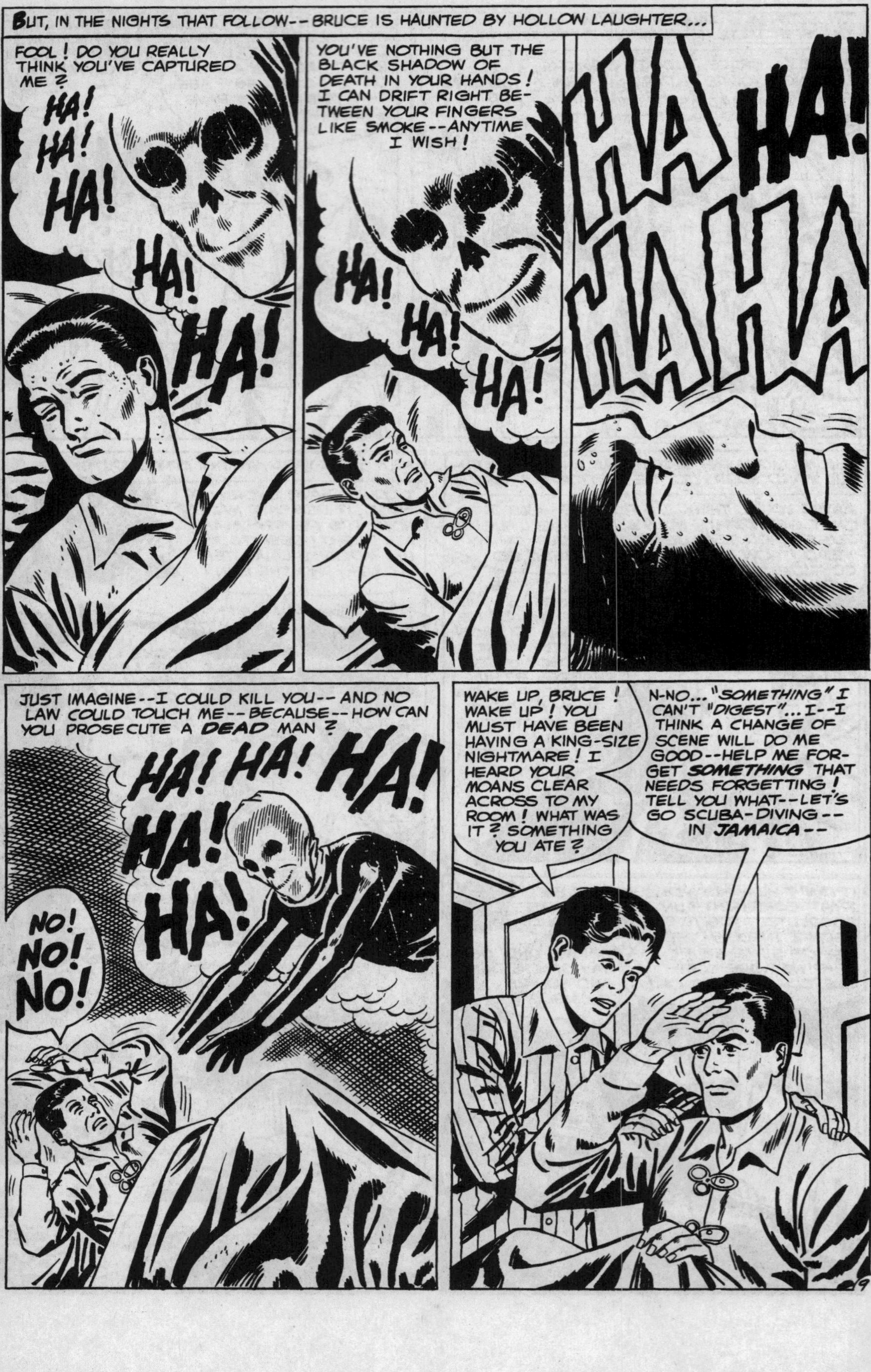
BUT, IN THE NIGHTS THAT FOLLOW--BRUCE IS HAUNTED BY HOLLOW LAUGHTER...
FOOL! DO YOU REALLY THINK YOU'VE CAPTURED ME?
HA! HA! HA!
HA! HA!
YOU'VE NOTHING BUT THE BLACK SHADOW OF DEATH IN YOUR HANDS! I CAN DRIFT RIGHT BETWEEN YOUR FINGERS LIKE SMOKE--ANYTIME I WISH!
HA! HA! HA!
HA HA! HA HA
JUST IMAGINE--I COULD KILL YOU--AND NO LAW COULD TOUCH ME--BECAUSE--HOW CAN YOU PROSECUTE A DEAD MAN?
HA! HA! HA! HA! HA!
NO! NO! NO!
WAKE UP, BRUCE! WAKE UP! YOU MUST HAVE BEEN HAVING A KING-SIZE NIGHTMARE! I HEARD YOUR MOANS CLEAR ACROSS TO MY ROOM! WHAT WAS IT? SOMETHING YOU ATE?
N-NO... "SOMETHING" I CAN'T "DIGEST"... I--I THINK A CHANGE OF SCENE WILL DO ME GOOD--HELP ME FORGET SOMETHING THAT NEEDS FORGETTING! TELL YOU WHAT--LET'S GO SCUBA-DIVING--IN JAMAICA--

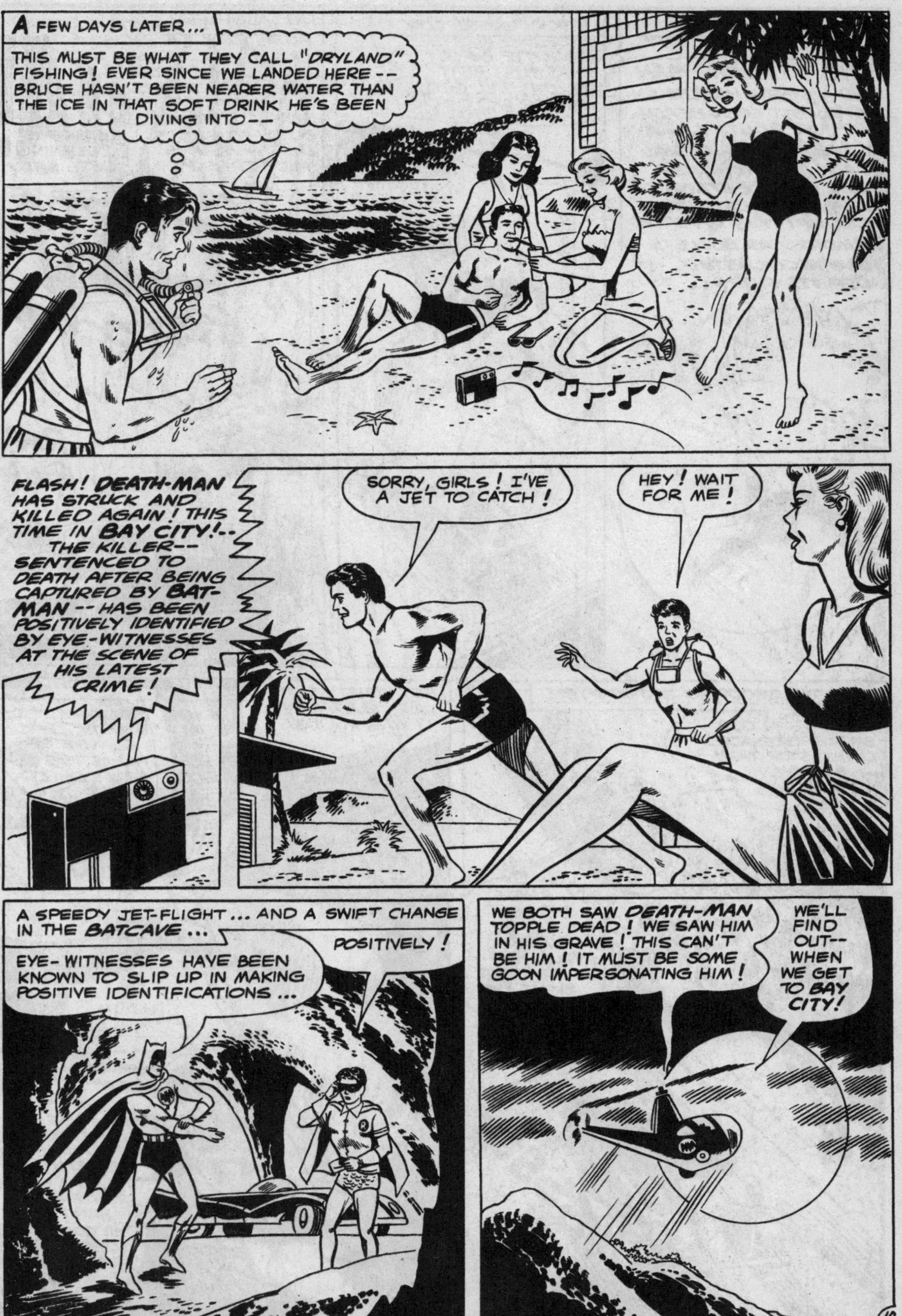
A FEW DAYS LATER...
THIS MUST BE WHAT THEY CALL "DRYLAND" FISHING! EVER SINCE WE LANDED HERE -- BRUCE HASN'T BEEN NEARER WATER THAN THE ICE IN THAT SOFT DRINK HE'S BEEN DIVING INTO--
FLASH! DEATH-MAN HAS STRUCK AND KILLED AGAIN! THIS TIME IN BAY CITY!-- THE KILLER-- SENTENCED TO DEATH AFTER BEING CAPTURED BY BATMAN -- HAS BEEN POSITIVELY IDENTIFIED BY EYE-WITNESSES AT THE SCENE OF HIS LATEST CRIME!
SORRY, GIRLS! I'VE A JET TO CATCH!
HEY! WAIT FOR ME!
A SPEEDY JET-FLIGHT ... AND A SWIFT CHANGE IN THE BATCAVE ...
EYE-WITNESSES HAVE BEEN KNOWN TO SLIP UP IN MAKING POSITIVE IDENTIFICATIONS ...
POSITIVELY!
WE BOTH SAW DEATH-MAN TOPPLE DEAD! WE SAW HIM IN HIS GRAVE! THIS CAN'T BE HIM! IT MUST BE SOME GOON IMPERSONATING HIM!
WE'LL FIND OUT-- WHEN WE GET TO BAY CITY!
10

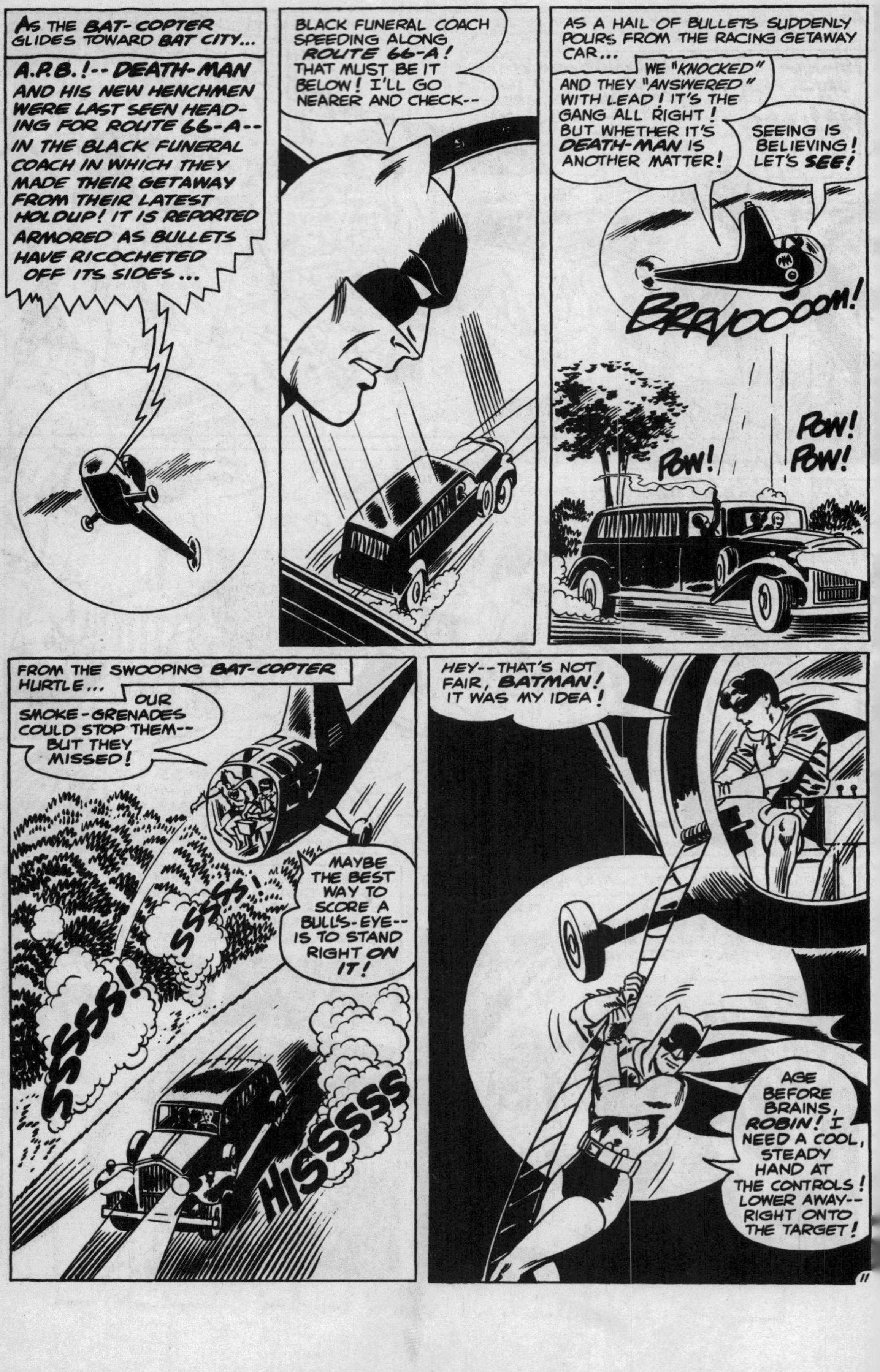
AS THE BAT-COPTER GLIDES TOWARD BAT CITY...
A.P.B.!--DEATH-MAN AND HIS NEW HENCHMEN WERE LAST SEEN HEADING FOR ROUTE 66-A--IN THE BLACK FUNERAL COACH IN WHICH THEY MADE THEIR GETAWAY FROM THEIR LATEST HOLDUP! IT IS REPORTED ARMORED AS BULLETS HAVE RICOCHETED OFF ITS SIDES...
BLACK FUNERAL COACH SPEEDING ALONG ROUTE 66-A! THAT MUST BE IT BELOW! I'LL GO NEARER AND CHECK--
AS A HAIL OF BULLETS SUDDENLY POURS FROM THE RACING GETAWAY CAR...
WE "KNOCKED" AND THEY "ANSWERED" WITH LEAD! IT'S THE GANG ALL RIGHT! BUT WHETHER IT'S DEATH-MAN IS ANOTHER MATTER!
SEEING IS BELIEVING! LET'S SEE!
BRRVOOOOOM!
POW!
POW! POW!
FROM THE SWOOPING BAT-COPTER HURTLE...
OUR SMOKE-GRENADES COULD STOP THEM--BUT THEY MISSED!
MAYBE THE BEST WAY TO SCORE A BULL'S-EYE--IS TO STAND RIGHT ON IT!
SSSSS!
SSSSS!
HISSSSSS
HEY--THAT'S NOT FAIR, BATMAN! IT WAS MY IDEA!
AGE BEFORE BRAINS, ROBIN! I NEED A COOL, STEADY HAND AT THE CONTROLS! LOWER AWAY--RIGHT ONTO THE TARGET!
11

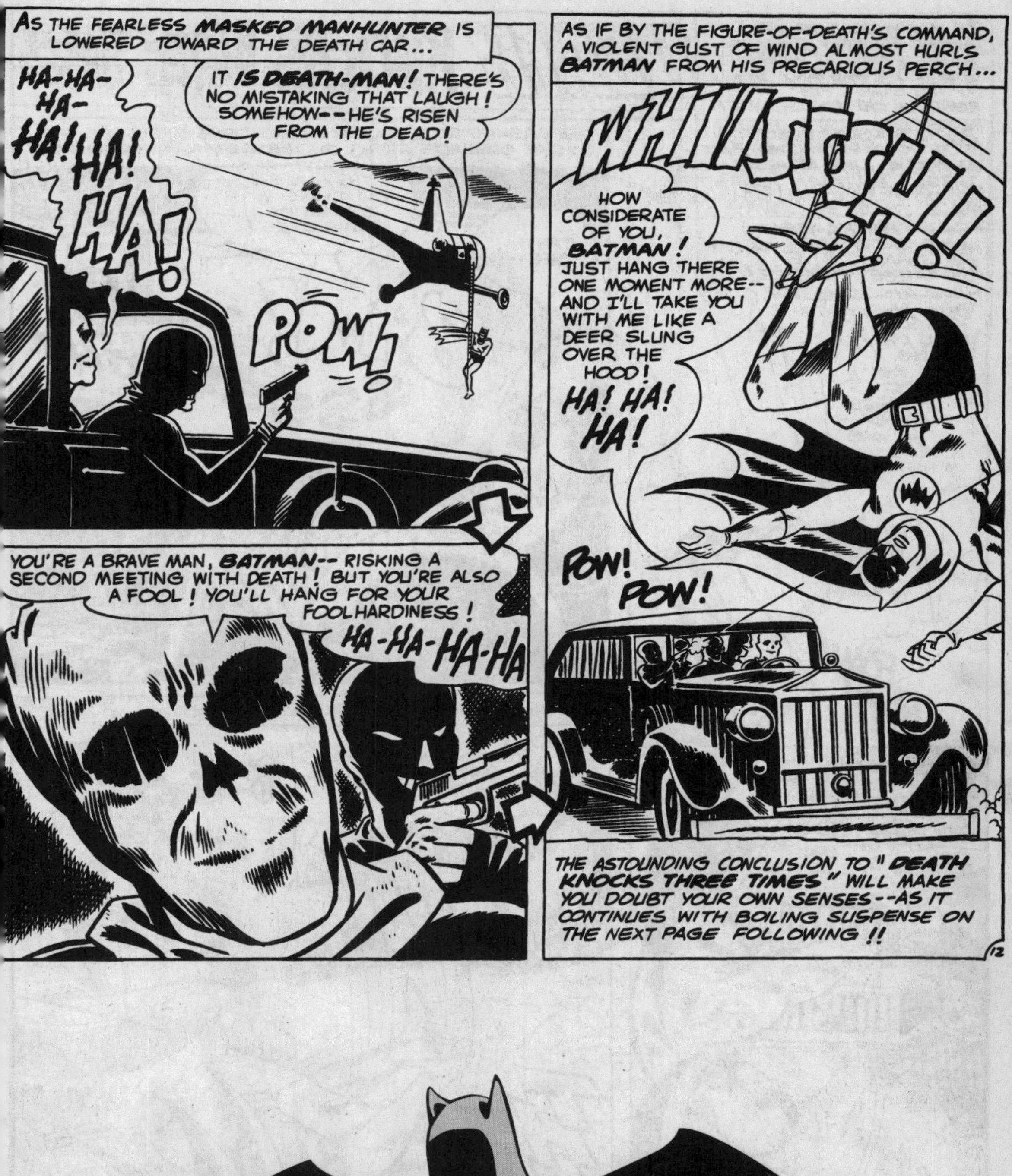
AS THE FEARLESS MASKED MANHUNTER IS LOWERED TOWARD THE DEATH CAR...
HA-HA-HA-HA! HA! HA!
IT IS DEATH-MAN! THERE'S NO MISTAKING THAT LAUGH! SOMEHOW--HE'S RISEN FROM THE DEAD!
POW!
AS IF BY THE FIGURE-OF-DEATH'S COMMAND, A VIOLENT GUST OF WIND ALMOST HURLS BATMAN FROM HIS PRECARIOUS PERCH...
WHIISSSH!!
HOW CONSIDERATE OF YOU, BATMAN! JUST HANG THERE ONE MOMENT MORE--AND I'LL TAKE YOU WITH ME LIKE A DEER SLUNG OVER THE HOOD! HA! HA! HA!
POW! POW!
YOU'RE A BRAVE MAN, BATMAN-- RISKING A SECOND MEETING WITH DEATH! BUT YOU'RE ALSO A FOOL! YOU'LL HANG FOR YOUR FOOLHARDINESS!
HA-HA-HA-HA
THE ASTOUNDING CONCLUSION TO "DEATH KNOCKS THREE TIMES" WILL MAKE YOU DOUBT YOUR OWN SENSES--AS IT CONTINUES WITH BOILING SUSPENSE ON THE NEXT PAGE FOLLOWING!!
12

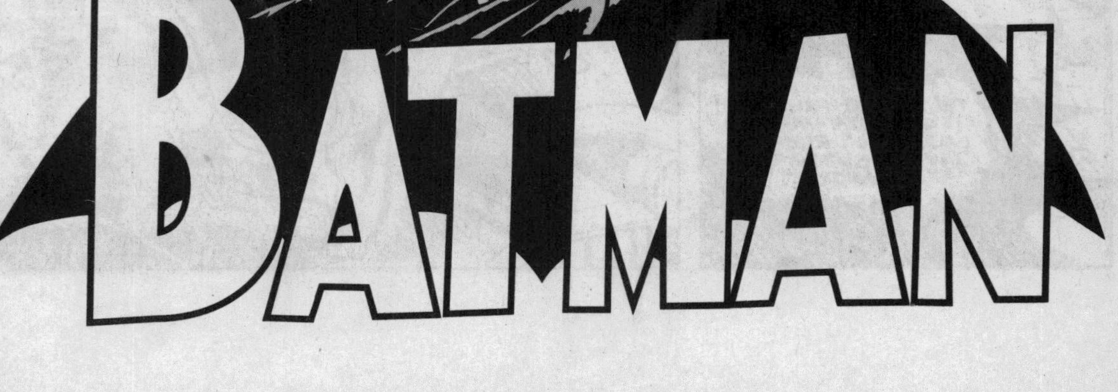
BATMAN

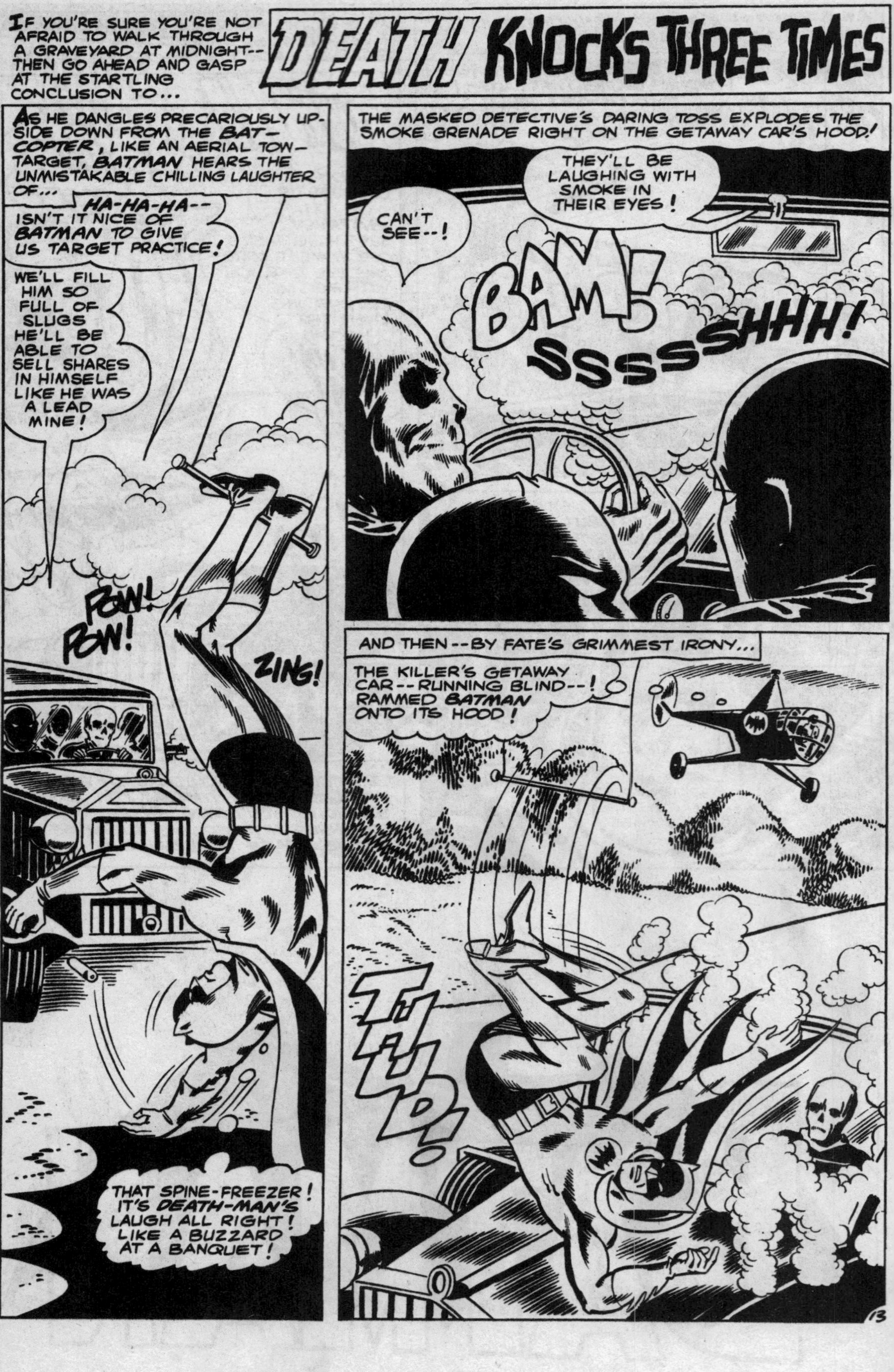
IF YOU'RE SURE YOU'RE NOT AFRAID TO WALK THROUGH A GRAVEYARD AT MIDNIGHT-- THEN GO AHEAD AND GASP AT THE STARTLING CONCLUSION TO...
DEATH KNOCKS THREE TIMES
AS HE DANGLES PRECARIOUSLY UPSIDE DOWN FROM THE BAT-COPTER, LIKE AN AERIAL TOW-TARGET, BATMAN HEARS THE UNMISTAKABLE CHILLING LAUGHTER OF...
HA-HA-HA-- ISN'T IT NICE OF BATMAN TO GIVE US TARGET PRACTICE!
WE'LL FILL HIM SO FULL OF SLUGS HE'LL BE ABLE TO SELL SHARES IN HIMSELF LIKE HE WAS A LEAD MINE!
POW! POW!
ZING!
THAT SPINE-FREEZER! IT'S DEATH-MAN'S LAUGH ALL RIGHT! LIKE A BUZZARD AT A BANQUET!
THE MASKED DETECTIVE'S DARING TOSS EXPLODES THE SMOKE GRENADE RIGHT ON THE GETAWAY CAR'S HOOD!
THEY'LL BE LAUGHING WITH SMOKE IN THEIR EYES!
CAN'T SEE--!
BAM!
SSSSSHHH!
AND THEN--BY FATE'S GRIMMEST IRONY...
THE KILLER'S GETAWAY CAR--RUNNING BLIND--! RAMMED BATMAN ONTO ITS HOOD!
THUD!
13

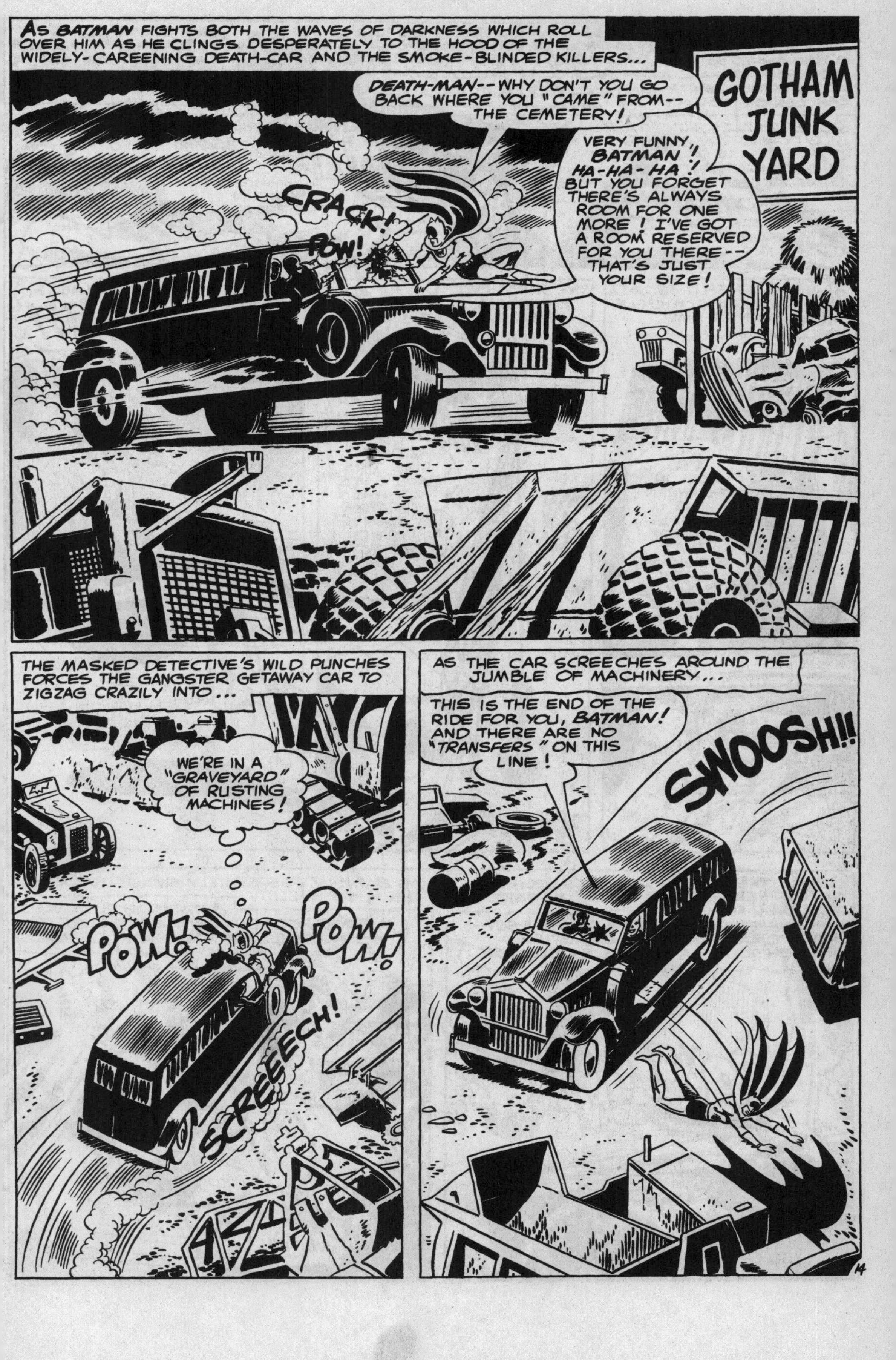
AS BATMAN FIGHTS BOTH THE WAVES OF DARKNESS WHICH ROLL OVER HIM AS HE CLINGS DESPERATELY TO THE HOOD OF THE WIDELY-CAREENING DEATH-CAR AND THE SMOKE-BLINDED KILLERS...
GOTHAM JUNK YARD
DEATH-MAN--WHY DON'T YOU GO BACK WHERE YOU "CAME" FROM--THE CEMETERY!
VERY FUNNY, BATMAN! HA-HA-HA! BUT YOU FORGET THERE'S ALWAYS ROOM FOR ONE MORE! I'VE GOT A ROOM RESERVED FOR YOU THERE--THAT'S JUST YOUR SIZE!
CRACK!
POW!
THE MASKED DETECTIVE'S WILD PUNCHES FORCES THE GANGSTER GETAWAY CAR TO ZIGZAG CRAZILY INTO...
WE'RE IN A "GRAVEYARD" OF RUSTING MACHINES!
POW!
POW!
SCREEECH!
AS THE CAR SCREECHES AROUND THE JUMBLE OF MACHINERY...
THIS IS THE END OF THE RIDE FOR YOU, BATMAN! AND THERE ARE NO "TRANSFERS" ON THIS LINE!
SWOOSH!!!
14

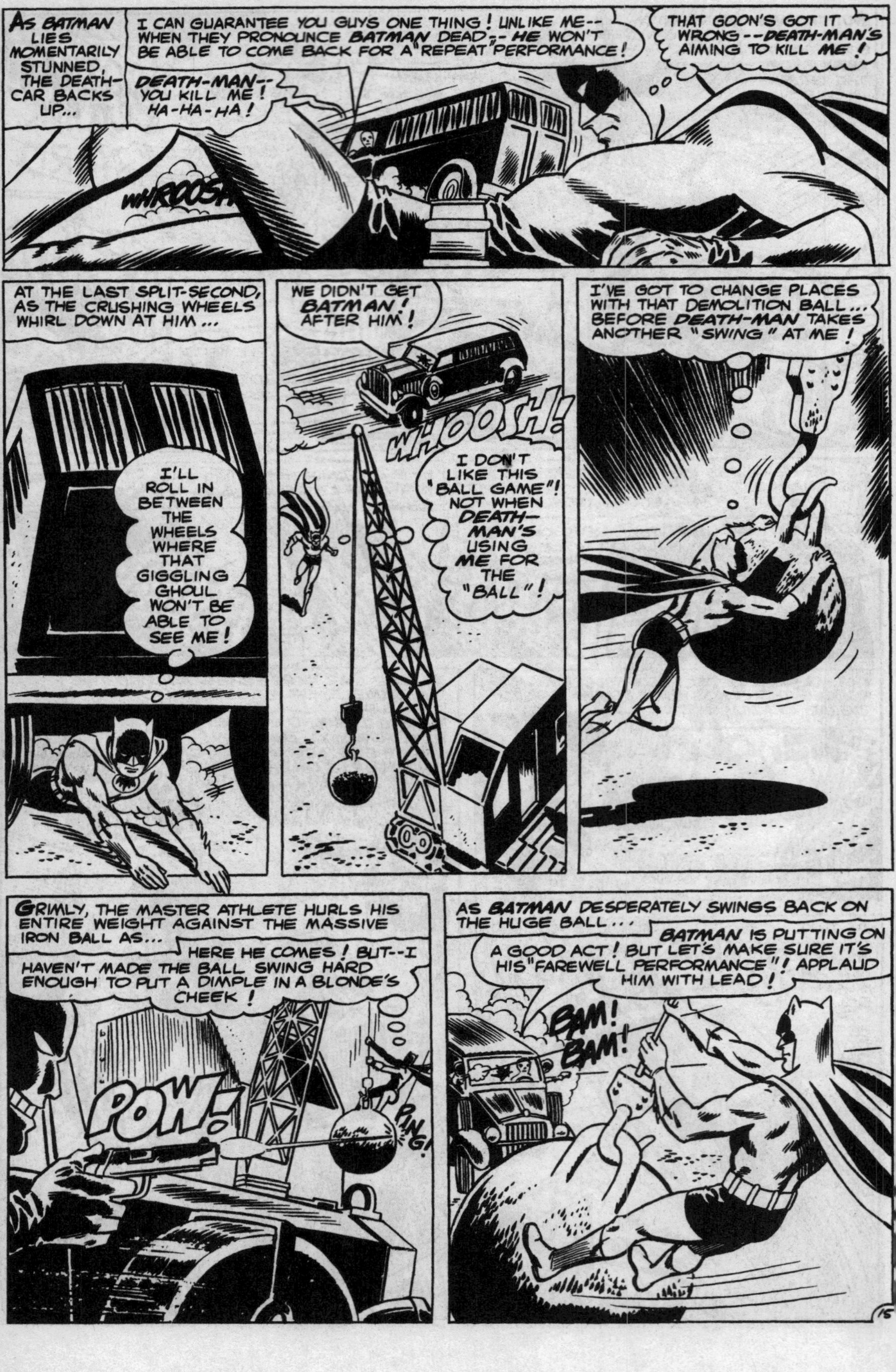
AS BATMAN LIES MOMENTARILY STUNNED, THE DEATH-CAR BACKS UP...
I CAN GUARANTEE YOU GUYS ONE THING! UNLIKE ME-- WHEN THEY PRONOUNCE BATMAN DEAD-- HE WON'T BE ABLE TO COME BACK FOR A "REPEAT PERFORMANCE"!
DEATH-MAN-- YOU KILL ME! HA-HA-HA!
THAT GOON'S GOT IT WRONG--DEATH-MAN'S AIMING TO KILL ME!
WHROOSH
AT THE LAST SPLIT-SECOND, AS THE CRUSHING WHEELS WHIRL DOWN AT HIM...
I'LL ROLL IN BETWEEN THE WHEELS WHERE THAT GIGGLING GHOUL WON'T BE ABLE TO SEE ME!
WE DIDN'T GET BATMAN! AFTER HIM!
WHOOSH!
I DON'T LIKE THIS "BALL GAME"! NOT WHEN DEATH-MAN'S USING ME FOR THE "BALL"!
I'VE GOT TO CHANGE PLACES WITH THAT DEMOLITION BALL... BEFORE DEATH-MAN TAKES ANOTHER "SWING" AT ME!
GRIMLY, THE MASTER ATHLETE HURLS HIS ENTIRE WEIGHT AGAINST THE MASSIVE IRON BALL AS...
HERE HE COMES! BUT--I HAVEN'T MADE THE BALL SWING HARD ENOUGH TO PUT A DIMPLE IN A BLONDE'S CHEEK!
POW!
PING!
AS BATMAN DESPERATELY SWINGS BACK ON THE HUGE BALL...
BATMAN IS PUTTING ON A GOOD ACT! BUT LET'S MAKE SURE IT'S HIS "FAREWELL PERFORMANCE"! APPLAUD HIM WITH LEAD!
BAM! BAM!
15

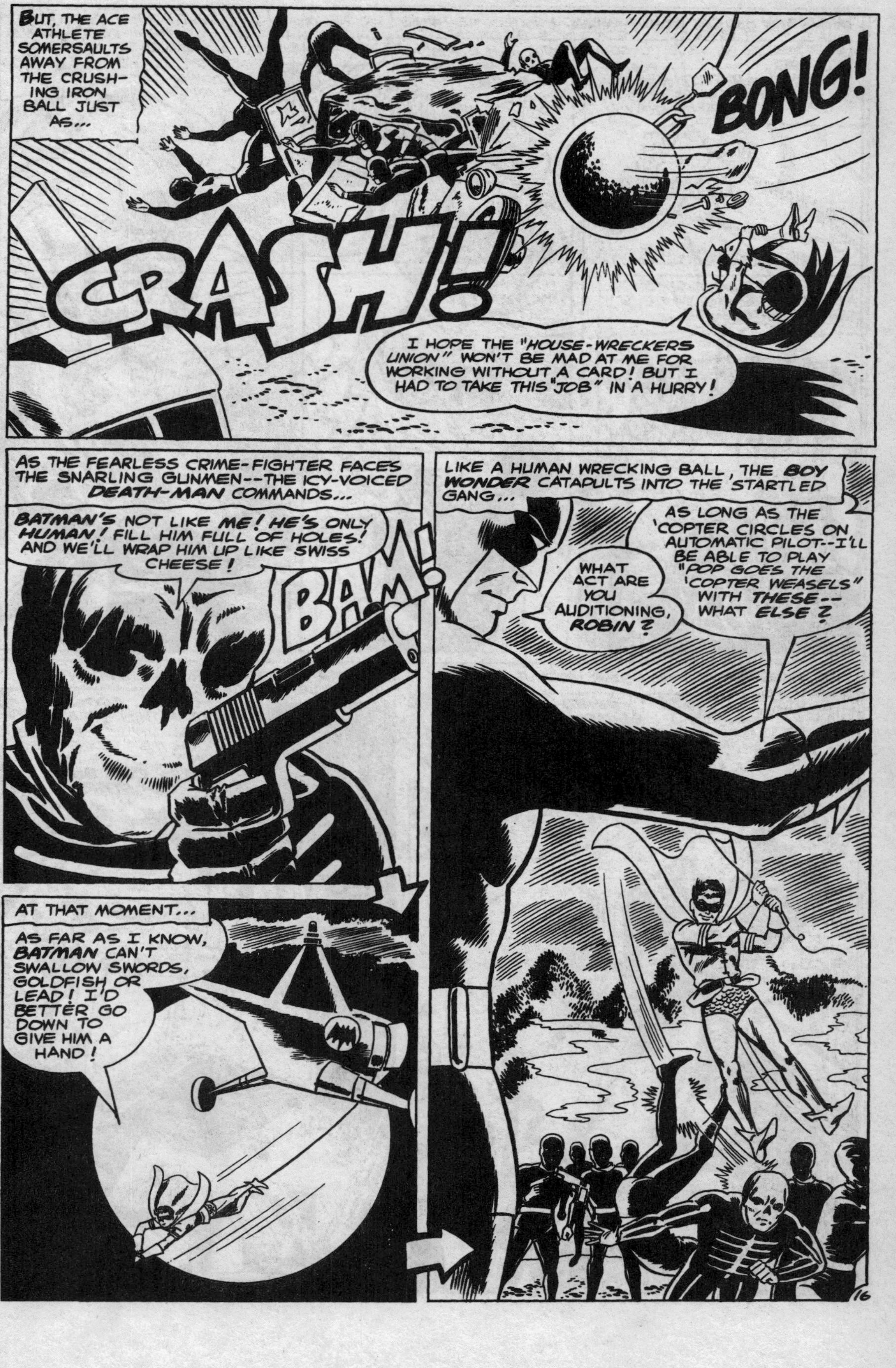
BUT, THE ACE ATHLETE SOMERSAULTS AWAY FROM THE CRUSHING IRON BALL JUST AS...
BONG!
CRASH!
I HOPE THE "HOUSE-WRECKERS UNION" WON'T BE MAD AT ME FOR WORKING WITHOUT A CARD! BUT I HAD TO TAKE THIS "JOB" IN A HURRY!
AS THE FEARLESS CRIME-FIGHTER FACES THE SNARLING GUNMEN--THE ICY-VOICED DEATH-MAN COMMANDS...
BATMAN'S NOT LIKE ME! HE'S ONLY HUMAN! FILL HIM FULL OF HOLES! AND WE'LL WRAP HIM UP LIKE SWISS CHEESE!
BAM!
AT THAT MOMENT...
AS FAR AS I KNOW, BATMAN CAN'T SWALLOW SWORDS, GOLDFISH OR LEAD! I'D BETTER GO DOWN TO GIVE HIM A HAND!
LIKE A HUMAN WRECKING BALL, THE BOY WONDER CATAPULTS INTO THE STARTLED GANG...
AS LONG AS THE 'COPTER CIRCLES ON AUTOMATIC PILOT--I'LL BE ABLE TO PLAY "POP GOES THE 'COPTER WEASELS" WITH THESE-- WHAT ELSE?
WHAT ACT ARE YOU AUDITIONING, ROBIN?
16

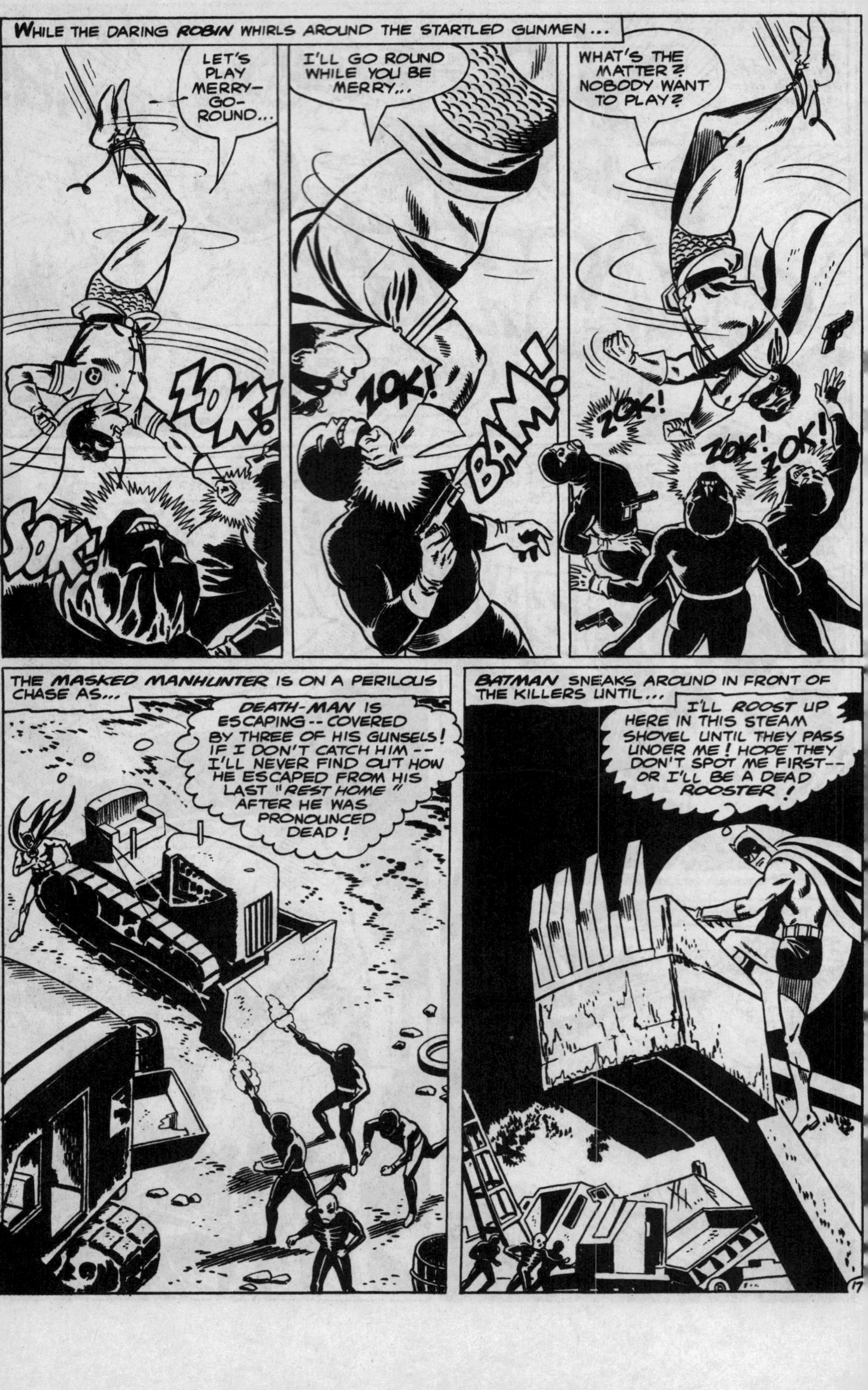
WHILE THE DARING ROBIN WHIRLS AROUND THE STARTLED GUNMEN...
LET'S PLAY MERRY-GO-ROUND...
ZOK!
SOK!
I'LL GO ROUND WHILE YOU BE MERRY...
ZOK!
BAM!
WHAT'S THE MATTER? NOBODY WANT TO PLAY?
ZOK!
ZOK!
ZOK!
THE MASKED MANHUNTER IS ON A PERILOUS CHASE AS...
DEATH-MAN IS ESCAPING--COVERED BY THREE OF HIS GUNSELS! IF I DON'T CATCH HIM--I'LL NEVER FIND OUT HOW HE ESCAPED FROM HIS LAST "REST HOME" AFTER HE WAS PRONOUNCED DEAD!
BATMAN SNEAKS AROUND IN FRONT OF THE KILLERS UNTIL...
I'LL ROOST UP HERE IN THIS STEAM SHOVEL UNTIL THEY PASS UNDER ME! HOPE THEY DON'T SPOT ME FIRST--OR I'LL BE A DEAD ROOSTER!
17

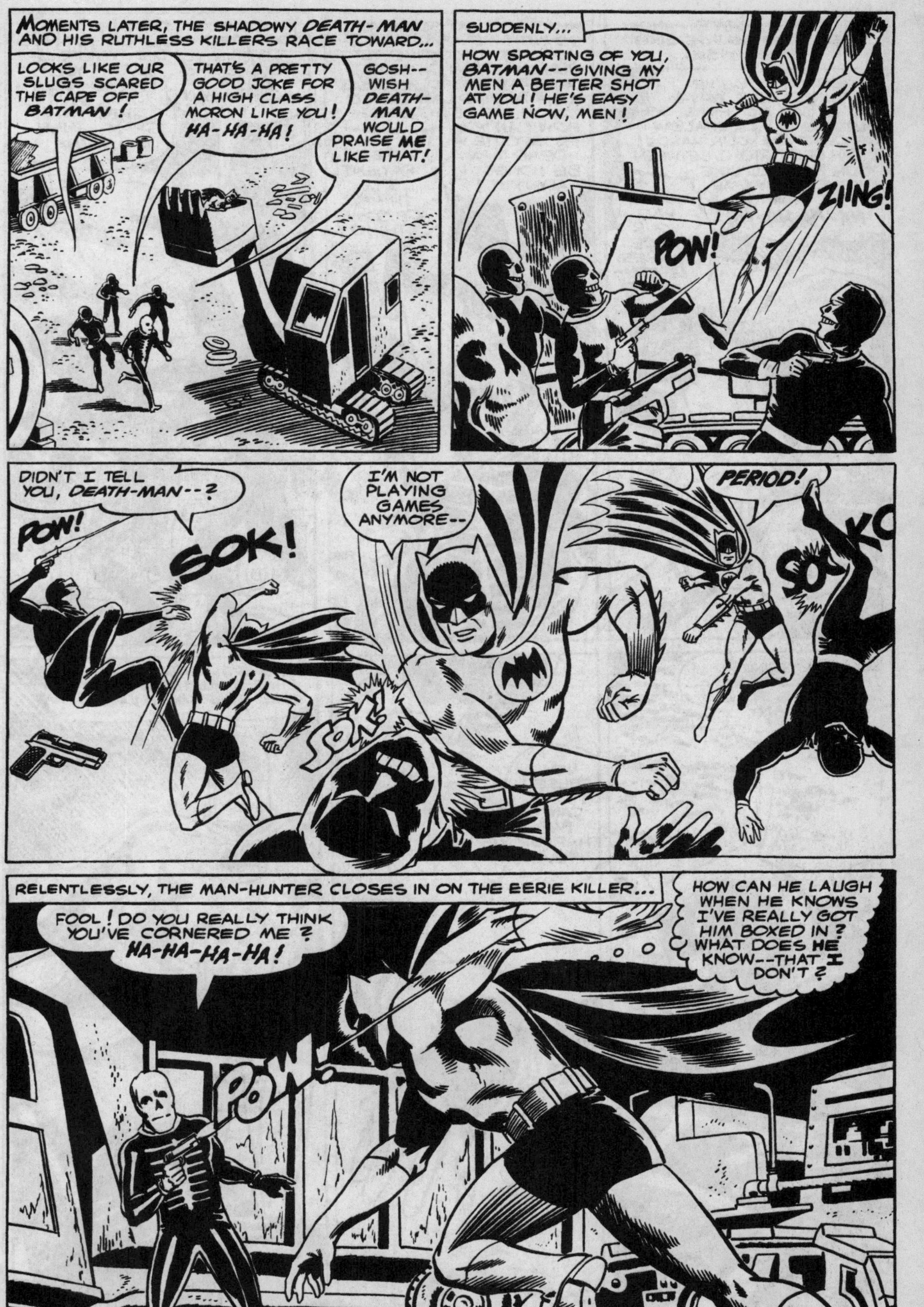
MOMENTS LATER, THE SHADOWY DEATH-MAN AND HIS RUTHLESS KILLERS RACE TOWARD...
LOOKS LIKE OUR SLUGS SCARED THE CAPE OFF BATMAN!
THAT'S A PRETTY GOOD JOKE FOR A HIGH CLASS MORON LIKE YOU! HA-HA-HA!
GOSH-- WISH DEATH-MAN WOULD PRAISE ME LIKE THAT!
SUDDENLY...
HOW SPORTING OF YOU, BATMAN--GIVING MY MEN A BETTER SHOT AT YOU! HE'S EASY GAME NOW, MEN!
ZIING!
POW!
DIDN'T I TELL YOU, DEATH-MAN--?
POW!
SOK!
I'M NOT PLAYING GAMES ANYMORE--
SOK!
PERIOD!
SOCK
RELENTLESSLY, THE MAN-HUNTER CLOSES IN ON THE EERIE KILLER...
FOOL! DO YOU REALLY THINK YOU'VE CORNERED ME? HA-HA-HA-HA!
HOW CAN HE LAUGH WHEN HE KNOWS I'VE REALLY GOT HIM BOXED IN? WHAT DOES HE KNOW--THAT I DON'T?
POW!
18

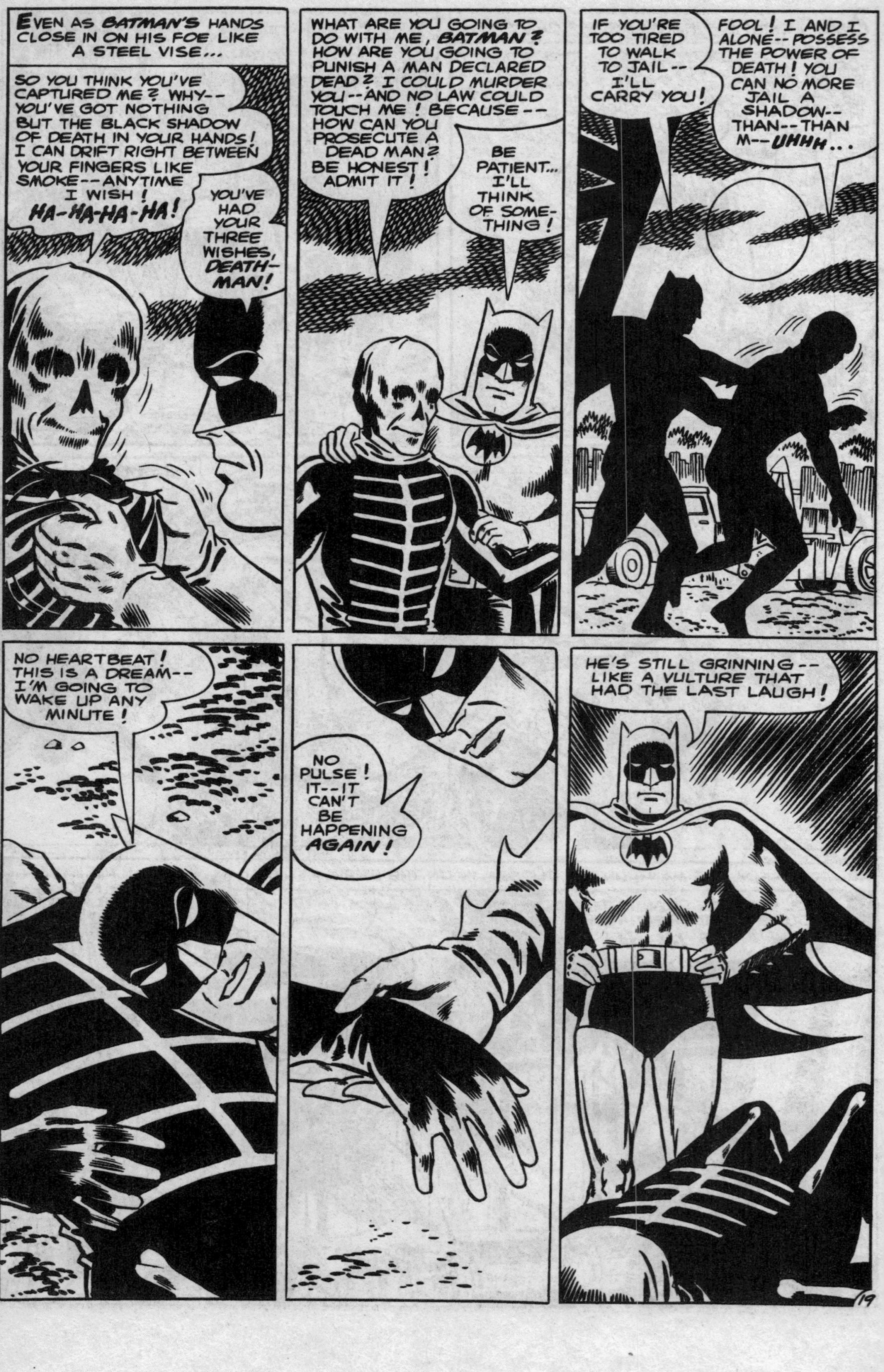
EVEN AS BATMAN'S HANDS CLOSE IN ON HIS FOE LIKE A STEEL VISE...
SO YOU THINK YOU'VE CAPTURED ME? WHY-- YOU'VE GOT NOTHING BUT THE BLACK SHADOW OF DEATH IN YOUR HANDS! I CAN DRIFT RIGHT BETWEEN YOUR FINGERS LIKE SMOKE--ANYTIME I WISH! HA-HA-HA-HA!
YOU'VE HAD YOUR THREE WISHES, DEATH-MAN!
WHAT ARE YOU GOING TO DO WITH ME, BATMAN? HOW ARE YOU GOING TO PUNISH A MAN DECLARED DEAD? I COULD MURDER YOU--AND NO LAW COULD TOUCH ME! BECAUSE-- HOW CAN YOU PROSECUTE A DEAD MAN? BE HONEST! ADMIT IT!
BE PATIENT... I'LL THINK OF SOME-THING!
IF YOU'RE TOO TIRED TO WALK TO JAIL-- I'LL CARRY YOU!
FOOL! I AND I ALONE--POSSESS THE POWER OF DEATH! YOU CAN NO MORE JAIL A SHADOW-- THAN--THAN M--UHHH...
NO HEARTBEAT! THIS IS A DREAM-- I'M GOING TO WAKE UP ANY MINUTE!
NO PULSE! IT--IT CAN'T BE HAPPENING AGAIN!
HE'S STILL GRINNING-- LIKE A VULTURE THAT HAD THE LAST LAUGH!
19

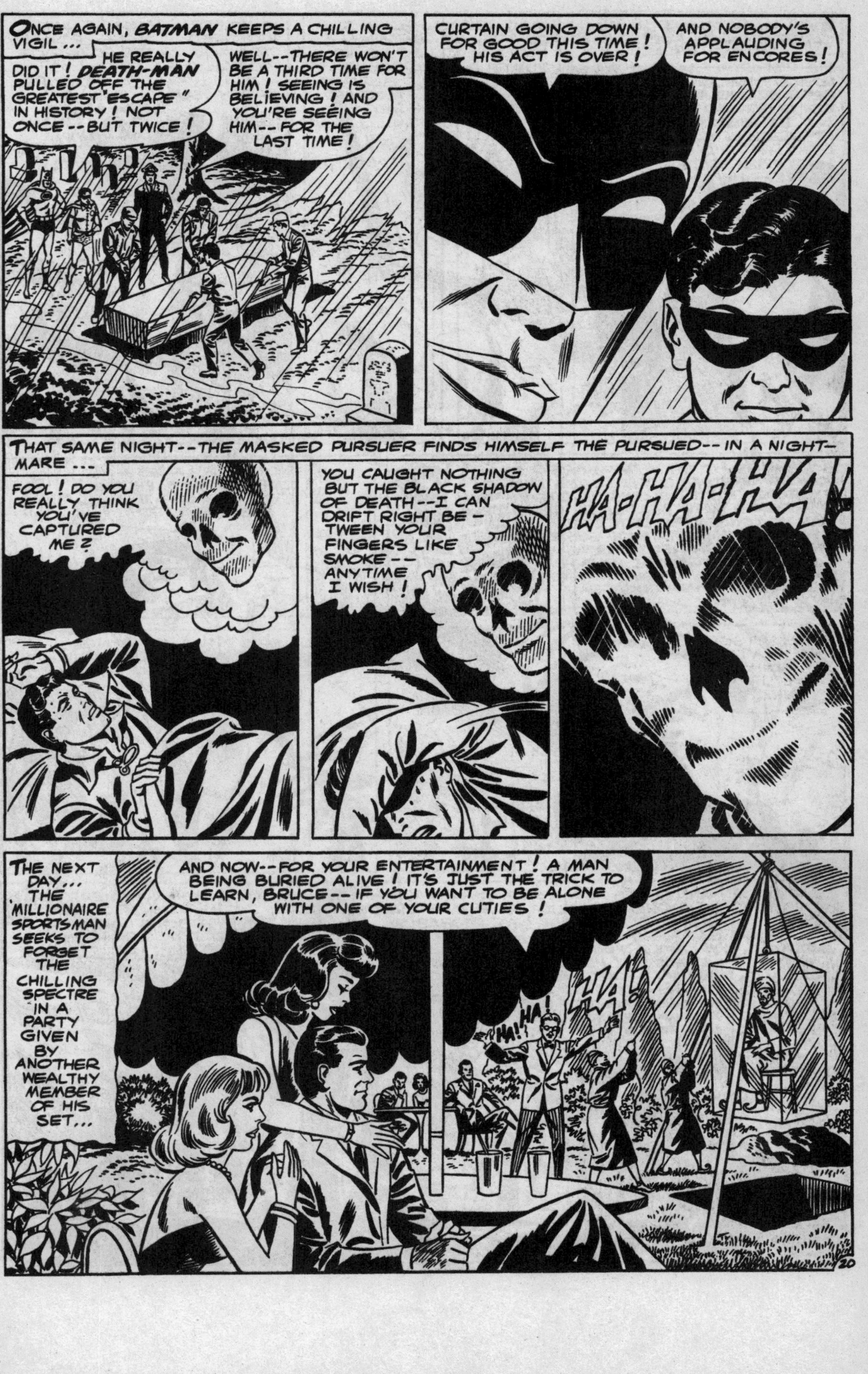
ONCE AGAIN, BATMAN KEEPS A CHILLING VIGIL...
HE REALLY DID IT! DEATH-MAN PULLED OFF THE GREATEST "ESCAPE" IN HISTORY! NOT ONCE--BUT TWICE!
WELL--THERE WON'T BE A THIRD TIME FOR HIM! SEEING IS BELIEVING! AND YOU'RE SEEING HIM--FOR THE LAST TIME!
CURTAIN GOING DOWN FOR GOOD THIS TIME! HIS ACT IS OVER!
AND NOBODY'S APPLAUDING FOR ENCORES!
THAT SAME NIGHT--THE MASKED PURSUER FINDS HIMSELF THE PURSUED--IN A NIGHT-MARE...
FOOL! DO YOU REALLY THINK YOU'VE CAPTURED ME?
YOU CAUGHT NOTHING BUT THE BLACK SHADOW OF DEATH--I CAN DRIFT RIGHT BE-TWEEN YOUR FINGERS LIKE SMOKE--ANYTIME I WISH!
HA-HA-HA!
THE NEXT DAY... THE MILLIONAIRE SPORTSMAN SEEKS TO FORGET THE CHILLING SPECTRE IN A PARTY GIVEN BY ANOTHER WEALTHY MEMBER OF HIS SET...
AND NOW--FOR YOUR ENTERTAINMENT! A MAN BEING BURIED ALIVE! IT'S JUST THE TRICK TO LEARN, BRUCE--IF YOU WANT TO BE ALONE WITH ONE OF YOUR CUTIES!
HA!
HA!
HA!
20

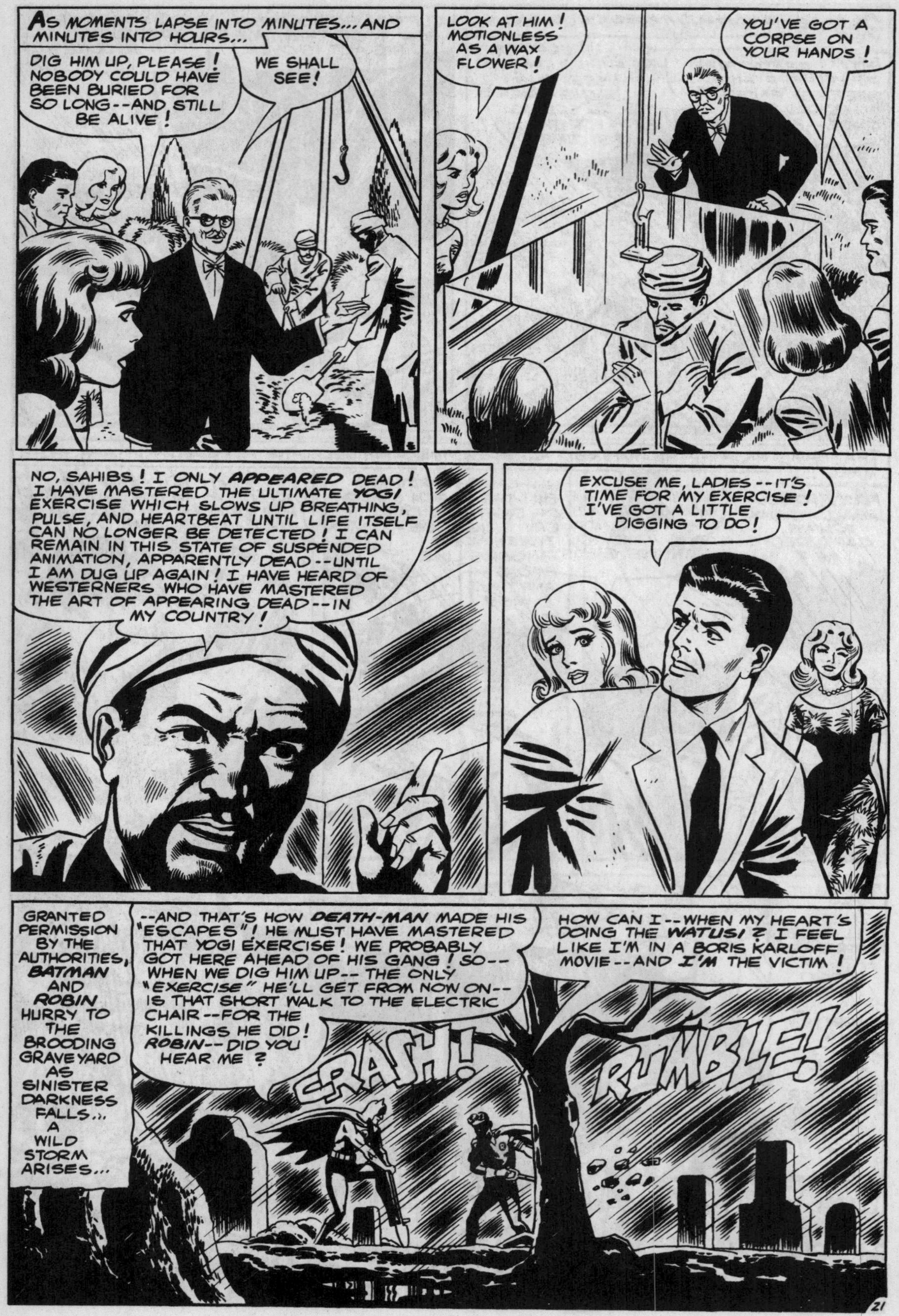
AS MOMENTS LAPSE INTO MINUTES... AND MINUTES INTO HOURS...
DIG HIM UP, PLEASE! NOBODY COULD HAVE BEEN BURIED FOR SO LONG--AND STILL BE ALIVE!
WE SHALL SEE!
LOOK AT HIM! MOTIONLESS AS A WAX FLOWER!
YOU'VE GOT A CORPSE ON YOUR HANDS!
NO, SAHIBS! I ONLY APPEARED DEAD! I HAVE MASTERED THE ULTIMATE YOGI EXERCISE WHICH SLOWS UP BREATHING, PULSE, AND HEARTBEAT UNTIL LIFE ITSELF CAN NO LONGER BE DETECTED! I CAN REMAIN IN THIS STATE OF SUSPENDED ANIMATION, APPARENTLY DEAD--UNTIL I AM DUG UP AGAIN! I HAVE HEARD OF WESTERNERS WHO HAVE MASTERED THE ART OF APPEARING DEAD--IN MY COUNTRY!
EXCUSE ME, LADIES--IT'S TIME FOR MY EXERCISE! I'VE GOT A LITTLE DIGGING TO DO!
GRANTED PERMISSION BY THE AUTHORITIES, BATMAN AND ROBIN HURRY TO THE BROODING GRAVEYARD AS SINISTER DARKNESS FALLS... A WILD STORM ARISES...
--AND THAT'S HOW DEATH-MAN MADE HIS "ESCAPES"! HE MUST HAVE MASTERED THAT YOGI EXERCISE! WE PROBABLY GOT HERE AHEAD OF HIS GANG! SO--WHEN WE DIG HIM UP-- THE ONLY "EXERCISE" HE'LL GET FROM NOW ON--IS THAT SHORT WALK TO THE ELECTRIC CHAIR--FOR THE KILLINGS HE DID! ROBIN--DID YOU HEAR ME?
HOW CAN I--WHEN MY HEART'S DOING THE WATUSI? I FEEL LIKE I'M IN A BORIS KARLOFF MOVIE--AND I'M THE VICTIM!
CRASH!
RUMBLE!
21

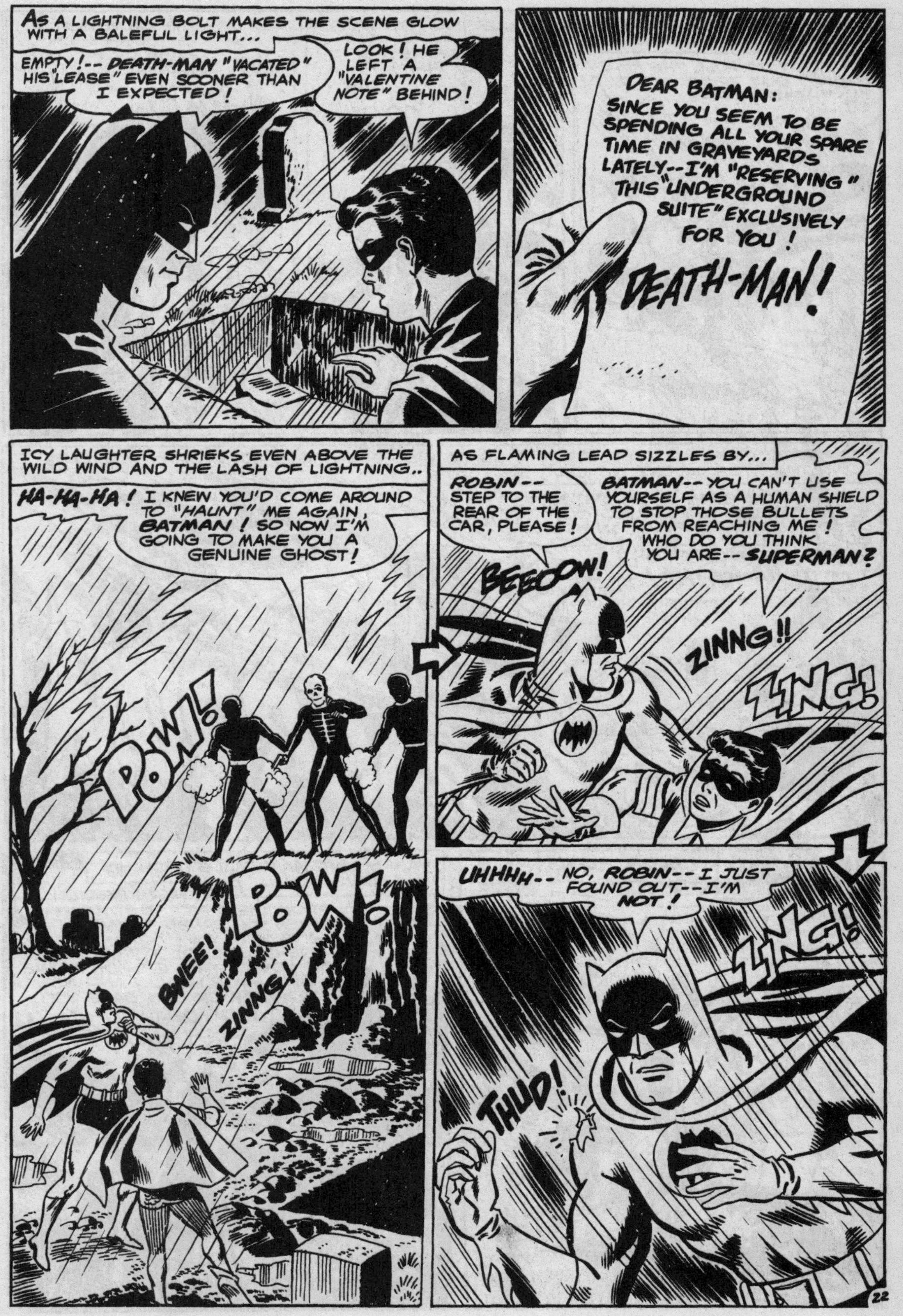
AS A LIGHTNING BOLT MAKES THE SCENE GLOW WITH A BALEFUL LIGHT...
EMPTY!-- DEATH-MAN "VACATED" HIS "LEASE" EVEN SOONER THAN I EXPECTED!
LOOK! HE LEFT A "VALENTINE NOTE" BEHIND!
DEAR BATMAN: SINCE YOU SEEM TO BE SPENDING ALL YOUR SPARE TIME IN GRAVEYARDS LATELY--I'M "RESERVING" THIS "UNDERGROUND SUITE" EXCLUSIVELY FOR YOU! DEATH-MAN!
ICY LAUGHTER SHRIEKS EVEN ABOVE THE WILD WIND AND THE LASH OF LIGHTNING..
HA-HA-HA! I KNEW YOU'D COME AROUND TO "HAUNT" ME AGAIN, BATMAN! SO NOW I'M GOING TO MAKE YOU A GENUINE GHOST!
POW!
POW!
BWEE!
ZINNG!
AS FLAMING LEAD SIZZLES BY...
ROBIN-- STEP TO THE REAR OF THE CAR, PLEASE!
BATMAN-- YOU CAN'T USE YOURSELF AS A HUMAN SHIELD TO STOP THOSE BULLETS FROM REACHING ME! WHO DO YOU THINK YOU ARE-- SUPERMAN?
BEEOOW!
ZINNG!!
ZING!
UHHHH-- NO, ROBIN-- I JUST FOUND OUT--I'M NOT!
ZING!
THUD!
22

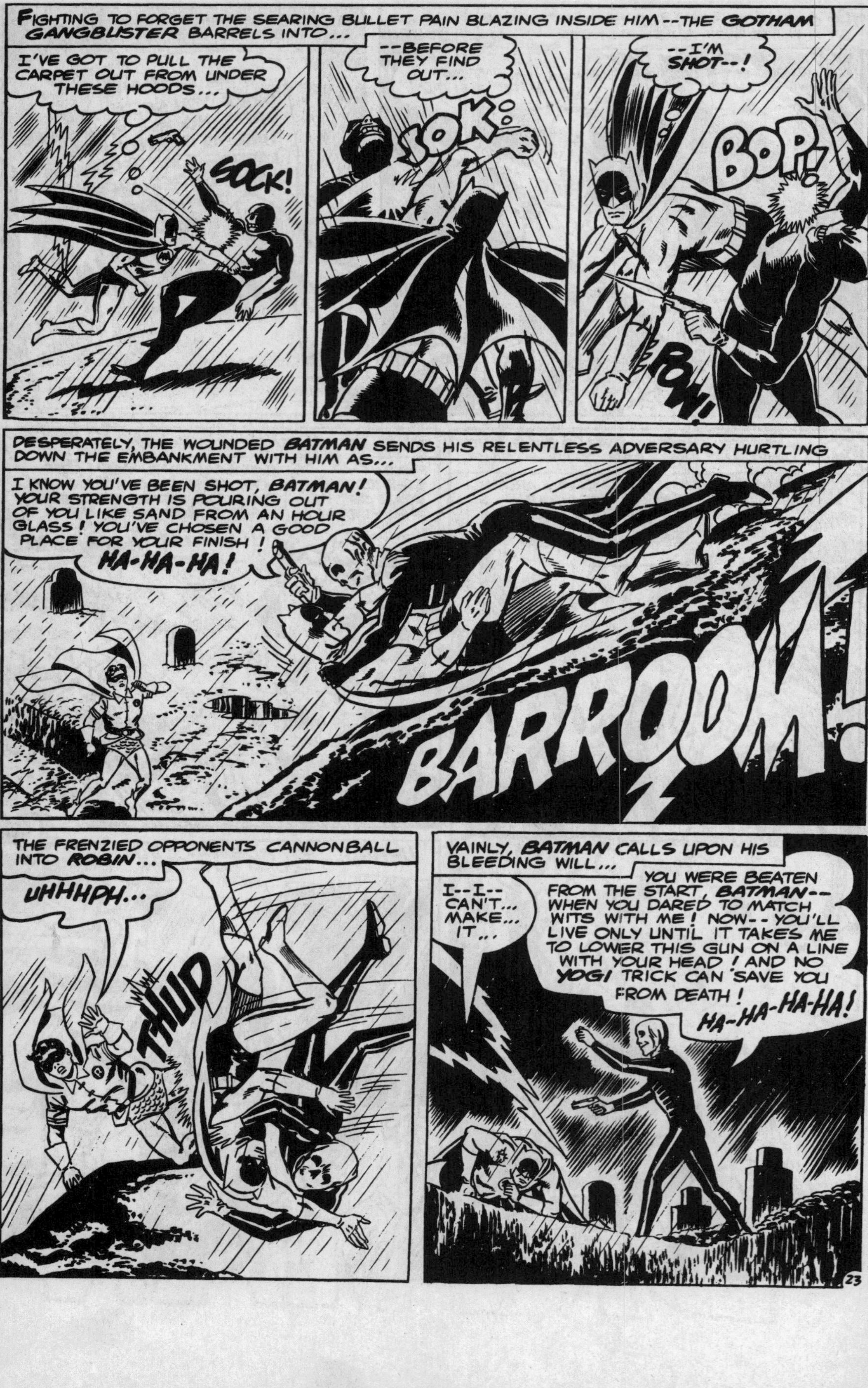
FIGHTING TO FORGET THE SEARING BULLET PAIN BLAZING INSIDE HIM--THE GOTHAM GANGBUSTER BARRELS INTO...
I'VE GOT TO PULL THE CARPET OUT FROM UNDER THESE HOODS...
SOCK!
--BEFORE THEY FIND OUT...
SOK
--I'M SHOT--!
BOP!
POW!
DESPERATELY, THE WOUNDED BATMAN SENDS HIS RELENTLESS ADVERSARY HURTLING DOWN THE EMBANKMENT WITH HIM AS...
I KNOW YOU'VE BEEN SHOT, BATMAN! YOUR STRENGTH IS POURING OUT OF YOU LIKE SAND FROM AN HOUR GLASS! YOU'VE CHOSEN A GOOD PLACE FOR YOUR FINISH! HA-HA-HA!
BARROOM!
THE FRENZIED OPPONENTS CANNONBALL INTO ROBIN...
UHHHPH...
THUD
VAINLY, BATMAN CALLS UPON HIS BLEEDING WILL...
I--I--CAN'T... MAKE... IT...
YOU WERE BEATEN FROM THE START, BATMAN--WHEN YOU DARED TO MATCH WITS WITH ME! NOW--YOU'LL LIVE ONLY UNTIL IT TAKES ME TO LOWER THIS GUN ON A LINE WITH YOUR HEAD! AND NO YOGI TRICK CAN SAVE YOU FROM DEATH! HA-HA-HA-HA!
23

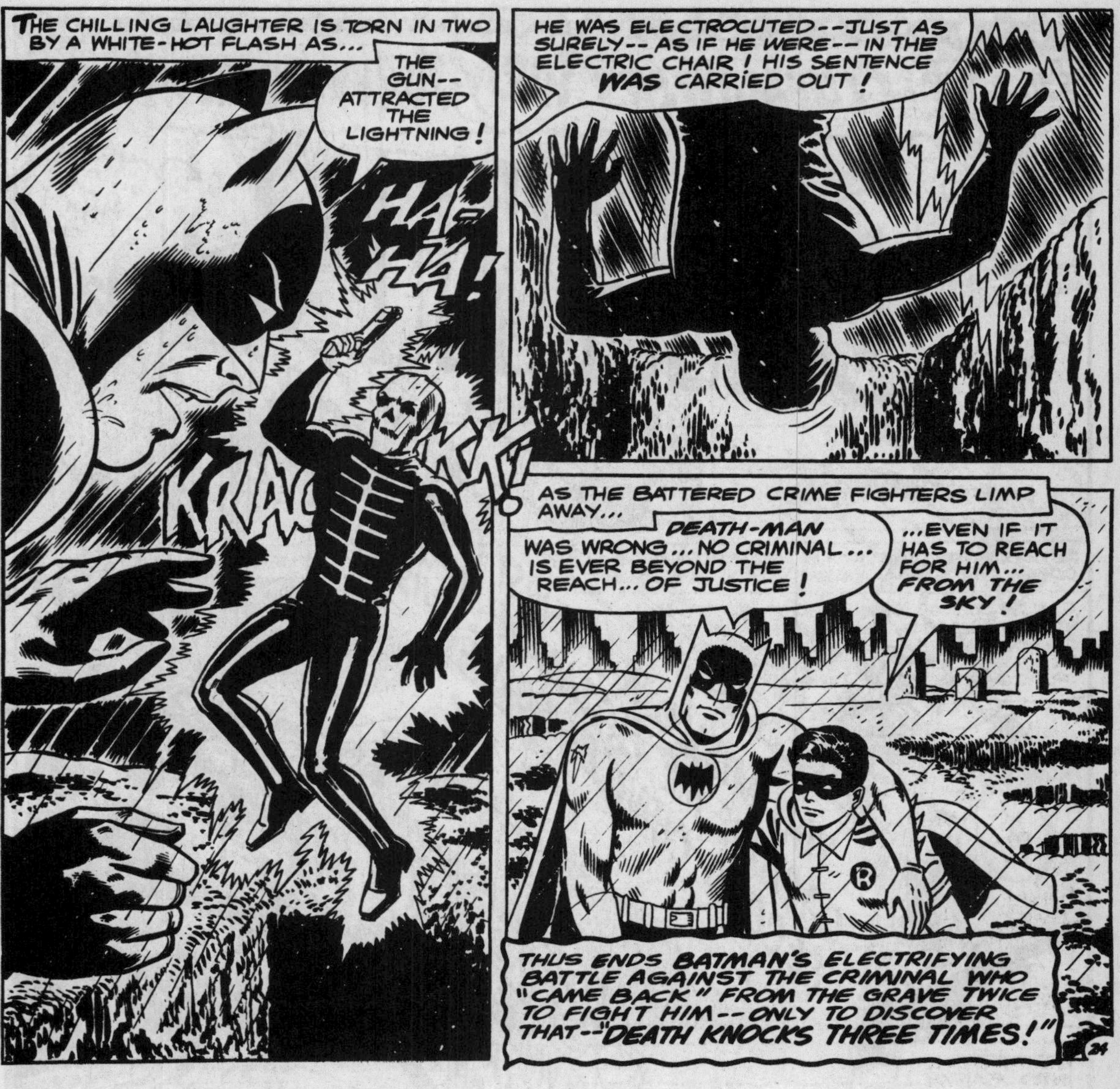
THE CHILLING LAUGHTER IS TORN IN TWO BY A WHITE-HOT FLASH AS...
THE GUN-- ATTRACTED THE LIGHTNING!
HA-HA!
KRACKKK!
HE WAS ELECTROCUTED--JUST AS SURELY-- AS IF HE WERE-- IN THE ELECTRIC CHAIR! HIS SENTENCE WAS CARRIED OUT!
AS THE BATTERED CRIME FIGHTERS LIMP AWAY...
DEATH-MAN WAS WRONG... NO CRIMINAL... IS EVER BEYOND THE REACH... OF JUSTICE!
...EVEN IF IT HAS TO REACH FOR HIM... FROM THE SKY!
THUS ENDS BATMAN'S ELECTRIFYING BATTLE AGAINST THE CRIMINAL WHO "CAME BACK" FROM THE GRAVE TWICE TO FIGHT HIM--ONLY TO DISCOVER THAT--"DEATH KNOCKS THREE TIMES!"
24

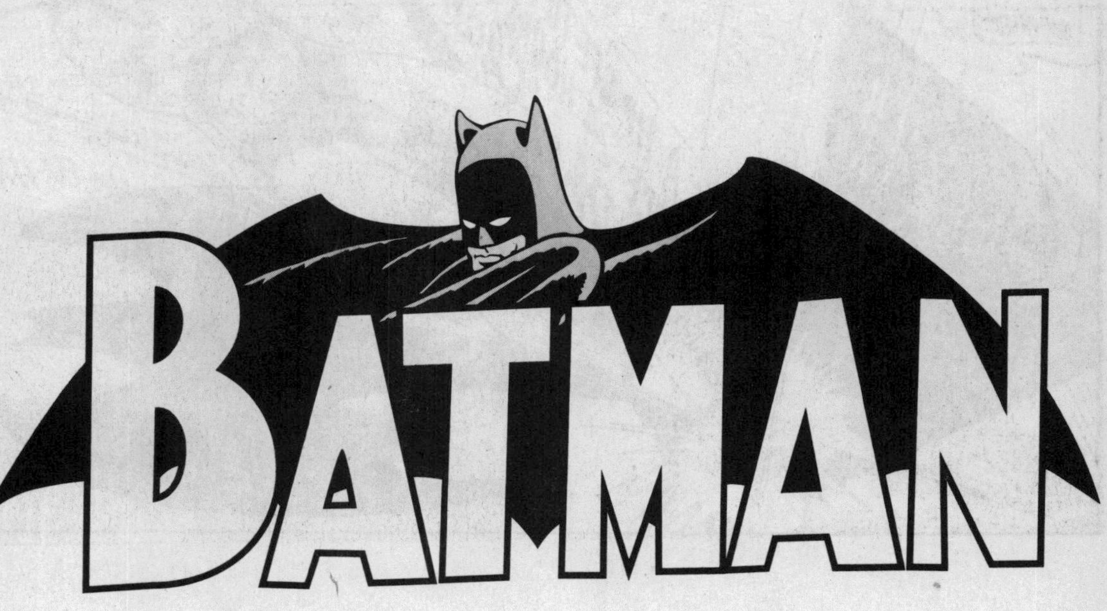
BATMAN

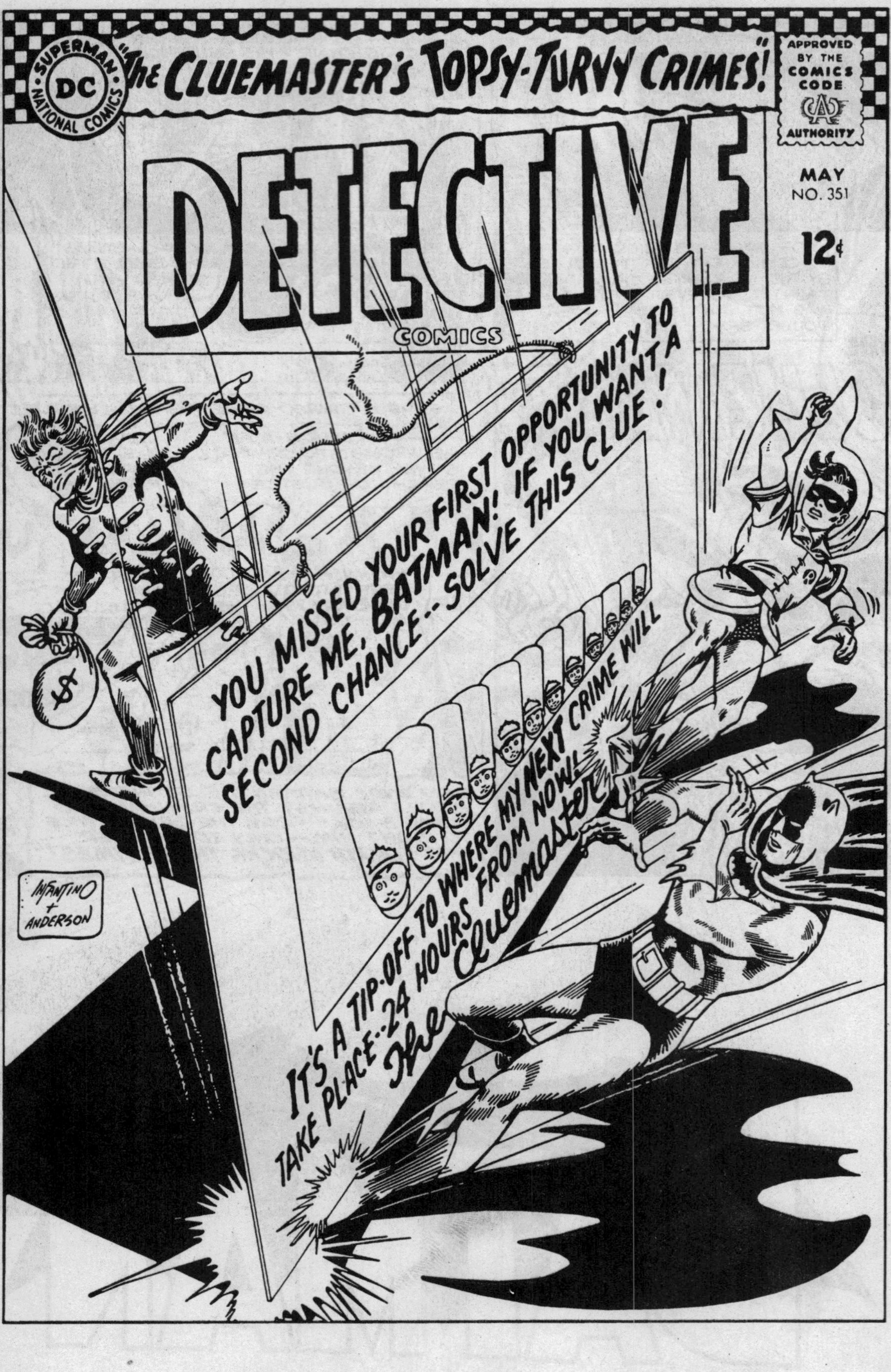
SUPERMAN DC NATIONAL COMICS
"The CLUEMASTER's TOPSY-TURVY CRIMES!"
APPROVED BY THE COMICS CODE AUTHORITY
DETECTIVE COMICS
MAY NO. 351
12¢
YOU MISSED YOUR FIRST OPPORTUNITY TO CAPTURE ME, BATMAN! IF YOU WANT A SECOND CHANCE--SOLVE THIS CLUE!
IT'S A TIP-OFF TO WHERE MY NEXT CRIME WILL TAKE PLACE--24 HOURS FROM NOW!
The Cluemaster
$
INFANTINO + ANDERSON

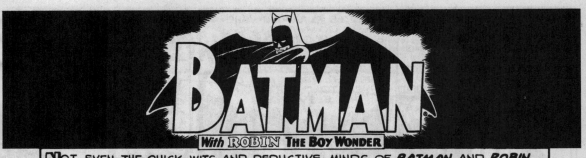

BATMAN
With ROBIN The Boy Wonder

NOT EVEN THE QUICK WITS AND DEDUCTIVE MINDS OF *BATMAN* AND *ROBIN* COULD FATHOM THE CLUES LEFT FOR THEM AT EVERY CRIME COMMITTED BY THE NEW ARCH-CRIMINAL, *THE CLUEMASTER!* THEY WERE TRICKED AND TAUNTED AT EVERY TURN BY THIS STRANGEST OF CROOKS-- WHOSE MOTIVE WAS NOT JUST ROBBERY BUT SOMETHING SO DARINGLY DIFFERENT THAT IT WOULD BRING ABOUT A MONUMENTAL FIRST IN CRIMEDOM !

THE CLUEMASTER'S TOPSY-TURVY CRIMES!

HA! HA! HA! BATMAN--YOU'VE JUST BEEN INTRODUCED TO *THE CLUEMASTER!* YOU'VE FOUND ME--ONLY TO LOSE ME! BUT DON'T DESPAIR-- I'LL LEAVE A *CLUE* FOR YOU TO TRACK ME DOWN-- IF YOU *DARE!*

CRAAAASHH

As aunt harriet goes about her daily chores of keeping the bruce wayne mansion spick-and-span, she uses some extra "elbow grease" on a wall -- and ...

OH, MY GOODNESS-- A PANEL IN THE WALL'S SLIDING OPEN!

A little fearfully, she peers down the long elevator shaft...

WHERE IN THE WORLD DOES *THIS* GO? ODD THAT NEITHER BRUCE NOR DICK EVER TOLD ME ABOUT THIS *ELEVATOR*!

She presses the button for the car and moments later, rides it down into a great sprawling cave...

WHERE AM I? OH MY GOODNESS. A SCIENTIFIC LABORATORY--*BATARANGS* ON THE WALL--*BATMAN* AND *ROBIN* COSTUMES! I MUST BE IN THEIR SECRET HIDE-OUT--THE FAMOUS *BATCAVE*!

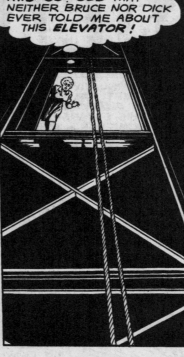

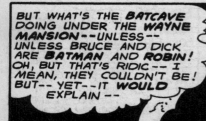

BUT WHAT'S THE *BATCAVE* DOING UNDER THE *WAYNE* MANSION--UNLESS-- UNLESS BRUCE AND DICK ARE *BATMAN* AND *ROBIN*! OH, BUT THAT'S RIDIC-- I MEAN, THEY COULDN'T BE! BUT-- YET--IT *WOULD* EXPLAIN --

Suddenly, the roar of an automobile motor startles the woman...

VRRR ROOMMMM

SOMEBODY'S COMING IN ANOTHER WAY! I DON'T WANT TO BE CAUGHT IN HERE! I'LL PRETEND NOTHING'S HAPPENED

She rides the elevator upstairs, makes a hurried exit --

HOLD IT, HATTIE! DON'T PANIC! YOU CAN'T LEAVE THE CAR UP HERE! BETTER SEND IT DOWN AS IT WAS ORIGINALLY-- OR THEY'LL SUSPECT WHAT I'VE FOUND OUT!

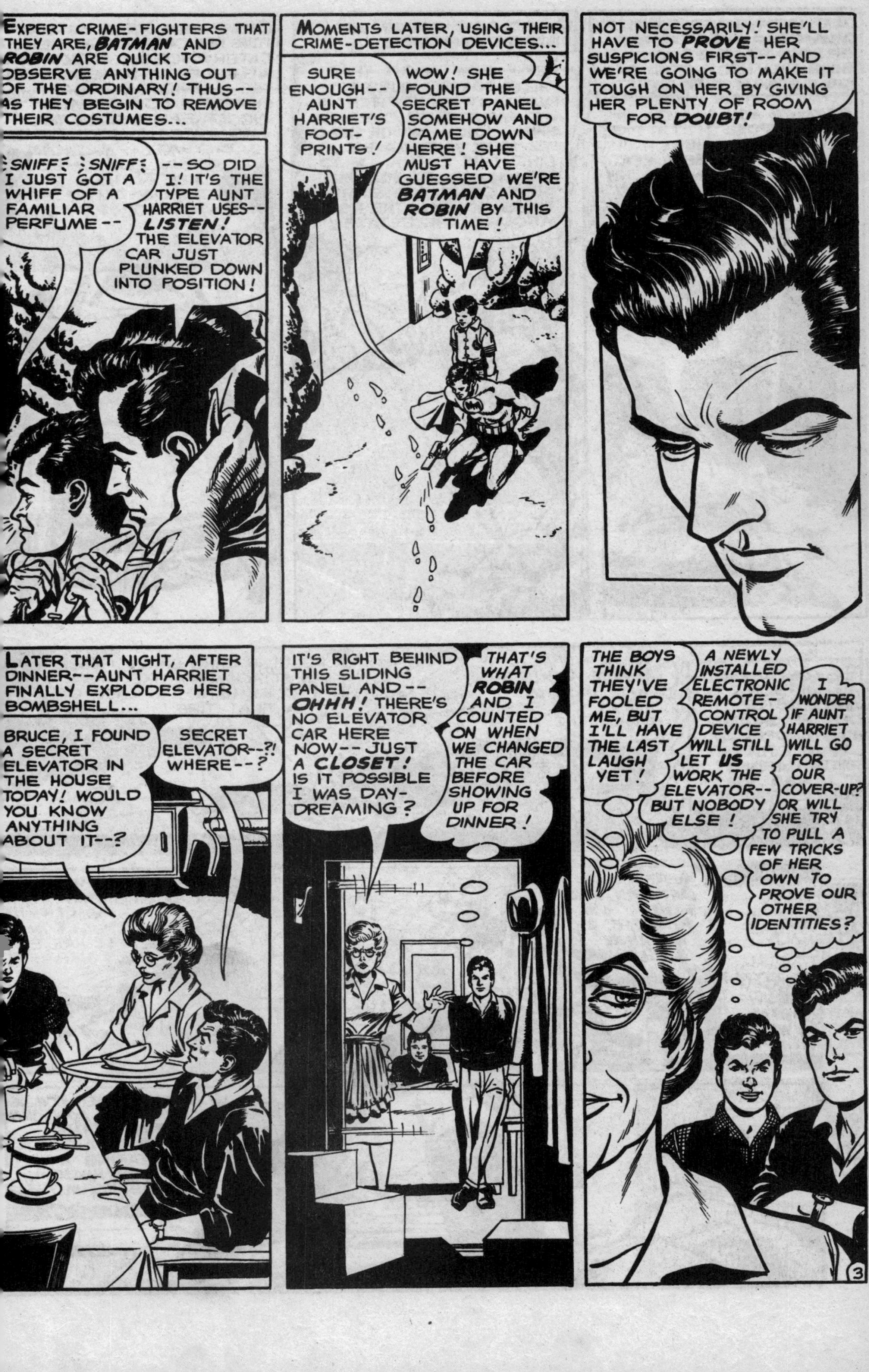
EXPERT CRIME-FIGHTERS THAT THEY ARE, BATMAN AND ROBIN ARE QUICK TO OBSERVE ANYTHING OUT OF THE ORDINARY! THUS-- AS THEY BEGIN TO REMOVE THEIR COSTUMES...
SNIFF SNIFF I JUST GOT A WHIFF OF A FAMILIAR PERFUME--
--SO DID I! IT'S THE TYPE AUNT HARRIET USES-- LISTEN! THE ELEVATOR CAR JUST PLUNKED DOWN INTO POSITION!
MOMENTS LATER, USING THEIR CRIME-DETECTION DEVICES...
SURE ENOUGH--AUNT HARRIET'S FOOT-PRINTS!
WOW! SHE FOUND THE SECRET PANEL SOMEHOW AND CAME DOWN HERE! SHE MUST HAVE GUESSED WE'RE BATMAN AND ROBIN BY THIS TIME!
NOT NECESSARILY! SHE'LL HAVE TO PROVE HER SUSPICIONS FIRST--AND WE'RE GOING TO MAKE IT TOUGH ON HER BY GIVING HER PLENTY OF ROOM FOR DOUBT!
LATER THAT NIGHT, AFTER DINNER--AUNT HARRIET FINALLY EXPLODES HER BOMBSHELL...
BRUCE, I FOUND A SECRET ELEVATOR IN THE HOUSE TODAY! WOULD YOU KNOW ANYTHING ABOUT IT--?
SECRET ELEVATOR--?! WHERE--?
IT'S RIGHT BEHIND THIS SLIDING PANEL AND--OHHH! THERE'S NO ELEVATOR CAR HERE NOW--JUST A CLOSET! IS IT POSSIBLE I WAS DAY-DREAMING?
THAT'S WHAT ROBIN AND I COUNTED ON WHEN WE CHANGED THE CAR BEFORE SHOWING UP FOR DINNER!
THE BOYS THINK THEY'VE FOOLED ME, BUT I'LL HAVE THE LAST LAUGH YET!
A NEWLY INSTALLED ELECTRONIC REMOTE-CONTROL DEVICE WILL STILL LET US WORK THE ELEVATOR--BUT NOBODY ELSE!
I WONDER IF AUNT HARRIET WILL GO FOR OUR COVER-UP? OR WILL SHE TRY TO PULL A FEW TRICKS OF HER OWN TO PROVE OUR OTHER IDENTITIES?
3

NEXT EVENING AS THE *COWLED CRUSADER* AND *BOY WONDER* PREPARE TO LEAVE ON THEIR NIGHTLY PATROL OF THE *GOTHAM CITY* STREETS...

BATMAN, YOU DON'T SUPPOSE AUNT HARRIET WOULD GO SO FAR AS TO HAVE GIMMICKED UP THE ROAD-WAY OUT OF THE *BATCAVE,* DO YOU?

I WOULDN'T PUT IT PAST HER! IT'D BE A NEAT WAY TO TRY AND FIND THE ENTRANCE TO THE *BATCAVE* FROM *OUTSIDE,* SINCE SHE CAN NO LONGER WORK THE ELEVATOR! CHECK THAT, *ROBIN!*

OUTSIDE THE CONCEALED HILLSIDE ENTRANCE...

HEYYY, HOW ABOUT THAT! SHE'S COATED OUR EXIT ROAD WITH WET PITCH! IF WE HAD DRIVEN OVER IT, SHE'D KNOW WHICH ROAD WE TOOK AND MAYBE FIND *THIS* ENTRANCE TO THE *BATCAVE!* I'LL BET SHE'S DONE THE SAME THING TO *ALL* THE ROADS AROUND THE ESTATE!

OKAY! WE'LL TAKE CARE OF THIS "EMERGENCY" BY USING THE HYDROFOIL ATTACHMENT WE RECENTLY FITTED UNDER THE *BATMOBILE*-- THAT SHOOTS A COMPRESSED AIR STREAM UNDER US AND LETS US MOVE ALONG ON THAT!

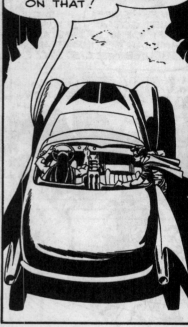

THE COMPRESSED AIR LIFTS THE *BATMOBILE* OFF THE GROUND AS A PROPELLER WHICH EJECTS FROM BEHIND IT, MOVES THE VEHICLE FORWARD...

WHEN WE'VE GONE A MILE ALONG THE MAIN HIGHWAY WE'LL LET DOWN ONTO THE TIRES!

REGULAR CARS SHOULD HAVE AN ATTACHMENT LIKE THIS-- IT'D BE HANDY IN CASE OF A FLAT TIRE!

AHEAD OF THEM IN *GOTHAM CITY* HALF AN HOUR LATER, UNSEEN IN THE ROOF-TOP SHADOWS, WAITS A MAN WITH A WALKIE-TALKIE...

HERE COME *BATMAN* AND *ROBIN* NOW, STRAIGHT UP *MARINE BOULEVARD!*

IT'S ABOUT TIME! WE'VE BEEN WAITING A WEEK FOR THEM TO TAKE THIS ROUTE!

ONE HUNDRED YARDS FURTHER ON...

BATMAN! MEN COMING OUT OF THE *LOWLAND TRUST BANK*-- LED BY A GUY WEARING A CRAZY MIXED-UP UNIFORM!

4

I'VE REHEARSED THIS MEETING TOO LONG TO MESS IT UP NOW! OFF COMES THIS GLASS-PELLET FROM MY UNIFORM--

SNAP!

A PERFECT PITCH-- RIGHT IN FRONT OF THE *BATMOBILE!*

CRAAAAASHH!

INSTANTLY THE NIGHT TURNS INTO CONCENTRATED EYE-DAZZLING BRIGHTNESS...

HA! HA! HA! *BATMAN--* YOU'VE JUST BEEN INTRODUCED TO-- *THE CLUEMASTER!* YOU'VE FOUND ME--ONLY TO LOSE ME! BUT DON'T DESPAIR-- I'LL LEAVE A *CLUE* FOR YOU TO TRACK ME DOWN--IF YOU *DARE!*

AS IF THOSE TAUNTING WORDS ARE A SPUR TO THEIR PRIDE, THE *MASKED MANHUNTER* AND *TEEN-AGE THUNDER-BOLT* LEAP FROM THE *BATMOBILE...*

LUCKILY OUR SPECIALLY TREATED WINDSHIELD REDUCED MOST OF THAT GLARE!

I CAN SEE WELL ENOUGH TO ZERO IN ON SOMEBODY'S JAW--

-- JUST LIKE A GUIDED MISSILE WITH WARHEAD KNUCKLES!

ZOK

5

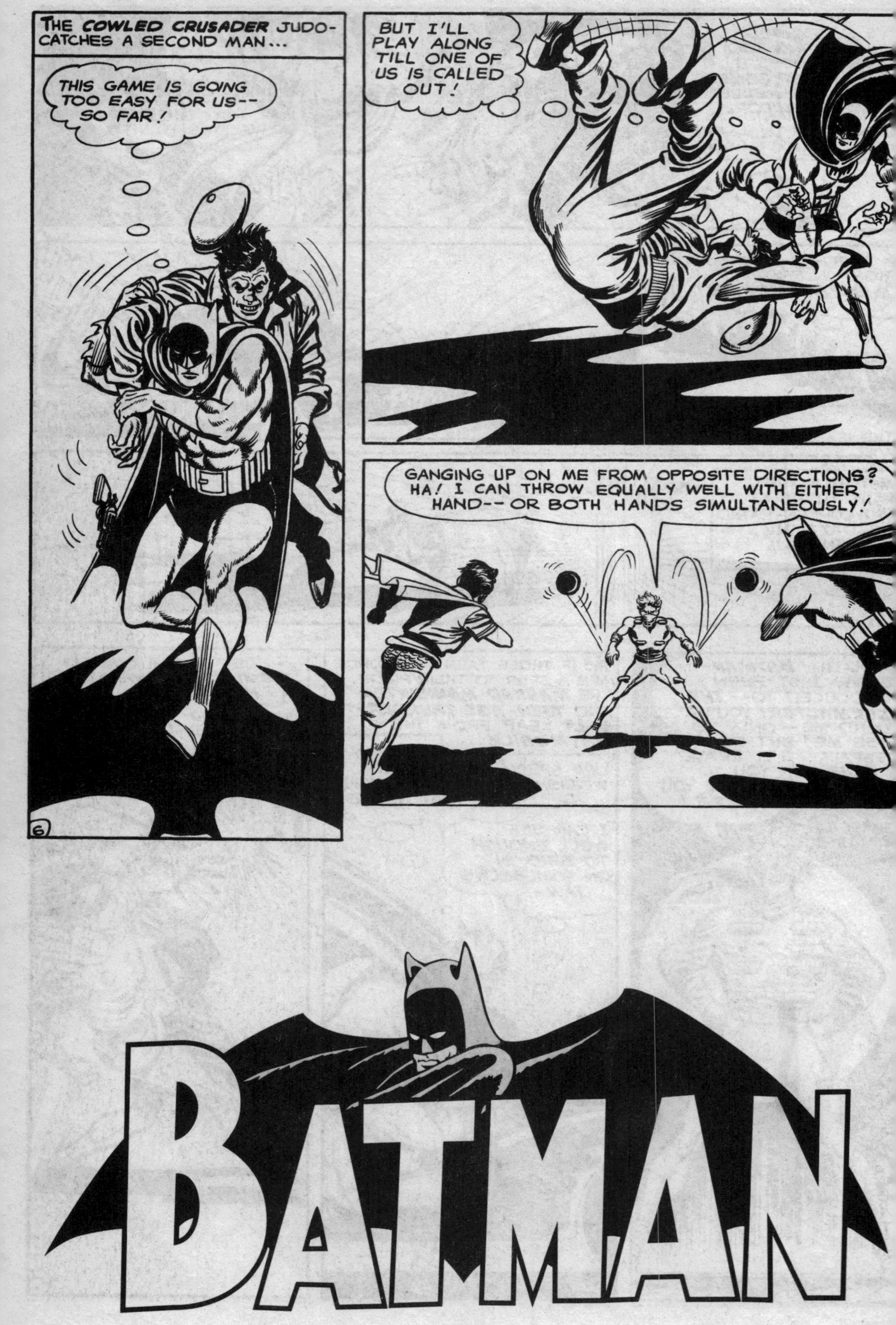
THE COWLED CRUSADER JUDO-CATCHES A SECOND MAN...
THIS GAME IS GOING TOO EASY FOR US-- SO FAR!
BUT I'LL PLAY ALONG TILL ONE OF US IS CALLED OUT!
GANGING UP ON ME FROM OPPOSITE DIRECTIONS? HA! I CAN THROW EQUALLY WELL WITH EITHER HAND-- OR BOTH HANDS SIMULTANEOUSLY!
6

BATMAN

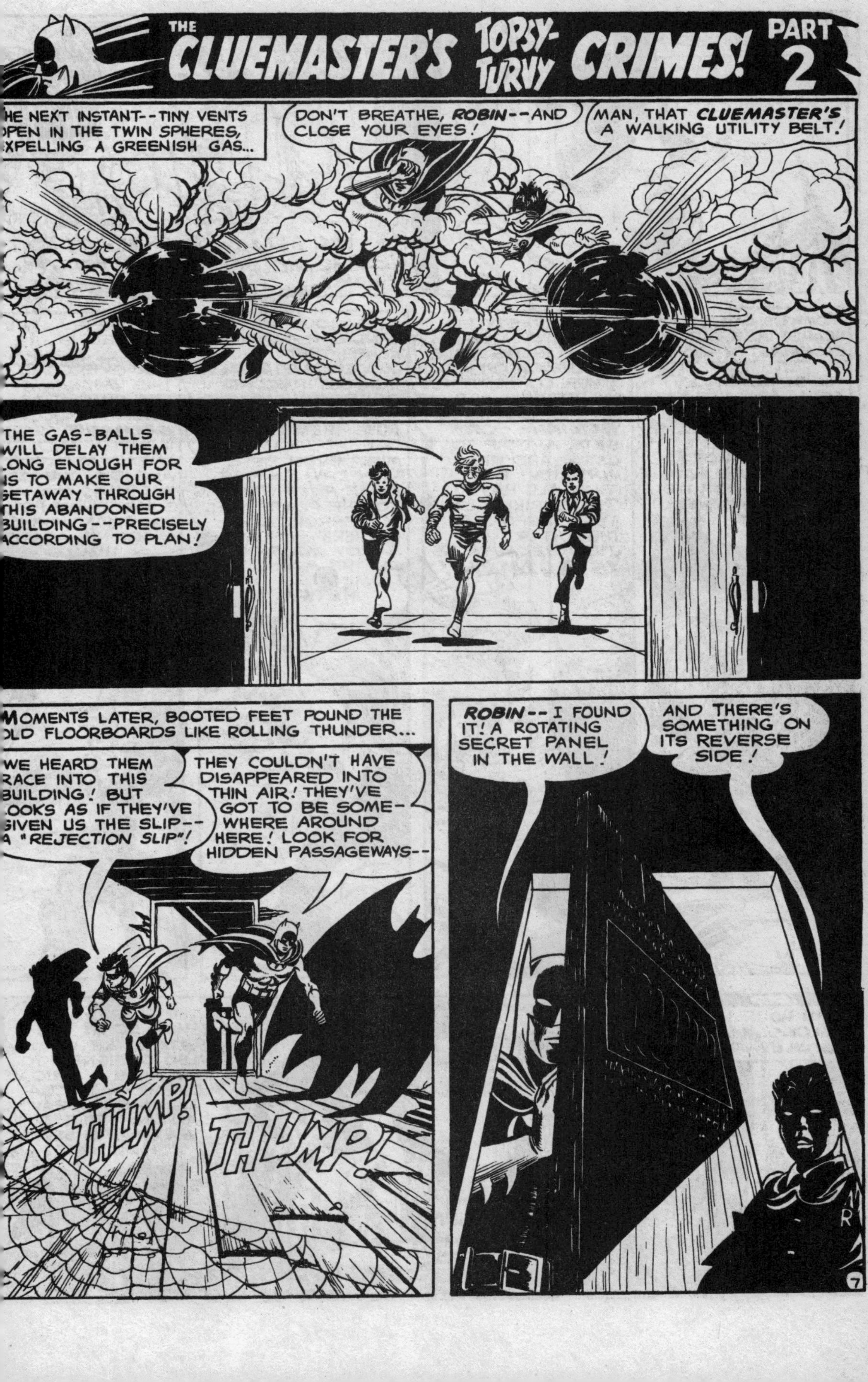
THE CLUEMASTER'S TOPSY-TURVY CRIMES! PART 2
THE NEXT INSTANT--TINY VENTS OPEN IN THE TWIN SPHERES, EXPELLING A GREENISH GAS...
DON'T BREATHE, ROBIN--AND CLOSE YOUR EYES!
MAN, THAT CLUEMASTER'S A WALKING UTILITY BELT!
THE GAS-BALLS WILL DELAY THEM LONG ENOUGH FOR US TO MAKE OUR GETAWAY THROUGH THIS ABANDONED BUILDING--PRECISELY ACCORDING TO PLAN!
MOMENTS LATER, BOOTED FEET POUND THE OLD FLOORBOARDS LIKE ROLLING THUNDER...
WE HEARD THEM RACE INTO THIS BUILDING! BUT LOOKS AS IF THEY'VE GIVEN US THE SLIP--A "REJECTION SLIP"!
THEY COULDN'T HAVE DISAPPEARED INTO THIN AIR! THEY'VE GOT TO BE SOMEWHERE AROUND HERE! LOOK FOR HIDDEN PASSAGEWAYS--
THUMP! THUMP!
ROBIN--I FOUND IT! A ROTATING SECRET PANEL IN THE WALL!
AND THERE'S SOMETHING ON ITS REVERSE SIDE!
7

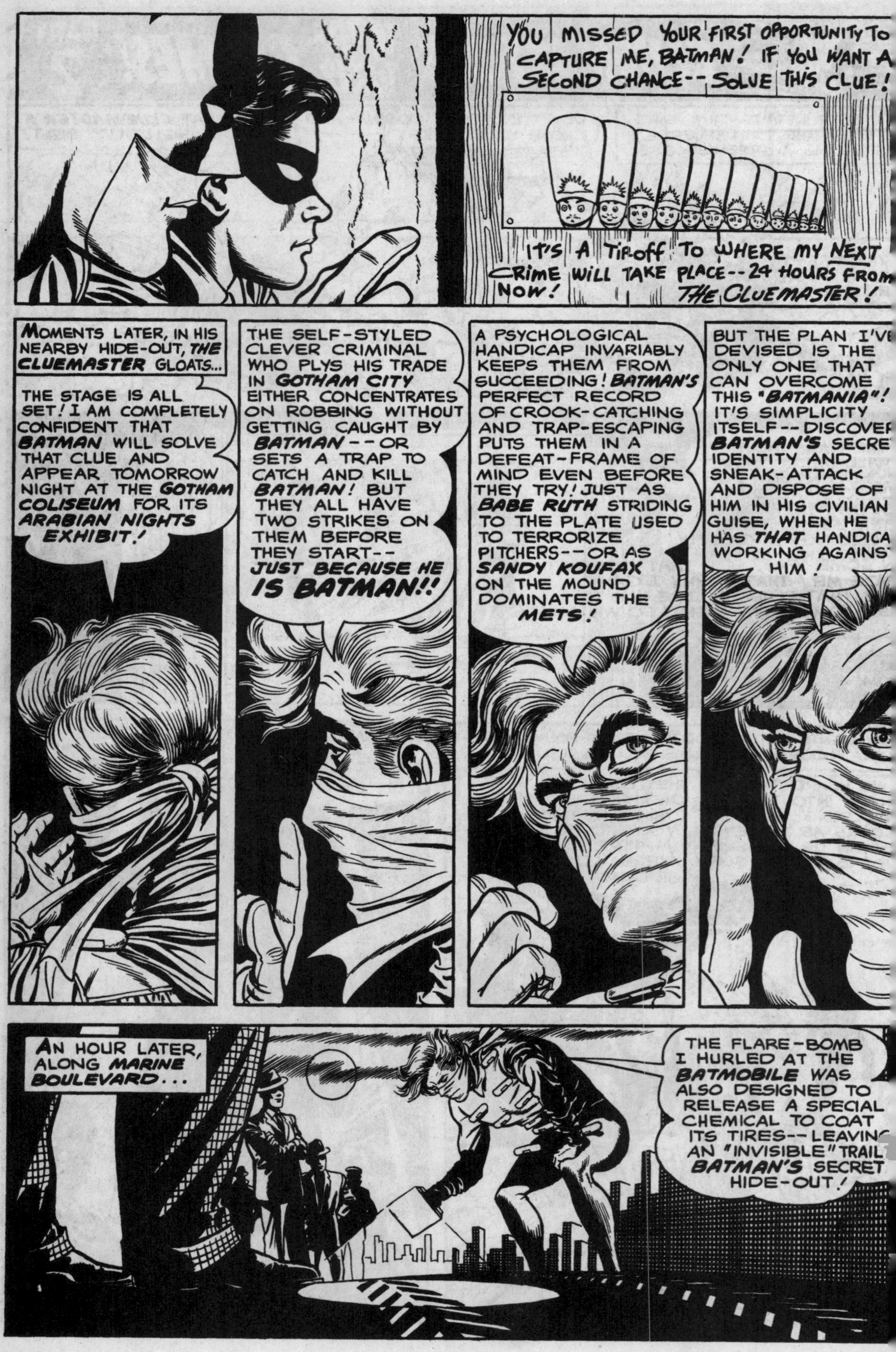
YOU MISSED YOUR FIRST OPPORTUNITY TO CAPTURE ME, BATMAN! IF YOU WANT A SECOND CHANCE-- SOLVE THIS CLUE!
IT'S A TIP-OFF TO WHERE MY NEXT CRIME WILL TAKE PLACE-- 24 HOURS FROM NOW! THE CLUEMASTER!
MOMENTS LATER, IN HIS NEARBY HIDE-OUT, THE CLUEMASTER GLOATS...
THE STAGE IS ALL SET! I AM COMPLETELY CONFIDENT THAT BATMAN WILL SOLVE THAT CLUE AND APPEAR TOMORROW NIGHT AT THE GOTHAM COLISEUM FOR ITS ARABIAN NIGHTS EXHIBIT!
THE SELF-STYLED CLEVER CRIMINAL WHO PLYS HIS TRADE IN GOTHAM CITY EITHER CONCENTRATES ON ROBBING WITHOUT GETTING CAUGHT BY BATMAN--OR SETS A TRAP TO CATCH AND KILL BATMAN! BUT THEY ALL HAVE TWO STRIKES ON THEM BEFORE THEY START-- JUST BECAUSE HE IS BATMAN!!
A PSYCHOLOGICAL HANDICAP INVARIABLY KEEPS THEM FROM SUCCEEDING! BATMAN'S PERFECT RECORD OF CROOK-CATCHING AND TRAP-ESCAPING PUTS THEM IN A DEFEAT-FRAME OF MIND EVEN BEFORE THEY TRY! JUST AS BABE RUTH STRIDING TO THE PLATE USED TO TERRORIZE PITCHERS--OR AS SANDY KOUFAX ON THE MOUND DOMINATES THE METS!
BUT THE PLAN I'VE DEVISED IS THE ONLY ONE THAT CAN OVERCOME THIS "BATMANIA"! IT'S SIMPLICITY ITSELF--DISCOVER BATMAN'S SECRET IDENTITY AND SNEAK-ATTACK AND DISPOSE OF HIM IN HIS CIVILIAN GUISE, WHEN HE HAS THAT HANDICAP WORKING AGAINST HIM!
AN HOUR LATER, ALONG MARINE BOULEVARD...
THE FLARE-BOMB I HURLED AT THE BATMOBILE WAS ALSO DESIGNED TO RELEASE A SPECIAL CHEMICAL TO COAT ITS TIRES--LEAVING AN "INVISIBLE" TRAIL BATMAN'S SECRET HIDE-OUT!

SOON *THE CLUEMASTER'S* CAR IS HURTLING ALONG THE MAIN HIGHWAY ON THE BETRAYING TIRE-TREAD TRAIL...

ONCE I LEARN WHERE HIS *BATCAVE* IS, IT'LL BE A CINCH TO SEE HIS MASK-LESS FEATURES AND DISCOVER HIS CIVILIAN IDENTITY! THEN I'LL GET RID OF--*HUH?*

THE TIRE-TRACKS-- COME TO AN ABRUPT END IN THE MIDDLE OF THE HIGHWAY!

MAYBE *BATMAN* AND *ROBIN* ARE *ALIENS* FROM ANOTHER WORLD AND THE *BATMOBILE* IS REALLY A *SPACESHIP* THAT SUDDENLY TOOK OFF!

NONSENSE! ALREADY YOU'RE LETTING YOUR SUBCONSCIOUS FEAR OF *BATMAN* GRAB YOU! I TELL YOU-- *BATMAN'S* SMART! OBVIOUSLY, HE FIGURED OUT WHAT I DID TO HIS TIRES AND CONCEALED THE TRACKS IN SOME WAY! BUT THAT DOESN'T FAZE ME! THAT'S WHY I GAVE HIM THAT CLUE TO LURE HIM TO US-- TOMORROW NIGHT! SO WE CAN TRY AGAIN!

MEANTIME, ON A CUSHION OF COMPRESSED AIR, THE *BAT-MOBILE* FLOATS SAFELY INTO THE *BATCAVE*, LEAVING *BATMAN* AND *ROBIN* UNAWARE THAT THEY HAVE MISLED NO MORE THAN AUNT HARRIET...

FOR A LONG WHILE THEY STUDY THE CLUE OF THE PANEL PAINTING THEY HAVE BROUGHT WITH THEM...

HOW YOU DOIN'? I'M BATTING ZERO--

SAME HERE! MAYBE OUR NEW FOE'S TRYING TO CROSS US UP WITH A "NOTHING" CLUE!

NEXT EVENING FINDS THE *DYNAMIC DUO* ONCE AGAIN ON PATROL, WHEN...

BATMAN--OVER THERE! GLASS BREAKING IN THAT TELEVISION STORE FRONT!

TTINNKKLL

9

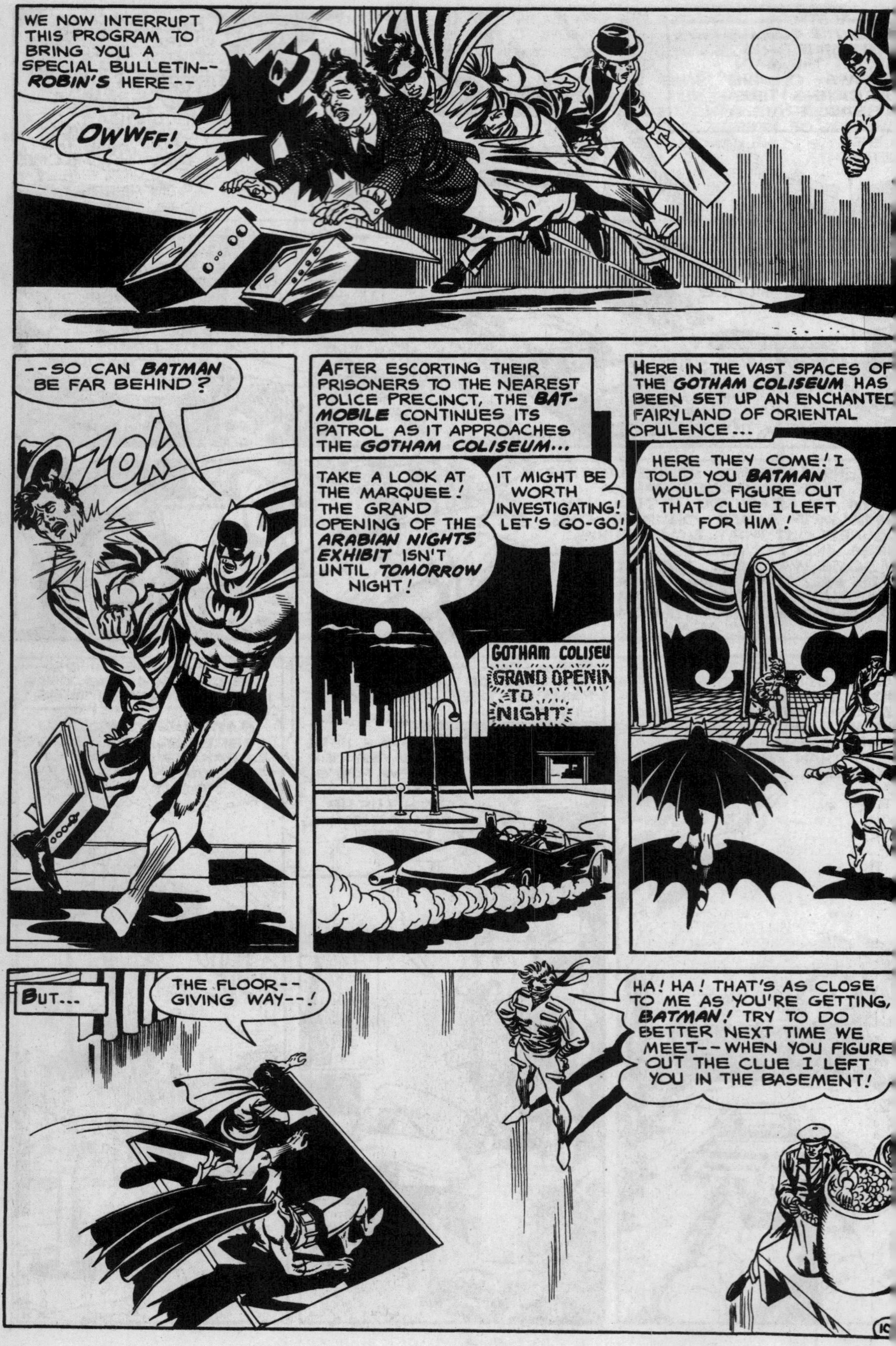
WE NOW INTERRUPT THIS PROGRAM TO BRING YOU A SPECIAL BULLETIN-- ROBIN'S HERE--
OWWFF!
--SO CAN BATMAN BE FAR BEHIND?
ZOK
AFTER ESCORTING THEIR PRISONERS TO THE NEAREST POLICE PRECINCT, THE BAT-MOBILE CONTINUES ITS PATROL AS IT APPROACHES THE GOTHAM COLISEUM...
TAKE A LOOK AT THE MARQUEE! THE GRAND OPENING OF THE ARABIAN NIGHTS EXHIBIT ISN'T UNTIL TOMORROW NIGHT!
IT MIGHT BE WORTH INVESTIGATING! LET'S GO-GO!
GOTHAM COLISEU
GRAND OPENIN
TO
NIGHT
HERE IN THE VAST SPACES OF THE GOTHAM COLISEUM HAS BEEN SET UP AN ENCHANTED FAIRYLAND OF ORIENTAL OPULENCE...
HERE THEY COME! I TOLD YOU BATMAN WOULD FIGURE OUT THAT CLUE I LEFT FOR HIM!
BUT...
THE FLOOR-- GIVING WAY--!
HA! HA! THAT'S AS CLOSE TO ME AS YOU'RE GETTING, BATMAN! TRY TO DO BETTER NEXT TIME WE MEET--WHEN YOU FIGURE OUT THE CLUE I LEFT YOU IN THE BASEMENT!

IN THE STYGIAN DARKNESS BELOW...

THERE'S THE CLUE-- A LUMINOUS PAINTING OF A SEA SERPENT!

WHY IS HE BRAZENLY LEAVING US THESE CLUES? HE COULD ROB AND WE'D NEVER KNOW IT! WHAT DEEPER GAME IS HE PLAYING?

WHEN THEY MAKE THEIR WAY BACK TO THE BATCAVE...

WE MUST BE SLIPPIN'! TWO CLUES TO WORK ON--AND WE CAN'T MAKE HEAD OR TAIL OF THEM!

HEAD OR TAIL-- BUT HOW ABOUT OTHER POSSIBLE ANGLES?

OKAY! I'LL TURN THIS THING ON ITS SIDE-- THEN UPSIDE DOWN--

HOLD IT! WHAT WE THOUGHT WAS A SEA SERPENT-- IS NOW A DUCK! IN A TOPSY-TURVY POSITION, THE DRAWING BECOMES COMPLETELY DIFFERENT!

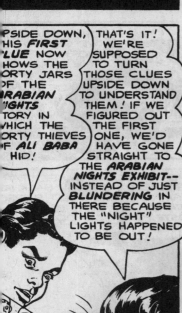

UPSIDE DOWN, THIS FIRST CLUE NOW SHOWS THE FORTY JARS OF THE ARABIAN NIGHTS STORY IN WHICH THE FORTY THIEVES OF ALI BABA HID!

THAT'S IT! WE'RE SUPPOSED TO TURN THOSE CLUES UPSIDE DOWN TO UNDERSTAND THEM! IF WE FIGURED OUT THE FIRST ONE, WE'D HAVE GONE STRAIGHT TO THE ARABIAN NIGHTS EXHIBIT-- INSTEAD OF JUST BLUNDERING IN THERE BECAUSE THE "NIGHT" LIGHTS HAPPENED TO BE OUT!

LATER, AS THEY LEAVE THE "CLOSET-ELEVATOR" BY THE SLIDING WALL PANEL...

THERE'S A DUCK MARINA ALONG THE THE WATER- FRONT! WE'LL BE ALL SET FOR THE CLUEMASTER TOMORROW NIGHT--

WHIRRR

LISTEN! YOU HEAR THAT? SOUNDS LIKE A MOVIE CAMERA--

FOUND IT, BRUCE-- HIDDEN IN THIS CHANDELIER! IT WAS TAKING PICTURES OF US AS WE LEFT THE ELEVATOR--

IT'S AUNT HARRIET'S WORK-- PLAYING DETECTIVE! COME ON BACK TO THE BATCAVE! SHE ISN'T GOING TO EXPOSE US THAT EASILY!

11

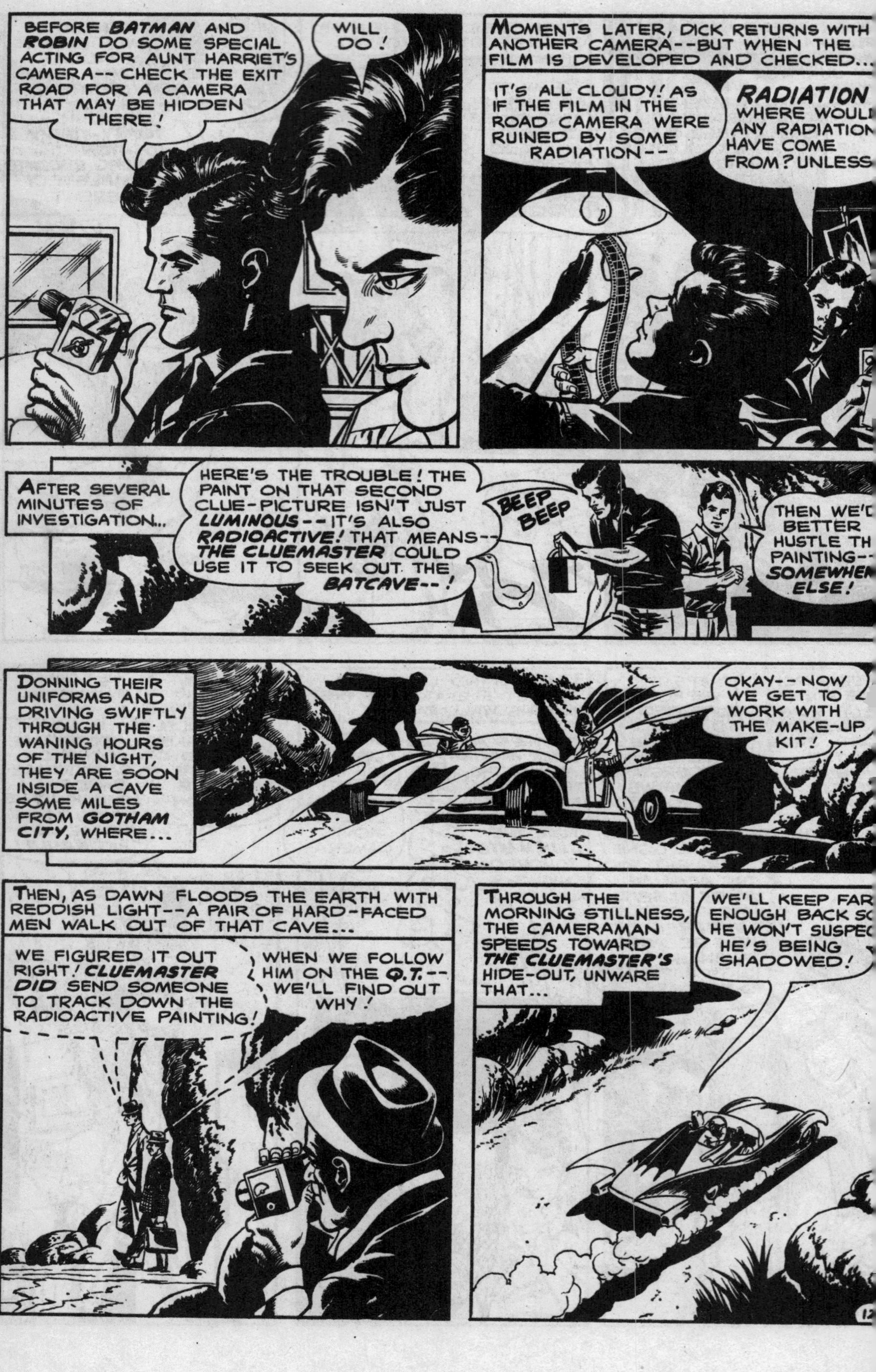
BEFORE BATMAN AND ROBIN DO SOME SPECIAL ACTING FOR AUNT HARRIET'S CAMERA-- CHECK THE EXIT ROAD FOR A CAMERA THAT MAY BE HIDDEN THERE!
WILL DO!
MOMENTS LATER, DICK RETURNS WITH ANOTHER CAMERA--BUT WHEN THE FILM IS DEVELOPED AND CHECKED...
IT'S ALL CLOUDY! AS IF THE FILM IN THE ROAD CAMERA WERE RUINED BY SOME RADIATION--
RADIATION WHERE WOUL ANY RADIATION HAVE COME FROM? UNLESS
AFTER SEVERAL MINUTES OF INVESTIGATION...
HERE'S THE TROUBLE! THE PAINT ON THAT SECOND CLUE-PICTURE ISN'T JUST LUMINOUS--IT'S ALSO RADIOACTIVE! THAT MEANS--THE CLUEMASTER COULD USE IT TO SEEK OUT THE BATCAVE--!
BEEP BEEP
THEN WE'D BETTER HUSTLE TH PAINTING--SOMEWHE ELSE!
DONNING THEIR UNIFORMS AND DRIVING SWIFTLY THROUGH THE WANING HOURS OF THE NIGHT, THEY ARE SOON INSIDE A CAVE SOME MILES FROM GOTHAM CITY, WHERE...
OKAY--NOW WE GET TO WORK WITH THE MAKE-UP KIT!
THEN, AS DAWN FLOODS THE EARTH WITH REDDISH LIGHT--A PAIR OF HARD-FACED MEN WALK OUT OF THAT CAVE...
WE FIGURED IT OUT RIGHT! CLUEMASTER DID SEND SOMEONE TO TRACK DOWN THE RADIOACTIVE PAINTING!
WHEN WE FOLLOW HIM ON THE Q.T.-- WE'LL FIND OUT WHY!
THROUGH THE MORNING STILLNESS, THE CAMERAMAN SPEEDS TOWARD THE CLUEMASTER'S HIDE-OUT, UNWARE THAT...
WE'LL KEEP FAR ENOUGH BACK SO HE WON'T SUSPEC HE'S BEING SHADOWED!
12

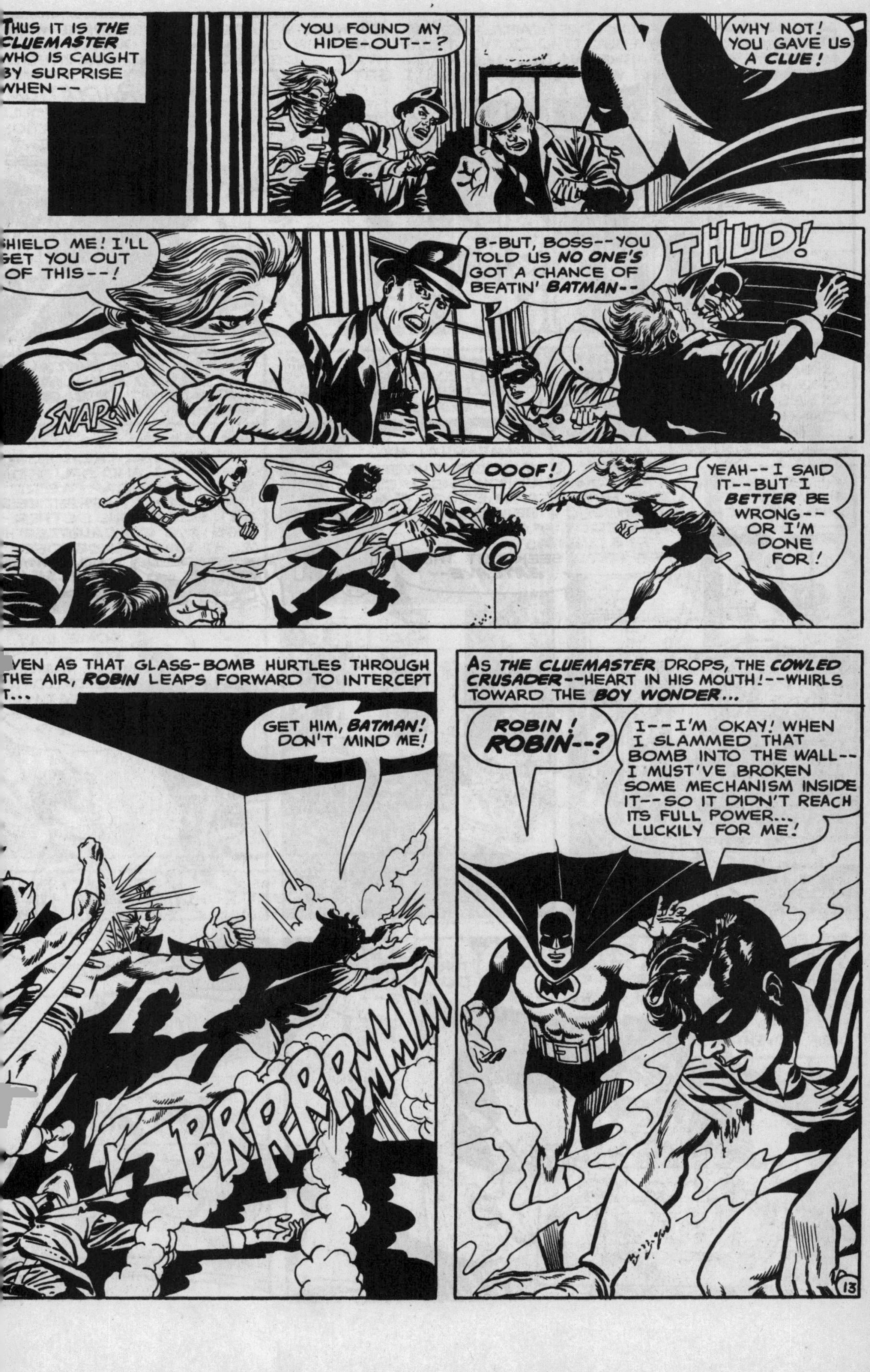
THUS IT IS THE CLUEMASTER WHO IS CAUGHT BY SURPRISE WHEN --
YOU FOUND MY HIDE-OUT--?
WHY NOT! YOU GAVE US A CLUE!
SHIELD ME! I'LL GET YOU OUT OF THIS--!
SNAP!
B-BUT, BOSS--YOU TOLD US NO ONE'S GOT A CHANCE OF BEATIN' BATMAN--
THUD!
OOOF!
YEAH--I SAID IT--BUT I BETTER BE WRONG-- OR I'M DONE FOR!
EVEN AS THAT GLASS-BOMB HURTLES THROUGH THE AIR, ROBIN LEAPS FORWARD TO INTERCEPT IT...
GET HIM, BATMAN! DON'T MIND ME!
BRRRRMMM
AS THE CLUEMASTER DROPS, THE COWLED CRUSADER--HEART IN HIS MOUTH!--WHIRLS TOWARD THE BOY WONDER...
ROBIN! ROBIN--?
I--I'M OKAY! WHEN I SLAMMED THAT BOMB INTO THE WALL-- I MUST'VE BROKEN SOME MECHANISM INSIDE IT--SO IT DIDN'T REACH ITS FULL POWER... LUCKILY FOR ME!
13

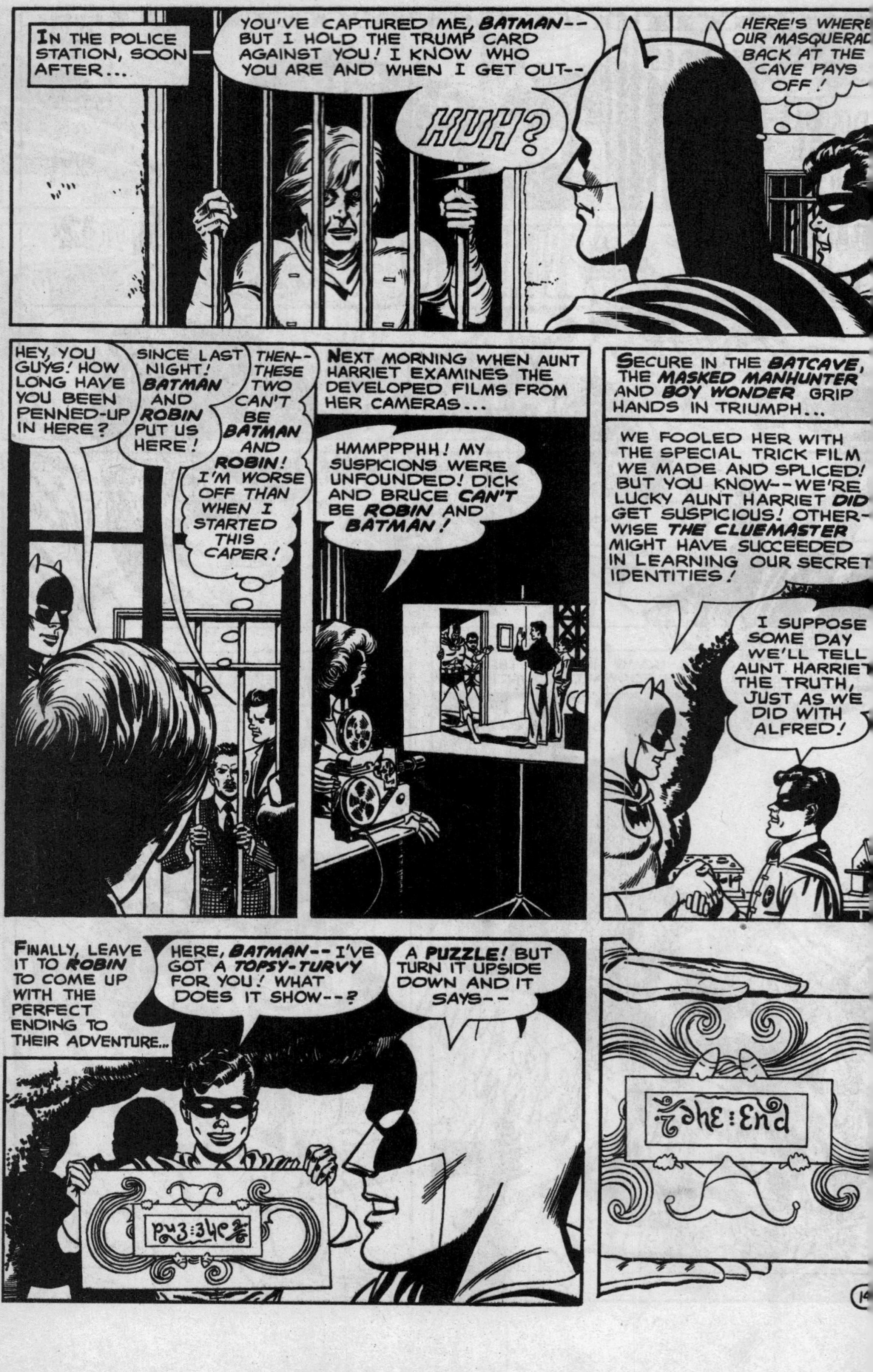
IN THE POLICE STATION, SOON AFTER...
YOU'VE CAPTURED ME, BATMAN-- BUT I HOLD THE TRUMP CARD AGAINST YOU! I KNOW WHO YOU ARE AND WHEN I GET OUT--
HUH?
HERE'S WHERE OUR MASQUERAD BACK AT THE CAVE PAYS OFF!
HEY, YOU GUYS! HOW LONG HAVE YOU BEEN PENNED-UP IN HERE?
SINCE LAST NIGHT! BATMAN AND ROBIN PUT US HERE!
THEN-- THESE TWO CAN'T BE BATMAN AND ROBIN! I'M WORSE OFF THAN WHEN I STARTED THIS CAPER!
NEXT MORNING WHEN AUNT HARRIET EXAMINES THE DEVELOPED FILMS FROM HER CAMERAS...
HMMPPPHH! MY SUSPICIONS WERE UNFOUNDED! DICK AND BRUCE CAN'T BE ROBIN AND BATMAN!
SECURE IN THE BATCAVE, THE MASKED MANHUNTER AND BOY WONDER GRIP HANDS IN TRIUMPH...
WE FOOLED HER WITH THE SPECIAL TRICK FILM WE MADE AND SPLICED! BUT YOU KNOW--WE'RE LUCKY AUNT HARRIET DID GET SUSPICIOUS! OTHERWISE THE CLUEMASTER MIGHT HAVE SUCCEEDED IN LEARNING OUR SECRET IDENTITIES!
I SUPPOSE SOME DAY WE'LL TELL AUNT HARRIET THE TRUTH, JUST AS WE DID WITH ALFRED!
FINALLY, LEAVE IT TO ROBIN TO COME UP WITH THE PERFECT ENDING TO THEIR ADVENTURE...
HERE, BATMAN-- I'VE GOT A TOPSY-TURVY FOR YOU! WHAT DOES IT SHOW--?
A PUZZLE! BUT TURN IT UPSIDE DOWN AND IT SAYS--
The End
14

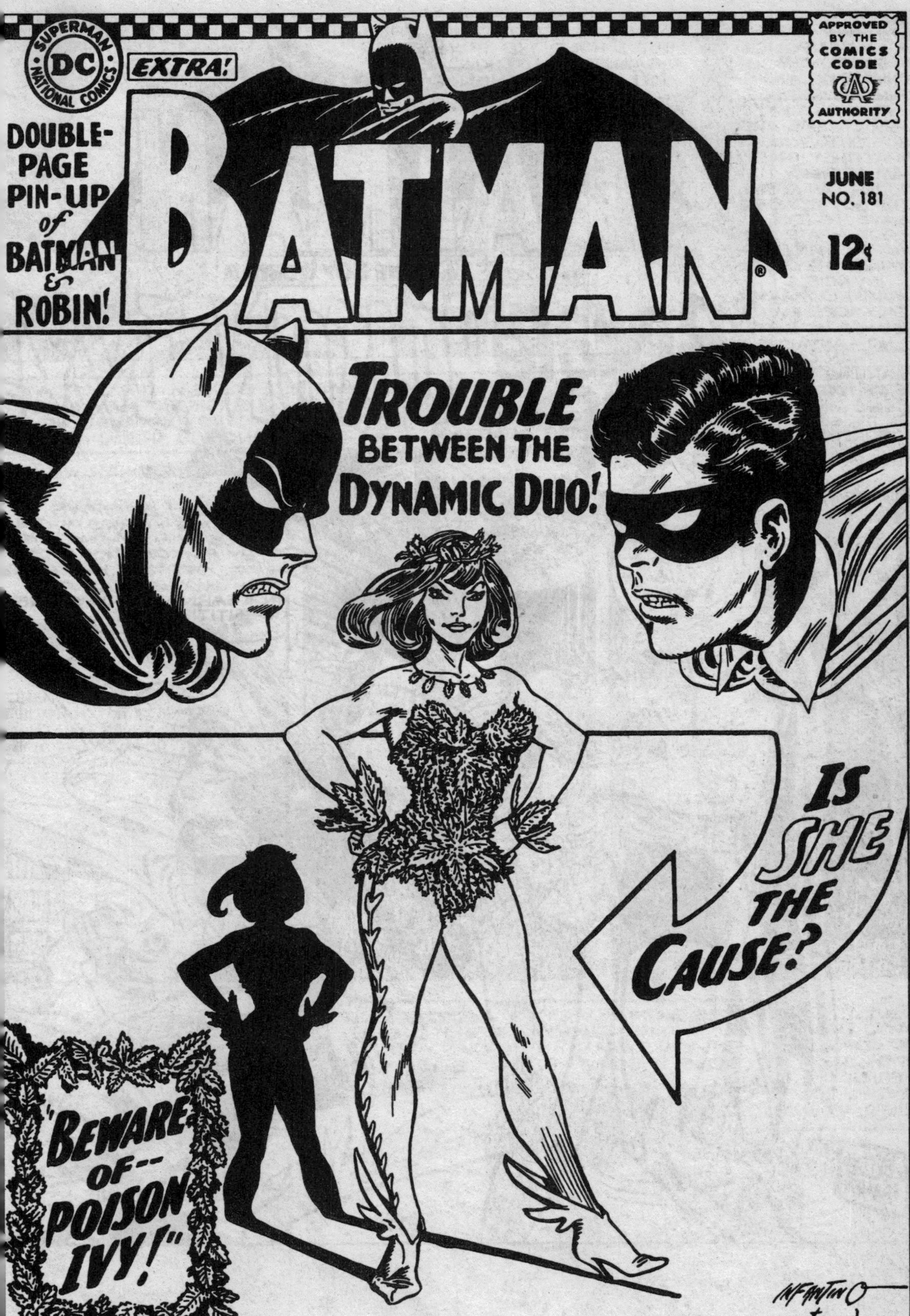
SUPERMAN DC NATIONAL COMICS
EXTRA!
APPROVED BY THE COMICS CODE AUTHORITY
DOUBLE-PAGE PIN-UP of BATMAN & ROBIN!
BATMAN
JUNE NO. 181
12¢
TROUBLE BETWEEN THE DYNAMIC DUO!
IS SHE THE CAUSE?
"BEWARE OF--POISON IVY!"
INFANTINO + ANDERSON

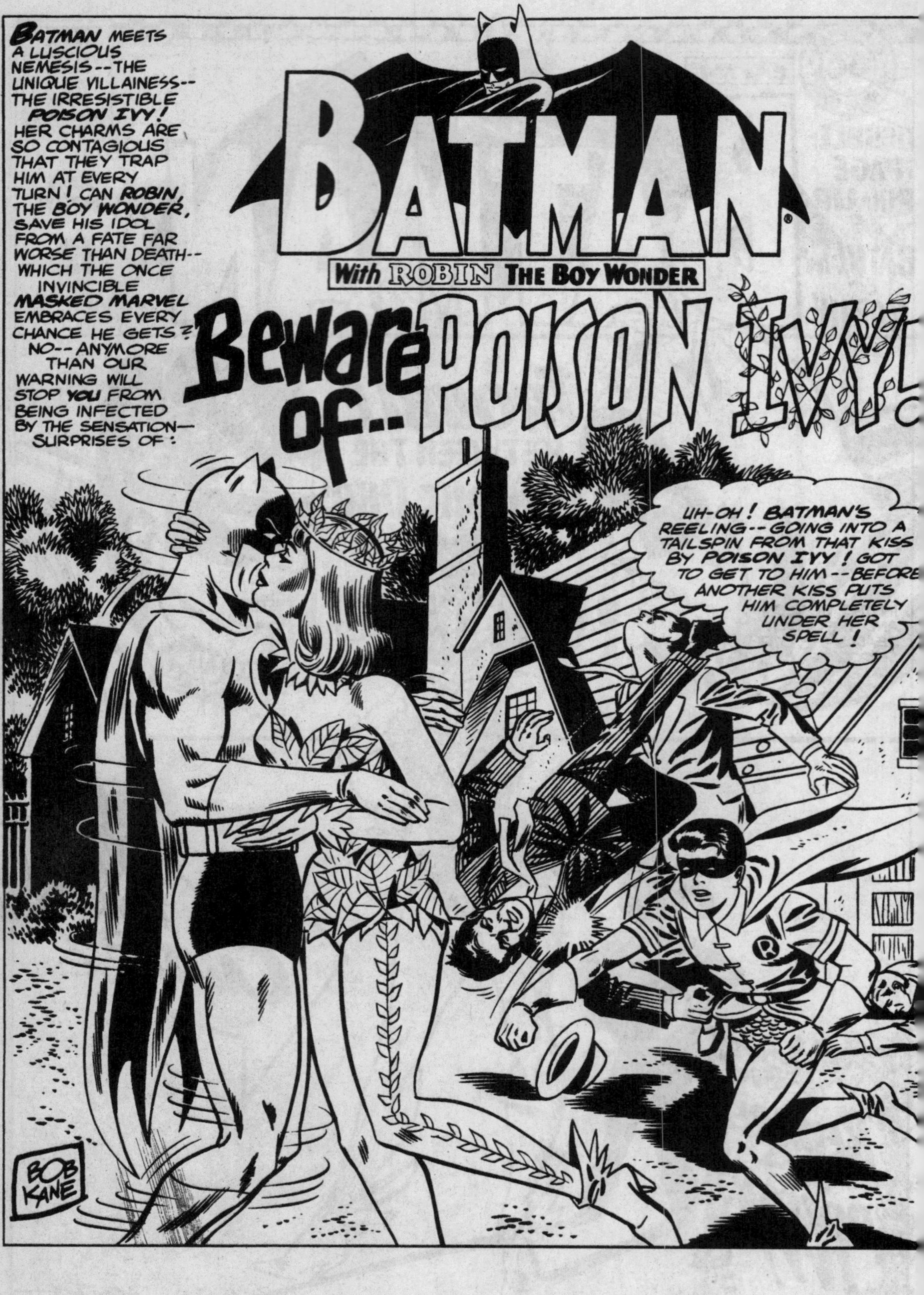
BATMAN MEETS A LUSCIOUS NEMESIS--THE UNIQUE VILLAINESS--THE IRRESISTIBLE POISON IVY! HER CHARMS ARE SO CONTAGIOUS THAT THEY TRAP HIM AT EVERY TURN! CAN ROBIN, THE BOY WONDER, SAVE HIS IDOL FROM A FATE FAR WORSE THAN DEATH--WHICH THE ONCE INVINCIBLE MASKED MARVEL EMBRACES EVERY CHANCE HE GETS? NO--ANYMORE THAN OUR WARNING WILL STOP YOU FROM BEING INFECTED BY THE SENSATION-SURPRISES OF:
BATMAN
With ROBIN THE BOY WONDER
Beware of... POISON IVY!
UH-OH! BATMAN'S REELING--GOING INTO A TAILSPIN FROM THAT KISS BY POISON IVY! GOT TO GET TO HIM--BEFORE ANOTHER KISS PUTS HIM COMPLETELY UNDER HER SPELL!
BOB KANE

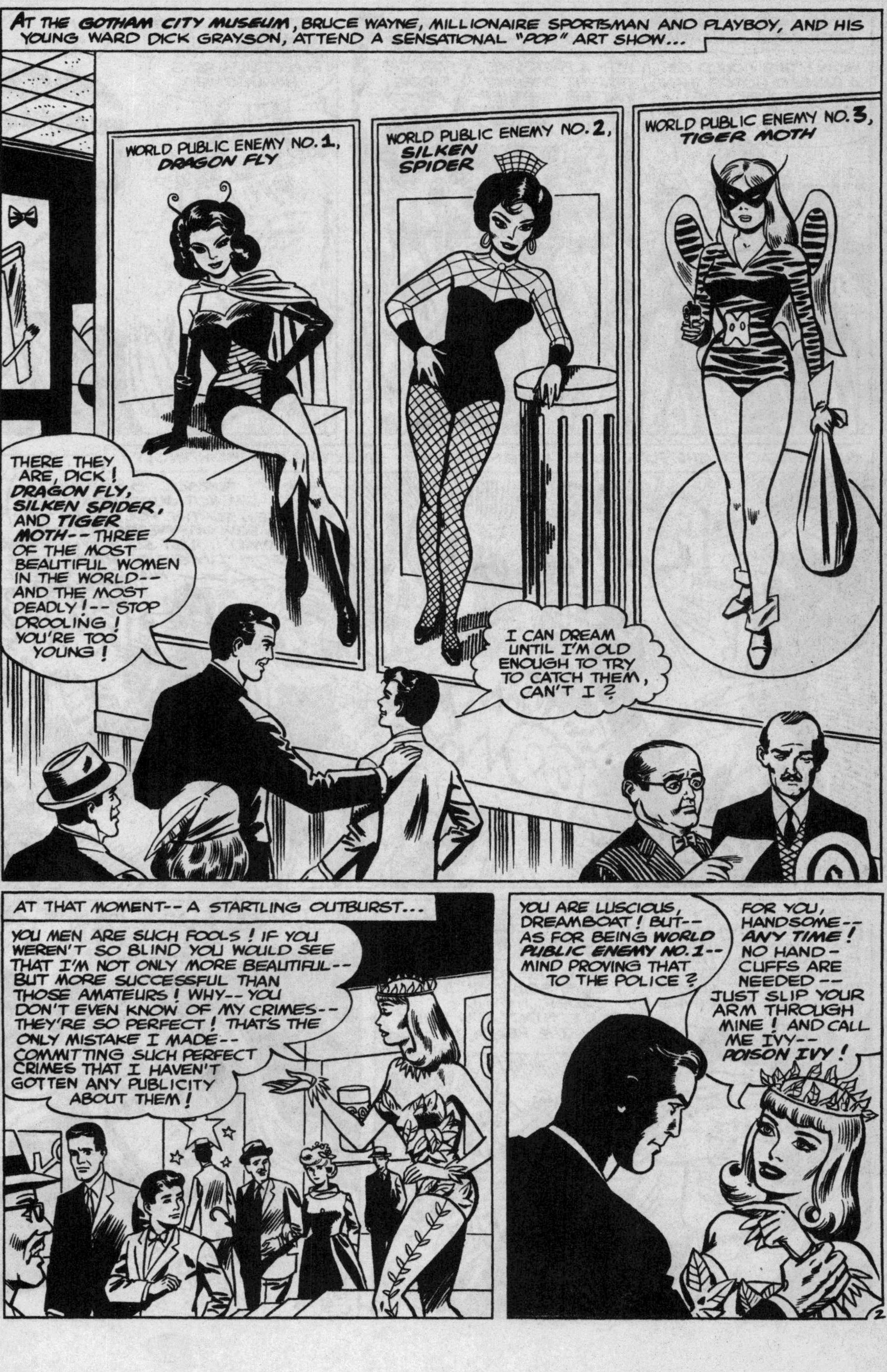
AT THE GOTHAM CITY MUSEUM, BRUCE WAYNE, MILLIONAIRE SPORTSMAN AND PLAYBOY, AND HIS YOUNG WARD DICK GRAYSON, ATTEND A SENSATIONAL "POP" ART SHOW...
WORLD PUBLIC ENEMY NO. 1, DRAGON FLY
WORLD PUBLIC ENEMY NO. 2, SILKEN SPIDER
WORLD PUBLIC ENEMY NO. 3, TIGER MOTH
THERE THEY ARE, DICK! DRAGON FLY, SILKEN SPIDER, AND TIGER MOTH-- THREE OF THE MOST BEAUTIFUL WOMEN IN THE WORLD-- AND THE MOST DEADLY!-- STOP DROOLING! YOU'RE TOO YOUNG!
I CAN DREAM UNTIL I'M OLD ENOUGH TO TRY TO CATCH THEM, CAN'T I?
AT THAT MOMENT-- A STARTLING OUTBURST...
YOU MEN ARE SUCH FOOLS! IF YOU WEREN'T SO BLIND YOU WOULD SEE THAT I'M NOT ONLY MORE BEAUTIFUL-- BUT MORE SUCCESSFUL THAN THOSE AMATEURS! WHY-- YOU DON'T EVEN KNOW OF MY CRIMES-- THEY'RE SO PERFECT! THAT'S THE ONLY MISTAKE I MADE-- COMMITTING SUCH PERFECT CRIMES THAT I HAVEN'T GOTTEN ANY PUBLICITY ABOUT THEM!
YOU ARE LUSCIOUS, DREAMBOAT! BUT-- AS FOR BEING WORLD PUBLIC ENEMY NO. 1-- MIND PROVING THAT TO THE POLICE?
FOR YOU, HANDSOME-- ANY TIME! NO HAND-CUFFS ARE NEEDED-- JUST SLIP YOUR ARM THROUGH MINE! AND CALL ME IVY-- POISON IVY!
2

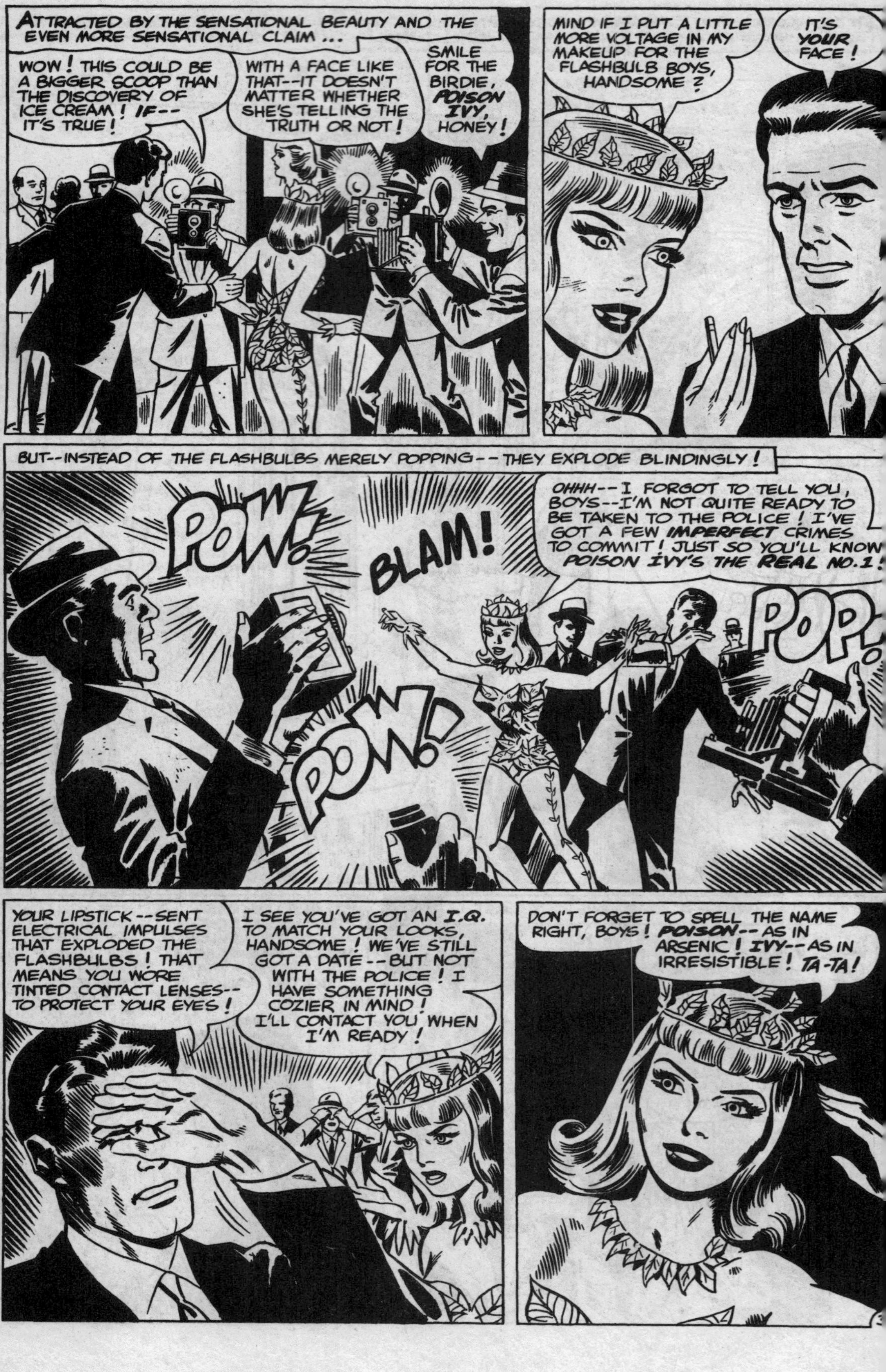
ATTRACTED BY THE SENSATIONAL BEAUTY AND THE EVEN MORE SENSATIONAL CLAIM ...
WOW! THIS COULD BE A BIGGER SCOOP THAN THE DISCOVERY OF ICE CREAM! IF-- IT'S TRUE!
WITH A FACE LIKE THAT--IT DOESN'T MATTER WHETHER SHE'S TELLING THE TRUTH OR NOT!
SMILE FOR THE BIRDIE, POISON IVY, HONEY!
MIND IF I PUT A LITTLE MORE VOLTAGE IN MY MAKEUP FOR THE FLASHBULB BOYS, HANDSOME?
IT'S YOUR FACE!
BUT--INSTEAD OF THE FLASHBULBS MERELY POPPING--THEY EXPLODE BLINDINGLY!
POW!
BLAM!
OHHH--I FORGOT TO TELL YOU, BOYS--I'M NOT QUITE READY TO BE TAKEN TO THE POLICE! I'VE GOT A FEW IMPERFECT CRIMES TO COMMIT! JUST SO YOU'LL KNOW POISON IVY'S THE REAL NO.1!
POP
POW!
YOUR LIPSTICK--SENT ELECTRICAL IMPULSES THAT EXPLODED THE FLASHBULBS! THAT MEANS YOU WORE TINTED CONTACT LENSES-- TO PROTECT YOUR EYES!
I SEE YOU'VE GOT AN I.Q. TO MATCH YOUR LOOKS, HANDSOME! WE'VE STILL GOT A DATE--BUT NOT WITH THE POLICE! I HAVE SOMETHING COZIER IN MIND! I'LL CONTACT YOU WHEN I'M READY!
DON'T FORGET TO SPELL THE NAME RIGHT, BOYS! POISON--AS IN ARSENIC! IVY--AS IN IRRESISTIBLE! TA-TA!

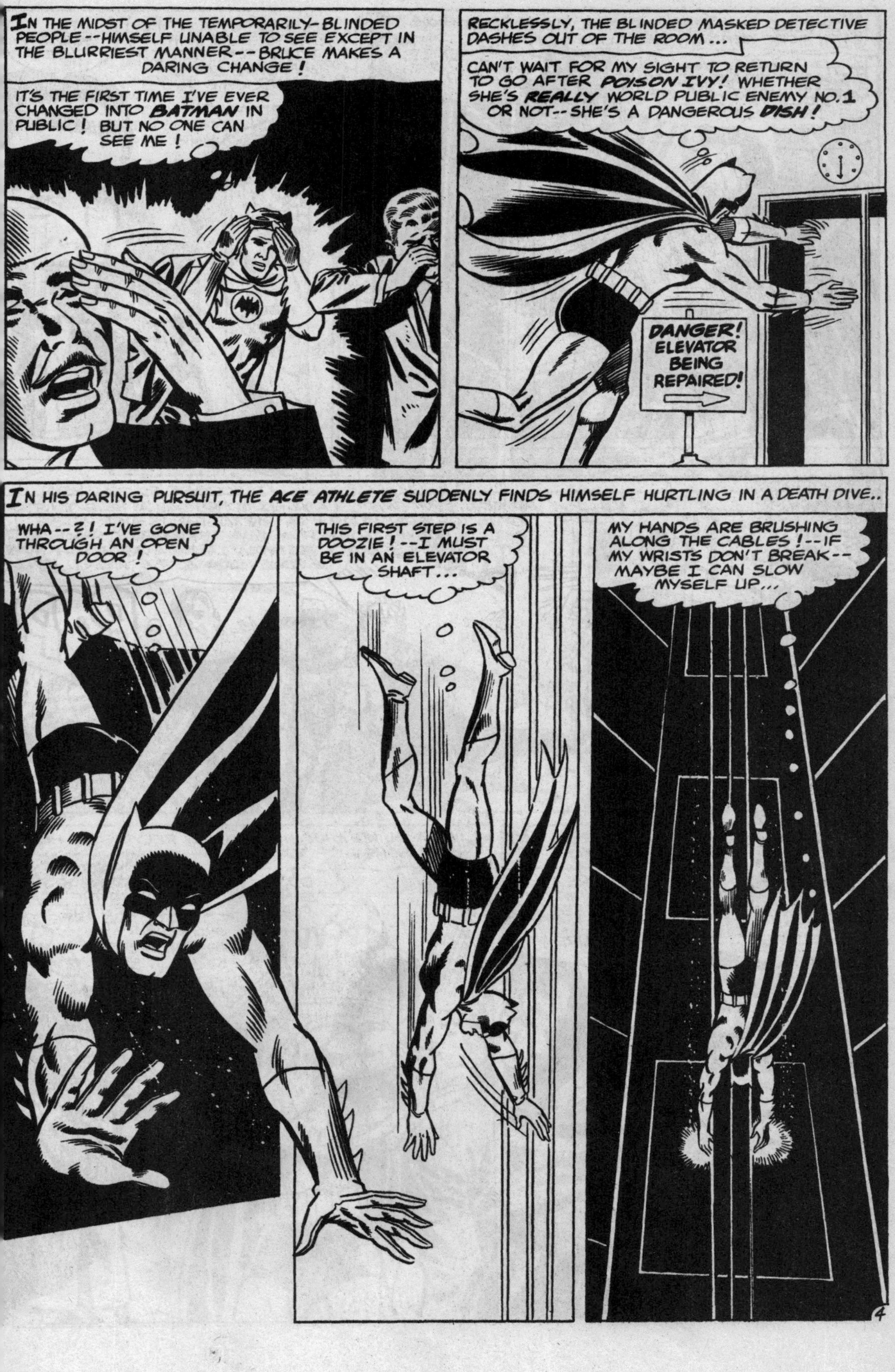
IN THE MIDST OF THE TEMPORARILY-BLINDED PEOPLE--HIMSELF UNABLE TO SEE EXCEPT IN THE BLURRIEST MANNER--BRUCE MAKES A DARING CHANGE!
IT'S THE FIRST TIME I'VE EVER CHANGED INTO BATMAN IN PUBLIC! BUT NO ONE CAN SEE ME!
RECKLESSLY, THE BLINDED MASKED DETECTIVE DASHES OUT OF THE ROOM...
CAN'T WAIT FOR MY SIGHT TO RETURN TO GO AFTER POISON IVY! WHETHER SHE'S REALLY WORLD PUBLIC ENEMY NO.1 OR NOT--SHE'S A DANGEROUS DISH!
DANGER! ELEVATOR BEING REPAIRED!
IN HIS DARING PURSUIT, THE ACE ATHLETE SUDDENLY FINDS HIMSELF HURTLING IN A DEATH DIVE..
WHA--?! I'VE GONE THROUGH AN OPEN DOOR!
THIS FIRST STEP IS A DOOZIE!--I MUST BE IN AN ELEVATOR SHAFT...
MY HANDS ARE BRUSHING ALONG THE CABLES!--IF MY WRISTS DON'T BREAK--MAYBE I CAN SLOW MYSELF UP...
4

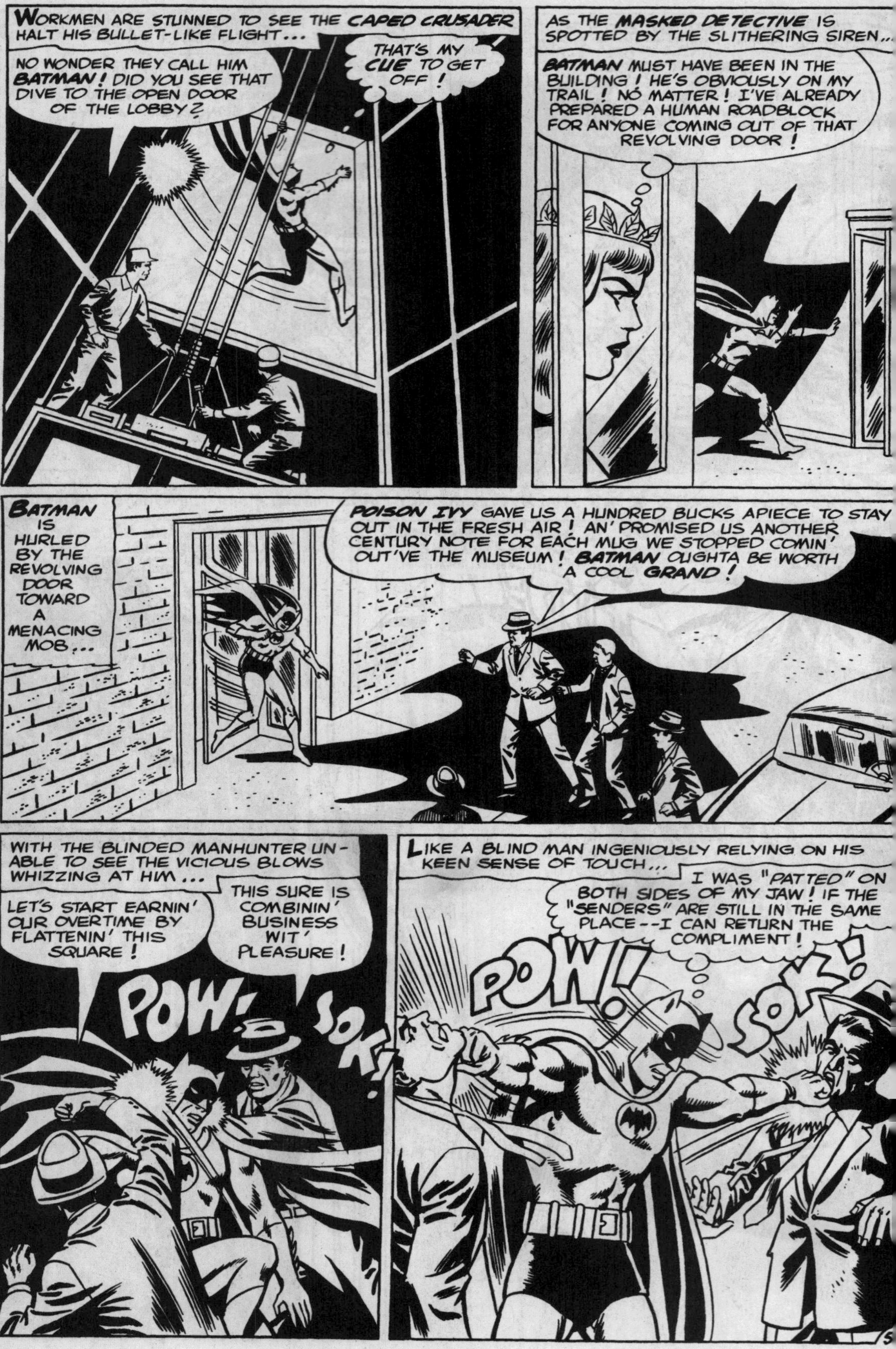
WORKMEN ARE STUNNED TO SEE THE CAPED CRUSADER HALT HIS BULLET-LIKE FLIGHT...
NO WONDER THEY CALL HIM BATMAN! DID YOU SEE THAT DIVE TO THE OPEN DOOR OF THE LOBBY?
THAT'S MY CUE TO GET OFF!
AS THE MASKED DETECTIVE IS SPOTTED BY THE SLITHERING SIREN...
BATMAN MUST HAVE BEEN IN THE BUILDING! HE'S OBVIOUSLY ON MY TRAIL! NO MATTER! I'VE ALREADY PREPARED A HUMAN ROADBLOCK FOR ANYONE COMING OUT OF THAT REVOLVING DOOR!
BATMAN IS HURLED BY THE REVOLVING DOOR TOWARD A MENACING MOB...
POISON IVY GAVE US A HUNDRED BUCKS APIECE TO STAY OUT IN THE FRESH AIR! AN' PROMISED US ANOTHER CENTURY NOTE FOR EACH MUG WE STOPPED COMIN' OUT'VE THE MUSEUM! BATMAN OUGHTA BE WORTH A COOL GRAND!
WITH THE BLINDED MANHUNTER UN-ABLE TO SEE THE VICIOUS BLOWS WHIZZING AT HIM...
LET'S START EARNIN' OUR OVERTIME BY FLATTENIN' THIS SQUARE!
THIS SURE IS COMBININ' BUSINESS WIT' PLEASURE!
POW!
SOK!
LIKE A BLIND MAN INGENIOUSLY RELYING ON HIS KEEN SENSE OF TOUCH...
I WAS "PATTED" ON BOTH SIDES OF MY JAW! IF THE "SENDERS" ARE STILL IN THE SAME PLACE--I CAN RETURN THE COMPLIMENT!
POW!
SOK!

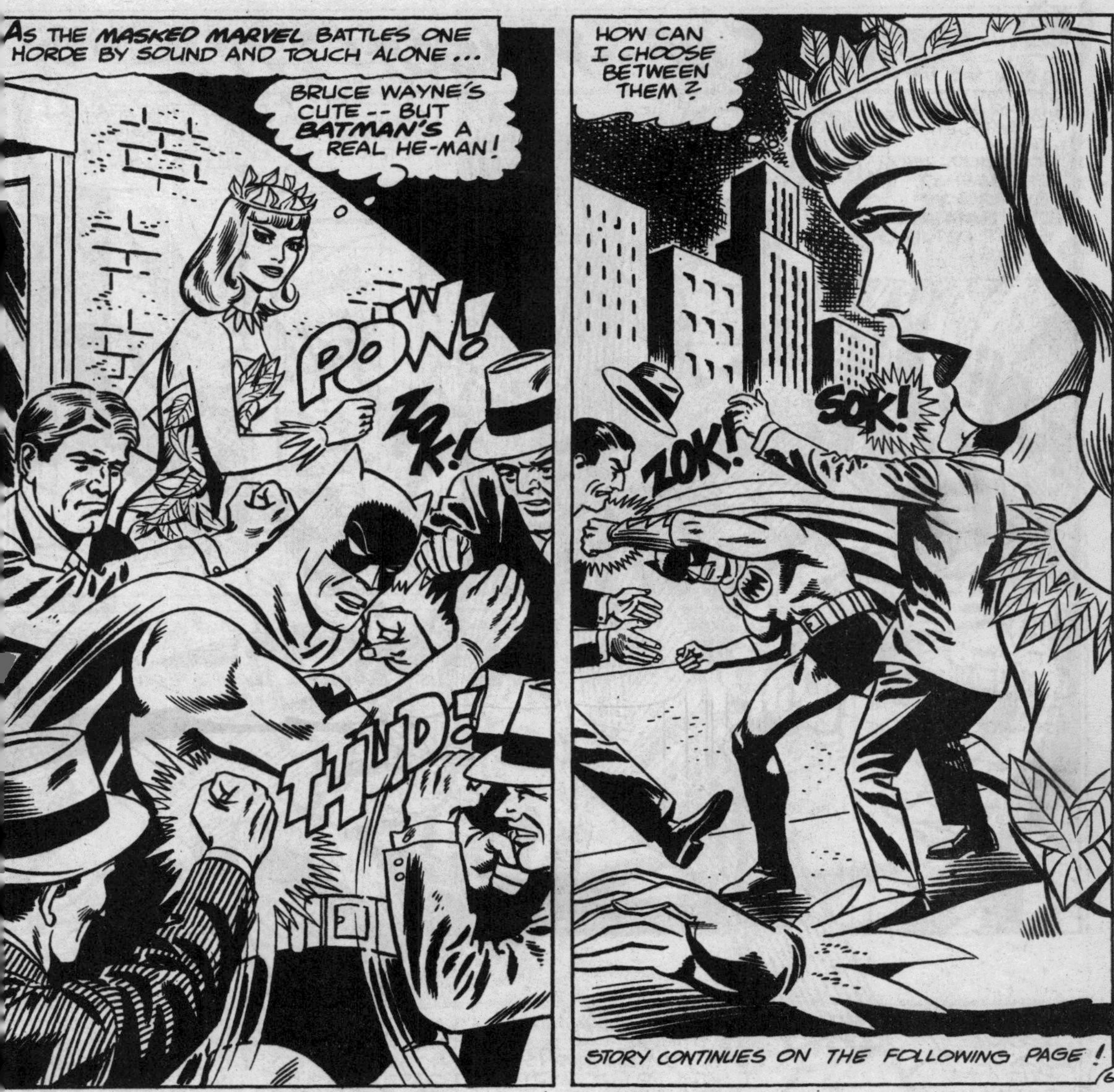
AS THE MASKED MARVEL BATTLES ONE HORDE BY SOUND AND TOUCH ALONE ...
BRUCE WAYNE'S CUTE -- BUT BATMAN'S A REAL HE-MAN!
POW!
ZOK!
THUD!
HOW CAN I CHOOSE BETWEEN THEM?
SOK!
ZOK!
STORY CONTINUES ON THE FOLLOWING PAGE!
6

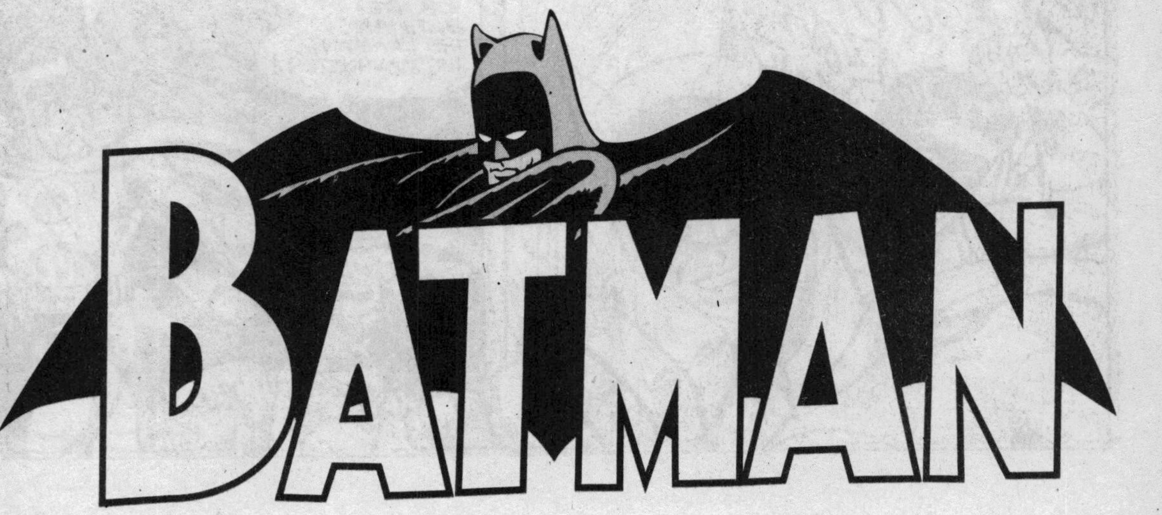
BATMAN

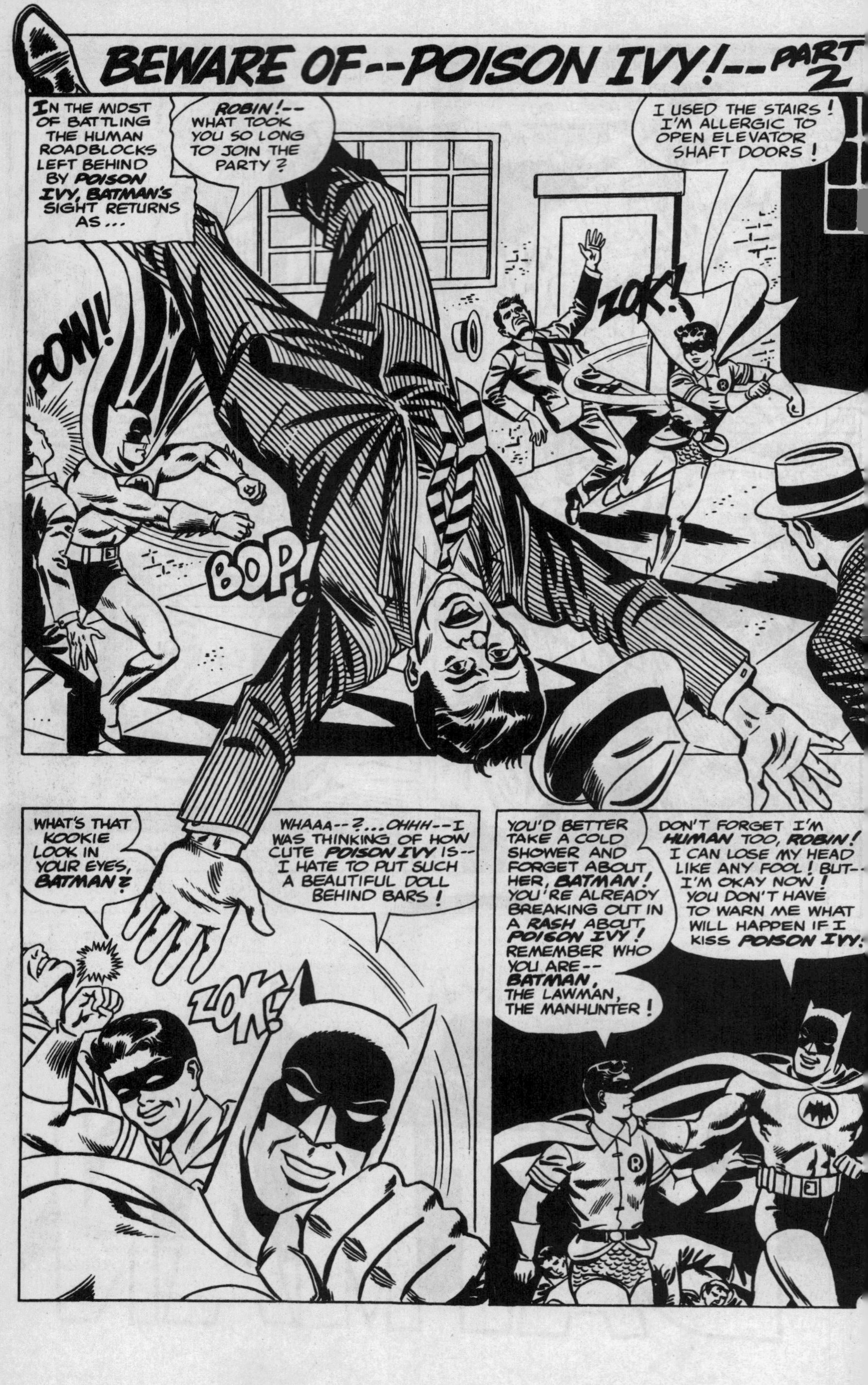
BEWARE OF--POISON IVY!--PART 2
IN THE MIDST OF BATTLING THE HUMAN ROADBLOCKS LEFT BEHIND BY POISON IVY, BATMAN'S SIGHT RETURNS AS...
ROBIN!-- WHAT TOOK YOU SO LONG TO JOIN THE PARTY?
I USED THE STAIRS! I'M ALLERGIC TO OPEN ELEVATOR SHAFT DOORS!
POW!
ZOK!
BOP!
WHAT'S THAT KOOKIE LOOK IN YOUR EYES, BATMAN?
WHAAA--?...OHHH--I WAS THINKING OF HOW CUTE POISON IVY IS-- I HATE TO PUT SUCH A BEAUTIFUL DOLL BEHIND BARS!
ZOK!
YOU'D BETTER TAKE A COLD SHOWER AND FORGET ABOUT HER, BATMAN! YOU'RE ALREADY BREAKING OUT IN A RASH ABOUT POISON IVY! REMEMBER WHO YOU ARE-- BATMAN, THE LAWMAN, THE MANHUNTER!
DON'T FORGET I'M HUMAN TOO, ROBIN! I CAN LOSE MY HEAD LIKE ANY FOOL! BUT-- I'M OKAY NOW! YOU DON'T HAVE TO WARN ME WHAT WILL HAPPEN IF I KISS POISON IVY!

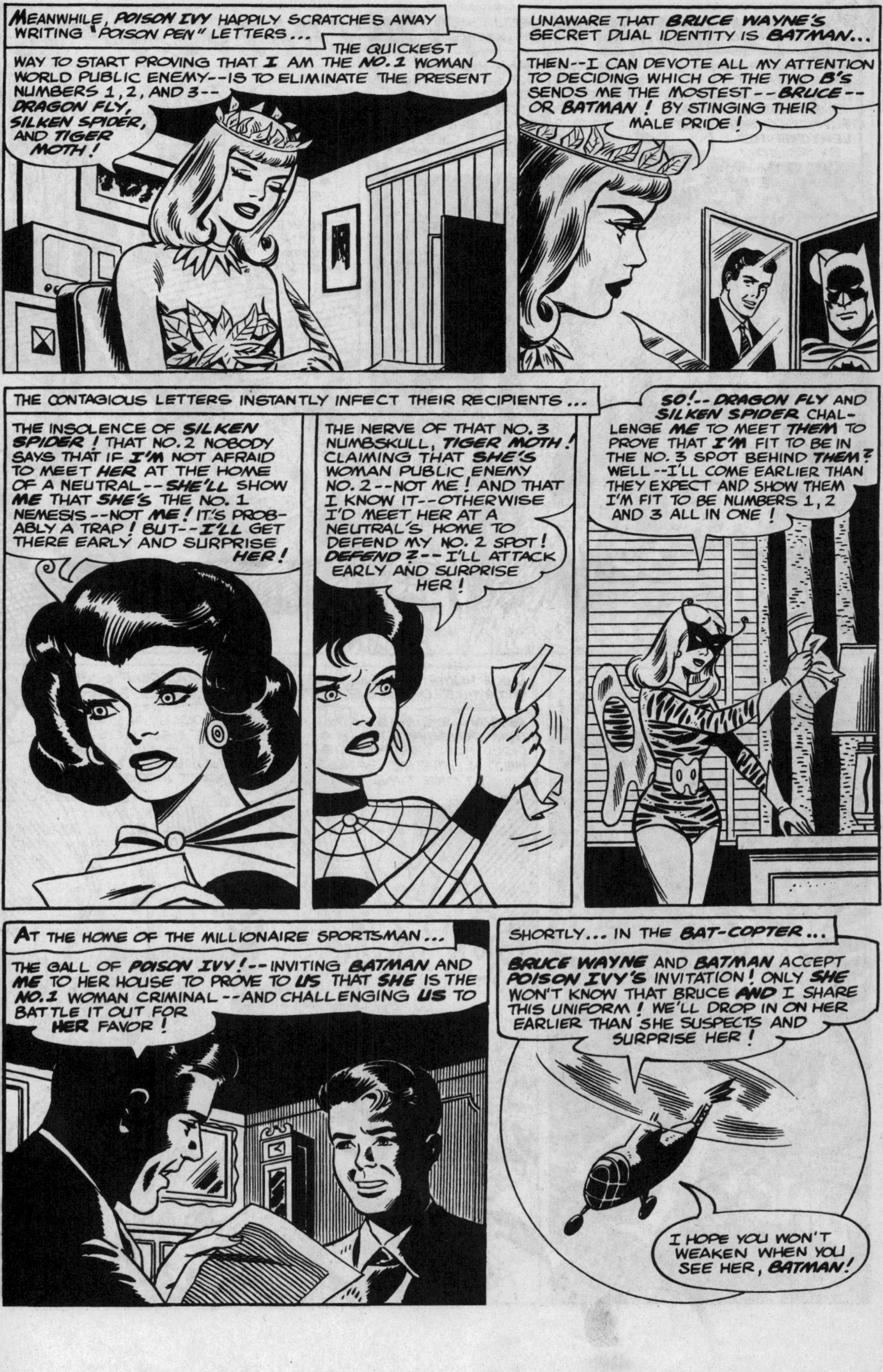
MEANWHILE, POISON IVY HAPPILY SCRATCHES AWAY WRITING "POISON PEN" LETTERS...
THE QUICKEST WAY TO START PROVING THAT I AM THE NO.1 WOMAN WORLD PUBLIC ENEMY--IS TO ELIMINATE THE PRESENT NUMBERS 1, 2, AND 3-- DRAGON FLY, SILKEN SPIDER, AND TIGER MOTH!
UNAWARE THAT BRUCE WAYNE'S SECRET DUAL IDENTITY IS BATMAN...
THEN--I CAN DEVOTE ALL MY ATTENTION TO DECIDING WHICH OF THE TWO B'S SENDS ME THE MOSTEST--BRUCE--OR BATMAN! BY STINGING THEIR MALE PRIDE!
THE CONTAGIOUS LETTERS INSTANTLY INFECT THEIR RECIPIENTS...
THE INSOLENCE OF SILKEN SPIDER! THAT NO.2 NOBODY SAYS THAT IF I'M NOT AFRAID TO MEET HER AT THE HOME OF A NEUTRAL--SHE'LL SHOW ME THAT SHE'S THE NO.1 NEMESIS--NOT ME! IT'S PROBABLY A TRAP! BUT--I'LL GET THERE EARLY AND SURPRISE HER!
THE NERVE OF THAT NO.3 NUMBSKULL, TIGER MOTH! CLAIMING THAT SHE'S WOMAN PUBLIC ENEMY NO.2--NOT ME! AND THAT I KNOW IT--OTHERWISE I'D MEET HER AT A NEUTRAL'S HOME TO DEFEND MY NO.2 SPOT! DEFEND?--I'LL ATTACK EARLY AND SURPRISE HER!
SO!--DRAGON FLY AND SILKEN SPIDER CHALLENGE ME TO MEET THEM TO PROVE THAT I'M FIT TO BE IN THE NO.3 SPOT BEHIND THEM? WELL--I'LL COME EARLIER THAN THEY EXPECT AND SHOW THEM I'M FIT TO BE NUMBERS 1, 2 AND 3 ALL IN ONE!
AT THE HOME OF THE MILLIONAIRE SPORTSMAN...
THE GALL OF POISON IVY!--INVITING BATMAN AND ME TO HER HOUSE TO PROVE TO US THAT SHE IS THE NO.1 WOMAN CRIMINAL--AND CHALLENGING US TO BATTLE IT OUT FOR HER FAVOR!
SHORTLY... IN THE BAT-COPTER...
BRUCE WAYNE AND BATMAN ACCEPT POISON IVY'S INVITATION! ONLY SHE WON'T KNOW THAT BRUCE AND I SHARE THIS UNIFORM! WE'LL DROP IN ON HER EARLIER THAN SHE SUSPECTS AND SURPRISE HER!
I HOPE YOU WON'T WEAKEN WHEN YOU SEE HER, BATMAN!

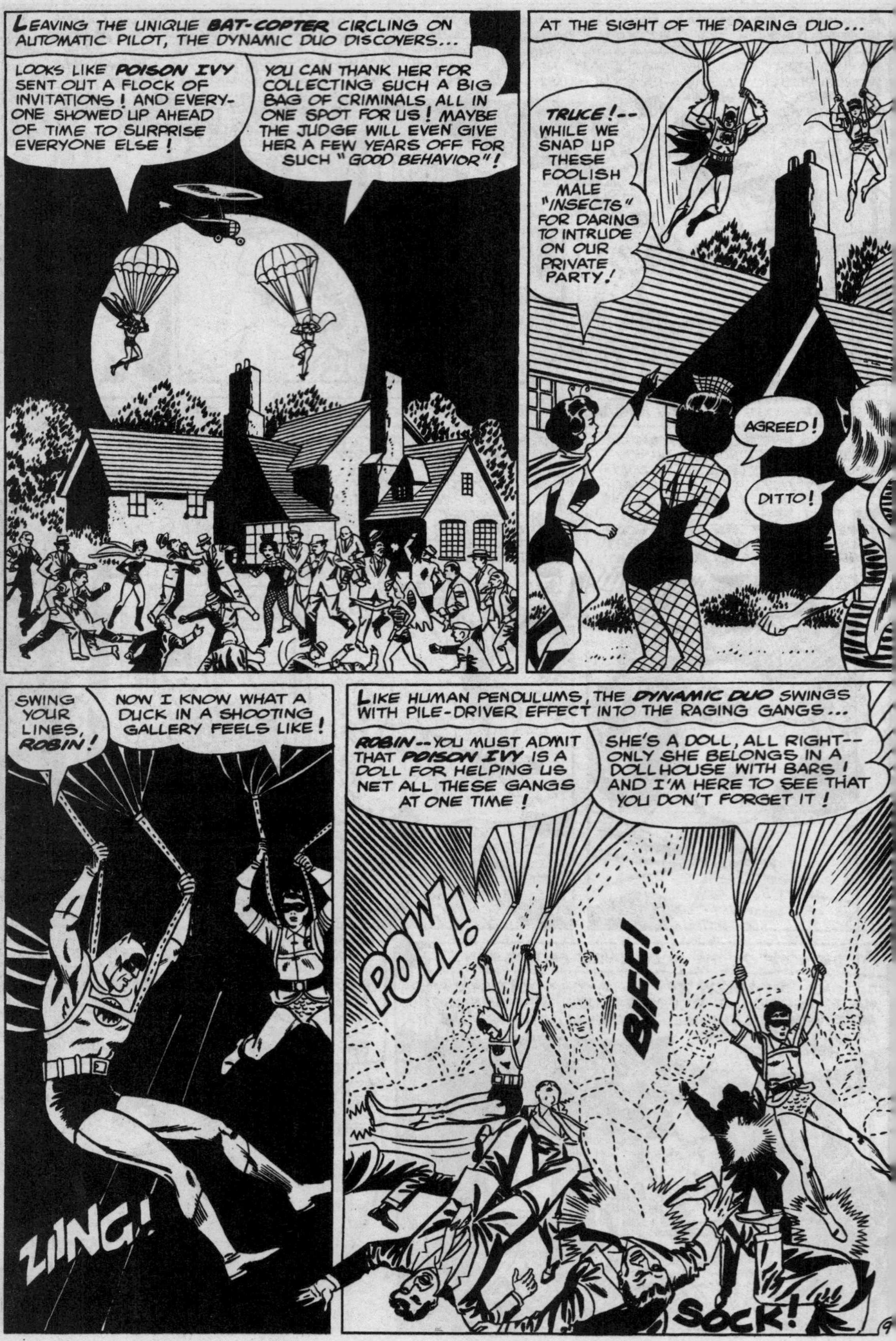
LEAVING THE UNIQUE BAT-COPTER CIRCLING ON AUTOMATIC PILOT, THE DYNAMIC DUO DISCOVERS...
LOOKS LIKE POISON IVY SENT OUT A FLOCK OF INVITATIONS! AND EVERYONE SHOWED UP AHEAD OF TIME TO SURPRISE EVERYONE ELSE!
YOU CAN THANK HER FOR COLLECTING SUCH A BIG BAG OF CRIMINALS ALL IN ONE SPOT FOR US! MAYBE THE JUDGE WILL EVEN GIVE HER A FEW YEARS OFF FOR SUCH "GOOD BEHAVIOR"!
AT THE SIGHT OF THE DARING DUO...
TRUCE!-- WHILE WE SNAP UP THESE FOOLISH MALE "INSECTS" FOR DARING TO INTRUDE ON OUR PRIVATE PARTY!
AGREED!
DITTO!
SWING YOUR LINES, ROBIN!
NOW I KNOW WHAT A DUCK IN A SHOOTING GALLERY FEELS LIKE!
ZIING!
LIKE HUMAN PENDULUMS, THE DYNAMIC DUO SWINGS WITH PILE-DRIVER EFFECT INTO THE RAGING GANGS...
ROBIN--YOU MUST ADMIT THAT POISON IVY IS A DOLL FOR HELPING US NET ALL THESE GANGS AT ONE TIME!
SHE'S A DOLL, ALL RIGHT-- ONLY SHE BELONGS IN A DOLLHOUSE WITH BARS! AND I'M HERE TO SEE THAT YOU DON'T FORGET IT!
POW!
BIFF!
SOCK!

AS THE THREE BALEFUL BEAUTIES FLEE...

OHHHH--MUST YOU LEAVE SO SOON? I WAS GOING TO PRESENT THIS PRICELESS *CROWN* TO WHICHEVER ONE OF YOU PROVED THAT *SHE* AND SHE *ALONE* WAS WORTHY TO BE THE *REAL* NO. 1 WANTED WOMAN CRIMINAL OF THE WORLD!

I'M ELECTING MYSELF NO. 1--IT BELONGS TO ME! LET GO!

I'M DEPOSING *YOU* AS OF RIGHT NOW!

NEITHER OF YOU WILL GET IT AS LONG AS I'VE GOT *MY* HANDS ON IT!

HOW THOUGHTLESS OF ME NOT TO MENTION THAT I USED *SHOCK-PROOF GLOVES* TO HOLD THE CROWN! IT'S ELECTRIFIED JUST ENOUGH TO KEEP YOU DANCING A SIZZLING *FRUG* UNTIL THE POLICE GET HERE! BUT--LONG BEFORE THEY DO-- I'LL START SHOWING THE WORLD WHAT THE REAL *NO. 1* CAN DO IN CRIMES A LITTLE *LESS* THAN *PERFECT*--SO EVERYONE WILL KNOW THAT THEY WERE COMMITTED BY THE QUEEN OF CRIME-- ME--POISON IVY!!

OHWOOO-- OHHHHHH--!

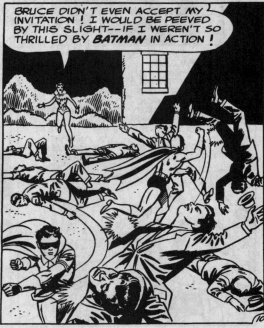

BRUCE DIDN'T EVEN ACCEPT MY INVITATION! I WOULD BE PEEVED BY THIS SLIGHT--IF I WEREN'T SO THRILLED BY *BATMAN* IN ACTION!

10

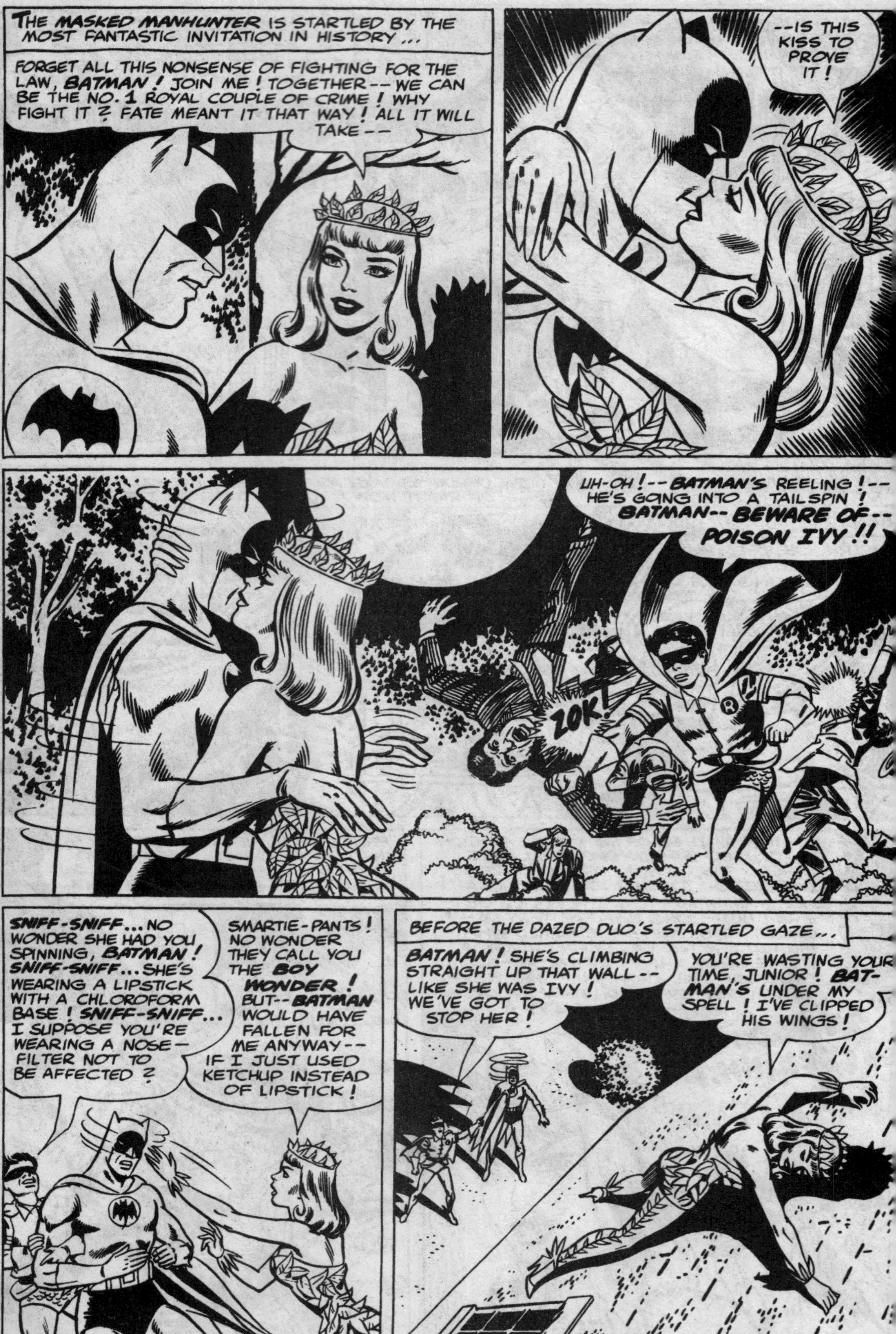

THE MASKED MANHUNTER IS STARTLED BY THE MOST FANTASTIC INVITATION IN HISTORY...
FORGET ALL THIS NONSENSE OF FIGHTING FOR THE LAW, BATMAN! JOIN ME! TOGETHER-- WE CAN BE THE NO. 1 ROYAL COUPLE OF CRIME! WHY FIGHT IT? FATE MEANT IT THAT WAY! ALL IT WILL TAKE--
--IS THIS KISS TO PROVE IT!
UH-OH!--BATMAN'S REELING!-- HE'S GOING INTO A TAILSPIN! BATMAN-- BEWARE OF-- POISON IVY!!
ZOK!
SNIFF-SNIFF... NO WONDER SHE HAD YOU SPINNING, BATMAN! SNIFF-SNIFF... SHE'S WEARING A LIPSTICK WITH A CHLOROFORM BASE! SNIFF-SNIFF... I SUPPOSE YOU'RE WEARING A NOSE-FILTER NOT TO BE AFFECTED?
SMARTIE-PANTS! NO WONDER THEY CALL YOU THE BOY WONDER! BUT--BATMAN WOULD HAVE FALLEN FOR ME ANYWAY-- IF I JUST USED KETCHUP INSTEAD OF LIPSTICK!
BEFORE THE DAZED DUO'S STARTLED GAZE...
BATMAN! SHE'S CLIMBING STRAIGHT UP THAT WALL-- LIKE SHE WAS IVY! WE'VE GOT TO STOP HER!
YOU'RE WASTING YOUR TIME, JUNIOR! BATMAN'S UNDER MY SPELL! I'VE CLIPPED HIS WINGS!

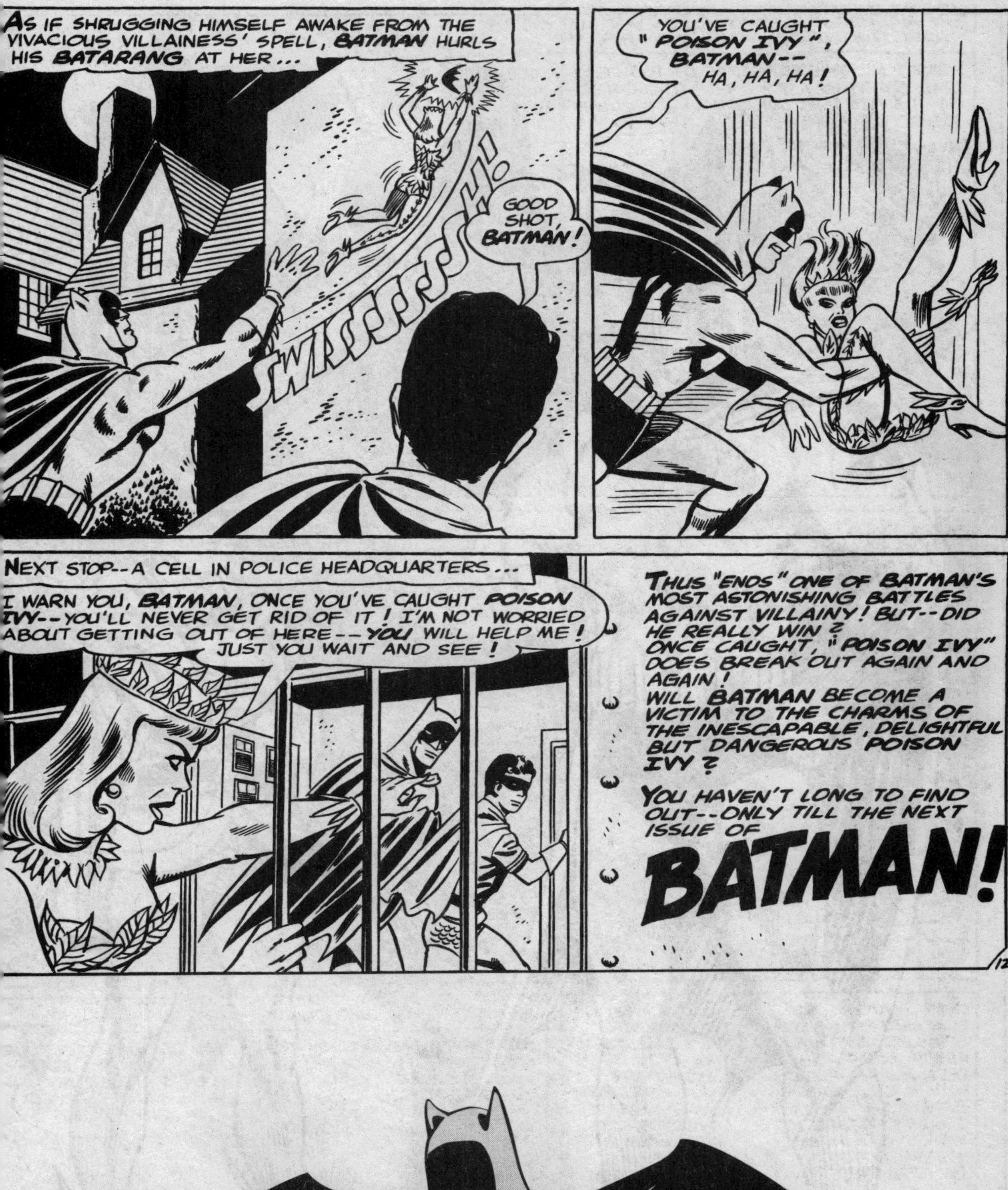
AS IF SHRUGGING HIMSELF AWAKE FROM THE VIVACIOUS VILLAINESS' SPELL, BATMAN HURLS HIS BATARANG AT HER...
SWISSSSSSH!
GOOD SHOT, BATMAN!
YOU'VE CAUGHT "POISON IVY", BATMAN-- HA, HA, HA!
NEXT STOP--A CELL IN POLICE HEADQUARTERS...
I WARN YOU, BATMAN, ONCE YOU'VE CAUGHT POISON IVY--YOU'LL NEVER GET RID OF IT! I'M NOT WORRIED ABOUT GETTING OUT OF HERE--YOU WILL HELP ME! JUST YOU WAIT AND SEE!
THUS "ENDS" ONE OF BATMAN'S MOST ASTONISHING BATTLES AGAINST VILLAINY! BUT--DID HE REALLY WIN?
ONCE CAUGHT, "POISON IVY" DOES BREAK OUT AGAIN AND AGAIN!
WILL BATMAN BECOME A VICTIM TO THE CHARMS OF THE INESCAPABLE, DELIGHTFUL BUT DANGEROUS POISON IVY?
YOU HAVEN'T LONG TO FIND OUT--ONLY TILL THE NEXT ISSUE OF
BATMAN!
12

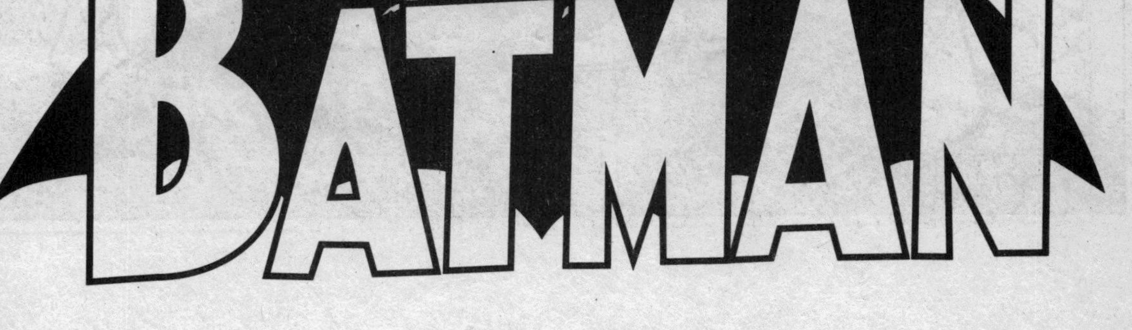
BATMAN

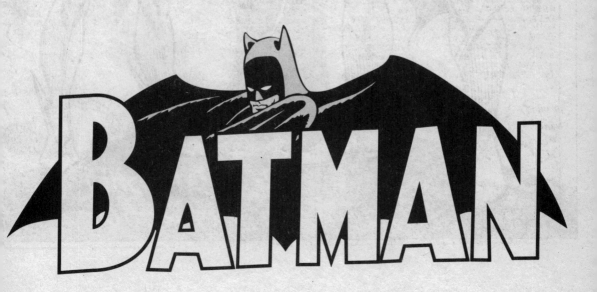

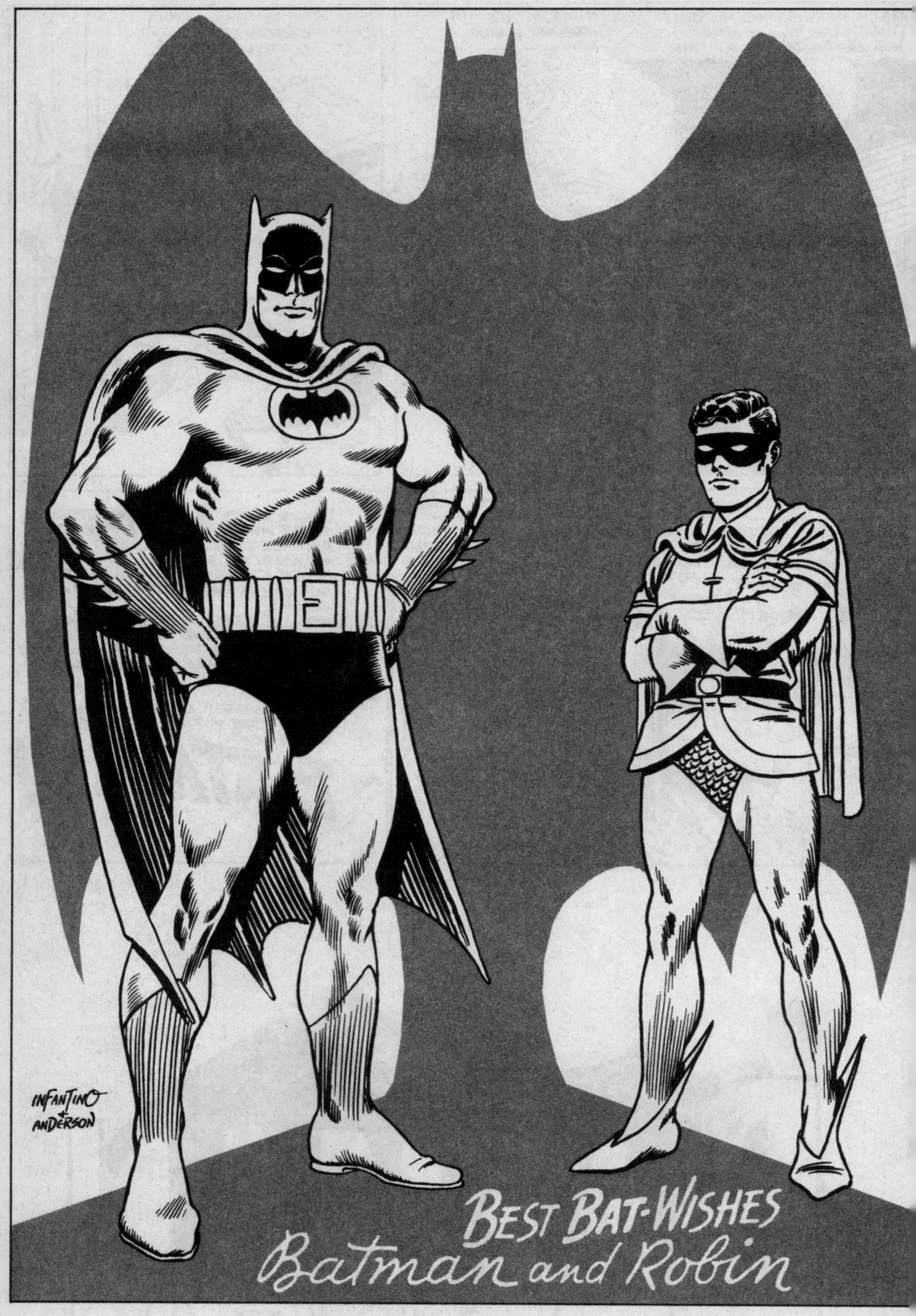
INFANTINO + ANDERSON
BEST BAT-WISHES
Batman and Robin

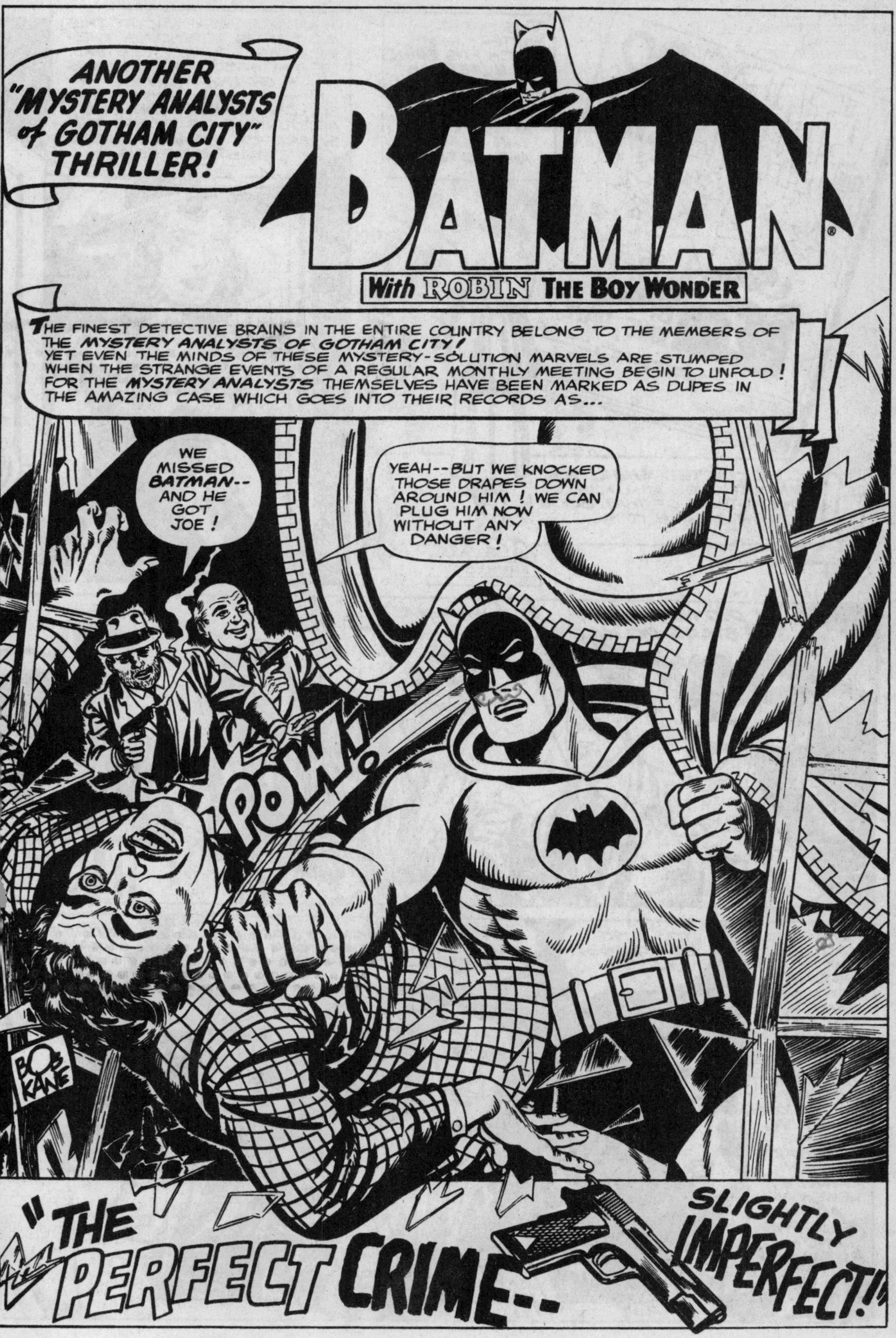
ANOTHER "MYSTERY ANALYSTS of GOTHAM CITY" THRILLER!
BATMAN®
With ROBIN THE BOY WONDER
THE FINEST DETECTIVE BRAINS IN THE ENTIRE COUNTRY BELONG TO THE MEMBERS OF THE MYSTERY ANALYSTS OF GOTHAM CITY! YET EVEN THE MINDS OF THESE MYSTERY-SOLUTION MARVELS ARE STUMPED WHEN THE STRANGE EVENTS OF A REGULAR MONTHLY MEETING BEGIN TO UNFOLD! FOR THE MYSTERY ANALYSTS THEMSELVES HAVE BEEN MARKED AS DUPES IN THE AMAZING CASE WHICH GOES INTO THEIR RECORDS AS...
WE MISSED BATMAN-- AND HE GOT JOE!
YEAH--BUT WE KNOCKED THOSE DRAPES DOWN AROUND HIM! WE CAN PLUG HIM NOW WITHOUT ANY DANGER!
POW!
BOB KANE
"THE PERFECT CRIME-- SLIGHTLY IMPERFECT!"

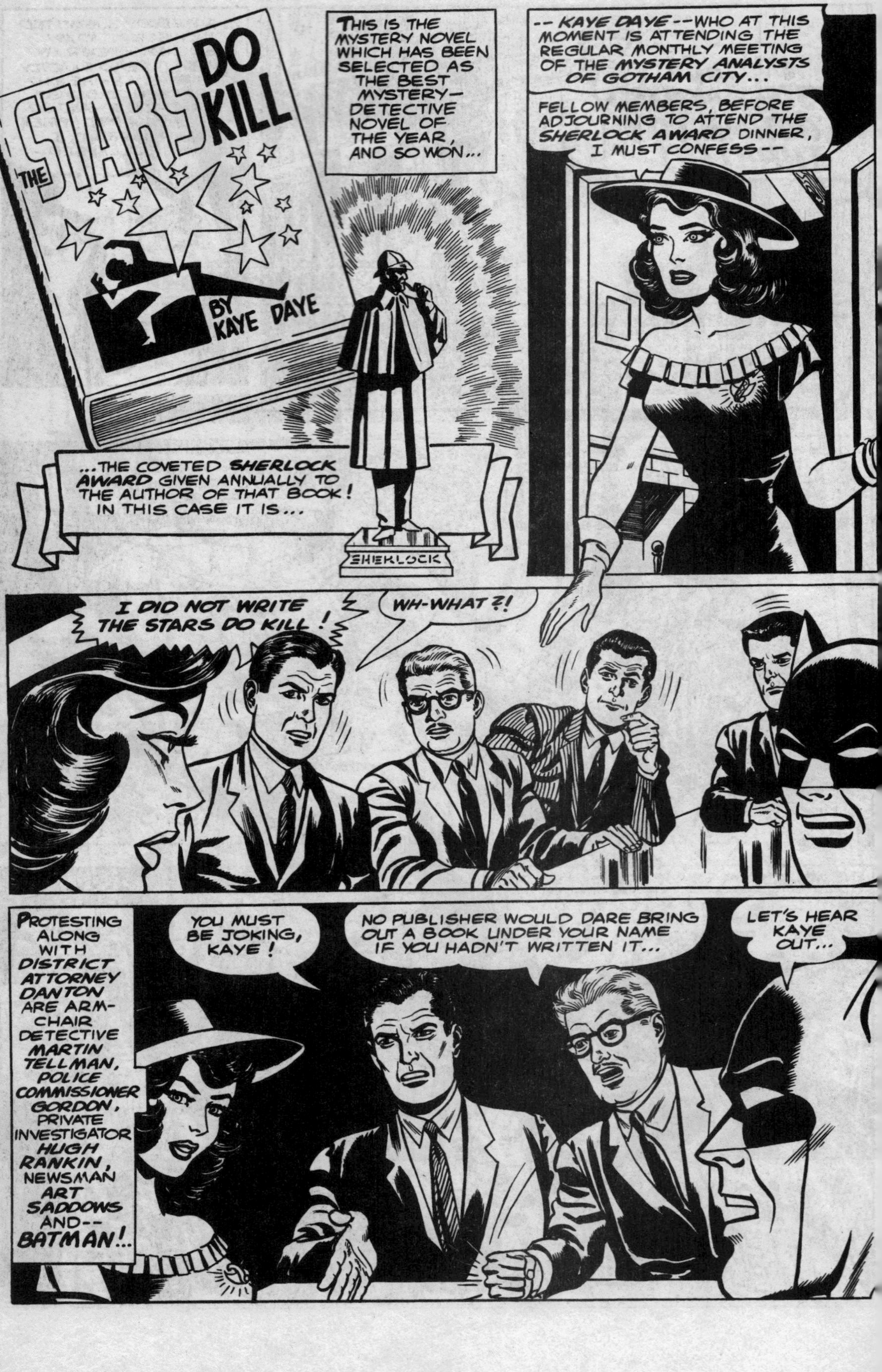
THE STARS DO KILL
BY KAYE DAYE
THIS IS THE MYSTERY NOVEL WHICH HAS BEEN SELECTED AS THE BEST MYSTERY-DETECTIVE NOVEL OF THE YEAR, AND SO WON...
...THE COVETED SHERLOCK AWARD GIVEN ANNUALLY TO THE AUTHOR OF THAT BOOK! IN THIS CASE IT IS...
SHERLOCK
-- KAYE DAYE --WHO AT THIS MOMENT IS ATTENDING THE REGULAR MONTHLY MEETING OF THE MYSTERY ANALYSTS OF GOTHAM CITY...
FELLOW MEMBERS, BEFORE ADJOURNING TO ATTEND THE SHERLOCK AWARD DINNER, I MUST CONFESS--
I DID NOT WRITE THE STARS DO KILL!
WH-WHAT?!
PROTESTING ALONG WITH DISTRICT ATTORNEY DANTON ARE ARM-CHAIR DETECTIVE MARTIN TELLMAN, POLICE COMMISSIONER GORDON, PRIVATE INVESTIGATOR HUGH RANKIN, NEWSMAN ART SADDOWS AND-- BATMAN!...
YOU MUST BE JOKING, KAYE!
NO PUBLISHER WOULD DARE BRING OUT A BOOK UNDER YOUR NAME IF YOU HADN'T WRITTEN IT...
LET'S HEAR KAYE OUT...

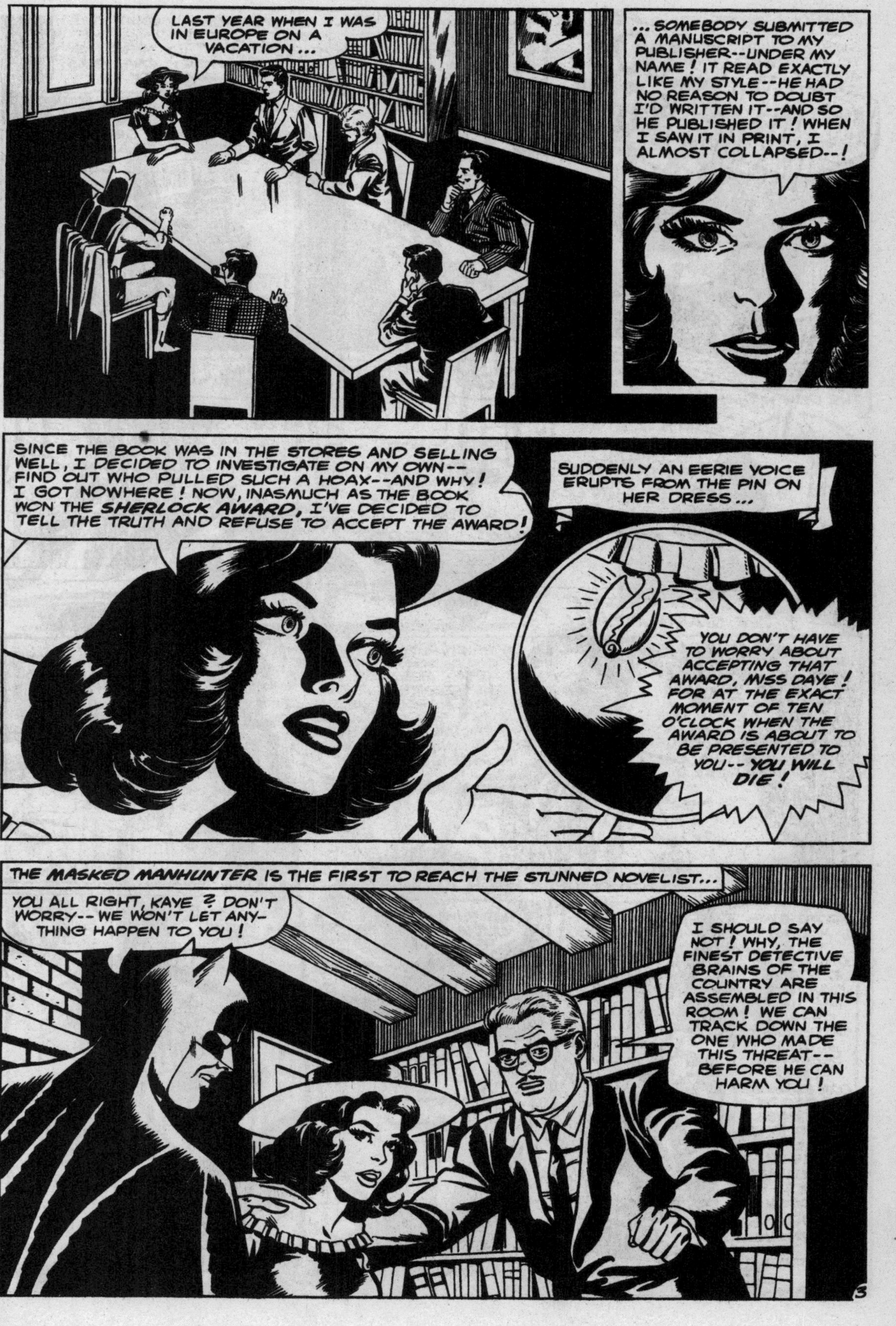
LAST YEAR WHEN I WAS IN EUROPE ON A VACATION...
...SOMEBODY SUBMITTED A MANUSCRIPT TO MY PUBLISHER--UNDER MY NAME! IT READ EXACTLY LIKE MY STYLE--HE HAD NO REASON TO DOUBT I'D WRITTEN IT--AND SO HE PUBLISHED IT! WHEN I SAW IT IN PRINT, I ALMOST COLLAPSED--!
SINCE THE BOOK WAS IN THE STORES AND SELLING WELL, I DECIDED TO INVESTIGATE ON MY OWN--FIND OUT WHO PULLED SUCH A HOAX--AND WHY! I GOT NOWHERE! NOW, INASMUCH AS THE BOOK WON THE SHERLOCK AWARD, I'VE DECIDED TO TELL THE TRUTH AND REFUSE TO ACCEPT THE AWARD!
SUDDENLY AN EERIE VOICE ERUPTS FROM THE PIN ON HER DRESS...
YOU DON'T HAVE TO WORRY ABOUT ACCEPTING THAT AWARD, MISS DAYE! FOR AT THE EXACT MOMENT OF TEN O'CLOCK WHEN THE AWARD IS ABOUT TO BE PRESENTED TO YOU--YOU WILL DIE!
THE MASKED MANHUNTER IS THE FIRST TO REACH THE STUNNED NOVELIST...
YOU ALL RIGHT, KAYE? DON'T WORRY--WE WON'T LET ANYTHING HAPPEN TO YOU!
I SHOULD SAY NOT! WHY, THE FINEST DETECTIVE BRAINS OF THE COUNTRY ARE ASSEMBLED IN THIS ROOM! WE CAN TRACK DOWN THE ONE WHO MADE THIS THREAT--BEFORE HE CAN HARM YOU!
3

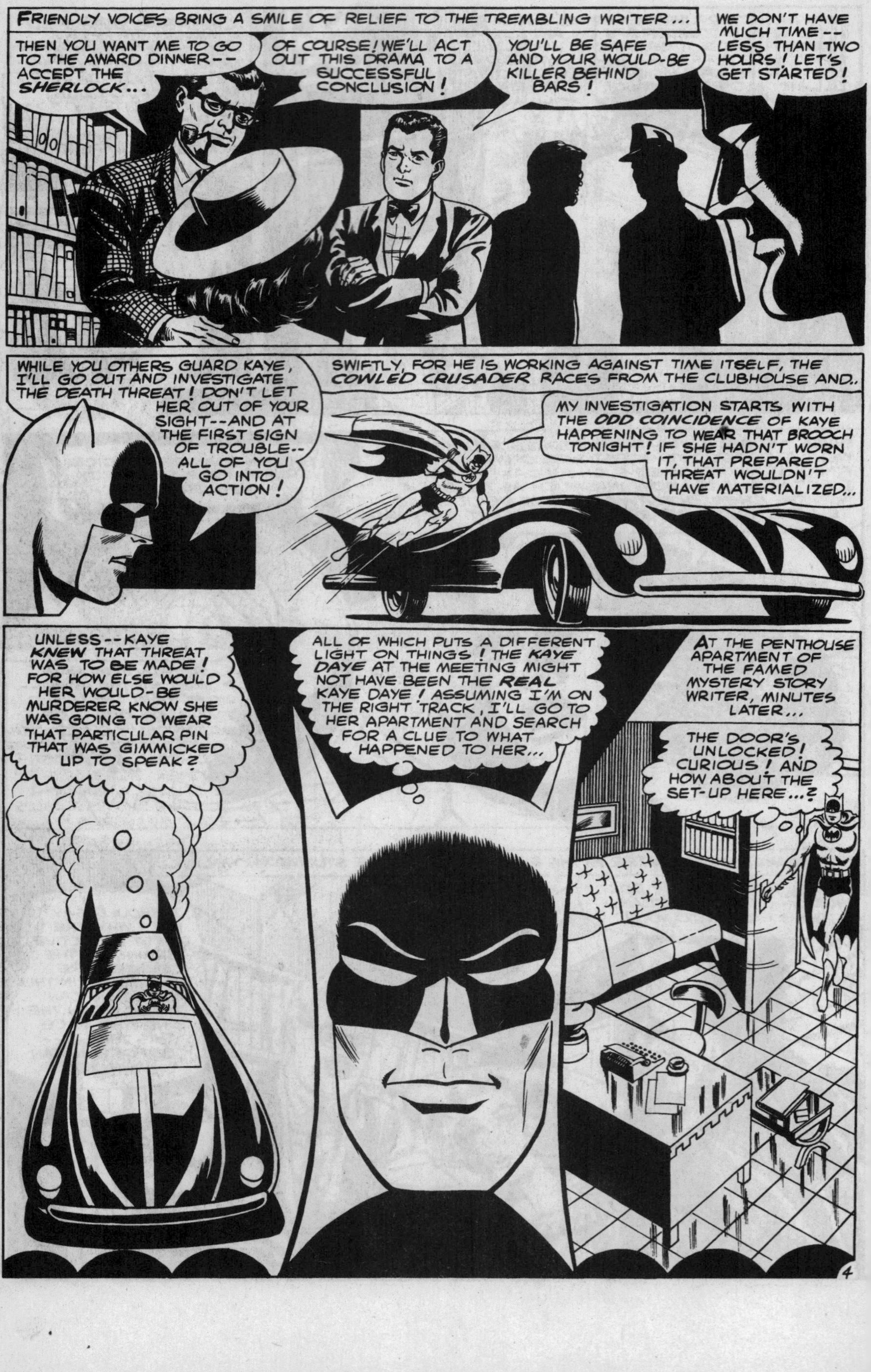
FRIENDLY VOICES BRING A SMILE OF RELIEF TO THE TREMBLING WRITER...
THEN YOU WANT ME TO GO TO THE AWARD DINNER-- ACCEPT THE SHERLOCK...
OF COURSE! WE'LL ACT OUT THIS DRAMA TO A SUCCESSFUL CONCLUSION!
YOU'LL BE SAFE AND YOUR WOULD-BE KILLER BEHIND BARS!
WE DON'T HAVE MUCH TIME-- LESS THAN TWO HOURS! LET'S GET STARTED!
WHILE YOU OTHERS GUARD KAYE, I'LL GO OUT AND INVESTIGATE THE DEATH THREAT! DON'T LET HER OUT OF YOUR SIGHT--AND AT THE FIRST SIGN OF TROUBLE-- ALL OF YOU GO INTO ACTION!
SWIFTLY, FOR HE IS WORKING AGAINST TIME ITSELF, THE COWLED CRUSADER RACES FROM THE CLUBHOUSE AND..
MY INVESTIGATION STARTS WITH THE ODD COINCIDENCE OF KAYE HAPPENING TO WEAR THAT BROOCH TONIGHT! IF SHE HADN'T WORN IT, THAT PREPARED THREAT WOULDN'T HAVE MATERIALIZED...
UNLESS--KAYE KNEW THAT THREAT WAS TO BE MADE! FOR HOW ELSE WOULD HER WOULD-BE MURDERER KNOW SHE WAS GOING TO WEAR THAT PARTICULAR PIN THAT WAS GIMMICKED UP TO SPEAK?
ALL OF WHICH PUTS A DIFFERENT LIGHT ON THINGS! THE KAYE DAYE AT THE MEETING MIGHT NOT HAVE BEEN THE REAL KAYE DAYE! ASSUMING I'M ON THE RIGHT TRACK, I'LL GO TO HER APARTMENT AND SEARCH FOR A CLUE TO WHAT HAPPENED TO HER...
AT THE PENTHOUSE APARTMENT OF THE FAMED MYSTERY STORY WRITER, MINUTES LATER...
THE DOOR'S UNLOCKED! CURIOUS! AND HOW ABOUT THE SET-UP HERE...?
4

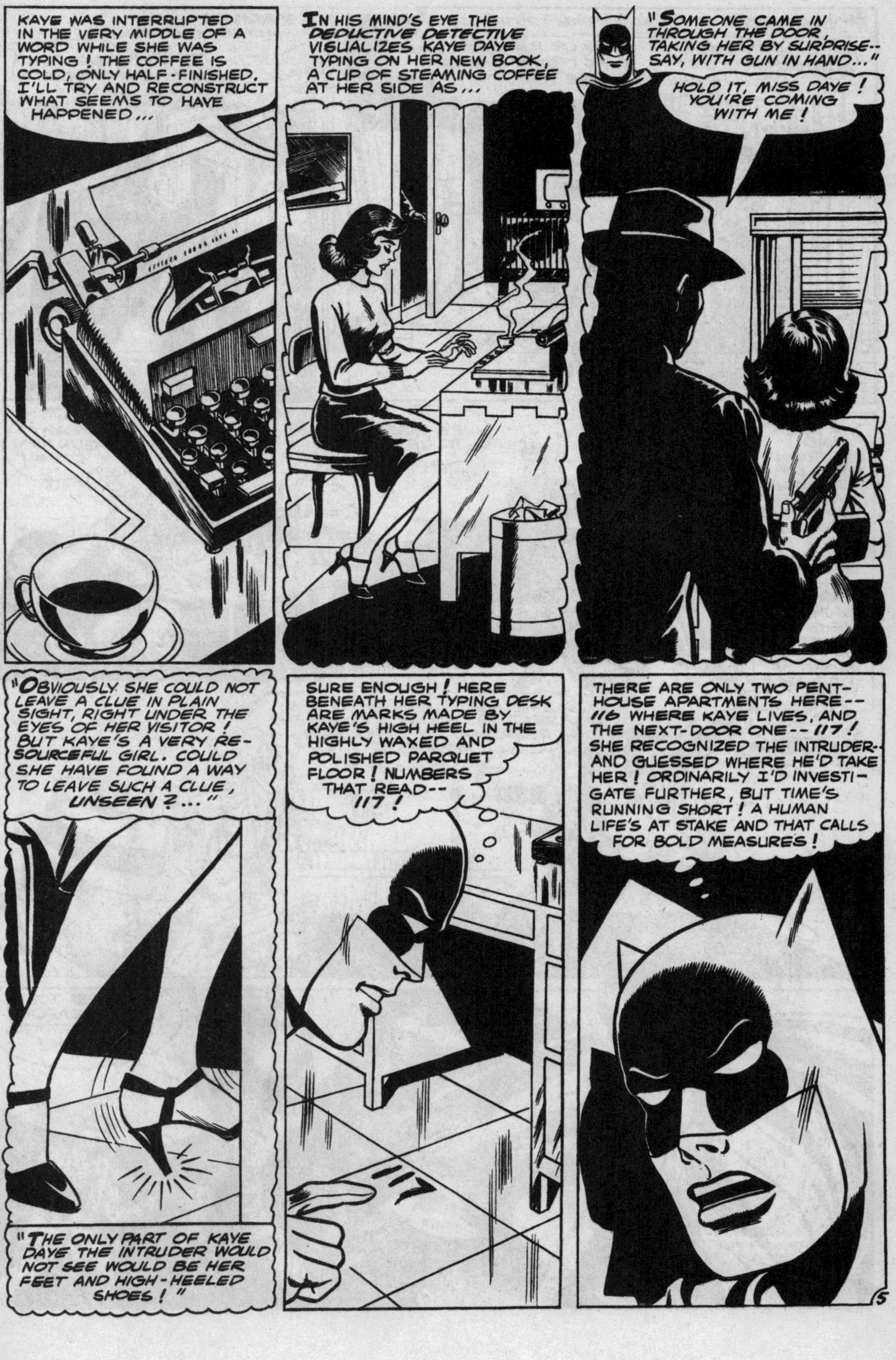
KAYE WAS INTERRUPTED IN THE VERY MIDDLE OF A WORD WHILE SHE WAS TYPING ! THE COFFEE IS COLD, ONLY HALF-FINISHED. I'LL TRY AND RECONSTRUCT WHAT SEEMS TO HAVE HAPPENED...
IN HIS MIND'S EYE THE DEDUCTIVE DETECTIVE VISUALIZES KAYE DAYE TYPING ON HER NEW BOOK, A CUP OF STEAMING COFFEE AT HER SIDE AS...
"SOMEONE CAME IN THROUGH THE DOOR, TAKING HER BY SURPRISE-- SAY, WITH GUN IN HAND..."
HOLD IT, MISS DAYE ! YOU'RE COMING WITH ME !
"OBVIOUSLY SHE COULD NOT LEAVE A CLUE IN PLAIN SIGHT, RIGHT UNDER THE EYES OF HER VISITOR ! BUT KAYE'S A VERY RESOURCEFUL GIRL. COULD SHE HAVE FOUND A WAY TO LEAVE SUCH A CLUE, UNSEEN ?..."
"THE ONLY PART OF KAYE DAYE THE INTRUDER WOULD NOT SEE WOULD BE HER FEET AND HIGH-HEELED SHOES !"
SURE ENOUGH ! HERE BENEATH HER TYPING DESK ARE MARKS MADE BY KAYE'S HIGH HEEL IN THE HIGHLY WAXED AND POLISHED PARQUET FLOOR ! NUMBERS THAT READ-- 117 !
117
THERE ARE ONLY TWO PENT-HOUSE APARTMENTS HERE-- 116 WHERE KAYE LIVES, AND THE NEXT-DOOR ONE-- 117 ! SHE RECOGNIZED THE INTRUDER-- AND GUESSED WHERE HE'D TAKE HER ! ORDINARILY I'D INVESTIGATE FURTHER, BUT TIME'S RUNNING SHORT ! A HUMAN LIFE'S AT STAKE AND THAT CALLS FOR BOLD MEASURES !
5

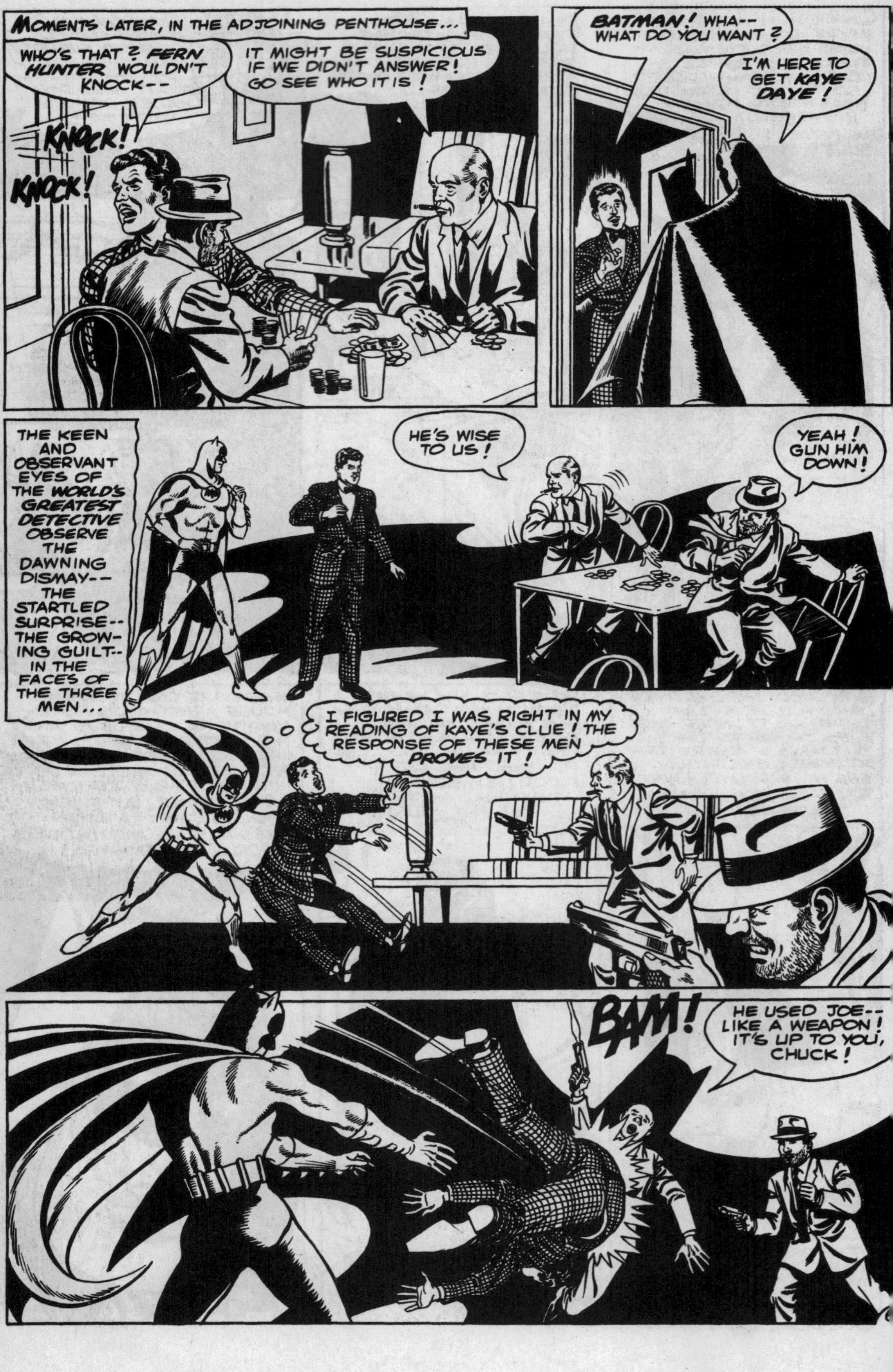
MOMENTS LATER, IN THE ADJOINING PENTHOUSE...
WHO'S THAT? FERN HUNTER WOULDN'T KNOCK--
KNOCK! KNOCK!
IT MIGHT BE SUSPICIOUS IF WE DIDN'T ANSWER! GO SEE WHO IT IS!
BATMAN! WHA-- WHAT DO YOU WANT?
I'M HERE TO GET KAYE DAYE!
THE KEEN AND OBSERVANT EYES OF THE WORLD'S GREATEST DETECTIVE OBSERVE THE DAWNING DISMAY-- THE STARTLED SURPRISE-- THE GROWING GUILT-- IN THE FACES OF THE THREE MEN...
HE'S WISE TO US!
YEAH! GUN HIM DOWN!
I FIGURED I WAS RIGHT IN MY READING OF KAYE'S CLUE! THE RESPONSE OF THESE MEN PROVES IT!
BAM!
HE USED JOE-- LIKE A WEAPON! IT'S UP TO YOU, CHUCK!

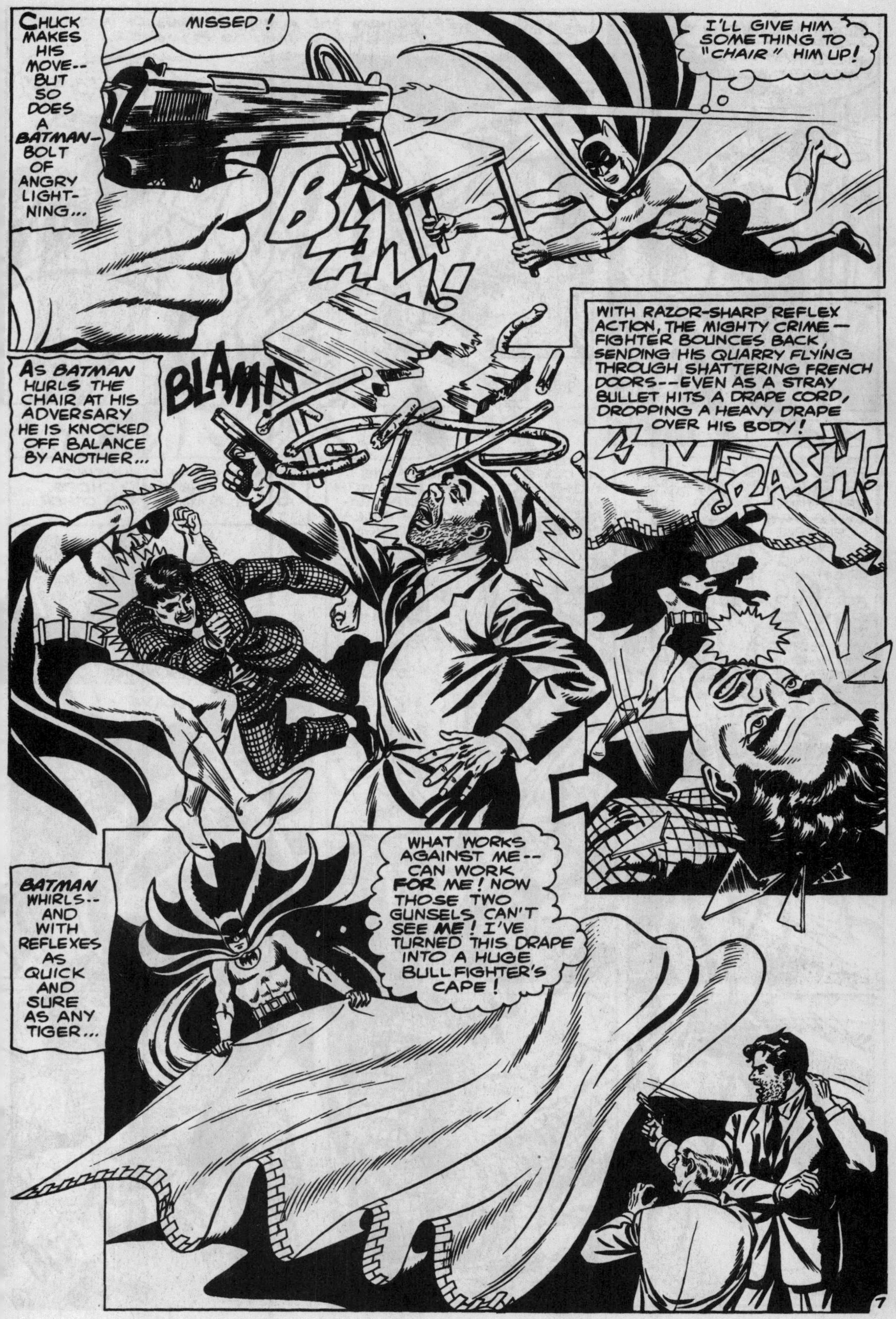
CHUCK MAKES HIS MOVE-- BUT SO DOES A BATMAN-BOLT OF ANGRY LIGHTNING...
MISSED!
I'LL GIVE HIM SOMETHING TO "CHAIR" HIM UP!
BLAM!
AS BATMAN HURLS THE CHAIR AT HIS ADVERSARY HE IS KNOCKED OFF BALANCE BY ANOTHER...
BLAM!
WITH RAZOR-SHARP REFLEX ACTION, THE MIGHTY CRIME-FIGHTER BOUNCES BACK, SENDING HIS QUARRY FLYING THROUGH SHATTERING FRENCH DOORS--EVEN AS A STRAY BULLET HITS A DRAPE CORD, DROPPING A HEAVY DRAPE OVER HIS BODY!
CRASH!
BATMAN WHIRLS-- AND WITH REFLEXES AS QUICK AND SURE AS ANY TIGER...
WHAT WORKS AGAINST ME-- CAN WORK FOR ME! NOW THOSE TWO GUNSELS CAN'T SEE ME! I'VE TURNED THIS DRAPE INTO A HUGE BULLFIGHTER'S CAPE!
7

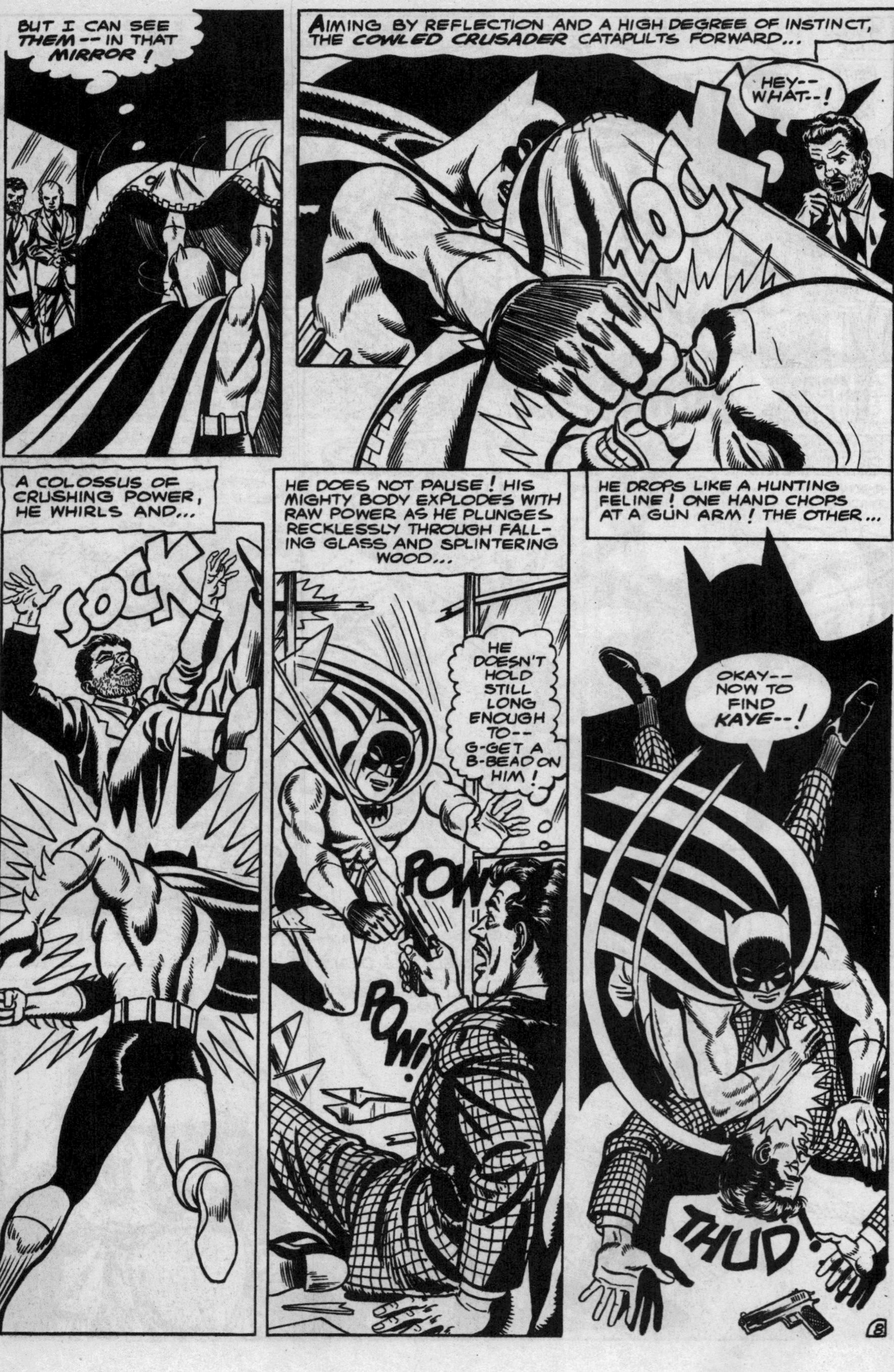
BUT I CAN SEE THEM -- IN THAT MIRROR!
AIMING BY REFLECTION AND A HIGH DEGREE OF INSTINCT, THE COWLED CRUSADER CATAPULTS FORWARD...
HEY-- WHAT--!
SOCK
A COLOSSUS OF CRUSHING POWER, HE WHIRLS AND...
SOCK
HE DOES NOT PAUSE! HIS MIGHTY BODY EXPLODES WITH RAW POWER AS HE PLUNGES RECKLESSLY THROUGH FALLING GLASS AND SPLINTERING WOOD...
HE DOESN'T HOLD STILL LONG ENOUGH TO-- G-GET A B-BEAD ON HIM!
POW
POW!
HE DROPS LIKE A HUNTING FELINE! ONE HAND CHOPS AT A GUN ARM! THE OTHER...
OKAY-- NOW TO FIND KAYE--!
THUD!
8

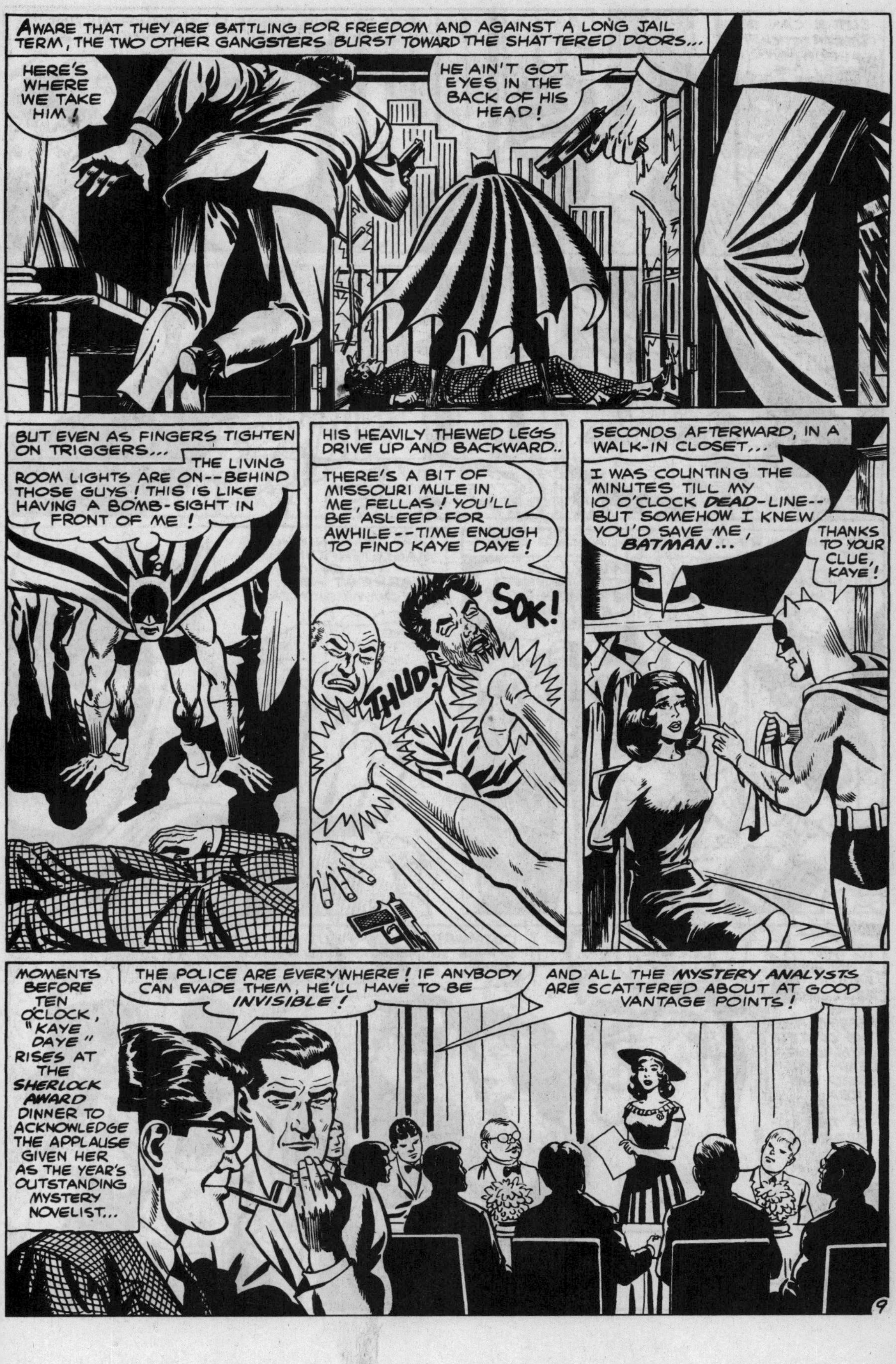
AWARE THAT THEY ARE BATTLING FOR FREEDOM AND AGAINST A LONG JAIL TERM, THE TWO OTHER GANGSTERS BURST TOWARD THE SHATTERED DOORS...
HERE'S WHERE WE TAKE HIM!
HE AIN'T GOT EYES IN THE BACK OF HIS HEAD!
BUT EVEN AS FINGERS TIGHTEN ON TRIGGERS...
THE LIVING ROOM LIGHTS ARE ON--BEHIND THOSE GUYS! THIS IS LIKE HAVING A BOMB-SIGHT IN FRONT OF ME!
HIS HEAVILY THEWED LEGS DRIVE UP AND BACKWARD..
THERE'S A BIT OF MISSOURI MULE IN ME, FELLAS! YOU'LL BE ASLEEP FOR AWHILE--TIME ENOUGH TO FIND KAYE DAYE!
SOK!
THUD!
SECONDS AFTERWARD, IN A WALK-IN CLOSET...
I WAS COUNTING THE MINUTES TILL MY 10 O'CLOCK DEAD-LINE--BUT SOMEHOW I KNEW YOU'D SAVE ME, BATMAN...
THANKS TO YOUR CLUE, KAYE!
MOMENTS BEFORE TEN O'CLOCK, "KAYE DAYE" RISES AT THE SHERLOCK AWARD DINNER TO ACKNOWLEDGE THE APPLAUSE GIVEN HER AS THE YEAR'S OUTSTANDING MYSTERY NOVELIST...
THE POLICE ARE EVERYWHERE! IF ANYBODY CAN EVADE THEM, HE'LL HAVE TO BE INVISIBLE!
AND ALL THE MYSTERY ANALYSTS ARE SCATTERED ABOUT AT GOOD VANTAGE POINTS!
9

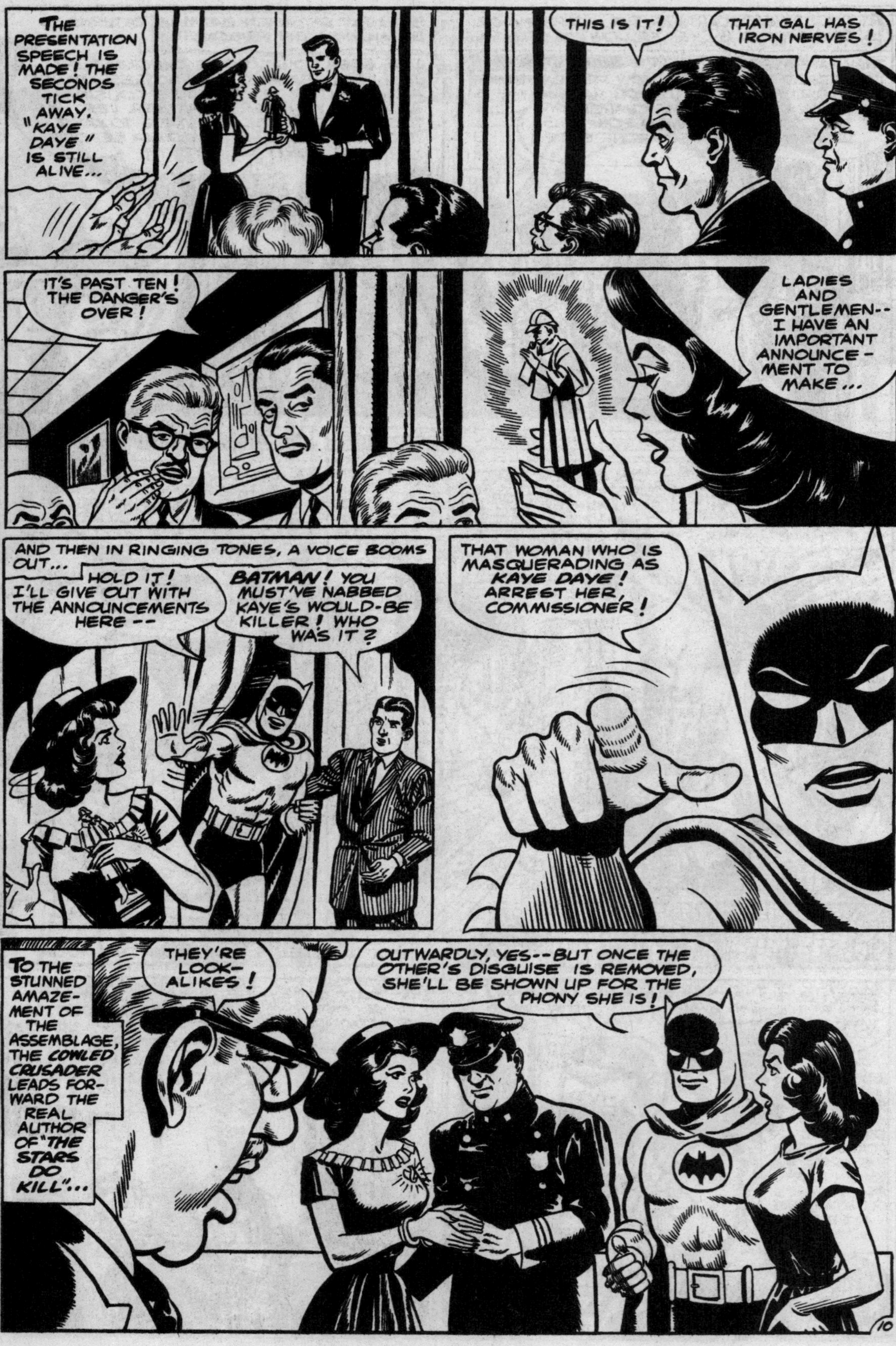
THE PRESENTATION SPEECH IS MADE! THE SECONDS TICK AWAY. "KAYE DAYE" IS STILL ALIVE...
THIS IS IT!
THAT GAL HAS IRON NERVES!
IT'S PAST TEN! THE DANGER'S OVER!
LADIES AND GENTLEMEN-- I HAVE AN IMPORTANT ANNOUNCEMENT TO MAKE...
AND THEN IN RINGING TONES, A VOICE BOOMS OUT...
HOLD IT! I'LL GIVE OUT WITH THE ANNOUNCEMENTS HERE --
BATMAN! YOU MUST'VE NABBED KAYE'S WOULD-BE KILLER! WHO WAS IT?
THAT WOMAN WHO IS MASQUERADING AS KAYE DAYE! ARREST HER, COMMISSIONER!
TO THE STUNNED AMAZEMENT OF THE ASSEMBLAGE, THE COWLED CRUSADER LEADS FORWARD THE REAL AUTHOR OF "THE STARS DO KILL"...
THEY'RE LOOK-ALIKES!
OUTWARDLY, YES--BUT ONCE THE OTHER'S DISGUISE IS REMOVED, SHE'LL BE SHOWN UP FOR THE PHONY SHE IS!
10

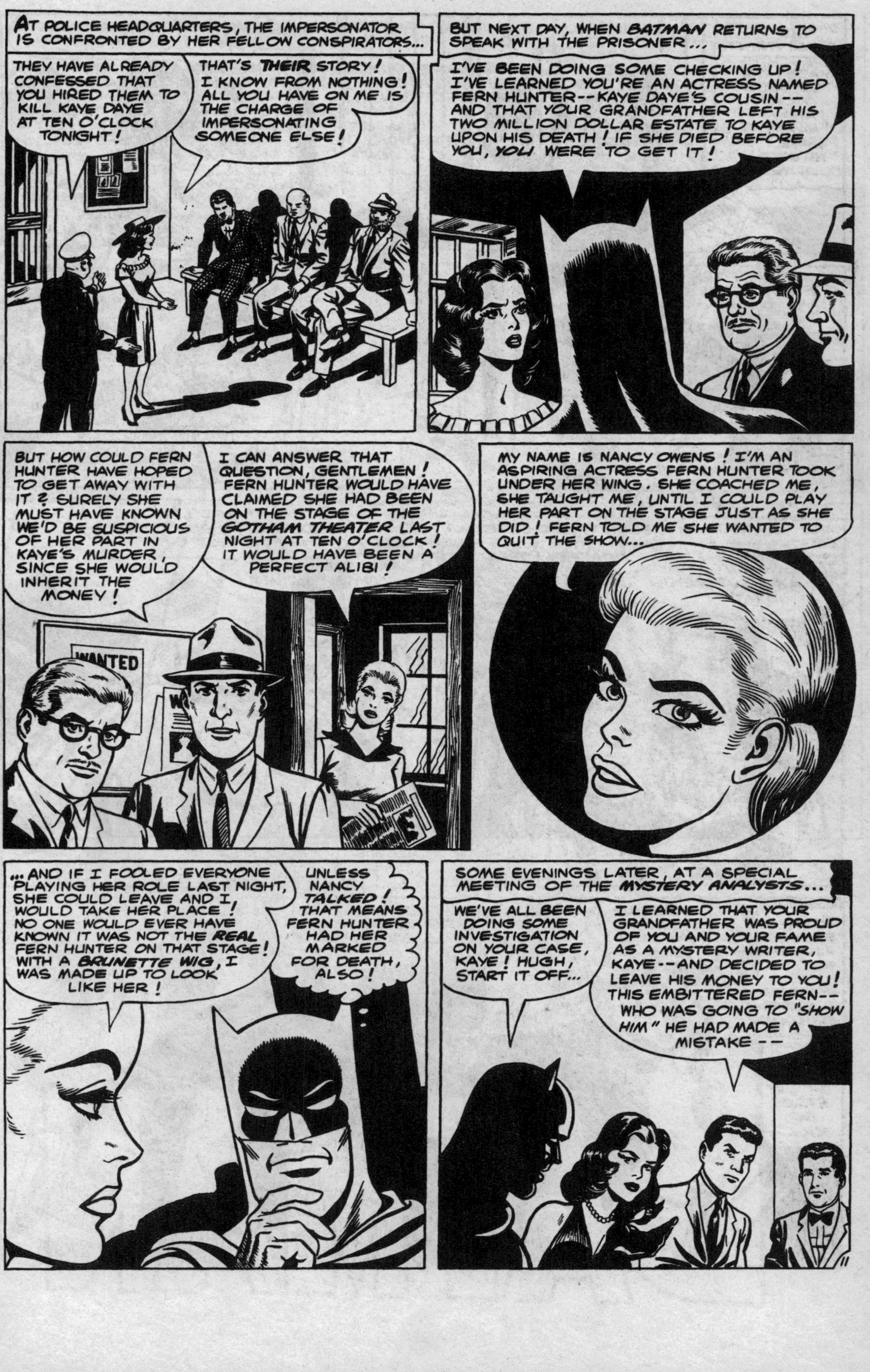
AT POLICE HEADQUARTERS, THE IMPERSONATOR IS CONFRONTED BY HER FELLOW CONSPIRATORS...
THEY HAVE ALREADY CONFESSED THAT YOU HIRED THEM TO KILL KAYE DAYE AT TEN O'CLOCK TONIGHT!
THAT'S THEIR STORY! I KNOW FROM NOTHING! ALL YOU HAVE ON ME IS THE CHARGE OF IMPERSONATING SOMEONE ELSE!
BUT NEXT DAY, WHEN BATMAN RETURNS TO SPEAK WITH THE PRISONER...
I'VE BEEN DOING SOME CHECKING UP! I'VE LEARNED YOU'RE AN ACTRESS NAMED FERN HUNTER--KAYE DAYE'S COUSIN--AND THAT YOUR GRANDFATHER LEFT HIS TWO MILLION DOLLAR ESTATE TO KAYE UPON HIS DEATH! IF SHE DIED BEFORE YOU, YOU WERE TO GET IT!
BUT HOW COULD FERN HUNTER HAVE HOPED TO GET AWAY WITH IT? SURELY SHE MUST HAVE KNOWN WE'D BE SUSPICIOUS OF HER PART IN KAYE'S MURDER, SINCE SHE WOULD INHERIT THE MONEY!
I CAN ANSWER THAT QUESTION, GENTLEMEN! FERN HUNTER WOULD HAVE CLAIMED SHE HAD BEEN ON THE STAGE OF THE GOTHAM THEATER LAST NIGHT AT TEN O'CLOCK! IT WOULD HAVE BEEN A PERFECT ALIBI!
WANTED
MY NAME IS NANCY OWENS! I'M AN ASPIRING ACTRESS FERN HUNTER TOOK UNDER HER WING. SHE COACHED ME, SHE TAUGHT ME, UNTIL I COULD PLAY HER PART ON THE STAGE JUST AS SHE DID! FERN TOLD ME SHE WANTED TO QUIT THE SHOW...
...AND IF I FOOLED EVERYONE PLAYING HER ROLE LAST NIGHT, SHE COULD LEAVE AND I WOULD TAKE HER PLACE! NO ONE WOULD EVER HAVE KNOWN IT WAS NOT THE REAL FERN HUNTER ON THAT STAGE! WITH A BRUNETTE WIG, I WAS MADE UP TO LOOK LIKE HER!
UNLESS NANCY TALKED! THAT MEANS FERN HUNTER HAD HER MARKED FOR DEATH, ALSO!
SOME EVENINGS LATER, AT A SPECIAL MEETING OF THE MYSTERY ANALYSTS...
WE'VE ALL BEEN DOING SOME INVESTIGATION ON YOUR CASE, KAYE! HUGH, START IT OFF...
I LEARNED THAT YOUR GRANDFATHER WAS PROUD OF YOU AND YOUR FAME AS A MYSTERY WRITER, KAYE--AND DECIDED TO LEAVE HIS MONEY TO YOU! THIS EMBITTERED FERN--WHO WAS GOING TO "SHOW HIM" HE HAD MADE A MISTAKE--
11

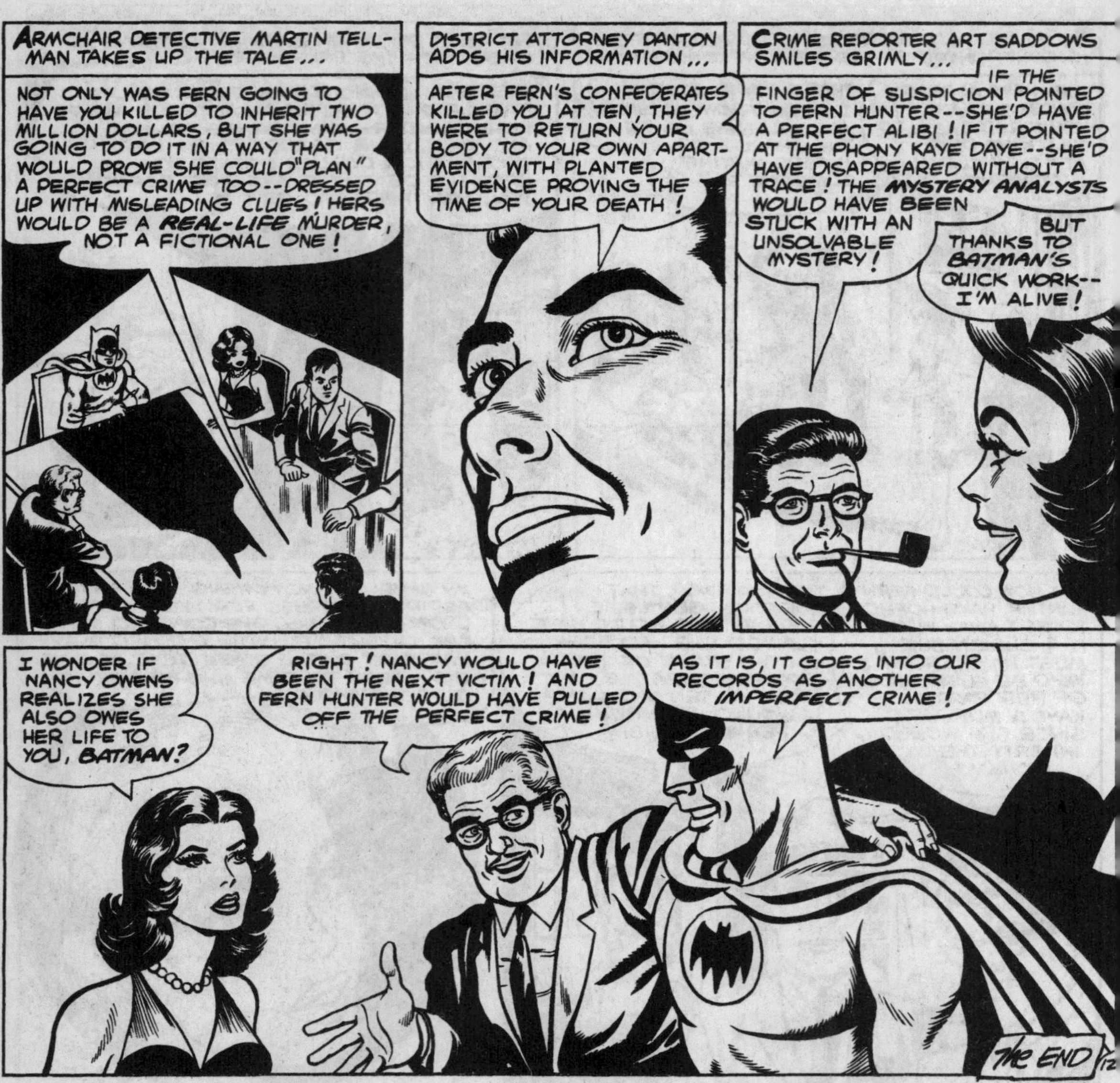
ARMCHAIR DETECTIVE MARTIN TELLMAN TAKES UP THE TALE...
NOT ONLY WAS FERN GOING TO HAVE YOU KILLED TO INHERIT TWO MILLION DOLLARS, BUT SHE WAS GOING TO DO IT IN A WAY THAT WOULD PROVE SHE COULD "PLAN" A PERFECT CRIME TOO--DRESSED UP WITH MISLEADING CLUES! HERS WOULD BE A REAL-LIFE MURDER, NOT A FICTIONAL ONE!
DISTRICT ATTORNEY DANTON ADDS HIS INFORMATION...
AFTER FERN'S CONFEDERATES KILLED YOU AT TEN, THEY WERE TO RETURN YOUR BODY TO YOUR OWN APARTMENT, WITH PLANTED EVIDENCE PROVING THE TIME OF YOUR DEATH!
CRIME REPORTER ART SADDOWS SMILES GRIMLY...
IF THE FINGER OF SUSPICION POINTED TO FERN HUNTER--SHE'D HAVE A PERFECT ALIBI! IF IT POINTED AT THE PHONY KAYE DAYE--SHE'D HAVE DISAPPEARED WITHOUT A TRACE! THE MYSTERY ANALYSTS WOULD HAVE BEEN STUCK WITH AN UNSOLVABLE MYSTERY!
BUT THANKS TO BATMAN'S QUICK WORK--I'M ALIVE!
I WONDER IF NANCY OWENS REALIZES SHE ALSO OWES HER LIFE TO YOU, BATMAN?
RIGHT! NANCY WOULD HAVE BEEN THE NEXT VICTIM! AND FERN HUNTER WOULD HAVE PULLED OFF THE PERFECT CRIME!
AS IT IS, IT GOES INTO OUR RECORDS AS ANOTHER IMPERFECT CRIME!
THE END
12

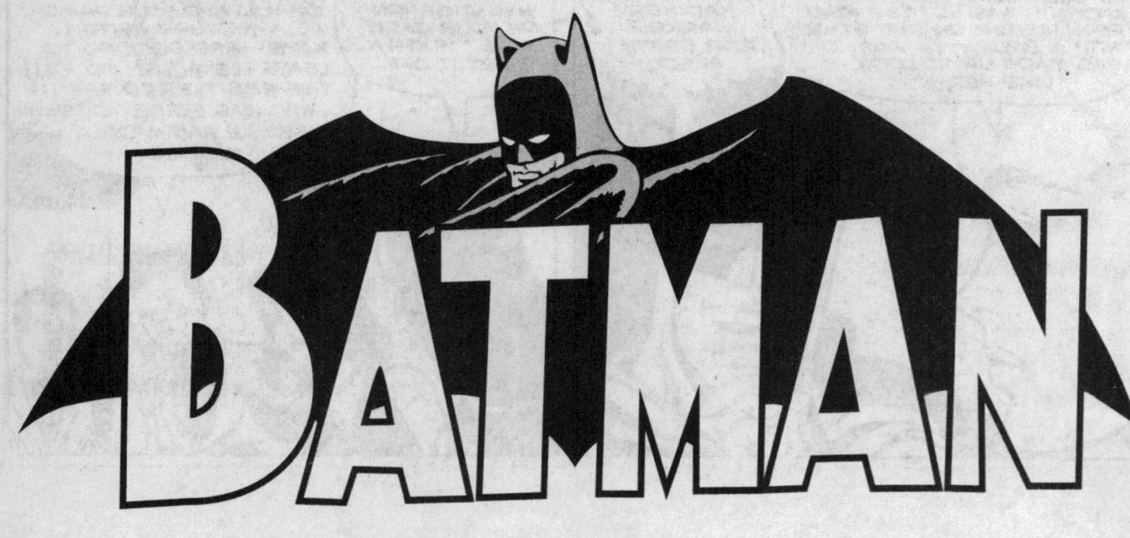
BATMAN

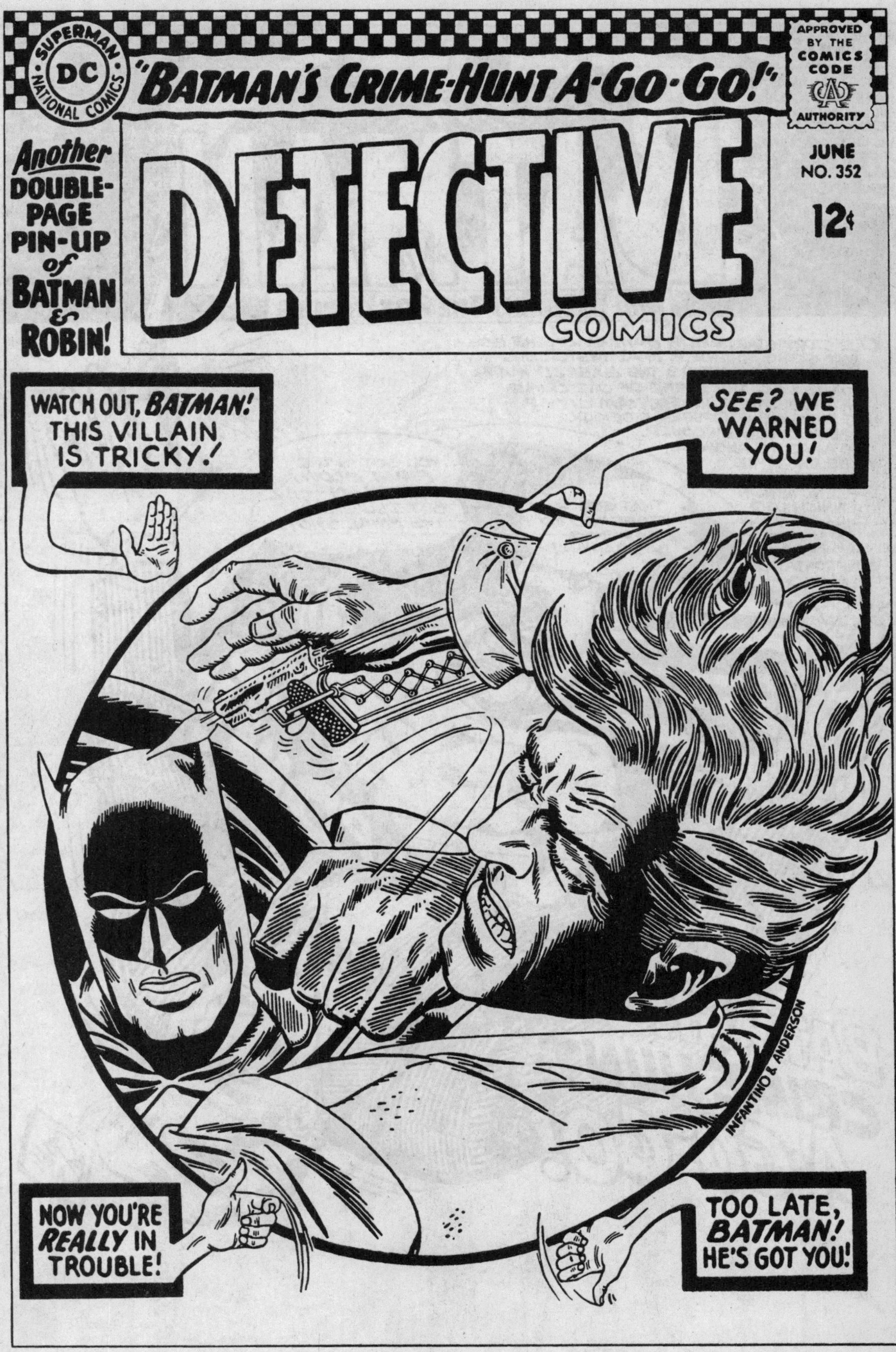
SUPERMAN DC NATIONAL COMICS
"BATMAN'S CRIME-HUNT A-GO-GO!"
APPROVED BY THE COMICS CODE AUTHORITY
Another DOUBLE-PAGE PIN-UP of BATMAN & ROBIN!
DETECTIVE COMICS
JUNE NO. 352
12¢
WATCH OUT, BATMAN! THIS VILLAIN IS TRICKY!
SEE? WE WARNED YOU!
NOW YOU'RE REALLY IN TROUBLE!
TOO LATE, BATMAN! HE'S GOT YOU!
INFANTINO & ANDERSON

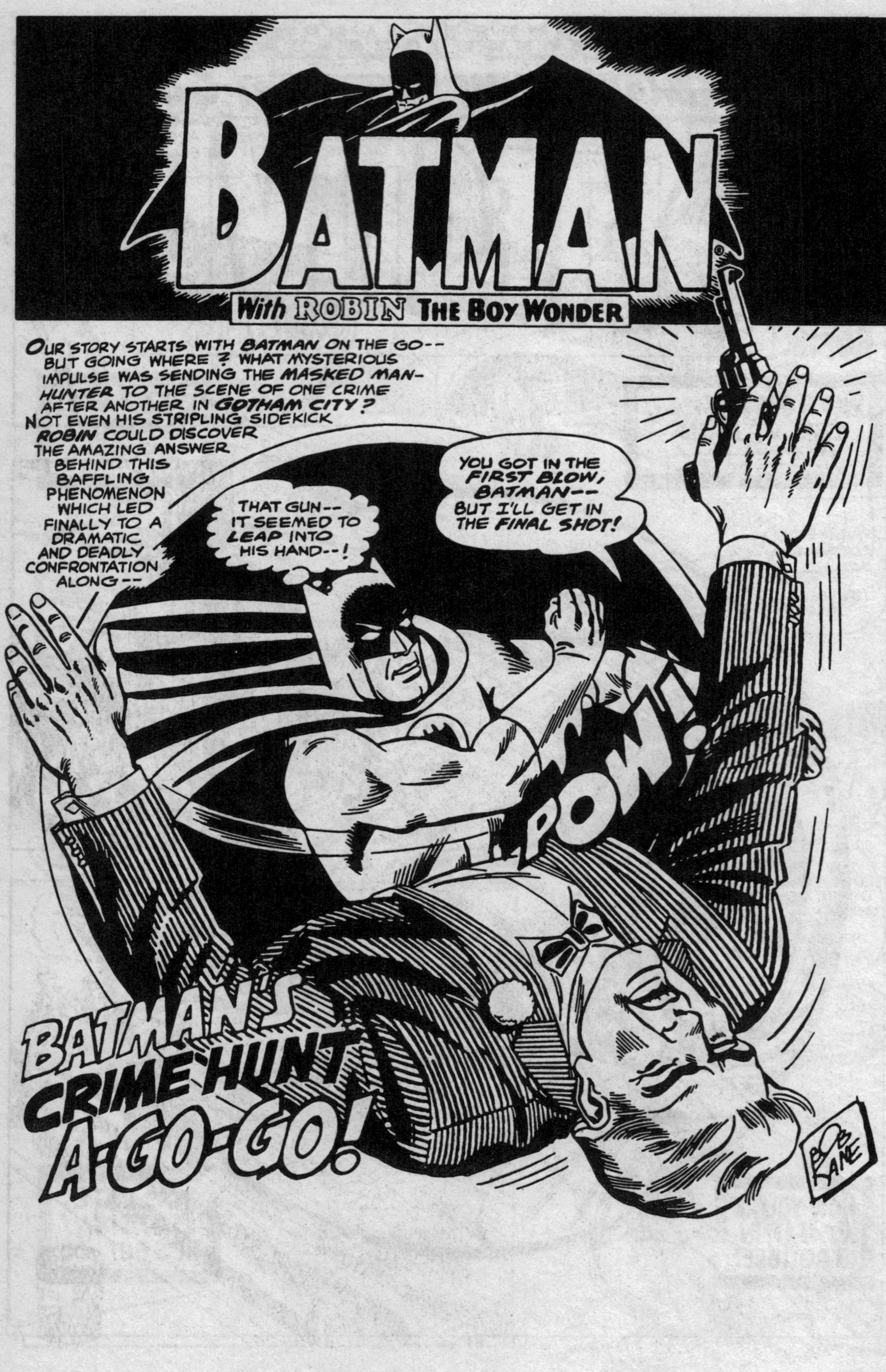
BATMAN
With ROBIN THE BOY WONDER
OUR STORY STARTS WITH BATMAN ON THE GO-- BUT GOING WHERE ? WHAT MYSTERIOUS IMPULSE WAS SENDING THE MASKED MAN-HUNTER TO THE SCENE OF ONE CRIME AFTER ANOTHER IN GOTHAM CITY? NOT EVEN HIS STRIPLING SIDEKICK ROBIN COULD DISCOVER THE AMAZING ANSWER BEHIND THIS BAFFLING PHENOMENON WHICH LED FINALLY TO A DRAMATIC AND DEADLY CONFRONTATION ALONG--
THAT GUN-- IT SEEMED TO LEAP INTO HIS HAND--!
YOU GOT IN THE FIRST BLOW, BATMAN-- BUT I'LL GET IN THE FINAL SHOT!
POW!
BATMAN'S CRIME-HUNT A-GO-GO!
BOB KANE

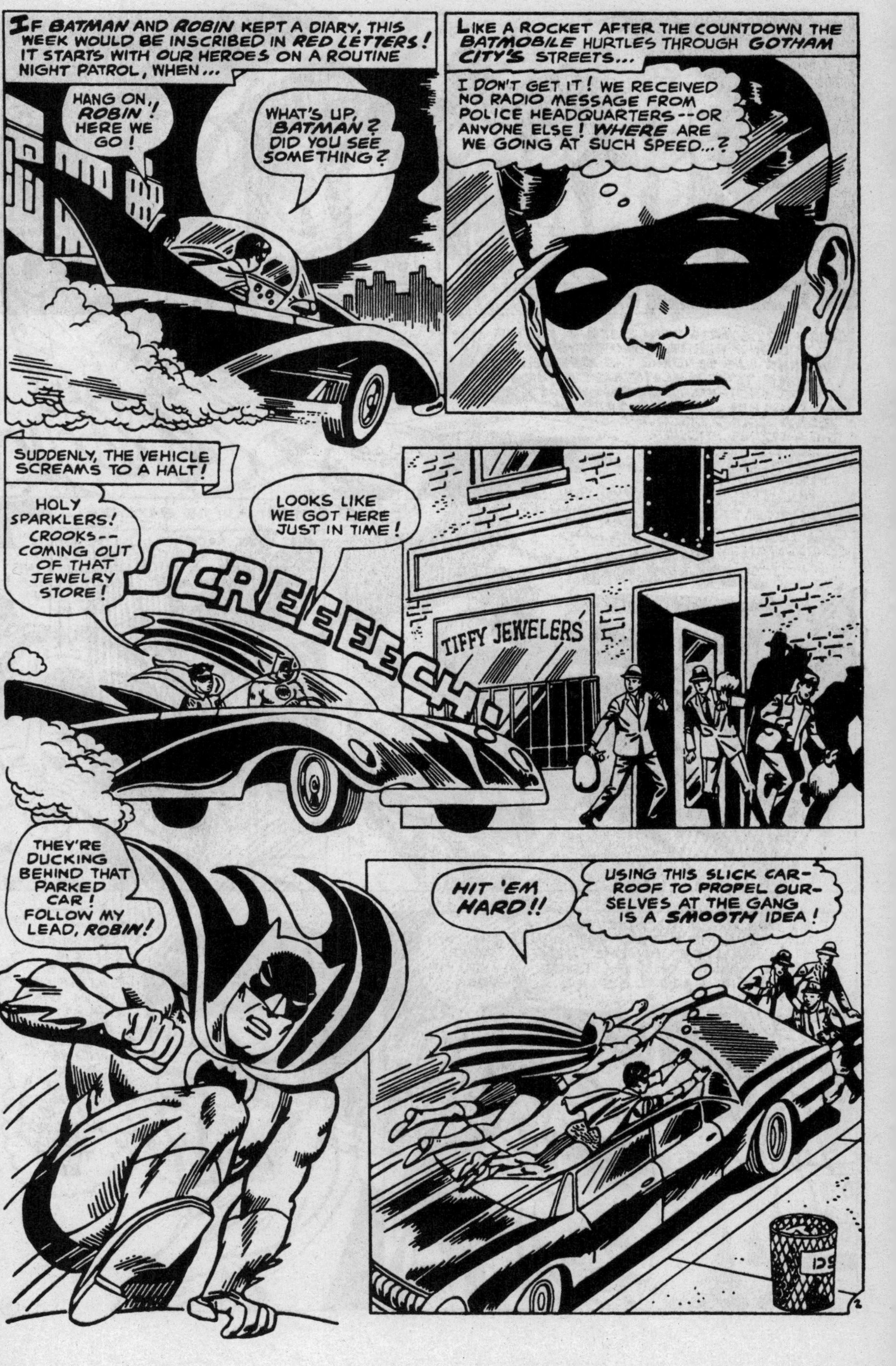
IF BATMAN AND ROBIN KEPT A DIARY, THIS WEEK WOULD BE INSCRIBED IN RED LETTERS! IT STARTS WITH OUR HEROES ON A ROUTINE NIGHT PATROL, WHEN...
HANG ON, ROBIN! HERE WE GO!
WHAT'S UP, BATMAN? DID YOU SEE SOMETHING?
LIKE A ROCKET AFTER THE COUNTDOWN THE BATMOBILE HURTLES THROUGH GOTHAM CITY'S STREETS...
I DON'T GET IT! WE RECEIVED NO RADIO MESSAGE FROM POLICE HEADQUARTERS--OR ANYONE ELSE! WHERE ARE WE GOING AT SUCH SPEED...?
SUDDENLY, THE VEHICLE SCREAMS TO A HALT!
HOLY SPARKLERS! CROOKS--COMING OUT OF THAT JEWELRY STORE!
LOOKS LIKE WE GOT HERE JUST IN TIME!
SCREEEECH!
TIFFY JEWELERS
THEY'RE DUCKING BEHIND THAT PARKED CAR! FOLLOW MY LEAD, ROBIN!
HIT 'EM HARD!!
USING THIS SLICK CAR-ROOF TO PROPEL OURSELVES AT THE GANG IS A SMOOTH IDEA!
2

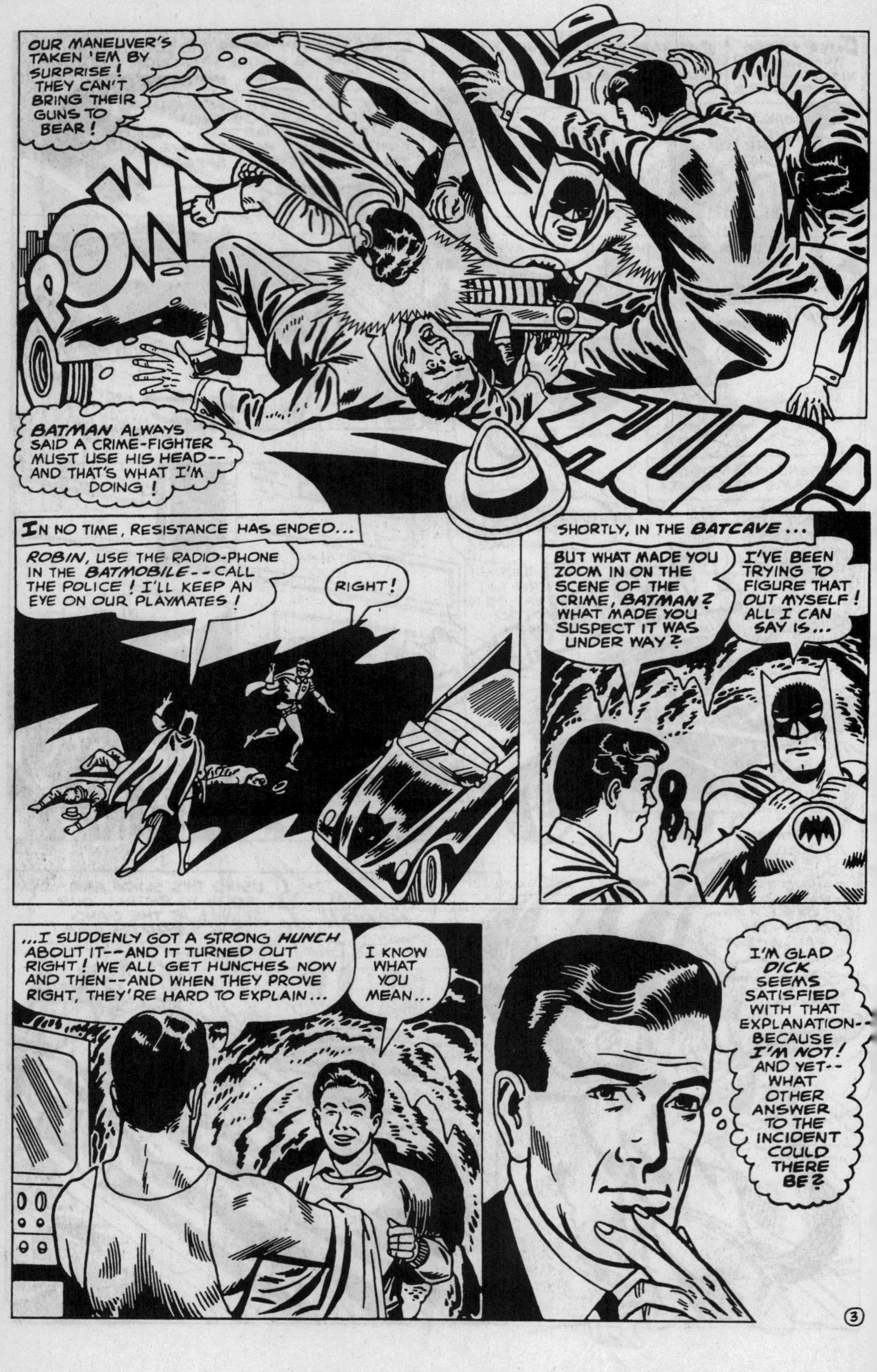
OUR MANEUVER'S TAKEN 'EM BY SURPRISE! THEY CAN'T BRING THEIR GUNS TO BEAR!
POW
BATMAN ALWAYS SAID A CRIME-FIGHTER MUST USE HIS HEAD--AND THAT'S WHAT I'M DOING!
THUD!
IN NO TIME, RESISTANCE HAS ENDED...
ROBIN, USE THE RADIO-PHONE IN THE BATMOBILE--CALL THE POLICE! I'LL KEEP AN EYE ON OUR PLAYMATES!
RIGHT!
SHORTLY, IN THE BATCAVE...
BUT WHAT MADE YOU ZOOM IN ON THE SCENE OF THE CRIME, BATMAN? WHAT MADE YOU SUSPECT IT WAS UNDER WAY?
I'VE BEEN TRYING TO FIGURE THAT OUT MYSELF! ALL I CAN SAY IS...
...I SUDDENLY GOT A STRONG HUNCH ABOUT IT--AND IT TURNED OUT RIGHT! WE ALL GET HUNCHES NOW AND THEN--AND WHEN THEY PROVE RIGHT, THEY'RE HARD TO EXPLAIN...
I KNOW WHAT YOU MEAN...
I'M GLAD DICK SEEMS SATISFIED WITH THAT EXPLANATION--BECAUSE I'M NOT! AND YET--WHAT OTHER ANSWER TO THE INCIDENT COULD THERE BE?
3

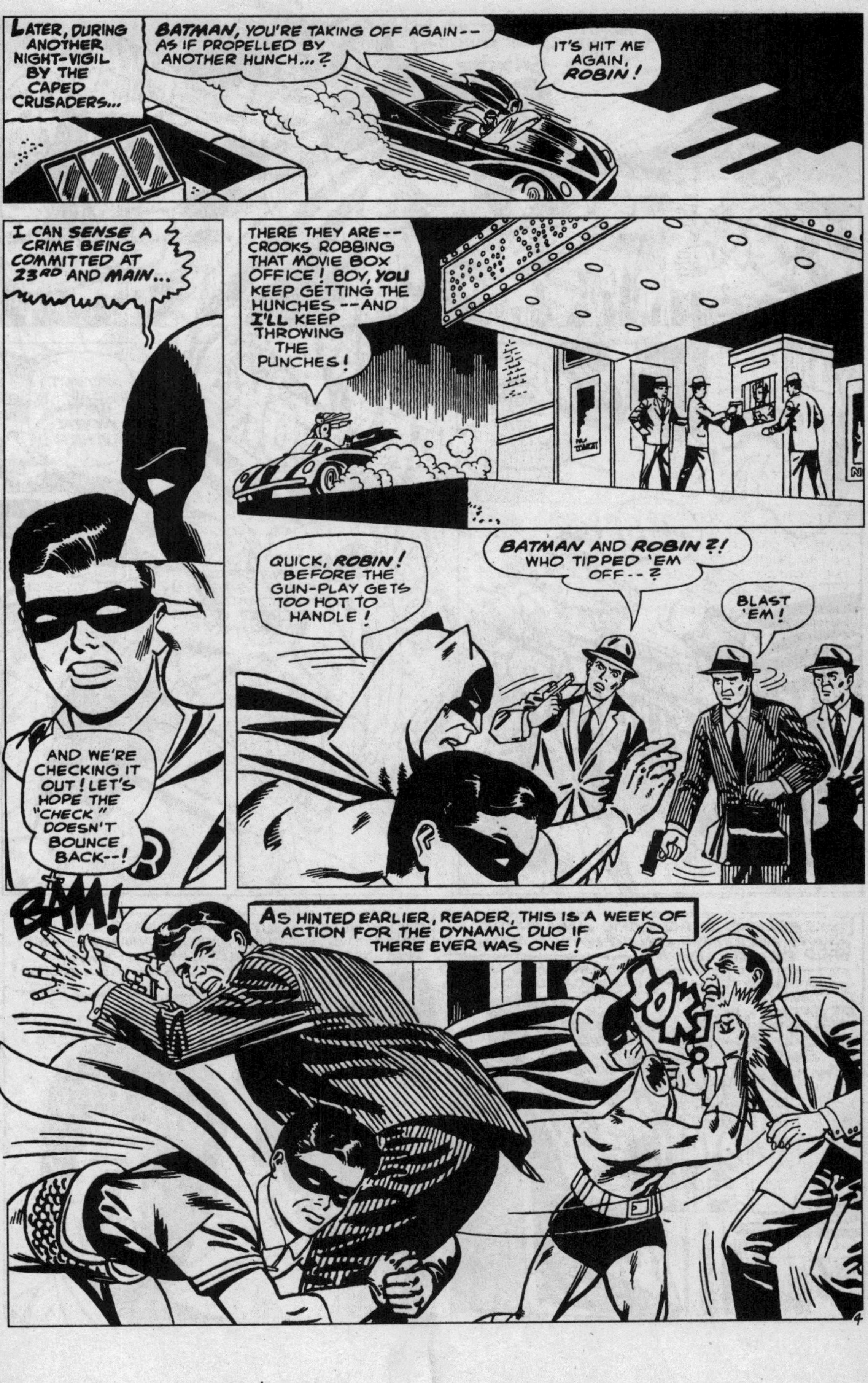
LATER, DURING ANOTHER NIGHT-VIGIL BY THE CAPED CRUSADERS...
BATMAN, YOU'RE TAKING OFF AGAIN-- AS IF PROPELLED BY ANOTHER HUNCH...?
IT'S HIT ME AGAIN, ROBIN!
I CAN SENSE A CRIME BEING COMMITTED AT 23RD AND MAIN...
AND WE'RE CHECKING IT OUT! LET'S HOPE THE "CHECK" DOESN'T BOUNCE BACK--!
THERE THEY ARE-- CROOKS ROBBING THAT MOVIE BOX OFFICE! BOY, YOU KEEP GETTING THE HUNCHES --AND I'LL KEEP THROWING THE PUNCHES!
QUICK, ROBIN! BEFORE THE GUN-PLAY GETS TOO HOT TO HANDLE!
BATMAN AND ROBIN?! WHO TIPPED 'EM OFF--?
BLAST 'EM!
BAM!
AS HINTED EARLIER, READER, THIS IS A WEEK OF ACTION FOR THE DYNAMIC DUO IF THERE EVER WAS ONE!
SOK!
4

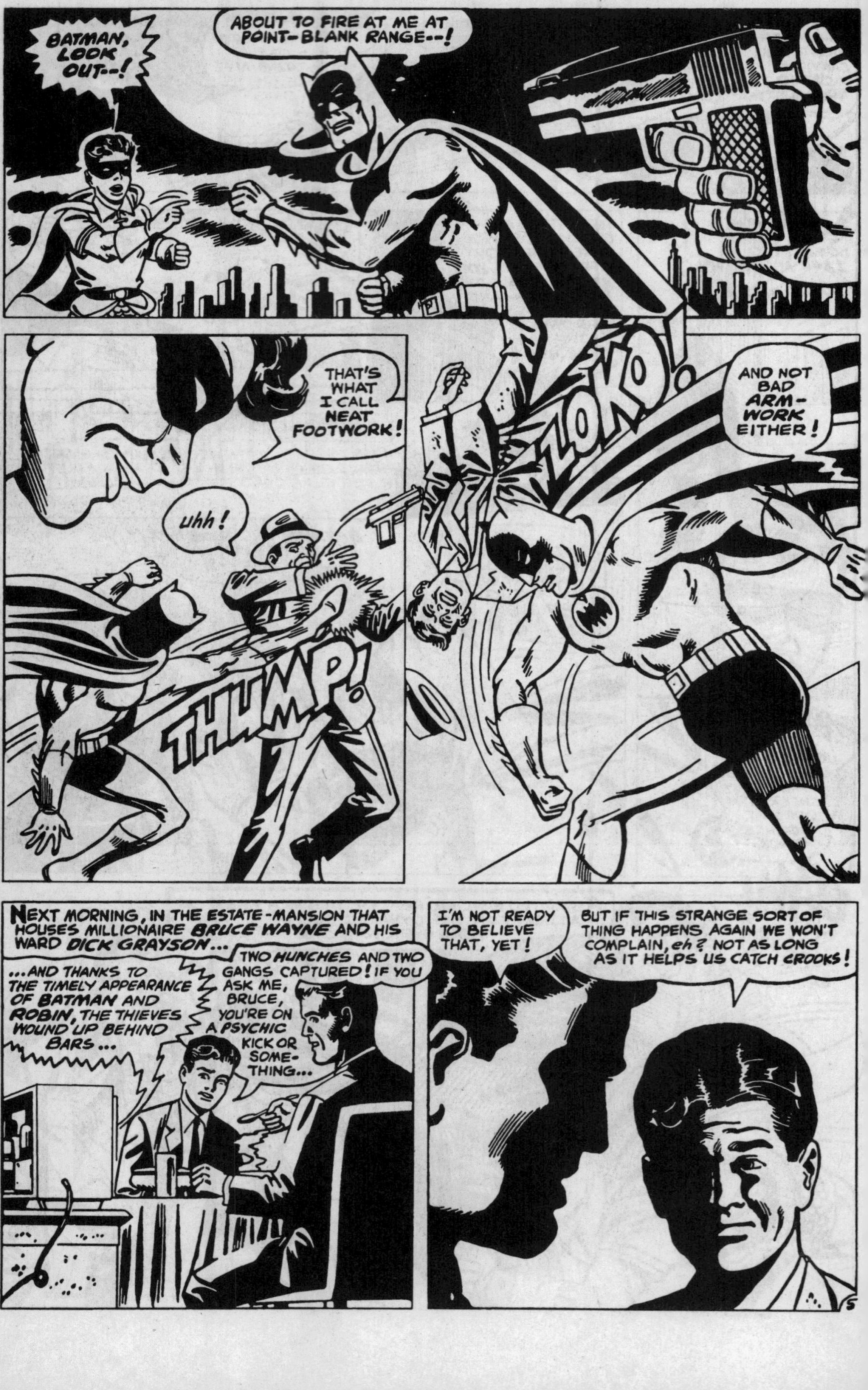
BATMAN, LOOK OUT--!
ABOUT TO FIRE AT ME AT POINT-BLANK RANGE--!
THAT'S WHAT I CALL NEAT FOOTWORK!
uhh!
THUMP!
ZOK!
AND NOT BAD ARM-WORK EITHER!
NEXT MORNING, IN THE ESTATE-MANSION THAT HOUSES MILLIONAIRE BRUCE WAYNE AND HIS WARD DICK GRAYSON...
...AND THANKS TO THE TIMELY APPEARANCE OF BATMAN AND ROBIN, THE THIEVES WOUND UP BEHIND BARS...
TWO HUNCHES AND TWO GANGS CAPTURED! IF YOU ASK ME, BRUCE, YOU'RE ON A PSYCHIC KICK OR SOME-THING...
I'M NOT READY TO BELIEVE THAT, YET!
BUT IF THIS STRANGE SORT OF THING HAPPENS AGAIN WE WON'T COMPLAIN, eh? NOT AS LONG AS IT HELPS US CATCH CROOKS!
5

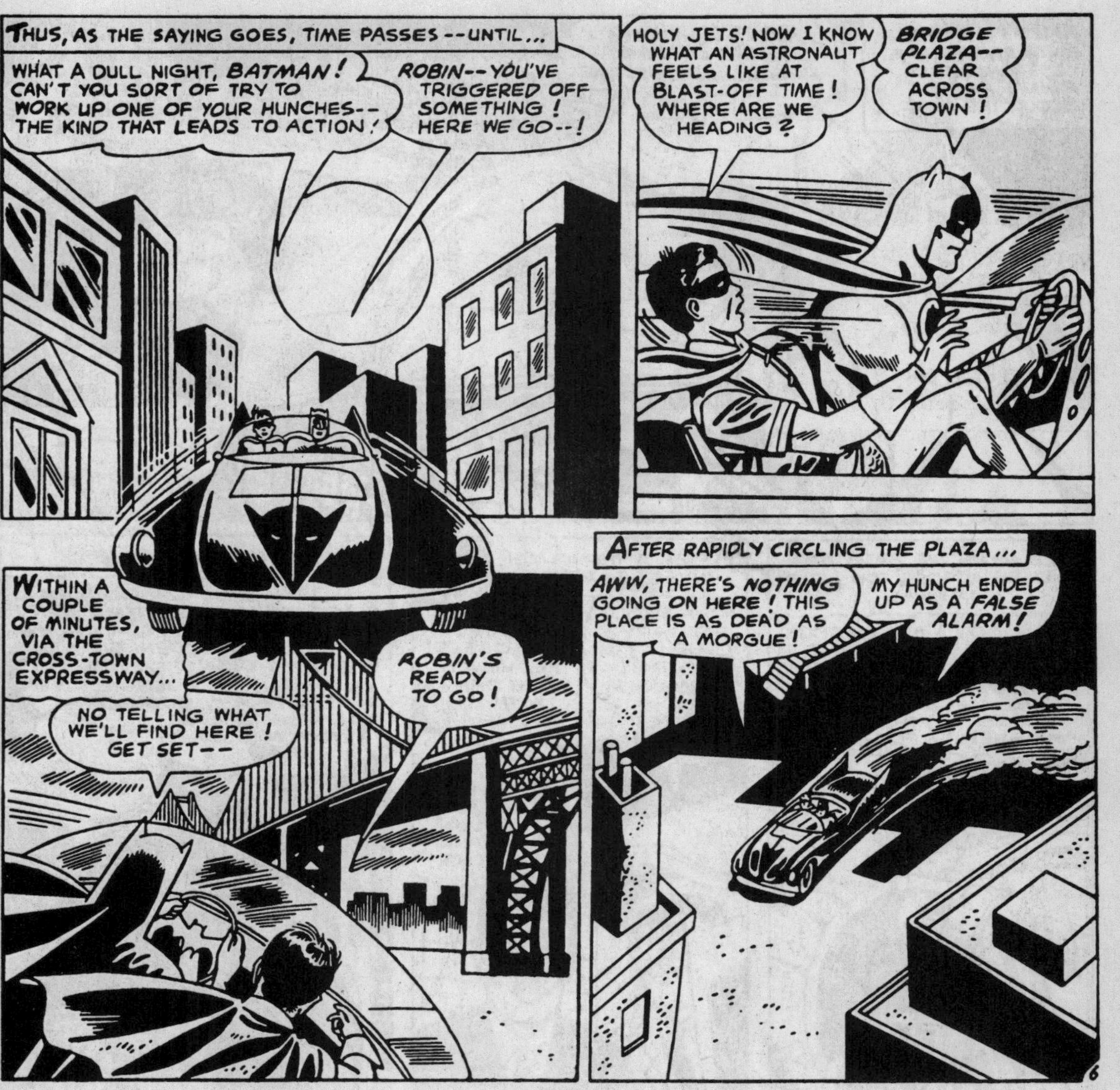
THUS, AS THE SAYING GOES, TIME PASSES--UNTIL...
WHAT A DULL NIGHT, BATMAN! CAN'T YOU SORT OF TRY TO WORK UP ONE OF YOUR HUNCHES-- THE KIND THAT LEADS TO ACTION!
ROBIN--YOU'VE TRIGGERED OFF SOMETHING! HERE WE GO--!
HOLY JETS! NOW I KNOW WHAT AN ASTRONAUT FEELS LIKE AT BLAST-OFF TIME! WHERE ARE WE HEADING?
BRIDGE PLAZA-- CLEAR ACROSS TOWN!
WITHIN A COUPLE OF MINUTES, VIA THE CROSS-TOWN EXPRESSWAY...
NO TELLING WHAT WE'LL FIND HERE! GET SET--
ROBIN'S READY TO GO!
AFTER RAPIDLY CIRCLING THE PLAZA...
AWW, THERE'S NOTHING GOING ON HERE! THIS PLACE IS AS DEAD AS A MORGUE!
MY HUNCH ENDED UP AS A FALSE ALARM!
6

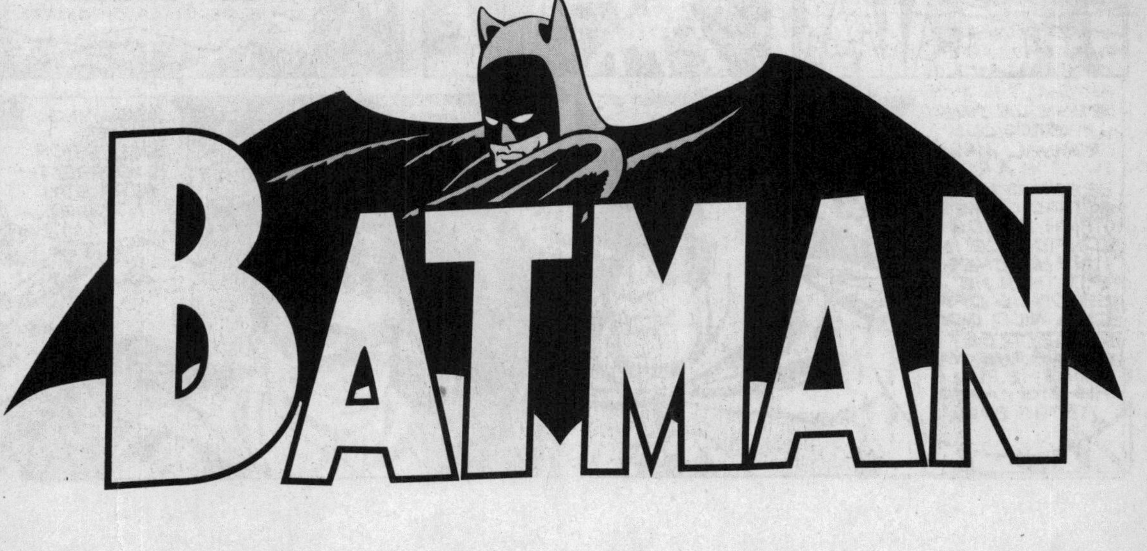
BATMAN

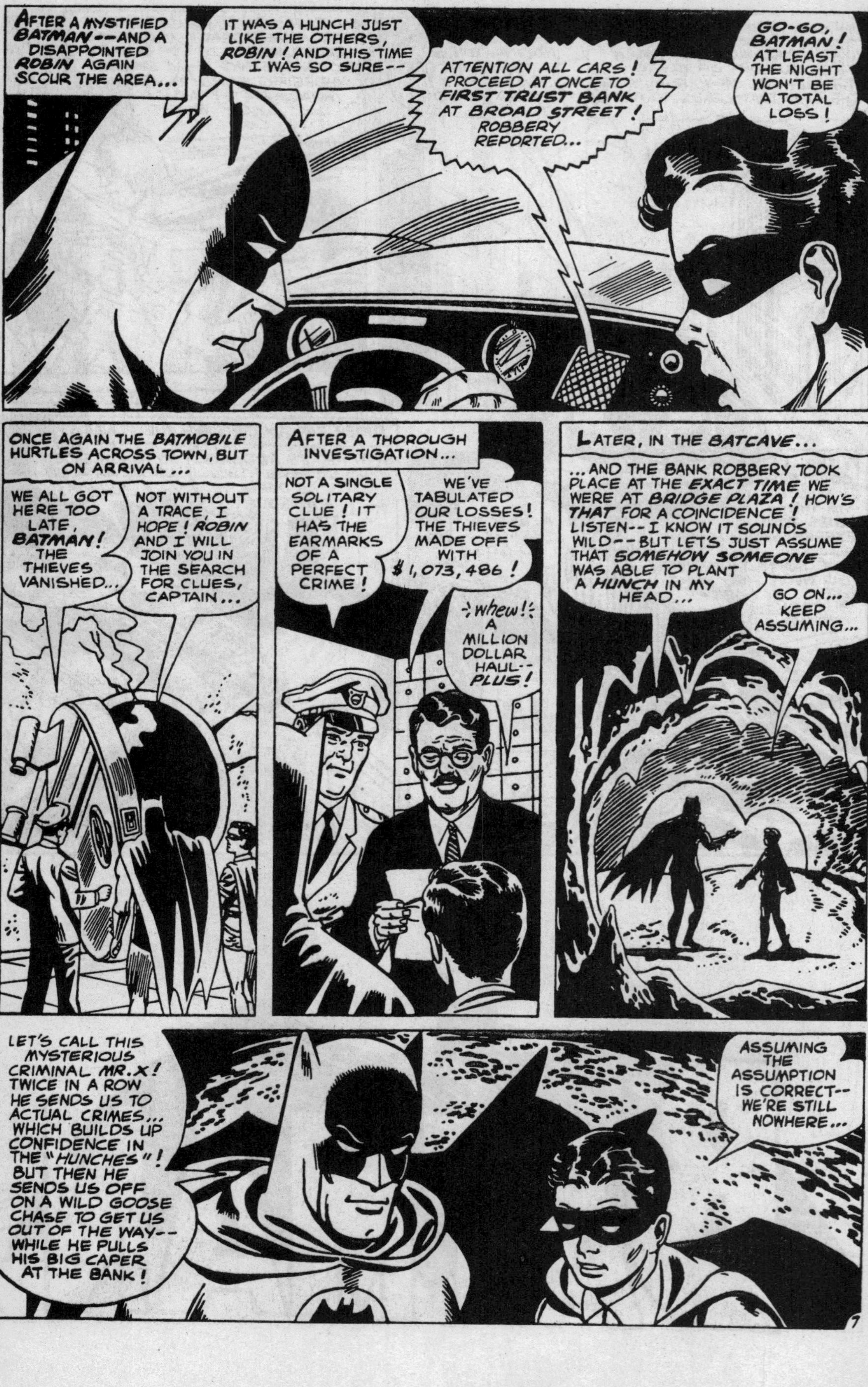
AFTER A MYSTIFIED BATMAN--AND A DISAPPOINTED ROBIN AGAIN SCOUR THE AREA...
IT WAS A HUNCH JUST LIKE THE OTHERS, ROBIN! AND THIS TIME I WAS SO SURE--
ATTENTION ALL CARS! PROCEED AT ONCE TO FIRST TRUST BANK AT BROAD STREET! ROBBERY REPORTED...
GO-GO, BATMAN! AT LEAST THE NIGHT WON'T BE A TOTAL LOSS!
ONCE AGAIN THE BATMOBILE HURTLES ACROSS TOWN, BUT ON ARRIVAL...
WE ALL GOT HERE TOO LATE, BATMAN! THE THIEVES VANISHED...
NOT WITHOUT A TRACE, I HOPE! ROBIN AND I WILL JOIN YOU IN THE SEARCH FOR CLUES, CAPTAIN...
AFTER A THOROUGH INVESTIGATION...
NOT A SINGLE SOLITARY CLUE! IT HAS THE EARMARKS OF A PERFECT CRIME!
WE'VE TABULATED OUR LOSSES! THE THIEVES MADE OFF WITH $1,073,486!
whew! A MILLION DOLLAR HAUL--PLUS!
LATER, IN THE BATCAVE...
...AND THE BANK ROBBERY TOOK PLACE AT THE EXACT TIME WE WERE AT BRIDGE PLAZA! HOW'S THAT FOR A COINCIDENCE! LISTEN--I KNOW IT SOUNDS WILD--BUT LET'S JUST ASSUME THAT SOMEHOW SOMEONE WAS ABLE TO PLANT A HUNCH IN MY HEAD...
GO ON... KEEP ASSUMING...
LET'S CALL THIS MYSTERIOUS CRIMINAL MR. X! TWICE IN A ROW HE SENDS US TO ACTUAL CRIMES... WHICH BUILDS UP CONFIDENCE IN THE "HUNCHES"! BUT THEN HE SENDS US OFF ON A WILD GOOSE CHASE TO GET US OUT OF THE WAY--WHILE HE PULLS HIS BIG CAPER AT THE BANK!
ASSUMING THE ASSUMPTION IS CORRECT--WE'RE STILL NOWHERE...
7

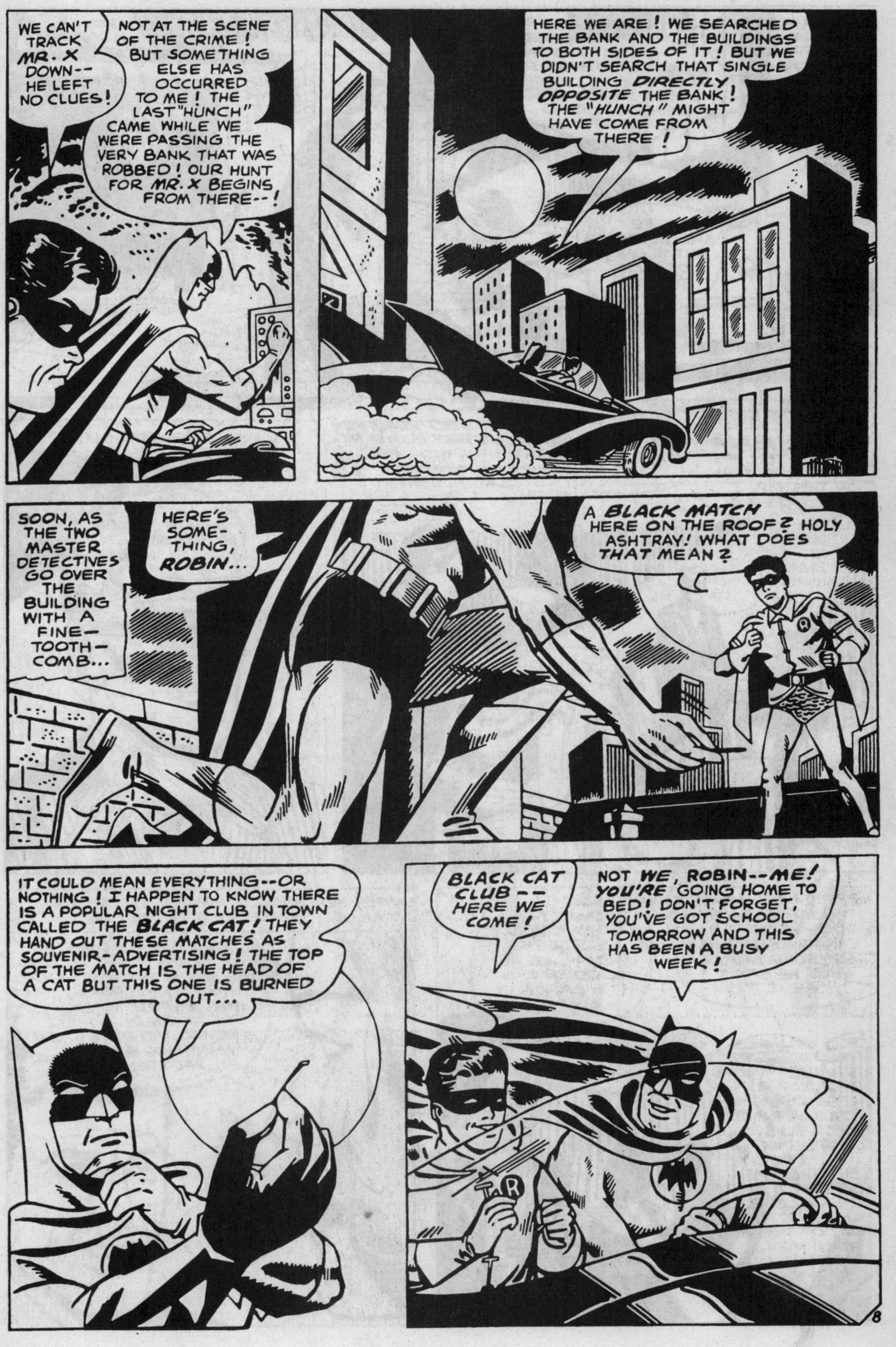
WE CAN'T TRACK MR. X DOWN-- HE LEFT NO CLUES!
NOT AT THE SCENE OF THE CRIME! BUT SOMETHING ELSE HAS OCCURRED TO ME! THE LAST "HUNCH" CAME WHILE WE WERE PASSING THE VERY BANK THAT WAS ROBBED! OUR HUNT FOR MR. X BEGINS FROM THERE--!
HERE WE ARE! WE SEARCHED THE BANK AND THE BUILDINGS TO BOTH SIDES OF IT! BUT WE DIDN'T SEARCH THAT SINGLE BUILDING DIRECTLY OPPOSITE THE BANK! THE "HUNCH" MIGHT HAVE COME FROM THERE!
SOON, AS THE TWO MASTER DETECTIVES GO OVER THE BUILDING WITH A FINE-TOOTH-COMB...
HERE'S SOME-THING, ROBIN...
A BLACK MATCH HERE ON THE ROOF? HOLY ASHTRAY! WHAT DOES THAT MEAN?
IT COULD MEAN EVERYTHING--OR NOTHING! I HAPPEN TO KNOW THERE IS A POPULAR NIGHT CLUB IN TOWN CALLED THE BLACK CAT! THEY HAND OUT THESE MATCHES AS SOUVENIR-ADVERTISING! THE TOP OF THE MATCH IS THE HEAD OF A CAT BUT THIS ONE IS BURNED OUT...
BLACK CAT CLUB-- HERE WE COME!
NOT WE, ROBIN--ME! YOU'RE GOING HOME TO BED! DON'T FORGET, YOU'VE GOT SCHOOL TOMORROW AND THIS HAS BEEN A BUSY WEEK!
8

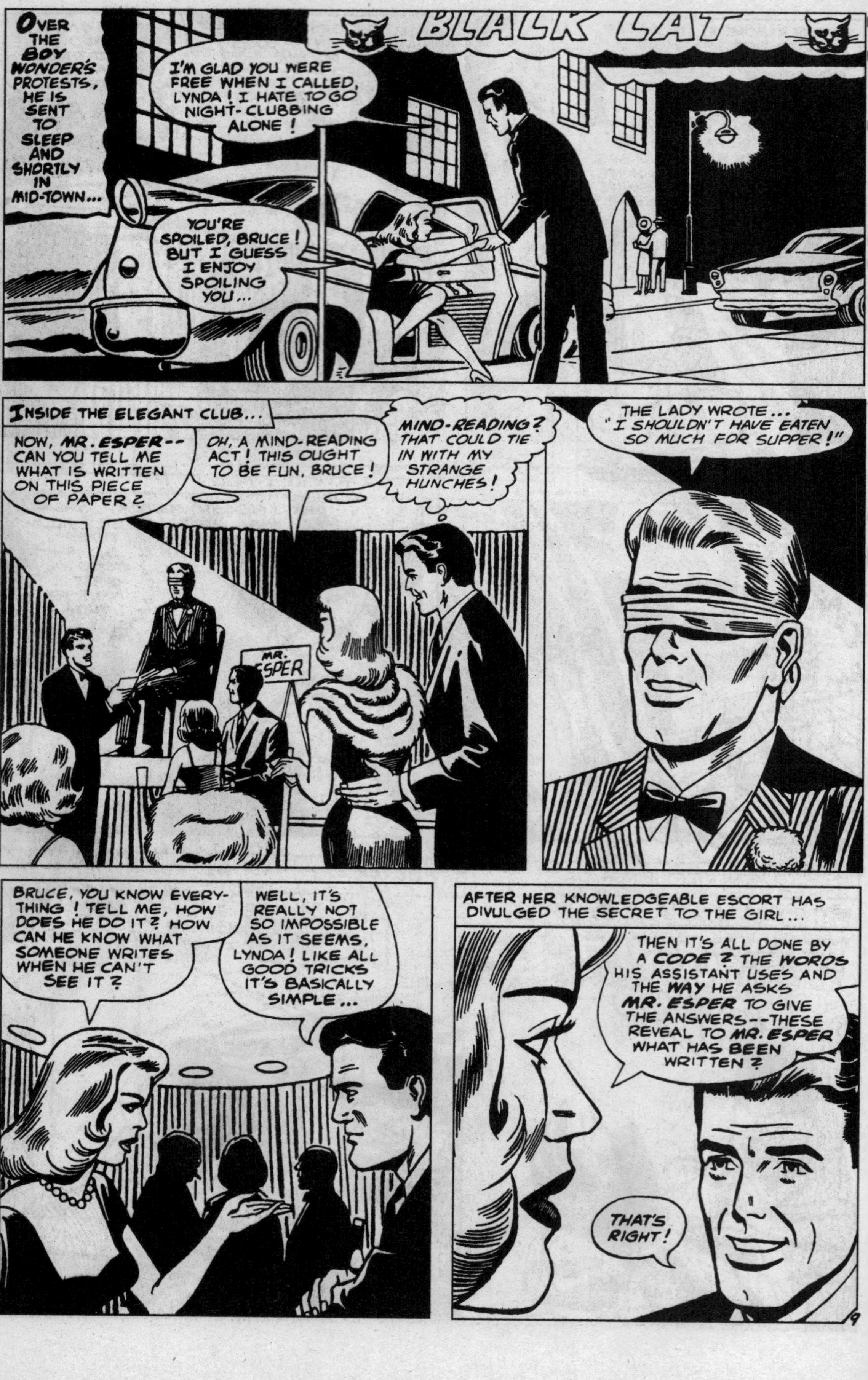
BLACK CAT
OVER THE BOY WONDER'S PROTESTS, HE IS SENT TO SLEEP AND SHORTLY IN MID-TOWN...
I'M GLAD YOU WERE FREE WHEN I CALLED, LYNDA! I HATE TO GO NIGHT-CLUBBING ALONE!
YOU'RE SPOILED, BRUCE! BUT I GUESS I ENJOY SPOILING YOU...
INSIDE THE ELEGANT CLUB...
NOW, MR. ESPER-- CAN YOU TELL ME WHAT IS WRITTEN ON THIS PIECE OF PAPER?
OH, A MIND-READING ACT! THIS OUGHT TO BE FUN, BRUCE!
MIND-READING? THAT COULD TIE IN WITH MY STRANGE HUNCHES!
MR. ESPER
THE LADY WROTE... "I SHOULDN'T HAVE EATEN SO MUCH FOR SUPPER!"
BRUCE, YOU KNOW EVERYTHING! TELL ME, HOW DOES HE DO IT? HOW CAN HE KNOW WHAT SOMEONE WRITES WHEN HE CAN'T SEE IT?
WELL, IT'S REALLY NOT SO IMPOSSIBLE AS IT SEEMS, LYNDA! LIKE ALL GOOD TRICKS IT'S BASICALLY SIMPLE...
AFTER HER KNOWLEDGEABLE ESCORT HAS DIVULGED THE SECRET TO THE GIRL...
THEN IT'S ALL DONE BY A CODE? THE WORDS HIS ASSISTANT USES AND THE WAY HE ASKS MR. ESPER TO GIVE THE ANSWERS--THESE REVEAL TO MR. ESPER WHAT HAS BEEN WRITTEN?
THAT'S RIGHT!
9

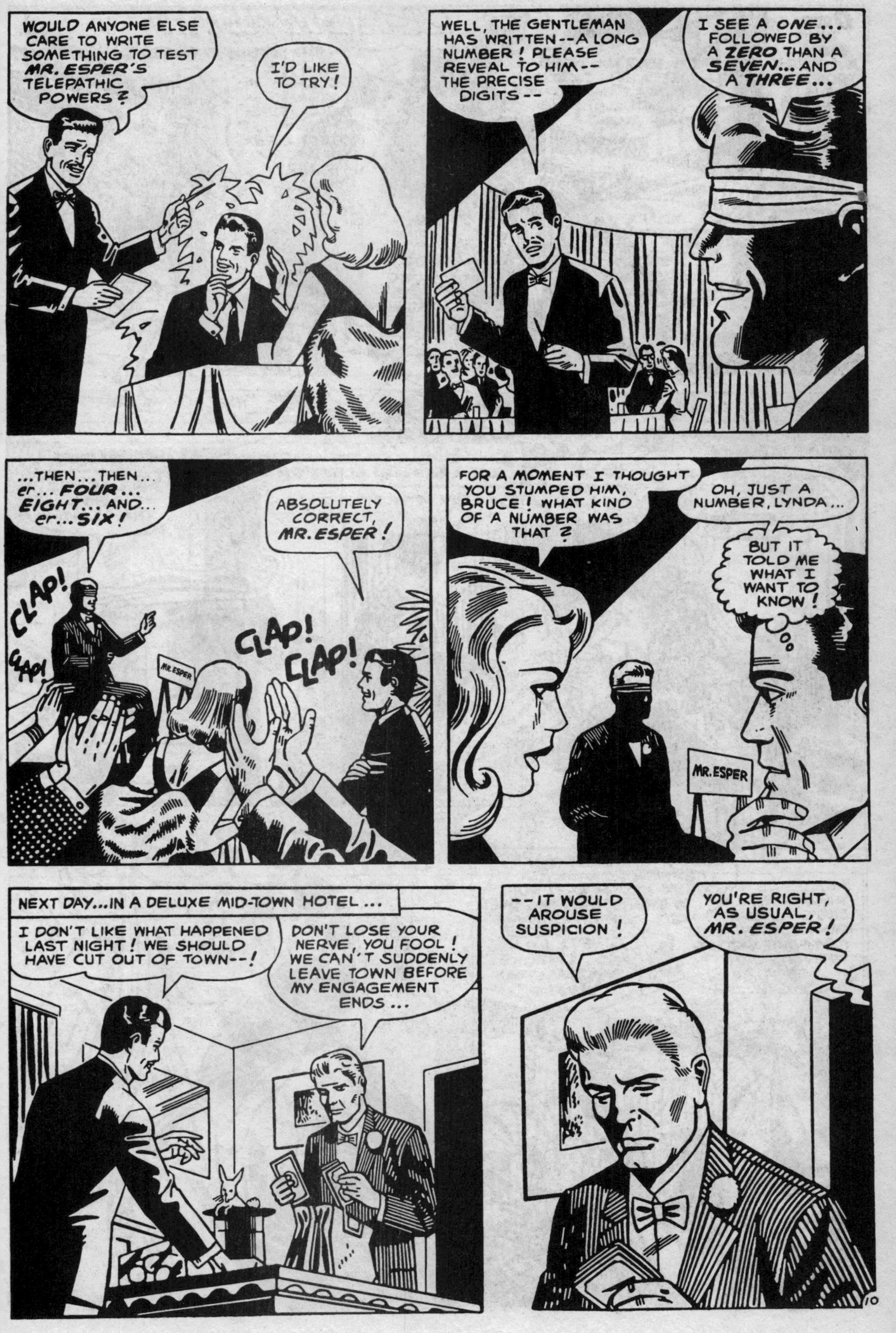
WOULD ANYONE ELSE CARE TO WRITE SOMETHING TO TEST MR. ESPER'S TELEPATHIC POWERS?
I'D LIKE TO TRY!
WELL, THE GENTLEMAN HAS WRITTEN--A LONG NUMBER! PLEASE REVEAL TO HIM--THE PRECISE DIGITS--
I SEE A ONE... FOLLOWED BY A ZERO THAN A SEVEN... AND A THREE...
...THEN...THEN... er... FOUR... EIGHT... AND... er...SIX!
ABSOLUTELY CORRECT, MR. ESPER!
CLAP!
CLAP!
CLAP!
CLAP!
MR. ESPER
FOR A MOMENT I THOUGHT YOU STUMPED HIM, BRUCE! WHAT KIND OF A NUMBER WAS THAT?
OH, JUST A NUMBER, LYNDA...
BUT IT TOLD ME WHAT I WANT TO KNOW!
MR. ESPER
NEXT DAY...IN A DELUXE MID-TOWN HOTEL ...
I DON'T LIKE WHAT HAPPENED LAST NIGHT! WE SHOULD HAVE CUT OUT OF TOWN--!
DON'T LOSE YOUR NERVE, YOU FOOL! WE CAN'T SUDDENLY LEAVE TOWN BEFORE MY ENGAGEMENT ENDS ...
--IT WOULD AROUSE SUSPICION!
YOU'RE RIGHT, AS USUAL, MR. ESPER!
10

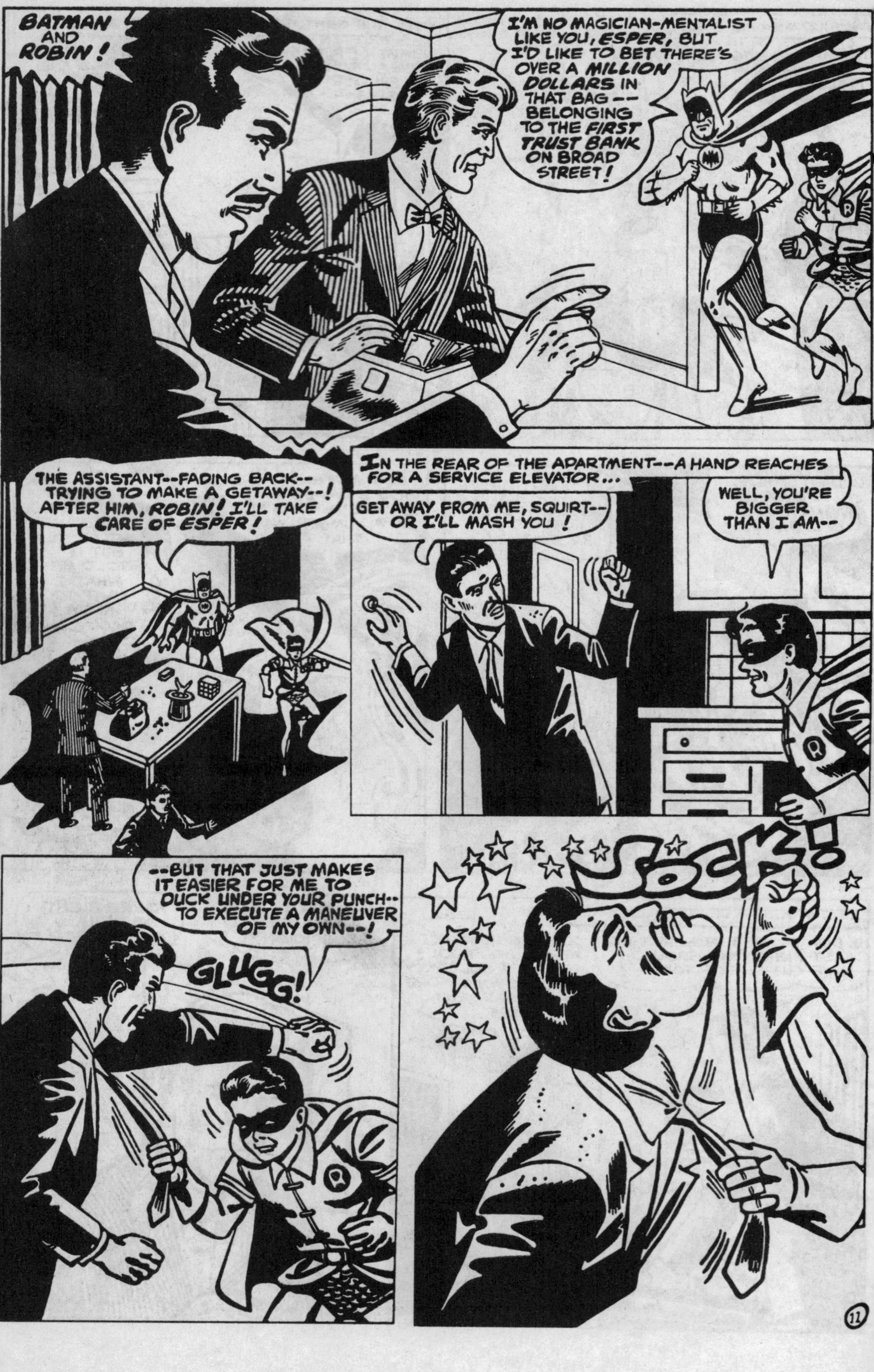
BATMAN AND ROBIN!
I'M NO MAGICIAN-MENTALIST LIKE YOU, ESPER, BUT I'D LIKE TO BET THERE'S OVER A MILLION DOLLARS IN THAT BAG -- BELONGING TO THE FIRST TRUST BANK ON BROAD STREET!
THE ASSISTANT--FADING BACK--TRYING TO MAKE A GETAWAY--! AFTER HIM, ROBIN! I'LL TAKE CARE OF ESPER!
IN THE REAR OF THE APARTMENT--A HAND REACHES FOR A SERVICE ELEVATOR...
GET AWAY FROM ME, SQUIRT--OR I'LL MASH YOU!
WELL, YOU'RE BIGGER THAN I AM--
--BUT THAT JUST MAKES IT EASIER FOR ME TO DUCK UNDER YOUR PUNCH--TO EXECUTE A MANEUVER OF MY OWN--!
GLUGG!
SOCK!
11

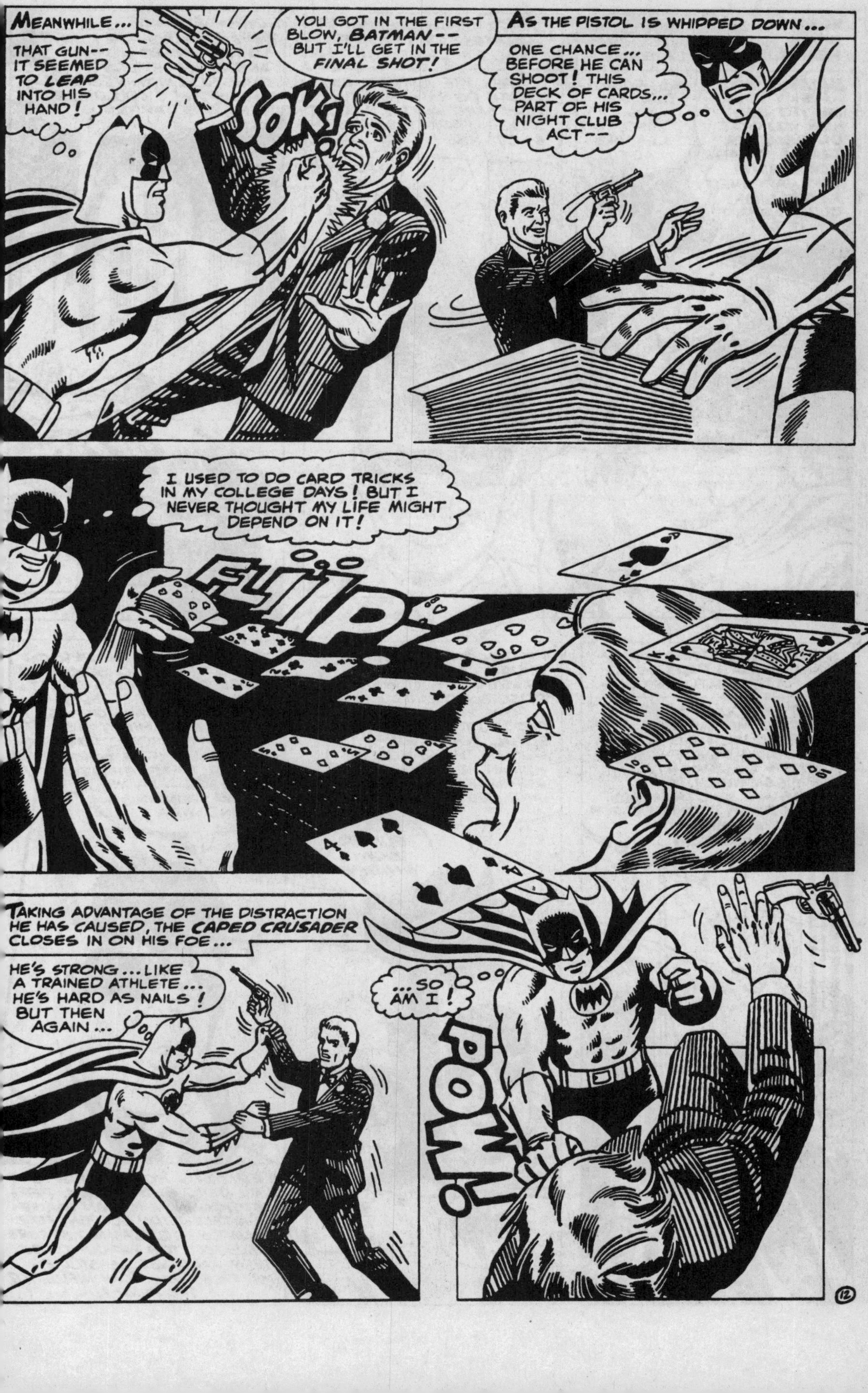
MEANWHILE...
THAT GUN--
IT SEEMED
TO LEAP
INTO HIS
HAND!
YOU GOT IN THE FIRST
BLOW, BATMAN--
BUT I'LL GET IN THE
FINAL SHOT!
SOK!
AS THE PISTOL IS WHIPPED DOWN...
ONE CHANCE...
BEFORE HE CAN
SHOOT! THIS
DECK OF CARDS...
PART OF HIS
NIGHT CLUB
ACT--
I USED TO DO CARD TRICKS
IN MY COLLEGE DAYS! BUT I
NEVER THOUGHT MY LIFE MIGHT
DEPEND ON IT!
FLIP!
TAKING ADVANTAGE OF THE DISTRACTION
HE HAS CAUSED, THE CAPED CRUSADER
CLOSES IN ON HIS FOE...
HE'S STRONG...LIKE
A TRAINED ATHLETE...
HE'S HARD AS NAILS!
BUT THEN
AGAIN...
...SO
AM I!
POW!
12

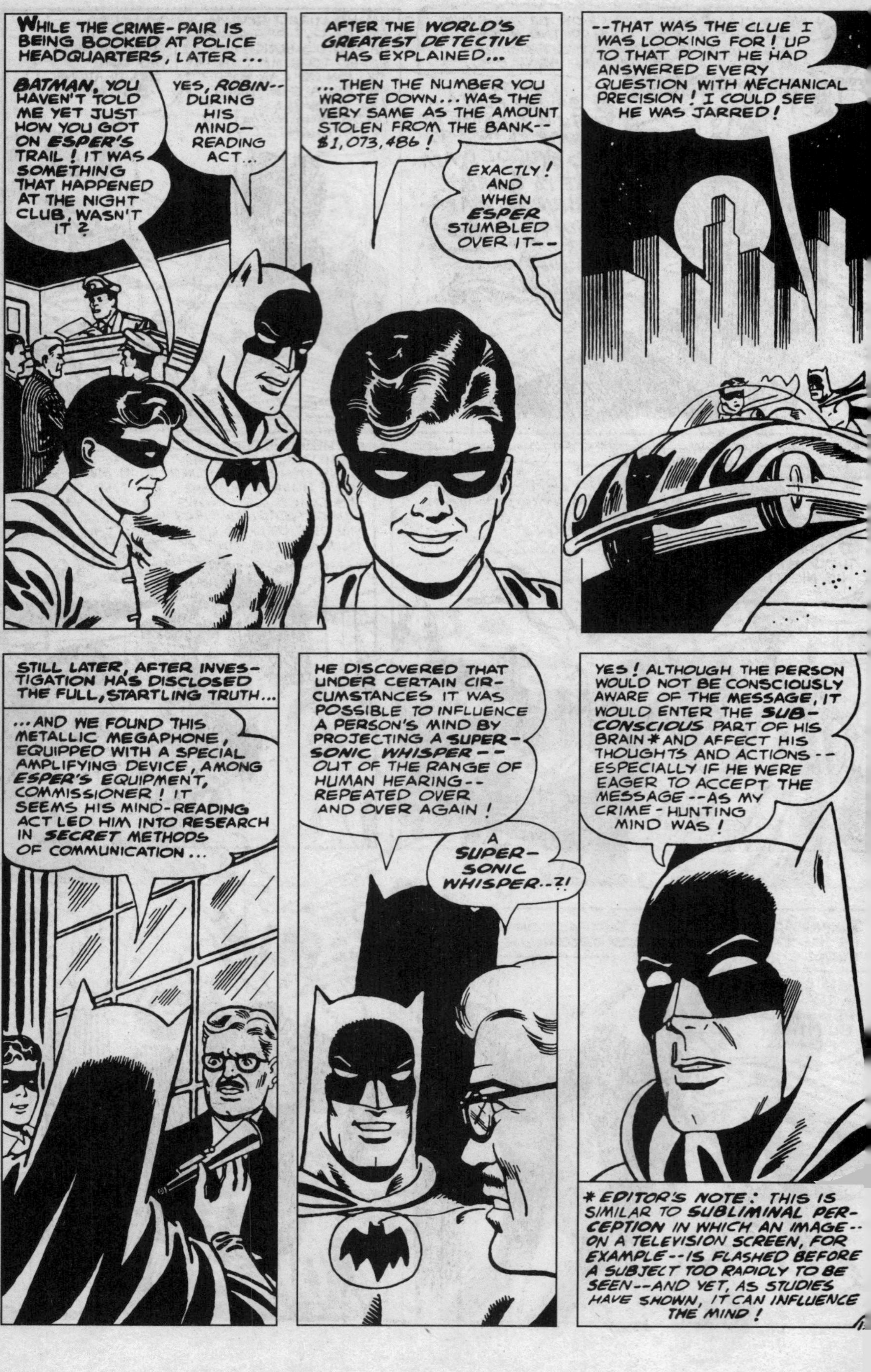
WHILE THE CRIME-PAIR IS BEING BOOKED AT POLICE HEADQUARTERS, LATER...
BATMAN, YOU HAVEN'T TOLD ME YET JUST HOW YOU GOT ON ESPER'S TRAIL! IT WAS SOMETHING THAT HAPPENED AT THE NIGHT CLUB, WASN'T IT?
YES, ROBIN--DURING HIS MIND-READING ACT...
AFTER THE WORLD'S GREATEST DETECTIVE HAS EXPLAINED...
...THEN THE NUMBER YOU WROTE DOWN...WAS THE VERY SAME AS THE AMOUNT STOLEN FROM THE BANK--$1,073,486!
EXACTLY! AND WHEN ESPER STUMBLED OVER IT--
--THAT WAS THE CLUE I WAS LOOKING FOR! UP TO THAT POINT HE HAD ANSWERED EVERY QUESTION WITH MECHANICAL PRECISION! I COULD SEE HE WAS JARRED!
STILL LATER, AFTER INVESTIGATION HAS DISCLOSED THE FULL, STARTLING TRUTH...
...AND WE FOUND THIS METALLIC MEGAPHONE, EQUIPPED WITH A SPECIAL AMPLIFYING DEVICE, AMONG ESPER'S EQUIPMENT, COMMISSIONER! IT SEEMS HIS MIND-READING ACT LED HIM INTO RESEARCH IN SECRET METHODS OF COMMUNICATION...
HE DISCOVERED THAT UNDER CERTAIN CIRCUMSTANCES IT WAS POSSIBLE TO INFLUENCE A PERSON'S MIND BY PROJECTING A SUPER-SONIC WHISPER--OUT OF THE RANGE OF HUMAN HEARING--REPEATED OVER AND OVER AGAIN!
A SUPER-SONIC WHISPER..?!
YES! ALTHOUGH THE PERSON WOULD NOT BE CONSCIOUSLY AWARE OF THE MESSAGE, IT WOULD ENTER THE SUB-CONSCIOUS PART OF HIS BRAIN* AND AFFECT HIS THOUGHTS AND ACTIONS--ESPECIALLY IF HE WERE EAGER TO ACCEPT THE MESSAGE--AS MY CRIME-HUNTING MIND WAS!
*EDITOR'S NOTE: THIS IS SIMILAR TO SUBLIMINAL PERCEPTION IN WHICH AN IMAGE--ON A TELEVISION SCREEN, FOR EXAMPLE--IS FLASHED BEFORE A SUBJECT TOO RAPIDLY TO BE SEEN--AND YET, AS STUDIES HAVE SHOWN, IT CAN INFLUENCE THE MIND!

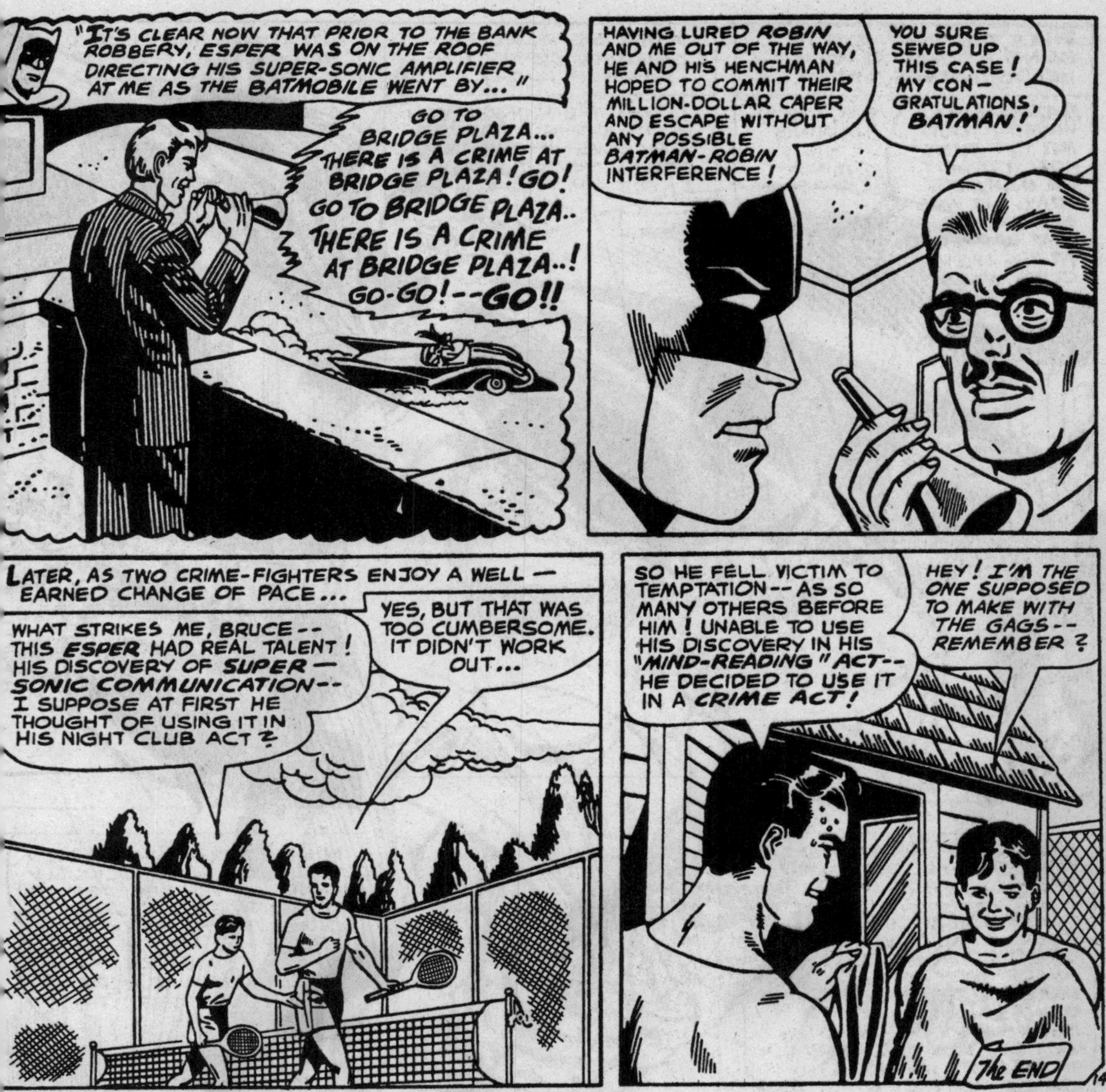
"IT'S CLEAR NOW THAT PRIOR TO THE BANK ROBBERY, ESPER WAS ON THE ROOF DIRECTING HIS SUPER-SONIC AMPLIFIER AT ME AS THE BATMOBILE WENT BY..."
GO TO BRIDGE PLAZA... THERE IS A CRIME AT BRIDGE PLAZA! GO! GO TO BRIDGE PLAZA.. THERE IS A CRIME AT BRIDGE PLAZA..! GO-GO!--GO!!
HAVING LURED ROBIN AND ME OUT OF THE WAY, HE AND HIS HENCHMAN HOPED TO COMMIT THEIR MILLION-DOLLAR CAPER AND ESCAPE WITHOUT ANY POSSIBLE BATMAN-ROBIN INTERFERENCE!
YOU SURE SEWED UP THIS CASE! MY CON-GRATULATIONS, BATMAN!
LATER, AS TWO CRIME-FIGHTERS ENJOY A WELL-EARNED CHANGE OF PACE...
WHAT STRIKES ME, BRUCE-- THIS ESPER HAD REAL TALENT! HIS DISCOVERY OF SUPER-SONIC COMMUNICATION-- I SUPPOSE AT FIRST HE THOUGHT OF USING IT IN HIS NIGHT CLUB ACT?
YES, BUT THAT WAS TOO CUMBERSOME. IT DIDN'T WORK OUT...
SO HE FELL VICTIM TO TEMPTATION--AS SO MANY OTHERS BEFORE HIM! UNABLE TO USE HIS DISCOVERY IN HIS "MIND-READING" ACT-- HE DECIDED TO USE IT IN A CRIME ACT!
HEY! I'M THE ONE SUPPOSED TO MAKE WITH THE GAGS-- REMEMBER?
The END
14

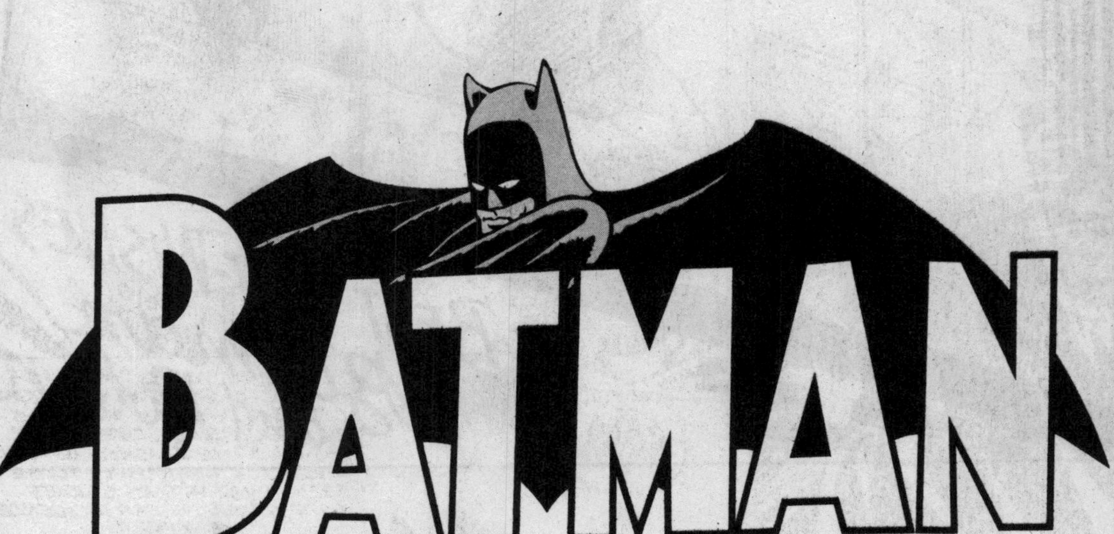

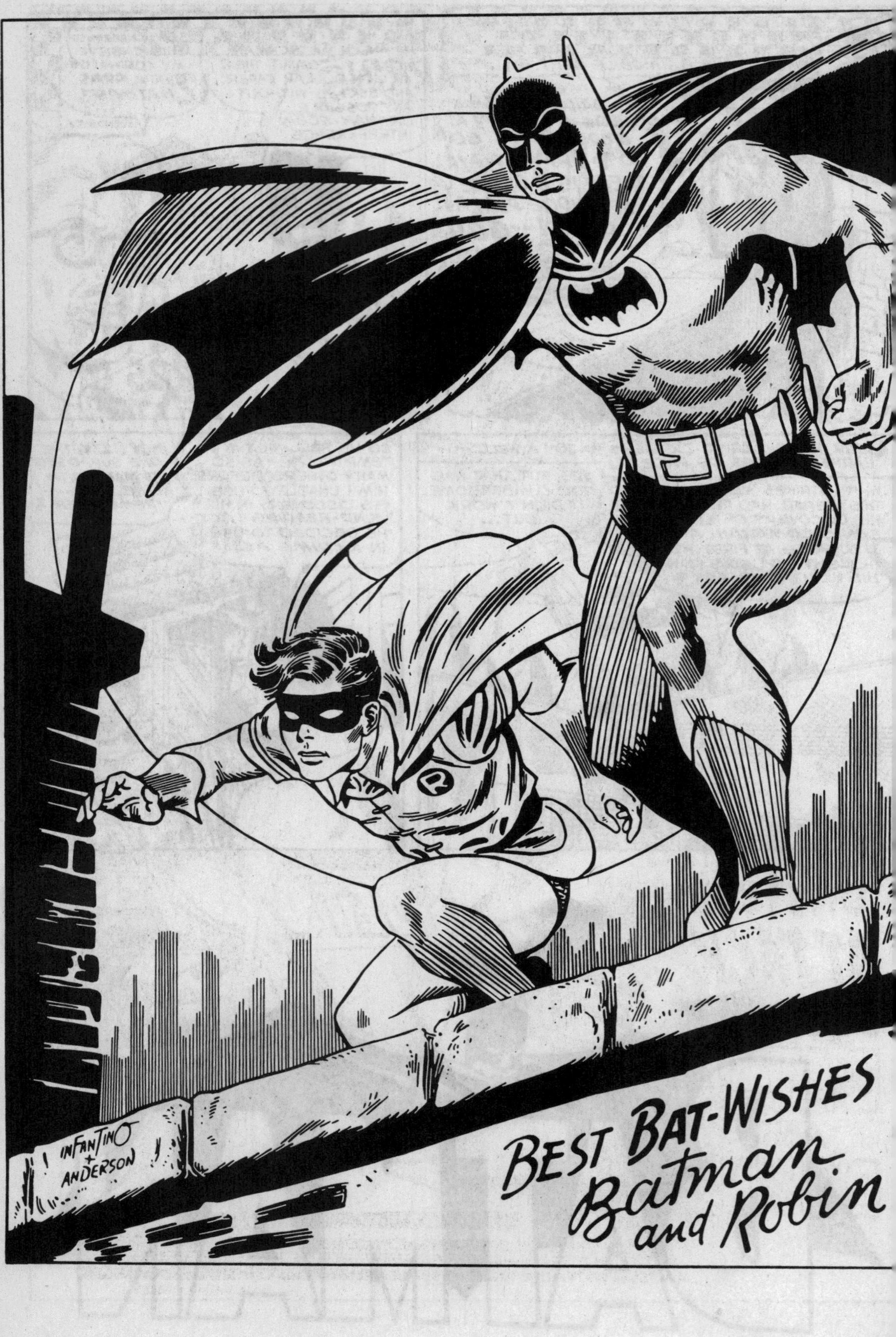
INFANTINO + ANDERSON
BEST BAT-WISHES
Batman and Robin

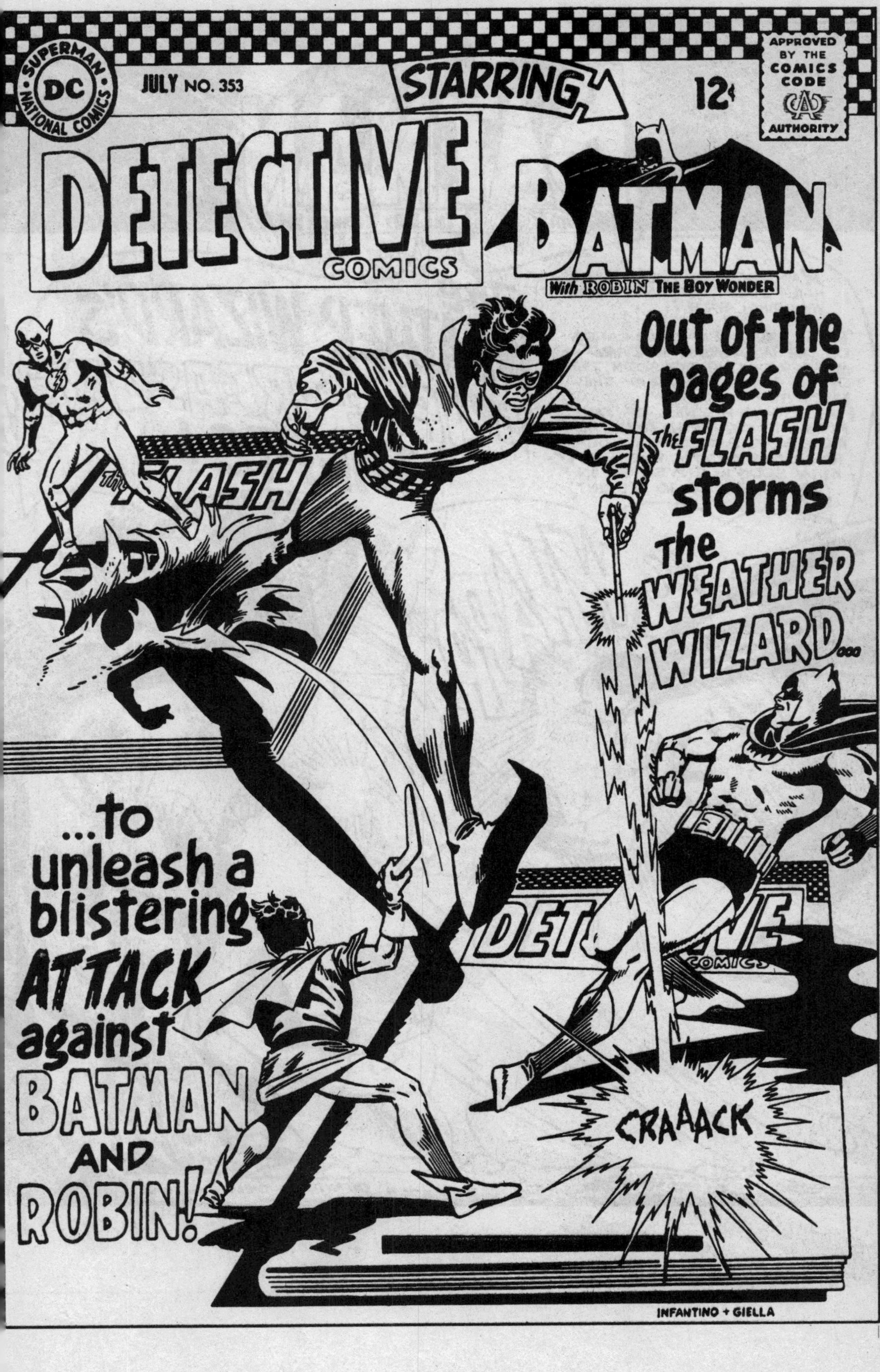
SUPERMAN DC NATIONAL COMICS
JULY NO. 353
STARRING
12¢
APPROVED BY THE COMICS CODE AUTHORITY
DETECTIVE COMICS
BATMAN
With ROBIN THE BOY WONDER
Out of the pages of The FLASH storms The WEATHER WIZARD...
THE FLASH
...to unleash a blistering ATTACK against BATMAN AND ROBIN!
CRAAACK
INFANTINO + GIELLA

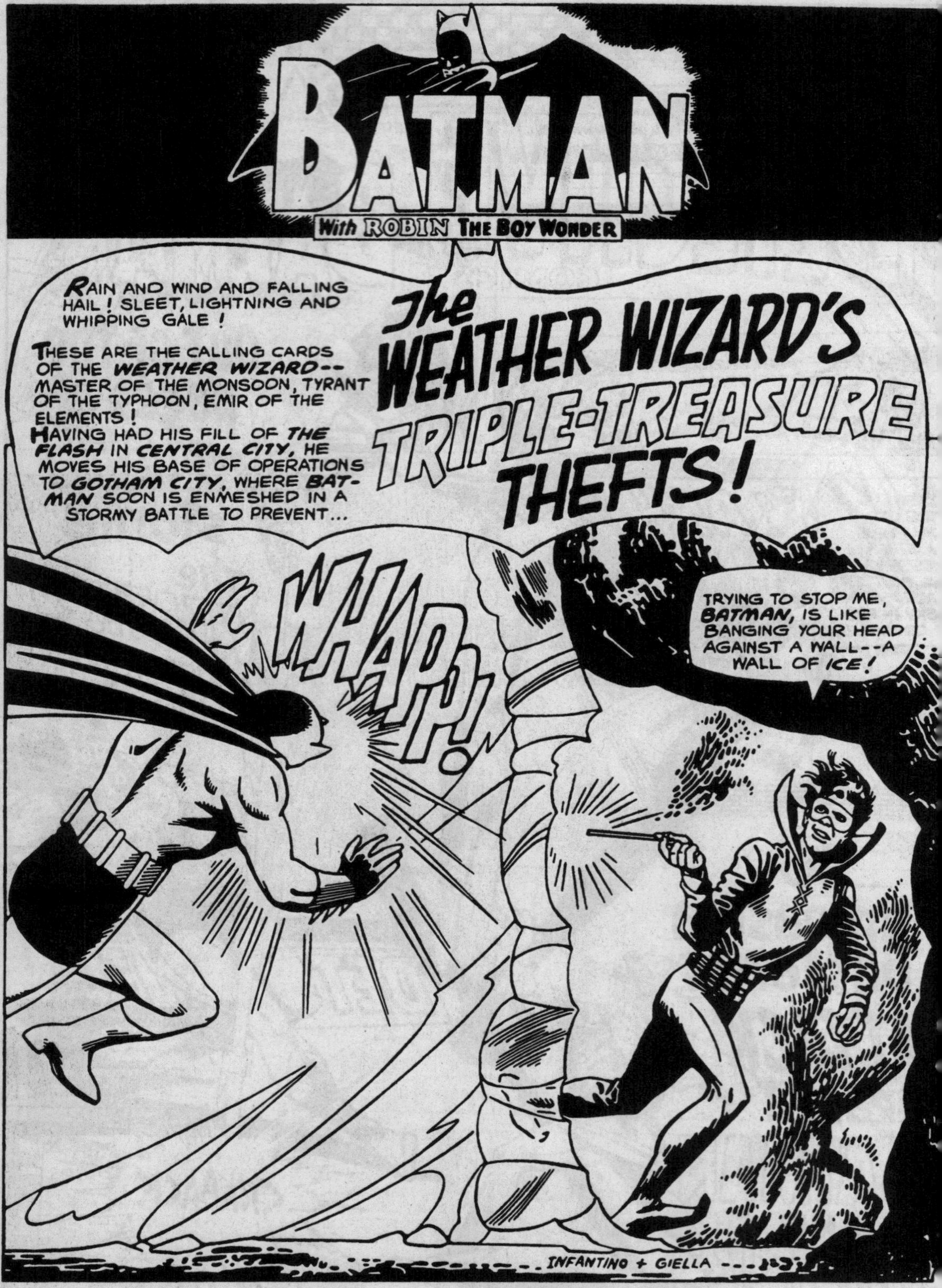

BATMAN
With ROBIN THE BOY WONDER
RAIN AND WIND AND FALLING HAIL! SLEET, LIGHTNING AND WHIPPING GALE!
THESE ARE THE CALLING CARDS OF THE WEATHER WIZARD-- MASTER OF THE MONSOON, TYRANT OF THE TYPHOON, EMIR OF THE ELEMENTS!
HAVING HAD HIS FILL OF THE FLASH IN CENTRAL CITY, HE MOVES HIS BASE OF OPERATIONS TO GOTHAM CITY, WHERE BATMAN SOON IS ENMESHED IN A STORMY BATTLE TO PREVENT...
The WEATHER WIZARD'S TRIPLE-TREASURE THEFTS!
WHAPP!
TRYING TO STOP ME, BATMAN, IS LIKE BANGING YOUR HEAD AGAINST A WALL--A WALL OF ICE!
INFANTINO + GIELLA

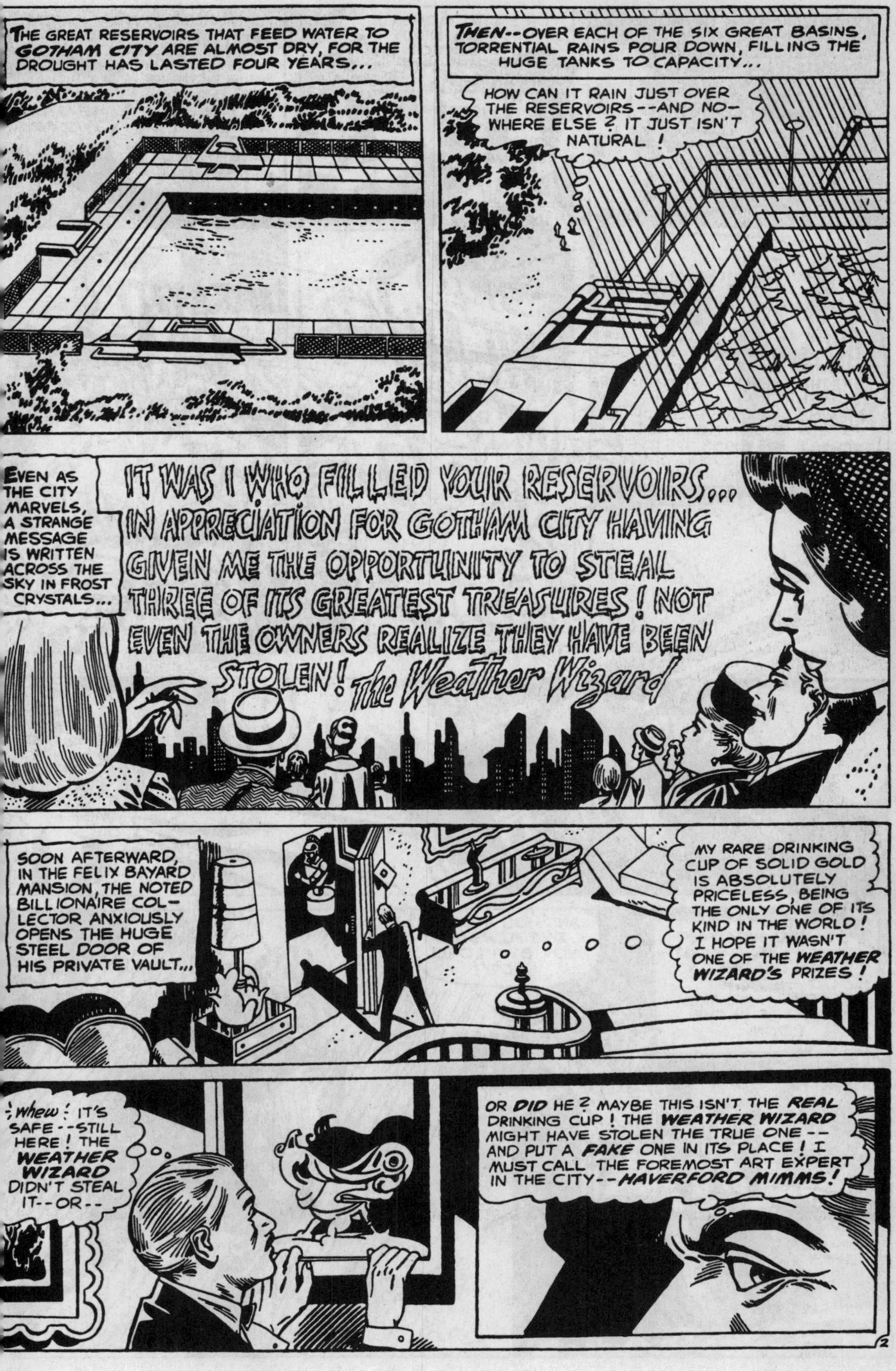
THE GREAT RESERVOIRS THAT FEED WATER TO GOTHAM CITY ARE ALMOST DRY, FOR THE DROUGHT HAS LASTED FOUR YEARS...
THEN--OVER EACH OF THE SIX GREAT BASINS, TORRENTIAL RAINS POUR DOWN, FILLING THE HUGE TANKS TO CAPACITY...
HOW CAN IT RAIN JUST OVER THE RESERVOIRS--AND NOWHERE ELSE? IT JUST ISN'T NATURAL!
EVEN AS THE CITY MARVELS, A STRANGE MESSAGE IS WRITTEN ACROSS THE SKY IN FROST CRYSTALS...
IT WAS I WHO FILLED YOUR RESERVOIRS... IN APPRECIATION FOR GOTHAM CITY HAVING GIVEN ME THE OPPORTUNITY TO STEAL THREE OF ITS GREATEST TREASURES! NOT EVEN THE OWNERS REALIZE THEY HAVE BEEN STOLEN! the Weather Wizard
SOON AFTERWARD, IN THE FELIX BAYARD MANSION, THE NOTED BILLIONAIRE COLLECTOR ANXIOUSLY OPENS THE HUGE STEEL DOOR OF HIS PRIVATE VAULT...
MY RARE DRINKING CUP OF SOLID GOLD IS ABSOLUTELY PRICELESS, BEING THE ONLY ONE OF ITS KIND IN THE WORLD! I HOPE IT WASN'T ONE OF THE WEATHER WIZARD'S PRIZES!
WHEW! IT'S SAFE--STILL HERE! THE WEATHER WIZARD DIDN'T STEAL IT--OR--
OR DID HE? MAYBE THIS ISN'T THE REAL DRINKING CUP! THE WEATHER WIZARD MIGHT HAVE STOLEN THE TRUE ONE--AND PUT A FAKE ONE IN ITS PLACE! I MUST CALL THE FOREMOST ART EXPERT IN THE CITY--HAVERFORD MIMMS!
2

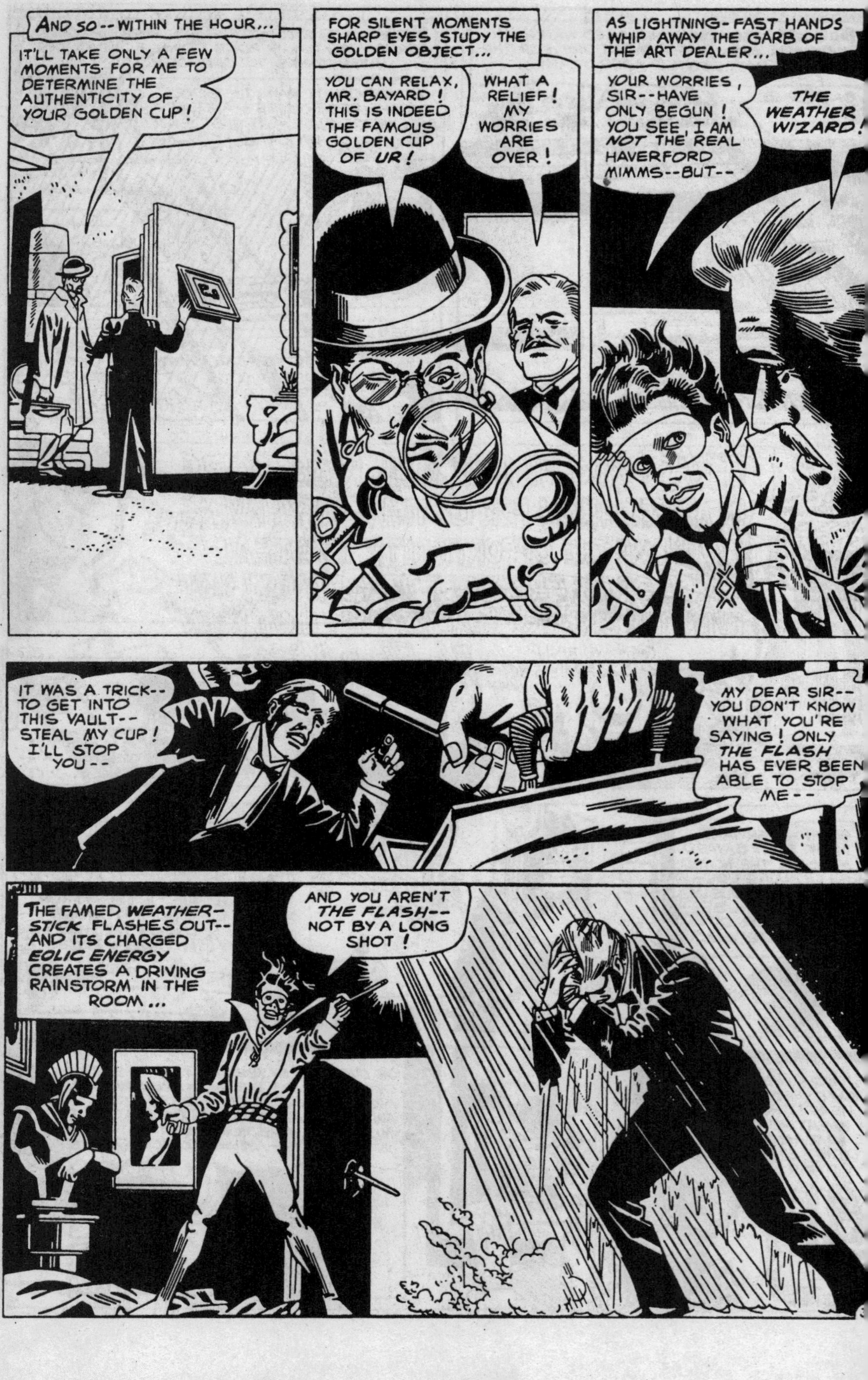
AND SO--WITHIN THE HOUR...
IT'LL TAKE ONLY A FEW MOMENTS FOR ME TO DETERMINE THE AUTHENTICITY OF YOUR GOLDEN CUP!
FOR SILENT MOMENTS SHARP EYES STUDY THE GOLDEN OBJECT...
YOU CAN RELAX, MR. BAYARD! THIS IS INDEED THE FAMOUS GOLDEN CUP OF UR!
WHAT A RELIEF! MY WORRIES ARE OVER!
AS LIGHTNING-FAST HANDS WHIP AWAY THE GARB OF THE ART DEALER...
YOUR WORRIES, SIR--HAVE ONLY BEGUN! YOU SEE, I AM NOT THE REAL HAVERFORD MIMMS--BUT--
THE WEATHER WIZARD!
IT WAS A TRICK--TO GET INTO THIS VAULT--STEAL MY CUP! I'LL STOP YOU--
MY DEAR SIR--YOU DON'T KNOW WHAT YOU'RE SAYING! ONLY THE FLASH HAS EVER BEEN ABLE TO STOP ME--
THE FAMED WEATHER-STICK FLASHES OUT--AND ITS CHARGED EOLIC ENERGY CREATES A DRIVING RAINSTORM IN THE ROOM...
AND YOU AREN'T THE FLASH--NOT BY A LONG SHOT!

BUFFETED BY THAT AWESOME DELUGE, FELIX BAYARD IS HELPLESS TO INTERVENE AS...

HA! HA! HA! I CAME TO *GOTHAM CITY* TO STEAL THREE OF ITS MOST VALUABLE TREASURES-- AND NOW I HAVE ONE OF THEM!

THEN--A GETAWAY ALONG A RAINBOW OF SOLID HUES...

I DIDN'T HAVE THE SLIGHTEST IDEA IN ADVANCE WHAT THOSE GREATEST TREASURES WERE-- SO I PUT THAT MESSAGE OF THANKS IN THE SKY TO LURE LEERY OWNERS OF PRICELESS OBJECTS TO CHECK THEIR POSSESSIONS -- AND UNWITTINGLY TIP ME OFF ABOUT THEM!

I SIMPLY TAPPED THE PHONE OF *HAVINGFORD MIMMS*, THE MOST FAMOUS ART EXPERT OF THEM ALL --AND WHEN FELIX BAYARD PHONED, I WAYLAID MIMMS AND POSED AS HIM TO GET MY HANDS ON THE GOLD DRINKING CUP TREASURE!

IN THE *BATCAVE*, SOON AFTER, A SCOWLING *BATMAN* IS DRESSING FOR HIS NIGHT PATROL... THE *WEATHER WIZARD* STOLE THREE OBJECTS--BUT WHICH ONES? I HAVEN'T A SINGLE CLUE TO GO ON! NO ONE'S EVEN REPORTED A THEFT!

I'LL GET THAT *HOT-LINE* CALL, DICK! YOU'VE GOT TO REST THOSE WRISTS YOU INJURED PLAYING BASKET-BALL WITH YOUR SCHOOL TEAM!

AWW, THEY DON'T BOTHER ME *THAT* MUCH!

BRINGG RINGG

AS USUAL, IT IS POLICE COMMISSIONER GORDON AT THE OTHER END OF THE WIRE...

...AND WE'VE BEEN FLOODED BY CALLS FROM PEOPLE OWN-ING UNUSUAL AND VALUABLE OBJECTS! BUT THE ONE THAT'LL INTEREST *YOU* CAME FROM FELIX BAYARD! HE'S JUST BEEN ROBBED-- BY THE *WEATHER WIZARD!*

I'LL BE RIGHT OVER, COM-MISSIONER.

4

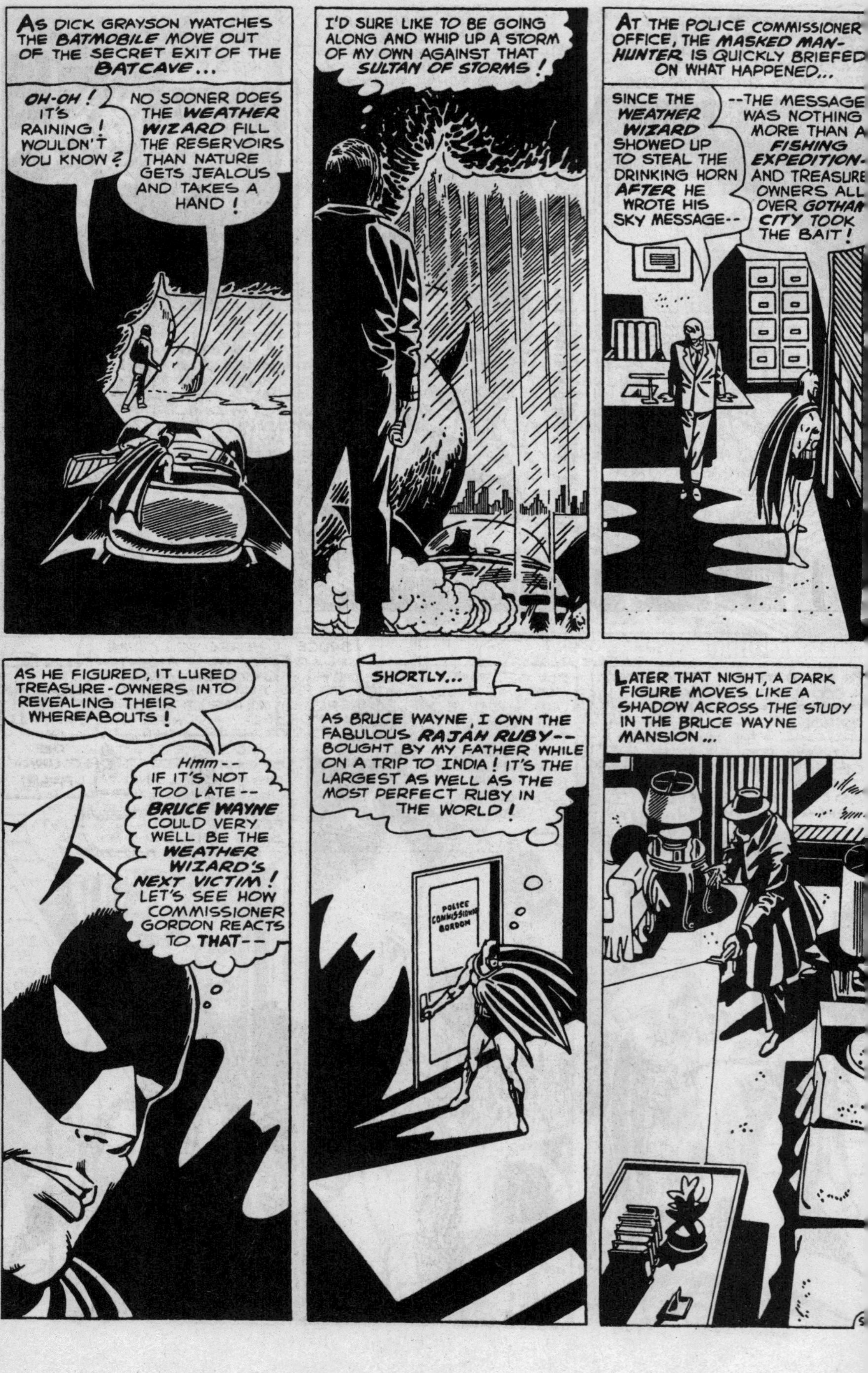

AS DICK GRAYSON WATCHES THE BATMOBILE MOVE OUT OF THE SECRET EXIT OF THE BATCAVE...
OH-OH! IT'S RAINING! WOULDN'T YOU KNOW?
NO SOONER DOES THE WEATHER WIZARD FILL THE RESERVOIRS THAN NATURE GETS JEALOUS AND TAKES A HAND!
I'D SURE LIKE TO BE GOING ALONG AND WHIP UP A STORM OF MY OWN AGAINST THAT SULTAN OF STORMS!
AT THE POLICE COMMISSIONER OFFICE, THE MASKED MAN-HUNTER IS QUICKLY BRIEFED ON WHAT HAPPENED...
SINCE THE WEATHER WIZARD SHOWED UP TO STEAL THE DRINKING HORN AFTER HE WROTE HIS SKY MESSAGE--
--THE MESSAGE WAS NOTHING MORE THAN A FISHING EXPEDITION-- AND TREASURE OWNERS ALL OVER GOTHAM CITY TOOK THE BAIT!
AS HE FIGURED, IT LURED TREASURE-OWNERS INTO REVEALING THEIR WHEREABOUTS!
Hmm-- IF IT'S NOT TOO LATE-- BRUCE WAYNE COULD VERY WELL BE THE WEATHER WIZARD'S NEXT VICTIM! LET'S SEE HOW COMMISSIONER GORDON REACTS TO THAT--
SHORTLY...
AS BRUCE WAYNE, I OWN THE FABULOUS RAJAH RUBY-- BOUGHT BY MY FATHER WHILE ON A TRIP TO INDIA! IT'S THE LARGEST AS WELL AS THE MOST PERFECT RUBY IN THE WORLD!
LATER THAT NIGHT, A DARK FIGURE MOVES LIKE A SHADOW ACROSS THE STUDY IN THE BRUCE WAYNE MANSION...

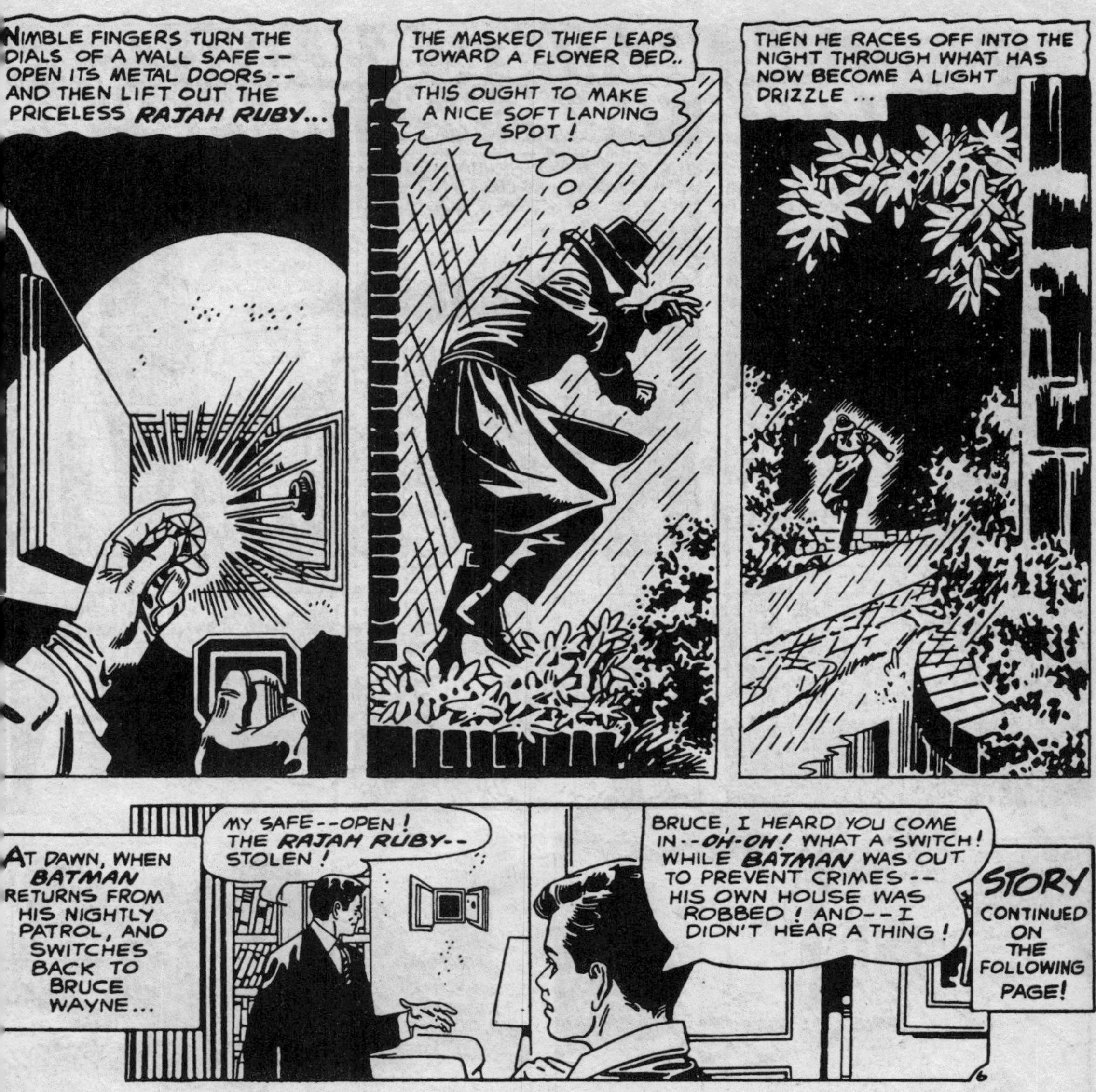
NIMBLE FINGERS TURN THE DIALS OF A WALL SAFE-- OPEN ITS METAL DOORS-- AND THEN LIFT OUT THE PRICELESS RAJAH RUBY...
THE MASKED THIEF LEAPS TOWARD A FLOWER BED..
THIS OUGHT TO MAKE A NICE SOFT LANDING SPOT!
THEN HE RACES OFF INTO THE NIGHT THROUGH WHAT HAS NOW BECOME A LIGHT DRIZZLE ...
AT DAWN, WHEN BATMAN RETURNS FROM HIS NIGHTLY PATROL, AND SWITCHES BACK TO BRUCE WAYNE...
MY SAFE--OPEN! THE RAJAH RUBY-- STOLEN!
BRUCE, I HEARD YOU COME IN--OH-OH! WHAT A SWITCH! WHILE BATMAN WAS OUT TO PREVENT CRIMES-- HIS OWN HOUSE WAS ROBBED! AND--I DIDN'T HEAR A THING!
STORY CONTINUED ON THE FOLLOWING PAGE!
6

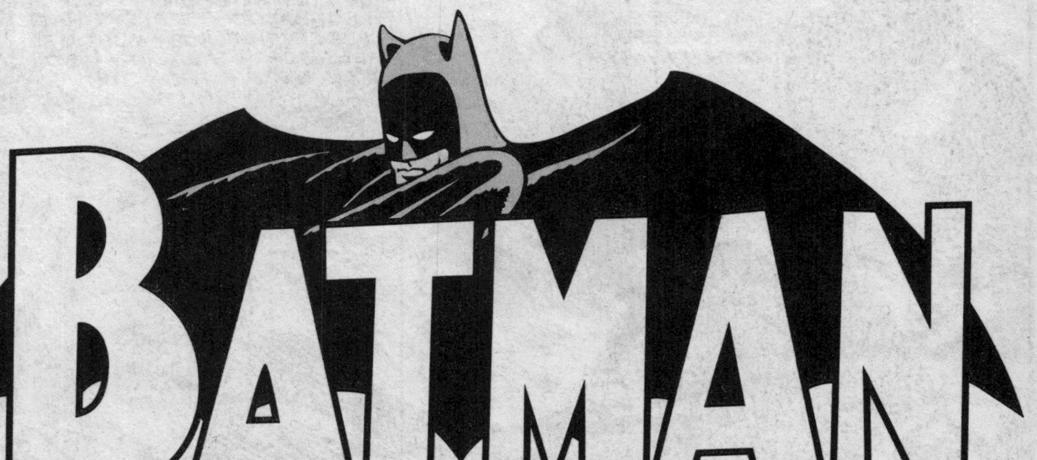
BATMAN

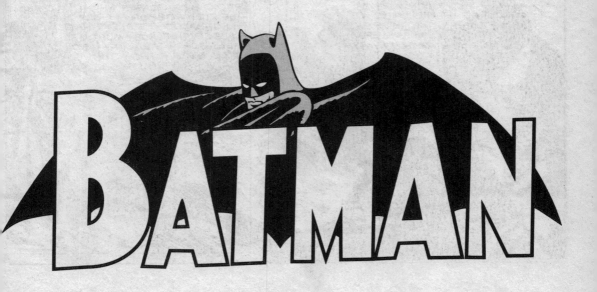

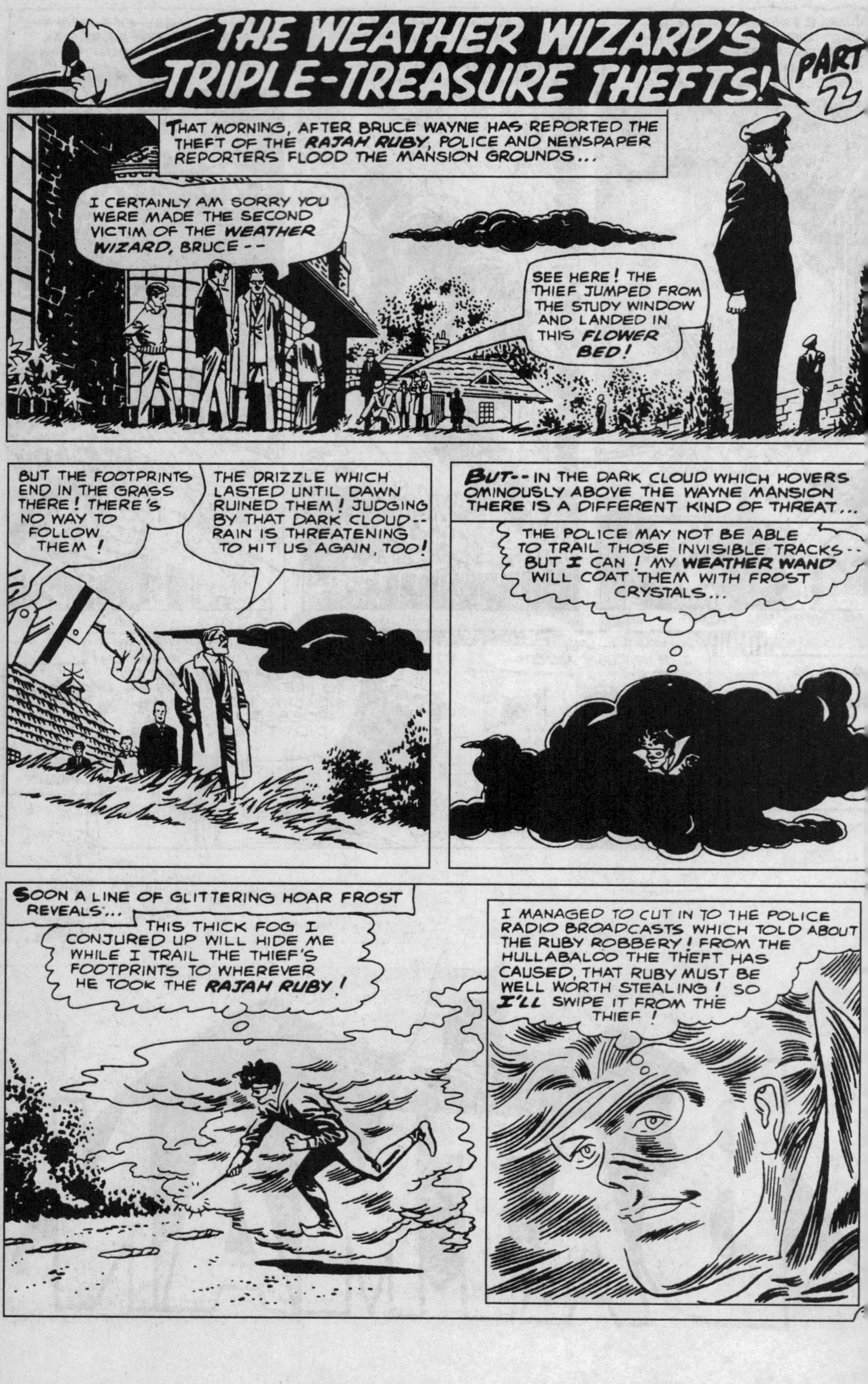
THE WEATHER WIZARD'S TRIPLE-TREASURE THEFTS!
PART 2
THAT MORNING, AFTER BRUCE WAYNE HAS REPORTED THE THEFT OF THE RAJAH RUBY, POLICE AND NEWSPAPER REPORTERS FLOOD THE MANSION GROUNDS...
I CERTAINLY AM SORRY YOU WERE MADE THE SECOND VICTIM OF THE WEATHER WIZARD, BRUCE --
SEE HERE! THE THIEF JUMPED FROM THE STUDY WINDOW AND LANDED IN THIS FLOWER BED!
BUT THE FOOTPRINTS END IN THE GRASS THERE! THERE'S NO WAY TO FOLLOW THEM!
THE DRIZZLE WHICH LASTED UNTIL DAWN RUINED THEM! JUDGING BY THAT DARK CLOUD-- RAIN IS THREATENING TO HIT US AGAIN, TOO!
BUT-- IN THE DARK CLOUD WHICH HOVERS OMINOUSLY ABOVE THE WAYNE MANSION THERE IS A DIFFERENT KIND OF THREAT...
THE POLICE MAY NOT BE ABLE TO TRAIL THOSE INVISIBLE TRACKS-- BUT I CAN! MY WEATHER WAND WILL COAT THEM WITH FROST CRYSTALS...
SOON A LINE OF GLITTERING HOAR FROST REVEALS...
THIS THICK FOG I CONJURED UP WILL HIDE ME WHILE I TRAIL THE THIEF'S FOOTPRINTS TO WHEREVER HE TOOK THE RAJAH RUBY!
I MANAGED TO CUT IN TO THE POLICE RADIO BROADCASTS WHICH TOLD ABOUT THE RUBY ROBBERY! FROM THE HULLABALOO THE THEFT HAS CAUSED, THAT RUBY MUST BE WELL WORTH STEALING! SO I'LL SWIPE IT FROM THE THIEF!

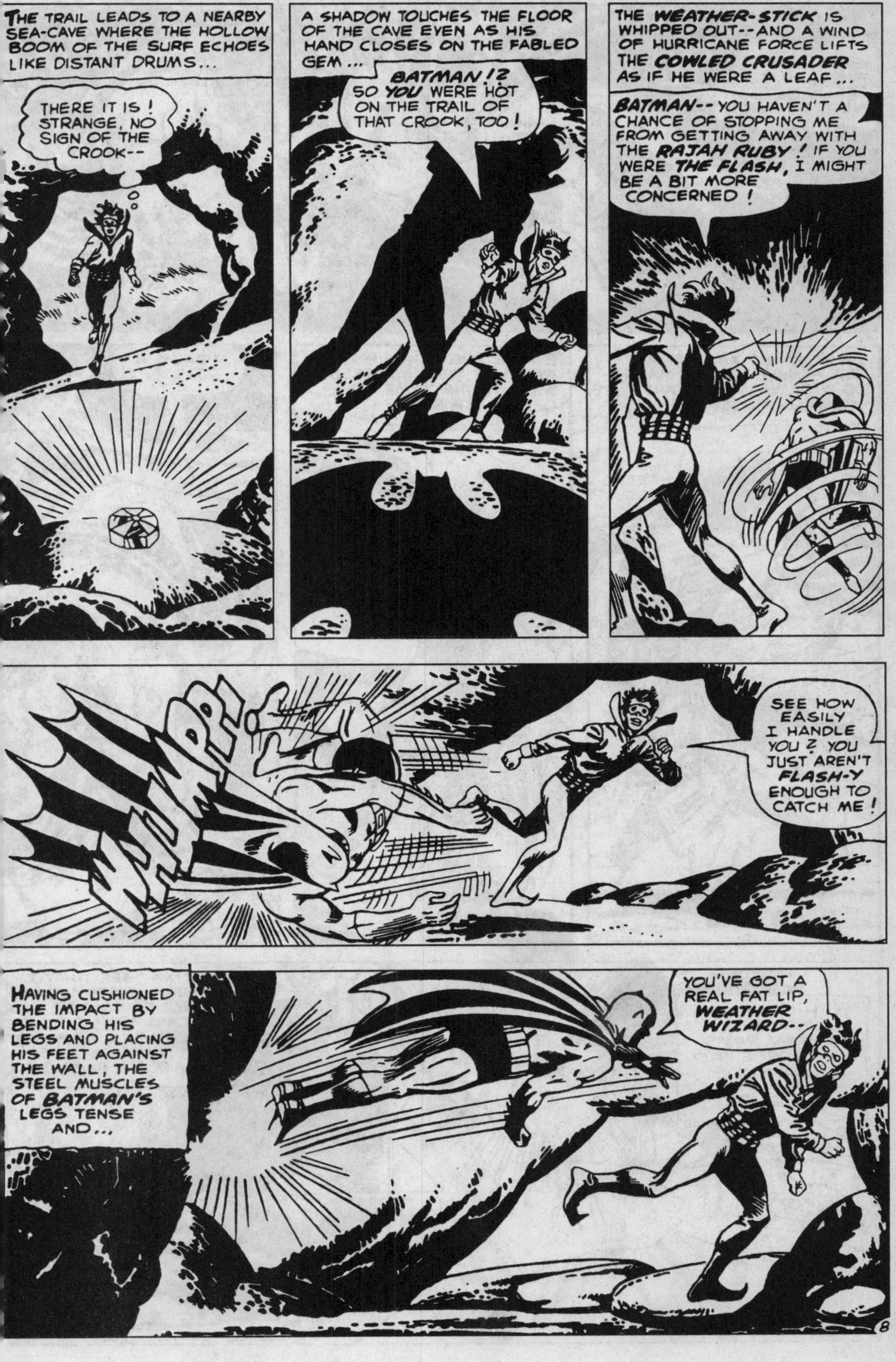
THE TRAIL LEADS TO A NEARBY SEA-CAVE WHERE THE HOLLOW BOOM OF THE SURF ECHOES LIKE DISTANT DRUMS...
THERE IT IS! STRANGE, NO SIGN OF THE CROOK--
A SHADOW TOUCHES THE FLOOR OF THE CAVE EVEN AS HIS HAND CLOSES ON THE FABLED GEM...
BATMAN!? SO YOU WERE HOT ON THE TRAIL OF THAT CROOK, TOO!
THE WEATHER-STICK IS WHIPPED OUT--AND A WIND OF HURRICANE FORCE LIFTS THE COWLED CRUSADER AS IF HE WERE A LEAF...
BATMAN-- YOU HAVEN'T A CHANCE OF STOPPING ME FROM GETTING AWAY WITH THE RAJAH RUBY! IF YOU WERE THE FLASH, I MIGHT BE A BIT MORE CONCERNED!
WHUMP!
SEE HOW EASILY I HANDLE YOU? YOU JUST AREN'T FLASH-Y ENOUGH TO CATCH ME!
HAVING CUSHIONED THE IMPACT BY BENDING HIS LEGS AND PLACING HIS FEET AGAINST THE WALL, THE STEEL MUSCLES OF BATMAN'S LEGS TENSE AND...
YOU'VE GOT A REAL FAT LIP, WEATHER WIZARD--

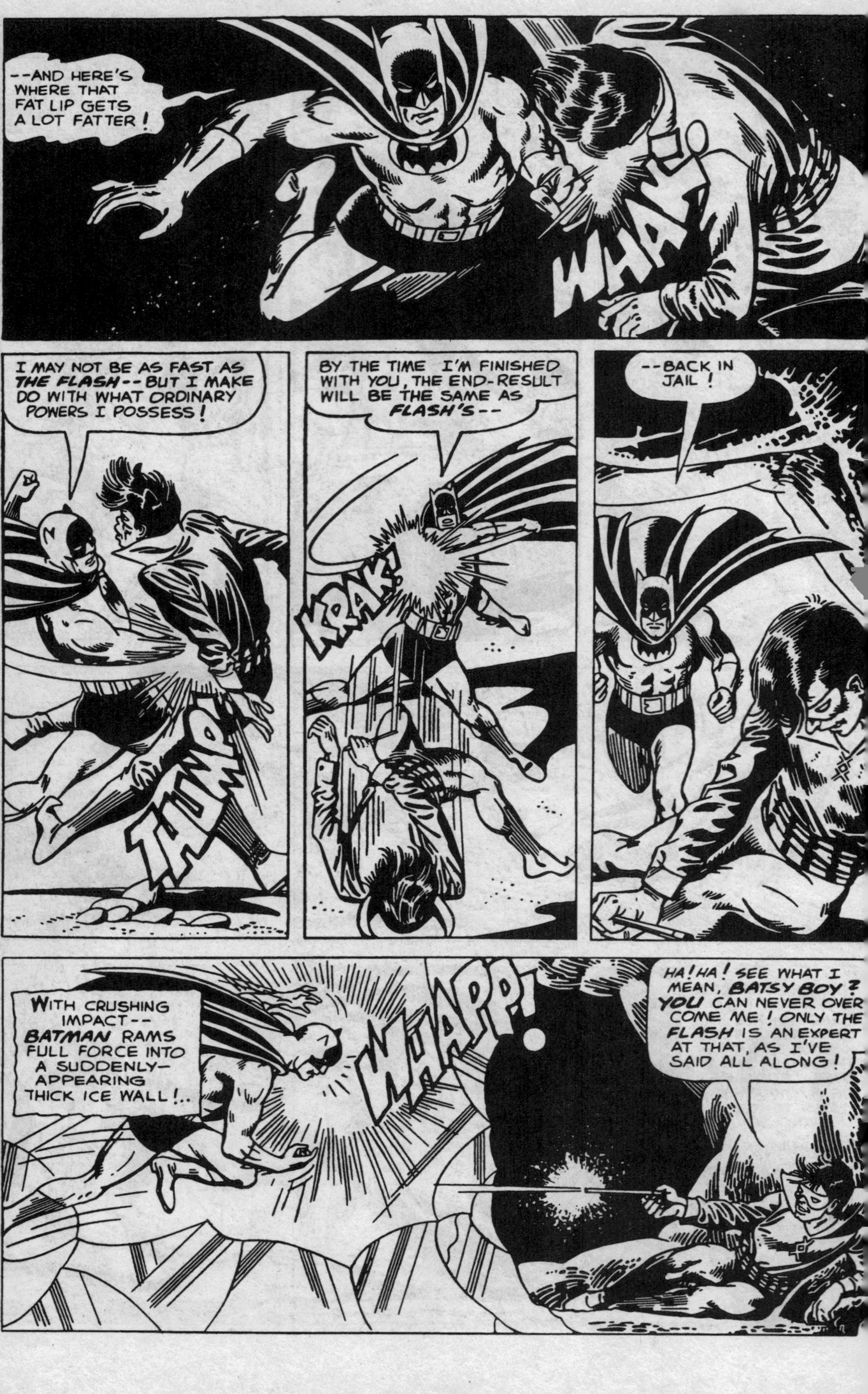
--AND HERE'S WHERE THAT FAT LIP GETS A LOT FATTER!
WHAP
I MAY NOT BE AS FAST AS THE FLASH--BUT I MAKE DO WITH WHAT ORDINARY POWERS I POSSESS!
THUMP
BY THE TIME I'M FINISHED WITH YOU, THE END-RESULT WILL BE THE SAME AS FLASH'S--
KRAK!
--BACK IN JAIL!
WITH CRUSHING IMPACT--BATMAN RAMS FULL FORCE INTO A SUDDENLY-APPEARING THICK ICE WALL!..
WHAPP!
HA! HA! SEE WHAT I MEAN, BATSY BOY? YOU CAN NEVER OVER COME ME! ONLY THE FLASH IS AN EXPERT AT THAT, AS I'VE SAID ALL ALONG!

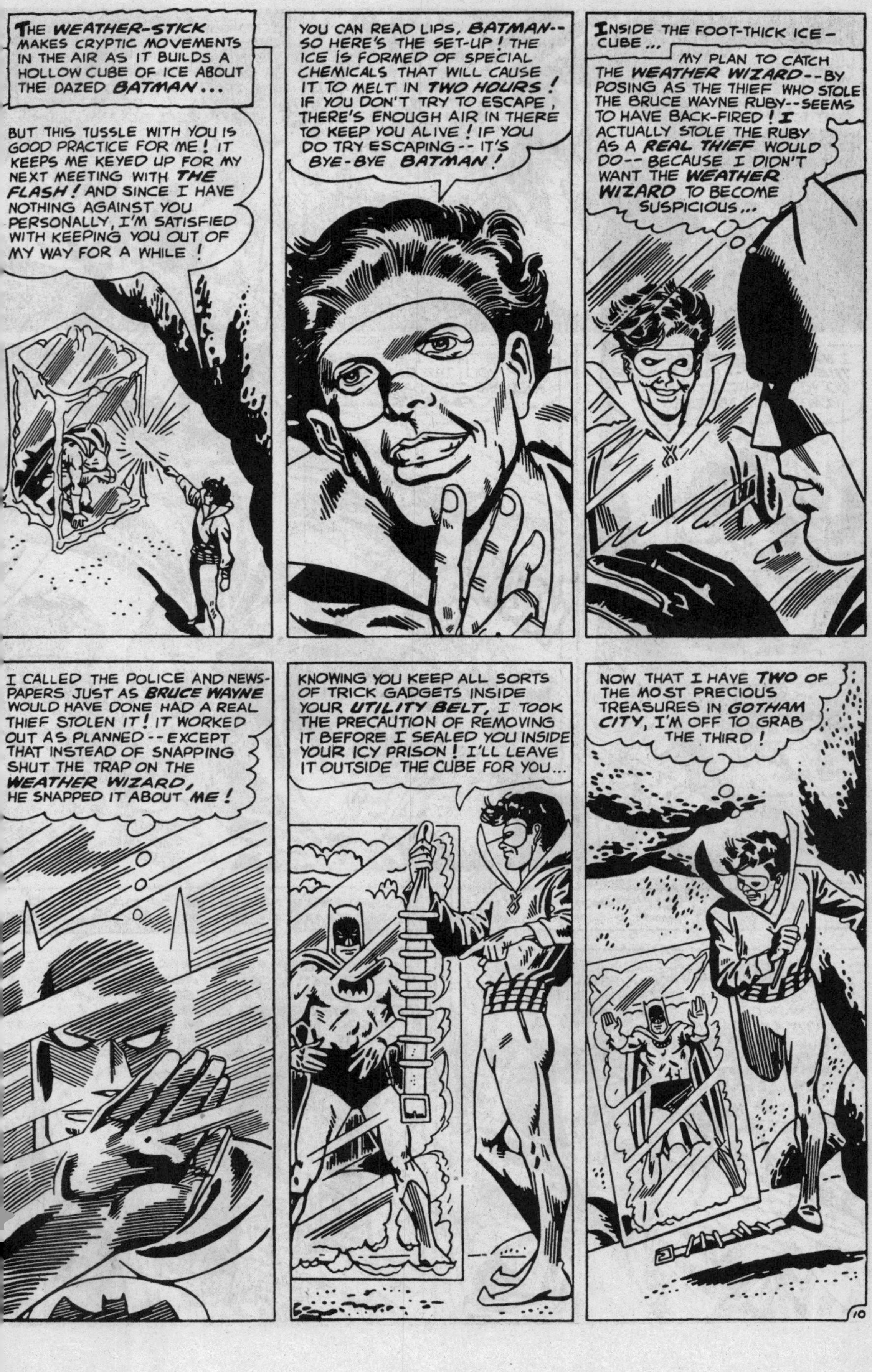
THE WEATHER-STICK MAKES CRYPTIC MOVEMENTS IN THE AIR AS IT BUILDS A HOLLOW CUBE OF ICE ABOUT THE DAZED BATMAN...
BUT THIS TUSSLE WITH YOU IS GOOD PRACTICE FOR ME! IT KEEPS ME KEYED UP FOR MY NEXT MEETING WITH THE FLASH! AND SINCE I HAVE NOTHING AGAINST YOU PERSONALLY, I'M SATISFIED WITH KEEPING YOU OUT OF MY WAY FOR A WHILE!
YOU CAN READ LIPS, BATMAN-- SO HERE'S THE SET-UP! THE ICE IS FORMED OF SPECIAL CHEMICALS THAT WILL CAUSE IT TO MELT IN TWO HOURS! IF YOU DON'T TRY TO ESCAPE, THERE'S ENOUGH AIR IN THERE TO KEEP YOU ALIVE! IF YOU DO TRY ESCAPING-- IT'S BYE-BYE BATMAN!
INSIDE THE FOOT-THICK ICE-CUBE...
MY PLAN TO CATCH THE WEATHER WIZARD--BY POSING AS THE THIEF WHO STOLE THE BRUCE WAYNE RUBY--SEEMS TO HAVE BACK-FIRED! I ACTUALLY STOLE THE RUBY AS A REAL THIEF WOULD DO-- BECAUSE I DIDN'T WANT THE WEATHER WIZARD TO BECOME SUSPICIOUS...
I CALLED THE POLICE AND NEWS-PAPERS JUST AS BRUCE WAYNE WOULD HAVE DONE HAD A REAL THIEF STOLEN IT! IT WORKED OUT AS PLANNED--EXCEPT THAT INSTEAD OF SNAPPING SHUT THE TRAP ON THE WEATHER WIZARD, HE SNAPPED IT ABOUT ME!
KNOWING YOU KEEP ALL SORTS OF TRICK GADGETS INSIDE YOUR UTILITY BELT, I TOOK THE PRECAUTION OF REMOVING IT BEFORE I SEALED YOU INSIDE YOUR ICY PRISON! I'LL LEAVE IT OUTSIDE THE CUBE FOR YOU...
NOW THAT I HAVE TWO OF THE MOST PRECIOUS TREASURES IN GOTHAM CITY, I'M OFF TO GRAB THE THIRD!
10

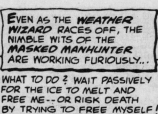

EVEN AS THE *WEATHER WIZARD* RACES OFF, THE NIMBLE WITS OF THE *MASKED MANHUNTER* ARE WORKING FURIOUSLY...

WHAT TO DO? WAIT PASSIVELY FOR THE ICE TO MELT AND FREE ME--OR RISK DEATH BY TRYING TO FREE MYSELF! WELL, THE CHOICE IS CLEAR...

THE *WEATHER WIZARD* IS ALSO DOING SOME DEEP THINKING...

IT SURE WAS EASY, DEFEATING *BATMAN*-- *Hmmm!* MAYBE IT WAS *TOO* EASY! I KIDDED HIM ABOUT NOT HAVING *FLASH'S* SPEED--BUT *BATMAN* IS NOTED FOR USING HIS *WITS*-- AND BEING A TRICKY GUY--

I WONDER IF THIS *RAJAH RUBY* COULD POSSIBLY BE GIMMICKED UP IN SOME WAY? IF IT IS--AND IF *BATMAN* SHOULD ESCAPE MY ICE-TRAP--HE COULD EASILY FOLLOW ME! I BETTER TEST IT BEFORE I GO ANY FURTHER...

WITH A WAVE OF THE WONDER *WEATHER-STICK*, AN ASSORTMENT OF RAYS BATHES THE RUBY...

SURE ENOUGH! *BATMAN* COATED THE RUBY WITH A CHEMICAL WHICH CREATES A COLUMN OF LIGHT VISIBLE ONLY IN THE INFRA-RED WAVE BAND! NEAT, NEAT!

WELL, I KNOW HOW TO HANDLE THAT! YESSIREE-- THIS SESSION WITH *BATMAN* IS REALLY SHARPENING MY WITS FOR A FUTURE ENCOUNTER WITH *THE FLASH*, ALL RIGHT!

ENCASED WITHIN THE CUBE OF ICE, THE *COWLED CRUSADER* TAKES STOCK OF WHAT LITTLE FACTS HE HAS IN HIS FAVOR...

THIS ISN'T *NORMAL* ICE--IT'LL MELT IN TWO SHORT HOURS! IT MUST HAVE BEEN FORMED WITH SOME SPECIAL *HEAT-ABSORBING CHEMICAL!* BY ABSORBING HEAT FROM THE AIR AROUND IT, THE ICE WILL MELT FASTER! IN THAT CASE--

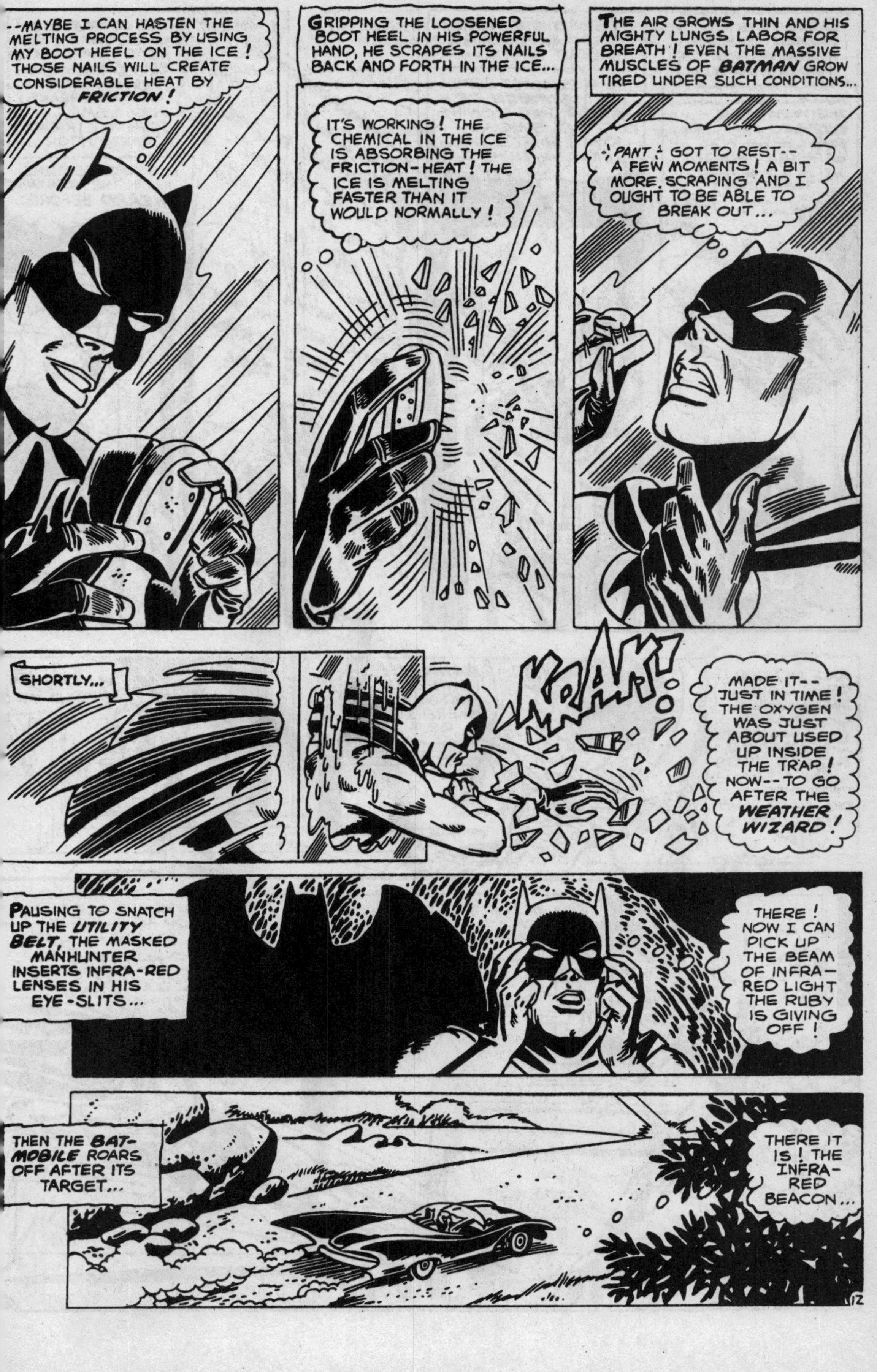
--MAYBE I CAN HASTEN THE MELTING PROCESS BY USING MY BOOT HEEL ON THE ICE! THOSE NAILS WILL CREATE CONSIDERABLE HEAT BY FRICTION!
GRIPPING THE LOOSENED BOOT HEEL IN HIS POWERFUL HAND, HE SCRAPES ITS NAILS BACK AND FORTH IN THE ICE...
IT'S WORKING! THE CHEMICAL IN THE ICE IS ABSORBING THE FRICTION-HEAT! THE ICE IS MELTING FASTER THAN IT WOULD NORMALLY!
THE AIR GROWS THIN AND HIS MIGHTY LUNGS LABOR FOR BREATH! EVEN THE MASSIVE MUSCLES OF BATMAN GROW TIRED UNDER SUCH CONDITIONS...
PANT GOT TO REST-- A FEW MOMENTS! A BIT MORE SCRAPING AND I OUGHT TO BE ABLE TO BREAK OUT...
SHORTLY...
KRAK!
MADE IT-- JUST IN TIME! THE OXYGEN WAS JUST ABOUT USED UP INSIDE THE TRAP! NOW--TO GO AFTER THE WEATHER WIZARD!
PAUSING TO SNATCH UP THE UTILITY BELT, THE MASKED MANHUNTER INSERTS INFRA-RED LENSES IN HIS EYE-SLITS...
THERE! NOW I CAN PICK UP THE BEAM OF INFRA-RED LIGHT THE RUBY IS GIVING OFF!
THEN THE BAT-MOBILE ROARS OFF AFTER ITS TARGET...
THERE IT IS! THE INFRA-RED BEACON...
12

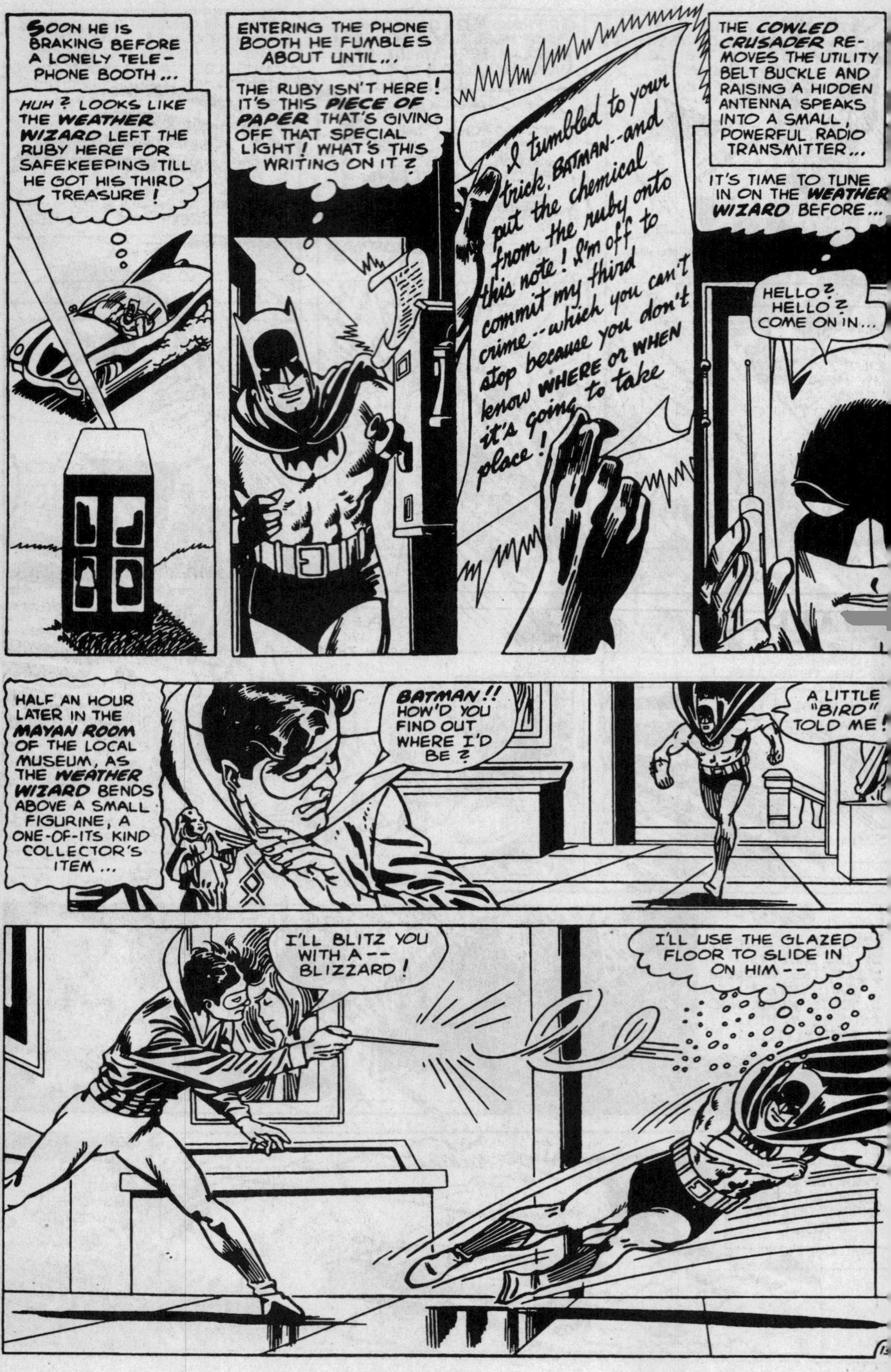
SOON HE IS BRAKING BEFORE A LONELY TELE-PHONE BOOTH...
HUH? LOOKS LIKE THE WEATHER WIZARD LEFT THE RUBY HERE FOR SAFEKEEPING TILL HE GOT HIS THIRD TREASURE!
ENTERING THE PHONE BOOTH HE FUMBLES ABOUT UNTIL...
THE RUBY ISN'T HERE! IT'S THIS PIECE OF PAPER THAT'S GIVING OFF THAT SPECIAL LIGHT! WHAT'S THIS WRITING ON IT?
I tumbled to your trick, BATMAN--and put the chemical from the ruby onto this note! I'm off to commit my third crime--which you can't stop because you don't know WHERE or WHEN it's going to take place!
THE COWLED CRUSADER REMOVES THE UTILITY BELT BUCKLE AND RAISING A HIDDEN ANTENNA SPEAKS INTO A SMALL, POWERFUL RADIO TRANSMITTER...
IT'S TIME TO TUNE IN ON THE WEATHER WIZARD BEFORE...
HELLO? HELLO? COME ON IN...
HALF AN HOUR LATER IN THE MAYAN ROOM OF THE LOCAL MUSEUM, AS THE WEATHER WIZARD BENDS ABOVE A SMALL FIGURINE, A ONE-OF-ITS KIND COLLECTOR'S ITEM...
BATMAN!! HOW'D YOU FIND OUT WHERE I'D BE?
A LITTLE "BIRD" TOLD ME!
I'LL BLITZ YOU WITH A--BLIZZARD!
I'LL USE THE GLAZED FLOOR TO SLIDE IN ON HIM--

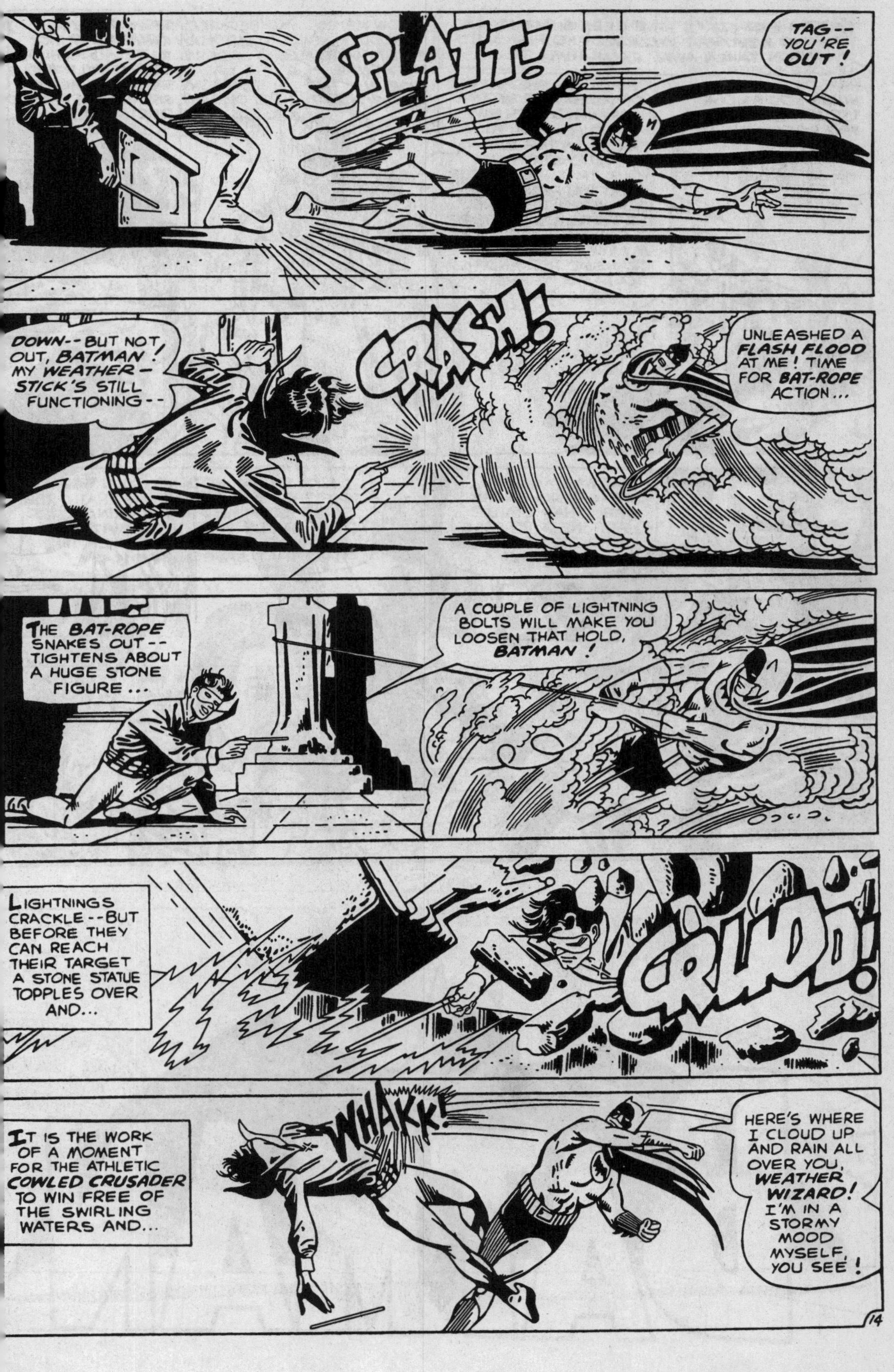
SPLATT!
TAG-- YOU'RE OUT!
DOWN--BUT NOT OUT, BATMAN! MY WEATHER-STICK'S STILL FUNCTIONING--
CRASH!
UNLEASHED A FLASH FLOOD AT ME! TIME FOR BAT-ROPE ACTION...
THE BAT-ROPE SNAKES OUT--TIGHTENS ABOUT A HUGE STONE FIGURE...
A COUPLE OF LIGHTNING BOLTS WILL MAKE YOU LOOSEN THAT HOLD, BATMAN!
LIGHTNINGS CRACKLE--BUT BEFORE THEY CAN REACH THEIR TARGET A STONE STATUE TOPPLES OVER AND...
CRUDD!
IT IS THE WORK OF A MOMENT FOR THE ATHLETIC COWLED CRUSADER TO WIN FREE OF THE SWIRLING WATERS AND...
WHAKK!
HERE'S WHERE I CLOUD UP AND RAIN ALL OVER YOU, WEATHER WIZARD! I'M IN A STORMY MOOD MYSELF, YOU SEE!
14

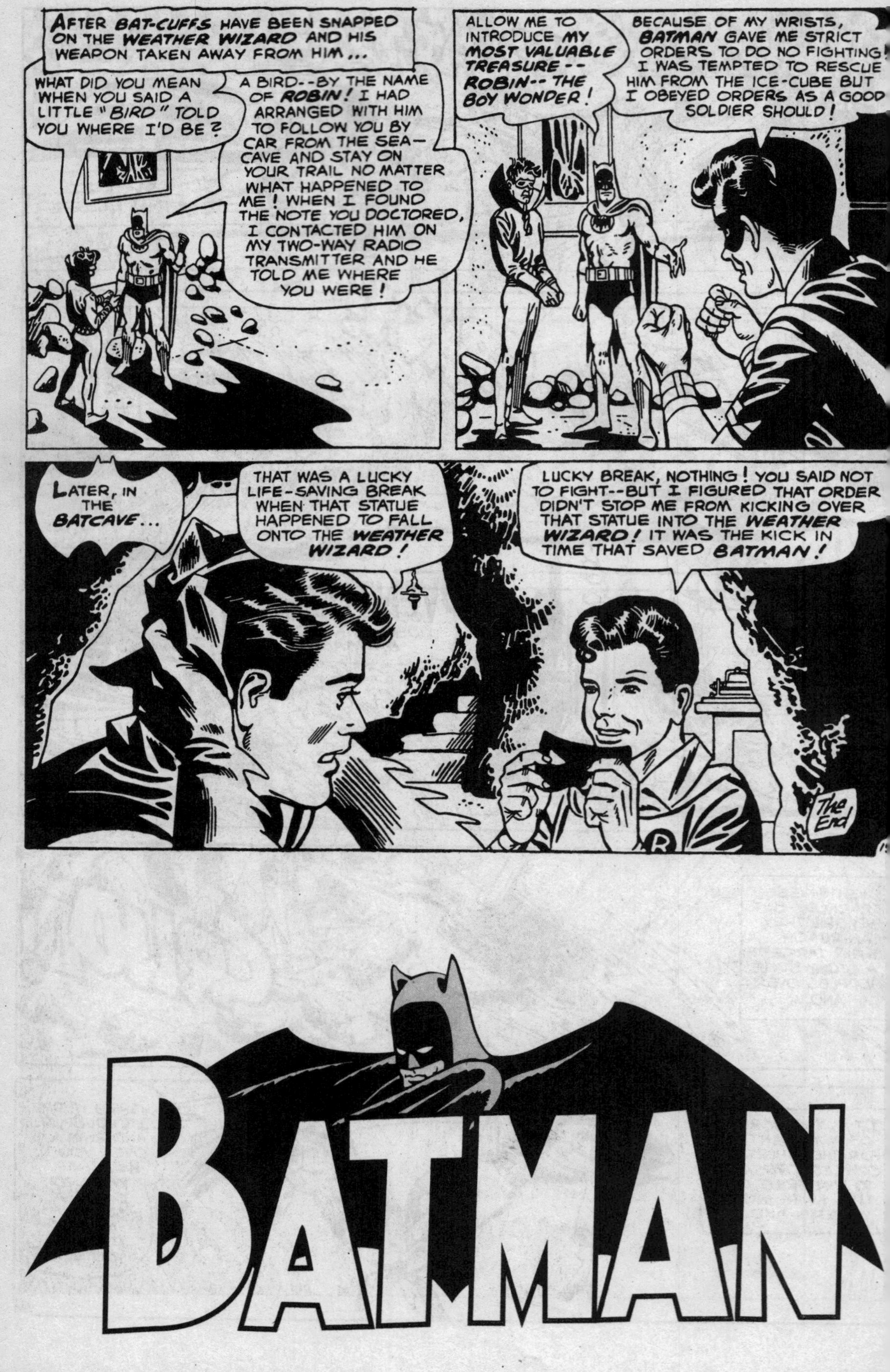
AFTER BAT-CUFFS HAVE BEEN SNAPPED ON THE WEATHER WIZARD AND HIS WEAPON TAKEN AWAY FROM HIM...
WHAT DID YOU MEAN WHEN YOU SAID A LITTLE "BIRD" TOLD YOU WHERE I'D BE?
A BIRD--BY THE NAME OF ROBIN! I HAD ARRANGED WITH HIM TO FOLLOW YOU BY CAR FROM THE SEA-CAVE AND STAY ON YOUR TRAIL NO MATTER WHAT HAPPENED TO ME! WHEN I FOUND THE NOTE YOU DOCTORED, I CONTACTED HIM ON MY TWO-WAY RADIO TRANSMITTER AND HE TOLD ME WHERE YOU WERE!
ALLOW ME TO INTRODUCE MY MOST VALUABLE TREASURE -- ROBIN -- THE BOY WONDER!
BECAUSE OF MY WRISTS, BATMAN GAVE ME STRICT ORDERS TO DO NO FIGHTING! I WAS TEMPTED TO RESCUE HIM FROM THE ICE-CUBE BUT I OBEYED ORDERS AS A GOOD SOLDIER SHOULD!
LATER, IN THE BATCAVE...
THAT WAS A LUCKY LIFE-SAVING BREAK WHEN THAT STATUE HAPPENED TO FALL ONTO THE WEATHER WIZARD!
LUCKY BREAK, NOTHING! YOU SAID NOT TO FIGHT--BUT I FIGURED THAT ORDER DIDN'T STOP ME FROM KICKING OVER THAT STATUE INTO THE WEATHER WIZARD! IT WAS THE KICK IN TIME THAT SAVED BATMAN!
The End

BATMAN

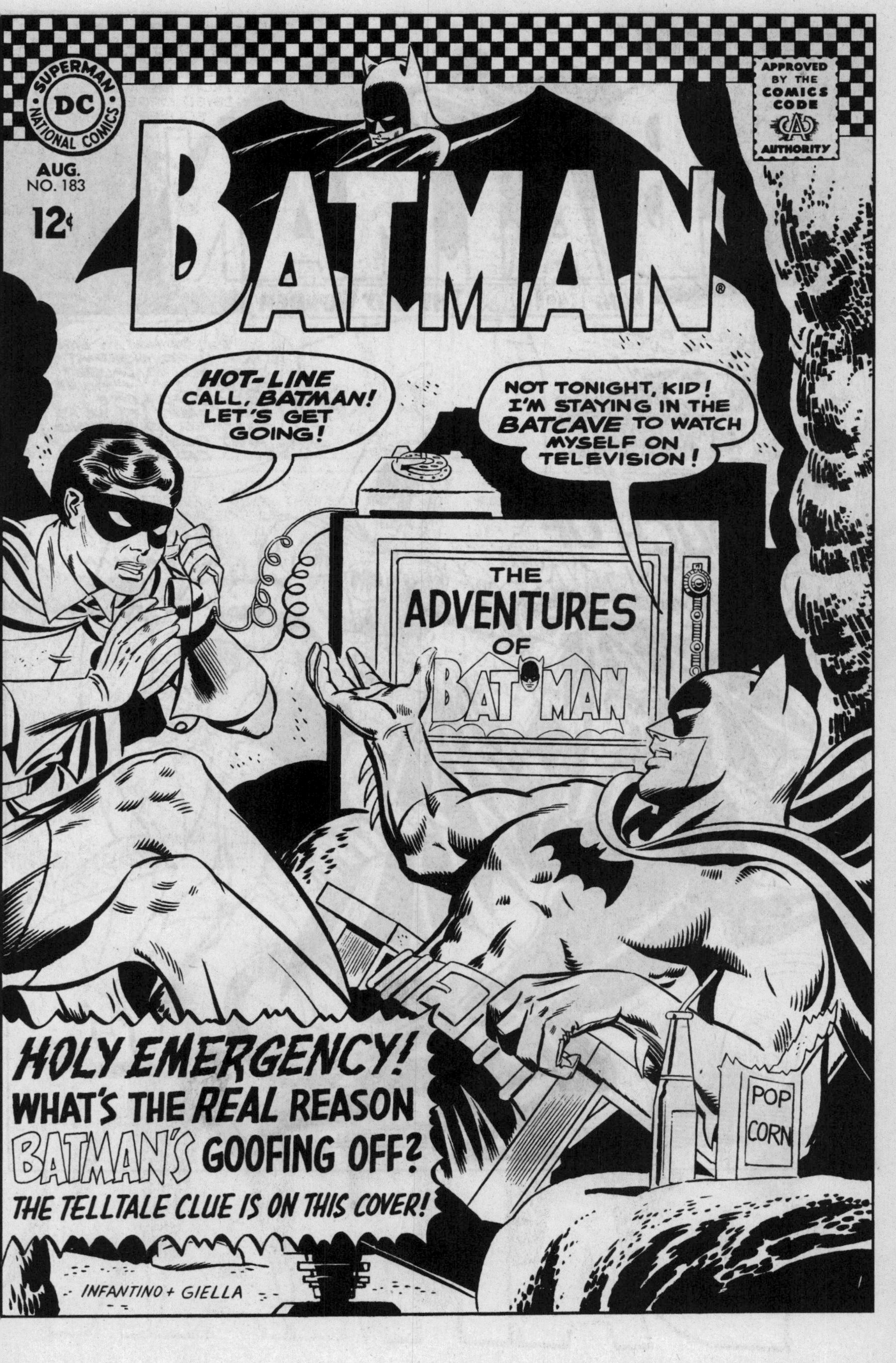
SUPERMAN DC NATIONAL COMICS
AUG. NO. 183
12¢
BATMAN®
APPROVED BY THE COMICS CODE AUTHORITY
HOT-LINE CALL, BATMAN! LET'S GET GOING!
NOT TONIGHT, KID! I'M STAYING IN THE BATCAVE TO WATCH MYSELF ON TELEVISION!
THE ADVENTURES OF BATMAN
HOLY EMERGENCY!
WHAT'S THE REAL REASON
BATMAN'S GOOFING OFF?
THE TELLTALE CLUE IS ON THIS COVER!
POP CORN
INFANTINO + GIELLA

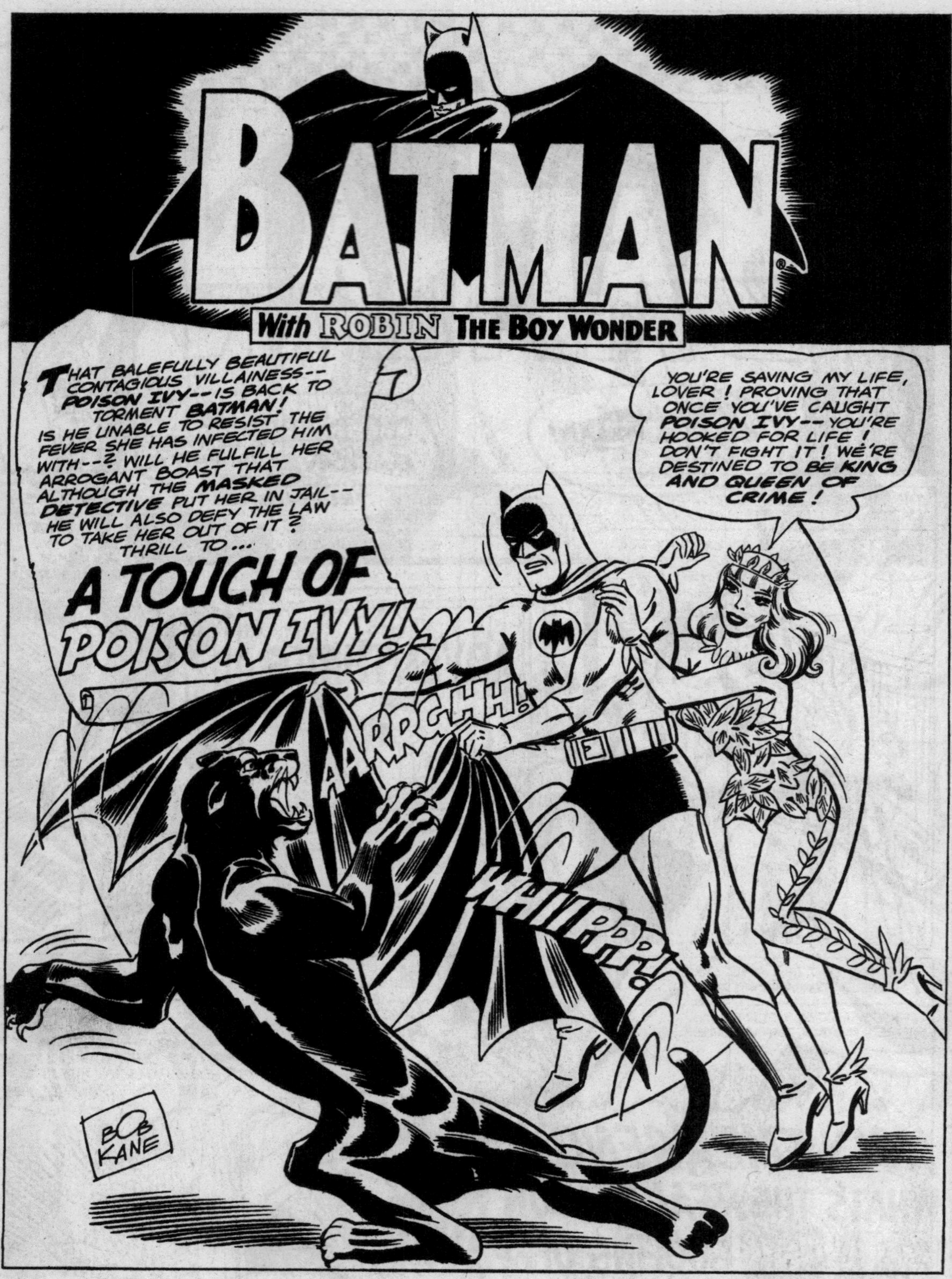
BATMAN
With ROBIN THE BOY WONDER
THAT BALEFULLY BEAUTIFUL CONTAGIOUS VILLAINESS-- POISON IVY--IS BACK TO TORMENT BATMAN! IS HE UNABLE TO RESIST THE FEVER SHE HAS INFECTED HIM WITH--? WILL HE FULFILL HER ARROGANT BOAST THAT ALTHOUGH THE MASKED DETECTIVE PUT HER IN JAIL-- HE WILL ALSO DEFY THE LAW TO TAKE HER OUT OF IT? THRILL TO...
A TOUCH OF POISON IVY!
YOU'RE SAVING MY LIFE, LOVER! PROVING THAT ONCE YOU'VE CAUGHT POISON IVY--YOU'RE HOOKED FOR LIFE! DON'T FIGHT IT! WE'RE DESTINED TO BE KING AND QUEEN OF CRIME!
AARRGHH!
WHIIPPP!
BOB KANE

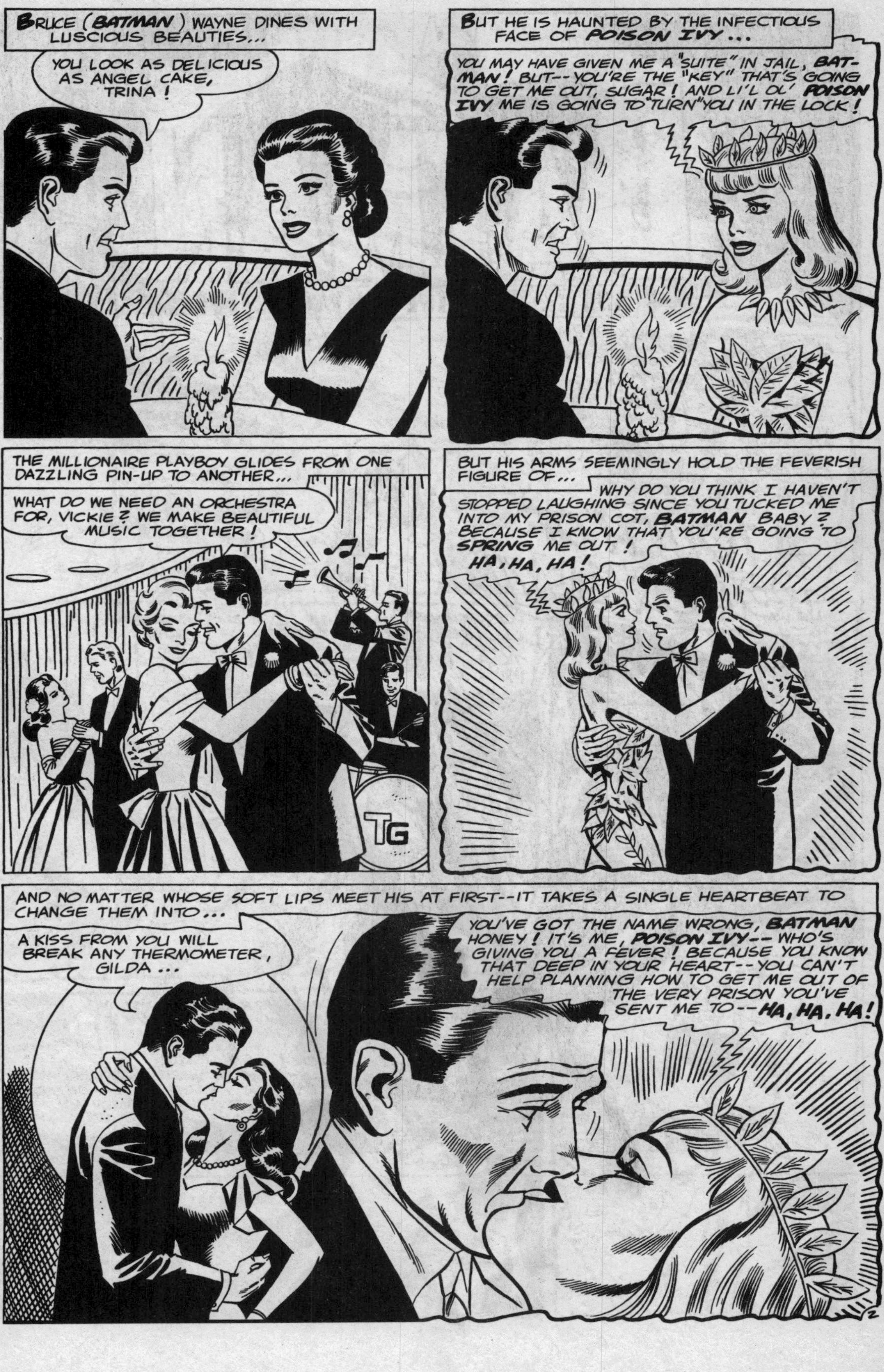
BRUCE (BATMAN) WAYNE DINES WITH LUSCIOUS BEAUTIES...
YOU LOOK AS DELICIOUS AS ANGEL CAKE, TRINA!
BUT HE IS HAUNTED BY THE INFECTIOUS FACE OF POISON IVY...
YOU MAY HAVE GIVEN ME A "SUITE" IN JAIL, BATMAN! BUT--YOU'RE THE "KEY" THAT'S GOING TO GET ME OUT, SUGAR! AND LI'L OL' POISON IVY ME IS GOING TO "TURN" YOU IN THE LOCK!
THE MILLIONAIRE PLAYBOY GLIDES FROM ONE DAZZLING PIN-UP TO ANOTHER...
WHAT DO WE NEED AN ORCHESTRA FOR, VICKIE? WE MAKE BEAUTIFUL MUSIC TOGETHER!
TG
BUT HIS ARMS SEEMINGLY HOLD THE FEVERISH FIGURE OF...
WHY DO YOU THINK I HAVEN'T STOPPED LAUGHING SINCE YOU TUCKED ME INTO MY PRISON COT, BATMAN BABY? BECAUSE I KNOW THAT YOU'RE GOING TO SPRING ME OUT!
HA, HA, HA!
AND NO MATTER WHOSE SOFT LIPS MEET HIS AT FIRST--IT TAKES A SINGLE HEARTBEAT TO CHANGE THEM INTO...
A KISS FROM YOU WILL BREAK ANY THERMOMETER, GILDA...
YOU'VE GOT THE NAME WRONG, BATMAN HONEY! IT'S ME, POISON IVY--WHO'S GIVING YOU A FEVER! BECAUSE YOU KNOW THAT DEEP IN YOUR HEART--YOU CAN'T HELP PLANNING HOW TO GET ME OUT OF THE VERY PRISON YOU'VE SENT ME TO--HA, HA, HA!
2

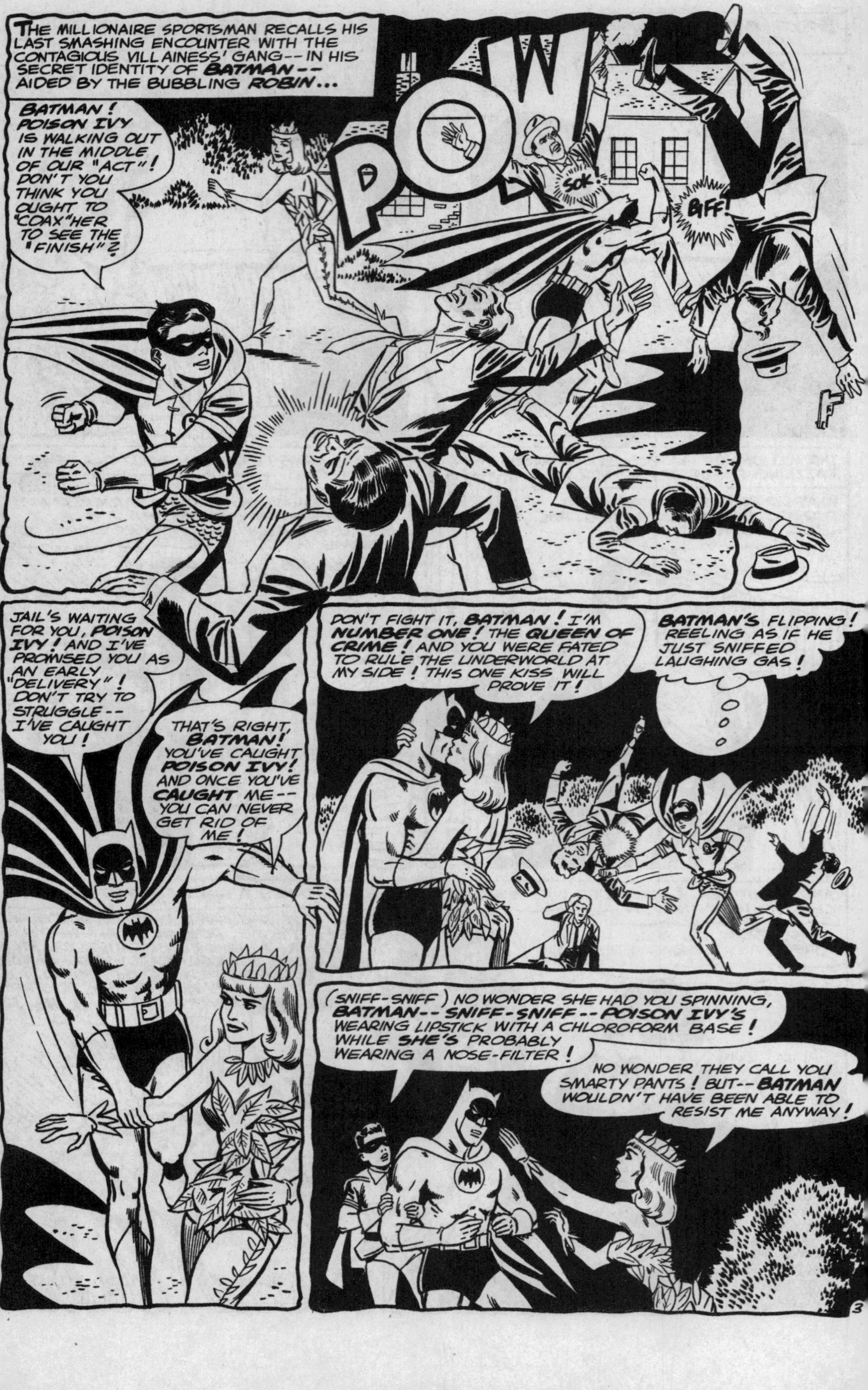
THE MILLIONAIRE SPORTSMAN RECALLS HIS LAST SMASHING ENCOUNTER WITH THE CONTAGIOUS VILLAINESS' GANG-- IN HIS SECRET IDENTITY OF BATMAN -- AIDED BY THE BUBBLING ROBIN...
POW!
BATMAN! POISON IVY IS WALKING OUT IN THE MIDDLE OF OUR "ACT"! DON'T YOU THINK YOU OUGHT TO "COAX" HER TO SEE THE "FINISH"?
SOK
BIFF!
JAIL'S WAITING FOR YOU, POISON IVY! AND I'VE PROMISED YOU AS AN EARLY "DELIVERY"! DON'T TRY TO STRUGGLE -- I'VE CAUGHT YOU!
THAT'S RIGHT, BATMAN! YOU'VE CAUGHT POISON IVY! AND ONCE YOU'VE CAUGHT ME -- YOU CAN NEVER GET RID OF ME!
DON'T FIGHT IT, BATMAN! I'M NUMBER ONE! THE QUEEN OF CRIME! AND YOU WERE FATED TO RULE THE UNDERWORLD AT MY SIDE! THIS ONE KISS WILL PROVE IT!
BATMAN'S FLIPPING! REELING AS IF HE JUST SNIFFED LAUGHING GAS!
(SNIFF-SNIFF) NO WONDER SHE HAD YOU SPINNING, BATMAN-- SNIFF-SNIFF -- POISON IVY'S WEARING LIPSTICK WITH A CHLOROFORM BASE! WHILE SHE'S PROBABLY WEARING A NOSE-FILTER!
NO WONDER THEY CALL YOU SMARTY PANTS! BUT-- BATMAN WOULDN'T HAVE BEEN ABLE TO RESIST ME ANYWAY!
3

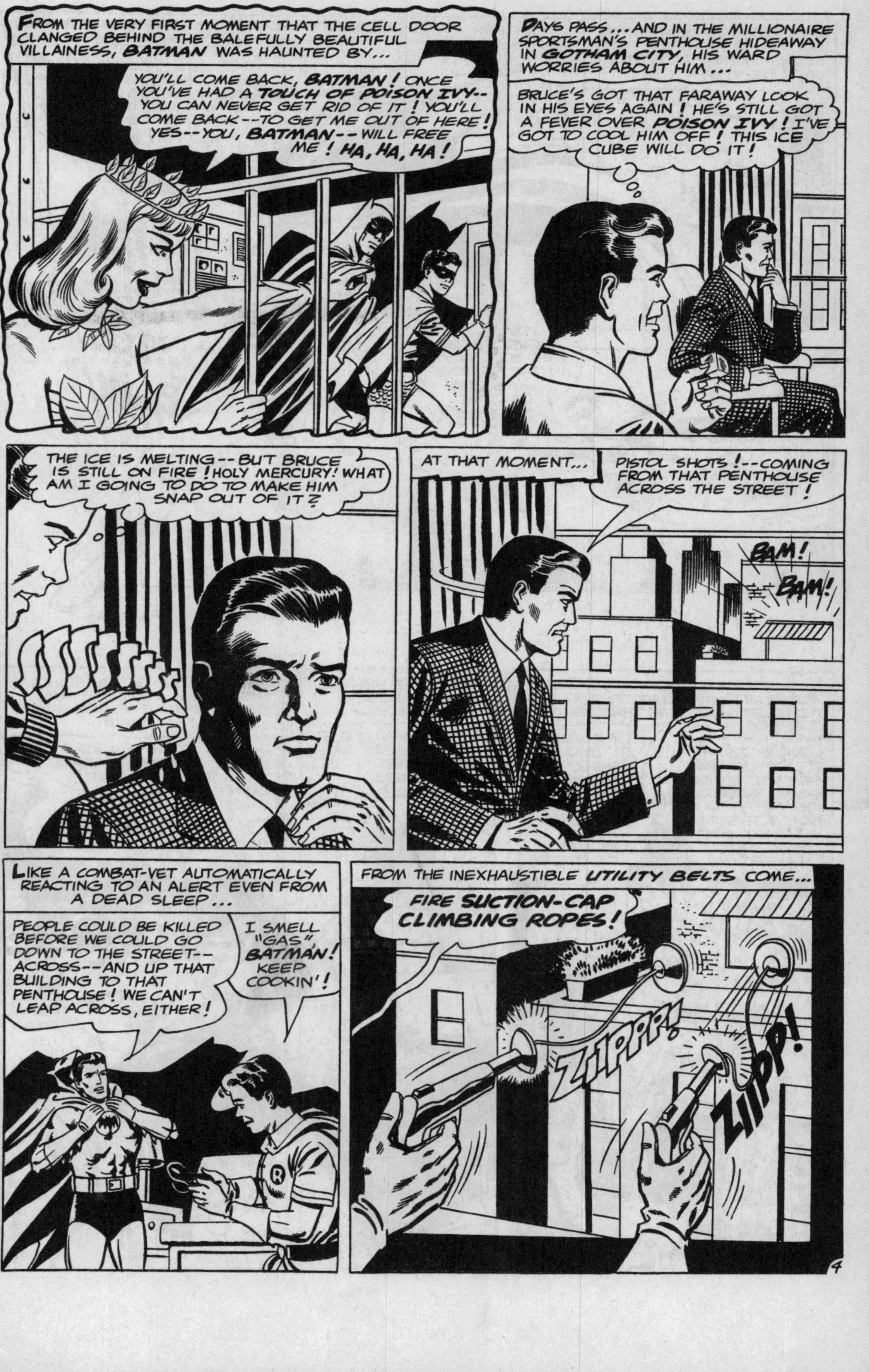
FROM THE VERY FIRST MOMENT THAT THE CELL DOOR CLANGED BEHIND THE BALEFULLY BEAUTIFUL VILLAINESS, BATMAN WAS HAUNTED BY...
YOU'LL COME BACK, BATMAN! ONCE YOU'VE HAD A TOUCH OF POISON IVY-- YOU CAN NEVER GET RID OF IT! YOU'LL COME BACK--TO GET ME OUT OF HERE! YES--YOU, BATMAN--WILL FREE ME! HA, HA, HA!
DAYS PASS...AND IN THE MILLIONAIRE SPORTSMAN'S PENTHOUSE HIDEAWAY IN GOTHAM CITY, HIS WARD WORRIES ABOUT HIM...
BRUCE'S GOT THAT FARAWAY LOOK IN HIS EYES AGAIN! HE'S STILL GOT A FEVER OVER POISON IVY! I'VE GOT TO COOL HIM OFF! THIS ICE CUBE WILL DO IT!
THE ICE IS MELTING--BUT BRUCE IS STILL ON FIRE! HOLY MERCURY! WHAT AM I GOING TO DO TO MAKE HIM SNAP OUT OF IT?
AT THAT MOMENT...
PISTOL SHOTS!--COMING FROM THAT PENTHOUSE ACROSS THE STREET!
BAM!
BAM!
LIKE A COMBAT-VET AUTOMATICALLY REACTING TO AN ALERT EVEN FROM A DEAD SLEEP...
PEOPLE COULD BE KILLED BEFORE WE COULD GO DOWN TO THE STREET--ACROSS--AND UP THAT BUILDING TO THAT PENTHOUSE! WE CAN'T LEAP ACROSS, EITHER!
I SMELL "GAS" BATMAN! KEEP COOKIN'!
FROM THE INEXHAUSTIBLE UTILITY BELTS COME...
FIRE SUCTION-CAP CLIMBING ROPES!
ZIIPPP!
ZIIPP!
4

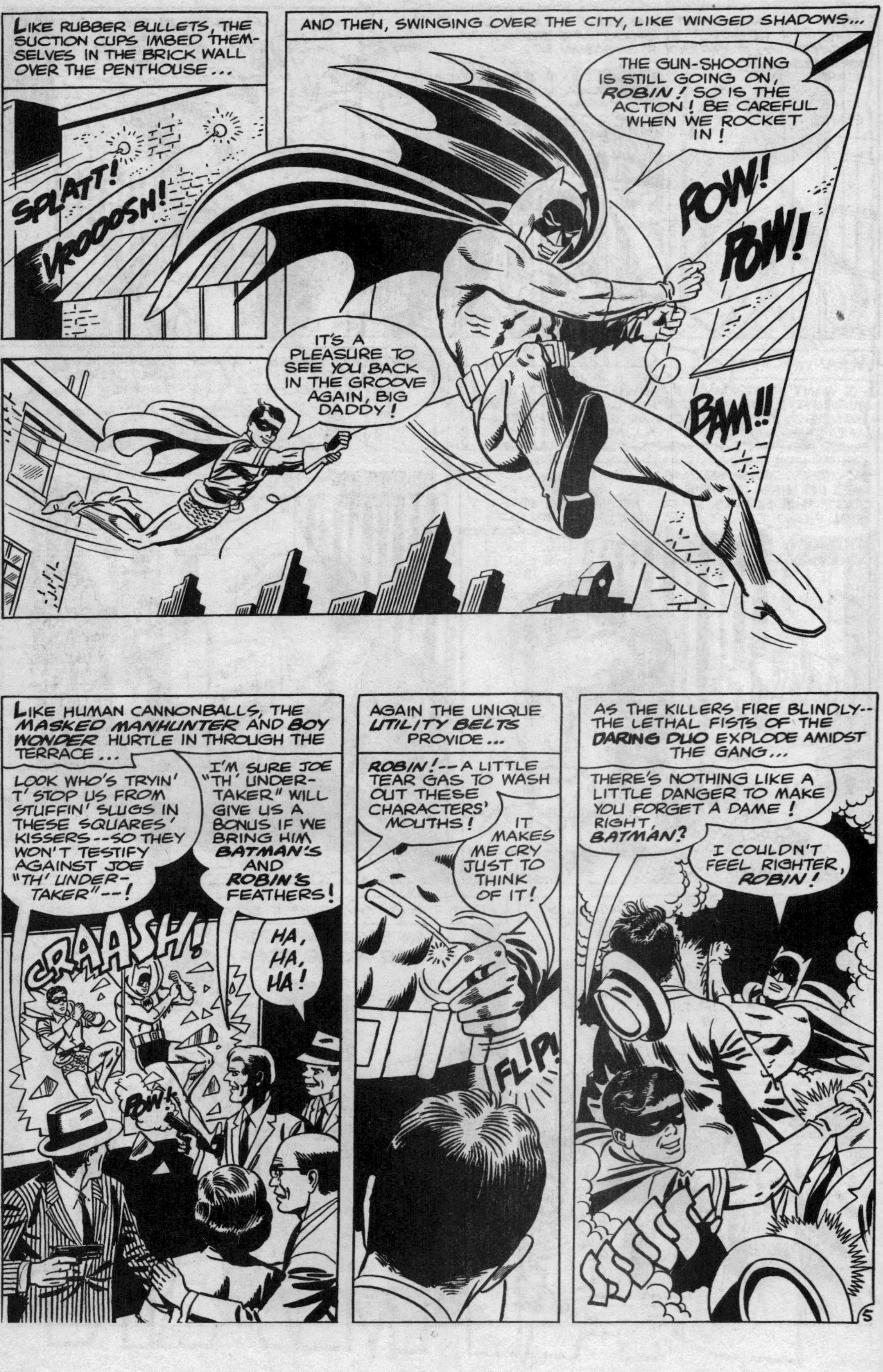
LIKE RUBBER BULLETS, THE SUCTION CUPS IMBED THEMSELVES IN THE BRICK WALL OVER THE PENTHOUSE...
SPLATT!
VROOOOSH!
AND THEN, SWINGING OVER THE CITY, LIKE WINGED SHADOWS...
THE GUN-SHOOTING IS STILL GOING ON, ROBIN! SO IS THE ACTION! BE CAREFUL WHEN WE ROCKET IN!
POW!
POW!
IT'S A PLEASURE TO SEE YOU BACK IN THE GROOVE AGAIN, BIG DADDY!
BAM!!
LIKE HUMAN CANNONBALLS, THE MASKED MANHUNTER AND BOY WONDER HURTLE IN THROUGH THE TERRACE...
LOOK WHO'S TRYIN' T' STOP US FROM STUFFIN' SLUGS IN THESE SQUARES' KISSERS--SO THEY WON'T TESTIFY AGAINST JOE "TH' UNDER-TAKER"--!
I'M SURE JOE "TH' UNDER-TAKER" WILL GIVE US A BONUS IF WE BRING HIM BATMAN'S AND ROBIN'S FEATHERS!
CRAASH!
HA, HA, HA!
POW!
AGAIN THE UNIQUE UTILITY BELTS PROVIDE...
ROBIN!--A LITTLE TEAR GAS TO WASH OUT THESE CHARACTERS' MOUTHS!
IT MAKES ME CRY JUST TO THINK OF IT!
FLIP!
AS THE KILLERS FIRE BLINDLY--THE LETHAL FISTS OF THE DARING DUO EXPLODE AMIDST THE GANG...
THERE'S NOTHING LIKE A LITTLE DANGER TO MAKE YOU FORGET A DAME! RIGHT, BATMAN?
I COULDN'T FEEL RIGHTER, ROBIN!
SSSSS
5

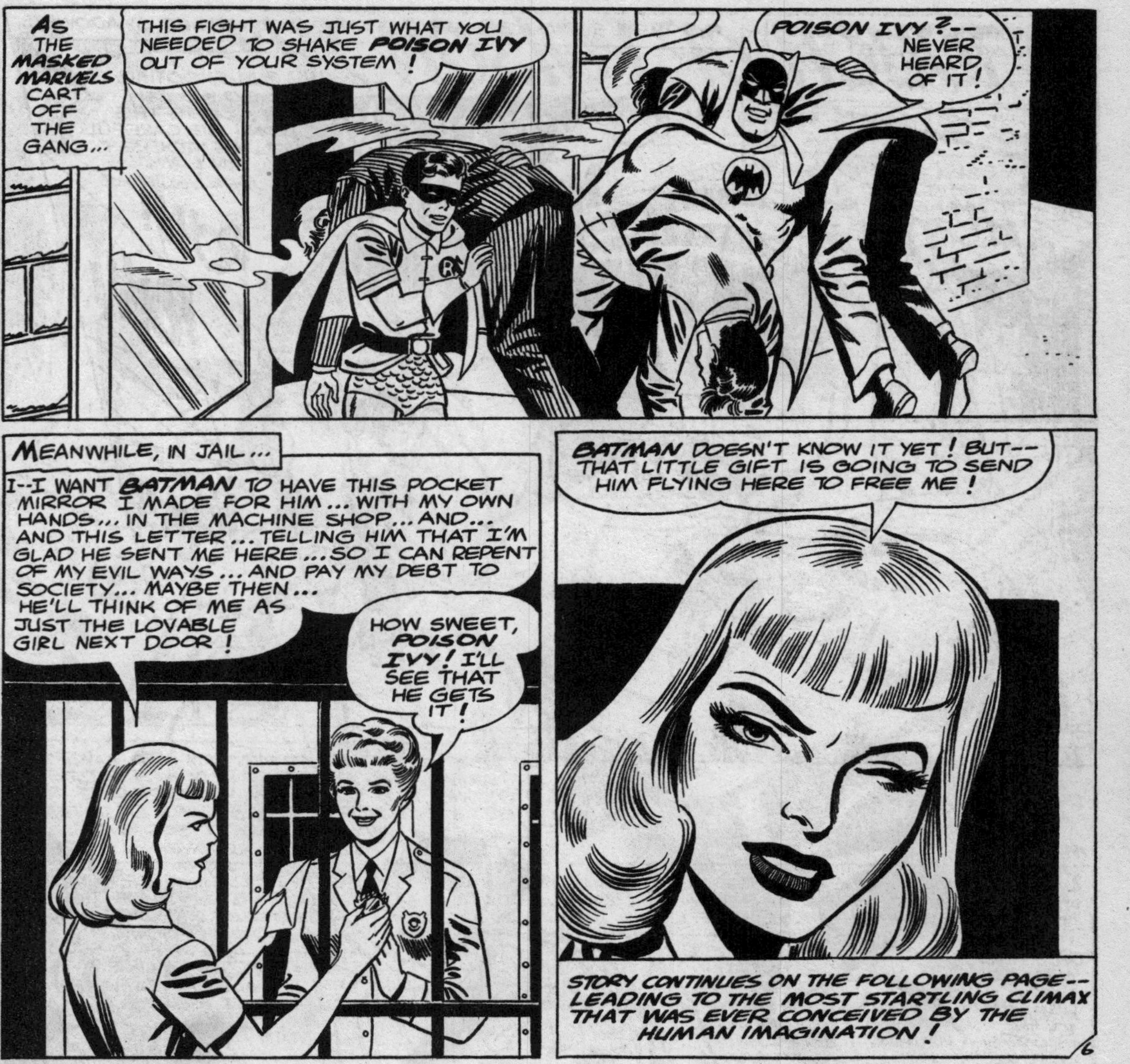
AS THE MASKED MARVELS CART OFF THE GANG...
THIS FIGHT WAS JUST WHAT YOU NEEDED TO SHAKE POISON IVY OUT OF YOUR SYSTEM!
POISON IVY?-- NEVER HEARD OF IT!
MEANWHILE, IN JAIL...
I--I WANT BATMAN TO HAVE THIS POCKET MIRROR I MADE FOR HIM... WITH MY OWN HANDS... IN THE MACHINE SHOP... AND... AND THIS LETTER... TELLING HIM THAT I'M GLAD HE SENT ME HERE... SO I CAN REPENT OF MY EVIL WAYS... AND PAY MY DEBT TO SOCIETY... MAYBE THEN... HE'LL THINK OF ME AS JUST THE LOVABLE GIRL NEXT DOOR!
HOW SWEET, POISON IVY! I'LL SEE THAT HE GETS IT!
BATMAN DOESN'T KNOW IT YET! BUT-- THAT LITTLE GIFT IS GOING TO SEND HIM FLYING HERE TO FREE ME!
STORY CONTINUES ON THE FOLLOWING PAGE-- LEADING TO THE MOST STARTLING CLIMAX THAT WAS EVER CONCEIVED BY THE HUMAN IMAGINATION!
6

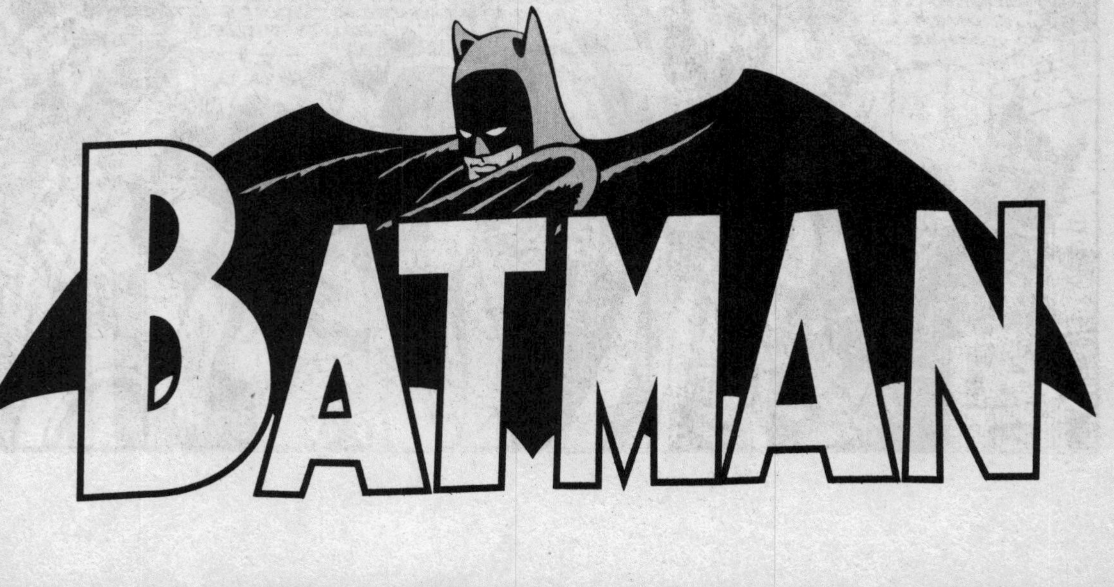
BATMAN

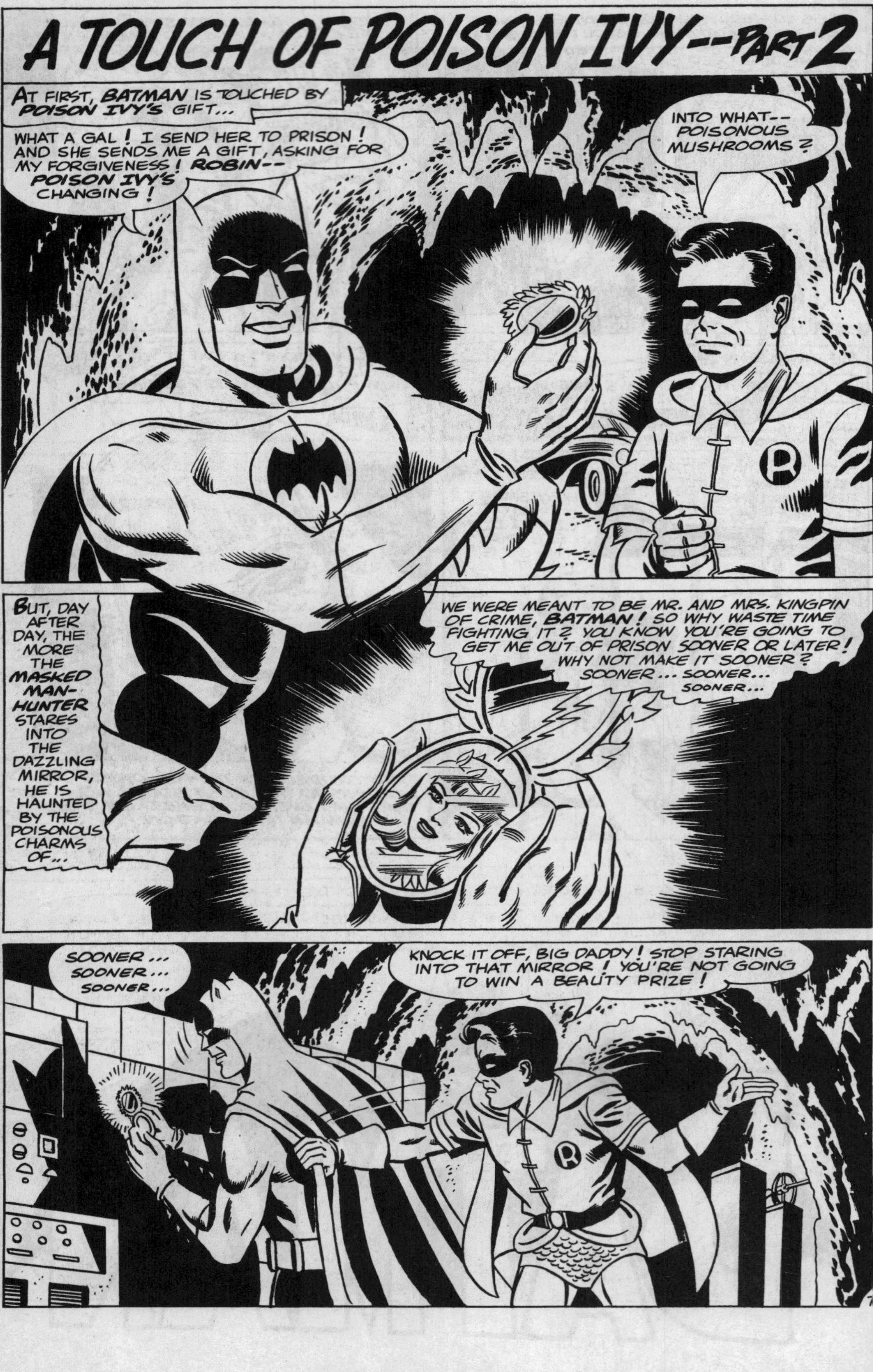
A TOUCH OF POISON IVY--PART 2
AT FIRST, BATMAN IS TOUCHED BY POISON IVY'S GIFT...
WHAT A GAL! I SEND HER TO PRISON! AND SHE SENDS ME A GIFT, ASKING FOR MY FORGIVENESS! ROBIN-- POISON IVY'S CHANGING!
INTO WHAT-- POISONOUS MUSHROOMS?
BUT, DAY AFTER DAY, THE MORE THE MASKED MAN-HUNTER STARES INTO THE DAZZLING MIRROR, HE IS HAUNTED BY THE POISONOUS CHARMS OF...
WE WERE MEANT TO BE MR. AND MRS. KINGPIN OF CRIME, BATMAN! SO WHY WASTE TIME FIGHTING IT? YOU KNOW YOU'RE GOING TO GET ME OUT OF PRISON SOONER OR LATER! WHY NOT MAKE IT SOONER? SOONER... SOONER... SOONER...
SOONER... SOONER... SOONER...
KNOCK IT OFF, BIG DADDY! STOP STARING INTO THAT MIRROR! YOU'RE NOT GOING TO WIN A BEAUTY PRIZE!

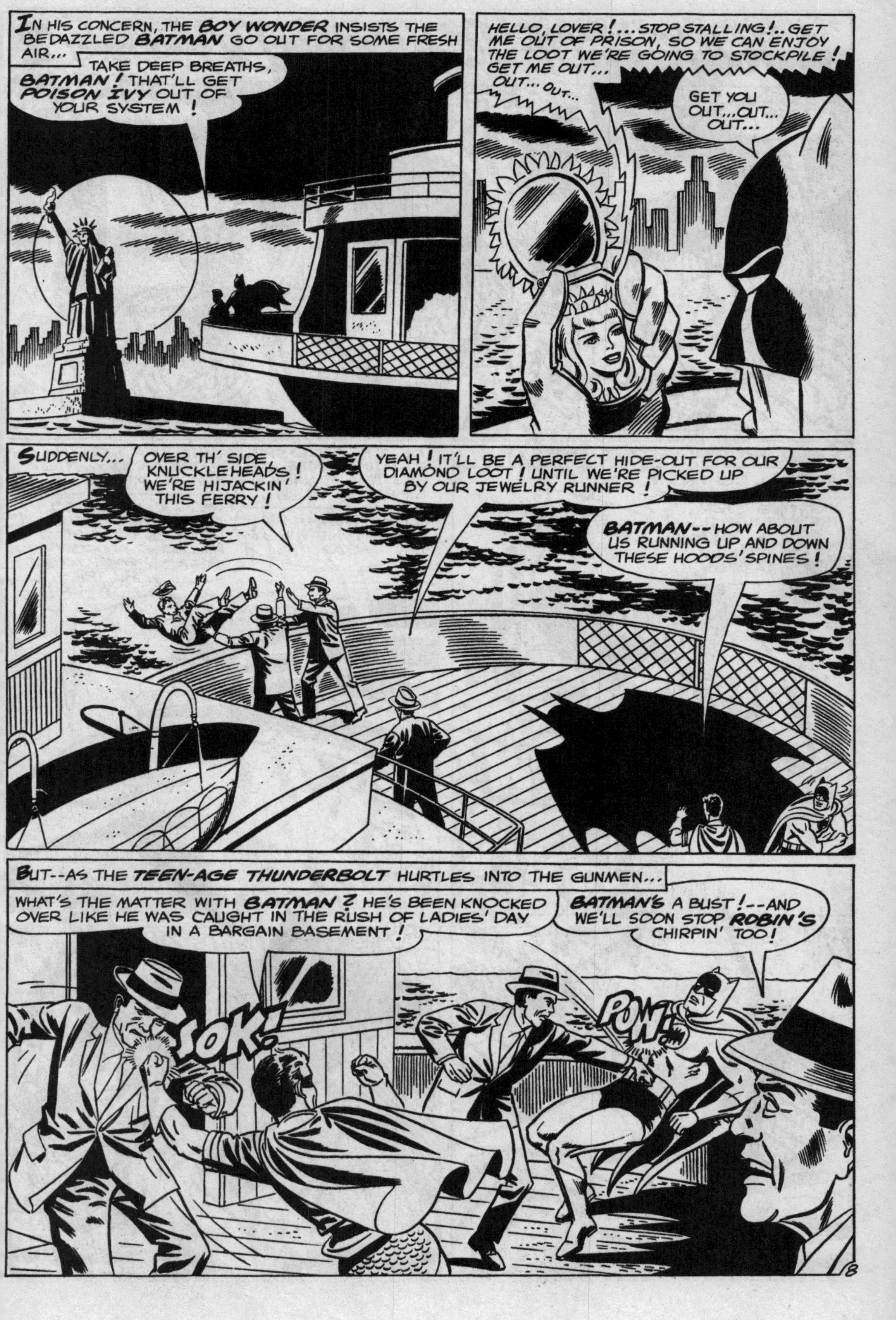
IN HIS CONCERN, THE BOY WONDER INSISTS THE BEDAZZLED BATMAN GO OUT FOR SOME FRESH AIR...
TAKE DEEP BREATHS, BATMAN! THAT'LL GET POISON IVY OUT OF YOUR SYSTEM!
HELLO, LOVER!... STOP STALLING!.. GET ME OUT OF PRISON, SO WE CAN ENJOY THE LOOT WE'RE GOING TO STOCKPILE! GET ME OUT... OUT... OUT...
GET YOU OUT...OUT... OUT...
SUDDENLY...
OVER TH' SIDE, KNUCKLEHEADS! WE'RE HIJACKIN' THIS FERRY!
YEAH! IT'LL BE A PERFECT HIDE-OUT FOR OUR DIAMOND LOOT! UNTIL WE'RE PICKED UP BY OUR JEWELRY RUNNER!
BATMAN-- HOW ABOUT US RUNNING UP AND DOWN THESE HOODS' SPINES!
BUT--AS THE TEEN-AGE THUNDERBOLT HURTLES INTO THE GUNMEN...
WHAT'S THE MATTER WITH BATMAN? HE'S BEEN KNOCKED OVER LIKE HE WAS CAUGHT IN THE RUSH OF LADIES' DAY IN A BARGAIN BASEMENT!
BATMAN'S A BUST!--AND WE'LL SOON STOP ROBIN'S CHIRPIN' TOO!
SOK!
POW!
8

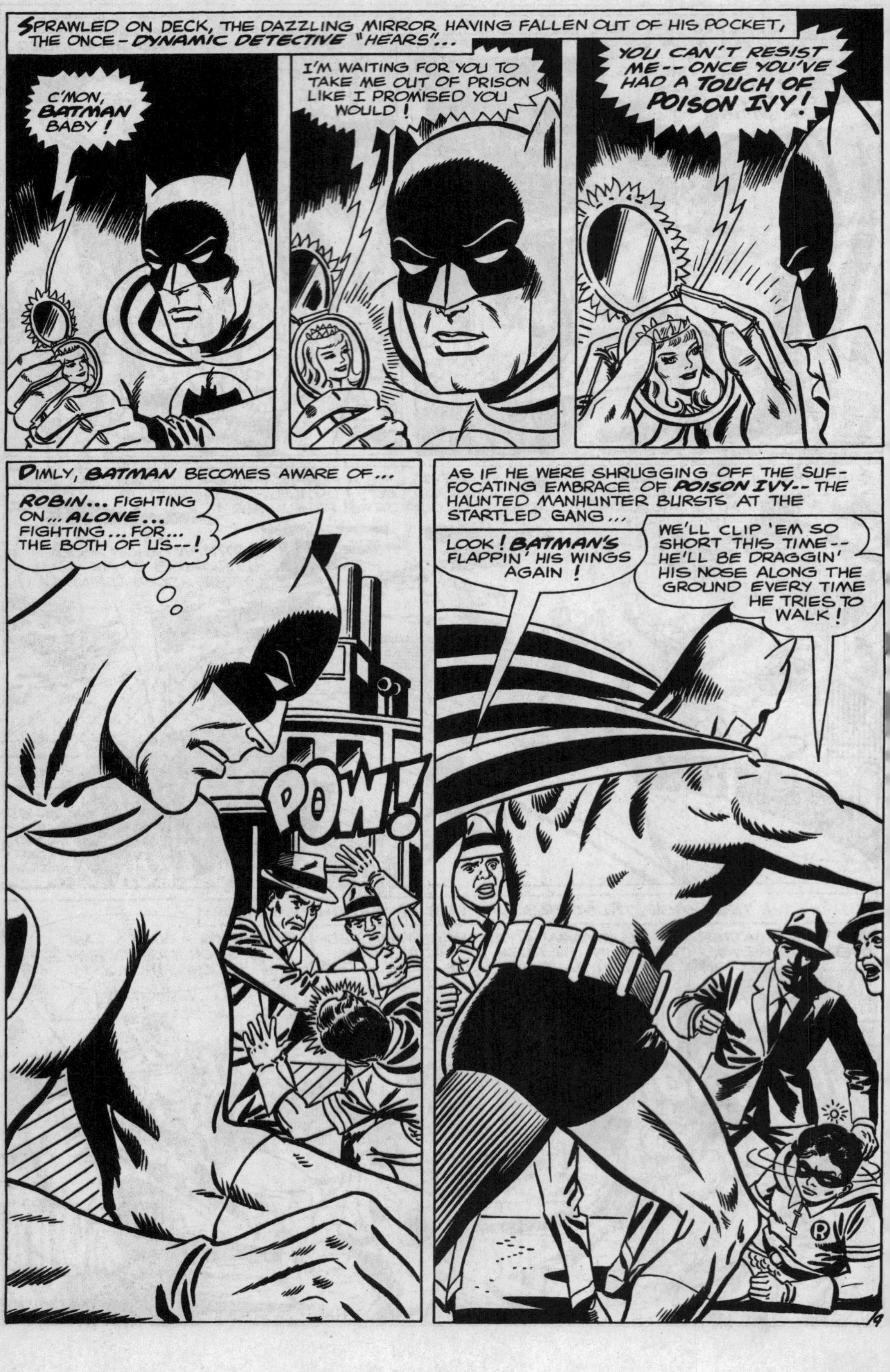
SPRAWLED ON DECK, THE DAZZLING MIRROR HAVING FALLEN OUT OF HIS POCKET, THE ONCE-DYNAMIC DETECTIVE "HEARS"...
C'MON, BATMAN BABY!
I'M WAITING FOR YOU TO TAKE ME OUT OF PRISON LIKE I PROMISED YOU WOULD!
YOU CAN'T RESIST ME--ONCE YOU'VE HAD A TOUCH OF POISON IVY!
DIMLY, BATMAN BECOMES AWARE OF...
ROBIN... FIGHTING ON... ALONE... FIGHTING... FOR... THE BOTH OF US--!
POW!
AS IF HE WERE SHRUGGING OFF THE SUFFOCATING EMBRACE OF POISON IVY-- THE HAUNTED MANHUNTER BURSTS AT THE STARTLED GANG...
LOOK! BATMAN'S FLAPPIN' HIS WINGS AGAIN!
WE'LL CLIP 'EM SO SHORT THIS TIME--HE'LL BE DRAGGIN' HIS NOSE ALONG THE GROUND EVERY TIME HE TRIES TO WALK!
19

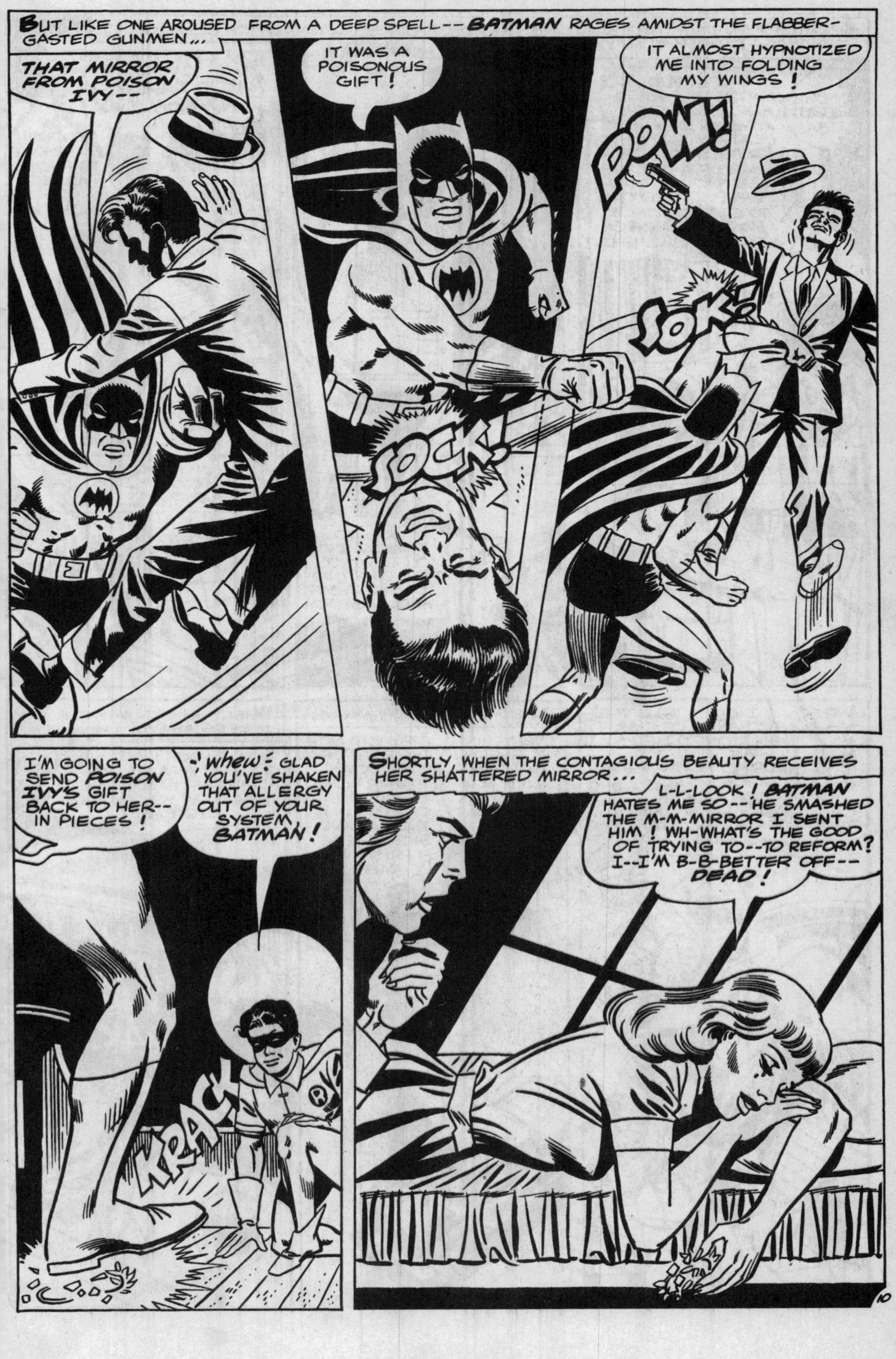
BUT LIKE ONE AROUSED FROM A DEEP SPELL-- BATMAN RAGES AMIDST THE FLABBERGASTED GUNMEN...
THAT MIRROR FROM POISON IVY--
IT WAS A POISONOUS GIFT!
IT ALMOST HYPNOTIZED ME INTO FOLDING MY WINGS!
POW!
SOK!
SOCK!
I'M GOING TO SEND POISON IVY'S GIFT BACK TO HER-- IN PIECES!
WHEW! GLAD YOU'VE SHAKEN THAT ALLERGY OUT OF YOUR SYSTEM, BATMAN!
KRACK
SHORTLY, WHEN THE CONTAGIOUS BEAUTY RECEIVES HER SHATTERED MIRROR...
L-L-LOOK! BATMAN HATES ME SO--HE SMASHED THE M-M-MIRROR I SENT HIM! WH-WHAT'S THE GOOD OF TRYING TO--TO REFORM? I--I'M B-B-BETTER OFF-- DEAD!
10

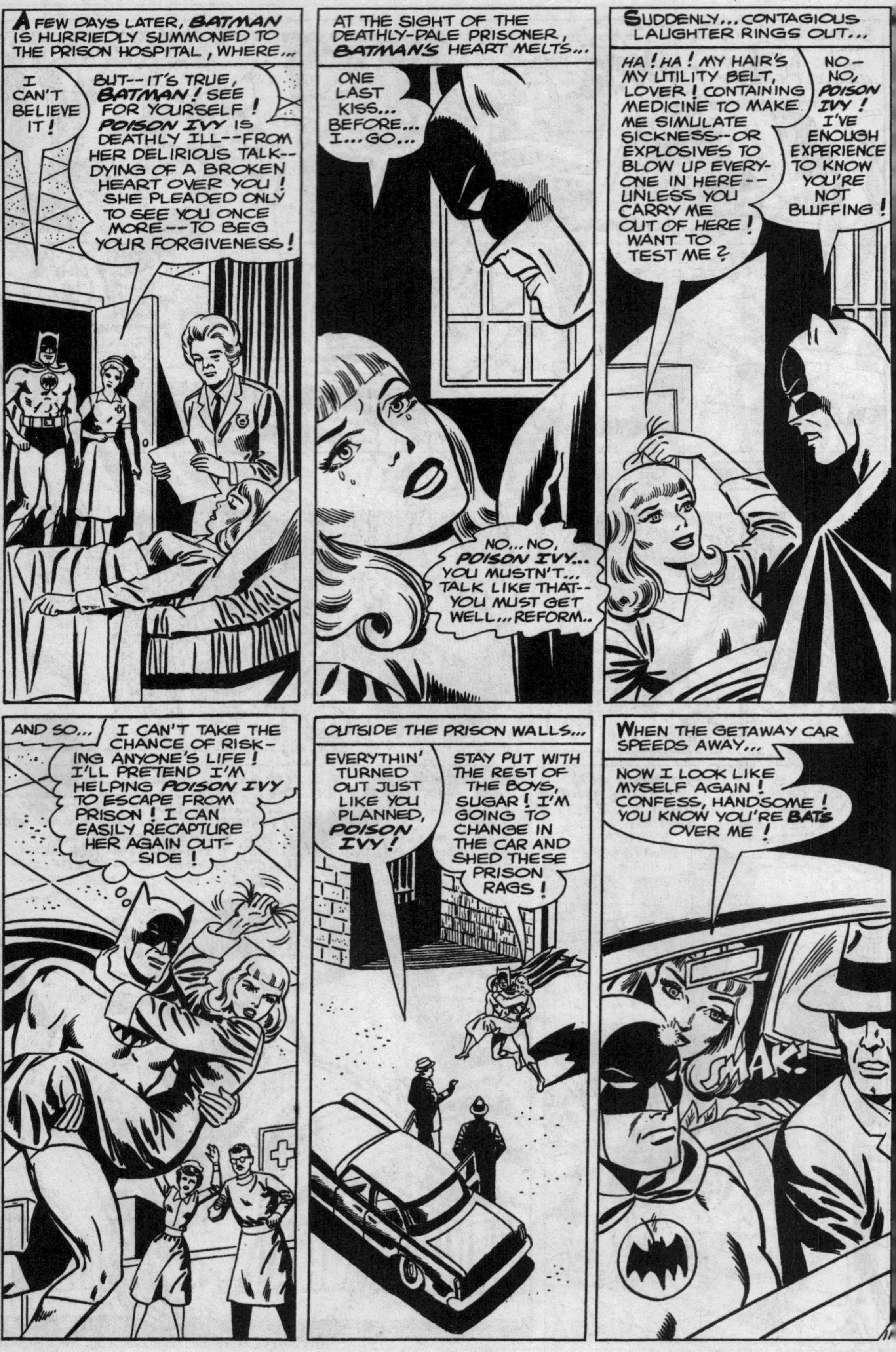
A FEW DAYS LATER, BATMAN IS HURRIEDLY SUMMONED TO THE PRISON HOSPITAL, WHERE...
I CAN'T BELIEVE IT!
BUT--IT'S TRUE, BATMAN! SEE FOR YOURSELF! POISON IVY IS DEATHLY ILL--FROM HER DELIRIOUS TALK--DYING OF A BROKEN HEART OVER YOU! SHE PLEADED ONLY TO SEE YOU ONCE MORE--TO BEG YOUR FORGIVENESS!
AT THE SIGHT OF THE DEATHLY-PALE PRISONER, BATMAN'S HEART MELTS...
ONE LAST KISS... BEFORE... I...GO...
NO...NO, POISON IVY... YOU MUSTN'T... TALK LIKE THAT--YOU MUST GET WELL...REFORM..
SUDDENLY...CONTAGIOUS LAUGHTER RINGS OUT...
HA! HA! MY HAIR'S MY UTILITY BELT, LOVER! CONTAINING MEDICINE TO MAKE ME SIMULATE SICKNESS--OR EXPLOSIVES TO BLOW UP EVERYONE IN HERE--UNLESS YOU CARRY ME OUT OF HERE! WANT TO TEST ME?
NO--NO, POISON IVY! I'VE ENOUGH EXPERIENCE TO KNOW YOU'RE NOT BLUFFING!
AND SO...
I CAN'T TAKE THE CHANCE OF RISKING ANYONE'S LIFE! I'LL PRETEND I'M HELPING POISON IVY TO ESCAPE FROM PRISON! I CAN EASILY RECAPTURE HER AGAIN OUTSIDE!
OUTSIDE THE PRISON WALLS...
EVERYTHIN' TURNED OUT JUST LIKE YOU PLANNED, POISON IVY!
STAY PUT WITH THE REST OF THE BOYS, SUGAR! I'M GOING TO CHANGE IN THE CAR AND SHED THESE PRISON RAGS!
WHEN THE GETAWAY CAR SPEEDS AWAY...
NOW I LOOK LIKE MYSELF AGAIN! CONFESS, HANDSOME! YOU KNOW YOU'RE BATS OVER ME!
SMAK!

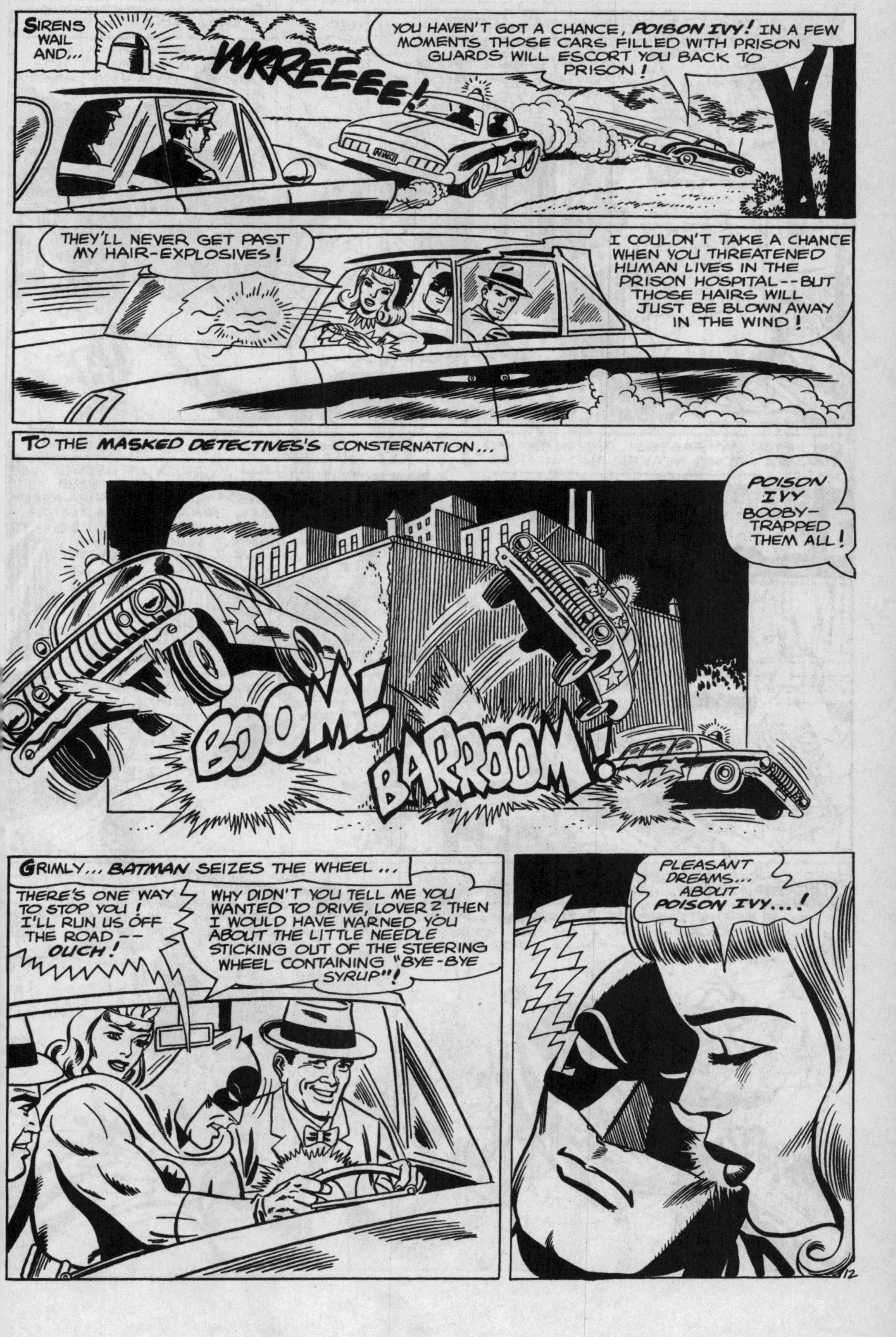
SIRENS WAIL AND...
WRREEEEE!
YOU HAVEN'T GOT A CHANCE, POISON IVY! IN A FEW MOMENTS THOSE CARS FILLED WITH PRISON GUARDS WILL ESCORT YOU BACK TO PRISON!
THEY'LL NEVER GET PAST MY HAIR-EXPLOSIVES!
I COULDN'T TAKE A CHANCE WHEN YOU THREATENED HUMAN LIVES IN THE PRISON HOSPITAL--BUT THOSE HAIRS WILL JUST BE BLOWN AWAY IN THE WIND!
TO THE MASKED DETECTIVES'S CONSTERNATION...
POISON IVY BOOBY-TRAPPED THEM ALL!
BOOM!
BARROOM!
GRIMLY... BATMAN SEIZES THE WHEEL...
THERE'S ONE WAY TO STOP YOU! I'LL RUN US OFF THE ROAD-- OUCH!
WHY DIDN'T YOU TELL ME YOU WANTED TO DRIVE, LOVER? THEN I WOULD HAVE WARNED YOU ABOUT THE LITTLE NEEDLE STICKING OUT OF THE STEERING WHEEL CONTAINING "BYE-BYE SYRUP"!
PLEASANT DREAMS... ABOUT POISON IVY...!
12

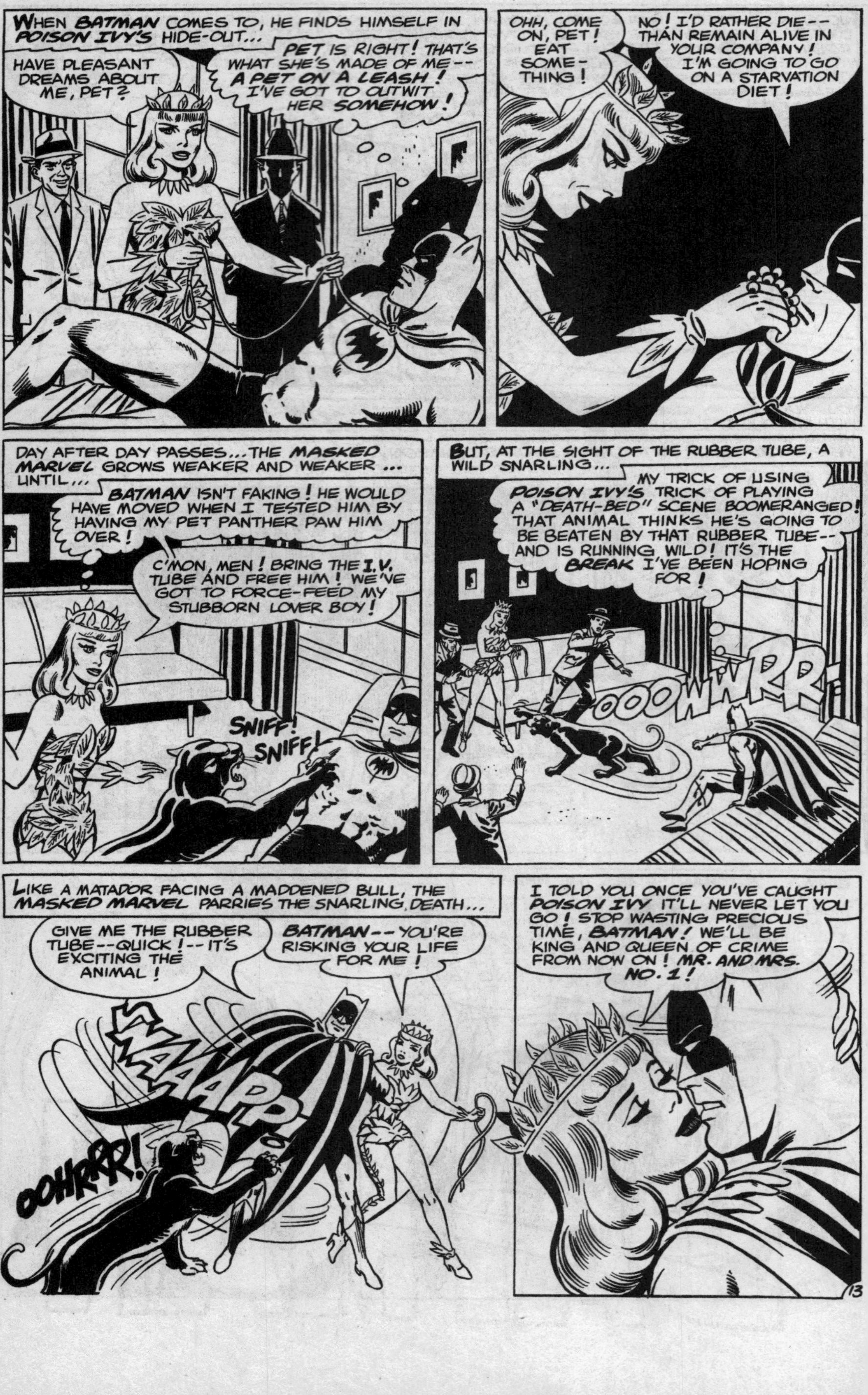
WHEN BATMAN COMES TO, HE FINDS HIMSELF IN POISON IVY'S HIDE-OUT...
HAVE PLEASANT DREAMS ABOUT ME, PET?
PET IS RIGHT! THAT'S WHAT SHE'S MADE OF ME-- A PET ON A LEASH! I'VE GOT TO OUTWIT HER SOMEHOW!
OHH, COME ON, PET! EAT SOME-THING!
NO! I'D RATHER DIE-- THAN REMAIN ALIVE IN YOUR COMPANY! I'M GOING TO GO ON A STARVATION DIET!
DAY AFTER DAY PASSES... THE MASKED MARVEL GROWS WEAKER AND WEAKER ... UNTIL...
BATMAN ISN'T FAKING! HE WOULD HAVE MOVED WHEN I TESTED HIM BY HAVING MY PET PANTHER PAW HIM OVER!
C'MON, MEN! BRING THE I.V. TUBE AND FREE HIM! WE'VE GOT TO FORCE-FEED MY STUBBORN LOVER BOY!
SNIFF! SNIFF!
BUT, AT THE SIGHT OF THE RUBBER TUBE, A WILD SNARLING...
MY TRICK OF USING POISON IVY'S TRICK OF PLAYING A "DEATH-BED" SCENE BOOMERANGED! THAT ANIMAL THINKS HE'S GOING TO BE BEATEN BY THAT RUBBER TUBE-- AND IS RUNNING WILD! IT'S THE BREAK I'VE BEEN HOPING FOR!
OOOONWRR
LIKE A MATADOR FACING A MADDENED BULL, THE MASKED MARVEL PARRIES THE SNARLING DEATH...
GIVE ME THE RUBBER TUBE--QUICK!--IT'S EXCITING THE ANIMAL!
BATMAN--YOU'RE RISKING YOUR LIFE FOR ME!
SWAAAPP
OOHRRR!
I TOLD YOU ONCE YOU'VE CAUGHT POISON IVY IT'LL NEVER LET YOU GO! STOP WASTING PRECIOUS TIME, BATMAN! WE'LL BE KING AND QUEEN OF CRIME FROM NOW ON! MR. AND MRS. NO. 1!
13

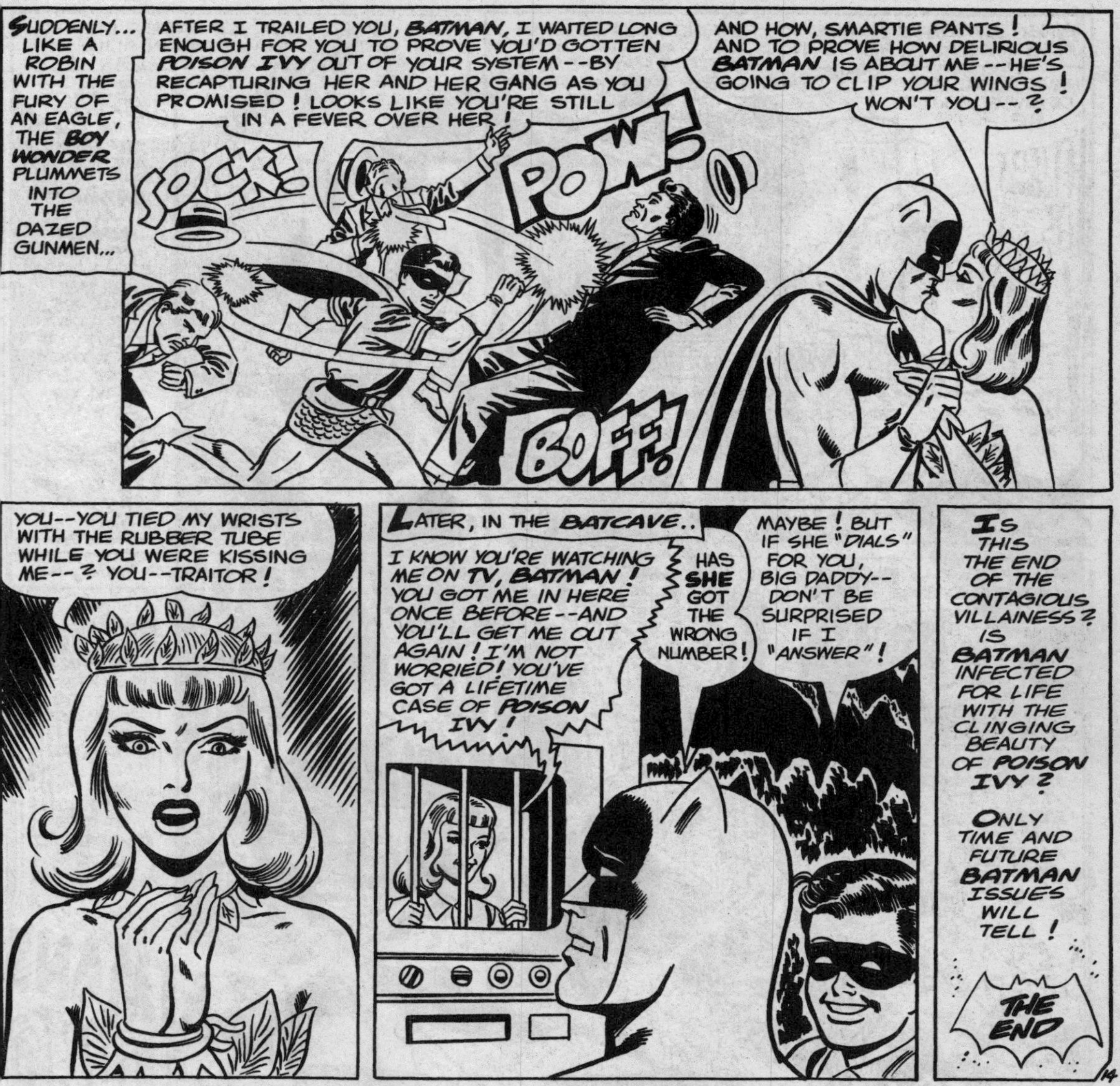
SUDDENLY... LIKE A ROBIN WITH THE FURY OF AN EAGLE, THE BOY WONDER PLUMMETS INTO THE DAZED GUNMEN...
AFTER I TRAILED YOU, BATMAN, I WAITED LONG ENOUGH FOR YOU TO PROVE YOU'D GOTTEN POISON IVY OUT OF YOUR SYSTEM--BY RECAPTURING HER AND HER GANG AS YOU PROMISED! LOOKS LIKE YOU'RE STILL IN A FEVER OVER HER!
SOCK!
POW!
BOFF!
AND HOW, SMARTIE PANTS! AND TO PROVE HOW DELIRIOUS BATMAN IS ABOUT ME--HE'S GOING TO CLIP YOUR WINGS! WON'T YOU--?
YOU--YOU TIED MY WRISTS WITH THE RUBBER TUBE WHILE YOU WERE KISSING ME--? YOU--TRAITOR!
LATER, IN THE BATCAVE..
I KNOW YOU'RE WATCHING ME ON TV, BATMAN! YOU GOT ME IN HERE ONCE BEFORE--AND YOU'LL GET ME OUT AGAIN! I'M NOT WORRIED! YOU'VE GOT A LIFETIME CASE OF POISON IVY!
HAS SHE GOT THE WRONG NUMBER!
MAYBE! BUT IF SHE "DIALS" FOR YOU, BIG DADDY--DON'T BE SURPRISED IF I "ANSWER"!
IS THIS THE END OF THE CONTAGIOUS VILLAINESS? IS BATMAN INFECTED FOR LIFE WITH THE CLINGING BEAUTY OF POISON IVY?
ONLY TIME AND FUTURE BATMAN ISSUES WILL TELL!
THE END
14

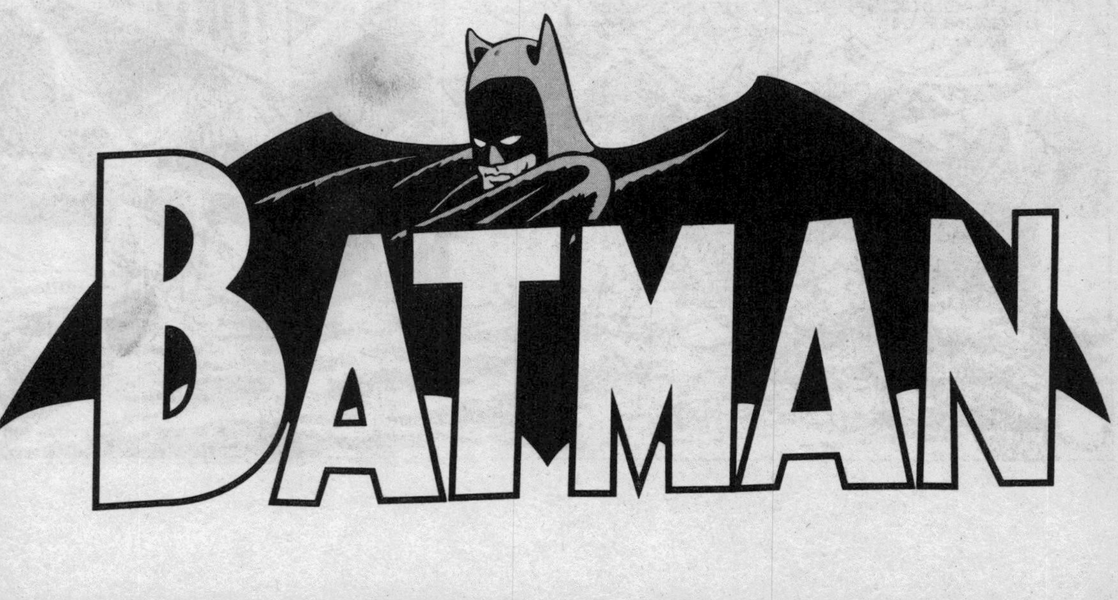
BATMAN

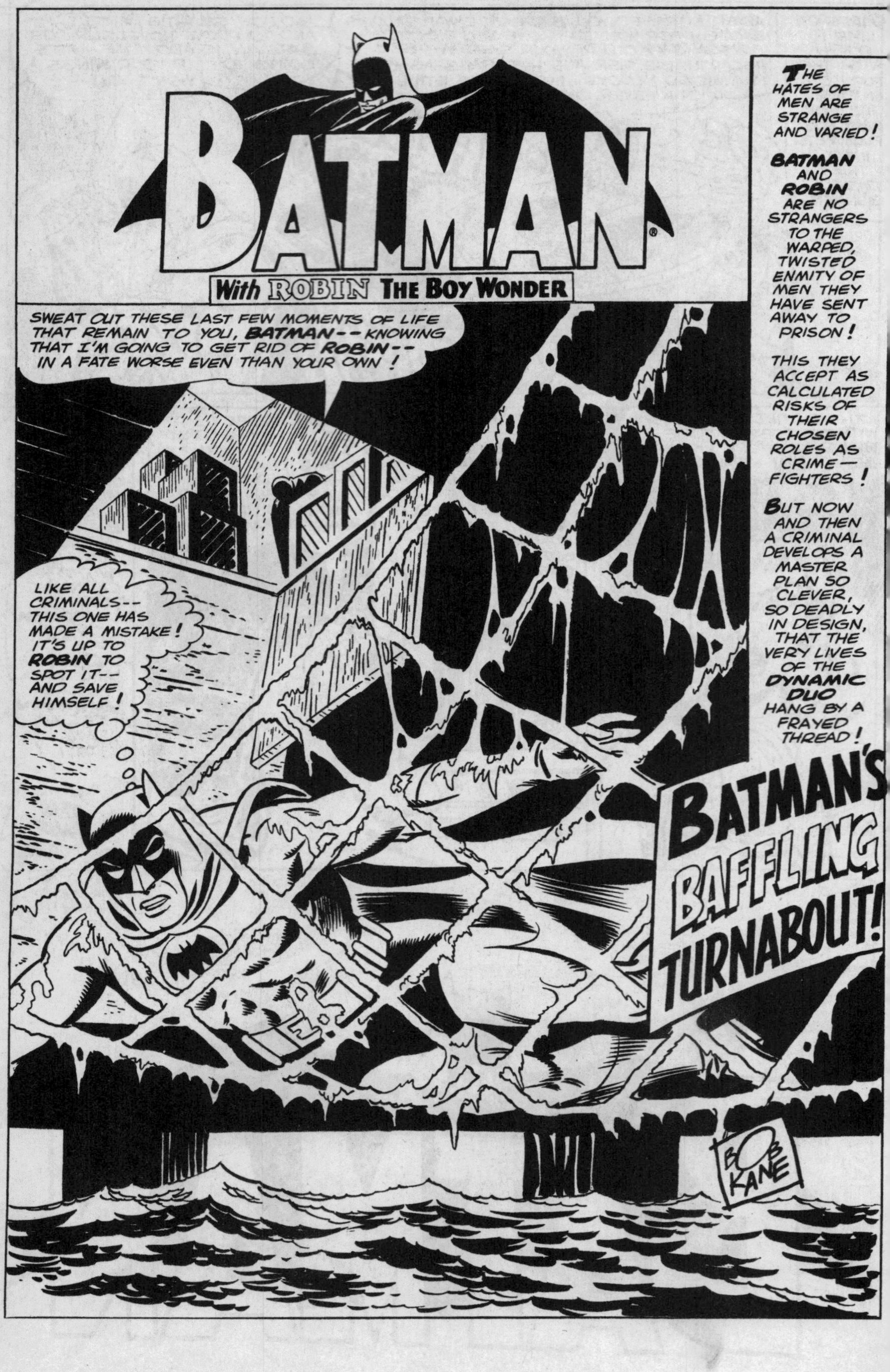

BATMAN
With ROBIN THE BOY WONDER
THE HATES OF MEN ARE STRANGE AND VARIED! BATMAN AND ROBIN ARE NO STRANGERS TO THE WARPED, TWISTED ENMITY OF MEN THEY HAVE SENT AWAY TO PRISON!
THIS THEY ACCEPT AS CALCULATED RISKS OF THEIR CHOSEN ROLES AS CRIME-FIGHTERS!
BUT NOW AND THEN A CRIMINAL DEVELOPS A MASTER PLAN SO CLEVER, SO DEADLY IN DESIGN, THAT THE VERY LIVES OF THE DYNAMIC DUO HANG BY A FRAYED THREAD!
SWEAT OUT THESE LAST FEW MOMENTS OF LIFE THAT REMAIN TO YOU, BATMAN--KNOWING THAT I'M GOING TO GET RID OF ROBIN--IN A FATE WORSE EVEN THAN YOUR OWN!
LIKE ALL CRIMINALS--THIS ONE HAS MADE A MISTAKE! IT'S UP TO ROBIN TO SPOT IT--AND SAVE HIMSELF!
BATMAN'S BAFFLING TURNABOUT!
BOB KANE

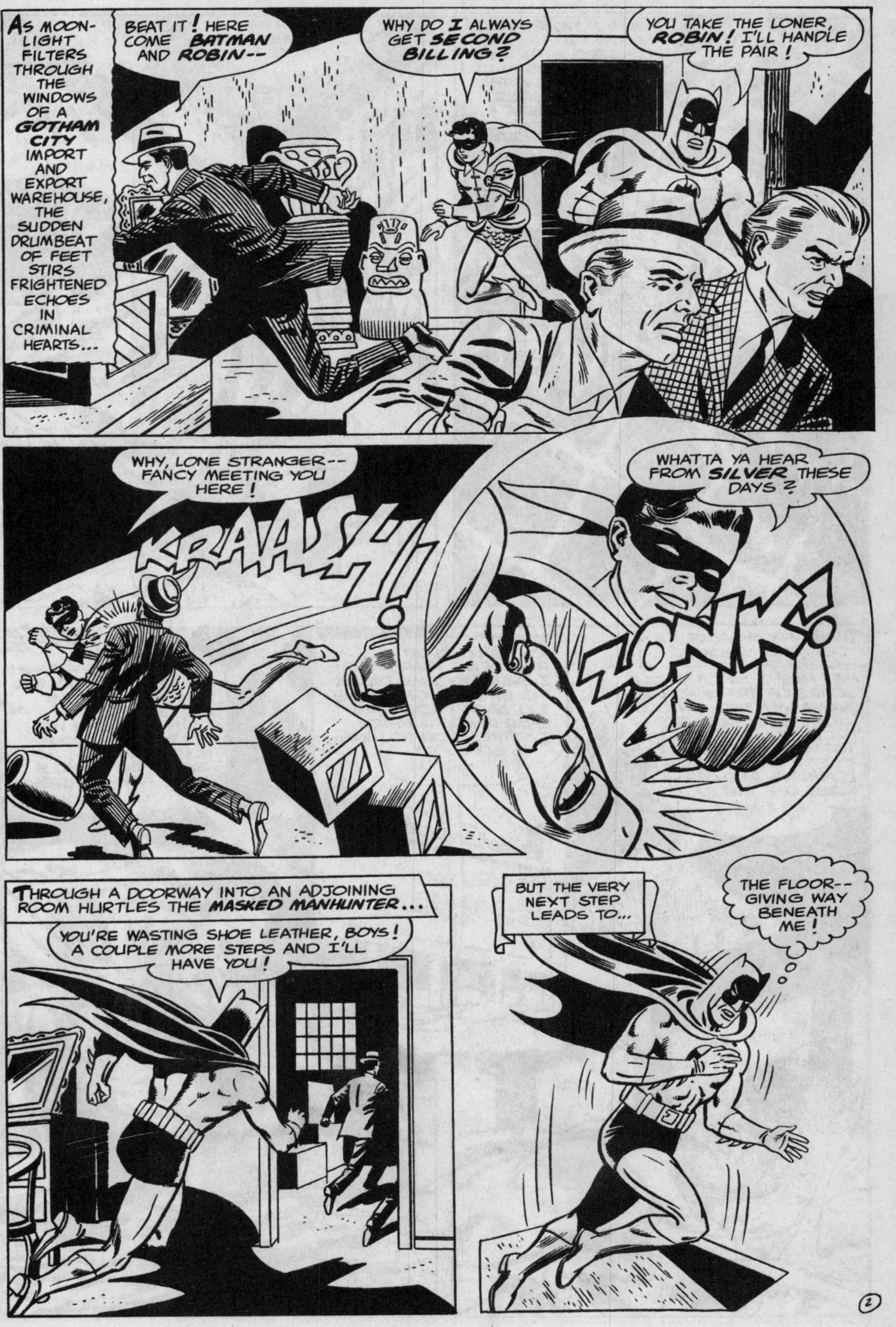
AS MOON-LIGHT FILTERS THROUGH THE WINDOWS OF A GOTHAM CITY IMPORT AND EXPORT WAREHOUSE, THE SUDDEN DRUMBEAT OF FEET STIRS FRIGHTENED ECHOES IN CRIMINAL HEARTS...
BEAT IT! HERE COME BATMAN AND ROBIN--
WHY DO I ALWAYS GET SECOND BILLING?
YOU TAKE THE LONER, ROBIN! I'LL HANDLE THE PAIR!
WHY, LONE STRANGER-- FANCY MEETING YOU HERE!
KRAASH!
WHATTA YA HEAR FROM SILVER THESE DAYS?
WONK!
THROUGH A DOORWAY INTO AN ADJOINING ROOM HURTLES THE MASKED MANHUNTER...
YOU'RE WASTING SHOE LEATHER, BOYS! A COUPLE MORE STEPS AND I'LL HAVE YOU!
BUT THE VERY NEXT STEP LEADS TO...
THE FLOOR-- GIVING WAY BENEATH ME!
2

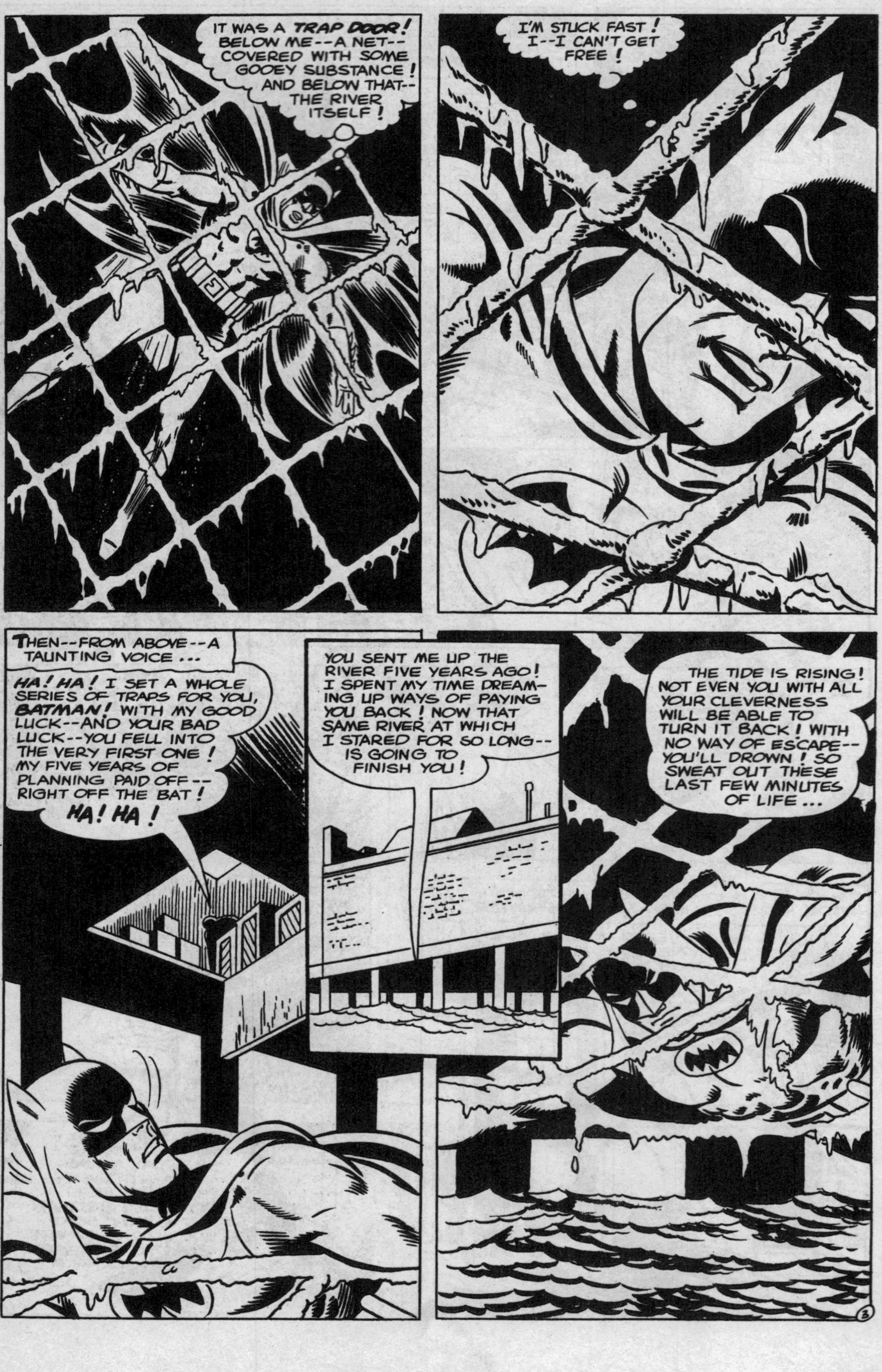
IT WAS A TRAP DOOR! BELOW ME--A NET--COVERED WITH SOME GOOEY SUBSTANCE! AND BELOW THAT--THE RIVER ITSELF!
I'M STUCK FAST! I--I CAN'T GET FREE!
THEN--FROM ABOVE--A TAUNTING VOICE...
HA! HA! I SET A WHOLE SERIES OF TRAPS FOR YOU, BATMAN! WITH MY GOOD LUCK--AND YOUR BAD LUCK--YOU FELL INTO THE VERY FIRST ONE! MY FIVE YEARS OF PLANNING PAID OFF--RIGHT OFF THE BAT! HA! HA!
YOU SENT ME UP THE RIVER FIVE YEARS AGO! I SPENT MY TIME DREAMING UP WAYS OF PAYING YOU BACK! NOW THAT SAME RIVER AT WHICH I STARED FOR SO LONG--IS GOING TO FINISH YOU!
THE TIDE IS RISING! NOT EVEN YOU WITH ALL YOUR CLEVERNESS WILL BE ABLE TO TURN IT BACK! WITH NO WAY OF ESCAPE--YOU'LL DROWN! SO SWEAT OUT THESE LAST FEW MINUTES OF LIFE...
3

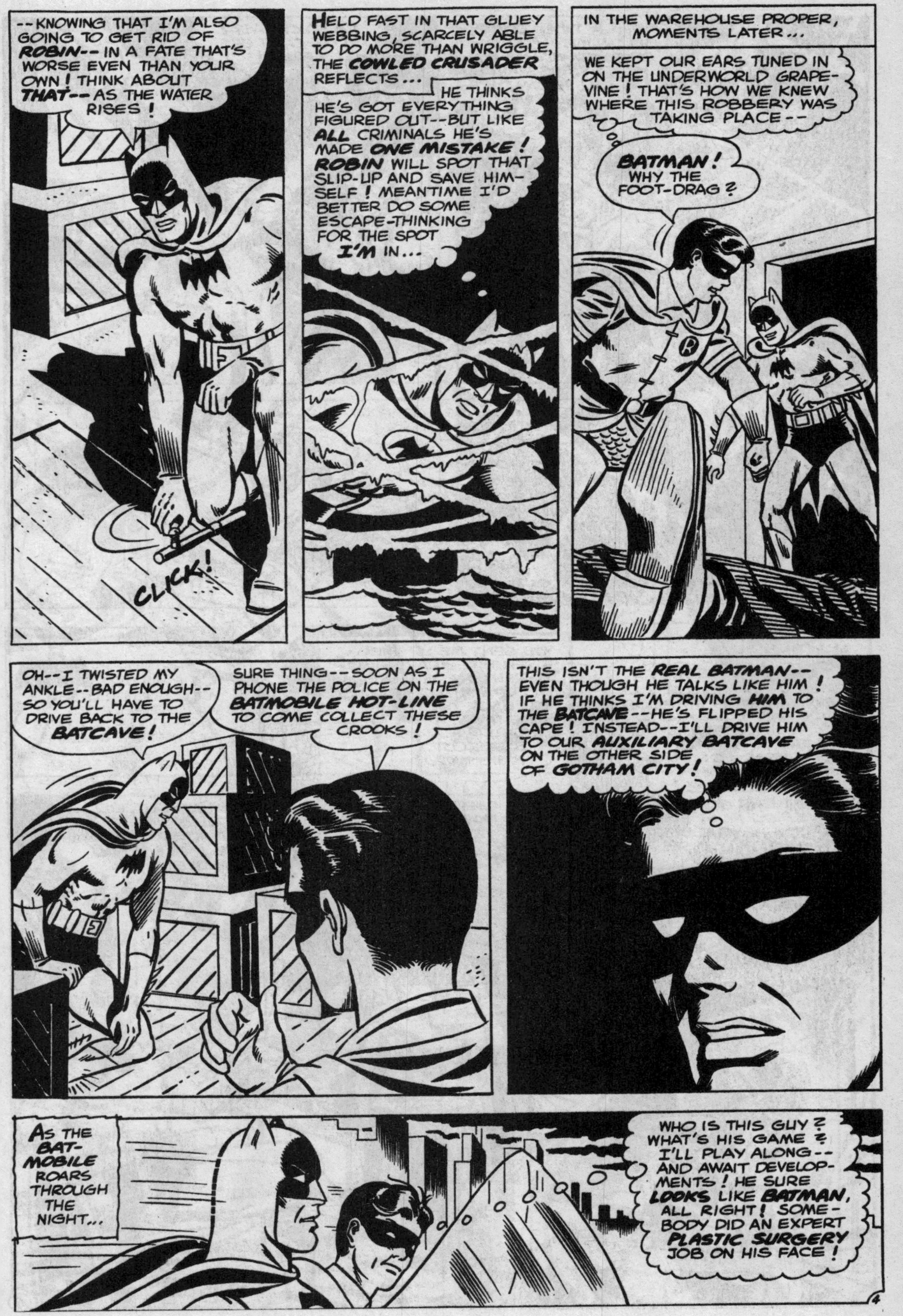
--KNOWING THAT I'M ALSO GOING TO GET RID OF ROBIN-- IN A FATE THAT'S WORSE EVEN THAN YOUR OWN! THINK ABOUT THAT-- AS THE WATER RISES!
CLICK!
HELD FAST IN THAT GLUEY WEBBING, SCARCELY ABLE TO DO MORE THAN WRIGGLE, THE COWLED CRUSADER REFLECTS...
HE THINKS HE'S GOT EVERYTHING FIGURED OUT--BUT LIKE ALL CRIMINALS HE'S MADE ONE MISTAKE! ROBIN WILL SPOT THAT SLIP-UP AND SAVE HIMSELF! MEANTIME I'D BETTER DO SOME ESCAPE-THINKING FOR THE SPOT I'M IN...
IN THE WAREHOUSE PROPER, MOMENTS LATER...
WE KEPT OUR EARS TUNED IN ON THE UNDERWORLD GRAPE-VINE! THAT'S HOW WE KNEW WHERE THIS ROBBERY WAS TAKING PLACE--
BATMAN! WHY THE FOOT-DRAG?
OH--I TWISTED MY ANKLE--BAD ENOUGH-- SO YOU'LL HAVE TO DRIVE BACK TO THE BATCAVE!
SURE THING--SOON AS I PHONE THE POLICE ON THE BATMOBILE HOT-LINE TO COME COLLECT THESE CROOKS!
THIS ISN'T THE REAL BATMAN-- EVEN THOUGH HE TALKS LIKE HIM! IF HE THINKS I'M DRIVING HIM TO THE BATCAVE--HE'S FLIPPED HIS CAPE! INSTEAD--I'LL DRIVE HIM TO OUR AUXILIARY BATCAVE ON THE OTHER SIDE OF GOTHAM CITY!
AS THE BAT-MOBILE ROARS THROUGH THE NIGHT...
WHO IS THIS GUY? WHAT'S HIS GAME? I'LL PLAY ALONG-- AND AWAIT DEVELOP-MENTS! HE SURE LOOKS LIKE BATMAN, ALL RIGHT! SOME-BODY DID AN EXPERT PLASTIC SURGERY JOB ON HIS FACE!
4

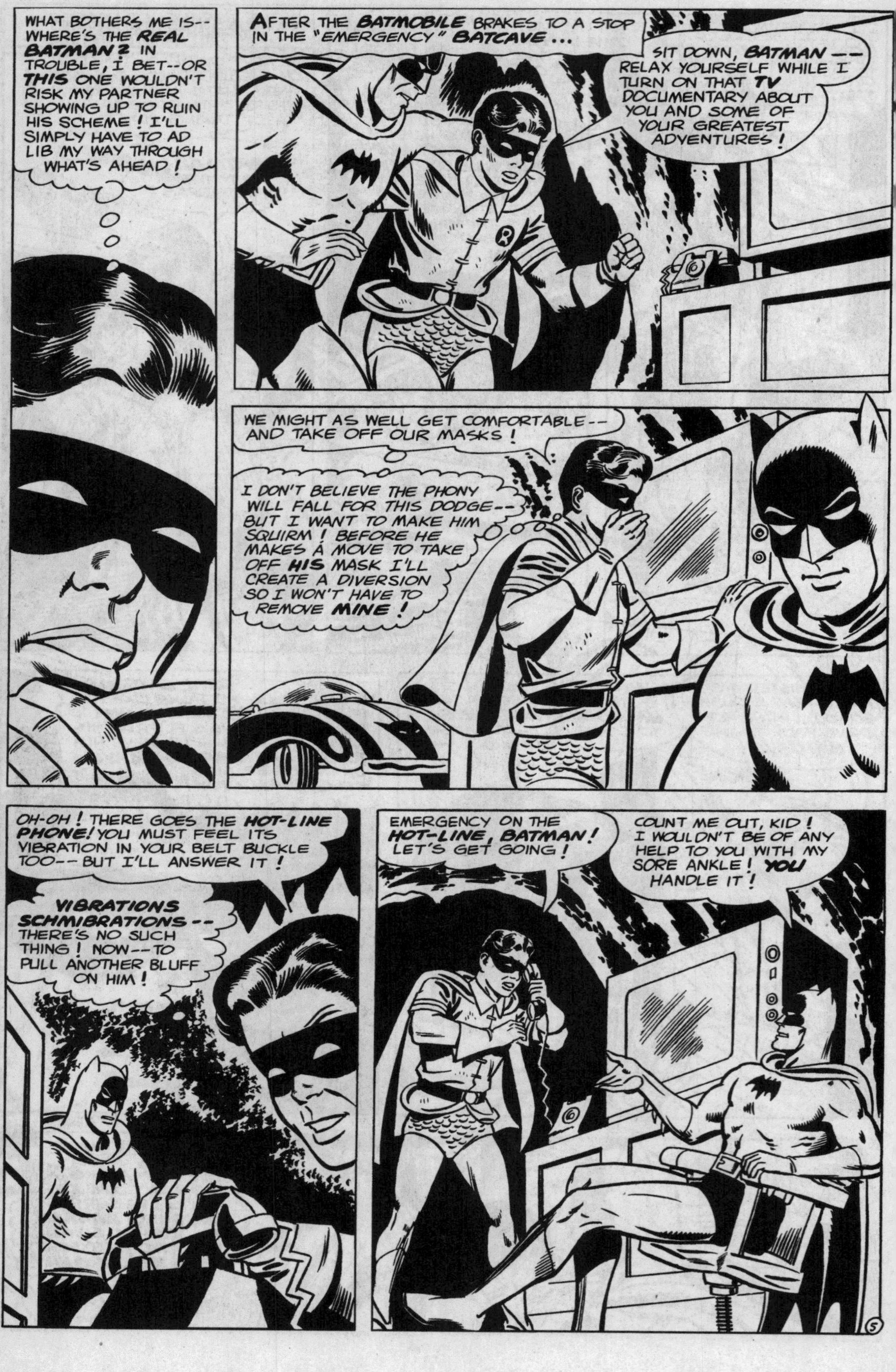
WHAT BOTHERS ME IS-- WHERE'S THE REAL BATMAN? IN TROUBLE, I BET--OR THIS ONE WOULDN'T RISK MY PARTNER SHOWING UP TO RUIN HIS SCHEME! I'LL SIMPLY HAVE TO AD LIB MY WAY THROUGH WHAT'S AHEAD!
AFTER THE BATMOBILE BRAKES TO A STOP IN THE "EMERGENCY" BATCAVE...
SIT DOWN, BATMAN -- RELAX YOURSELF WHILE I TURN ON THAT TV DOCUMENTARY ABOUT YOU AND SOME OF YOUR GREATEST ADVENTURES!
WE MIGHT AS WELL GET COMFORTABLE-- AND TAKE OFF OUR MASKS!
I DON'T BELIEVE THE PHONY WILL FALL FOR THIS DODGE-- BUT I WANT TO MAKE HIM SQUIRM! BEFORE HE MAKES A MOVE TO TAKE OFF HIS MASK I'LL CREATE A DIVERSION SO I WON'T HAVE TO REMOVE MINE!
OH-OH! THERE GOES THE HOT-LINE PHONE! YOU MUST FEEL ITS VIBRATION IN YOUR BELT BUCKLE TOO-- BUT I'LL ANSWER IT!
VIBRATIONS SCHMIBRATIONS-- THERE'S NO SUCH THING! NOW--TO PULL ANOTHER BLUFF ON HIM!
EMERGENCY ON THE HOT-LINE, BATMAN! LET'S GET GOING!
COUNT ME OUT, KID! I WOULDN'T BE OF ANY HELP TO YOU WITH MY SORE ANKLE! YOU HANDLE IT!
5

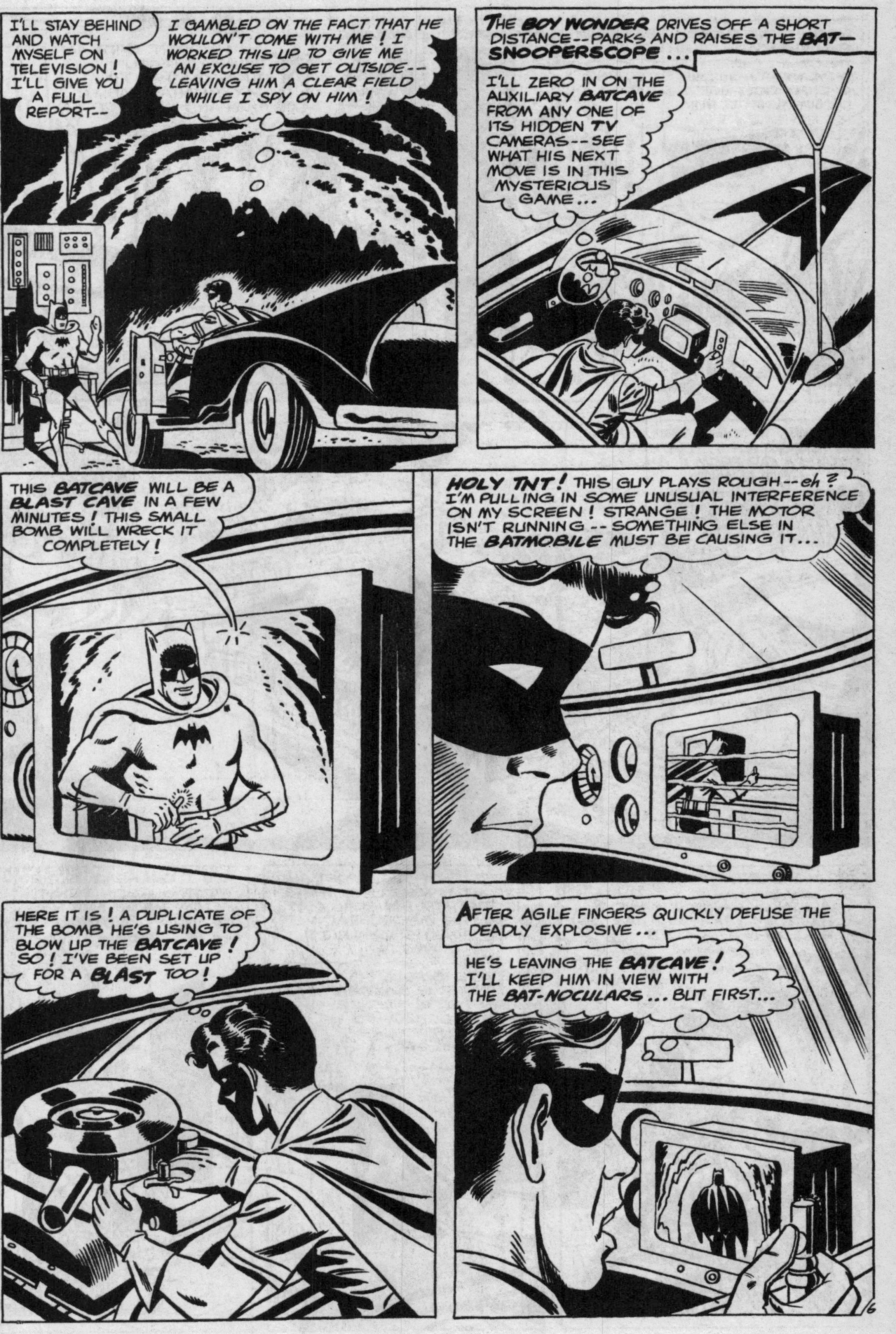
I'LL STAY BEHIND AND WATCH MYSELF ON TELEVISION! I'LL GIVE YOU A FULL REPORT--
I GAMBLED ON THE FACT THAT HE WOULDN'T COME WITH ME! I WORKED THIS UP TO GIVE ME AN EXCUSE TO GET OUTSIDE--LEAVING HIM A CLEAR FIELD WHILE I SPY ON HIM!
THE BOY WONDER DRIVES OFF A SHORT DISTANCE--PARKS AND RAISES THE BAT-SNOOPERSCOPE...
I'LL ZERO IN ON THE AUXILIARY BATCAVE FROM ANY ONE OF ITS HIDDEN TV CAMERAS--SEE WHAT HIS NEXT MOVE IS IN THIS MYSTERIOUS GAME...
THIS BATCAVE WILL BE A BLAST CAVE IN A FEW MINUTES! THIS SMALL BOMB WILL WRECK IT COMPLETELY!
HOLY TNT! THIS GUY PLAYS ROUGH--eh? I'M PULLING IN SOME UNUSUAL INTERFERENCE ON MY SCREEN! STRANGE! THE MOTOR ISN'T RUNNING--SOMETHING ELSE IN THE BATMOBILE MUST BE CAUSING IT...
HERE IT IS! A DUPLICATE OF THE BOMB HE'S USING TO BLOW UP THE BATCAVE! SO! I'VE BEEN SET UP FOR A BLAST TOO!
AFTER AGILE FINGERS QUICKLY DEFUSE THE DEADLY EXPLOSIVE...
HE'S LEAVING THE BATCAVE! I'LL KEEP HIM IN VIEW WITH THE BAT-NOCULARS... BUT FIRST...
6

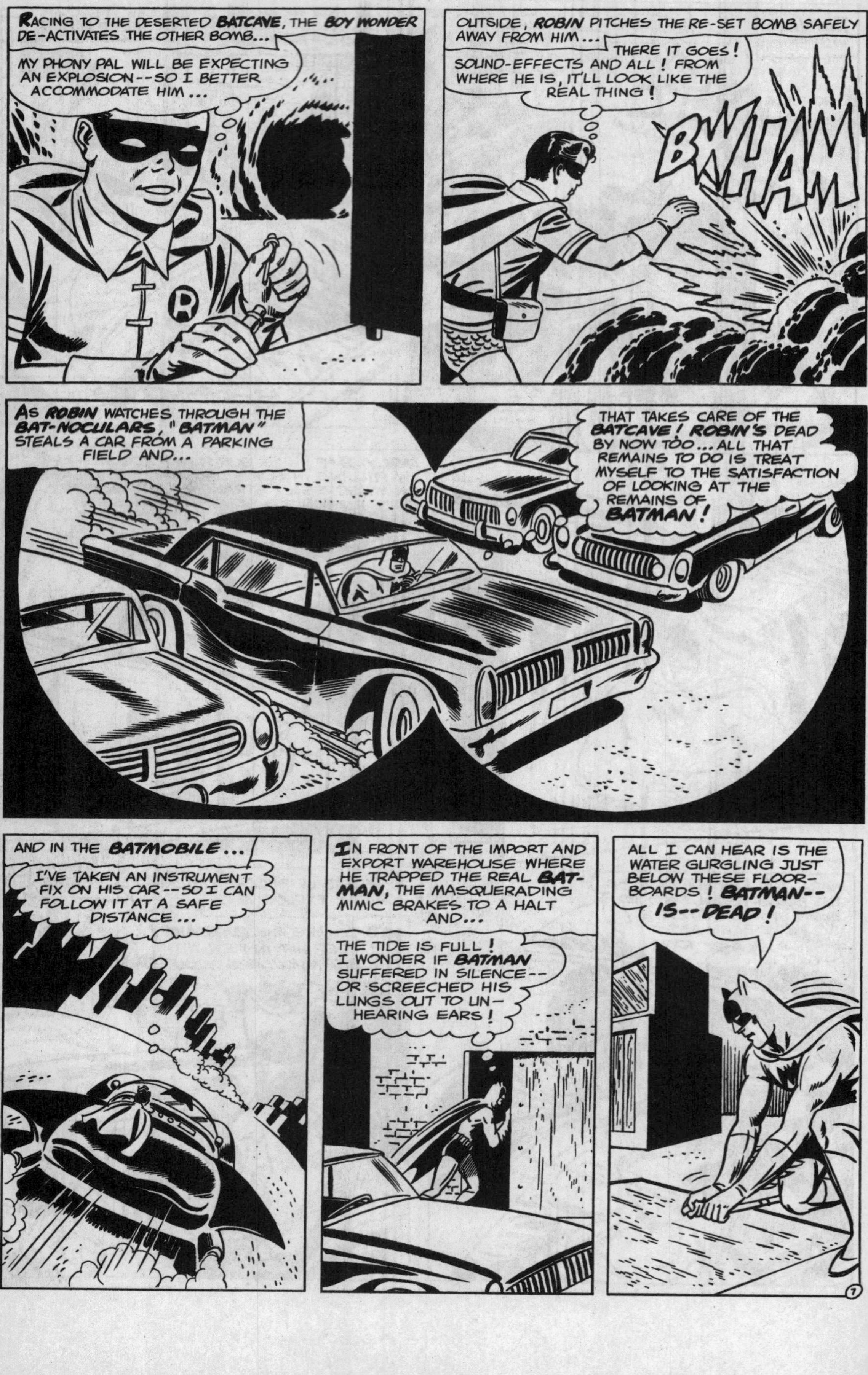
RACING TO THE DESERTED BATCAVE, THE BOY WONDER DE-ACTIVATES THE OTHER BOMB...
MY PHONY PAL WILL BE EXPECTING AN EXPLOSION--SO I BETTER ACCOMMODATE HIM...
OUTSIDE, ROBIN PITCHES THE RE-SET BOMB SAFELY AWAY FROM HIM...
THERE IT GOES! SOUND-EFFECTS AND ALL! FROM WHERE HE IS, IT'LL LOOK LIKE THE REAL THING!
B-WHAM
AS ROBIN WATCHES THROUGH THE BAT-NOCULARS, "BATMAN" STEALS A CAR FROM A PARKING FIELD AND...
THAT TAKES CARE OF THE BATCAVE! ROBIN'S DEAD BY NOW TOO... ALL THAT REMAINS TO DO IS TREAT MYSELF TO THE SATISFACTION OF LOOKING AT THE REMAINS OF BATMAN!
AND IN THE BATMOBILE...
I'VE TAKEN AN INSTRUMENT FIX ON HIS CAR--SO I CAN FOLLOW IT AT A SAFE DISTANCE...
IN FRONT OF THE IMPORT AND EXPORT WAREHOUSE WHERE HE TRAPPED THE REAL BATMAN, THE MASQUERADING MIMIC BRAKES TO A HALT AND...
THE TIDE IS FULL! I WONDER IF BATMAN SUFFERED IN SILENCE--OR SCREECHED HIS LUNGS OUT TO UN-HEARING EARS!
ALL I CAN HEAR IS THE WATER GURGLING JUST BELOW THESE FLOOR-BOARDS! BATMAN--IS--DEAD!
7

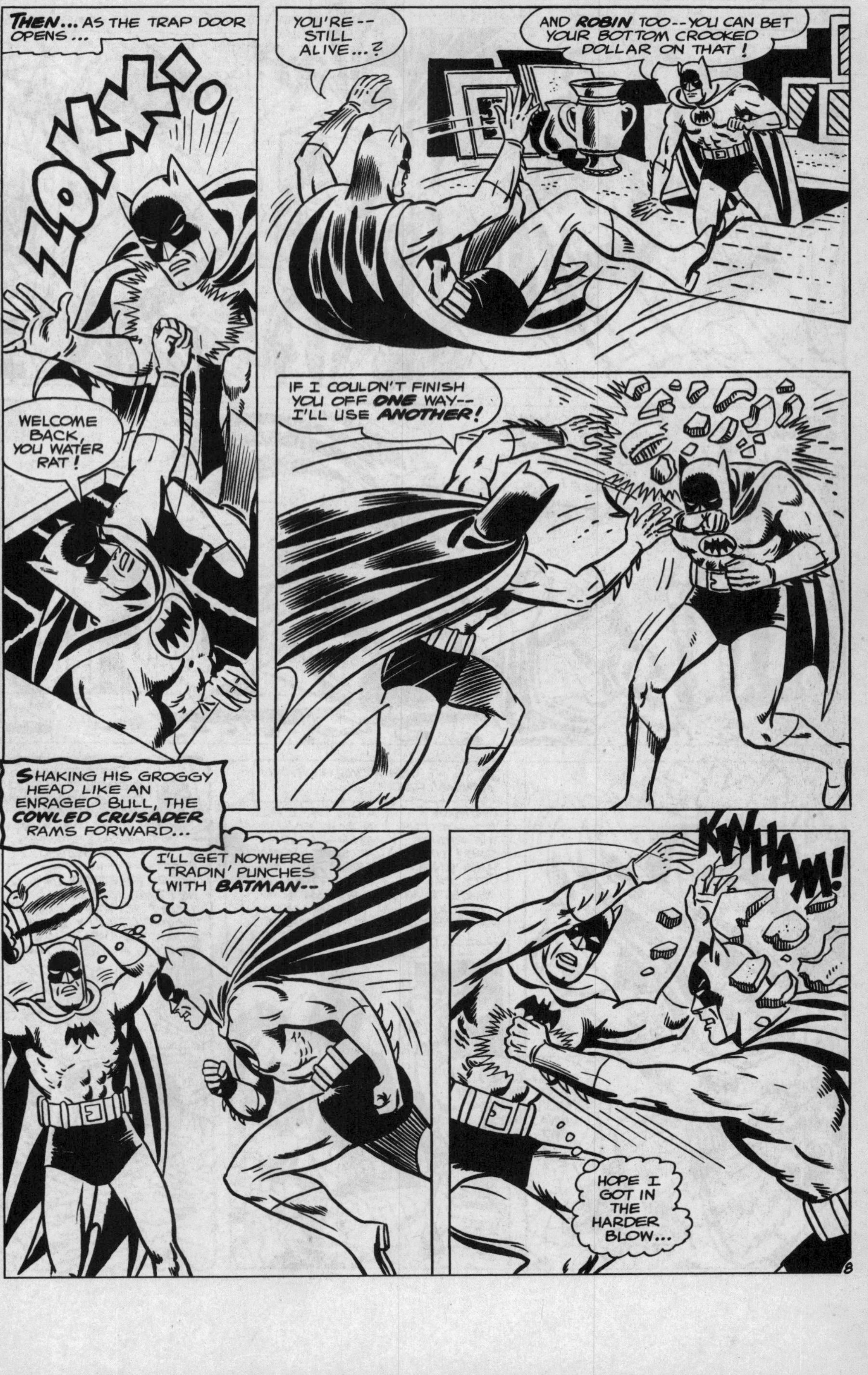
THEN... AS THE TRAP DOOR OPENS...
ZOKK!
WELCOME BACK, YOU WATER RAT!
YOU'RE -- STILL ALIVE...?
AND ROBIN TOO-- YOU CAN BET YOUR BOTTOM CROOKED DOLLAR ON THAT!
IF I COULDN'T FINISH YOU OFF ONE WAY-- I'LL USE ANOTHER!
SHAKING HIS GROGGY HEAD LIKE AN ENRAGED BULL, THE COWLED CRUSADER RAMS FORWARD...
I'LL GET NOWHERE TRADIN' PUNCHES WITH BATMAN--
KWHAM!
HOPE I GOT IN THE HARDER BLOW...
8

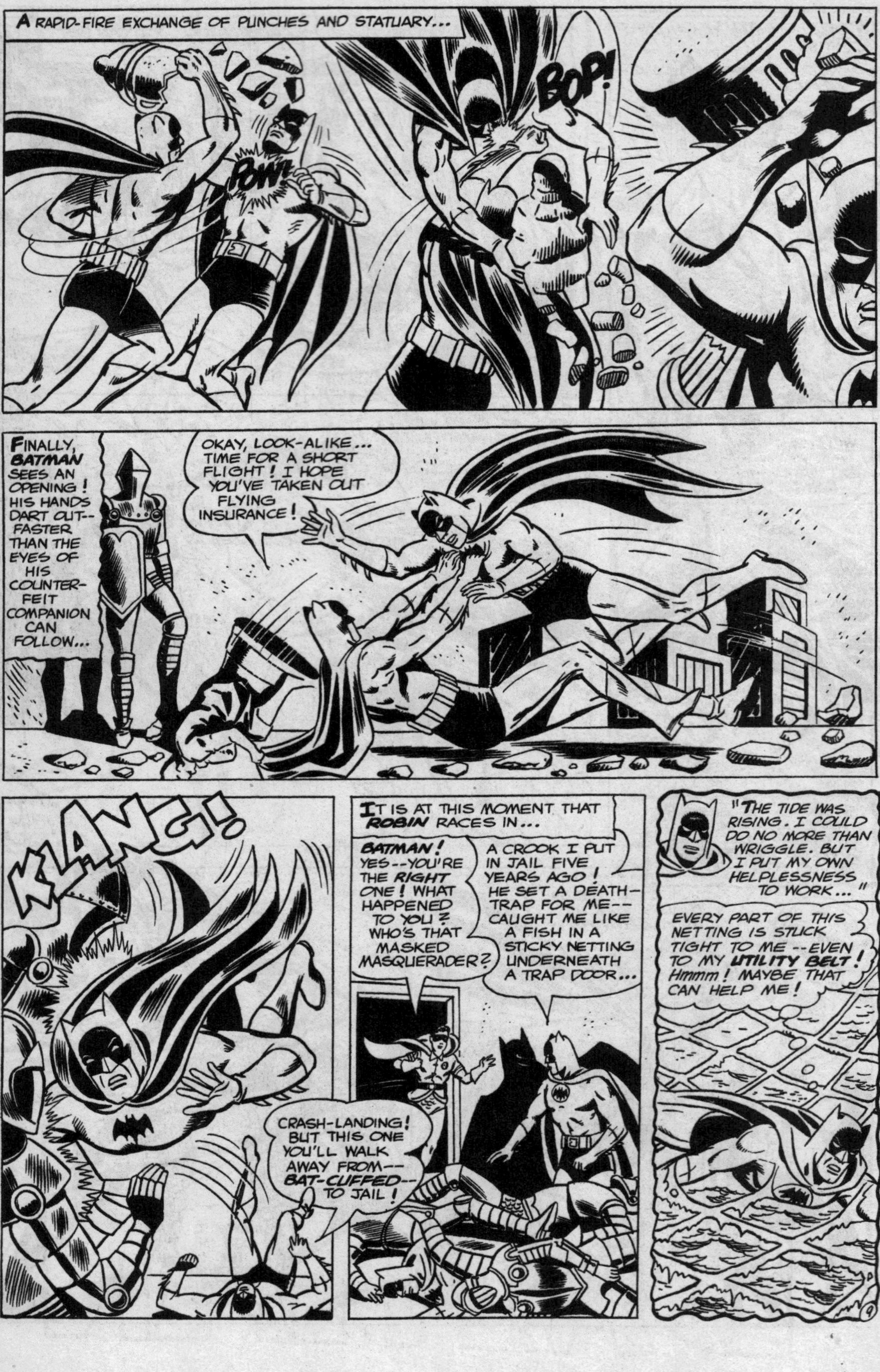
A RAPID-FIRE EXCHANGE OF PUNCHES AND STATUARY...
POW!
BOP!
FINALLY, BATMAN SEES AN OPENING! HIS HANDS DART OUT--FASTER THAN THE EYES OF HIS COUNTERFEIT COMPANION CAN FOLLOW...
OKAY, LOOK-ALIKE... TIME FOR A SHORT FLIGHT! I HOPE YOU'VE TAKEN OUT FLYING INSURANCE!
KLANG!
CRASH-LANDING! BUT THIS ONE YOU'LL WALK AWAY FROM--BAT-CUFFED--TO JAIL!
IT IS AT THIS MOMENT THAT ROBIN RACES IN...
BATMAN! YES--YOU'RE THE RIGHT ONE! WHAT HAPPENED TO YOU? WHO'S THAT MASKED MASQUERADER?
A CROOK I PUT IN JAIL FIVE YEARS AGO! HE SET A DEATH-TRAP FOR ME--CAUGHT ME LIKE A FISH IN A STICKY NETTING UNDERNEATH A TRAP DOOR...
"THE TIDE WAS RISING. I COULD DO NO MORE THAN WRIGGLE. BUT I PUT MY OWN HELPLESSNESS TO WORK..."
EVERY PART OF THIS NETTING IS STUCK TIGHT TO ME --EVEN TO MY UTILITY BELT! Hmmm! MAYBE THAT CAN HELP ME!
9

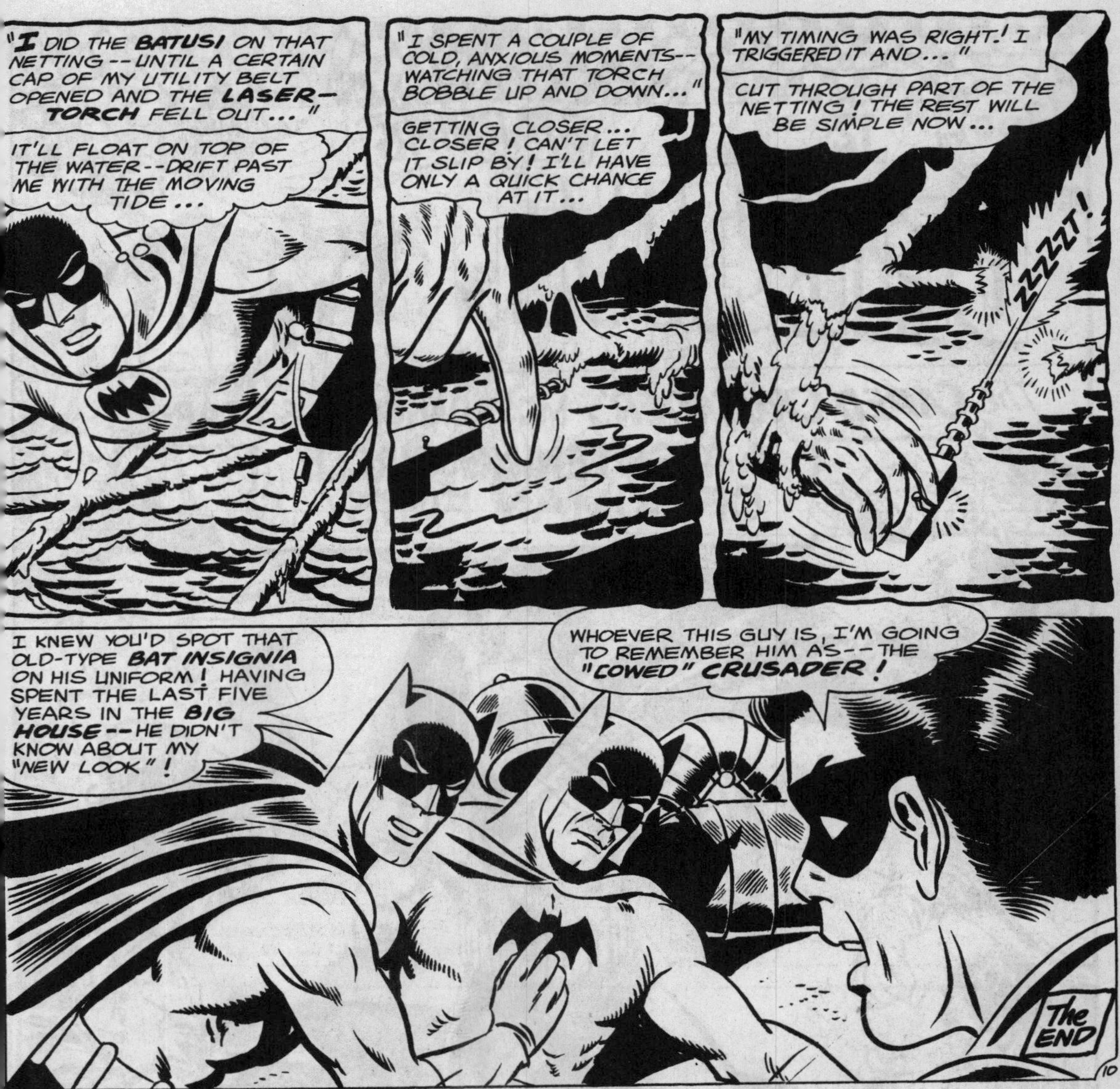
"I DID THE BATUSI ON THAT NETTING -- UNTIL A CERTAIN CAP OF MY UTILITY BELT OPENED AND THE LASER-TORCH FELL OUT..."
IT'LL FLOAT ON TOP OF THE WATER--DRIFT PAST ME WITH THE MOVING TIDE...
"I SPENT A COUPLE OF COLD, ANXIOUS MOMENTS-- WATCHING THAT TORCH BOBBLE UP AND DOWN..."
GETTING CLOSER... CLOSER! CAN'T LET IT SLIP BY! I'LL HAVE ONLY A QUICK CHANCE AT IT...
"MY TIMING WAS RIGHT! I TRIGGERED IT AND..."
CUT THROUGH PART OF THE NETTING! THE REST WILL BE SIMPLE NOW...
ZZZZZT!
I KNEW YOU'D SPOT THAT OLD-TYPE BAT INSIGNIA ON HIS UNIFORM! HAVING SPENT THE LAST FIVE YEARS IN THE BIG HOUSE--HE DIDN'T KNOW ABOUT MY "NEW LOOK"!
WHOEVER THIS GUY IS, I'M GOING TO REMEMBER HIM AS--THE "COWED" CRUSADER!
The END
10

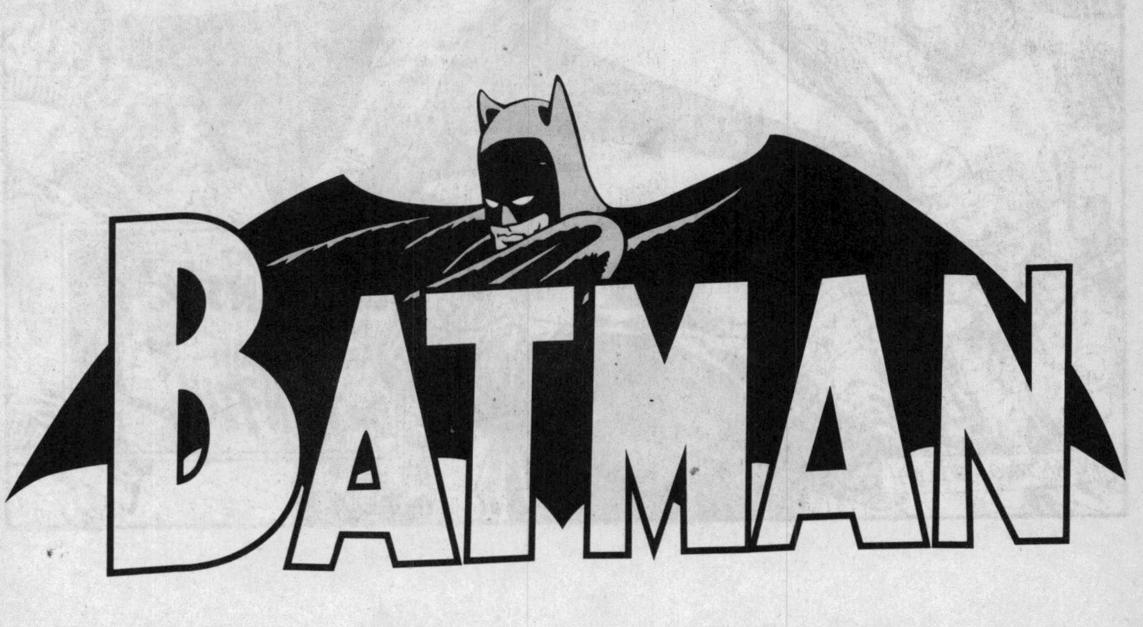
BATMAN

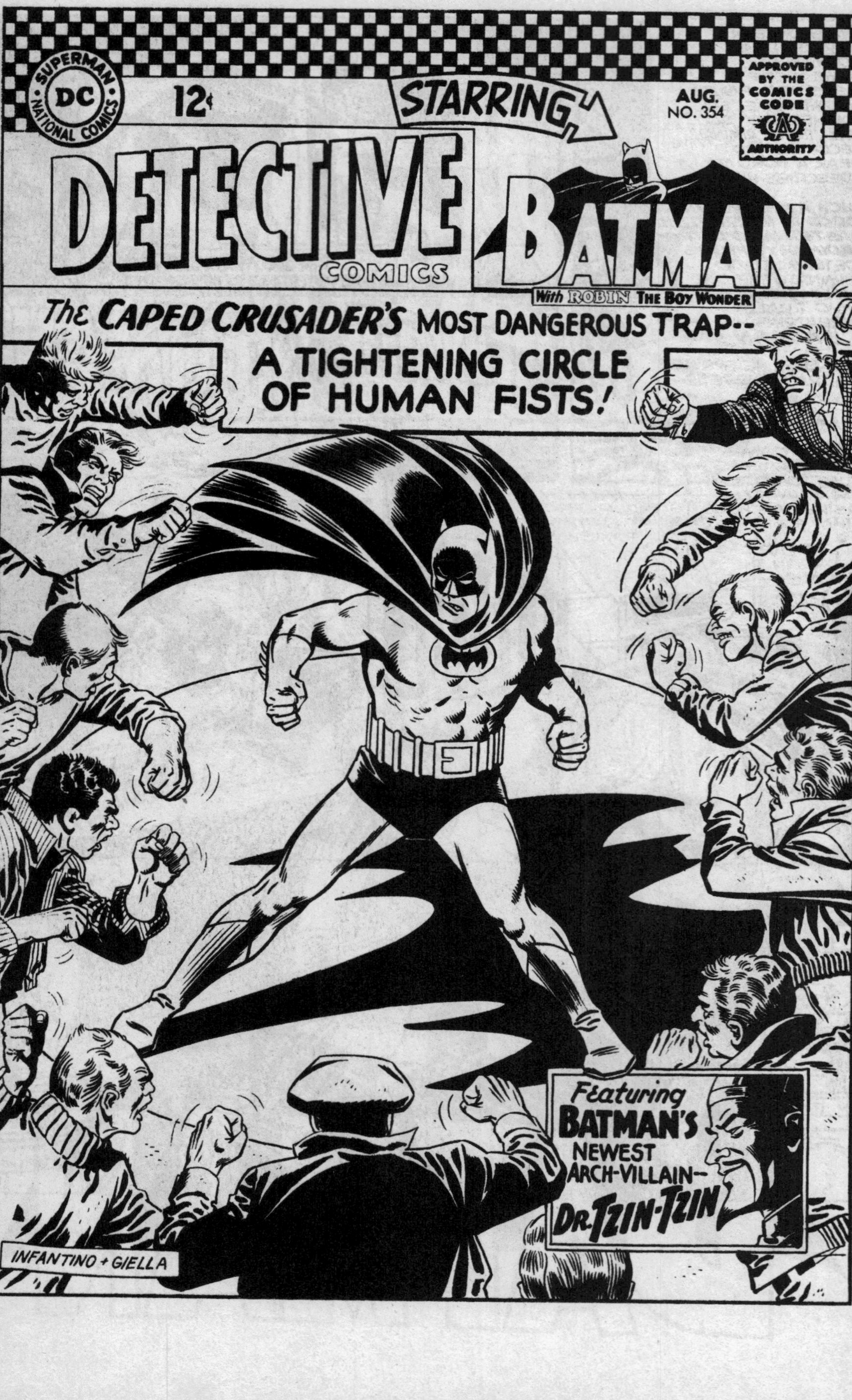
SUPERMAN DC NATIONAL COMICS
12¢
STARRING
AUG. NO. 354
APPROVED BY THE COMICS CODE AUTHORITY
DETECTIVE COMICS
BATMAN
With ROBIN THE BOY WONDER
The CAPED CRUSADER'S MOST DANGEROUS TRAP--
A TIGHTENING CIRCLE OF HUMAN FISTS!
Featuring BATMAN'S NEWEST ARCH-VILLAIN-- DR. TZIN-TZIN
INFANTINO + GIELLA

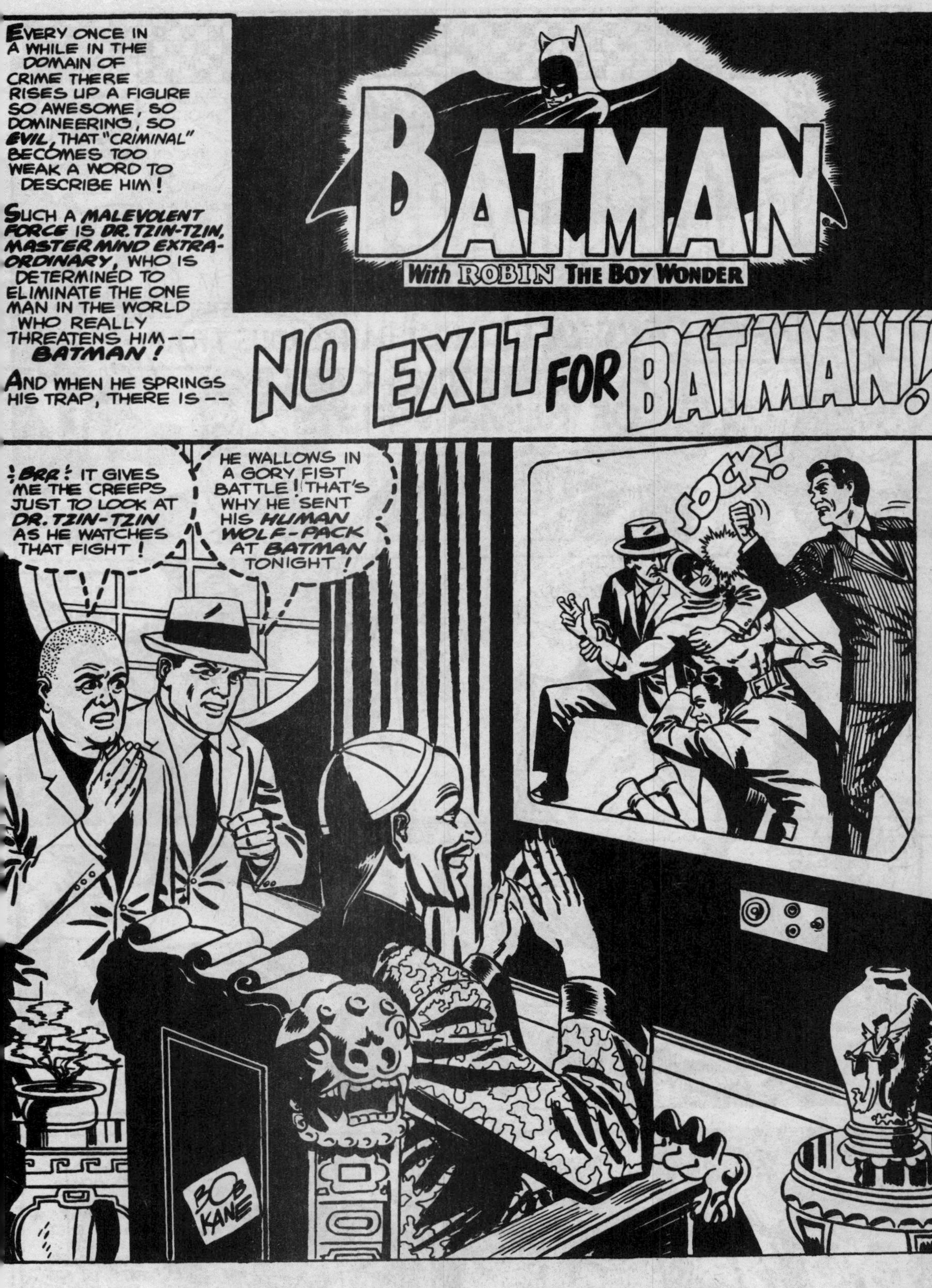
EVERY ONCE IN A WHILE IN THE DOMAIN OF CRIME THERE RISES UP A FIGURE SO AWESOME, SO DOMINEERING, SO EVIL, THAT "CRIMINAL" BECOMES TOO WEAK A WORD TO DESCRIBE HIM!
SUCH A MALEVOLENT FORCE IS DR. TZIN-TZIN, MASTERMIND EXTRA-ORDINARY, WHO IS DETERMINED TO ELIMINATE THE ONE MAN IN THE WORLD WHO REALLY THREATENS HIM-- BATMAN!
AND WHEN HE SPRINGS HIS TRAP, THERE IS --
BATMAN
With ROBIN THE BOY WONDER
NO EXIT FOR BATMAN!
BRR! IT GIVES ME THE CREEPS JUST TO LOOK AT DR. TZIN-TZIN AS HE WATCHES THAT FIGHT!
HE WALLOWS IN A GORY FIST BATTLE! THAT'S WHY HE SENT HIS HUMAN WOLF-PACK AT BATMAN TONIGHT!
SOCK!
BOB KANE

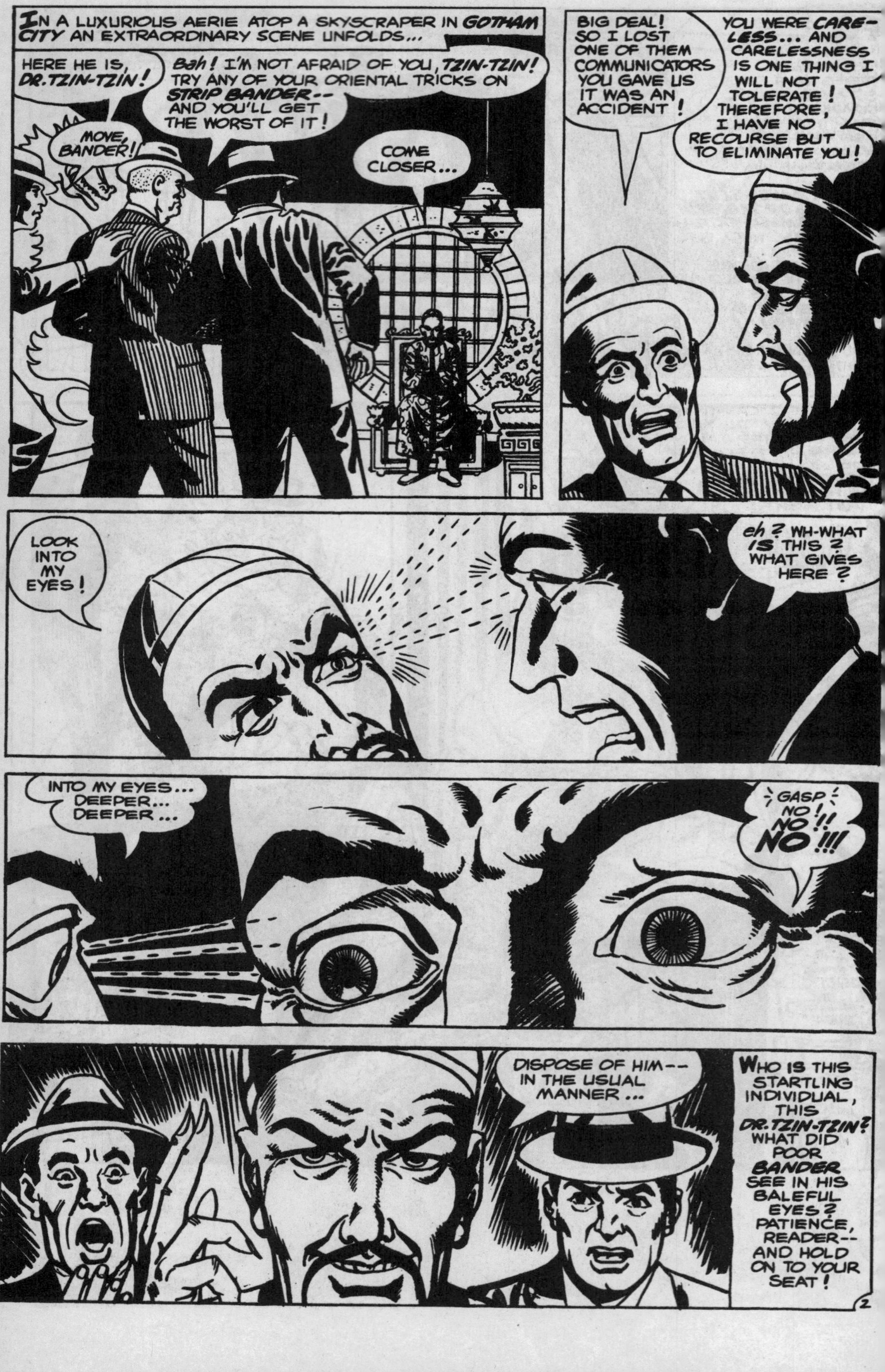
IN A LUXURIOUS AERIE ATOP A SKYSCRAPER IN GOTHAM CITY AN EXTRAORDINARY SCENE UNFOLDS...
HERE HE IS, DR. TZIN-TZIN!
Bah! I'M NOT AFRAID OF YOU, TZIN-TZIN! TRY ANY OF YOUR ORIENTAL TRICKS ON STRIP BANDER-- AND YOU'LL GET THE WORST OF IT!
MOVE, BANDER!
COME CLOSER...
BIG DEAL! SO I LOST ONE OF THEM COMMUNICATORS YOU GAVE US IT WAS AN ACCIDENT!
YOU WERE CARE-LESS... AND CARELESSNESS IS ONE THING I WILL NOT TOLERATE! THEREFORE, I HAVE NO RECOURSE BUT TO ELIMINATE YOU!
LOOK INTO MY EYES!
eh? WH-WHAT IS THIS? WHAT GIVES HERE?
INTO MY EYES... DEEPER... DEEPER...
GASP NO! NO!! NO!!!
DISPOSE OF HIM-- IN THE USUAL MANNER...
WHO IS THIS STARTLING INDIVIDUAL, THIS DR. TZIN-TZIN? WHAT DID POOR BANDER SEE IN HIS BALEFUL EYES? PATIENCE, READER-- AND HOLD ON TO YOUR SEAT!
2

SOON AFTER, IN THE BLEAK, CHEERLESS SURROUNDINGS OF THE *GOTHAM CITY MORGUE*...

HE WAS FOUND UNDER THE DOCKS, *BATMAN*-- A SMALL-TIME CROOK NAMED *STRIP BANDER*! I WANTED YOU AND *ROBIN* TO HEAR THE VERDICT OF THE *MEDICAL EXAMINER* ON HIS DEATH! GO AHEAD, DR. COREY...

AS NEAR AS I CAN MAKE OUT, *BATMAN*, THE AUTOPSY SHOWS THAT THIS MAN WAS *FRIGHTENED TO DEATH!* THERE ARE NO MARKS... NOTHING UNUSUAL... EXCEPT THAT *LOOK* ON HIS FACE...

YOU MEAN--?

I MEAN HE DIED OF *SHEER FRIGHT*--UNDER UNKNOWN CIRCUMSTANCES!

ROBIN--I SUSPECT THAT'S WHY COMMISSIONER GORDON SUMMONED US HERE--TO FIND OUT *HOW!*

WE'LL GO BACK TO MY OFFICE NOW...

AND ACCORDING TO OUR CONTACTS ABROAD, ONE YEAR AGO A MAN WAS FOUND IN *ISTANBUL* WHO APPARENTLY SUFFERED THE SAME FATE AS BANDER-- DEATH FROM *PURE TERROR!* AT THAT TIME A MYSTERIOUS CHARACTER NAMED *DR. TZIN-TZIN* WAS IN ISTANBUL...

DR. TZIN-TZIN--?

WHAT A SWINGING NAME--!

NO ONE KNOWS HIS REAL NAME! FROM *INTERPOL* WE LEARNED THAT HE'S REALLY AN AMERICAN-- AN ORPHAN FOUND YEARS AGO BY CHINESE BANDITS AND RAISED BY THEM! HE ADOPTED THEIR WAYS--THEN ENTERED THE WESTERN WORLD TO ROB AND PILLAGE IN A GRAND STYLE!

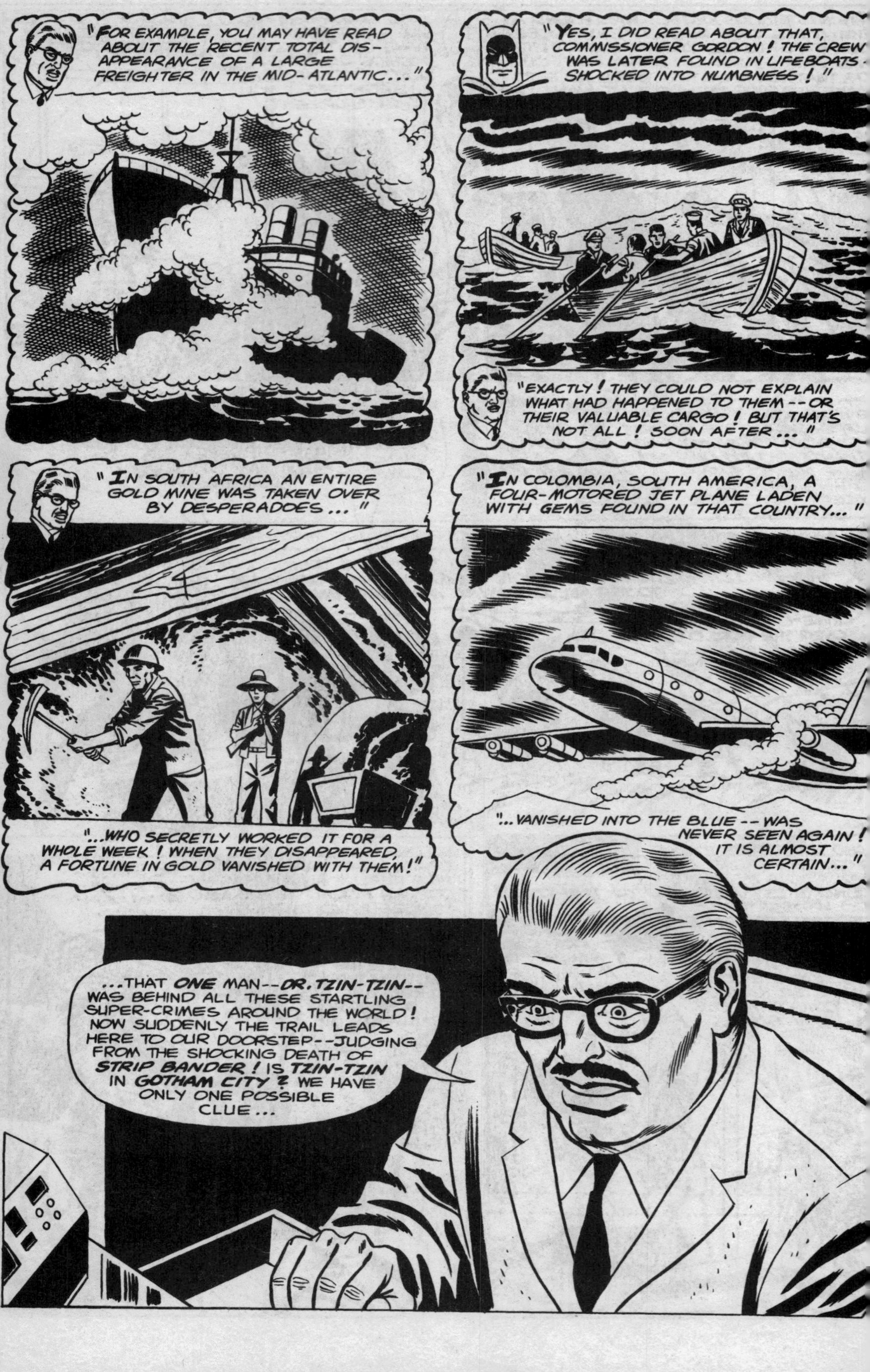
"FOR EXAMPLE, YOU MAY HAVE READ ABOUT THE RECENT TOTAL DIS-APPEARANCE OF A LARGE FREIGHTER IN THE MID-ATLANTIC..."
"YES, I DID READ ABOUT THAT, COMMISSIONER GORDON! THE CREW WAS LATER FOUND IN LIFEBOATS -- SHOCKED INTO NUMBNESS!"
"EXACTLY! THEY COULD NOT EXPLAIN WHAT HAD HAPPENED TO THEM -- OR THEIR VALUABLE CARGO! BUT THAT'S NOT ALL! SOON AFTER..."
"IN SOUTH AFRICA AN ENTIRE GOLD MINE WAS TAKEN OVER BY DESPERADOES..."
"...WHO SECRETLY WORKED IT FOR A WHOLE WEEK! WHEN THEY DISAPPEARED, A FORTUNE IN GOLD VANISHED WITH THEM!"
"IN COLOMBIA, SOUTH AMERICA, A FOUR-MOTORED JET PLANE LADEN WITH GEMS FOUND IN THAT COUNTRY..."
"...VANISHED INTO THE BLUE -- WAS NEVER SEEN AGAIN! IT IS ALMOST CERTAIN..."
...THAT ONE MAN--DR. TZIN-TZIN--WAS BEHIND ALL THESE STARTLING SUPER-CRIMES AROUND THE WORLD! NOW SUDDENLY THE TRAIL LEADS HERE TO OUR DOORSTEP--JUDGING FROM THE SHOCKING DEATH OF STRIP BANDER! IS TZIN-TZIN IN GOTHAM CITY? WE HAVE ONLY ONE POSSIBLE CLUE...

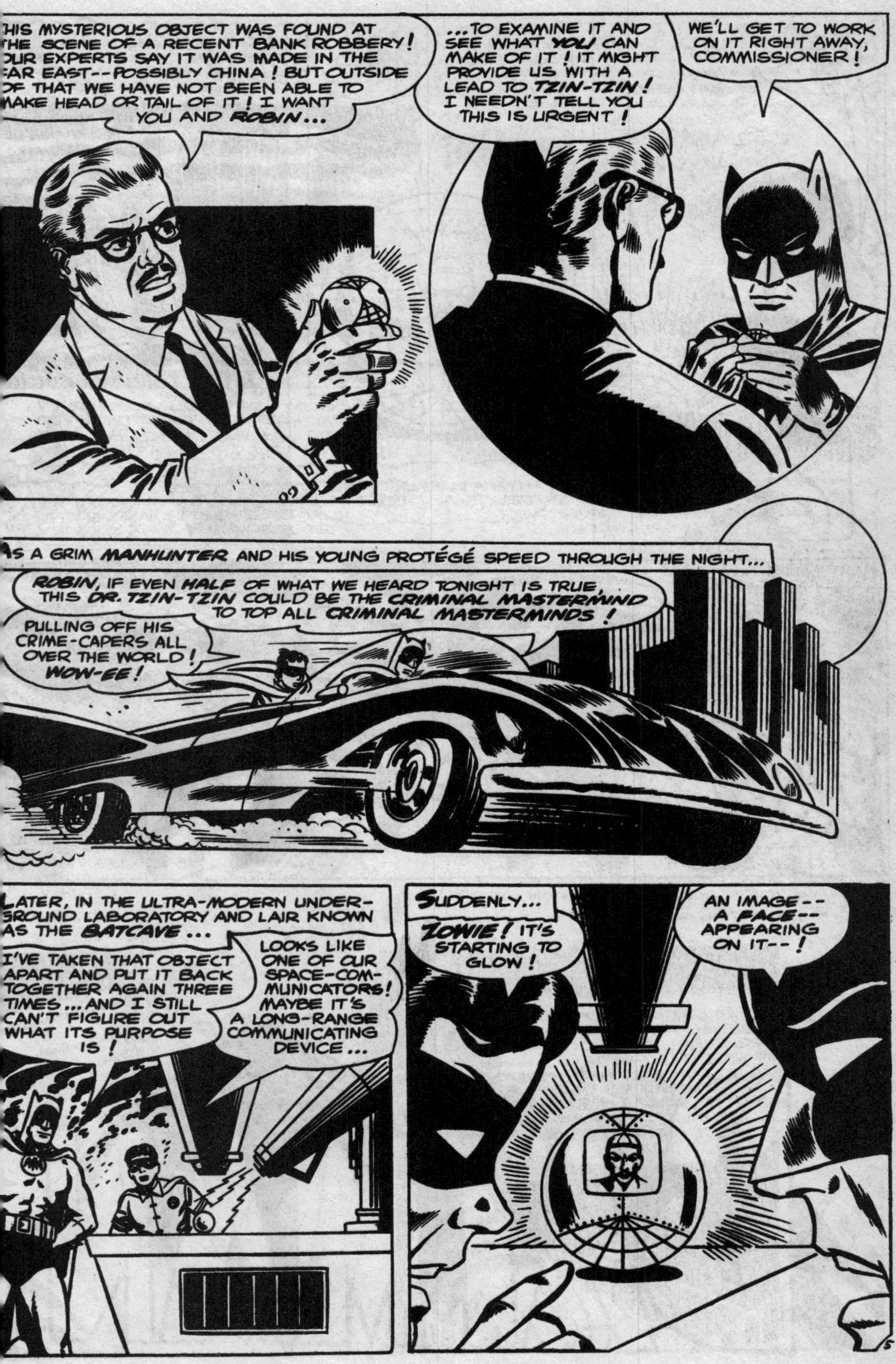
THIS MYSTERIOUS OBJECT WAS FOUND AT THE SCENE OF A RECENT BANK ROBBERY! OUR EXPERTS SAY IT WAS MADE IN THE FAR EAST--POSSIBLY CHINA! BUT OUTSIDE OF THAT WE HAVE NOT BEEN ABLE TO MAKE HEAD OR TAIL OF IT! I WANT YOU AND ROBIN...
...TO EXAMINE IT AND SEE WHAT YOU CAN MAKE OF IT! IT MIGHT PROVIDE US WITH A LEAD TO TZIN-TZIN! I NEEDN'T TELL YOU THIS IS URGENT!
WE'LL GET TO WORK ON IT RIGHT AWAY, COMMISSIONER!
AS A GRIM MANHUNTER AND HIS YOUNG PROTÉGÉ SPEED THROUGH THE NIGHT...
ROBIN, IF EVEN HALF OF WHAT WE HEARD TONIGHT IS TRUE, THIS DR. TZIN-TZIN COULD BE THE CRIMINAL MASTERMIND TO TOP ALL CRIMINAL MASTERMINDS!
PULLING OFF HIS CRIME-CAPERS ALL OVER THE WORLD! WOW-EE!
LATER, IN THE ULTRA-MODERN UNDERGROUND LABORATORY AND LAIR KNOWN AS THE BATCAVE...
I'VE TAKEN THAT OBJECT APART AND PUT IT BACK TOGETHER AGAIN THREE TIMES...AND I STILL CAN'T FIGURE OUT WHAT ITS PURPOSE IS!
LOOKS LIKE ONE OF OUR SPACE-COMMUNICATORS! MAYBE IT'S A LONG-RANGE COMMUNICATING DEVICE...
SUDDENLY...
ZOWIE! IT'S STARTING TO GLOW!
AN IMAGE--A FACE--APPEARING ON IT--!
5

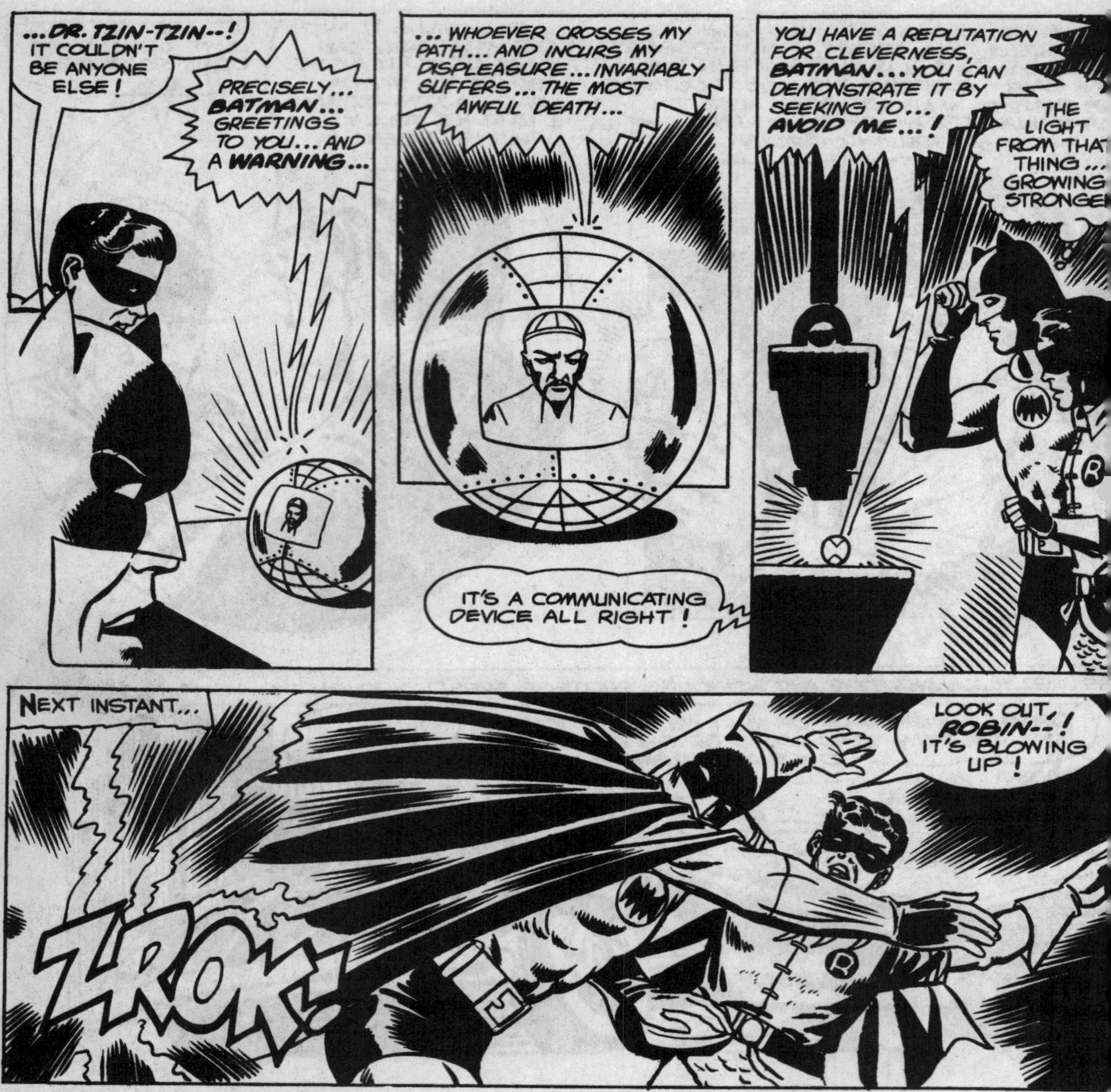
...DR. TZIN-TZIN--! IT COULDN'T BE ANYONE ELSE!
PRECISELY... BATMAN... GREETINGS TO YOU... AND A WARNING...
... WHOEVER CROSSES MY PATH... AND INCURS MY DISPLEASURE... INVARIABLY SUFFERS... THE MOST AWFUL DEATH...
IT'S A COMMUNICATING DEVICE ALL RIGHT!
YOU HAVE A REPUTATION FOR CLEVERNESS, BATMAN... YOU CAN DEMONSTRATE IT BY SEEKING TO... AVOID ME...!
THE LIGHT FROM THA THING... GROWING STRONGE
NEXT INSTANT...
LOOK OUT, ROBIN--! IT'S BLOWING UP!
ZROK!

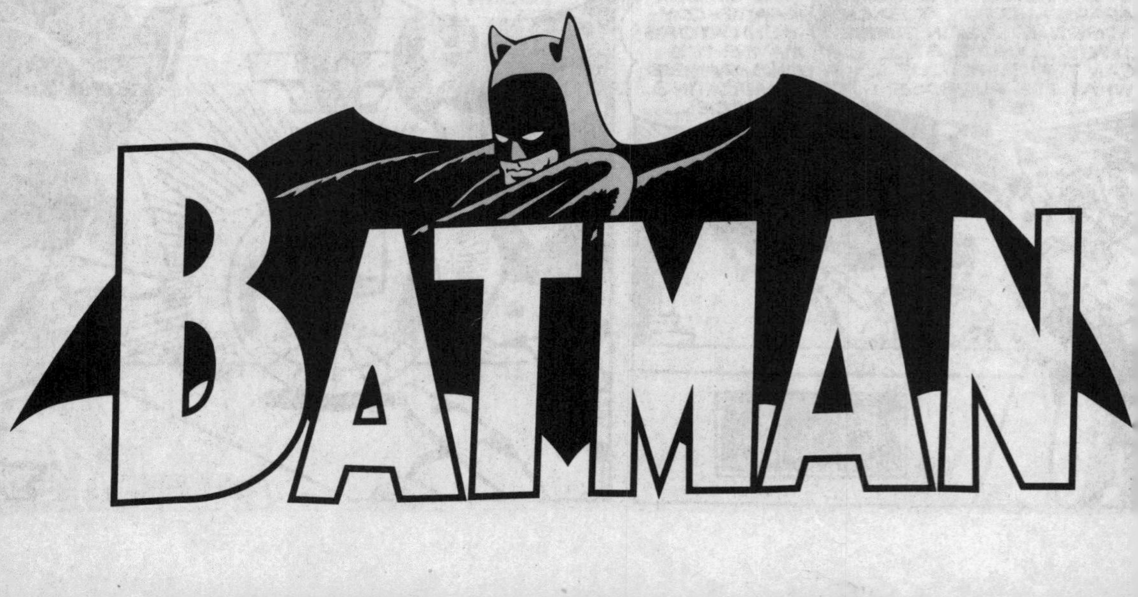
BATMAN

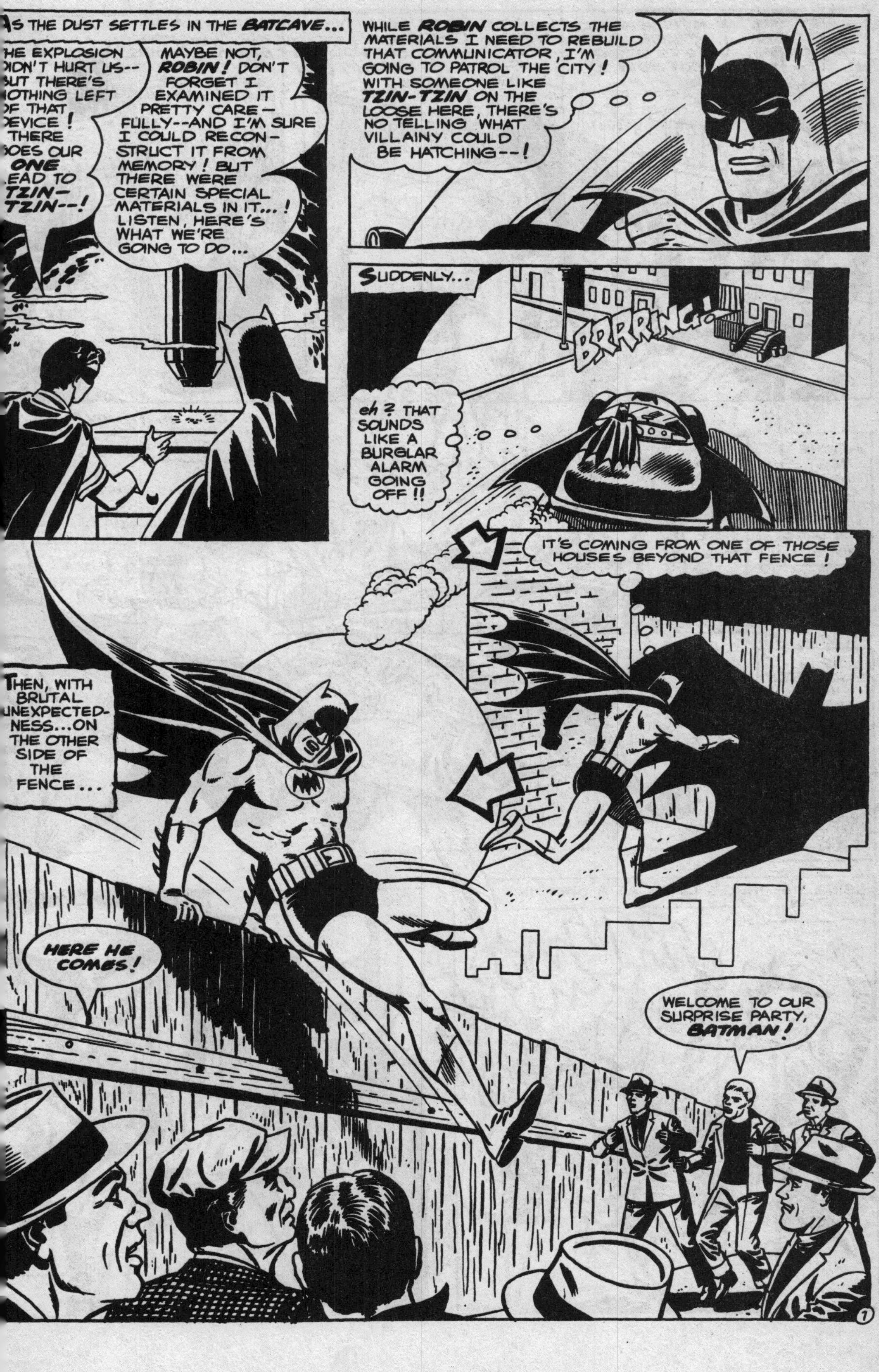
AS THE DUST SETTLES IN THE BATCAVE...
THE EXPLOSION DIDN'T HURT US--BUT THERE'S NOTHING LEFT OF THAT DEVICE! THERE GOES OUR ONE LEAD TO TZIN-TZIN--!
MAYBE NOT, ROBIN! DON'T FORGET I EXAMINED IT PRETTY CARE-FULLY--AND I'M SURE I COULD RECON-STRUCT IT FROM MEMORY! BUT THERE WERE CERTAIN SPECIAL MATERIALS IN IT...! LISTEN, HERE'S WHAT WE'RE GOING TO DO...
WHILE ROBIN COLLECTS THE MATERIALS I NEED TO REBUILD THAT COMMUNICATOR, I'M GOING TO PATROL THE CITY! WITH SOMEONE LIKE TZIN-TZIN ON THE LOOSE HERE, THERE'S NO TELLING WHAT VILLAINY COULD BE HATCHING--!
SUDDENLY...
BRRRING!
eh? THAT SOUNDS LIKE A BURGLAR ALARM GOING OFF!!
IT'S COMING FROM ONE OF THOSE HOUSES BEYOND THAT FENCE!
THEN, WITH BRUTAL UNEXPECTED-NESS...ON THE OTHER SIDE OF THE FENCE...
HERE HE COMES!
WELCOME TO OUR SURPRISE PARTY, BATMAN!
7

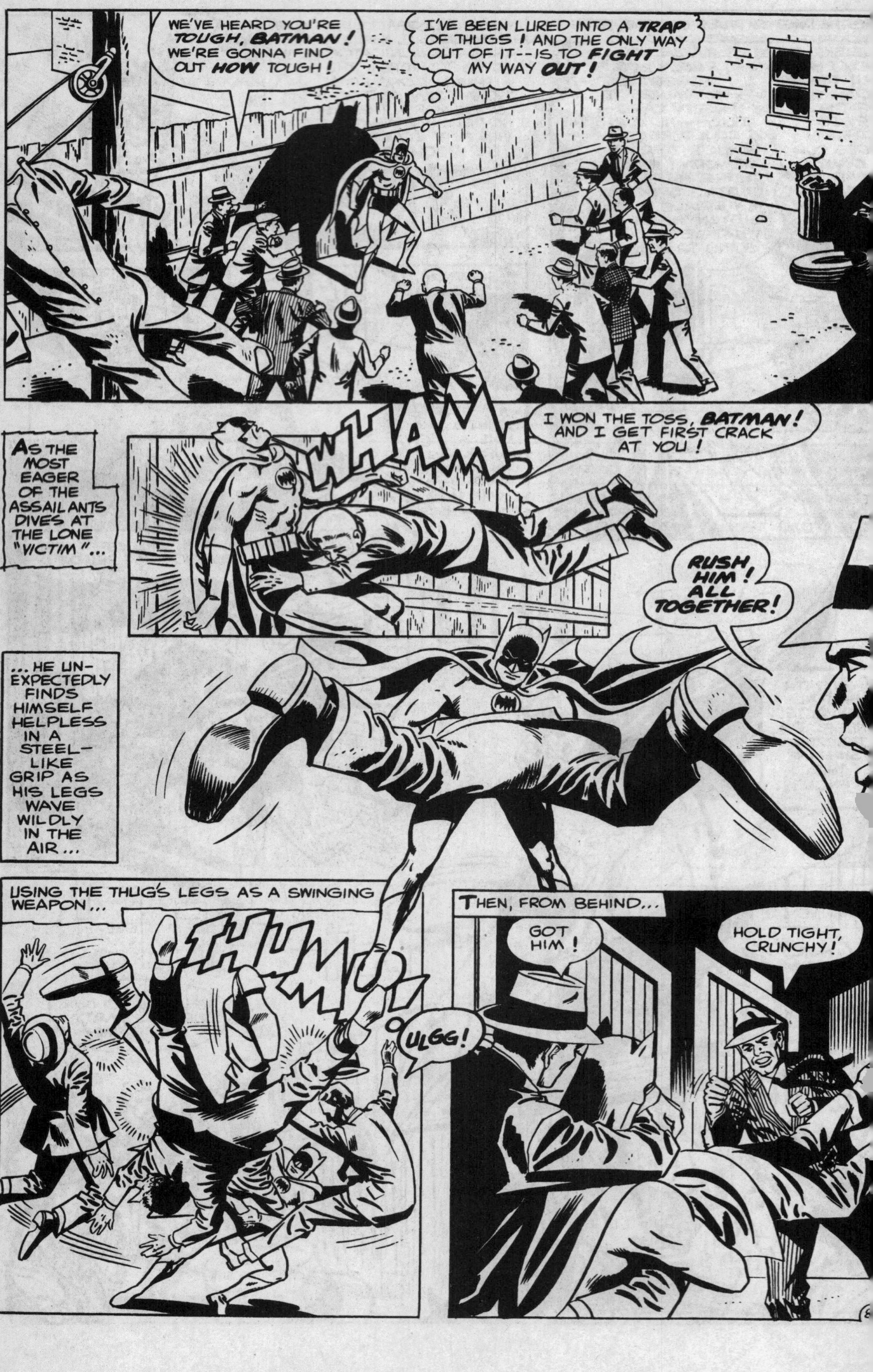
WE'VE HEARD YOU'RE TOUGH, BATMAN! WE'RE GONNA FIND OUT HOW TOUGH!
I'VE BEEN LURED INTO A TRAP OF THUGS! AND THE ONLY WAY OUT OF IT--IS TO FIGHT MY WAY OUT!
AS THE MOST EAGER OF THE ASSAILANTS DIVES AT THE LONE "VICTIM"...
WHAM!
I WON THE TOSS, BATMAN! AND I GET FIRST CRACK AT YOU!
...HE UNEXPECTEDLY FINDS HIMSELF HELPLESS IN A STEEL-LIKE GRIP AS HIS LEGS WAVE WILDLY IN THE AIR...
RUSH HIM! ALL TOGETHER!
USING THE THUG'S LEGS AS A SWINGING WEAPON...
THUMP!
ULGG!
THEN, FROM BEHIND...
GOT HIM!
HOLD TIGHT, CRUNCHY!

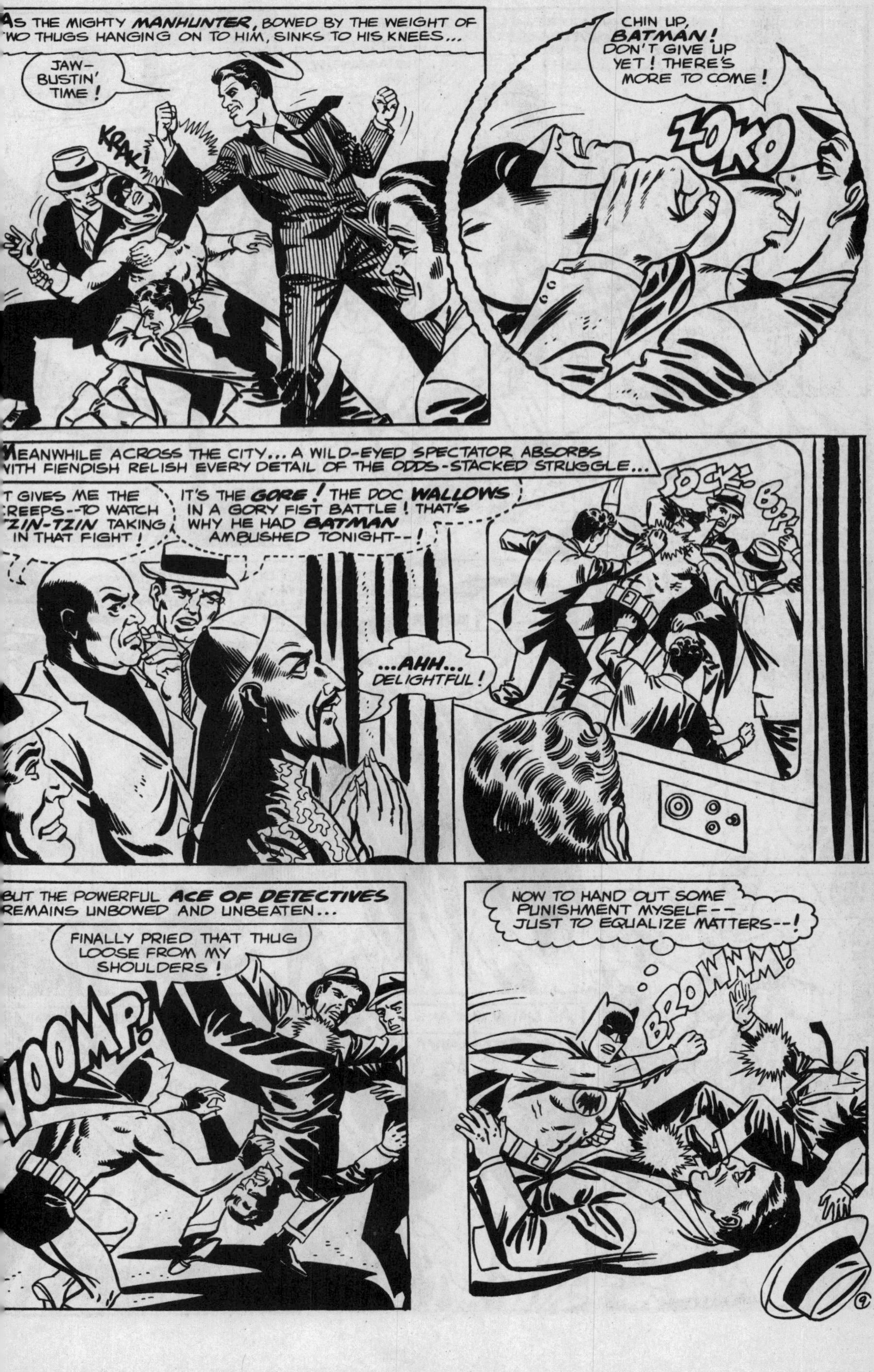
AS THE MIGHTY MANHUNTER, BOWED BY THE WEIGHT OF TWO THUGS HANGING ON TO HIM, SINKS TO HIS KNEES...
JAW-BUSTIN' TIME!
KRAK!
CHIN UP, BATMAN! DON'T GIVE UP YET! THERE'S MORE TO COME!
ZOKO
MEANWHILE ACROSS THE CITY... A WILD-EYED SPECTATOR ABSORBS WITH FIENDISH RELISH EVERY DETAIL OF THE ODDS-STACKED STRUGGLE...
IT GIVES ME THE CREEPS--TO WATCH TZIN-TZIN TAKING IN THAT FIGHT!
IT'S THE GORE! THE DOC WALLOWS IN A GORY FIST BATTLE! THAT'S WHY HE HAD BATMAN AMBUSHED TONIGHT--!
SOCK! BOP!
...AHH... DELIGHTFUL!
BUT THE POWERFUL ACE OF DETECTIVES REMAINS UNBOWED AND UNBEATEN...
FINALLY PRIED THAT THUG LOOSE FROM MY SHOULDERS!
VOOMP!
NOW TO HAND OUT SOME PUNISHMENT MYSELF-- JUST TO EQUALIZE MATTERS--!
BROWNM!
9

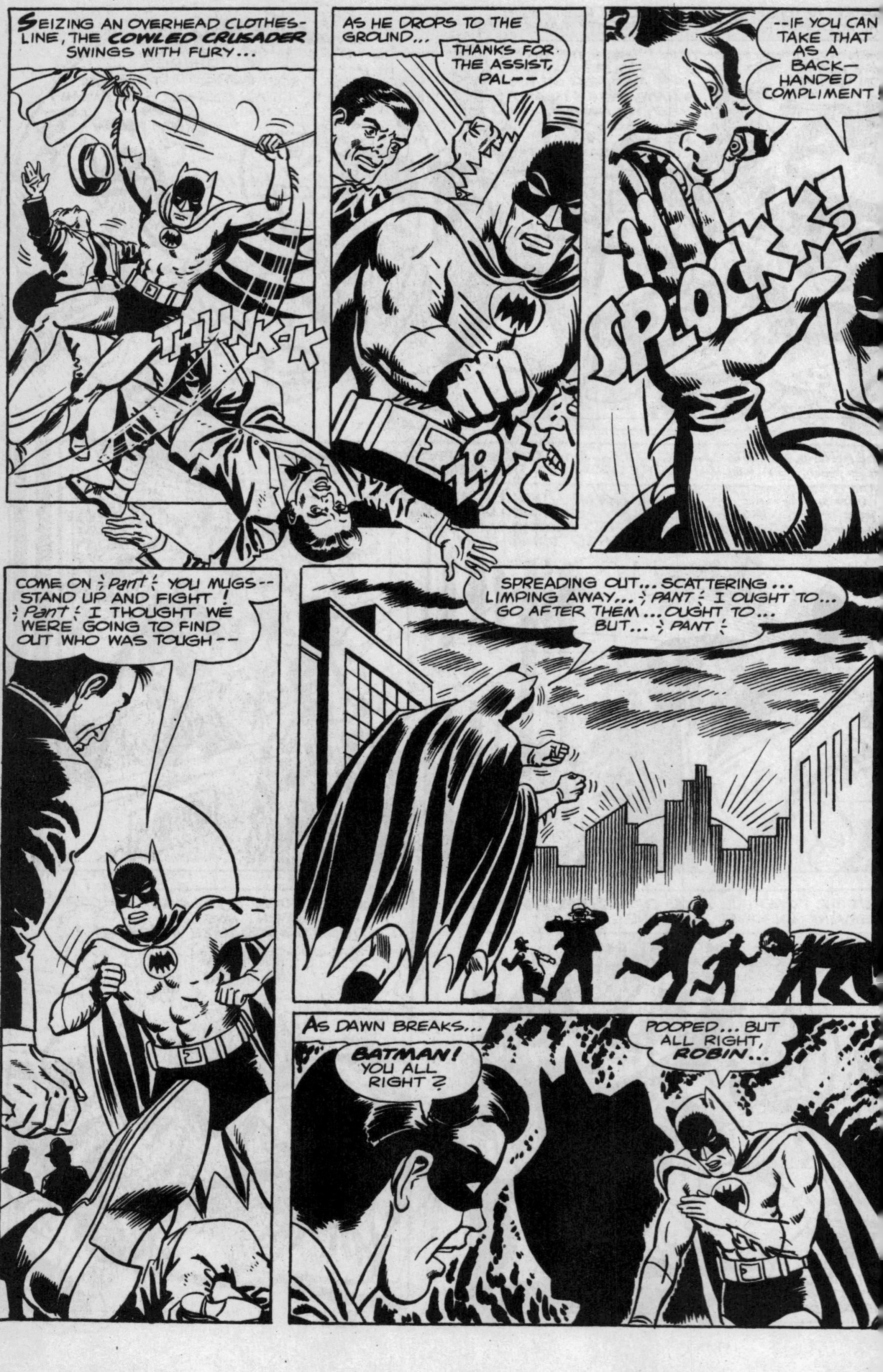
SEIZING AN OVERHEAD CLOTHES-LINE, THE COWLED CRUSADER SWINGS WITH FURY...
THUNK-K
AS HE DROPS TO THE GROUND...
THANKS FOR THE ASSIST, PAL--
ZOK
--IF YOU CAN TAKE THAT AS A BACK-HANDED COMPLIMENT!
SPLOCK!
COME ON ; pant ; YOU MUGS--STAND UP AND FIGHT! ; Pant ; I THOUGHT WE WERE GOING TO FIND OUT WHO WAS TOUGH--
SPREADING OUT... SCATTERING... LIMPING AWAY... ; PANT ; I OUGHT TO... GO AFTER THEM... OUGHT TO... BUT... ; PANT ;
AS DAWN BREAKS...
BATMAN! YOU ALL RIGHT?
POOPED... BUT ALL RIGHT, ROBIN...

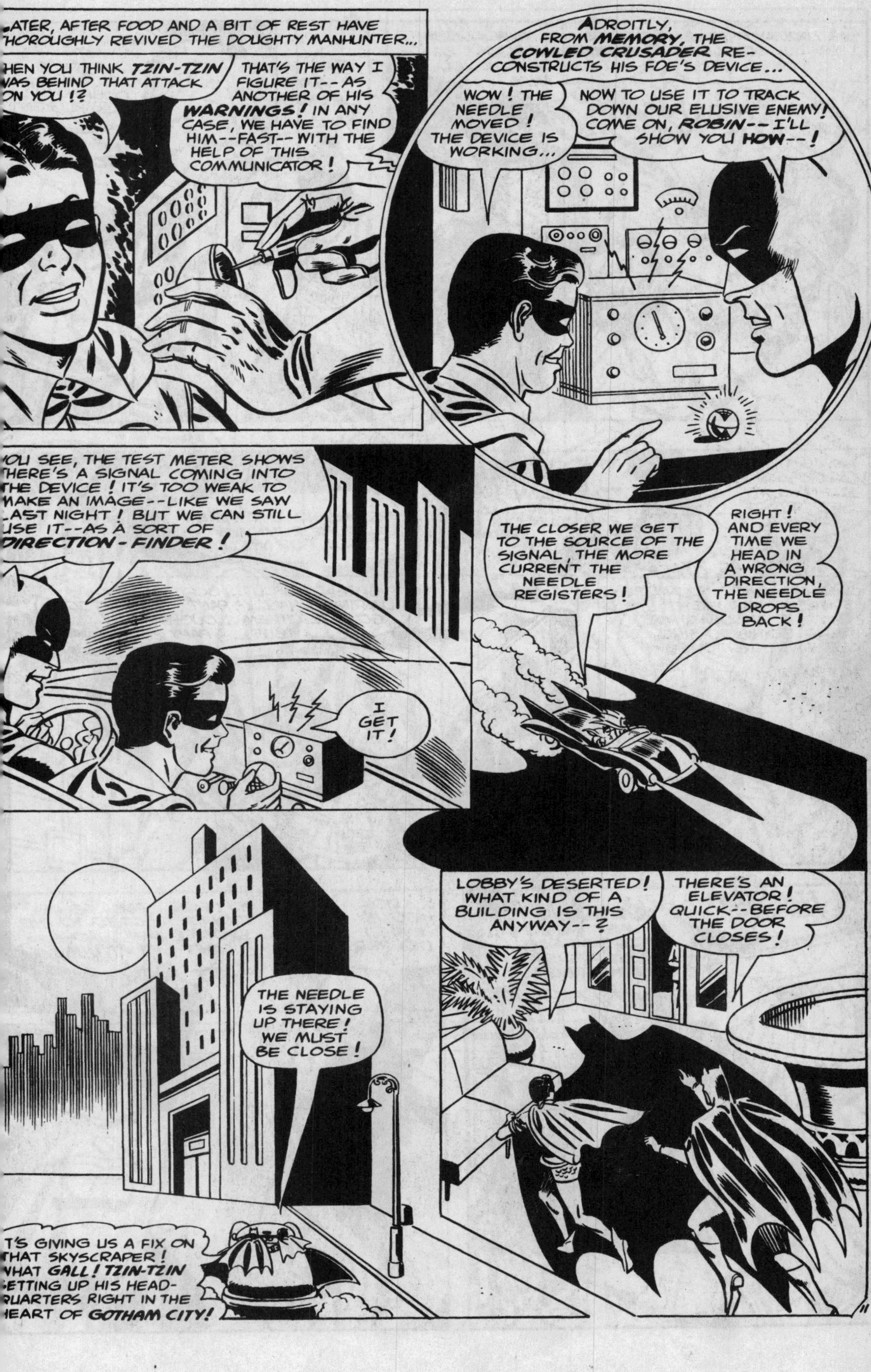
LATER, AFTER FOOD AND A BIT OF REST HAVE THOROUGHLY REVIVED THE DOUGHTY MANHUNTER...
THEN YOU THINK TZIN-TZIN WAS BEHIND THAT ATTACK ON YOU !?
THAT'S THE WAY I FIGURE IT-- AS ANOTHER OF HIS WARNINGS! IN ANY CASE, WE HAVE TO FIND HIM--FAST-- WITH THE HELP OF THIS COMMUNICATOR!
ADROITLY, FROM MEMORY, THE COWLED CRUSADER RE-CONSTRUCTS HIS FOE'S DEVICE...
WOW! THE NEEDLE MOVED! THE DEVICE IS WORKING...
NOW TO USE IT TO TRACK DOWN OUR ELUSIVE ENEMY! COME ON, ROBIN-- I'LL SHOW YOU HOW--!
YOU SEE, THE TEST METER SHOWS THERE'S A SIGNAL COMING INTO THE DEVICE! IT'S TOO WEAK TO MAKE AN IMAGE--LIKE WE SAW LAST NIGHT! BUT WE CAN STILL USE IT--AS A SORT OF DIRECTION-FINDER!
I GET IT!
THE CLOSER WE GET TO THE SOURCE OF THE SIGNAL, THE MORE CURRENT THE NEEDLE REGISTERS!
RIGHT! AND EVERY TIME WE HEAD IN A WRONG DIRECTION, THE NEEDLE DROPS BACK!
THE NEEDLE IS STAYING UP THERE! WE MUST BE CLOSE!
IT'S GIVING US A FIX ON THAT SKYSCRAPER! WHAT GALL! TZIN-TZIN SETTING UP HIS HEAD-QUARTERS RIGHT IN THE HEART OF GOTHAM CITY!
LOBBY'S DESERTED! WHAT KIND OF A BUILDING IS THIS ANYWAY--?
THERE'S AN ELEVATOR! QUICK--BEFORE THE DOOR CLOSES!
11

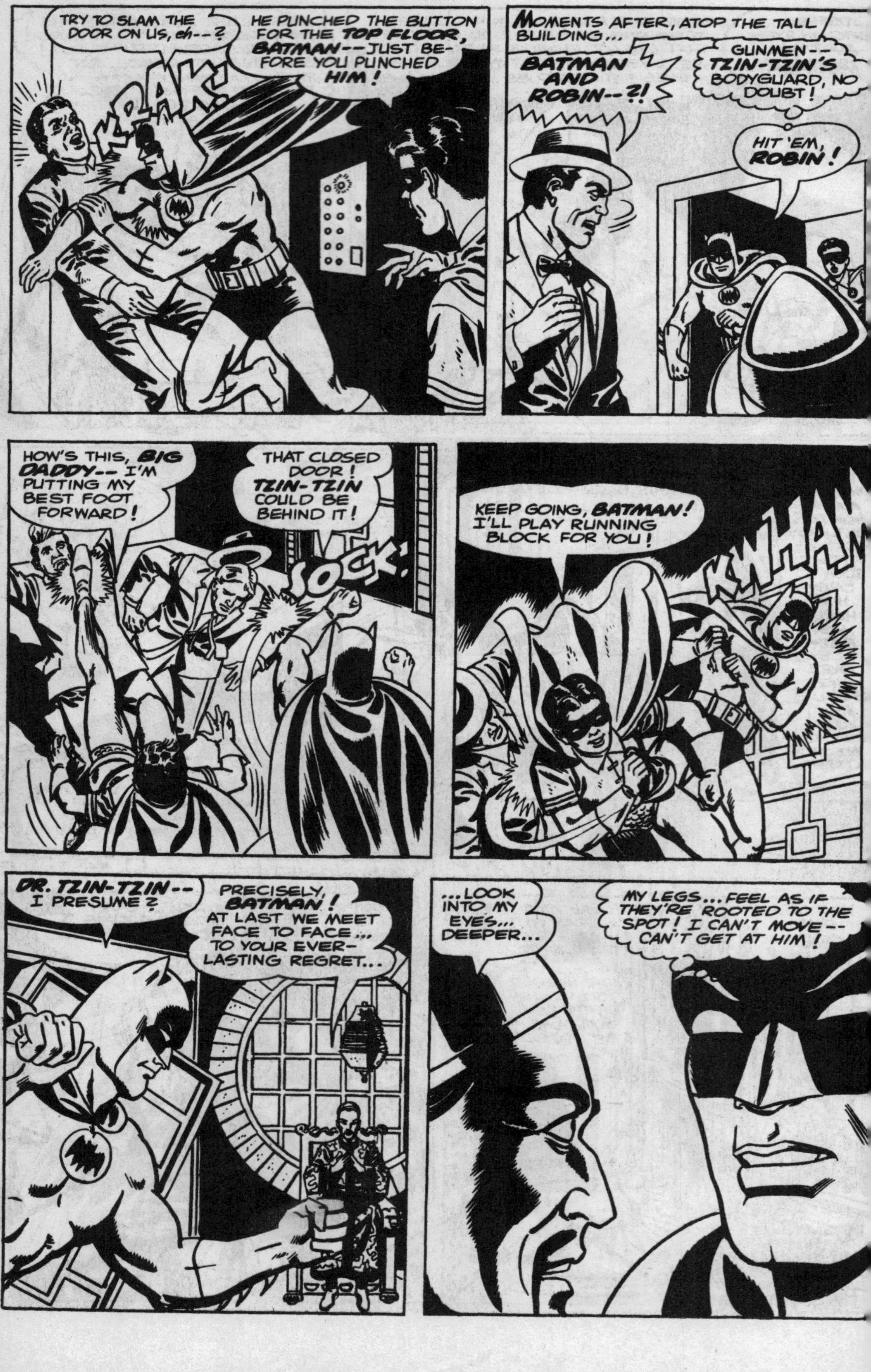
TRY TO SLAM THE DOOR ON US, eh--?
KRAK!
HE PUNCHED THE BUTTON FOR THE TOP FLOOR, BATMAN--JUST BEFORE YOU PUNCHED HIM!
MOMENTS AFTER, ATOP THE TALL BUILDING...
BATMAN AND ROBIN--?!
GUNMEN--TZIN-TZIN'S BODYGUARD, NO DOUBT!
HIT 'EM, ROBIN!
HOW'S THIS, BIG DADDY--I'M PUTTING MY BEST FOOT FORWARD!
THAT CLOSED DOOR! TZIN-TZIN COULD BE BEHIND IT!
SOCK!
KEEP GOING, BATMAN! I'LL PLAY RUNNING BLOCK FOR YOU!
KWHAM
DR. TZIN-TZIN--I PRESUME?
PRECISELY, BATMAN! AT LAST WE MEET FACE TO FACE... TO YOUR EVERLASTING REGRET...
...LOOK INTO MY EYES... DEEPER...
MY LEGS... FEEL AS IF THEY'RE ROOTED TO THE SPOT! I CAN'T MOVE--CAN'T GET AT HIM!

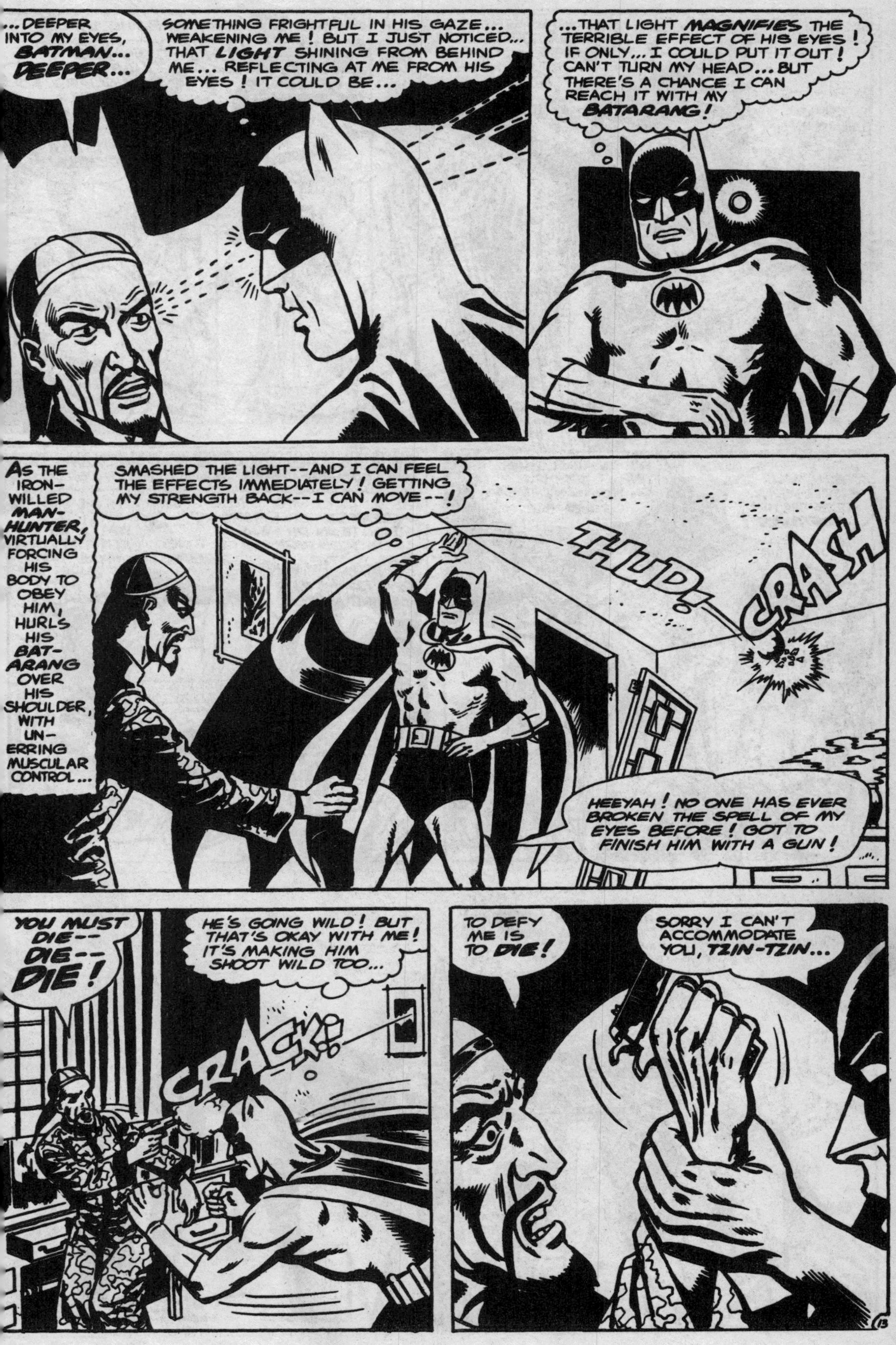
...DEEPER INTO MY EYES, BATMAN... DEEPER...
SOMETHING FRIGHTFUL IN HIS GAZE... WEAKENING ME! BUT I JUST NOTICED... THAT LIGHT SHINING FROM BEHIND ME... REFLECTING AT ME FROM HIS EYES! IT COULD BE...
...THAT LIGHT MAGNIFIES THE TERRIBLE EFFECT OF HIS EYES! IF ONLY... I COULD PUT IT OUT! CAN'T TURN MY HEAD... BUT THERE'S A CHANCE I CAN REACH IT WITH MY BATARANG!
AS THE IRON-WILLED MAN-HUNTER, VIRTUALLY FORCING HIS BODY TO OBEY HIM, HURLS HIS BAT-ARANG OVER HIS SHOULDER, WITH UN-ERRING MUSCULAR CONTROL...
SMASHED THE LIGHT--AND I CAN FEEL THE EFFECTS IMMEDIATELY! GETTING MY STRENGTH BACK--I CAN MOVE--!
THUD!
CRASH
HEEYAH! NO ONE HAS EVER BROKEN THE SPELL OF MY EYES BEFORE! GOT TO FINISH HIM WITH A GUN!
YOU MUST DIE--DIE--DIE!
HE'S GOING WILD! BUT THAT'S OKAY WITH ME! IT'S MAKING HIM SHOOT WILD TOO...
CRACK!
CRACK
TO DEFY ME IS TO DIE!
SORRY I CAN'T ACCOMMODATE YOU, TZIN-TZIN...
13

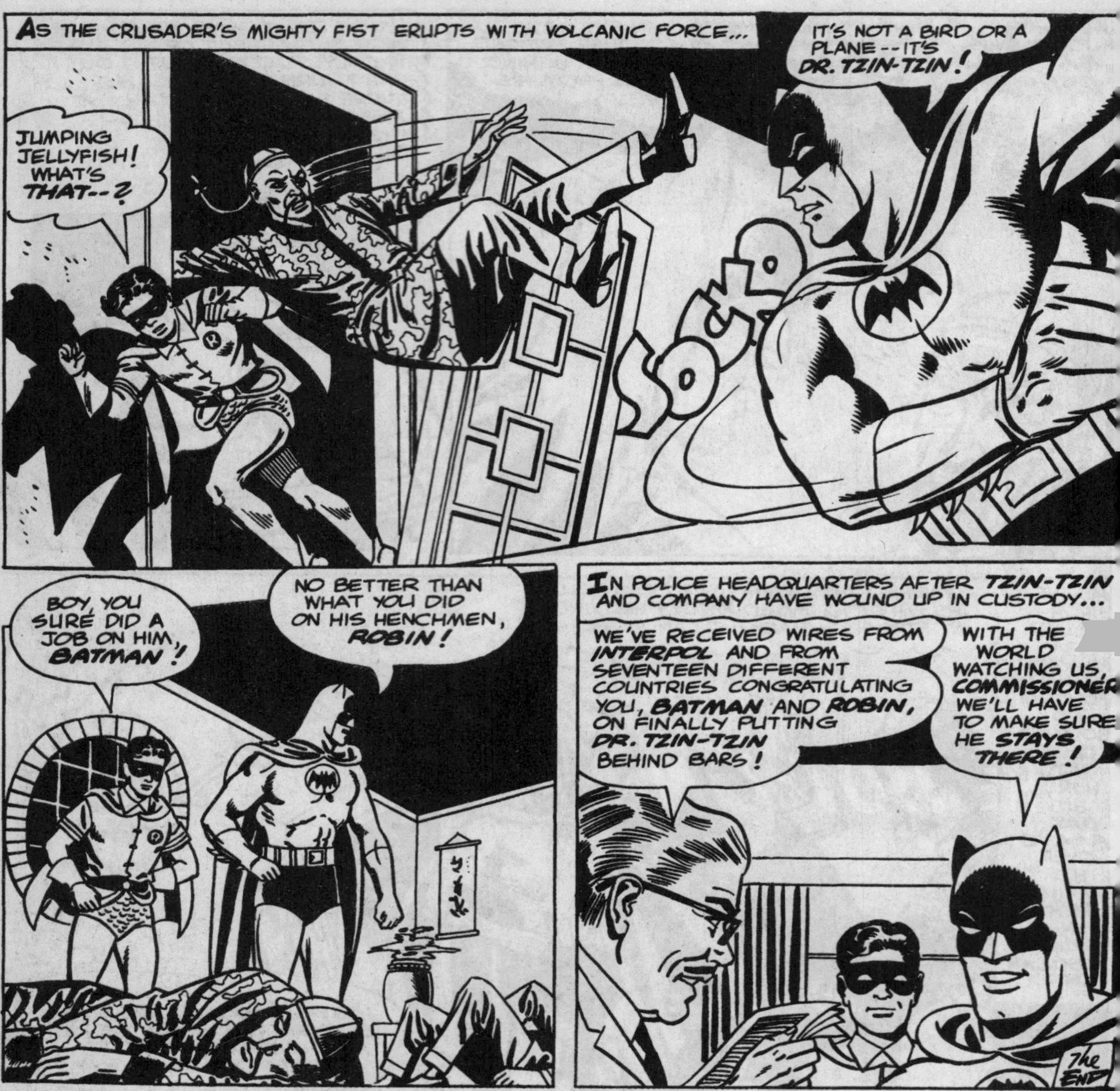
AS THE CRUSADER'S MIGHTY FIST ERUPTS WITH VOLCANIC FORCE...
IT'S NOT A BIRD OR A PLANE -- IT'S DR. TZIN-TZIN!
JUMPING JELLYFISH! WHAT'S THAT--?
SOCKO
BOY, YOU SURE DID A JOB ON HIM, BATMAN!
NO BETTER THAN WHAT YOU DID ON HIS HENCHMEN, ROBIN!
IN POLICE HEADQUARTERS AFTER TZIN-TZIN AND COMPANY HAVE WOUND UP IN CUSTODY...
WE'VE RECEIVED WIRES FROM INTERPOL AND FROM SEVENTEEN DIFFERENT COUNTRIES CONGRATULATING YOU, BATMAN AND ROBIN, ON FINALLY PUTTING DR. TZIN-TZIN BEHIND BARS!
WITH THE WORLD WATCHING US, COMMISSIONER WE'LL HAVE TO MAKE SURE HE STAYS THERE!
The END

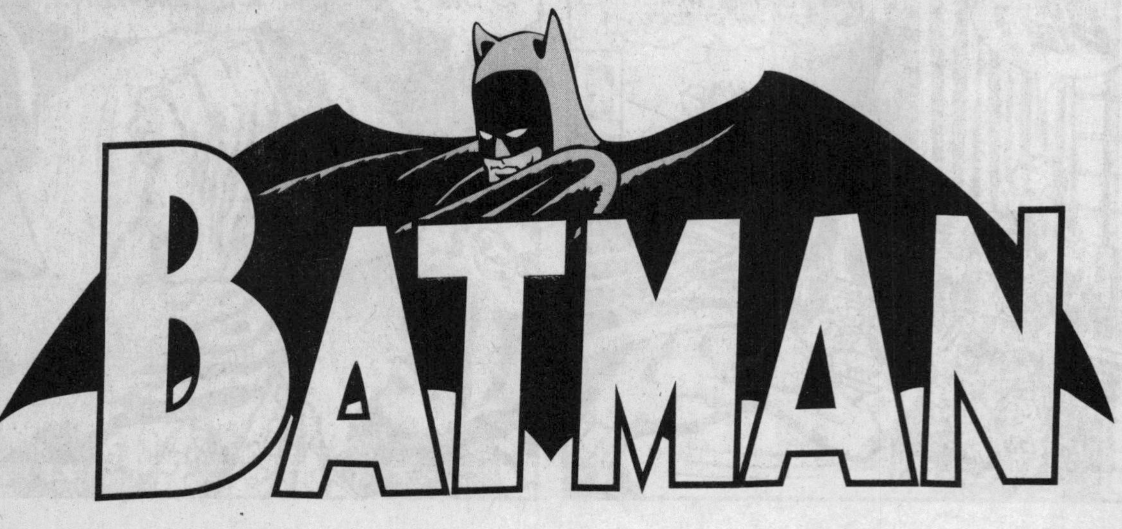
BATMAN

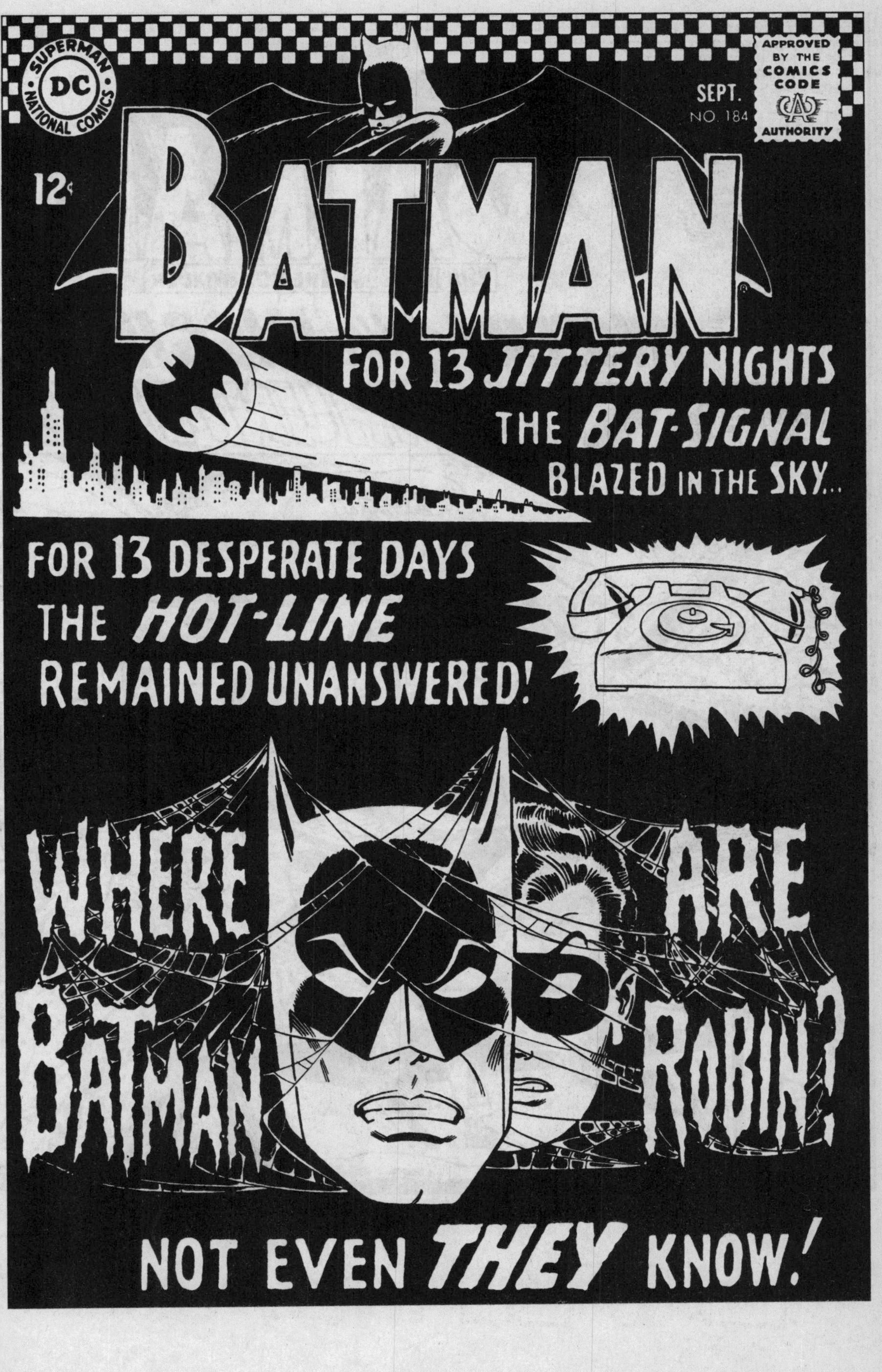
SUPERMAN DC NATIONAL COMICS
APPROVED BY THE COMICS CODE AUTHORITY
SEPT.
NO. 184
12¢
BATMAN
FOR 13 JITTERY NIGHTS
THE BAT-SIGNAL
BLAZED IN THE SKY...
FOR 13 DESPERATE DAYS
THE HOT-LINE
REMAINED UNANSWERED!
WHERE ARE
BATMAN ROBIN?
NOT EVEN THEY KNOW.!

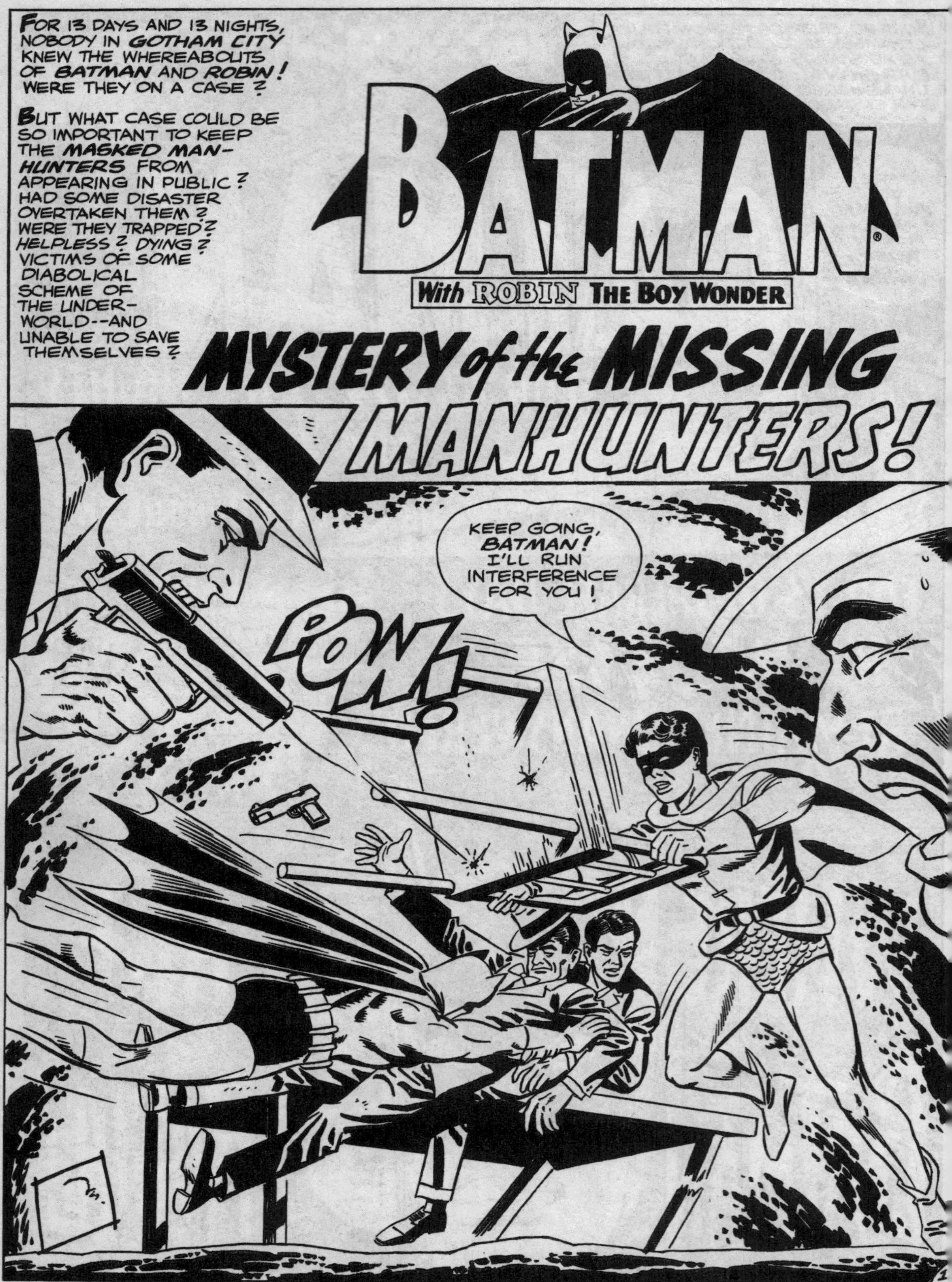
FOR 13 DAYS AND 13 NIGHTS, NOBODY IN GOTHAM CITY KNEW THE WHEREABOUTS OF BATMAN AND ROBIN! WERE THEY ON A CASE?
BUT WHAT CASE COULD BE SO IMPORTANT TO KEEP THE MASKED MAN-HUNTERS FROM APPEARING IN PUBLIC? HAD SOME DISASTER OVERTAKEN THEM? WERE THEY TRAPPED? HELPLESS? DYING? VICTIMS OF SOME DIABOLICAL SCHEME OF THE UNDER-WORLD--AND UNABLE TO SAVE THEMSELVES?
BATMAN®
With ROBIN THE BOY WONDER
MYSTERY of the MISSING MANHUNTERS!
KEEP GOING, BATMAN! I'LL RUN INTERFERENCE FOR YOU!
POW!
1

WORRIED CREASES FURROW POLICE COMMISSIONER GORDON'S BROW AS HE STARES UPWARD AT A *BAT-SIGNAL* THAT HAS GLITTERED UNANSWERED FOR 13 NIGHTS IN THE SKY ABOVE *GOTHAM CITY...*

WHERE ARE *BATMAN* AND *ROBIN*? WHERE? WHERE?

FOR 13 DAYS IN THE *BATCAVE*, THE *HOT-LINE* PHONE GLOWS-- WITH NO RESPONSE...

IN THE BRUCE WAYNE MANSION ABOVE THE *BATCAVE*, THE *HOT-LINE* PHONE RINGS INCESSANTLY WITH ONLY AUNT HARRIET THERE TO COMPLAIN...

THERE IT GOES AGAIN--THAT SAME MYSTERIOUS CALL WITH NOBODY EVER AT THE OTHER END OF THE LINE!

R-R-RING!

AND IN THE *BATMOBILE*, YET ANOTHER *HOT-LINE* PHONE SCREAMS ITS MESSAGE! BUT--NOW-- AT LONG LAST--AFTER A 13 DAY-AND-NIGHT SILENCE, A FAMILIAR GLOVED HAND REACHES FORWARD...

I'LL TAKE THAT, *ROBIN*!

BATMAN! WE'VE BEEN TRYING TO CONTACT YOU FOR ALMOST TWO WEEKS! WHERE IN BLAZES HAVE YOU BEEN?

I DON'T KNOW, COMMISSIONER! I--JUST-- DON'T-- KNOW!

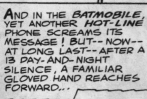

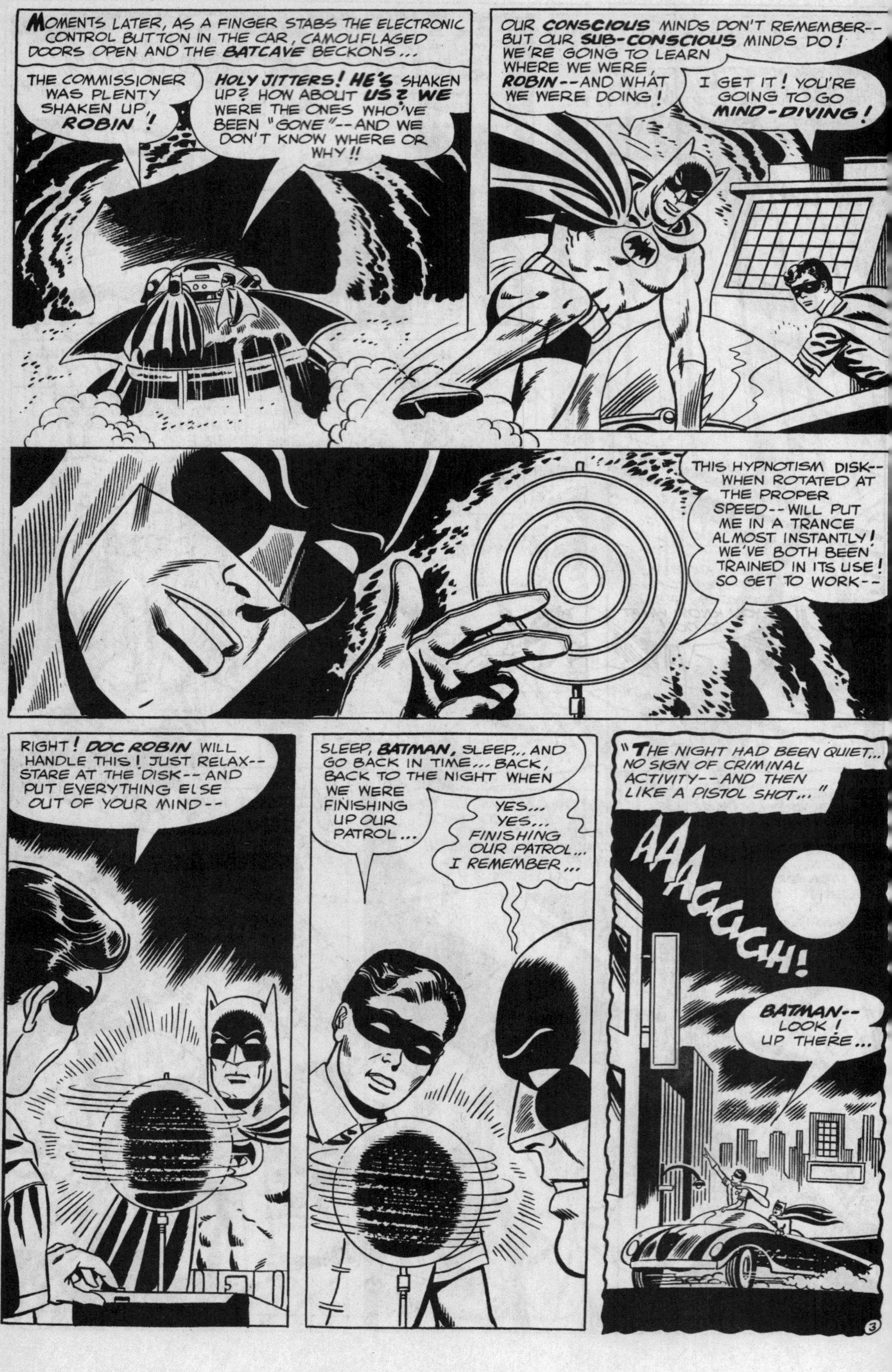
MOMENTS LATER, AS A FINGER STABS THE ELECTRONIC CONTROL BUTTON IN THE CAR, CAMOUFLAGED DOORS OPEN AND THE BATCAVE BECKONS...
THE COMMISSIONER WAS PLENTY SHAKEN UP, ROBIN!
HOLY JITTERS! HE'S SHAKEN UP? HOW ABOUT US? WE WERE THE ONES WHO'VE BEEN "GONE"--AND WE DON'T KNOW WHERE OR WHY!!
OUR CONSCIOUS MINDS DON'T REMEMBER--BUT OUR SUB-CONSCIOUS MINDS DO! WE'RE GOING TO LEARN WHERE WE WERE, ROBIN--AND WHAT WE WERE DOING!
I GET IT! YOU'RE GOING TO GO MIND-DIVING!
THIS HYPNOTISM DISK--WHEN ROTATED AT THE PROPER SPEED--WILL PUT ME IN A TRANCE ALMOST INSTANTLY! WE'VE BOTH BEEN TRAINED IN ITS USE! SO GET TO WORK--
RIGHT! DOC ROBIN WILL HANDLE THIS! JUST RELAX--STARE AT THE DISK--AND PUT EVERYTHING ELSE OUT OF YOUR MIND--
SLEEP, BATMAN, SLEEP... AND GO BACK IN TIME... BACK, BACK TO THE NIGHT WHEN WE WERE FINISHING UP OUR PATROL...
YES... YES... FINISHING OUR PATROL... I REMEMBER...
"THE NIGHT HAD BEEN QUIET... NO SIGN OF CRIMINAL ACTIVITY--AND THEN LIKE A PISTOL SHOT..."
AAAAGGGH!
BATMAN--LOOK! UP THERE...
3

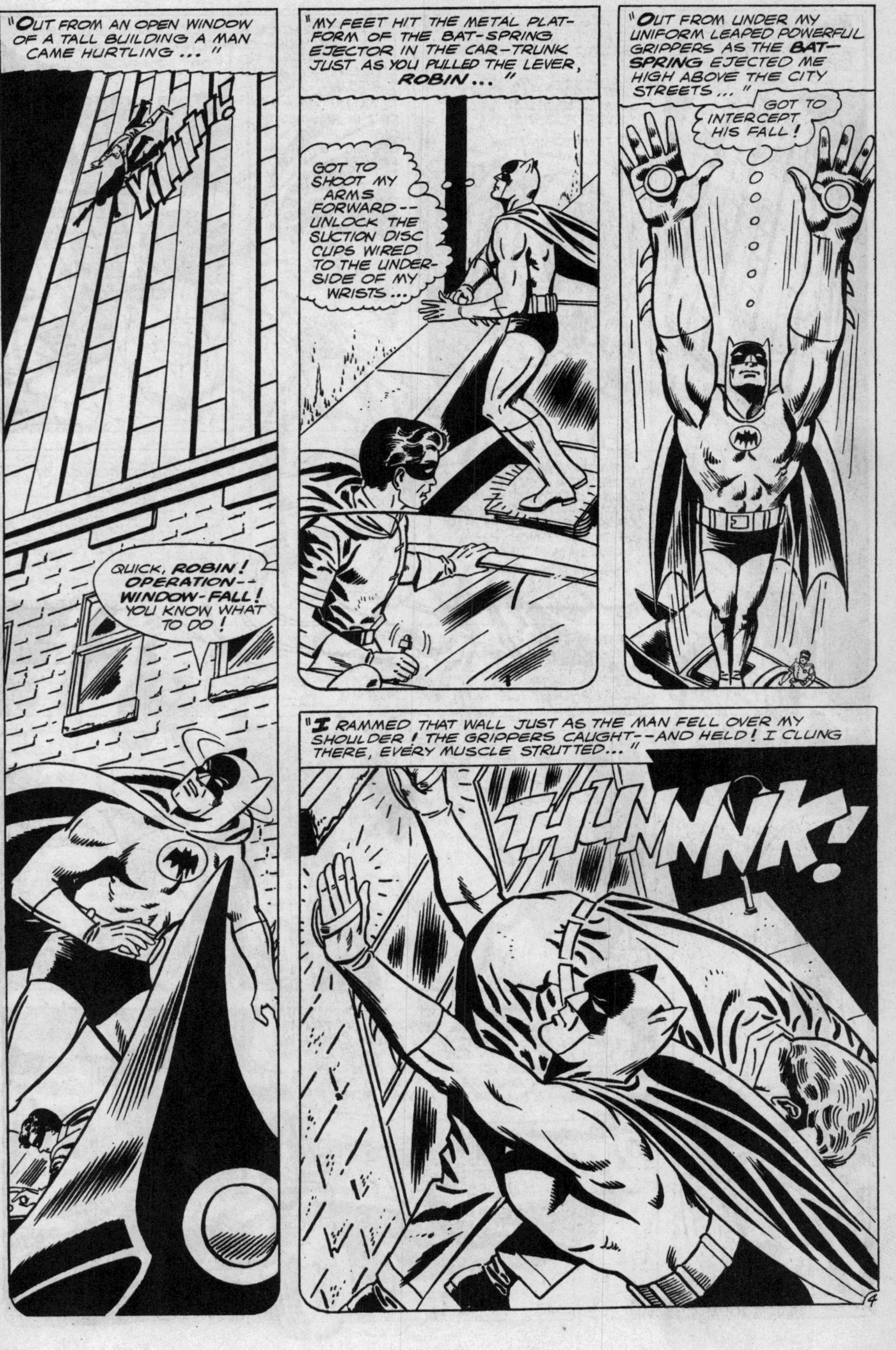
"OUT FROM AN OPEN WINDOW OF A TALL BUILDING A MAN CAME HURTLING ..."
QUICK, ROBIN! OPERATION--WINDOW-FALL! YOU KNOW WHAT TO DO!
"MY FEET HIT THE METAL PLATFORM OF THE BAT-SPRING EJECTOR IN THE CAR-TRUNK JUST AS YOU PULLED THE LEVER, ROBIN ..."
GOT TO SHOOT MY ARMS FORWARD--UNLOCK THE SUCTION DISC CUPS WIRED TO THE UNDERSIDE OF MY WRISTS ...
"OUT FROM UNDER MY UNIFORM LEAPED POWERFUL GRIPPERS AS THE BAT-SPRING EJECTED ME HIGH ABOVE THE CITY STREETS ..."
GOT TO INTERCEPT HIS FALL!
"I RAMMED THAT WALL JUST AS THE MAN FELL OVER MY SHOULDER! THE GRIPPERS CAUGHT--AND HELD! I CLUNG THERE, EVERY MUSCLE STRUTTED ..."
THUNNNK!

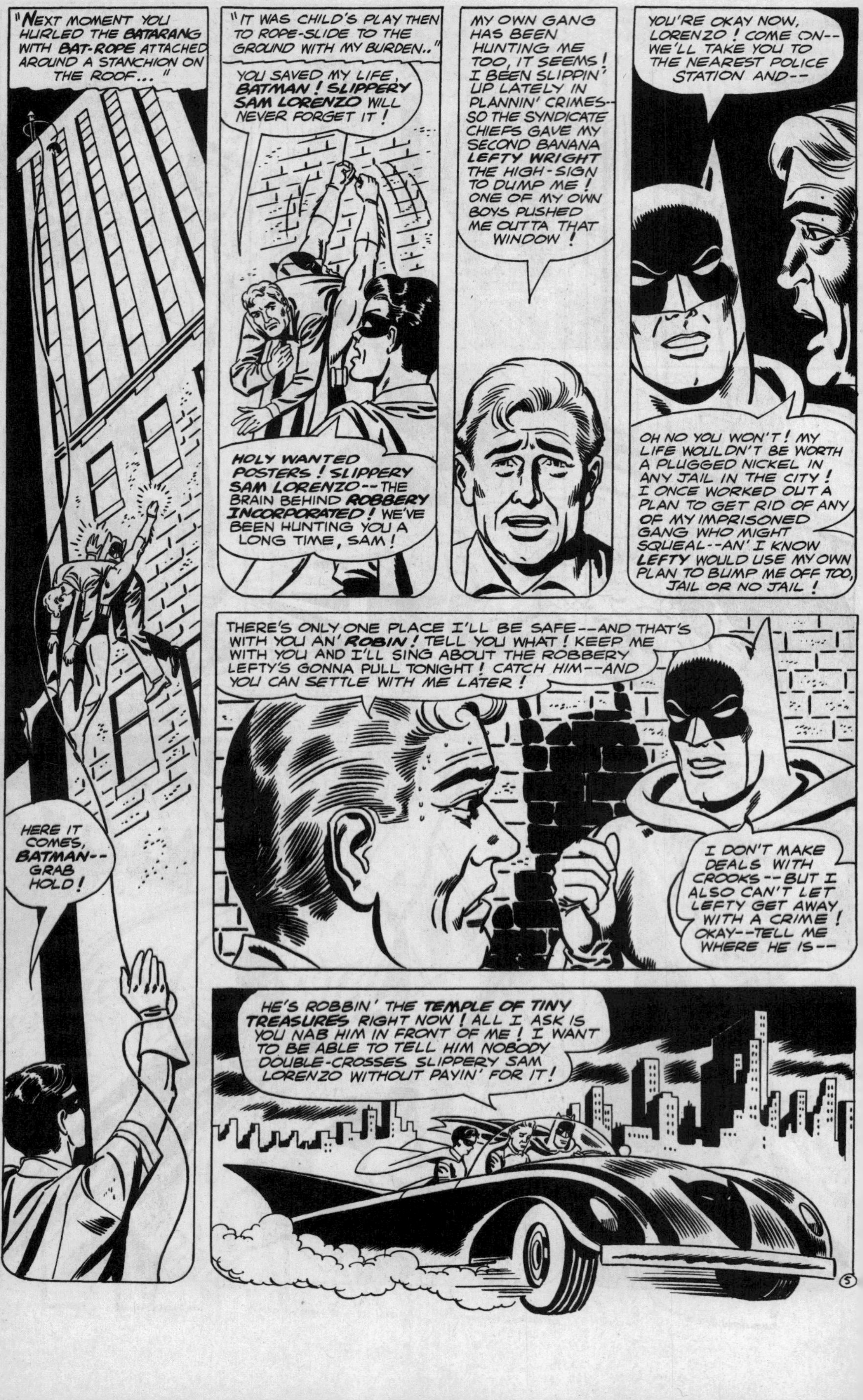
"NEXT MOMENT YOU HURLED THE BATARANG WITH BAT-ROPE ATTACHED AROUND A STANCHION ON THE ROOF..."
HERE IT COMES, BATMAN--GRAB HOLD!
"IT WAS CHILD'S PLAY THEN TO ROPE-SLIDE TO THE GROUND WITH MY BURDEN.."
YOU SAVED MY LIFE, BATMAN! SLIPPERY SAM LORENZO WILL NEVER FORGET IT!
HOLY WANTED POSTERS! SLIPPERY SAM LORENZO--THE BRAIN BEHIND ROBBERY INCORPORATED! WE'VE BEEN HUNTING YOU A LONG TIME, SAM!
MY OWN GANG HAS BEEN HUNTING ME TOO, IT SEEMS! I BEEN SLIPPIN' UP LATELY IN PLANNIN' CRIMES--SO THE SYNDICATE CHIEFS GAVE MY SECOND BANANA LEFTY WRIGHT THE HIGH-SIGN TO DUMP ME! ONE OF MY OWN BOYS PUSHED ME OUTTA THAT WINDOW!
YOU'RE OKAY NOW, LORENZO! COME ON--WE'LL TAKE YOU TO THE NEAREST POLICE STATION AND--
OH NO YOU WON'T! MY LIFE WOULDN'T BE WORTH A PLUGGED NICKEL IN ANY JAIL IN THE CITY! I ONCE WORKED OUT A PLAN TO GET RID OF ANY OF MY IMPRISONED GANG WHO MIGHT SQUEAL--AN' I KNOW LEFTY WOULD USE MY OWN PLAN TO BUMP ME OFF TOO, JAIL OR NO JAIL!
THERE'S ONLY ONE PLACE I'LL BE SAFE--AND THAT'S WITH YOU AN' ROBIN! TELL YOU WHAT! KEEP ME WITH YOU AND I'LL SING ABOUT THE ROBBERY LEFTY'S GONNA PULL TONIGHT! CATCH HIM--AND YOU CAN SETTLE WITH ME LATER!
I DON'T MAKE DEALS WITH CROOKS--BUT I ALSO CAN'T LET LEFTY GET AWAY WITH A CRIME! OKAY--TELL ME WHERE HE IS--
HE'S ROBBIN' THE TEMPLE OF TINY TREASURES RIGHT NOW! ALL I ASK IS YOU NAB HIM IN FRONT OF ME! I WANT TO BE ABLE TO TELL HIM NOBODY DOUBLE-CROSSES SLIPPERY SAM LORENZO WITHOUT PAYIN' FOR IT!
5

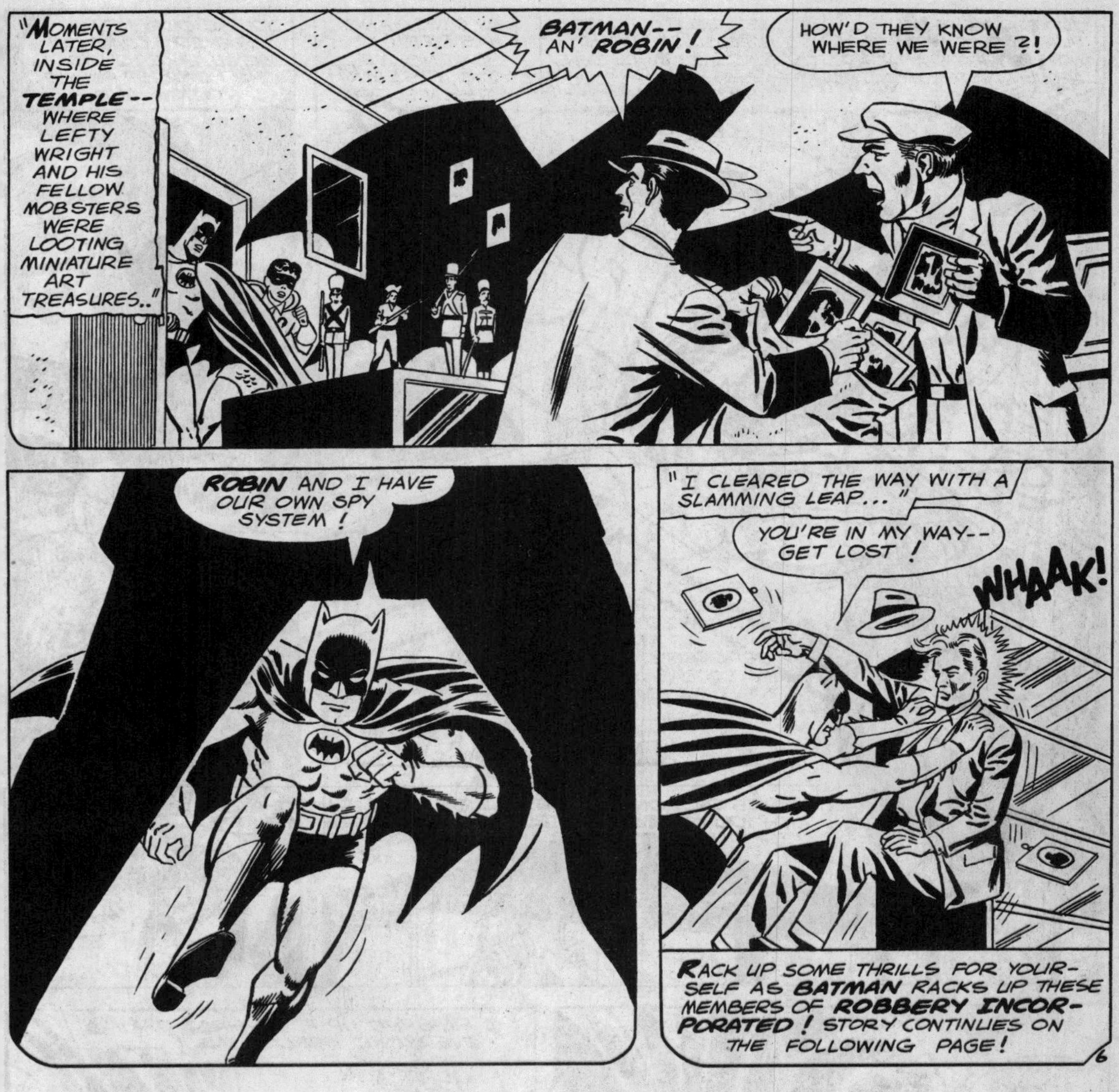
"MOMENTS LATER, INSIDE THE TEMPLE-- WHERE LEFTY WRIGHT AND HIS FELLOW MOBSTERS WERE LOOTING MINIATURE ART TREASURES.."
BATMAN-- AN' ROBIN!
HOW'D THEY KNOW WHERE WE WERE ?!
ROBIN AND I HAVE OUR OWN SPY SYSTEM!
"I CLEARED THE WAY WITH A SLAMMING LEAP..."
YOU'RE IN MY WAY-- GET LOST!
WHAAK!
RACK UP SOME THRILLS FOR YOURSELF AS BATMAN RACKS UP THESE MEMBERS OF ROBBERY INCORPORATED! STORY CONTINUES ON THE FOLLOWING PAGE!
6

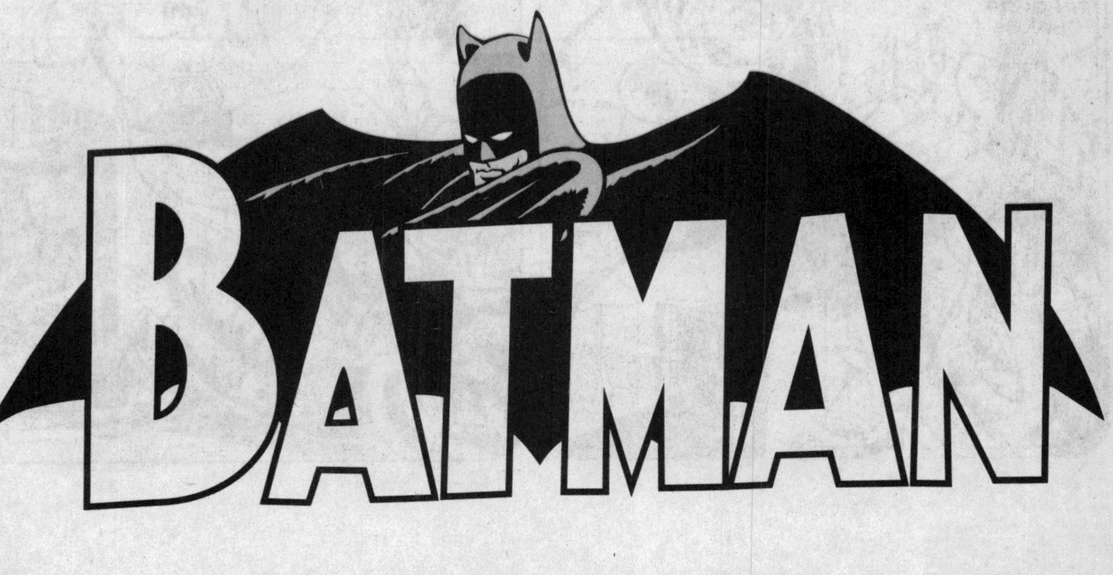
BATMAN

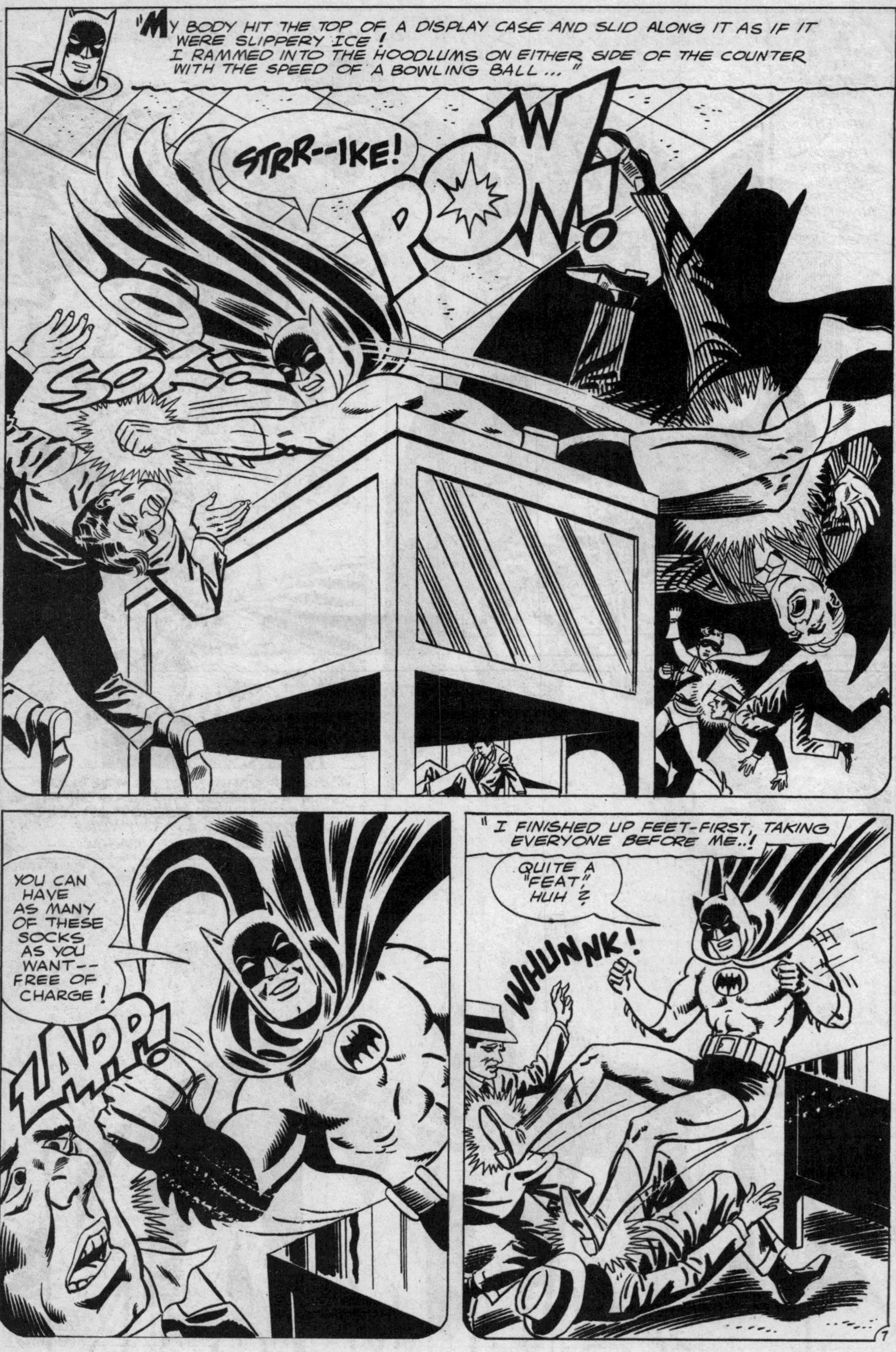
"MY BODY HIT THE TOP OF A DISPLAY CASE AND SLID ALONG IT AS IF IT WERE SLIPPERY ICE!
I RAMMED INTO THE HOODLUMS ON EITHER SIDE OF THE COUNTER WITH THE SPEED OF A BOWLING BALL..."
STRR--IKE!
POW!
SOK!
YOU CAN HAVE AS MANY OF THESE SOCKS AS YOU WANT-- FREE OF CHARGE!
ZAPP!
"I FINISHED UP FEET-FIRST, TAKING EVERYONE BEFORE ME..!
QUITE A "FEAT," HUH?
WHUNNK!
7

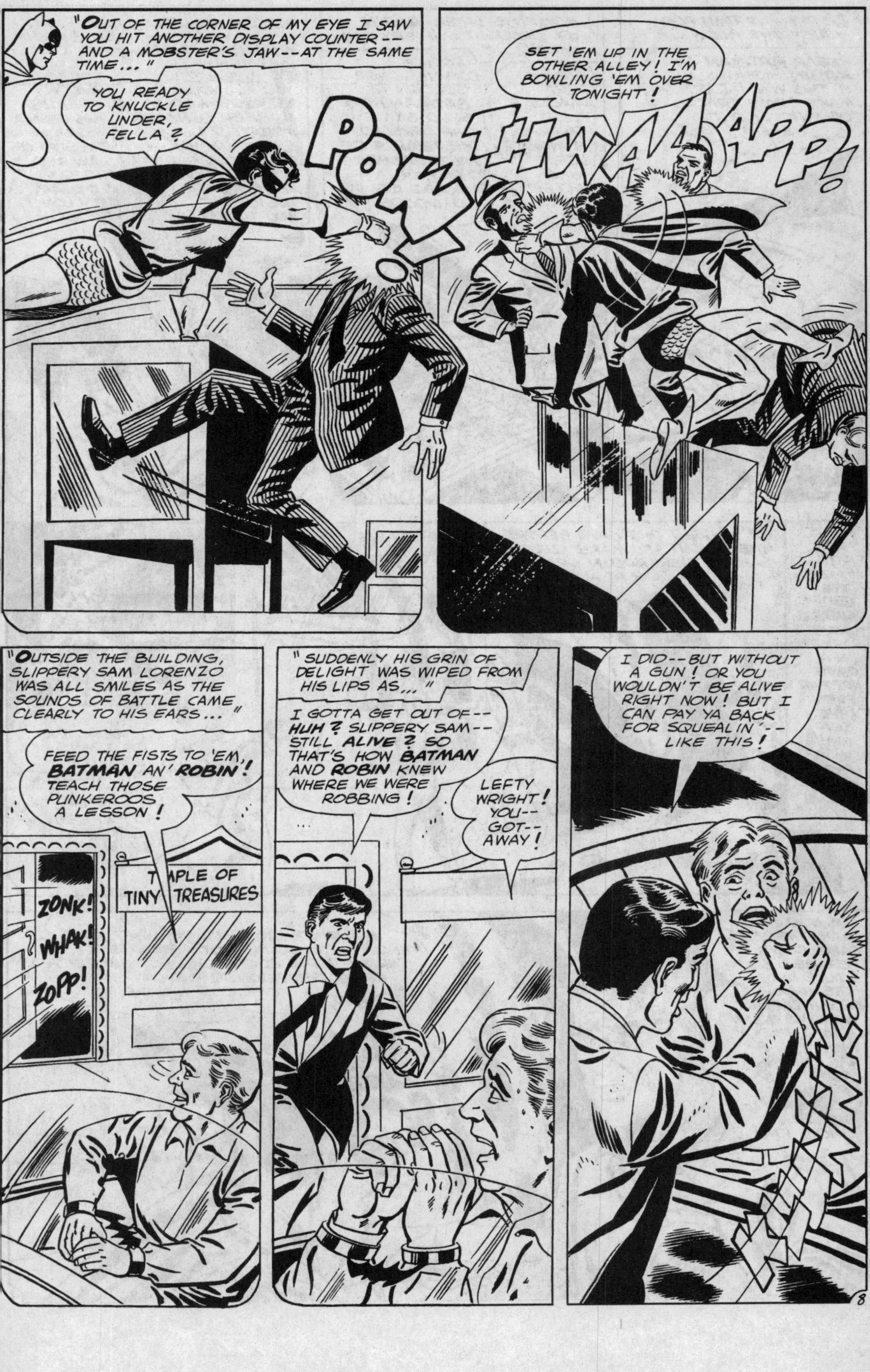
"OUT OF THE CORNER OF MY EYE I SAW YOU HIT ANOTHER DISPLAY COUNTER -- AND A MOBSTER'S JAW--AT THE SAME TIME..."
YOU READY TO KNUCKLE UNDER, FELLA?
POW!
SET 'EM UP IN THE OTHER ALLEY! I'M BOWLING 'EM OVER TONIGHT!
THWAAAPP!
"OUTSIDE THE BUILDING, SLIPPERY SAM LORENZO WAS ALL SMILES AS THE SOUNDS OF BATTLE CAME CLEARLY TO HIS EARS..."
FEED THE FISTS TO 'EM, BATMAN AN' ROBIN! TEACH THOSE PUNKEROOS A LESSON!
TEMPLE OF TINY TREASURES
ZONK!
WHAK!
ZOPP!
"SUDDENLY HIS GRIN OF DELIGHT WAS WIPED FROM HIS LIPS AS..."
I GOTTA GET OUT OF-- HUH? SLIPPERY SAM--STILL ALIVE? SO THAT'S HOW BATMAN AND ROBIN KNEW WHERE WE WERE ROBBING!
LEFTY WRIGHT! YOU--GOT--AWAY!
I DID--BUT WITHOUT A GUN! OR YOU WOULDN'T BE ALIVE RIGHT NOW! BUT I CAN PAY YA BACK FOR SQUEALIN'--LIKE THIS!
8

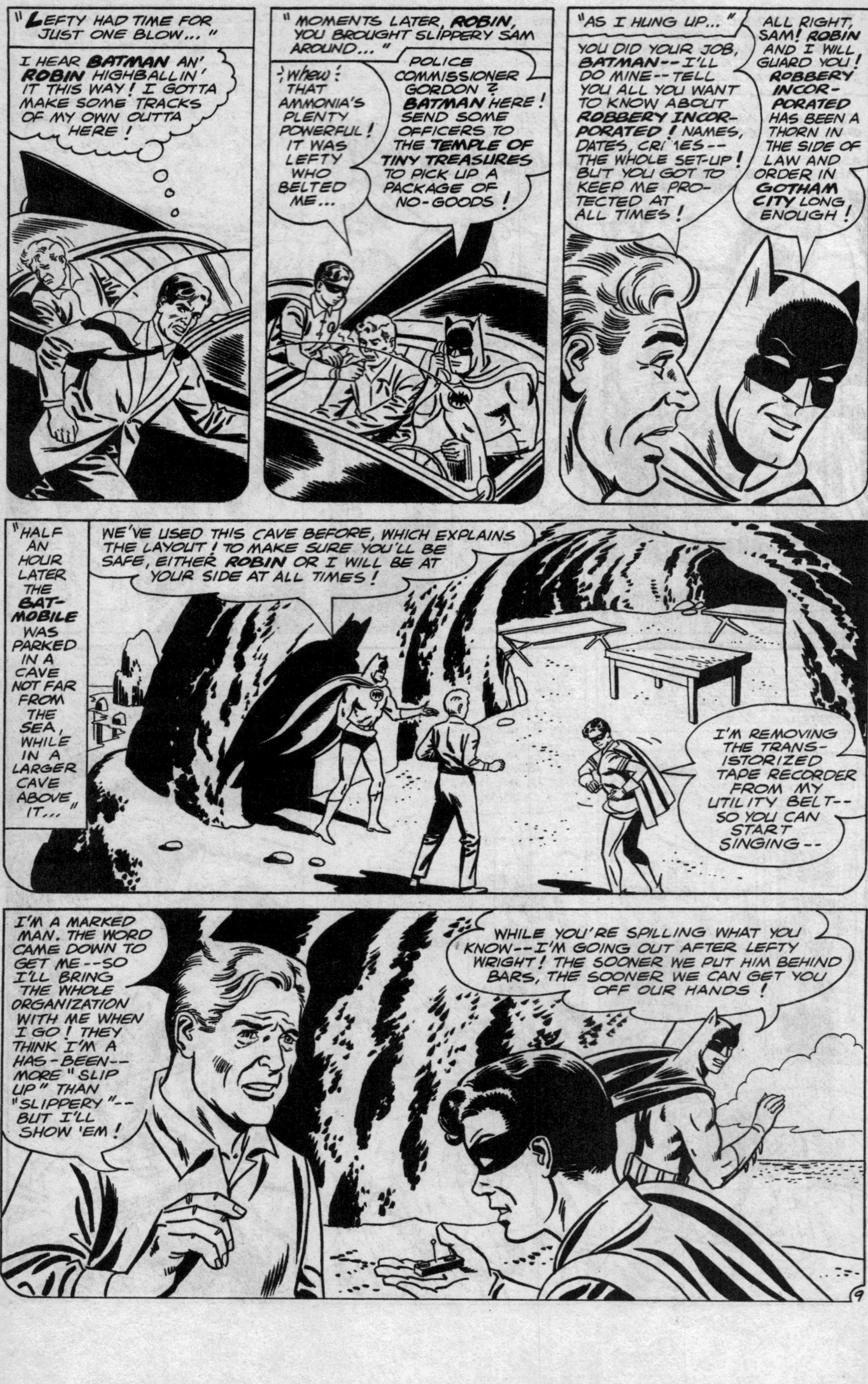
"LEFTY HAD TIME FOR JUST ONE BLOW..."
I HEAR BATMAN AN' ROBIN HIGHBALLIN' IT THIS WAY! I GOTTA MAKE SOME TRACKS OF MY OWN OUTTA HERE!
"MOMENTS LATER, ROBIN, YOU BROUGHT SLIPPERY SAM AROUND..."
WHEW! THAT AMMONIA'S PLENTY POWERFUL! IT WAS LEFTY WHO BELTED ME...
POLICE COMMISSIONER GORDON? BATMAN HERE! SEND SOME OFFICERS TO THE TEMPLE OF TINY TREASURES TO PICK UP A PACKAGE OF NO-GOODS!
"AS I HUNG UP..."
YOU DID YOUR JOB, BATMAN--I'LL DO MINE--TELL YOU ALL YOU WANT TO KNOW ABOUT ROBBERY INCORPORATED! NAMES, DATES, CRIMES--THE WHOLE SET-UP! BUT YOU GOT TO KEEP ME PROTECTED AT ALL TIMES!
ALL RIGHT, SAM! ROBIN AND I WILL GUARD YOU! ROBBERY INCORPORATED HAS BEEN A THORN IN THE SIDE OF LAW AND ORDER IN GOTHAM CITY LONG ENOUGH!
"HALF AN HOUR LATER THE BATMOBILE WAS PARKED IN A CAVE NOT FAR FROM THE SEA, WHILE IN A LARGER CAVE ABOVE IT..."
WE'VE USED THIS CAVE BEFORE, WHICH EXPLAINS THE LAYOUT! TO MAKE SURE YOU'LL BE SAFE, EITHER ROBIN OR I WILL BE AT YOUR SIDE AT ALL TIMES!
I'M REMOVING THE TRANSISTORIZED TAPE RECORDER FROM MY UTILITY BELT--SO YOU CAN START SINGING--
I'M A MARKED MAN. THE WORD CAME DOWN TO GET ME--SO I'LL BRING THE WHOLE ORGANIZATION WITH ME WHEN I GO! THEY THINK I'M A HAS-BEEN--MORE "SLIP UP" THAN "SLIPPERY"--BUT I'LL SHOW 'EM!
WHILE YOU'RE SPILLING WHAT YOU KNOW--I'M GOING OUT AFTER LEFTY WRIGHT! THE SOONER WE PUT HIM BEHIND BARS, THE SOONER WE CAN GET YOU OFF OUR HANDS!
9

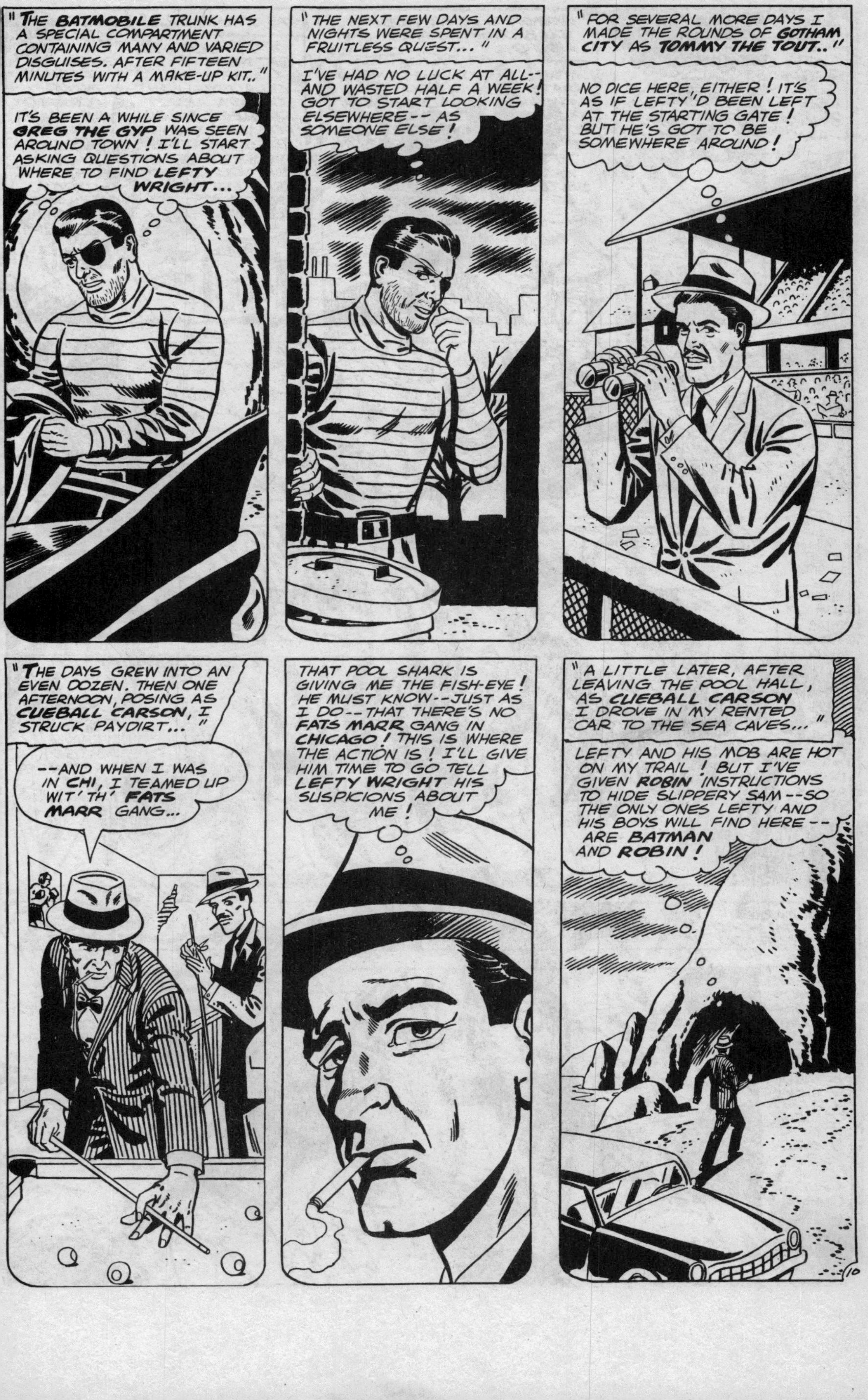
"THE BATMOBILE TRUNK HAS A SPECIAL COMPARTMENT CONTAINING MANY AND VARIED DISGUISES. AFTER FIFTEEN MINUTES WITH A MAKE-UP KIT.."
IT'S BEEN A WHILE SINCE GREG THE GYP WAS SEEN AROUND TOWN! I'LL START ASKING QUESTIONS ABOUT WHERE TO FIND LEFTY WRIGHT...
"THE NEXT FEW DAYS AND NIGHTS WERE SPENT IN A FRUITLESS QUEST..."
I'VE HAD NO LUCK AT ALL--AND WASTED HALF A WEEK! GOT TO START LOOKING ELSEWHERE--AS SOMEONE ELSE!
"FOR SEVERAL MORE DAYS I MADE THE ROUNDS OF GOTHAM CITY AS TOMMY THE TOUT.."
NO DICE HERE, EITHER! IT'S AS IF LEFTY'D BEEN LEFT AT THE STARTING GATE! BUT HE'S GOT TO BE SOMEWHERE AROUND!
"THE DAYS GREW INTO AN EVEN DOZEN. THEN ONE AFTERNOON, POSING AS CUEBALL CARSON, I STRUCK PAYDIRT..."
--AND WHEN I WAS IN CHI, I TEAMED UP WIT' TH' FATS MARR GANG...
THAT POOL SHARK IS GIVING ME THE FISH-EYE! HE MUST KNOW--JUST AS I DO--THAT THERE'S NO FATS MARR GANG IN CHICAGO! THIS IS WHERE THE ACTION IS! I'LL GIVE HIM TIME TO GO TELL LEFTY WRIGHT HIS SUSPICIONS ABOUT ME!
"A LITTLE LATER, AFTER LEAVING THE POOL HALL, AS CUEBALL CARSON I DROVE IN MY RENTED CAR TO THE SEA CAVES..."
LEFTY AND HIS MOB ARE HOT ON MY TRAIL! BUT I'VE GIVEN ROBIN INSTRUCTIONS TO HIDE SLIPPERY SAM--SO THE ONLY ONES LEFTY AND HIS BOYS WILL FIND HERE--ARE BATMAN AND ROBIN!
10

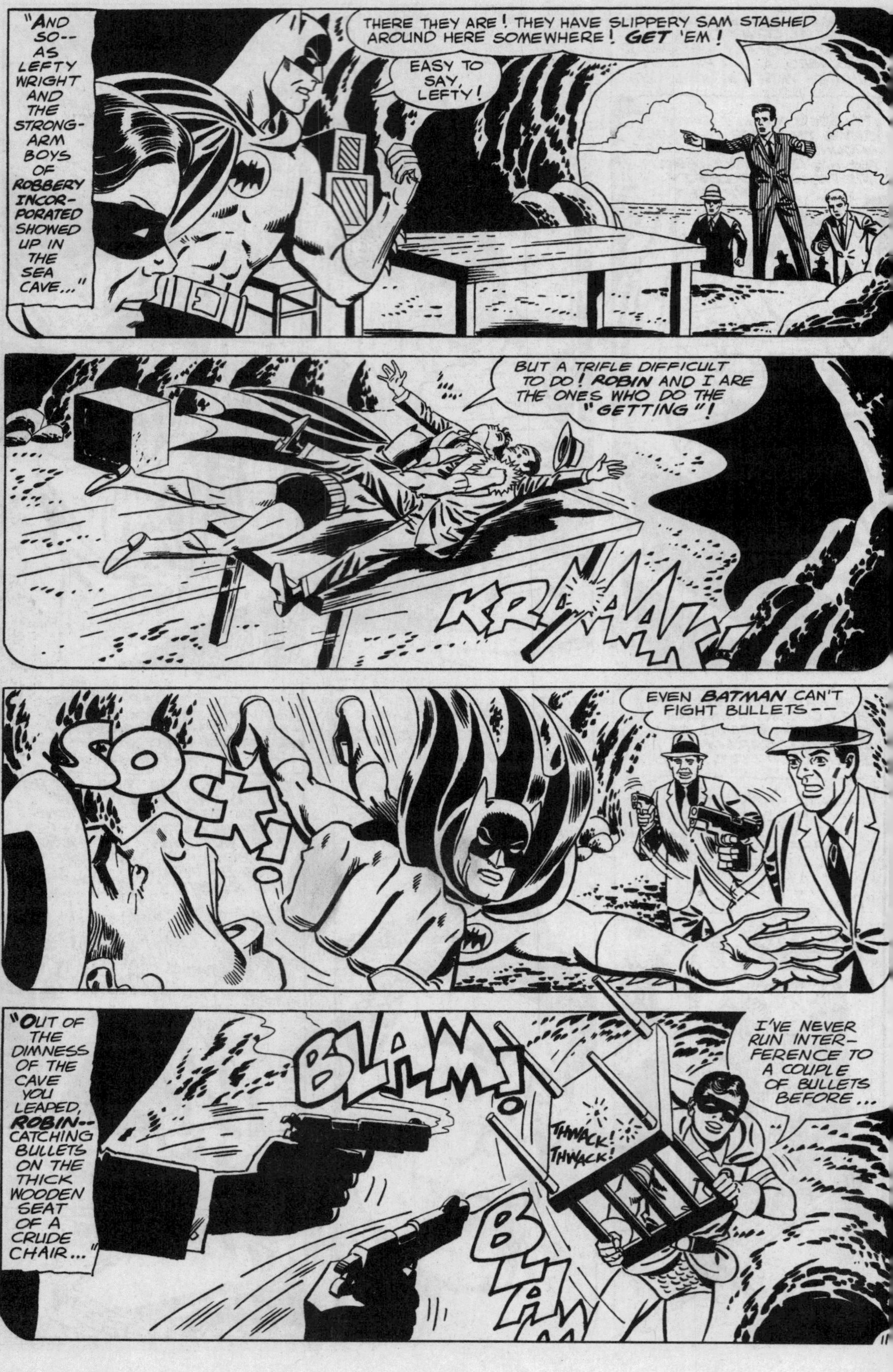
"AND SO-- AS LEFTY WRIGHT AND THE STRONG-ARM BOYS OF ROBBERY INCORPORATED SHOWED UP IN THE SEA CAVE..."
THERE THEY ARE! THEY HAVE SLIPPERY SAM STASHED AROUND HERE SOMEWHERE! GET 'EM!
EASY TO SAY, LEFTY!
BUT A TRIFLE DIFFICULT TO DO! ROBIN AND I ARE THE ONES WHO DO THE "GETTING"!
KRAAAK!
SOCK!
EVEN BATMAN CAN'T FIGHT BULLETS--
"OUT OF THE DIMNESS OF THE CAVE YOU LEAPED, ROBIN-- CATCHING BULLETS ON THE THICK WOODEN SEAT OF A CRUDE CHAIR..."
BLAM!
I'VE NEVER RUN INTERFERENCE TO A COUPLE OF BULLETS BEFORE...
THWACK! THWACK!
BLAM

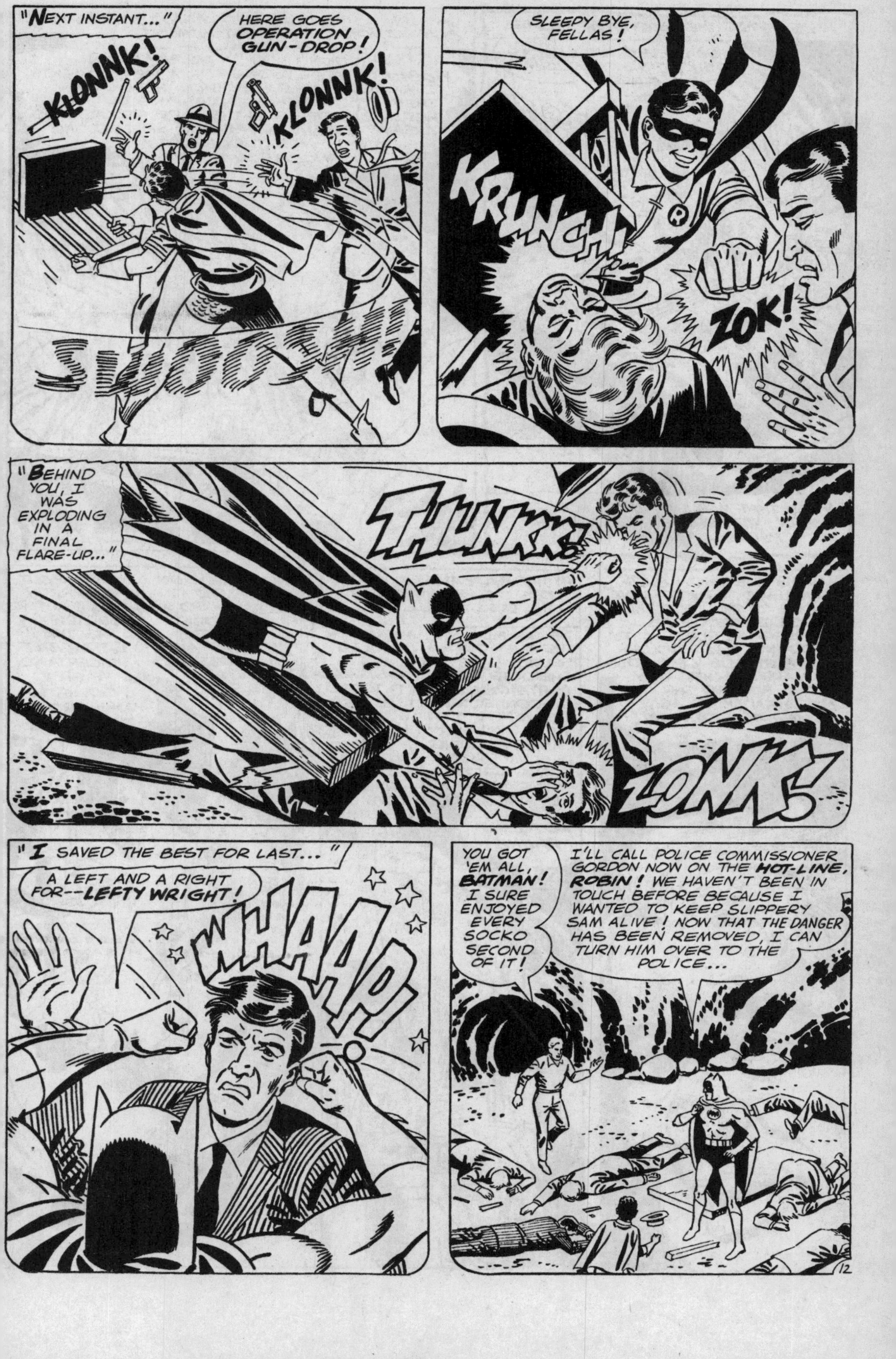
"NEXT INSTANT..."
HERE GOES OPERATION GUN-DROP!
KLONNK!
KLONNK!
SWOOSH!
SLEEPY BYE, FELLAS!
KRUNCH
ZOK!
"BEHIND YOU, I WAS EXPLODING IN A FINAL FLARE-UP..."
THUNKK!
ZONK!
"I SAVED THE BEST FOR LAST..."
A LEFT AND A RIGHT FOR--LEFTY WRIGHT!
WHAAP!
YOU GOT 'EM ALL, BATMAN! I SURE ENJOYED EVERY SOCKO SECOND OF IT!
I'LL CALL POLICE COMMISSIONER GORDON NOW ON THE HOT-LINE, ROBIN! WE HAVEN'T BEEN IN TOUCH BEFORE BECAUSE I WANTED TO KEEP SLIPPERY SAM ALIVE! NOW THAT THE DANGER HAS BEEN REMOVED, I CAN TURN HIM OVER TO THE POLICE...
12

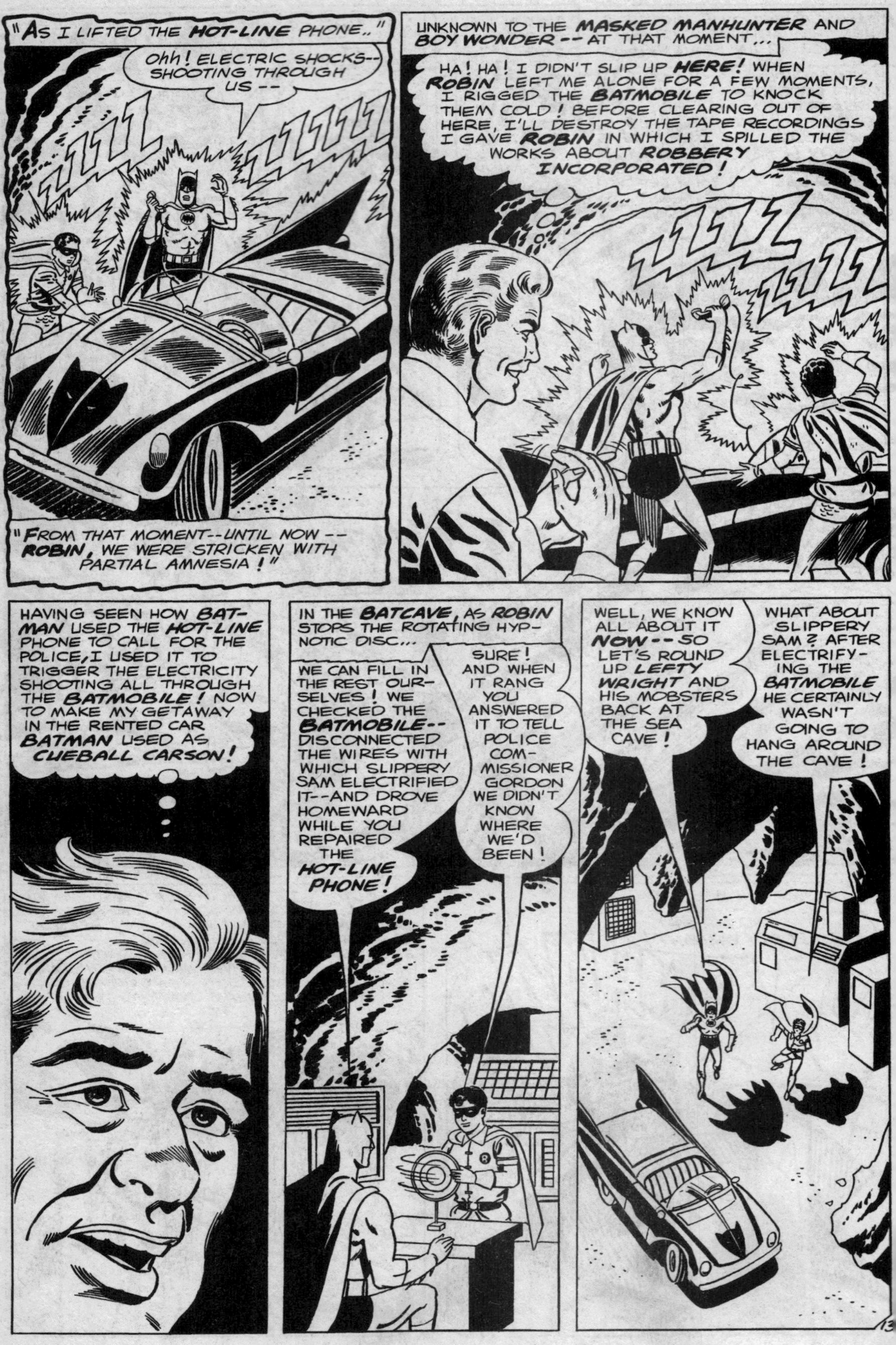

"AS I LIFTED THE HOT-LINE PHONE.."
OHH! ELECTRIC SHOCKS-- SHOOTING THROUGH US --
ZZZZ ZZZZZ
"FROM THAT MOMENT--UNTIL NOW -- ROBIN, WE WERE STRICKEN WITH PARTIAL AMNESIA!"
UNKNOWN TO THE MASKED MANHUNTER AND BOY WONDER -- AT THAT MOMENT,...
HA! HA! I DIDN'T SLIP UP HERE! WHEN ROBIN LEFT ME ALONE FOR A FEW MOMENTS, I RIGGED THE BATMOBILE TO KNOCK THEM COLD! BEFORE CLEARING OUT OF HERE, I'LL DESTROY THE TAPE RECORDINGS I GAVE ROBIN IN WHICH I SPILLED THE WORKS ABOUT ROBBERY INCORPORATED!
ZZZZ ZZZZ
HAVING SEEN HOW BATMAN USED THE HOT-LINE PHONE TO CALL FOR THE POLICE, I USED IT TO TRIGGER THE ELECTRICITY SHOOTING ALL THROUGH THE BATMOBILE! NOW TO MAKE MY GETAWAY IN THE RENTED CAR BATMAN USED AS CUEBALL CARSON!
IN THE BATCAVE, AS ROBIN STOPS THE ROTATING HYPNOTIC DISC...
WE CAN FILL IN THE REST OURSELVES! WE CHECKED THE BATMOBILE--DISCONNECTED THE WIRES WITH WHICH SLIPPERY SAM ELECTRIFIED IT--AND DROVE HOMEWARD WHILE YOU REPAIRED THE HOT-LINE PHONE!
SURE! AND WHEN IT RANG YOU ANSWERED IT TO TELL POLICE COMMISSIONER GORDON WE DIDN'T KNOW WHERE WE'D BEEN!
WELL, WE KNOW ALL ABOUT IT NOW -- SO LET'S ROUND UP LEFTY WRIGHT AND HIS MOBSTERS BACK AT THE SEA CAVE!
WHAT ABOUT SLIPPERY SAM? AFTER ELECTRIFYING THE BATMOBILE HE CERTAINLY WASN'T GOING TO HANG AROUND THE CAVE!
13

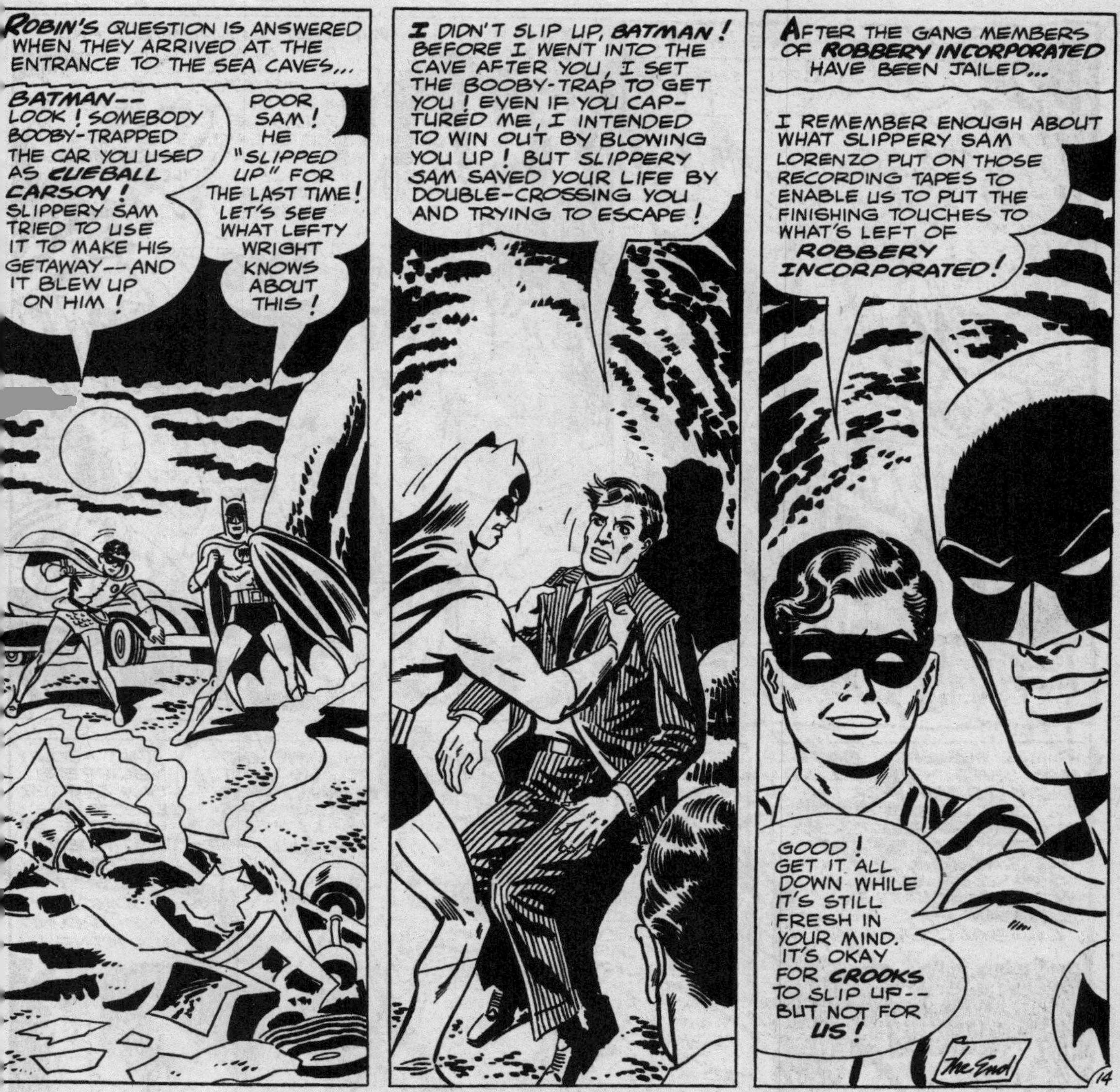
ROBIN'S QUESTION IS ANSWERED WHEN THEY ARRIVED AT THE ENTRANCE TO THE SEA CAVES...
BATMAN-- LOOK! SOMEBODY BOOBY-TRAPPED THE CAR YOU USED AS CUEBALL CARSON! SLIPPERY SAM TRIED TO USE IT TO MAKE HIS GETAWAY-- AND IT BLEW UP ON HIM!
POOR SAM! HE "SLIPPED UP" FOR THE LAST TIME! LET'S SEE WHAT LEFTY WRIGHT KNOWS ABOUT THIS!
I DIDN'T SLIP UP, BATMAN! BEFORE I WENT INTO THE CAVE AFTER YOU, I SET THE BOOBY-TRAP TO GET YOU! EVEN IF YOU CAPTURED ME, I INTENDED TO WIN OUT BY BLOWING YOU UP! BUT SLIPPERY SAM SAVED YOUR LIFE BY DOUBLE-CROSSING YOU AND TRYING TO ESCAPE!
AFTER THE GANG MEMBERS OF ROBBERY INCORPORATED HAVE BEEN JAILED...
I REMEMBER ENOUGH ABOUT WHAT SLIPPERY SAM LORENZO PUT ON THOSE RECORDING TAPES TO ENABLE US TO PUT THE FINISHING TOUCHES TO WHAT'S LEFT OF ROBBERY INCORPORATED!
GOOD! GET IT ALL DOWN WHILE IT'S STILL FRESH IN YOUR MIND. IT'S OKAY FOR CROOKS TO SLIP UP-- BUT NOT FOR US!
The End
14

BATMAN

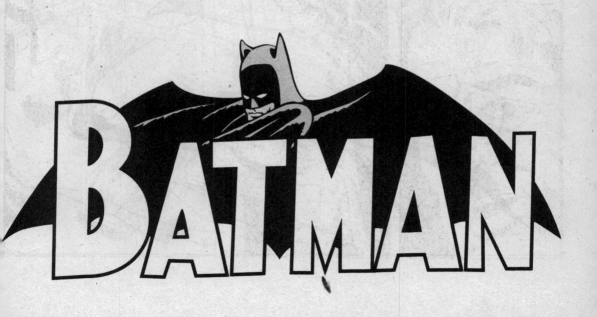

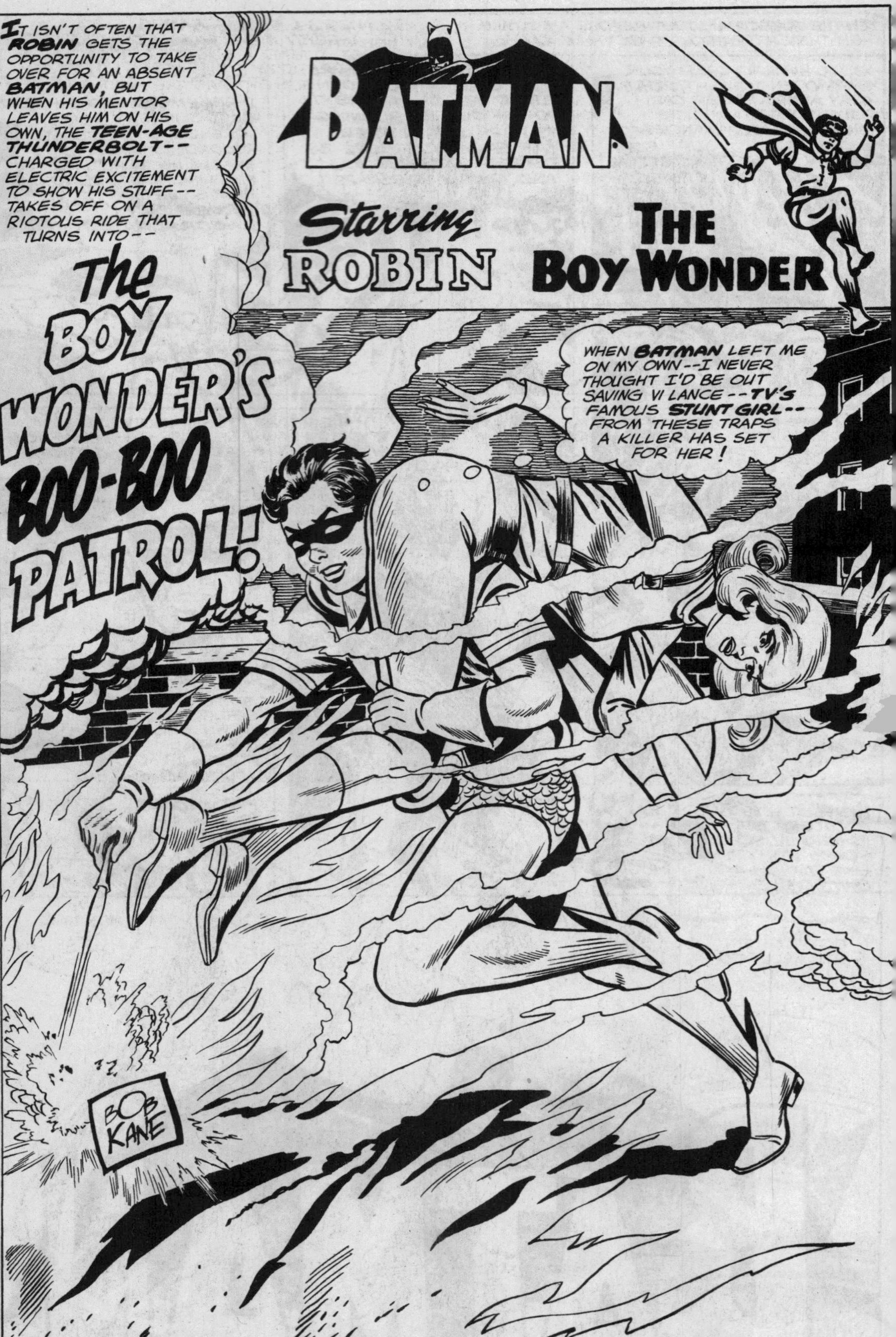
IT ISN'T OFTEN THAT ROBIN GETS THE OPPORTUNITY TO TAKE OVER FOR AN ABSENT BATMAN, BUT WHEN HIS MENTOR LEAVES HIM ON HIS OWN, THE TEEN-AGE THUNDERBOLT-- CHARGED WITH ELECTRIC EXCITEMENT TO SHOW HIS STUFF-- TAKES OFF ON A RIOTOUS RIDE THAT TURNS INTO--
BATMAN
Starring ROBIN THE BOY WONDER
The BOY WONDER'S BOO-BOO PATROL!
WHEN BATMAN LEFT ME ON MY OWN--I NEVER THOUGHT I'D BE OUT SAVING VI LANCE --TV'S FAMOUS STUNT GIRL-- FROM THESE TRAPS A KILLER HAS SET FOR HER!
BOB KANE

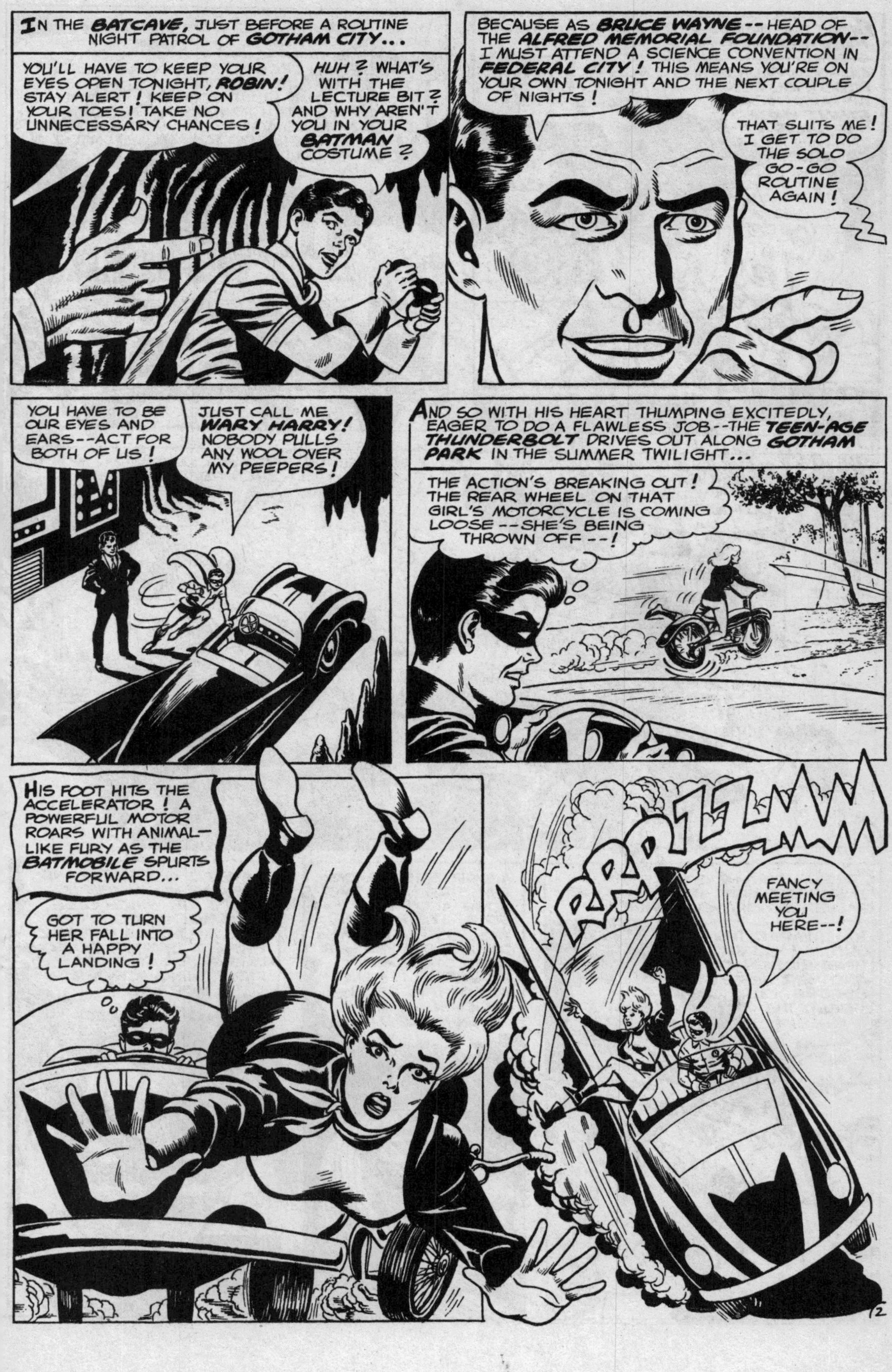
IN THE BATCAVE, JUST BEFORE A ROUTINE NIGHT PATROL OF GOTHAM CITY...
YOU'LL HAVE TO KEEP YOUR EYES OPEN TONIGHT, ROBIN! STAY ALERT! KEEP ON YOUR TOES! TAKE NO UNNECESSARY CHANCES!
HUH? WHAT'S WITH THE LECTURE BIT? AND WHY AREN'T YOU IN YOUR BATMAN COSTUME?
BECAUSE AS BRUCE WAYNE--HEAD OF THE ALFRED MEMORIAL FOUNDATION--I MUST ATTEND A SCIENCE CONVENTION IN FEDERAL CITY! THIS MEANS YOU'RE ON YOUR OWN TONIGHT AND THE NEXT COUPLE OF NIGHTS!
THAT SUITS ME! I GET TO DO THE SOLO GO-GO ROUTINE AGAIN!
YOU HAVE TO BE OUR EYES AND EARS--ACT FOR BOTH OF US!
JUST CALL ME WARY HARRY! NOBODY PULLS ANY WOOL OVER MY PEEPERS!
AND SO WITH HIS HEART THUMPING EXCITEDLY, EAGER TO DO A FLAWLESS JOB--THE TEEN-AGE THUNDERBOLT DRIVES OUT ALONG GOTHAM PARK IN THE SUMMER TWILIGHT...
THE ACTION'S BREAKING OUT! THE REAR WHEEL ON THAT GIRL'S MOTORCYCLE IS COMING LOOSE--SHE'S BEING THROWN OFF--!
HIS FOOT HITS THE ACCELERATOR! A POWERFUL MOTOR ROARS WITH ANIMAL-LIKE FURY AS THE BATMOBILE SPURTS FORWARD...
GOT TO TURN HER FALL INTO A HAPPY LANDING!
RRRZZZMMM
FANCY MEETING YOU HERE--!
12

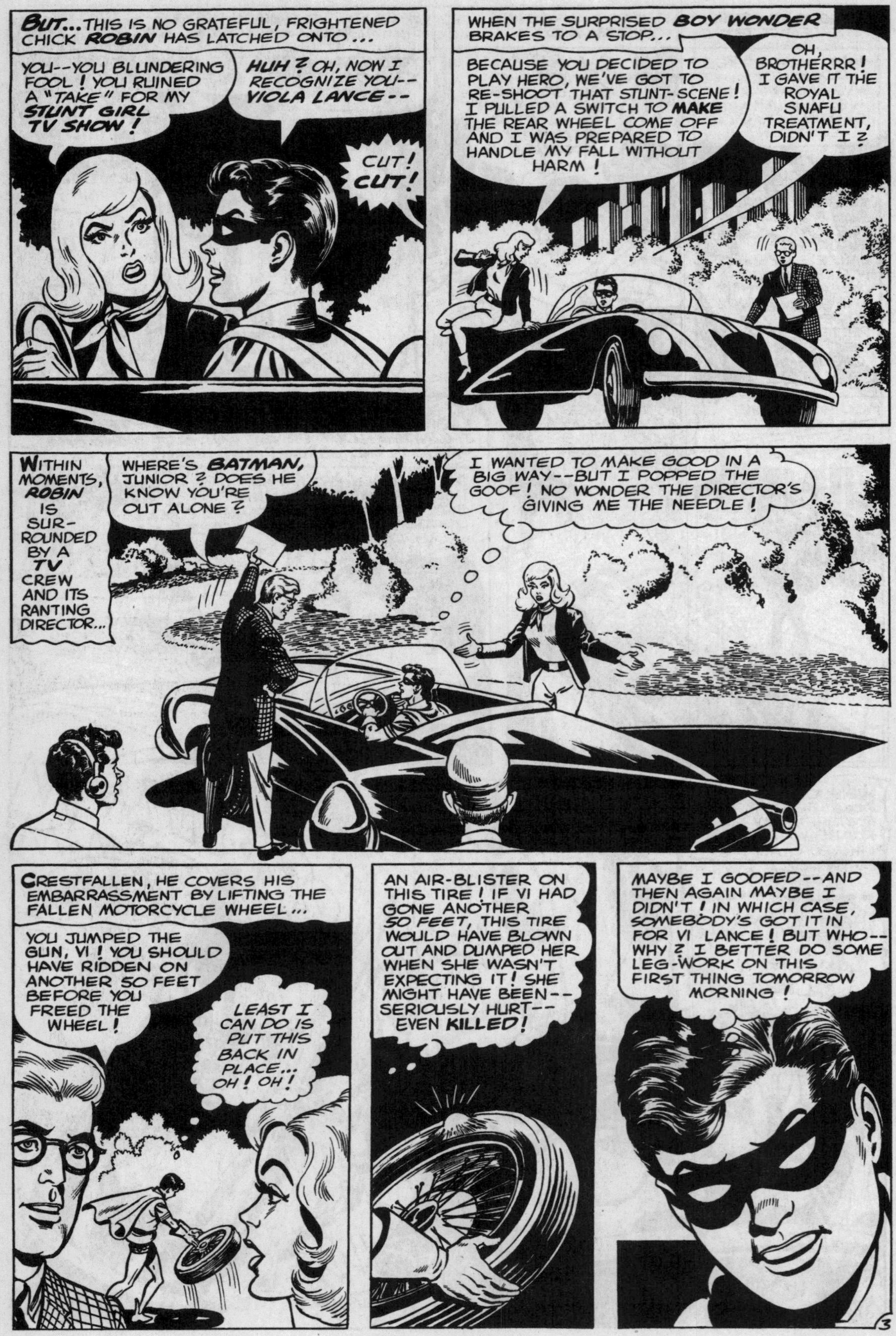
BUT... THIS IS NO GRATEFUL, FRIGHTENED CHICK ROBIN HAS LATCHED ONTO...
YOU--YOU BLUNDERING FOOL! YOU RUINED A "TAKE" FOR MY STUNT GIRL TV SHOW!
HUH? OH, NOW I RECOGNIZE YOU-- VIOLA LANCE--
CUT! CUT!
WHEN THE SURPRISED BOY WONDER BRAKES TO A STOP...
BECAUSE YOU DECIDED TO PLAY HERO, WE'VE GOT TO RE-SHOOT THAT STUNT-SCENE! I PULLED A SWITCH TO MAKE THE REAR WHEEL COME OFF AND I WAS PREPARED TO HANDLE MY FALL WITHOUT HARM!
OH, BROTHERRR! I GAVE IT THE ROYAL SNAFU TREATMENT, DIDN'T I?
WITHIN MOMENTS, ROBIN IS SURROUNDED BY A TV CREW AND ITS RANTING DIRECTOR...
WHERE'S BATMAN, JUNIOR? DOES HE KNOW YOU'RE OUT ALONE?
I WANTED TO MAKE GOOD IN A BIG WAY--BUT I POPPED THE GOOF! NO WONDER THE DIRECTOR'S GIVING ME THE NEEDLE!
CRESTFALLEN, HE COVERS HIS EMBARRASSMENT BY LIFTING THE FALLEN MOTORCYCLE WHEEL...
YOU JUMPED THE GUN, VI! YOU SHOULD HAVE RIDDEN ON ANOTHER 50 FEET BEFORE YOU FREED THE WHEEL!
LEAST I CAN DO IS PUT THIS BACK IN PLACE... OH! OH!
AN AIR-BLISTER ON THIS TIRE! IF VI HAD GONE ANOTHER 50 FEET, THIS TIRE WOULD HAVE BLOWN OUT AND DUMPED HER WHEN SHE WASN'T EXPECTING IT! SHE MIGHT HAVE BEEN--SERIOUSLY HURT--EVEN KILLED!
MAYBE I GOOFED--AND THEN AGAIN MAYBE I DIDN'T! IN WHICH CASE, SOMEBODY'S GOT IT IN FOR VI LANCE! BUT WHO--WHY? I BETTER DO SOME LEG-WORK ON THIS FIRST THING TOMORROW MORNING!
3

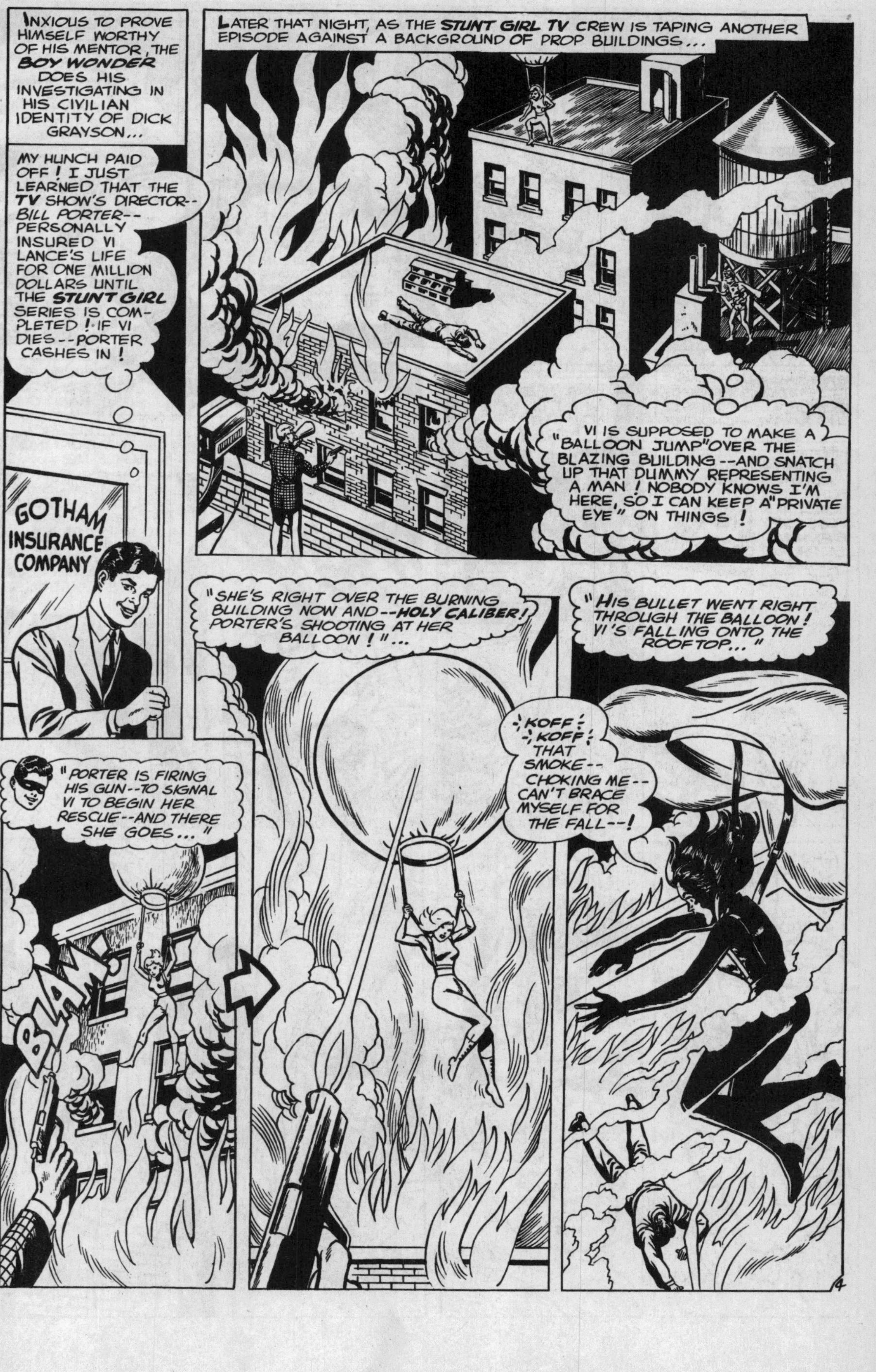
ANXIOUS TO PROVE HIMSELF WORTHY OF HIS MENTOR, THE BOY WONDER DOES HIS INVESTIGATING IN HIS CIVILIAN IDENTITY OF DICK GRAYSON...
MY HUNCH PAID OFF! I JUST LEARNED THAT THE TV SHOW'S DIRECTOR--BILL PORTER--PERSONALLY INSURED VI LANCE'S LIFE FOR ONE MILLION DOLLARS UNTIL THE STUNT GIRL SERIES IS COMPLETED! IF VI DIES--PORTER CASHES IN!
GOTHAM INSURANCE COMPANY
LATER THAT NIGHT, AS THE STUNT GIRL TV CREW IS TAPING ANOTHER EPISODE AGAINST A BACKGROUND OF PROP BUILDINGS...
VI IS SUPPOSED TO MAKE A "BALLOON JUMP" OVER THE BLAZING BUILDING--AND SNATCH UP THAT DUMMY REPRESENTING A MAN! NOBODY KNOWS I'M HERE, SO I CAN KEEP A "PRIVATE EYE" ON THINGS!
"PORTER IS FIRING HIS GUN--TO SIGNAL VI TO BEGIN HER RESCUE--AND THERE SHE GOES..."
BLAM
"SHE'S RIGHT OVER THE BURNING BUILDING NOW AND--HOLY CALIBER! PORTER'S SHOOTING AT HER BALLOON!"...
"HIS BULLET WENT RIGHT THROUGH THE BALLOON! VI'S FALLING ONTO THE ROOFTOP..."
KOFF KOFF THAT SMOKE--CHOKING ME--CAN'T BRACE MYSELF FOR THE FALL--!
4

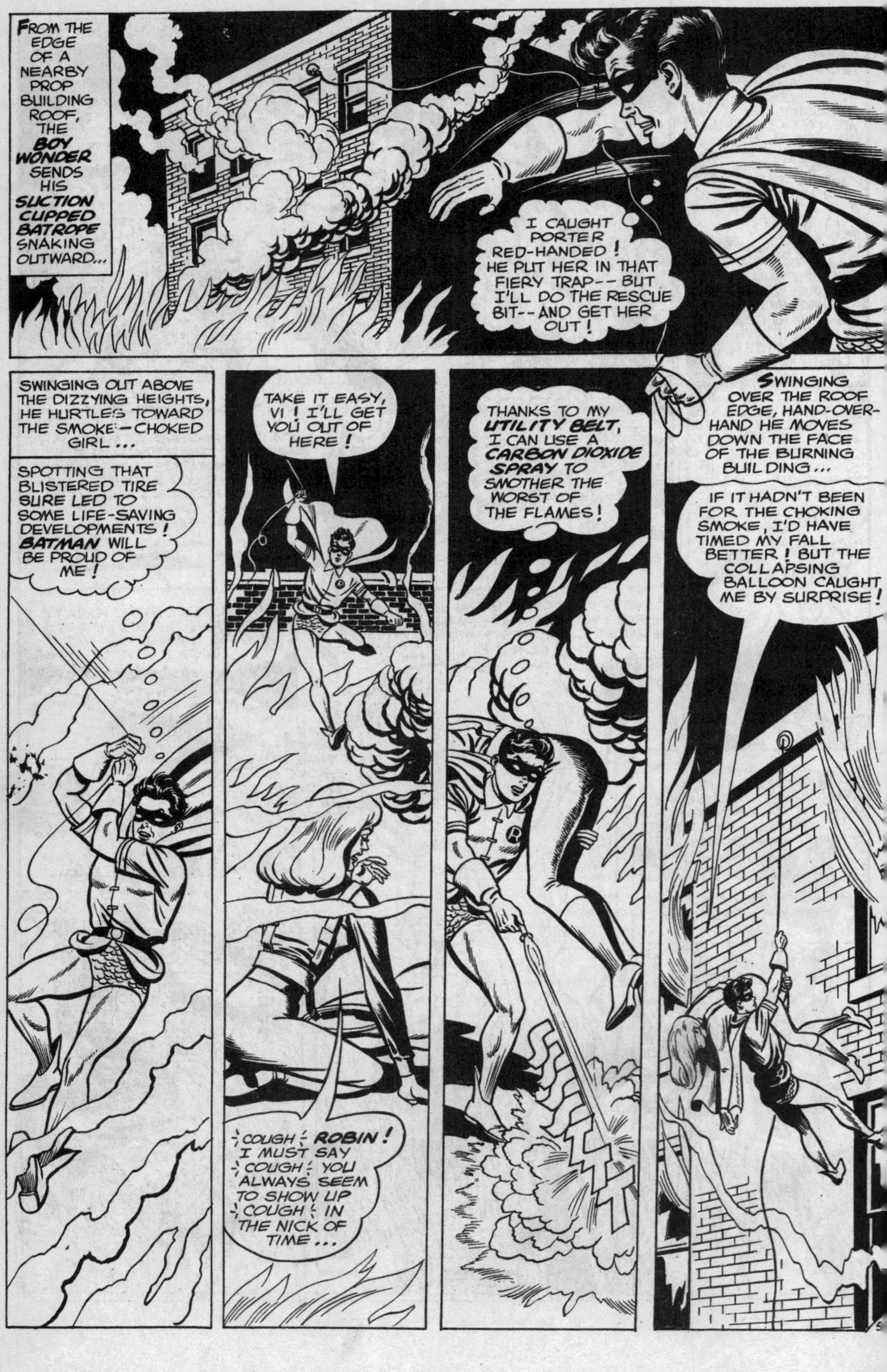

FROM THE EDGE OF A NEARBY PROP BUILDING ROOF, THE BOY WONDER SENDS HIS SUCTION CUPPED BATROPE SNAKING OUTWARD...
I CAUGHT PORTER RED-HANDED! HE PUT HER IN THAT FIERY TRAP-- BUT I'LL DO THE RESCUE BIT-- AND GET HER OUT!
SWINGING OUT ABOVE THE DIZZYING HEIGHTS, HE HURTLES TOWARD THE SMOKE-CHOKED GIRL...
SPOTTING THAT BLISTERED TIRE SURE LED TO SOME LIFE-SAVING DEVELOPMENTS! BATMAN WILL BE PROUD OF ME!
TAKE IT EASY, VI! I'LL GET YOU OUT OF HERE!
-COUGH- ROBIN! I MUST SAY -COUGH- YOU ALWAYS SEEM TO SHOW UP -COUGH- IN THE NICK OF TIME...
THANKS TO MY UTILITY BELT, I CAN USE A CARBON DIOXIDE SPRAY TO SMOTHER THE WORST OF THE FLAMES!
SWINGING OVER THE ROOF EDGE, HAND-OVER-HAND HE MOVES DOWN THE FACE OF THE BURNING BUILDING...
IF IT HADN'T BEEN FOR THE CHOKING SMOKE, I'D HAVE TIMED MY FALL BETTER! BUT THE COLLAPSING BALLOON CAUGHT ME BY SURPRISE!

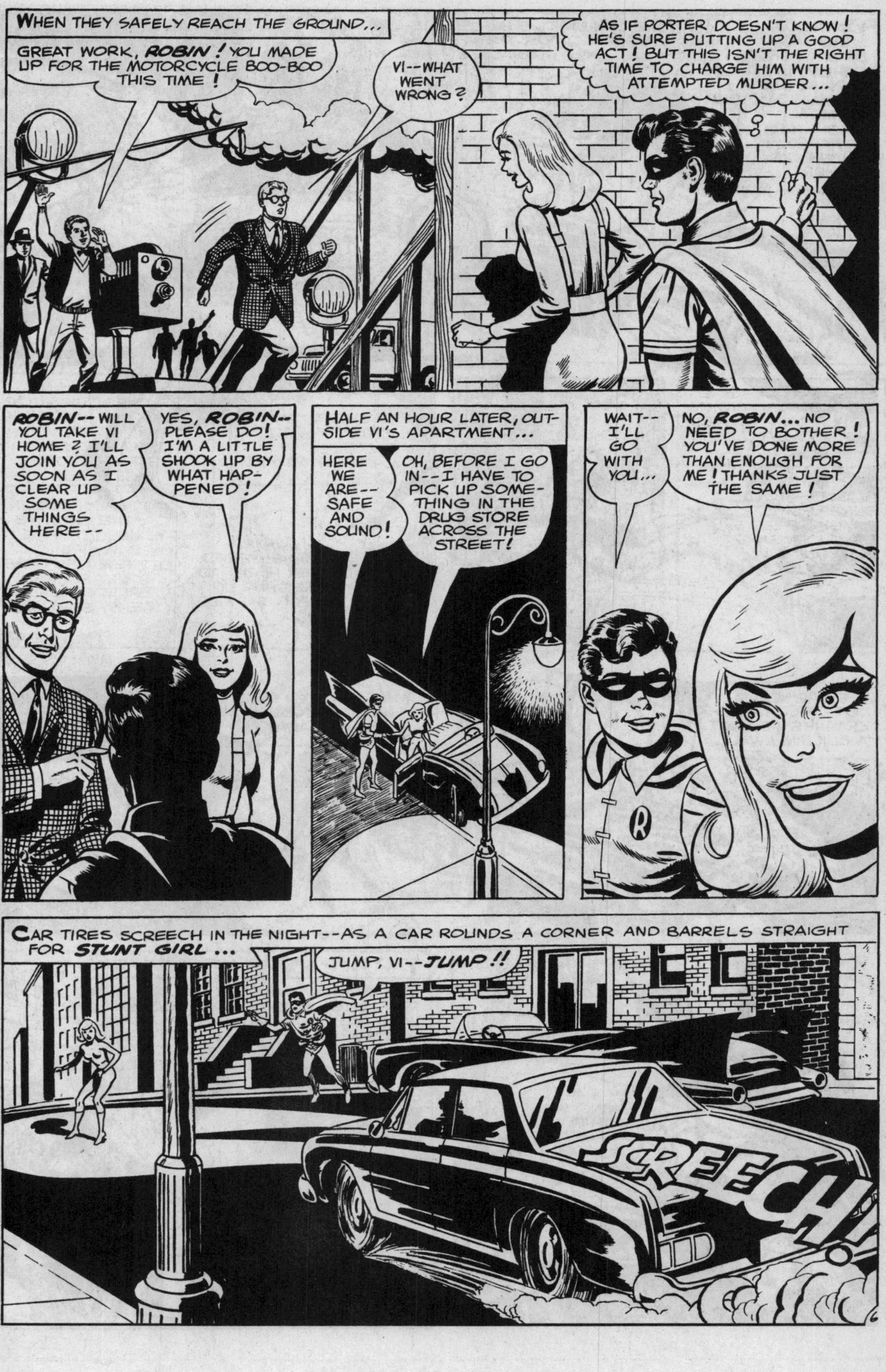
WHEN THEY SAFELY REACH THE GROUND...
GREAT WORK, ROBIN! YOU MADE UP FOR THE MOTORCYCLE BOO-BOO THIS TIME!
VI--WHAT WENT WRONG?
AS IF PORTER DOESN'T KNOW! HE'S SURE PUTTING UP A GOOD ACT! BUT THIS ISN'T THE RIGHT TIME TO CHARGE HIM WITH ATTEMPTED MURDER...
ROBIN--WILL YOU TAKE VI HOME? I'LL JOIN YOU AS SOON AS I CLEAR UP SOME THINGS HERE--
YES, ROBIN--PLEASE DO! I'M A LITTLE SHOOK UP BY WHAT HAPPENED!
HALF AN HOUR LATER, OUTSIDE VI'S APARTMENT...
HERE WE ARE--SAFE AND SOUND!
OH, BEFORE I GO IN--I HAVE TO PICK UP SOMETHING IN THE DRUG STORE ACROSS THE STREET!
WAIT--I'LL GO WITH YOU...
NO, ROBIN... NO NEED TO BOTHER! YOU'VE DONE MORE THAN ENOUGH FOR ME! THANKS JUST THE SAME!
CAR TIRES SCREECH IN THE NIGHT--AS A CAR ROUNDS A CORNER AND BARRELS STRAIGHT FOR STUNT GIRL...
JUMP, VI--JUMP!!
SCREECH!

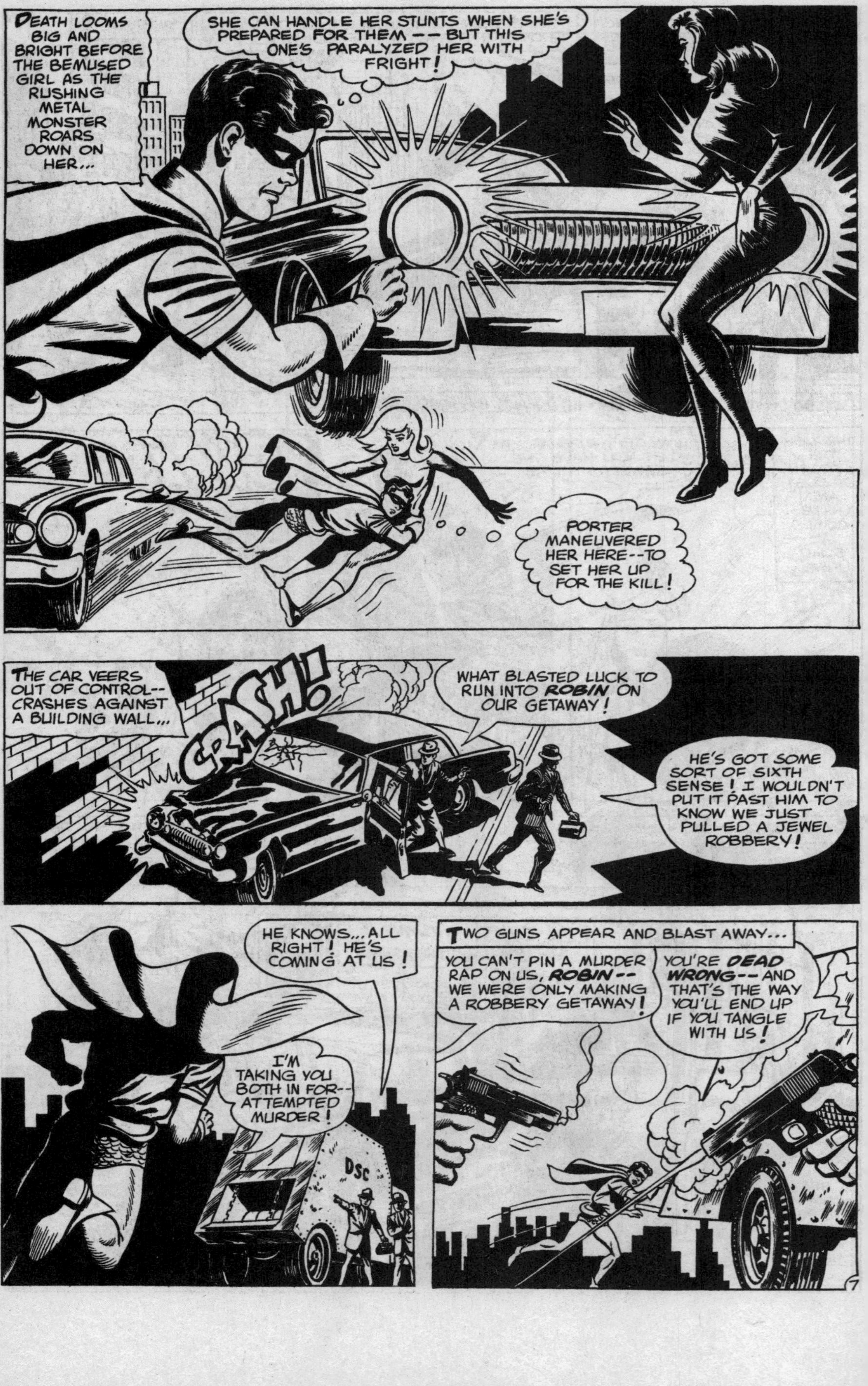
DEATH LOOMS BIG AND BRIGHT BEFORE THE BEMUSED GIRL AS THE RUSHING METAL MONSTER ROARS DOWN ON HER...
SHE CAN HANDLE HER STUNTS WHEN SHE'S PREPARED FOR THEM -- BUT THIS ONE'S PARALYZED HER WITH FRIGHT!
PORTER MANEUVERED HER HERE--TO SET HER UP FOR THE KILL!
THE CAR VEERS OUT OF CONTROL-- CRASHES AGAINST A BUILDING WALL...
CRASH!
WHAT BLASTED LUCK TO RUN INTO ROBIN ON OUR GETAWAY!
HE'S GOT SOME SORT OF SIXTH SENSE! I WOULDN'T PUT IT PAST HIM TO KNOW WE JUST PULLED A JEWEL ROBBERY!
HE KNOWS... ALL RIGHT! HE'S COMING AT US!
I'M TAKING YOU BOTH IN FOR-- ATTEMPTED MURDER!
DSC
TWO GUNS APPEAR AND BLAST AWAY...
YOU CAN'T PIN A MURDER RAP ON US, ROBIN-- WE WERE ONLY MAKING A ROBBERY GETAWAY!
YOU'RE DEAD WRONG-- AND THAT'S THE WAY YOU'LL END UP IF YOU TANGLE WITH US!
7

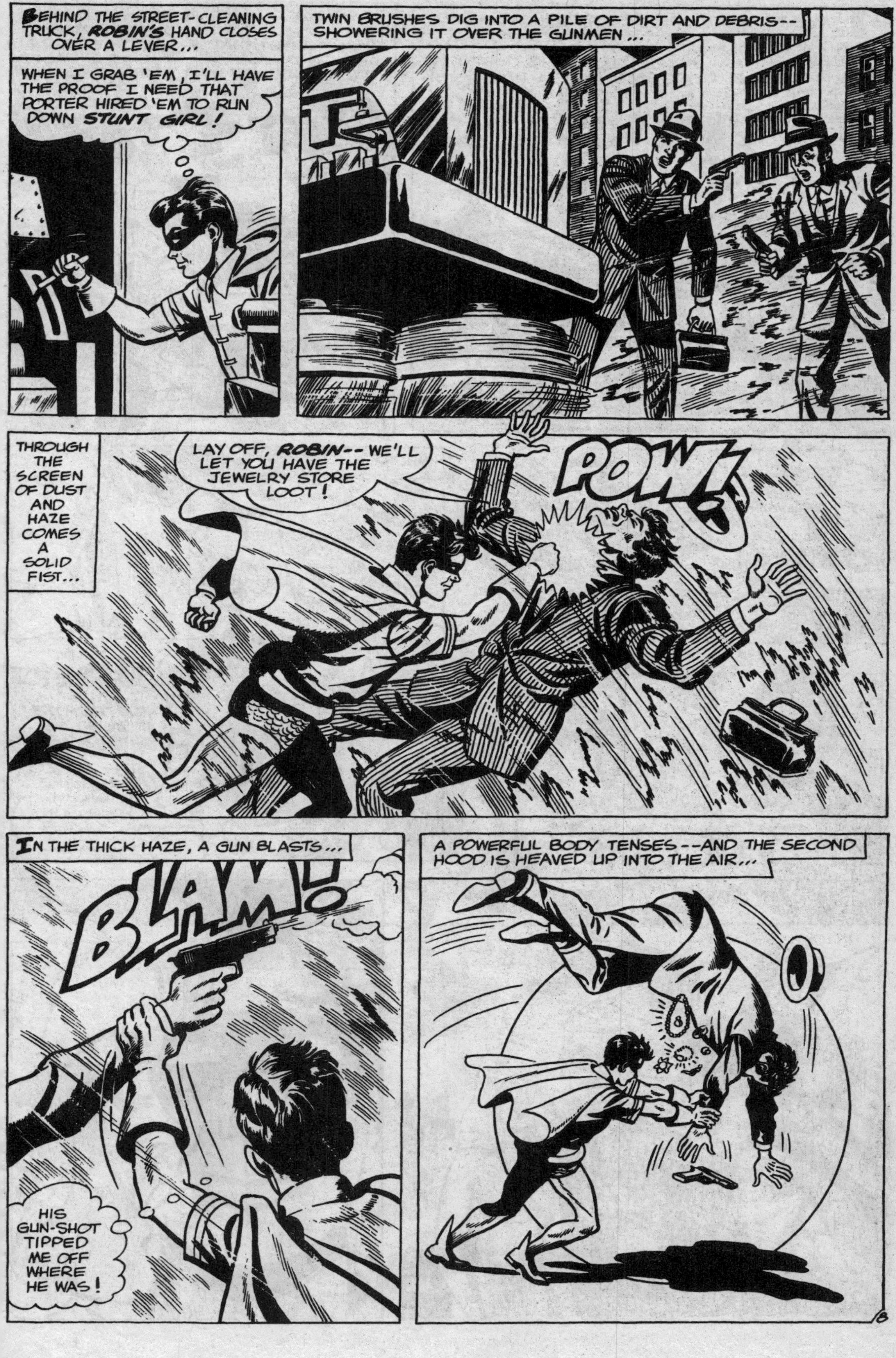
BEHIND THE STREET-CLEANING TRUCK, ROBIN'S HAND CLOSES OVER A LEVER...
WHEN I GRAB 'EM, I'LL HAVE THE PROOF I NEED THAT PORTER HIRED 'EM TO RUN DOWN STUNT GIRL!
TWIN BRUSHES DIG INTO A PILE OF DIRT AND DEBRIS--SHOWERING IT OVER THE GUNMEN...
THROUGH THE SCREEN OF DUST AND HAZE COMES A SOLID FIST...
LAY OFF, ROBIN--WE'LL LET YOU HAVE THE JEWELRY STORE LOOT!
POW!
IN THE THICK HAZE, A GUN BLASTS...
BLAM!
HIS GUN-SHOT TIPPED ME OFF WHERE HE WAS!
A POWERFUL BODY TENSES--AND THE SECOND HOOD IS HEAVED UP INTO THE AIR...
8

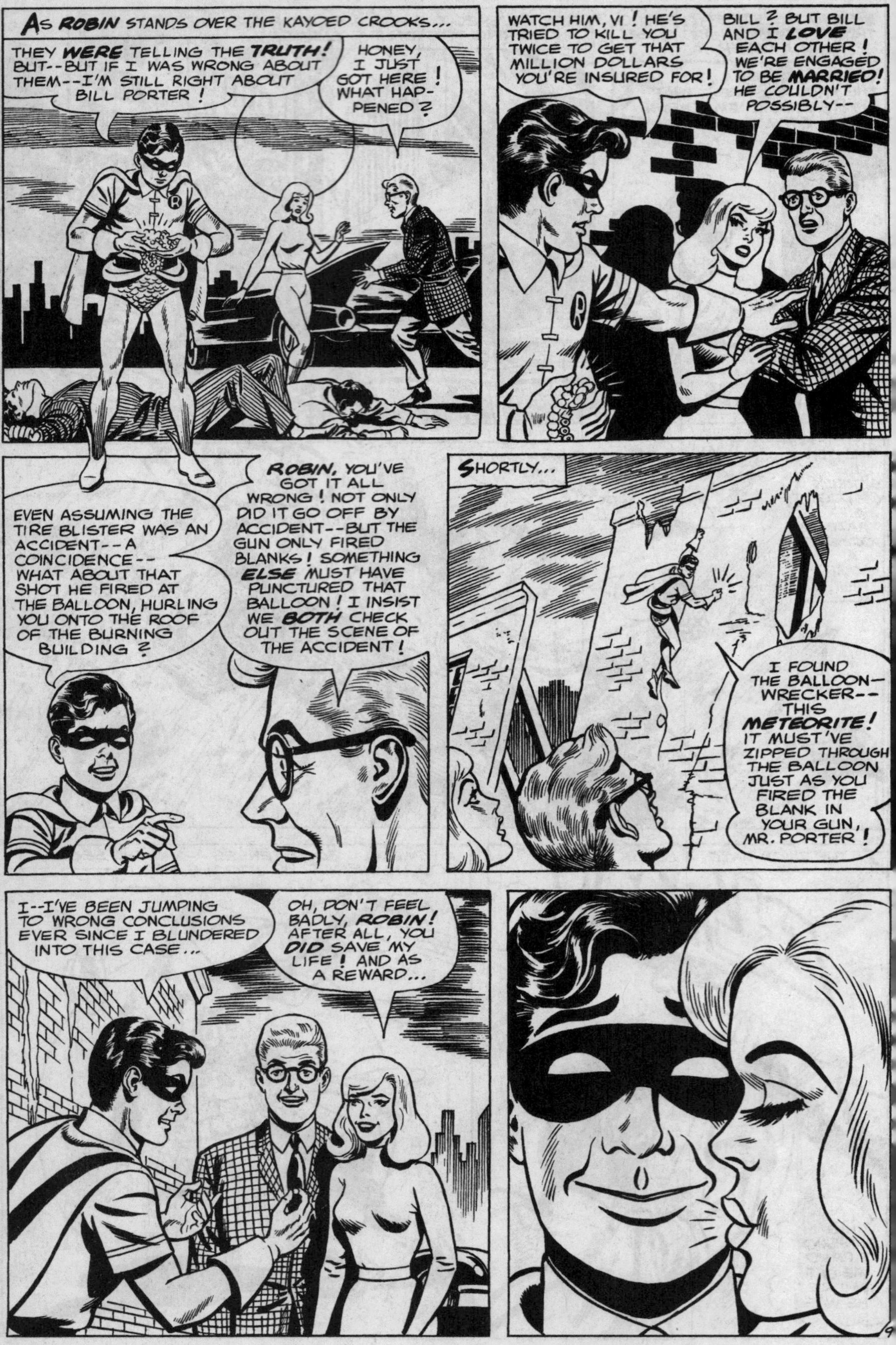
AS ROBIN STANDS OVER THE KAYOED CROOKS...
THEY WERE TELLING THE TRUTH! BUT--BUT IF I WAS WRONG ABOUT THEM--I'M STILL RIGHT ABOUT BILL PORTER!
HONEY, I JUST GOT HERE! WHAT HAPPENED?
WATCH HIM, VI! HE'S TRIED TO KILL YOU TWICE TO GET THAT MILLION DOLLARS YOU'RE INSURED FOR!
BILL? BUT BILL AND I LOVE EACH OTHER! WE'RE ENGAGED TO BE MARRIED! HE COULDN'T POSSIBLY--
EVEN ASSUMING THE TIRE BLISTER WAS AN ACCIDENT--A COINCIDENCE--WHAT ABOUT THAT SHOT HE FIRED AT THE BALLOON, HURLING YOU ONTO THE ROOF OF THE BURNING BUILDING?
ROBIN, YOU'VE GOT IT ALL WRONG! NOT ONLY DID IT GO OFF BY ACCIDENT--BUT THE GUN ONLY FIRED BLANKS! SOMETHING ELSE MUST HAVE PUNCTURED THAT BALLOON! I INSIST WE BOTH CHECK OUT THE SCENE OF THE ACCIDENT!
SHORTLY...
I FOUND THE BALLOON-WRECKER--THIS METEORITE! IT MUST'VE ZIPPED THROUGH THE BALLOON JUST AS YOU FIRED THE BLANK IN YOUR GUN, MR. PORTER!
I--I'VE BEEN JUMPING TO WRONG CONCLUSIONS EVER SINCE I BLUNDERED INTO THIS CASE...
OH, DON'T FEEL BADLY, ROBIN! AFTER ALL, YOU DID SAVE MY LIFE! AND AS A REWARD...
9

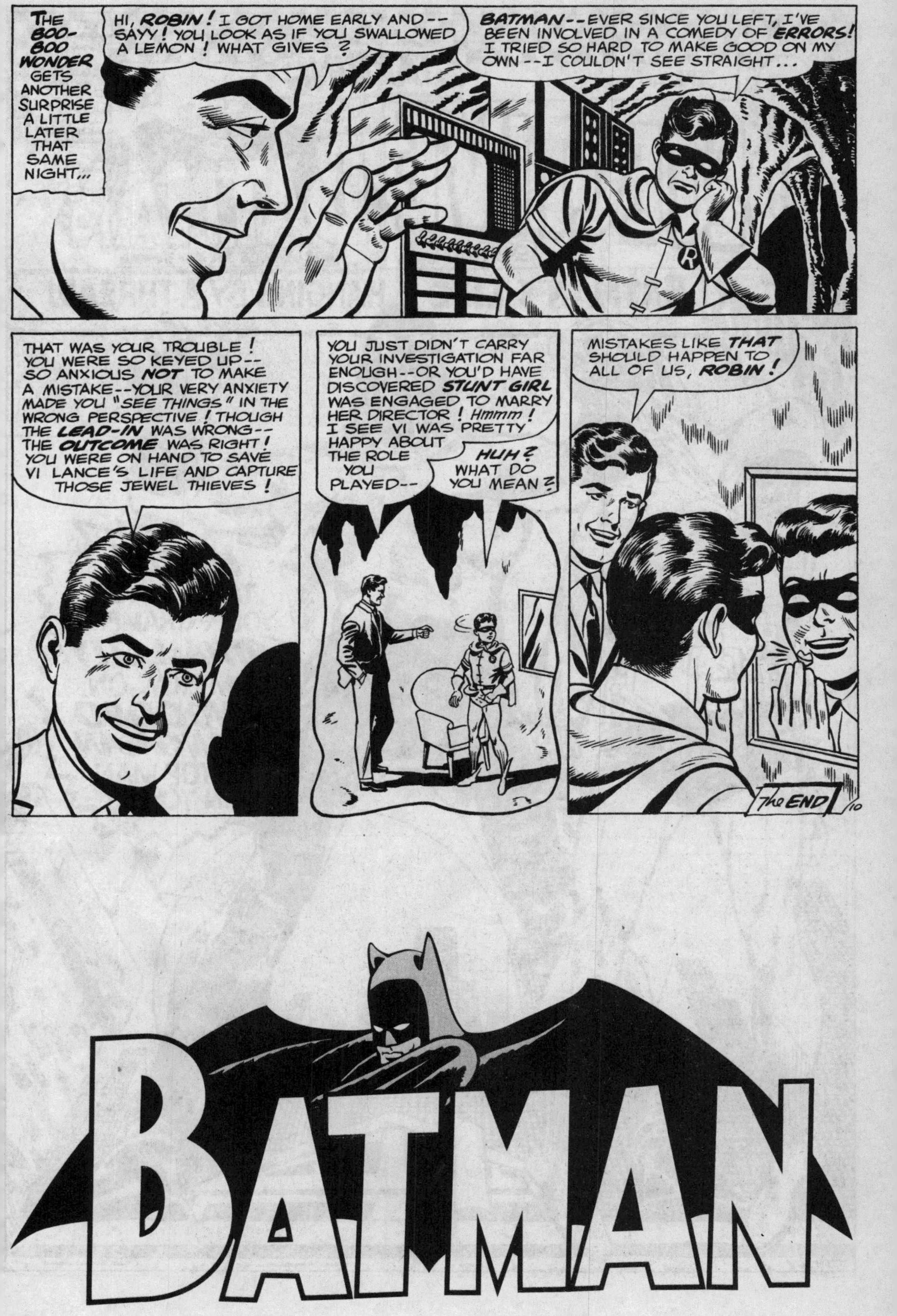
THE BOO-BOO WONDER GETS ANOTHER SURPRISE A LITTLE LATER THAT SAME NIGHT...
HI, ROBIN! I GOT HOME EARLY AND-- SAYY! YOU LOOK AS IF YOU SWALLOWED A LEMON! WHAT GIVES?
BATMAN--EVER SINCE YOU LEFT, I'VE BEEN INVOLVED IN A COMEDY OF ERRORS! I TRIED SO HARD TO MAKE GOOD ON MY OWN--I COULDN'T SEE STRAIGHT...
THAT WAS YOUR TROUBLE! YOU WERE SO KEYED UP-- SO ANXIOUS NOT TO MAKE A MISTAKE--YOUR VERY ANXIETY MADE YOU "SEE THINGS" IN THE WRONG PERSPECTIVE! THOUGH THE LEAD-IN WAS WRONG-- THE OUTCOME WAS RIGHT! YOU WERE ON HAND TO SAVE VI LANCE'S LIFE AND CAPTURE THOSE JEWEL THIEVES!
YOU JUST DIDN'T CARRY YOUR INVESTIGATION FAR ENOUGH--OR YOU'D HAVE DISCOVERED STUNT GIRL WAS ENGAGED TO MARRY HER DIRECTOR! Hmmm! I SEE VI WAS PRETTY HAPPY ABOUT THE ROLE YOU PLAYED--
HUH? WHAT DO YOU MEAN?
MISTAKES LIKE THAT SHOULD HAPPEN TO ALL OF US, ROBIN!
The END
10

BATMAN

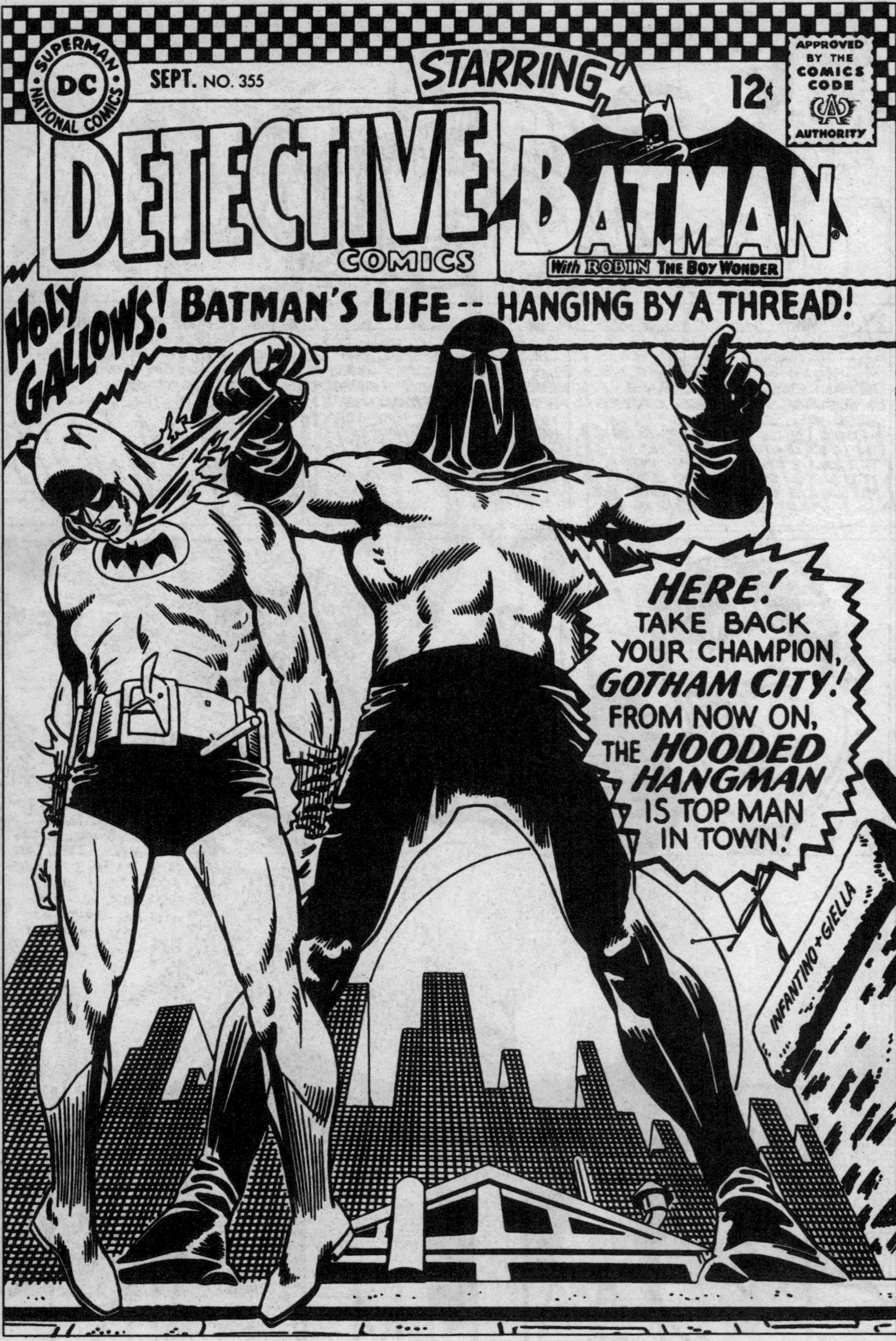
SUPERMAN DC NATIONAL COMICS
SEPT. NO. 355
STARRING
12¢
APPROVED BY THE COMICS CODE AUTHORITY
DETECTIVE COMICS
BATMAN
With ROBIN THE BOY WONDER
HOLY GALLOWS! BATMAN'S LIFE-- HANGING BY A THREAD!
HERE! TAKE BACK YOUR CHAMPION, GOTHAM CITY! FROM NOW ON, THE HOODED HANGMAN IS TOP MAN IN TOWN!
INFANTINO + GIELLA

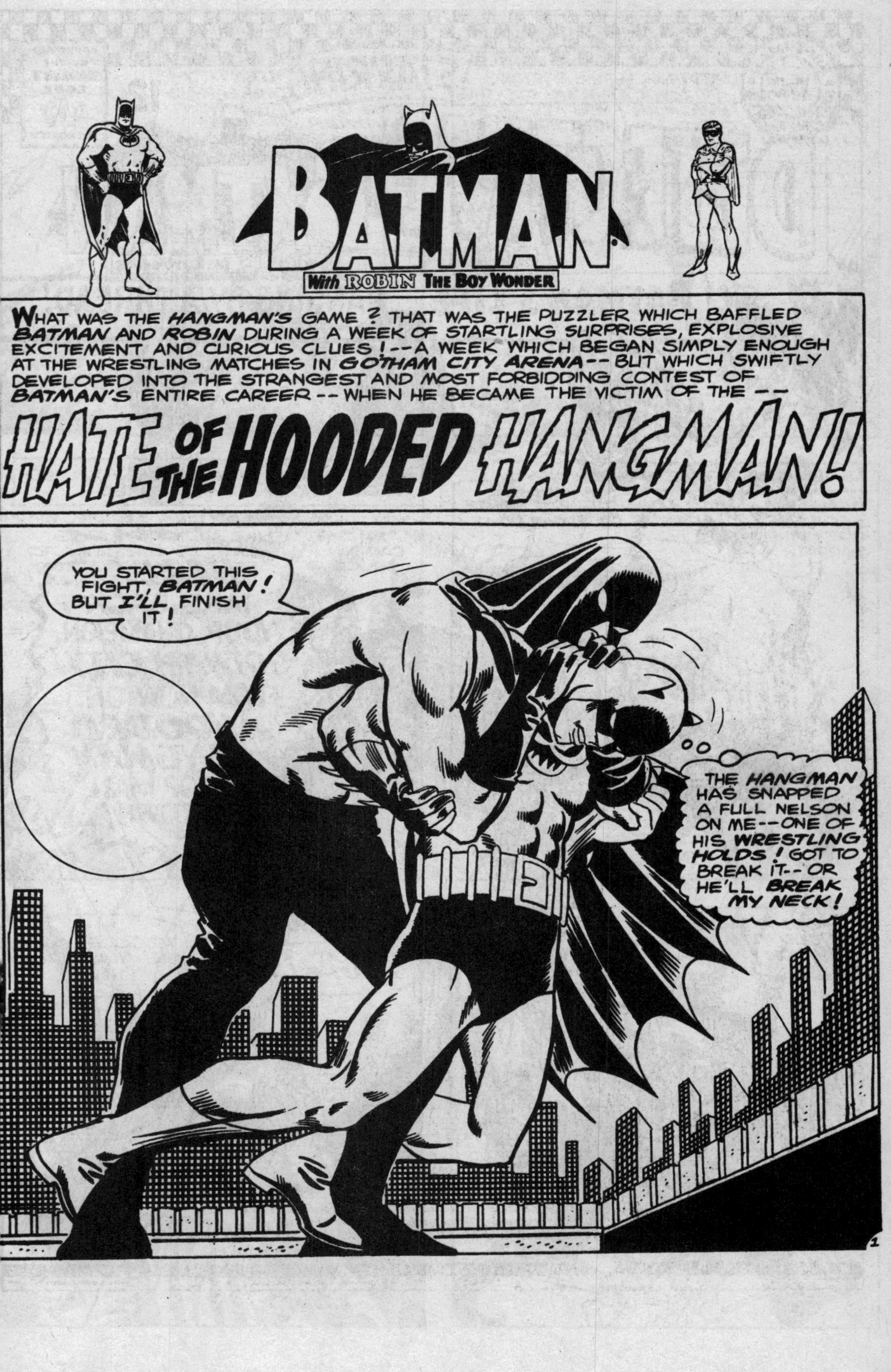
BATMAN
With ROBIN THE BOY WONDER
WHAT WAS THE HANGMAN'S GAME ? THAT WAS THE PUZZLER WHICH BAFFLED BATMAN AND ROBIN DURING A WEEK OF STARTLING SURPRISES, EXPLOSIVE EXCITEMENT AND CURIOUS CLUES ! -- A WEEK WHICH BEGAN SIMPLY ENOUGH AT THE WRESTLING MATCHES IN GOTHAM CITY ARENA -- BUT WHICH SWIFTLY DEVELOPED INTO THE STRANGEST AND MOST FORBIDDING CONTEST OF BATMAN'S ENTIRE CAREER -- WHEN HE BECAME THE VICTIM OF THE --
HATE OF THE HOODED HANGMAN!
YOU STARTED THIS FIGHT, BATMAN! BUT I'LL FINISH IT!
THE HANGMAN HAS SNAPPED A FULL NELSON ON ME--ONE OF HIS WRESTLING HOLDS! GOT TO BREAK IT--OR HE'LL BREAK MY NECK!
1

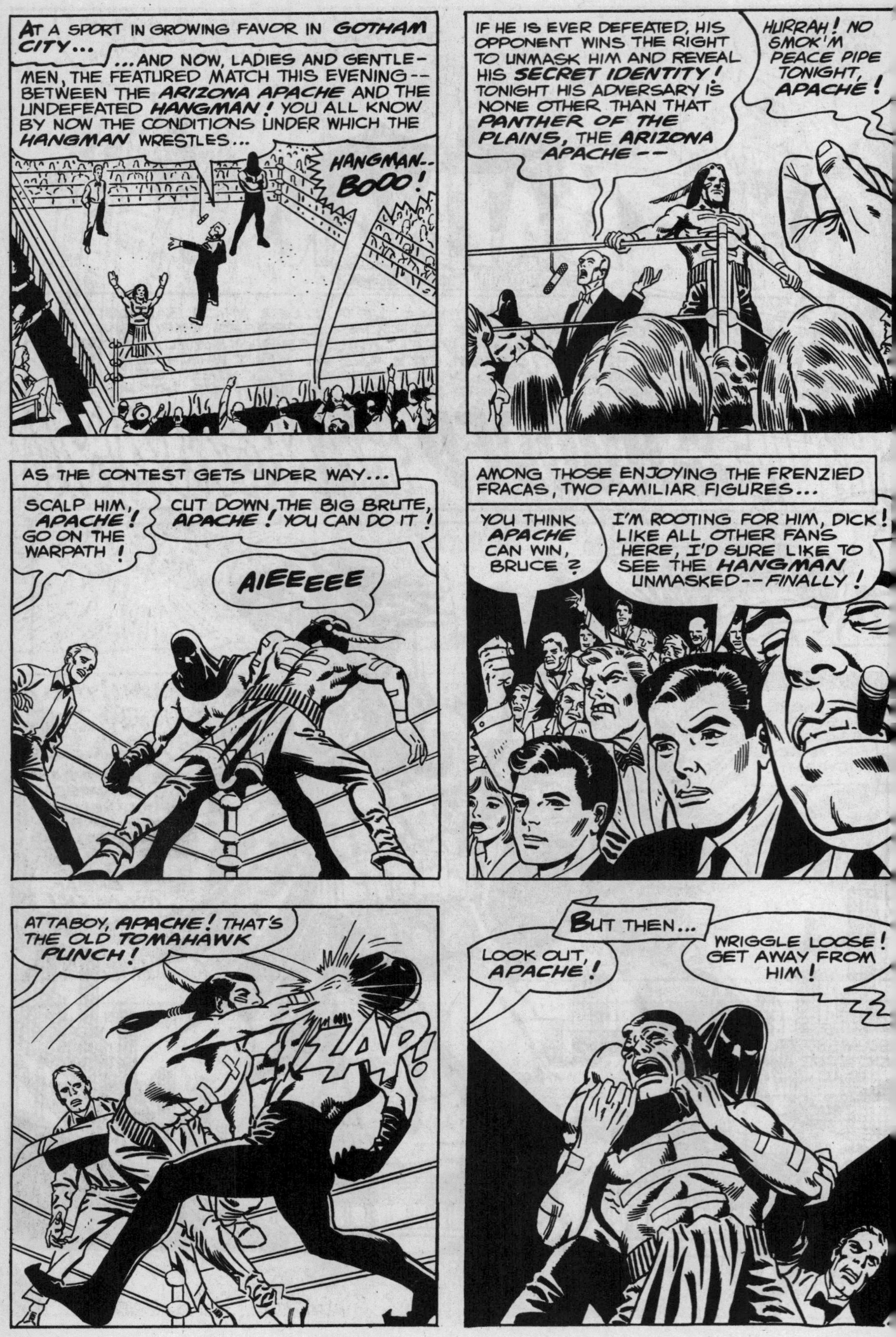
AT A SPORT IN GROWING FAVOR IN GOTHAM CITY...
...AND NOW, LADIES AND GENTLEMEN, THE FEATURED MATCH THIS EVENING--BETWEEN THE ARIZONA APACHE AND THE UNDEFEATED HANGMAN! YOU ALL KNOW BY NOW THE CONDITIONS UNDER WHICH THE HANGMAN WRESTLES...
HANGMAN.. BOOO!
IF HE IS EVER DEFEATED, HIS OPPONENT WINS THE RIGHT TO UNMASK HIM AND REVEAL HIS SECRET IDENTITY! TONIGHT HIS ADVERSARY IS NONE OTHER THAN THAT PANTHER OF THE PLAINS, THE ARIZONA APACHE--
HURRAH! NO SMOK'M PEACE PIPE TONIGHT, APACHE!
AS THE CONTEST GETS UNDER WAY...
SCALP HIM, APACHE! GO ON THE WARPATH!
CUT DOWN THE BIG BRUTE, APACHE! YOU CAN DO IT!
AIEEEEEE
AMONG THOSE ENJOYING THE FRENZIED FRACAS, TWO FAMILIAR FIGURES...
YOU THINK APACHE CAN WIN, BRUCE?
I'M ROOTING FOR HIM, DICK! LIKE ALL OTHER FANS HERE, I'D SURE LIKE TO SEE THE HANGMAN UNMASKED--FINALLY!
ATTABOY, APACHE! THAT'S THE OLD TOMAHAWK PUNCH!
ZAP!
BUT THEN...
LOOK OUT, APACHE!
WRIGGLE LOOSE! GET AWAY FROM HIM!

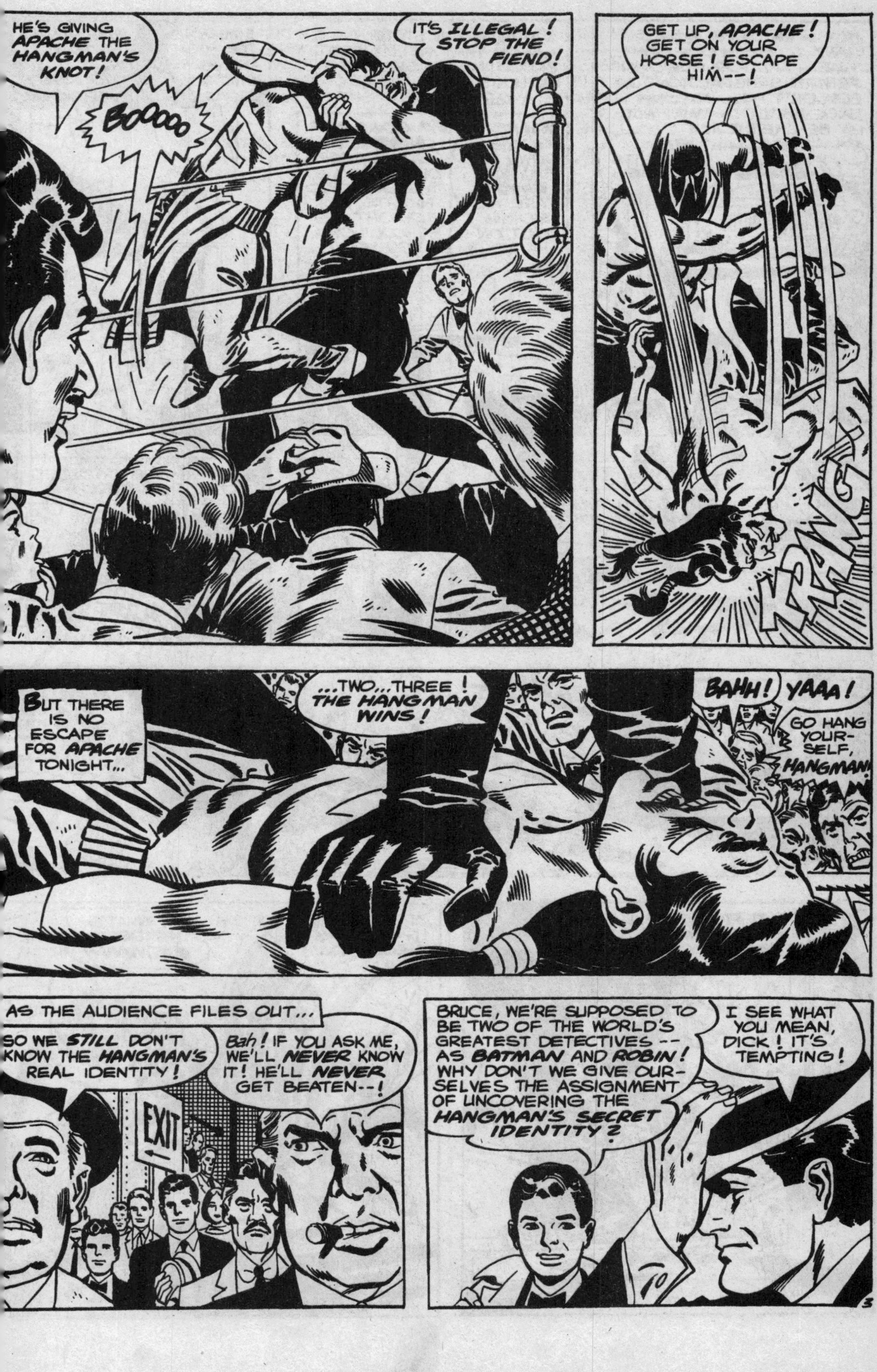

HE'S GIVING APACHE THE HANGMAN'S KNOT!
BOOOOO
IT'S ILLEGAL! STOP THE FIEND!
GET UP, APACHE! GET ON YOUR HORSE! ESCAPE HIM--!
KRANG
BUT THERE IS NO ESCAPE FOR APACHE TONIGHT...
...TWO...THREE! THE HANGMAN WINS!
BAHH! YAAA!
GO HANG YOURSELF, HANGMAN!
AS THE AUDIENCE FILES OUT...
SO WE STILL DON'T KNOW THE HANGMAN'S REAL IDENTITY!
Bah! IF YOU ASK ME, WE'LL NEVER KNOW IT! HE'LL NEVER GET BEATEN--!
EXIT
BRUCE, WE'RE SUPPOSED TO BE TWO OF THE WORLD'S GREATEST DETECTIVES -- AS BATMAN AND ROBIN! WHY DON'T WE GIVE OURSELVES THE ASSIGNMENT OF UNCOVERING THE HANGMAN'S SECRET IDENTITY?
I SEE WHAT YOU MEAN, DICK! IT'S TEMPTING!
3

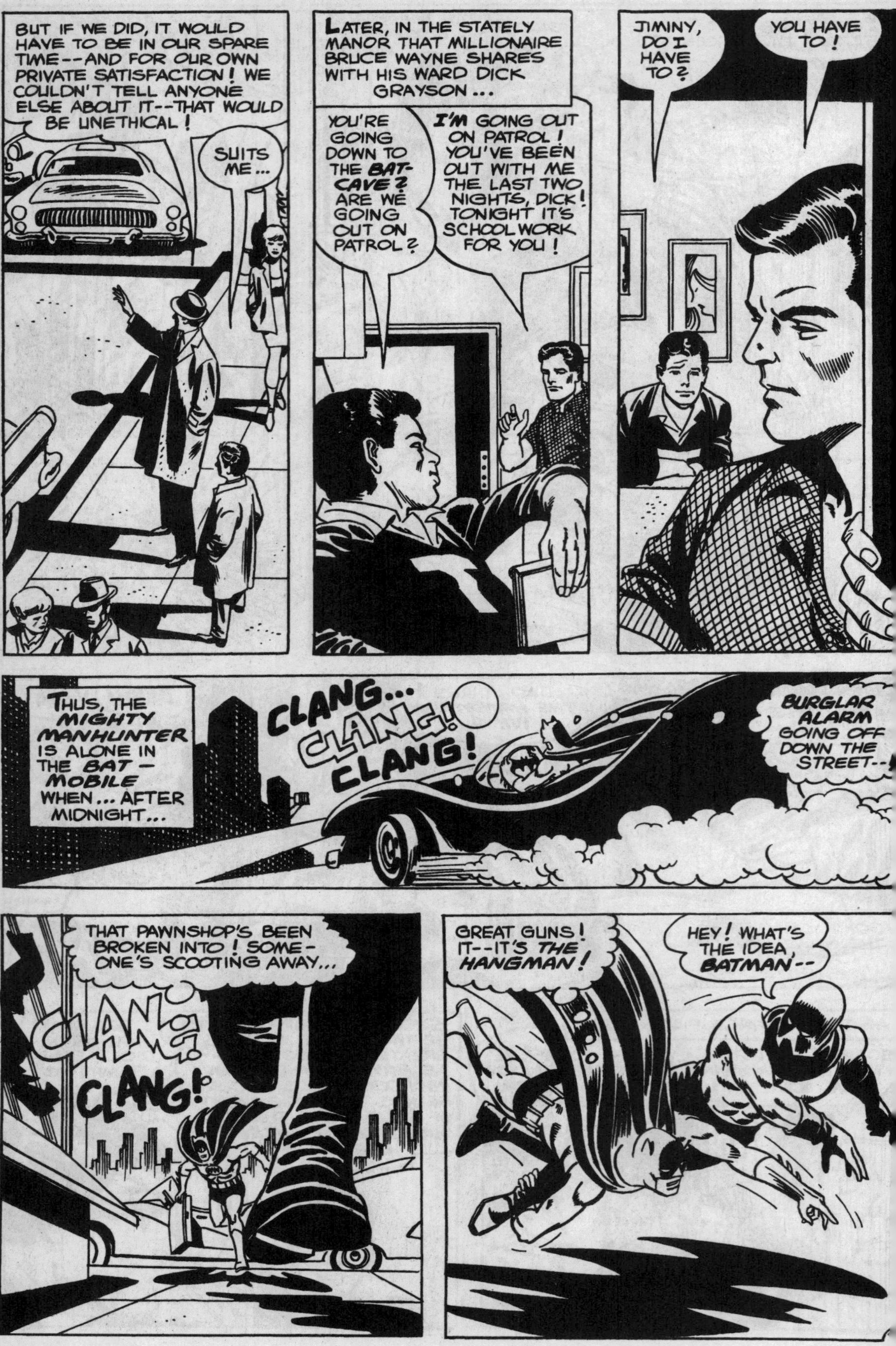
BUT IF WE DID, IT WOULD HAVE TO BE IN OUR SPARE TIME--AND FOR OUR OWN PRIVATE SATISFACTION! WE COULDN'T TELL ANYONE ELSE ABOUT IT--THAT WOULD BE UNETHICAL!
SUITS ME...
LATER, IN THE STATELY MANOR THAT MILLIONAIRE BRUCE WAYNE SHARES WITH HIS WARD DICK GRAYSON...
YOU'RE GOING DOWN TO THE BAT-CAVE? ARE WE GOING OUT ON PATROL?
I'M GOING OUT ON PATROL! YOU'VE BEEN OUT WITH ME THE LAST TWO NIGHTS, DICK! TONIGHT IT'S SCHOOLWORK FOR YOU!
JIMINY, DO I HAVE TO?
YOU HAVE TO!
THUS, THE MIGHTY MANHUNTER IS ALONE IN THE BAT-MOBILE WHEN... AFTER MIDNIGHT...
CLANG... CLANG! CLANG!
BURGLAR ALARM GOING OFF DOWN THE STREET--!
THAT PAWNSHOP'S BEEN BROKEN INTO! SOME-ONE'S SCOOTING AWAY...
CLANG! CLANG!
GREAT GUNS! IT--IT'S THE HANGMAN!
HEY! WHAT'S THE IDEA, BATMAN--

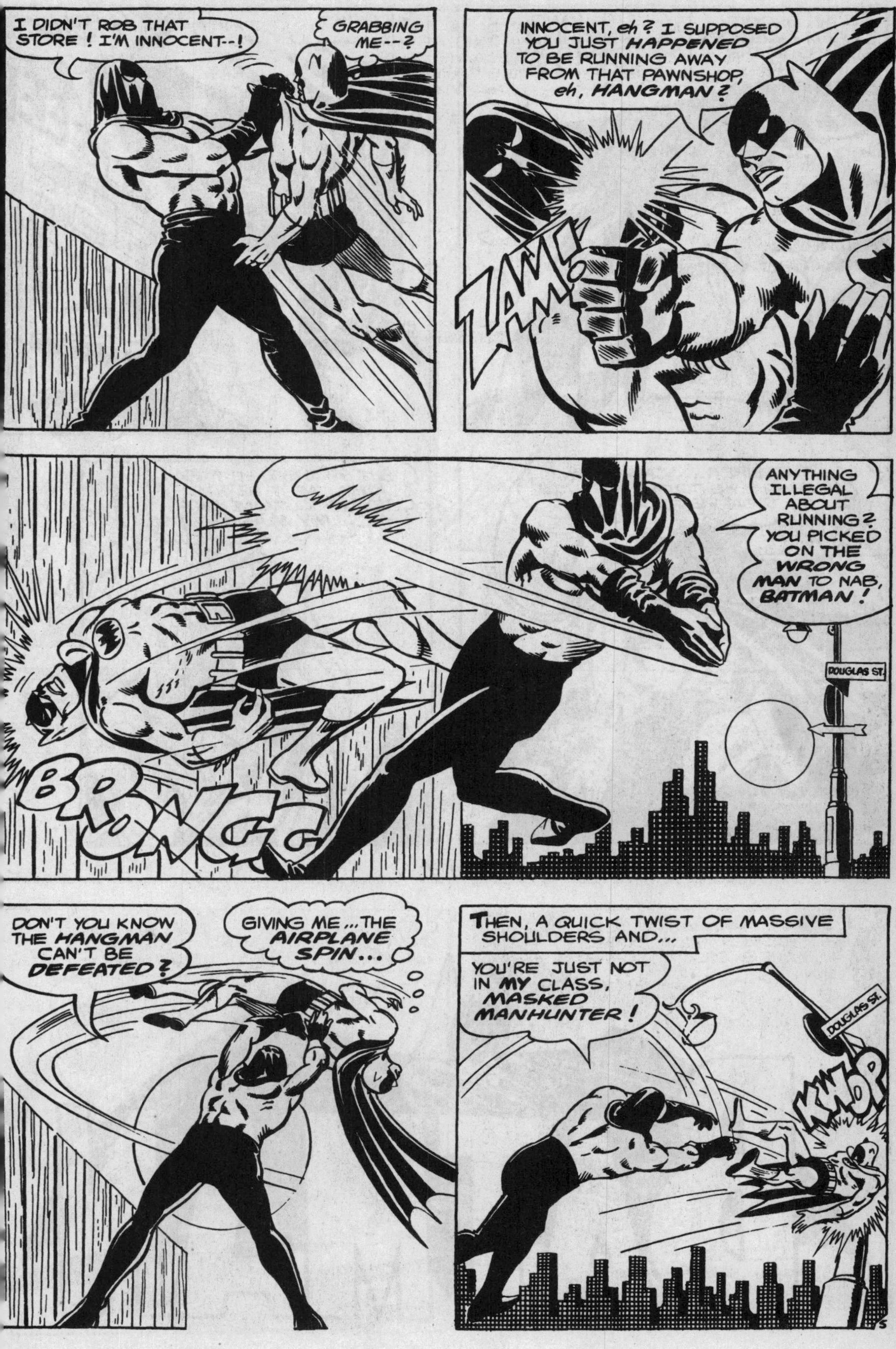
I DIDN'T ROB THAT STORE ! I'M INNOCENT--!
GRABBING ME--?
INNOCENT, eh? I SUPPOSED YOU JUST HAPPENED TO BE RUNNING AWAY FROM THAT PAWNSHOP, eh, HANGMAN?
ZAM!
ANYTHING ILLEGAL ABOUT RUNNING? YOU PICKED ON THE WRONG MAN TO NAB, BATMAN!
DOUGLAS ST.
BRONGG
DON'T YOU KNOW THE HANGMAN CAN'T BE DEFEATED?
GIVING ME... THE AIRPLANE SPIN...
THEN, A QUICK TWIST OF MASSIVE SHOULDERS AND...
YOU'RE JUST NOT IN MY CLASS, MASKED MANHUNTER!
DOUGLAS ST.
KWOP
5

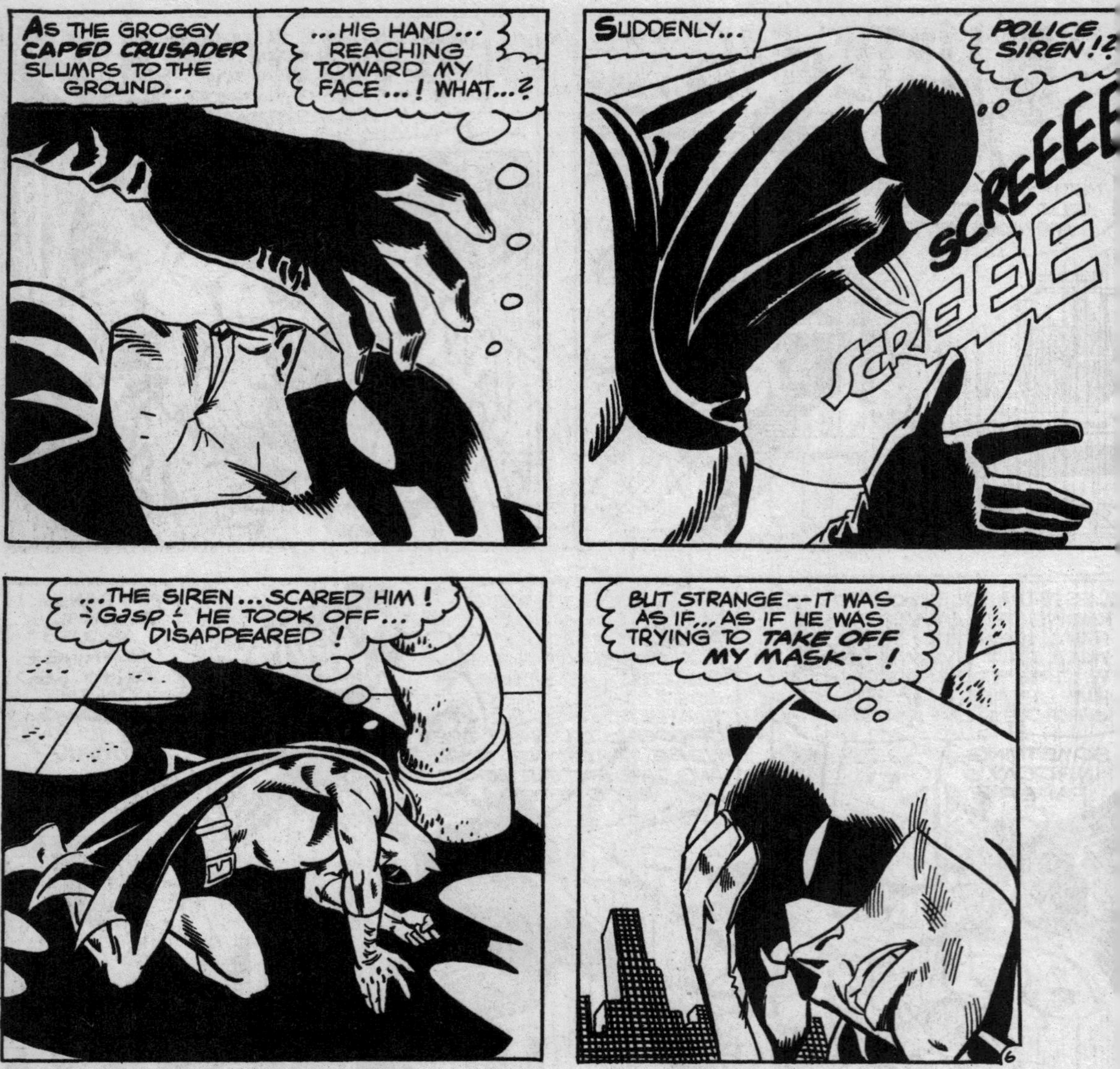
AS THE GROGGY **CAPED CRUSADER** SLUMPS TO THE GROUND...
...HIS HAND... REACHING TOWARD MY FACE...! WHAT...?
SUDDENLY...
POLICE SIREN!?
SCREEEE
SCREEEE
...THE SIREN...SCARED HIM! -Gasp- HE TOOK OFF... DISAPPEARED!
BUT STRANGE--IT WAS AS IF... AS IF HE WAS TRYING TO **TAKE OFF MY MASK**--!
6

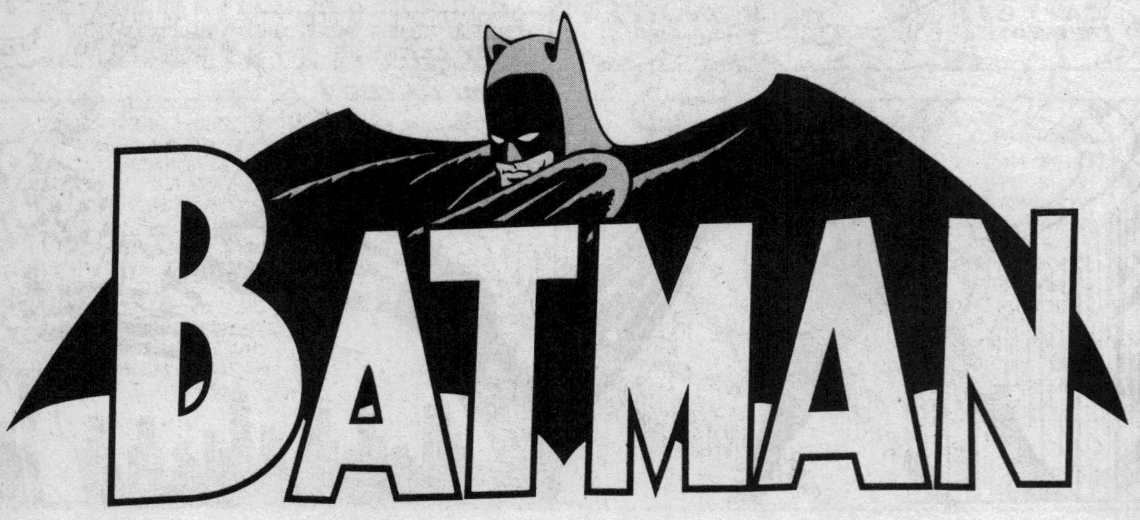
BATMAN

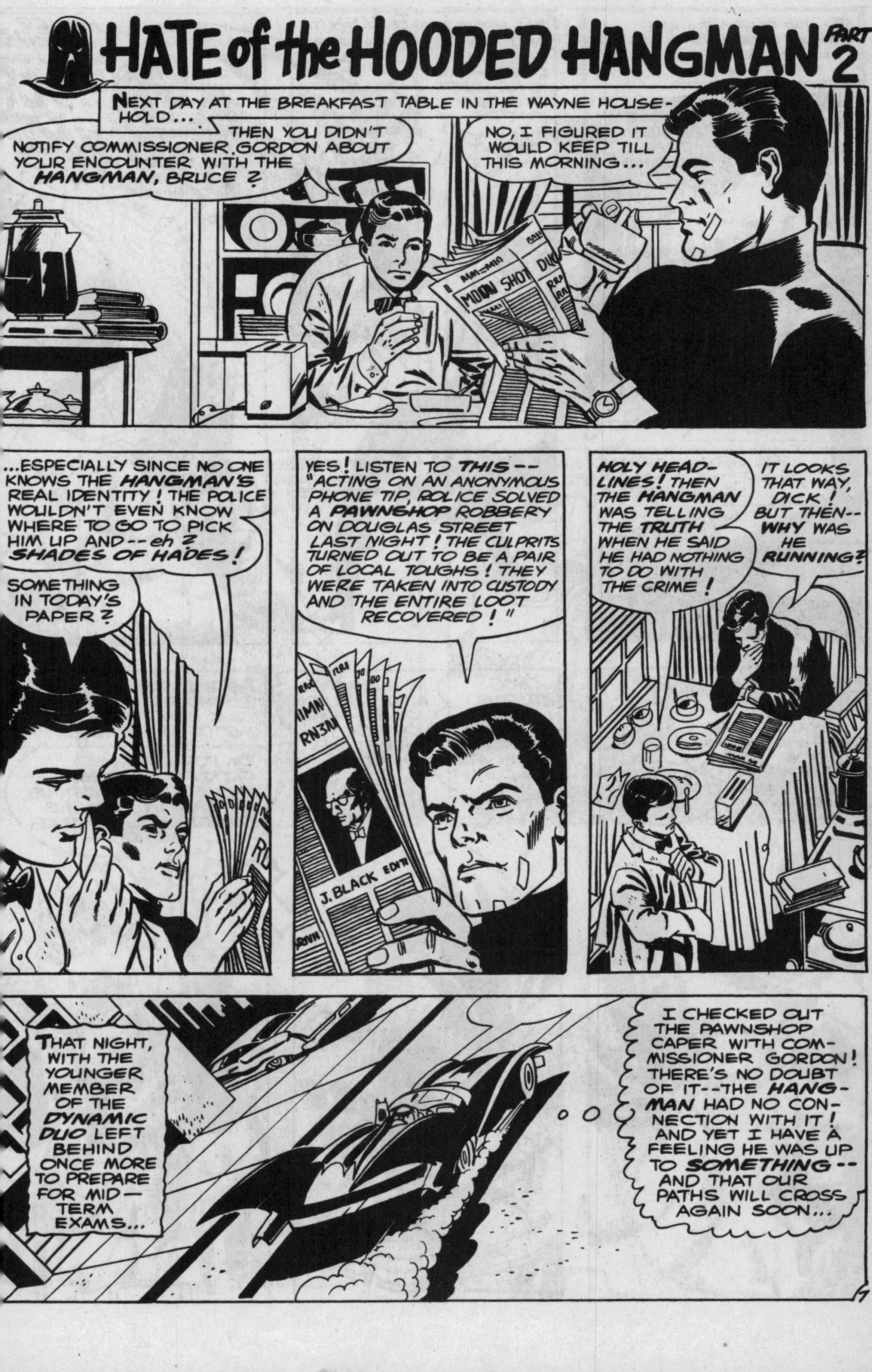
HATE of the HOODED HANGMAN PART 2
NEXT DAY AT THE BREAKFAST TABLE IN THE WAYNE HOUSEHOLD...
THEN YOU DIDN'T NOTIFY COMMISSIONER GORDON ABOUT YOUR ENCOUNTER WITH THE HANGMAN, BRUCE?
NO, I FIGURED IT WOULD KEEP TILL THIS MORNING...
MOON SHOT
...ESPECIALLY SINCE NO ONE KNOWS THE HANGMAN'S REAL IDENTITY! THE POLICE WOULDN'T EVEN KNOW WHERE TO GO TO PICK HIM UP AND--eh? SHADES OF HADES!
SOMETHING IN TODAY'S PAPER?
YES! LISTEN TO THIS-- "ACTING ON AN ANONYMOUS PHONE TIP, POLICE SOLVED A PAWNSHOP ROBBERY ON DOUGLAS STREET LAST NIGHT! THE CULPRITS TURNED OUT TO BE A PAIR OF LOCAL TOUGHS! THEY WERE TAKEN INTO CUSTODY AND THE ENTIRE LOOT RECOVERED!"
J. BLACK EDIT
HOLY HEADLINES! THEN THE HANGMAN WAS TELLING THE TRUTH WHEN HE SAID HE HAD NOTHING TO DO WITH THE CRIME!
IT LOOKS THAT WAY, DICK! BUT THEN--WHY WAS HE RUNNING?
THAT NIGHT, WITH THE YOUNGER MEMBER OF THE DYNAMIC DUO LEFT BEHIND ONCE MORE TO PREPARE FOR MID-TERM EXAMS...
I CHECKED OUT THE PAWNSHOP CAPER WITH COMMISSIONER GORDON! THERE'S NO DOUBT OF IT--THE HANGMAN HAD NO CONNECTION WITH IT! AND YET I HAVE A FEELING HE WAS UP TO SOMETHING--AND THAT OUR PATHS WILL CROSS AGAIN SOON...
7

AS THE SLEEK VEHICLE RIDES THROUGH A SLEEPING CITY, THE DARKNESS IS SPLIT BY AN OUTCRY...

HELP! POLICE! HELP!

SOMEONE IN TROUBLE -- BEHIND THAT BUILDING!

THE *HANGMAN!* AND THAT WINDOW BEHIND HIM *OPEN*-- AS IF HE JUST CLIMBED OUT OF IT!

YOU AGAIN, *BAT-MAN!?* YOU MUST HAVE HEARD THAT CRY FOR HELP! I HEARD IT TOO-- AND DASHED HERE!

WHAT'S THE MATTER, DON'T YOU BELIEVE ME? YOU'RE NOT THINKING OF TANGLING WITH ME AGAIN, *BATMAN?* NOT AFTER LAST NIGHT--

STRANGE... THAT *VOICE* OF HIS! IT'S *FAMILIAR*-- AND YET IT *ISN'T!* AS IF HE'S TRYING TO *DISGUISE* HIS *REAL* VOICE!

YOU'RE COMING WITH ME --TO THE POLICE! IF YOU'VE DONE NOTHING WRONG, YOU'VE GOT NOTHING TO BE AFRAID OF!

PULLING ME --!?

YOU STARTED THIS, *BATMAN!* YOU CAN'T YANK *ME* AROUND!

HE'S SNAPPED A FULL NELSON ON ME --ONE OF HIS WRESTLING HOLDS!

AS THE STEELY MUSCLES BEHIND THE *MANHUNTER'S* NECK REACT WITH TRE-MENDOUS POWER...

I'M PERFORMING A *CITIZEN'S ARREST*-- AND YOU'RE RESISTING, *HANGMAN!* YOU'RE *FORCING* ME TO TAKE ACTION --!

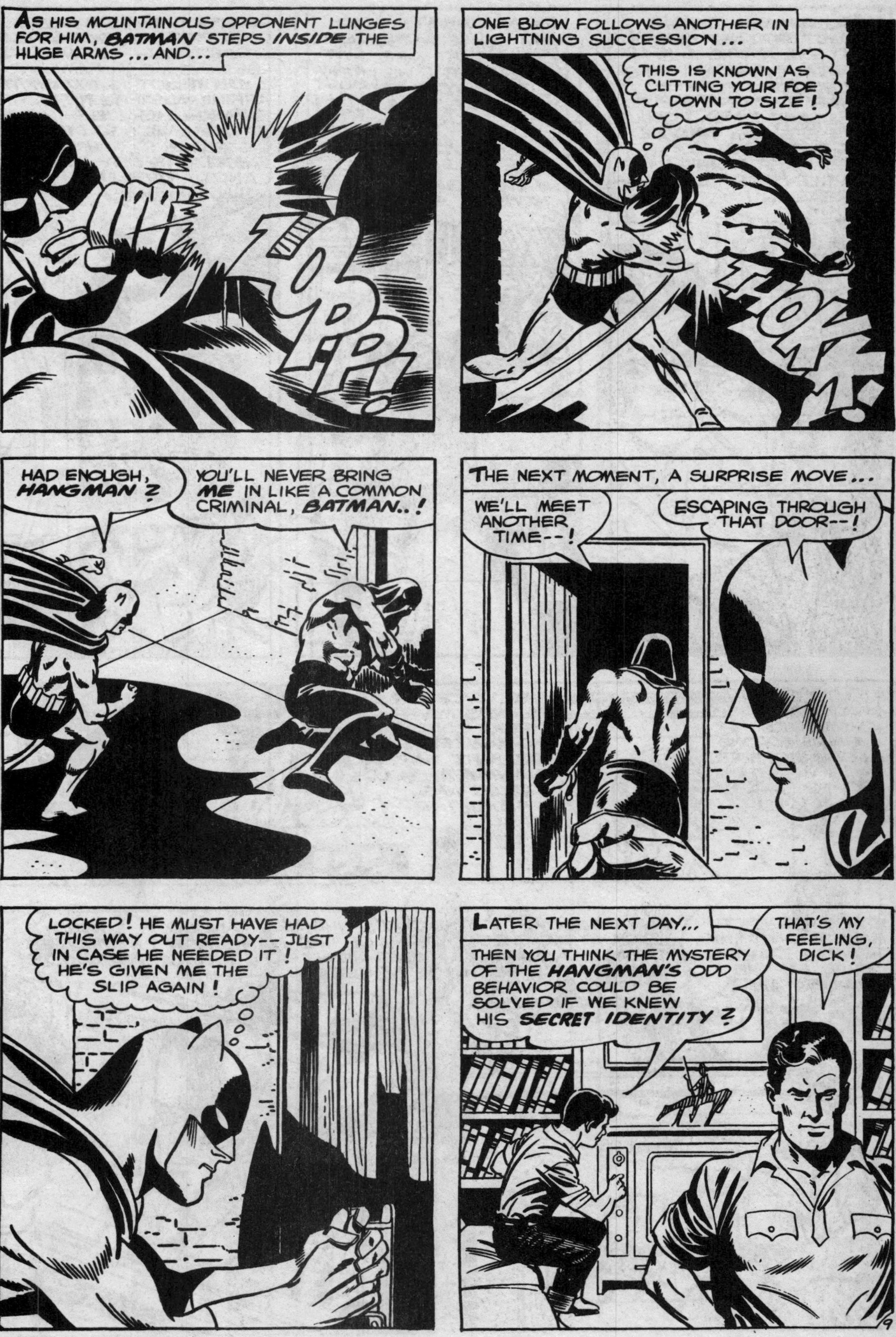
AS HIS MOUNTAINOUS OPPONENT LUNGES FOR HIM, BATMAN STEPS INSIDE THE HUGE ARMS ... AND...
ZOPP!
ONE BLOW FOLLOWS ANOTHER IN LIGHTNING SUCCESSION...
THIS IS KNOWN AS CUTTING YOUR FOE DOWN TO SIZE!
THOK!
HAD ENOUGH, HANGMAN ?
YOU'LL NEVER BRING ME IN LIKE A COMMON CRIMINAL, BATMAN..!
THE NEXT MOMENT, A SURPRISE MOVE...
WE'LL MEET ANOTHER TIME--!
ESCAPING THROUGH THAT DOOR--!
LOCKED! HE MUST HAVE HAD THIS WAY OUT READY-- JUST IN CASE HE NEEDED IT! HE'S GIVEN ME THE SLIP AGAIN!
LATER THE NEXT DAY...
THEN YOU THINK THE MYSTERY OF THE HANGMAN'S ODD BEHAVIOR COULD BE SOLVED IF WE KNEW HIS SECRET IDENTITY ?
THAT'S MY FEELING, DICK!
9

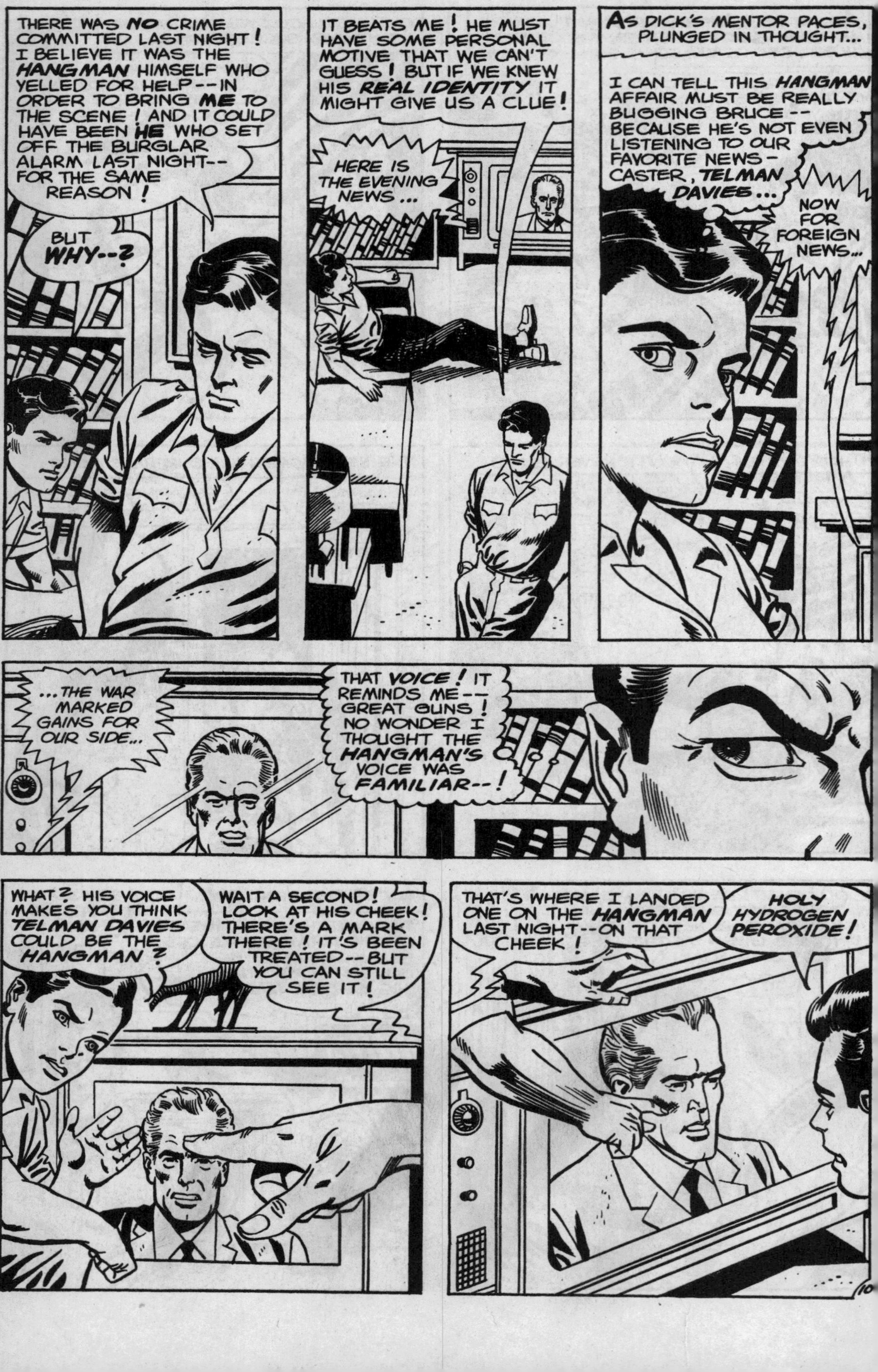
THERE WAS NO CRIME COMMITTED LAST NIGHT! I BELIEVE IT WAS THE HANGMAN HIMSELF WHO YELLED FOR HELP--IN ORDER TO BRING ME TO THE SCENE! AND IT COULD HAVE BEEN HE WHO SET OFF THE BURGLAR ALARM LAST NIGHT--FOR THE SAME REASON!
BUT WHY--?
IT BEATS ME! HE MUST HAVE SOME PERSONAL MOTIVE THAT WE CAN'T GUESS! BUT IF WE KNEW HIS REAL IDENTITY IT MIGHT GIVE US A CLUE!
HERE IS THE EVENING NEWS...
AS DICK'S MENTOR PACES, PLUNGED IN THOUGHT...
I CAN TELL THIS HANGMAN AFFAIR MUST BE REALLY BUGGING BRUCE--BECAUSE HE'S NOT EVEN LISTENING TO OUR FAVORITE NEWS-CASTER, TELMAN DAVIES...
NOW FOR FOREIGN NEWS...
...THE WAR MARKED GAINS FOR OUR SIDE...
THAT VOICE! IT REMINDS ME--GREAT GUNS! NO WONDER I THOUGHT THE HANGMAN'S VOICE WAS FAMILIAR--!
WHAT? HIS VOICE MAKES YOU THINK TELMAN DAVIES COULD BE THE HANGMAN?
WAIT A SECOND! LOOK AT HIS CHEEK! THERE'S A MARK THERE! IT'S BEEN TREATED--BUT YOU CAN STILL SEE IT!
THAT'S WHERE I LANDED ONE ON THE HANGMAN LAST NIGHT--ON THAT CHEEK!
HOLY HYDROGEN PEROXIDE!
10

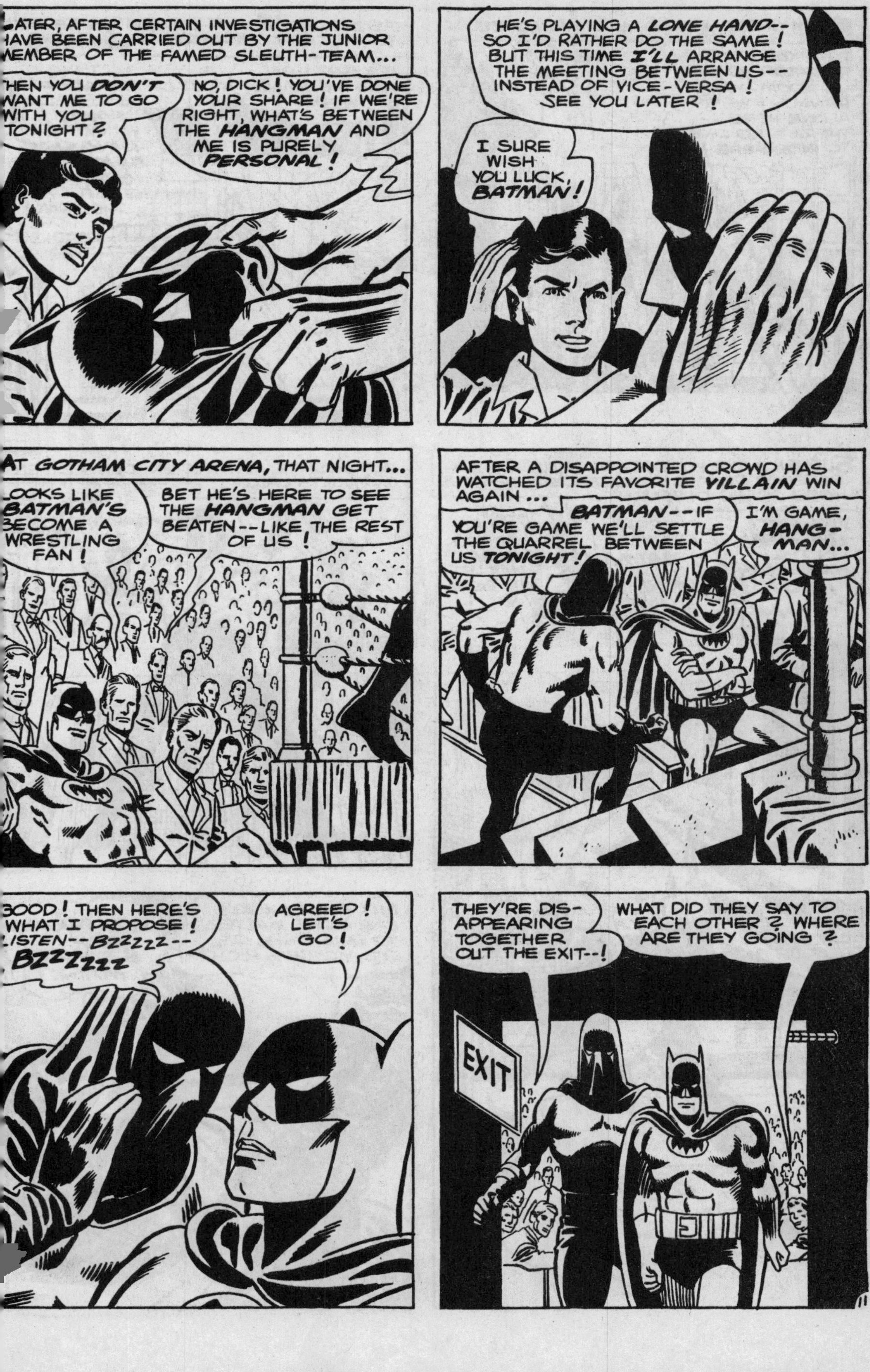
LATER, AFTER CERTAIN INVESTIGATIONS HAVE BEEN CARRIED OUT BY THE JUNIOR MEMBER OF THE FAMED SLEUTH-TEAM...
THEN YOU DON'T WANT ME TO GO WITH YOU TONIGHT?
NO, DICK! YOU'VE DONE YOUR SHARE! IF WE'RE RIGHT, WHAT'S BETWEEN THE HANGMAN AND ME IS PURELY PERSONAL!
HE'S PLAYING A LONE HAND-- SO I'D RATHER DO THE SAME! BUT THIS TIME I'LL ARRANGE THE MEETING BETWEEN US-- INSTEAD OF VICE-VERSA! SEE YOU LATER!
I SURE WISH YOU LUCK, BATMAN!
AT GOTHAM CITY ARENA, THAT NIGHT...
LOOKS LIKE BATMAN'S BECOME A WRESTLING FAN!
BET HE'S HERE TO SEE THE HANGMAN GET BEATEN--LIKE THE REST OF US!
AFTER A DISAPPOINTED CROWD HAS WATCHED ITS FAVORITE VILLAIN WIN AGAIN...
BATMAN--IF YOU'RE GAME WE'LL SETTLE THE QUARREL BETWEEN US TONIGHT!
I'M GAME, HANGMAN...
GOOD! THEN HERE'S WHAT I PROPOSE! LISTEN--BZZZZZ-- BZZZZZZ
AGREED! LET'S GO!
THEY'RE DISAPPEARING TOGETHER OUT THE EXIT--!
WHAT DID THEY SAY TO EACH OTHER? WHERE ARE THEY GOING?
EXIT
11

SOON UNDER A PALE MOON IN MID-CITY...

I PICKED ON THIS ROOFTOP TO GIVE US ROOM--AND PRIVACY! WE'RE ALONE HERE-- THERE'S NO ONE TO INTERFERE!

I'M READY!

AS THE SOUNDS OF COMBAT CAUSE LIGHTS TO GO ON ROUNDABOUT...

IT'S BATMAN AND THE HANGMAN!

THEY'RE BATTLING IT OUT ON THE ROOF!

WOWIE! WE GOT A RINGSIDE SEAT TO THE GREATEST FIGHT OF THE YEAR!

SUDDENLY THE HOODED WRESTLER MANAGES TO OBTAIN HIS DREADED, INFAMOUS HOLD ON HIS OPPONENT...

HE'S GOT BATMAN IN THE HANGMAN'S KNOT!!

BREAK LOOSE, BATMAN!

WE'RE ROOTING FOR YOU, BATMAN! DON'T LET HIM BEAT YOU!

BUT DESPITE ALL THE ENCOURAGEMENT, MOMENTS LATER...

HERE! TAKE BACK YOUR CHAMPION GOTHAM CITY! I'M FINISHED WITH HIM! HA HA!

BUT FIRST THERE'S ONE MORE MATTER TO TAKE CARE OF... THE VICTOR'S RIGHT--!

HE'S TAKING OFF BATMAN'S MASK!

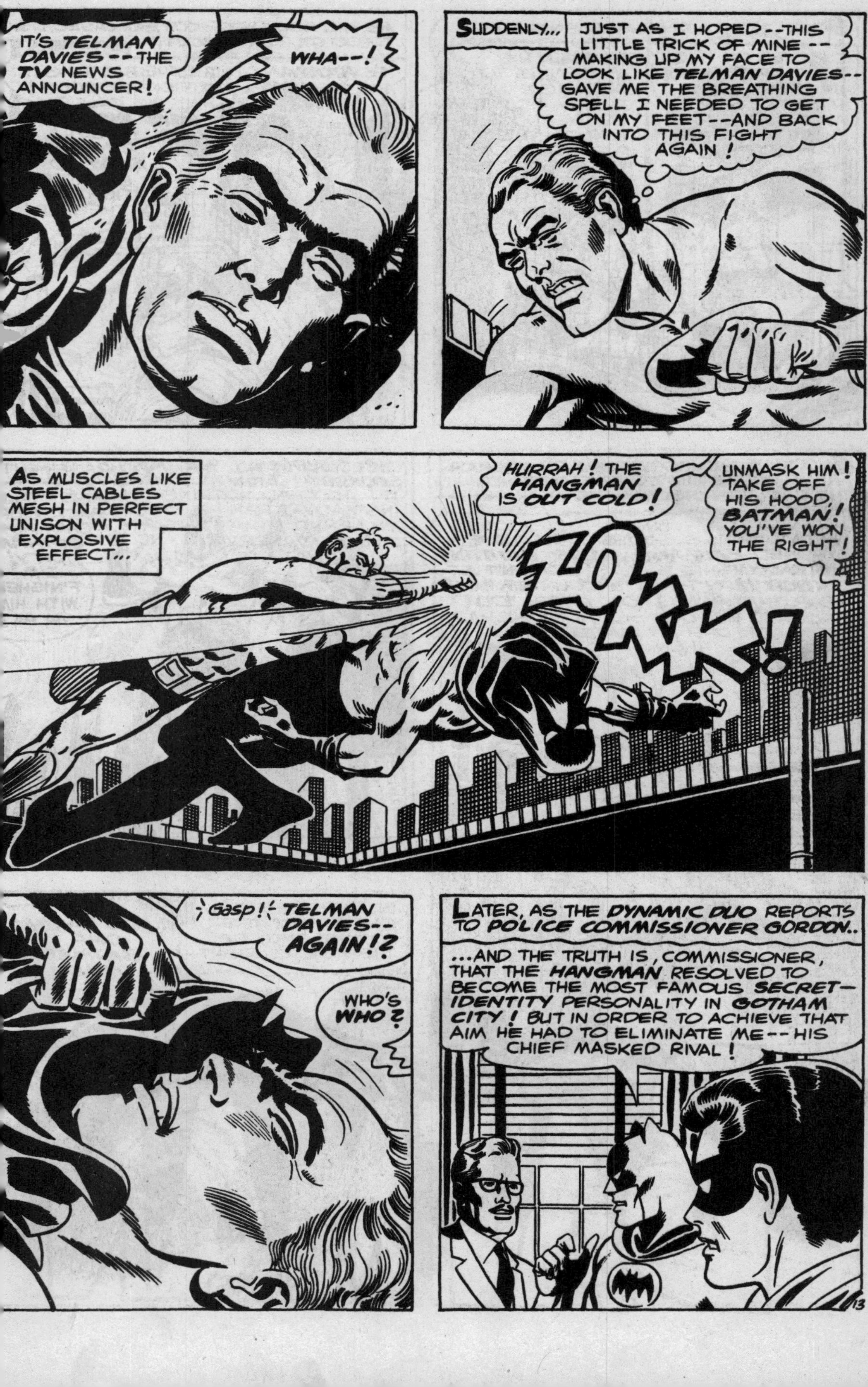
IT'S TELMAN DAVIES -- THE TV NEWS ANNOUNCER!
WHA--!
SUDDENLY...
JUST AS I HOPED--THIS LITTLE TRICK OF MINE -- MAKING UP MY FACE TO LOOK LIKE TELMAN DAVIES-- GAVE ME THE BREATHING SPELL I NEEDED TO GET ON MY FEET--AND BACK INTO THIS FIGHT AGAIN!
AS MUSCLES LIKE STEEL CABLES MESH IN PERFECT UNISON WITH EXPLOSIVE EFFECT...
HURRAH! THE HANGMAN IS OUT COLD!
UNMASK HIM! TAKE OFF HIS HOOD, BATMAN! YOU'VE WON THE RIGHT!
ZOKK!
Gasp! TELMAN DAVIES-- AGAIN!?
WHO'S WHO?
LATER, AS THE DYNAMIC DUO REPORTS TO POLICE COMMISSIONER GORDON..
...AND THE TRUTH IS, COMMISSIONER, THAT THE HANGMAN RESOLVED TO BECOME THE MOST FAMOUS SECRET-IDENTITY PERSONALITY IN GOTHAM CITY! BUT IN ORDER TO ACHIEVE THAT AIM HE HAD TO ELIMINATE ME--HIS CHIEF MASKED RIVAL!
13

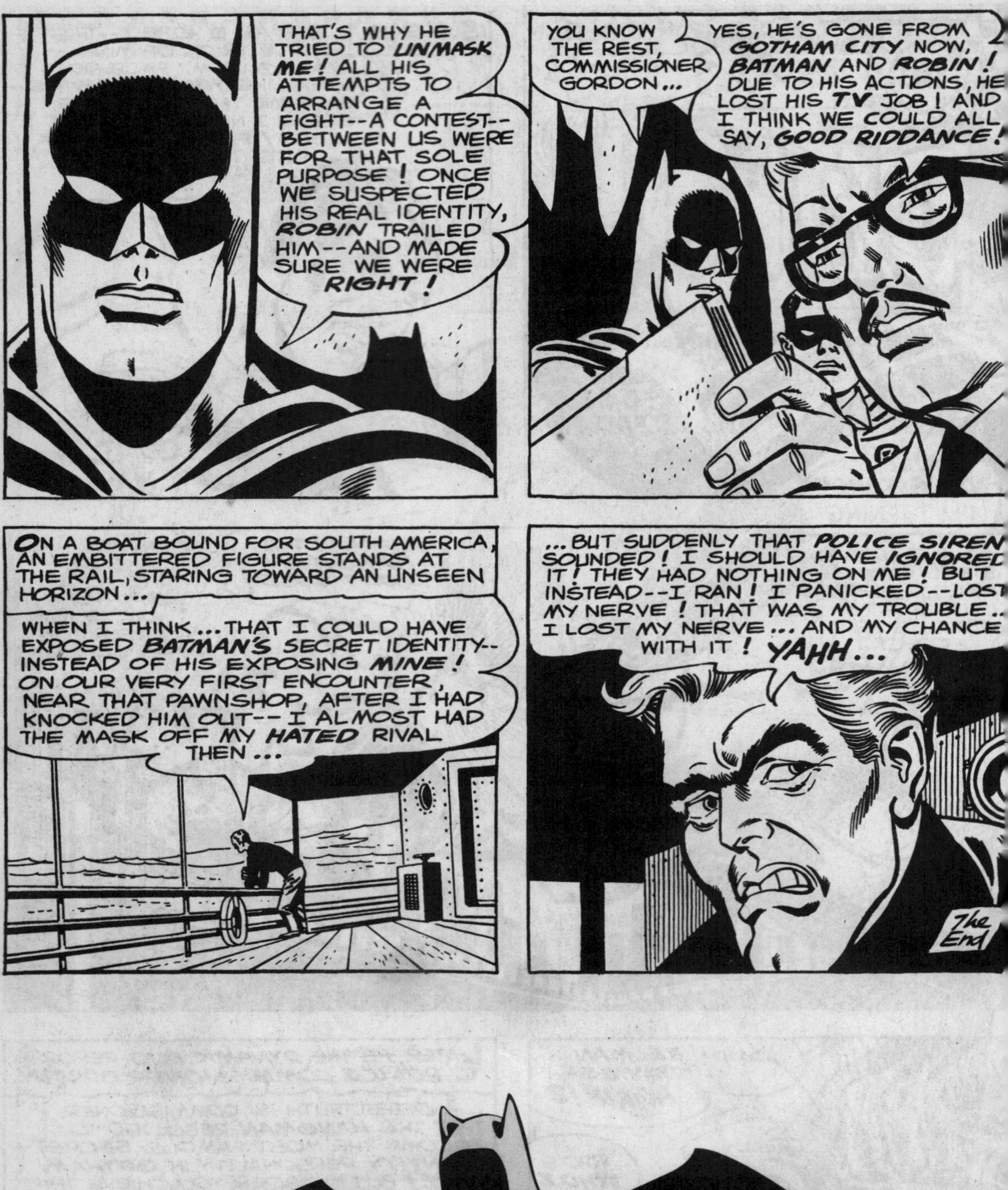
THAT'S WHY HE TRIED TO UNMASK ME! ALL HIS ATTEMPTS TO ARRANGE A FIGHT--A CONTEST--BETWEEN US WERE FOR THAT SOLE PURPOSE! ONCE WE SUSPECTED HIS REAL IDENTITY, ROBIN TRAILED HIM--AND MADE SURE WE WERE RIGHT!
YOU KNOW THE REST, COMMISSIONER GORDON...
YES, HE'S GONE FROM GOTHAM CITY NOW, BATMAN AND ROBIN! DUE TO HIS ACTIONS, HE LOST HIS TV JOB! AND I THINK WE COULD ALL SAY, GOOD RIDDANCE!
ON A BOAT BOUND FOR SOUTH AMERICA, AN EMBITTERED FIGURE STANDS AT THE RAIL, STARING TOWARD AN UNSEEN HORIZON...
WHEN I THINK...THAT I COULD HAVE EXPOSED BATMAN'S SECRET IDENTITY--INSTEAD OF HIS EXPOSING MINE! ON OUR VERY FIRST ENCOUNTER, NEAR THAT PAWNSHOP, AFTER I HAD KNOCKED HIM OUT--I ALMOST HAD THE MASK OFF MY HATED RIVAL THEN...
...BUT SUDDENLY THAT POLICE SIREN SOUNDED! I SHOULD HAVE IGNORED IT! THEY HAD NOTHING ON ME! BUT INSTEAD--I RAN! I PANICKED--LOST MY NERVE! THAT WAS MY TROUBLE... I LOST MY NERVE... AND MY CHANCE WITH IT! YAHH...
The End

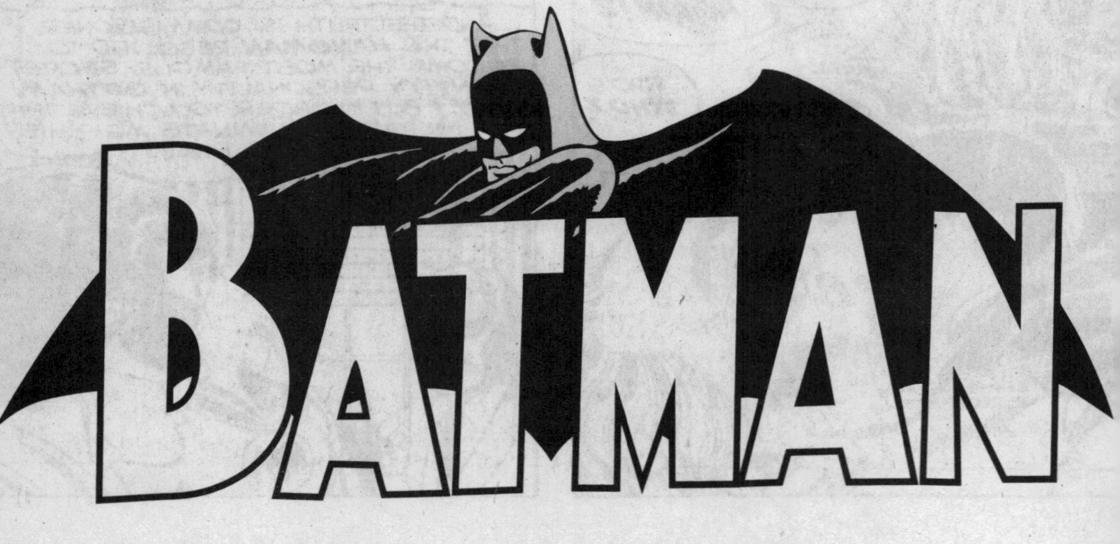
BATMAN

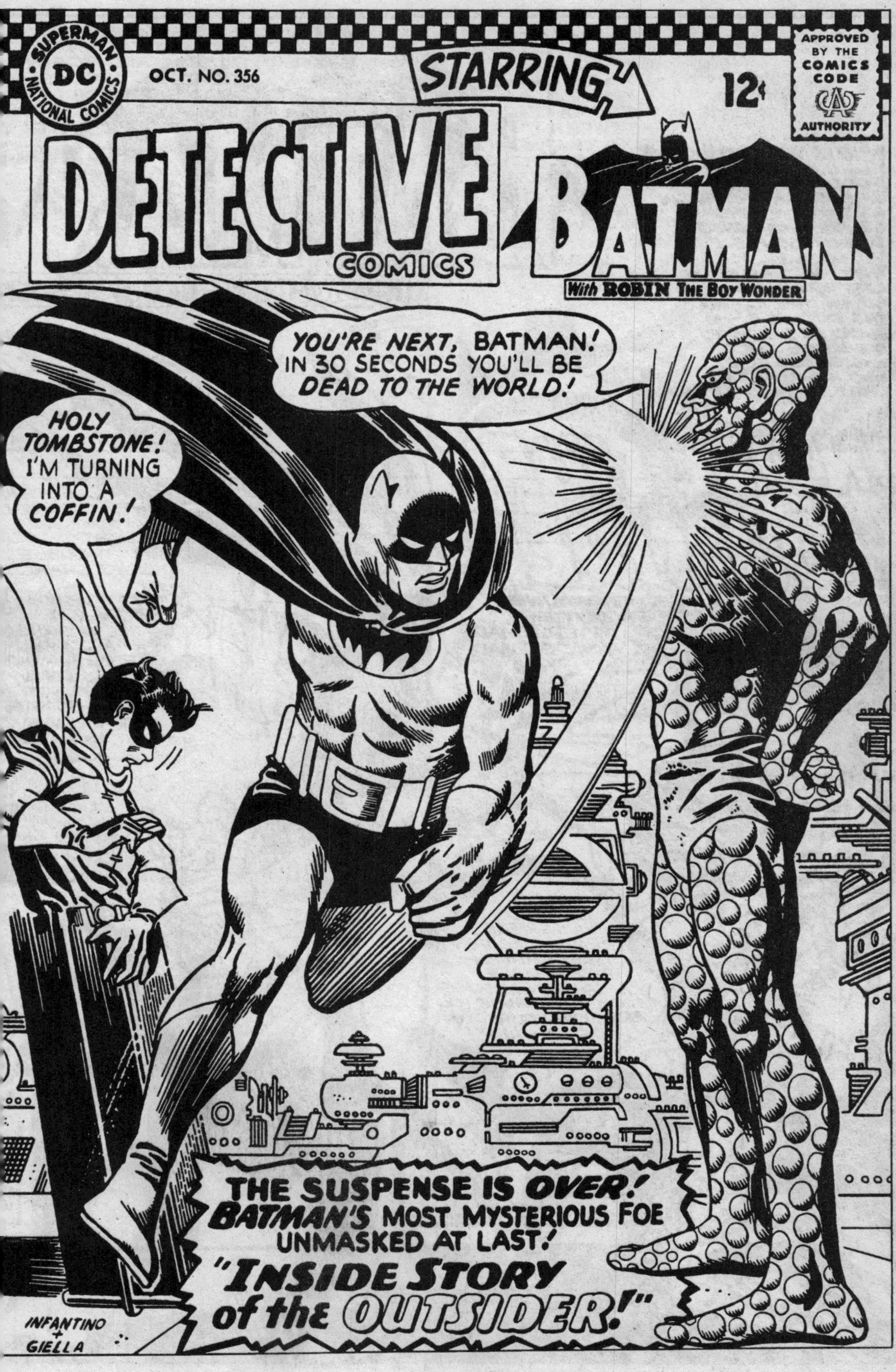
SUPERMAN DC NATIONAL COMICS
OCT. NO. 356
STARRING
12¢
APPROVED BY THE COMICS CODE AUTHORITY
DETECTIVE COMICS
BATMAN
With ROBIN THE BOY WONDER
YOU'RE NEXT, BATMAN! IN 30 SECONDS YOU'LL BE DEAD TO THE WORLD!
HOLY TOMBSTONE! I'M TURNING INTO A COFFIN!
THE SUSPENSE IS OVER! BATMAN'S MOST MYSTERIOUS FOE UNMASKED AT LAST!
"INSIDE STORY of the OUTSIDER!"
INFANTINO + GIELLA

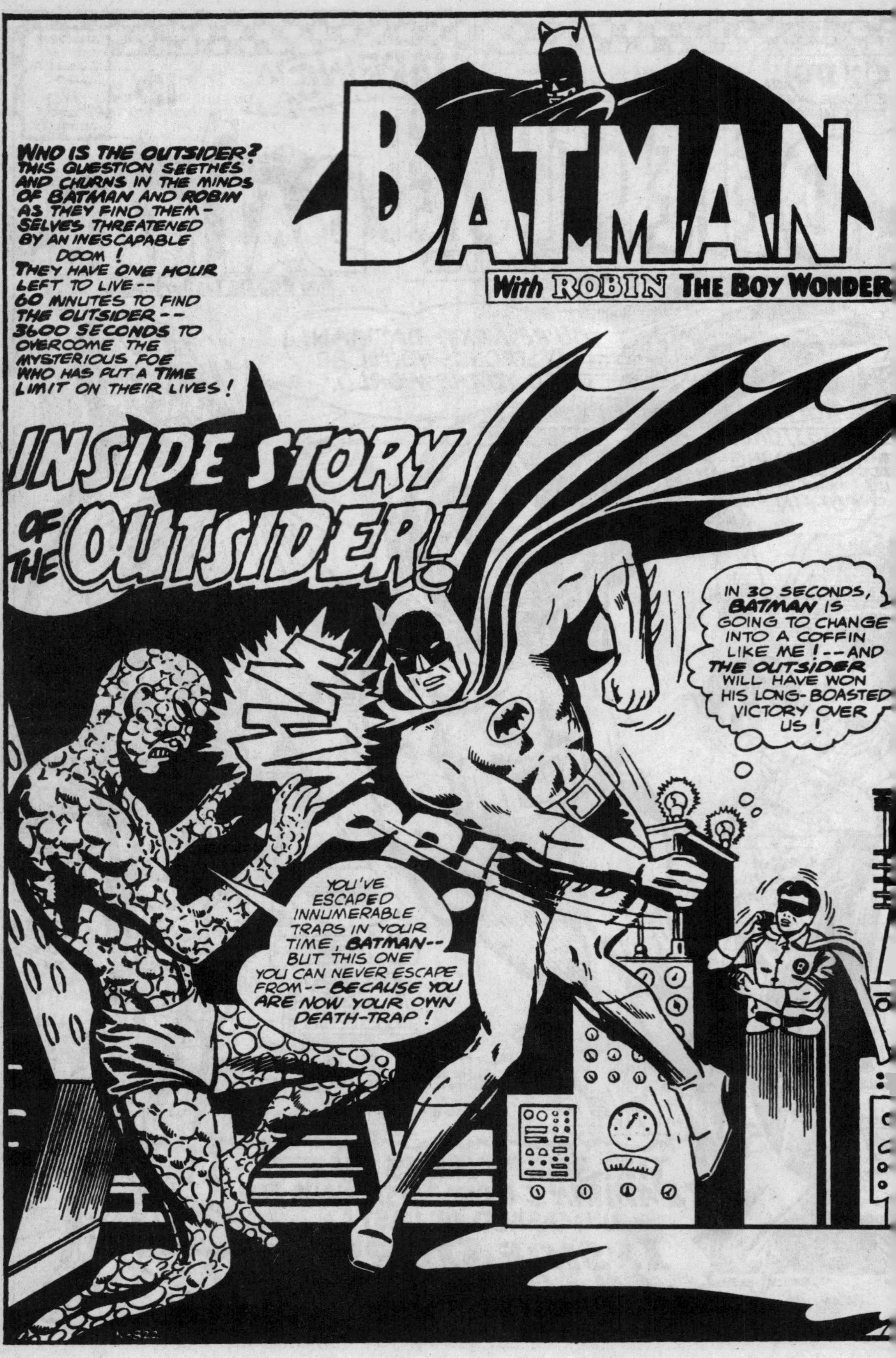
BATMAN
With ROBIN THE BOY WONDER
WHO IS THE OUTSIDER? THIS QUESTION SEETHES AND CHURNS IN THE MINDS OF BATMAN AND ROBIN AS THEY FIND THEMSELVES THREATENED BY AN INESCAPABLE DOOM! THEY HAVE ONE HOUR LEFT TO LIVE -- 60 MINUTES TO FIND THE OUTSIDER -- 3600 SECONDS TO OVERCOME THE MYSTERIOUS FOE WHO HAS PUT A TIME LIMIT ON THEIR LIVES!
INSIDE STORY OF THE OUTSIDER!
IN 30 SECONDS, BATMAN IS GOING TO CHANGE INTO A COFFIN LIKE ME! -- AND THE OUTSIDER WILL HAVE WON HIS LONG-BOASTED VICTORY OVER US!
YOU'VE ESCAPED INNUMERABLE TRAPS IN YOUR TIME, BATMAN -- BUT THIS ONE YOU CAN NEVER ESCAPE FROM -- BECAUSE YOU ARE NOW YOUR OWN DEATH-TRAP!

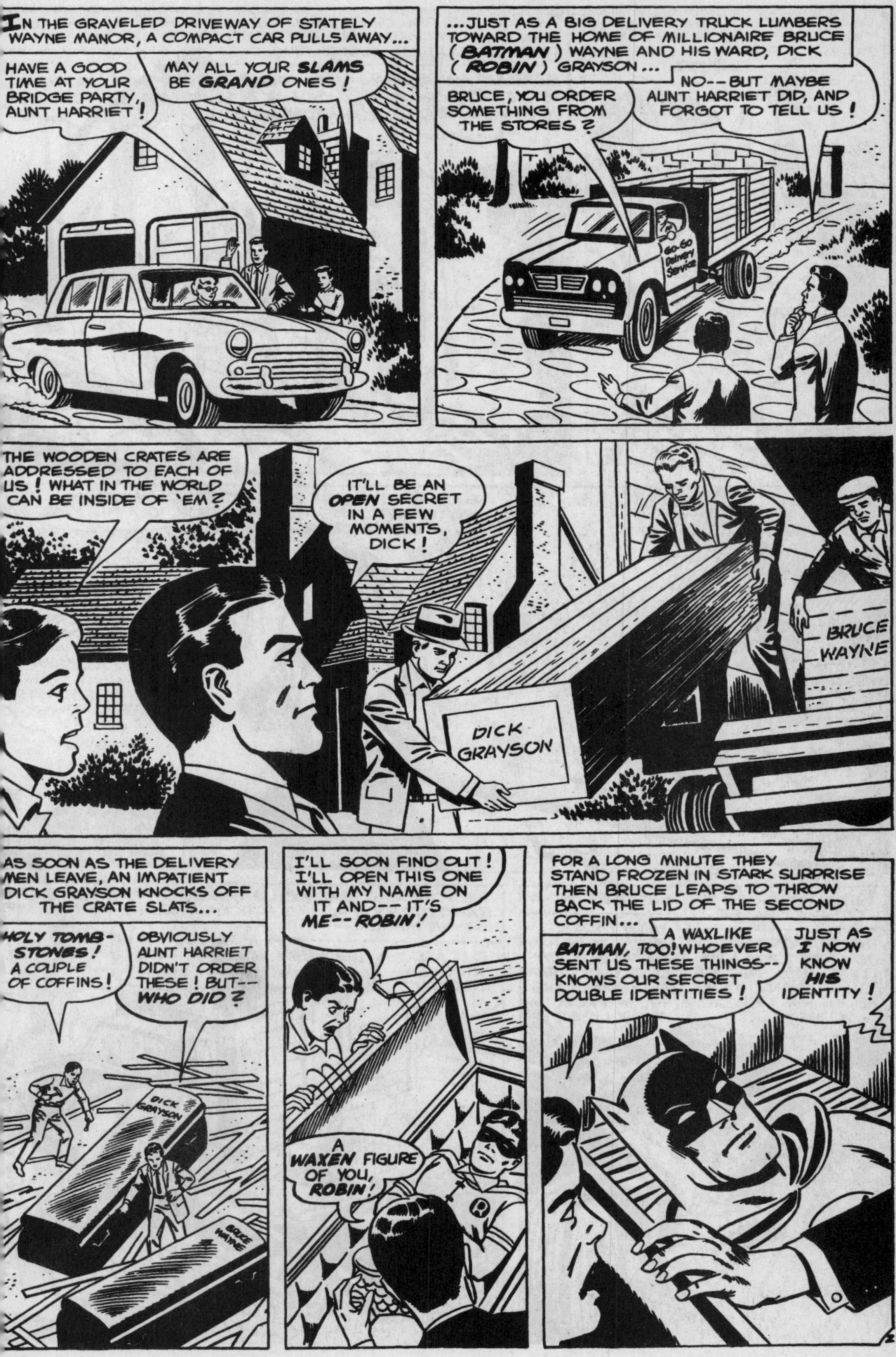
IN THE GRAVELED DRIVEWAY OF STATELY WAYNE MANOR, A COMPACT CAR PULLS AWAY...
HAVE A GOOD TIME AT YOUR BRIDGE PARTY, AUNT HARRIET!
MAY ALL YOUR SLAMS BE GRAND ONES!
...JUST AS A BIG DELIVERY TRUCK LUMBERS TOWARD THE HOME OF MILLIONAIRE BRUCE (BATMAN) WAYNE AND HIS WARD, DICK (ROBIN) GRAYSON...
BRUCE, YOU ORDER SOMETHING FROM THE STORES?
NO--BUT MAYBE AUNT HARRIET DID, AND FORGOT TO TELL US!
Go-Go Delivery Service
THE WOODEN CRATES ARE ADDRESSED TO EACH OF US! WHAT IN THE WORLD CAN BE INSIDE OF 'EM?
IT'LL BE AN OPEN SECRET IN A FEW MOMENTS, DICK!
BRUCE WAYNE
DICK GRAYSON
AS SOON AS THE DELIVERY MEN LEAVE, AN IMPATIENT DICK GRAYSON KNOCKS OFF THE CRATE SLATS...
HOLY TOMB-STONES! A COUPLE OF COFFINS!
OBVIOUSLY AUNT HARRIET DIDN'T ORDER THESE! BUT--WHO DID?
DICK GRAYSON
BRUCE WAYNE
I'LL SOON FIND OUT! I'LL OPEN THIS ONE WITH MY NAME ON IT AND--IT'S ME--ROBIN!
A WAXEN FIGURE OF YOU, ROBIN!
FOR A LONG MINUTE THEY STAND FROZEN IN STARK SURPRISE THEN BRUCE LEAPS TO THROW BACK THE LID OF THE SECOND COFFIN...
A WAXLIKE BATMAN, TOO! WHOEVER SENT US THESE THINGS--KNOWS OUR SECRET DOUBLE IDENTITIES!
JUST AS I NOW KNOW HIS IDENTITY!
2

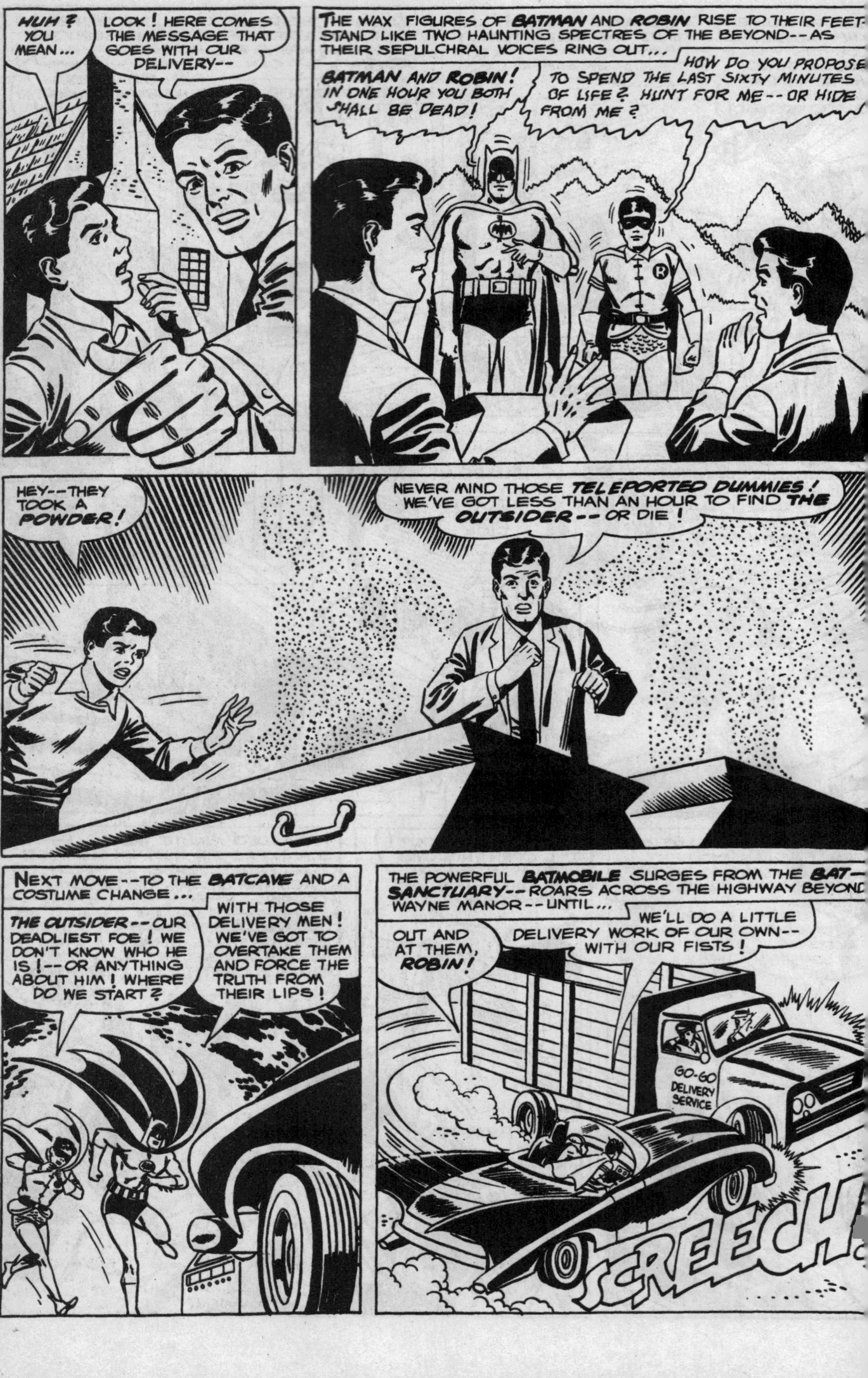
HUH? YOU MEAN...
LOOK! HERE COMES THE MESSAGE THAT GOES WITH OUR DELIVERY--
THE WAX FIGURES OF BATMAN AND ROBIN RISE TO THEIR FEET-- STAND LIKE TWO HAUNTING SPECTRES OF THE BEYOND--AS THEIR SEPULCHRAL VOICES RING OUT...
BATMAN AND ROBIN! IN ONE HOUR YOU BOTH SHALL BE DEAD!
HOW DO YOU PROPOSE TO SPEND THE LAST SIXTY MINUTES OF LIFE? HUNT FOR ME--OR HIDE FROM ME?
HEY--THEY TOOK A POWDER!
NEVER MIND THOSE TELEPORTED DUMMIES! WE'VE GOT LESS THAN AN HOUR TO FIND THE OUTSIDER--OR DIE!
NEXT MOVE--TO THE BATCAVE AND A COSTUME CHANGE...
THE OUTSIDER--OUR DEADLIEST FOE! WE DON'T KNOW WHO HE IS!--OR ANYTHING ABOUT HIM! WHERE DO WE START?
WITH THOSE DELIVERY MEN! WE'VE GOT TO OVERTAKE THEM AND FORCE THE TRUTH FROM THEIR LIPS!
THE POWERFUL BATMOBILE SURGES FROM THE BAT-SANCTUARY--ROARS ACROSS THE HIGHWAY BEYOND WAYNE MANOR--UNTIL...
OUT AND AT THEM, ROBIN!
WE'LL DO A LITTLE DELIVERY WORK OF OUR OWN--WITH OUR FISTS!
GO-GO DELIVERY SERVICE
SCREECH

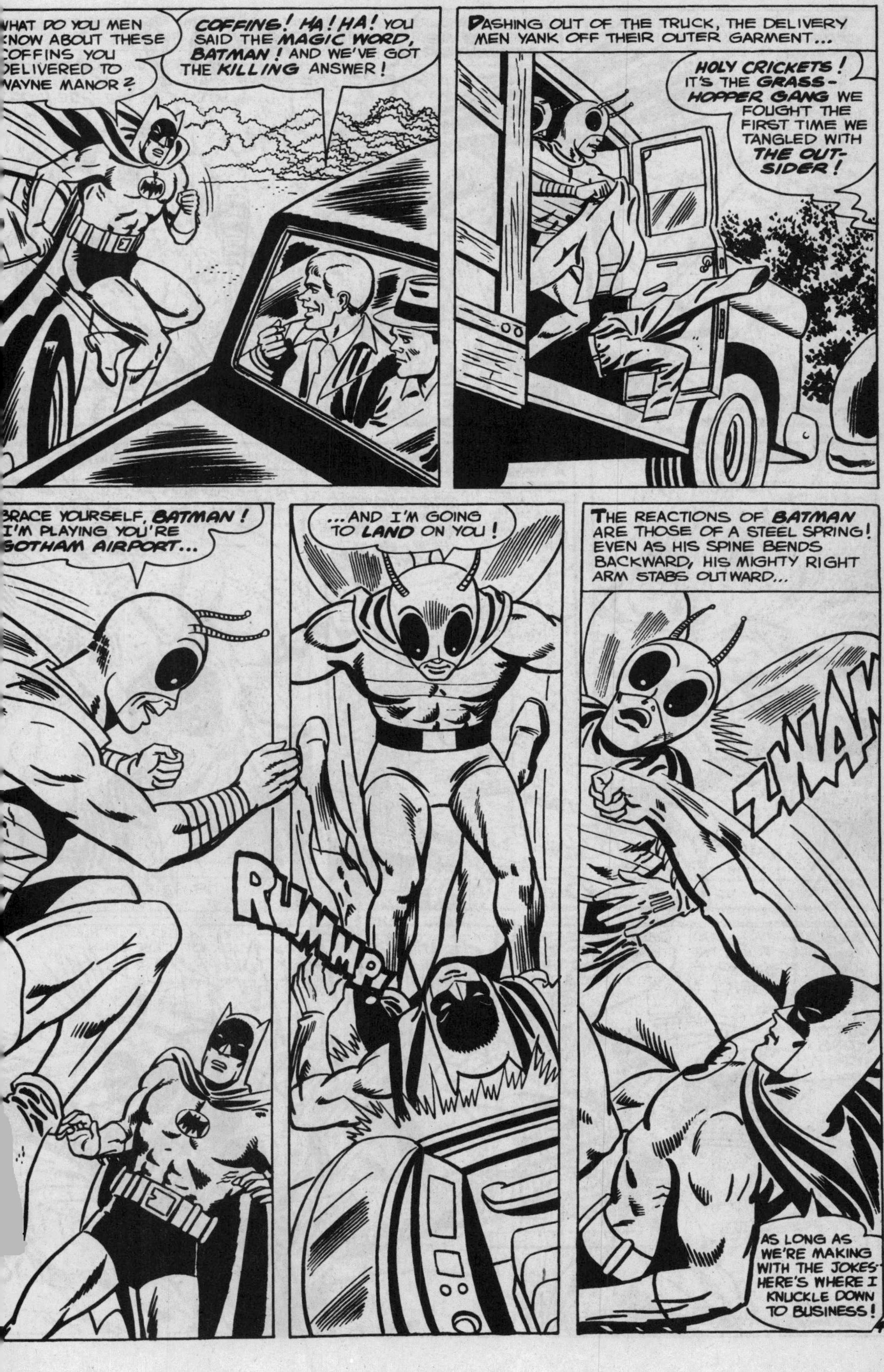
WHAT DO YOU MEN KNOW ABOUT THESE COFFINS YOU DELIVERED TO WAYNE MANOR?
COFFINS! HA! HA! YOU SAID THE MAGIC WORD, BATMAN! AND WE'VE GOT THE KILLING ANSWER!
DASHING OUT OF THE TRUCK, THE DELIVERY MEN YANK OFF THEIR OUTER GARMENT...
HOLY CRICKETS! IT'S THE GRASS-HOPPER GANG WE FOUGHT THE FIRST TIME WE TANGLED WITH THE OUT-SIDER!
BRACE YOURSELF, BATMAN! I'M PLAYING YOU'RE GOTHAM AIRPORT...
...AND I'M GOING TO LAND ON YOU!
RUMMP!
THE REACTIONS OF BATMAN ARE THOSE OF A STEEL SPRING! EVEN AS HIS SPINE BENDS BACKWARD, HIS MIGHTY RIGHT ARM STABS OUTWARD...
ZWAK
AS LONG AS WE'RE MAKING WITH THE JOKES-- HERE'S WHERE I KNUCKLE DOWN TO BUSINESS!
4

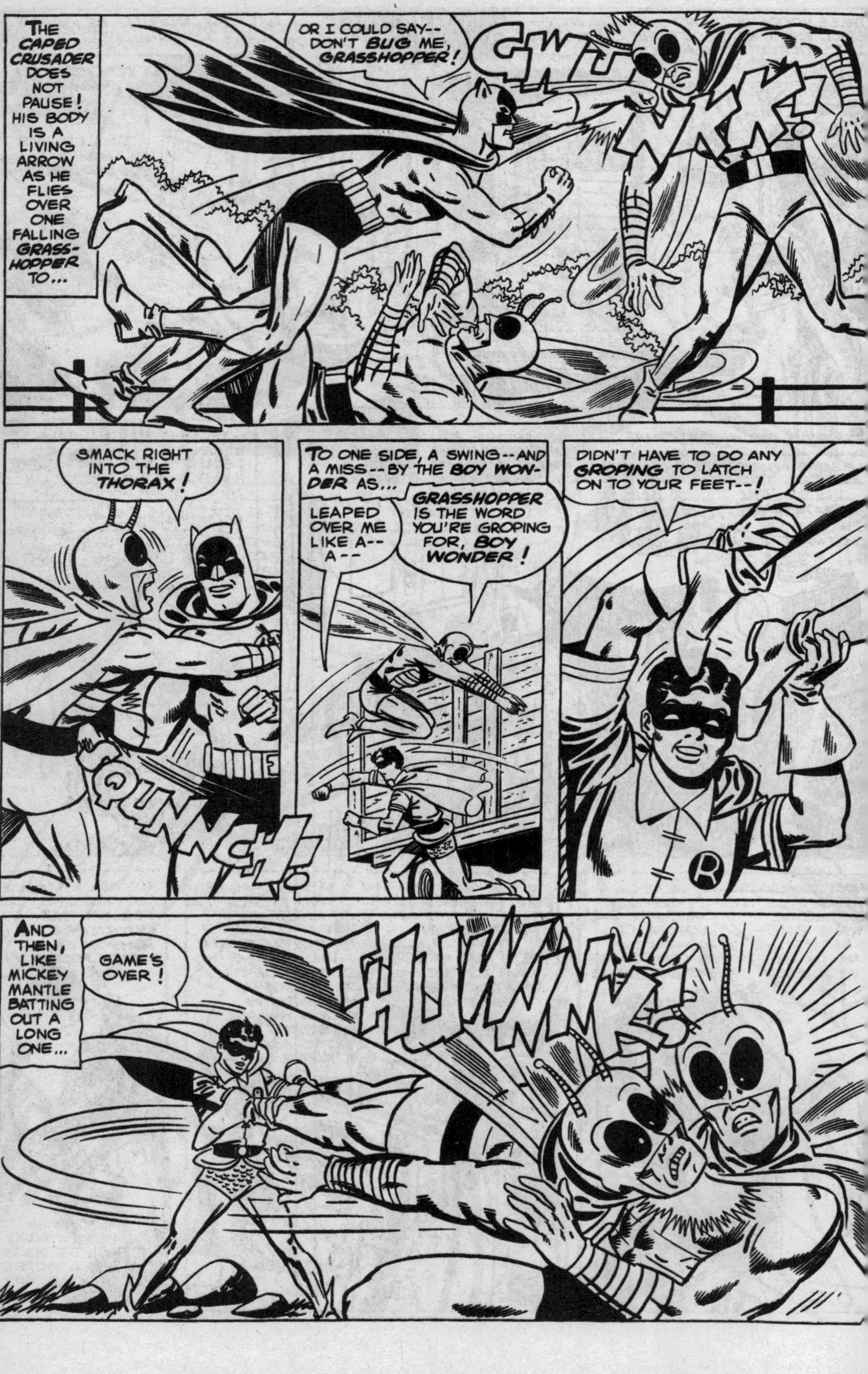
THE CAPED CRUSADER DOES NOT PAUSE! HIS BODY IS A LIVING ARROW AS HE FLIES OVER ONE FALLING GRASSHOPPER TO...
OR I COULD SAY-- DON'T BUG ME, GRASSHOPPER!
GWUNKK!
SMACK RIGHT INTO THE THORAX!
QUNNCH!
TO ONE SIDE, A SWING--AND A MISS--BY THE BOY WONDER AS...
LEAPED OVER ME LIKE A-- A--
GRASSHOPPER IS THE WORD YOU'RE GROPING FOR, BOY WONDER!
DIDN'T HAVE TO DO ANY GROPING TO LATCH ON TO YOUR FEET--!
AND THEN, LIKE MICKEY MANTLE BATTING OUT A LONG ONE...
GAME'S OVER!
THWNK!

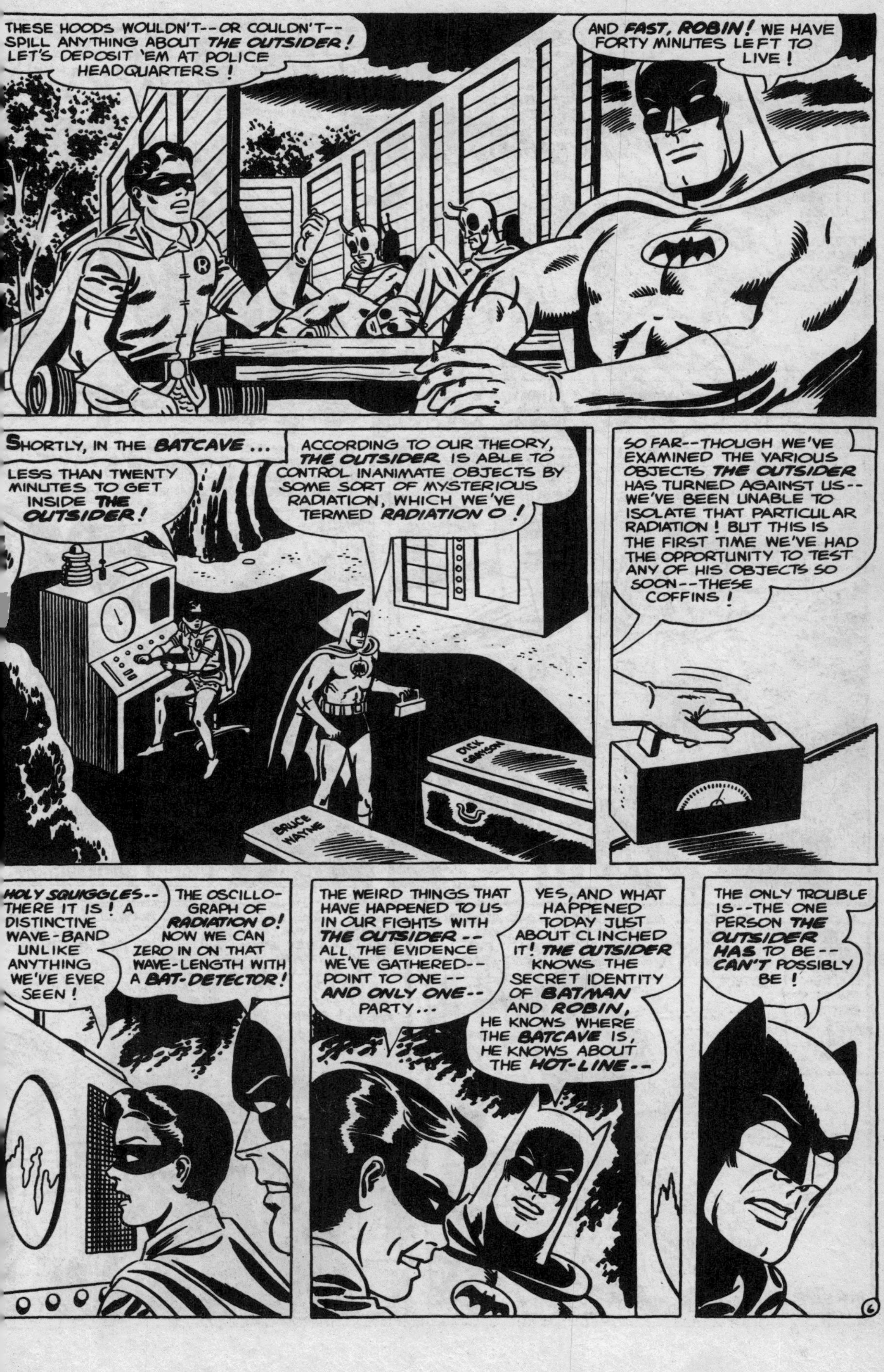
THESE HOODS WOULDN'T--OR COULDN'T--SPILL ANYTHING ABOUT THE OUTSIDER! LET'S DEPOSIT 'EM AT POLICE HEADQUARTERS!
AND FAST, ROBIN! WE HAVE FORTY MINUTES LEFT TO LIVE!
SHORTLY, IN THE BATCAVE ...
LESS THAN TWENTY MINUTES TO GET INSIDE THE OUTSIDER!
ACCORDING TO OUR THEORY, THE OUTSIDER IS ABLE TO CONTROL INANIMATE OBJECTS BY SOME SORT OF MYSTERIOUS RADIATION, WHICH WE'VE TERMED RADIATION O!
DICK GRAYSON
BRUCE WAYNE
SO FAR--THOUGH WE'VE EXAMINED THE VARIOUS OBJECTS THE OUTSIDER HAS TURNED AGAINST US--WE'VE BEEN UNABLE TO ISOLATE THAT PARTICULAR RADIATION! BUT THIS IS THE FIRST TIME WE'VE HAD THE OPPORTUNITY TO TEST ANY OF HIS OBJECTS SO SOON--THESE COFFINS!
HOLY SQUIGGLES--THERE IT IS! A DISTINCTIVE WAVE-BAND UNLIKE ANYTHING WE'VE EVER SEEN!
THE OSCILLOGRAPH OF RADIATION O! NOW WE CAN ZERO IN ON THAT WAVE-LENGTH WITH A BAT-DETECTOR!
THE WEIRD THINGS THAT HAVE HAPPENED TO US IN OUR FIGHTS WITH THE OUTSIDER--ALL THE EVIDENCE WE'VE GATHERED--POINT TO ONE--AND ONLY ONE--PARTY...
YES, AND WHAT HAPPENED TODAY JUST ABOUT CLINCHED IT! THE OUTSIDER KNOWS THE SECRET IDENTITY OF BATMAN AND ROBIN, HE KNOWS WHERE THE BATCAVE IS, HE KNOWS ABOUT THE HOT-LINE--
THE ONLY TROUBLE IS--THE ONE PERSON THE OUTSIDER HAS TO BE--CAN'T POSSIBLY BE!
6

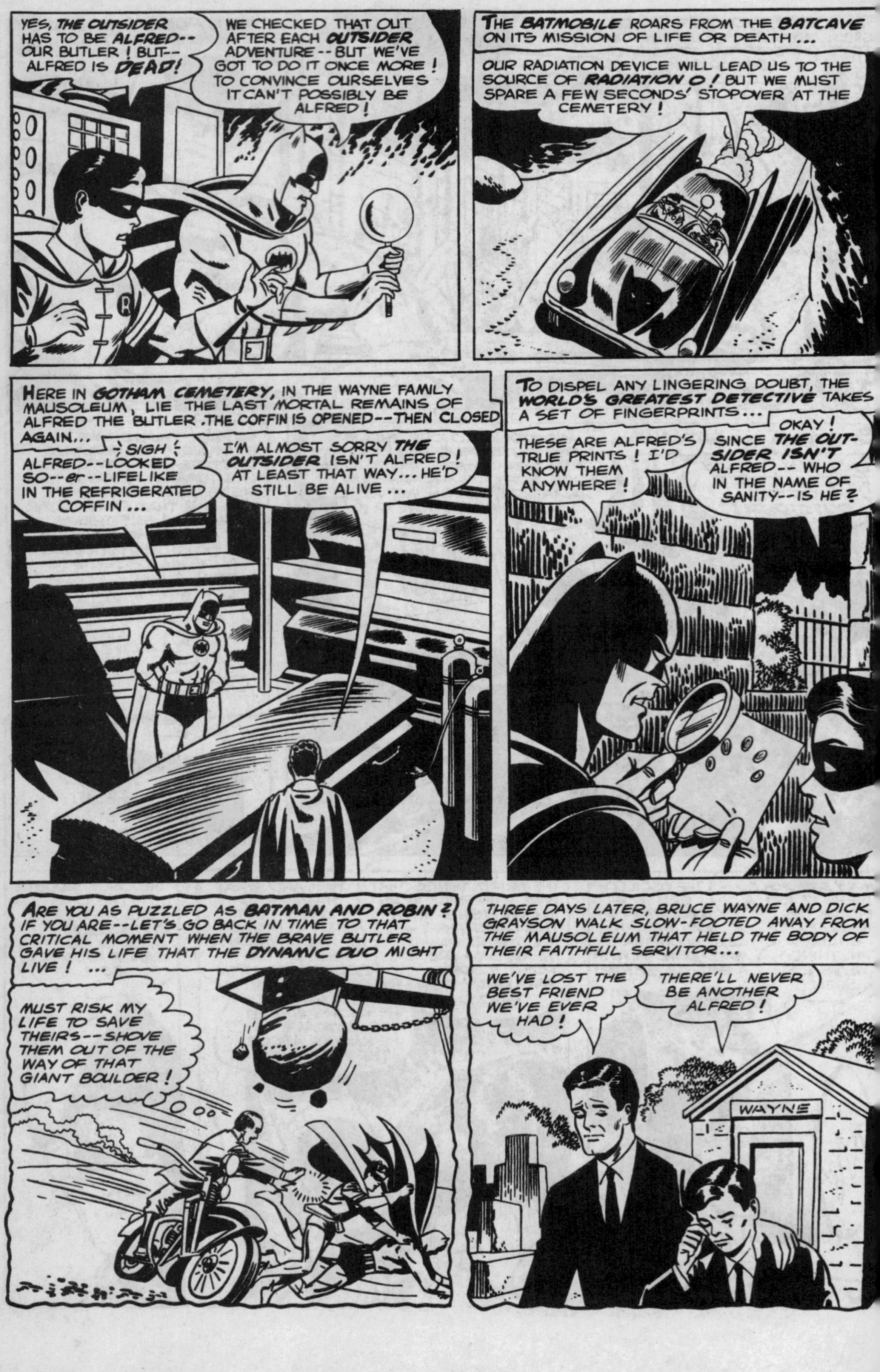
YES, THE OUTSIDER HAS TO BE ALFRED-- OUR BUTLER! BUT-- ALFRED IS DEAD!
WE CHECKED THAT OUT AFTER EACH OUTSIDER ADVENTURE--BUT WE'VE GOT TO DO IT ONCE MORE! TO CONVINCE OURSELVES IT CAN'T POSSIBLY BE ALFRED!
THE BATMOBILE ROARS FROM THE BATCAVE ON ITS MISSION OF LIFE OR DEATH...
OUR RADIATION DEVICE WILL LEAD US TO THE SOURCE OF RADIATION O! BUT WE MUST SPARE A FEW SECONDS' STOPOVER AT THE CEMETERY!
HERE IN GOTHAM CEMETERY, IN THE WAYNE FAMILY MAUSOLEUM, LIE THE LAST MORTAL REMAINS OF ALFRED THE BUTLER. THE COFFIN IS OPENED--THEN CLOSED AGAIN...
SIGH
ALFRED--LOOKED SO--er--LIFELIKE IN THE REFRIGERATED COFFIN...
I'M ALMOST SORRY THE OUTSIDER ISN'T ALFRED! AT LEAST THAT WAY... HE'D STILL BE ALIVE...
TO DISPEL ANY LINGERING DOUBT, THE WORLD'S GREATEST DETECTIVE TAKES A SET OF FINGERPRINTS...
THESE ARE ALFRED'S TRUE PRINTS! I'D KNOW THEM ANYWHERE!
OKAY! SINCE THE OUTSIDER ISN'T ALFRED-- WHO IN THE NAME OF SANITY--IS HE?
ARE YOU AS PUZZLED AS BATMAN AND ROBIN? IF YOU ARE--LET'S GO BACK IN TIME TO THAT CRITICAL MOMENT WHEN THE BRAVE BUTLER GAVE HIS LIFE THAT THE DYNAMIC DUO MIGHT LIVE! ...
MUST RISK MY LIFE TO SAVE THEIRS--SHOVE THEM OUT OF THE WAY OF THAT GIANT BOULDER!
THREE DAYS LATER, BRUCE WAYNE AND DICK GRAYSON WALK SLOW-FOOTED AWAY FROM THE MAUSOLEUM THAT HELD THE BODY OF THEIR FAITHFUL SERVITOR...
WE'VE LOST THE BEST FRIEND WE'VE EVER HAD!
THERE'LL NEVER BE ANOTHER ALFRED!
WAYNE

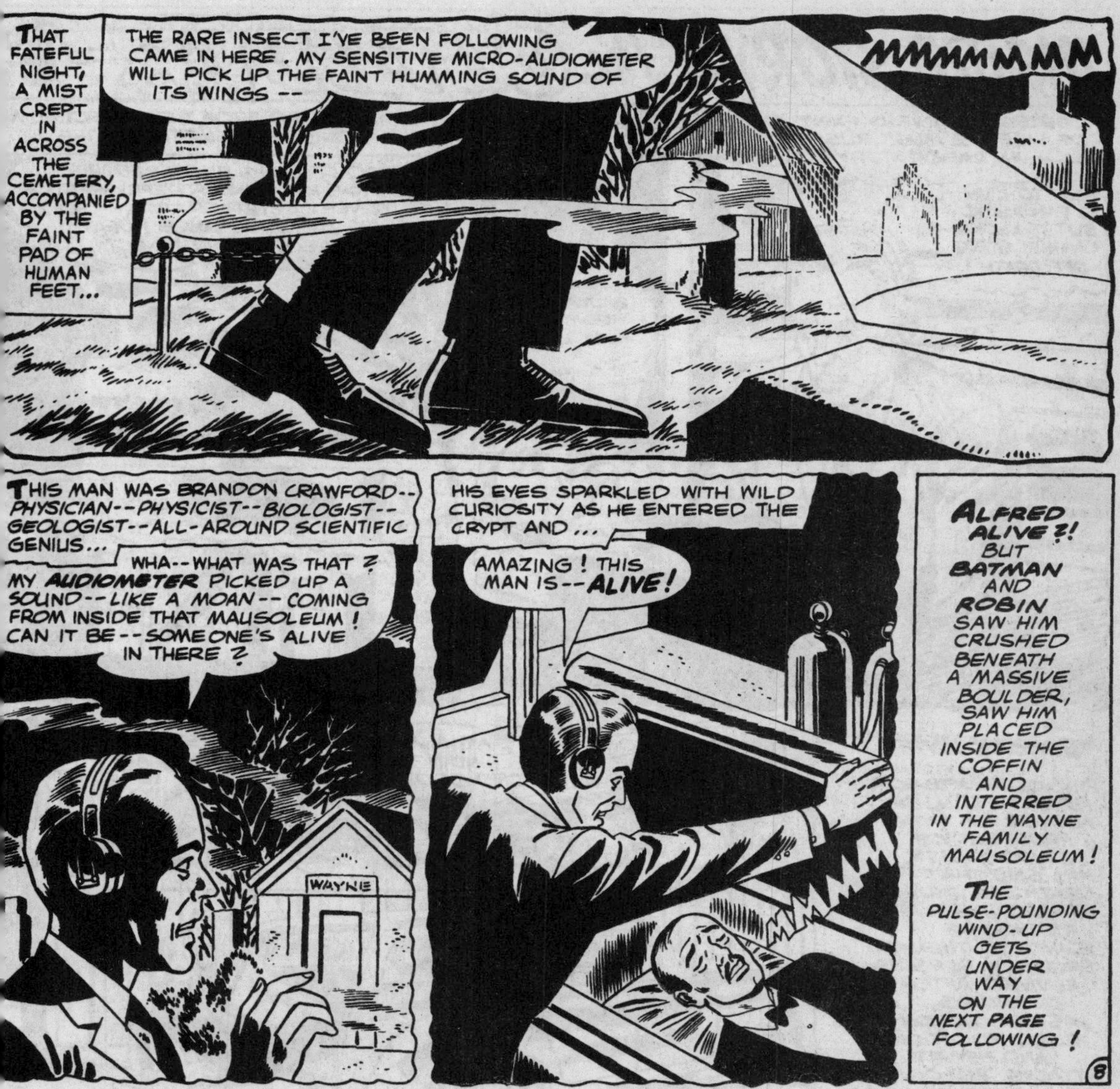
THAT FATEFUL NIGHT, A MIST CREPT IN ACROSS THE CEMETERY, ACCOMPANIED BY THE FAINT PAD OF HUMAN FEET...
THE RARE INSECT I'VE BEEN FOLLOWING CAME IN HERE. MY SENSITIVE MICRO-AUDIOMETER WILL PICK UP THE FAINT HUMMING SOUND OF ITS WINGS --
MMMMMMMM
THIS MAN WAS BRANDON CRAWFORD-- PHYSICIAN--PHYSICIST--BIOLOGIST-- GEOLOGIST--ALL-AROUND SCIENTIFIC GENIUS...
WHA--WHAT WAS THAT? MY AUDIOMETER PICKED UP A SOUND--LIKE A MOAN--COMING FROM INSIDE THAT MAUSOLEUM! CAN IT BE--SOMEONE'S ALIVE IN THERE?
WAYNE
HIS EYES SPARKLED WITH WILD CURIOSITY AS HE ENTERED THE CRYPT AND...
AMAZING! THIS MAN IS--ALIVE!
ALFRED ALIVE?! BUT BATMAN AND ROBIN SAW HIM CRUSHED BENEATH A MASSIVE BOULDER, SAW HIM PLACED INSIDE THE COFFIN AND INTERRED IN THE WAYNE FAMILY MAUSOLEUM!
THE PULSE-POUNDING WIND-UP GETS UNDER WAY ON THE NEXT PAGE FOLLOWING!
8

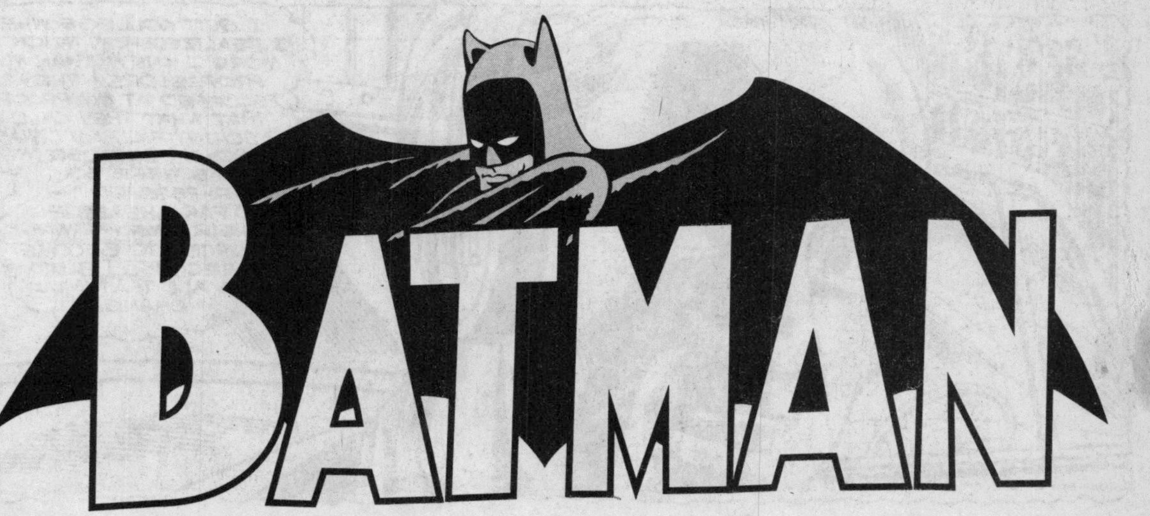
BATMAN

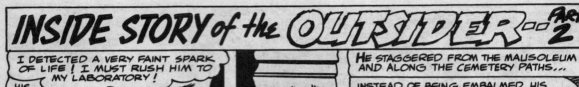

INSIDE STORY of the OUTSIDER--Part 2

I DETECTED A VERY FAINT SPARK OF LIFE! I MUST RUSH HIM TO MY LABORATORY!

HIS WILL TO LIVE IS FANTASTIC-- BUT IT ALONE CANNOT STAVE OFF DEATH!

...SAVE BATMAN AND ROBIN... MUST LIVE...

HE STAGGERED FROM THE MAUSOLEUM AND ALONG THE CEMETERY PATHS...

INSTEAD OF BEING EMBALMED, HIS BODY WAS KEPT UNDER REFRIGERATION TO PREVENT DETERIORATION -- SO THERE'S STILL A CHANCE! DEATH CAN DECEIVE EVEN THE FINEST DOCTORS! *

*EDITOR'S NOTE:

PHYSICS PROFESSOR ROBERT ETTINGER, AUTHOR OF "THE PROSPECT OF IMMORTALITY," HAS SAID THAT DEATH CAN ONLY BE DEFINED IN RELATIVE TERMS. HE POINTS TO THE HUNDREDS OF PERSONS REVIVED AFTER DROWNING, ASPHYXIATION, ELECTROCUTION, AND HEART ATTACKS. "BIOLOGICAL DEATH DEPENDS NOT ONLY ON THE STATE OF THE BODY," ETTINGER SAYS, "BUT ALSO ON THE STATE OF MEDICAL ART!"

PERHAPS I ALONE--FOR I AM A RADICAL INDIVIDUALIST, ALWAYS EXPERIMENTING, ALWAYS FINDING NEW LAWS OF NATURE AND SCIENCE--LAWS WHICH ORTHODOX SCIENTISTS DO NOT YET ADMIT-- CAN BRING HIM BACK TO LIFE!

I QUIT COLLEGE WHEN I REALIZED HOW MUCH MORE I KNEW THAN MY PROFESSORS! THEY SCOFFED AT MY PROOF THAT WHAT THEY CALL "SCIENTIFIC FACT" WAS WRONG! BECAUSE MY IDEAS WERE SO "FAR-FETCHED"-- SO FAR AHEAD OF THEIR TIME--I WAS FORCED TO BECOME A RECLUSE! BUT NOW ALL THAT WILL CHANGE!

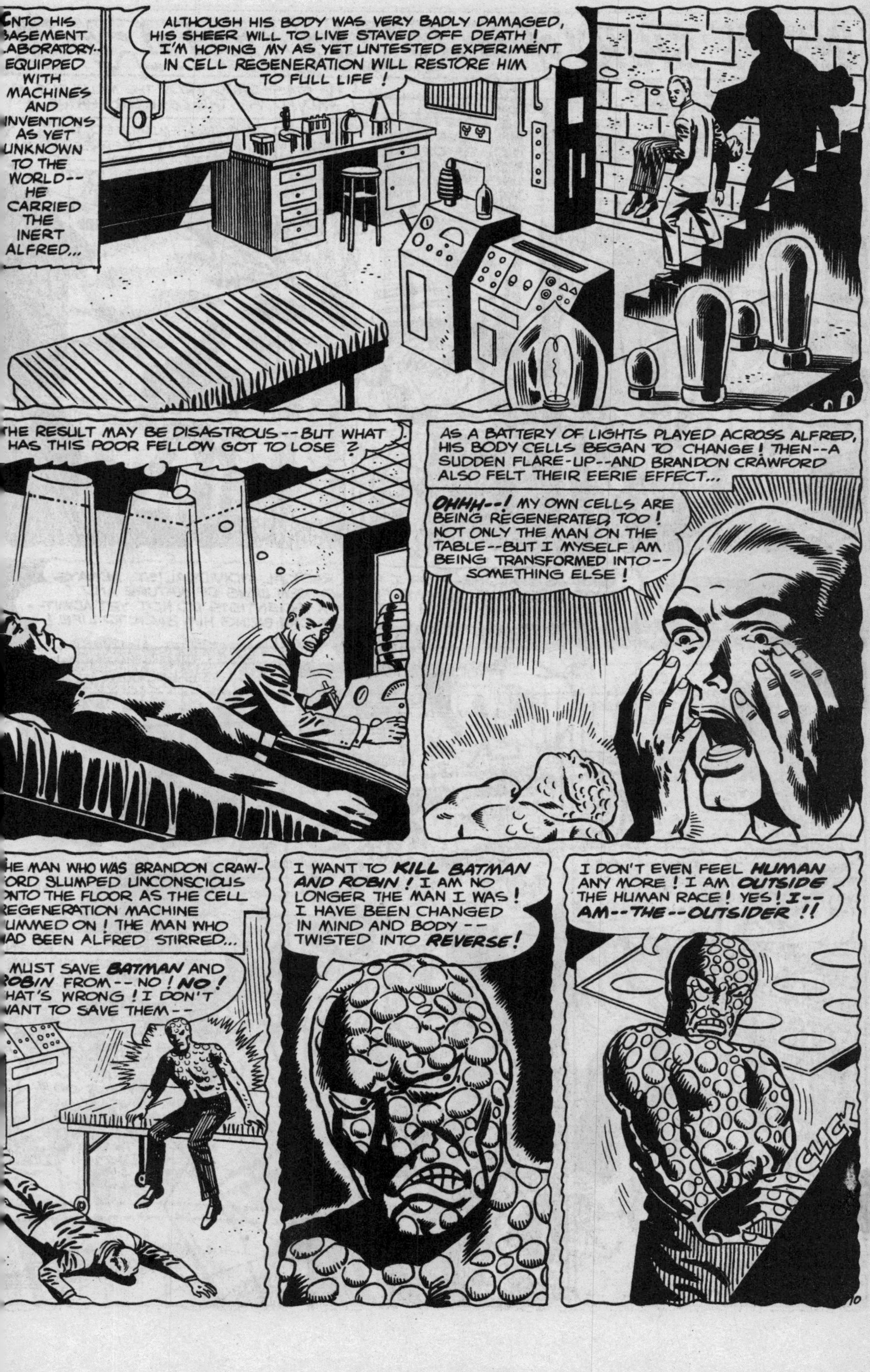
INTO HIS BASEMENT LABORATORY--EQUIPPED WITH MACHINES AND INVENTIONS AS YET UNKNOWN TO THE WORLD--HE CARRIED THE INERT ALFRED...
ALTHOUGH HIS BODY WAS VERY BADLY DAMAGED, HIS SHEER WILL TO LIVE STAVED OFF DEATH! I'M HOPING MY AS YET UNTESTED EXPERIMENT IN CELL REGENERATION WILL RESTORE HIM TO FULL LIFE!
THE RESULT MAY BE DISASTROUS--BUT WHAT HAS THIS POOR FELLOW GOT TO LOSE?
AS A BATTERY OF LIGHTS PLAYED ACROSS ALFRED, HIS BODY CELLS BEGAN TO CHANGE! THEN--A SUDDEN FLARE-UP--AND BRANDON CRAWFORD ALSO FELT THEIR EERIE EFFECT...
OHHH--! MY OWN CELLS ARE BEING REGENERATED, TOO! NOT ONLY THE MAN ON THE TABLE--BUT I MYSELF AM BEING TRANSFORMED INTO--SOMETHING ELSE!
THE MAN WHO WAS BRANDON CRAWFORD SLUMPED UNCONSCIOUS ONTO THE FLOOR AS THE CELL REGENERATION MACHINE HUMMED ON! THE MAN WHO HAD BEEN ALFRED STIRRED...
I MUST SAVE BATMAN AND ROBIN FROM--NO! NO! WHAT'S WRONG! I DON'T WANT TO SAVE THEM--
I WANT TO KILL BATMAN AND ROBIN! I AM NO LONGER THE MAN I WAS! I HAVE BEEN CHANGED IN MIND AND BODY--TWISTED INTO REVERSE!
I DON'T EVEN FEEL HUMAN ANY MORE! I AM OUTSIDE THE HUMAN RACE! YES! I--AM--THE--OUTSIDER!!
CLICK
10

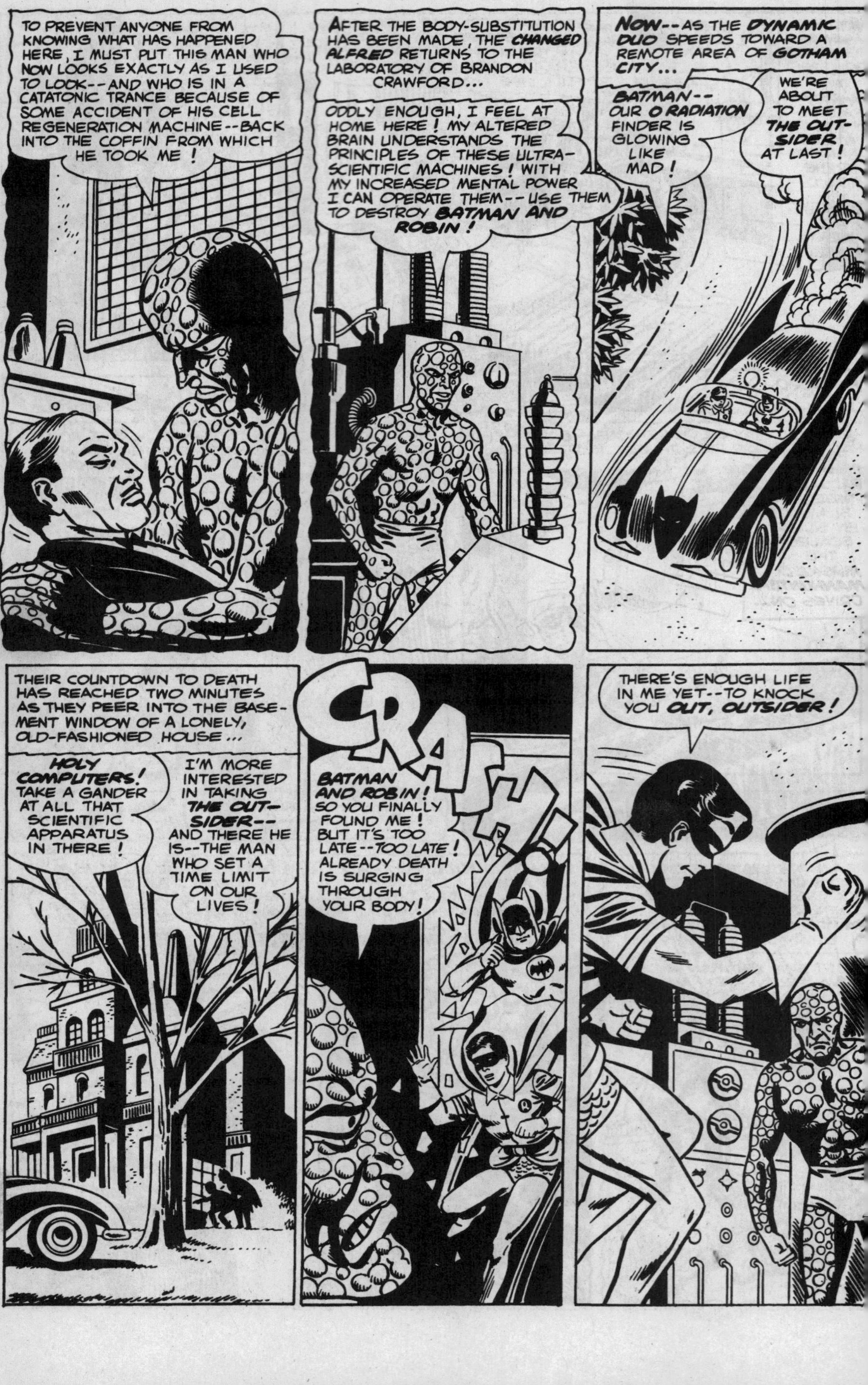
TO PREVENT ANYONE FROM KNOWING WHAT HAS HAPPENED HERE, I MUST PUT THIS MAN WHO NOW LOOKS EXACTLY AS I USED TO LOOK--AND WHO IS IN A CATATONIC TRANCE BECAUSE OF SOME ACCIDENT OF HIS CELL REGENERATION MACHINE--BACK INTO THE COFFIN FROM WHICH HE TOOK ME!
AFTER THE BODY-SUBSTITUTION HAS BEEN MADE, THE CHANGED ALFRED RETURNS TO THE LABORATORY OF BRANDON CRAWFORD...
ODDLY ENOUGH, I FEEL AT HOME HERE! MY ALTERED BRAIN UNDERSTANDS THE PRINCIPLES OF THESE ULTRA-SCIENTIFIC MACHINES! WITH MY INCREASED MENTAL POWER I CAN OPERATE THEM--USE THEM TO DESTROY BATMAN AND ROBIN!
NOW--AS THE DYNAMIC DUO SPEEDS TOWARD A REMOTE AREA OF GOTHAM CITY...
BATMAN--OUR O RADIATION FINDER IS GLOWING LIKE MAD!
WE'RE ABOUT TO MEET THE OUT-SIDER AT LAST!
THEIR COUNTDOWN TO DEATH HAS REACHED TWO MINUTES AS THEY PEER INTO THE BASE-MENT WINDOW OF A LONELY, OLD-FASHIONED HOUSE...
HOLY COMPUTERS! TAKE A GANDER AT ALL THAT SCIENTIFIC APPARATUS IN THERE!
I'M MORE INTERESTED IN TAKING THE OUT-SIDER--AND THERE HE IS--THE MAN WHO SET A TIME LIMIT ON OUR LIVES!
CRASH!
BATMAN AND ROBIN! SO YOU FINALLY FOUND ME! BUT IT'S TOO LATE--TOO LATE! ALREADY DEATH IS SURGING THROUGH YOUR BODY!
THERE'S ENOUGH LIFE IN ME YET--TO KNOCK YOU OUT, OUTSIDER!

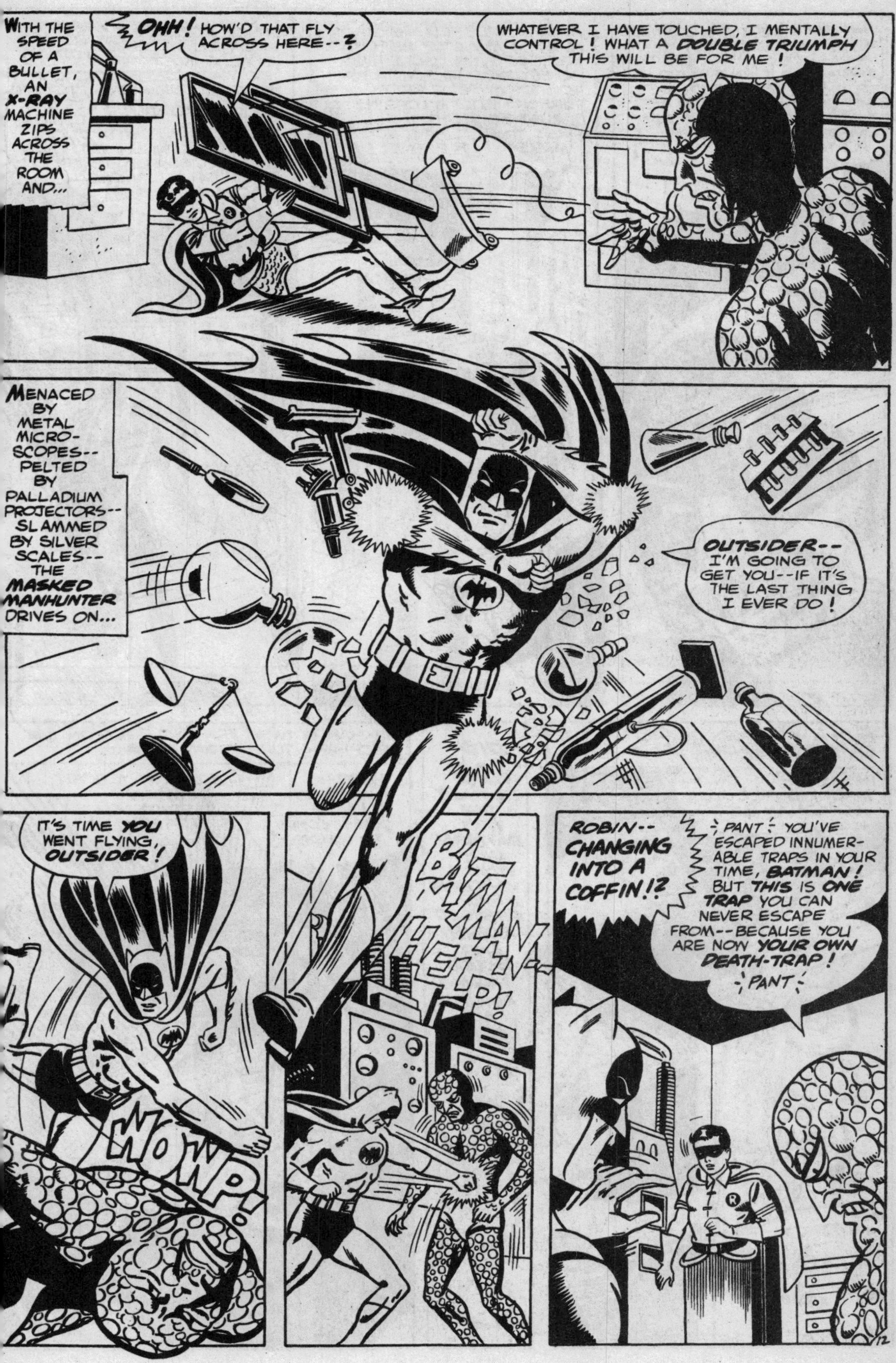
WITH THE SPEED OF A BULLET, AN X-RAY MACHINE ZIPS ACROSS THE ROOM AND...
OHH! HOW'D THAT FLY ACROSS HERE--?
WHATEVER I HAVE TOUCHED, I MENTALLY CONTROL! WHAT A DOUBLE TRIUMPH THIS WILL BE FOR ME!
MENACED BY METAL MICRO-SCOPES--PELTED BY PALLADIUM PROJECTORS--SLAMMED BY SILVER SCALES--THE MASKED MANHUNTER DRIVES ON...
OUTSIDER--I'M GOING TO GET YOU--IF IT'S THE LAST THING I EVER DO!
IT'S TIME YOU WENT FLYING, OUTSIDER!
WOWP!
BAT-MAN-HELP!
ROBIN--CHANGING INTO A COFFIN!?
-PANT- YOU'VE ESCAPED INNUMER-ABLE TRAPS IN YOUR TIME, BATMAN! BUT THIS IS ONE TRAP YOU CAN NEVER ESCAPE FROM--BECAUSE YOU ARE NOW YOUR OWN DEATH-TRAP! -PANT-
12

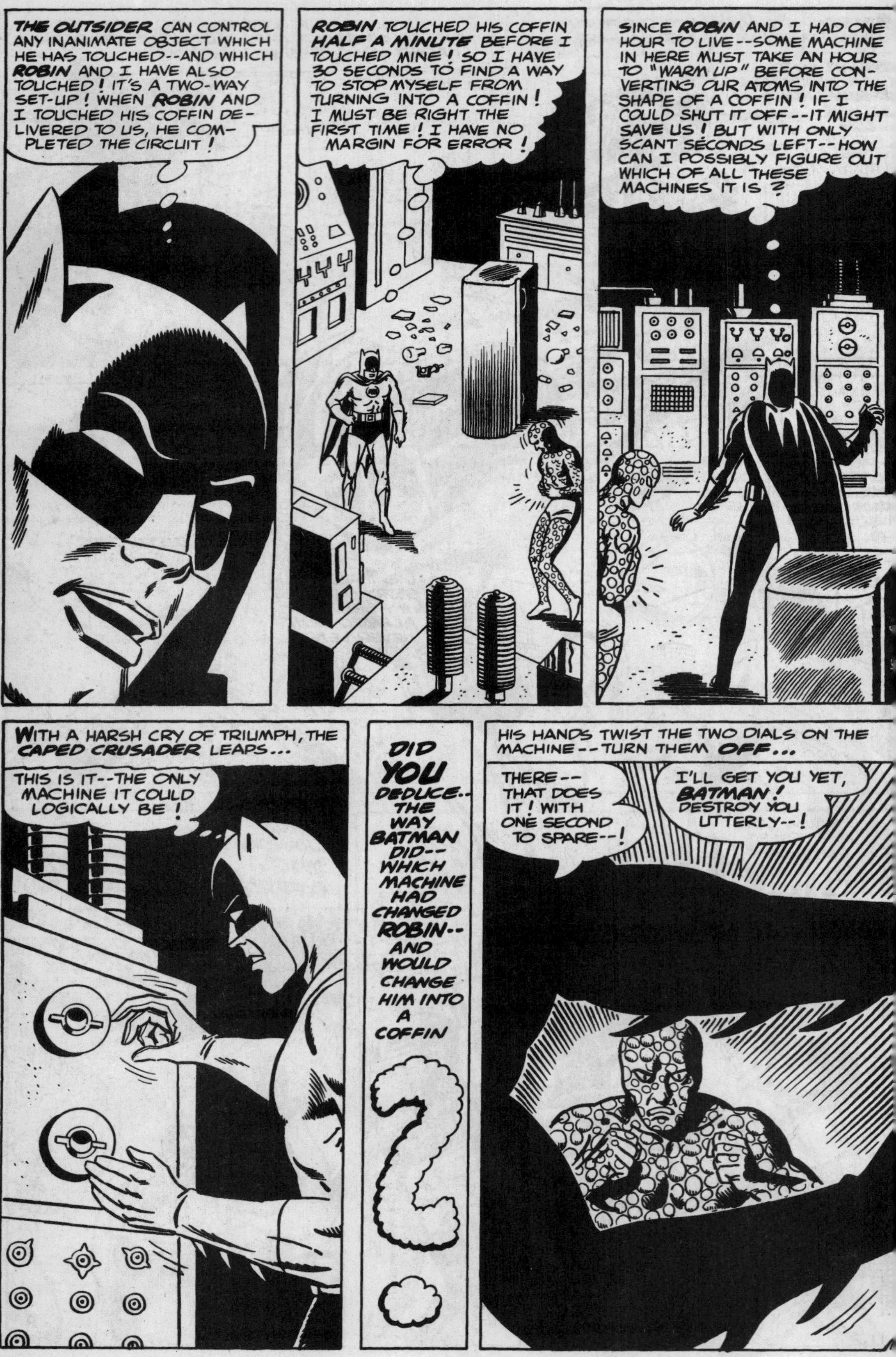
THE OUTSIDER CAN CONTROL ANY INANIMATE OBJECT WHICH HE HAS TOUCHED--AND WHICH ROBIN AND I HAVE ALSO TOUCHED! IT'S A TWO-WAY SET-UP! WHEN ROBIN AND I TOUCHED HIS COFFIN DELIVERED TO US, HE COMPLETED THE CIRCUIT!
ROBIN TOUCHED HIS COFFIN HALF A MINUTE BEFORE I TOUCHED MINE! SO I HAVE 30 SECONDS TO FIND A WAY TO STOP MYSELF FROM TURNING INTO A COFFIN! I MUST BE RIGHT THE FIRST TIME! I HAVE NO MARGIN FOR ERROR!
SINCE ROBIN AND I HAD ONE HOUR TO LIVE--SOME MACHINE IN HERE MUST TAKE AN HOUR TO "WARM UP" BEFORE CONVERTING OUR ATOMS INTO THE SHAPE OF A COFFIN! IF I COULD SHUT IT OFF--IT MIGHT SAVE US! BUT WITH ONLY SCANT SECONDS LEFT--HOW CAN I POSSIBLY FIGURE OUT WHICH OF ALL THESE MACHINES IT IS?
WITH A HARSH CRY OF TRIUMPH, THE CAPED CRUSADER LEAPS...
THIS IS IT--THE ONLY MACHINE IT COULD LOGICALLY BE!
DID YOU DEDUCE.. THE WAY BATMAN DID--WHICH MACHINE HAD CHANGED ROBIN--AND WOULD CHANGE HIM INTO A COFFIN
?
HIS HANDS TWIST THE TWO DIALS ON THE MACHINE--TURN THEM OFF...
THERE--THAT DOES IT! WITH ONE SECOND TO SPARE--!
I'LL GET YOU YET, BATMAN! DESTROY YOU UTTERLY--!

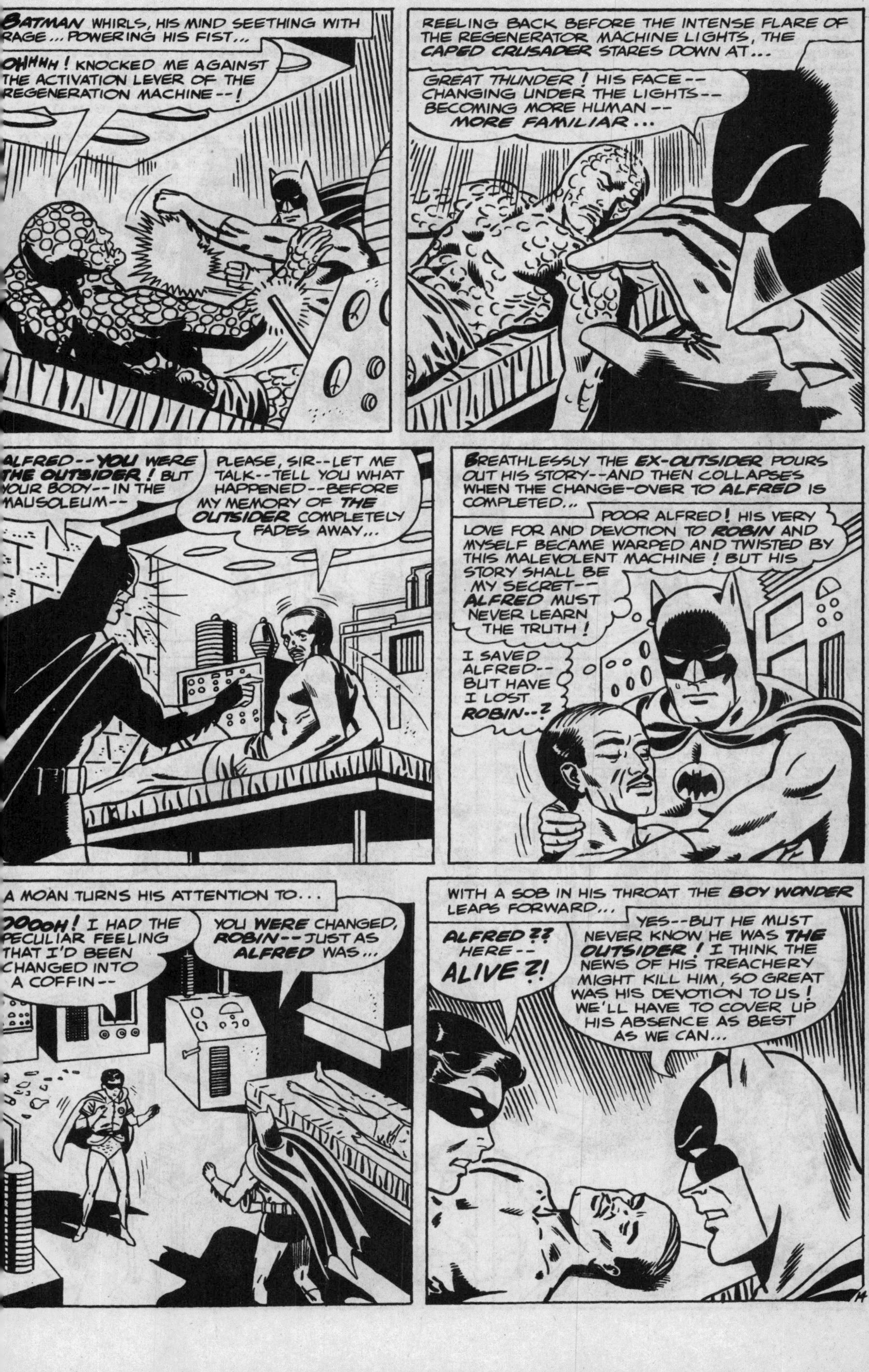
BATMAN WHIRLS, HIS MIND SEETHING WITH RAGE... POWERING HIS FIST...
OHHHH! KNOCKED ME AGAINST THE ACTIVATION LEVER OF THE REGENERATION MACHINE--!
REELING BACK BEFORE THE INTENSE FLARE OF THE REGENERATOR MACHINE LIGHTS, THE CAPED CRUSADER STARES DOWN AT...
GREAT THUNDER! HIS FACE-- CHANGING UNDER THE LIGHTS-- BECOMING MORE HUMAN -- MORE FAMILIAR...
ALFRED--YOU WERE THE OUTSIDER! BUT YOUR BODY--IN THE MAUSOLEUM--
PLEASE, SIR--LET ME TALK--TELL YOU WHAT HAPPENED--BEFORE MY MEMORY OF THE OUTSIDER COMPLETELY FADES AWAY...
BREATHLESSLY THE EX-OUTSIDER POURS OUT HIS STORY--AND THEN COLLAPSES WHEN THE CHANGE-OVER TO ALFRED IS COMPLETED...
POOR ALFRED! HIS VERY LOVE FOR AND DEVOTION TO ROBIN AND MYSELF BECAME WARPED AND TWISTED BY THIS MALEVOLENT MACHINE! BUT HIS STORY SHALL BE MY SECRET-- ALFRED MUST NEVER LEARN THE TRUTH!
I SAVED ALFRED-- BUT HAVE I LOST ROBIN--?
A MOAN TURNS HIS ATTENTION TO...
OOOOH! I HAD THE PECULIAR FEELING THAT I'D BEEN CHANGED INTO A COFFIN--
YOU WERE CHANGED, ROBIN--JUST AS ALFRED WAS...
WITH A SOB IN HIS THROAT THE BOY WONDER LEAPS FORWARD...
ALFRED?? HERE-- ALIVE?!
YES--BUT HE MUST NEVER KNOW HE WAS THE OUTSIDER! I THINK THE NEWS OF HIS TREACHERY MIGHT KILL HIM, SO GREAT WAS HIS DEVOTION TO US! WE'LL HAVE TO COVER UP HIS ABSENCE AS BEST AS WE CAN...
14

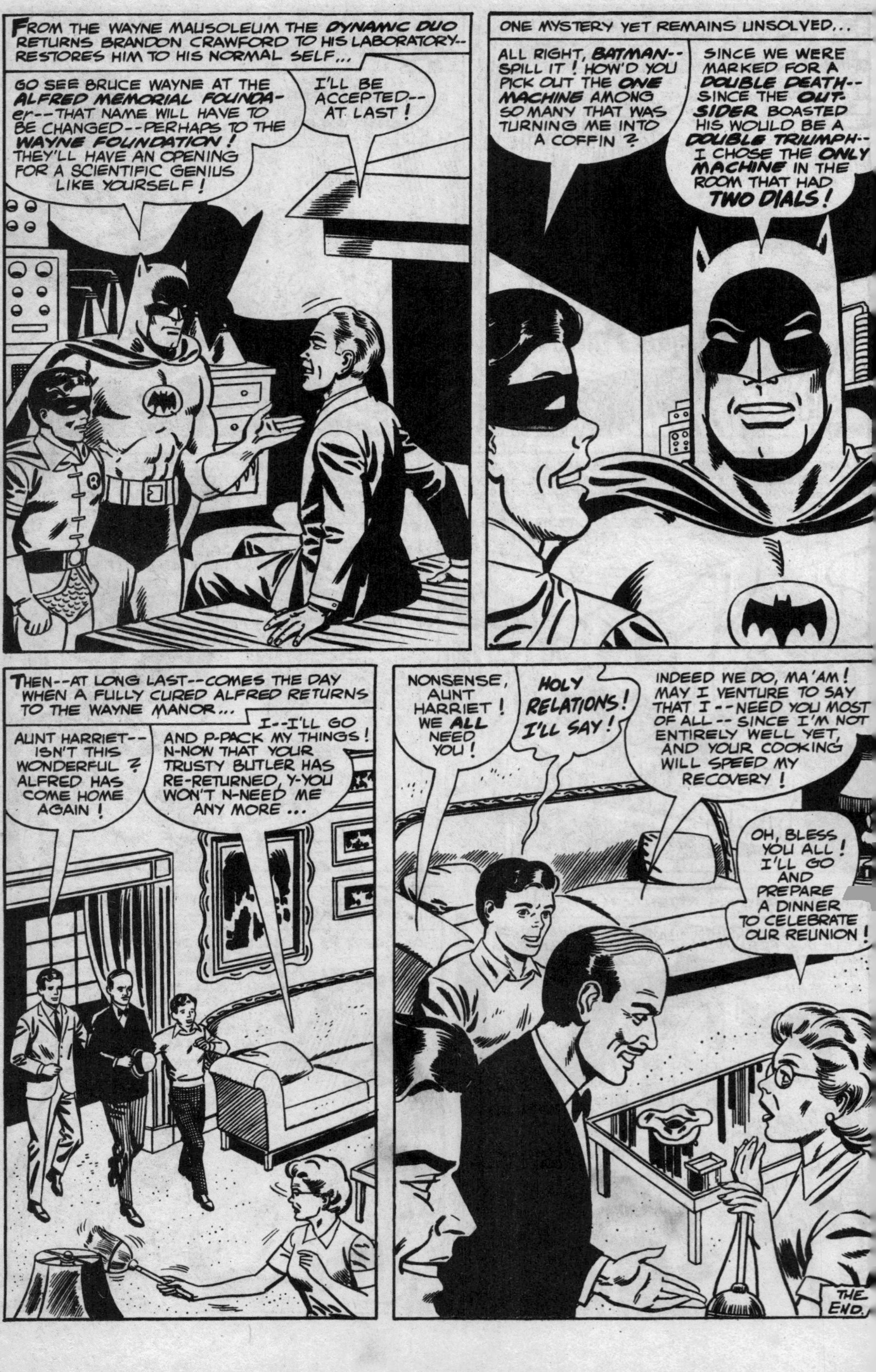
FROM THE WAYNE MAUSOLEUM THE DYNAMIC DUO RETURNS BRANDON CRAWFORD TO HIS LABORATORY-- RESTORES HIM TO HIS NORMAL SELF...
GO SEE BRUCE WAYNE AT THE ALFRED MEMORIAL FOUNDAer--THAT NAME WILL HAVE TO BE CHANGED--PERHAPS TO THE WAYNE FOUNDATION! THEY'LL HAVE AN OPENING FOR A SCIENTIFIC GENIUS LIKE YOURSELF!
I'LL BE ACCEPTED-- AT LAST!
ONE MYSTERY YET REMAINS UNSOLVED...
ALL RIGHT, BATMAN-- SPILL IT! HOW'D YOU PICK OUT THE ONE MACHINE AMONG SO MANY THAT WAS TURNING ME INTO A COFFIN?
SINCE WE WERE MARKED FOR A DOUBLE DEATH-- SINCE THE OUTSIDER BOASTED HIS WOULD BE A DOUBLE TRIUMPH-- I CHOSE THE ONLY MACHINE IN THE ROOM THAT HAD TWO DIALS!
THEN--AT LONG LAST--COMES THE DAY WHEN A FULLY CURED ALFRED RETURNS TO THE WAYNE MANOR...
AUNT HARRIET-- ISN'T THIS WONDERFUL? ALFRED HAS COME HOME AGAIN!
I--I'LL GO AND P-PACK MY THINGS! N-NOW THAT YOUR TRUSTY BUTLER HAS RE-RETURNED, Y-YOU WON'T N-NEED ME ANY MORE...
NONSENSE, AUNT HARRIET! WE ALL NEED YOU!
HOLY RELATIONS! I'LL SAY!
INDEED WE DO, MA'AM! MAY I VENTURE TO SAY THAT I--NEED YOU MOST OF ALL--SINCE I'M NOT ENTIRELY WELL YET, AND YOUR COOKING WILL SPEED MY RECOVERY!
OH, BLESS YOU ALL! I'LL GO AND PREPARE A DINNER TO CELEBRATE OUR REUNION!
THE END.

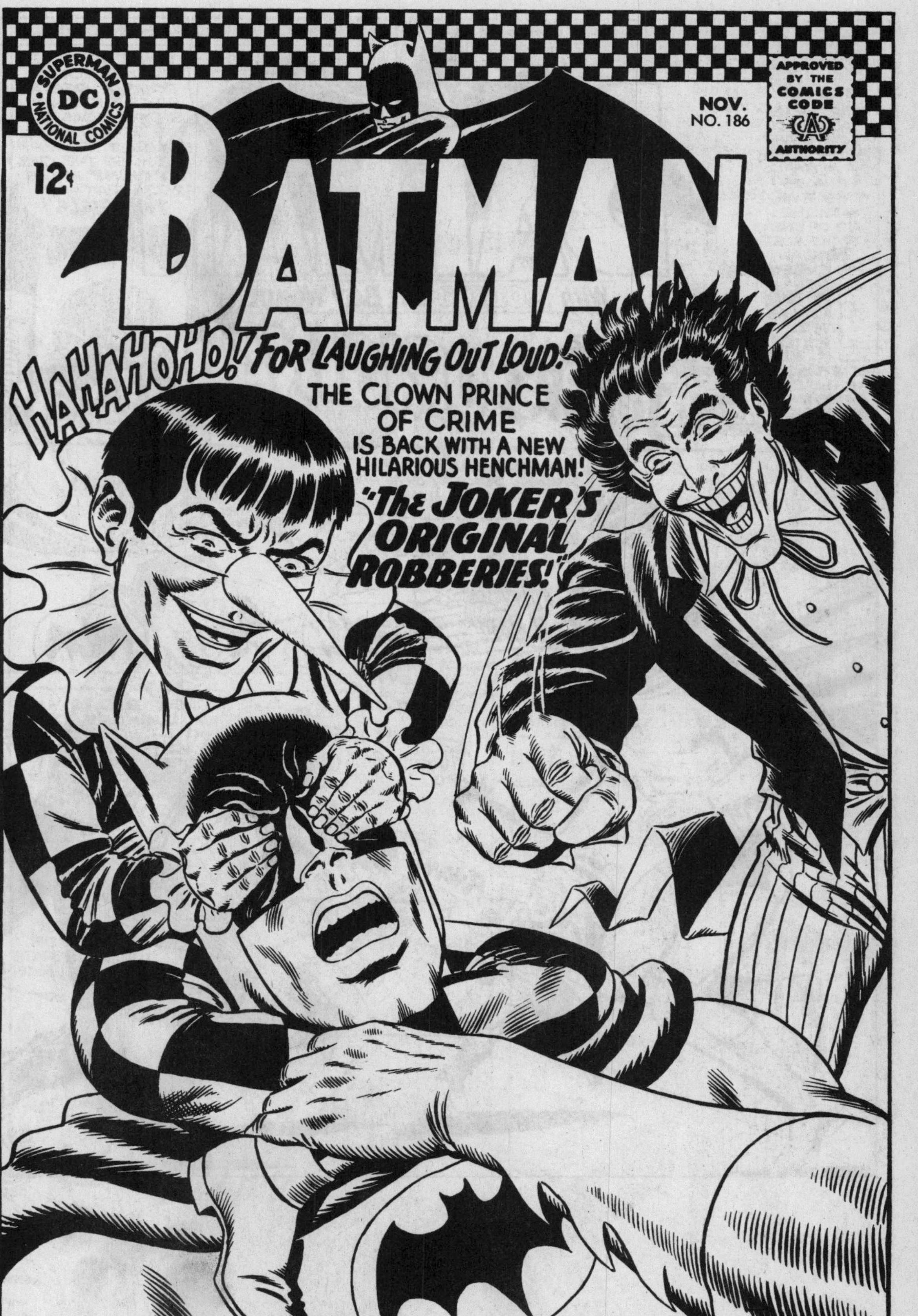
SUPERMAN DC NATIONAL COMICS
12¢
NOV. NO. 186
APPROVED BY THE COMICS CODE AUTHORITY
BATMAN
HAHAHOHO! FOR LAUGHING OUT LOUD!
THE CLOWN PRINCE OF CRIME IS BACK WITH A NEW HILARIOUS HENCHMAN!
"The JOKER'S ORIGINAL ROBBERIES!"

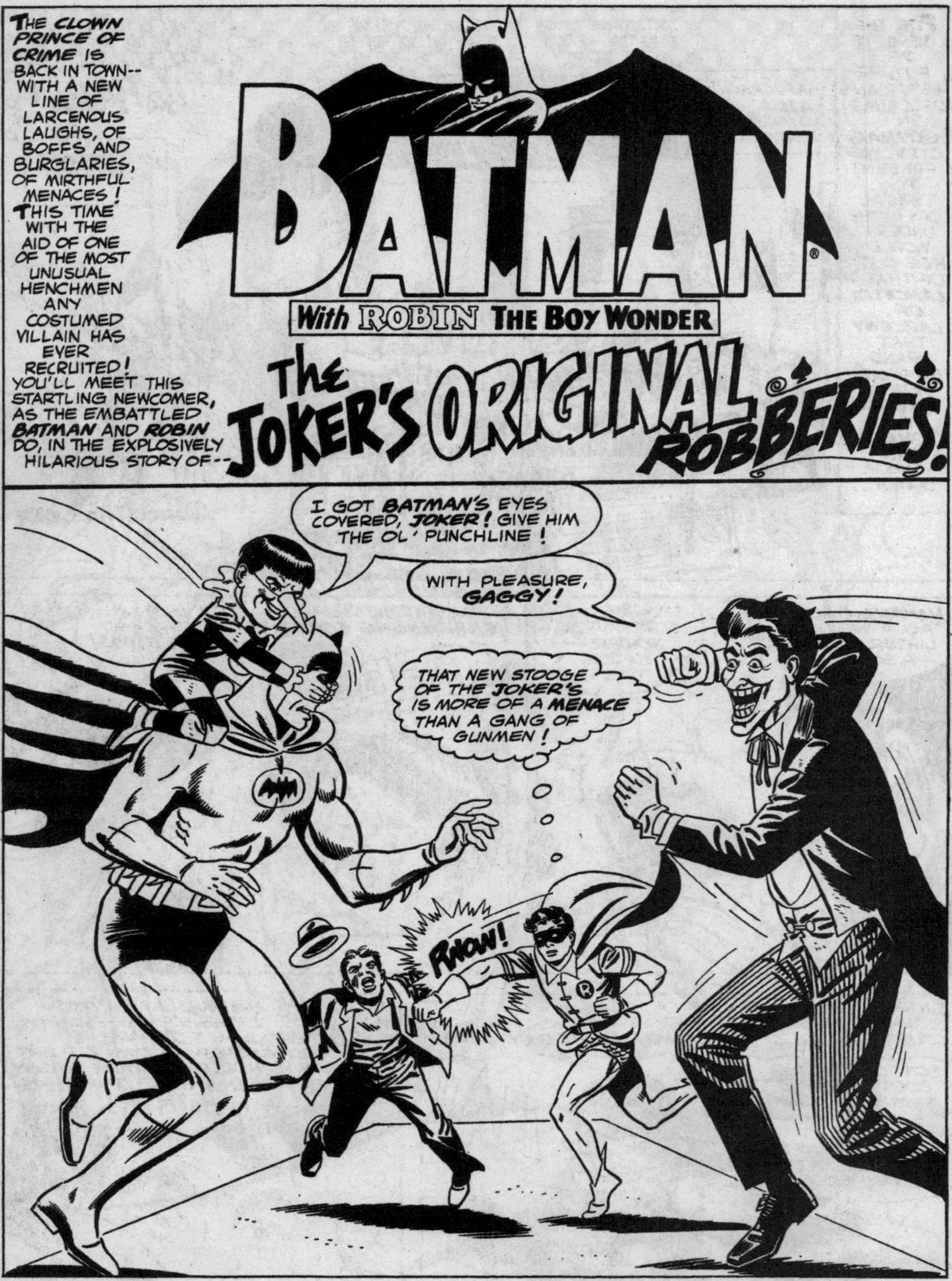
THE CLOWN PRINCE OF CRIME IS BACK IN TOWN-- WITH A NEW LINE OF LARCENOUS LAUGHS, OF BOFFS AND BURGLARIES, OF MIRTHFUL MENACES! THIS TIME WITH THE AID OF ONE OF THE MOST UNUSUAL HENCHMEN ANY COSTUMED VILLAIN HAS EVER RECRUITED! YOU'LL MEET THIS STARTLING NEWCOMER, AS THE EMBATTLED BATMAN AND ROBIN DO, IN THE EXPLOSIVELY HILARIOUS STORY OF--
BATMAN
With ROBIN THE BOY WONDER
The JOKER'S ORIGINAL ROBBERIES!
I GOT BATMAN'S EYES COVERED, JOKER! GIVE HIM THE OL' PUNCHLINE!
WITH PLEASURE, GAGGY!
THAT NEW STOOGE OF THE JOKER'S IS MORE OF A MENACE THAN A GANG OF GUNMEN!
RHOW!

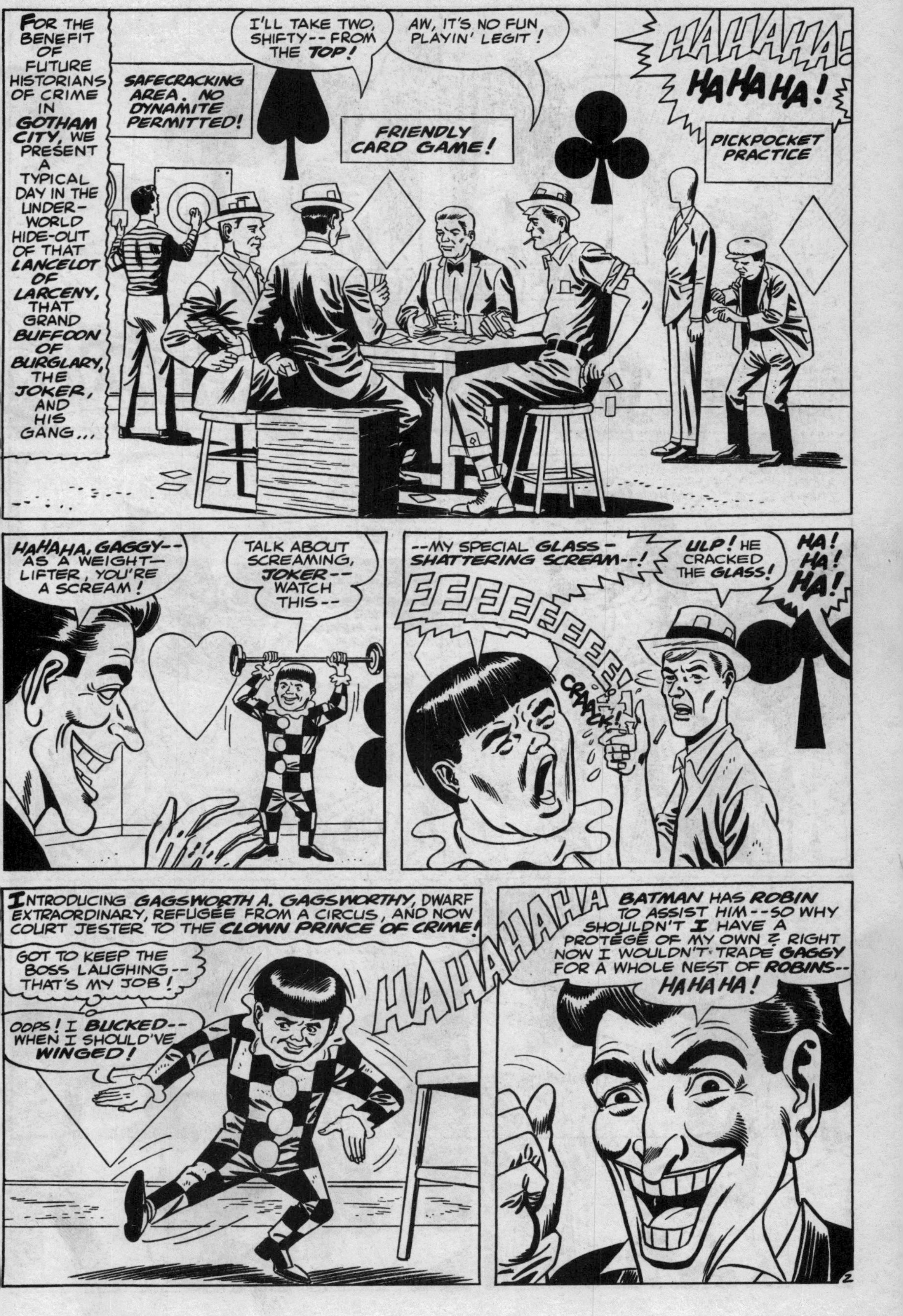
FOR THE BENEFIT OF FUTURE HISTORIANS OF CRIME IN GOTHAM CITY, WE PRESENT A TYPICAL DAY IN THE UNDER-WORLD HIDE-OUT OF THAT LANCELOT OF LARCENY, THAT GRAND BUFFOON OF BURGLARY, THE JOKER, AND HIS GANG...
SAFECRACKING AREA. NO DYNAMITE PERMITTED!
I'LL TAKE TWO, SHIFTY-- FROM THE TOP!
AW, IT'S NO FUN PLAYIN' LEGIT!
FRIENDLY CARD GAME!
HAHAHA! HAHAHA!
PICKPOCKET PRACTICE
HAHAHA, GAGGY-- AS A WEIGHT-LIFTER, YOU'RE A SCREAM!
TALK ABOUT SCREAMING, JOKER-- WATCH THIS--
--MY SPECIAL GLASS-SHATTERING SCREAM--!
EEEEEEEEEEE!
CRAAACK!
ULP! HE CRACKED THE GLASS!
HA! HA! HA!
INTRODUCING GAGSWORTH A. GAGSWORTHY, DWARF EXTRAORDINARY, REFUGEE FROM A CIRCUS, AND NOW COURT JESTER TO THE CLOWN PRINCE OF CRIME!
GOT TO KEEP THE BOSS LAUGHING-- THAT'S MY JOB!
OOPS! I BUCKED-- WHEN I SHOULD'VE WINGED!
HAHAHAHAHA
BATMAN HAS ROBIN TO ASSIST HIM--SO WHY SHOULDN'T I HAVE A PROTÉGÉ OF MY OWN? RIGHT NOW I WOULDN'T TRADE GAGGY FOR A WHOLE NEST OF ROBINS-- HAHAHA!
2

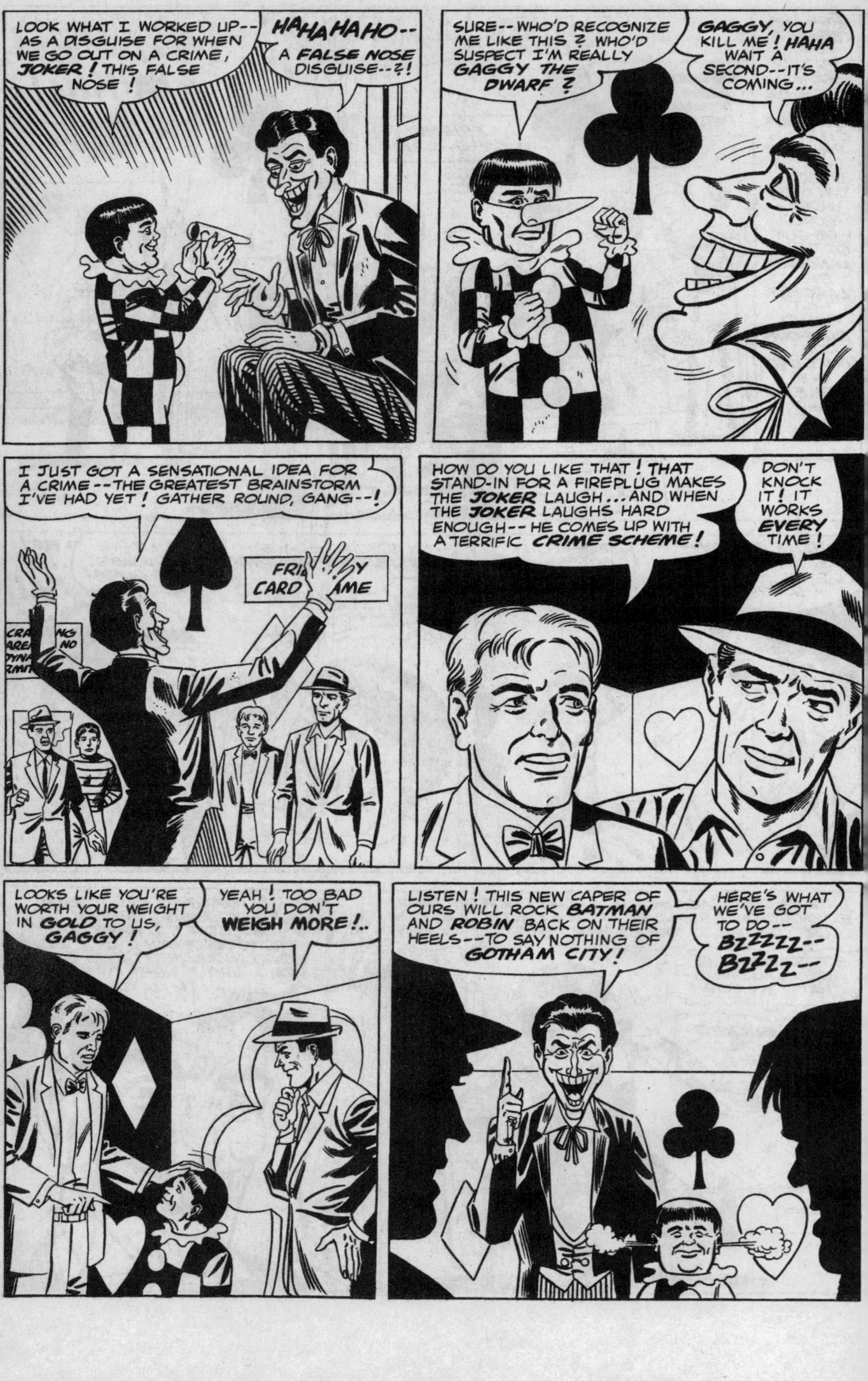
LOOK WHAT I WORKED UP-- AS A DISGUISE FOR WHEN WE GO OUT ON A CRIME, JOKER! THIS FALSE NOSE!
HAHAHAHAHO-- A FALSE NOSE DISGUISE--?!
SURE--WHO'D RECOGNIZE ME LIKE THIS? WHO'D SUSPECT I'M REALLY GAGGY THE DWARF?
GAGGY, YOU KILL ME! HAHA WAIT A SECOND--IT'S COMING...
I JUST GOT A SENSATIONAL IDEA FOR A CRIME--THE GREATEST BRAINSTORM I'VE HAD YET! GATHER ROUND, GANG--!
HOW DO YOU LIKE THAT! THAT STAND-IN FOR A FIREPLUG MAKES THE JOKER LAUGH...AND WHEN THE JOKER LAUGHS HARD ENOUGH--HE COMES UP WITH A TERRIFIC CRIME SCHEME!
DON'T KNOCK IT! IT WORKS EVERY TIME!
LOOKS LIKE YOU'RE WORTH YOUR WEIGHT IN GOLD TO US, GAGGY!
YEAH! TOO BAD YOU DON'T WEIGH MORE!..
LISTEN! THIS NEW CAPER OF OURS WILL ROCK BATMAN AND ROBIN BACK ON THEIR HEELS--TO SAY NOTHING OF GOTHAM CITY!
HERE'S WHAT WE'VE GOT TO DO-- BZZZZZ-- BZZZZ--

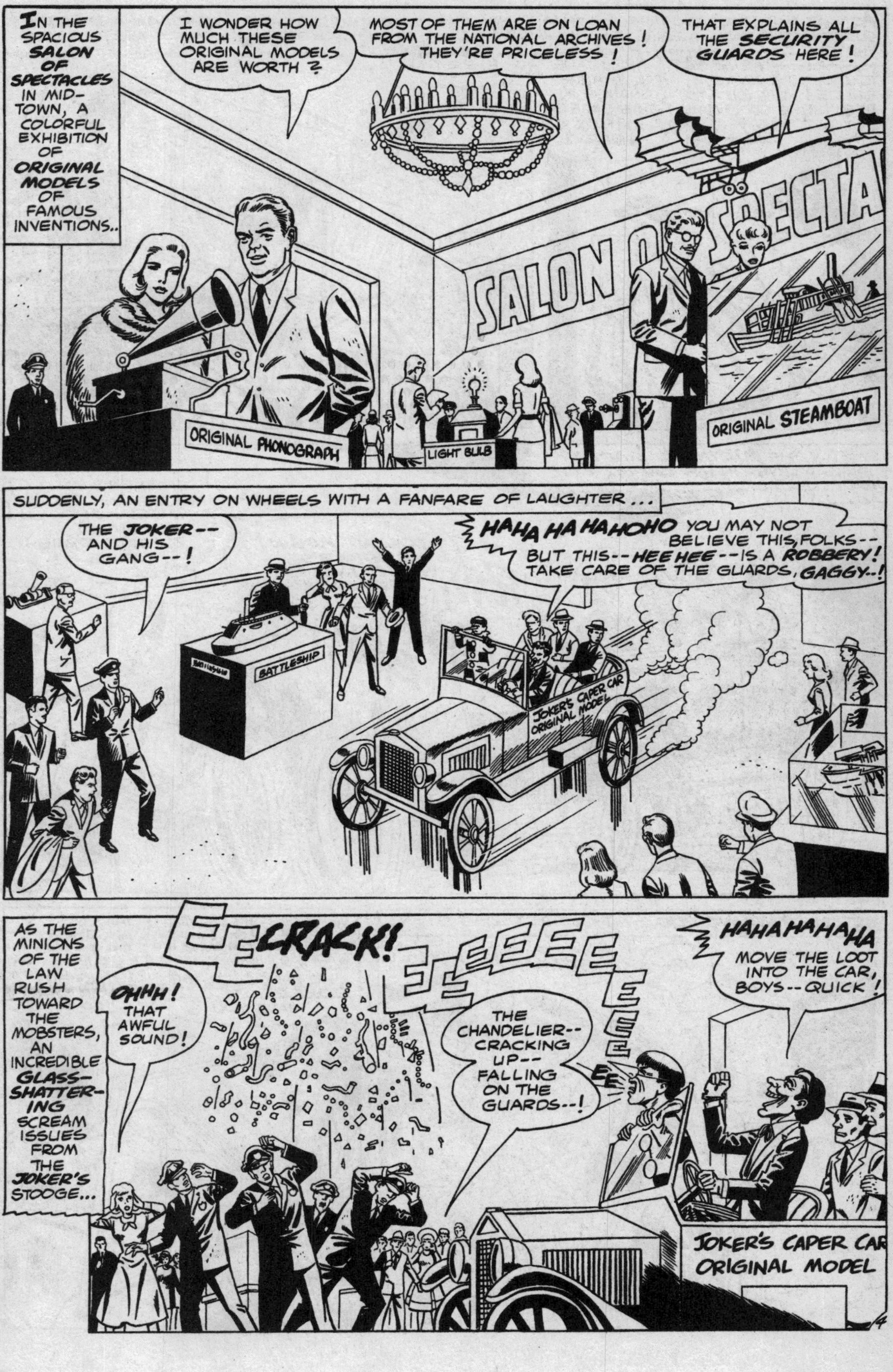
IN THE SPACIOUS SALON OF SPECTACLES IN MID-TOWN, A COLORFUL EXHIBITION OF ORIGINAL MODELS OF FAMOUS INVENTIONS..
I WONDER HOW MUCH THESE ORIGINAL MODELS ARE WORTH ?
MOST OF THEM ARE ON LOAN FROM THE NATIONAL ARCHIVES ! THEY'RE PRICELESS !
THAT EXPLAINS ALL THE SECURITY GUARDS HERE !
SALON OF SPECTA
ORIGINAL PHONOGRAPH
LIGHT BULB
ORIGINAL STEAMBOAT
SUDDENLY, AN ENTRY ON WHEELS WITH A FANFARE OF LAUGHTER ...
THE JOKER-- AND HIS GANG--!
HAHAHA HAHAHOHO YOU MAY NOT BELIEVE THIS, FOLKS-- BUT THIS--HEE HEE--IS A ROBBERY! TAKE CARE OF THE GUARDS, GAGGY..!
BATTLESHIP
JOKER'S CAPER CAR ORIGINAL MODEL
AS THE MINIONS OF THE LAW RUSH TOWARD THE MOBSTERS, AN INCREDIBLE GLASS-SHATTERING SCREAM ISSUES FROM THE JOKER'S STOOGE...
EE CRACK! EEEEEEEEEEEE
OHHH! THAT AWFUL SOUND!
THE CHANDELIER-- CRACKING UP-- FALLING ON THE GUARDS--!
HAHAHAHAHAHA MOVE THE LOOT INTO THE CAR, BOYS--QUICK !
JOKER'S CAPER CAR ORIGINAL MODEL

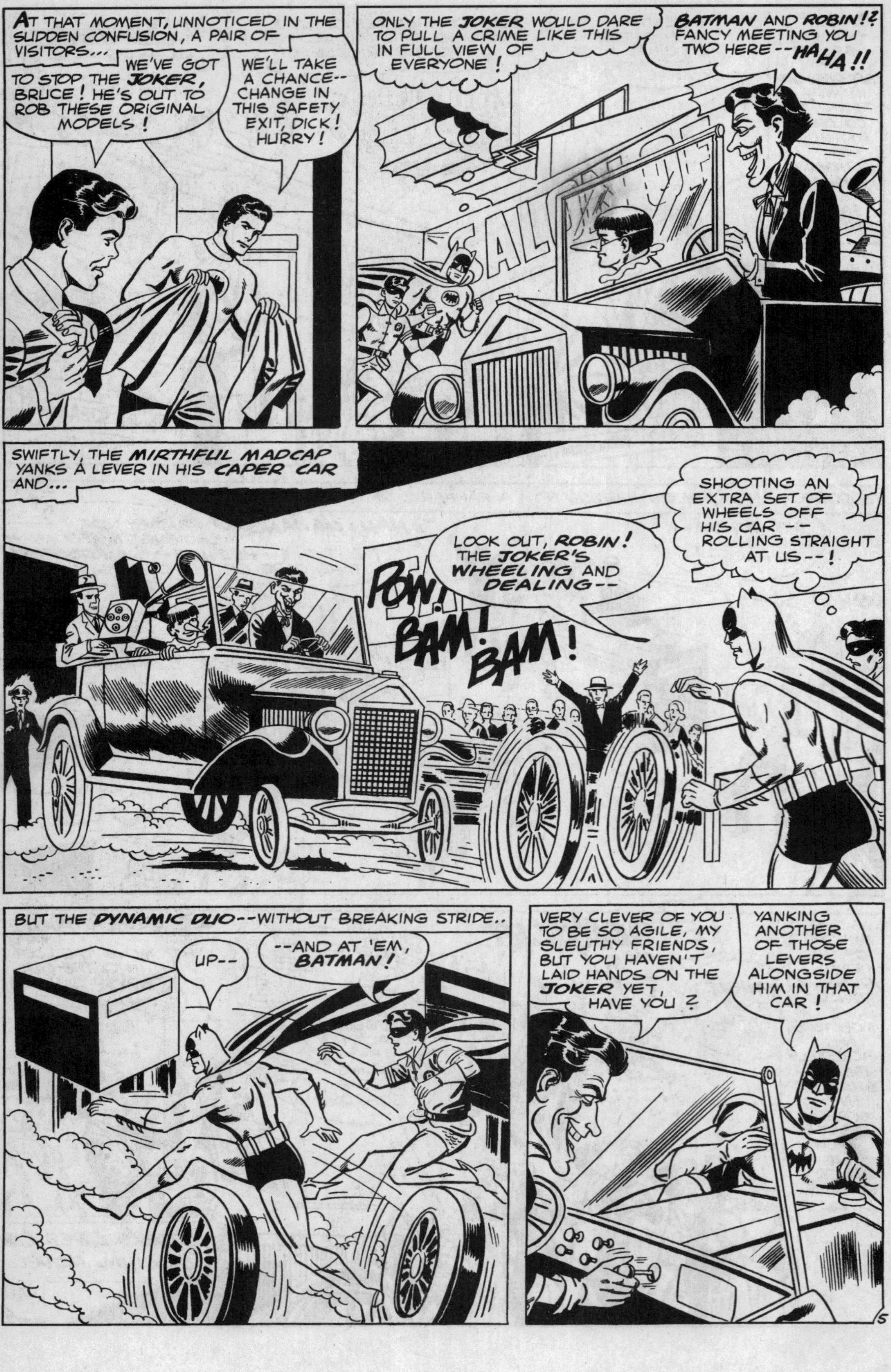
AT THAT MOMENT, UNNOTICED IN THE SUDDEN CONFUSION, A PAIR OF VISITORS...
WE'VE GOT TO STOP THE JOKER, BRUCE! HE'S OUT TO ROB THESE ORIGINAL MODELS!
WE'LL TAKE A CHANCE-- CHANGE IN THIS SAFETY EXIT, DICK! HURRY!
ONLY THE JOKER WOULD DARE TO PULL A CRIME LIKE THIS IN FULL VIEW OF EVERYONE!
BATMAN AND ROBIN!? FANCY MEETING YOU TWO HERE--HAHA!!
SWIFTLY, THE MIRTHFUL MADCAP YANKS A LEVER IN HIS CAPER CAR AND...
LOOK OUT, ROBIN! THE JOKER'S WHEELING AND DEALING--
SHOOTING AN EXTRA SET OF WHEELS OFF HIS CAR -- ROLLING STRAIGHT AT US--!
POW! BAM! BAM!
BUT THE DYNAMIC DUO--WITHOUT BREAKING STRIDE..
UP--
--AND AT 'EM, BATMAN!
VERY CLEVER OF YOU TO BE SO AGILE, MY SLEUTHY FRIENDS, BUT YOU HAVEN'T LAID HANDS ON THE JOKER YET, HAVE YOU?
YANKING ANOTHER OF THOSE LEVERS ALONGSIDE HIM IN THAT CAR!
5

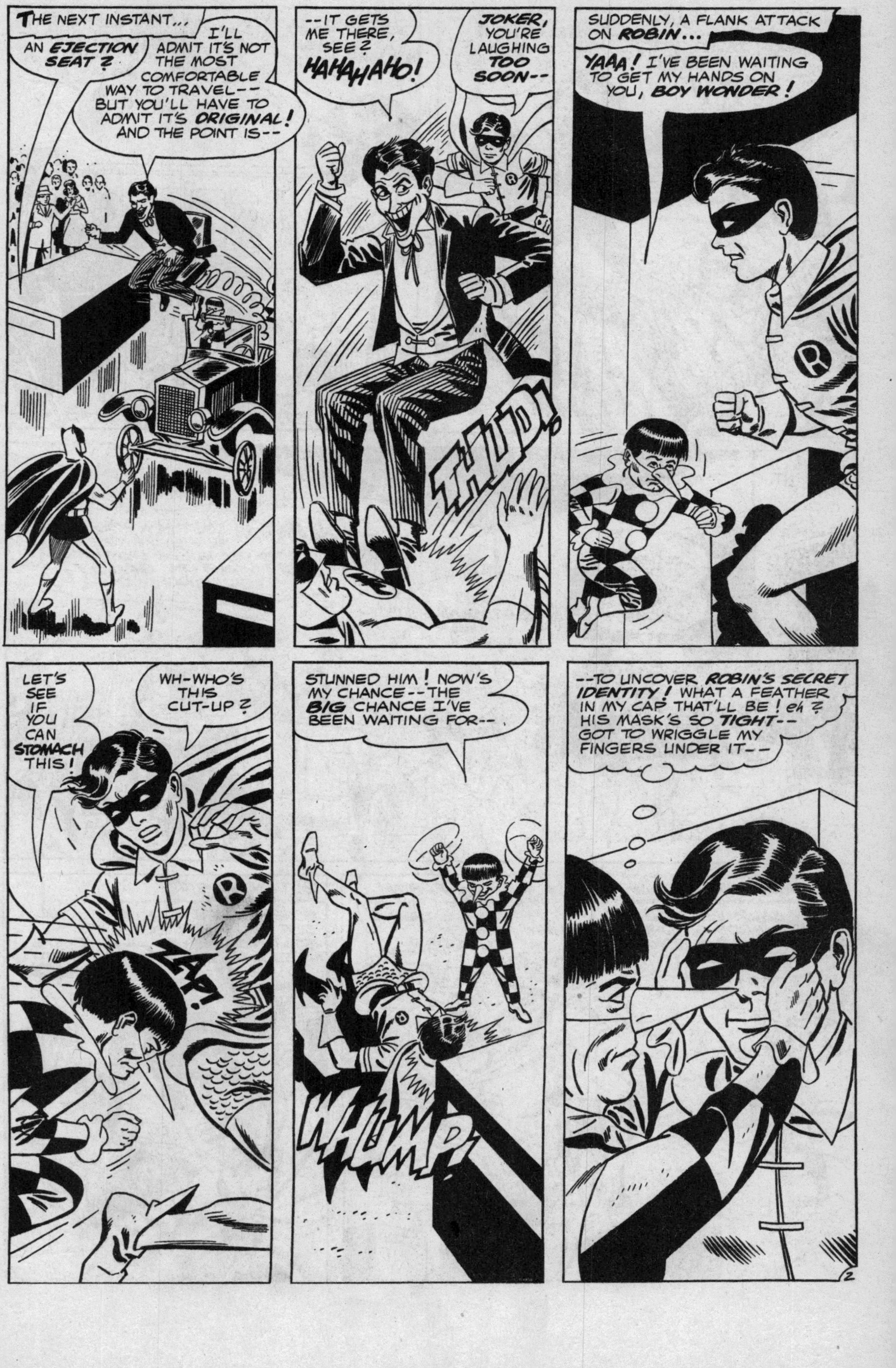
THE NEXT INSTANT...
AN EJECTION SEAT?
I'LL ADMIT IT'S NOT THE MOST COMFORTABLE WAY TO TRAVEL-- BUT YOU'LL HAVE TO ADMIT IT'S ORIGINAL! AND THE POINT IS--
--IT GETS ME THERE, SEE? HAHAHAHO!
JOKER, YOU'RE LAUGHING TOO SOON--
THUD!
SUDDENLY, A FLANK ATTACK ON ROBIN...
YAAA! I'VE BEEN WAITING TO GET MY HANDS ON YOU, BOY WONDER!
LET'S SEE IF YOU CAN STOMACH THIS!
WH-WHO'S THIS CUT-UP?
ZAP!
STUNNED HIM! NOW'S MY CHANCE--THE BIG CHANCE I'VE BEEN WAITING FOR--
WHUMP!
--TO UNCOVER ROBIN'S SECRET IDENTITY! WHAT A FEATHER IN MY CAP THAT'LL BE! eh? HIS MASK'S SO TIGHT-- GOT TO WRIGGLE MY FINGERS UNDER IT--
2

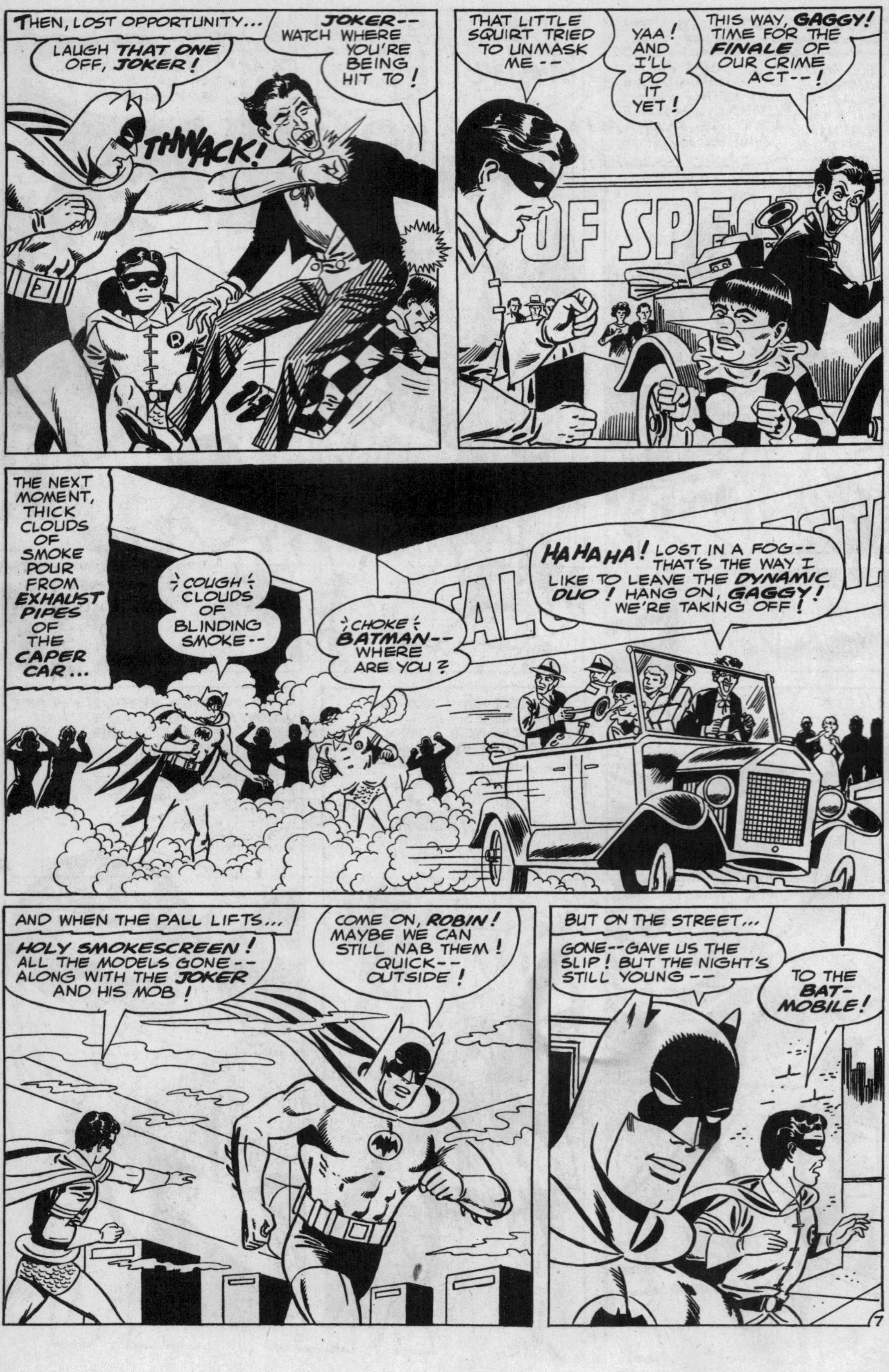
THEN, LOST OPPORTUNITY...
LAUGH THAT ONE OFF, JOKER!
JOKER-- WATCH WHERE YOU'RE BEING HIT TO!
THWACK!
THAT LITTLE SQUIRT TRIED TO UNMASK ME--
YAA! AND I'LL DO IT YET!
THIS WAY, GAGGY! TIME FOR THE FINALE OF OUR CRIME ACT--!
THE NEXT MOMENT, THICK CLOUDS OF SMOKE POUR FROM EXHAUST PIPES OF THE CAPER CAR...
COUGH CLOUDS OF BLINDING SMOKE--
CHOKE BATMAN-- WHERE ARE YOU?
HAHAHA! LOST IN A FOG-- THAT'S THE WAY I LIKE TO LEAVE THE DYNAMIC DUO! HANG ON, GAGGY! WE'RE TAKING OFF!
AND WHEN THE PALL LIFTS...
HOLY SMOKESCREEN! ALL THE MODELS GONE-- ALONG WITH THE JOKER AND HIS MOB!
COME ON, ROBIN! MAYBE WE CAN STILL NAB THEM! QUICK-- OUTSIDE!
BUT ON THE STREET...
GONE--GAVE US THE SLIP! BUT THE NIGHT'S STILL YOUNG--
TO THE BAT-MOBILE!
7

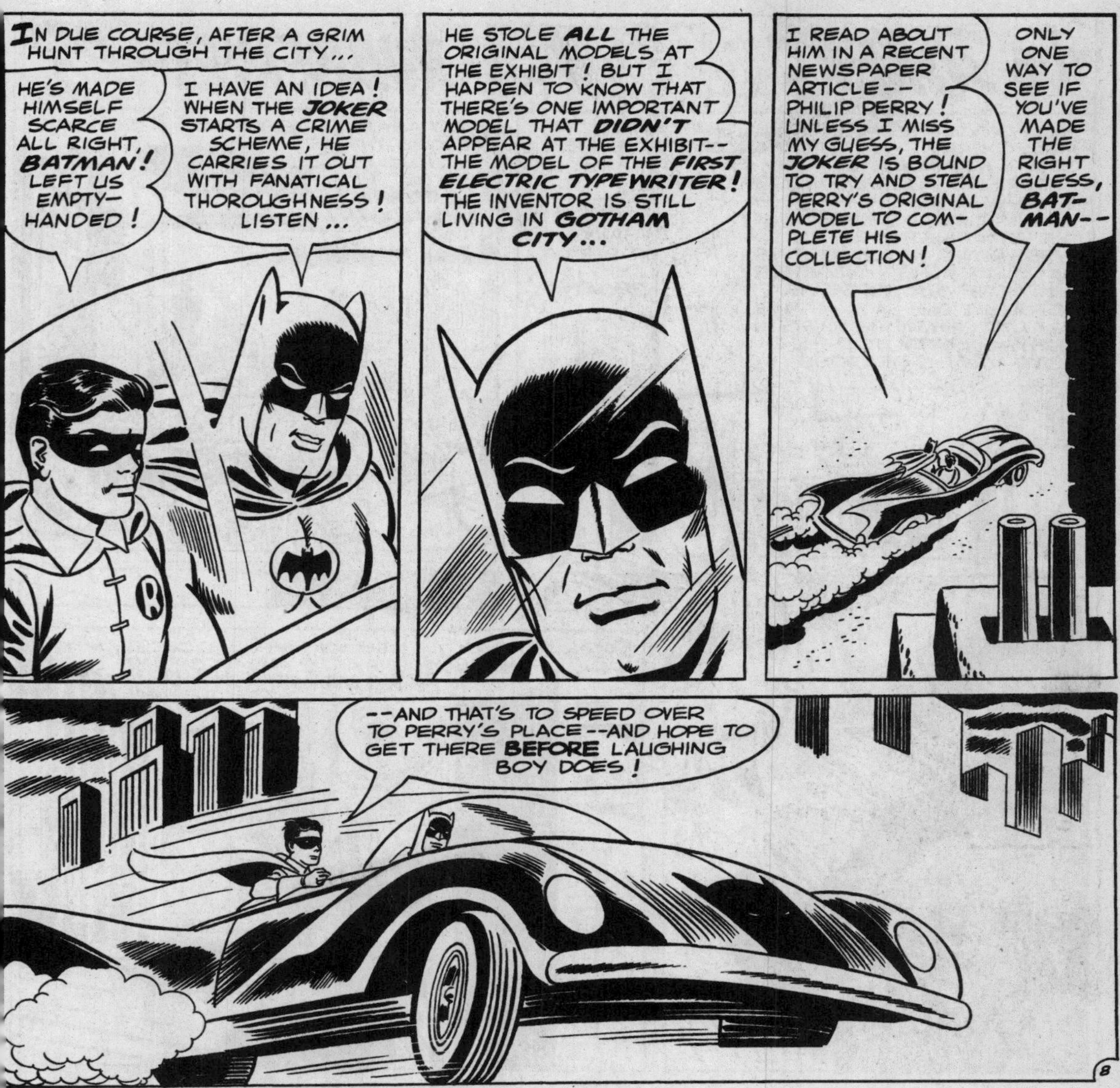
IN DUE COURSE, AFTER A GRIM HUNT THROUGH THE CITY...
HE'S MADE HIMSELF SCARCE ALL RIGHT, BATMAN! LEFT US EMPTY-HANDED!
I HAVE AN IDEA! WHEN THE JOKER STARTS A CRIME SCHEME, HE CARRIES IT OUT WITH FANATICAL THOROUGHNESS! LISTEN...
HE STOLE ALL THE ORIGINAL MODELS AT THE EXHIBIT! BUT I HAPPEN TO KNOW THAT THERE'S ONE IMPORTANT MODEL THAT DIDN'T APPEAR AT THE EXHIBIT-- THE MODEL OF THE FIRST ELECTRIC TYPEWRITER! THE INVENTOR IS STILL LIVING IN GOTHAM CITY...
I READ ABOUT HIM IN A RECENT NEWSPAPER ARTICLE-- PHILIP PERRY! UNLESS I MISS MY GUESS, THE JOKER IS BOUND TO TRY AND STEAL PERRY'S ORIGINAL MODEL TO COMPLETE HIS COLLECTION!
ONLY ONE WAY TO SEE IF YOU'VE MADE THE RIGHT GUESS, BATMAN--
--AND THAT'S TO SPEED OVER TO PERRY'S PLACE--AND HOPE TO GET THERE BEFORE LAUGHING BOY DOES!
8

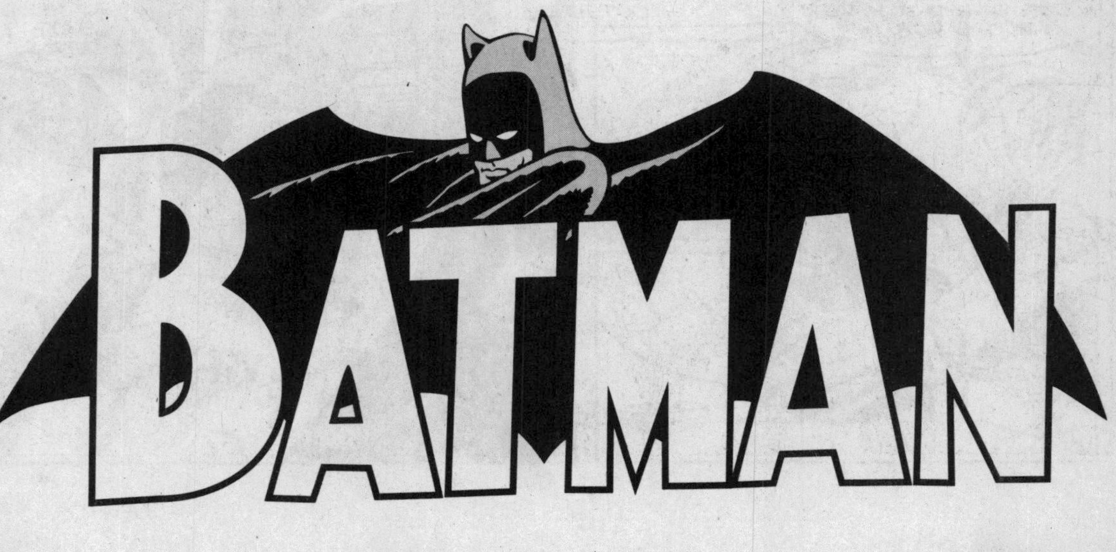
BATMAN

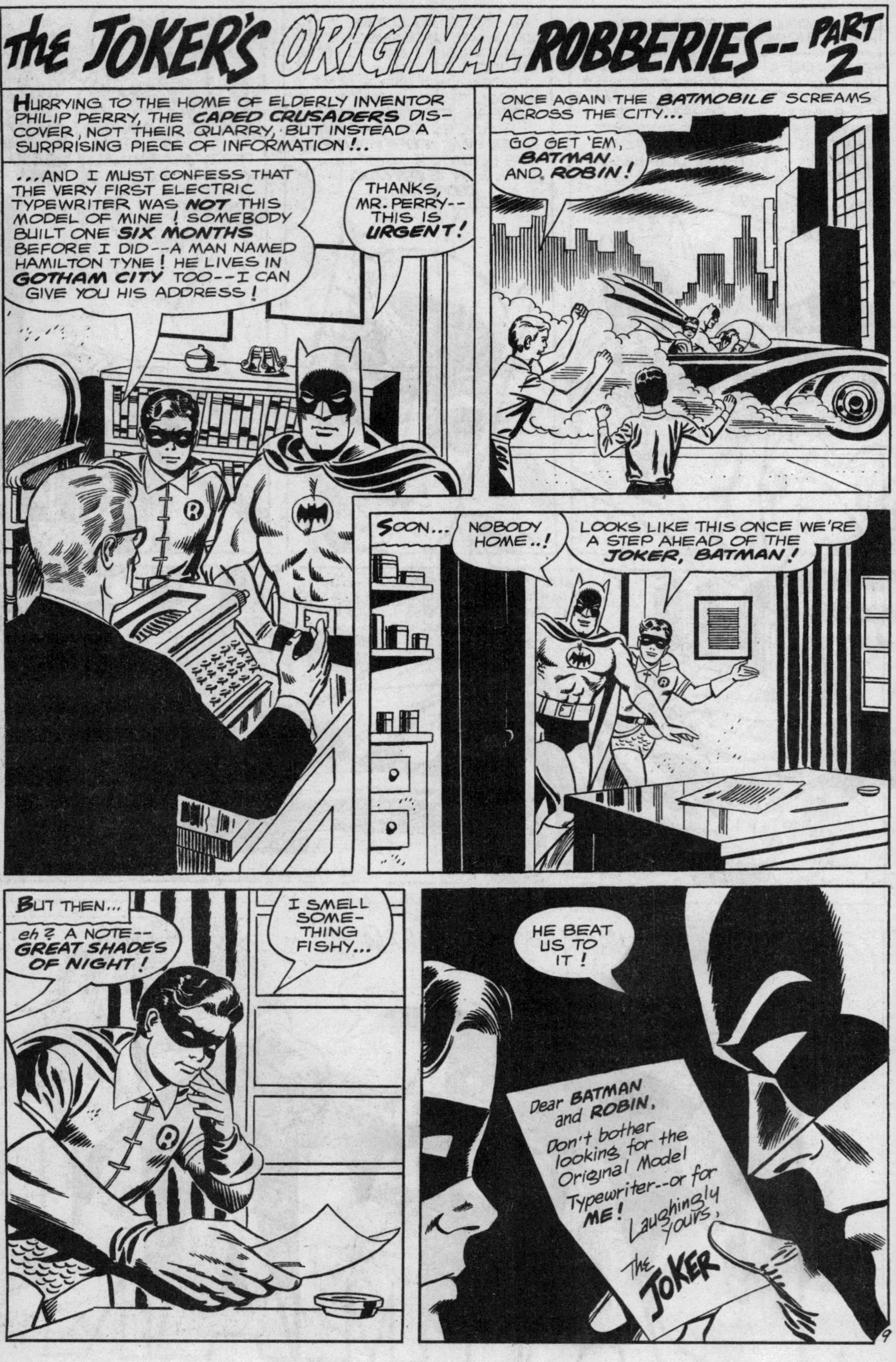
THE JOKER'S ORIGINAL ROBBERIES-- PART 2
HURRYING TO THE HOME OF ELDERLY INVENTOR PHILIP PERRY, THE CAPED CRUSADERS DISCOVER, NOT THEIR QUARRY, BUT INSTEAD A SURPRISING PIECE OF INFORMATION!..
...AND I MUST CONFESS THAT THE VERY FIRST ELECTRIC TYPEWRITER WAS NOT THIS MODEL OF MINE! SOMEBODY BUILT ONE SIX MONTHS BEFORE I DID--A MAN NAMED HAMILTON TYNE! HE LIVES IN GOTHAM CITY TOO--I CAN GIVE YOU HIS ADDRESS!
THANKS, MR. PERRY-- THIS IS URGENT!
ONCE AGAIN THE BATMOBILE SCREAMS ACROSS THE CITY...
GO GET 'EM, BATMAN AND ROBIN!
SOON...
NOBODY HOME..!
LOOKS LIKE THIS ONCE WE'RE A STEP AHEAD OF THE JOKER, BATMAN!
BUT THEN...
eh? A NOTE-- GREAT SHADES OF NIGHT!
I SMELL SOMETHING FISHY...
HE BEAT US TO IT!
Dear BATMAN and ROBIN, Don't bother looking for the Original Model Typewriter--or for ME! Laughingly yours, The JOKER
9

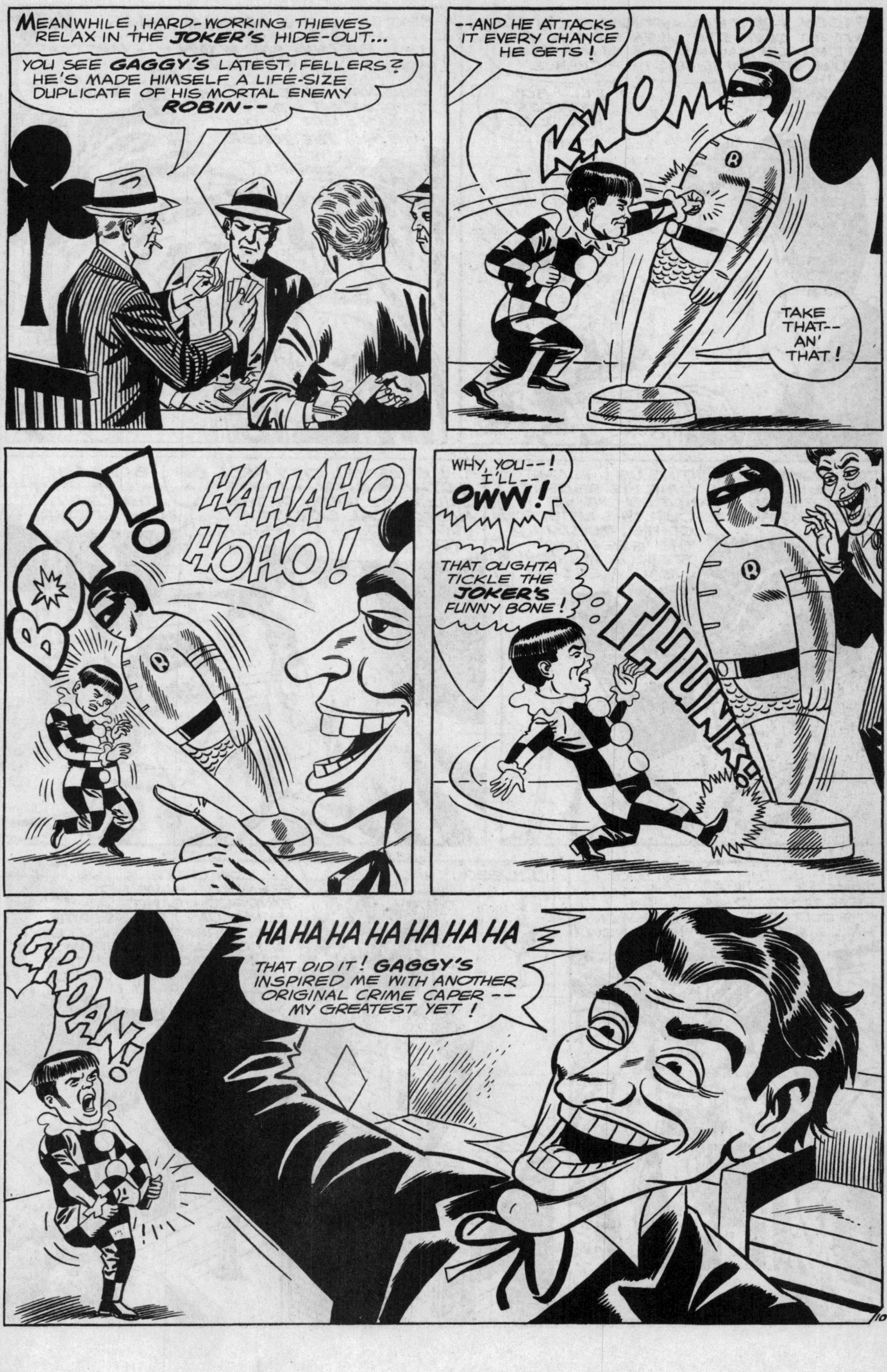
MEANWHILE, HARD-WORKING THIEVES RELAX IN THE JOKER'S HIDE-OUT...
YOU SEE GAGGY'S LATEST, FELLERS? HE'S MADE HIMSELF A LIFE-SIZE DUPLICATE OF HIS MORTAL ENEMY ROBIN--
--AND HE ATTACKS IT EVERY CHANCE HE GETS!
KWOMP!
TAKE THAT-- AN' THAT!
BOP!
HAHAHO HOHO!
WHY, YOU--! I'LL-- OWW!
THAT OUGHTA TICKLE THE JOKER'S FUNNY BONE!
THUNK!
GROAN!
HA HA HA HA HA HA HA HA
THAT DID IT! GAGGY'S INSPIRED ME WITH ANOTHER ORIGINAL CRIME CAPER -- MY GREATEST YET!
10

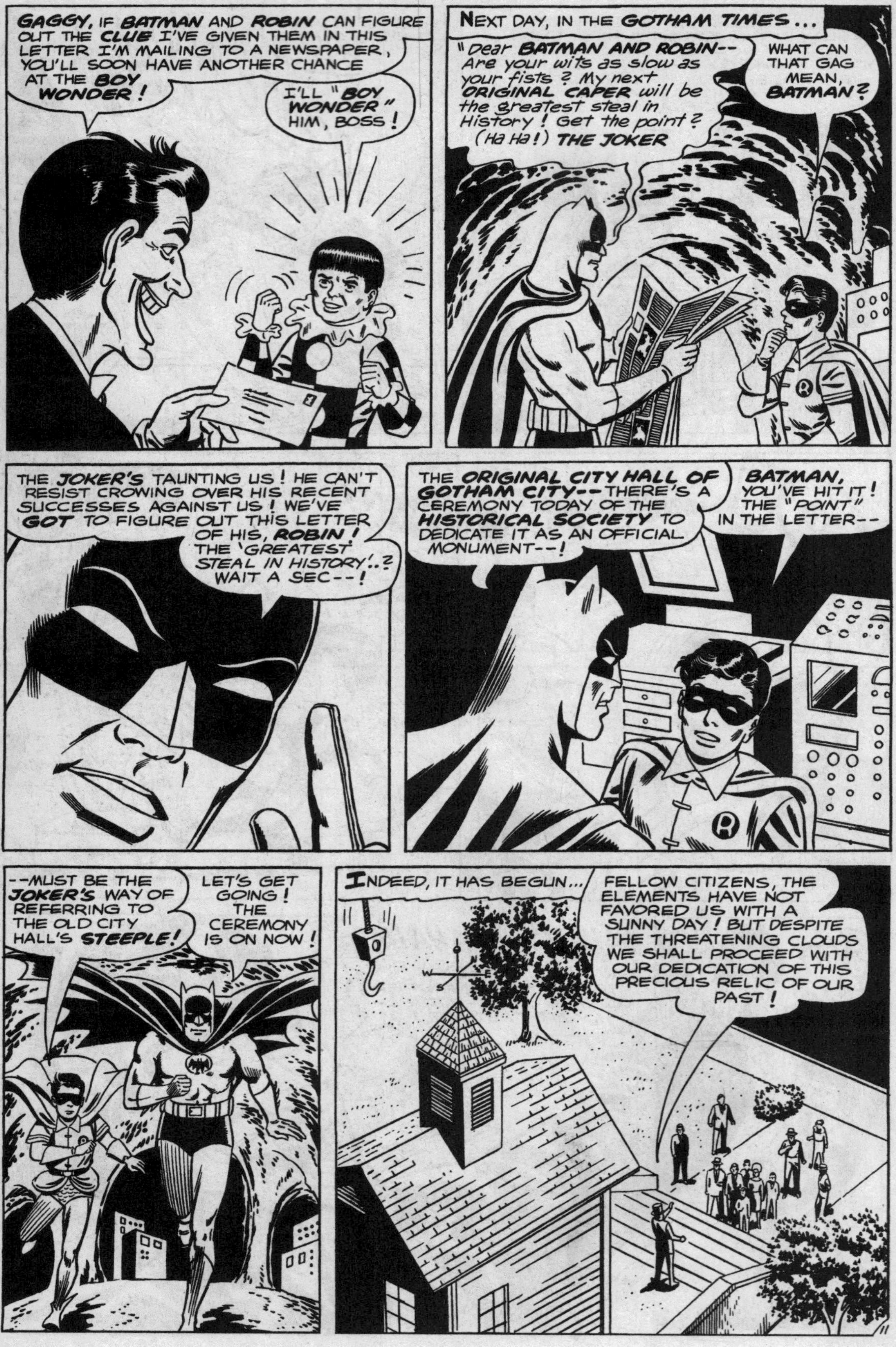
GAGGY, IF BATMAN AND ROBIN CAN FIGURE OUT THE CLUE I'VE GIVEN THEM IN THIS LETTER I'M MAILING TO A NEWSPAPER, YOU'LL SOON HAVE ANOTHER CHANCE AT THE BOY WONDER!
I'LL "BOY WONDER" HIM, BOSS!
NEXT DAY, IN THE GOTHAM TIMES...
"Dear BATMAN AND ROBIN-- Are your wits as slow as your fists? My next ORIGINAL CAPER will be the greatest steal in History! Get the point? (Ha Ha!) THE JOKER
WHAT CAN THAT GAG MEAN, BATMAN?
THE JOKER'S TAUNTING US! HE CAN'T RESIST CROWING OVER HIS RECENT SUCCESSES AGAINST US! WE'VE GOT TO FIGURE OUT THIS LETTER OF HIS, ROBIN! THE 'GREATEST STEAL IN HISTORY'..? WAIT A SEC--!
THE ORIGINAL CITY HALL OF GOTHAM CITY--THERE'S A CEREMONY TODAY OF THE HISTORICAL SOCIETY TO DEDICATE IT AS AN OFFICIAL MONUMENT--!
BATMAN, YOU'VE HIT IT! THE "POINT" IN THE LETTER--
--MUST BE THE JOKER'S WAY OF REFERRING TO THE OLD CITY HALL'S STEEPLE!
LET'S GET GOING! THE CEREMONY IS ON NOW!
INDEED, IT HAS BEGUN...
FELLOW CITIZENS, THE ELEMENTS HAVE NOT FAVORED US WITH A SUNNY DAY! BUT DESPITE THE THREATENING CLOUDS WE SHALL PROCEED WITH OUR DEDICATION OF THIS PRECIOUS RELIC OF OUR PAST!
11

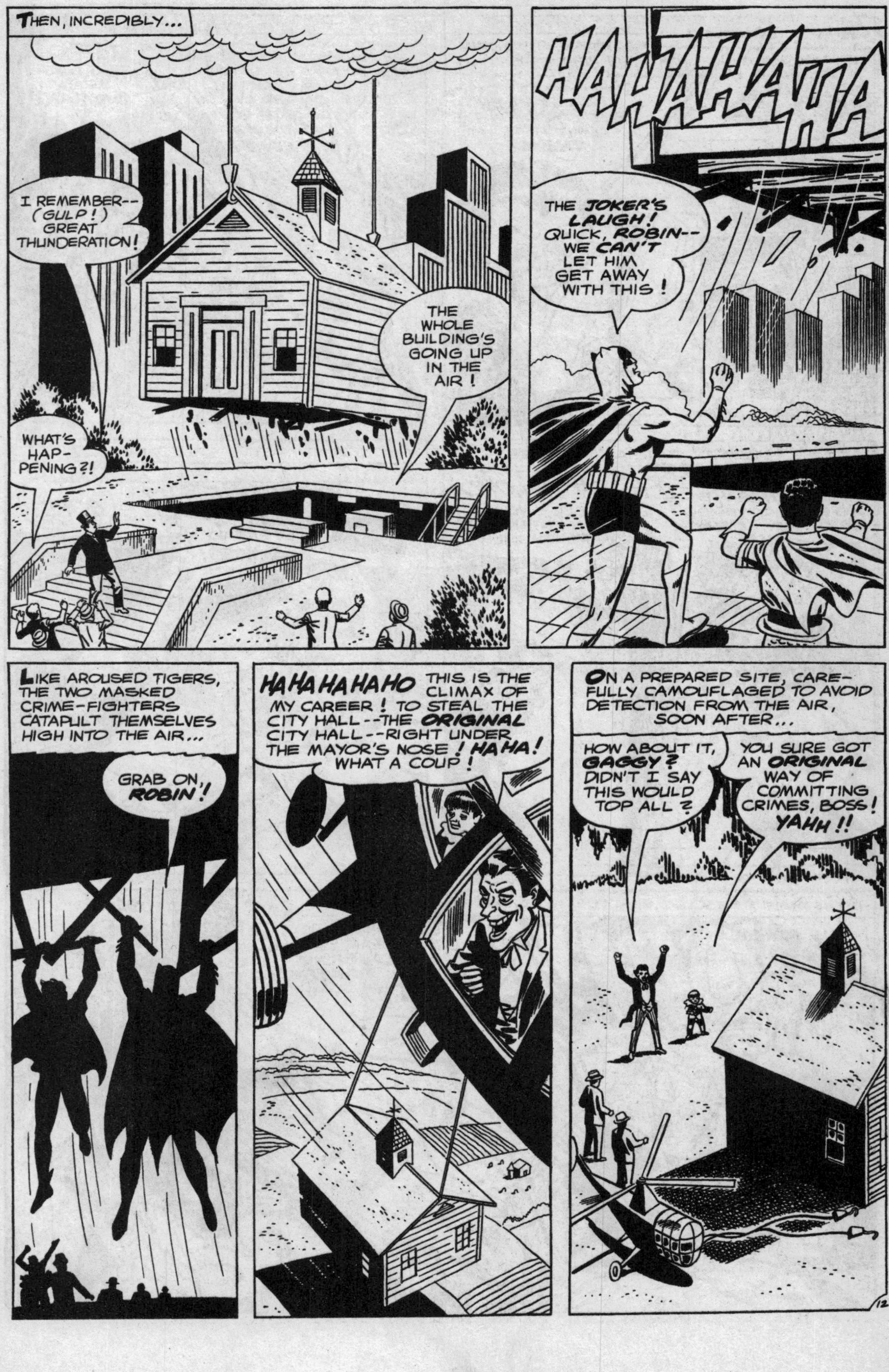
THEN, INCREDIBLY...
I REMEMBER-- (GULP!) GREAT THUNDERATION!
THE WHOLE BUILDING'S GOING UP IN THE AIR!
WHAT'S HAP-PENING?!
HAHAHAHAHA
THE JOKER'S LAUGH! QUICK, ROBIN-- WE CAN'T LET HIM GET AWAY WITH THIS!
LIKE AROUSED TIGERS, THE TWO MASKED CRIME-FIGHTERS CATAPULT THEMSELVES HIGH INTO THE AIR...
GRAB ON, ROBIN!
HAHAHAHAHO THIS IS THE CLIMAX OF MY CAREER! TO STEAL THE CITY HALL--THE ORIGINAL CITY HALL--RIGHT UNDER THE MAYOR'S NOSE! HAHA! WHAT A COUP!
ON A PREPARED SITE, CAREFULLY CAMOUFLAGED TO AVOID DETECTION FROM THE AIR, SOON AFTER...
HOW ABOUT IT, GAGGY? DIDN'T I SAY THIS WOULD TOP ALL?
YOU SURE GOT AN ORIGINAL WAY OF COMMITTING CRIMES, BOSS! YAHH!!
12

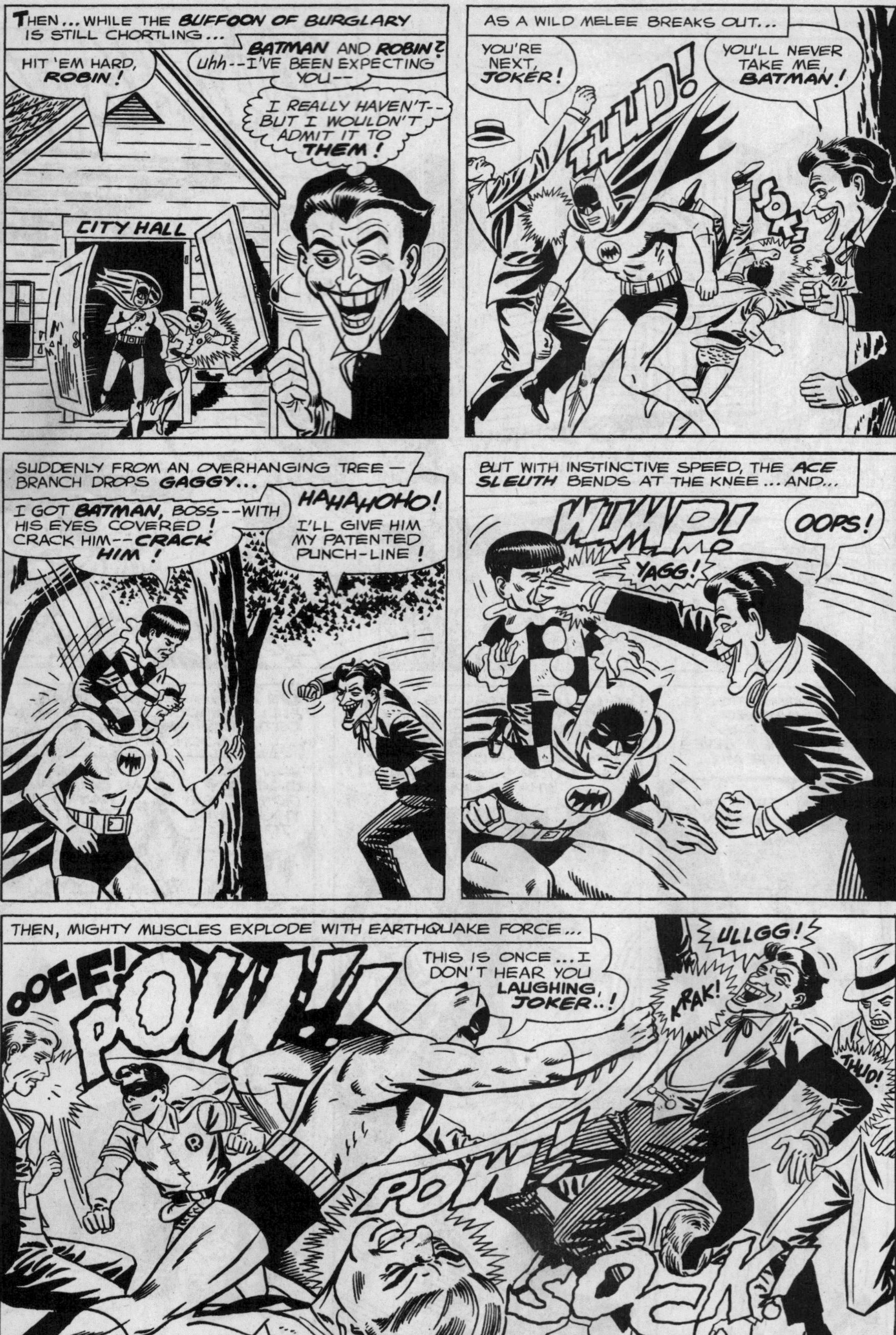
THEN... WHILE THE BUFFOON OF BURGLARY IS STILL CHORTLING...
HIT 'EM HARD, ROBIN!
BATMAN AND ROBIN? uhh--I'VE BEEN EXPECTING YOU--
I REALLY HAVEN'T--BUT I WOULDN'T ADMIT IT TO THEM!
CITY HALL
AS A WILD MELEE BREAKS OUT...
YOU'RE NEXT, JOKER!
THUD!
YOU'LL NEVER TAKE ME, BATMAN!
SOK!
SUDDENLY FROM AN OVERHANGING TREE-BRANCH DROPS GAGGY...
I GOT BATMAN, BOSS--WITH HIS EYES COVERED! CRACK HIM--CRACK HIM!
HAHAHOHO! I'LL GIVE HIM MY PATENTED PUNCH-LINE!
BUT WITH INSTINCTIVE SPEED, THE ACE SLEUTH BENDS AT THE KNEE... AND...
WUMP!
YAGG!
OOPS!
THEN, MIGHTY MUSCLES EXPLODE WITH EARTHQUAKE FORCE...
OOFF!
POW!!
THIS IS ONCE... I DON'T HEAR YOU LAUGHING, JOKER..!
ULLGG!
KRAK!
THUD!
POW!
SOCK!
13

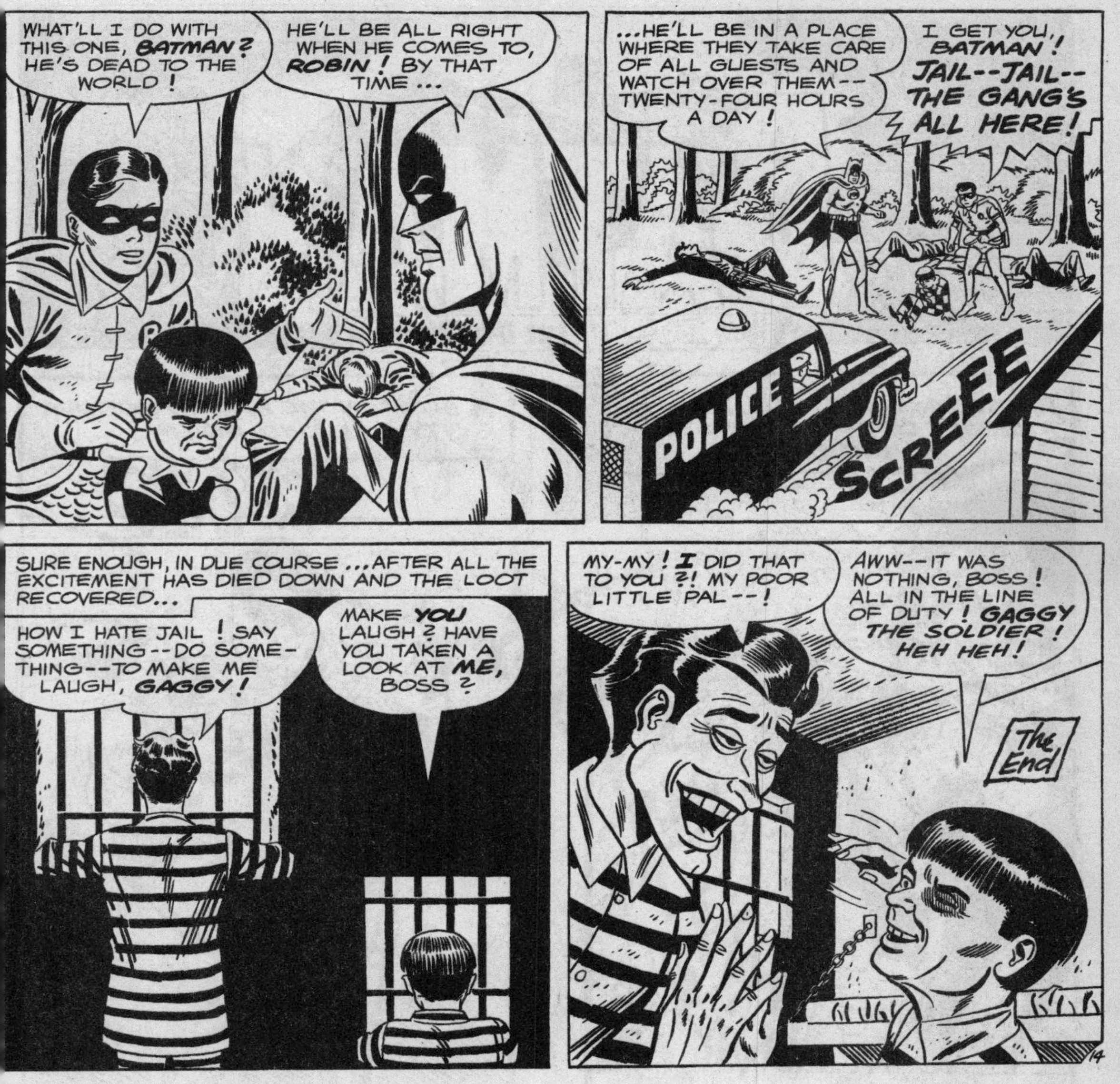
WHAT'LL I DO WITH THIS ONE, BATMAN? HE'S DEAD TO THE WORLD!
HE'LL BE ALL RIGHT WHEN HE COMES TO, ROBIN! BY THAT TIME...
...HE'LL BE IN A PLACE WHERE THEY TAKE CARE OF ALL GUESTS AND WATCH OVER THEM--TWENTY-FOUR HOURS A DAY!
I GET YOU, BATMAN! JAIL--JAIL--THE GANG'S ALL HERE!
POLICE
SCREEEE
SURE ENOUGH, IN DUE COURSE...AFTER ALL THE EXCITEMENT HAS DIED DOWN AND THE LOOT RECOVERED...
HOW I HATE JAIL! SAY SOMETHING--DO SOMETHING--TO MAKE ME LAUGH, GAGGY!
MAKE YOU LAUGH? HAVE YOU TAKEN A LOOK AT ME, BOSS?
MY-MY! I DID THAT TO YOU?! MY POOR LITTLE PAL--!
AWW--IT WAS NOTHING, BOSS! ALL IN THE LINE OF DUTY! GAGGY THE SOLDIER! HEH HEH!
The End
14

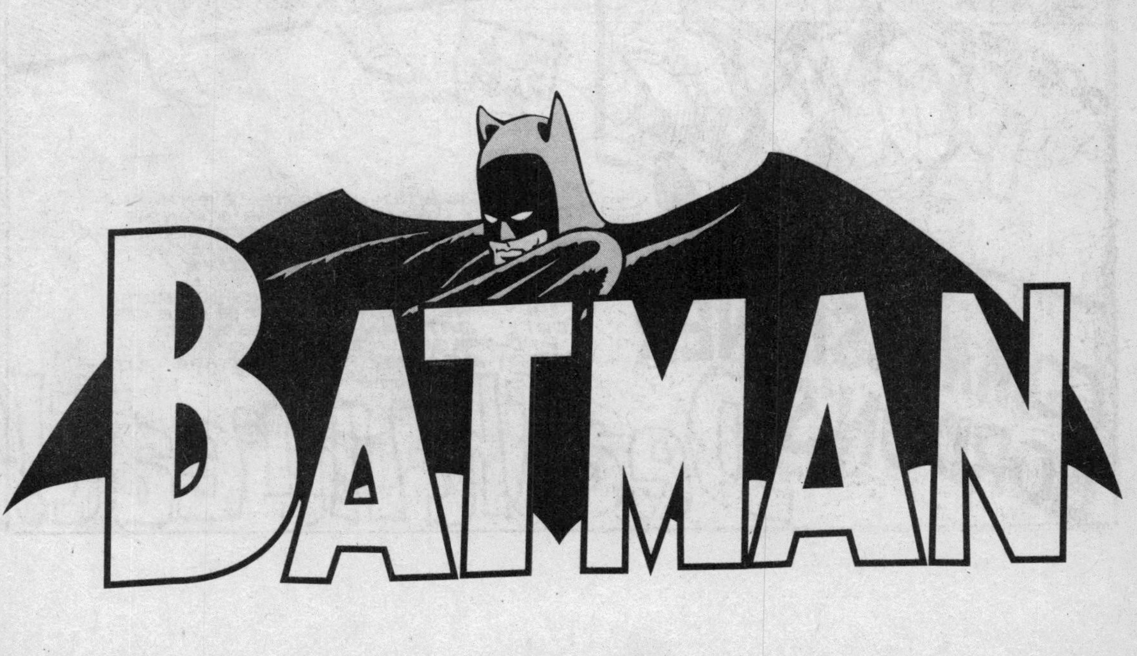
BATMAN

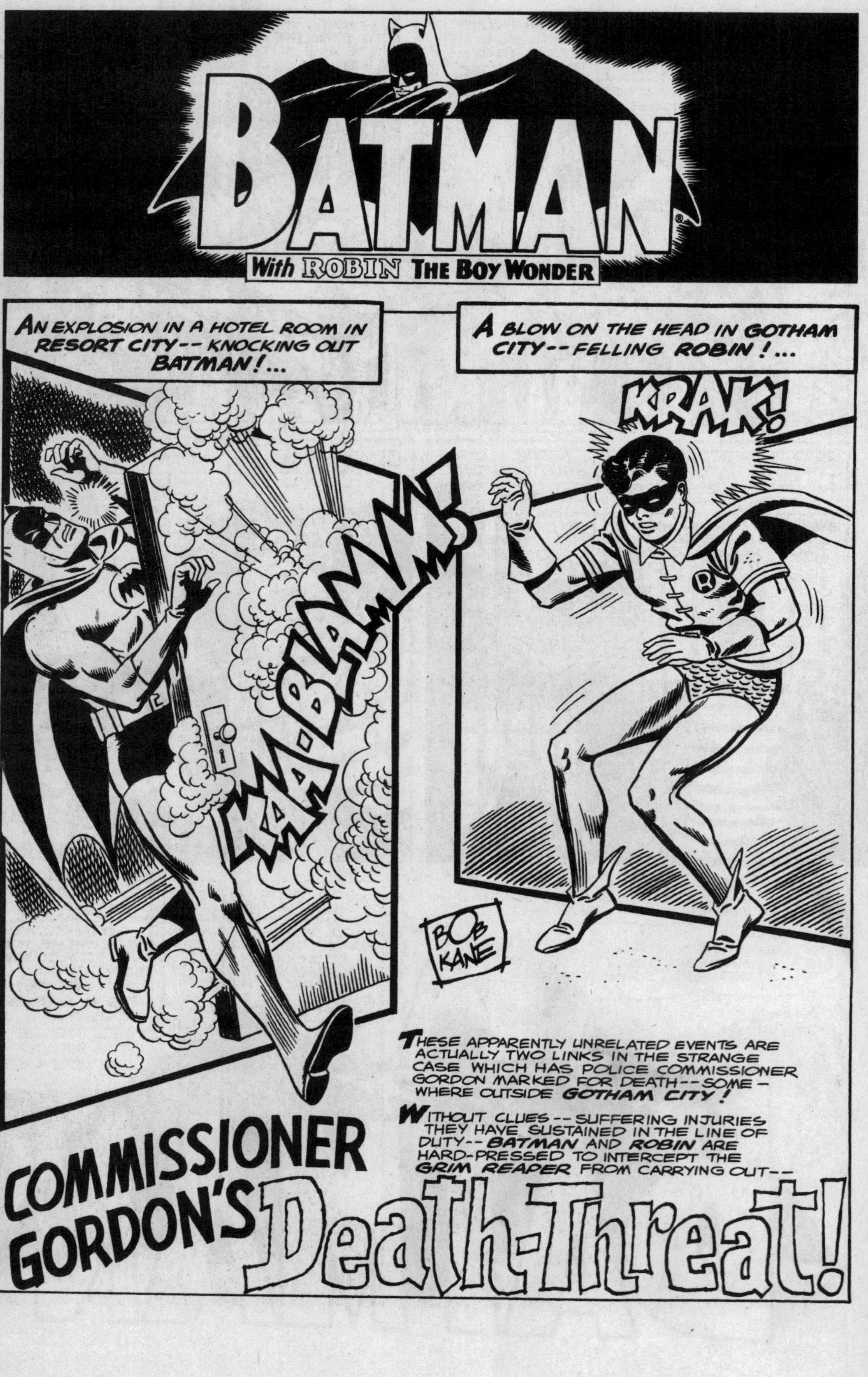
BATMAN
With ROBIN THE BOY WONDER
AN EXPLOSION IN A HOTEL ROOM IN RESORT CITY-- KNOCKING OUT BATMAN!...
KA-BLAMM!
A BLOW ON THE HEAD IN GOTHAM CITY-- FELLING ROBIN!...
KRAK!
BOB KANE
THESE APPARENTLY UNRELATED EVENTS ARE ACTUALLY TWO LINKS IN THE STRANGE CASE WHICH HAS POLICE COMMISSIONER GORDON MARKED FOR DEATH-- SOME-WHERE OUTSIDE GOTHAM CITY!
WITHOUT CLUES-- SUFFERING INJURIES THEY HAVE SUSTAINED IN THE LINE OF DUTY-- BATMAN AND ROBIN ARE HARD-PRESSED TO INTERCEPT THE GRIM REAPER FROM CARRYING OUT--
COMMISSIONER GORDON'S Death-Threat!

IT IS EARLY EVENING IN THE *GOTHAM CITY* POLICE HEADQUARTERS. A DARK, GRIM FIGURE STRIDES DOWN THE CORRIDOR -- AS A VOICE RINGS OUT...

BATMAN! COMMISSIONER GORDON JUST PHONED FROM *RESORT CITY* ASKING YOU TO CALL HIM -- ON A MATTER OF LIFE AND DEATH!

HE SAYS TO TELL YOU -- IT'S *HIS* LIFE AND *HIS* DEATH!

; wheww ; I'LL CALL FROM HIS PRIVATE OFFICE! CONNECT ME WITH HIM, PLEASE!

AS THE CALL IS PUT THROUGH -- IN THE HOTEL ROOM WHERE THE POLICE COMMISSIONER IS VACATIONING...

BATMAN! THANK HEAVEN! MY LIFE IS IN DEADLY DANGER! I'M IN ROOM 721, HIDING OUT--BECAUSE FORTY YEARS AGO WHEN I WAS A ROOKIE COP, I CAUGHT A CROOK NAMED FRED PURLEY ROBBING THE *FOXCROFT JEWEL SALON!*

THAT MADE HIM A FOUR-TIME LOSER...

"*JUDGE PARKER THREW THE BOOK AT HIM...*"

I HEREBY SENTENCE YOU IN ACCORDANCE WITH THE LAW ON *FOURTH OFFENDERS*-- TO LIFE IM-PRISONMENT!

"*THEN, AS PURLEY RANTED AND RAGED WHILE BEING TAKEN FROM THE COURT-ROOM...*"

THIS IS ALL YOUR FAULT, GORDON! I'M GONNA GET YOU FOR THIS-- SOMEDAY... SOMEHOW...

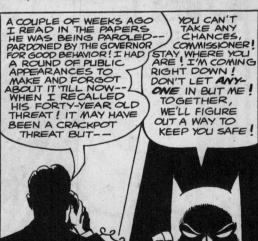

A COUPLE OF WEEKS AGO I READ IN THE PAPERS HE WAS BEING PAROLED-- PARDONED BY THE GOVERNOR FOR GOOD BEHAVIOR! I HAD A ROUND OF PUBLIC APPEARANCES TO MAKE AND FORGOT ABOUT IT 'TILL NOW-- WHEN I RECALLED HIS FORTY-YEAR OLD THREAT! IT MAY HAVE BEEN A CRACKPOT THREAT BUT--

YOU CAN'T TAKE ANY CHANCES, COMMISSIONER! STAY WHERE YOU ARE! I'M COMING RIGHT DOWN! DON'T LET *ANY-ONE* IN BUT ME! TOGETHER, WE'LL FIGURE OUT A WAY TO KEEP YOU SAFE!

2

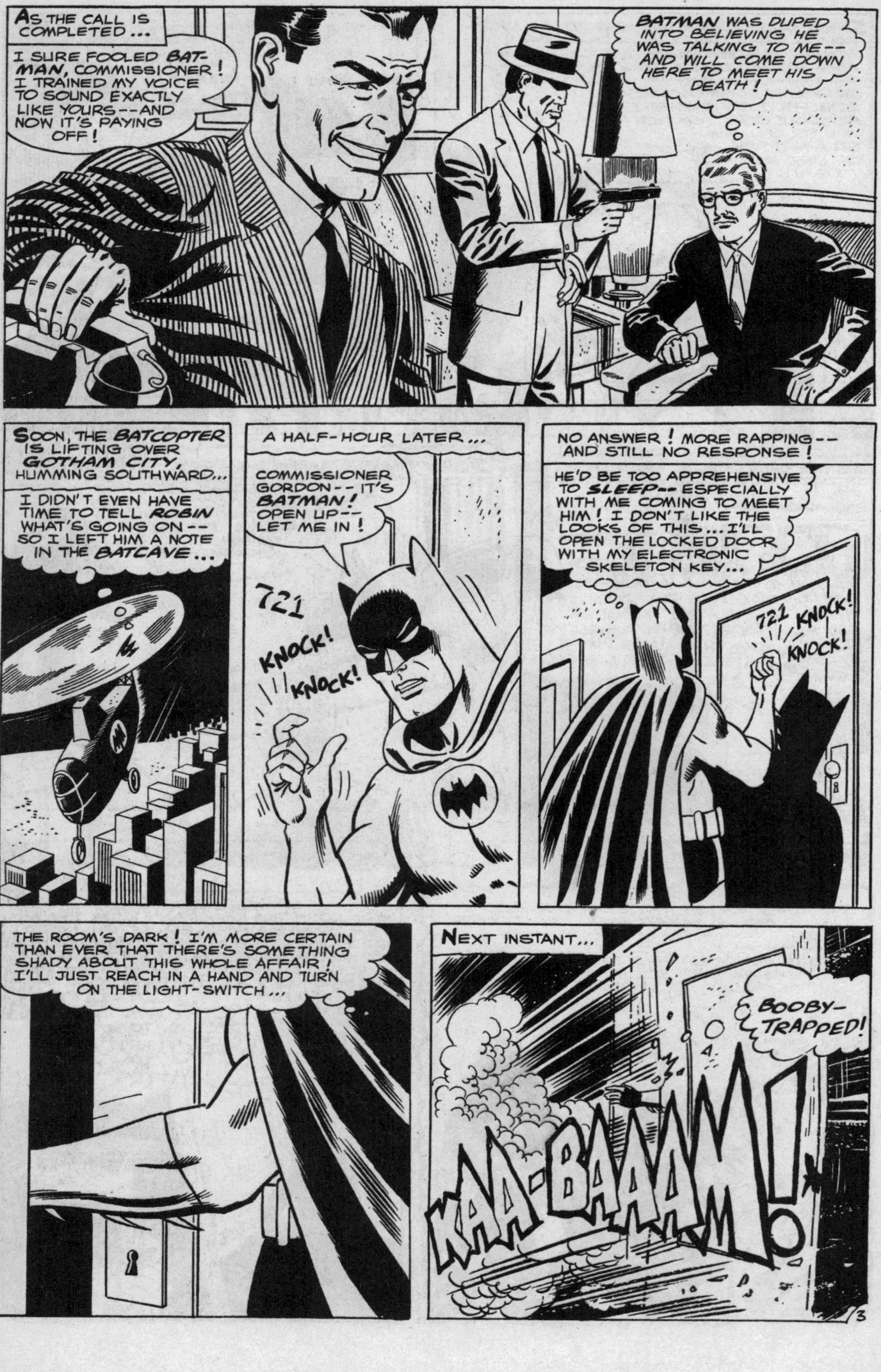
AS THE CALL IS COMPLETED...
I SURE FOOLED BATMAN, COMMISSIONER! I TRAINED MY VOICE TO SOUND EXACTLY LIKE YOURS--AND NOW IT'S PAYING OFF!
BATMAN WAS DUPED INTO BELIEVING HE WAS TALKING TO ME--AND WILL COME DOWN HERE TO MEET HIS DEATH!
SOON, THE BATCOPTER IS LIFTING OVER GOTHAM CITY, HUMMING SOUTHWARD...
I DIDN'T EVEN HAVE TIME TO TELL ROBIN WHAT'S GOING ON--SO I LEFT HIM A NOTE IN THE BATCAVE...
A HALF-HOUR LATER...
COMMISSIONER GORDON--IT'S BATMAN! OPEN UP--LET ME IN!
721
KNOCK! KNOCK!
NO ANSWER! MORE RAPPING--AND STILL NO RESPONSE!
HE'D BE TOO APPREHENSIVE TO SLEEP--ESPECIALLY WITH ME COMING TO MEET HIM! I DON'T LIKE THE LOOKS OF THIS...I'LL OPEN THE LOCKED DOOR WITH MY ELECTRONIC SKELETON KEY...
721
KNOCK! KNOCK!
THE ROOM'S DARK! I'M MORE CERTAIN THAN EVER THAT THERE'S SOMETHING SHADY ABOUT THIS WHOLE AFFAIR! I'LL JUST REACH IN A HAND AND TURN ON THE LIGHT-SWITCH...
NEXT INSTANT...
BOOBY-TRAPPED!
KAA-BAAAM!
3

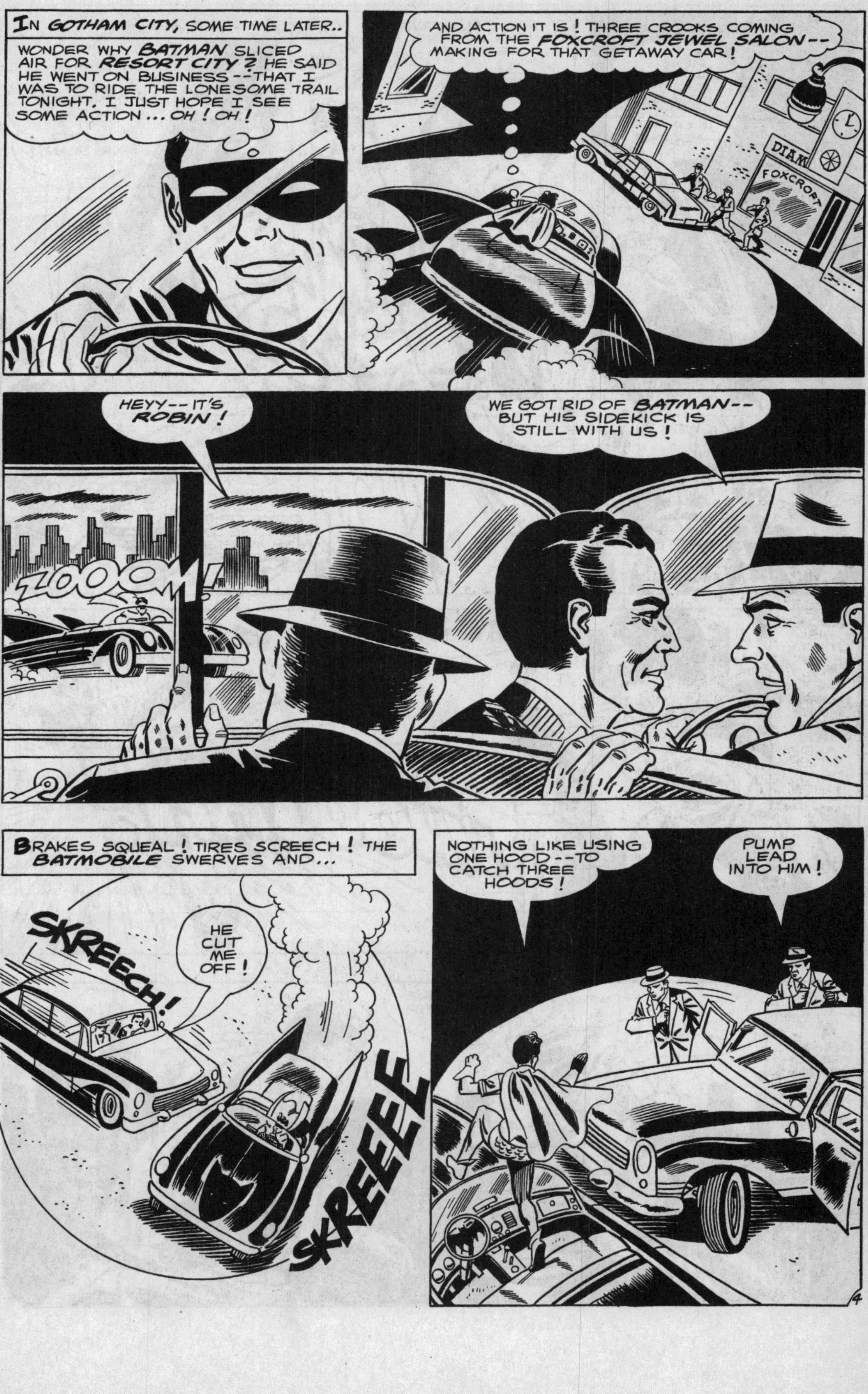

IN GOTHAM CITY, SOME TIME LATER..
WONDER WHY BATMAN SLICED AIR FOR RESORT CITY? HE SAID HE WENT ON BUSINESS--THAT I WAS TO RIDE THE LONESOME TRAIL TONIGHT. I JUST HOPE I SEE SOME ACTION ... OH! OH!
AND ACTION IT IS! THREE CROOKS COMING FROM THE FOXCROFT JEWEL SALON--MAKING FOR THAT GETAWAY CAR!
DIAM
FOXCROFT
HEYY--IT'S ROBIN!
WE GOT RID OF BATMAN--BUT HIS SIDEKICK IS STILL WITH US!
ZOOOM!
BRAKES SQUEAL! TIRES SCREECH! THE BATMOBILE SWERVES AND...
SKREECH!
HE CUT ME OFF!
SKREEEE
NOTHING LIKE USING ONE HOOD--TO CATCH THREE HOODS!
PUMP LEAD INTO HIM!
4

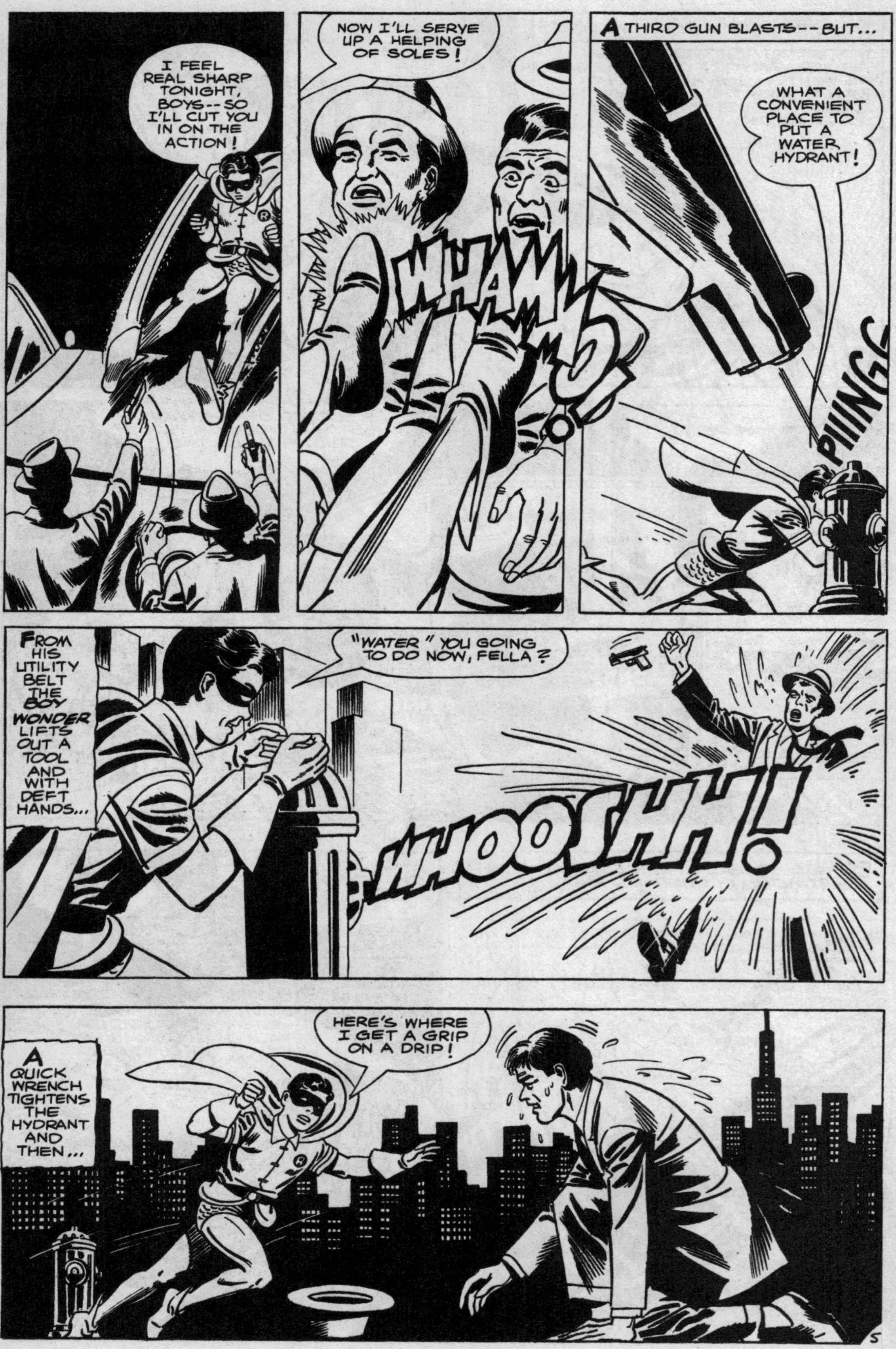
I FEEL REAL SHARP TONIGHT, BOYS--SO I'LL CUT YOU IN ON THE ACTION!
NOW I'LL SERVE UP A HELPING OF SOLES!
WHAM!
A THIRD GUN BLASTS--BUT...
WHAT A CONVENIENT PLACE TO PUT A WATER HYDRANT!
PIINGG
FROM HIS UTILITY BELT THE BOY WONDER LIFTS OUT A TOOL AND WITH DEFT HANDS...
"WATER" YOU GOING TO DO NOW, FELLA?
WHOOSHH!
A QUICK WRENCH TIGHTENS THE HYDRANT AND THEN...
HERE'S WHERE I GET A GRIP ON A DRIP!
5

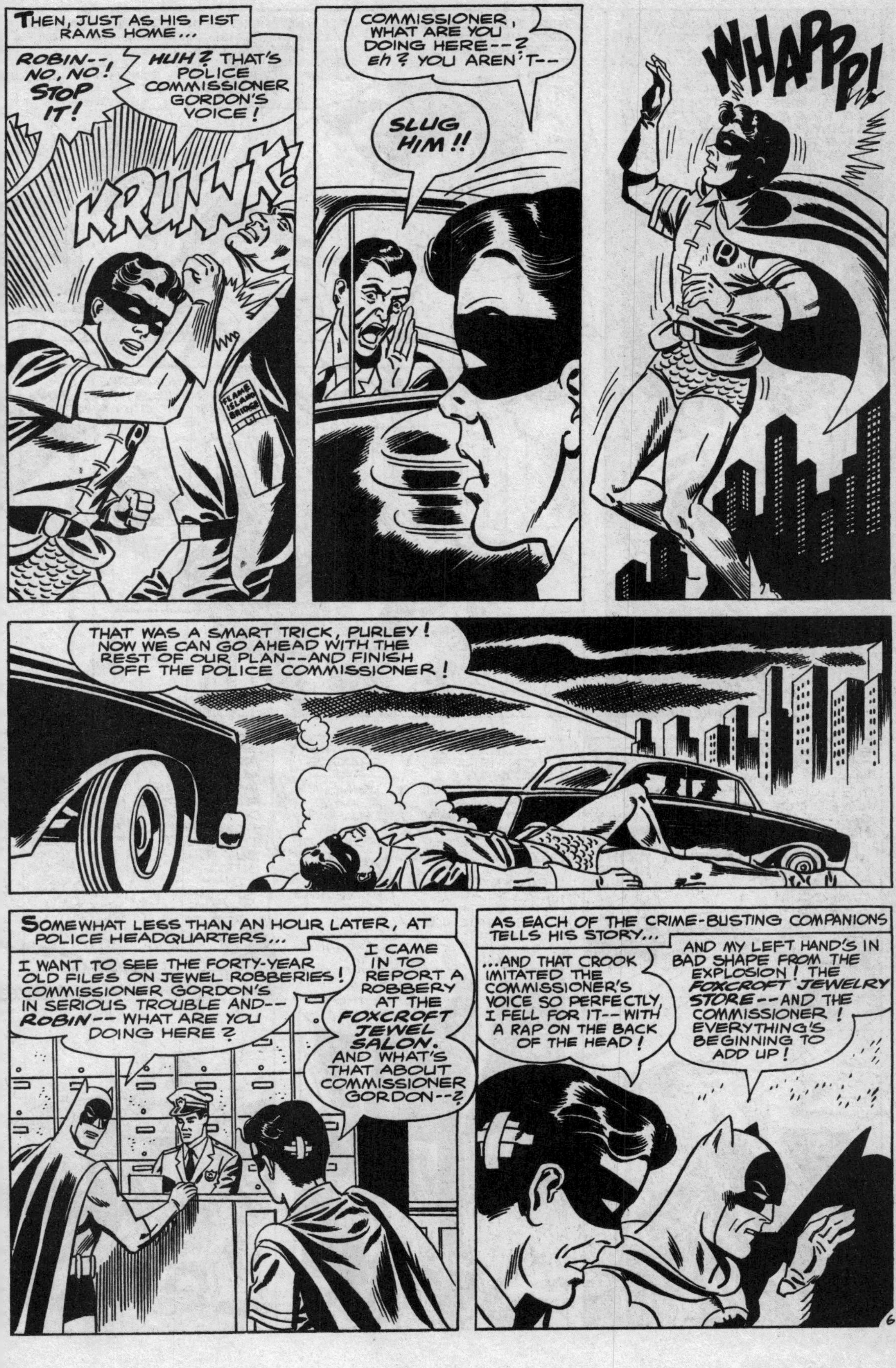
THEN, JUST AS HIS FIST RAMS HOME...
ROBIN-- NO, NO! STOP IT!
HUH? THAT'S POLICE COMMISSIONER GORDON'S VOICE!
KRUNK!
COMMISSIONER, WHAT ARE YOU DOING HERE--? Eh? YOU AREN'T--
SLUG HIM!!
WHAPP!
THAT WAS A SMART TRICK, PURLEY! NOW WE CAN GO AHEAD WITH THE REST OF OUR PLAN--AND FINISH OFF THE POLICE COMMISSIONER!
SOMEWHAT LESS THAN AN HOUR LATER, AT POLICE HEADQUARTERS...
I WANT TO SEE THE FORTY-YEAR OLD FILES ON JEWEL ROBBERIES! COMMISSIONER GORDON'S IN SERIOUS TROUBLE AND-- ROBIN-- WHAT ARE YOU DOING HERE?
I CAME IN TO REPORT A ROBBERY AT THE FOXCROFT JEWEL SALON. AND WHAT'S THAT ABOUT COMMISSIONER GORDON--?
AS EACH OF THE CRIME-BUSTING COMPANIONS TELLS HIS STORY...
...AND THAT CROOK IMITATED THE COMMISSIONER'S VOICE SO PERFECTLY, I FELL FOR IT-- WITH A RAP ON THE BACK OF THE HEAD!
AND MY LEFT HAND'S IN BAD SHAPE FROM THE EXPLOSION! THE FOXCROFT JEWELRY STORE--AND THE COMMISSIONER! EVERYTHING'S BEGINNING TO ADD UP!
6

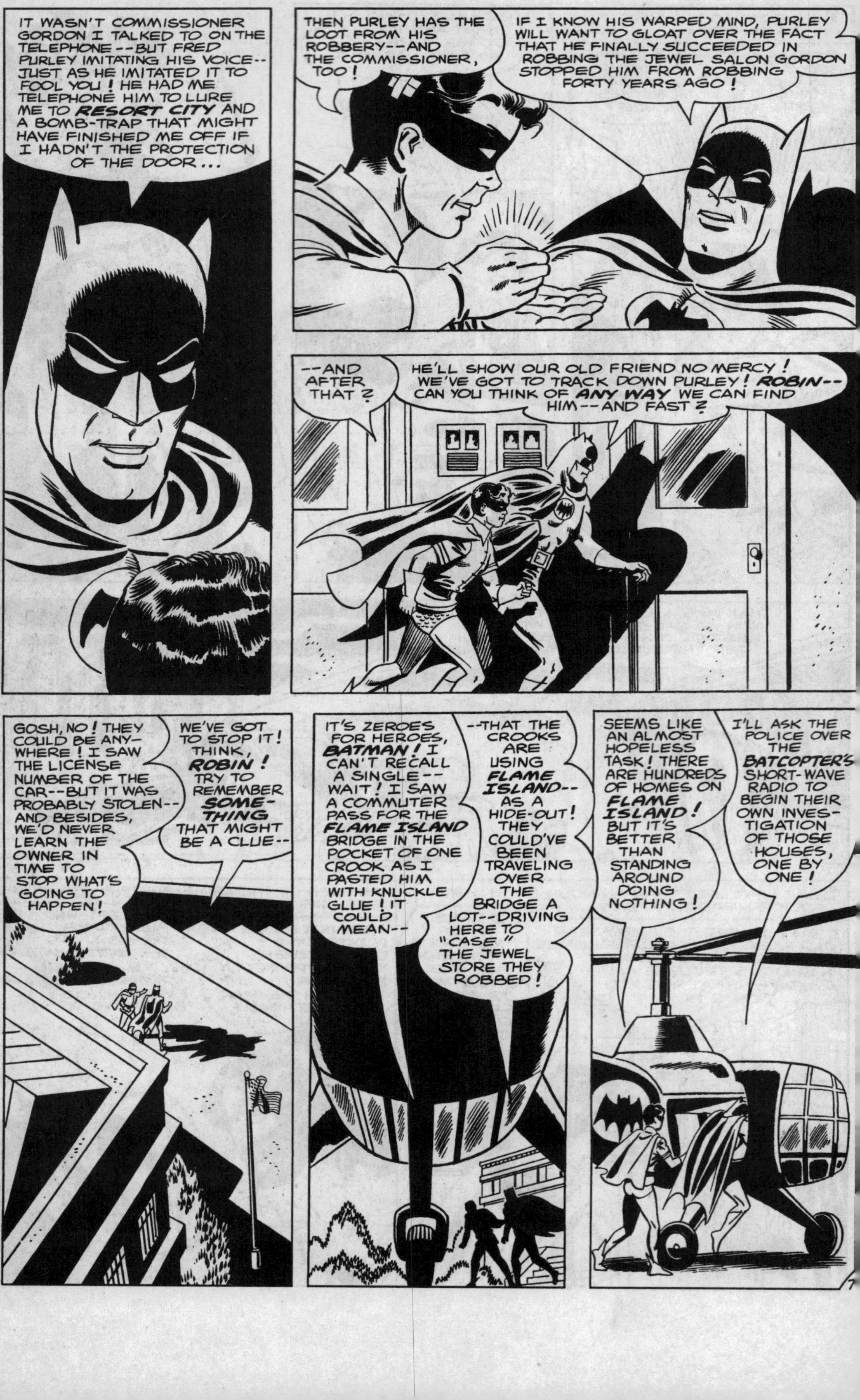
IT WASN'T COMMISSIONER GORDON I TALKED TO ON THE TELEPHONE--BUT FRED PURLEY IMITATING HIS VOICE--JUST AS HE IMITATED IT TO FOOL YOU! HE HAD ME TELEPHONE HIM TO LURE ME TO RESORT CITY AND A BOMB-TRAP THAT MIGHT HAVE FINISHED ME OFF IF I HADN'T THE PROTECTION OF THE DOOR...
THEN PURLEY HAS THE LOOT FROM HIS ROBBERY--AND THE COMMISSIONER, TOO!
IF I KNOW HIS WARPED MIND, PURLEY WILL WANT TO GLOAT OVER THE FACT THAT HE FINALLY SUCCEEDED IN ROBBING THE JEWEL SALON GORDON STOPPED HIM FROM ROBBING FORTY YEARS AGO!
--AND AFTER THAT?
HE'LL SHOW OUR OLD FRIEND NO MERCY! WE'VE GOT TO TRACK DOWN PURLEY! ROBIN--CAN YOU THINK OF ANY WAY WE CAN FIND HIM--AND FAST?
GOSH, NO! THEY COULD BE ANYWHERE! I SAW THE LICENSE NUMBER OF THE CAR--BUT IT WAS PROBABLY STOLEN--AND BESIDES, WE'D NEVER LEARN THE OWNER IN TIME TO STOP WHAT'S GOING TO HAPPEN!
WE'VE GOT TO STOP IT! THINK, ROBIN! TRY TO REMEMBER SOMETHING THAT MIGHT BE A CLUE--
IT'S ZEROES FOR HEROES, BATMAN! I CAN'T RECALL A SINGLE--WAIT! I SAW A COMMUTER PASS FOR THE FLAME ISLAND BRIDGE IN THE POCKET OF ONE CROOK AS I PASTED HIM WITH KNUCKLE GLUE! IT COULD MEAN--
--THAT THE CROOKS ARE USING FLAME ISLAND--AS A HIDE-OUT! THEY COULD'VE BEEN TRAVELING OVER THE BRIDGE A LOT--DRIVING HERE TO "CASE" THE JEWEL STORE THEY ROBBED!
SEEMS LIKE AN ALMOST HOPELESS TASK! THERE ARE HUNDREDS OF HOMES ON FLAME ISLAND! BUT IT'S BETTER THAN STANDING AROUND DOING NOTHING!
I'LL ASK THE POLICE OVER THE BATCOPTER'S SHORT-WAVE RADIO TO BEGIN THEIR OWN INVESTIGATION OF THOSE HOUSES, ONE BY ONE!
7

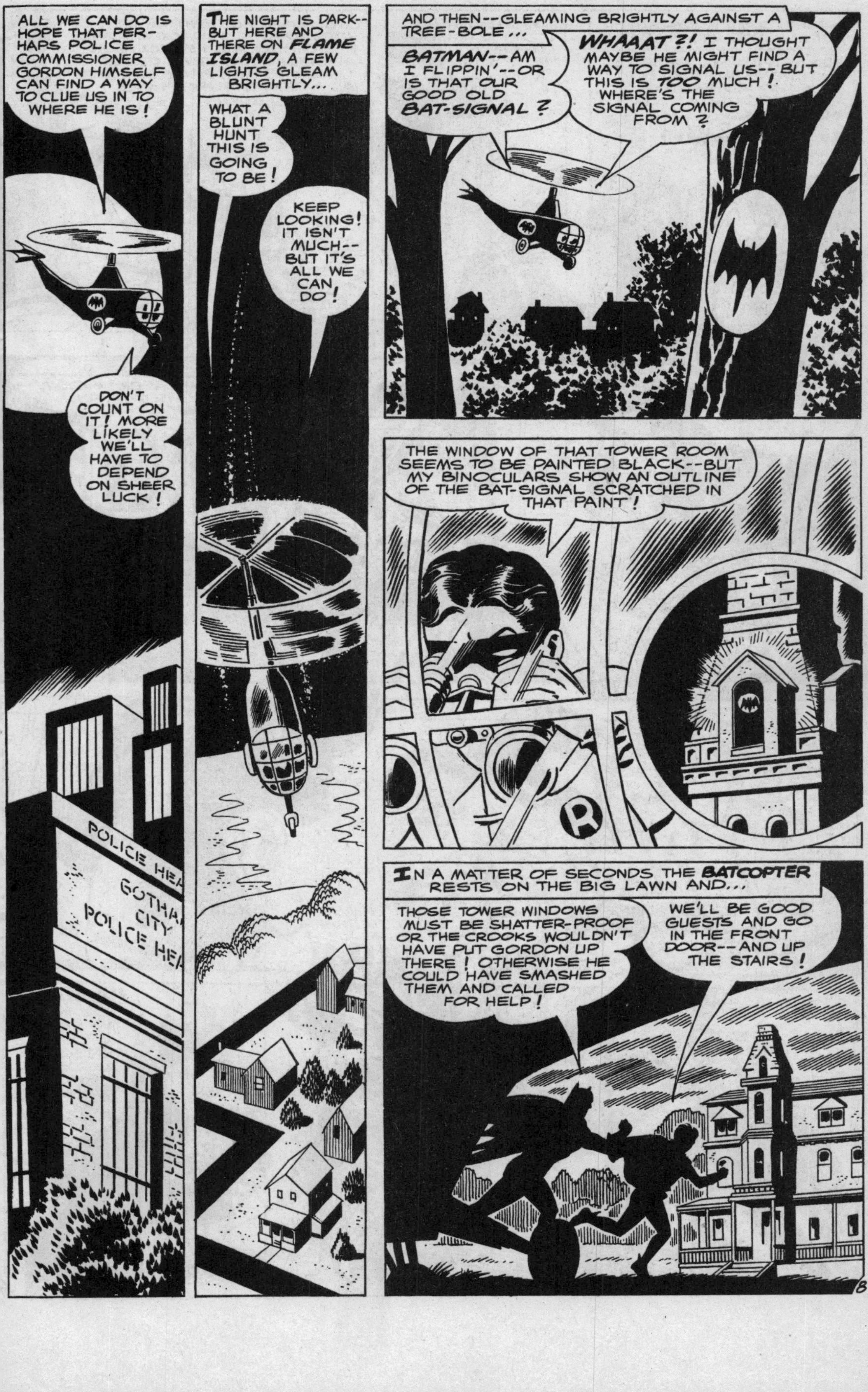
ALL WE CAN DO IS HOPE THAT PERHAPS POLICE COMMISSIONER GORDON HIMSELF CAN FIND A WAY TO CLUE US IN TO WHERE HE IS!
DON'T COUNT ON IT! MORE LIKELY WE'LL HAVE TO DEPEND ON SHEER LUCK!
POLICE HEA
GOTHAM CITY POLICE HEA
THE NIGHT IS DARK--BUT HERE AND THERE ON FLAME ISLAND, A FEW LIGHTS GLEAM BRIGHTLY...
WHAT A BLUNT HUNT THIS IS GOING TO BE!
KEEP LOOKING! IT ISN'T MUCH--BUT IT'S ALL WE CAN DO!
AND THEN--GLEAMING BRIGHTLY AGAINST A TREE-BOLE...
BATMAN--AM I FLIPPIN'--OR IS THAT OUR GOOD OLD BAT-SIGNAL?
WHAAAT?! I THOUGHT MAYBE HE MIGHT FIND A WAY TO SIGNAL US--BUT THIS IS TOO MUCH! WHERE'S THE SIGNAL COMING FROM?
THE WINDOW OF THAT TOWER ROOM SEEMS TO BE PAINTED BLACK--BUT MY BINOCULARS SHOW AN OUTLINE OF THE BAT-SIGNAL SCRATCHED IN THAT PAINT!
IN A MATTER OF SECONDS THE BATCOPTER RESTS ON THE BIG LAWN AND...
THOSE TOWER WINDOWS MUST BE SHATTER-PROOF OR THE CROOKS WOULDN'T HAVE PUT GORDON UP THERE! OTHERWISE HE COULD HAVE SMASHED THEM AND CALLED FOR HELP!
WE'LL BE GOOD GUESTS AND GO IN THE FRONT DOOR--AND UP THE STAIRS!
8

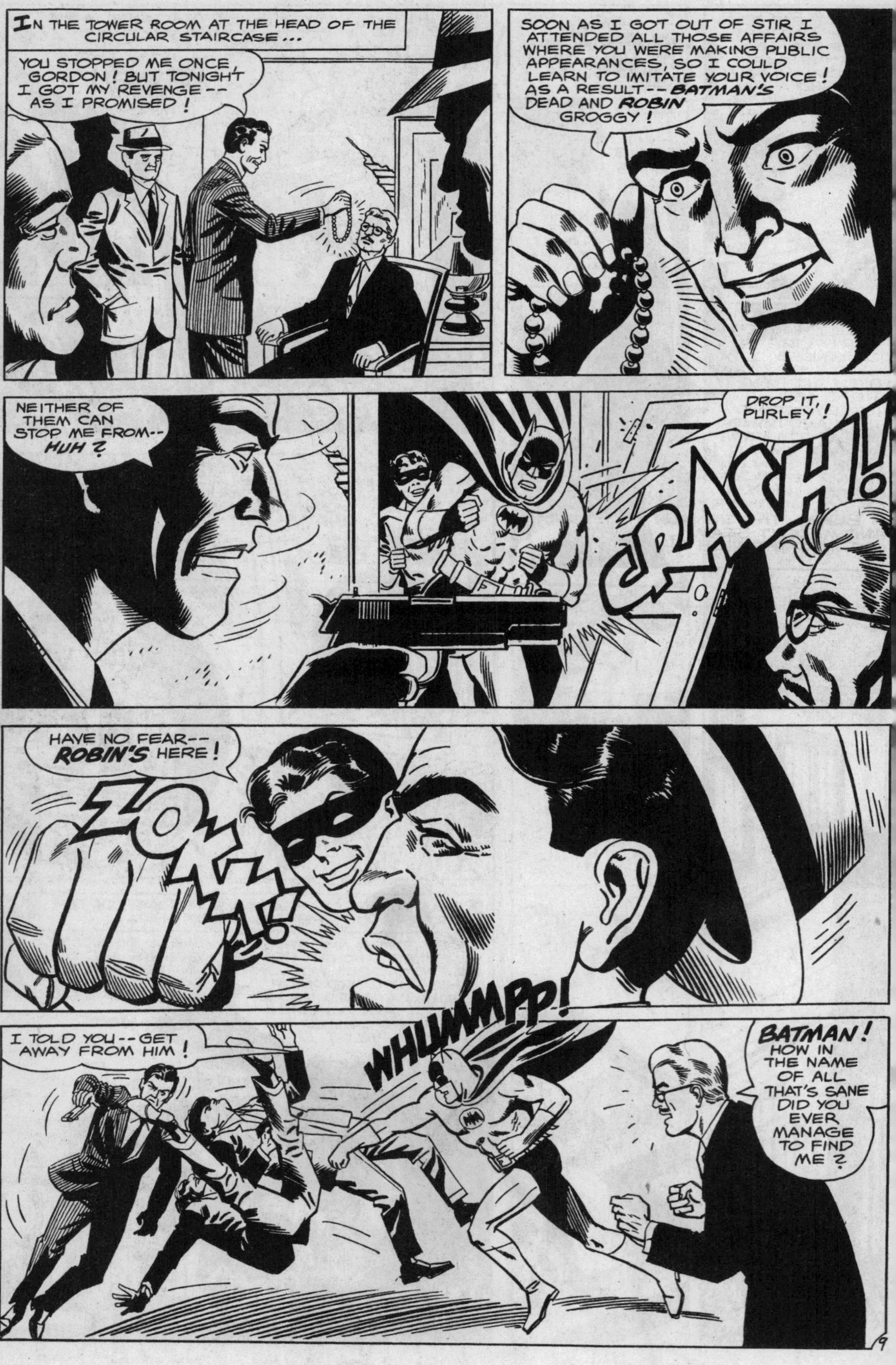
IN THE TOWER ROOM AT THE HEAD OF THE CIRCULAR STAIRCASE...
YOU STOPPED ME ONCE, GORDON! BUT TONIGHT I GOT MY REVENGE -- AS I PROMISED!
SOON AS I GOT OUT OF STIR I ATTENDED ALL THOSE AFFAIRS WHERE YOU WERE MAKING PUBLIC APPEARANCES, SO I COULD LEARN TO IMITATE YOUR VOICE! AS A RESULT -- BATMAN'S DEAD AND ROBIN GROGGY!
NEITHER OF THEM CAN STOP ME FROM-- HUH?
DROP IT, PURLEY!
CRASH!
HAVE NO FEAR-- ROBIN'S HERE!
ZOK!
WHUMMPP!
I TOLD YOU--GET AWAY FROM HIM!
BATMAN! HOW IN THE NAME OF ALL THAT'S SANE DID YOU EVER MANAGE TO FIND ME?
9

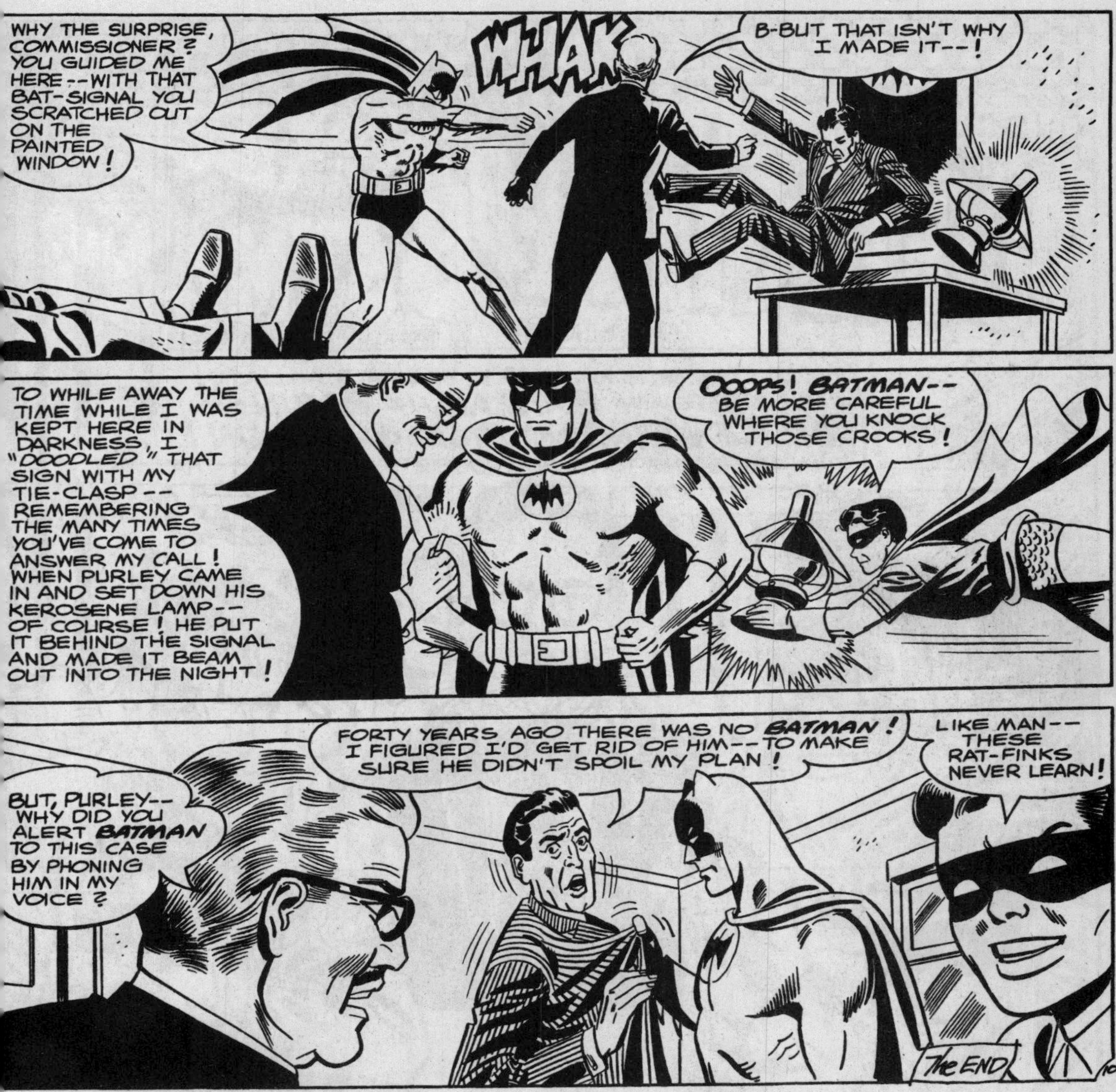
WHY THE SURPRISE, COMMISSIONER ? YOU GUIDED ME HERE--WITH THAT BAT-SIGNAL YOU SCRATCHED OUT ON THE PAINTED WINDOW !
WHAK
B-BUT THAT ISN'T WHY I MADE IT--!
TO WHILE AWAY THE TIME WHILE I WAS KEPT HERE IN DARKNESS, I "DOODLED" THAT SIGN WITH MY TIE-CLASP--REMEMBERING THE MANY TIMES YOU'VE COME TO ANSWER MY CALL ! WHEN PURLEY CAME IN AND SET DOWN HIS KEROSENE LAMP--OF COURSE ! HE PUT IT BEHIND THE SIGNAL AND MADE IT BEAM OUT INTO THE NIGHT !
OOOPS ! BATMAN--BE MORE CAREFUL WHERE YOU KNOCK THOSE CROOKS !
BUT, PURLEY--WHY DID YOU ALERT BATMAN TO THIS CASE BY PHONING HIM IN MY VOICE ?
FORTY YEARS AGO THERE WAS NO BATMAN ! I FIGURED I'D GET RID OF HIM--TO MAKE SURE HE DIDN'T SPOIL MY PLAN !
LIKE MAN--THESE RAT-FINKS NEVER LEARN !
The END
10

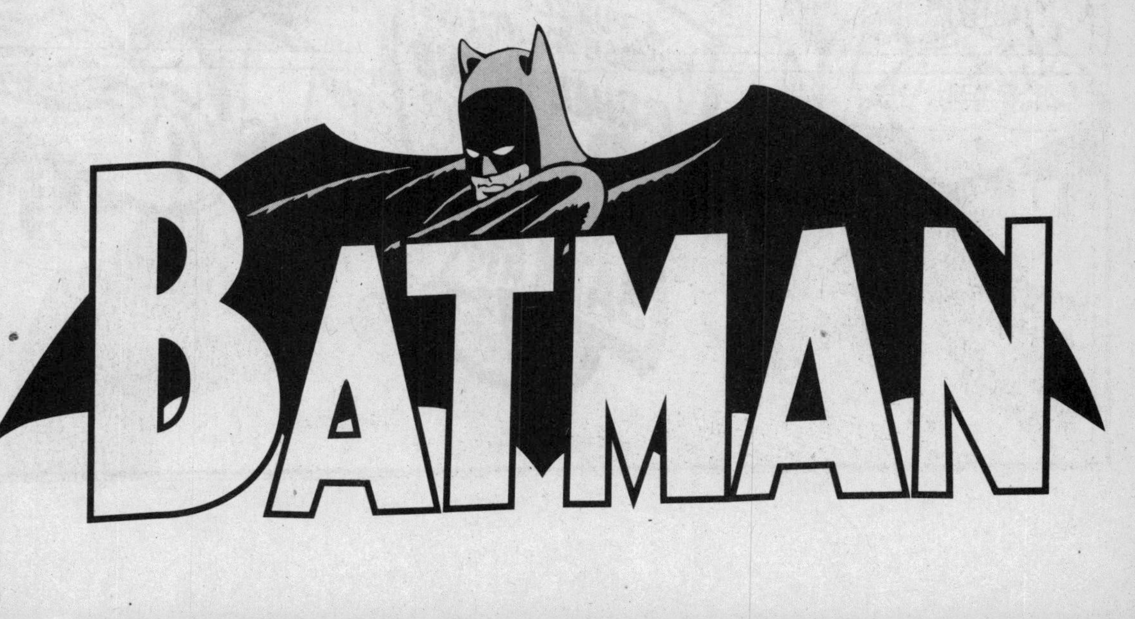
BATMAN

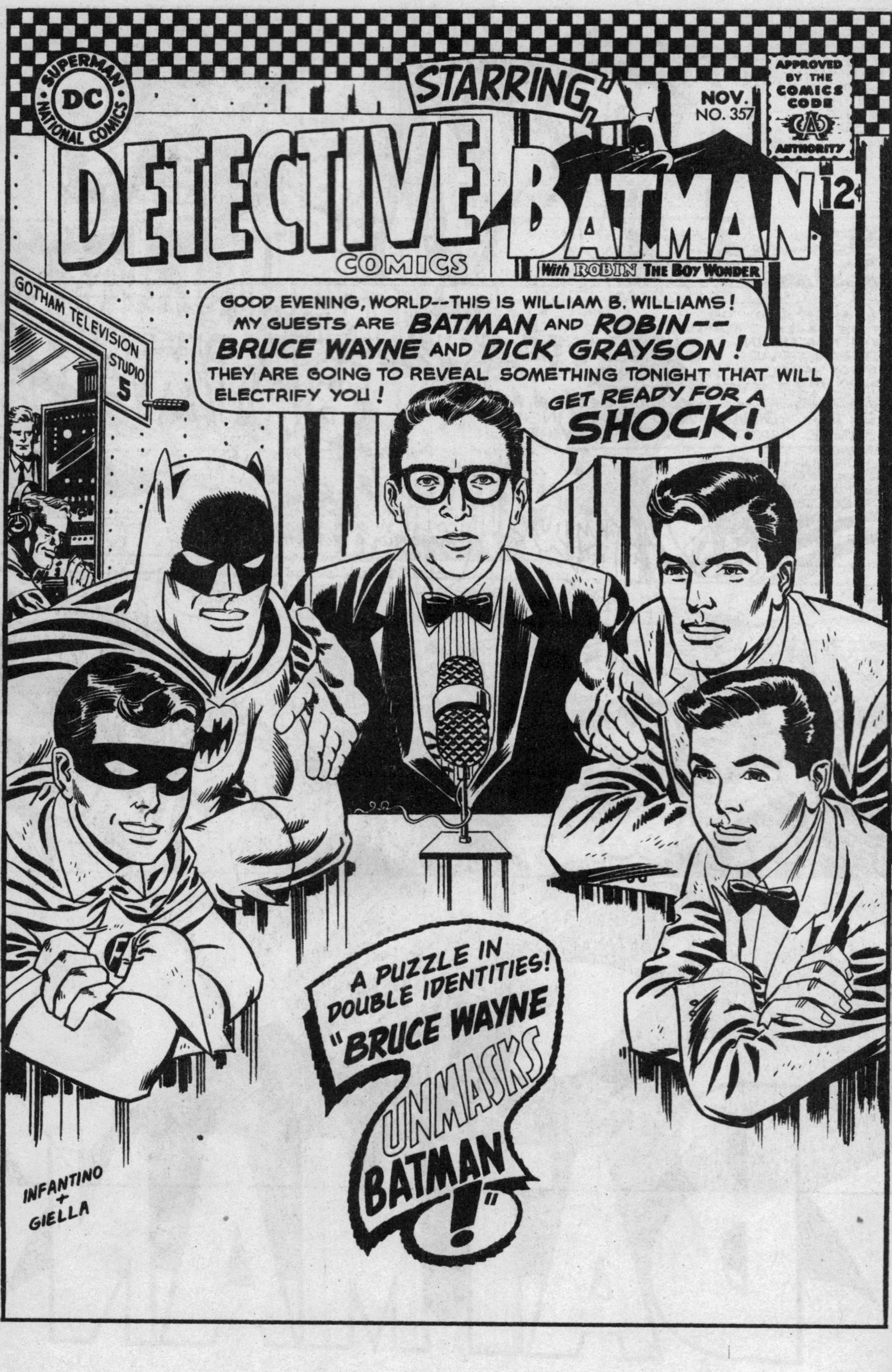
SUPERMAN DC NATIONAL COMICS
STARRING
DETECTIVE COMICS
BATMAN
With ROBIN THE BOY WONDER
NOV. NO. 357
12¢
APPROVED BY THE COMICS CODE AUTHORITY
GOTHAM TELEVISION STUDIO 5
GOOD EVENING, WORLD--THIS IS WILLIAM B. WILLIAMS! MY GUESTS ARE BATMAN AND ROBIN-- BRUCE WAYNE AND DICK GRAYSON! THEY ARE GOING TO REVEAL SOMETHING TONIGHT THAT WILL ELECTRIFY YOU! GET READY FOR A SHOCK!
A PUZZLE IN DOUBLE IDENTITIES! "BRUCE WAYNE UNMASKS BATMAN!"
INFANTINO + GIELLA

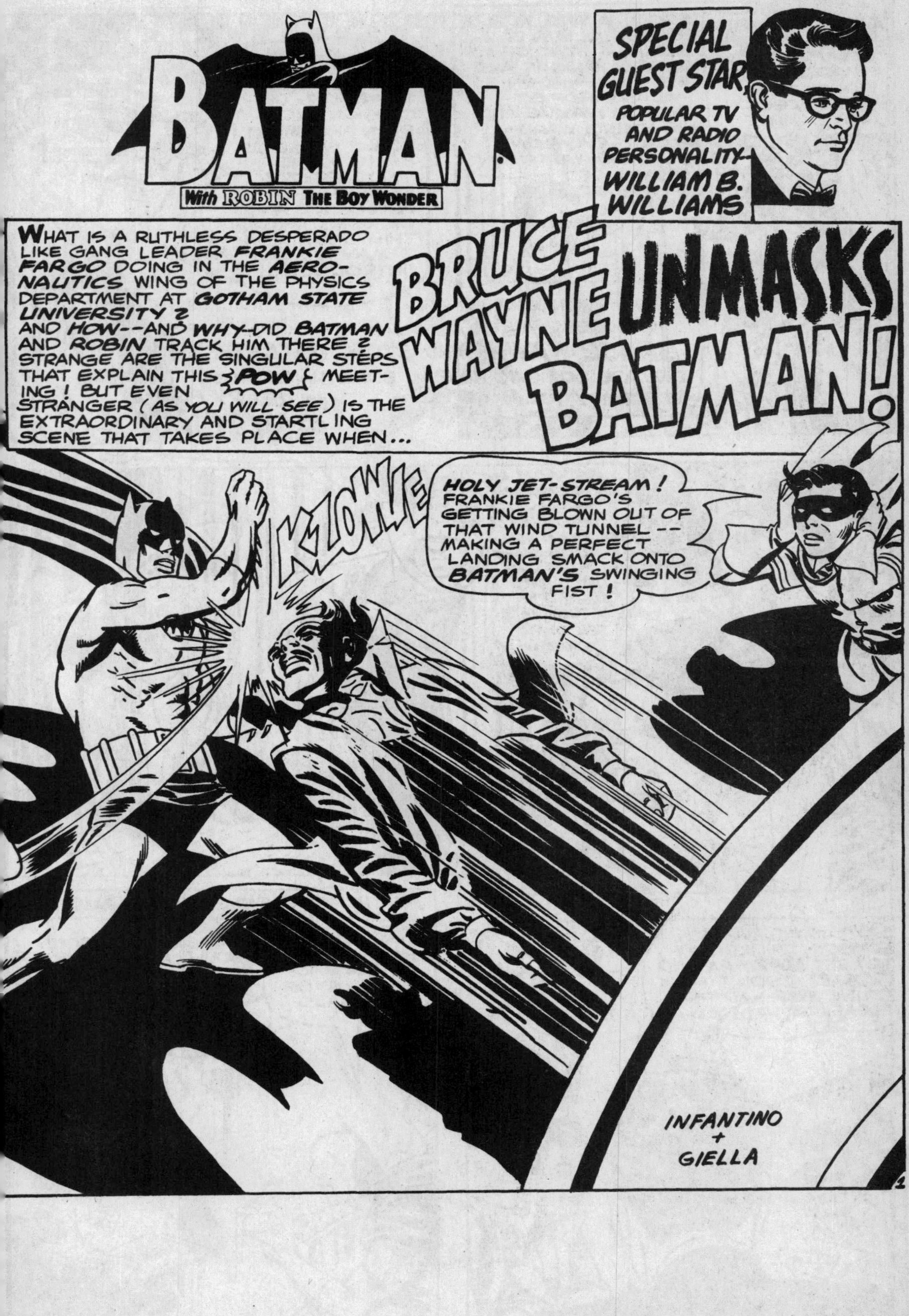
BATMAN
With ROBIN THE BOY WONDER
SPECIAL GUEST STAR, POPULAR TV AND RADIO PERSONALITY-- WILLIAM B. WILLIAMS
WHAT IS A RUTHLESS DESPERADO LIKE GANG LEADER FRANKIE FARGO DOING IN THE AERONAUTICS WING OF THE PHYSICS DEPARTMENT AT GOTHAM STATE UNIVERSITY ? AND HOW--AND WHY--DID BATMAN AND ROBIN TRACK HIM THERE ? STRANGE ARE THE SINGULAR STEPS THAT EXPLAIN THIS POW MEETING ! BUT EVEN STRANGER (AS YOU WILL SEE) IS THE EXTRAORDINARY AND STARTLING SCENE THAT TAKES PLACE WHEN...
BRUCE WAYNE UNMASKS BATMAN!
K-ZOWIE
HOLY JET-STREAM! FRANKIE FARGO'S GETTING BLOWN OUT OF THAT WIND TUNNEL -- MAKING A PERFECT LANDING SMACK ONTO BATMAN'S SWINGING FIST!
INFANTINO + GIELLA
1

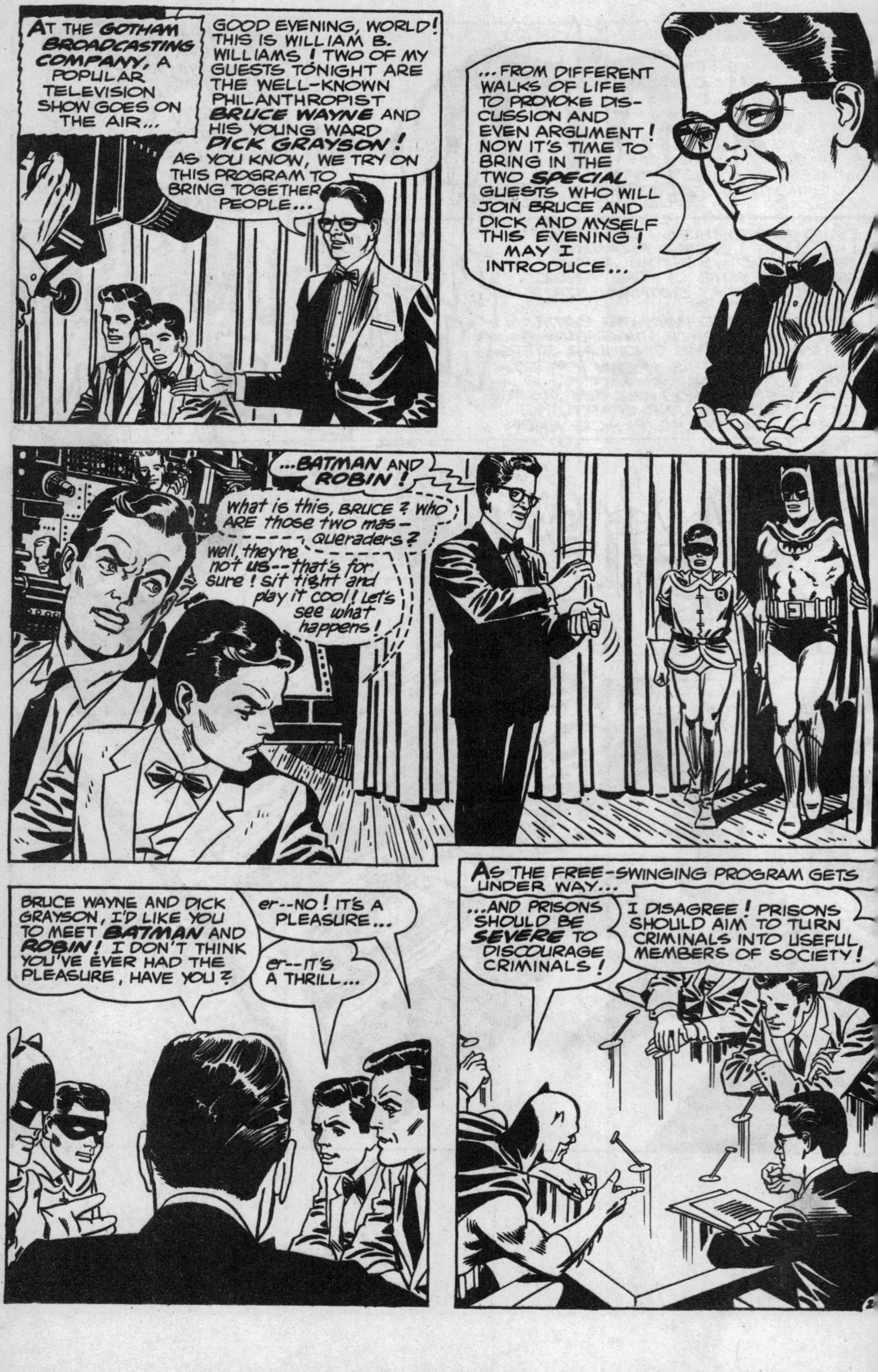
AT THE GOTHAM BROADCASTING COMPANY, A POPULAR TELEVISION SHOW GOES ON THE AIR...
GOOD EVENING, WORLD! THIS IS WILLIAM B. WILLIAMS! TWO OF MY GUESTS TONIGHT ARE THE WELL-KNOWN PHILANTHROPIST BRUCE WAYNE AND HIS YOUNG WARD DICK GRAYSON!
AS YOU KNOW, WE TRY ON THIS PROGRAM TO BRING TOGETHER PEOPLE...
...FROM DIFFERENT WALKS OF LIFE TO PROVOKE DISCUSSION AND EVEN ARGUMENT! NOW IT'S TIME TO BRING IN THE TWO SPECIAL GUESTS WHO WILL JOIN BRUCE AND DICK AND MYSELF THIS EVENING! MAY I INTRODUCE...
...BATMAN AND ROBIN!
what is this, BRUCE? who ARE those two masqueraders?
well, they're not us--that's for sure! sit tight and play it cool! let's see what happens!
BRUCE WAYNE AND DICK GRAYSON, I'D LIKE YOU TO MEET BATMAN AND ROBIN! I DON'T THINK YOU'VE EVER HAD THE PLEASURE, HAVE YOU?
er--NO! IT'S A PLEASURE...
er--IT'S A THRILL...
AS THE FREE-SWINGING PROGRAM GETS UNDER WAY...
...AND PRISONS SHOULD BE SEVERE TO DISCOURAGE CRIMINALS!
I DISAGREE! PRISONS SHOULD AIM TO TURN CRIMINALS INTO USEFUL MEMBERS OF SOCIETY!

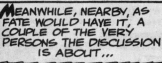

MEANWHILE, NEARBY, AS FATE WOULD HAVE IT, A COUPLE OF THE VERY PERSONS THE DISCUSSION IS ABOUT...

A FINE PAIR O' CROOKS WE ARE, BOO-BOO! THE REST OF THE GANG GOES ON A JOB--AND LEAVES US BEHIND!

YEAH! 'CAUSE THEY SAY WE ALWAYS GUM UP THE JOB!

I SURE WISH THERE WAS SOME WAY WE COULD SHOW THOSE PROS WE'RE NOT THE AMATEURS THEY THINK!

THERE'S NO JUSTICE, THAT'S ALL!

AS THE IMAGE ON THE TV SET CLEARS... CRIMINALS ARE MISGUIDED INDIVIDUALS WHO--

HUH? WHO'S THE WISE GUY TALKING THAT WAY ABOUT US?

TAKE A LOOK, BEEFY--

WELL, WHATTA YA KNOW-- THE DYNAMIC DUO! BATMAN AND ROBIN!

YEAH! BEEFY, LIKE THEY SAY IN COMIC MAGS--THIS GIVES ME AN IDEA! THE ANSWER TO OUR WISH--!

THE TWO OF US ARE GONNA PULL SOMETHING THAT WILL SHOW THE REST O' THE GANG WHAT WE CAN DO! THAT STUDIO BUILDING IS ONLY A COUPLE BLOCKS FROM HERE! NOW LISTEN...

BZZZZZ-- BZZZZZ-- BZZZ

BOO-BOO, THAT'S ABSOLUTELY A STREAK OF GENIUS! IN FACT-- IT'S A GOOD IDEA!

COME ON! GRAB THAT CONTAINER OF SLEEPING GAS THE OTHERS LEFT BEHIND-- WE CAN USE IT!

WE PULL THIS OFF AN' WE'LL GO DOWN IN HISTORY!

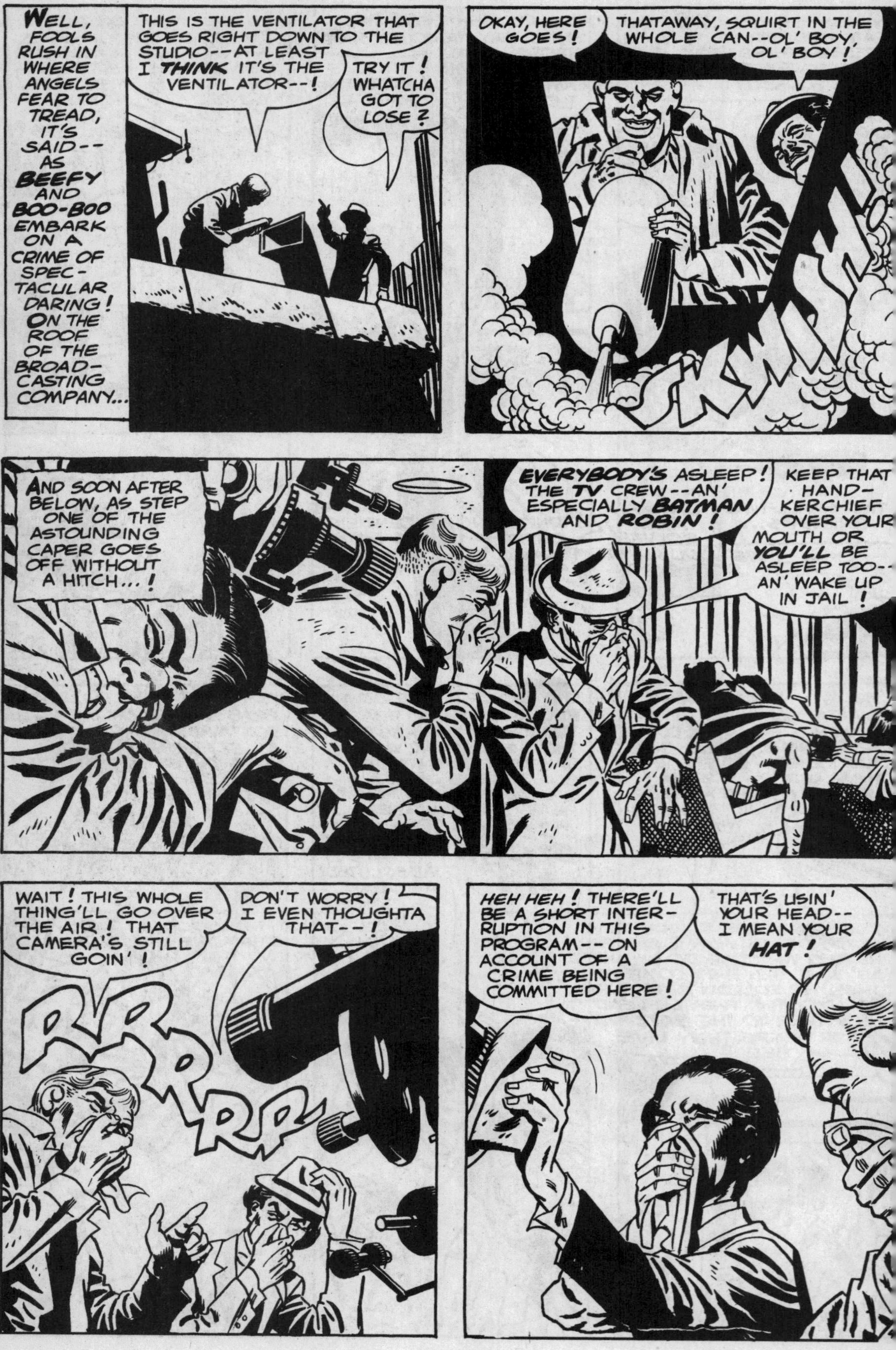
WELL, FOOLS RUSH IN WHERE ANGELS FEAR TO TREAD, IT'S SAID-- AS BEEFY AND BOO-BOO EMBARK ON A CRIME OF SPECTACULAR DARING! ON THE ROOF OF THE BROADCASTING COMPANY...
THIS IS THE VENTILATOR THAT GOES RIGHT DOWN TO THE STUDIO--AT LEAST I THINK IT'S THE VENTILATOR--!
TRY IT! WHATCHA GOT TO LOSE?
OKAY, HERE GOES!
THATAWAY, SQUIRT IN THE WHOLE CAN--OL' BOY, OL' BOY!
AND SOON AFTER BELOW, AS STEP ONE OF THE ASTOUNDING CAPER GOES OFF WITHOUT A HITCH...!
EVERYBODY'S ASLEEP! THE TV CREW--AN' ESPECIALLY BATMAN AND ROBIN!
KEEP THAT HANDKERCHIEF OVER YOUR MOUTH OR YOU'LL BE ASLEEP TOO--AN' WAKE UP IN JAIL!
WAIT! THIS WHOLE THING'LL GO OVER THE AIR! THAT CAMERA'S STILL GOIN'!
DON'T WORRY! I EVEN THOUGHTA THAT--!
HEH HEH! THERE'LL BE A SHORT INTERRUPTION IN THIS PROGRAM--ON ACCOUNT OF A CRIME BEING COMMITTED HERE!
THAT'S USIN' YOUR HEAD--I MEAN YOUR HAT!

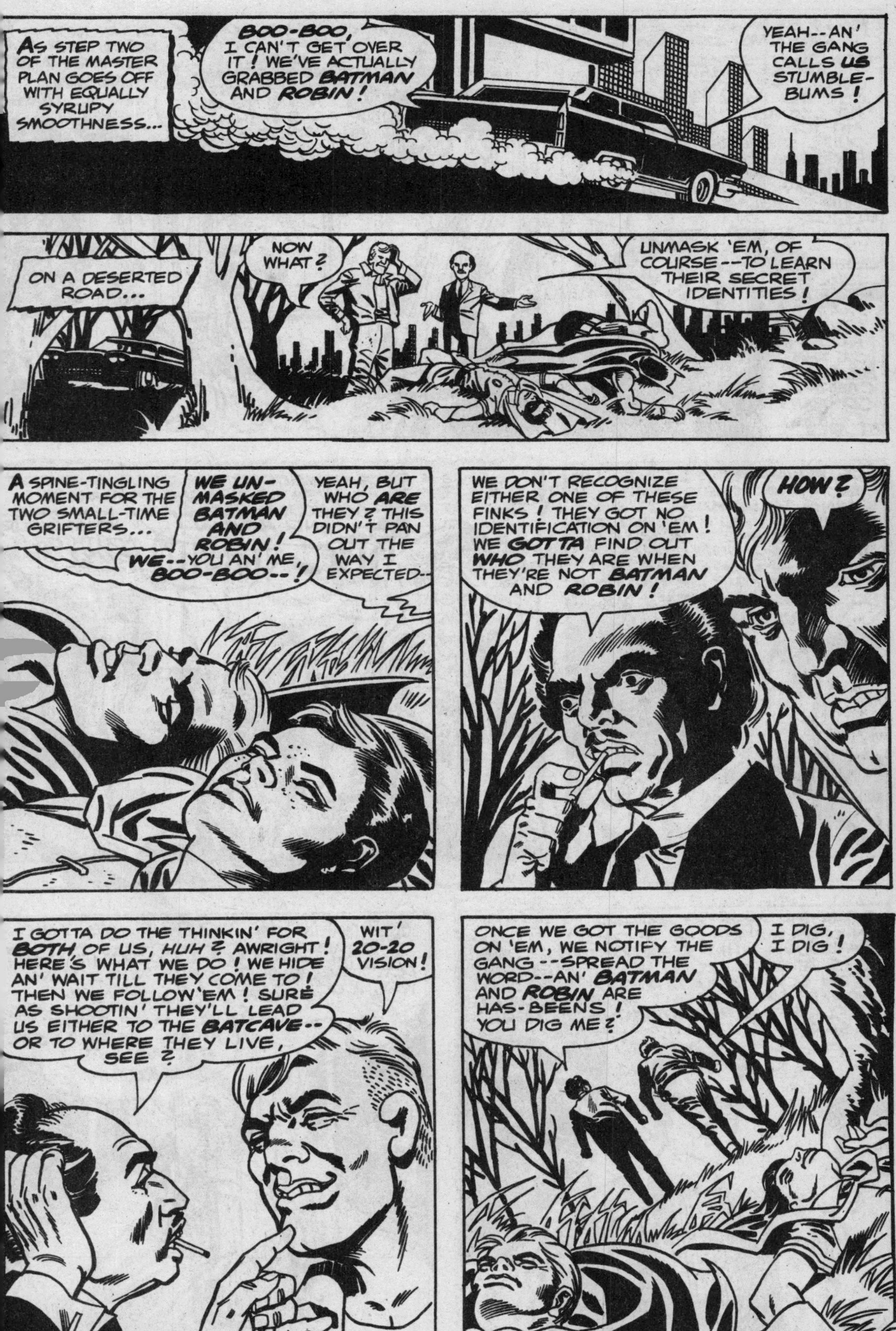
AS STEP TWO OF THE MASTER PLAN GOES OFF WITH EQUALLY SYRUPY SMOOTHNESS...
BOO-BOO, I CAN'T GET OVER IT! WE'VE ACTUALLY GRABBED BATMAN AND ROBIN!
YEAH--AN' THE GANG CALLS US STUMBLE-BUMS!
ON A DESERTED ROAD...
NOW WHAT?
UNMASK 'EM, OF COURSE--TO LEARN THEIR SECRET IDENTITIES!
A SPINE-TINGLING MOMENT FOR THE TWO SMALL-TIME GRIFTERS...
WE UN-MASKED BATMAN AND ROBIN! WE--YOU AN' ME, BOO-BOO--!
YEAH, BUT WHO ARE THEY? THIS DIDN'T PAN OUT THE WAY I EXPECTED--
WE DON'T RECOGNIZE EITHER ONE OF THESE FINKS! THEY GOT NO IDENTIFICATION ON 'EM! WE GOTTA FIND OUT WHO THEY ARE WHEN THEY'RE NOT BATMAN AND ROBIN!
HOW?
I GOTTA DO THE THINKIN' FOR BOTH OF US, HUH? AWRIGHT! HERE'S WHAT WE DO! WE HIDE AN' WAIT TILL THEY COME TO! THEN WE FOLLOW 'EM! SURE AS SHOOTIN' THEY'LL LEAD US EITHER TO THE BATCAVE--OR TO WHERE THEY LIVE, SEE?
WIT' 20-20 VISION!
ONCE WE GOT THE GOODS ON 'EM, WE NOTIFY THE GANG--SPREAD THE WORD--AN' BATMAN AND ROBIN ARE HAS-BEENS! YOU DIG ME?
I DIG, I DIG!
5

WHILE BACK AT THE *BROADCASTING COMPANY*...

WE REGRET THAT--*er*--UNFORESEEN CIRCUMSTANCES CUT THE *WILLIAM B. WILLIAMS* SHOW OFF THE AIR TONIGHT! WE ASSURE OUR LISTENERS THAT THE PROGRAM WILL GO ON AS USUAL TOMORROW NIGHT! WE NOW CONTINUE WITH OUR REGULAR SCHEDULE...

AND IN A PRIVATE ROOM IN THE STUDIO...

FORTUNATELY NO ONE WAS HURT! AND THE POLICE ARE NOW LOOKING FOR THOSE TWO WHO WERE DRESSED UP AS *BATMAN* AND *ROBIN*--!

OH? JUST DRESSED AS *BATMAN* AND *ROBIN*, MR. WILLIAMS?

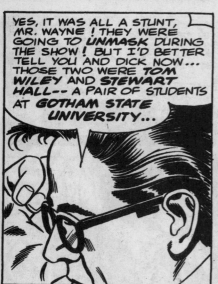

YES, IT WAS ALL A STUNT, MR. WAYNE! THEY WERE GOING TO *UNMASK* DURING THE SHOW! BUT I'D BETTER TELL YOU AND DICK NOW... THOSE TWO WERE *TOM WILEY* AND *STEWART HALL*--A PAIR OF STUDENTS AT *GOTHAM STATE UNIVERSITY*...

"DURING A RECENT VISIT TO THE CAMPUS, I SAW THEM PUT ON AN IMITATION OF THE *DYNAMIC DUO* AT A FRATERNITY PARTY..."

IT'S "*MEAT HOOK*", THE ICEBOX RAIDER! NO DOUBT OF IT, *ROBIN*! THE CHICKEN BONES LED RIGHT TO HIS ROOM!

HOLY WISHBONE!

HAHA! THEY'RE A GREAT TEAM!

I INVITED THEM TO APPEAR IN COSTUME ON THE SHOW! OF COURSE, THE *SLEEPING GAS* ATTACK COULD HAVE BEEN SOME *FRATERNITY PRANK*! THAT MIGHT ALSO EXPLAIN THEIR MYSTERIOUS DISAPPEARANCE...

I'LL HAVE TO MAKE SOME EXCUSE TO CUT OUT OF HERE...

AND WHEN THE TWO PANELISTS TAKE OFF...

THEN YOU DON'T BELIEVE IT WAS A COLLEGE BOY PRANK, BRUCE?

I DOUBT IT, DICK! BUT WE'LL HAVE TO CHECK OUT THAT THEORY OF WILLIAMS RIGHT AWAY--AS THE *REAL BATMAN* AND *ROBIN*!

6

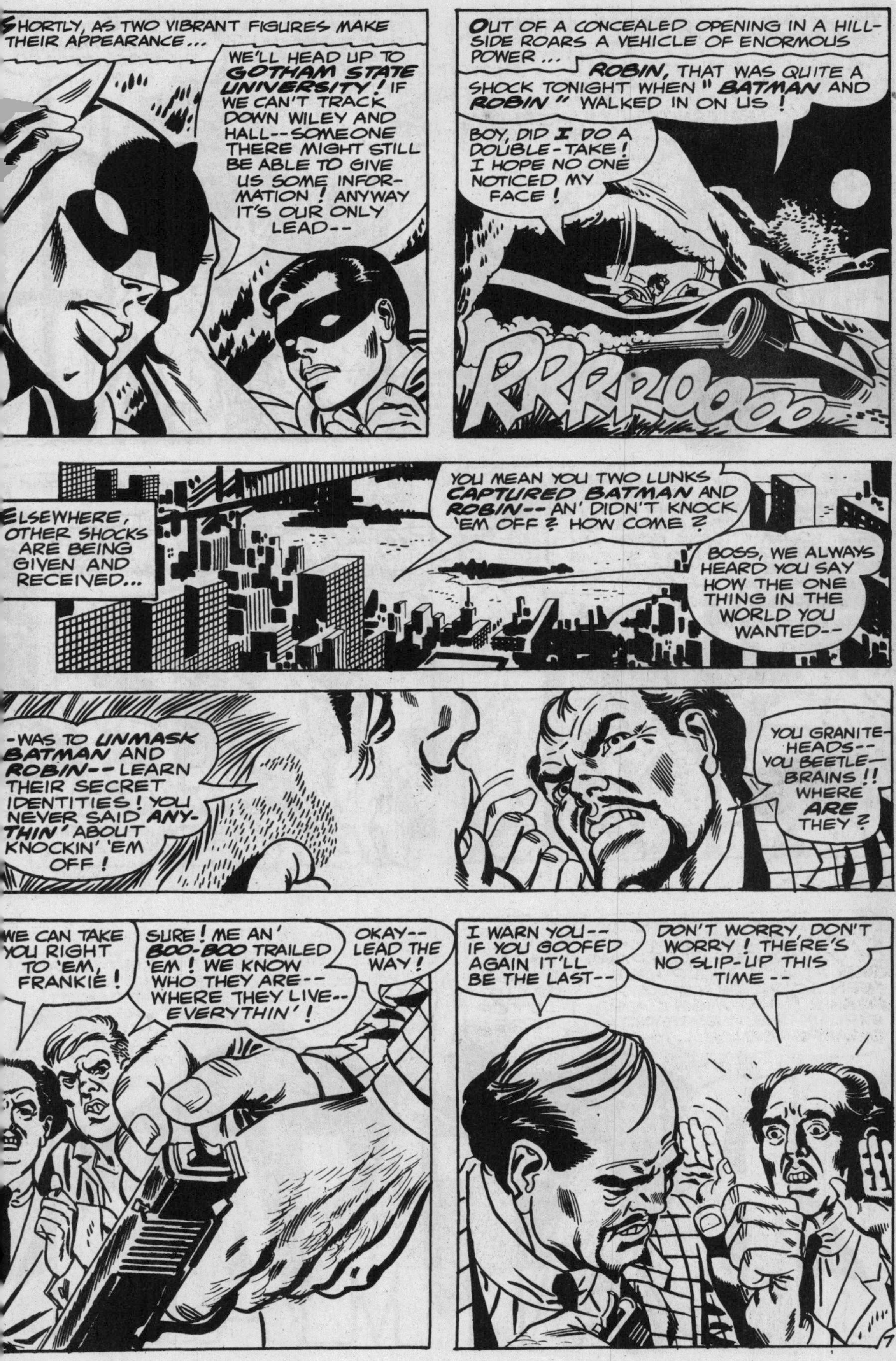
SHORTLY, AS TWO VIBRANT FIGURES MAKE THEIR APPEARANCE...
WE'LL HEAD UP TO GOTHAM STATE UNIVERSITY! IF WE CAN'T TRACK DOWN WILEY AND HALL--SOMEONE THERE MIGHT STILL BE ABLE TO GIVE US SOME INFORMATION! ANYWAY IT'S OUR ONLY LEAD--
OUT OF A CONCEALED OPENING IN A HILLSIDE ROARS A VEHICLE OF ENORMOUS POWER...
ROBIN, THAT WAS QUITE A SHOCK TONIGHT WHEN "BATMAN AND ROBIN" WALKED IN ON US!
BOY, DID I DO A DOUBLE-TAKE! I HOPE NO ONE NOTICED MY FACE!
RRRROOOOO
ELSEWHERE, OTHER SHOCKS ARE BEING GIVEN AND RECEIVED...
YOU MEAN YOU TWO LUNKS CAPTURED BATMAN AND ROBIN-- AN' DIDN'T KNOCK 'EM OFF? HOW COME?
BOSS, WE ALWAYS HEARD YOU SAY HOW THE ONE THING IN THE WORLD YOU WANTED--
-WAS TO UNMASK BATMAN AND ROBIN--LEARN THEIR SECRET IDENTITIES! YOU NEVER SAID ANYTHIN' ABOUT KNOCKIN' 'EM OFF!
YOU GRANITE-HEADS--YOU BEETLE-BRAINS!! WHERE ARE THEY?
WE CAN TAKE YOU RIGHT TO 'EM, FRANKIE!
SURE! ME AN' BOO-BOO TRAILED 'EM! WE KNOW WHO THEY ARE--WHERE THEY LIVE--EVERYTHIN'!
OKAY--LEAD THE WAY!
I WARN YOU--IF YOU GOOFED AGAIN IT'LL BE THE LAST--
DON'T WORRY, DON'T WORRY! THERE'S NO SLIP-UP THIS TIME--
7

ON THE CAMPUS OF GOTHAM STATE UNIVERSITY...
THIS IS THE PLACE!
"ETA PI"? IT'S ONE O' THEM FRATERNITIES!
YOU TRYIN' TO TELL US BATMAN AND ROBIN ARE FRATERNITY BROTHERS?
ETA PI
DON'TCHA GET IT? IT'S A TERRIFIC COVER-UP! THEY'RE COLLEGE GUYS-- THE TWO OF 'EM!
C'M HERE, FRANKIE! THEY'RE INSIDE NOW!
THERE THEY ARE--THE DYNAMIC DUO!
IN THEIR UNDERWEAR-- EATING HERO SANDWICHES IN FRONT OF A FIREPLACE? IT'S HARD TO TELL ONE HERO FROM ANOTHER-- HA HA! GIMME THE TOMMYGUN!
AS A DEADLY FINGER TIGHTENS ON THE TRIGGER...
Y'KNOW... I ALWAYS FIGURED BATMAN AN' ROBIN WOULD DIE WITH THEIR BOOTS ON!
THEY AIN'T EVEN GOT THEIR PANTS ON! HAW! HAW! HAW!
STORY CONTINUES ON THE FOLLOWING PAGE!

BATMAN

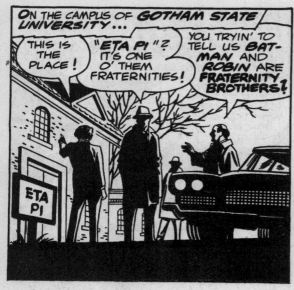

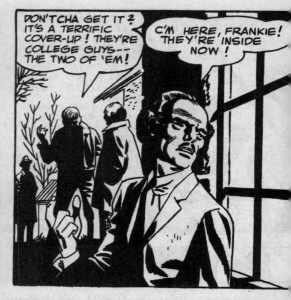

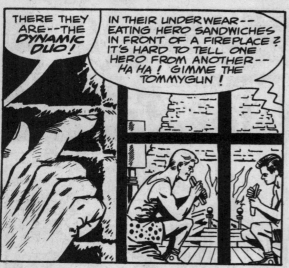

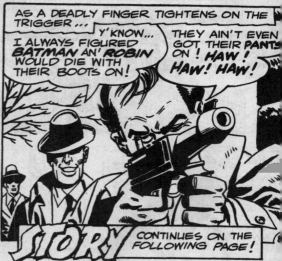

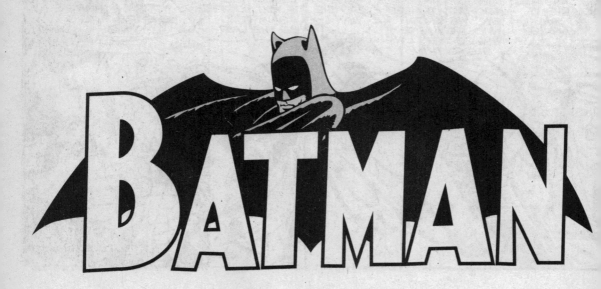

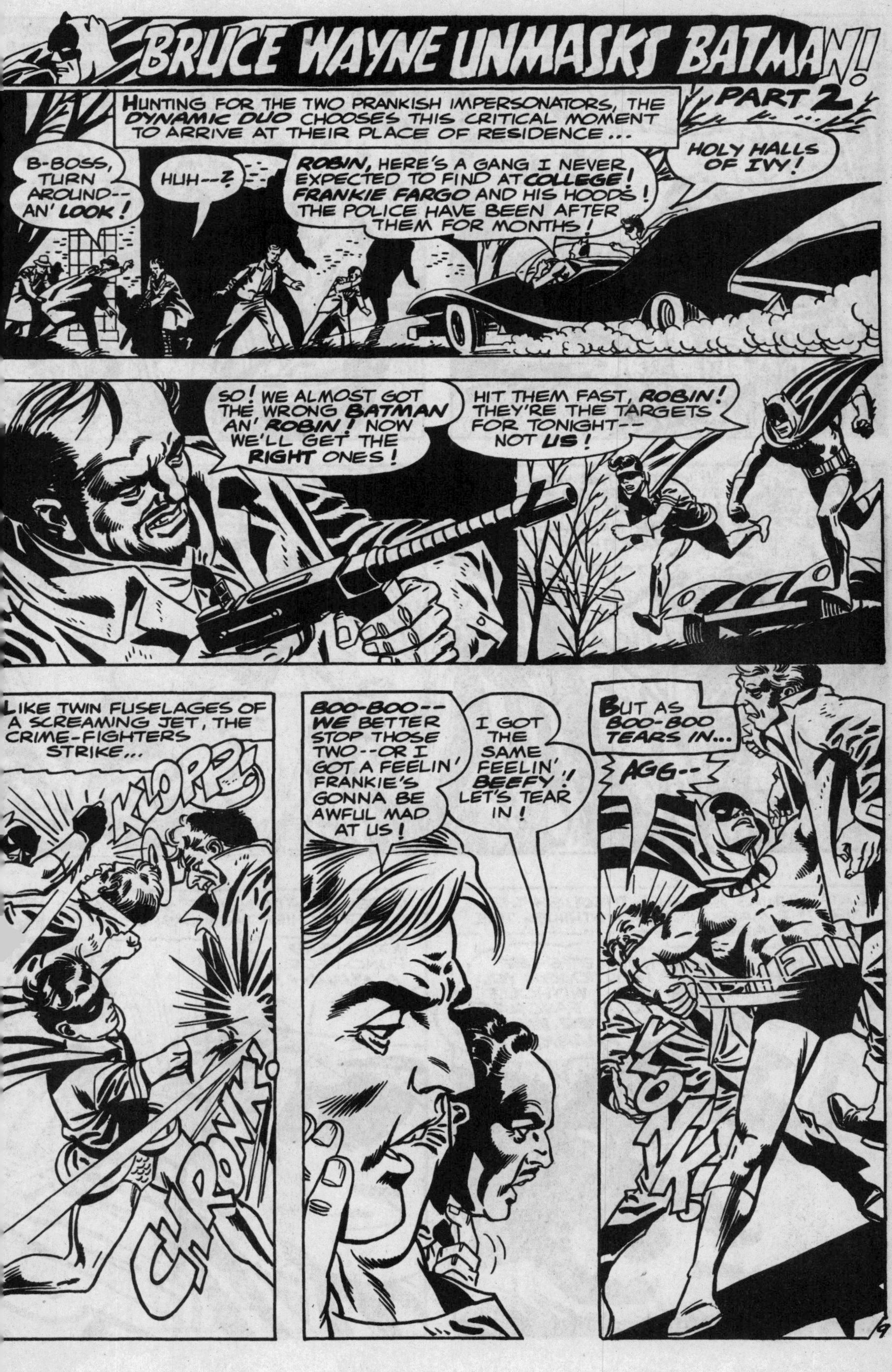
BRUCE WAYNE UNMASKS BATMAN!
PART 2
HUNTING FOR THE TWO PRANKISH IMPERSONATORS, THE DYNAMIC DUO CHOOSES THIS CRITICAL MOMENT TO ARRIVE AT THEIR PLACE OF RESIDENCE...
B-BOSS, TURN AROUND-- AN' LOOK!
HUH--?
ROBIN, HERE'S A GANG I NEVER EXPECTED TO FIND AT COLLEGE! FRANKIE FARGO AND HIS HOODS! THE POLICE HAVE BEEN AFTER THEM FOR MONTHS!
HOLY HALLS OF IVY!
SO! WE ALMOST GOT THE WRONG BATMAN AN' ROBIN! NOW WE'LL GET THE RIGHT ONES!
HIT THEM FAST, ROBIN! THEY'RE THE TARGETS FOR TONIGHT-- NOT US!
LIKE TWIN FUSELAGES OF A SCREAMING JET, THE CRIME-FIGHTERS STRIKE...
KLOPP!
CHRONK!
BOO-BOO-- WE BETTER STOP THOSE TWO--OR I GOT A FEELIN' FRANKIE'S GONNA BE AWFUL MAD AT US!
I GOT THE SAME FEELIN' BEEFY! LET'S TEAR IN!
BUT AS BOO-BOO TEARS IN...
AGG--
9

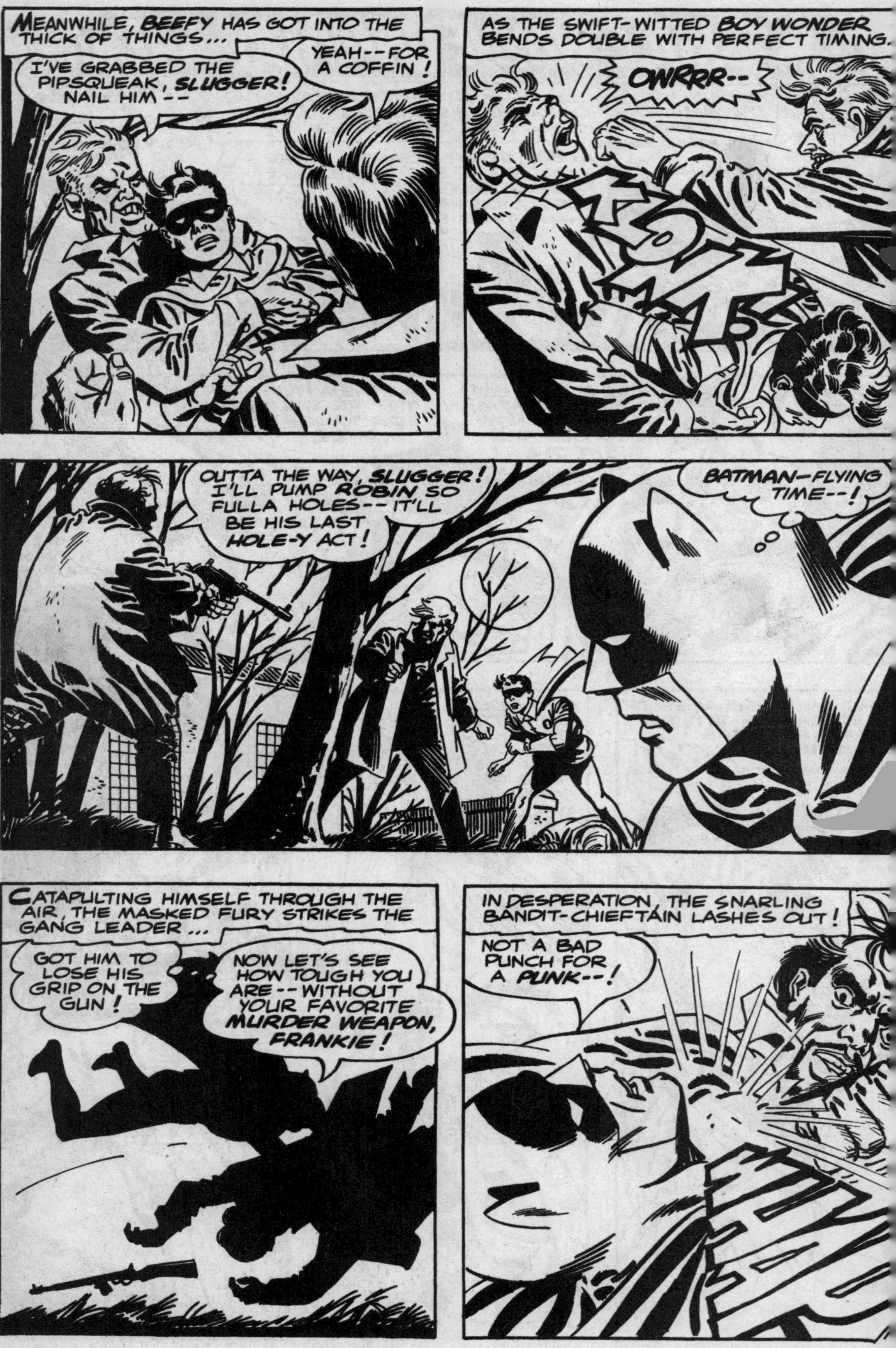
MEANWHILE, BEEFY HAS GOT INTO THE THICK OF THINGS...
I'VE GRABBED THE PIPSQUEAK, SLUGGER! NAIL HIM--
YEAH--FOR A COFFIN!
AS THE SWIFT-WITTED BOY WONDER BENDS DOUBLE WITH PERFECT TIMING...
OWRRR--
OUTTA THE WAY, SLUGGER! I'LL PUMP ROBIN SO FULLA HOLES--IT'LL BE HIS LAST HOLE-Y ACT!
BATMAN--FLYING TIME--!
CATAPULTING HIMSELF THROUGH THE AIR, THE MASKED FURY STRIKES THE GANG LEADER...
GOT HIM TO LOSE HIS GRIP ON THE GUN!
NOW LET'S SEE HOW TOUGH YOU ARE--WITHOUT YOUR FAVORITE MURDER WEAPON, FRANKIE!
IN DESPERATION, THE SNARLING BANDIT-CHIEFTAIN LASHES OUT!
NOT A BAD PUNCH FOR A PUNK--!

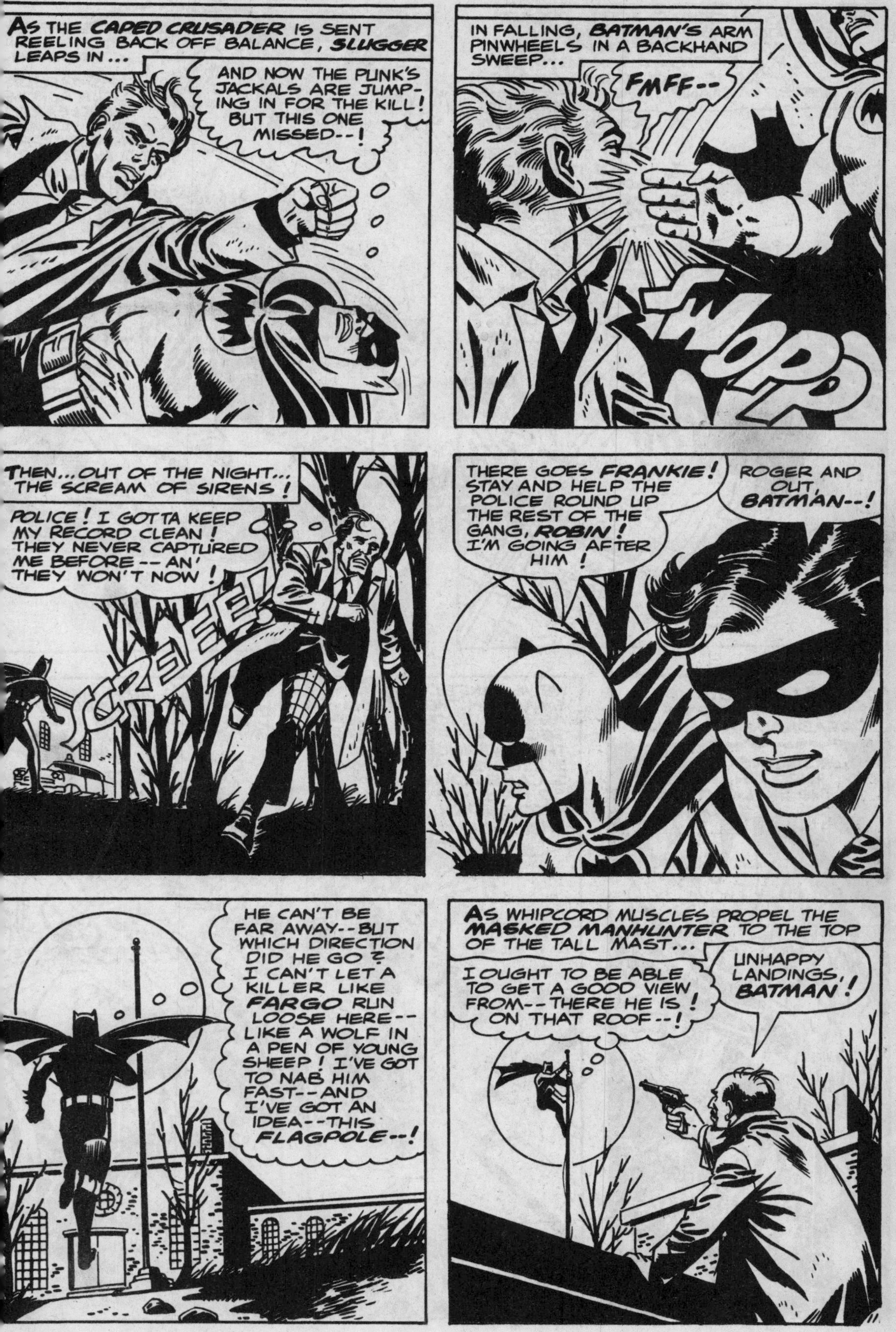
AS THE CAPED CRUSADER IS SENT REELING BACK OFF BALANCE, SLUGGER LEAPS IN...
AND NOW THE PUNK'S JACKALS ARE JUMPING IN FOR THE KILL! BUT THIS ONE MISSED--!
IN FALLING, BATMAN'S ARM PINWHEELS IN A BACKHAND SWEEP...
FMFF--
WHOPP
THEN...OUT OF THE NIGHT... THE SCREAM OF SIRENS!
POLICE! I GOTTA KEEP MY RECORD CLEAN! THEY NEVER CAPTURED ME BEFORE--AN' THEY WON'T NOW!
SCREEE!
THERE GOES FRANKIE! STAY AND HELP THE POLICE ROUND UP THE REST OF THE GANG, ROBIN! I'M GOING AFTER HIM!
ROGER AND OUT, BATMAN--!
HE CAN'T BE FAR AWAY--BUT WHICH DIRECTION DID HE GO? I CAN'T LET A KILLER LIKE FARGO RUN LOOSE HERE--LIKE A WOLF IN A PEN OF YOUNG SHEEP! I'VE GOT TO NAB HIM FAST--AND I'VE GOT AN IDEA--THIS FLAGPOLE--!
AS WHIPCORD MUSCLES PROPEL THE MASKED MANHUNTER TO THE TOP OF THE TALL MAST...
I OUGHT TO BE ABLE TO GET A GOOD VIEW FROM--THERE HE IS! ON THAT ROOF--!
UNHAPPY LANDINGS, BATMAN!
11

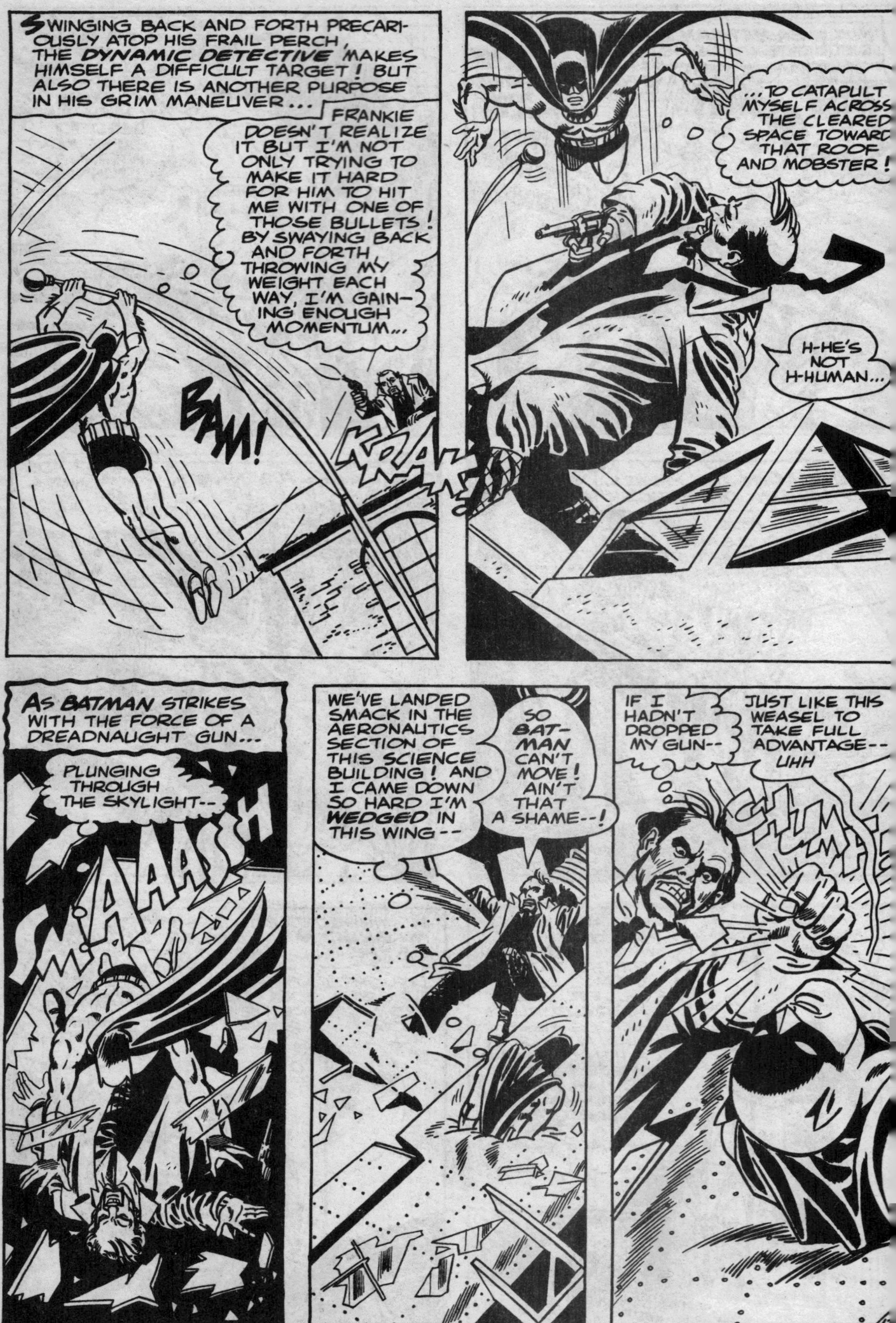
SWINGING BACK AND FORTH PRECARIOUSLY ATOP HIS FRAIL PERCH, THE DYNAMIC DETECTIVE MAKES HIMSELF A DIFFICULT TARGET! BUT ALSO THERE IS ANOTHER PURPOSE IN HIS GRIM MANEUVER...
FRANKIE DOESN'T REALIZE IT BUT I'M NOT ONLY TRYING TO MAKE IT HARD FOR HIM TO HIT ME WITH ONE OF THOSE BULLETS! BY SWAYING BACK AND FORTH THROWING MY WEIGHT EACH WAY, I'M GAINING ENOUGH MOMENTUM...
BAM!
KRAK
...TO CATAPULT MYSELF ACROSS THE CLEARED SPACE TOWARD THAT ROOF AND MOBSTER!
H-HE'S NOT H-HUMAN...
AS BATMAN STRIKES WITH THE FORCE OF A DREADNAUGHT GUN...
PLUNGING THROUGH THE SKYLIGHT--
SMAAASH
WE'VE LANDED SMACK IN THE AERONAUTICS SECTION OF THIS SCIENCE BUILDING! AND I CAME DOWN SO HARD I'M WEDGED IN THIS WING--
SO BATMAN CAN'T MOVE! AIN'T THAT A SHAME--!
IF I HADN'T DROPPED MY GUN--
JUST LIKE THIS WEASEL TO TAKE FULL ADVANTAGE-- UHH

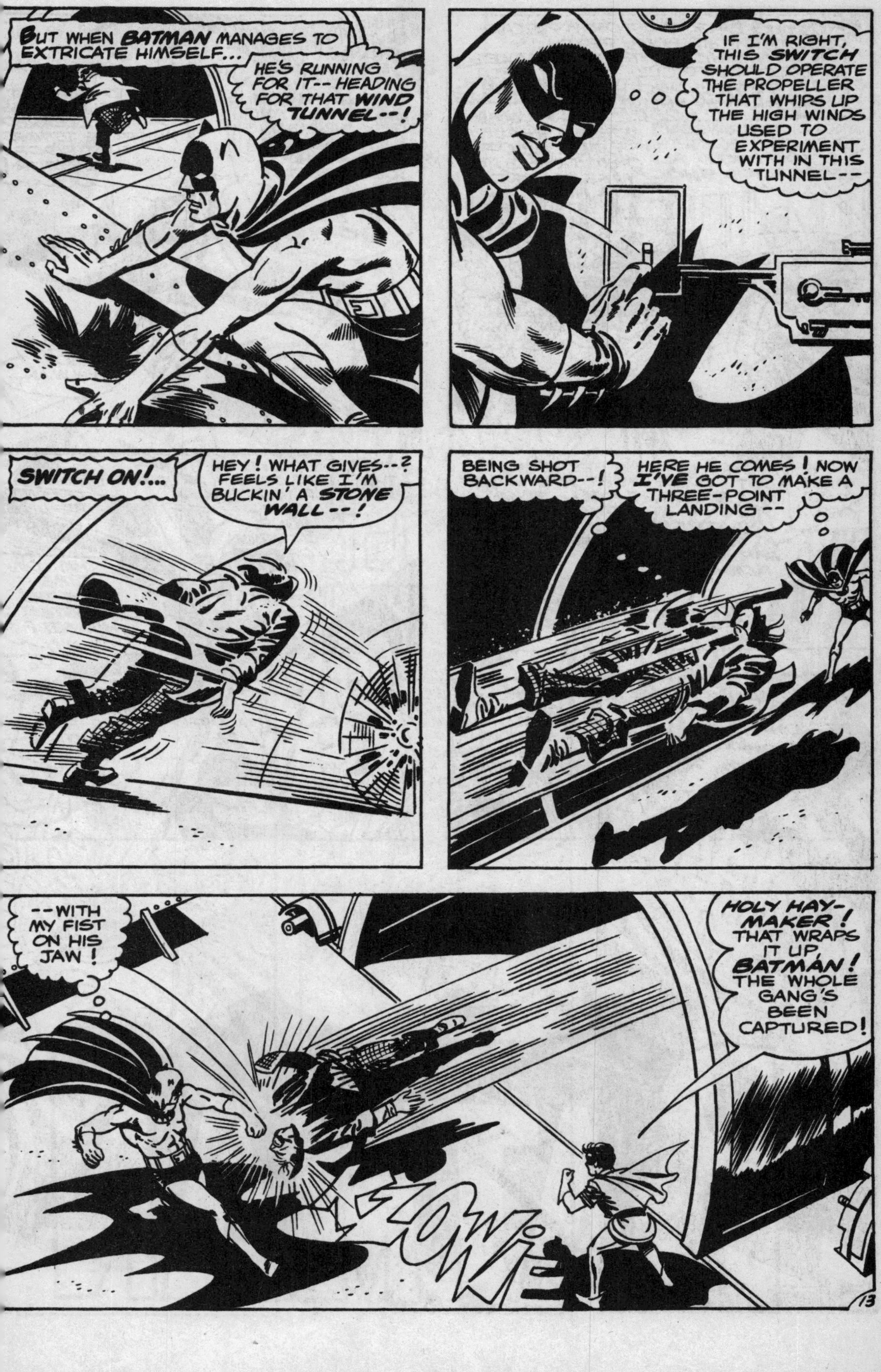
BUT WHEN BATMAN MANAGES TO EXTRICATE HIMSELF...
HE'S RUNNING FOR IT-- HEADING FOR THAT WIND TUNNEL--!
IF I'M RIGHT, THIS SWITCH SHOULD OPERATE THE PROPELLER THAT WHIPS UP THE HIGH WINDS USED TO EXPERIMENT WITH IN THIS TUNNEL--
SWITCH ON!...
HEY! WHAT GIVES--? FEELS LIKE I'M BUCKIN' A STONE WALL--!
BEING SHOT BACKWARD--!
HERE HE COMES! NOW I'VE GOT TO MAKE A THREE-POINT LANDING--
--WITH MY FIST ON HIS JAW!
HOLY HAYMAKER! THAT WRAPS IT UP, BATMAN! THE WHOLE GANG'S BEEN CAPTURED!
POW
13

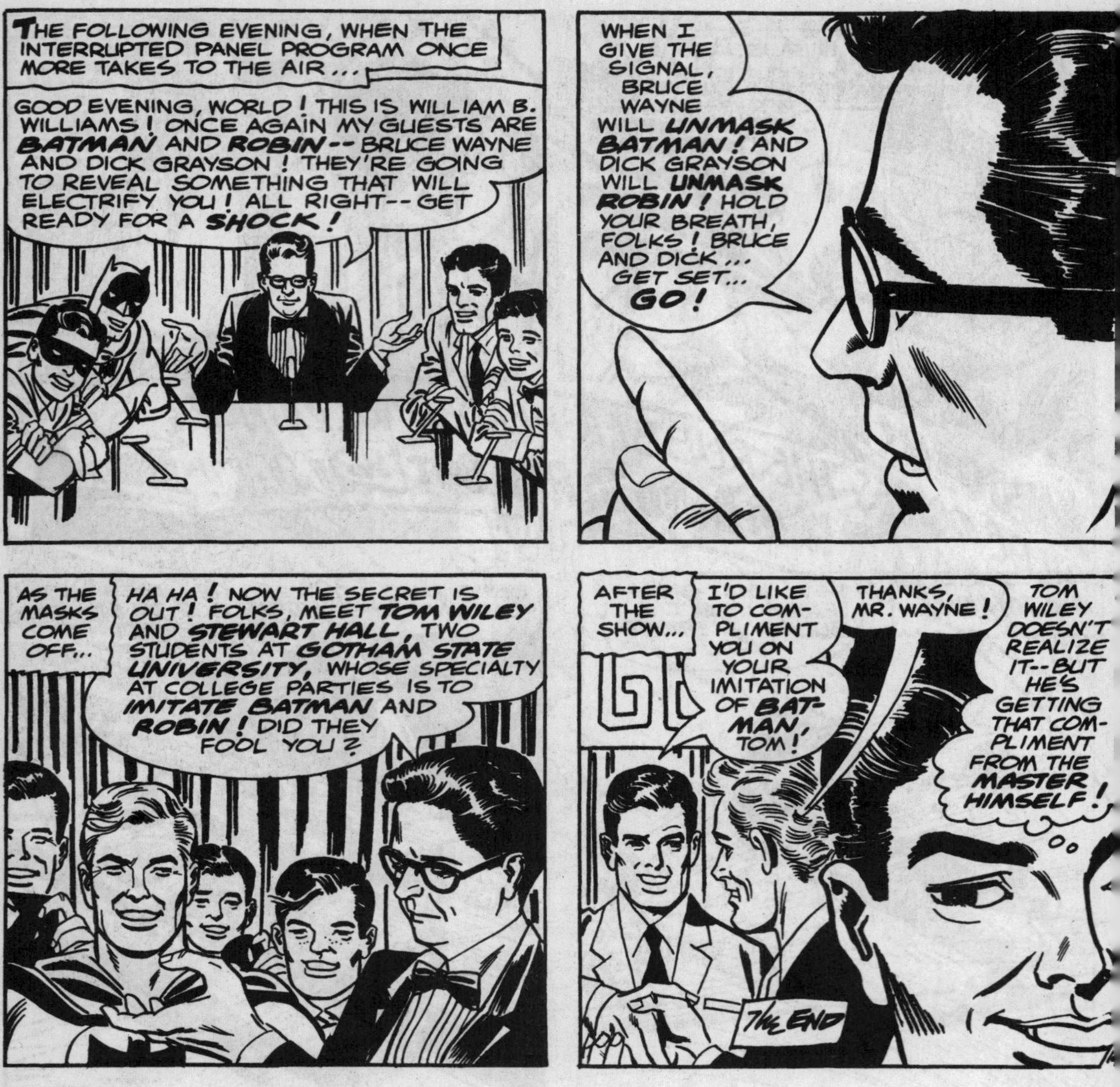
THE FOLLOWING EVENING, WHEN THE INTERRUPTED PANEL PROGRAM ONCE MORE TAKES TO THE AIR...
GOOD EVENING, WORLD! THIS IS WILLIAM B. WILLIAMS! ONCE AGAIN MY GUESTS ARE BATMAN AND ROBIN -- BRUCE WAYNE AND DICK GRAYSON! THEY'RE GOING TO REVEAL SOMETHING THAT WILL ELECTRIFY YOU! ALL RIGHT -- GET READY FOR A SHOCK!
WHEN I GIVE THE SIGNAL, BRUCE WAYNE WILL UNMASK BATMAN! AND DICK GRAYSON WILL UNMASK ROBIN! HOLD YOUR BREATH, FOLKS! BRUCE AND DICK... GET SET... GO!
AS THE MASKS COME OFF...
HA HA! NOW THE SECRET IS OUT! FOLKS, MEET TOM WILEY AND STEWART HALL, TWO STUDENTS AT GOTHAM STATE UNIVERSITY, WHOSE SPECIALTY AT COLLEGE PARTIES IS TO IMITATE BATMAN AND ROBIN! DID THEY FOOL YOU?
AFTER THE SHOW...
I'D LIKE TO COMPLIMENT YOU ON YOUR IMITATION OF BATMAN, TOM!
THANKS, MR. WAYNE!
TOM WILEY DOESN'T REALIZE IT -- BUT HE'S GETTING THAT COMPLIMENT FROM THE MASTER HIMSELF!
THE END

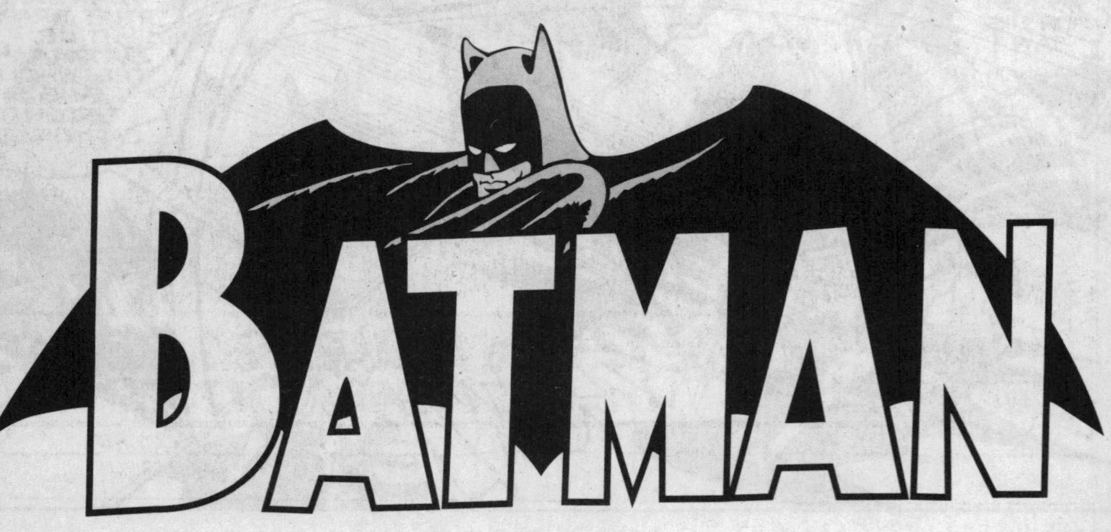
BATMAN

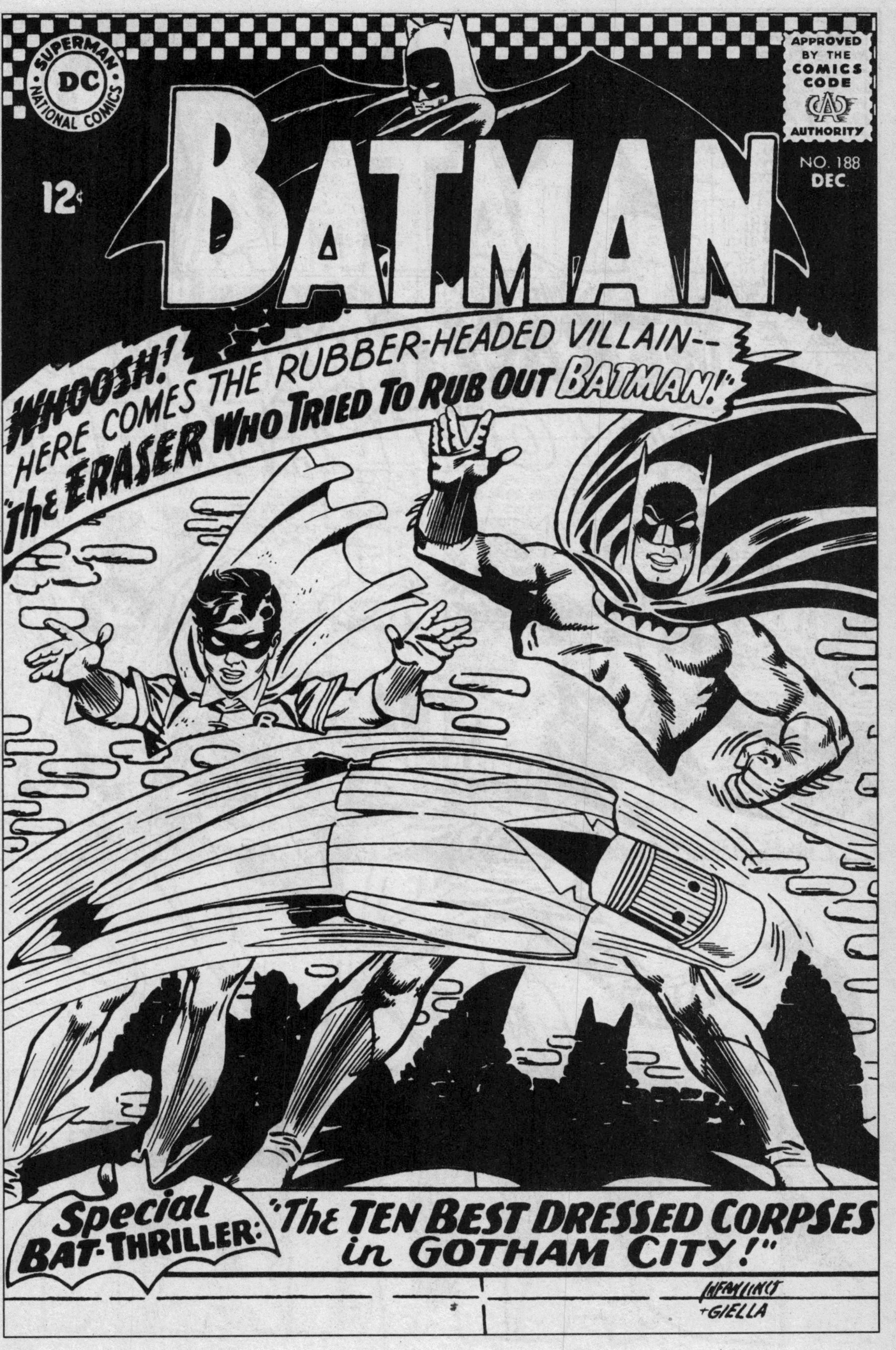
SUPERMAN DC NATIONAL COMICS
APPROVED BY THE COMICS CODE AUTHORITY
12¢
BATMAN
NO. 188 DEC
WHOOSH! HERE COMES THE RUBBER-HEADED VILLAIN--
"The ERASER WHO TRIED TO RUB OUT BATMAN!"
Special BAT-THRILLER:
"The TEN BEST DRESSED CORPSES in GOTHAM CITY!"
+GIELLA

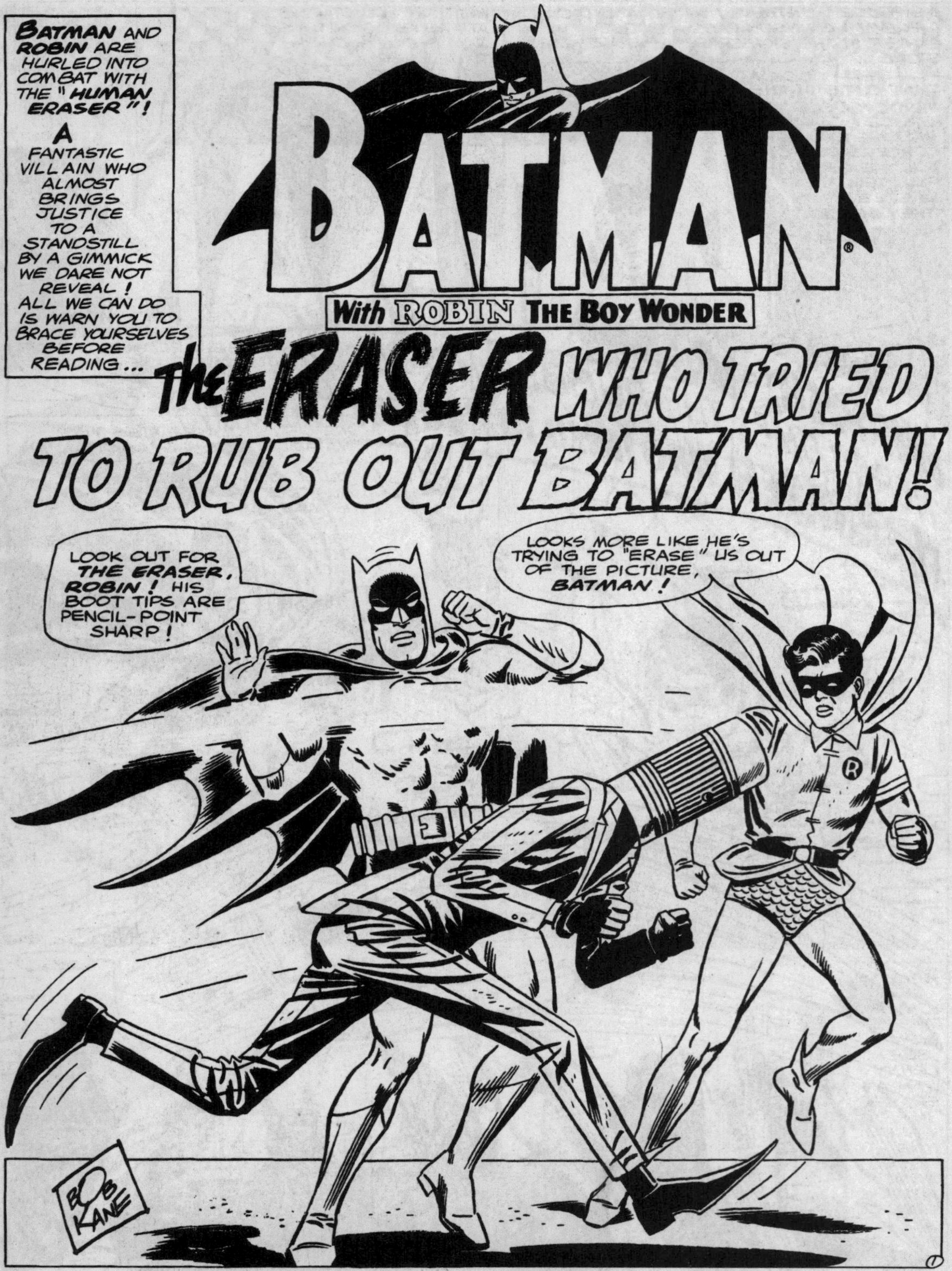

BATMAN AND ROBIN ARE HURLED INTO COMBAT WITH THE "HUMAN ERASER"! A FANTASTIC VILLAIN WHO ALMOST BRINGS JUSTICE TO A STANDSTILL BY A GIMMICK WE DARE NOT REVEAL! ALL WE CAN DO IS WARN YOU TO BRACE YOURSELVES BEFORE READING...
BATMAN®
With ROBIN THE BOY WONDER
The ERASER WHO TRIED TO RUB OUT BATMAN!
LOOK OUT FOR THE ERASER, ROBIN! HIS BOOT TIPS ARE PENCIL-POINT SHARP!
LOOKS MORE LIKE HE'S TRYING TO "ERASE" US OUT OF THE PICTURE, BATMAN!
BOB KANE
1

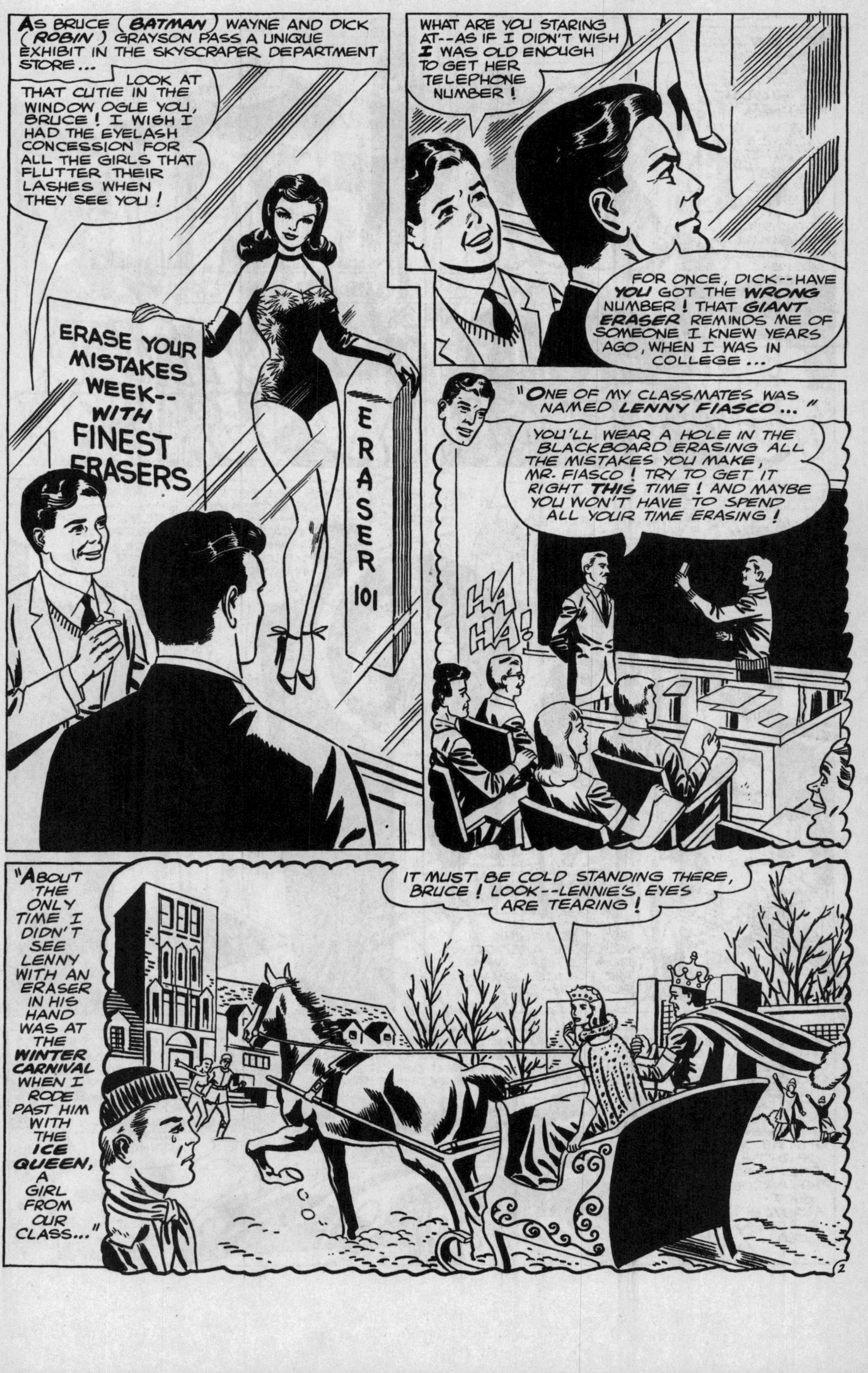
AS BRUCE (BATMAN) WAYNE AND DICK (ROBIN) GRAYSON PASS A UNIQUE EXHIBIT IN THE SKYSCRAPER DEPARTMENT STORE...
LOOK AT THAT CUTIE IN THE WINDOW OGLE YOU, BRUCE! I WISH I HAD THE EYELASH CONCESSION FOR ALL THE GIRLS THAT FLUTTER THEIR LASHES WHEN THEY SEE YOU!
ERASE YOUR MISTAKES WEEK--WITH FINEST ERASERS
ERASER 101
WHAT ARE YOU STARING AT--AS IF I DIDN'T WISH I WAS OLD ENOUGH TO GET HER TELEPHONE NUMBER!
FOR ONCE, DICK--HAVE YOU GOT THE WRONG NUMBER! THAT GIANT ERASER REMINDS ME OF SOMEONE I KNEW YEARS AGO, WHEN I WAS IN COLLEGE...
"ONE OF MY CLASSMATES WAS NAMED LENNY FIASCO..."
YOU'LL WEAR A HOLE IN THE BLACKBOARD ERASING ALL THE MISTAKES YOU MAKE, MR. FIASCO! TRY TO GET IT RIGHT THIS TIME! AND MAYBE YOU WON'T HAVE TO SPEND ALL YOUR TIME ERASING!
HA HA!
"ABOUT THE ONLY TIME I DIDN'T SEE LENNY WITH AN ERASER IN HIS HAND WAS AT THE WINTER CARNIVAL WHEN I RODE PAST HIM WITH THE ICE QUEEN, A GIRL FROM OUR CLASS..."
IT MUST BE COLD STANDING THERE, BRUCE! LOOK--LENNIE'S EYES ARE TEARING!
2

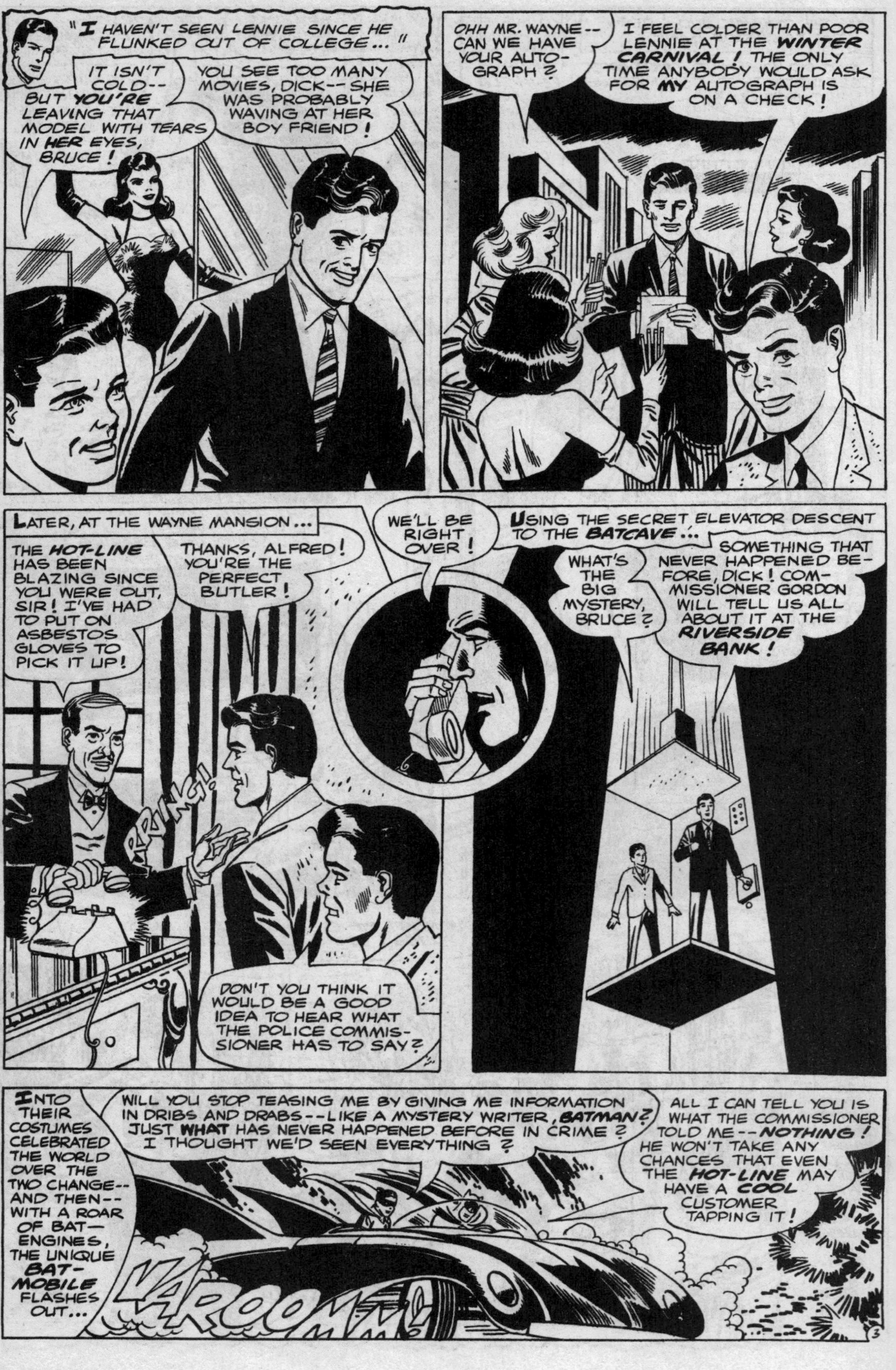
"I HAVEN'T SEEN LENNIE SINCE HE FLUNKED OUT OF COLLEGE..."
IT ISN'T COLD-- BUT YOU'RE LEAVING THAT MODEL WITH TEARS IN HER EYES, BRUCE!
YOU SEE TOO MANY MOVIES, DICK--SHE WAS PROBABLY WAVING AT HER BOY FRIEND!
OHH MR. WAYNE-- CAN WE HAVE YOUR AUTO-GRAPH?
I FEEL COLDER THAN POOR LENNIE AT THE WINTER CARNIVAL! THE ONLY TIME ANYBODY WOULD ASK FOR MY AUTOGRAPH IS ON A CHECK!
LATER, AT THE WAYNE MANSION...
THE HOT-LINE HAS BEEN BLAZING SINCE YOU WERE OUT, SIR! I'VE HAD TO PUT ON ASBESTOS GLOVES TO PICK IT UP!
THANKS, ALFRED! YOU'RE THE PERFECT BUTLER!
BRRING!
WE'LL BE RIGHT OVER!
DON'T YOU THINK IT WOULD BE A GOOD IDEA TO HEAR WHAT THE POLICE COMMISSIONER HAS TO SAY?
USING THE SECRET ELEVATOR DESCENT TO THE BATCAVE...
WHAT'S THE BIG MYSTERY, BRUCE?
SOMETHING THAT NEVER HAPPENED BEFORE, DICK! COMMISSIONER GORDON WILL TELL US ALL ABOUT IT AT THE RIVERSIDE BANK!
INTO THEIR COSTUMES CELEBRATED THE WORLD OVER THE TWO CHANGE-- AND THEN-- WITH A ROAR OF BAT-ENGINES, THE UNIQUE BAT-MOBILE FLASHES OUT...
WILL YOU STOP TEASING ME BY GIVING ME INFORMATION IN DRIBS AND DRABS--LIKE A MYSTERY WRITER, BATMAN? JUST WHAT HAS NEVER HAPPENED BEFORE IN CRIME? I THOUGHT WE'D SEEN EVERYTHING?
ALL I CAN TELL YOU IS WHAT THE COMMISSIONER TOLD ME--NOTHING! HE WON'T TAKE ANY CHANCES THAT EVEN THE HOT-LINE MAY HAVE A COOL CUSTOMER TAPPING IT!
VAROOMM!
3

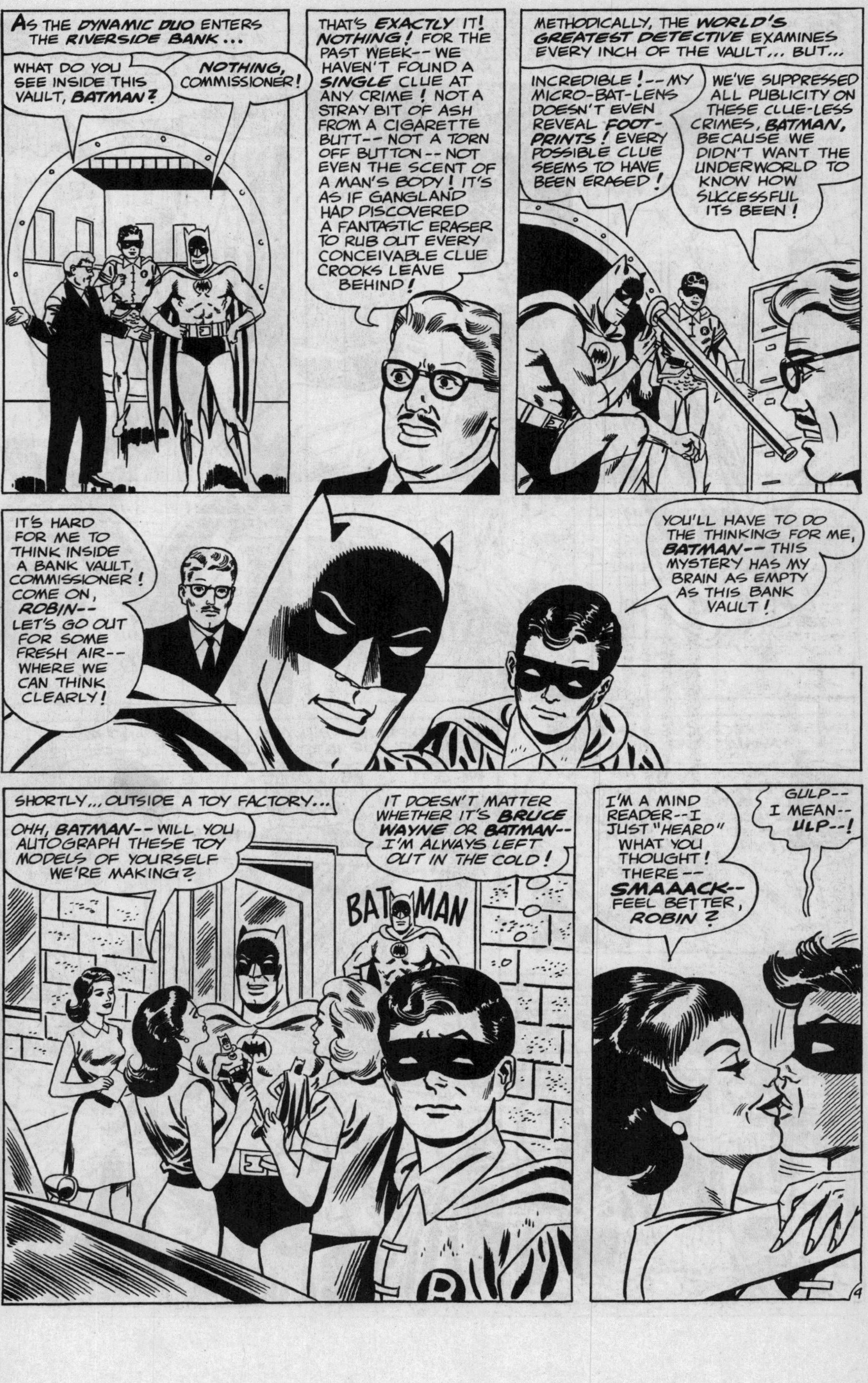
AS THE DYNAMIC DUO ENTERS THE RIVERSIDE BANK...
WHAT DO YOU SEE INSIDE THIS VAULT, BATMAN?
NOTHING, COMMISSIONER!
THAT'S EXACTLY IT! NOTHING! FOR THE PAST WEEK-- WE HAVEN'T FOUND A SINGLE CLUE AT ANY CRIME! NOT A STRAY BIT OF ASH FROM A CIGARETTE BUTT-- NOT A TORN OFF BUTTON-- NOT EVEN THE SCENT OF A MAN'S BODY! IT'S AS IF GANGLAND HAD DISCOVERED A FANTASTIC ERASER TO RUB OUT EVERY CONCEIVABLE CLUE CROOKS LEAVE BEHIND!
METHODICALLY, THE WORLD'S GREATEST DETECTIVE EXAMINES EVERY INCH OF THE VAULT... BUT...
INCREDIBLE!-- MY MICRO-BAT-LENS DOESN'T EVEN REVEAL FOOT-PRINTS! EVERY POSSIBLE CLUE SEEMS TO HAVE BEEN ERASED!
WE'VE SUPPRESSED ALL PUBLICITY ON THESE CLUE-LESS CRIMES, BATMAN, BECAUSE WE DIDN'T WANT THE UNDERWORLD TO KNOW HOW SUCCESSFUL ITS BEEN!
IT'S HARD FOR ME TO THINK INSIDE A BANK VAULT, COMMISSIONER! COME ON, ROBIN-- LET'S GO OUT FOR SOME FRESH AIR-- WHERE WE CAN THINK CLEARLY!
YOU'LL HAVE TO DO THE THINKING FOR ME, BATMAN-- THIS MYSTERY HAS MY BRAIN AS EMPTY AS THIS BANK VAULT!
SHORTLY... OUTSIDE A TOY FACTORY...
OHH, BATMAN-- WILL YOU AUTOGRAPH THESE TOY MODELS OF YOURSELF WE'RE MAKING?
IT DOESN'T MATTER WHETHER IT'S BRUCE WAYNE OR BATMAN-- I'M ALWAYS LEFT OUT IN THE COLD!
BATMAN
I'M A MIND READER-- I JUST "HEARD" WHAT YOU THOUGHT! THERE-- SMAAACK-- FEEL BETTER, ROBIN?
GULP-- I MEAN-- ULP--!
4

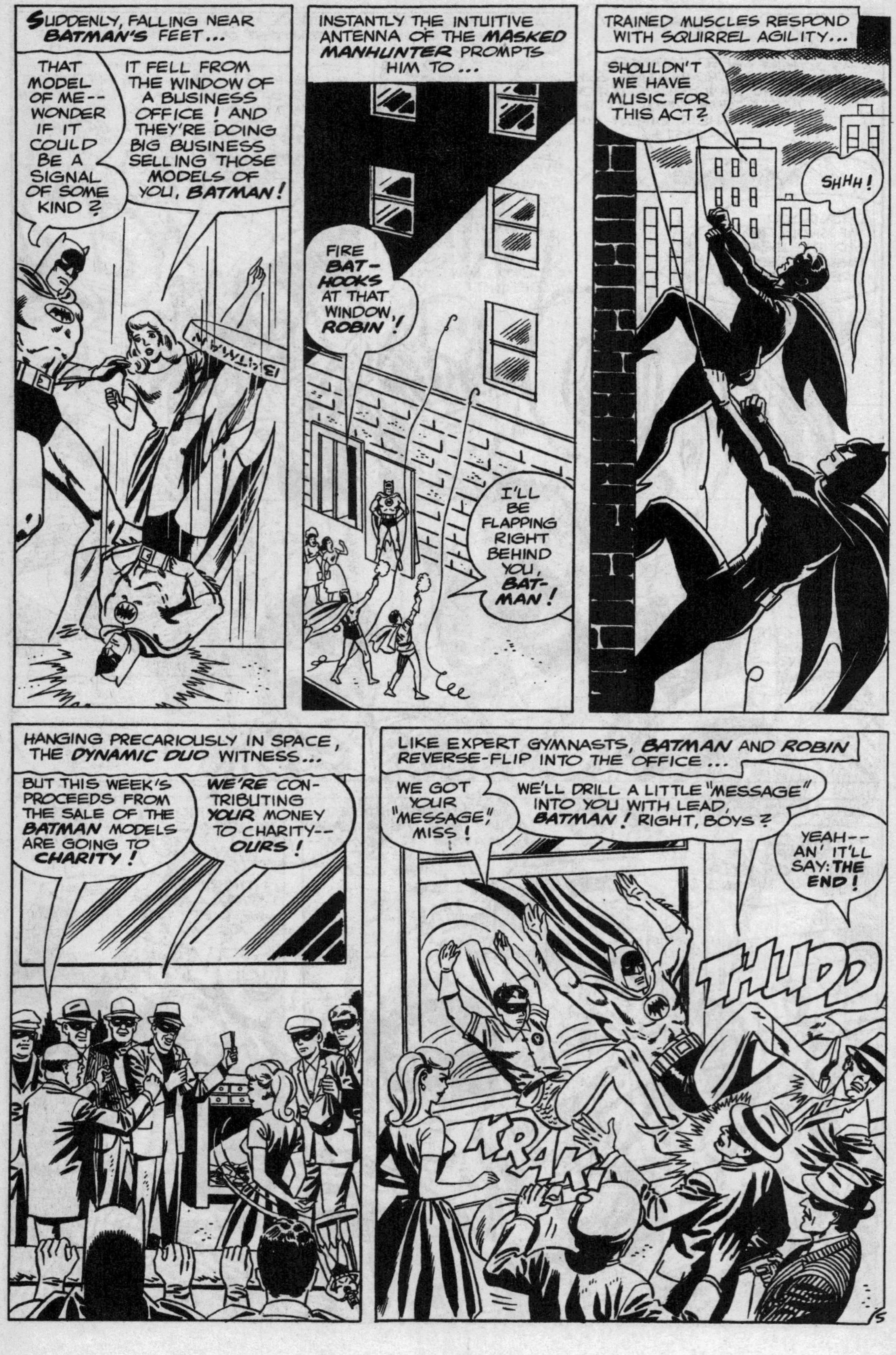
SUDDENLY, FALLING NEAR BATMAN'S FEET...
THAT MODEL OF ME--WONDER IF IT COULD BE A SIGNAL OF SOME KIND?
IT FELL FROM THE WINDOW OF A BUSINESS OFFICE! AND THEY'RE DOING BIG BUSINESS SELLING THOSE MODELS OF YOU, BATMAN!
INSTANTLY THE INTUITIVE ANTENNA OF THE MASKED MANHUNTER PROMPTS HIM TO...
FIRE BAT-HOOKS AT THAT WINDOW, ROBIN!
I'LL BE FLAPPING RIGHT BEHIND YOU, BAT-MAN!
TRAINED MUSCLES RESPOND WITH SQUIRREL AGILITY...
SHOULDN'T WE HAVE MUSIC FOR THIS ACT?
SHHH!
HANGING PRECARIOUSLY IN SPACE, THE DYNAMIC DUO WITNESS...
BUT THIS WEEK'S PROCEEDS FROM THE SALE OF THE BATMAN MODELS ARE GOING TO CHARITY!
WE'RE CONTRIBUTING YOUR MONEY TO CHARITY--OURS!
LIKE EXPERT GYMNASTS, BATMAN AND ROBIN REVERSE-FLIP INTO THE OFFICE...
WE GOT YOUR "MESSAGE," MISS!
WE'LL DRILL A LITTLE "MESSAGE" INTO YOU WITH LEAD, BATMAN! RIGHT, BOYS?
YEAH--AN' IT'LL SAY: THE END!
THUDD
KRAK!
5

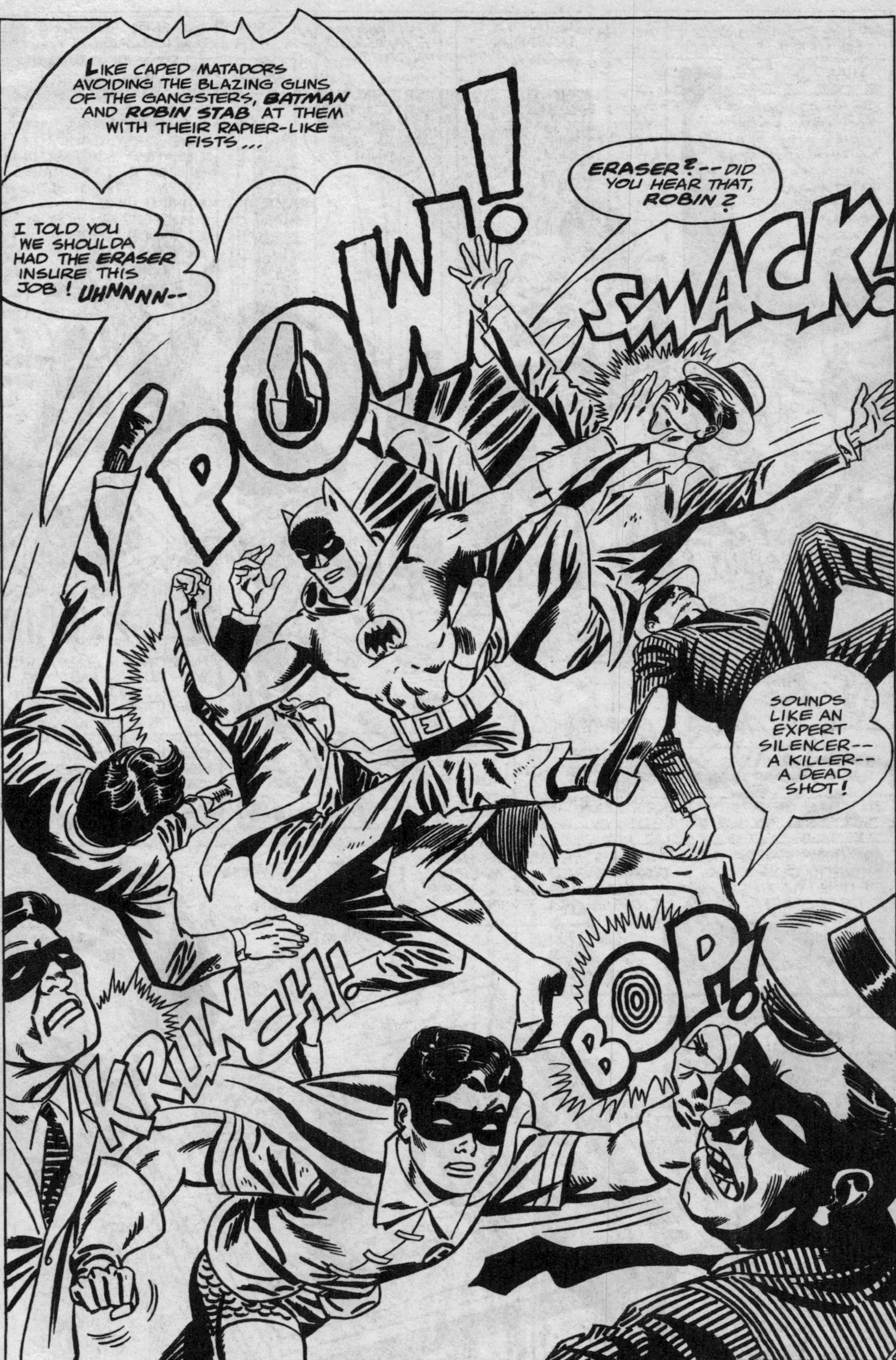
LIKE CAPED MATADORS AVOIDING THE BLAZING GUNS OF THE GANGSTERS, BATMAN AND ROBIN STAB AT THEM WITH THEIR RAPIER-LIKE FISTS...
I TOLD YOU WE SHOULDA HAD THE ERASER INSURE THIS JOB! UHHNNNN--
POW!
ERASER?--DID YOU HEAR THAT, ROBIN?
SMACK!
SOUNDS LIKE AN EXPERT SILENCER-- A KILLER-- A DEAD SHOT!
KRUNCH!
BOP!
6

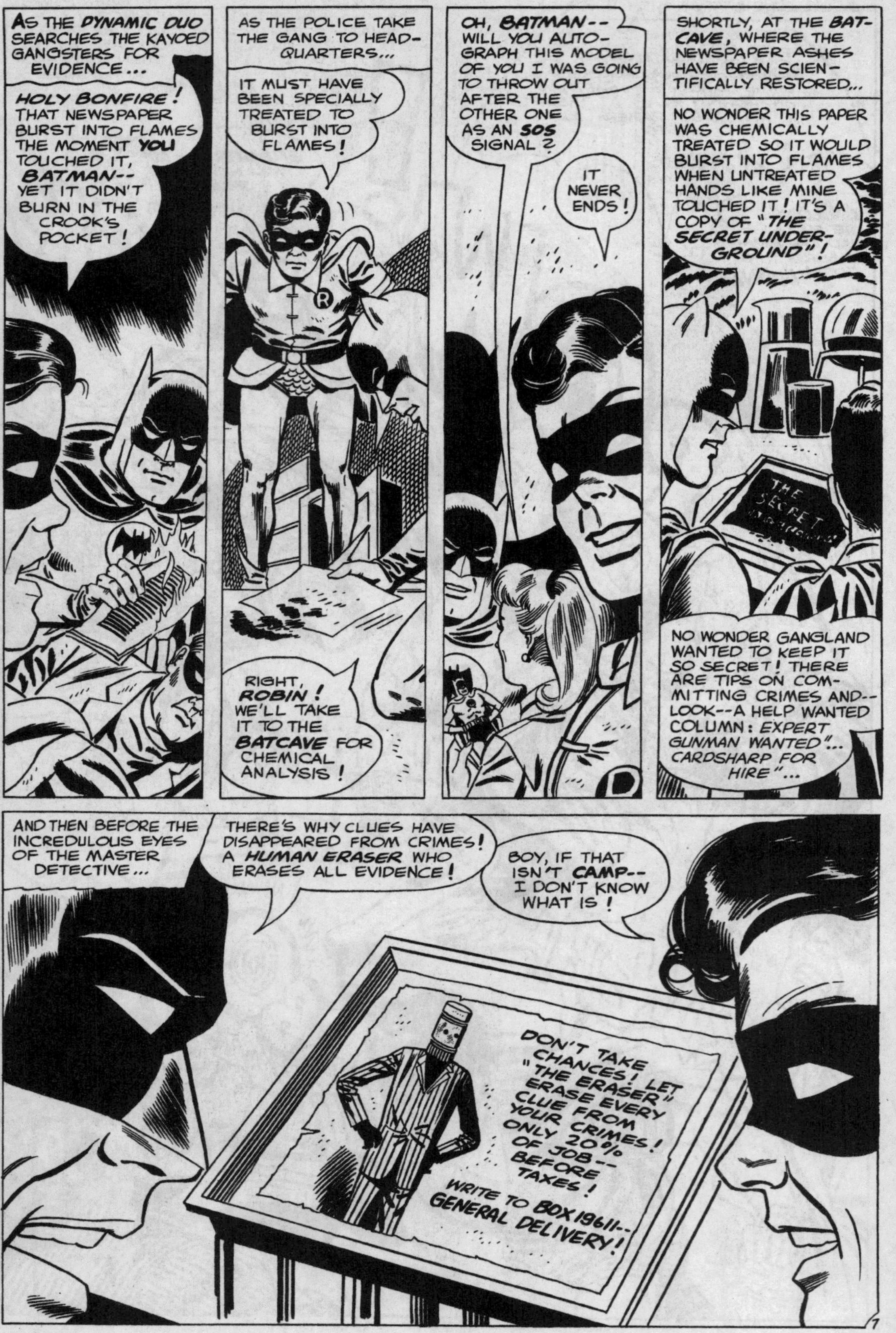
AS THE DYNAMIC DUO SEARCHES THE KAYOED GANGSTERS FOR EVIDENCE...
HOLY BONFIRE! THAT NEWSPAPER BURST INTO FLAMES THE MOMENT YOU TOUCHED IT, BATMAN--YET IT DIDN'T BURN IN THE CROOK'S POCKET!
AS THE POLICE TAKE THE GANG TO HEAD-QUARTERS...
IT MUST HAVE BEEN SPECIALLY TREATED TO BURST INTO FLAMES!
RIGHT, ROBIN! WE'LL TAKE IT TO THE BATCAVE FOR CHEMICAL ANALYSIS!
OH, BATMAN--WILL YOU AUTO-GRAPH THIS MODEL OF YOU I WAS GOING TO THROW OUT AFTER THE OTHER ONE AS AN SOS SIGNAL?
IT NEVER ENDS!
SHORTLY, AT THE BAT-CAVE, WHERE THE NEWSPAPER ASHES HAVE BEEN SCIEN-TIFICALLY RESTORED...
NO WONDER THIS PAPER WAS CHEMICALLY TREATED SO IT WOULD BURST INTO FLAMES WHEN UNTREATED HANDS LIKE MINE TOUCHED IT! IT'S A COPY OF "THE SECRET UNDER-GROUND"!
THE SECRET
NO WONDER GANGLAND WANTED TO KEEP IT SO SECRET! THERE ARE TIPS ON COM-MITTING CRIMES AND--LOOK--A HELP WANTED COLUMN: EXPERT GUNMAN WANTED"... CARDSHARP FOR HIRE"...
AND THEN BEFORE THE INCREDULOUS EYES OF THE MASTER DETECTIVE...
THERE'S WHY CLUES HAVE DISAPPEARED FROM CRIMES! A HUMAN ERASER WHO ERASES ALL EVIDENCE!
BOY, IF THAT ISN'T CAMP--I DON'T KNOW WHAT IS!
DON'T TAKE CHANCES! LET "THE ERASER" ERASE EVERY CLUE FROM YOUR CRIMES! ONLY 20% OF JOB--BEFORE TAXES!
WRITE TO BOX 19611--GENERAL DELIVERY!
7

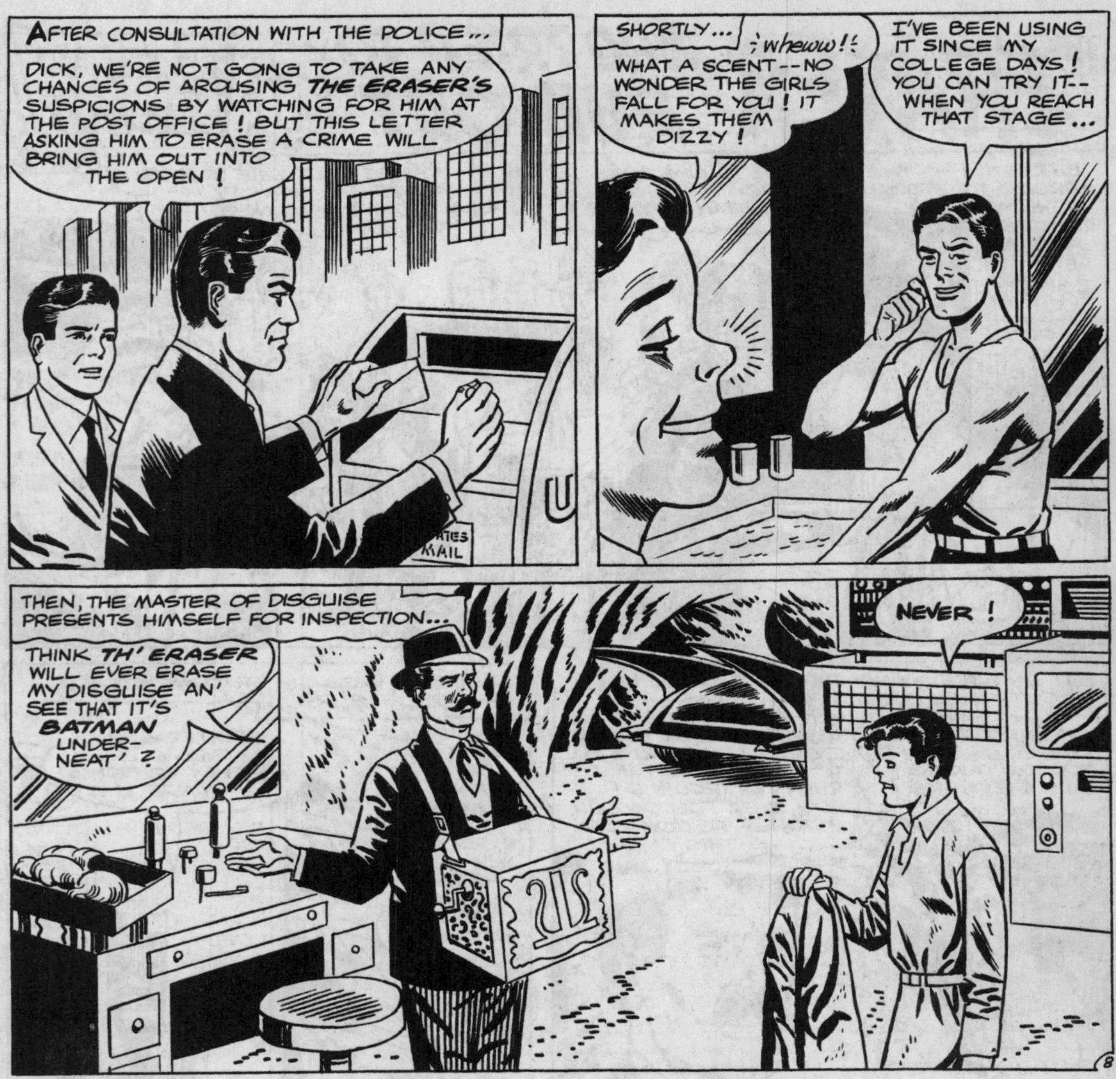
AFTER CONSULTATION WITH THE POLICE...
DICK, WE'RE NOT GOING TO TAKE ANY CHANCES OF AROUSING THE ERASER'S SUSPICIONS BY WATCHING FOR HIM AT THE POST OFFICE! BUT THIS LETTER ASKING HIM TO ERASE A CRIME WILL BRING HIM OUT INTO THE OPEN!
SHORTLY...
;wheww!;
WHAT A SCENT--NO WONDER THE GIRLS FALL FOR YOU! IT MAKES THEM DIZZY!
I'VE BEEN USING IT SINCE MY COLLEGE DAYS! YOU CAN TRY IT--WHEN YOU REACH THAT STAGE...
THEN, THE MASTER OF DISGUISE PRESENTS HIMSELF FOR INSPECTION...
THINK TH' ERASER WILL EVER ERASE MY DISGUISE AN' SEE THAT IT'S BATMAN UNDER-NEAT'?
NEVER!

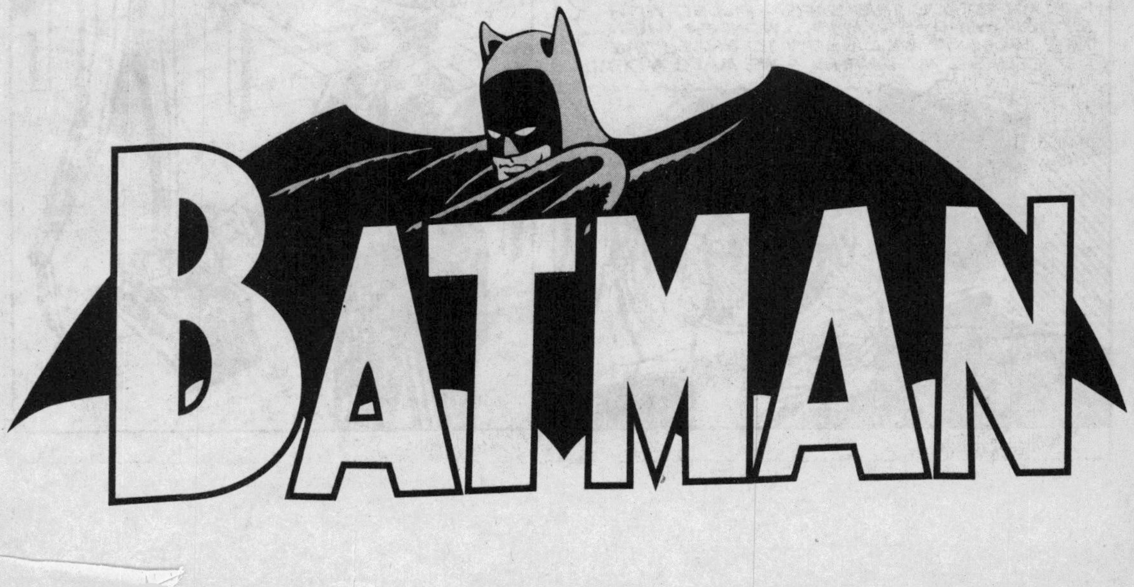
BATMAN

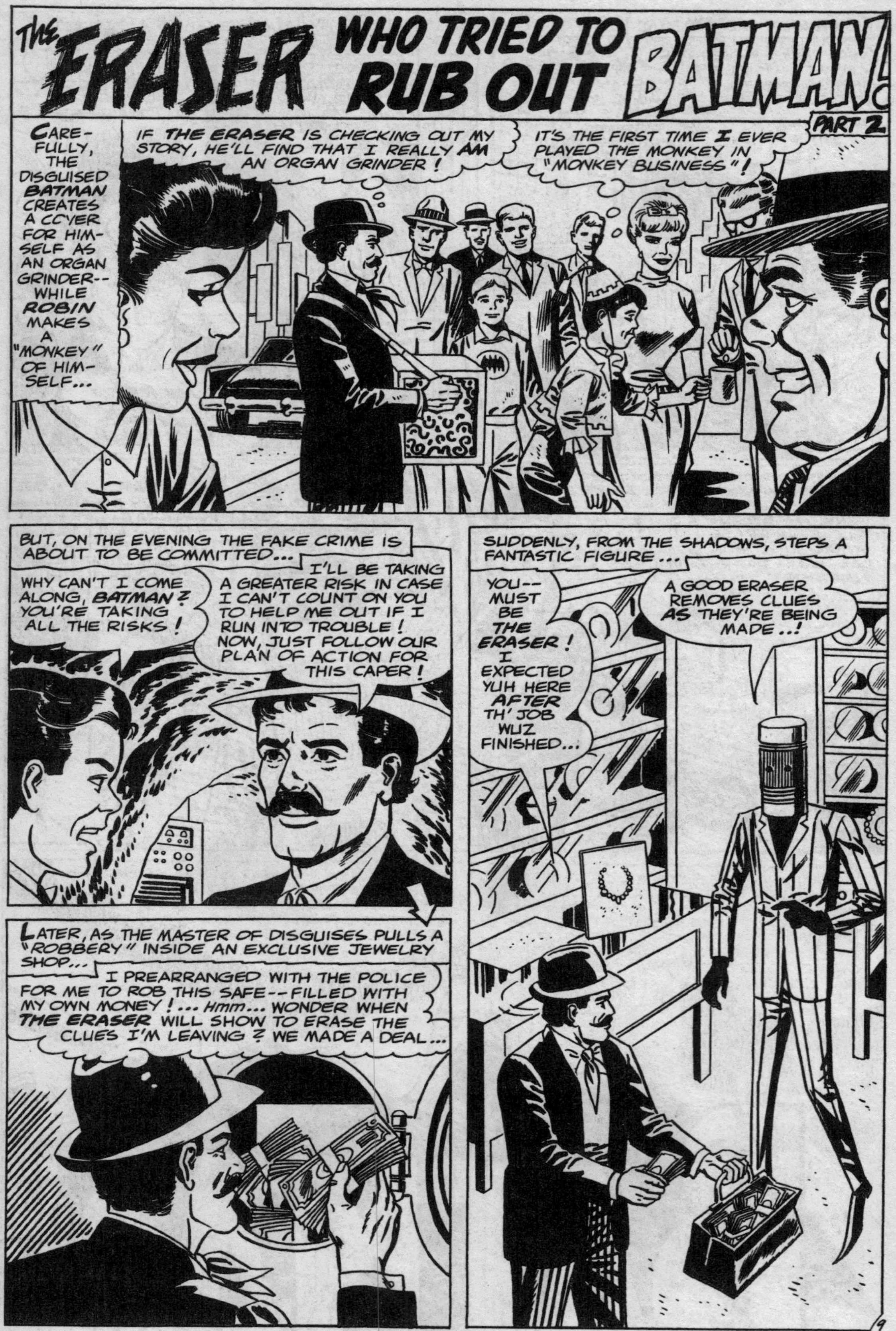
THE ERASER WHO TRIED TO RUB OUT BATMAN!
PART 2
CAREFULLY, THE DISGUISED BATMAN CREATES A COVER FOR HIMSELF AS AN ORGAN GRINDER--WHILE ROBIN MAKES A "MONKEY" OF HIMSELF...
IF THE ERASER IS CHECKING OUT MY STORY, HE'LL FIND THAT I REALLY AM AN ORGAN GRINDER!
IT'S THE FIRST TIME I EVER PLAYED THE MONKEY IN "MONKEY BUSINESS"!
BUT, ON THE EVENING THE FAKE CRIME IS ABOUT TO BE COMMITTED...
WHY CAN'T I COME ALONG, BATMAN? YOU'RE TAKING ALL THE RISKS!
I'LL BE TAKING A GREATER RISK IN CASE I CAN'T COUNT ON YOU TO HELP ME OUT IF I RUN INTO TROUBLE! NOW, JUST FOLLOW OUR PLAN OF ACTION FOR THIS CAPER!
LATER, AS THE MASTER OF DISGUISES PULLS A "ROBBERY" INSIDE AN EXCLUSIVE JEWELRY SHOP...
I PREARRANGED WITH THE POLICE FOR ME TO ROB THIS SAFE--FILLED WITH MY OWN MONEY! ... Hmm... WONDER WHEN THE ERASER WILL SHOW TO ERASE THE CLUES I'M LEAVING? WE MADE A DEAL...
SUDDENLY, FROM THE SHADOWS, STEPS A FANTASTIC FIGURE...
YOU--MUST BE THE ERASER! I EXPECTED YUH HERE AFTER TH' JOB WUZ FINISHED...
A GOOD ERASER REMOVES CLUES AS THEY'RE BEING MADE...!
9

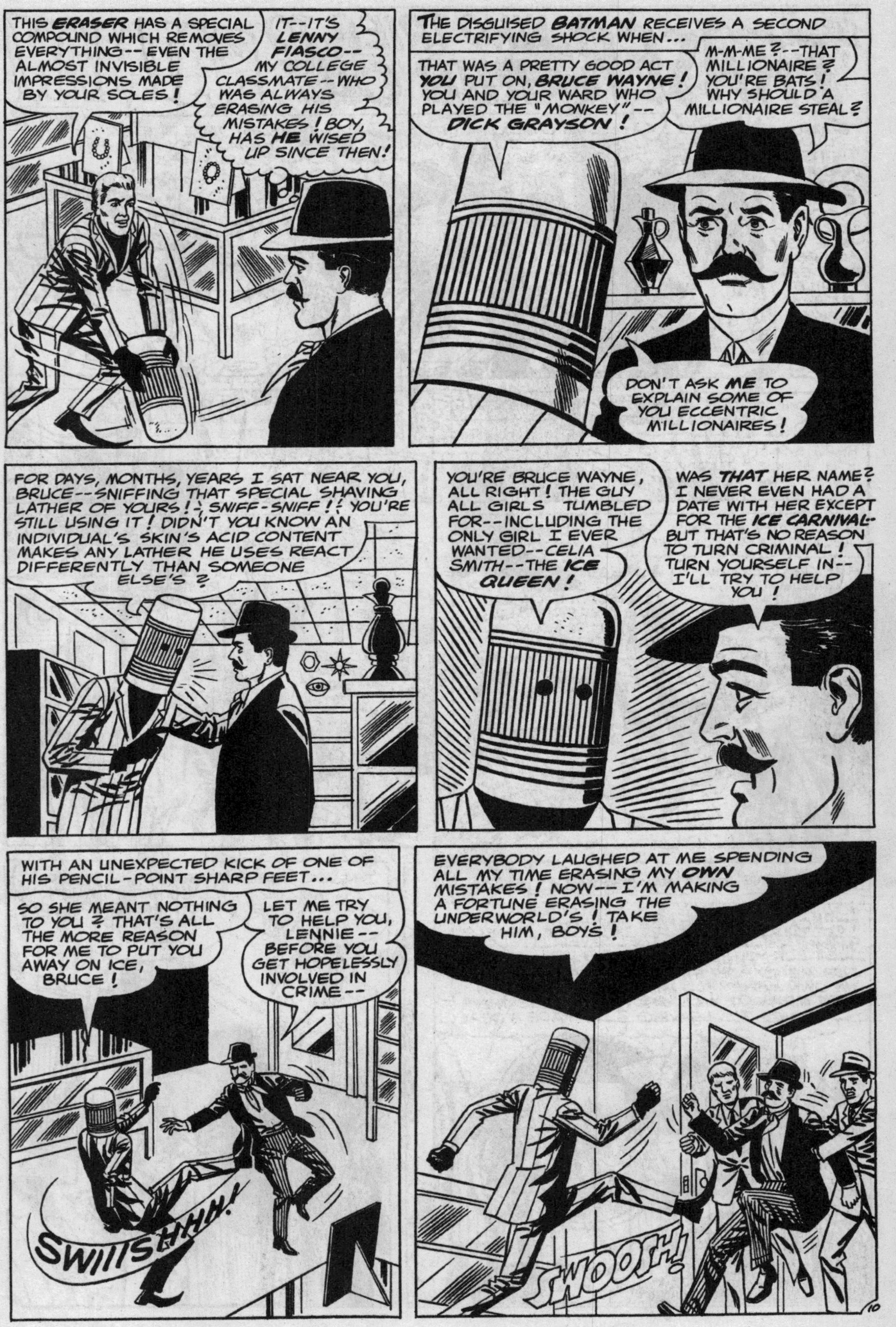
THIS ERASER HAS A SPECIAL COMPOUND WHICH REMOVES EVERYTHING-- EVEN THE ALMOST INVISIBLE IMPRESSIONS MADE BY YOUR SOLES!
IT--IT'S LENNY FIASCO-- MY COLLEGE CLASSMATE--WHO WAS ALWAYS ERASING HIS MISTAKES! BOY, HAS HE WISED UP SINCE THEN!
THE DISGUISED BATMAN RECEIVES A SECOND ELECTRIFYING SHOCK WHEN...
THAT WAS A PRETTY GOOD ACT YOU PUT ON, BRUCE WAYNE! YOU AND YOUR WARD WHO PLAYED THE "MONKEY"-- DICK GRAYSON!
M-M-ME?--THAT MILLIONAIRE? YOU'RE BATS! WHY SHOULD A MILLIONAIRE STEAL?
DON'T ASK ME TO EXPLAIN SOME OF YOU ECCENTRIC MILLIONAIRES!
FOR DAYS, MONTHS, YEARS I SAT NEAR YOU, BRUCE--SNIFFING THAT SPECIAL SHAVING LATHER OF YOURS! -SNIFF-SNIFF!- YOU'RE STILL USING IT! DIDN'T YOU KNOW AN INDIVIDUAL'S SKIN'S ACID CONTENT MAKES ANY LATHER HE USES REACT DIFFERENTLY THAN SOMEONE ELSE'S?
YOU'RE BRUCE WAYNE, ALL RIGHT! THE GUY ALL GIRLS TUMBLED FOR--INCLUDING THE ONLY GIRL I EVER WANTED--CELIA SMITH--THE ICE QUEEN!
WAS THAT HER NAME? I NEVER EVEN HAD A DATE WITH HER EXCEPT FOR THE ICE CARNIVAL-BUT THAT'S NO REASON TO TURN CRIMINAL! TURN YOURSELF IN-- I'LL TRY TO HELP YOU!
WITH AN UNEXPECTED KICK OF ONE OF HIS PENCIL-POINT SHARP FEET...
SO SHE MEANT NOTHING TO YOU? THAT'S ALL THE MORE REASON FOR ME TO PUT YOU AWAY ON ICE, BRUCE!
LET ME TRY TO HELP YOU, LENNIE-- BEFORE YOU GET HOPELESSLY INVOLVED IN CRIME--
SWIIISHHH!
EVERYBODY LAUGHED AT ME SPENDING ALL MY TIME ERASING MY OWN MISTAKES! NOW--I'M MAKING A FORTUNE ERASING THE UNDERWORLD'S! TAKE HIM, BOYS!
SWOOSH!
10

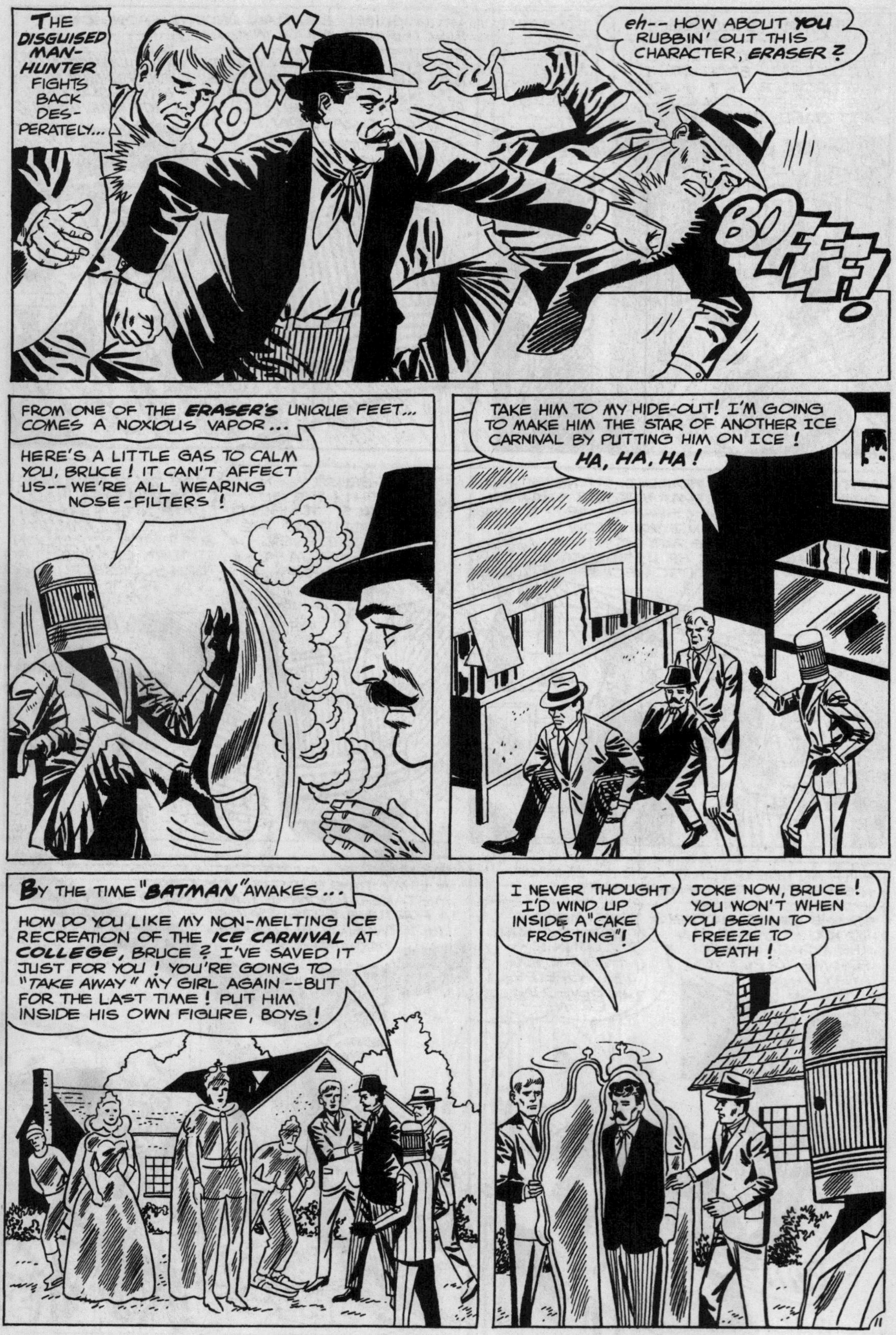
THE DISGUISED MAN-HUNTER FIGHTS BACK DES-PERATELY...
SOCK
eh-- HOW ABOUT YOU RUBBIN' OUT THIS CHARACTER, ERASER?
BOFFF!
FROM ONE OF THE ERASER'S UNIQUE FEET... COMES A NOXIOUS VAPOR...
HERE'S A LITTLE GAS TO CALM YOU, BRUCE! IT CAN'T AFFECT US-- WE'RE ALL WEARING NOSE-FILTERS!
TAKE HIM TO MY HIDE-OUT! I'M GOING TO MAKE HIM THE STAR OF ANOTHER ICE CARNIVAL BY PUTTING HIM ON ICE! HA, HA, HA!
BY THE TIME "BATMAN" AWAKES...
HOW DO YOU LIKE MY NON-MELTING ICE RECREATION OF THE ICE CARNIVAL AT COLLEGE, BRUCE? I'VE SAVED IT JUST FOR YOU! YOU'RE GOING TO "TAKE AWAY" MY GIRL AGAIN --BUT FOR THE LAST TIME! PUT HIM INSIDE HIS OWN FIGURE, BOYS!
I NEVER THOUGHT I'D WIND UP INSIDE A "CAKE FROSTING"!
JOKE NOW, BRUCE! YOU WON'T WHEN YOU BEGIN TO FREEZE TO DEATH!
11

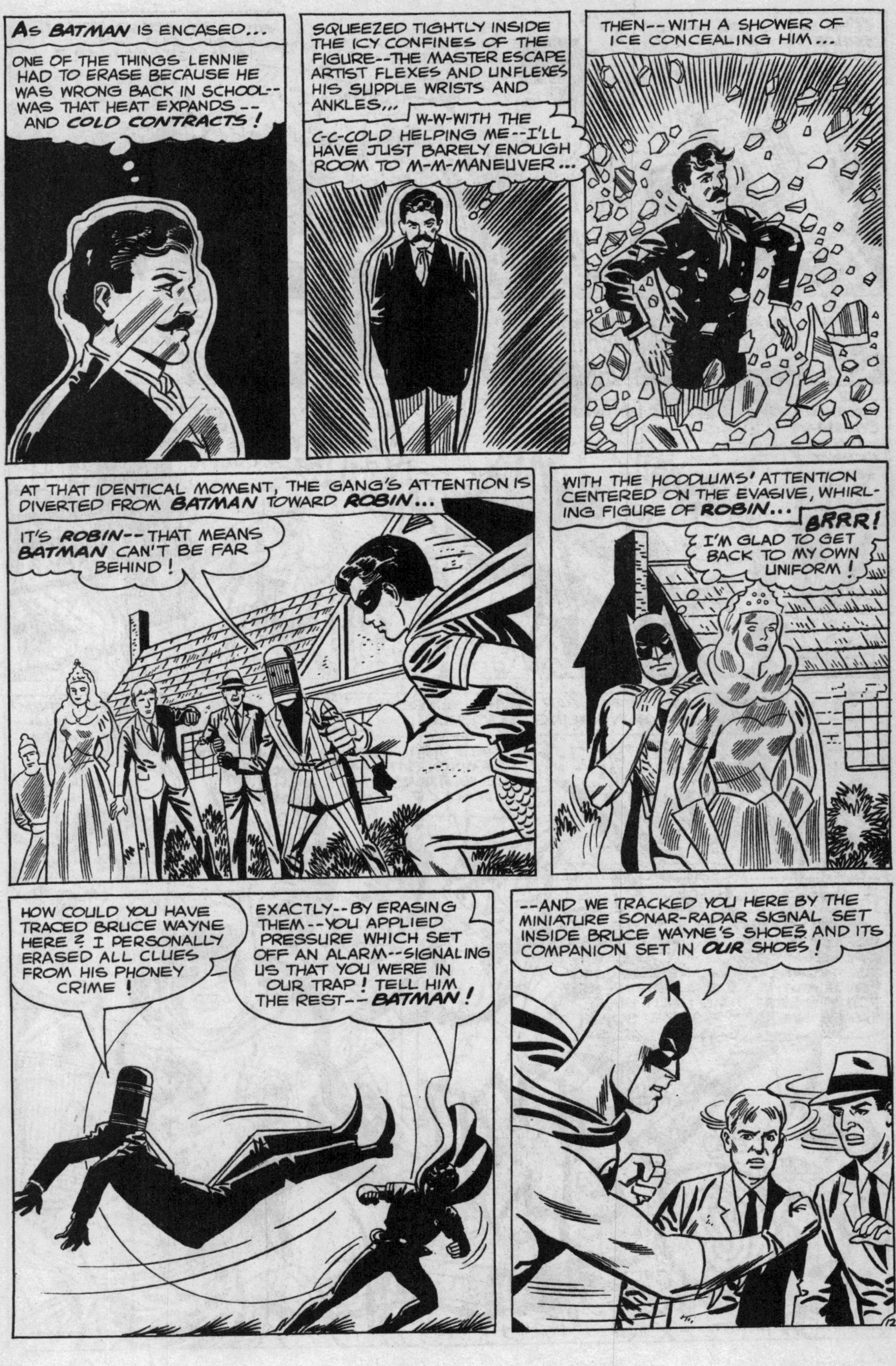
AS BATMAN IS ENCASED...
ONE OF THE THINGS LENNIE HAD TO ERASE BECAUSE HE WAS WRONG BACK IN SCHOOL--WAS THAT HEAT EXPANDS --AND COLD CONTRACTS!
SQUEEZED TIGHTLY INSIDE THE ICY CONFINES OF THE FIGURE--THE MASTER ESCAPE ARTIST FLEXES AND UNFLEXES HIS SUPPLE WRISTS AND ANKLES...
W-W-WITH THE C-C-COLD HELPING ME--I'LL HAVE JUST BARELY ENOUGH ROOM TO M-M-MANEUVER...
THEN--WITH A SHOWER OF ICE CONCEALING HIM...
AT THAT IDENTICAL MOMENT, THE GANG'S ATTENTION IS DIVERTED FROM BATMAN TOWARD ROBIN...
IT'S ROBIN--THAT MEANS BATMAN CAN'T BE FAR BEHIND!
WITH THE HOODLUMS' ATTENTION CENTERED ON THE EVASIVE, WHIRLING FIGURE OF ROBIN...
BRRR! I'M GLAD TO GET BACK TO MY OWN UNIFORM!
HOW COULD YOU HAVE TRACED BRUCE WAYNE HERE? I PERSONALLY ERASED ALL CLUES FROM HIS PHONEY CRIME!
EXACTLY--BY ERASING THEM--YOU APPLIED PRESSURE WHICH SET OFF AN ALARM--SIGNALING US THAT YOU WERE IN OUR TRAP! TELL HIM THE REST--BATMAN!
--AND WE TRACKED YOU HERE BY THE MINIATURE SONAR-RADAR SIGNAL SET INSIDE BRUCE WAYNE'S SHOES AND ITS COMPANION SET IN OUR SHOES!
12

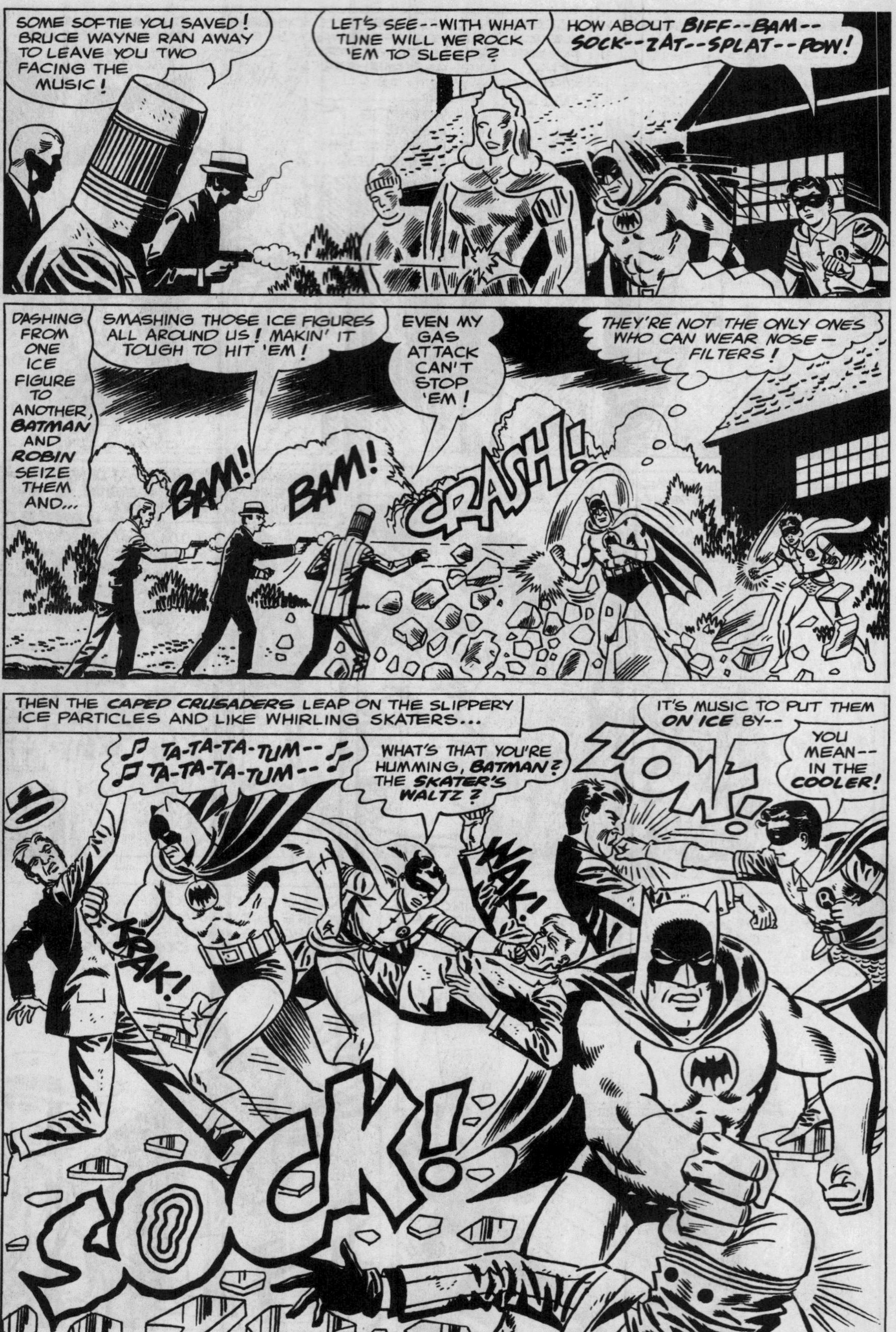
SOME SOFTIE YOU SAVED! BRUCE WAYNE RAN AWAY TO LEAVE YOU TWO FACING THE MUSIC!
LET'S SEE--WITH WHAT TUNE WILL WE ROCK 'EM TO SLEEP?
HOW ABOUT BIFF--BAM--SOCK--ZAT--SPLAT--POW!
DASHING FROM ONE ICE FIGURE TO ANOTHER, BATMAN AND ROBIN SEIZE THEM AND...
SMASHING THOSE ICE FIGURES ALL AROUND US! MAKIN' IT TOUGH TO HIT 'EM!
EVEN MY GAS ATTACK CAN'T STOP 'EM!
THEY'RE NOT THE ONLY ONES WHO CAN WEAR NOSE-FILTERS!
BAM!
BAM!
CRASH!
THEN THE CAPED CRUSADERS LEAP ON THE SLIPPERY ICE PARTICLES AND LIKE WHIRLING SKATERS...
♪ TA-TA-TA-TUM-- ♪ TA-TA-TA-TUM-- ♪
WHAT'S THAT YOU'RE HUMMING, BATMAN? THE SKATER'S WALTZ?
IT'S MUSIC TO PUT THEM ON ICE BY--
YOU MEAN--IN THE COOLER!
ZOK!
WAK!
KRAK!
SOCK!
13

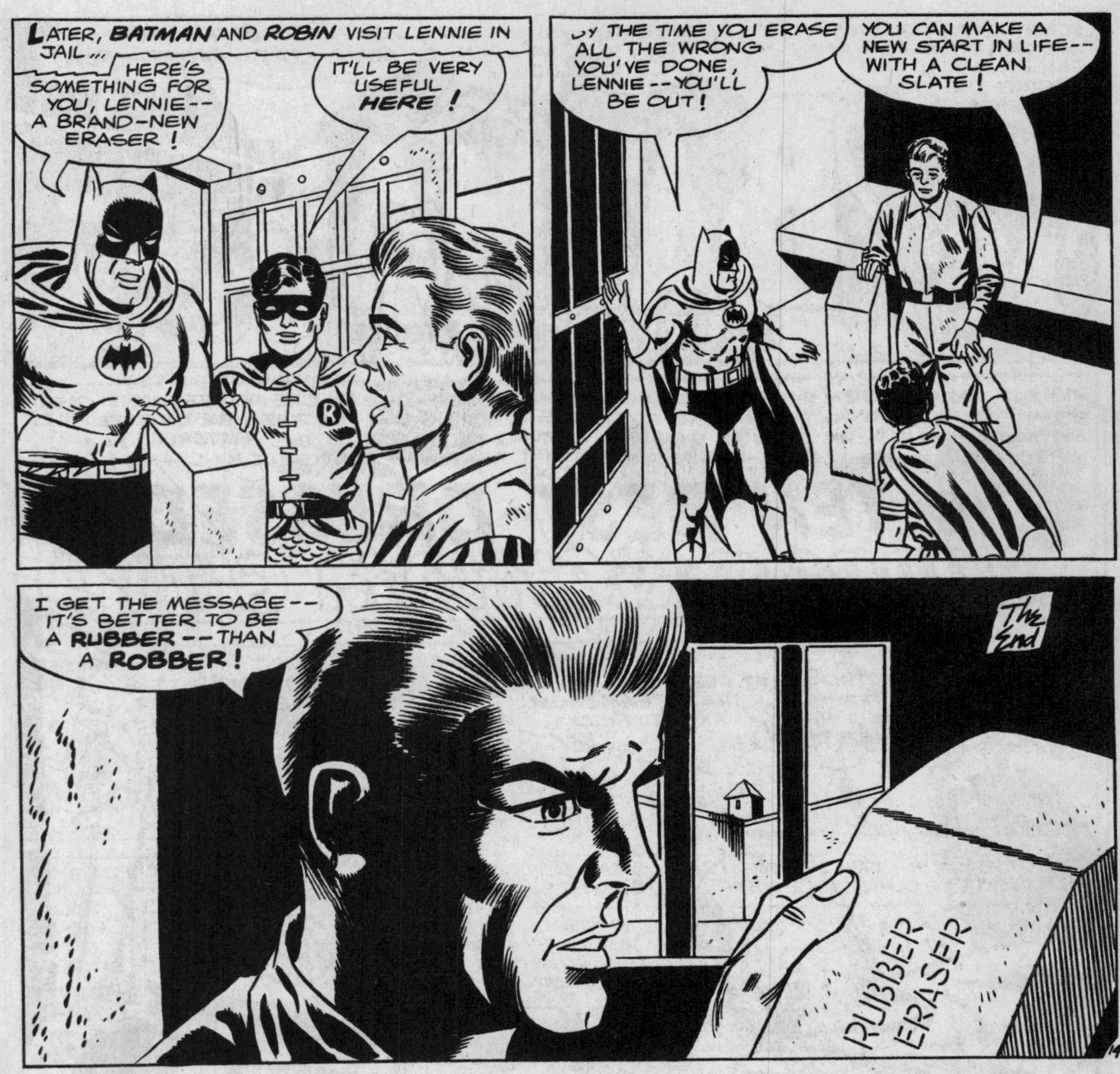
LATER, BATMAN AND ROBIN VISIT LENNIE IN JAIL...
HERE'S SOMETHING FOR YOU, LENNIE-- A BRAND-NEW ERASER!
IT'LL BE VERY USEFUL HERE!
BY THE TIME YOU ERASE ALL THE WRONG YOU'VE DONE, LENNIE--YOU'LL BE OUT!
YOU CAN MAKE A NEW START IN LIFE-- WITH A CLEAN SLATE!
I GET THE MESSAGE-- IT'S BETTER TO BE A RUBBER--THAN A ROBBER!
The End
RUBBER ERASER
14

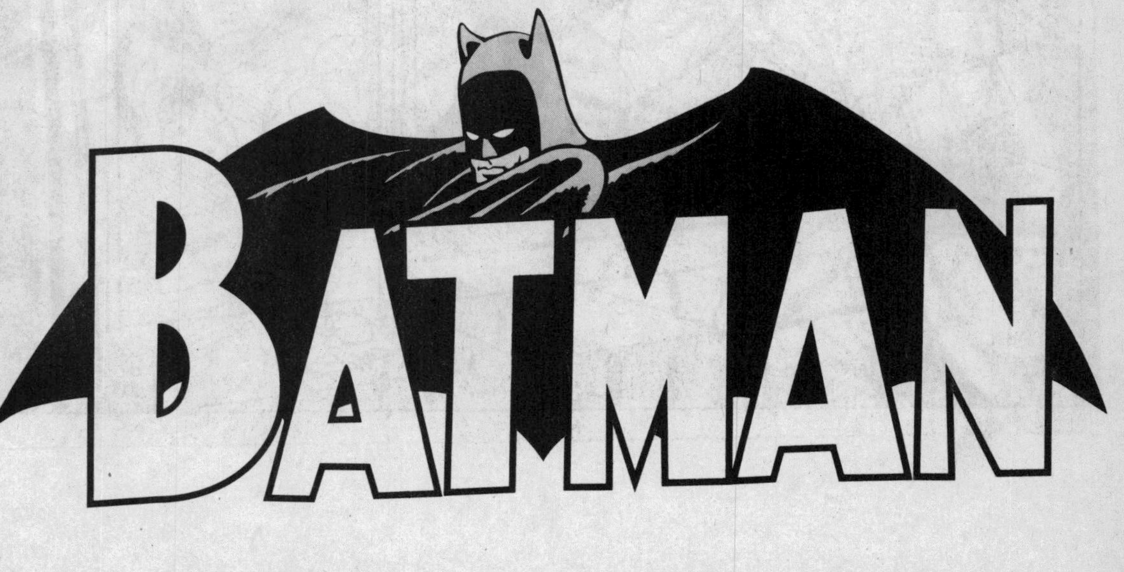
BATMAN

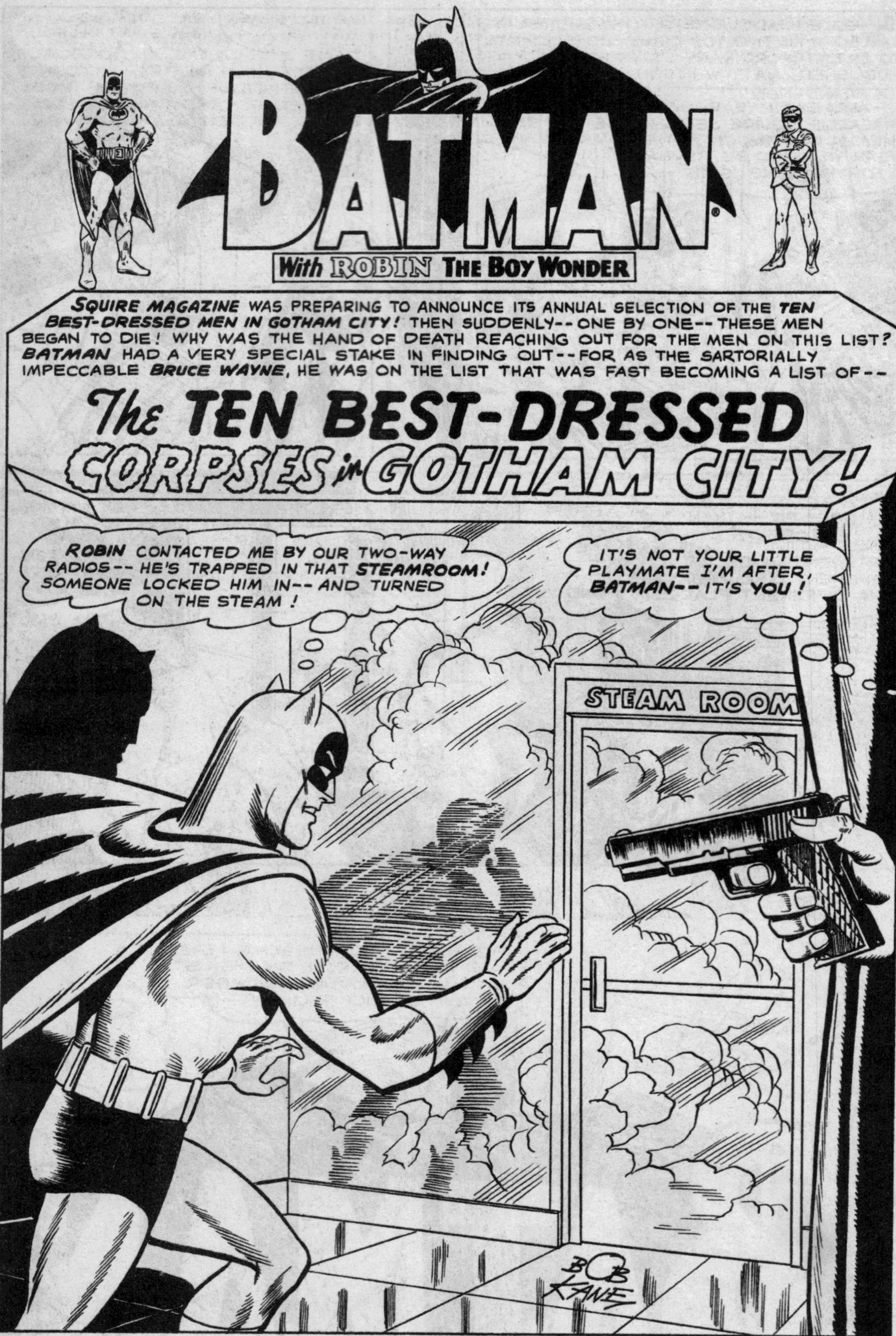
BATMAN
With ROBIN THE BOY WONDER
SQUIRE MAGAZINE WAS PREPARING TO ANNOUNCE ITS ANNUAL SELECTION OF THE TEN BEST-DRESSED MEN IN GOTHAM CITY! THEN SUDDENLY-- ONE BY ONE-- THESE MEN BEGAN TO DIE! WHY WAS THE HAND OF DEATH REACHING OUT FOR THE MEN ON THIS LIST? BATMAN HAD A VERY SPECIAL STAKE IN FINDING OUT--FOR AS THE SARTORIALLY IMPECCABLE BRUCE WAYNE, HE WAS ON THE LIST THAT WAS FAST BECOMING A LIST OF--
The TEN BEST-DRESSED CORPSES in GOTHAM CITY!
ROBIN CONTACTED ME BY OUR TWO-WAY RADIOS-- HE'S TRAPPED IN THAT STEAMROOM! SOMEONE LOCKED HIM IN-- AND TURNED ON THE STEAM!
IT'S NOT YOUR LITTLE PLAYMATE I'M AFTER, BATMAN-- IT'S YOU!
STEAM ROOM
BOB KANE

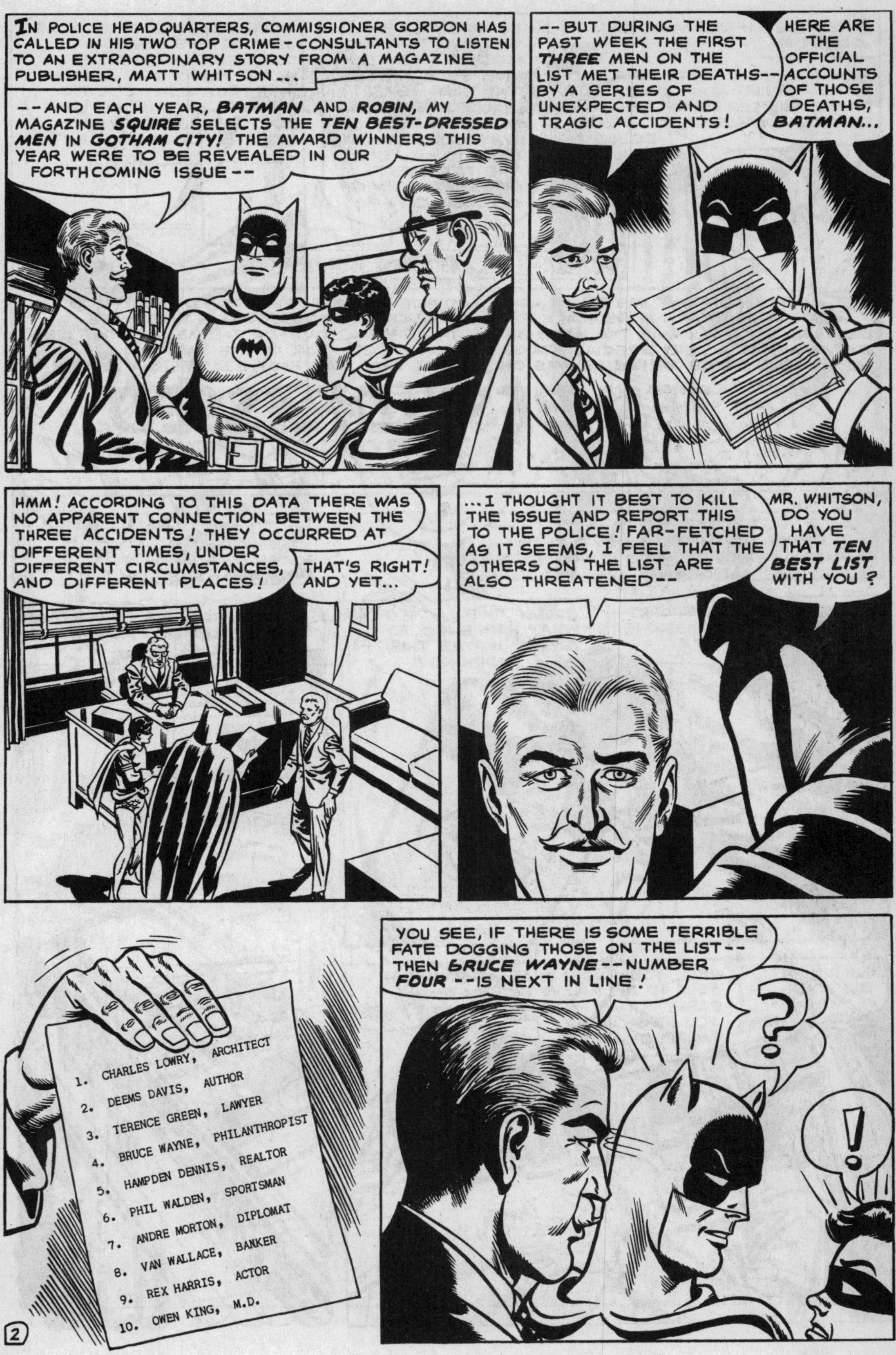
IN POLICE HEADQUARTERS, COMMISSIONER GORDON HAS CALLED IN HIS TWO TOP CRIME-CONSULTANTS TO LISTEN TO AN EXTRAORDINARY STORY FROM A MAGAZINE PUBLISHER, MATT WHITSON...
--AND EACH YEAR, BATMAN AND ROBIN, MY MAGAZINE SQUIRE SELECTS THE TEN BEST-DRESSED MEN IN GOTHAM CITY! THE AWARD WINNERS THIS YEAR WERE TO BE REVEALED IN OUR FORTHCOMING ISSUE--
--BUT DURING THE PAST WEEK THE FIRST THREE MEN ON THE LIST MET THEIR DEATHS--BY A SERIES OF UNEXPECTED AND TRAGIC ACCIDENTS!
HERE ARE THE OFFICIAL ACCOUNTS OF THOSE DEATHS, BATMAN...
HMM! ACCORDING TO THIS DATA THERE WAS NO APPARENT CONNECTION BETWEEN THE THREE ACCIDENTS! THEY OCCURRED AT DIFFERENT TIMES, UNDER DIFFERENT CIRCUMSTANCES, AND DIFFERENT PLACES!
THAT'S RIGHT! AND YET...
...I THOUGHT IT BEST TO KILL THE ISSUE AND REPORT THIS TO THE POLICE! FAR-FETCHED AS IT SEEMS, I FEEL THAT THE OTHERS ON THE LIST ARE ALSO THREATENED--
MR. WHITSON, DO YOU HAVE THAT TEN BEST LIST WITH YOU?
1. CHARLES LOWRY, ARCHITECT
2. DEEMS DAVIS, AUTHOR
3. TERENCE GREEN, LAWYER
4. BRUCE WAYNE, PHILANTHROPIST
5. HAMPDEN DENNIS, REALTOR
6. PHIL WALDEN, SPORTSMAN
7. ANDRE MORTON, DIPLOMAT
8. VAN WALLACE, BANKER
9. REX HARRIS, ACTOR
10. OWEN KING, M.D.
2
YOU SEE, IF THERE IS SOME TERRIBLE FATE DOGGING THOSE ON THE LIST--THEN BRUCE WAYNE--NUMBER FOUR--IS NEXT IN LINE!
?
!

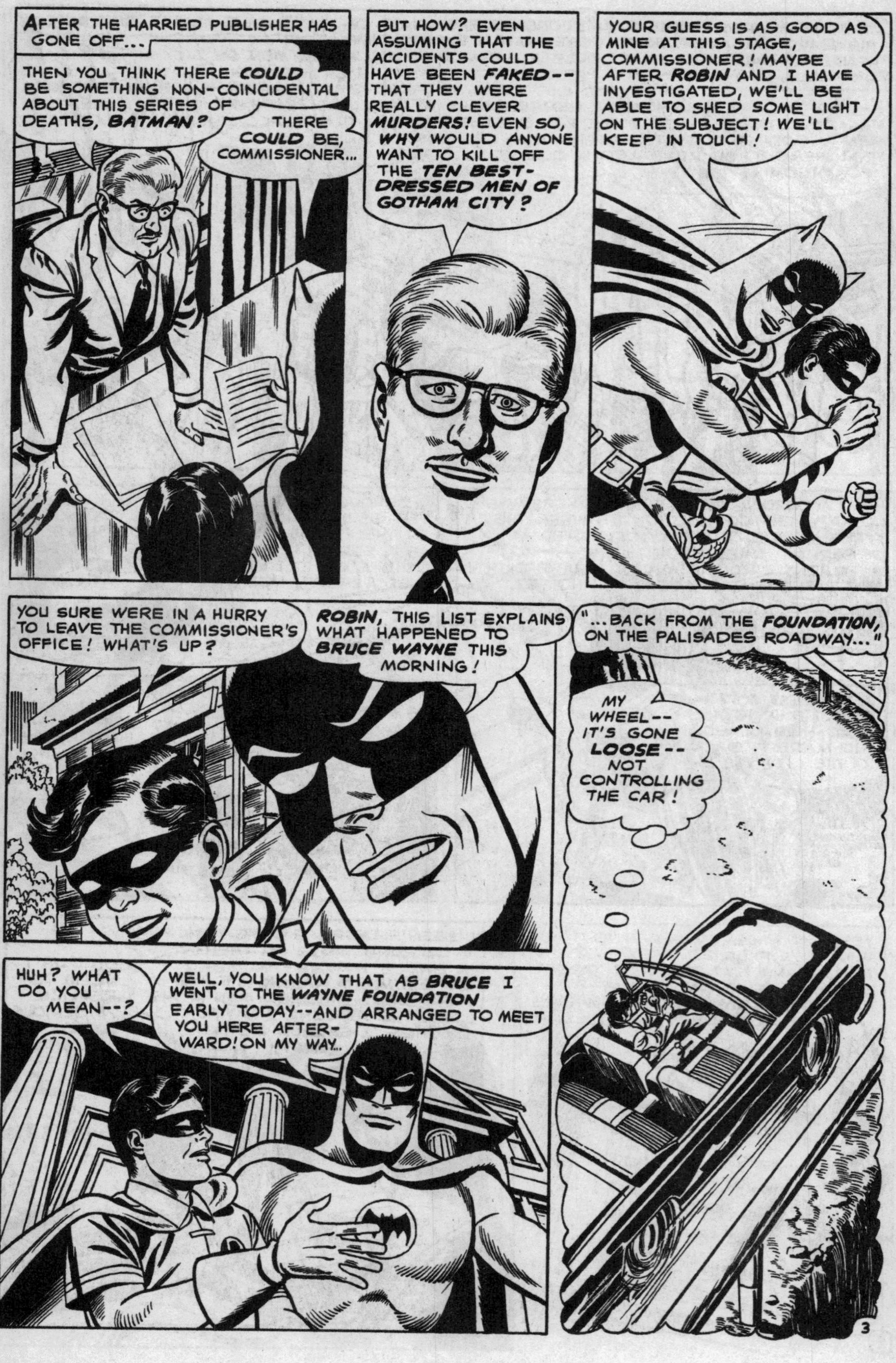
AFTER THE HARRIED PUBLISHER HAS GONE OFF...
THEN YOU THINK THERE COULD BE SOMETHING NON-COINCIDENTAL ABOUT THIS SERIES OF DEATHS, BATMAN?
THERE COULD BE, COMMISSIONER...
BUT HOW? EVEN ASSUMING THAT THE ACCIDENTS COULD HAVE BEEN FAKED--THAT THEY WERE REALLY CLEVER MURDERS! EVEN SO, WHY WOULD ANYONE WANT TO KILL OFF THE TEN BEST-DRESSED MEN OF GOTHAM CITY?
YOUR GUESS IS AS GOOD AS MINE AT THIS STAGE, COMMISSIONER! MAYBE AFTER ROBIN AND I HAVE INVESTIGATED, WE'LL BE ABLE TO SHED SOME LIGHT ON THE SUBJECT! WE'LL KEEP IN TOUCH!
YOU SURE WERE IN A HURRY TO LEAVE THE COMMISSIONER'S OFFICE! WHAT'S UP?
ROBIN, THIS LIST EXPLAINS WHAT HAPPENED TO BRUCE WAYNE THIS MORNING!
HUH? WHAT DO YOU MEAN--?
WELL, YOU KNOW THAT AS BRUCE I WENT TO THE WAYNE FOUNDATION EARLY TODAY--AND ARRANGED TO MEET YOU HERE AFTER-WARD! ON MY WAY...
"...BACK FROM THE FOUNDATION, ON THE PALISADES ROADWAY..."
MY WHEEL--IT'S GONE LOOSE--NOT CONTROLLING THE CAR!
3

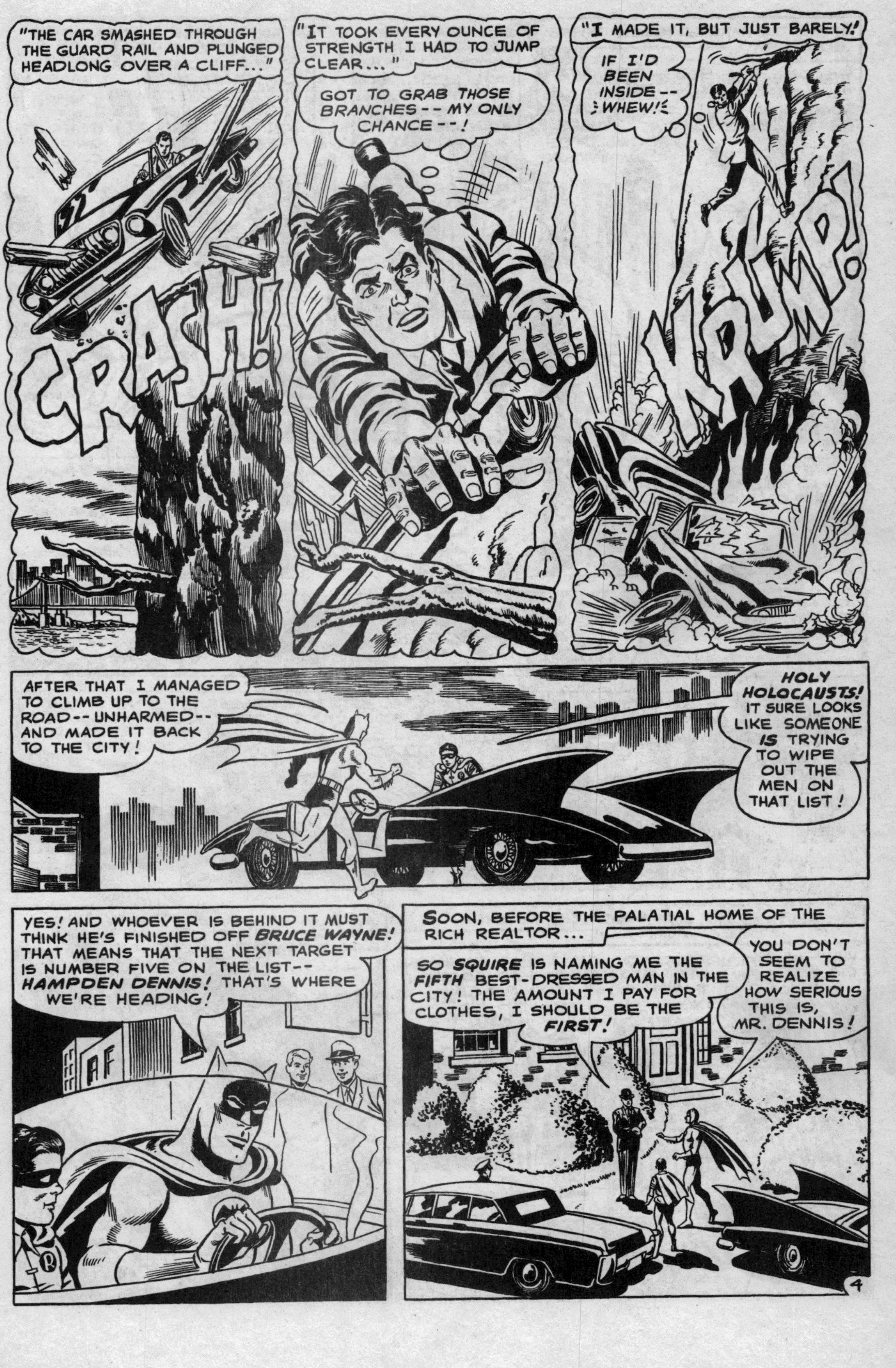
"THE CAR SMASHED THROUGH THE GUARD RAIL AND PLUNGED HEADLONG OVER A CLIFF..."
CRASH!
"IT TOOK EVERY OUNCE OF STRENGTH I HAD TO JUMP CLEAR..."
GOT TO GRAB THOSE BRANCHES -- MY ONLY CHANCE --!
"I MADE IT, BUT JUST BARELY!
IF I'D BEEN INSIDE -- WHEW!
KRUMP!
AFTER THAT I MANAGED TO CLIMB UP TO THE ROAD -- UNHARMED -- AND MADE IT BACK TO THE CITY!
HOLY HOLOCAUSTS! IT SURE LOOKS LIKE SOMEONE IS TRYING TO WIPE OUT THE MEN ON THAT LIST!
YES! AND WHOEVER IS BEHIND IT MUST THINK HE'S FINISHED OFF BRUCE WAYNE! THAT MEANS THAT THE NEXT TARGET IS NUMBER FIVE ON THE LIST-- HAMPDEN DENNIS! THAT'S WHERE WE'RE HEADING!
SOON, BEFORE THE PALATIAL HOME OF THE RICH REALTOR...
SO SQUIRE IS NAMING ME THE FIFTH BEST-DRESSED MAN IN THE CITY! THE AMOUNT I PAY FOR CLOTHES, I SHOULD BE THE FIRST!
YOU DON'T SEEM TO REALIZE HOW SERIOUS THIS IS, MR. DENNIS!
4

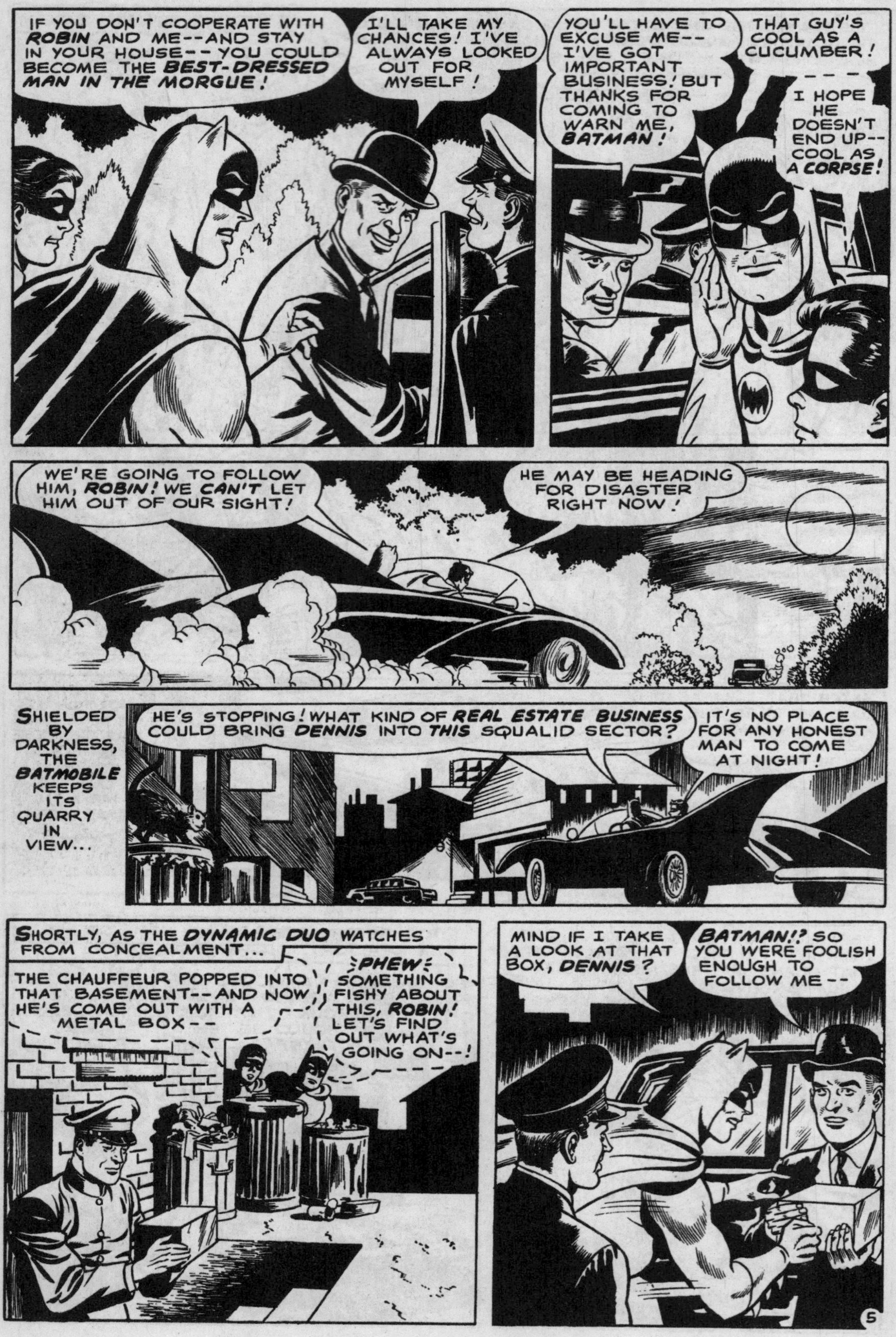
IF YOU DON'T COOPERATE WITH ROBIN AND ME--AND STAY IN YOUR HOUSE-- YOU COULD BECOME THE BEST-DRESSED MAN IN THE MORGUE!
I'LL TAKE MY CHANCES! I'VE ALWAYS LOOKED OUT FOR MYSELF!
YOU'LL HAVE TO EXCUSE ME-- I'VE GOT IMPORTANT BUSINESS! BUT THANKS FOR COMING TO WARN ME, BATMAN!
THAT GUY'S COOL AS A CUCUMBER!
I HOPE HE DOESN'T END UP--COOL AS A CORPSE!
WE'RE GOING TO FOLLOW HIM, ROBIN! WE CAN'T LET HIM OUT OF OUR SIGHT!
HE MAY BE HEADING FOR DISASTER RIGHT NOW!
SHIELDED BY DARKNESS, THE BATMOBILE KEEPS ITS QUARRY IN VIEW...
HE'S STOPPING! WHAT KIND OF REAL ESTATE BUSINESS COULD BRING DENNIS INTO THIS SQUALID SECTOR?
IT'S NO PLACE FOR ANY HONEST MAN TO COME AT NIGHT!
SHORTLY, AS THE DYNAMIC DUO WATCHES FROM CONCEALMENT...
THE CHAUFFEUR POPPED INTO THAT BASEMENT--AND NOW HE'S COME OUT WITH A METAL BOX--
PHEW SOMETHING FISHY ABOUT THIS, ROBIN! LET'S FIND OUT WHAT'S GOING ON--!
MIND IF I TAKE A LOOK AT THAT BOX, DENNIS?
BATMAN!? SO YOU WERE FOOLISH ENOUGH TO FOLLOW ME--
5

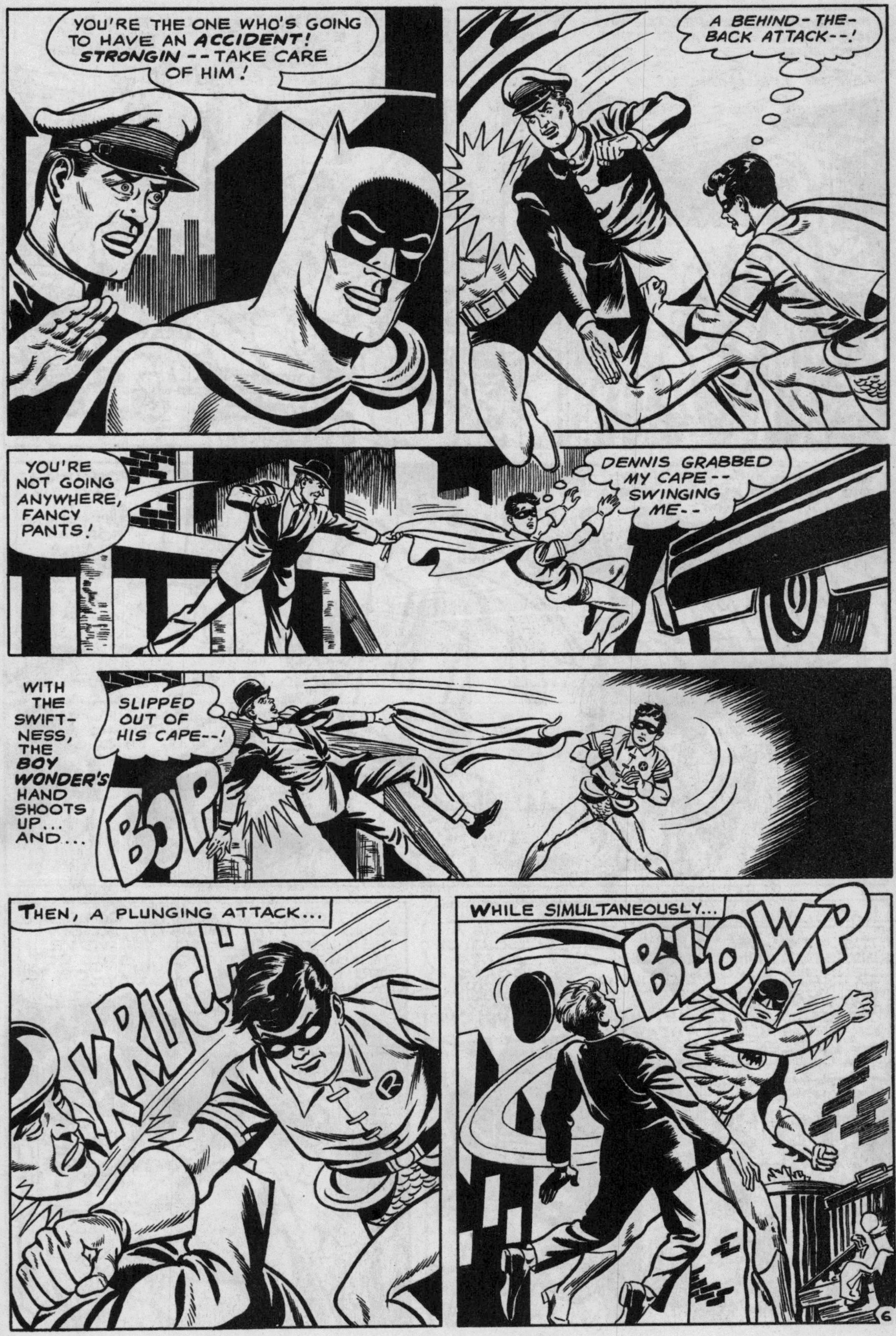
YOU'RE THE ONE WHO'S GOING TO HAVE AN ACCIDENT! STRONGIN --TAKE CARE OF HIM!
A BEHIND-THE-BACK ATTACK--!
YOU'RE NOT GOING ANYWHERE, FANCY PANTS!
DENNIS GRABBED MY CAPE-- SWINGING ME--
WITH THE SWIFTNESS, THE BOY WONDER'S HAND SHOOTS UP... AND...
SLIPPED OUT OF HIS CAPE--!
BOP!
THEN, A PLUNGING ATTACK...
KRUCH
WHILE SIMULTANEOUSLY...
BLOWP
6

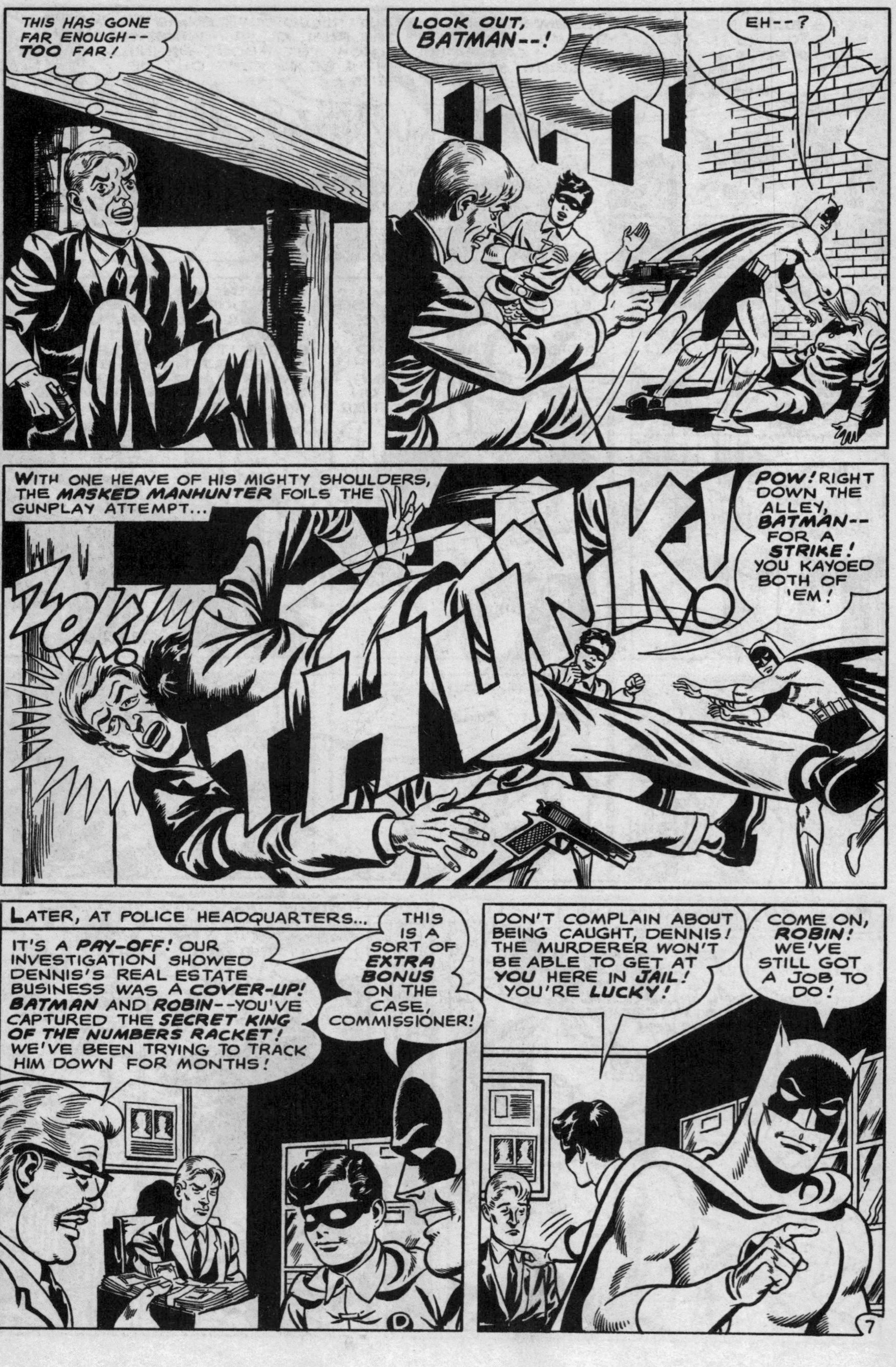
THIS HAS GONE FAR ENOUGH-- TOO FAR!
LOOK OUT, BATMAN--!
EH--?
WITH ONE HEAVE OF HIS MIGHTY SHOULDERS, THE MASKED MANHUNTER FOILS THE GUNPLAY ATTEMPT...
ZOK!
THUNK!
POW! RIGHT DOWN THE ALLEY, BATMAN-- FOR A STRIKE! YOU KAYOED BOTH OF 'EM!
LATER, AT POLICE HEADQUARTERS...
IT'S A PAY-OFF! OUR INVESTIGATION SHOWED DENNIS'S REAL ESTATE BUSINESS WAS A COVER-UP! BATMAN AND ROBIN--YOU'VE CAPTURED THE SECRET KING OF THE NUMBERS RACKET! WE'VE BEEN TRYING TO TRACK HIM DOWN FOR MONTHS!
THIS IS A SORT OF EXTRA BONUS ON THE CASE, COMMISSIONER!
DON'T COMPLAIN ABOUT BEING CAUGHT, DENNIS! THE MURDERER WON'T BE ABLE TO GET AT YOU HERE IN JAIL! YOU'RE LUCKY!
COME ON, ROBIN! WE'VE STILL GOT A JOB TO DO!
7

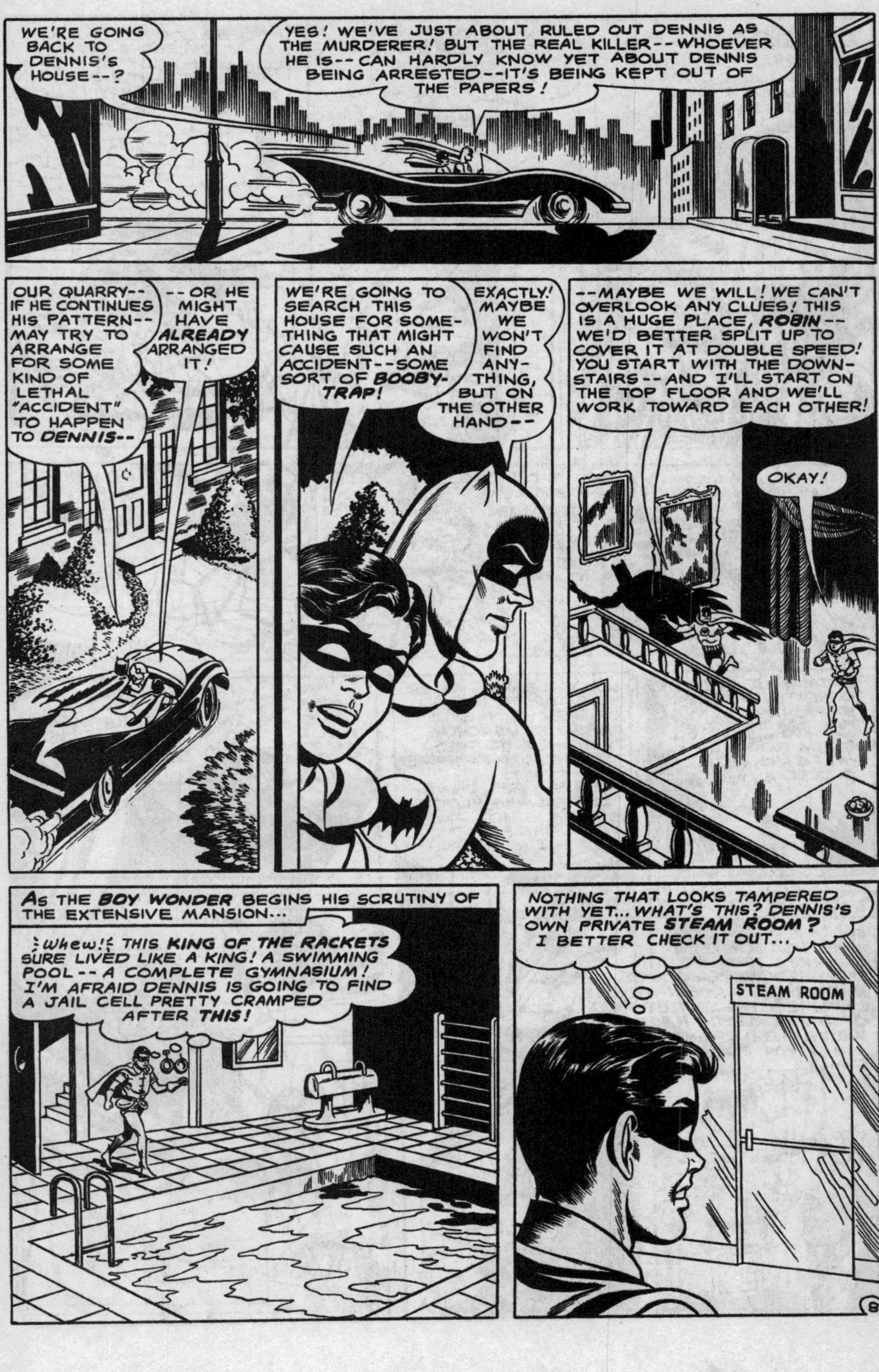
WE'RE GOING BACK TO DENNIS'S HOUSE--?
YES! WE'VE JUST ABOUT RULED OUT DENNIS AS THE MURDERER! BUT THE REAL KILLER--WHOEVER HE IS--CAN HARDLY KNOW YET ABOUT DENNIS BEING ARRESTED--IT'S BEING KEPT OUT OF THE PAPERS!
OUR QUARRY--IF HE CONTINUES HIS PATTERN--MAY TRY TO ARRANGE FOR SOME KIND OF LETHAL "ACCIDENT" TO HAPPEN TO DENNIS--
--OR HE MIGHT HAVE ALREADY ARRANGED IT!
WE'RE GOING TO SEARCH THIS HOUSE FOR SOMETHING THAT MIGHT CAUSE SUCH AN ACCIDENT--SOME SORT OF BOOBY-TRAP!
EXACTLY! MAYBE WE WON'T FIND ANYTHING, BUT ON THE OTHER HAND--
--MAYBE WE WILL! WE CAN'T OVERLOOK ANY CLUES! THIS IS A HUGE PLACE, ROBIN--WE'D BETTER SPLIT UP TO COVER IT AT DOUBLE SPEED! YOU START WITH THE DOWNSTAIRS--AND I'LL START ON THE TOP FLOOR AND WE'LL WORK TOWARD EACH OTHER!
OKAY!
AS THE BOY WONDER BEGINS HIS SCRUTINY OF THE EXTENSIVE MANSION...
Whew! THIS KING OF THE RACKETS SURE LIVED LIKE A KING! A SWIMMING POOL--A COMPLETE GYMNASIUM! I'M AFRAID DENNIS IS GOING TO FIND A JAIL CELL PRETTY CRAMPED AFTER THIS!
NOTHING THAT LOOKS TAMPERED WITH YET... WHAT'S THIS? DENNIS'S OWN PRIVATE STEAM ROOM? I BETTER CHECK IT OUT...
STEAM ROOM
8

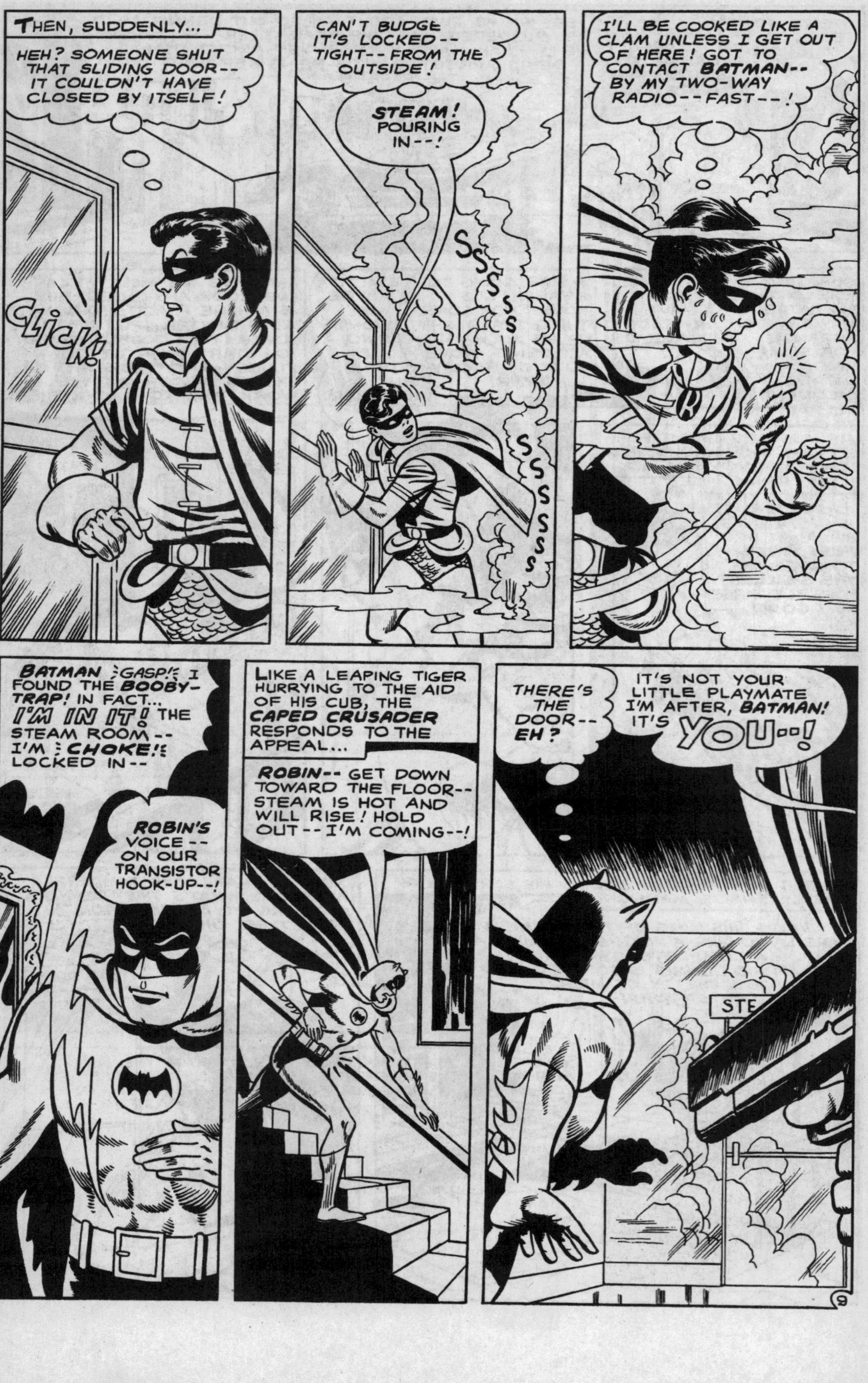
THEN, SUDDENLY...
HEH? SOMEONE SHUT THAT SLIDING DOOR-- IT COULDN'T HAVE CLOSED BY ITSELF!
CLICK!
CAN'T BUDGE IT'S LOCKED-- TIGHT--FROM THE OUTSIDE!
STEAM! POURING IN--!
SSSSSS
SSSSSSSS
I'LL BE COOKED LIKE A CLAM UNLESS I GET OUT OF HERE! GOT TO CONTACT BATMAN-- BY MY TWO-WAY RADIO--FAST--!
BATMAN :GASP!: I FOUND THE BOOBY-TRAP! IN FACT... I'M IN IT! THE STEAM ROOM-- I'M :CHOKE!: LOCKED IN--
ROBIN'S VOICE-- ON OUR TRANSISTOR HOOK-UP--!
LIKE A LEAPING TIGER HURRYING TO THE AID OF HIS CUB, THE CAPED CRUSADER RESPONDS TO THE APPEAL...
ROBIN-- GET DOWN TOWARD THE FLOOR-- STEAM IS HOT AND WILL RISE! HOLD OUT--I'M COMING--!
THERE'S THE DOOR-- EH?
IT'S NOT YOUR LITTLE PLAYMATE I'M AFTER, BATMAN! IT'S YOU--!
STE
9

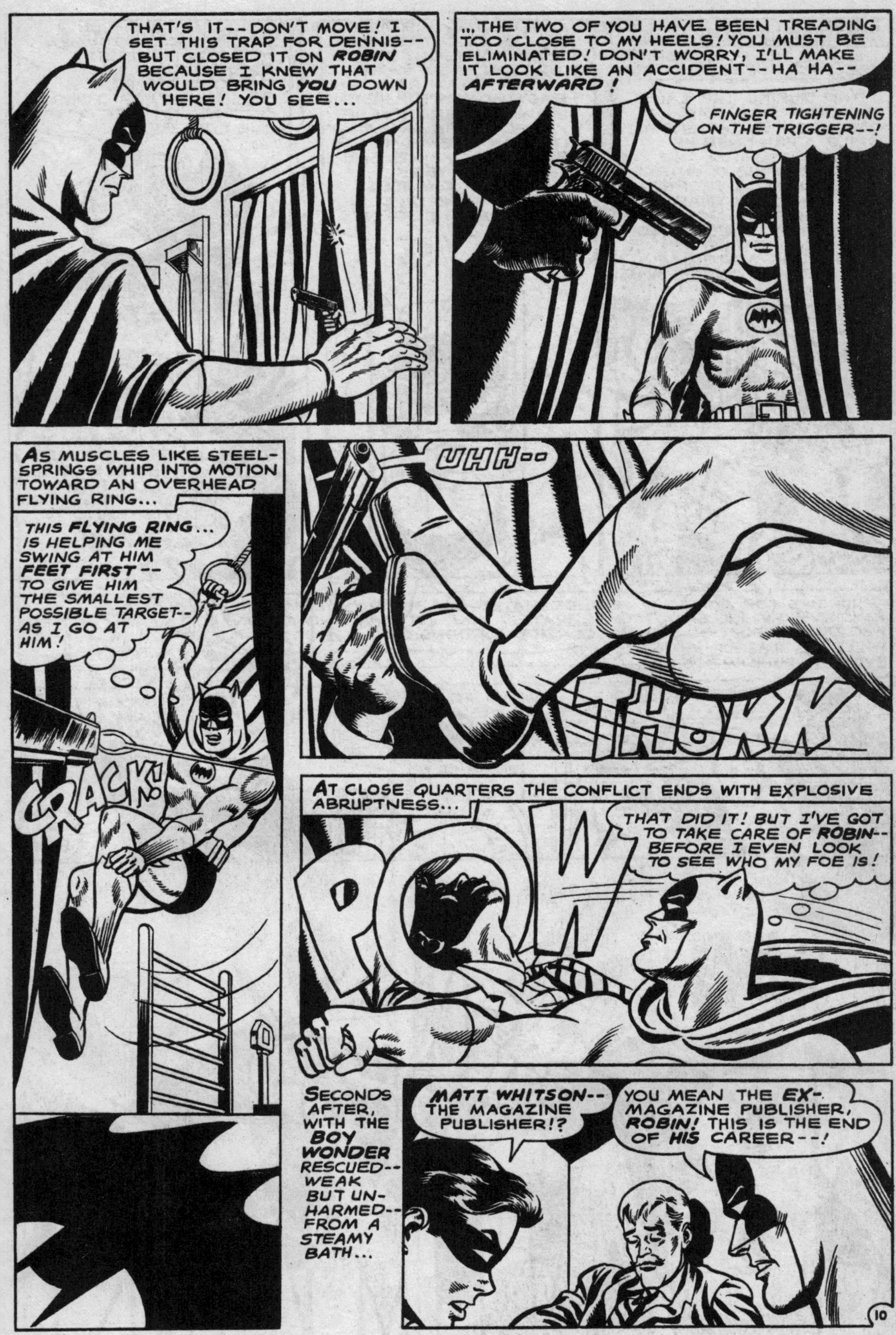
THAT'S IT--DON'T MOVE! I SET THIS TRAP FOR DENNIS--BUT CLOSED IT ON ROBIN BECAUSE I KNEW THAT WOULD BRING YOU DOWN HERE! YOU SEE...
...THE TWO OF YOU HAVE BEEN TREADING TOO CLOSE TO MY HEELS! YOU MUST BE ELIMINATED! DON'T WORRY, I'LL MAKE IT LOOK LIKE AN ACCIDENT--HA HA--AFTERWARD!
FINGER TIGHTENING ON THE TRIGGER--!
AS MUSCLES LIKE STEEL-SPRINGS WHIP INTO MOTION TOWARD AN OVERHEAD FLYING RING...
THIS FLYING RING... IS HELPING ME SWING AT HIM FEET FIRST--TO GIVE HIM THE SMALLEST POSSIBLE TARGET--AS I GO AT HIM!
CRACK!
UHH--
THOKK
AT CLOSE QUARTERS THE CONFLICT ENDS WITH EXPLOSIVE ABRUPTNESS...
POW
THAT DID IT! BUT I'VE GOT TO TAKE CARE OF ROBIN--BEFORE I EVEN LOOK TO SEE WHO MY FOE IS!
SECONDS AFTER, WITH THE BOY WONDER RESCUED--WEAK BUT UNHARMED--FROM A STEAMY BATH...
MATT WHITSON--THE MAGAZINE PUBLISHER!?
YOU MEAN THE EX-MAGAZINE PUBLISHER, ROBIN! THIS IS THE END OF HIS CAREER--!
10

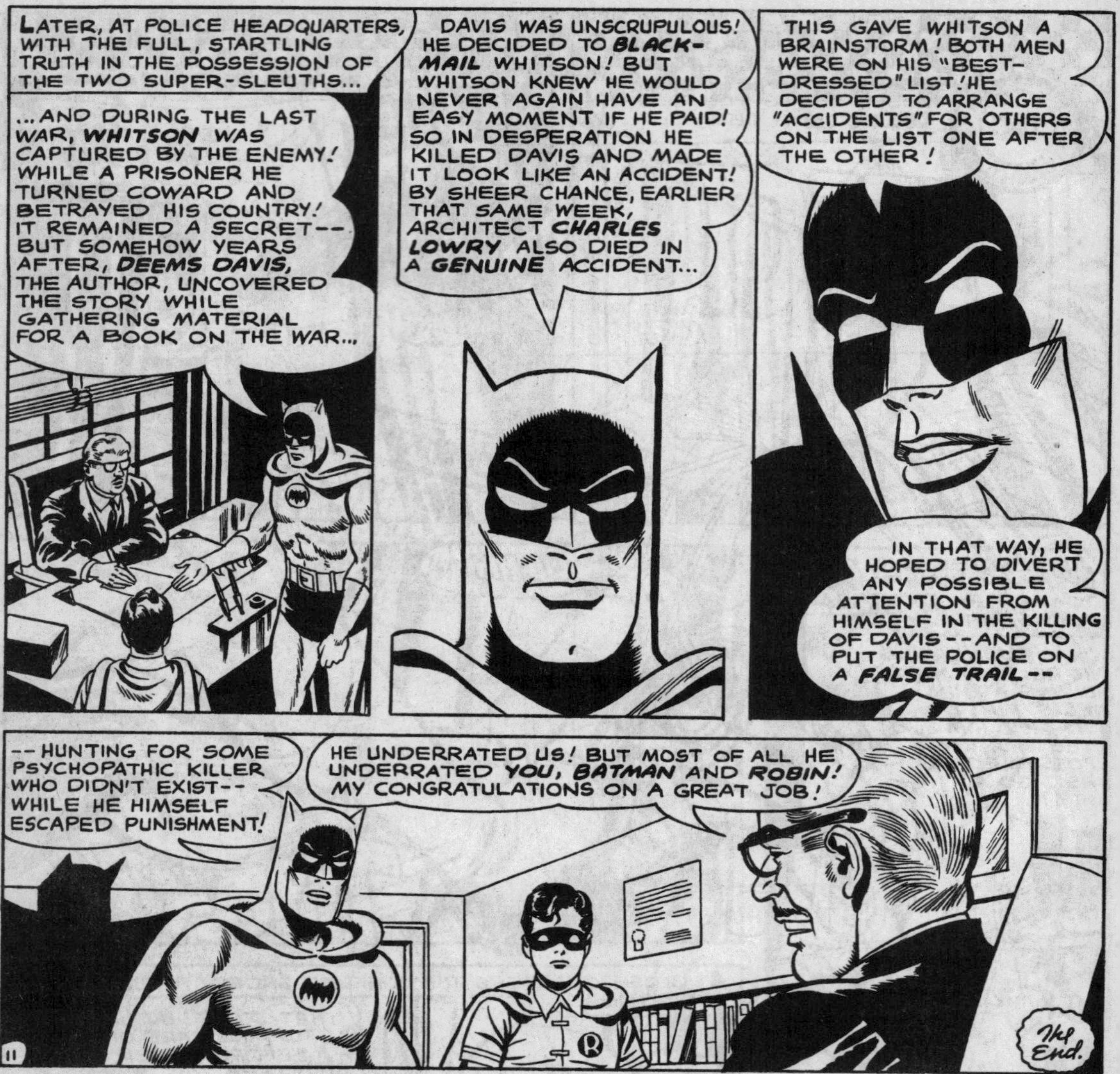
LATER, AT POLICE HEADQUARTERS, WITH THE FULL, STARTLING TRUTH IN THE POSSESSION OF THE TWO SUPER-SLEUTHS...
...AND DURING THE LAST WAR, WHITSON WAS CAPTURED BY THE ENEMY! WHILE A PRISONER HE TURNED COWARD AND BETRAYED HIS COUNTRY! IT REMAINED A SECRET-- BUT SOMEHOW YEARS AFTER, DEEMS DAVIS, THE AUTHOR, UNCOVERED THE STORY WHILE GATHERING MATERIAL FOR A BOOK ON THE WAR...
DAVIS WAS UNSCRUPULOUS! HE DECIDED TO BLACKMAIL WHITSON! BUT WHITSON KNEW HE WOULD NEVER AGAIN HAVE AN EASY MOMENT IF HE PAID! SO IN DESPERATION HE KILLED DAVIS AND MADE IT LOOK LIKE AN ACCIDENT! BY SHEER CHANCE, EARLIER THAT SAME WEEK, ARCHITECT CHARLES LOWRY ALSO DIED IN A GENUINE ACCIDENT...
THIS GAVE WHITSON A BRAINSTORM! BOTH MEN WERE ON HIS "BEST-DRESSED" LIST! HE DECIDED TO ARRANGE "ACCIDENTS" FOR OTHERS ON THE LIST ONE AFTER THE OTHER!
IN THAT WAY, HE HOPED TO DIVERT ANY POSSIBLE ATTENTION FROM HIMSELF IN THE KILLING OF DAVIS--AND TO PUT THE POLICE ON A FALSE TRAIL--
--HUNTING FOR SOME PSYCHOPATHIC KILLER WHO DIDN'T EXIST--WHILE HE HIMSELF ESCAPED PUNISHMENT!
HE UNDERRATED US! BUT MOST OF ALL HE UNDERRATED YOU, BATMAN AND ROBIN! MY CONGRATULATIONS ON A GREAT JOB!
11
The End.

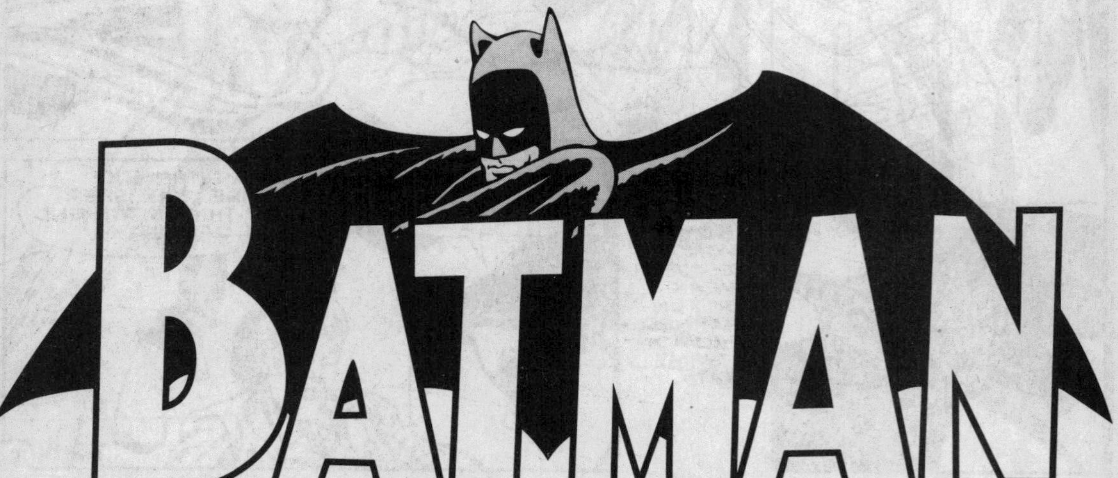
BATMAN

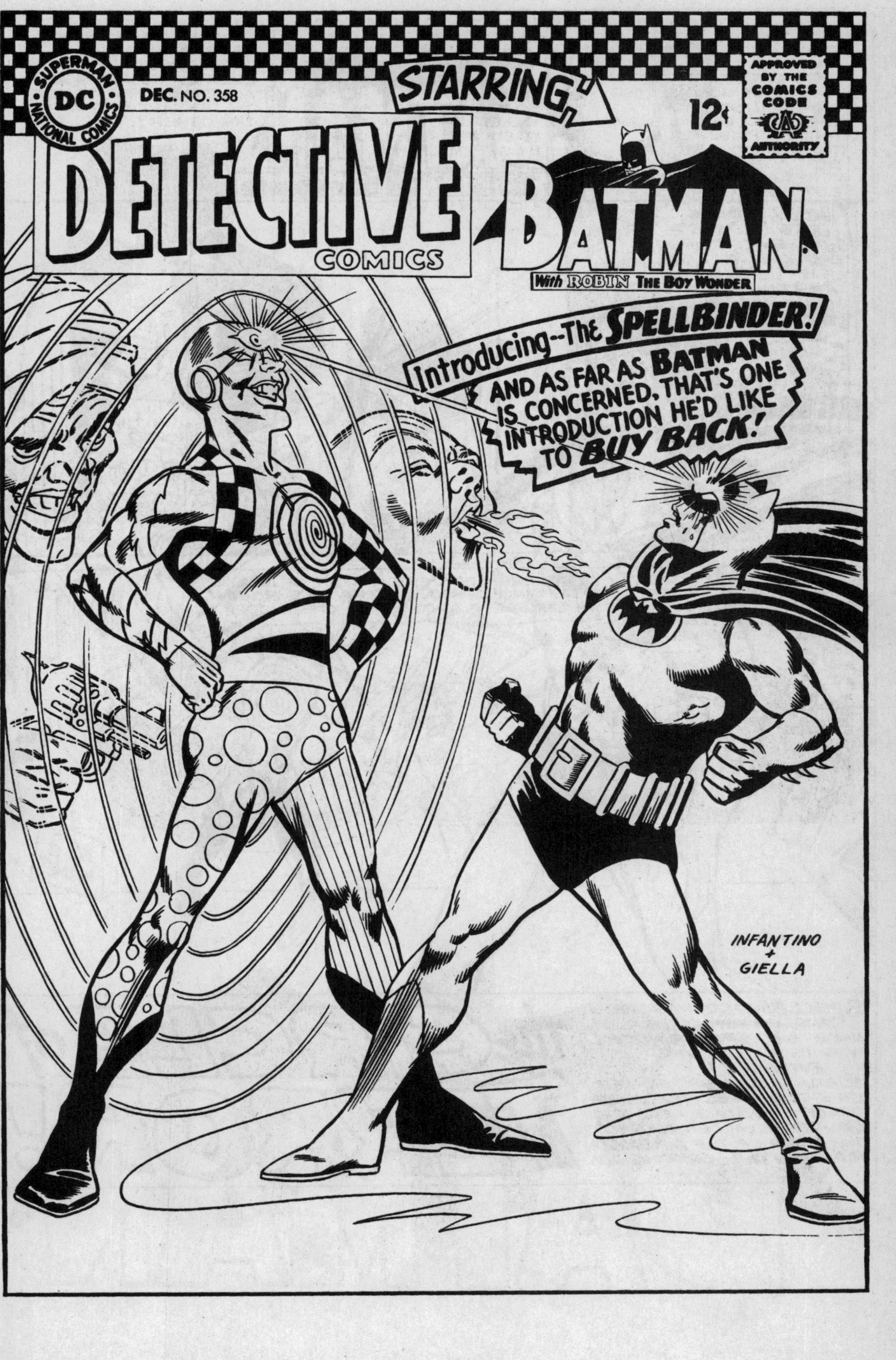
SUPERMAN DC NATIONAL COMICS
DEC. NO. 358
STARRING
12¢
APPROVED BY THE COMICS CODE AUTHORITY
DETECTIVE COMICS
BATMAN
With ROBIN The Boy Wonder
Introducing--The SPELLBINDER!
AND AS FAR AS BATMAN IS CONCERNED, THAT'S ONE INTRODUCTION HE'D LIKE TO BUY BACK!
INFANTINO + GIELLA

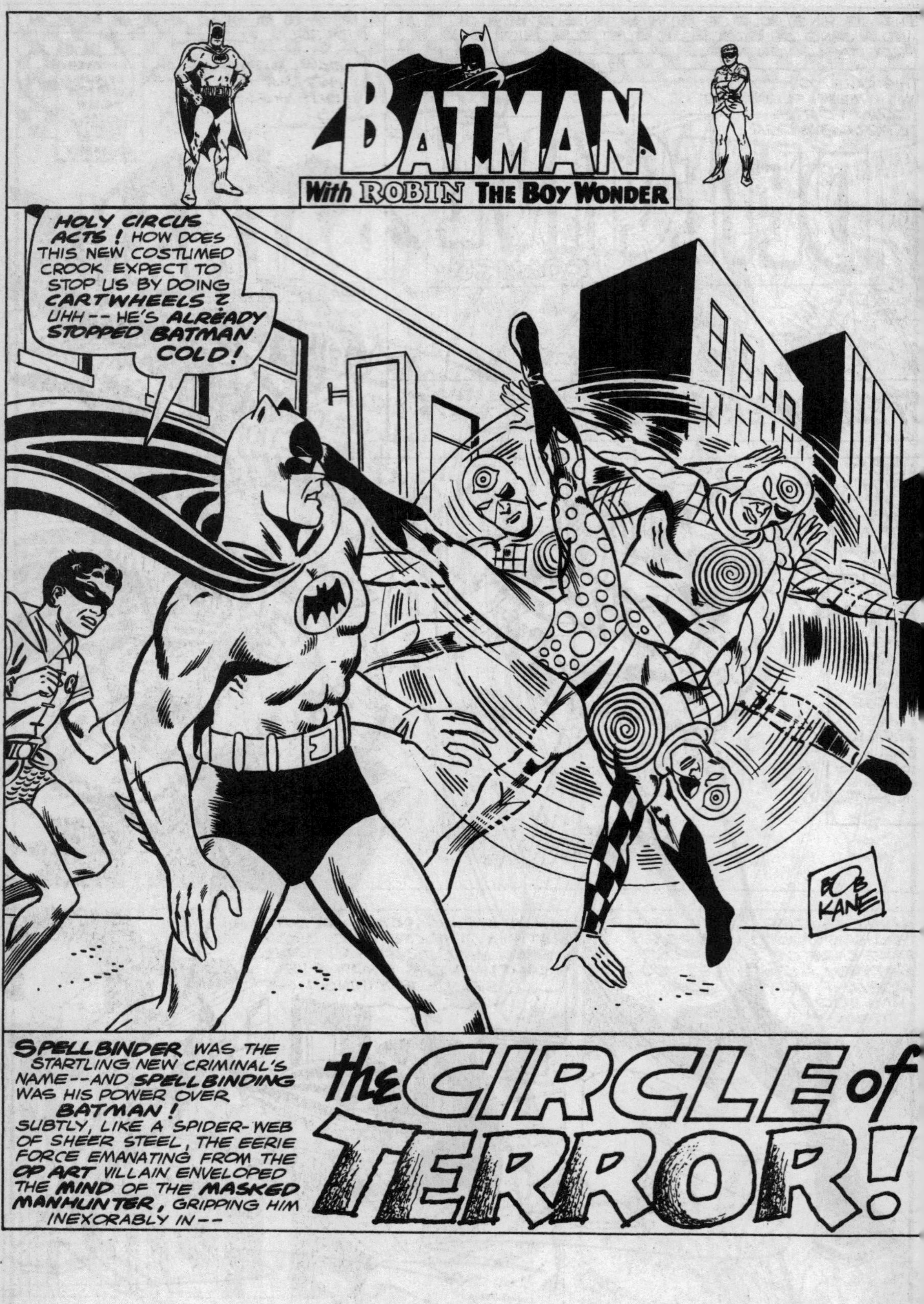
BATMAN
With ROBIN THE BOY WONDER
HOLY CIRCUS ACTS! HOW DOES THIS NEW COSTUMED CROOK EXPECT TO STOP US BY DOING CARTWHEELS? UHH--HE'S ALREADY STOPPED BATMAN COLD!
BOB KANE
SPELLBINDER WAS THE STARTLING NEW CRIMINAL'S NAME--AND SPELLBINDING WAS HIS POWER OVER BATMAN! SUBTLY, LIKE A SPIDER-WEB OF SHEER STEEL, THE EERIE FORCE EMANATING FROM THE OP ART VILLAIN ENVELOPED THE MIND OF THE MASKED MANHUNTER, GRIPPING HIM INEXORABLY IN--
the CIRCLE of TERROR!

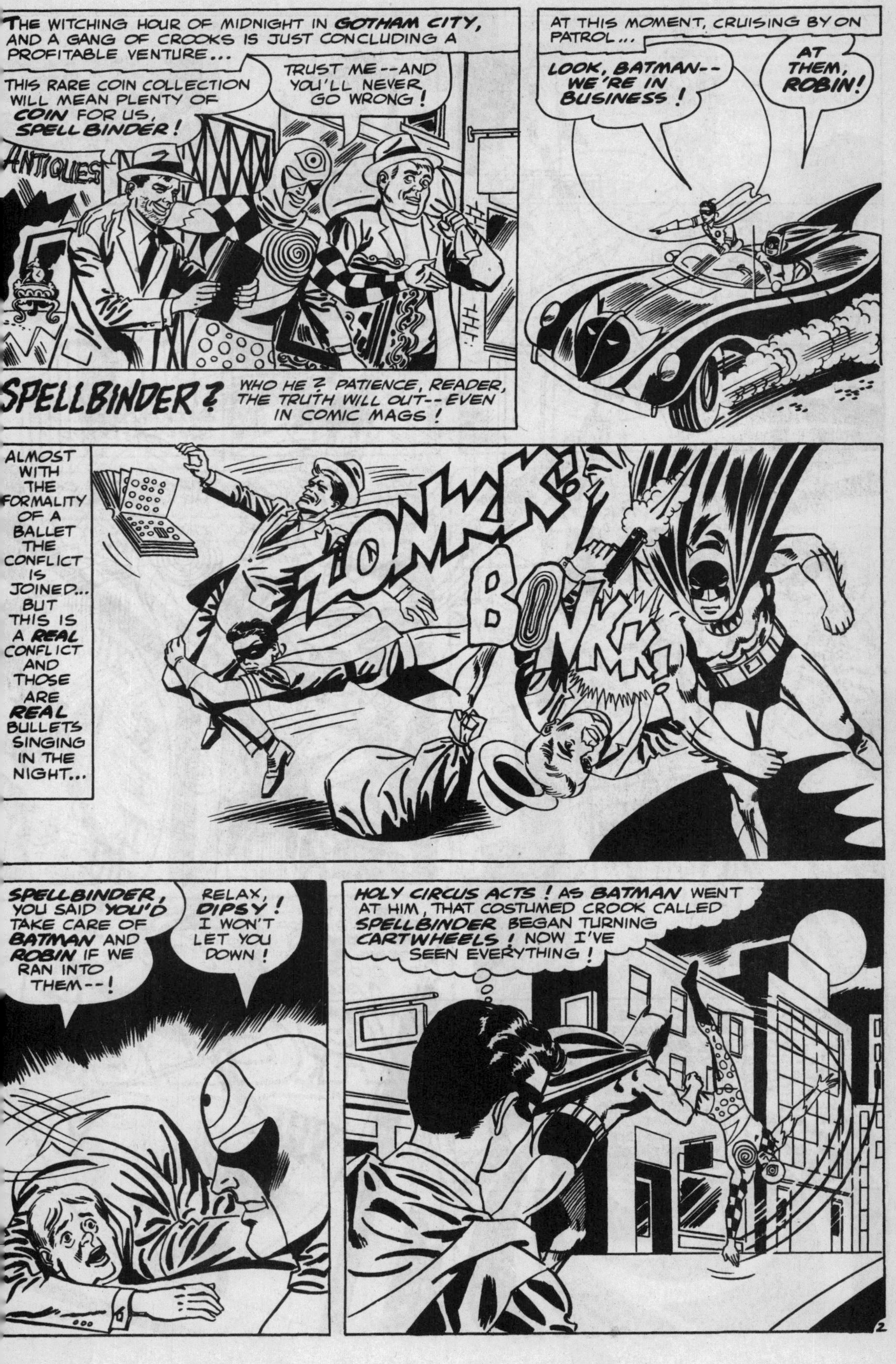

THE WITCHING HOUR OF MIDNIGHT IN GOTHAM CITY, AND A GANG OF CROOKS IS JUST CONCLUDING A PROFITABLE VENTURE...
THIS RARE COIN COLLECTION WILL MEAN PLENTY OF COIN FOR US, SPELLBINDER!
TRUST ME--AND YOU'LL NEVER GO WRONG!
ANTIQUES
SPELLBINDER? WHO HE? PATIENCE, READER, THE TRUTH WILL OUT--EVEN IN COMIC MAGS!
AT THIS MOMENT, CRUISING BY ON PATROL...
LOOK, BATMAN--WE'RE IN BUSINESS!
AT THEM, ROBIN!
ALMOST WITH THE FORMALITY OF A BALLET THE CONFLICT IS JOINED... BUT THIS IS A REAL CONFLICT AND THOSE ARE REAL BULLETS SINGING IN THE NIGHT...
ZONKK!
BONKK!
SPELLBINDER, YOU SAID YOU'D TAKE CARE OF BATMAN AND ROBIN IF WE RAN INTO THEM--!
RELAX, DIPSY! I WON'T LET YOU DOWN!
HOLY CIRCUS ACTS! AS BATMAN WENT AT HIM, THAT COSTUMED CROOK CALLED SPELLBINDER BEGAN TURNING CARTWHEELS! NOW I'VE SEEN EVERYTHING!
2

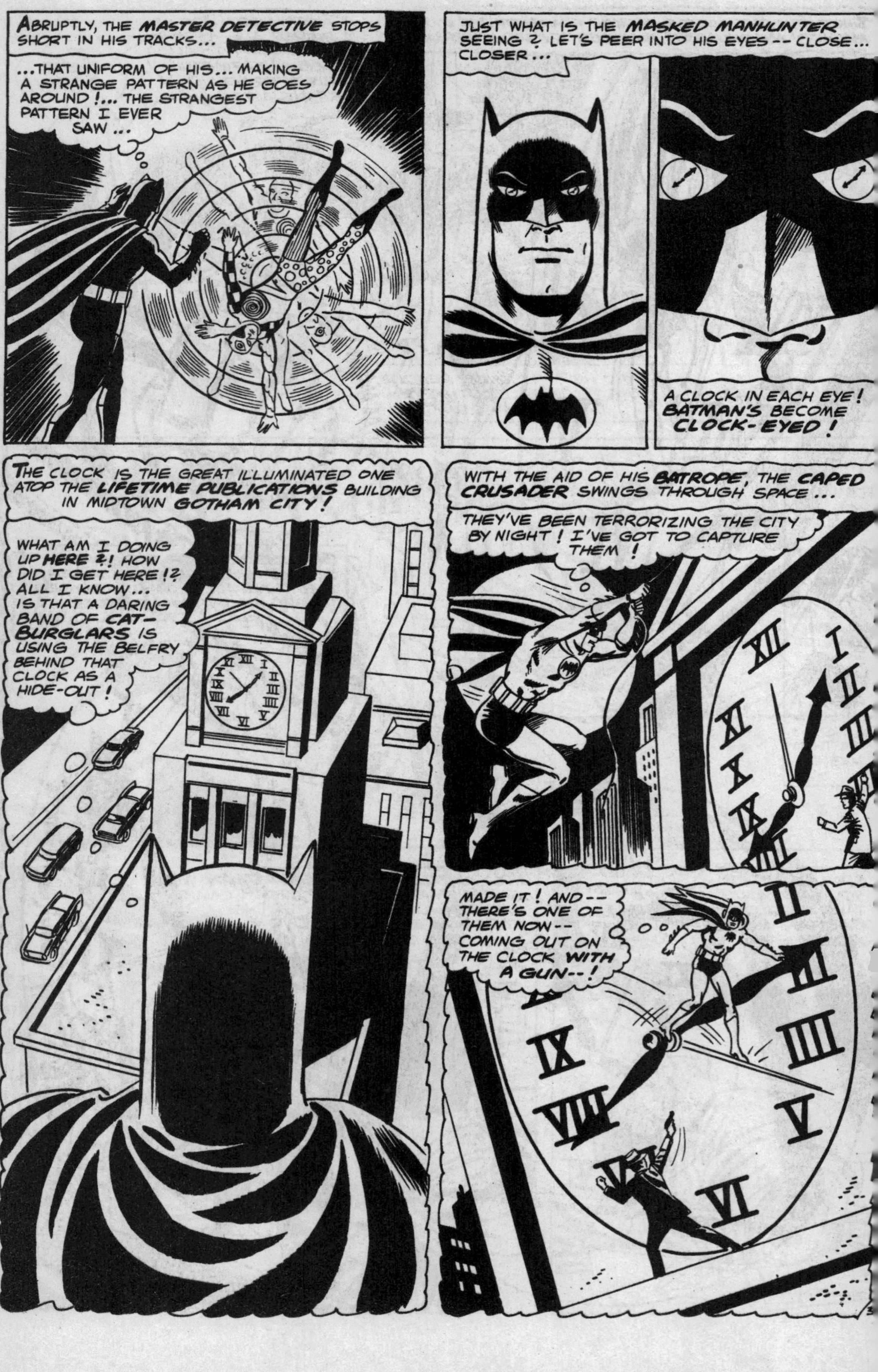
ABRUPTLY, THE MASTER DETECTIVE STOPS SHORT IN HIS TRACKS...
...THAT UNIFORM OF HIS... MAKING A STRANGE PATTERN AS HE GOES AROUND!... THE STRANGEST PATTERN I EVER SAW...
JUST WHAT IS THE MASKED MANHUNTER SEEING? LET'S PEER INTO HIS EYES -- CLOSE... CLOSER...
A CLOCK IN EACH EYE! BATMAN'S BECOME CLOCK-EYED!
THE CLOCK IS THE GREAT ILLUMINATED ONE ATOP THE LIFETIME PUBLICATIONS BUILDING IN MIDTOWN GOTHAM CITY!
WHAT AM I DOING UP HERE?! HOW DID I GET HERE!? ALL I KNOW... IS THAT A DARING BAND OF CAT-BURGLARS IS USING THE BELFRY BEHIND THAT CLOCK AS A HIDE-OUT!
WITH THE AID OF HIS BATROPE, THE CAPED CRUSADER SWINGS THROUGH SPACE...
THEY'VE BEEN TERRORIZING THE CITY BY NIGHT! I'VE GOT TO CAPTURE THEM!
MADE IT! AND -- THERE'S ONE OF THEM NOW -- COMING OUT ON THE CLOCK WITH A GUN--!

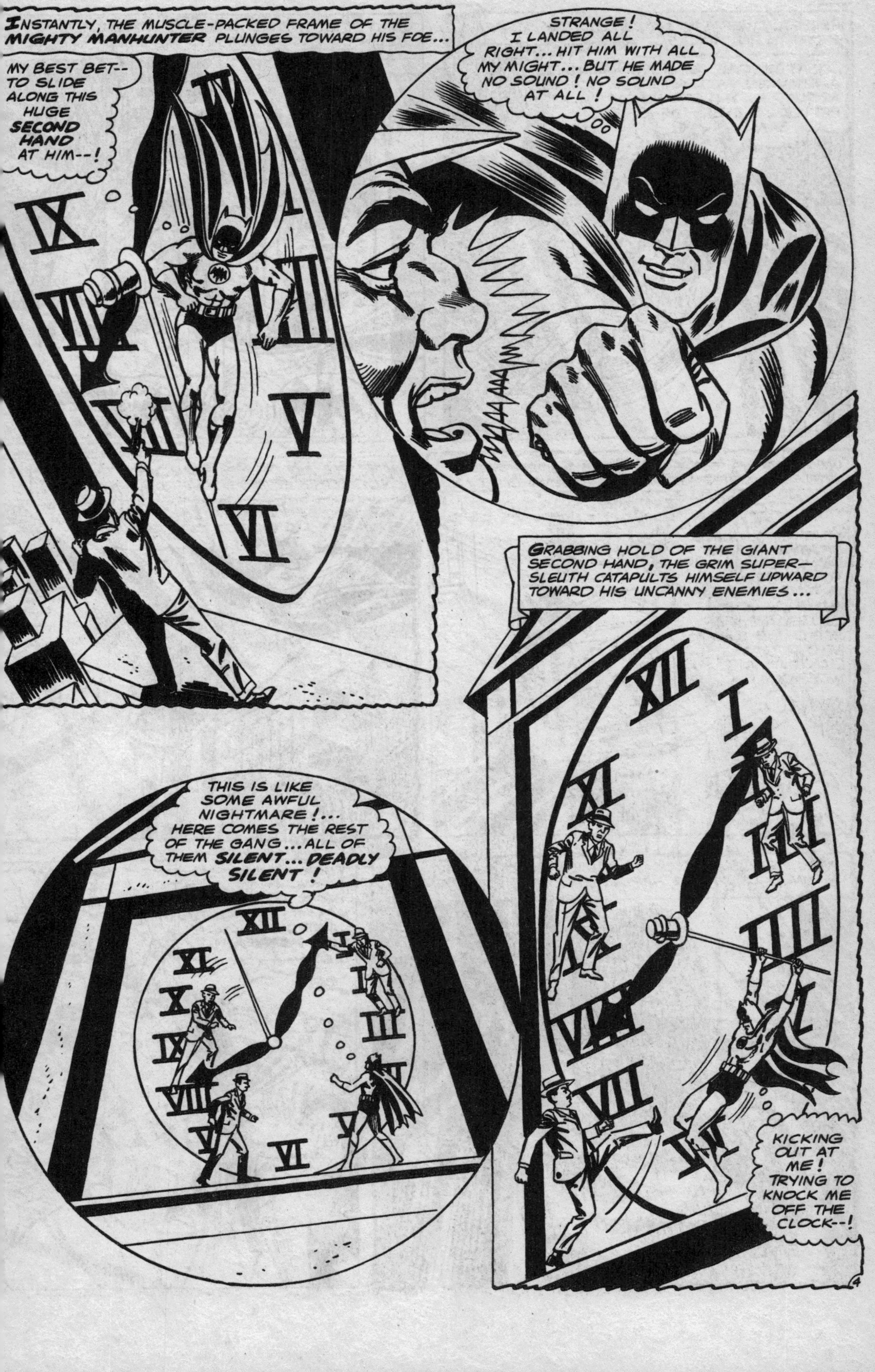
INSTANTLY, THE MUSCLE-PACKED FRAME OF THE MIGHTY MANHUNTER PLUNGES TOWARD HIS FOE...
MY BEST BET-- TO SLIDE ALONG THIS HUGE SECOND HAND AT HIM--!
STRANGE! I LANDED ALL RIGHT... HIT HIM WITH ALL MY MIGHT... BUT HE MADE NO SOUND! NO SOUND AT ALL!
GRABBING HOLD OF THE GIANT SECOND HAND, THE GRIM SUPER-SLEUTH CATAPULTS HIMSELF UPWARD TOWARD HIS UNCANNY ENEMIES...
THIS IS LIKE SOME AWFUL NIGHTMARE!... HERE COMES THE REST OF THE GANG... ALL OF THEM SILENT... DEADLY SILENT!
KICKING OUT AT ME! TRYING TO KNOCK ME OFF THE CLOCK--!
4

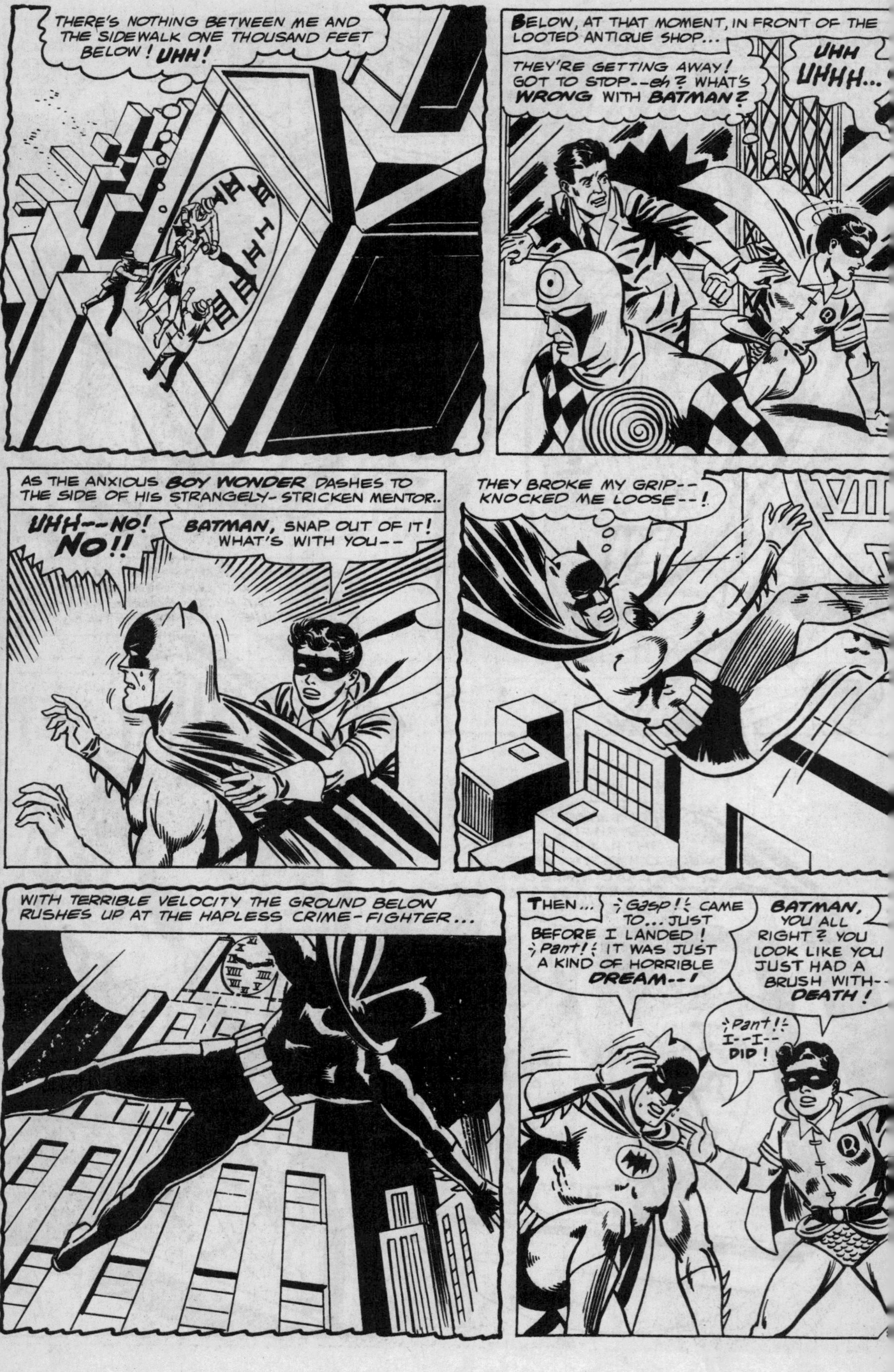
THERE'S NOTHING BETWEEN ME AND THE SIDEWALK ONE THOUSAND FEET BELOW! UHH!
BELOW, AT THAT MOMENT, IN FRONT OF THE LOOTED ANTIQUE SHOP...
THEY'RE GETTING AWAY! GOT TO STOP--eh? WHAT'S WRONG WITH BATMAN?
UHH UHHH...
AS THE ANXIOUS BOY WONDER DASHES TO THE SIDE OF HIS STRANGELY-STRICKEN MENTOR..
UHH--NO! NO!!
BATMAN, SNAP OUT OF IT! WHAT'S WITH YOU--
THEY BROKE MY GRIP--KNOCKED ME LOOSE--!
WITH TERRIBLE VELOCITY THE GROUND BELOW RUSHES UP AT THE HAPLESS CRIME-FIGHTER...
THEN...
-Gasp!- CAME TO... JUST BEFORE I LANDED! -Pant!- IT WAS JUST A KIND OF HORRIBLE DREAM--!
BATMAN, YOU ALL RIGHT? YOU LOOK LIKE YOU JUST HAD A BRUSH WITH--DEATH!
-Pant!- I--I--DID!

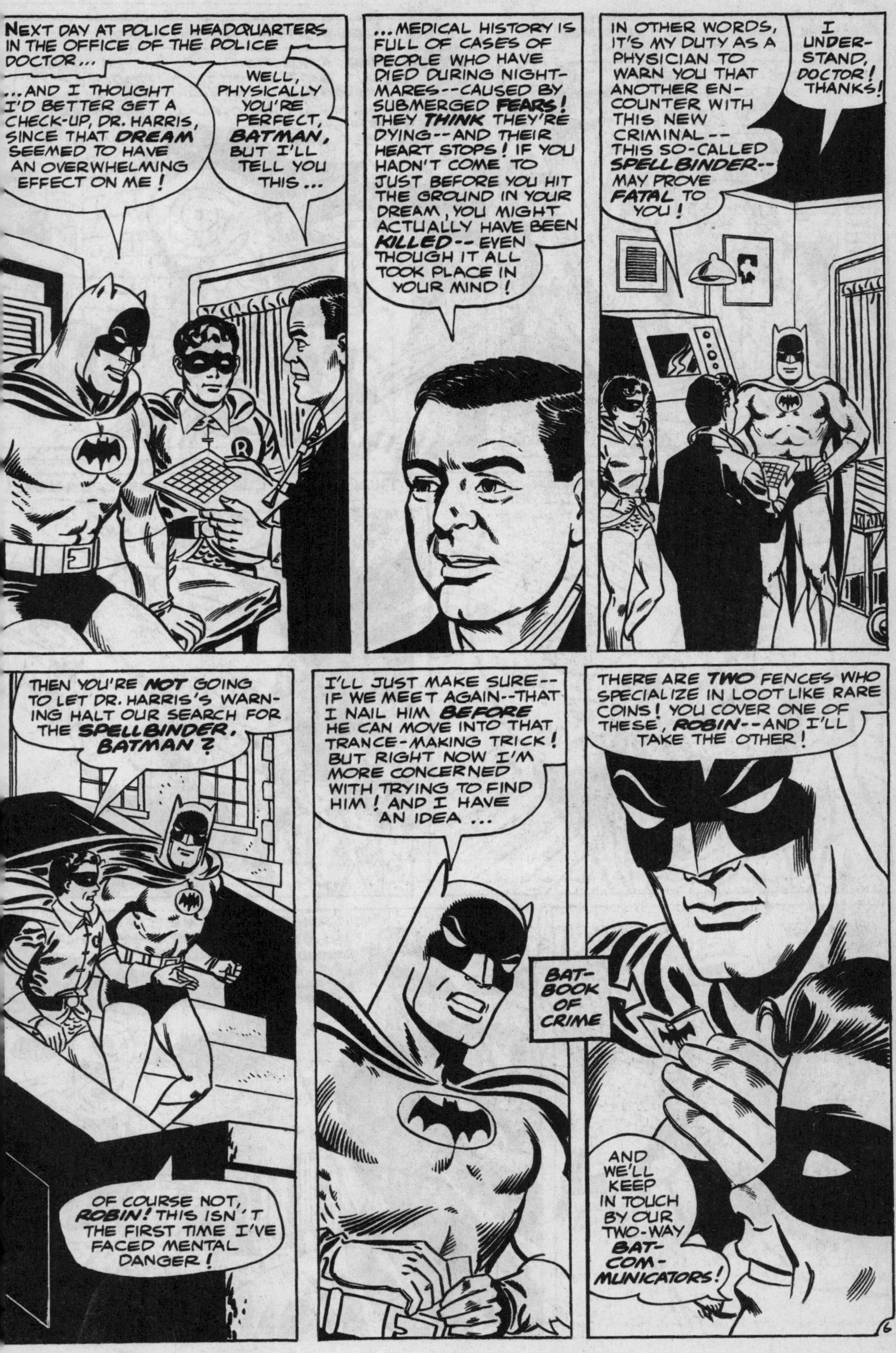
NEXT DAY AT POLICE HEADQUARTERS IN THE OFFICE OF THE POLICE DOCTOR...
...AND I THOUGHT I'D BETTER GET A CHECK-UP, DR. HARRIS, SINCE THAT DREAM SEEMED TO HAVE AN OVERWHELMING EFFECT ON ME!
WELL, PHYSICALLY YOU'RE PERFECT, BATMAN, BUT I'LL TELL YOU THIS...
...MEDICAL HISTORY IS FULL OF CASES OF PEOPLE WHO HAVE DIED DURING NIGHT-MARES--CAUSED BY SUBMERGED FEARS! THEY THINK THEY'RE DYING--AND THEIR HEART STOPS! IF YOU HADN'T COME TO JUST BEFORE YOU HIT THE GROUND IN YOUR DREAM, YOU MIGHT ACTUALLY HAVE BEEN KILLED--EVEN THOUGH IT ALL TOOK PLACE IN YOUR MIND!
IN OTHER WORDS, IT'S MY DUTY AS A PHYSICIAN TO WARN YOU THAT ANOTHER EN-COUNTER WITH THIS NEW CRIMINAL--THIS SO-CALLED SPELLBINDER--MAY PROVE FATAL TO YOU!
I UNDER-STAND, DOCTOR! THANKS!
THEN YOU'RE NOT GOING TO LET DR. HARRIS'S WARN-ING HALT OUR SEARCH FOR THE SPELLBINDER, BATMAN?
OF COURSE NOT, ROBIN! THIS ISN'T THE FIRST TIME I'VE FACED MENTAL DANGER!
I'LL JUST MAKE SURE--IF WE MEET AGAIN--THAT I NAIL HIM BEFORE HE CAN MOVE INTO THAT TRANCE-MAKING TRICK! BUT RIGHT NOW I'M MORE CONCERNED WITH TRYING TO FIND HIM! AND I HAVE AN IDEA...
BAT-BOOK OF CRIME
THERE ARE TWO FENCES WHO SPECIALIZE IN LOOT LIKE RARE COINS! YOU COVER ONE OF THESE, ROBIN--AND I'LL TAKE THE OTHER!
AND WE'LL KEEP IN TOUCH BY OUR TWO-WAY BAT-COM-MUNICATORS!
6

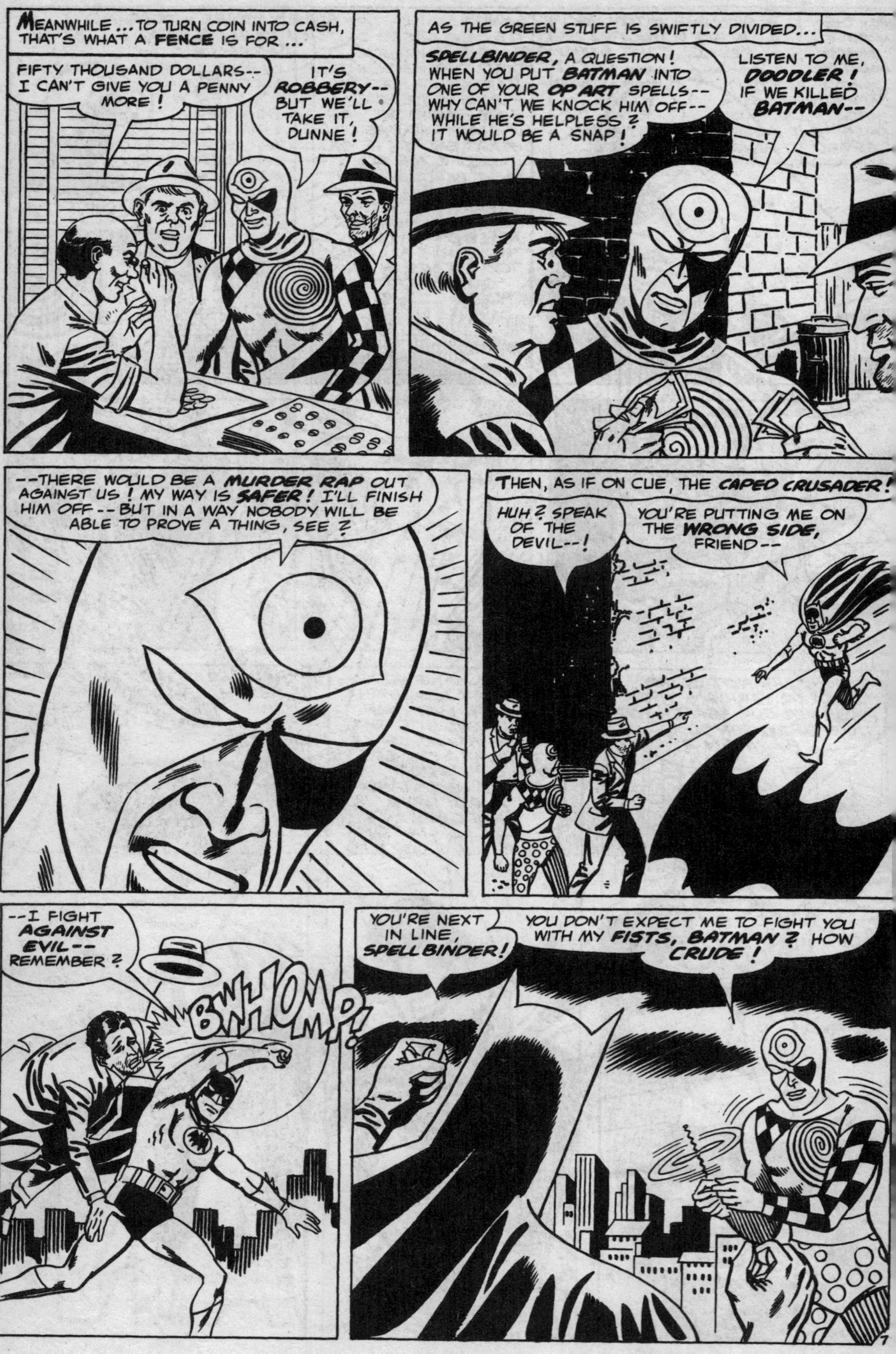
MEANWHILE ... TO TURN COIN INTO CASH, THAT'S WHAT A FENCE IS FOR ...
FIFTY THOUSAND DOLLARS-- I CAN'T GIVE YOU A PENNY MORE!
IT'S ROBBERY-- BUT WE'LL TAKE IT, DUNNE!
AS THE GREEN STUFF IS SWIFTLY DIVIDED...
SPELLBINDER, A QUESTION! WHEN YOU PUT BATMAN INTO ONE OF YOUR OP ART SPELLS-- WHY CAN'T WE KNOCK HIM OFF-- WHILE HE'S HELPLESS? IT WOULD BE A SNAP!
LISTEN TO ME, DOODLER! IF WE KILLED BATMAN--
--THERE WOULD BE A MURDER RAP OUT AGAINST US! MY WAY IS SAFER! I'LL FINISH HIM OFF-- BUT IN A WAY NOBODY WILL BE ABLE TO PROVE A THING, SEE?
THEN, AS IF ON CUE, THE CAPED CRUSADER!
HUH? SPEAK OF THE DEVIL--!
YOU'RE PUTTING ME ON THE WRONG SIDE, FRIEND--
--I FIGHT AGAINST EVIL-- REMEMBER?
BWHOMP!
YOU'RE NEXT IN LINE, SPELLBINDER!
YOU DON'T EXPECT ME TO FIGHT YOU WITH MY FISTS, BATMAN? HOW CRUDE!
7

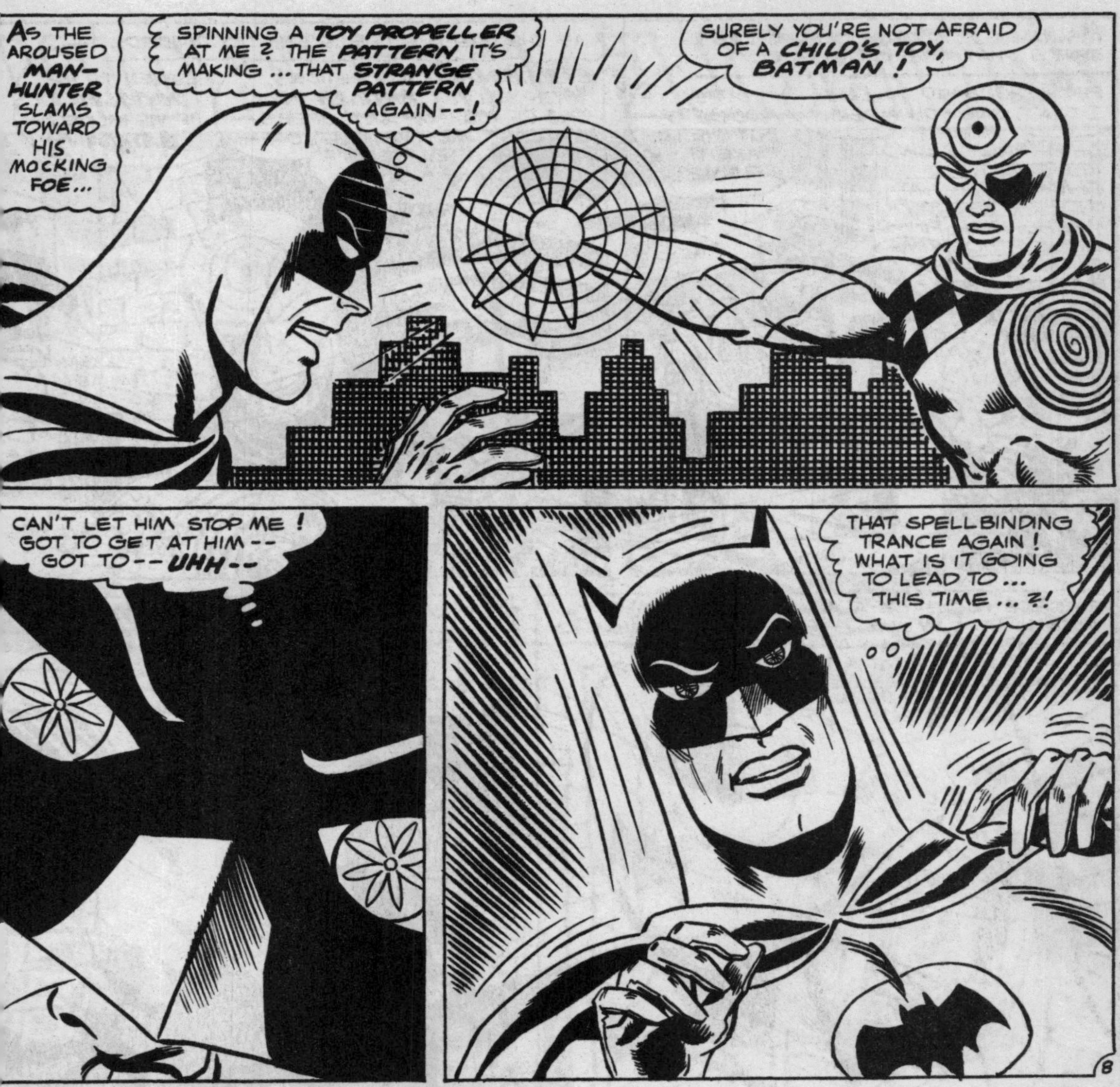
AS THE AROUSED MAN-HUNTER SLAMS TOWARD HIS MOCKING FOE...
SPINNING A TOY PROPELLER AT ME? THE PATTERN IT'S MAKING ... THAT STRANGE PATTERN AGAIN--!
SURELY YOU'RE NOT AFRAID OF A CHILD'S TOY, BATMAN!
CAN'T LET HIM STOP ME! GOT TO GET AT HIM -- GOT TO -- UHH--
THAT SPELLBINDING TRANCE AGAIN! WHAT IS IT GOING TO LEAD TO ... THIS TIME ...?!
8

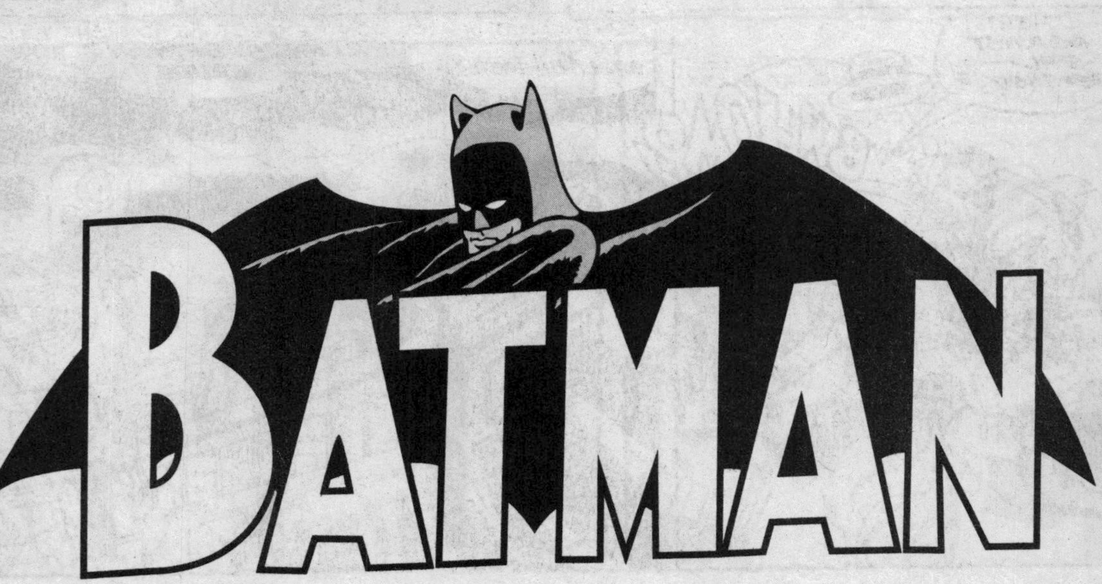
BATMAN

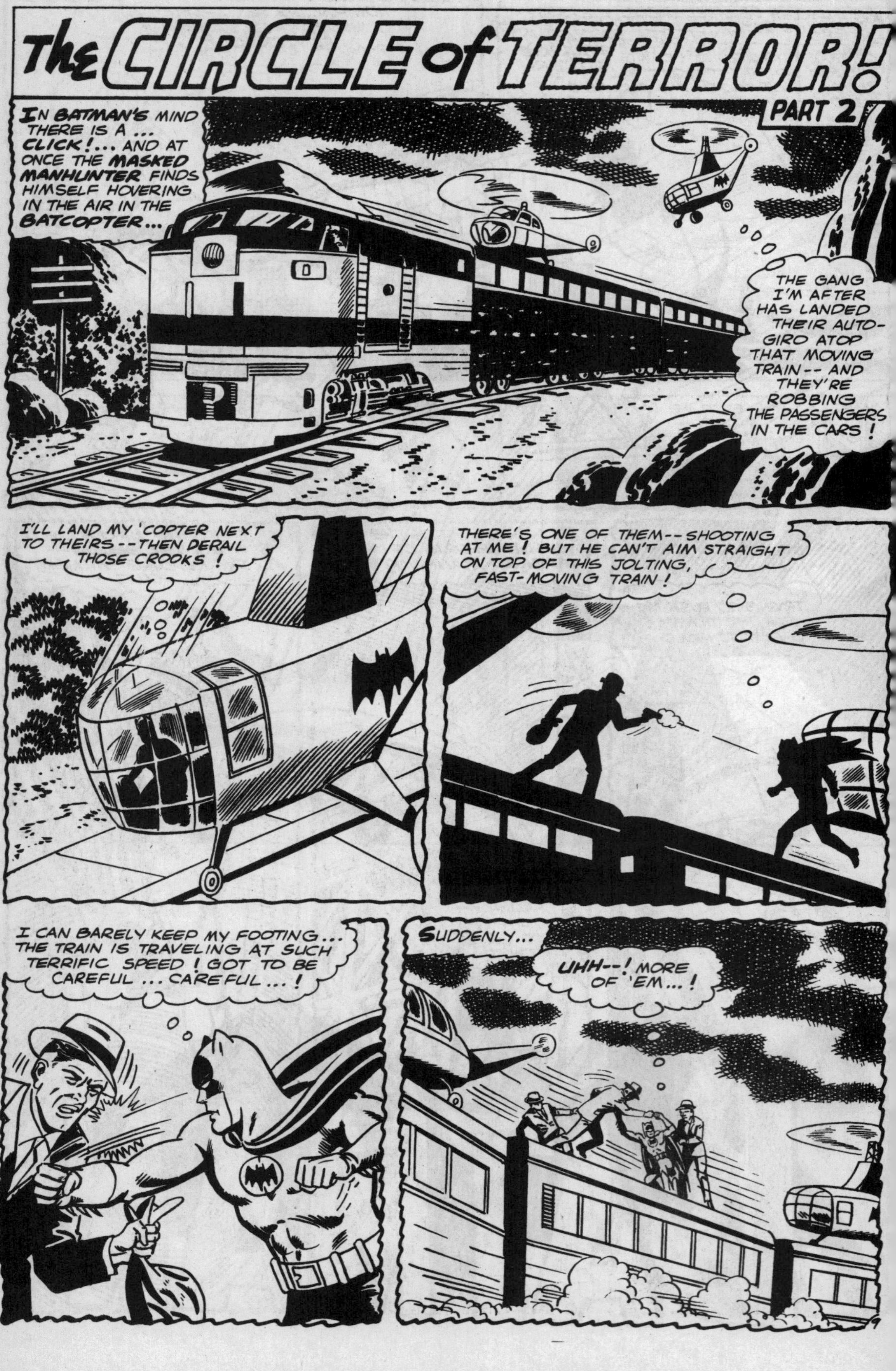
The CIRCLE of TERROR!
PART 2
IN BATMAN'S MIND THERE IS A ... CLICK! ... AND AT ONCE THE MASKED MANHUNTER FINDS HIMSELF HOVERING IN THE AIR IN THE BATCOPTER...
THE GANG I'M AFTER HAS LANDED THEIR AUTO-GIRO ATOP THAT MOVING TRAIN -- AND THEY'RE ROBBING THE PASSENGERS IN THE CARS!
I'LL LAND MY 'COPTER NEXT TO THEIRS -- THEN DERAIL THOSE CROOKS!
THERE'S ONE OF THEM -- SHOOTING AT ME! BUT HE CAN'T AIM STRAIGHT ON TOP OF THIS JOLTING, FAST-MOVING TRAIN!
I CAN BARELY KEEP MY FOOTING... THE TRAIN IS TRAVELING AT SUCH TERRIFIC SPEED! GOT TO BE CAREFUL ... CAREFUL ...!
SUDDENLY...
UHH--! MORE OF 'EM ...!

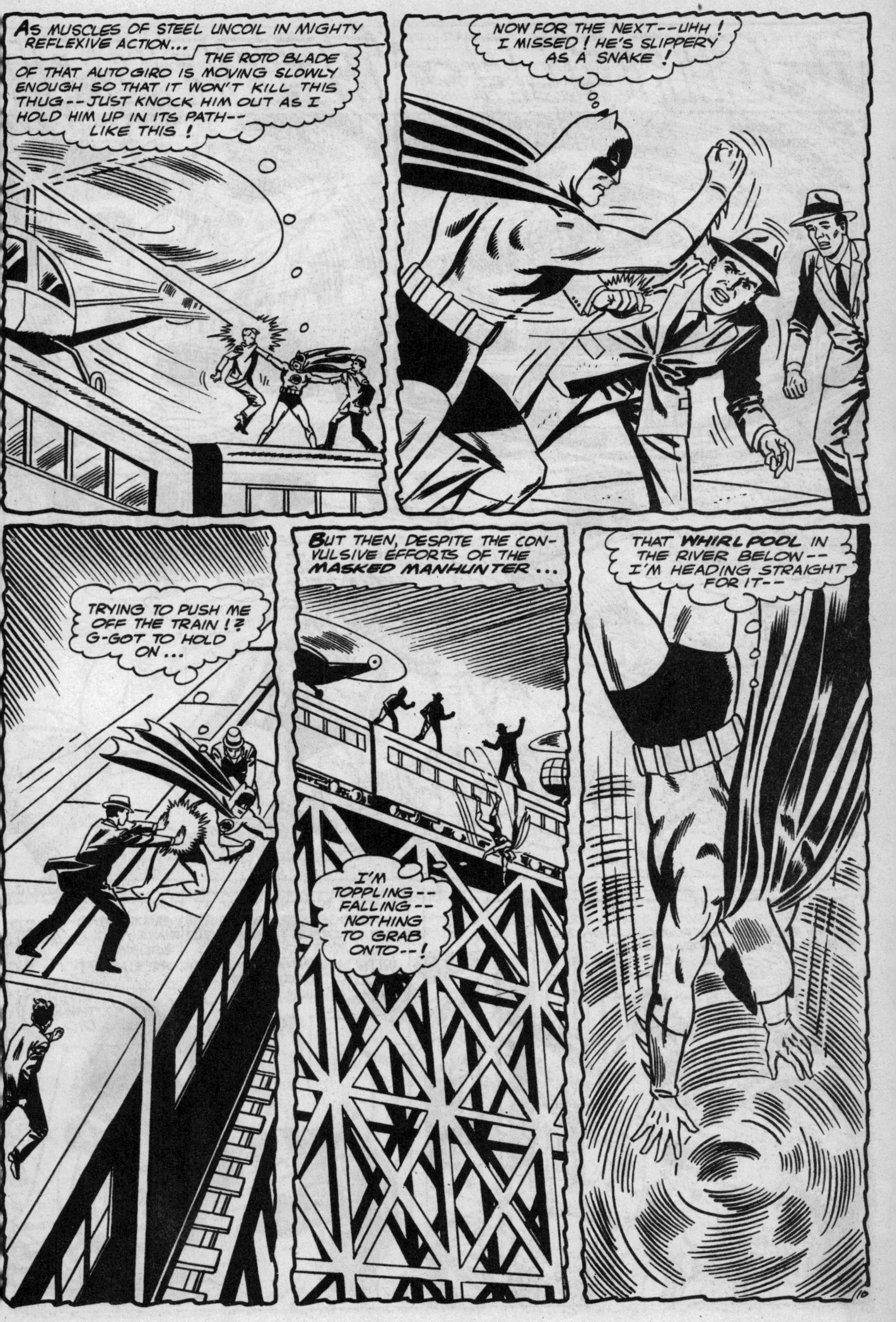
AS MUSCLES OF STEEL UNCOIL IN MIGHTY REFLEXIVE ACTION...
THE ROTO BLADE OF THAT AUTOGIRO IS MOVING SLOWLY ENOUGH SO THAT IT WON'T KILL THIS THUG--JUST KNOCK HIM OUT AS I HOLD HIM UP IN ITS PATH--LIKE THIS !
NOW FOR THE NEXT--UHH ! I MISSED ! HE'S SLIPPERY AS A SNAKE !
TRYING TO PUSH ME OFF THE TRAIN !? G-GOT TO HOLD ON...
BUT THEN, DESPITE THE CONVULSIVE EFFORTS OF THE MASKED MANHUNTER...
I'M TOPPLING--FALLING--NOTHING TO GRAB ONTO--!
THAT WHIRLPOOL IN THE RIVER BELOW--I'M HEADING STRAIGHT FOR IT--
10

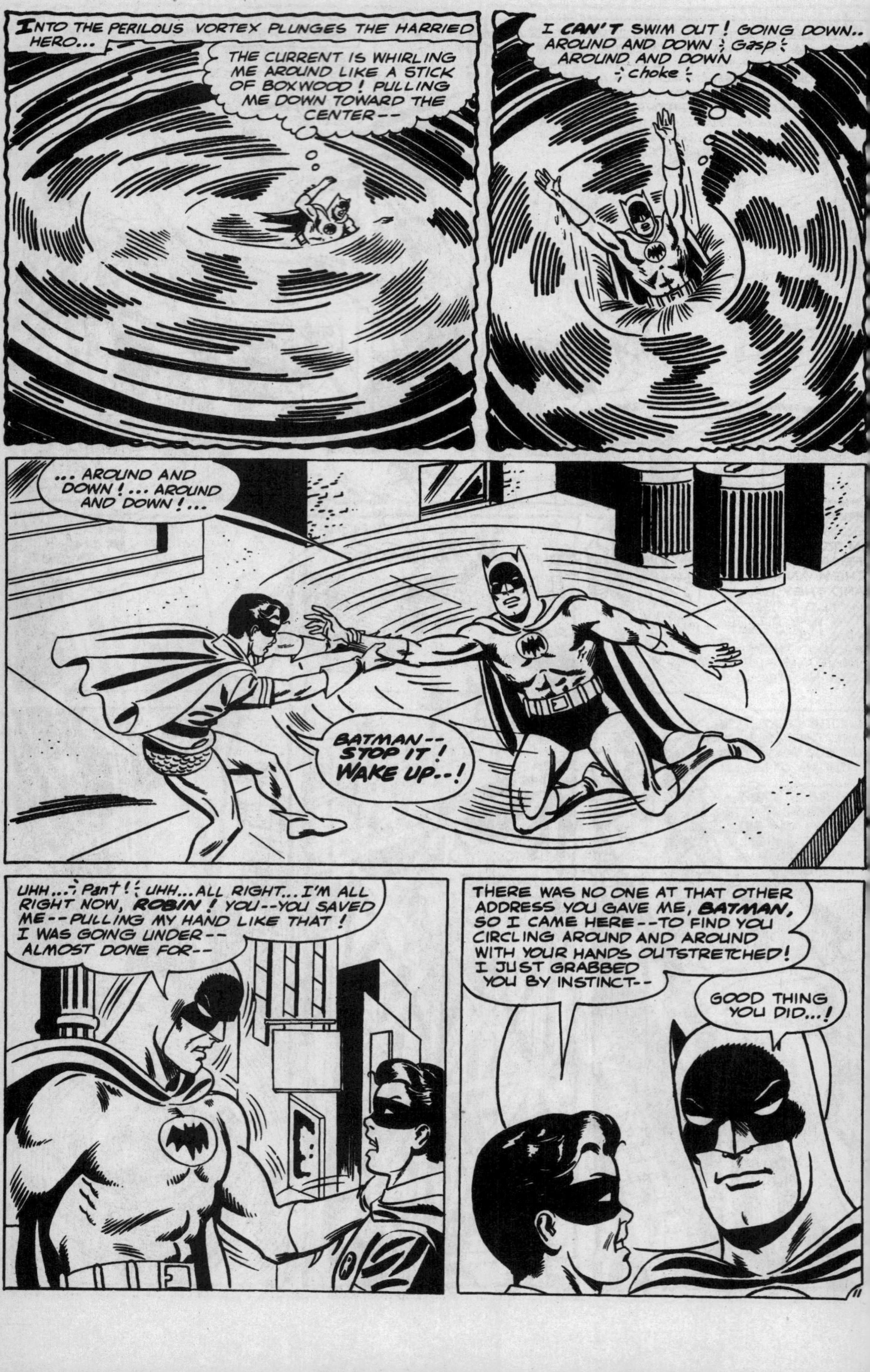
INTO THE PERILOUS VORTEX PLUNGES THE HARRIED HERO...
THE CURRENT IS WHIRLING ME AROUND LIKE A STICK OF BOXWOOD! PULLING ME DOWN TOWARD THE CENTER--
I CAN'T SWIM OUT! GOING DOWN.. AROUND AND DOWN -Gasp- AROUND AND DOWN -choke-
... AROUND AND DOWN! ... AROUND AND DOWN! ...
BATMAN-- STOP IT! WAKE UP--!
UHH...-Pant!- UHH... ALL RIGHT... I'M ALL RIGHT NOW, ROBIN! YOU--YOU SAVED ME--PULLING MY HAND LIKE THAT! I WAS GOING UNDER-- ALMOST DONE FOR--
THERE WAS NO ONE AT THAT OTHER ADDRESS YOU GAVE ME, BATMAN, SO I CAME HERE--TO FIND YOU CIRCLING AROUND AND AROUND WITH YOUR HANDS OUTSTRETCHED! I JUST GRABBED YOU BY INSTINCT--
GOOD THING YOU DID...!

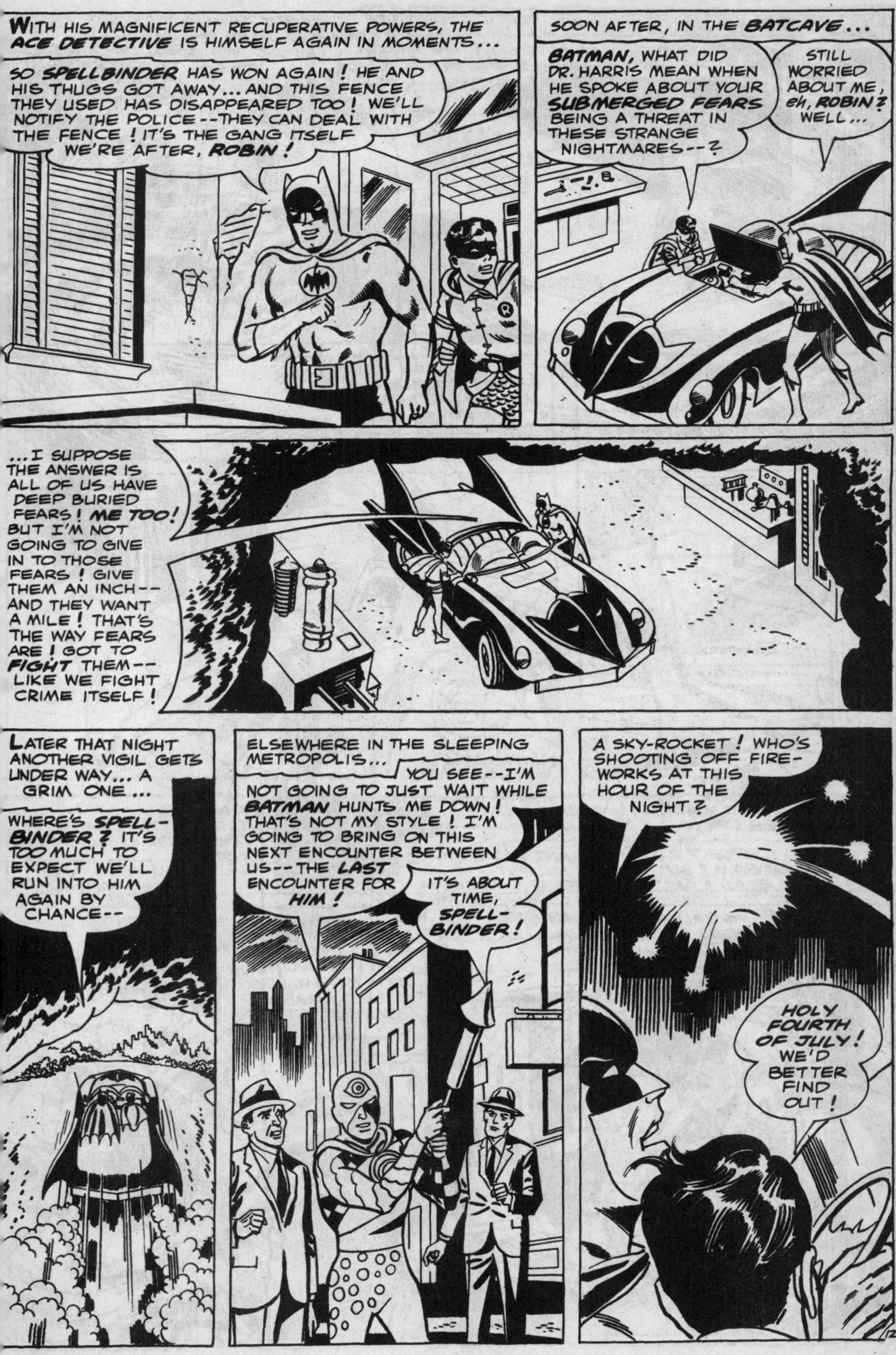
WITH HIS MAGNIFICENT RECUPERATIVE POWERS, THE ACE DETECTIVE IS HIMSELF AGAIN IN MOMENTS...
SO SPELLBINDER HAS WON AGAIN! HE AND HIS THUGS GOT AWAY... AND THIS FENCE THEY USED HAS DISAPPEARED TOO! WE'LL NOTIFY THE POLICE--THEY CAN DEAL WITH THE FENCE! IT'S THE GANG ITSELF WE'RE AFTER, ROBIN!
SOON AFTER, IN THE BATCAVE...
BATMAN, WHAT DID DR. HARRIS MEAN WHEN HE SPOKE ABOUT YOUR SUBMERGED FEARS BEING A THREAT IN THESE STRANGE NIGHTMARES--?
STILL WORRIED ABOUT ME, eh, ROBIN? WELL...
...I SUPPOSE THE ANSWER IS ALL OF US HAVE DEEP BURIED FEARS! ME TOO! BUT I'M NOT GOING TO GIVE IN TO THOSE FEARS! GIVE THEM AN INCH--AND THEY WANT A MILE! THAT'S THE WAY FEARS ARE! GOT TO FIGHT THEM--LIKE WE FIGHT CRIME ITSELF!
LATER THAT NIGHT ANOTHER VIGIL GETS UNDER WAY... A GRIM ONE...
WHERE'S SPELLBINDER? IT'S TOO MUCH TO EXPECT WE'LL RUN INTO HIM AGAIN BY CHANCE--
ELSEWHERE IN THE SLEEPING METROPOLIS...
YOU SEE--I'M NOT GOING TO JUST WAIT WHILE BATMAN HUNTS ME DOWN! THAT'S NOT MY STYLE! I'M GOING TO BRING ON THIS NEXT ENCOUNTER BETWEEN US--THE LAST ENCOUNTER FOR HIM!
IT'S ABOUT TIME, SPELLBINDER!
A SKY-ROCKET! WHO'S SHOOTING OFF FIRE-WORKS AT THIS HOUR OF THE NIGHT?
HOLY FOURTH OF JULY! WE'D BETTER FIND OUT!
12

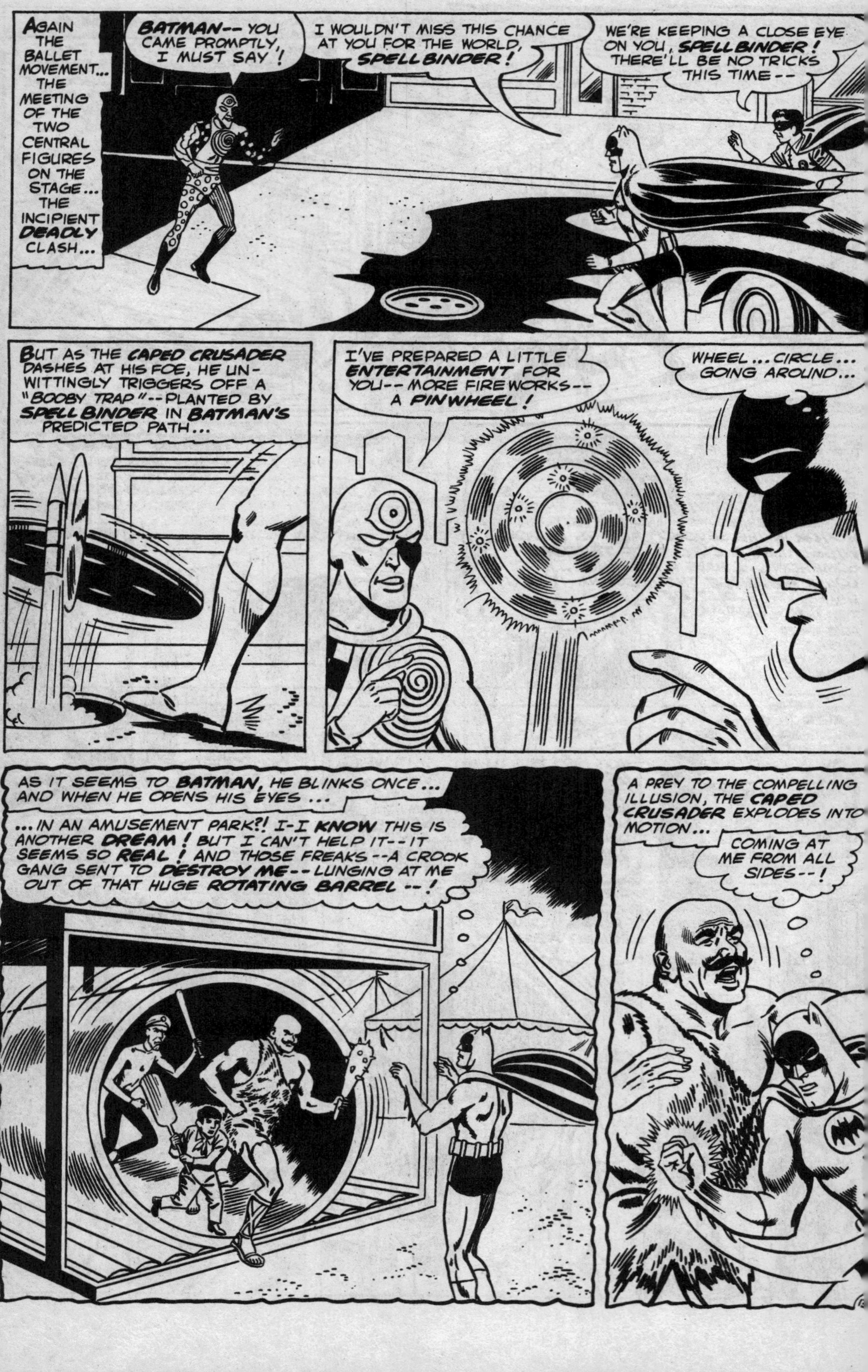
AGAIN THE BALLET MOVEMENT... THE MEETING OF THE TWO CENTRAL FIGURES ON THE STAGE... THE INCIPIENT DEADLY CLASH...
BATMAN-- YOU CAME PROMPTLY, I MUST SAY!
I WOULDN'T MISS THIS CHANCE AT YOU FOR THE WORLD, SPELLBINDER!
WE'RE KEEPING A CLOSE EYE ON YOU, SPELLBINDER! THERE'LL BE NO TRICKS THIS TIME--
BUT AS THE CAPED CRUSADER DASHES AT HIS FOE, HE UNWITTINGLY TRIGGERS OFF A "BOOBY TRAP"--PLANTED BY SPELLBINDER IN BATMAN'S PREDICTED PATH...
I'VE PREPARED A LITTLE ENTERTAINMENT FOR YOU-- MORE FIREWORKS-- A PINWHEEL!
WHEEL... CIRCLE... GOING AROUND...
AS IT SEEMS TO BATMAN, HE BLINKS ONCE... AND WHEN HE OPENS HIS EYES...
...IN AN AMUSEMENT PARK?! I-I KNOW THIS IS ANOTHER DREAM! BUT I CAN'T HELP IT-- IT SEEMS SO REAL! AND THOSE FREAKS--A CROOK GANG SENT TO DESTROY ME-- LUNGING AT ME OUT OF THAT HUGE ROTATING BARREL--!
A PREY TO THE COMPELLING ILLUSION, THE CAPED CRUSADER EXPLODES INTO MOTION...
COMING AT ME FROM ALL SIDES--!

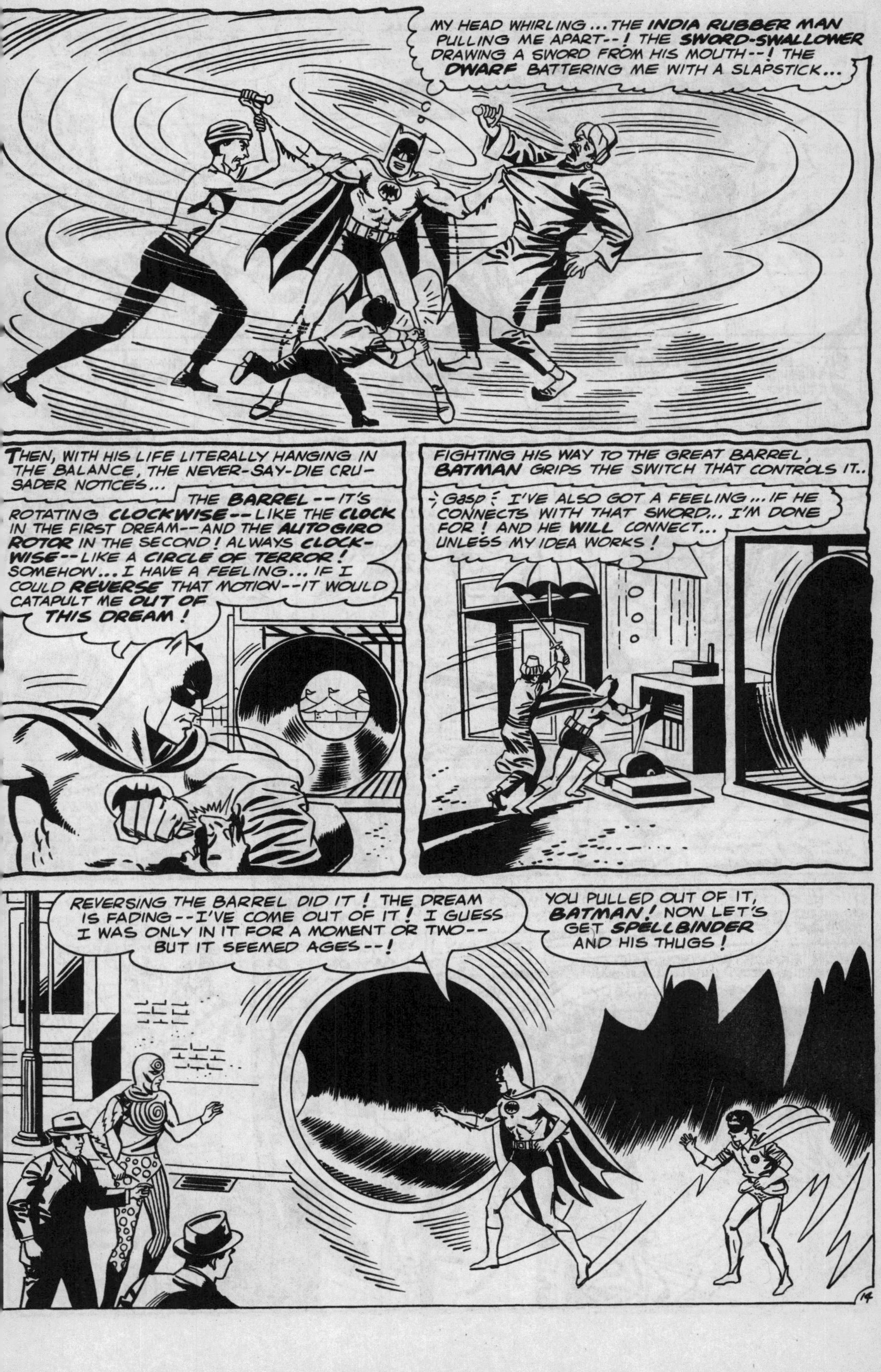
MY HEAD WHIRLING... THE INDIA RUBBER MAN PULLING ME APART--! THE SWORD-SWALLOWER DRAWING A SWORD FROM HIS MOUTH--! THE DWARF BATTERING ME WITH A SLAPSTICK...
THEN, WITH HIS LIFE LITERALLY HANGING IN THE BALANCE, THE NEVER-SAY-DIE CRUSADER NOTICES...
THE BARREL--IT'S ROTATING CLOCKWISE--LIKE THE CLOCK IN THE FIRST DREAM--AND THE AUTOGIRO ROTOR IN THE SECOND! ALWAYS CLOCKWISE--LIKE A CIRCLE OF TERROR! SOMEHOW... I HAVE A FEELING... IF I COULD REVERSE THAT MOTION--IT WOULD CATAPULT ME OUT OF THIS DREAM!
FIGHTING HIS WAY TO THE GREAT BARREL, BATMAN GRIPS THE SWITCH THAT CONTROLS IT..
Gasp! I'VE ALSO GOT A FEELING... IF HE CONNECTS WITH THAT SWORD... I'M DONE FOR! AND HE WILL CONNECT... UNLESS MY IDEA WORKS!
REVERSING THE BARREL DID IT! THE DREAM IS FADING--I'VE COME OUT OF IT! I GUESS I WAS ONLY IN IT FOR A MOMENT OR TWO--BUT IT SEEMED AGES--!
YOU PULLED OUT OF IT, BATMAN! NOW LET'S GET SPELLBINDER AND HIS THUGS!
14

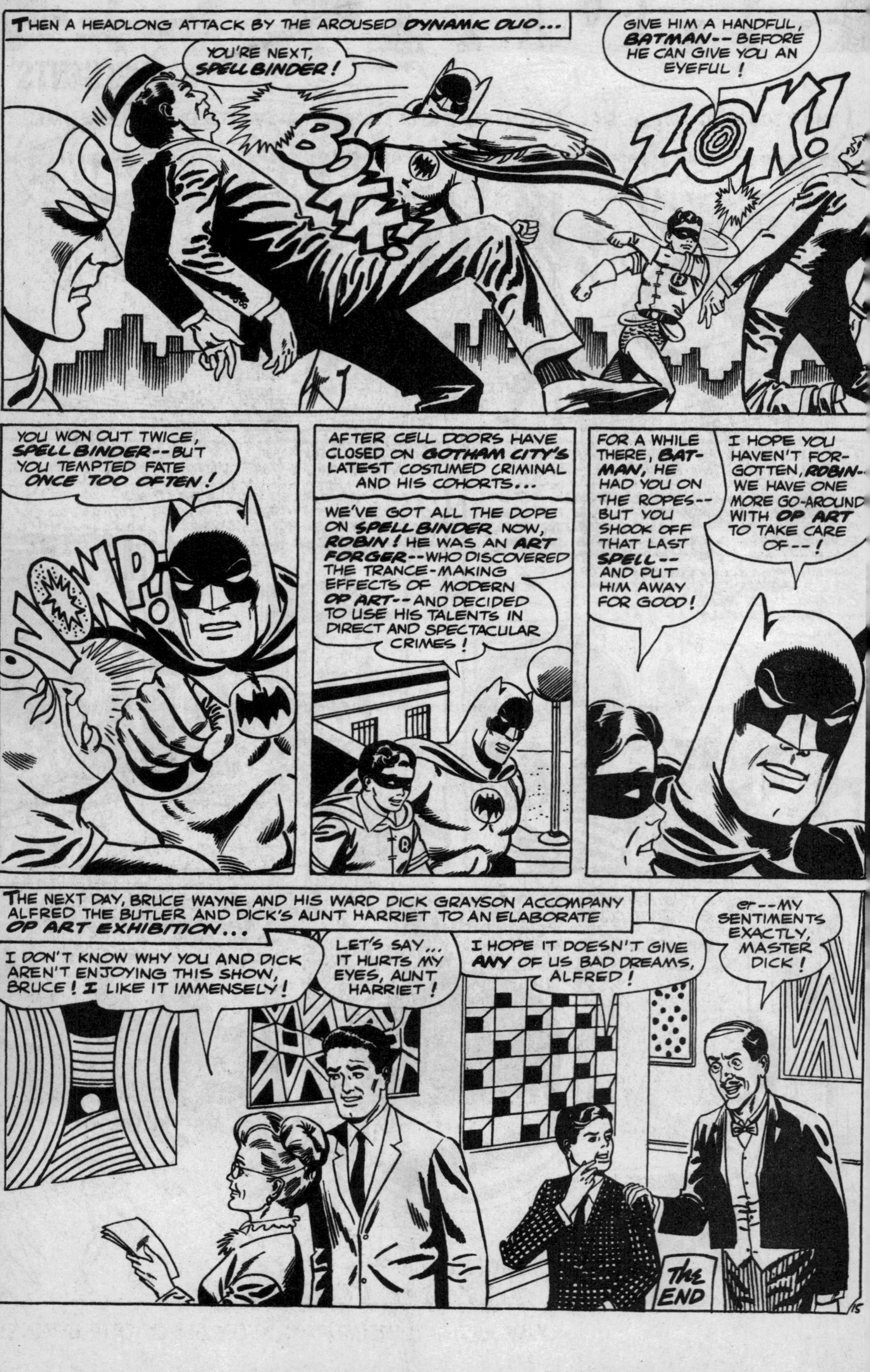
THEN A HEADLONG ATTACK BY THE AROUSED DYNAMIC DUO...
YOU'RE NEXT, SPELLBINDER!
BOK!
GIVE HIM A HANDFUL, BATMAN-- BEFORE HE CAN GIVE YOU AN EYEFUL!
ZOK!
YOU WON OUT TWICE, SPELLBINDER-- BUT YOU TEMPTED FATE ONCE TOO OFTEN!
WHAP!
AFTER CELL DOORS HAVE CLOSED ON GOTHAM CITY'S LATEST COSTUMED CRIMINAL AND HIS COHORTS...
WE'VE GOT ALL THE DOPE ON SPELLBINDER NOW, ROBIN! HE WAS AN ART FORGER-- WHO DISCOVERED THE TRANCE-MAKING EFFECTS OF MODERN OP ART-- AND DECIDED TO USE HIS TALENTS IN DIRECT AND SPECTACULAR CRIMES!
FOR A WHILE THERE, BATMAN, HE HAD YOU ON THE ROPES-- BUT YOU SHOOK OFF THAT LAST SPELL-- AND PUT HIM AWAY FOR GOOD!
I HOPE YOU HAVEN'T FORGOTTEN, ROBIN-- WE HAVE ONE MORE GO-AROUND WITH OP ART TO TAKE CARE OF--!
THE NEXT DAY, BRUCE WAYNE AND HIS WARD DICK GRAYSON ACCOMPANY ALFRED THE BUTLER AND DICK'S AUNT HARRIET TO AN ELABORATE OP ART EXHIBITION...
I DON'T KNOW WHY YOU AND DICK AREN'T ENJOYING THIS SHOW, BRUCE! I LIKE IT IMMENSELY!
LET'S SAY... IT HURTS MY EYES, AUNT HARRIET!
I HOPE IT DOESN'T GIVE ANY OF US BAD DREAMS, ALFRED!
er-- MY SENTIMENTS EXACTLY, MASTER DICK!
THE END
15

SHOWCASE
PRESENTS

OVER 500 PAGES OF DC'S CLASSIC HEROES AND STORIES PRESENTED IN EACH VOLUME!

**GREEN LANTERN
VOL. 1**

**SUPERMAN
VOL. 1**

**SUPERMAN
VOL. 2**

**SUPERMAN FAMILY
VOL. 1**

**JONAH HEX
VOL. 1**

**METAMORPHO
VOL. 1**

SEARCH THE GRAPHIC NOVELS SECTION OF
WWW.DCCOMICS.COM
FOR ART AND INFORMATION ON ALL OF OUR BOOKS!